P9-DGQ-204

INTERNATIONAL ENCYCLOPEDIA OF DANCE

INTERNATIONAL ENCYCLOPEDIA OF

DANCE

A project of Dance Perspectives Foundation, Inc.

FOUNDING EDITOR

Selma Jeanne Cohen

AREA EDITORS

George Dorris   Nancy Goldner   Beate Gordon
Nancy Reynolds   David Vaughan
Suzanne Youngerman

CONSULTANTS

Thomas F. Kelly   Horst Koegler   Richard Ralph
Elizabeth Souritz

VOLUME 5

OXFORD UNIVERSITY PRESS

New York   1998   Oxford

OXFORD UNIVERSITY PRESS

Oxford New York
Athens Auckland Bangkok Bogotá Bombay
Buenos Aires Calcutta Cape Town Dar es Salaam
Delhi Florence Hong Kong Istanbul Karachi
Kuala Lumpur Madras Madrid Melbourne
Mexico City Nairobi Paris Singapore
Taipei Tokyo Toronto Warsaw
and associated companies in
Berlin Ibadan

Published by Oxford University Press, Inc.,
198 Madison Avenue, New York, New York 10016

This work was initiated with funds granted by the National Endowment for the Humanities, a federal agency

Library of Congress Cataloging-in-Publication Data
International encyclopedia of dance : a project of Dance Perspectives Foundation, Inc. / founding editor, Selma Jeanne Cohen; area editors, George Dorris et al.; consultants, Thomas F. Kelly et al.
p. cm.
Includes bibliographical references and index.
1. Dance—Encyclopedias. 2. Ballet—Encyclopedias. I. Cohen, Selma Jeanne, 1920-. II. Dance Perspectives Foundation.
GV1585.I586 1998 97-36562 792.6′2′03—dc21 CIP
ISBN 0-19-509462-X (set)
ISBN 0-19-512309-3 (vol. 5)

Printing (last digit): 9 8 7 6 5 4 3 2

Printed in the United States of America
on acid-free paper

N

CONTINUED

NOZZE DEGLI DEI, LE. Choreography: Agnioli Ricci. Director: Ferdinando Sarcinelli. Music: Five unknown composers. Libretto: Abbé Giovanni Carlo Coppola. Scenery, costumes, and machinery: Alfonso Parigi the younger. First performance: 8 July 1637, courtyard of the Pitti Palace, Florence.

This spectacle, the title of which means "The Wedding of the Gods," was presented on the occasion of the wedding of the grand duke of Tuscany, Ferdinand II de' Medici, to Vittoria della Rovere, princess of Urbino. The wedding was given great publicity by the printing in 1637 of four celebratory publications. *Le Nozze degli Dei,* a booklet by the librettist, G. C. Coppola, included eight engravings by Stefano Della Bella illustrating the sets and stage effects. *Argomento delle Nozze degli Dei,* by an anonymous author, and *Relazione delle Nozze degli Dei* by F. Rondinelli also appeared. *Descrizione delle feste date in Firenze* (Description of the Festivals Given in Florence), by F. de' Bardi with an engraving by S. Della Bella, documents the tournament presented after the performance of *Le Nozze degli Dei,* inspired by the episode of Armida in *Gerusalemme Liberata* (Jerusalem Liberated) by Torquato Tasso.

The exceptional prominence given to the celebration was perhaps motivated by the desire to mask an unhappy political situation. In 1631 the small but strategically and culturally important duchy of Urbino was annexed to the Vatican State by Pope Urban VIII Barberini. Vittoria della Rovere, the last descendant of the dukes of Urbino, was thus the princess of a nonexistent realm, and the wedding sanctioned the waiver of all her claims to her ancestral domain. It is no accident that a panorama of Florence is shown in the prologue to *Le Nozze degli Dei;* this is not only a courtly allusion but also a consoling image for the bride, to whom a new and stable realm is being offered.

The plot of *Le Nozze degli Dei* is very slender: Jove, the chief deity, decides to give wives to the gods of Olympus, but his choices cause many conflicts, which are finally resolved to general satisfaction. To this thread are attached various mythological episodes, including the rape of Persephone, the descent of the Centaurs to Tartarus, the battle between the followers of Mars and Vulcan, the ascent of Venus to Heaven, and the maritime wedding of Neptune and Amphitrite. The scenes represented the Wood of Diana, the Garden of Venus, the Sea, Vulcan's Grotto, Tartarus, and Heaven ("scene of the whole heaven"). The spectacle thus depicted an imaginary voyage through the three realms of human, divine, and infernal, which together with an allegory of the four elements (air, water, earth, and fire), composed the magical number seven.

There were also seven scenes, including the view of Florence in the prologue. In the course of the action each scene appeared twice, except for the view of Florence and the final vision of Heaven. There were therefore twelve changes of scenery, possibly symbolic of the months of the year. Certainly symbolic was the choice of the two nonrepeated subjects, Florence and Heaven—establishing an exact relationship between the seat of the ruler and the seat of the gods. In this way, the ruler defined himself as representing divinity on earth, and his private happiness was identified with the public happiness of his subjects. This allusive metaphor recurs frequently in court spectacles of the seventeenth century.

In this respect, *Le Nozze degli Dei* is no different from similar presentations, except for the invention of a "pattern title" (Zorzi, 1977). Its innovative elements lie elsewhere—in certain scenes or choreographic formulas, and in the relationship of the action to the theatrical environment. Most of the scenes are within the Florentine theatrical tradition. For example, the Garden of Venus and the Sea have precedents in the Garden of Calypso and in the Ship of Amerigo Vespucci, as conceived by Giulio Parigi for *Il Giudizio di Paride* (The Judgment of Paris; Florence, 1608). The inferno recalls the descent of Circe to Tartarus, a scene by Giulio Parigi for *La Liberazione di Tirreno* (Florence, 1616) documented in an engraving by Jacques Callot.

A new element is the "scene of the whole heaven," obscured by two pillars of dark clouds in the foreground. The pillars emphasize the luminosity of the celestial vision in the background and divide it like an altar triptych, as if wishing to establish a liturgical image of the sovereign power. The novelty of this type of scene was quickly assimilated by contemporary scene painters: in the English masque *Salmacida Spolia* (1640), Inigo Jones introduced a "scene of the whole heaven"; in *Gridelino,* a court ballet presented in Turin in 1653, the pillars of clouds reappear.

The splendid quality of the engravings by Stefano Della Bella makes them valuable as documentation not only for the scenery but also for the choreography. Della Bella unites different episodes in a single image, but he is very accurate in reproducing the steps, figures, and costumes. The choreography for *Le Nozze degli Dei* is unusual in combining different types of dances in a single spectacle. These include pastoral dance, in Diana's Wood; children's ballet, in the ballet of the little Amors in the Garden of Venus; the grotesque ballet in the dance of the Centaurs in Tartarus; the so-called overthrow, the warriors' battle in the Grotto of Vulcan), and the equestrian ballet and the figures of the tournament in the Heavens. The last scene has remarkable choreography, arranged vertically on superimposed levels. Against all the rules, the heavier group of the equestrian ballet is above; under it, the dancers are configured (just as was done in real tournaments) to form the initial and final letters of the names of the bridal couple—F and O on the left, and V and A on the right. The spectacle was thus an encyclopedia of the various contemporary forms of theatrical expression.

The environment in which *Le Nozze degli Dei* was presented is also significant. In Florence, the courtyard of the Pitti Palace was transformed into a theater. A platform was erected in it for the bridal pair and the most illustrious guests; many spectators were in the courtyard itself, used as theater pit and surrounded by balconies; other spectators watched from windows and balconies on the second floor of the palace, around three sides. The fourth side was the stage, delimited by a large scenic arch which supported the curtain. Zorzi (1977) sees this arrangement as "the archetype of a modern theater" and an anticipation of the "structure of the opera, surrounded by several superimposed ranks of boxes." In reality, in 1637 there were already theaters with boxes in Venice, but these were

LE NOZZE DEGLI DEI. *(below)* The Garden of Venus, the third scene, and *(opposite page)* the Heavens, the sixth scene, from *Le Nozze degli Dei,* first performed on 8 July 1637 in the courtyard of the Pitti Palace, Florence, in honor of the marriage of Ferdinand II de' Medici and Vittoria della Rovere. The etchings are by Stefano Della Bella after Alfonso Parigi the younger. (Courtesy of Madison U. Sowell and Debra H. Sowell, Brigham Young University, Provo, Utah.)

halls operated by theater managers and open to the paying public. Only at the end of the seventeenth century did the theater with balconies, prefigured in the presentation of *Le Nozze degli Dei,* become standard for public, private, and court theaters in Italy.

BIBLIOGRAPHY

Argomento delle nozze degli dei. Florence, 1637.

Bardi, Ferdinando. *Descrizione delle feste fatte in Firenze per le reali nozze de serenissimi sposi Ferdinando II gran duca di Toscana, e Vittoria principessa d'Urbino.* Florence, 1637.

Coppola, Giovanni Carlo. *Le nozze degli dei favola . . . rappresentata in musica in Firenze nelle reali nozze de serenismi. gran duchi di Toschana Ferdinando II. e Vittoria principessa d'Urbino.* Florence, 1637.

Fabbri, Mario, et al., eds. *Il luogo teatrale a Firenze.* Milan, 1975.

Forlani Tempesti, Anna. *Mostra di incisioni di Stefano Della Bella.* Florence, 1973.

Molinari, Cesare. *Le nozze degli dei.* Rome, 1968.

Nagler, A. M. *Theatre Festivals of the Medici, 1539–1637.* New Haven, 1964.

Rondinelli, Francesco. *Relazione delle nozze degli dei: Favola.* Florence, 1637.

Zorzi, Ludovico. *Il teatro e la città.* Turin, 1977.

MERCEDES VIALE FERRERO

NUBA DANCE. The dances of the Nuba peoples of Kordofan Province in Sudan are typical of East African dance genres only in the great complexity of the types and the contexts in which they are performed. Community dances of several types are characteristic of these small hill farmers. Each village has a common social dance, usually performed by mature boys and girls. While facing each other, they dance with small rhythmic steps and extended upper-body motion and display to virtuoso drumming by a single drummer striking any available resonating surface. These dances are performed spontaneously—usually during the dry season when farmwork is finished—at evening gatherings of young unmarried men and women. Such social dances are known as *bul.*

Other Nuba dances are more specialized. For example, the *nyertuŋ* is a dance that commonly accompanies praise-song cycles executed by male drummers and female choruses. These songs exalt the men's wrestling and fighting prowess and agricultural successes. The accompanying dances are performed around a community men's hut by nubile girls under the tutelage of older

women. From time to time, the men rise and prance in response to the praise of themselves and their kinsmen.

The *nyertuŋ* praise-song dance is the most choreographically elaborate of the Nuba dances. It also manifests an overt female sensuality in the dancers' graceful long strides and dramatic hip-swaying poses. Even more explicitly, at a specific drum cadence a dancer may honor one of the young men being praised by putting a leg over his shoulder. This may also be an invitation to a later rendezvous. The men, on hearing their praises, perform a slow, preening step and work themselves into an emotional, almost trancelike state that culminates in a screamed challenge, usually directed toward the drummers and chorus.

Some southeastern Nuba communities have mature women's a cappella singing and dancing groups known as *kama*. They perform on request, for payment, or on occasions such as the funerals of their members or other important people in the community. The songs are usually paeans, with stylized lyrics, which often involve archaic and rhetorical references that commonly celebrate the successes of men. The choreography is relatively simple, sometimes involving graceful lunges and retreating motions, reminiscent of those used in spearing.

Drumming for dances may involve as many as three or four voices, each with a separate but harmonizing rhythmic function. Only men drum, but both men and women sing praise songs and dance.

The increasing Islamic influence in the Nuba territories will probably mean the demise, or at least the change, of many dances—just as the spread of Christianity has altered or repressed indigenous dance elsewhere in Africa.

[*For related discussion, see* Central and East Africa; and Sub-Saharan Africa.]

BIBLIOGRAPHY

Faris, James C. *Nuba Personal Art.* London, 1972.

Faris, James C. "Nuba." In *Muslim Peoples: A World Ethnographic Survey,* edited by Richard V. Weekes. Westport, Conn., 1984.

Faris, James C. *Southeast Nuba Social Relations.* Aachen, 1989.

Riefenstahl, Leni. *The People of Kau.* Translated by J. Maxwell Brownjohn. New York, 1976.

FILM. *Southeast Nuba,* produced by C. Curling (BBC, Bristol, 1982).

JAMES C. FARIS

NUBIAN DANCE. *See* Egypt, *article on* Traditional Dance.

NUREYEV, RUDOLF (Rudol'f Khametovich Nureev; born 17 March 1938 in Siberia, near Irkutsk, died 5 January 1993 in Paris), ballet dancer, choreographer, and company director. It is possible that the dancing of Rudolf Nureyev was seen by more people than that of any other dancer in history. During much of his career, which spanned more than twenty-five years, he regularly danced more than 250 performances a year. He danced for television and in films and also acted in films. He choreographed original ballets, restaged ballets from the Russian nineteenth-century repertory for Western companies, and presented ballet on Broadway. His repertory included more than one hundred roles. After he died at age fifty-four from complications from AIDS, it was learned he had danced for ten years after being infected with the illness.

Nureyev's brilliant but often erratic dancing and his flamboyance made him a controversial figure. He presented not merely his dancing but also himself as a work of art, and his career belongs as much to the history of publicity as to the history of ballet. In his prime, from about 1963 to about 1973, he was an exotically beautiful man who emanated sensitivity and animality, intelligence and blind instinct. The furious abandon of his dancing and his presentation of himself onstage as a sex object are without parallel in the world of dance. He became a folk hero and a symbol of his era. The unevenness of his technique disqualified him as a true virtuoso, yet his dancing commanded virtuoso elements of unsurpassed grandeur—specifically, a variety of enormous, slow jumps and air turns that elicited gasps of surprise and spontaneous applause from audiences for nearly a decade. One of his teachers during the early 1960s reported that Nureyev could jump ten feet into the air from a simple *plié.* His bravura delivery was modulated by a highly poetic style and eloquent legato phrasing based on an acute musical awareness.

Nureyev was born in Siberia and raised in Ufa, then the capital city of the Bashkir A.S.S.R., a part of the Soviet Union. Both his parents were Bashkir Tatars. His first memories were of the excitement of hearing music on the radio, an excitement that escalated when he learned a few Bashkirian folk dances at school. The first time he saw a ballet, *The Cranes' Song,* at the Ufa Opera House when he was seven, he felt called to devote his life to dancing. His early training consisted of learning folk dances as a member of his Young Pioneers group. He studied with local teachers until the age of seventeen, when he won admission to the Vaganova Choreographic Institute in Leningrad and soon became a much-favored pupil of Aleksandr Pushkin. During the last of his three years at the conservatory, he was accorded the school's highest honor—appearances with the Kirov Ballet in the lead parts of nine different ballets. For his graduation he danced the *Le Corsaire* pas de deux with Alla Sizova. He gave his first appearance as a member of the Kirov, as a principal dancer, in November 1958, partnering Natalia Dudinskaya, then the Kirov's leading ballerina, in *Lauren-*

cia, a performance said to have entered legend before it was over. Critics and the public quickly hailed Nureyev as successor to the heroically poetic style of Soviet male dancing as evinced by Aleksei Yermolayev and Vakhtang Chabukiani. He soon acquired a cult following among the public, although Soviet authorities considered his individuality and his curiosity about unorthodox interpretations and performing styles the expression of a pathological personality. Other notable performances in the Soviet Union included appearances with Ninel Kurgapkina and Alla Shelest.

In his years with the Kirov, Nureyev amassed a large repertory, dancing the leading male roles in nineteenth-century classics, experimental works such as Leonid Yakobson's *Valse Volonté,* and nationalist ballets such as Nina Anisimova's *Gayané* and Vasily Vainonen's *The Flames of Paris.* He altered costumes to maximize his appearance, revised the steps in his variations, and refused to wear any of the then-customary wigs. While this behavior was tolerated, his "above the law" status made him enemies, especially among rival male dancers, and alienated the Kirov's director, Konstantin Sergeyev. His friendships were outside the theater, arousing the suspicion of the authorities.

Efforts were made to keep Nureyev away from contact with foreigners, and when the Kirov scheduled a tour to Paris in 1961, Nureyev was included only at the insistence of presenters. Once in Paris, Nureyev cultivated new, Western friends. When the Kirov was about to depart for another stop in London, Nureyev was informed he was being sent back to Russia on the next flight. He could claim asylum only by approaching the French police, who could not intervene unsolicited; while he waited, guarded by two KGB agents, in the departure lounge, a pair of French policemen were alerted to the situation and placed themselves a few feet away. Nureyev found an opportunity to run to them and ask for the protection of the French government, which was instantly granted. It was the first political defection by a Soviet artist and a defining moment in the Cold War.

Within a week of Nureyev's defection he was dancing again in Paris with the Grand Ballet du Marquis de Cuevas, alternating as Prince Florimund and the Bluebird in *The Sleeping Beauty.*

Nureyev made his American debut in Chicago in October 1961 as a guest artist with the Chicago Opera Ballet. His New York debut at the Brooklyn Academy of Music—partnering Sonia Arova in the *Don Quixote* pas de deux—followed a few weeks later. His London debut occurred later that fall when he danced in Margot Fonteyn's annual gala benefit performance at the Theatre Royal, Drury Lane. His Covent Garden debut with the Royal Ballet on 21 February 1962 marked his first performance with Fonteyn and the beginning of an alliance that became one

NUREYEV. Prior to his defection to the West, Nureyev appeared with Irina Kolpakova in a Kirov Ballet production of *Giselle.* This publicity photograph was taken about 1960. (Photograph by M. Gershmaya; from the Dance Collection, New York Public Library for the Performing Arts.)

of the most celebrated in ballet. Soon afterward Ninette de Valois invited him to work regularly with the Royal Ballet as a guest artist.

For the next ten years Nureyev appeared in virtually every Covent Garden season of the Royal Ballet. He also danced with the Royal Ballet in New York in nine seasons from 1963 to 1976, seasons often followed by extensive tours of the United States. During his early tenure with the Royal Ballet he danced a wide range of parts, including Frederick Ashton's *Symphonic Variations* and works by Kenneth MacMillan, but the English ballet masters were dubious about Nureyev's idiosyncratic readings of English ballets. After his enormous successes in New York with Fonteyn, the company began to exploit, with his consent, his star appeal by showing him almost exclusively in classical Romantic ballets. Most often he was opposite Fonteyn, but he also danced with Nadia Nerina, Svetlana Beriosova, Merle Park, Antoinette Sibley, and Monica Mason.

NUREYEV. The Royal Ballet's production of Kenneth MacMillan's *Romeo and Juliet* (1965) provided Nureyev and Margot Fonteyn with another pair of ideal roles in which to display their celebrated partnership. (Photograph from the Dance Collection, New York Public Library for the Performing Arts.)

Two of the biggest hits were Kenneth MacMillan's *Romeo and Juliet* (1965), which the company expropriated for Nureyev and Fonteyn, the piece having been choreographed for Lynn Seymour and Christopher Gable, and Frederick Ashton's *Marguerite and Armand* (1963). The latter piece capitalized on the popular sentiment surrounding the two lead dancers. Fonteyn, nearing the end of her career, relived the life of the dying courtesan, while Nureyev, whose defection the press had called a "leap to freedom," executed his famous leaps around the stage. In effect, Ashton presented Nureyev in this ballet as the live version of a movie star: his entrance was announced by the projection of a series of close-up photographs of his face on a scrim that covered the entire stage opening.

Nureyev achieved his most distinguished dancing during the years he worked regularly with the Royal Ballet. His partnership with Fonteyn was one of the artistic highlights of the era: his rejuvenating effect on her helped her to extend her career for another decade. Fonteyn had a taming effect on Nureyev without squelching his spontaneous excitement; her quiet nobility was juxtaposed against his incendiary intensity. Nureyev's dancing with the prestigious Royal Ballet and his dutiful, impassioned attendance on Fonteyn in such ballets as *Swan Lake* and *The Sleeping Beauty* also lent him a kind of legitimacy, a validation of his seriousness of purpose that, because of his notoriety in the press, he might not have otherwise achieved.

Acting as an unofficial ballet master, Nureyev also staged several important works and individual dances for the company: *Raymonda,* act 3; the Kingdom of the Shades scene from *La Bayadère;* the pas de six from *Laurencia;* the pas de deux from *Gayané, Le Corsaire,* and *Diana and Actaeon;* an act 1 polonaise and an act 3 mazurka from *Swan Lake;* and a male solo from act 1 of *Swan Lake* that subsequently became a virtually obligatory feature of *Swan Lake* productions worldwide. His staging of the Shades scene from *La Bayadère* (1963), after his recollection of the Kirov Ballet's production, was, as Western audiences later discovered, superior to the Soviet productions. *La Bayadère,* more than a vehicle for Nureyev and Fonteyn, was an exercise in eloquence for the entire company. It became the hallmark of the Royal Ballet's lyric, legato style and remained so for as long as they performed it.

Nureyev persuaded the Royal Ballet to rethink its ideas about how ballerinas were cast for roles. Until his intervention, the company favored a casting policy based almost entirely on considerations of physique and temperament, the equivalent of typecasting in the movies. He encouraged the company to give dancers opportunities, most often in ballets that he had staged, out of concern for their ability to execute the technique required for an effective demonstration of the role. This expansion of plastic possibilities greatly enhanced the company's texture and profile. If this period was a high-water mark for Nureyev, it was no less than that for the Royal Ballet, whose style was never more sharply focused than when he was an integral part of the company.

It is ironic that Nureyev made his greatest impact as a dancer in *La Bayadère, Swan Lake, Giselle, The Sleeping Beauty, Les Sylphides, La Fille Mal Gardée,* and pas de deux showpieces from *Le Corsaire* and *Diana and Actaeon*—ballets in which the man is required to do little more than partner the ballerina and dance a variation. Although he worked sporadically with all the most important choreographers in the West (including an opera ballet with George Balanchine), he never had an important role created for him, nor did he ever have a substantial collaboration with any choreographer. His triumphs in ballets not designed to give him central importance are all the more dramatic, because he engendered those triumphs himself.

Nureyev's readings of these Romantic ballets were without rival in his time and have become the models with which present and future interpreters must contend. Besides his solo dancing, he was a sensitive partner who brought a Byronic élan to his readings of the prince roles. His wide-eyed, transfixed air of amazement on first seeing the Swan Queen; the rash, impulsive gestures he made as he tried to embrace her; his gentleness and courtliness with her: these actions did more than vivify what was at best a secondary role; they sharpened our attention on the ballerina, and we saw her through his eyes. In so doing, Nureyev restated for our time, in a novel and daring way, the controlling metaphor of classical Romantic ballet: man is the poet, the seeker; the ballerina is music, poetry, enchantment itself, the prize sought.

Nureyev was never a permanent member of any ballet company, nor was he ever invited to become one. He did not want to confine himself to a single repertory or style, and no important company wanted to present itself merely as a showcase for Nureyev at the expense of its other dancers' development. By allowing himself to be exploited by impresarios and managements, he found that the demands of the public escalated. People wanted to see more of him in the kinds of ballets for which he was famous or in other types of performances in which he was always present on stage. Because of this public demand and because he had no choreographer to create roles for him that would enhance his development, Nureyev began to make ballets for himself. These were usually revisions of the nineteenth-century ballets in which he inflated the male role with his own choreography and truncated the ballerina's significance. He revised, among others, *The Sleeping Beauty, Swan Lake, Raymonda* in several versions other than the act 3 dances produced by the Royal Ballet, and *Don Quixote*. His original ballets include *The Nutcracker, Tancredi, Romeo and Juliet, The Tempest,* and *Washington Square*.

Nureyev always danced with many different ballet companies, even when he worked regularly with the Royal Ballet. But by the mid-1970s when his bravura abilities had begun to fade, he received even fewer invitations to work with the Royal Ballet. Increasingly from that point on, he began making numerous tours with mediocre companies that featured him prominently. He even danced with modern dance companies—including those of Martha Graham (who created *The Scarlet Letter* for him), Paul Taylor, and Murray Louis—and with Maurice Béjart's Ballet du XXe Siècle. He danced with American Ballet Theatre, La Scala Ballet, New York City Opera Ballet, London Festival Ballet, the Royal Swedish Ballet, the Vienna State Opera Ballet, the Australian Ballet, the National Ballet of Canada, the Dutch National Ballet, the Joffrey Ballet, the Berlin Opera Ballet, and the Paris Opera Ballet. Under the headline "Nureyev and Friends," he appeared several times on Broadway in New York and in various other cities in America and Europe. His movie credits include *A Leap of the Soul, Swan Lake, Romeo and Juliet, I Am a Dancer, Don Quixote, Valentino,* and *Exposed*. (In the latter two films he had straight acting parts.)

In 1983 Nureyev became the artistic director of the Paris Opera Ballet. He produced new and experimental work by choreographers from many countries, brought in guest teachers from important schools and companies, and provided challenging opportunities for the artists who were his responsibility. The central core of his curriculum, however, remained an emphasis on the classical style.

Nureyev had a pronounced, nearly immediate impact on the Paris Opera's roster, finding a way to promote young talent quickly despite the institution's entrenched "trial by jury" examination system. Among the dancers he brought to prominence were Sylvie Guillem, Elisabeth Platel, Isabelle Guerin, Charles Jude, Laurent Hilaire, and Manuel Legris. In 1984, when Guillem was nineteen, Nureyev made her the youngest *étoile* in the company's history. His policies also had a major impact on repertory; in addition to choreographing or staging many works himself, he acquired works by Merce Cunningham, Paul Taylor, and Jerome Robbins and commissioned pieces by

NUREYEV. As Prince Désiré in his 1972 production of *The Sleeping Beauty*, for the National Ballet of Canada, Nureyev demonstrates his sublime aristocratic poise. (Photograph by Anthony Crickmay; used by permission of the Board of Trustees of the Theatre Museum, London.)

NUREYEV. Choreographer Murray Louis worked with Nureyev in 1975 and again in 1978. With Bill Hollahan (left), Nureyev is seen here in a 1978 revival of Louis's *Moments,* which premiered with the Scottish Ballet in 1975. (Photograph © 1978 by Jack Vartoogian; used by permission.)

young groundbreakers such as Maguy Marin, William Forsythe, Karole Armitage, and David Parsons.

During the entire period of his tenure at the Paris Opera, Nureyev was ill with AIDS. He was diagnosed in 1984 after a period of recurrent illnesses. He sought the newest treatments available and continued a punishing performing schedule, keeping the knowledge of his diagnosis private while rumors circulated.

In 1987, when his mother was dying in Ufa, Nureyev, who had not seen her in twenty-seven years, was permitted a brief visit by the government of Mikhail Gorbachev. Two years later, he returned to Leningrad to dance with the Kirov. He was very ill but danced all five scheduled performances.

Despite a directorship viewed throughout the ballet world as a remarkable success, relations between Nureyev and the management of the Paris Opera frayed beyond repair by the end of the 1988/89 season. For one thing, although he had agreed to a certain (minimal) number of days annual residence at the Opera, peripatetic Nureyev was not quite able to fulfill this part of his contract. The flashpoint was his wish to promote a green corps dancer, the handsome twenty-one-year-old Dane Kenneth Greve, almost overnight to the status of *étoile.* The company threatened a strike, and Nureyev departed to undertake a nine-month tour of the musical *The King and I.* After the tour, he returned to Nureyev and Friends, but his weak condition was unmistakable. He performed for the last time in February 1992.

His last artistic project consisted of staging a three-act version of *La Bayadère* for the Paris Opera Ballet. The rehearsal process was interrupted for his frequent hospital stays, but the production had its premiere on 8 October 1992. Nureyev, who attended in a wheelchair, was awarded the medal of the Legion of Honor at the end of the evening.

Nureyev's career, outstanding in many respects, was further notable for the extraordinary financial fortune he amassed: he was renowned as the wealthiest man in ballet, with an estate, its amount closely guarded, estimated to be between $25 million and $80 million. He was a thrifty millionaire with a profound distaste for paying taxes and a talent for picking financial advisers. At the time of his death, his estate included a Mediterranean island, museum-quality furnishing for his several homes, and numerous classical and European art treasures worth upward of $250,000 each.

BIBLIOGRAPHY

Ballet Review 21 (Winter 1993): 27–37. Section entitled "A Tribute to Rudolf Nureyev."

Barnes, Clive. *Nureyev.* New York, 1982.

Bland, Alexander. *The Nureyev Image.* London and New York, 1976.

Bland, Alexander. *Fonteyn and Nureyev: The Story of a Partnership.* London and New York, 1979.

Gosling, Maude. "Nureyev in the West." *Ballet Review* 22 (Spring 1994): 32–40.

Gruen, John. *People Who Dance: Twenty-two Dancers Tell Their Own Stories.* Princeton, N.J., 1988.

Houseal, Joseph. "Peter Brinson: About Nureyev." *Ballet Review* 22 (Summer 1994): 59–63.

Houseal, Joseph. "Dame Ninette de Valois: Remembering Rudolf Nureyev." *Ballet Review* 22 (Summer 1994): 52–58.

Money, Keith. *Fonteyn and Nureyev: The Great Years.* London, 1994.

Nureyev, Rudolf. *Nureyev: An Autobiography with Pictures.* London, 1962. Includes an introduction and afterword by Alexander Bland, and photographs by Richard Avedon et al.

Percival, John. *Nureyev: Aspects of the Dancer.* New York, 1975.

Pierpont, Claudia Roth. "Nouvelles Cendrillons." *Ballet Review* 15 (Summer 1987): 93–100.

Stuart, Otis. *Perpetual Motion: The Public and Private Lives of Rudolf Nureyev.* New York, 1994.

Verdy, Violette, and David Daniel. "Speaking of Nureyev." *Ballet Review* 5.2 (1975–1976): 45–53.

Watson, Peter. *Nureyev: A Biography.* London, 1994.

INTERVIEWS. Merle Park, Alexander Minz, and Frederick Ashton, by David Daniel (New York).

VIDEOTAPE. See Virginia Loring Brooks, "Dance on Screen," *Ballet Review* 22 (Summer 1994): 85–95, for a list of documentary programs and performances recorded on videotape.

DAVID DANIEL
Amended by Anita Finkel

NUTCRACKER, THE. [*This entry comprises two articles on ballets choreographed to the score for "The Nutcracker," written by Petr Ilich Tchaikovsky: the first is a description of the original production in Saint Petersburg in 1892 and a survey of subsequent productions in Russia; the second is a survey of productions outside Russia.*]

Productions in Russia

In 1888, Ivan Vsevolozhsky, director of the Imperial Theaters in Russia, asked Tchaikovsky to compose a score for a ballet based on an outline he had made of Charles Perrault's fairy tale "The Sleeping Beauty." The success of this work, choreographed by Marius Petipa and presented at the Maryinsky Theater in Saint Petersburg in January 1890, led Vsevolozhsky to approach Tchaikovsky again, toward the end of 1890, with a proposal for a two-act ballet based on a fairy tale by E. T. A. Hoffmann. The resulting work, *The Nutcracker,* first presented at the Maryinsky in 1892, would join Tchaikovsky's earlier works, *Swan Lake* and *The Sleeping Beauty,* to form a trio of the best-loved and most frequently performed ballets of all time.

Original Production. Russian title: *Shchelkunchik.* Ballet in two acts. Choreography: Lev Ivanov. Music: Petr Ilich Tchaikovsky. Libretto: Ivan Vsevolozhsky and Marius Petipa, based on E. T. A. Hoffmann's "The Nutcracker and the Mouse King." Scenery: Konstantin Ivanov. First performance: 6 [18] December 1892, Maryinsky Theater, Saint Petersburg. Principals: Stanislava Belinskaya (Clara), Sergei Legat (The Nutcracker), Antonietta Dell'Era (The Sugarplum Fairy), Pavel Gerdt (Prince Coqueluche), Timofei Stukolkin (Drosselmeyer).

The musical and choreographic plan of the new ballet was made by Marius Petipa. The unsophisticated plot, based on a story by E. T. A. Hoffmann, allowed for quite a few spectacular stage effects: a children's party (in the first act), a large *divertissement* (in the second act), a battle scene, scenes of a journey, changes of the seasons, and a blend of genre and fairy-tale life. Seeking to overcome the psychological uncertainty of the libretto, the fragmented character of its scenes, and the gaps between its acts, Tchaikovsky emphasized detail, down to observing the length and number of bars in the dance numbers. He opposed the conception of the ballet as a whimsical piece and a doll festival, reinterpreting the plan and the libretto and creating, as musicologist Boris Asafiev put it, a "superlative artistic masterpiece . . . a symphony of childhood" about the first anticipation of adulthood and a dream of happiness. *The Nutcracker* was closely linked with Tchaikovsky's early compositions for children, primarily his *Children's Album.*

THE NUTCRACKER: Productions in Russia. A scene from act 1 of the original production, with Stanislava Belinskaya as Clara and, probably, Vasily Stukolkin as her brother Fritz and Lydia Rubtsova as Marianna, their cousin. All three were students at the Imperial Theater School at the time of the premiere, as was Sergei Legat, who played the role of the Nutcracker. Act 1 began with the scene of a holiday party at the home of President Silberhaus and his wife, parents of Clara and Fritz, featuring the lighting of the Christmas tree, the giving of gifts to the children, and dancing and games by the assembled company. (Photograph from the A. A. Bakrushin Central State Theatrical Museum, Moscow.)

THE NUTCRACKER: Productions in Russia. The "Waltz of the Flowers" from the Vainonen production of 1934, as performed by the Kirov Ballet in 1961. This famous waltz, danced by the female ensemble, led choreographically to the *grand pas de deux* near the end of the second act. When performed together on a program of *divertissements*, these two dances were billed as *The Rose Waltz*. (Photograph from a Leningrad Kirov Ballet souvenir program, 1961.)

Petipa fell ill before rehearsals began and handed over his plan of the production to his assistant, Lev Ivanov, a choreographer of rare musicality. However, Ivanov was handicapped by Petipa's plan and denied effective support by Vsevolozhsky, who was prone to dictate his own terms, and thus he failed to find the right dance images for the first scene. Moreover, in the second act, he overemphasized the sugary fairy scenes. The child's dreamworld that he created was not a longing for happiness or a quest for an ideal, but rather a rich and expensive sweetmeats shop: after various adventures, the protagonists find themselves in a kingdom of coffee, nuts, sugarplums, lemonade, and candies. This contradicted the music and its message of struggle for happiness. Nevertheless, in the "Waltz of Snowflakes" (the second scene of the first act), Ivanov managed to reveal the hidden meaning of the score. By creating a mood of anxiety and anticipation of the future, he conveyed the lyrical content of the music as a story about the destiny of the characters and a poetic reflection of their spirit. Unfortunately, Ivanov's choreography to this waltz has not survived.

Subsequent Productions. The perceived flaws of the first production of *The Nutcracker* induced later choreographers to seek new interpretations and to renounce in principal even the most valuable innovations of the Saint Petersburg production. Among those who mounted notable productions in Russia were Aleksandr Gorsky, Fedor Lopukhov, Vasily Vainonen, and Yuri Grigorovich.

Gorsky production. In the twentieth century, the stage history of *The Nutcracker* began with Aleksandr Gorsky, who staged the ballet at Moscow's Bolshoi Theater in 1919. As choreographer, Gorsky intensified the elements of fairy-tale fantasy, making a three-act ballet for children. He isolated the "Waltz of Snowflakes" in a separate act, to which he transferred the *grand pas de deux* from the original second act. Gorsky was the first to initiate a genre tendency in the interpretations of *The Nutcracker*. In the first scene he portrayed Drosselmeyer as an old, burgher-like man whose wife (a character invented by Gorsky) was courted by young men. Clara fell asleep near an enormous window covered with hoarfrost patterns. The miracles of the fairy tale became the play of a child's imagination, which had its source in real life; the Snowflakes, for example, were dressed in fur coats and fur caps, and Santa Clauses marched across the stage.

Lopukhov production. The next milestone in the Russian history of *The Nutcracker* was Fedor Lopukhov's version at the Kirov Theater in Leningrad in 1929. It was a controversial experimental production that was almost immediately dropped from the repertory and unanimously denounced by the public and the critics. Nevertheless, the experience proved edifying, its influence on all later interpretations of the ballet not yet fully appreciated.

Relying on the experience of the drama theater of Vsevolod Meyerhold and Evgeny Vakhtangov, the choreographer devised the production as a revue, a form that was popular in those years. The ballet was broken up into twenty-two episodes, each of which was a complete scene that contrasted a child's world of play and fantasy to the world of middle-class pragmatism, presented in a panorama of masked images of Old Russia that included a tsarist general, a landlady, the tsarina, a maid of honor, and an official with a briefcase. The child's fantasy appeared in grotesque colors with acrobatic elements, the action developed against a background of moving colored panels designed by the artist Vladimir Dmitriev, the Snowflakes appeared as showgirls, and the leads in a winter waltz rode on a barrier, while in the second-act waltz cyclists rode around the stage. This satirical approach to the poetic conflict of the ballet naturally led the choreographer away from the lyrical, psychologically nuanced music. Lopukhov arbitrarily mingled episodes from the fairy tale with contemporary motifs, using a recital of Hoffmann's text to accompany the dances.

In spite of these quirks, Lopukhov's version introduced elements that became standard in successive productions: the role of Clara was renamed Masha and was danced by a ballerina, in this case, Olga Mungalova; the second-act pas de deux was performed by the protagonists, rather than the Sugarplum Fairy and her cavalier; the action defined the polarity between reality and Masha's dream, from which she awakens in the finale. In essence, Lopukhov was seeking a way back to the ballet's literary source.

Vainonen production. In the next version of the ballet, produced by the choreographer Vasily Vainonen at the Kirov Opera and Ballet Theater in Leningrad in 1934, a different approach to the music was used. The action unfolded in a realistic, authentically depicted environment, in which all the miraculous transformations and fantastic adventures of the fairy tale were motivated by Masha's dream. Vainonen continued in part Gorsky's innovation and used some of Lopukhov's ideas as well. In contrast to the latter, however, he avoided confusion of genre scenes and fantasy. The first act presented a genre episode: a Christmas party in a respectable burgher's home. In attempting to describe the event realistically, Vainonen lost the poetry and lyricism characteristic of Tchaikovsky's score, which was devoted to events that were extraordinary. The choreographer had failed to take this into account; in his interpretation Masha was an ordinary girl, and the world around her harbored nothing fantastic. Therefore, her dream did not extend beyond the limits of the everyday.

Although Vainonen largely followed Gorsky's version, seeking to present the ballet as a classical performance in three acts, it was also oriented to an audience of children and included children in the cast. The choreographer had thoroughly planned all the genre motivations of the action, then gave free rein to his fantasy in two large dance

THE NUTCRACKER: Productions in Russia. A scene from Masha's Journey in the Grigorovich production of 1966, as performed by the Bolshoi Ballet in the late 1960s. The ensemble performs a dramatic dance before the ever-present Christmas tree, atop which blazes the star of hope and happiness. (Photograph from the Dance Collection, New York Public Library for the Performing Arts.)

scenes: the "Waltz of Snowflakes" in the first act, and the Waltz of the Flowers with a pas de deux in the second act. These episodes were plastically varied, very complex technically, and rather independent in form. In the "Waltz of Snowflakes," however, Vainonen intensified its imitative features, while in the pas de deux, looking back to *The Sleeping Beauty* and Aurora's adagio with four cavaliers (Masha performs an adagio with partners), he used acrobatic supports suggested by Lopukhov's version. These fragments of virtuosic classical choreography were egregious and lent a degree of uncertainty to its genre nature; most important, their contemplative mood made them alien to the music.

Nevertheless, Vainonen's logically impeccable version remained for more than thirty years the only acceptable version of the ballet. It was invariably in the repertory of all leading Soviet ballet companies and is still extant at some theaters. The greatest modern ballerinas, ranging from Galina Ulanova to Irina Kolpakova, danced the role of Masha in this version.

Grigorovich production. In 1966 *The Nutcracker* was produced by Yuri Grigorovich for Moscow's Bolshoi Ballet. He returned to the two-act version and completely restored the composer's original score. Relying upon the music, the dramatic movement and imagery suggested by it, Grigorovich carefully revised the libretto, taking into account the experience of all his predecessors. No schoolchildren danced in the ballet, and the roles of Masha's friends, her brother, and his friends were entrusted to professional dancers. In this way he was able to build the first scene on continuous dancing, without adapting it to the needs of child dancers. This scene was in harmony with the music as a poetic narrative of the world of childhood. Furthermore, the image of Drosselmeyer as one of Hoffmann's eccentric dreamers endowed with mysterious demonic power assumed significance.

The episode of the growth of the Christmas tree and Masha's journey to a fantastic world was depicted not by imitative means (by replacing a child with an adult ballerina, as had been the case in Vainonen's production) but by a dramatic ritual dance. Without losing sight of the destiny of the protagonists, Grigorovich introduced them into the scene of the "Waltz of Snowflakes," which then reflected new love. The choreographer sensed the thrust of Tchaikovsky's music: its poetry, its central theme of a quest for an ideal, the brief discovery of this ideal, and the end of a dream in the return to ordinary life. The set designer, Simon Virsaladze, created the image of a constantly changing Christmas tree that ran throughout the production. The plot of the ballet, after the Nutcracker's liberation from his monstrous mask, was interpreted by Grigorovich as the hero's journey to the top of the Christmas tree, toward the star of hope and happiness and the shining expanses of the sky. The journey was crowned in the concluding pas de deux with a solemn though slightly sad wedding. Grigorovich's achievement was the reinterpretation of *The Nutcracker* as a ballet for adult audiences, without changing its fantastic nature. He preserved its sharp humor and grotesquerie, which blended with the overall lyrical atmosphere of the action. This production served to showcase the talent of many leading Soviet dancers, among them Vladimir Vasiliev, Mikhail Lavrovsky, Ekaterina Maximova, Natalia Bessmertnova, Yuri Vladimirov, and Ludmila Semenyaka.

Other versions. At the end of the 1960s new versions of *The Nutcracker* followed two trends. One was in the tradition of Ivanov and Vainonen, for whom *The Nutcracker* was a children's fairy tale. The other reverted to Hoffmann, evoking the dramatic if not tragic meaning of the story. The version by Igor Chernyshev (Odessa in 1969, Kuibyshev in 1978) stressed the idea that middle-class neutrality ruins all real values in life. Igor Belsky at the Maly Theater in Leningrad (1969) speculated on hopes that were never to be fulfilled. In 1989 Nikolai Boyarchikov created in Perm a new version, which included some of the Vainonen choreography.

[*See also the entries on the principal choreographers mentioned herein.*]

BIBLIOGRAPHY

Beaumont, Cyril W. *Complete Book of Ballets.* Rev. ed. London, 1951.

Brown, David. "Tchaikovsky's Ballets: *The Nutcracker.*" *Dance Now* 2 (Autumn 1993): 28–39.

Demidov, Alexander P. "Kukolny Dom." *Teatr,* no. 3 (1970).

Dobrovolskaya, Galina N. *Shchelkunchik.* Saint Petersberg, 1996.

Grigorovich, Yuri, and Alexander Demidov. *The Official Bolshoi Ballet Book of the Nutcracker.* Translated by Yuri S. Shirokov. Neptune, N.J., 1986.

Maynard, Olga. "The Ballet of *The Nutcracker.*" In Maynard's *The Ballet Companion.* Philadelphia, 1957.

Maynard, Olga. "*The Nutcracker* History." *Dance Magazine* (December 1982): HC6–HC12.

Maynard, Olga. "*The Nutcracker* Story." *Dance Magazine* (December 1982): HC1–HC6.

Slonimsky, Yuri. *P. I. Chaikovskii i baletnyi teatr ego vremeni.* Moscow, 1956.

Souritz, Elizabeth. *Soviet Choreographers in the 1920s.* Translated by Lynn Visson. Durham, N.C., 1990.

Souritz, Elizabeth. "One Hundred Years of *The Nutcracker* in Russia." *Ballet Review* 20 (Fall 1992): 77–84.

Swinson, Cyril, ed. *The Nutcracker.* London, 1960.

Vanslov, Victor V. *Balety Grigorovicha i problemy khoreografii.* 2d ed. Moscow, 1971.

Wiley, Roland John. "On Meaning in *Nutcracker.*" *Dance Research* 3 (Autumn 1984): 3–38.

Wiley, Roland John, comp. *A Production Plan for Nutcracker.* N.p., 1984.

Wiley, Roland John. *Tchaikovsky's Ballets: "Swan Lake," "Sleeping Beauty," "Nutcracker."* Oxford, 1985.

Wiley, Roland John. *The Life and Ballets of Lev Ivanov, Choreographer of "The Nutcracker" and "Swan Lake."* Oxford, 1997.

ALEXANDER P. DEMIDOV
Translated from Russian

Productions outside Russia

In the West, *The Nutcracker* has become considered by many a Christmas entertainment, with its act 1 an essay on the virtues and support of family life and its act 2 a vision of the risks and powers of imagination. Clara has remained the heroine of the tale (though some productions call her Marie), and it is her character that the ballet develops as it concurrently plumbs deeper, more elusive themes: the nostalgia for innocence, the permeable nature of dreams.

Western conceptions of *The Nutcracker* divide along fairly consistent lines. Those *Nutcracker*s aimed at a younger audience tend to retain the traditional staging. Modeled on the original Maryinsky version brought to the West in the memories of Russian dancers and the notebooks of Nicholas Sergeyev, these productions generally use a child in the role of Clara. The role of Sugarplum Fairy is taken by a ballerina (as is the role of Snow Queen, if one is included) and given a classical pas de deux in the act 2 *divertissements*. The model of these *Nutcracker*s is the production that George Balanchine mounted for the New York City Ballet in 1954. Balanchine sought not only to restore Hoffmann's dark and poetic undertones (which had been lost in the Dumas translation used by Petipa) but strove as well to re-create the *Nutcracker* of his childhood. His *Nutcracker* act 1, lovingly detailed and cozily realistic, contains breathtaking scenes of transformation, which then give way to a sumptuous, grandly scaled act 2 of *divertissement*. While the production was an instant box-office success, early critical reaction was skeptical, worried that the ballet was not appropriate for a modern company. Balanchine's *Nutcracker*, however, served as the blueprint for innumerable American productions, and by the 1980s more than three hundred *Nutcrackers* were performed in the United States each year. Furthermore, it is often the sold-out performances of *Nutcracker* that finance a company's more adventurous productions.

*Nutcracker*s that depart from tradition usually do so in an attempt to create a more satisfying, adult entertainment. Stressing the psychoanalytic elements of the story, they seek to integrate acts 1 and 2 with thematic density and to extract a worldly story from Petipa's sugary ballet. The ballet's break between acts is not just a jump from reality to make-believe; it becomes a subtle shift from the conscious to the subconscious. These *Nutcracker*s invariably choose to place an adult dancer in the role of Clara, a substitution that makes it a ballerina role, allowing her to dance the Sugarplum pas de deux with her Prince.

In a traditional *Nutcracker*, Drosselmeyer may be presented in a range of ways: from loving uncle to tinkering old fool to ominous family friend. But as the version becomes less orthodox, it is usually Drosselmeyer on whom the change hinges. In Rudolf Nureyev's "Freudian" production, Drosselmeyer is identified with the Prince, so it becomes a double role for the lead male. Mikhail Baryshnikov's version presents Drosselmeyer as a patriarch with a puppet master's control over Clara's dream. She follows her Prince into act 2 and finally loosens Drosselmeyer's hold on her imagination. John Neumeier's version, possibly the most eccentric of all, turns Drosselmeyer into a ballet master who choreographs a series of dances that are, in effect, act 2.

THE NUTCRACKER: Productions outside Russia. Marilyn Burr and Flemming Flindt in a 1955 performance of the "Waltz of the Snowflakes" with London's Festival Ballet. This production was mounted by Nicholas Beriozoff, after Ivanov, in 1951. (Photograph by Blick; reprinted from Koegler, *Ballett International*, Berlin, 1960, fig. 2.)

The emergence of *The Nutcracker* in the Western world can be likened to a tiny rivulet that becomes a flood. Bits and pieces of *The Nutcracker* first turned up in the repertory of Serge Diaghilev's Ballets Russes. These included a solo *trepak* to the "Buffoon's Dance," choreographed by Mikhail Fokine for Georgi Rosai in 1909, and a Fokine-arranged solo for Vaslav Nijinsky to the Sugarplum Fairy celesta variation, inserted in, of all things, *Swan Lake* (featuring Matilda Kshessinska) during the 1911 London season. Still later, in London in 1920, the Sugarplum Fairy solo was added to the Lilac Fairy's role (danced by Lydia Lopokova) in Diaghilev's revival of *The Sleeping Princess*, while fairy-tale visitors were inserted into the last act to the music of "Danse Arabe" and "Danse Chinoise" (choreographed by Bronislava Nijinska). In 1931, also in London, the Ballet de L'Opéra Russe à Paris presented Felia Doubrovska and Valentin Froman in the adagio from the snowflake scene of *The Nutcracker.* Meanwhile, Americans had a taste of *The Nutcracker* when Anna Pavlova's company presented *Snowflakes* in 1915 at the Manhattan Opera House. Staged by Ivan Clustine and using music from both *Swan Lake* and *The Nutcracker*'s snow scene, it presented Pavlova and Alexandre Volinine as a Snow Queen and her Prince. These were the first Western incarnations of *The Nutcracker,* fragmentary and adulterated.

The first full-length production of *The Nutcracker* in the West was produced on 30 January 1934 by the Vic-Wells Ballet. Looking for ballets to show off the great English ballerina Alicia Markova, company head Ninette de Valois contracted Sergeyev, the former *régisseur* of the Maryinsky Ballet and possessor of notated scores of Maryinsky productions, to stage some classics for the company. This *Nutcracker* (or *Casse-Noisette,* as it was called) used an ensemble augmented by child actors who appeared as toy soldiers and mice. The company occasionally performed just act 2 (and Sadler's Wells Theatre Ballet inherited this act 2 in 1947). In 1937, Vic-Wells had remounted the ballet with new décor and costumes; Margot Fonteyn and Robert Helpmann starred.

There have been many restagings of *The Nutcracker* in the West. Boris Romanov restaged the ballet in 1936 for Blum's Ballets de Monte Carlo, London. Romanov introduced the Snow Queen into the snow scene (possibly influenced by Pavlova's *Snowflakes*). Margarita Froman's production in 1938 at Teatro alla Scala, Milan (conceived and designed by Alexandre Benois), had Drosselmeyer return in act 2 as King of the Land of Sweets.

In 1940, Alexandra Fedorova staged the ballet (after Ivanov) for the Ballet Russe de Monte Carlo. This was a long one-act *Nutcracker,* premiering in New York City, with Benois scenery. Alicia Markova and André Eglevsky danced both the Snow and Sugarplum pas de deux. Eventually the first scene was dropped (it had dwindled to five minutes) and Snowflakes was deleted, leaving just the act 2 *divertissement.* Touring through the 1940s and

THE NUTCRACKER: Productions outside Russia. Celia Franca staged her version for the National Ballet of Canada in 1955. Here the Snow Queen (Lois Smith, held aloft at left) waves farewell to the transformed Nutcracker Prince (David Adams, standing at right) and Clara (seated in the sleigh) as they continue their journey to the Kingdom of Sweets. (Photograph by Ken Bell; used by permission of the National Ballet of Canada.)

1950s, this version was the first experience of *The Nutcracker* for many Americans.

William Christensen staged the first full-length *Nutcracker* in the United States (1944; San Francisco Ballet) without ever having seen a complete production of the ballet. He learned much from Alexandra Danilova and George Balanchine when, in town with the Ballet Russe de Monte Carlo, they spent a night with him describing their memories of the ballet and its staging. Danilova even danced all the female roles for Christensen. His production was a huge success and became a Christmas tradition. The Christensen version is now in the repertory of Ballet West. The San Francisco Ballet maintains a rechoreographed version of Lew Christensen (1954), which was made to appeal to children as much as possible.

Nicholas Beriozoff produced the ballet in 1950 for the London Festival Ballet. The premiere starred Markova and Anton Dolin. The production was altered a bit until 1957 when it was reproduced by David Lichine, with Dolin taking the role of Drosselmeyer. Lichine's choreography was much admired for its clarity and discretion, and the production was distinguished by Benois's sets. In this version, the Nutcracker was transformed into the Sugarplum Fairy's cavalier.

Frederick Ashton's 1951 production for Sadler's Wells Theatre Ballet was a single-act version that dispensed with narrative and nightmare and presented only the Snowflake scene and the act 2 *divertissement.* Sections of the Sugarplum pas de deux and the "Chinese Dance" were left unchanged (after Ivanov), while the rest was rechoreographed "freely based on Ivanov." Cecil Beaton designed the black and white costumes.

In 1966, John Cranko staged the ballet for the Stuttgart Ballet. Cranko changed the act 1 Christmas setting to the birthday party of a young girl. Drosselmeyer became an eccentric old aunt who, also a fairy godmother, manipulates the plot. In act 2, she sends Clara on a magic journey with the soldier that Clara loves. At the end of the journey, he realizes that he loves Clara.

Rudolf Nureyev's 1968 version for The Royal Ballet (danced first at the Royal Swedish Ballet in Stockholm on 17 November 1967, set and costumes by Nicholas Georgiadis) was frequently revived, although it was not in the company's repertory. Nureyev's *Nutcracker* uses children in act 1 but casts a small ballerina in the role of Clara. Except for one male solo (that was kept from Vainonen's Leningrad version), Nureyev rechoreographed the entire ballet. This much-debated version casts a colder eye on the story, seizing on its petty cruelties and frightening visions. The lead male doubles as Drosselmeyer and Prince, while the lead ballerina dances Clara as a child and as the adult she will become. The ballet gives them three pas de deux. Nureyev has also staged *Nutcrackers* in Milan and Buenos Aires.

THE NUTCRACKER: Productions outside Russia. Fernand Nault mounted his production for Les Grands Ballets Canadiens in 1965. In this publicity photograph, Anton Dolin as Herr Drosselmeyer presents the Nutcracker doll to Fritz and Clara, portrayed by students at the Académie des Grands Ballets Canadiens. (Photograph by Barrie Flakelar; from the archives of Les Grands Ballets Canadiens.)

John Neumeier produced *The Nutcracker* in 1971 for the Frankfurt Ballet. Using Cranko's version as a starting point, Neumeier created a web of relationships in act 1: At her twelfth-birthday party, Clara falls in love with her brother's guest, a captain. Drosselmeyer, another guest, is her ballerina sister's odd little ballet master. The act 2 dream is of a theater, and there Clara dances with the captain to steps choreographed by Drosselmeyer. Neumeier's *Nutcracker,* an elaborate metaphor for life in the theater, was set on the Royal Winnipeg Ballet in 1972.

In Roland Petit's 1976 version for Les Ballets de Marseilles, Drosselmeyer is an elegant young man who leads Clara to love. The production includes sophisticated touches in the *divertissement.* Elisabetta Terabust was its first Clara.

Mikhail Baryshnikov restaged the ballet in 1976 for American Ballet Theatre. Except for Vainonen's "Waltz of the Snowflakes," the choreography was entirely Baryshnikov's. His Drosselmeyer was omniscient and mysterious, seemingly in command of all the action, and the final pas de deux became a pas de trois, with him, the Nutcracker Prince, and Clara. Here Clara prevailed, if only for a time. The ballet premiered in Washington, D.C., starring Marianna Tcherkassky and Baryshnikov, but Gelsey Kirkland's portrayal set the dramatic tone of the role. Children were not used in this production.

The *Nutcracker* of 1991 was Mark Morris's *The Hard Nut,* produced in Brussels. In a 1960s household, Dr. Drosselmeyer tells Marie about a trip around the world, which occasions the national dances that Alistair Macaulay called "corny, inauthentic, cute, silly, and delicious." The Nutcracker turns into Drosselmeyer's young nephew, and Marie falls in love with him.

Various productions of *The Nutcracker* have been filmed (including Balanchine's, Neumeier's, Willam Christensen's, and Baryshnikov's), but the most famous film treatment may still be Walt Disney's animation of the *Nutcracker Suite* as it appeared in the film *Fantasia* (1940).

[*See also entries on principal figures and companies mentioned herein.*]

BIBLIOGRAPHY

Anderson, Jack. *The Nutcracker Ballet.* New York, 1979.

Ballet Review 16 (Fall 1988): 82–99. Proceedings of a symposium entitled "Balanchine's *Nutcracker.*"

Christout, Marie-Françoise, et al. "*The Nutcracker* in France and England." *Dance and Dancers* (March 1977): 19–27.

Dance Magazine (December 1983). Special issue devoted to the ballet.

Macaulay, Alastair. "All You Need Is Love." *The Dancing Times* (April 1991): 658–660.

Maynard, Olga. "*The Nutcracker.*" *Dance Magazine* (December 1973): 52–74.

Meyerowitz, Joel. *George Balanchine's "The Nutcracker."* Boston, 1993.

Switzer, Ellen. *The Nutcracker: A Story & A Ballet.* New York, 1985.

Volkov, Solomon. *Balanchine's Tchaikovsky: Interviews with George Balanchine.* Translated by Antonina W. Bouis. New York, 1985.

LAURA A. JACOBS

O

OBOUKHOFF, ANATOLE (Anatolii Nikolaevich Obukhov; born 3 [15] January 1896 in Saint Petersburg, Russia, died 25 February 1962 in New York), Russian dancer and teacher. Oboukhoff was a member of a family of dancers and singers, among them his uncle Mikhail, teacher of Vaslav Nijinsky. Oboukhoff graduated from the Imperial School in Saint Petersburg in 1913, dancing the waltz from *Chopiniana* with Olga Spessivtseva at their graduation performance. He partnered Anna Pavlova in her last performances in Russia in 1914. He joined the Imperial Ballet at the Maryinsky Theater and was promoted to principal in 1917, partnering Tamara Karsavina, among others. His roles included Albrecht in *Giselle,* Basilio in *Don Quixote,* Lord Wilson/Ta-Hor in *La Fille du Pharaon,* Jean de Brienne in *Raymonda,* Siegfried in *Swan Lake,* Harlequin in *Les Millions d'Arlequin,* and the Bluebird and Prince Désiré in *The Sleeping Beauty.*

In 1920 Oboukhoff left the Soviet Union; he danced first at the Bucharest Opera and then in Berlin with Boris Romanov's Russian Romantic Ballet. In 1931 he danced in ballets choreographed by Romanov for Colonel Wassily de Basil's first company, Opéra Russe, in Monte Carlo and London. Vera Nemchinova (whom Oboukhoff married) was also in that company. Together they danced in Riga, Latvia, in 1930, then joined the Lithuanian State Ballet in Kaunas, of which Oboukhoff was also ballet master. This company appeared in London in 1935 with a repertory of classical ballets including *Raymonda,* which had not before been seen in its entirety in the West. When the Ballets Russes de Monte Carlo split into two companies, Oboukhoff joined the faction headed by René Blum with Michel Fokine as ballet master. He danced such roles as Petrouchka, Franz in *Coppélia,* and the Poet in *Les Sylphides,* and he created the role of the Ambassador in Fokine's *L'Épreuve d'Amour,* a performance described by dance critic Cyril W. Beaumont as being "in the finest tradition of the Imperial Ballet."

In 1939 Oboukhoff went to Australia with Colonel de Basil's Original Ballet Russe as ballet master and teacher. In Sydney he staged a two-act version of *Coppélia* (after the original choreographer, Marius Petipa) in August 1940, with Tamara Toumanova, Tatiana Riabouchinska, and Nemchinova alternating as Swanilda. Later that year he and Nemchinova made their way to the United States, and in 1941 he joined the faculty of the School of American Ballet in New York, where he taught until his death. In 1944 he staged the pas de deux from Petipa's *Don Quixote* for Ballet Theatre, with Toumanova and Anton Dolin, introducing that showpiece to the contemporary Western repertory. In 1946 he choreographed an original pas de deux to Nikolai Tcherepnin's music from *Le Pavillon d'Armide,* with Alicia Alonso and André Eglevsky, also for Ballet Theatre.

Oboukhoff was one of the greatest *danseurs nobles* of his time, and "the finest tradition of the Imperial Ballet" was what he also imparted to his students. His classes were rigorous and beautiful, and through them he inspired his students with his own love of classical ballet in its purest form.

BIBLIOGRAPHY

Beaumont, Cyril W. *Complete Book of Ballets.* London, 1937.

Dunning, Jennifer. *"But First a School": The First Fifty Years of the School of American Ballet.* New York, 1985.

Sorley Walker, Kathrine. *De Basil's Ballets Russes.* New York, 1983.

Vaughan, David. "'Beautifully Dance': Anatole Obukhov." *Ballet Review* 24.4 (Winter 1996): 17–32.

DAVID VAUGHAN

OCEAN. Choreography: Merce Cunningham. Music: David Tudor, *Ocean Diary;* Andrew Culver, *Ocean 1–95.* Costumes and lighting: Marsha Skinner. First performance: 18 May 1994, Cirque Royal, Brussels, Belgium, Merce Cunningham Dance Company. Dancers: Kimberly Bartosik, Thomas Caley, Michael Cole, Emma Diamond, Jean Freebury, Frédéric Gafner, China Laudisio, Matthew Mohr, Banu Ogan, Jared Phillips, Glen Rumsey, Jeannie Steele, Robert Swinston, Cheryl Therrien, Jenifer Weaver.

Exactly ninety minutes long, to the second, *Ocean* is a very great choreographer's grandest work, epic yet intimate. Taking place on a circular stage, it provides an equally valid experience for viewers watching from any point on its 360-degree periphery: *Ocean* is completely and perfectly a dance without front, back, or sides. After the opening night performance Cunningham remarked, "Now all my dances look flat to me." (His next dance, *Ground Level Overlay,* 1995, would marvelously recreate the multidirectional effect of *Ocean* on the proscenium stage.)

Ocean is, in essence, the final collaboration between Cunningham and John Cage, his companion and collaborator of some fifty years. The original program contains the following opening credit: "conception: John Cage and Merce Cunningham." At the time of his death in 1992, Cage had already made many suggestions concerning the work, including the title, which he believed would have been the title of James Joyce's next novel after *Finnegan's Wake.* At least four other titles of Cunningham's dances come from the *Wake,* including *In the Name of the Holocaust* (1943), *Tossed as it is Untroubled* (1944), *Sounddance* (1975), and *Roaratorio* (1984). Cage had long steeped himself in Joyce's work, and there are suggestive parallels between Cunningham's methods and Joyce's. Similar correspondences—whether subliminal or overt—exist between Cunningham's choreography and the choreography of George Balanchine, to which he frequently seems to allude, in this work and others; and between images in Cunningham's works and the iconography of the Catholic Church, in which he was raised.

As ever with Cunningham and Cage, the music here was conceived apart from the dance, having in common with it only duration in time. There is, however, a rare congruity of thematic material, namely the watery setting, similar to the congruity between Cage's score and Cunningham's choreography for *Inlets* (1977). The orchestral musicians, 112 in number, are seated around the periphery of the audience, enclosing the viewers in a circle of sound. The electronic equipment and its players are ranged immediately inside or outside the circle of musicians, at "twelve o'clock." The music blends slowly shifting, atonal drones and washes of strings and woodwinds with eruptions of percussion and brass (organized according to extremely complex chance procedures by Andrew Culver, using "time brackets" provided by Cage) and incursions of the electronically processed oceanic sounds (sonar, moving ice, shipping, whales and dolphins, and the like) in David Tudor's score.

Like several other Cunningham works (for instance, *August Pace,* 1989), *Ocean* unfolds as a series of duets. Here they occur alongside other activity, but separate from it. Also notable in *Ocean* are recurrent full-cast sections of great complexity (from above these look like the inner workings of a clock, or the stars rotating in a clear night sky; one such segment is a jig, as at a country fair), as well as a section for men, a section for women (plus one man), and a wealth of other figures and patterns. Nonetheless, the duets are a key to what might be considered the dance's interior meaning, with each duet representing a different period in a long companionship, undertaken in youth, and continued until a final parting. For example, one duet celebrates the youthful exuberance of youth, while another suggests temple sculpture in India, where the Cunningham company toured in the 1960s. The last of the duets is danced side by side, in parallel, suggesting oneness of mind.

Like all of Cunningham's works, *Ocean* itself offers no explicit narrative (indeed some would argue that there are no narratives or meanings in Cunningham's choreography whatsoever, however subliminal, submerged, or subconscious.) Viewers are simply free to interpret the dances as they will. But it is not accidental that another segment of this beautiful work (occurring at the one hour mark) reveals two stationary groups of dancers clumped together and intertwined, suggesting coral reefs or the like, while between and around them travel two dancers (both women); suddenly, one exits, leaving the other to continue on alone.

BIBLIOGRAPHY. Obvious sources for information about Merce Cunningham include his own writings and transcriptions of conversations with him, such as his *Changes/Notes on Choreography,* edited by Frances Starr (New York, 1968) and *The Dancer and the Dance, Merce Cunningham in Conversation with Jacqueline Lesschaeve* (New York and London, 1985). A comprehensive Cunningham overview, including some texts by the choreographer, has been prepared by the Merce Cunningham Dance Foundation archivist David Vaughan (scheduled for publication in New York, 1997), whose numerous individual articles are invaluable. In addition there is a comprehensive Cunningham web site (http://www.merce.org./home.html), originally constructed under the supervision of Michael Bloom. In thinking about Cunningham, one should also consider sources perhaps more indirect, but profoundly helpful. Among these is the *Dao De jing* (*Tao Te ching),* used as a choreographic tool for decades by Cunningham, who has said he prefers an unpublished translation by Edwin Denby (see the interview by Nancy Dalva in *The Village Voice,* March 14, 1995, "Re *Rune*"). William Anastasi, an artistic adviser to Cunningham who was a great friend of John Cage and also part of the chess-playing circle that included Marcel Duchamp and his wife Alexina (Teeny), recommends a translation by Stephen Mitchell (New York, 1988; personal communication); as with any translated texts, different versions also have their virtues.

Another source of illumination are scientific writings on chaos theory and other aspects of contemporary physics, which bears interesting comparison with Cunningham's use of aleatory procedures. For several relevant articles accessible to the general reader published roughly contemporaneously with the making of *Ocean,* see *Science News* (no. 139, 1991, and no. 140, 1991.) For a discussion with the choreographer about his use of change procedures, see Dalva's "The I Ching and Me," *Dance Magazine* (1988). See also the same author's general essay "The Way of Merce," originally published in *Dance Ink* (vol. 3, no. 1, Spring 1992) and subsequently collected in *Merce Cunningham, Dancing in Time and Space,* edited by Richard Kostelanetz (Pennington, N. J., 1992); and "La Ronde," *Dance Ink* (vol. 5, no. 3, Fall 1994), a chronological description of the first performance of *Ocean,* including exact timing. This is accompanied by a reproduction of a page from the choreographer's notes for the dance.

Concerning the relationship between Cunningham and Cage, see Elliot Caplan's film (available on videotape) *Cage/Cunningham* (1991), which was produced under Cage's guidance. For an obituary/appreciation of John Cage from a dancegoer's point of view see Dalva's "John Cage," *Dance Ink,* (vol. 3, no. 4, Winter 1992/93). Finally, for an interview with Cunningham and a description of the first performance (in Paris in 1992) of *Enter,* a dance Cunningham was making when Cage died, see her article "Cunningham in New York and Paris: Enter Merce, Laughing" in *Dance Magazine* (March 1993). See also her

"Credo in Us" (forthcoming), an essay concerning how images of Cage's death emerged in Cunningham's dances, which tracks a particular figure from *Roaratorio* to *Enter* to *Ocean,* and its subsequent reappearance in Cunningham's Events.

NANCY DALVA

OCEANIC DANCE TRADITIONS. Although the Pacific Ocean covers nearly one-third of the earth's surface, the land area within it is relatively small. A series of volcanoes rims the Pacific. Along the Asian shore the coast is low and fringed with islands rising from a wide continental shelf. The shore of the Americas has a narrow continental shelf, with high mountains rising abruptly from a deep sea floor. The Pacific islands consist of only about 486,700 square miles (1.4 million square kilometers), encompassing Polynesia, Micronesia, and Melanesia (which includes the large island of New Guinea). The islands are geologically and geographically diverse: continental, volcanic, and coral islands stretch over tropical, subtropical, and temperate climatic zones, encompassing a range of environments that vary from permanent snowfields to tropical rain forests. The nearly ten thousand islands are widely distributed—some isolated from their nearest neighbors by hundreds of miles, while others lie in groups or chains called *archipelagos.* A large number of distinctive sociocultural groups, aligned in various ways among themselves and with non-Pacific nations, have emerged as a result of the complex migrations that brought seafaring peoples into the open ocean, the subsequent isolation of the island peoples from their ancestral homelands, and their interaction with neighboring groups and colonial powers. An understanding of these prehistoric, historic, and present-day links is crucial for understanding dance as it exists today in its myriad forms in the Pacific islands.

Eighteenth- and nineteenth-century geographers divided Oceania into three large areas, which are also useful culturally: Melanesia ("black islands"), Micronesia ("small islands"), and Polynesia ("many islands"). Although these classifications become less useful when the complex culture history of any individual island is considered, they are helpful in distinguishing the main dance traditions in the area.

The earliest written descriptions of dance in the Pacific islands come from seventeenth- and eighteenth-century European explorers from Spain, Holland, France, and Britain. The best of these, from Captain Cook's expedition, focus primarily on Polynesia. Nineteenth-century descriptions by German, Russian, and American explorers were supplemented by reports from whalers, beachcombers, traders, and missionaries. Twentieth-century anthropologists reported in even more detail. Most of these writers, however, had little acquaintance with the description or recording of human movement; they focused primarily on the context of the dances they observed, or on their "heathen" character. These eyewitness accounts join the early drawings of the eighteenth century, the still photographs of the nineteenth and twentieth centuries, and the films and videotapes of the twentieth century as valuable sources when used in conjunction with the detailed studies of dance and music for these areas today. Few such studies, however, have yet been carried out, and most of the contributions to our knowledge have been made by ethnomusicologists and anthropologists who focus primarily on the music or the context of the dances, not on the movement itself.

Before Europeans arrived in the Pacific islands—bringing with them new religions, rituals, visual images, and sociopolitical forms—dance was an inextricable part of religious ritual and social celebrations; it was used primarily in those contexts. There were no dance dramas like those of Indonesia or India, nor was there an attempt to portray or convey abstract morals. Although gods might be worshiped or stories told with the help of human

OCEANIC DANCE TRADITIONS. A 1946 studio portrait of an Iatmul masked dancer from the central Sepik River region, Papua New Guinea. The mask is a woven structure, painted and decorated with bird feathers; the full-length body-skirt is made of grass. (Photograph by T. L. Bierwert; from the Department of Library Services, American Museum of Natural History, New York [no. 320363]; used by permission.)

OCEANIC DANCE TRADITIONS. Since the 1960s, New Zealand has seen a revived interest in the traditional performing arts of the islands in its territory. Local festivals often feature displays by a wide range of indigenous culture groups. Pictured here are members of the Tokelan Island Community Group performing a Polynesian dance at the Wellington Pacific Drum Festival in Naenae, New Zealand, 1989. (Photograph by Helena Hughes; courtesy of Jennifer Shennan; used by permission.)

movement, this was done in the service of living people and their ancestors—focusing on the past and present—not on the future or afterlife.

Most of the Malayo-Polynesian Pacific languages did not have terms or concepts that corresponded to the English word *dance,* although some have now adopted such a word. Seldom was a sequence of beautiful movements put together simply for aesthetic enjoyment or entertainment. More often, movement sequences were embedded in ritual or based on a composer-choreographer's challenge to an audience to understand the deeper cultural meaning behind the movements. A distinction might be made between dances of participation, which were likely to occur in ritual, and dances of presentation, which were usually tied to social and political contexts. Even dances of presentation, however, required the spectator to engage in active mental participation to fully enjoy their content; dances of participation might require that there be observers, such as members of the opposite sex, who were forbidden to participate actively.

Dance traditions were of three main types, corresponding roughly to the three large geographical–cultural divisions. Two of these traditions—Polynesia and Micronesia—were oriented toward texts; the third—Melanesia—focused on the visual enhancement of rhythm. In Polynesia, a text was rendered melodically and rhythmically; it was accompanied by hand and arm movements that alluded to and interpreted the text, while leg and body movements kept the rhythmic pulse. In Micronesia, a text was enhanced (rather than interpreted) by hands, arms, and sometimes other parts of the body; the text might not be understood by the dancers or audience. In Melanesia, up-and-down movements of the legs and body were performed as the dancers moved from place to place or in a circle (usually clockwise); movements often changed the orientation of the group from one side to another. Legs and body were more important than arms and hands, and they functioned along with costumes and masks to enhance rhythmic pulse and to convey meaning in ritual contexts.

Today, although some of these functions of human movement are still important in the social, political, and ritual life of Pacific Islanders, many of the contexts of the movements and the movements themselves have evolved along with changes in lifestyles. For many, dance performances have become part of cultural events and competitions (such as the yearly Heiva [formerly the Bastille Day fête] in the Society Islands) or independence celebrations (as in Vauatu, formerly the New Hebrides). For others, the most important dance event is the Pacific Festival of Arts, which takes place in a different island area every four years. For these occasions, dance troupes representing twenty to thirty island nations and territories gather to perform in an atmosphere of mutual respect for one another's traditions. In nearly every Pacific area, dance has also become part of tourist entertainment—sometimes to the detriment of tradition. Despite these changes, dance is highly regarded by Pacific Islanders as an important part of past traditions and as an enhancement of present-day ethnic identity.

[*See also* Melanesia; Micronesia; Polynesia; *and* Music for Dance, *article on* Oceanic Music.]

BIBLIOGRAPHY

Christensen, Dieter, and Adrienne L. Kaeppler. "Oceania, Arts of (Music and Dance)." In *Encyclopaedia Britannica,* 15th ed. Chicago, 1974.

Kaeppler, Adrienne L. "Movement in the Performing Arts of the Pacific Islands." In *Theatrical Movement: A Bibliographical Anthology,* edited by Bob Fleshman. Metuchen, N.J., 1986.

Kaeppler, Adrienne L., and Jacob Love, eds. *Australia and the Pacific Islands.* Volume of *Garland Encyclopedia of World Music.* New York, 1997.

McLean, Mervyn. *An Annotated Bibliography of Oceanic Music and Dance.* Auckland, 1977–1981, 1995.

Moyle, Alice M., ed. *Music and Dance of Aboriginal Australia and the South Pacific: The Effects of Documentation on the Living Tradition.* Sydney, 1992.

Shennan, Jennifer. "Approaches to the Study of Dance in Oceania: Is the Dancer Carrying an Umbrella or Not?" *Journal of the Polynesian Society* 90.2 (1981).

Smith, Barbara B., et al. "Melanesia," "Micronesia," "Pacific Islands," and "Polynesia." In *The New Grove Dictionary of Music and Musicians.* London, 1980.

ADRIENNE L. KAEPPLER

O'CONNOR, DONALD (Donald David Dixon Ronald O'Connor; born 30 August 1925 in Chicago, Illinois), tap dancer, singer, and actor. O'Connor has played to generations in vaudeville, films, musical shows, and on television. An outstanding performer of comedy tap dance, he claims to have put comedy into his dancing because he could not tap well.

O'Connor came from a circus family. His father was an Irish dancer-comedian, one of Ringling Brothers' greatest acrobats, and his mother was a circus tightrope walker and bareback rider. O'Connor was their seventh child and, by the time he came along, his family was performing on variety circuits billed as "The O'Connor Family—The Royal Family of Vaudeville." His first professional appearance with the act was at age thirteen months, for which he was paid $25 a week to dance the popular Black Bottom. As he recalled, "I couldn't actually dance, but they held me up by the back of my skirt, and I moved my feet like crazy!" (Frank, 1994). O'Connor spent his childhood traveling the United States, performing with his family. Their act included remnants of its circus days (hand balancing, barrel jumping), as well as such familiar vaudeville standards as singing and dancing. O'Connor's specialty was his "knock 'em dead" tap dance.

O'Connor was first discovered by Hollywood in 1937. His early films include *Melody For Two* (1937), *Sing, You Sinners* (1938), *Beau Geste* (1939), *Death of a Champion* (1939), and *On Your Toes* (1939). After a brief return to what was left of vaudeville, he was back in Hollywood in 1942 for a series of Universal Studios B musicals, starring the popular teen dance group the Jivin' Jacks and Jills. These young dancers were some of the most talented in the business, and many grew up to be principal dancers and instructors on Broadway and in Hollywood (e.g., Peggy Ryan, Tommy Rall, Roland Dupree, Bobby Scheerer). Most of these films and O'Connor's later work were choreographed by the legendary Hollywood dance director Louis DaPron. Of this string of musicals, O'Connor appeared in *What's Cookin'?* (1942), *Private Buckaroo* (1942), *Give Out, Sisters* (1942), *It Comes Up Love* and *Get Hep to Love* (both in 1942), and *Mister Big* (1943). In the midst of the series, O'Connor was drafted for military service during World War II.

After the war, O'Connor returned to Hollywood to carry on his career in films, which included the popular *Francis, the Talking Mule* series. During the 1950s, he delighted audiences with his dancing in such films as *The Milkman* (1950), *Call Me Madam* (1953), *There's No Business Like Show Business* (1954), and *Anything Goes* (1956). This brilliant comic dancer reached his zenith in 1952, when he was teamed with Gene Kelly and Debby Reynolds to co-star in what became the film classic *Singin' in the Rain.* In it, he and Kelly performed thrilling tap duets to "Moses Supposes" and "Fit as a Fiddle." O'Connor's sensational "Make 'Em Laugh," which he choreographed using many of the stage "bits" he had seen during his

O'CONNOR. Gene Kelly sits on O'Connor's knee in the "Fit as a Fiddle" number from the film *Singin' in the Rain* (MGM, 1952). (Photograph from the collection of Rusty E. Frank.)

youth in vaudeville, may yet be the most hilarious dance routine recorded on film.

[*See also* Tap Dance.]

BIBLIOGRAPHY

Frank, Rusty E. *Tap! The Greatest Tap Dance Stars and Their Stories, 1900–1955.* Rev. ed. New York, 1994.

Thomas, Tony. *That's Dancing.* New York, 1984.

RUSTY E. FRANK

OḌISSI. The earliest known representation of Oḍissi dance, in the Ranigumpha and Udaygiri caves of Orissa in northeastern India, is a scene in a dance hall that dates from the second century BCE. This scene is part of the large number of sculptures, inscriptions, and palm-leaf manuscripts related to dance rituals that span approximately nine centuries in the temples of Orissa. The countless dance sculptures from the seventh century CE on speak of the highly evolved technique of this dance style.

Like other Indian classical dance traditions, Oḍissi is closely linked with religion, in this case with movements that developed in Orissa from the second century BCE to the thirteenth century CE. Dynasties and rulers supported dance as a part of ritual in the temples. The dance rituals were performed by *devadāsīs*, dancing girls attached to the temples, and by *gōtipūas*, boy dancers dressed as girls. [*See* Devadāsī.]

ODISSI. Sanjukta Panigrahi, seen here in *darpana* ("mirror") *bhaṅgi*, a pure dance pose, is a well-known exponent of Oḍissi dance. (Photograph from the archives of The Asia Society, New York.)

The Jagannath temple at Puri in Orissa became a major religious center, and dance was until recently an integral part of its rituals. The Konaraka temple (thirteenth century) has a dance hall with many sculptures which form a veritable lexicon of dance. In the eleventh century, the poet Jayadeva wrote the *Gīta Govinda;* it is even now sung at the Jagannath temple, and the *devadāsīs* used to dance to its songs. It forms an integral part of the contemporary Oḍissi expressive dance works. The tradition of the *gōtipūa* dancers saved Oḍissi dance from oblivion; today's great Oḍissi masters are *gōtipūa* dancers.

The quintessence of Oḍissi is its sculptural quality: no other Indian classical dance style has such a close resemblance to sculpture. The *tribhaṅga* pose of sculpture has been exploited to the maximum in Oḍissi dance; *tribhaṅga* is a stance in which the torso is moved in the direction opposite to that of the head and the hips. It gives the dance form a sensuous and rhythmic quality. The six *padabhedas* (basic positions of the feet), the five basic *bhūmis* (manner of moving), the *bhaṅgis* (basic postures with relevant movements), the *karaṇas* (basic dance units consisting of a stance, pose, hand gestures, and movement), and the *hastas* (hand gestures), all indicate that Oḍissi is classical in all its aspects. The palm-leaf manuscript *Abhinayacandrikā*, by Maheshwara Mahapatra (seventeenth century), gives details of the dance technique.

The body movements retaining the visual quality of sculpture and broken into different units (torso, hips, legs, and hands) are a distinct feature of Oḍissi. The use of geometric rectangles, squares, and circles creates fascinating patterns. Movement done on the heels is another characteristic peculiar to Oḍissi and is also found in the neighboring Kuchipudi style: the dancer, balancing only on his or her heels, moves backward or describes a circle while the body remains erect and the hands are kept in front.

Like other Indian classical dance styles, Oḍissi has two main divisions: *nṛtta,* pure dance, and *nṛtya,* expressive dance. Oḍissi has been mainly revived as solo dance, although attempts have been made to use the technique in dance drama and ballet.

The Oḍissi repertory includes *Bhūmi-praṇām,* an obeisance to the goddess of the earth and a prayer; *Baṭu-nṛtya,* a pure dance incorporating the motifs of dance and music sculptures; and *Pallavi,* in which pure dance is presented in sculpturesque movements set to a certain *tāla* (metrical cycle) and *rāga* (melody). The finale is called *Mokhya,* which also features pure dance. The *abhinaya,* or expressive dances, are set to the songs of the *Gīta Govinda* and lyrics of Oriya poets such as Banamali, Kavisurya Baladeva Rah, and Gopalakrishna. They center around the various states of mental agony and ecstasy of the heroine, arising from separation or union with her beloved lord. The songs are in Sanskrit and Oriya; recently, songs from Hindi, Brajbhasha, and Avadhi have been used for new compositions.

The music for Oḍissi is soft, lilting, and melodious, employing the northern Indian classical Hindustani style; it is also influenced by Karnatic music. The instruments used are a pair of small cymbals, a *pakhavaj* (a drum played on both sides and held horizontally), and a flute or violin. The lyrics are set to a particular *rāga* and are sung by the vocalist; the dancer mimes them during the *abhinaya* portions of the performance.

The palm-leaf manuscripts give details of the costumes and ornaments used in Oḍissi. In the past the *devadāsīs* adorned themselves with many ornaments, but now the dancers wear what suits them best for the dance movements they will perform.

Since its revival in 1956, Oḍissi has come into its own. Yamini Krishnamurthi, Ritha Devi, and Sonal Mansingh contributed to arousing interest in this form. Among the better-known Oḍissi exponents are Sanjukta Panigrahi and Kum Kum Mohanty (née Das). Three gurus—Pankajcharan Das, Kelucharan Mahapatra, and Debuprasad Das—have trained Oḍissi dancers. Other young teachers, such as Suredranath Jena, Mayadhar Raut, Harekrishna Behra, Ramaniranjan, and Raghu Dutta, train dancers in the cities. A state College of Dance and Music in Bhubaneshwar and Kala Vikasha Kendra in Cuttack have rendered pioneering service in the propagation of Oḍissi. In recent times, the *māhārī* style as performed by Pankajcharan Das and the *gōtipūa* style of Kelucharan Mahapatra have become popular.

[*For general discussion, see* India, *article on* History of Indian Dance. *See also the entries on Indrani, Kermani, Krishnamurthi, Mahapatra, Mansingh, Panigrahi, and Ritha Devi.*]

BIBLIOGRAPHY

Citaristi, Ileana. "Devadasis of the Jagannath Temple: Precursors of Odissi Music and Dance." *Sruti* (Madras), no. 33–34 (July–July 1987): 51–57.

Gaston, Anne-Marie. *Śiva in Dance, Myth, and Iconography.* Delhi, 1982.

Kothari, Sunil. "Odissi Dance." *Quarterly Journal of the National Centre for the Performing Arts* 3 (June 1974): 37–49.

Kothari, Sunil, and Avinash Pasricha. *Odissi: Indian Classical Dance Art.* Bombay, 1990.

Massey, Reginald, and Jamila Massey. *The Dances of India: A General Survey and Dancer's Guide.* London, 1989.

Patnaik, Dhirendranath. *Odissi Dance.* Bhubaneswar, Orissa, 1971.

Ragini Devi. *Dance Dialects of India.* 2d rev. ed. Delhi, 1990.

Samson, Leela. *Rhythm in Joy: Classical Indian Dance Traditions.* New Delhi, 1987.

SUNIL KOTHARI

OGOUN, LUBOŠ (born 18 February 1924 in Prague), Czech dancer and choreographer. In his youth, Ogoun divided his interests between dance and sports (light athletics, gymnastics) and later was coach of the Czechoslovak women's gymnastics team. He learned ballet basics from Robert Braun and Helena Štěpáková, and in 1945 he became a member of the ballet corps at the National Theater in Prague. At the same time he studied to become a professor of physical education. A physically mature dancer with powerful leaps and a comic streak, Ogoun interpreted several of the smaller solo roles in the repertory.

In 1951 Ogoun joined the Military Artistic Company and the Military Opera, where he became director of the dance section and a choreographer. In the late 1950s he was back at the National Theater, as a teacher and choreographer. His choreographic work included *The Flames of Paris,* to music by Boris Asafiev, in 1956; and *Prometheus,* to Beethoven, in 1957. From 1957 to 1961, as *chef de ballet* in Pilsen, Ogoun began to form his own choreographic style. The programmatic piece in which he fully realized his ideas about modern poetic ballet—speaking to the viewer through movement metaphor rather than dry, descriptive works—was *Ballad of a Sailor,* to the music of Zdeněk Křížek, in 1961; Ogoun wrote his own libretto. Ogoun's repertory developed further in Brno, where he was ballet director from 1961 to 1964. He created several progressive works at Brno and stood at the head of the "new wave" of Czech choreography, which uncompromisingly worked for the modernization of ballet in Czechoslovakia. His works in this period included *Leningrad Symphony,* to music by Dmitri Shostakovich, in 1962; *Hiroshima,* set to the music of Viliam Bukový, in 1963; *Taras Bulba,* to the music of Leoš Janáček, also in 1963; and Igor Stravinsky's *The Rite of Spring,* in 1964.

Ogoun's choreography went far beyond the classical vocabulary; it was full of new movement shapes, often inspired by acrobatics but always serving to express thought and content. The culmination of Ogoun's reforming work was the establishment of Ballet Prague, which together with choreographer Pavel Šmok and dance critic Vladimír Vašut he founded in 1964. Ogoun was artistic director of the company until 1968, and he toured with the ensemble on several trips abroad. The most important works from this period were *The Miraculous Mandarin,* set to music by Béla Bartók, in 1964, and a new version of Bukový's *Hiroshima,* which the company performed 219 times; at the Paris Dance Festival in 1967, *Hiroshima* received the Serge Lifar Prize. In the 1968/69 season Ogoun returned to Brno as ballet director, staging Richard Strauss's *Don Juan* in 1969; afterward Ogoun was for a short time director of the Laterna Magica Theater in Prague.

In 1970, early in the Soviet occupation, Ogoun was removed as director and returned to Brno, where he worked as choreographer and collaborated in directing opera as well as dramatic and musical theater. His work with the ballet was only occasional; however, he did choreograph *Concertino,* to music by Janáček, in 1978; *Check to the King,* set to music by Bohuslav Martinů, in 1980; *A Summer Night's Dream,* to music by Václav Trojan, in 1984; *Lady among the Shadows,* to music by Zdeněk Pololáník, in 1987; and *The Strangler,* set to music by Martinů, in 1990. After the so-called Velvet Revolution, Ogoun was named *chef de ballet* of the Brno State Ballet, a position he held until 1991.

[*See also* Brno Ballet; Czech Republic and Slovak Republic, *article on* Theatrical Dance.]

BIBLIOGRAPHY

Brno State Theater. *Almanach 66–69.* Brno, 1969.

100 let českého divadla v plzni. 1965.

Schmidová, Lidka. *Československý balet.* Prague, 1962.

Spindler-Brown, Angela. "Letter from Czechoslovakia." *Dance and Dancers* (May 1987): 36–37.

Studio Balet Praha. Mexico City, 1968. In Spanish and English.

Vašut, Vladimír. "Prága Balett." *Tánctudományi Tanulmánok* (1975): 95–112.

Vladimír Vašut
Translated from Czech

OHIO BALLET. At its founding in 1968, the Ohio Ballet was named the Chamber Ballet. Eight years later it acquired its current title. Under the guidance of founding director Heinz Poll, it has remained true to the original concept. The company has twenty close-knit dancers, all selected for their strength and versatility. Nearly 80 percent of the repertory consists of original ballets by Poll. These are performed in simple, carefully designed costumes by A. Christina Giannini and in a theatrical environment achieved principally through imaginative lighting. Until his death in 1994, lighting designer Thomas R. Skelton was Poll's close collaborator. He also was the company's co-founder and associate director.

Just as the company remains close to its roots, so does Poll's choreography. Three early influences are constant. Poll is inspired by clear, unfettered space and by the athleticism of his dancers, both of which are reminiscent of his own days as an ice skater in his native city of Oberhausen in the Ruhr Valley. In addition, Poll's approach to performing technique is balanced between the classical and contemporary vocabularies to which he was exposed as a scholarship student at the Essen Folkwang Schule directed by Kurt Jooss and Sigurd Leeder. The same stylistic amalgam characterized his own dancing in the National Ballet of Chile, directed by former Jooss artists Ernst Uthoff and Lola Botka.

In 1962, Poll, who had moved to New York, was invited to teach during the summer in Akron, Ohio. Under the aegis of the University of Akron, he developed a modest ensemble of dancers. Poll's most memorable ballet, *Elegaic Song,* was created on that initial nucleus of students.

OHIO BALLET. Negotiating long, elegant dresses while standing atop naked men, Jane Startzman and Pandora Robertson are seen with Miguel Romero and Scott Heinzerling in *Untitled,* choreographed by Pilobolus Dance Theatre. (Photograph by Ott Gangl; used by permission.)

The Ohio Ballet is part of the small minority of American ballet companies that does not offer a Christmas production of *The Nutcracker.* Instead, it sometimes presents Poll's version of *The Little Match Girl.* And although Poll admires and is influenced by the choreography of George Balanchine, the company dances relatively few of his works. The choice of ballets by outside choreographers generally complements the ballets that Poll has created for a given season. Works by Laura Dean and Lynne Taylor-Corbett are frequent choices. Lucinda Childs and Charles Moulton have been contributors to the repertory. Poll also favors Paul Taylor's *Aureole* and *Big Bertha,* Jooss's *The Green Table* and *The Big City,* and Antony Tudor's *Dark Elegies.* Company members, among them Stephani Achuff, Luc Vanier, and David Shimotakahara, also are encouraged to create.

Poll himself is not an innovator. His ballets, although soundly constructed and confidently danced, often allude to similar themes used by more mainstream choreographers. There are romantic waltz ballets, such as *Summer Night* and *Concert Dances;* suites to the music of popular composers, among them *Eight by Benny Goodman* and *In Full Swing;* and other, more independent excursions, such as *Planes/Configurations* and *Cascade.*

The familial structure of the Ohio Ballet extends to its administrative personnel. Associate director Barbara S. Schubert is a former trustee, and artistic administrator Jane Startzman is a former company dancer. The company maintains a modest budget of $1.5 million. Within this stricture it has toured in more than 240 cities and performs biennially in New York City.

BIBLIOGRAPHY

Salisbury, Wilma. "Akron's Treasure: The Ohio Ballet." *Dance Magazine* (October 1978): 50–55.

Salisbury, Wilma. "Ohio Ballet Celebrates Anniversary." *Dance Magazine* (May 1985): 125–126.

Salisbury, Wilma. "One Man's Vision." *Ballet News* 7 (February 1986): 20–24.

Tobias, Tobi. "To Each His Own." *New York Magazine* (22 February 1993).

DORIS HERING

OISEAU DE FEU, L'. *See* Firebird, The.

OKINAWA. Also known as the Ryukyu Islands, Okinawa is located in the Ryukyu archipelago at the southwest tip of Japan, just east of the island of Taiwan. Okinawans share an ethnicity with the people of the main islands of Japan, but their history was independent from that of the mainstream of Japan and they maintained their own identity. Its unique location has placed Okinawa at the crossroads of trade between Japan and Southeast Asia and contributed to its various political and economic occupations through the centuries. Begining in 1372, trade and political relations with China were established by Okinawa's King Satto. In 1609, following an invasion of Shimazu, lord of Satsuma in Kyushu, the Ryukyu kingdom maintained two tributary relations—with both China and the Tokugawa Shogunate in Edo, represented by Shimazu. With the fall of the kingdom, Okinawa entered the sovereignty of Japan in 1879. In recent history, Okinawa was the scene of severe battles during World War II and postwar occupation by the United States. In 1972, Okinawa was returned to Japan as Okinawa Prefecture.

Okinawans have a distinct and diverse dance tradition. It remains a vital part of their lives, coming from ancient religious rites, various folk traditions, and classical dances that have developed into a high art form over several centuries. Some scholars of Okinawan history and the arts believe that Okinawan dance was imported from other Asian countries, but others assert that Okinawan dance originated in the islands' indigenous dance forms. Both views focus their arguments on the particular

OKINAWA. A small, hand-held drum (called *ku-daiku*) is a typical accompaniment for many Okinawan songs and dances. The women pictured here accompany themselves in a staged presentation of a traditional folk dance. (Photograph © 1986 by Jack Vartoogian; used by permission.)

twirling motion of the hands, *koneri* or *konerite,* but the determination of the origins remains unresolved.

The oldest extant documentation of dance in Okinawa is found in an anthology of songs titled *Omorosōshi* (Collections of Omoro), edited in 1531, 1613, and 1623. The ninth volume of this extensive work (edited in 1623) contains various dance songs and footnotes alongside *omoro,* the songs, describing dance movements. The most notable movements are *koneri.* The term *koneri* was also used to denote dance in general at the time when *omoro* were sung, as well as *nayori.* The term *nayori* refers to a gradual and gentle circular movement of the entire body, which is prevalent in Okinawan dance, particulary in dances performed by women. Both terms remain in the current taxonomy of Okinawan dance. *Koneri,* in its present use, refers to the movement sequence that includes all three hand gestures of *ogamite* ("praying hand," or "worship hand"), *konerite* ("kneading hand"), and *oshite* ("pushing hand"). *Koneri* is also used as a shortened form for the term *konerite.*

Okinawan dance may be categorized into four groups: religious/ceremonial dance, folk dance, court dance, and contemporary dance. In Japanese, the term *Ryukyu buyō* ("Ryukyuan dance"), is often used to refer to the dances of Okinawa in general, in the widest sense of the term; it also refers specifically to the classical dance—court dance, both historical and current—and to contemporary dance that uses court dance technique.

OKINAWA. Miyagi, the director of the Miyagi Troupe, is seen here brandishing a fan and a sword in a court dance drama. (Photograph from the archives of The Asia Society, New York.)

Sairei buyō or *saishiki buyō* ("ceremonial dance") are performed by priestesses and shamans during Okinawan religious ceremonies. These dances use the prayer gestures of the hands. These Okinawan ceremonies are practiced yearly, based on the agricultural and fishing cycles, ancester worship, indigenous beliefs, and those beliefs syncretized with Buddhism. They include prayers and invocations for abundant crops and good fishing. Nana no Ūde, performed during the Ufuyumi festival on Iejima Island is an important example as it shows a clear execution of *konerite.* Other ceremonial dances include those performed during the festival of Izaihō on Kudaka Island and the festival of Uyagan in the Miyako Islands.

The folk dances of Okinawa, called *minzoku buyō,* are performed by villagers during festivals and celebrations that follow the successful completion of religious ceremonies. With the exception of the improvisational dance, *kachāshi,* all folk dances have recurrent patterns of movements. The popular dances among the folk forms are *kachāshi, ushidēku, eisā, kuichā, maki odori,* and *kwēna. Ushidēku* is performed during the Shinugu and Unjami festivals; this is a group dance performed only by women, and its movements and songs are considered to be the oldest among many. *Eisā* is a *bon odori* in Okinawa, a dance performed during Bon, the summer festival dedicated to ancestral spirits. *Kuichā* in the Miyako Islands is performed at festivals such as Amagoi, asking for rain during drought, and is characterized by vigorous jumping and stamping. *Maki odori* in the Yaeyama Islands is performed during the Pūri, Tantoi, and Kitsugan festivals and is noted for its rolling formation *(maki). Kwēna,* performed by women as a way of praying for a safe journey, is found mostly on the Okinawa Main Island.

Court dance developed under the patronage of the kingdom, known as Ryukyu Ofu, which governed the Ryukyu Islands from 1372 to 1869. Several names are used, including *kyutei buyō* ("court dance") and *ukanshin odori,* in Okinawan dialect *(ukanshin udui,* "coronation ship dance"). Its development is inseparable from the relationship between Ryukyu and China from as early as 1372, when the Chinese emissaries *(sappōshi)* were honored with banquets and theatrical entertainments hosted by the kings of Ryukyu. These entertainments, which included dance, music, and drama, became known as *ukanshin odori,* taking the name from the ship on which the Chinese emissaries sailed to Okinawa. The Chinese delegations' documents relate that Okinawan court dance developed over time from ceremonial and folk forms into a refined art form. The final transformation, although an

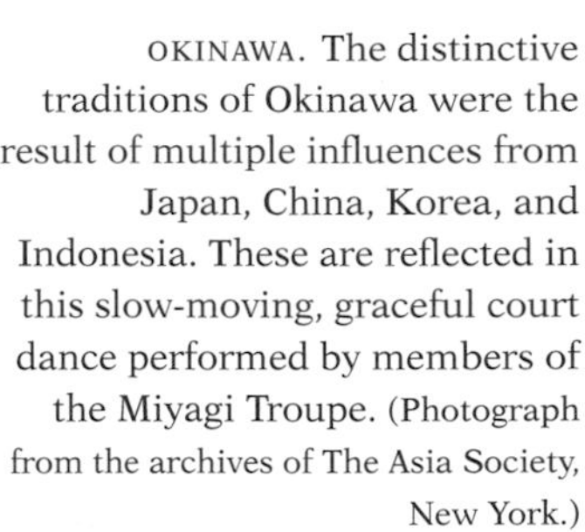

OKINAWA. The distinctive traditions of Okinawa were the result of multiple influences from Japan, China, Korea, and Indonesia. These are reflected in this slow-moving, graceful court dance performed by members of the Miyagi Troupe. (Photograph from the archives of The Asia Society, New York.)

evolutionary one, can officially be credited to the genius of the eighteenth-century artist, Tamagusuku Chokun (1684–1743).

The complete details of *ukanshin* performances are unknown at this time but included are two basic categories, *kumi odori* ("combined dance/drama") and *ha odori* ("short or fragmentary dance"), with references to precursors of the *ukanshin odori* known as *chigo mai* ("children's dance"). *Kumi odori* is the Ryukyuan dance drama—a form using speech, music, and dance. It was first produced by the court dance master Tamagusuku Chokun in 1719 and is still performed today. In 1972, *kumi odori* was designated as an Intangible National Treasure by the Japanese government. Each four-line verse of the narrative has an 8-8-8-6 syllable structure. Music is the central element, metaphorically depicting scenes and expressing the changes of mood, emotions, and thoughts of the characters in the drama. Dance may be performed as an independent section or during the entrance, journey, and exit dances; it may also be used to express the actions of characters through choreographed and stylized movements.

There are two styles of *ha odori* dances: men's and women's. These include *rōjin odori* ("old man's dance"), *wakashū odori* ("boy's dance"), *nisē odori* ("young man's dance"), and *on'na odori* ("woman's dance"). In general, *ha odori* dances are characterized by a gliding walk, and symbolic hand gestures depict the meaning of the lyrics. Integral elements of the structure of *ha odori* are known as *deha* ("entrance"), *naka odori* ("middle dance"), and *iriha* ("exit"); but it is *on'na odori* that uses the structure most aesthetically and dramatically. *Deha* creates the general mood of the theme of the dance. In *naka odori* the theme is fully developed—it is here that the story is told or the theme evolves. *Iriha* provides the conclusion of the story line or theme, or it may be merely a simple exit walk. The structure of *deha* and *iriha* is similar to that of the early *kabuki* dance, then called *kouta odori*. Using *kouta odori* as an example, one theory claims that Okinawan court dance is diretly influenced by the *nō* and *kabuki* of the main islands of Japan. This seems to be an easy and oversimplified assumption, similar to the way it is claimed that Okinawan dance originated in Indonesian or other Southeast Asian countries, based merely on some observable similarities. Okinawan dances reflect the people's history, lifestyle, and indigenous beliefs and traditions—all of which make their dance genres uniquely Okinawan.

Rōjin odori is performed as an opening number of a dance program, and it is an essential part of any performance in Okinawa. In its solemn dignity, *rōjin odori* is identical with the *chōja no ufushu* ("the old man") of folk village performances, since the old man symbolizes a god, bringing happiness and longevity. *Wakashū odori,* the boy's dance, is closer to *rōjin odori* than to *nisē odori,* other men's-style dances, in the sense that both are celebratory and auspicious dances. *Wakashū odori* costumes are as colorful as those of women's. *Nisē odori* is a manly, boistereous dance with the black costume of a journey, incorporating *kata* (the movement pattern) of *karate* (the martial art) in the dance.

The beauty and grace of the *on'na odori* is comparable to those of Japan's *nō,* while the dance is characterized by hand gestures of soft undulating movements. Their costumes, *bingata,* are highly praised works of art. *On'na odori's* themes center around love—in many cases, unrequited love. Here, the techniques of *koneri* and *nayori* are most effectively woven into the dance, complemented by the melancholy music of *Ryuka* (Ryukyuan song) and *sanshin* (the three-stringed instrument, also known as *jabisen*). The best classics of *on'na odori* are called *Nana Odori* (The Seven Dances): they include "Shudun" (Memories), "Nuha Bushi" (Nuha Melody), "Tsukuten Bushi" (Tsukuten Melody), "Yanaji" (A Willow Tree), "Amakawa" (The Amakawa Pond), "Kashikaki" (Looming of Thread), and "Nuchibana" (Strings of Flowers). Although Chokun is often cited as the choreographer of *nana odori,* a clear record of this has not been found. Still it is possible to credit Chokun as the one who established the base of *on'na odori.* Since the court dance and drama were performed only by men, female impersonators first performed *on'na odori,* and this tradition continued into the early 1900s.

Gendai Okinawa buyō ("contemporary Okinawan dance") is a dance form using techniques of the court dance but choreographed to a new theme. A distinguishable category of contemporary Okinawan dance is *zō odori* ("miscellaneous dance"), the themes of which are taken from folk traditions. These were first choreographed for popular theater productions by artists who lost their patronage because of the fall of the court during the Meiji era (1868–1913). Using the elements of Okinawan folk dances, the tempo of the music and dance movements were made faster than those of the preceding dance forms, which greatly appealed to the taste of the general public. As the result of the popularization—from the court restriction to the general public's access—since that time, *Ryukyu buyō* has been studied as a serious art form by the people, particulary young women.

[*See also* Bon Odori.]

BIBLIOGRAPHY

Higa Shuncho. *Higa Shuncho Zenshu.* Naha, 1971.

Iha Fuyu. "Kochu ryukyu gikyokushu." In *Iha Fuyu Zenshu.* Vol. 3. Tokyo, 1929.

Ikemiya Masaharu. "Ryukyu Buyo no Gaikan." In *Ryukyu Buyo.* Naha, 1985.

Ito, Sachiyo. "The Origins of Traditional Okinawan Dance." Ph.D. diss., New York University, 1988.

Majikina Anko. "Kumi Odori to Nohgaku no Kosatsu." In *Iha Fuyu Zenshu.* Vol. 3. Tokyo, 1929.

Masato, Matsui, et al. *Ryukyu: An Annotated Bibliography.* Honolulu, 1981.

Misumi Haruo. *Gen Nihon Okinawa.* Tokyo, 1972.

Yano Teruo. *Okinawa Geino shiwa.* Tokyo, 1974.

ARCHIVES. The *Shi Liu-Chiu Lu* (Reports of Missions), written by delegations of Chinese emissaries to Okinawa in 1534, 1606, 1633, 1683, and 1721, are held in the Hawley Collection, University of Hawaii. *Chung-shan Ch'uan-hsin* (The Reports on Chuzan Kingdom), written by Hsu Pao-kuang in 1721, is housed at the Prefectural Museum of Okinawa, Naha. A copy may be obtained from the Hawley Collection. The Shoke-bon Manuscript copy of the *Omorososhi* is located at the Prefectural Museum of Okinawa, Naha, while the Nakayoshi-bon Manuscript copy is housed at the University of Ryukyu, Naha.

SACHIYO ITO

OKUNI (flourished early seventeenth century), the semilegendary founder of *kabuki.* Okuni was a female shrine attendant at the Grand (Shintō) Shrine of Izumo. She is often referred to as Izumo no Okuni. At the end of the sixteenth century, she went about Japan performing her eroticized interpretations of popular and religious dances. As her fame grew, she organized a troupe of mainly female dancers. She was joined by a masterless *kyōgen* player named Sankurō (or Sanjūro), who acted as her manager. Sankurō advised her to include comic sketches, based on *kyōgen* farces and usually set in the pleasure quarters, in her repertory.

Okuni was a daring performer, and audiences liked to see her portray male characters; she often appeared doing a religious dance, the *nembutsu odori,* with cropped hair, a pair of swords in her sash, a priest's robe over her shoulders, a Catholic rosary and crucifix about her neck, and holding a brass gong that she beat with a metal stick as she sang and moved about.

Her troupe played in the dry riverbed of Kyoto's Kamo River in 1603 and gained great popularity. Because of their offbeat nature, the dances came to be called *kabuki,* a word derived from a term then applied to anything that was decidedly unconventional. Okuni's *kabuki* satisfied a need of the urban population for new forms of diversion, since Japan had just been pacified under the rule of the Tokugawa shogunate (in 1603). Okuni's sketches used both contemporary and classical materials. In one extremely well-liked sketch, a young, dead samurai named Nagoya Sanzaburō was irresistably drawn from his resting place in the underworld by Okuni's voice; he danced with her in remembrance of past amours. (Nagoya Sanzaburō was a real person, a samurai who died in 1603. He was somehow linked to Okuni because of his reputation as a romantic antiestablishment figure, or *kabukimono.* The actual relationship between him and Okuni has been much discussed, although many now feel that she exploited his reputation but was not in fact his lover.)

It is not clear when Okuni died; some say 1610, others 1614, and others much later. Her fame was so great that it was not long before rival troupes of women dancers appeared, giving rise to *onna kabuki,* or "women's *kabuki.*" These women plied the arts of the courtesan, their appeal heightened by the male dress they wore while performing. *Kabuki* (or *yujō kabuki*) was another name by which their shows were known. Although a nationwide phenomenon, in 1629, for a number of (mainly political) reasons, women were banned from the professional stage and did not return to it until the late nineteenth century.

[*See also* Kabuki Theater.]

BIBLIOGRAPHY

Ariyoshi, Sawako. *Kabuki Dancer.* Translated by James R. Brandon. Tokyo, 1994.

Kurata Yoshiro et al. *Nihon Geinō Jinmei Jiten.* Tokyo, 1995.

Ortolani, Benito. *The Japanese Theatre: From Shamanistic Ritual to Contemporary Pluralism.* Rev. ed. Princeton, 1995.

SAMUEL L. LEITER

ONDINE. Full title: *Ondine, ou La Naïade.* Ballet in six scenes. Choreography: Jules Perrot and Fanny Cerrito. Music: Cesare Pugni. Libretto: Jules Perrot. Scenery: William Grieve. First performance: 22 June 1843, Her Majesty's Theatre, London. Principals: Fanny Cerrito (Ondine), Jules Perrot (Matteo).

One of the most beautiful images in the history of the Romantic ballet was created by Jules Perrot in the *pas de l'ombre,* the "shadow dance" in *Ondine.* The idea of this dance apparently originated with Perrot; nothing like it occurs in the ballet's literary source, Friedrich de la Motte Fouqué's novel *Undine* (1811), or in Guilbert de Pixérécourt's *féerie* called *Ondine, ou La Nymphe des Eaux* (1830), from which Perrot drew many of his theatrical ideas.

Ondine provided a twist on the popular Romantic theme of a mortal in love with a supernatural being by having the water sprite Ondine pursue the human Matteo. She assumes mortal flesh for his sake (hence the shadow dance, illustrating her delight in her newfound substantiality), but she cannot sustain a mortal's ills and relinquishes Matteo to his human sweetheart.

The Catanian (Sicilian) setting provided a pretext for lively Italian dances and a colorful folk festival. Matteo's dream of the undersea realm of the water sprites was comparable to the "white acts" of *La Sylphide* or *Giselle.* Fanny Cerrito, who danced the title role, choreographed the pas de six in this scene.

In 1851 Perrot staged the ballet in Saint Petersburg, where it enjoyed a long life. William Dollar's *Ondine* (1949) revived Perrot's libretto. In 1958 Frederick Ashton included a shadow dance in the Royal Ballet's new *Ondine,* danced to a new score by Hans Werner Henze.

BIBLIOGRAPHY

Au, Susan. "The Shadow of Herself: Some Sources of Jules Perrot's *Ondine.*" *Dance Chronicle* 2.3 (1978): 159–171.

Beaumont, Cyril W. *Complete Book of Ballets.* London, 1937.

Gautier, Théophile, et al. *Les beautés de l'Opéra.* Paris, 1845.

Guest, Ivor. *"Undine:* The Pure Gold of Romanticism." *Ballet Annual* 13 (1959): 64–74.

Guest, Ivor. *The Romantic Ballet in England.* London, 1972.

Guest, Ivor. *Fanny Cerrito.* 2d rev. ed. London, 1974.

Guest, Ivor. *Jules Perrot: Master of the Romantic Ballet.* London, 1984.

Heath, Charles. *Beauties of the Opera and Ballet* (1845). New York, 1977.

Moore, Lillian. "Cerrito and *Ondine.*" *The Dancing Times* 33 (June 1943): 408–410.

SUSAN AU

ONNAGATA. Also called *oyama,* an *onnagata* is a highly trained *kabuki* actor who specializes in the performance of female roles. The term combines the word for "woman" *(onna)* with a word (*gata,* from *kata*) meaning "person," "form," or "pattern."

Female impersonation became a necessary adjunct of *kabuki* when actresses were banned from the stage in 1629 by the Tokugawa shogunate, because fights broke out in the audience over the women, who were also prostitutes. The early female impersonators were pretty *wakashu,* young men (under fifteen years of age), who were more interested in their own homosexual prostitution than their art, and public disturbances continued. In 1652 *wakashu kabuki* was banned and a series of government edicts resulted in the legitimizing of *kabuki;* one required each actor in a troupe to be registered as a player of either male or female roles. This forced specialization led to the rapid development of the *onnagata*'s art, and

ONNAGATA. Bandō Tamasaburō V, one of the great contemporary *onnagata*s (female impersonators), in *Kurokami* (Jet Black Hair). (Photograph © 1984 by Jack Vartoogian; used by permission.)

plays were soon written that enabled actors to exploit their insights into female psychology and behavior. Ultimately, they were so successful that Japanese women were greatly influenced by their costuming and carriage.

The *onnagata* learns to be feminine in every detail of his movement and behavior onstage; he wears elaborate female costumes and wigs and is artfully made up to resemble a woman as closely as possible. He speaks in a falsetto that normally fails to disguise his true sex completely, and this trace of masculinity is deemed a satisfyingly erotic touch by connoisseurs. Numerous conventions for a wide variety of *onnagata* role-types have evolved; even if an actress were permitted to appear in a *kabuki* play, she would be expected to play her roles exactly as three centuries of male actors have decreed. The *onnagata* learns how to stand in a way that will emphasize his fragility and to walk with the delicate, pigeon-toed gait of the stage female. He even trains with a sheet of paper between his knees, which he must not drop, to capture the knee-to-knee shuffling manner of the onstage female.

Kabuki's onnagatas owe much of the accomplishment of their art to such early players as Yoshizawa Ayame I (1673–1729), Segawa Kikunonojō II (1693–1749), Iwai Hanshirō V (1776–1847), and many others, some of whom were the theatrical idols of their day—as the *onnagata* Bandō Tamasaburō V is today. [*See the entry on Bandō.*] In the past, the actors often lived their daily lives as women to enable them to bring great realism to the stage, but such practices are no longer in fashion. The *onnagata* remains the soul of *kabuki;* many believe that if the tradition should ever die, it will mean the end of *kabuki.*

[*For further general discussion, see also* Kabuki Theater.]

BIBLIOGRAPHY

Toita Yasuji. *Onnagata.* Tokyo, 1975.

Tsubouchi Shōyō and Yamatnoto Tirō. *History and Characteristics of Kabuki.* Edited and translated by Ryōzo, Matsumoto. Yokohama, 1960.

Watanabe Tamotsu. *Onnagata no Unmei.* Tokyo, 1965.

SAMUEL L. LEITER

ONOE BAIKŌ, name used by seven generations of *kabuki* actors. The name was first used as a pen name by members of the Onoe Kikugorō acting line, and apart from its brief use as a stage name by Onoe Kikugorō III, who was billed as Onoe Baikō III, it became significant as a theatrical name only with Onoe Baikō VI.

Onoe Baikō VI (born 15 October 1870 in Nagoya, died 8 November 1934 in Tokyo), son of Onoe Asjirō and grandson of Kikugorō III, was raised in his mother's geisha house. In 1876, he joined the household of dancer Nishikawa Koisaburō and debuted in Nagoya as Nishikawa Einosuke. He was adopted by Onoe Kikugorō V in 1882 and, with the name Onoe Einosuke I, trained as an *onnagata* (female impersonator). He held the name Onoe Eizaburō V before becoming Onoe Baikō VI in 1903. Baikō achieved considerable success playing in *sewamono* ("domestic plays") and in the Onoe family's specialty of *kaidan-mono* ("ghost plays"), as well as having many hits drawn from the family's play anthology, *Shinko Engeki Jūshū.* His work in new plays and dances was also memorable. He played leads against his adoptive father and created a sensation as the partner to Ichikawa Kakitsu VI (later known as Ichimura Uzaemon XV). In 1911, he joined the company at Tokyo's new Teikoku Gekijō (Imperial Theater) and became the artistic director.

Onoe Baikō VII (born 31 August 1915 in Tokyo, died 24 April 1995 in Tokyo), the adopted son of Onoe Kikugorō VI, received intensive training from his childhood onward. He made his debut at the Ichimura-za in 1921 under the name Onoe Ushinosuke, which he changed to Onoe Kikunosuke II in 1935. He spent a year at Keio University studying business before returning to the stage, taking his uncle's name, and becoming Onoe Baikō VII in 1947 at the Tokyo Gekijō. When his adoptive father died in 1949, Baikō VII, Ichikawa Sadanji II, Onoe Shōroku II, and others formed the Kikugorō Gekidan troupe, of which he became a central component. A National Living Treasure and a member of the Japan Arts Academy, he was, during his prime, considered one of the two greatest *onnagata* of his time, the other being Nakamura Utaemon VI. His finest classical roles included Masaoka in *Meiboku Sendai Hagi,* Tamate Gozen in *Sesshū Gappō ga Tsuji,* Agemaki in *Sukeroku,* Osono in *Hikosan Gongen Chikai no Sukedachi,* Chiyo in *Terakoya,* Omiwa in *Imoseyama,* Omitsu in *Nozaki Mura,* and so on. A brilliant dancer, he excelled in works such as *Onatsu Kyōran, Ysuna, Shiokumi,* and *Dōjōji.*

In new works of the 1950s, he created a splash playing Fuji no Tsubone in *Genji Monogatari* and the title role in *Nayotake.* On occasion, he played gentle young men like Katsuyori in *Honchō Nijūshikō,* Torazō in *Kikubatake,* Yoshitsune in *Kanjinchō,* Enya Hangan in *Chūshingura,* and Atsumori in *Ichinotani.* Somewhat stout of figure and, when in costume and makeup, not nearly so beautiful as Utaemon, he was known for both his grace and his largeheartedness. Unlike *onnagata* who carry their art with them even into private life, he remained resolutely masculine offstage, and was noted for his fondness for sports. His writings on acting include *Ume to Kiku* (Plum Blossoms and Chrysanthemums). Baikō VII also toured abroad frequently and even directed a small-scale production of *Narukami* at New York's Institute for Advanced Studies in the Theatre Arts (IASTA). His brother is Onoe Kuroemon II, and his son and artistic heir is Onoe Kikugorō VII.

[*See also* Japanese Traditional Schools *and* Kabuki Theater.]

BIBLIOGRAPHY

Akasaka Jiseki, ed. *Kabuki haiyū daihyakka.* Tokyo, 1993.

Bandō Tamasaburō and Sunaga Asahiko. *Tamasaburō: Butai no yume.* Tokyo, 1984.

Engekikai 52.2 (1993). Special issue: *kabuki* actors' directory.

Nojima Jusaburō. *Kabuki jinmei jiten.* Tokyo, 1988.

Toita Yasuji, ed. *Kabuki kanshō nyūmon.* 3d ed., rev. Tokyo, 1994.

SAMUEL L. LEITER

ONOE KIKUGORŌ, name used by seven generations of *kabuki* actors. This line holds what may be considered the second most influential position in the world of *kabuki,* after the Ichikawa Danjūrō line.

Onoe Kikugorō I (born 1717 in Kyoto, died 29 December 1783 in Osaka) debuted as Onoe Taketarō and became Onoe Kikugorō I in 1730. At first, he gained fame as an *onnagata* (female impersonator), making his first great success in 1743 as Princess Taema in *Narukami.* Subsequently, he achieved success as a player of leading male roles *(tachiyaku),* playing various great roles in *Chūshingura,* which subsequently became associated with the Kikugorō line. His greatest weakness was as a dancer.

Onoe Kikugorō II (born 1769 in Kyoto, died 12 July 1787), Kikugorō I's son, debuted as Onoe Ushinosuke I in Kyoto in 1776 and specialized in young male and female roles. He took the name Kikugorō II in 1785 but drowned two years later, at age eighteen while touring to Juo province.

Onoe Kikugorō III (born 1784, in Edo died 24 April 1849 in Kakegawa), an egocentric but brilliant star who could play any sort of role, was the adopted son of Onoe Matsusuke I (later Onoe Shōroku I) and debuted in 1788 as Onoe Shingaburō, which he soon changed to Onoe Eizaburō I. He held the names Onoe Matsusuke II and Onoe Baikō I before becoming Kikugorō III—which had been unused for nearly three decades. He made several temporary retirements during his career. Kikugorō III is remembered for his alliance with playwright Tsuruya Nanboku IV, who wrote such masterpieces as *Yotsuya Kaidan,* in which Kikugorō III played Oiwa. The playing of ghosts was one of his and his successors' specialties, as was the performance of multiple roles in a single play. He died while traveling to Eeo from Osaka.

Onoe Kikugorō IV (born 1808, died 28 June 1860 in Edo), the son-in-law of Kikugorō III, was the only pure *onnagata* in the line. He held the names Nakamura Kachō, Nakamura Tatsuzō, Onoe Eizaburō III, and Onoe Baikō IV before assuming the name Onoe Kikugorō IV in 1856.

Onoe Kikugorō V (born 4 June 1844 in Edo, died 18 February 1904 in Tokyo) was one of the greatest actors in Japanese history. Although not quite as versatile as his grandfather, Kikugorō III, he played with incredible skill and inventiveness in all types of roles. He was the son of impoverished theater-manager Ichimura Uzaemon XII. Debuting as Ichimura Kuro'emon II, he was recognized as a child actor of remarkable precocity. To rid himself of his debts, his father went into official retirement and the boy became a manager as Ichimura Uzaemon XIII. When his father died soon after, their theater had to be given up. Early in his career he was backed by the great Ichikawa Kodanji IV, who often became his co-star. In 1863, he became Ichimura Kakitsu IV and attained the name Onoe Kikugorō V in 1868. It was not long before he, Ichikawa Danjūrō IX, and Ichikawa Sadanji I became the three greatest Meiji period (1868–1912) stars, known collectively as Dan-Kiku-Sa. Kikugorō, however, was opposed to the pedantic "living history" *(katsureki)* plays being done by Danjūrō IX, and they did not act together for several years. In 1878 the two were reconciled when they played together at the first *kabuki* performance ever given before the emperor.

Kikugorō V's greatest roles included Kanpei in *Chūshingura,* Naojirō in *Naozamurai,* Benten Kozō, Sashichi in *Omatsuri Sodachi,* and the title role in *Kamiyui Shinza.* Although basically conservative, he pioneered the new "cropped hair" plays called *zangiri mono.* Kikugorō V also compiled the family play anthology, the *Shinko Engeki Jusshū,* made up mainly of dance plays performed in a style influenced by *nō* theater. In 1903, Kikugorō V attempted a comeback after suffering a stroke; another stroke that same year killed him.

Onoe Kikugorō VI (born 26 August 1885 in Tokyo, died 10 July 1949 in Tokyo) was one of the most potent forces in twentieth-century *kabuki.* He, too, was exceptionally versatile, although strongest in domestic plays *(sewamono).* He was a truly great dancer, bringing psychological realism to his work and even infusing elements of Western ballets, such as *Swan Lake* into certain interpretations.

"Rokudaime" ("the Sixth"), as he is remembered, made his debut at nine months, using his private name of Terajima Saizō. This was changed to Onoe Ushinosuke II in 1891. Ichikawa Danjūrō IX had a great influence during his formative years. Following his father's death, he became Onoe Kikugorō VI. After Danjūrō IX died in 1903, Rokudaime's career ran into problems because of the lack of a powerful patron, but his smashing success in a 1911 production requiring him to play seven roles made the theater world pay serious attention.

By the mid-1920s he had climbed to the top of the ladder, appearing in many new plays as well as classics. For a while, he had heavy business responsibilities as the major star at the Ichimura-za, where he and Nakamura Kichiemon I shared a golden age. Various setbacks, including the 1923 Kantō earthquake, placed the theater in the hands of the Shōchiku conglomerate. During the early years of World War II, he fell ill following a strenuous tour of Manchuria to play for the troops. Although weakened, he continued to play major roles in the postwar years. But the strain of working every month in straitened circumstances took its toll. This far-seeing actor had established in 1930 the Japan Actors' School, hoping to offer an appropriate education for the children of *kabuki* actors; lack of support led to its demise in 1933, however. His adopted sons were Onoe Baikō VII and Onoe Kuroemon II.

Onoe Kikugorō VII (born 12 October 1942 in Tokyo), the son of Onoe Baikō VII, is a worthy successor to the Kikugorō line, although he has not yet achieved the stature of his immediate predecessors. He debuted in 1948 as Onoe Ushinosuke V. During adolescence, he enjoyed sports more than acting, and he also had a reputation as a playboy. He began to find the stage interesting just before graduating from high school, when his parts started to improve. He used the name Onoe Kikunosuke IV before becoming Onoe Kikugorō VII in 1973. When he decided to devote himself to acting full time, he helped create a boom in *kabuki's* fortunes through his association with two peers, Ichikawa Shinnosuke VI (later Ichikawa Danjūrō XII) and Onoe Tatsunosuke I, who were often referred to as the "three Sukes." The 1960s brought a dramatic rise in his fame, largely because the handsome actor had become a television star. His marriage in 1972 to movie star Fuji Junko gave him national prominence. His success on television attracted many new fans to *kabuki,* but his stage work suffered because of his divided responsibilities. During the 1960s, his starring roles were mainly in small theaters, but in 1970 he, the future Danjūrō XII, and Tatsunosuke I created a sensation when they performed in *Genji Monogatari* at the Kabuki-za—playing the roles originated by their fathers at the same theater twenty years earlier.

Kikugorō VII is equally effective in male and female roles. He can shine as both Otomi and Yosaburō in *Kirare Yosa* or play either Sukeroku or Agemaki in *Sukeroku*—feats few others can match. During the first half of his career his male roles had been mainly those of young lovers, but since 1989 he has gradually undertaken more mature male roles, such as Gonta in the Sushi-ya scene of *Yoshitsune Senbon Zakura* and Okura in *Kiichi Hōgen,* completely changing his previous image and achieving considerable acclaim.

[*See also* Japanese Traditional Dance; Kabuki Theater; *and* Onnagata.]

BIBLIOGRAPHY

Akasaka Jiseki, ed. *Kabuki haiyū daihyakka.* Tokyo, 1993.
Blakeny, Ben Bruce. "Rokudaime." *Contemporary Japan* (October—December 1949).
Engekikai 52.2 (1993). Special issue: *kabuki* actors' directory.
Leiter, Samuel L. "Four Interviews with Kabuki Actors." *Educational Theatre Journal* (December 1966): 391–404.
Nojima Jusaburō. *Kabuki jinmei jiten.* Tokyo, 1988.
Onoe Kikugorō VI. *Gei.* Tokyo, 1947.
Toita Yasuji. *Onoe Kikugorō.* Tokyo, 1973.
Toita Yasuji, ed. *Kabuki kanshō nyūmon.* 3d ed., rev. Tokyo, 1994.

SAMUEL L. LEITER

ONOE SHŌROKU, name used by two generations of *kabuki* actor-dancers.

Onoe Shōroku I (born 1744 in Osaka, died 16 October 1815 in Edo [Tokyo]), debuted in 1755 and held the names Onoe Tokuzō and Onoe Matsusuke I before becoming Shōroku in 1809. He was best known as a player of mature male roles *(tachiyaku),* splitting his career between the Kyoto-Osaka (Kamigata) region and Edo. After he starred in Edo-author Tsuruya Nanboku IV's *Tengajaya Mura* in 1804, he became famous for the innovations he

ONOE SHŌROKU. Onoe Shōroku II as Nikki Danjō in *Sendai Hagi.* (Photograph courtesy of Samuel L. Leiter.)

made in acting in Nanboku IV's ghost plays *(kaidan-mono)*. A corpulent man, he became famous for villain roles in his later years.

Onoe Shōroku II (born 28 March 1913 in Tokyo, died 25 June 1989 in Tokyo), was the youngest son of Matsumoto Kōshirō VII. Together with his brothers Ichikawa Danjūrō XI and Matsumoto Hakuō I (better known as Matsumoto Kōshirō VIII), he was one of the giants of post–World War II *kabuki*. He debuted in 1918 as Matsumoto Toyo. In 1935, he became Shōroku II. He was well trained by Onoe Kikugorō VI (1885–1949) in the great domestic-play *(sewamono)* roles, such as Sakanaya Sōgorō in *Shin Sarayashiki*, the title role in *Kamiyui Shinza*, Matahei in *Domo Mata*, Dōgen in *Kaga Tobi*, and Tatsugorō in *Megumi no Kenka*, as well as in dance roles such as Tsuna in *Ibaraki* and the spider in *Tsuchigumo*. Some of his brilliant period-play *(jidaimono)* performances were in Kikugorō's tradition, others in his father's, and still others in that of Ichikawa Sadanji III (1898–1964). (Sadanji taught Shōroku parts in the bombastic *aragoto* style, including the role of Kumedera Danjō in *Kenuki* and the title role in *Narukami*.) Shōroku II was memorable in many other great roles; in *Yoshitsune Senbon Zakura*, he liked to play three characters—Tomomori, Tadanobu, and Gonta—in the same production. On several occasions, he and his elder brothers alternated the three main roles of Benkei, Togashi, and Yoshitsune in *Kanjinchō*. "New" *kabuki (shin kabuki)* plays in which he sparkled included *Ippon Gatana, Wakaki Hi no Nobunaga*, and *Kurayami no Ushimatsu*. Shōroku II also made several films and occasionally performed in Western plays, including Shakespeare's *Othello* and Rostand's *Cyrano de Bergerac*. Because of problems with his legs in his last years, he mostly played roles that did not require much standing.

Despite his stocky build, Shōroku II was a masterful dancer and choreographer. He became head *(iemoto)* of the Fujima school of dance in 1937 and used the dance name Fujima Kan'emon IV until 1975, when he became Fujima Kansai and handed his position over to his son Onoe Tatsunosuke I (1946–1987). Unhappily, the very promising Tatsunosuke predeceased him.

In 1960, Shōroku II was a leading member of the first postwar *kabuki* company to visit the West. He toured abroad again in 1969 and acted in China in 1979. He was the recipient of countless distinguished awards, including being named a National Living Treasure and being inducted into the Japan Arts Academy. His artistic methods, described in several books he wrote have been passed on to such present-day stars as Onoe Kikugorō VII and Ichikawa Danjūrō XII.

[*See also* Japanese Traditional Schools *and* Kabuki Theater.]

BIBLIOGRAPHY

Akasaka Jiseki, ed. *Kabuki haiyū daihyakka*. Tokyo, 1993.

Engekikai (January 1994). Special issue on *kabuki* actors.

Nojima Jusaburō. *Kabuki jinmei jiten*. Tokyo, 1988.

Toita Yasuji et al. "Tsuitō: Nidaime Onoe Shōroku." *Engekikai* (August 1989): 141–156.

Toita Yasuji, ed. *Kabuki kanshō nyūmon*. 3d ed., rev. Tokyo, 1994.

SAMUEL L. LEITER

ŌNO KAZUO (born 27 October 1906 in Hakodate, Hokkaido, Japan), Japanese modern dancer, *butō* performer, and choreographer. After graduating from the Nippon College of Physical Education, Ōno worked as a high school physical education teacher until he reached the compulsory retirement age. Meanwhile, he had been deeply impressed by the work of Spanish flamenco dancer La Argentina (Antonia Mercé) and German expressionist dancer Harald Kreutzberg. He began studying the German dance style known as *Neuer Tanz* with Ishii Baku, Eguchi Takaya, and Miya Misako. In his first concert, in 1949, Ōno danced three pieces: *Kikoku, Tango*, and *Rilke—First Flower of Linden Trees*.

After Ōno performed in the *Hijitaka Tatsumi 650 Dance Experience no Kai* in 1960 and 1961, he turned to *butō*. He joined Leda-no-Kai, an experimental dance group led by Hijikata, and danced in Hijikata's *ankoku butō* dances. In 1969, he appeared in the film *Portrait of Mr. O*, directed by Nagano Chiaki.

In 1977, at the age of seventy-one, Ōno presented his first *butō* work, *La Argentina Sho* (Admiring La Argentina). Performed again at the Nancy Performing Arts

ŌNO. *Ka Cho Fu Getsu* (Flowers-Birds-Wind-Moon), by Ōno Kazuo and his son Yoshito, was commissioned by the Italian city of Cremona and premiered there in May 1990. A recurring theme in Japanese art and literature, *Ka Cho Fu Getsu* deals with the relationship between humans and nature. In this scene, Kazuo becomes a tragicomic embodiment of enigmatic life forces. (Photograph © 1993 by Johan Elbers; used by permission.)

Festival in Nancy, France, in 1980, it received rave reviews from *Le monde* critic Colette Goddard. *La Argentina Sho* was based on Ōno's attempt to recreate his memory of La Argentina's beautiful dance, which he had seen fifty years earlier. Others of Ōno's works are *A Table, or Dreams of a Fetus* (1980), which was a prototype for a work entitled *My Mother,* presented the following year; *The Dead Sea—Vienna Waltz and Ghosts* (1985); *Water Lilies* (1987); and *Ka Cho Fu Getsu,* which premiered in Cremona, Italy, in 1990. Ōno has published a book on *butō* theory, *Ōno Kazuo butō no kotoba* (Ōno Kazuo's Words on *Butō,* 1989).

BIBLIOGRAPHY

Ichikawa, Miyabi. "Butoh: The Denial of the Body." *Ballett International* 12 (September 1989): 14–19.

Stein, Bonnie Sue. "Celebraing Hijikata: A Bow to the Butoh Master." *Dance Magazine* (May 1988): 44–47.

Tachiki Takashi. *Tennin keraku: Ōno Kazuo no sekai.* Tokyo, 1993.

HASEGAWA ROKU
Translated from Japanese

OPERA, BALLET IN. Although opera was developed in Florence at the end of the sixteenth century as a conscious attempt to revive the dramatic expressiveness of Greek tragedy, its theatrical style was determined primarily by the pageantry and ceremoniousness of late Renaissance court entertainments. From the earliest days of opera, its composers found ballet useful for enhancing the more spectacular characteristics of the new art form, especially in the virtually obligatory festive scene designed to bring each work to a joyous close, as in, for example, Jacopo Peri's *Euridice* (1600), Claudio Monteverdi's *Orfeo* (1607), and Marco da Gagliano's *Dafne* (1608).

The tendency to identify ballet with spectacle became even more pronounced during the second half of the seventeenth century, when, with the exception of France, Italian court opera flourished everywhere in Europe. During this time, scenic magnificence and vocal virtuosity gained undisputable ascendancy over affective action and psychological empathy. As a result, dance assumed an increasingly important diversionary role. Each of the five acts of Antonio Cesti's *Il Pomo d'Oro* (1668), staged with unstinting expenditure for the wedding in Vienna of Hungary's Leopold I and the infanta Margerita Teresa of Spain, contained several large-scale ballets, the aim of which was purely decorative.

In their court entertainments, the French, though even more devoted to dancing than the Italians and their admirers, paid greater attention to literary quality and dramatic unity, if not to plausibility. French opera, essentially the creation of Jean-Baptiste Lully, a dancer and a choreographer as well as a composer, invariably included ballet, the function of which was not only to divert the audience but also to reinforce the drama. In the third act of Lully's *Thésée* (1675), a dance by the denizens of hell becomes, in effect, a manifestation of Medea's vengeful feelings. In the fourth act of his *Roland* (1685), the eponymous hero, while watching a pastoral *divertissement* at a wedding celebration, discovers that the bride is his beloved and thus that he has been betrayed.

After Lully's death, the amount of dance in French opera increased. At the same time, the concern for unity of action and mood began to diminish rapidly. This shift in taste led to the birth of the *opéra-ballet,* a type of evening-length *divertissement* whose various acts were given a semblance of coherence by the use of a general theme, such as the four elements or the loves of the gods. Inaugurated by André Campra with *L'Europe Galante* (1697), the genre was brought to a climax by Jean-Philippe Rameau in works such as *Les Indes Galantes* (1735). Virtually the same in form as the *opéra-ballet,*

OPERA. In the late 1940s, Aurelio Milloss staged this ballet as the closing scene of a production of Claudio Monteverdi's *Orfeo* (1607), performed on an outdoor stage erected in the Boboli Gardens in Florence during the Maggio Musicale (May Music Festival). (Photograph by Marchiori; reprinted from Horst Koegler, *Ballett International,* Berlin, 1960, fig. 26.)

which it superseded without destroying, the *ballet-héroïque* testified to a growing interest in elevated themes, especially those drawn from classical antiquity.

The production in Paris of Christoph Wilibald Gluck's *Iphigénie en Aulide* (1774), a work whose subject accorded with the neoclassical inclinations of the time, ensured the triumph of Enlightenment principles in French opera. These, calling for a new emphasis on dramatic coherence and emotional directness, required that the dances display a narrative and stylistic kinship with the work as a whole. The operas that Gluck wrote, or rewrote, for Paris helped to remove ballet decisively from its origins as court ceremonial. In *Orphée* (1774), the well-received revision of his highly influential reform opera *Orfeo ed Euridice* (1762), Gluck extended the orchestral numbers to include ballets for the Furies and the Blessed Spirits in act 2 and for the celebrants in the Temple of Love in act 3. Choreographed by Maximilien Gardel and Gaëtan Vestris and performed by them and Marie-Madeleine Guimard, Anna Friedrike Heinel, Anne Dorival, and Pierre Gardel, the dance music that was added to the Paris production of the opera, especially in act 2, played a decisive role in creating the work's definitive character as a sustained lyrical utterance of noble solemnity.

Italian *opera seria* exercised a virtual hegemony throughout Europe, except France, until the mid-eighteenth century and, though in decline, survived until the early nineteenth century. Consisting mostly of a succession of virtuosic *da capo* arias, *opera seria* represented the triumph of music over drama. While it was rigorously formal and often had highly elaborate scenery, it was not inexpressive. In act 2 of George Frideric Handel's *Ariodante* (1735), for example, there is a powerful dream ballet in which we see into the heart of the heroine, by watching a battle between the forces of good and evil contending within her. The choreographer and principal dancer in *Ariodante,* first performed at Covent Garden in London, was Marie Sallé, on leave from the Paris Opera. More often than not, however, a ballet was used simply to augment the festive aspects of the production, as was the case with the finale of *Idomeneo* (1781), Wolfgang Amadeus Mozart's elegant *opera seria.*

During this period (and, indeed, until the twentieth century), even the most illustrious creators and executants in ballet tended to be members of opera companies—and thus accessories to an art generally considered more important and more inclusive than their own. Though they were given opportunities to create and appear in autonomous dance works—often used to fill out an evening otherwise devoted to opera—they devoted the larger part of their efforts to the *divertissements* incorporated into most large-scale operas.

The species of lyric theater that developed at the Paris Opera during the first decades of the nineteenth century

OPERA. Albert Lortzing's *Zar und Zimmerman* (Tsar and Carpenter; 1837) takes place in 1698 in a shipyard in Saardam, where Peter the Great has gone to work, incognito, as a carpenter to master trades he cannot learn in Russia. A festival scene in the third act features a jolly clog dance, performed in wooden shoes. For a production at the Basel Opera in 1977, Heinz Spoerli arranged the dance for members of the Basel Ballet. (Photograph by Peter Stöckli; courtesy of Heinz Spoerli.)

and that came to be associated with (the preexistent term) *grand opera,* was spectacular in manner, heroic in subject, and elevated in tone. It required a large cast of principals, a huge chorus, and a full-sized dance troupe—this last being necessary for the formal ballet considered indispensable at that house. Though the ballet, often placed in the third act, was likely to have a thematic, topographical, or stylistic connection to the subject of the opera, the relationship tended to be ornamental rather than organic. Such is the case with the pas de six in act 1 of Gioacchino Rossini's *Guillaume Tell* (1829), the Indian dances in act 4 of Giocomo Meyerbeer's *L'Africaine* (1865), "La Peregrina" in act 3 of Giuseppe Verdi's *Don Carlos* (1867), and the Spanish dances in act 2 of Jules Massenet's *Le Cid* (1885). Even in Daniel Auber's *La Muette de Portici* (1828), where the title role was conceived for a dancer-mime and there is no formal ballet sequence, the dances merely serve to intensify the local color.

But even in grand opera there were important exceptions to this tendency, the most celebrated being among the earliest: the ballet of ghostly nuns, who rise from their tombs in act 3 of Meyerbeer's *Robert le Diable* (1831). With this scene, Meyerbeer and his librettist Eugene Scribe (1791–1861) intensify the prevailing atmosphere of diabolism, while at the same time furthering the plot. The festive ballet in the previous act is, however, purely decorative.

Until after World War II, virtually any lyric work presented at the Paris Opera had to have a ballet, even if the composer had died without supplying one. In 1841, for the Opera's production of Carl Maria von Weber's *Der Freischütz* (1821)—which had only a single dance, a rustic waltz in act 1—Hector Berlioz concocted a ballet suite by orchestrating Weber's *Invitation to the Dance,* and arranging excerpts from the composer's incidental music for P. A. Wolff's play *Preciosa.*

For Charles Gounod's *Faust* (1859), transferred from the smaller Théâtre-Lyrique to the Paris Opera in 1869, the composer supplied his own ballet music, as he did again in 1888 for *Roméo et Juliette* (1867), when it, too, moved to the Opera. Several non-French composers also added ballet music to their operas for production in Paris: for example, Rossini in 1827 for *Mosè in Egitto* (1818), Wagner in 1861 for *Tannhäuser* (1845), and Verdi in 1857 for *Il Trovatore* (1853) and in 1894 for *Otello* (1887).

It was not only at the Paris Opera that the principles of grand opera prevailed. When Georges Bizet's *Carmen* (1874) was converted into a grand opera at the Vienna Court Opera in 1875 (four months after its Paris premiere as an *opéra comique*), a ballet was added by adapting music from *La Jolie Fille de Perth* (1866) and, *L'Arlésienne* (1872).

By the middle of the nineteenth century, most of the world's major lyric theaters possessed the kind of sizable and proficient ballet troupes required for works such as Richard Wagner's *Rienzi* (Dresden, 1842), Mikhail Glinka's *Ruslan and Ludmila* (Saint Petersburg, 1842), Stanisław Moniuszko's *Halka* (Vilnius, 1854), Ferenc Erkel's *Bánk Bán* (Budapest, 1861), Bedřich Smetana's *The Brandenburgers in Bohemia* (Prague, 1866), Giuseppe Verdi's *Aida* (Cairo, 1871), Amilcare Ponchielli's *La Gioconda* (Milan,

OPERA. Richard Wagner's *Tannhäuser* (1845) opens with the Venusberg scene, in which Tannhäuser sings of the pleasures afforded him in the realm of Venus. A production mounted in the 1950s by Wieland Wagner, the composer's grandson, at the Festspielhaus in Bayreuth, featured the abstract lighting effects that he favored and choreographic groupings arranged by Gertrud Wagner, his wife. (Photograph by Festspiele Bayreuth/Lauterwasser; reprinted from Horst Koegler, *Ballett International*, Berlin, 1960, fig. 141.)

1876), Camille Saint-Saëns's *Samson et Dalila* (Weimar, 1877), Carlos Gomes's *Lo Schiavo* (Rio de Janeiro, 1889), and César Franck's *Hulda* (Monte Carlo, 1894).

Although a ballet was not obligatory in *opéra-comique*, many examples of the genre included one, including Ferdinand Hérold's *Zampa* (1831), Georges Bizet's *Les Pêcheurs de Perles* (1863), Ambroise Thomas's *Mignon* (1866), Léo Delibes's *Lakmé* (1883), Jules Massenet's *Manon* (1884), and Henri Rabaud's *Mârouf, Savetier du Caire* (1914). Composers of operetta also made extensive use of ballet, as for example Jacques Offenbach in *Orphée aux Enfers* (1858) and Johann Strauss in *Die Fledermaus* (1874).

The style and technique of classical ballet dominated the dancing in nineteenth-century opera as a whole—in 1891 in Bayreuth, Cosima Wagner engaged Virginia Zucchi as choreographer and *prima ballerina* for the first *Tannhäuser* (1845) to be performed there. Nevertheless, the burgeoning nationalism that found expression in many eastern European operas during the nineteenth century led to an increasing emphasis on character dances, such as the *csárdás* in Erkel's *Bánk Bán*, the *lezghinka* in Glinka's *Ruslan and Ludmila*, and the *skocná* (a folk polka) in Smetana's *The Brandenburgers in Bohemia* and *The Bartered Bride* (1866).

Ballets, then, were not confined to grand opera. In German-speaking countries they were often a feature of *opéra-comique*, mainly in the guise of character dances—for example, in Albert Lortzing's *Zar und Zimmermann* (1837), Friedrich von Flotow's *Martha* (1847), and Wagner's *Die Meistersinger von Nürnberg* (1868), the world premiere of the latter being choreographed by the ballet mistress of the Munich Court Opera, Lucile Grahn.

In Russia, because of the popularity of ballet and the eminence of the dancers attached to the Imperial Theaters of Saint Petersburg and Moscow, dance found its way into operas of all kinds, its role in the work often as important as it had been at any time since the seventeenth century. Nikolai Rimsky-Korsakov's *Mlada* (1892), choreographed by Ivanov and Cecchetti and with the dancers led by Marie Petipa (as the shade of Mlada), was in fact conceived as an *opéra-ballet*. Other Russian operas with notable dance sequences are Tchaikovsky's *Eugene Onegin* (1879), Rimsky-Korsakov's *The Snow Maiden* (1882) and *Sadko* (1898), Modest Mussorgsky's *Khovanshchina* (1886), and Aleksandr Borodin's *Prince Igor* (1890).

In the first half of the twentieth century, opera continued to use dance, but (except in eastern Europe) more circumspectly than in the past. Several reasons account for this: a sharp increase in the cost of production made it impractical for most institutions to support a first-rate dance company merely to appear in opera-ballets; the use of the familiar balletic *divertissement* ran counter both to the long-prevailing Wagnerian ideal of opera and to the new seriousness with which Isadora Duncan and Serge Diaghilev had taught audiences to regard the art of dance; and the triumph of realism during the final decade of the nineteenth century, which made dance seem inappropriate in opera.

OPERA. Charles Gounod's *Faust* (1859), one of the most successful operas ever written, contains one of the most famous ballets in all of opera, the Walpurgis Night scene in act 5. At the Bolshoi Theater for Opera and Ballet in Leningrad, Leonid Lavrovsky's 1941 choreography established the standard for balletic revelry against which all later versions have been measured. In a 1961 performance, Ekaterina Maximova as the principal bacchante is lifted high above the heads of a crowd of gleeful nymphs and lecherous satyrs as they dance to celebrate Walpurgis Night, the eve of May Day. (Photograph by Eugene Umnov; reprinted from a Bolshoi Ballet souvenir program, 1962.)

Nevertheless, after World War I, when the inevitable reaction against both Wagnerism and realism gained momentum, dance no longer seemed so incompatible with operatic seriousness. By 1932, Arnold Schoenberg had completed act 2 of his *Moses und Aron* (1955), in which the orgiastic dance performed by the Children of Israel before the Golden Calf provides the work with a musical and dramatic climax of overwhelming power.

Since the end of World War II, other distinguished operatic composers have used dance as a means of enlarging their expressive resources—Benjamin Britten in *A Midsummer Night's Dream* (1960) and *Death in Venice* (1973); Hans Werner Henze in *Boulevard Solitude* (1952) and *The Bassarids* (1966); and Michael Tippett in *The Midsummer Marriage* (1955). In the 1970s and 1980s, dance has become a familiar feature of the mixed-media theatrical works that have outpaced opera in creative energy and that at least one of their prime creators, Robert Wilson, actually calls *operas.*

Though few new operas (in the older sense of the term) are added to the repertory these days, many long-neglected works have been successfully rediscovered. While musical authenticity is often sought in these revivals, grand operas are rarely produced with their ballet sequences intact. The Metropolitan Opera in New York, for example, regularly omits them from Verdi's *Les Vêpres Siciliennes* (1855) and *Don Carlos* (1867), at the same time reverting to Bizet's original *Carmen,* which it now presents as an *opéra-comique* with spoken dialogue and no ballet. In many cases (e.g., in *La Gioconda, Tannhäuser,* and the Russian repertory), the dance scenes, no matter how incidental, have become so much a part of the work's identity that omitting them is virtually unthinkable.

BIBLIOGRAPHY

Anthony, James R., et al. "Opera." In *The New Grove Dictionary of Music and Musicians.* London, 1980.

Grout, Donald Jay. *A Short History of Opera.* 2d ed. New York, 1965.

Guest, Ivor. *The Ballet of the Second Empire.* London, 1974.

Guest, Ivor. *The Romantic Ballet in Paris.* 2d rev. ed. London, 1980.

Searle, Humphrey. *Ballet Music.* 2d rev. ed. New York, 1973.

Sutton, Julia, et al. "Dance." In *The New Grove Dictionary of Music and Musicians.* London, 1980.

DALE HARRIS

OPÉRA-BALLET AND TRAGÉDIE LYRIQUE.

"All Europe knows the talent and taste of the French for dance and how this taste is admired and universally followed," wrote Luigi Riccoboni in 1738. The dance elements of rhythm and phrasing and the melodic shape of *menuets, gavottes, sarabandes, canaries, gigues, passepieds,* and *bourrées* transcended genre and medium and spread from court ballet to lyric stage, and there to chamber and to the foot of the altar itself. J. C. Nemeitz, an affluent young German visiting Paris in 1727, wrote "The music that is performed in churches is not too devout since the organ plays minuets and all types of worldly tunes."

Dance in the French lyric theater of the late seventeenth and early eighteenth centuries was affected by the creation of several different stage genres dominated by the *tragédie lyrique* and the *opéra-ballet.* The period began with Jean-Baptiste Lully's first operas in the 1670s and extended at least to Jean-Philippe Rameau's *tragédie lyrique* of 1733, *Hippolyte et Aricie.*

Lully gave France its national opera, the *tragédie en musique,* popularly known as the *tragédie lyrique.* Lully had witnessed Cardinal Jules Mazarin's ill-fated efforts between 1645 and his death in 1661 to establish a permanent Italian opera troupe in Paris. French audiences had accepted only the ballets (inserted between the acts), the choruses (singing music composed mostly by Frenchmen), and the elaborate machinery of these Italian operas. Lully was convinced that a judicious arrangement of these components had to figure in French opera.

Lully's tenure as a composer of French court ballets brought him face to face with the long history of French dance. He was credited with having introduced many fast dances *(airs de vitesse)* into court ballets, although he railed against the "stupidity of the greater part of the *grand seigneurs*" who could not master the more rapid steps (Pure, 1668). The dances Lully preferred in his court ballets were *menuets, sarabandes, gavottes, canaries, chaconnes, bourrées,* and *loures,* all of which later appeared on the operatic stage. Collaboration with Molière in creating the comic ballet taught Lully how to integrate dance with drama. Dances in the interludes of *Le Bourgeois Gentilhomme,* for example, penetrate the action with ease and conviction, thereby adding an important dimension to the comedy.

Dance in the Tragédie Lyrique. In March 1672 Lully was accorded dictatorial control over all French stage music. In the history of opera, Lully's power to direct public taste has been unequaled. Between 1673 and his death in 1687, he composed seventeen theatrical works for the Académie Royale de Musique. Of these, thirteen are *tragédies lyriques,* two are stage ballets, one is a *pastorale héroïque,* and one a *pastoral-pastiche.*

Always receptive to his audience, Lully determined that each act of his tragedies ought to contain a *divertissement* of songs and dances. He adroitly subordinated dance elements to dramatic continuity. "He did not overextend the dance," wrote Jean-Laurent Le Cerf de La Viéville, "unlike today [1705] where it makes up one quarter of the opera" (Le Cerf de La Viéville, 1904–1906).

Dance in a Lully *divertissement* is always a decorative element: sometimes it is inessential; sometimes it is an integral part of the dramatic action. A *divertissement* that combines both decorative and dramatic functions of dance is found in act 3, scenes 3–5, of *Roland,* where Roland learns his rival's identity during a bucolic village wedding.

The named dances used by Lully in his *tragédies lyriques* include *canaries, chaconnes, gavottes, gigues, menuets, rigaudons, sarabandes, bourrées, loures, passacailles,* and *passepieds* (Little, 1969). Their numbers could be increased by many untitled *airs de danse* that bear close resemblance to specific dance types. The *menuet* was by far the most popular stage dance during this period—a remarkable development given that in 1668 (just five years before Lully's first *tragédie lyrique*), the *menuet* was called a new invention (Pure, 1668).

Lully left the composition of *ballets ordinaires* to Pierre Beauchamps, dancing master to Louis XIV. Beauchamps retired from the Paris Opera in 1687, the year of Lully's death. He was succeeded by his student, Guillaume-Louis Pecour, who stopped dancing in 1703 but continued composing ballets for the Paris Opera until his death in 1729. In 1700 and 1704 respectively, Raoul-Auger Feuillet notated two collections of dance steps originally conceived by Beauchamps, most of which had been presented at the Opera.

Lully's most original contribution to dance in the *tragédie lyrique,* first employed by him in the comic ballet, was his concept of the dance as dramatic agent. "He imagined expressive steps which were related to the subject," wrote Le Cerf. Abbé Dubos added that Lully paid particular attention to pantomime and was aided in this by Louis-Hilaire d'Olivet, *maître de danse particulier.* Olivet was one of the thirteen original members of the Académie Royale de Danse, founded in 1661, and served for many years as its secretary.

Lully's approach to dance in opera influenced the development of French opera until the Revolution (1789), even influencing Christoph Willibald Gluck's French operas. Lully's and Olivet's choreography contributed to the excitement of the bellicose *divertissements* with trumpets and drums found in *Thésée, Bellérophon,* and *Amadis.* The Inhabitants of Hell in act 3 of *Thésée* must have danced to demonstrate the power of Medea over Aegeus. Dance must have conveyed the emotions of the grieving men and women in the funeral cortege in act 3, scenes 5 and 6, of *Alceste,* and dance must have lulled the unsuspecting Atys in the sleep scene (act 3, scene 4) of *Atys.*

Unfortunately, no choreography by Lully or Olivet survives for such scenes. It is possible that this innovative use of *danse en action* did not outlive Lully himself, but there are descriptions of the dances by Dubos, who wrote,

> I have heard tell of some ballets, almost without dances, that were composed of gestures instead, . . . in a word, pantomimes that Lully created for the funeral corteges in *Psyche* and *Alceste,* for the second act of *Thésée* where the poet had introduced dancing old men, for the ballet of the fourth act of *Atys,* and for the first scene of the fourth act of *Isis,* where Quinault had the inhabitants of the Hyperborean Regions come on stage. (Dubos, 1719)

Dubos added that the "shivering chorus" from *Isis* (including, one assumes, the preceding *ritournelle*) was composed "uniquely of the gestures and movements of people in a grip of cold. Not a single dance step from our ordinary dances was employed."

The lack of choreographic evidence dating from Lully's time undoubtedly contributed to the generally unfavorable comments by eighteenth-century dance historians concerning Lully's use of dance. In 1760 Jean-Georges Noverre wrote that Lully had composed "at the time when the Dance was slow *[tranquille]* and when Dancers were totally ignorant of what is meant by expression." One hundred years after the composer's death, Charles Compan characterized Lully's dance music as "cold, monotonous, without character." Louis de Cahusac, clearly ignorant of Lully's attempts to correlate dance with dramatic action, believed himself to be the first to have created the *danse en action* for the 1747 *opéra ballet* by Rameau, *Les Fêtes de l'Hymen et de l'Amour.*

After Lully's death, the clean, dramatic lines of the Lully-Quinault *tragédie en musique* were comprised of a proliferation of dances in purely decorative *divertissements.* André Campra was accused of "completely drown-

OPÉRA-BALLET AND TRAGÉDIE LYRIQUE. An engraving by Franz Ertinger of a scene from Jean-Baptiste Lully's *Bellérophon,* which premiered on 31 January 1679. Bellerophon, the protagonist of this *tragédie lyrique,* is shown riding Pegasus through the clouds as the Chimera lurks below. (Dance Collection, New York Public Library for the Performing Arts)

OPÉRA-BALLET AND TRAGÉDIE LYRIQUE. André Campra is credited with the creation of the *opéra-ballet,* a format popular with French audiences. The appeal of the genre lay in its variety, as each act featured a different plot and cast of characters. This print depicts a scene from Campra's *L'Europe Galante,* which premiered on 24 October 1697. (Dance Collection, New York Public Library for the Performing Arts.)

ing the subject in the *divertissements*" of his *tragédie lyrique Achille et Déidamie* (1735). The use of dance in the *tragédie lyrique* grew from Lully's time through Rameau's, as is evidenced by Lully's use of thirteen dances in *Amadis* (1684), Campra's use of twenty-three dances in *Tancrède* (1702), and Rameau's use of thirty dances in the revival of *Dardanus* (1744).

Dance in the Opéra-Ballet. In creating *L'Europe Galante* (1697), Campra created the *opéra-ballet.* Its format appealed to French audiences tired of the mythological deities, heroic posturing, and gallant intrigues of the Lullian *tragédie lyrique. Opéra-ballet* broke dramatic continuity by requiring a new plot and a new set of characters for each of three or four acts (the terms *acte* and *entrée* are synonomous in *opéra-ballet*). In the words of librettist Pierre-Charles Roy, *opéra-ballet* "pleases by its variety and sympathizes with French impatience."

In the *opéra-ballet,* Campra and his contemporaries substituted believable characters of their own times for the gods and goddesses of antiquity. Each *entrée* built toward its *divertissement.* No longer was there any need to justify songs and dances dramatically. "Each act," wrote Rémond de Saint-Mard, "must be made up of a fast-moving, light, and, if you wish, rather *galant* story . . . in two or three short scenes and the rest of the action in *ariettes, fêtes, spectacles.*" Cahusac (1754) was probably accurate when he pointed out that in *L'Europe Galante* "there are only *divertissements* in which one dances just to dance."

The *divertissements* of the *opéra-ballet* are a repository of the most popular stage dances of the early eighteenth century. In Campra's four *opéra-ballets* (*L'Europe Galante,* 1697; *Les Muses,* 1703; *Les Fêtes Venitiennes,* 1710; and *Les Ages,* 1718), there were sixteen kinds of named dances and sixty dances altogether: two *branles,* one *canarie,* five *chaconnes,* two *gavottes,* four *gigues,* ten *menuets,* six *rigaudons,* three *sarabandes,* two *bourrées,* two *contredanses,* three *forlanas,* three *loures,* two *musettes,* two *passacailles,* twelve *passepieds,* and a *villanelle.* The *menuet,* with ten dances, was challenged in popularity by the *rigaudon* and was surpassed by the faster *passepied.* Some of the other dances—the *forlana, contredanse,* and *villanelle*—were of foreign origin and new to the French lyric stage.

In addition to these sixty named dances and thirteen marches, Campra's four *opéra-ballets* included another 143 dances either bearing descriptive titles or simply called airs. In most instances, the dance was an ornament without dramatic function. The fact that each *entrée* had its own independent plot emphasized a measure of contrast between each *divertissement.* Occasionally, however, dance was involved in the dramatic action. In scene 3 of "Le Bal," in *Les Fêtes Venitiennes,* the dancing master uses dance to describe winds in turmoil and to conjure up the frightful aspect of demons. Rather than being a hiatus in the action, the masked ball in "L'Italie" (*L'Europe Galante,* scene 2) develops the plot to its critical point by revealing the identity of Olimpia's secret suitor to his jealous rival, Octavio.

Male dancers were more highly paid than female dancers. It was not until 1681 that professional female dancers were first permitted on stage at the Paris Opera, in Lully's stage ballet *Le Triomphe de l'Amour.* Mademoiselle de La Fontaine's solo dances created a sensation in this production. With her began the remarkable star system that dominated the French stage throughout the eighteenth century and brought forth such dancers as Françoise Prévost, Marie Sallé, Marie-Catherine Guyot, Marie Camargo, Michel Blondy, Claude Ballon, Louis Dupré, and the Dumoulin dynasty.

[*See also entries on the principal figures mentioned herein.*]

BIBLIOGRAPHY

Anthony, James R. *French Baroque Music from Beaujoyeulx to Rameau.* Rev. ed. London, 1978.

Anthony, James R. "Some Uses of the Dance in the French Opera-Ballet." *Recherches sur la Musique Francaise Classique* 11 (1969): 75–90.

Anthony, James R. "Lully, Jean-Baptiste." In *The New Grove Dictionary of Music and Musicians.* London, 1980.

Anthony, James R. "Opera: France—Tragédie Lyrique." In *The New Grove Dictionary of Music and Musicians.* London, 1980.

Cahusac, Louis de. *La danse ancienne et moderne, ou, Traité historique de la danse.* 3 vols. La Haye, 1754.

Dartois-Lapeyre, F. "La danse au temps de l'opéra-ballet." Ph.D. diss., University of Paris-Sorbonne, 1983.

Derra de Moroda, Friderica. "Chorégraphie, the Dance Notation of the Eighteenth Century: Beauchamp or Feuillet?" *Book Collector* 16 (Winter 1967): 450–476.

Dubos, Jean-Baptiste. *Réflexions critiques sur la poésie et sur la peinture.* 2 vols. Paris, 1719.

Durey de Noinville, Jacques Bernard. *Histoire du théâtre de l'Académie Royale de Musique en France.* 2 vols. in 1. 2d ed. Paris, 1757.

Harris-Warrick, Rebecca. "Intrepreting Pendulum Markings for French Baroque Dances." *Historical Performance* 6 (Spring 1993): 9–22.

Hilton, Wendy. *Dance of Court and Theatre: The French Noble Style, 1690–1725.* Princeton, 1981.

Hilton, Wendy. "Dances to Music by Jean-Baptiste Lully." *Early Music* 14 (February 1986): 51–63.

Le Cerf de la Viéville, Jean-Laurent, seigneur de Freneuse. *Comparaison de la musique italienne et de la musique françoise.* 3 vols. Paris, 1704–1706.

Levinson, André. "Les danseurs de Lully." *La Revue Musicale* 6 (January 1925).

Little, Meredith Ellis. "The Dances of J. B. Lully." Ph.D. diss., Stanford University, 1967.

Little, Meredith Ellis. "Inventory of the Dances of Jean-Baptiste Lully." *Recherches sur la Musique Française Classique* 9 (1969): 21–55.

Little, Meredith Ellis. "Dance under Louis XIV and XV." *Early Music* 3 (October 1975): 331–340.

Little, Meredith Ellis, and Carol G. Marsh. *La danse noble: an inventory of dances and sources.* Williamstown, Mass., 1992.

Mullins, Margaret. "Music and Dance in the French Baroque." *Studies in Music,* no. 12 (1978): 45–67.

Pure, Michel de. *Idée des spectacles anciens et nouveaux.* Paris, 1668.

Rosow, Lois. "Making Connections: Thoughts on Lully's Entr'actes." *Early Music* 21 (May 1993): 231–238.

Sadler, Graham. "The Paris Opera Dancers in Rameau's Day." In *Jean-Philippe Rameau: Colloque international, Dijon, 21–24 septembre 1983,* edited by Jérôme de La Gorce. Paris, 1987.

Witherell, Anne L. *Louis Pécour's 1700 Recueil des dances.* Ann Arbor, Mich., 1983.

JAMES R. ANTHONY

ORCHESTRA. Among all the early civilizations in the eastern Mediterranean, dance was a formal and regular part of religious and civic ceremony, and the place designated for its presentation acquired a special character. Requiring a functional minimum of a flat space for the performers and a viewing area for the spectators, the dance floor adopted a regularity of outline that made it possible for the dance movements to be set against and within a fixed frame. At the same time the combination of a flat floor and a naturally or artificially raked auditorium, which provided the best view of the action, influenced the nature of the dance, which was to some extent prescribed by its surroundings.

In Athenian theater of the sixth and fifth centuries BCE, the *orchēstra* was "the dancing place for the chorus," and the actors seldom encroached on it except for special effect. Located between the stage and the audience, the orchestra was the natural home for a chorus that could at some times interact with the actors, whose province was the stage area, and at times act as spectators.

The word *orchēstra* is rare in Classical Greek, although *orcheisthai,* "to dance," and other words derived from it, are common. Plato was the first to use *orchēstra* in surviving literature; in the *Apology* he has Socrates refer to the orchestra as a place where books and pamphlets can be bought. This may suggest that the Theater of Dionysus was used out of season as a commercial center, but it does not help us to divine anything about its nature as a theater space. For that it is necessary to go back to a time long before the first presentation of tragedy or comedy in Athens, since the history of the orchestra begins hundreds of years before the first use of the term.

The decoration on the shield of Achilles that Homer describes in the *Iliad* (18.590–592) includes "a dancing-floor like the one which Daedalus had fashioned for Ariadne of the lovely hair in the broad city of Knossos." The word Homer used for dancing-floor is *choros,* which at that time could also mean "dance," and which centuries later indicated the chorus of the tragedies and comedies performed during the Great Dionysia in Athens.

Extensive excavation in Crete since the late 1800s has located what Sir Arthur Evans identified as "theatral areas," not only in Knossos but also in Phaistos, Mallia, and Gournia, all dating from the late Minoan period (1600–1200 BCE). Rectangular in shape and flanked on at least two sides by steps, these "theatral areas" could be early forms of the orchestra that Homer refers to—but they could also serve a number of alternative civic functions and are far too small to accommodate the bull dancing so graphically depicted on the nearby frescoes in the palace of Minos.

As an early manifestation of the dance floor or theater space of Classical Greece, these paved Cretan areas, bounded by shallow steps, are less satisfactory than the circular threshing floor that many would posit as the home of religious dance connected with agricultural festivals. Both appear to share the basic physical relationship between performer and spectator that characterized the first recognizable dramas.

The tragedies of the sixth century BCE were performed in Athens in a temporary theater in the *Agora,* the commercial center. Drama found its first real home at the beginning of the fifth century BCE, when the site of the dramatic festivals was moved to the precinct of Dionysus, southeast of the Acropolis in Athens. This was the theater for which Aeschylus wrote all his surviving plays and that both Sophocles and Euripides knew in their early careers.

No more than the barest of traces remain of that theater, so the shape and dimension of the orchestra are matters of speculation. The common belief is that the orchestra was circular, with a diameter of between eighty and ninety feet (24 and 27 meters), and that the *theatron,* where the audience sat, followed the line of the circumference for over half its distance, with the actor playing at a tangent to the edge farthest from the audience. The stage relationship this suggests between dancer and actor fits well with what is known about those pre-Aeschylean tragedies as well as the surviving work of Aeschylus. Some scholars have suggested that it is unproven that the first Theater of Dionysus had a circular orchestra, as is found at Epidaurus, and implied that a circular orchestra was the exception among early theaters. If the pattern of the Theater of Dionysus was rectangular, like the orchestra of the theater at Thoricon, the current understanding of choral dance developing along a strictly cyclical form, around a central *thumele,* or "altar," might be questioned.

It is likely, however, that the orchestra of the first Theater of Dionysus in Athens, and that of the Periclean Theater constructed on the site of the first in the later fifth century BCE, were both circular, with a surface of beaten earth, featuring a central altar as the focal point; they probably differed mainly in that the size of the later orchestra was only about sixty-six feet (20 meters) in diameter rather than eighty to ninety feet (24 to 27 meters), and it was pushed farther into the hillside to allow for more elaborate stage buildings and a more steeply raked auditorium.

Later developments of the orchestra through late Classical, Hellenistic, and Roman times are comparatively easy to chart, if only because so many of these later theaters survive relatively intact. Changes of shape reflect changes of emphasis in the nature of the performances and in the dance element within the drama. The circular orchestra of Classical tragedy and comedy, in which the chorus was a principal feature, was replaced first by the horseshoe shape found at the fourth century BCE theater at Delphi, then by the simple semicircle of Roman times. The orchestra diminished in size as the chorus became less involved with the main action, finally becoming no more than an interlude. From the first century BCE onward, the orchestra was no longer the sole province of the performer but had been encroached upon by important members of the audience. Spectacle monopolized the theaters of Imperial Rome, and the orchestra might again become a focus of performance, when that performance was a bizarre form of entertainment—a beast fight, or a naval encounter—which the stage could not possibly accommodate.

As European drama, both tragic and comic, moved away from its initial concentration on dance and toward a reliance on the spoken word, so the shape of its home was adapted to fit the new emphasis. The theater building of Classical Athens kept the orchestra at its center because dance was central to the theater performance. As dance became less central, the orchestra shrank in size and architecturally lost its significance. With the change of emphasis away from the dance, European drama lost an impetus it was not to recover until the Renaissance.

[*For further discussion, see also* Greece, *article on* Dance in Ancient Greece; Roman Empire; Scenic Design; *and* Theaters for Dance.]

BIBLIOGRAPHY

Arnott, Peter D. *The Ancient Greek and Roman Theatre.* New York, 1971.

Beacham, R. C. *The Roman Theatre and Its Audience.* London, 1991.

Gebhard, E. R. *The Theater at Isthmia.* Chicago, 1973.

Lawler, Lillian B. *The Dance of the Ancient Greek Theatre.* Iowa City, 1964.

Leacroft, R., and H. Leacroft. *Theatre and Playhouse.* London, 1984.

Pickard-Cambridge, A. W. *The Theatre of Dionysus in Athens.* Oxford, 1946.

Thompson, H. A., and Wycherley, R. E. *The Athenian Agora,* vol. 14. Princeton, 1972.

J. MICHAEL WALTON

ORFF, CARL (born 10 July 1895 in Munich, died 29 March 1982 in Munich), German composer. Carl Orff received his first music lessons at home, then studied with Anton Beer-Walbrunn and Hermann Zilcher at the Munich Akademie der Tonkunst, graduating in 1914. He served as *Kapellmeister* at the Munich Kammerspiele (1915–1917) and at the Mannheim National Theater (1918–1919), after which he returned to Munich, continuing his composition studies with Heinrich Kaminski. In 1924, with Dorothee Günther, he established in Munich the Güntherschule for gymnastics, dance, and music, where the emphasis was on exploring the relationship between movement and music. There he started to develop the so-called Orff-Instrumentarium, which formed the base for his educational *Schulwerk,* published in several installments after 1930.

As the conductor of the Munich Bachverein, Orff was in

charge of a master class for composition at the Munich Musikhochschule (1950–1960), and in 1961 he established the Orff-Institut at the Akademie Mozarteum in Salzburg, where he continued to oversee the teaching and publication of his educational theories. Aiming for "total theater," Orff derived his musical elements from primitive sources throughout the world and especially from antiquity, which he studied thoroughly to integrate its elements into his musical language. Because he emphasized rhythm as one of the elementary forces of life, many kinds of percussion instruments dominate his musical works; as a result, his style has often been compared, usually unfavorably, to that of Igor Stravinsky, particularly to *Les Noces*.

It was not so much dance that Orff was interested in as movement *per se*, and his teaching aimed at the conscious development of the human being's musicality by linking it to the basic impulse to move, starting with improvisational exercises in both movement and percussive accompaniment. Because the distinction between stage movement and dance is vague in his stage works, the producer or director must decide whether the production should lean more toward stage movement or toward dance. Some directors eschew the participation of a choreographer, as did Jean-Pierre Ponnelle in his successful television production of Orff's *Carmina Burana*; and many choreographers, including John Butler, Norman Walker, and Peter Darrell, have refused the interference of a director. Orff himself intensely disliked completely choreographed productions of his works.

Orff's triptych of scenic cantatas based upon medieval German and Latin texts have repeatedly attracted choreographers. *Carmina Burana: Cantiones Profanae* (1937) was first choreographed by Inge Herting in 1937 and has since been staged by many others, including Mary Wigman (1943), John Butler (1959), Fernand Nault (1962), Peter Darrell (1969), Brydon Paige (1972), Youri Vámos (1985), David Bintley (1995), and Damian Woetzel (1997). The versions by Wigman, Butler, and Nault have been particularly admired. *Catulli Carmina: Ludi Scaenici* (1943) was first choreographed by Tatjana Gsovsky in 1943, the year of its composition; subsequent productions were staged by Wigman (1955), Erika Hanka (1957), Butler (1964), Darrell (1969), Heinz Spoerli (1979), and Johann Kresnik (1990). *Trionfo di Afrodite* (1953) was also first mounted by Gsovsky soon after its composition, in 1953; later productions include those of Heinz Rosen (1960), Norman Walker (1964), and Kresnik (1990). Of these, Walker's version is thought to be the most successful. Other works of Orff that have been choreographically treated include *Paradiesgärtlein* (based upon sixteenth-century lute music; choreographed by Sonia Korty, 1937) and *Entrata* (after William Byrd for orchestra and organ, 1930; choreographed by Heinz Rosen, 1963).

BIBLIOGRAPHY

Carl Orff und sein Werk: Dokumentation. 5 vols. to date. Tutzing, 1975–.

Liess, Andreas. *Carl Orff.* 2d ed. Zurich, 1977. English edition, London, 1966.

HORST KOEGLER

ORGANIZATIONS. Dance service organizations expanded throughout the world in the twentieth century. These groups serve many functions.

Some societies undertake a broad range of activities that include dance. An outstanding example is Sangeet Natak Akademi (the National Academy of Music, Dance and Drama), founded in India in 1953 to further all of India's performing arts. Its objectives are the following: to coordinate the activities of regional academies, to promote research, to encourage the exchange of ideas among the regions, to encourage the establishment of theater centers and schools, to sponsor festivals and seminars, to maintain standards in the arts, to award fellowships and prizes for outstanding achievement, and to promote cultural exchange with other countries.

Most organizations, however, concentrate on only one or two of these missions. Their activities generally include holding regular meetings and publishing newsletters for their members, as well as offering specific services to their field. The fields are numerous. Some examples follow.

An early function was encouraging public interest in dance performances. The Danish Ballet Club, started in 1949, sponsors tours to performances and also holds lecture demonstrations. In Germany, the New Society for Ballet and Dance, begun in 1983, organizes performances and arranges exhibitions.

A primary concern has been the welfare of dancers. Many countries have formed unions to support the interests of their performers. In 1937, the Union of Finnish Dance Artists was formed. In Brazil, the Association of Dance Professionals was established in 1982.

Support of education is another important concern. In Italy, the National Association of Dance Teachers was founded in 1956 to enable instructors to share experiences and to keep them informed of developments in the profession. In 1978, the New Zealand Association of Dance Teachers was formed to improve standards by sponsoring seminars and exchanges among various regions.

Different genres of dance receive special treatment. Since 1931 in England, the Royal Academy of Dancing has established standards for the teaching of ballet technique and has conducted worldwide examinations. Although its work is focused on a single choreographer, the Mary Wigman Society, founded in Germany in 1986, is devoted to perpetuating the legacy of Wigman by reporting on events in modern dance drama. The Philippine Folk Dance Society, founded in 1950, conducts annual workshops, documents unpublished dances, and offers assistance to folk dance groups and teachers.

Of increasing importance have been groups devoted to research and scholarship. The first was the American Congress on Research in Dance, founded in the United States in 1965; China, Japan, the Scandinavian countries, and the United Kingdom later founded their own. Growing interest led to the 1989 formation of the European Association of Dance Historians, which holds annual conferences, each year in another country.

The need to record choreography and performances stimulated the formation of the Dance Notation Bureau in the United States in 1940. The bureau trains notators and collaborates with dance companies in staging reconstructions.

The need to preserve archival materials has motivated the formation of organizations. Mexico's Center for Investigation, Information and Documentation of Dance was founded in 1983. The Dance Heritage Coalition, a consortium of performing arts libraries, was established in the United States in 1992 to better preserve and make accessible the historical materials of dance in America.

The dance world began to organize internationally in 1971 with the formation of the Dance Committee of the International Theatre Institute. In line with its parent organization, the committee aims to promote the exchange of knowledge and practice in order to consolidate peace and friendship among peoples. In 1973, the International Dance Council was established to protect and record the dance heritage; its annual meeting is held throughout the world. Dance and the Child International, founded in 1978, seeks to promote opportunities for children to experience dance as creators and performers as well as spectators.

An increasing number of international dance meetings were held in the 1980s. These occasions provided contacts and exchanges and thus stimulated interest in cooperative projects. At the Fifth Hong Kong International Dance Conference in 1990, director Carl Wolz proposed the formation of a single organization that would serve the multiple interests of the global dance community. All genres of dance would be involved, as would all methods of doing and dealing with them. Preliminary work on the World Dance Alliance began in 1989. Chapters were formed first in the Americas and Asia, then in Europe and Africa. Regional centers hold their own meetings, with leaders gathering to lay plans for the good of all.

ARCHIVE. Dance Collection, New York Public Library for the Performing Arts.

SELMA JEANNE COHEN

ORIENTALISM. The term *Orientalism* refers to the adaptation or affectation in Western art of what are assumed to be the customs, traits, or habits of expression characteristic of the people of the Near East and Asia. These are usually defined as different from or opposed to Western cultural characteristics. The term *Orientalism* entered popular usage in the late eighteenth and early nineteenth centuries because of broad political and academic interest in the languages, religions, histories, and social structures of Asian and Middle Eastern societies during that period.

Linked to the Western fascination with the exotic, orientalism in the arts developed as part of the nineteenth-century Romantic movement in poetry, literature, painting, music, theater, and dance. Orientalism spanned more than a century, as Europeans and Americans formed stereotypes of Asian and Middle Eastern dress and manners from illustrated translations and adaptations of Indian classics, Persian poetry, fables and folktales of China and Japan, and especially *The Thousand and One Nights* and *The Rubaiyat of Omar Khayyam.* The writings of colonial administrators and scholars and reports of merchants and travelers augmented popular notions of the East as a land of excessive riches, opulence, indolence, sensuality, and cruelty. Byron, Goethe, Chateaubriand, Victor Hugo, Gustav Flaubert, Théophile Gautier, Thomas Moore, and Samuel Taylor Coleridge used Oriental themes and characters, strengthening the role of the Orient as a setting for Western fantasies.

A well-defined Orientalist movement in the visual arts developed as European architects and designers borrowed Persian, Arabian, Chinese, Indian, and eventually Japanese symbolic and design motifs for clothing, jewelry, building decoration, furniture, and ornaments. Victorian Chinese furniture and bric-a-brac abounded, and the feminist and dress reformer Amelia Bloomer briefly advocated Turkish trousers for women.

Eugène Delacroix, Théodore Chassériau, and Eugène Fromentin led an array of French painters who established Orientalist art as a popular and prolific genre of the nineteenth century. European artists adopted Oriental trappings for nudes, portraits, and landscapes. These images in turn became models for the lavish costuming and sets used in theater, ballet, and opera productions.

Applied to performance, Orientalism denotes the use or the perception of Oriental elements in a performance (whether authentic, imitative, or derivative) as primarily exotic. Western theater had long incorporated themes and stories from the Orient, from early Greek tragedies *(The Persians, Oedipus Rex)* through Shakespeare *(Othello)* and Marlowe *(Tamurlaine).* Orientalism, however, took root in the extravagant staging practices of the nineteenth-century commercial theaters of Europe and America. Such popular spectacles as *Timour the Tartar* and *The Aethiop* were staples. "Turkish" and "Arab" horsemen, "Indian" fakirs, and "Asian" acrobats and tumblers were either imported or recruited locally for spectacular afterpieces such as *The Cataract of the Ganges, The Forty Thieves,* and *Bluebeard.* Entr'actes included high-wire artists and rope dancers who performed "Oriental" dances.

Court masques, *entrées* and ballets of the seventeenth and eighteenth centuries had used Eastern settings, characters, and hints of the appropriate costuming, adapted to court dance and dress, but Orientalism in dance flourished as the Romantic-era ballet became popular. By the latter part of the nineteenth century, Orientalized *divertissements* (for example, in *The Nutcracker*) and full-length ballets *(Le Corsaire, La Bayadère)* were standards of the Russian repertory. Serge Diaghilev's Ballets Russes had a profound effect on France, England, and the United States during the first decades of the twentieth century—alongside the modern, even outrageous ballets were the Orientalized *Schéhérazade, Cléopâtre,* and *Les Orientales.* Michel Fokine's vigorous choreography and Léon Bakst's sumptuous settings and costumes influenced both European and American fashion.

Anna Pavlova's ballet company also performed in Europe and America such Orientalized works as *La Péri* and *The Legend of Azyiade.* Uday Shankar, a member of the company, collaborated with Pavlova to produce romanticized versions of traditional dances from India.

The image of the Oriental dancing girl emerged from the profusion of stereotypes that made little distinction between Eastern popular dancers and the ancient class of sacred and ritual dancers, such as the *devadāsī* in India and the *almah* in the Near East. A few Parisian cafes presented Algerian dancers, but it was the importation of authentic Eastern performers to European and U.S. expositions and world's fairs that ignited popular interest in Oriental dance.

During the 1876 American Centenary Exposition in Philadelphia, a Turkish coffee house on the outskirts of the park grounds featured a group of traditional Turkish musicians and dancers. The troupe, prevented from performing by the police, appeared briefly in a Philadelphia vaudeville house and later in New York City.

On a larger scale, the Chicago World's Fair of 1893 exhibited several Eastern performance styles to a large segment of the American public. Moorish, Syrian, Turkish, and Persian groups performed, but the Algerian and Egyptian women presenting the *danse du ventre* (belly dance) became objects of protest by the clergy and the National Association of Dancing Masters. The protest enhanced the popularity of the performances, and the "shocking" and "indescribable" movements were promptly imitated in dance halls, vaudeville, and burlesque houses by a number of "Little Egypt" dancers doing their version of the "hootchy-kootchy."

ORIENTALISM. Anna Pavlova performed in numerous ballets and *divertissements* based on Oriental themes. She appears here with Laurent Novikoff in *Ajanta Frescoes* (1923), a one-act ballet inspired by her visit to the Ajanta caves in Hyderabad in southern Pakistan. Ivan Clustine created the choreography to a comissioned score by Alexander Tcherepnin. (Photograph by James Abbe; from the Dance Collection, New York Public Library for the Performing Arts.)

Circuses adopted orientalized themes to display exotic animals. P. T. Barnum engaged "Oriental freaks" for his American Museum in the mid-nineteenth century, and Pawnee Bill in the latter part of the century staged an "Oriental" Wild West Show.

The Paris Exposition of 1900 in particular provided a varied offering of Eastern dance genres. Egyptian *almées* were described as balancing candles and glasses on their heads and chests. The "Buddhist" dances by Sada Yakko preceded and were compared with the "Protestant" dances of Loie Fuller. Americans noted the submissive nature of the Turkish women's dances in contrast to the ferocity of the male Sinhala dances.

The pioneers of American modern dance were a part of the culmination of the Orientalist movement in dance. Although more interested in other aspects of production and other spheres of influence, both Loie Fuller *(The Salute of the Sun)* and Isadora Duncan *(The Rubaiyat)* used Oriental themes in their work. Maud Allan is best remembered for her *Vision of Salome.*

It was Ruth St. Denis, however, who epitomized Orientalism in American dance. Her early work with Augustine Daly, who had presented nautch dancers from Bombay, India, in the 1880s, plus the popularity of performers from India at New York's Coney Island, were reflected in her Indian themes—*Radha, Nautch, Incense, Dance of the Five Senses,* and *Cobra,* among others. St. Denis attempted to lend an air of authenticity by studying Hindu and Buddhist philosophy, researching visual source material, and using Asian performers in her company. She taught classes in Oriental dance in collaboration with Ted Shawn at the Denishawn school in California, where the founders of modern dance—Martha Graham, Doris Humphrey, and Charles Weidman—were exposed to concepts of Orientalism as an alternative to popular dance and ballet training. After touring Asia, St. Denis continued in the Orientalist tradition of combining stereotypes, using her increased awareness of authentic detail.

Michio Ito, a Japanese dancer and pupil of Émile Jaques-Dalcroze, drew on images of *kabuki* and *nō* drama to choreograph solo and group works in Europe and the United States. During the 1930s, he and his company appeared in Hollywood Bowl concerts.

Orientalism briefly revived after World War II, with a modernist interest in the Japanese aesthetics of design and visual arts. Since the 1950s a new type of interest in Asia has been reflected by dancers such as Laura Dean; they have followed the popular fascination with Eastern philosophies, religions, and martial arts by adapting Daoist, Sufi, Zen, yoga, karate and *taiji* techniques for training exercises and performance styles. In turn, Asian dancers and choreographers (Ritha Devi and Kei Takei, for example) have blended Eastern and Western themes and techniques into movement explorations. The strongest influence of the 1990s may be seen in the adaptation of Japanese *butō* in the work of such performers as Eiko and Koma.

Vestiges of Orientalism appear in films and on television, where today's Orientalized extravaganzas had their predecessors in the films *Intolerance* (1918), *Ben Hur* (1907, 1926, 1959) and *Cleopatra* (1934, 1963). The samurai and kung fu films of the 1980s continued to exploit the exoticism of Asian forms. A strong Orientalist influence may be seen in the Chinese, Japanese, and Moroccan villages at Epcot Center, Disney World, Orlando, Florida.

[*See also entries on the principal figures mentioned herein.*]

ORIENTALISM. The dances of Ruth St. Denis and Ted Shawn epitomized American Orientialism. *(left)* St. Denis posed, in Indian-style costume, with a large peacock feather fan. *(right)* Shawn as a Sufi dancer in his *Mevlevi Dervish,* c.1950. (Photograph at right by Constantine Photo, Los Angeles; both photographs from the archives at Jacob's Pillow, Becket, Massachusetts.)

BIBLIOGRAPHY

Chindahl, George L. *A History of the Circus in America.* Caldwell, Idaho, 1959.

Gilbert, Douglas. *American Vaudeville: Its Life and Times.* New York, 1940.

Jullian, Philippe. *The Orientalists: European Painters of Eastern Scenes.* Oxford, 1977.

McKechnie, Samuel. *Popular Entertainments through the Ages.* New York, 1969.

Odell, George C. D. *Annals of the New York Stage.* 15 vols. New York, 1927–1949.

Pronko, Leonard C. *Theater East and West: Towards a Total Theater.* Berkeley, 1967.

Rosenthal, Donald A. *Orientalism: The Near East in French Painting, 1800–1880.* Rochester, N.Y., 1982.

Said, Edward W. *Orientalism.* New York, 1978.

Schwab, Raymond. *The Oriental Renaissance: Europe's Rediscovery of India and the East, 1680–1880* (1950). New York, 1984.

Sinor, Denis, ed. *Orientalism and History.* Cambridge, 1954.

Spencer, Charles. *The World of Serge Diaghilev.* Chicago, 1974.

Truman, Ben C. *History of the World's Fair.* Chicago, 1893.

TRUDY SCOTT

ORIGINAL BALLET RUSSE. *See* Ballets Russes de Monte Carlo.

ORLANDO, MARIANE (born 1 June 1934 in Stockholm), Swedish dancer and teacher. Admitted to the ballet school of Royal Opera in Stockholm in 1942, Mariane Orlando was made *première élève* in 1948, having already danced important parts in school performances. She was nominated *première danseuse* in 1952, the youngest ever in Sweden. Her first important role was Odette-Odile in Mary Skeaping's *Swan Lake* (1953). Thereafter she danced all leading roles in the Royal Swedish Ballet's classical productions, such as *Les Sylphides, The Sleeping Beauty,* and *Giselle.* The most important parts for her development as a dramatic dancer were Aili in Birgit Cullberg's *Moon Reindeer* and Medea in her *Medea.* She danced the main roles in the repertory, including the Chosen One in *Le Sacre du Printemps,* the Miller's Wife in *Le Tricorne,* and the Glove Seller in *Gaîté Parisienne.* In Antony Tudor's *Pillar of Fire* she danced Hagar, in José Limón's *There Is a Time* the part of Silence, and in *The Moor's Pavane,* Emilia; in Eliot Feld's *At Midnight* she danced the Woman. There were many other leading roles, some created for her. Her teachers included Valborg Franchi, Albert and Nina Kozlovsky, and Lilian Karina, and she studied abroad at Sadler's Wells School and later at the Kirov Theater, Leningrad, with Naema Baltatsheva and Natalia Dudinskaya. Her partners included Teddy Rhodin, Caj Selling, Verner Klavsen, and famous foreign artists.

Orlando was a dancer of high technical skill; everything came easily to her. She had a very fine musical sense and a warm and natural stage presence. As the years passed, her interpretations deepened to express such deeply emotional parts as Hagar in *Pillar of Fire.* She toured with Royal Swedish Ballet to many countries and was given the title "Dancer of the Year" in Paris in 1959. In 1961 Orlando was guest artist with American Ballet Theatre for one year with her partner Caj Selling; she also toured the Soviet Union.

ORLANDO. Known for her technical skill and musicality, Orlando is seen here in a 1973 performance of Eliot Feld's *At Midnight.* (Photograph by Enar Merkel Rydberg; used by permission.)

After Orlando retired she worked for a few years as a teacher at Svenska Balettskolan (Swedish Ballet School) for the advanced classes of girls. Since 1992 she has been ballet mistress and *répétiteuse* at the Royal Opera, Stockholm. During the 1991/92 season she was on leave about six months to perform in a role especially created for her by Ingmar Bergman in his opera *Backanaterna* (after Euripides's *Bacchantes*), which premiered at the Royal Opera in November 1991 and which was later filmed for Swedish television.

Orlando has been awarded the Carina Ari Gold Medal, the Theater Union prize, and the Litteris et Artibus. She is a Member of the Vasaorden.

BIBLIOGRAPHY

Hood, Robin [Idestam-Almqvist, Bengt]. *Svensk balett/The Ballet in Sweden.* Malmö, 1951.

Palatsky, Eugene. "Interview in Stockholm." *Dance Magazine* (August 1960): 14–16.

LULLI SVEDIN

OSWALD, GENEVIEVE (born in Buffalo, New York), American dance researcher and archivist. Oswald was responsible for the development of the Dance Collection of the New York Public Library, an important center for the documentation of dance. She pioneered in techniques of collecting, cataloging, and maintaining a wide range of materials for this purpose.

While earning a bachelor's degree in music at the University of North Carolina, Oswald studied and performed modern dance. She did postgraduate work at the Juilliard School and at the New York University Graduate School of Music, and she attended the Columbia University School of Library Service. As a lyric soprano, she performed in concerts.

When Oswald began her work with the Dance Collection in 1947, it was part of the Music Division of the New York Public Library and had two shelves of materials. She felt the urgent need for an archive for dance, which, she pointed out in a 1968 article, "has no equivalent of the musical score or the written text; therein, indeed, lie the pleasure and the pain of documenting the art." Through her energy and determination, the Dance Collection grew to become an independent division of the library in 1964. The following year, it moved with other performing arts divisions from the main library building on Fifth Avenue at Forty-second Street to the Lincoln Center Library and Museum of the Performing Arts, where it now serves scholars, students, critics, choreographers, and other professionals from all parts of the world.

Oswald succeeded in acquiring large holdings through donations, beginning with important American collections such as those of Denishawn, Humphrey-Weidman, and Hanya Holm. An energetic fund-raiser, she acquired outside support for special projects: the Film Archive, begun in 1961, with a program since 1967 of original filming of dance works; the Oral History Project, begun in 1974 to initiate interviews with key figures; and the Asian Dance Archive, begun in 1975, for which she made an extensive visit to key countries. From the beginning, she recognized the need to preserve and make available diverse types of materials; the collection's holdings are now 95 percent non-book materials.

For a ten-year project for the creation of a fully automated book catalog of the collection, which preceded a similar project at the Library of Congress, it was necessary to devise a complete system with coding for input and eight thousand subject headings. The catalog, published in 1974, continuously updated, and now available on compact disc and the Internet, is an indispensable and unique research tool that groups holdings in all media under author and subject headings in one alphabetical listing.

The collection has organized numerous exhibitions and conferences, such as the Conference on Preservation and Dissemination of American Dance (1980) and the International Film and Videotape Dance Festival (1981), for which Oswald served as coordinator. Both these conferences were cosponsored by the International Dance Council (American Chapter of the Conseil International de la Danse), of which Oswald was president from 1979 to 1981. She retired from her library position in 1987. Since 1990 she has been coordinator of the Americas Center of the World Dance Alliance, and she continues as a member of the Library Committee of the Dance Collection.

Oswald has taught dance history at New York University, contributed to numerous publications, and served as lecturer and consultant to archival projects in many countries. Among her honors are a Capezio Dance Award (1956) and an American Dance Guild Award (1970).

BIBLIOGRAPHY

Hodgson, Moira. "Documenting the Ephemeral Art: The Dance Collection at Lincoln Center." *Dance News* (December 1976): 10–11.

Oswald, Genevieve. "Creating Tangible Records for an Intangible Art." *Special Libraries* (March 1968): 146–151.

Oswald, Genevieve, project dir. *Dictionary Catalog of the Dance Collection.* 10 vols. New York, 1974.

MARILYN HUNT

OTOZURU (*fl.* mid-fourteenth century in Nara area of Japan), shrine maiden, *shirabyōshi* and *kusemai* dancer. Although nearly nothing is known of Otozuru herself, records dating from 1349 at Kasuga Shrine in Nara indicate that a certain Otozuru Gozen served as a *miko* (shrine medium and dancer), and this is thought to have been the same Otozuru with whom Kan'ami, founder of the Kanze school of *nō*, studied *kusemai* dancing. (Kan'ami's troupe had strong ties with Kasuga Shrine.)

During the Heian period (794–1185), there had been a popular dance genre known as *shirabyōshi* (written with the characters for "white rhythm," originally it probably meant "simple rhythm"). In *shirabyōshi*, a young woman dressed in scarlet skirts over which she wore white, formal male robes (even to the sword girded at the waist) sang and danced long narrative works. Although the form degenerated (it became a popular dance among street entertainers who more often than not were also prostitutes), many *shirabyōshi* dancers became influential women of high rank, as, for example, Shizuka Gozen, the paramour of Genji general Minamoto no Yoshitsune (1159–1189?).

In the early fourteenth century a new genre called *kusemai* (meaning either "wild rhythm" or "lively rhythm") emerged from *shirabyōshi.* There were many types of *kusemai,* but the one that remained popular longest was that known as "Kaga-jo" (Women of Kaga Province), which had been developed by an extremely talented dancer named Hyakuman (*fl.* early fourteenth century), who lived in Nara. So famous was Hyakuman that she even figures in two *nō* plays, *Yamanba* (in which a young dancer named after her performs a special *kusemai* about the Old Woman of the Mountains—thought by many to represent an apotheosis of Otozuru) and *Hyakuman* (in which the dancer herself has been driven to madness by the disappearance of her only child).

The original *kusemai* is thought to have followed the formula apparent in the few *kuse* (dances derived from the ancient *kusemai*) of *nō* that seem to retain much of their original form. The *kuse* of *Hyakuman* is a good example. It begins with a *shidai,* a short thematic song in fixed rhythm, and continues with *kuri* and *sashi* sections, both sung in a freer, less rigid rhythm, during which the dancer starts to move (in what could be considered a dance version of the recitative before an aria). Then comes the *kuse* itself, a long narrative song chanted by the chorus in a fixed rhythm with strong accents, to which the dancer performs a beautiful dance (by extension of the analogy above, the aria itself). The *kuse* is often the highlight of the play. The dance ends with a repetition by the chorus of the thematic song.

Although not much is known about her, Otozuru had an enormous effect on Kan'ami. After studying her dance form diligently, he then added the interesting rhythms and new melodies of *kusemai* to his own performing art, the rustic form known as *sarugaku* (literally, "monkey entertainment"), transforming plebeian street entertainment into the stately, elegant dance drama known as *nō.* Otozuru's dancing must have been of an extremely high caliber to have brought about such an enormous change. If Kan'ami is considered the father of *nō,* Otozuru must be considered its mother.

[*See also* Nō *and the entry on Kan'ami.*]

BIBLIOGRAPHY

Dōmoto Masaki. *Zeami akutingu mesōdo.* Tokyo, 1987.

Keene, Donald. *Nō: The Classical Theatre of Japan.* New York, 1966.

Kodansha Encyclopedia of Japan. Tokyo, 1983. See the entries "Dance, Traditional," "Kan'ami," "Kusemai," "Nō," and "Sarugaku."

Komparu Kunio. *The Noh Theater: Principles and Perspectives.* Translated by Jane Corddry and Stephen Comee. New York, 1983.

Nishino Haruo and Hata Hisashi, eds. *Nō, kyōgen jiten* (Dictionary of Noh and Kyogen). 2d ed. Tokyo, 1988.

O'Neill, P. G. *Early Nō Drama.* London, 1958.

STEPHEN COMEE

OULED NAÏL, DANCES OF THE. During the nineteenth century, Algeria became familiar to the Western world through the paintings of the French Orientalists and, toward the end of the century, through photographs of the richly adorned dancers of the Ouled Naïl. A confederation of tribes, the Ouled Naïl occupy a large area of the mountainous high desert region; they often visit and sometimes reside in towns of the region, such as Bou Saâda, Biskra, and Chellala. They are nominally Muslim.

Until after World War II, in the Middle East and North Africa, it was assumed that any female dancer was also a prostitute. The dancers of the Ouled Naïl were, however, born into a tribe in which the arts of the courtesan were not only condoned but valued; its young girls approached this dual profession free of inhibitions. Their earnings, in the form of gold and silver coins, were made into necklaces and other jewelry that both ornamented their costumes and provided tangible evidence of their wealth. Once a sufficient dowry had been amassed, they found no difficulty in making a suitable marriage among their own people.

The dance arts of the Ouled Naïl reached a high point during French colonialism (1830–1962), when dancers attracted a large patronage from among French military personnel, who were sent to keep Algeria within France's domain. After Algeria won its independence in 1962, the

OULED NAÏL. A pair of dancers in the early twentieth century. (Photograph by Lehnert and Landrock, reprinted from *National Geographic Magazine* 25.1, January 1914; collection of Mardi Rollow.)

French army left, and demand declined for the diversions of the Naïlia, becoming limited to performances at weddings, festivals, and for a local clientele.

Few young Ouled Naïl women enter the profession today, so many of the dancers are in their middle years. Their costumes have not been modernized, but they are far less elaborate. The silk brocades, golden diadems, and festoons of coins are now rarely seen; today, dancers wear layers of diaphanous dresses, sometimes covered with a *palla* (an ancient Roman-style draped garment), and their turbans and head scarves are of nylon. Their only ornaments are a few gold or silver bracelets and a round pin to fasten a scarf beneath the chin. Some dancers completely cover their faces with transparent veils, while others wear small white embroidered triangles to cover the nose and mouth only; many wear no face covering at all.

In the 1970s, the best-known troupe of Ouled Naïl dancers and musicians was located at Bou Saâda, where a few tourists visited two luxury hotels. Both men and women perform; the men's repertory includes a rifle dance. When dancing, the men of the Ouled Naïl often cover the lower part of the face with a portion of their headwraps, in the manner of the nomadic Tuareg.

The musicians play the *ghayṭah* and a group of frame drums with snares *(bendirs)*. The performance generally begins with a procession led by the musicians. The exciting call of the *ghayṭah* and the women's high-pitched *zaghareet* (ululation) announce to all that there will be an entertainment, so an audience gathers. When they arrive at the stage area, the dancers and musicians sit together on a platform while the soloists and groups take turns performing.

The women sometimes form couples. As in the past they often danced side by side, occasionally with joined hands. In one dance figure still performed, they face each other with fingers linked and arms outstretched. During a solo, a Naïlia may stand poised with one leg extended and bend backward from the waist as far as possible. She sometimes sinks to one knee; then, holding her head scarf between her teeth, she moves her head from side to side, her shoulders quivering as she lifts the ends of her scarf with her fingertips.

Every performance includes several examples of the *danse du ventre*. With an impassive face and fluttering fingers, the dancer lifts and drops her abdomen by tilting her pelvis forward as she walks. [*See* Danse du Ventre.]

Many of the Ouled Naïl tribes gather at Chellala to set up their tents at festivals and holidays. At the rug festival, dancers perform informally for the buyers and sellers of carpets. Each tent shelters a different group of musicians, singers, and dancers. A man sometimes sits at the entrance to encourage passersby to enter. Here, the women also dance the *danse du ventre*. As in the past, dance performances continue to be occasions for displaying the attractions of the dancers to potential patrons.

[*See also* North Africa.]

BIBLIOGRAPHY

Dermenghem, Émile "Le Sahara des Ouled Naïl, des Larba et des Amars." *L'espèOce humaine* 18 (1960).

Johnson, Frank Edward. "Here and There in Northern Africa." *The National Geographic Magazine* (January 1914).

RECORDING. *Music of the Ouled Naïl* (Discs Araf 701, 1975).

AISHA ALI, LEONA WOOD, and MARDI ROLLOW

P

PACIFIC ISLANDS. *See* Oceanic Dance Traditions. *See also* Melanesia; Micronesia; *and* Polynesia. *For related discussion, see Music for Dance, article on* Oceanic Music.

PACIFIC NORTHWEST BALLET. The principal coastal cities of the United States are also homes to the nation's principal ballet companies: American Ballet Theatre and New York City Ballet in New York, Boston Ballet, Houston Ballet, San Francisco Ballet, and Pacific Northwest Ballet of Seattle. The Pacific Northwest Ballet (PNB) is the youngest of these, but under the direction of Kent Stowell and his wife, Francia Russell, its development has been rapid. The Seattle Opera was its catalyst, as the opera wanted a resident ballet corps. Leon Kalimos, executive director of the San Francisco Ballet, was engaged to guide the project. In 1973 he selected Janet Reed, a West Coast native, to become ballet mistress. By 1976, Melissa Hayden had taken over as company director. Her tenure lasted a year. The following year, Stowell became artistic director and principal choreographer; Russell was associate director and headed the school. She subsequently became co-director.

Stowell had began his performing career with the San Francisco Ballet. He and Russell had met when they were with the New York City Ballet. When the Pacific Northwest Ballet Association engaged them, they were artistic directors of the Frankfurt Ballet. Although Stowell's choreography became the backbone of the PNB repertory, the company also engaged a cross-section of guest choreographers, including, in the 1979/80 season, for example, Loyce Houlton, Jean-Paul Comelin, Michael Smuin, Charles Czarny, Ben Stevenson, and Lew Christensen. Stowell and Russell also initiated the "Summer Inventions" project, which welcomed emerging choreographers. Under Russell's guidance, the school rapidly achieved a heightened stature. By 1983 the company could boast thirty-two dancers, and the following year it attracted national attention with its new production of *The Nutcracker,* featuring decor and costumes by Maurice Sendak.

In accordance with the growing trend of companies establishing home bases in two cities, the Pacific Northwest Ballet tried in 1987 to merge with the Minnesota Dance Theater. The joint venture was to be known as the Northwest Ballet, but the project fell through.

By 1993 PNB had a new headquarters in Seattle and had grown to forty-five dancers; it also had an $8 million operating budget. The repertory had vastly increased as well. The bulwark was divided between Stowell's ballets and those of Balanchine. Stowell has staged versions of such standards as *Swan Lake, Cinderella, Romeo and Juliet,* and *The Firebird,* but the majority of his works deal with original themes, such as *Through Interior Worlds, Time and Ebb, Hail to the Conquering Hero,* and *Orpheus Portrait.* Because of Russell's familiarity with Balanchine's ballets, the company has about twenty. In addition to those often presented by regional companies, PNB performs *Chaconne, Agon, Divertimento No. 15, Mozartiana, La Valse,* and *A Midsummer Night's Dream.*

Pacific Northwest Ballet's choices of outside choreographers have been courageous, and the summer project, called PNB Offstage since 1990 and coordinated by former Paul Taylor Dance Company member Lila York, is the most iconoclastic on the West Coast. Their broad knowledge of the dance field's resources comes in part from the fact that both Stowell and Russell have, in turn, served on the National Endowment for the Arts dance panel. They know the current range of American dance, and they make it available to their dancers and audience.

BIBLIOGRAPHY

Aloff, Mindy. "Pacific Northwest Ballet." *Dance Magazine* (December 1978): 52–54.

Aloff, Mindy. "Seattle: Pacific Northwest Ballet." *Dance Magazine* (December 1980): 31–35.

Blake, Jon. "Pacific Northwest Ballet: Shooting for the Top Five." *Dance Magazine* (August 1983): 44–47.

Buchanan, Kathryn. "Dance in Seattle: Boom under the Bumbershoot." *Dance Magazine* (August 1978): 110–111.

Garafola, Lynn. "In the Best American Tradition." *Dance Magazine* (February 1992): 38–44.

Kendall, Elizabeth B. "A Company of Choice." *Dance Ink* 3 (Summer 1992): 12–15.

Doris Hering

PACT BALLET. In the northern regions of South Africa, few European settlers crossed the River Vaal before the Great Trek of the Boers (a Dutch word meaning "farmers") in 1836. The city of Pretoria, founded in 1855, became the seat of Boer government in the 1860s. In 1886 the discovery of rich deposits of gold led to the founding of the nearby city of Johannesburg, which became a boomtown, attracting many new immigrants. In the twentieth century, it was in Pretoria and Johannesburg, the two principal cities of the province of Transvaal, that South African ballet developed from its earliest beginnings in improvised studios to the country's first nationally subsidized professional company in 1963.

Origins and Background. Prior to 1963, several attempts were made to establish permanent professional companies in the Transvaal that could absorb the many talented dancers trained in the studios of teachers using the syllabuses of the Royal Academy of Dancing and the Cecchetti method. All these efforts failed, and the exodus of South African dancers to companies abroad continued. But each of these attempts helped to establish a foundation of public interest on which successors could build. One of the important attempts was the establishment of the Pretoria Ballet Club, followed by the Johannesburg Festival Ballet founded by Marjorie Sturman, Poppy Frames, and Ivy Conmee in 1946. This was followed in 1947 by the Johannesburg Ballet Theatre, with Faith de Villiers and Joyce van Geems directing. This company lasted less than a year, and no new company appeared until the well-known dancer and choreographer Frank Staff established the South African Ballet Company in 1955. Three years later, in 1958, it too came to an end, about a year after the Johannesburg Festival Ballet Society had closed. The last attempt, Johannesburg City Ballet, instituted in 1959 at the suggestion of Yvonne Mounsey, a former member of the New York City Ballet, was to become the final link between earlier efforts and PACT Ballet.

At the invitation of a sympathetic businessman, Fred Ziegler, a number of business leaders in Johannesburg accepted appointments to the board of directors of Johannesburg City Ballet, and the City Council responded with a measure of financial support. Also supportive were such prominent teachers and dancers as Faith de Villiers, Denise Schultz, Dulcie Howes, and Hermien Dommisse. But funds to establish the company on a professional level were not immediately available.

The first step in this direction was taken when Johannesburg City Ballet obtained an educational grant for school performances from the Transvaal Provincial Council. It was sufficient to cover not only basic production costs but also modest honoraria to be paid to the dancers for each performance. The second step was taken in 1962, when the company accepted an invitation to present a ballet during the opening festivities of Johannesburg's new Civic Theatre. This provided an ideal opportunity to demonstrate the dancers' professionalism. The company commissioned the Royal Ballet's David Blair to stage a production of *Coppélia* and to dance the role of Franz, partnering his South African–born wife, Maryon Lane, who alternated in the role of Swanilda with Denise Schultze, the company's ballerina.

The success of these performances enabled Deputy Minister John Vorster to secure financial support for a

PACT BALLET. Frank Staff's *Five Faces of Eurydice* (1965) was a jocular retelling of the Orpheus legend, with Orpheus, Eurydice, and Pluto each assuming new identities in different periods of history. Scene 4 took place in the restaurant of the Gare de Lyon, in the 1890s. In the center is Margo Wilson (Eurydice) as the Ballerina, with Bruce Merrill as her admirer; at far right is Philip Markham (Pluto) as the Impresario. Seated at an upstage table is Dawn Weller as a member of the corps de ballet. (Photograph courtesy of Claude Conyers.)

ballet company in the Transvaal. Hermien Dommisse, who had taken temporary leave of her career in theater and opera to assist the Johannesburg City Ballet in gaining a subsidy and achieving professional status, was appointed chair of the Ballet Committee of the newly formed Performing Arts Council of the Transvaal (PACT), also called, in Afrikaans, Transvaalse Raad vir die Uitvoerende Kunste (TRUK).

The first government-subsidized performance of ballet in South Africa subsequently took place in April 1963. In a production directed by Molly Lake, the famous French ballerina Yvette Chauviré danced the title role of *Giselle,* partnered by Gary Burne, the newly appointed ballet master and *premier danseur* of the company. A curtain raiser, *Capriccio,* was choreographed jointly by Dudley Davies and Gary Burne. The orchestra of the South African Broadcasting Company (SABC) was contracted to play for the performances.

After the *Giselle* season, the Johannesburg City Ballet was incorporated into PACT and given a new name, Ballet Transvaal. There were nineteen company members. With its professional future secured, the time had come for the appointment of a fully qualified artistic director. The board hoped that Vera Volkova, artistic adviser of the Royal Danish Ballet, would accept the appointment, and with this in mind she was invited to spend three months with the company, teaching the dancers and preparing them for her production of *Swan Lake.* To satisfy Johannesburg balletomanes, the company again invited a guest artist, Beryl Grey, who alternated in the role of Odette-Odile with the newly appointed *prima ballerina* of Ballet Transvaal, Phyllis Spira. Both were partnered by Gary Burne. At the end of the season, Volkova was unable to accept the proffered appointment, and the board was obliged to consider local candidates. Fortunately, among them was one who was ready, willing, and well-qualified to assume the post.

The de Villiers Period: 1964–1968. Faith de Villiers was appointed artistic manager at the beginning of 1964, and the company was renamed PACT Ballet, or TRUK Ballet. Although it had inherited the best dancing and teaching talents of the Johannesburg City Ballet, the new company was troubled by labor disputes. In a showdown between the dancers and the artistic director over working conditions, especially on tour, de Villiers stood firm, with the result that only nine dancers renewed their contracts for 1965. Undaunted, de Villiers quickly assembled a new company of thirty-three talented dancers, choosing women from various South African and Rhodesian schools and hiring men through her contacts in England, continental Europe, and the United States. Among the new dancers was Dawn Weller, a teenager who almost twenty years later would become artistic director of the company and a dominant force in South African ballet. [*See the entry on Weller.*]

PACT BALLET. Sandra Lipman, partnered by Claude Conyers, in Yvonne Mounsey's *Interplay,* created for the company in 1965. This short work, set to the jazzy score by Morton Gould, depicted a group of youngsters larking about after a ballet class. (Photograph by Tommy Murray; courtesy of Claude Conyers.)

In 1965, Basil Taylor began his long association with PACT Ballet as company organizer, and he and de Villiers formed an immediately effective team, working together to improve the dancers' benefits and raise their level of training. For the first time in South Africa's balletic history, company employees had the advantage of a pension fund, medical insurance, and annual paid holidays. The well-known teacher Marjorie Sturman was appointed honorary consultant to the company; Alexander Bennett, formerly a principal dancer with Sadler's Wells Theatre Ballet, was named ballet master; and Frank Staff accepted an appointment as resident choreographer and producer.

With this creative team on hand, the next few years of PACT Ballet were exceptionally fruitful. Major productions included Bennett's staging of *Coppélia* for the fall season (April–June) of 1965, with guest artists Claire Sombert and Milenko Banovitch as Swanilda and Franz; and de Villiers's restaging of Walter Gore's *The Nutcracker* for the following Christmas season, performed with alternative curtain raisers, Audrey King's *La Fenêtre* or Frank Staff's *Five Faces of Eurydice.* The following year saw productions of Roland Petit's *Carmen,* Frederick Ashton's *Façade* and *Les Patineurs,* Bennett's staging of *Aurora's Wedding,* and Françoise Adret's sumptuous production of *Cinderella,* with Galina Samsova in the title role and André Prokovsky as Prince Charming. Other works were choreographed by de Villiers herself, Audrey King, Yvonne Mounsey, and Lorna Haupt.

Important additions to the company's repertory were made by Frank Staff. In addition to new works such as *Spanish Encounter* and *Five Faces of Eurydice* (both 1965), he restaged two classic works that he had originally choreographed for Ballet Rambert in London, his comic masterpiece *Peter and the Wolf* (1940) and a third version of the whimsical and beautiful suite of dances he called *Czernyana* (1939, 1941). In 1967, working with the composer Graham Newcater and the designer Raimond Schoop, he made one of his most effective works, entitled *Raka*, based on an epic by the Afrikaans poet N. P. van Wyk Louw. [*See the entry on Staff.*]

Under de Villiers, the artistic policies of the company were clearly defined: the repertory would be based on the classic ballets, augmented by works by twentieth-century choreographers; the company would offer South African dancers the opportunity to pursue professional careers without having to leave the country, as had formerly been necessary; and guests artists from abroad would be imported from time to time to star in major new productions. These early principles were central to the development of PACT Ballet, shaping and defining the company's personality over the years.

PACT BALLET. The company has mounted three productions of *Cinderella*, with choreography by three quite different choreographers: Françoise Adret (1966), Frederick Ashton (1972), and Alfred Rodriguez (1979). Pictured here are Malcolm Burn as the Prince and Dawn Weller in the title role of the Rodriquez production. (Photograph © 1979 by Nan Melville; used by permission.)

PACT BALLET. Jeremy Hodges and Odette Millner in a 1990 performance of the pas de deux in George Balanchine's *Agon*, staged for the company by Brigitte Thom in 1987. (Photograph by Bob Martin; courtesy of PACT Ballet. Choreography by George Balanchine © The George Balanchine Trust.)

At the end of 1968, de Villiers resigned the directorship of the company, citing family pressures as her reason. During her tenure, an attractive repertory had emerged, including six full-length classics, and the company roster had boasted a number of outstanding South African dancers. In addition to *Sylvia, Coppélia, The Nutcracker, Cinderella, Giselle,* and *Swan Lake,* de Villiers had acquired productions of Michel Fokine's *The Firebird,* Jack Carter's *The Witch Boy,* and Ashton's *La Fille Mal Gardée.* Leading dancers during the de Villiers years were Phyllis Spira, Denise Schultze, Gary Burne, Sandra Lipman, Marijan Beyer, Noleen Nicol, and Juan Sanchez. Notable soloists included Annette van der Westhuizen, Marianne van der Merwe, Gillian Joubert, Philip Markham, Barbara Dunlop, and Dawn Weller.

Interim Managements: 1969–1972. De Villiers was succeeded as artistic director by Paul Grinwis, a Belgian born in South Africa, at the beginning of 1969. Denise Schultze, who had left the company, returned as ballet mistress and dancer. Grinwis, a faltering director and poor choreographer, remained for only one year and left no lasting impression. The most important productions during his tenure—Ashton's *La Fille Mal Gardée,* staged by John Hart, and a new *Swan Lake,* staged by Nicolas Beriozoff—were legacies from de Villiers.

At the beginning of 1970, PACT Ballet was without an artistic director, but the company management was strengthened by the appointment of Louis Godfrey as ballet master. The highlight of 1970 was the first production of *Romeo and Juliet,* mounted by Beriozoff. The following year, John Hart staged the company's first production of *The Sleeping Beauty,* with guest star Margot Fonteyn, as well as Ashton's *Les Rendezvous* and *The Dream.* Named artistic director at the start of 1972, Hart staged a new *Giselle,* with guest stars Natalia Makarova and Iván Nagy, and produced Ashton's *Cinderella,* with Ashton and Robert Helpmann in their famous roles as the Stepsisters. Leading dancers in 1969–1972 included Dawn Weller, Maxine Denys, Jo Savino, Milan Hatala, Edgardo Hartley, Christiaan Danhoff, and Keith Rossen.

The Schultze–Godfrey Years: 1973–1978. Hart's post with an American university allowed him to spend only twenty weeks a year in Johannesburg, and he was consequently replaced early in 1973 by Denise Schultze and Louis Godfrey as co–artistic directors. PACT Ballet, by then numbering nearly sixty dancers on full-time contract, thus entered its second decade under strong leadership. New productions of the classics were the focus of the company's work during this period, and, with Schultze's tutelage and encouragement, technical prowess became characteristic of the company's performance style, perhaps at the expense of dramatic and theatrical strengths.

Repertory additions included the Kingdom of the Shades scene from *La Bayadère,* staged by Keith Rossen; David Lichine's *Graduation Ball;* Ronald Hynd's *Dvořák Variations;* André Prokovsky's *Vespri,* and Ashton's *Monotones.* In 1973 Gary Burne choreographed the startling rock-music ballet *Nonquase,* based on a Xhosa legend, and for the 1978 season Ronald Hynd staged *Rosalinda,* based on Johann Strauss's operetta *Die Fledermaus,* with music arranged by John Lanchberry and set and costume designs by Peter Docherty. Among the guest artists who appeared with the company during the Schultze–Godfrey years were Galina Samsova, Anthony Dowell, Merle Park, Peter Breuer, Eva Evdokimova, and David Ashmole. The resident principals included Weller, Hartley, Malcolm Burn, Faye Daniel, and James Riveros.

The Haupt Years: 1979–1983. Following the resignation of Schultze and Godfrey in 1978, Pretoria ballet teacher Lorna Haupt took over as artistic director, with Ashley Killar as her ballet master. The chief event of Haupt's tenure was the move in 1981 of the company from Johannesburg to the splendid new State Theatre in Pretoria. A new direction in repertory building became evident with the acquisition of several full-length works recently created by various choreographers working on the international scene: Ronald Hynd's *Papillon,* mounted in 1979; André Prokovsky's *Anna Karenina* and *The Three Musketeers,* staged in 1980 and 1981; Valery Panov's *War and Peace,* mounted in 1981; and Hynd's *The Devil to Pay,* produced in 1982.

The Haupt years were, however, characterized by a general decline in standards. Although the company retained the services of a number of excellent dancers, there was a deterioration in production values and, notably, in the work of the corps de ballet. The guest-artist roster included Stephen Jefferies, Margaret Barbieri, Egon Madsen, Patricia Ruanne, Galina Panova, and Valery Panov. The resident company was led by Weller, Hartley, Burn, Bruce Simpson, Liane Lurie, Jeremy Coles, Ian Knowles, and Martin Raistrick.

The Weller Regime: 1983 to the Present. Early in 1983, ballerina Dawn Weller was named assistant artistic director, succeeding to the directorship upon Haupt's retirement in the middle of the year. Weller immediately imprinted her strong personality on PACT Ballet, which, under her direction, soon emerged as the country's leading ballet company, a position it sustained throughout the 1980s and 1990s. Weller succeeded to the directorship at a time of growing political unrest in South Africa and increasing isolation from abroad. A United Nations–sponsored cultural boycott reached its peak in the late

PACT BALLET. A scene from John Cranko's comic masterpiece *The Taming of the Shrew,* staged by Jane Bourne in 1992. From left to right, the dancers are Nigel Hannah (Gremio), Jeremy Coles (Petruchio), Johnny Bovang (Hortensio), David Palmer (Lucentio), Dianne Finch (Katherina), and Manuel Noram (Baptista). (Photograph by Bob Martin; courtesy of PACT Ballet.)

PACT BALLET. The company's senior principals, Tanja Graafland and Johnny Bovang, as Odette and Siegfried in a 1992 performance of *Swan Lake*. (Photograph by Edzard Meyberg; courtesy of PACT Ballet.)

1980s. In the arts there was an upsurge of resentment, particularly from black artists, toward the government-subsidized arts councils, and there emerged an ideology that propounded "Eurocentric" art forms as alien to Africa.

Despite the cultural boycott, Weller managed to enhance the company's repertory, particularly through acquisition of works by George Balanchine. She restored to the repertory works that had not been performed for many years, and she commissioned new productions of several classic works. Continuing Haupt's swing away from the importation of guest artists—a prominent feature before 1980—Weller endeavored to promote both the company as a whole as well as resident artists as South African models of excellence. This allowed the company to weather the storm of international isolation with more success than may have been possible in earlier years.

Important additions to the repertory under Weller included Rudolf Nureyev's *Don Quixote,* staged by Richard Nowotny (1985), Choo San Goh's *Variations Sérieuses,* staged by Janek Schergen (1985), August Bournonville's *La Sylphide,* staged by Poul Gnatt (1987), John Cranko's *The Taming of the Shrew,* staged by Jane Bourne (1992), Ronald Hynd's *The Merry Widow,* staged by Hynd and Colin Peasley (1993), David Bintley's *Still Life at the Penguin Café,* staged by Bintley and Grant Coyle (1994), and a full-length production of Marius Petipa's *La Bayadère,* staged by Weller (1996). Balanchine works added to the repertory included *Agon, Ballet Imperial, Rubies, Theme and Variations,* and *Who Cares?*. The principal dancers of the period were Jeremy Coles, Catherine Burnett, Johnny Bovang, Tanja Graafland, and Leticia Müller.

With the demise of the Nationalist government, with its policies of racial *apartheid* ("separateness"), and the advent of democracy in South Africa in the early 1990s, the future of state-subsidized ballet companies came to be a topic of increasing concern. By the spring of 1997, not only the subsidized status of PACT Ballet but its very name was in question, as the province of the Transvaal no longer exists, having been subdivided into four new provinces. Under the terms of legislation passed by the South African parliament late in 1996, subsidies to the arts councils of the former provinces, and to the ballet companies they have supported, will continue at decreasing levels until 1999, when it is expected that all dance companies in South Africa will compete for government funds on an equal basis.

[*See also* South Africa, *article on* Ballet.]

BIBLIOGRAPHY

Borland, Eve. "CAPAB and PACT Ballet South Africa." *Dance Gazette* (March 1985): 29–32.

Cooper, Montgomery, and Jane Allyn. *Dance for Life: Ballet in South Africa.* Cape Town, 1980. Photographs by Montogomery Cooper; text by Jane Allyn.

Grut, Marina. *The History of Ballet in South Africa.* Cape Town, 1981.

Hagemann, Fred. "The Politics of Dance in South Africa." *Ballett International* 13 (January 1990): 137–146.

Scimone, Diana. "Changes in South Africa." *Dance Teacher Now* 14 (April 1992): 52–57.

TRUK PACT Info. Pretoria, 1991–1996. A quarterly magazine published by the Performing Arts Council Transvaal; includes regular features on PACT Ballet.

ARCHIVES. Collections of photographs, souvenir programs, press clippings, and memorabilia are housed in the administrative offices of PACT Ballet in the State Theatre, Pretoria.

JONATHAN HURWITZ

PAEPER, VERONICA (born 9 April 1944 in Port Shepstone, Natal), South African ballet dancer, choreographer, and company director. Paeper received her dance training under the tutelage of Dulcie Howes at the University of Cape Town Ballet School, where she also studied with David Poole, Pamela Chrimes, and Frank Staff. Staff, whom she married in 1966, was to have a profound influence on her later work as a choreographer. During her performing career, Paeper rose to become a principal dancer with three South African companies, in the Cape

Province (CAPAB Ballet, also known as the University of Cape Town Ballet), in the Transvaal (PACT Ballet), and in the Orange Free State (PACOFS Ballet).

Paeper began choreographing in 1972. Her first work, created for CAPAB Ballet, was *John the Baptist,* a dramatic one-act ballet set to music by Ernest Bloch; scenery and costumes were designed by Peter Cazalet, an innovative, witty artist who would remain Paeper's most frequent artistic collaborator for the next twenty-five years. A prolific choreographer, Paeper has created more than forty ballets, among them sixteen full-length works. She has explored a variety of themes in her ballets and has drawn inspiration from sources as diverse as the works of Shakespeare and Dickens, fables, the Bible, mythology, and South African prose and poety. Her trademarks include a pronounced sense of humor, tender pas de deux, and skillfully created crowd scenes.

From the mid-1970s onward, Paeper created a steady stream of works for CAPAB, where she held the post of resident choreographer. Notable among the ballets she added to the company's repertory are *Funtastique* (1975) and *Concerto for Charlie* (1979), two one-act ballets set to music by Shostakovich; *Ohm* (1976), a pas de deux, and the one-act *Drie Diere* (Three Beasts; 1980), both set to music by the contemporary South African composer Peter Klatzow; and such full-length classics as *Romeo and Juliet* (1974), *Cinderella* (1975), and *Don Quixote* (1979).

The 1980s were an even more productive decade for Paeper. She continued to explore her interest in the music of Peter Klatzow, in *Still-Life with Moonbeams* (1981) and *Vespers* (1985), and she made two remarkable works to the music of David Earl, *The Return of the Soldier* (1982) and *Abelard and Heloise* (1985). In 1982, she also made two three-act works that must be counted as among her most successful productions, the rollicking *Orpheus in the Underworld,* set to the music of Jacques Offenbach, and *A Christmas Carol,* set to a score arranged by David Tidboald from music by various composers. These were followed by *Spartacus* (1984), *Nell Gwynne* (1984), which

PAEPER. Daria Klimentová as Ophelia and Hubert Essakow in the title role of Paeper's *Hamlet,* created for CAPAB Ballet in 1992. (Photograph by Pat Bromilow-Downing; used by permission.)

was set to music by Rossini, *The Tales of Hoffmann* (1985), *Carmen* (1987), and *The Merry Widow* (1988), all three-act works. On 1 October 1987, Paeper was appointed assistant director of CAPAB Ballet, retaining her position as resident choreographer, and in April 1990 she was appointed director designate to succeed David Poole. When he retired at the end of the year, she took up her post as director of CAPAB Ballet on 1 January 1991.

Administrative duties did not staunch the flow of Paeper's creativity. *Camille* (1990), a three-act work set to the music of Verdi, was followed by *Eine Kleine Nachtmusik* (1990), *The Nutcracker* (1991), *A Midsummer Night's Dream* (1993), and *Walpurgisnacht* (1993). Two exceptional works from the early 1990s were a two-act production of *Hamlet* (1992), set to a commissioned score by Peter Klatzow, and a three-act work of quite a different nature: *Sylvia in Hollywood* (1993), set to a score composed and arranged by Allan Stephenson, including his arrangements of the familiar ballet music of Léo Delibes.

For more than two decades, Paeper has been widely considered the most important ballet choreographer at work in South Africa. She has twice won the coveted Nederburg Award for Ballet in the Cape Province, in 1980 and 1992, and in 1993 she shared with Peter Klatzow the Artes Award for Best Contribution to Serious Music and Dance for their collaboration on *Hamlet*. In 1994 she gained international recognition for her company when it became the first South African ballet company to tour abroad. The repertory for the two-week season at the Sadler's Wells Theatre in London consisted entirely of works by South African choreographers.

[*See also* CAPAB Ballet.]

BIBLIOGRAPHY

Borland, Eve. "CAPAB and PACT Ballet, South Africa." *Dance Gazette* (March 1985).

Cooper, Montgomery, and Jane Allyn. *Dance for Life: Ballet in South Africa*. Cape Town, 1980. Photographs by Montgomery Cooper; text by Jane Allyn.

Glasstone, Richard. "The Cape Ballet." *The Dancing Times* (September 1994): 1153–1157.

NAN MELVILLE

PAGE, RUTH (born 22 March 1899 in Indianapolis, died 7 April 1991 in Chicago), American dancer, choreographer, company director, and writer. Ruth Page graduated from Tudor Hall School for Girls in Indianapolis in 1916. She had already studied "fancy dancing" and "skirt dancing" with Anna Stanton and ballet with Andreas Pavley and Serge Oukrainsky in Indianapolis, Elizavetta Menzeli in New York, and Jan Zalewski from the Anna Pavlova Company at Midway Gardens, Chicago.

While at Miss Williams and Miss McClellan's French School for Girls in New York, Page began training with Adolph Bolm, making her first professional appearance in Bolm's ballet *Falling Leaves* as part of the Victor Herbert revue *Miss 1917*. She interrupted her academic studies to join the corps de ballet of the Anna Pavlova Company for its tour of South America (January 1918 to February 1919). In December 1919, she danced the title role in Bolm's *The Birthday of the Infanta* at the Chicago Opera.

In 1920, while dancing with Bolm's Ballet Intime at the Coliseum in London, Page studied with Enrico Cecchetti. As *première danseuse* of the Ballet Intime, she toured the United States in Bolm's ballets and choreographed her first dances for the concert stage. In March 1922, she appeared with Bolm in Francis Brugier's film *Danse Macabre*, the first dance film with synchronized sound. From October 1922 to March 1924, she was the prima ballerina of Irving Berlin's *Music Box Revue* in New York City (1922–1923) and on its U.S. tour (1923–1924). Settling in Chicago to become *première danseuse* of Bolm's Chicago Allied Arts (1924–1927), she choreographed two of her most successful early dances for its repertory—*Peter Pan and the Butterfly* (1925) and *The Flapper and the Quarterback* (1926).

Following her marriage to Chicago lawyer Thomas Hart Fisher, Page danced briefly in early 1925 with Diaghilev's Ballets Russes in Monte Carlo—commissioning two dances from the young George Balanchine—and again studied with Cecchetti. As guest artist at the Teatro Colón, Buenos Aires, in the fall of 1925, she danced in Bolm's stagings of *Petrouchka* and *Le Coq d'Or* and in a command performance for Edward, prince of Wales.

In 1926 Page began her long association with opera ballet as ballet director, choreographer, and *première danseuse* of the Ravinia Opera (1926–1931), for which she choreographed new solo and group dances. In early 1927 and early 1928, she appeared as guest soloist with the Metropolitan Opera, New York; on 27 April 1928, she danced Terpsichore in the world premiere of Igor Stravinsky's *Apollon Musagète*, choreographed by Bolm for a festival of contemporary music in Washington, D.C.

Page ended her association with Bolm when she accepted an engagement to perform (with Edwin Strawbridge and a small group) during the coronation celebrations of Emperor Hirohito in Tokyo in October 1928. From November 1928 to April 1929 she toured, studied dance, and performed throughout Asia, the Middle East, and Europe. From 1926 to 1929 Page created primarily solos, duets, and trios, which she presented at Ravinia or in joint recitals with artists such as Strawbridge, Paul du Pont, Jacques Cartier, and Blake Scott. Starting in 1929 and continuing throughout the 1930s, she began to choreograph larger group works such as *Iberian Monotone* (1930); *Cinderella, Pavane,* and *La Valse* (1931); *Gold Standard* (1934); and *Love Song* (1935). Meanwhile, she con-

PAGE. Page choreographed *Billy Sunday* for her own company in 1946 but restaged it in 1948 for the Ballet Russe de Monte Carlo with Frederic Franklin in the title role. (Photograph reprinted from Page, 1973, p. 102.)

tinued to produce solo dances exploring a broad range of expression.

The 1930s were characteristic of most of Page's career—a whirlwind of simultaneous creating, performing, and touring, alone or with a company, throughout the United States and abroad, while maintaining a home base in Chicago with ties to the Chicago Opera. Her foreign tours included performances in Moscow (1930), Havana (1932), Japan (with Harald Kreutzberg, 1934), and Scandinavia (1937). The most significant events of this period were the beginning of her association with longtime partner Bentley Stone and the creation of a series of Americana ballets, most with commissioned scores by American composers: *Oak Street Beach* (music by Clarence Loomis, 1929); *Hear Ye! Hear Ye!* (Aaron Copland, 1934); *Americans in Paris* (George Gershwin, 1936); and *American Pattern* (1937) and *Frankie and Johnny* (1938) for the Federal Theatre Project, Chicago, both with music by Jerome Moross. There was also *La Guillablesse* (1933), a ballet danced by an African-American company (except for Page, at its premiere) and based on author Lafcadio Hearn's *Two Years in the French West Indies,* with a score by the African-American composer William Grant Still.

In the 1940s, Page's solo and duet concerts and company tours continued with Stone. She created three major ballets on American themes for the Original Ballet Russe—a revival of *Frankie and Johnny* (1945), *The Bells* (1946), and *Billy Sunday* (1948)—as well as *Dances with Words and Music,* a new series of danced poems, many to scores by Lehman Engel. Page made a brief foray into choreography for Broadway with *Music in My Heart* (1947). In 1950 she appeared in Paris with Les Ballets Américains, with Stone as co-director.

With *Guns and Castanets* (music by Moross, after Bizet; Federal Theatre Project, Chicago, 1939), Page transported *Carmen* to the Spanish Civil War of 1936 to 1939, and she made her first experiment with ballet versions of operas, a genre that became her trademark in the 1950s and 1960s. Significant examples of Page's ballet adaptations of operas are *Revenge* (1951, based on Verdi's *Il Trovatore*); *Susanna and the Barber* (1956, based on Rossini's *The Barber of Seville*); *Camille* (1957, based on Verdi's *La Traviata*); *Die Fledermaus* (1958); *Mephistophela* (1966, based on Gounod's *Faust*); and three versions of *Carmen* (1959, 1962, and 1972) among others. These ballets formed the basis of the repertory for Page's Chicago Opera Ballet in 1956 (after 1966, called Ruth Page's International Ballet), an offshoot of Page's association with the Chicago Lyric Opera (1955–1970). This company toured the United States with numerous international guest artists, including Rudolf Nureyev in his American stage debut at the Brooklyn Academy of Music on 10 March 1962. Other major works of Page's from the 1960s were *Carmina Burana* (1966, music by Carl Orff), *Boléro* (1968, music by Maurice Ravel), *Romeo and Juliet* (1969, music by Petr Ilich Tchaikovsky), and *The Nutcracker* (1965, music by Tchaikovsky).

Following the death of her husband in 1969, Page abandoned the International Ballet and toured with a small lecture-demonstration group, Ruth Page's Invitation to the Dance. In 1971 she formed the Ruth Page Foundation for Dance in Chicago, a school she co-directed with her

PAGE. Choreographed for the Chicago Opera Ballet, Page's *Mephistofela* (1963) was based on the Faust legend and set to music by Berlioz, Boito, and Gounod. Seen at center here are Patricia Klekovic, Kenneth Johnsonn, and Dolores Lipinski. (Photograph reprinted from Page, 1973, p. 121.)

longtime ballet master, Larry Long. In 1973 she formed a new company, the Chicago Ballet, which had various codirectors during its six-year existence.

In the 1970s Page continued to choreograph, producing, for example, *Catulli Carmina* (Pittsburgh Ballet Theatre, 1973), *Alice in the Garden* (Jacob's Pillow, 1970), and *Alice* (full-length version, Chicago Ballet, 1977). Her ballets were also staged, primarily by Frederic Franklin and Larry Long, for companies throughout the United States and Europe, including the Pittsburgh Ballet Theatre, Cincinnati Ballet, Milwaukee Ballet, Ballet du Rhin, Tulsa Ballet Theatre, and the Dance Theatre of Harlem.

New York Times dance critic John Martin commented, "No one has better ideas than Ruth Page." Throughout her career, an indefatigable urge to convey original ideas in dance led her to commission music for a majority of her works from an impressive array of composers, including Louis Horst, Copland, Moross, Darius Milhaud, Jacques Ibert, and Issac Van Grove, and costumes and decor from designers such as Nicholas Remisoff, Isamu Noguchi, John Pratt, Leonor Fini, Antoni Clave, José Basarte, Bernard Daydé, and André Delfau. Delfau, who had collaborated with Page on most of her ballets since 1961, married her in May 1984.

Along with her literary sources, sophisticated style, and tongue-in-cheek wit, Page's artistic restlessness is perhaps the most outstanding attribute of her work. Building on the foundation of her classical training, she gleaned a remarkably wide range of dance styles (modern, ethnic, jazz, and tap) from her travels and studies; she freely used these styles according to her choreographic needs, often in unorthodox ways in the same ballet. Her pragmatic yet eclectic approach to choreography was often successful, but ideas sometimes overwhelmed Page's choreography, confusing audiences and critics who expected the choreographer's style to be unified within the context of one ballet.

Another limitation of Page's career, despite her remarkable accomplishments, was her decision to remain in Chicago. Although Page toured throughout the United States from the outset of her career in 1920 and for fifteen years with the Chicago Opera Ballet, her primary influence was outside the mainstream of American dance in New York. Even so, the tours with Bolm and her early partners brought dance to audiences in the United States who had never seen ballet. Her work was nearly always successful with audiences, and her early solos, danced poems, and Americana ballets were pioneering works in American dance. For more than forty years her various companies gave first opportunities and exposure to countless talented American and international dance artists.

In recognition of her unique and distinguished career, Page received numerous civic and state honors. She was awarded honorary degrees from both Harvard University and Indiana University, and in 1985 she received an Illinois gubernatorial Award for Achievement in the Arts. She was twice honored with a *Dance Magazine* Award, in 1980 and 1990.

BIBLIOGRAPHY

Anderson, Jack. *The One and Only: The Ballet Russe de Monte Carlo.* New York, 1981.

Dorris, George. "*Frankie and Johnny* in Chicago and Some Problems of Attribution." *Dance Chronicle* 18.2 (1995): 179–188.

Martin, John. *Ruth Page: An Intimate Biography.* New York, 1977.

Page, Ruth. *Page by Page.* Edited by Andrew Mark Wentink. Brooklyn, 1978.

Page, Ruth. *Class: Notes on Dance Classes around the World, 1915–1980.* Edited by Andrew Mark Wentink. Princeton, 1984.

Wentink, Andrew Mark. "The Ruth Page Collection." *Bulletin of Research in the Humanities* (Spring 1980): 67–162.

FILM AND VIDEOTAPE. *Ruth Page: An American Original* (New York: Otter Productions, 1978). "The Merry Widow" (WTTW-TV, Chicago, 1983). "Billy Sunday: Baseball, Bible, and Ballet" (WCET-TV, Cincinnati, 1984).

ARCHIVES. Chicago Public Library. College of DuPage, Glen Ellyn, Illinois. Costume Collection, Chicago Art Institute. Harvard University. Newberry Library, Chicago. Ruth Page Collection, New York Public Library for the Performing Arts.

ANDREW MARK WENTINK

PAIGE, BRYDON (Brydone James Duncan; born 13 January 1933 in Vancouver, British Columbia), Canadian dancer, actor, teacher, choreographer, and company director. Brydone Duncan began his dance training with Kay Armstrong in 1950, when he was seventeen, and that same year appeared in a ballet choreographed by her at the third Canadian Ballet Festival, held in Montreal. In 1952 and 1953 Duncan again performed at the Canadian Ballet Festivals, appearing in Heiden's *Daphnis and Chloe* and *Pygmalion* at the 1953 festival in Ottawa. After Heiden's group was invited to Montreal to perform these two ballets on television for Radio-Canada, the French-language channel of the Canadian Broadcasting Corporation, Duncan remained in Montreal and joined a group of dancers formed by Ludmilla Chiriaeff to perform ballets on television. This small group eventually evolved into a theatrical troupe known first as Les Ballets Chiriaeff and then, in 1957, as Les Grands Ballets Canadiens. By then, Brydone Duncan had become well known under his adopted name of Brydon Paige.

For more than twenty years Paige served Les Ballets Chiriaeff and Les Grands Ballets Canadiens in a variety of posts, first as principal character dancer, then as resident choreographer, ballet master, and *répétiteur.* As a character dancer he excelled in such dramatic roles as Kastchei in *The Firebird,* Herr Drosselmeyer in *The Nutcracker,* and the Stranger in Eric Hyrst's *Sea Gallows* (1959). In lighter roles, his particular talent for comedy made him an ideal interpreter of Drusilla, one of the Ugly Stepsisters in *Cinderella,* as well as Il Dottore in Chiriaeff's *Farces* (*Commedia dell'Arte,* 1958) and the General in David Lichine's *Graduation Ball,* staged by Lichine for the company in 1963.

As a choreographer, Paige created two especially fine works for Les Grands Ballets Canadiens during the 1960s: *Médée* (1962), to a commissioned electronic score by Georges Savaria, and *La Corriveau* (1967), to music by Alexander Brott based on the popular songs of Giles Vigneault. The latter work, suggested by an incident that occurred in Saint-Valier, Quebec, in 1763, concerned a women convicted and hanged for the murder of her husband, after which her body was suspended in a cage in a tree for forty days. The ballet was mounted on Margery Lambert, a dramatic dancer who performed it to great effect during the company's Montreal season at the Expo 67 World Festival of Entertainment.

PAIGE. *Médée,* created for Les Grands Ballets Canadiens in 1962, featured Véronique Landory (kneeling, at left) as Medea, Armando Jorge (standing, at left) as Jason, Nicole Vachon (at right) as Creusa, and William Thompson as King Creon. Decor and costumes were designed by Silva de Nunes. (Photograph by Henry Kord; from the archives of Les Grands Ballets Canadiens; courtesy of Ludmilla Chiriaeff.)

Between 1969 and 1972, Paige also served as guest artistic director and choreographer for Ballet Guatemala and for one year directed the Guatemala Ballet Academy. For this company he mounted *Romeo and Juliet* (1971), to the Prokofiev score; *Salome* (1972), to music by Richard Strauss; and *Carmina Burana* (1972), to the choral setting by Carl Orff. In 1973 he rejoined Les Grands Ballets Canadiens and for two years directed their second company, Les Compagnons de la Danse. His choreographies during this period include *Songs for a Dark Voice* (1973), set to music by Harry Somers and created for the Summer Arts Festival at the Ottawa Arts Centre. In 1976 he was invited by Brian Macdonald to collaborate with him in choreographing *Lignes et Pointes*, created for the *hommage* to Canadian composer Pierre Mercure produced by Les Grands Ballets Canadiens in Montreal.

The year 1976 also brought a major challenge to Paige when he was appointed artistic director of the Alberta Ballet in Edmonton. He spent the next twelve years working to make this company worthy of international recognition. Among numerous ballets he mounted for the Alberta company were original works such as *Alice in Wonderland* (1978), to music by Glazunov, and productions of such standards as *The Firebird* (1980), *The Nutcracker* (1980), *Cinderella* (1983), and *Coppélia* (1985). In 1988 Paige was commissioned by the International Olympic Committee to mount a full-length version of *The Snow Maiden*, to be presented during the winter Olympic Games in Calgary later that year. Set to music by Tchaikovsky, Paige's version was acclaimed as a cultural highlight of the games.

Since 1980 Paige has served as a faculty member of the Banff Centre of Arts in Alberta as a teacher, coach, and choreographer, and he has continued to be a presence on the international ballet scene. He has worked with the Royal Winnipeg Ballet, the National Ballet of Portugal (Companhia Nacional de Bailado), the Louisville Ballet, the Baltimore Ballet, and the Ballet Nacional de Cuba. In the 1990s, Paige's career showed no signs of slowing down. In 1992 he returned to Guatemala to mount a full-length *Don Quixote* for the Festival of Antigua, and in 1995 he was named artistic director of Operama Productions, based in Madrid.

Paige's prolific and varied career as a Canadian artist has not gone unnoticed. He twice received grants from the Canada Council and once from the International Olympic Committee for study and research abroad, which he accomplished in Moscow, Saint Petersburg, and Kiev. He was also awarded the Canadian Centennial Medal and the Queen's Silver Jubilee Medal for his contribution to the arts in Canada.

BIBLIOGRAPHY

Maynard, Olga. "Purpose: Ludmilla Chiriaeff and Les Grands Ballets Canadiens." *Dance Magazine* (April 1971).

Wyman, Max. *Dance Canada: An Illustrated History.* Vancouver and Toronto, 1989.

CLAUDE CONYERS

PAINTING. *See* Artists and Dance.

PAKISTAN. When India gained independence from the British in 1947, it split into two countries, with two Muslim-majority regions in the northeast and northwest becoming the nation of Pakistan; the western part later became another independent country, Bangladesh. Much of Pakistan thus shares features of the broader culture of the Indian subcontinent, but some aspects of Pakistani culture derive specifically from within its territory. Additionally, since Pakistan was formed as a homeland for Muslims, albeit envisioned as a modern, secular state, Pakistanis have identified with the Islamic culture not only of India, but also of the larger Muslim world. As a part of the wider South Asian culture, Pakistanis have inherited the traditions of classical dance that developed in various parts of the subcontinent. The classical dance genres that have survived and developed in Pakistan are *bharata nāṭyam*, Oḍissi, and *kathak*, and to a lesser extent Manipuri. The interplay between Islamic and specifically Indian cultures has had the most influential role in determining the state of classical dance in Pakistan.

Patronage. Dance is the least developed of all the arts in Pakistan, largely as a result of a social stigma arising from the belief that dance is non-Islamic, a notion that has been gaining popularity since the 1970s. Nevertheless, several talented dancers chose to stay in or migrate to Pakistan in 1947, so classical dance managed to survive and develop despite the stigma. Before the 1971 civil war, especially during the 1960s, the official ideology of Pakistan was a secular one of economic growth and development. In this atmosphere dance was free to become prominent. Cabaret dancing in restaurants by dancers from all over the world, performances by touring foreign dance companies, especially those from India, and televised and stage performances by Pakistani dancers were common. Dancers were often asked to perform for state guests, and in 1966 the largely government-owned Pakistan International Airlines established an academy for Pakistan's folk and classical performing arts, with a company that traveled worldwide to project Pakistan's culture and publicize the airline.

A noteworthy example of state support for dance during this period was the invitation extended by Prime Minister G. H. Suhrawardy in 1956 to a husband-and-wife team of Indian dancers, the Ghanshyams, to establish an academy of music and dance in Pakistan. Suhrawardy has so far been the most supportive toward dance of all of the country's leaders. The Ghanshyams established their academy in Karachi, teaching *bhārata nāṭyam, kathak,* Oḍissi, and Manipuri dance, in addition to music and other related arts. Their academy operated for twenty-six years and was the only one of its scale in Pakistan. It was also during this time that Rafi Anwar, another *bharata nāṭyam* and *kathak* dancer from India, arrived to establish his career in Pakistan, encouraged by the positive prospects for dance there. [*See the entry on Anwar.*]

A series of events beginning in 1971, however, changed the atmosphere in the country. The 1971 civil war resulted in the break-up of East and West Pakistan into Bangladesh and Pakistan. In an effort to suppress the real reasons for the disintegration of the country, history was revised in a pan-Islamic, fundamentalist light. The new and truncated Pakistan now moved to claim old links with the Middle East and western Asia. The increasing income disparity precipitated by the official commitment to rapid economic growth was another factor that generated support for Islamization. By 1977 Prime Minister Zulfiqar Ali Bhutto had banned cabaret dancing in an effort to appease increasingly strong Islamic fundamentalist groups; soon after, under the military regime of General Muḥammad Zia ul-Haq (1977–1988), public performance of dance was banned—except for folk dancing by men—because it was considered inconsistent with the ideals of the Islamic society he sought to establish.

In the new, hostile atmosphere Islamic radicals threatened the Ghanshyam academy, forcing its staff to close it and flee the country. Nahid Siddiqui, at the time Pakistan's most promising proponent of *kathak,* was also forced to leave the country because of the lack of opportunities; she had to sign an official contract on her way out, promising not to claim to represent Pakistan when dancing abroad. [*See the entry on Siddiqui.*]

The country was drained of talented dancers not only because of the surge in religious sentiment but also because a substantial number of dancers chose to live in Bangladesh after the split. Pakistan's first television program focusing on dance, *Nrittya Tale Tale,* is an example of the quality of dance productions created by East Pakistanis. *Payal,* the only television dance program to be telecast after the 1971 war and the first one from the area that is now Pakistan, was terminated in 1978 by Zia's decree banning dance. The few dancers who remained after the passage of Zia's decree continued their efforts in the face of severe official opposition: their struggle to keep dance alive gained heroic status among the literati and certain segments of the elite, while also spurring boldly creative choreography.

With the return of democracy in 1988, the official ban on dance was lifted. Although the increase in the public performance of dance was considerable, it was still limited by conservative elements in society, many of whom held positions of power in the institutions responsible for supporting the arts. Public performances had tremendous turnouts, with many turned away because of full houses. All the governments since 1988 have shown some degree of support for dance, the most notable being the administration of Benazir Bhutto. The government's most prestigious award for artistic achievement, the Pride of Performance Award, was recently given to two *kathak* dancers, Maharaj Ghulam Husain Kathak and Nahid Siddiqui; never before had any Pakistani dancer received state recognition of this significance. A 1995 tourism conference, for which dancers from all over the country were flown into the capital to perform, is a more typical example of the kind of government patronage seen today. [*See the entry on Husain.*]

Choreographic Content and Style, 1977–1995. Choreography reached new levels of refinement and sophistication during the period of Zia ul Haq: for the first time in Pakistan, dance themes addressed some of the most painful issues facing Pakistani society, such as the lack of freedom of speech and democracy. Classical dance styles were often used to give modern interpretations to the poetry of some of Pakistan's most revolutionary poets, such as Faiz Ahmad Faiz and Fehmida Riaz. This development helped to widen the appeal of dance in Pakistan because poetry is a popular art form, with many indigenous poets being considered regional or national heroes. The setting in which these dances were performed—in the small spaces of private homes or occasionally in a few foreign diplomatic cultural institutes, always surrounded by fear of violent disruption by radical elements—intensified the impact of the choreography.

When the official ban on dance was lifted in 1988, the themes addressed by choreographers refocused. With freedom of speech and the press and the establishment of democracy, some of the earlier themes became irrelevant. One popular new theme focuses on the struggle to gain social acceptance for dance as an art form. Much of the new work of Nahid Siddiqui, who recently returned to Pakistan after a 15-year self-imposed exile, is inspired by the music, dance, and poetry of the Islamic mystical tradition. By linking dance with Islam, Siddiqui hopes to make it more widely accepted in Pakistan. In a recent work, *Dancing in the Mist,* she traced connections between the *faqirs,* or mystics, of the Punjab and the whirling dervishes at the shrine of the renowned Persian poet and Islamic mystic, Mawlana Jalāl al-Dīn Rūmī, in Konya, eastern Turkey. Sheema Kermani, in *The Song of Mohenjodaro,* attempted to show that dance is indigenous to the land that is now Pakistan, arguing that it existed as far back as the Indus Civilization (c.2500 to 1700 BCE). Nighat Chowdhry, one of Pakistan's most prominent *kathak* dancers, interpreted Sarmad Sehbai's poem "Ode to a Dancing Girl of Mohenjodaro" with a similar emphasis.

In a refreshingly different project titled *Kursi,* Nighat Chowdhry explored the politics and power dynamics of a patriarchal society in which the force of law affects private relationships. She alluded to the drastic changes in Pakistani laws that date from the Zia era, such as the Hudood Ordinances which make adultery a capital offense, and fornication a crime punishable by public lashing and imprisonment.

This thematic development has been accompanied by great experimentation with movement and music, to the extent that the post-Zia period might be termed a seminal one in the development of Pakistani modern dance. Nighat Chowdhry's *Kursi* incorporated innovative modern influences; Sheema Kermani, in her recent project with Marcos Matas—a French choreographer famous for his computer-assisted choreography, and the founder of the K Danse group in France—went even further. Her *Indus Europa,* with Indus signifying the East and Europa the West, blends classical Indian and Western modern and contemporary dance styles. The use of state-of-the-art stage and lighting techniques and multi-slide projections, coupled with the blend of diverse dance styles to depict diverse universal themes such as war, the drudgery of modern life, and the search for identity, resulted in a production that was the first of its kind in Pakistan. [*See the entry on Kermani.*]

The growing sophistication of themes addressed by choreographers, and the improvement in the overall quality of productions owing to enhanced technology, skill, and effort employed in stage and lighting techniques, have worked in tandem to elevate the status of all forms of dance in the country. Earlier, *kathak* had received the most recognition and patronage of the classical genres because its major development took place under the Muslim Mogul rulers of India, and *kathak* has been seen as more Pakistani than genres more closely tied to Hinduism. The close association of *kathak* with *mujra,* a lewd form into which *kathak* degenerated under British imperialism and which continues to be performed in some of the red-light districts in Pakistan, has not been as big a drawback for *kathak* as has the association with Hinduism for the other classical styles. The advances and innovations noted above, however, have reduced this strong preference for *kathak.*

Folk and Popular Dance. Despite its increased support and popularity, classical dance has remained an art enjoyed mostly by the elite and the literati. The fact that theater halls are packed for dance performances is more reflective of the size of the halls and the rarity of performances, than of the variety of backgrounds represented in the audience; only four or five choreographer–dancers actively organize shows, and the high price of tickets makes most performances out of reach for the majority of the population. Furthermore, the concentration of performances in the urban centers of Karachi, Lahore, and Rawalpindi-Islamabad excludes the majority of the population, who reside outside these areas. The biggest barrier to popularizing dance is posed by the restrictions preventing dance performances from being televised; despite the more liberal atmosphere, there seems little possibility of televised dance performances in the foreseeable future.

For the majority, exposure to dance has consisted of folk dancing and *"filmi"* dancing, the dancing performed in Pakistani cinema. *Mujra,* the lewd form of dance derived from *kathak,* is another, somewhat less popular form of dance that caters to the male Pakistani public.

PAKISTAN. After the death of Pakistan's military dictator, the Islamic fundamentalist Muḥammad Zia ul-Haq, the progressive, Western-educated Benazir Bhutto came to power. At the first public dance performance in eleven years, *The Palanquin Bearers* was mounted at the Karachi Arts Council Open Air Auditorium on 2 December 1988, with an audience of some two thousand. The dancers are Shayma Saiyid, choreographer Sheema Kermani, and Seema Kamal. (Photograph courtesy of Shayma Saiyid.)

While the trend in the development of classical dancing has been positive, *filmi* and folk dance have gradually deteriorated or been leached of their authenticity.

Folk dance, a diverse and rich tradition, occurs informally in a participatory way and is also performed by small professional folk dance troupes, most of which consist exclusively of men. Some of these professional groups have inherited the profession of folk dancing as part of their family tradition—that is, they are folk dancers by reason of their caste or ethnic group; the Mirasi of the Punjab are an example. Others have chosen folk dancing simply as a means of augmenting their income from other professions.

Originally these professional groups were patronized by the feudal landlords and by the public in general. Now, however, the government has stepped in with institutional sponsorship and, according to some, has been responsible for much loss of authenticity in the dances performed by these groups. In this view, when folk dancers from different regions and traditions are assembled at a few central venues under government auspices, they are trained together in such a way that their divergent regional styles become somewhat blended. This can be evident, for example, in the scant attention paid to the specific costumes and music that traditionally accompanied certain dances. The musical accompaniment to most dances has been reduced to the *tabla* and harmonium, and occasionally the *sitar*. Even *bhangra*, a popular folk dance from the Punjab which is traditionally performed to a *dhol*, a commonly available and easily played drum, is now performed mostly to the *tabla* at government functions.

The authenticity of folk dances has moreover been eroded by the surge of Islamic sentiment, in that many dances that were traditionally performed by men and women together are now performed in a sex-segregated fashion. Additionally, at the informal participatory level, traditional folk dancing has been undermined by the increasing availability of video cassette recorders and American and Indian film and music videos, and now through round-the-clock broadcasts of these via satellite dish antennas.

Dancing in Pakistani films, which in the 1950s and 1960s was tasteful and often artistic, has declined in a similar way to folk dancing. In the 1950s and 1960s *mujra* and folk dancing were commonly featured, and classical dancing was also frequently included. The dancers were usually talented and often accomplished professionals, such as Panna and Amy Minwalla. However, after the 1965 war with India, Indian movies were banned in Pakistan, and the consequent elimination of competition from the only other film industry making movies in Hindi–Urdu led to a general deterioration in the standard of Pakistani movies. Two other factors affected the quality and content of films: first the introduction of the VCR into homes, and second, the sharp increase in terrorist violence that targeted cinema halls during late 1970s and the early 1980s, resulted in upper-middle and middle-class audiences being replaced by poorer, semiliterate or illiterate ones. As a result, films became increasingly vulgar; dancing in today's movies mostly amounts to squirming and writhing, movements that do not require any serious training of the dancers.

BIBLIOGRAPHY

Alavi, Hamza A. "Pakistan." In *Encyclopaedia Britannica*. 15th ed. Chicago, 1980.

Dar, Shiv Nath. *Costumes of India and Pakistan*. Bombay, 1969.

Pasha, Mustapha Kamal. "Islamization, Civil Society, and the Politics of Transition in Pakistan." In *Religion and Political Conflict in South Asia*, edited by Douglas Allen. Delhi, 1993.

INTERVIEWS. Fauzia Saeed, United Nations Development Project and Lok Virsa (Islamabad); Imran Aslam, editor, *The News* (Karachi); Talat Aslam, editor, *The Herald* (Karachi); and Rehana Hakim, deputy editor, *Newsline* (Karachi), all January 1995 by the author.

SHAYMA SAIYID

PALAIS DE CRISTAL, LE. *See* Symphony in C.

PALUCCA, GRET (born 8 January 1902 in Munich, died 24 March 1993 in Dresden), German dancer and teacher. Palucca was one of the most prominent founders of German interpretive dance. As a young girl she studied classical dance with the ballet master Heinrich Kröller in Munich. After seeing one of Mary Wigman's dance evenings in Dresden, however, she decided to devote herself to modern dance. In 1920 she became one of Wigman's first students, and she helped in building up the Wigman school in Dresden. Together with Wigman, Yvonne Georgi, and Berthe Trümpy, Palucca appeared in Wigman's group dances and accompanied Wigman on her solo tours.

In 1922 Palucca danced in Berlin for the first time as a soloist. In 1923 and 1924 she appeared with the Wigman dance group. After this she became an independent dancer, and in 1925 she founded her own school in Dresden. Although influenced by her apprenticeship with Wigman, Palucca's style was quite different from Wigman's. Her dances, often inspired by music, are lighter, more carefree, and happier than Wigman's dramatic choreographies. Characteristic movements include wide-swinging, whirling series of steps and powerful, rhythmic, headlong combinations of leaps, the mastery of which contributed much to Palucca's fame. Improvisation was very important to her in finding a personal expression in dance movement and was the keystone of her pedagogical theory.

PALUCCA. A leading figure of *Ausdruckstanz,* German expressionist dancing, Palucca is caught here, c.1952, in a characteristically lighthearted moment. (Photograph by Höhne-Pohl, Dresden; from the Dance Collection, New York Public Library for the Performing Arts.)

Palucca became one of the most popular dancers of the 1920s and 1930s and gave as many as one hundred performances in a season. The American dance critic John Martin described her style in 1930 as follows:

> Palucca takes the simplest of all possible movements and develops them explosively through several forms: that is her dance. Her technique is tremendous and is never an end in itself. She is never a virtuoso, although she could be. There is charm of behavior, lightness of spirit, a lyric flight which replaces the weight of the Teutonic atmosphere with a leap, and although this is a studied change it is as welcome to the domestic audience as it is to foreigners.

Typical dances included *Walzer, In Weitem Schwung, Treibender Rhythmus, Stilles Lied, Appassionata,* and *Serenata.*

In 1936 Palucca participated in the dance festival at the Olympic Games. In 1939, because of the political situation, she was forbidden to perform in public, and her school was closed. In 1945 she resumed her teaching and her dancing, and in 1949 her school was incorporated into the state system of dance training.

After her last dance evening in 1950, Palucca devoted herself exclusively to teaching. Her school preserved the tradition of German interpretive (or expressionist) dance and attracted many international students to its summer courses. Advancing age eventually forced Palucca to limit her teaching activity, but she gave regular children's classes in her school well into her eighties. She was a founder of the German Academy of the Arts of the German Democratic Republic (East Germany) and in 1960 received the country's National Prize; she also received other awards.

In 1987 Palucca's eighty-fifth birthday was observed with an official celebration at the Semperoper and an exhibition entitled "Künstler um Palucca" (Artists on Palucca) presented by the Dresden Kupferstitch-Kabinett (Museum of Engravings). The exhibit included paintings, sketches and sculptures inspired by Palucca—by such artists as Wassily Kandinsky, Paul Klee, László Moholy-Nagy, and Oskar Schlemmer—juxtaposed with Charlotte Rudolph's photographs of Palucca dancing.

[*For related discussion, see* Germany, *article on* Theatrical Dance, 1600–1945.]

BIBLIOGRAPHY

"Ausdruckstanz and Ballet: Victor Gsovsky, Tatjana Gsovsky, Gret Palucca." *Ballett International* 10 (January 1987): 6–11.

Garske, Rolf. "Das Leben ist ein ewiger Tanz—Drei Kronzeugen geben Auskunft: Martha Graham, Tatjana Gsovsky, Gret Palucca." In *Ballet 1985: Chronik und Bilanz des Balletjahrs,* edited by Horst Koegler. Velber bei Hannover, 1985.

Kant, Marion. "Palucca." *Tanzforschung Jahrbuch* 5 (1994): 39–52.

Krull, Edith, and Werner Gommlich. *Palucca.* Berlin, 1964.

Schumann, Gerhard. *Palucca: Porträt einer Künstlerin.* Berlin, 1972.

HEDWIG MÜLLER
Translated from German

PANAMA. Situated at the Isthmus of Panama, The Republic of Panama is bordered by the Caribbean Sea to the north, the Pacific Ocean to the south, Costa Rica to the east, and Colombia to the west. Panama was discovered by Christopher Columbus on his fourth voyage and settled by the Spanish along the northern coast in the early 1500s. It was from here that Vasco Nuñez de Balboa crossed the isthmus to discover the Pacific Ocean. The short distance of the land mass between the two oceans has dominated Panama's history. During colonial times, this narrow neck of land provided a convenient land route for gold, silver, and Inca treasures taken from Peru and destined for Spain. Early settlers were under constant attack from pirates, such as Sir Francis Drake, seeking wealth, as well as rebellious slaves within the country known as the *cimarrones.* Panama was a part of the viceroyalty of Granada during the colonial period, and following independence in 1821, was a province of

Colombia. In 1903, with backing from the United States, Panama declared independence from Colombia. Early treaties with the United States enabled construction of the Panama Canal, first begun by the French, to continue without interruption. The Panama Canal was completed in 1914. The Carter-Torrijos treaty of 1979 transfers complete control of the Panama Canal to the Panamanians on 31 December 1999. A country of about 30,000 square miles (75,650 square kilometers), Panama has a Roman Catholic, mainly *mestizo* population of approximately three million.

Traditional Dance. Dancing is a national pastime in Panama during festivals and holidays. Traditional and contemporary dances are performed, but there is a special appreciation and cultivation of older dances. As rural areas modernize, traditional dances tend to disappear, but folklore festivals and performing groups help to preserve them. Equally important to this preservation effort are feelings of national pride and an emphasis on dance as a symbol of cultural uniqueness.

There are two broad categories of traditional dances—social dances in which anyone can participate, and dances performed for special celebrations such as the Roman Catholic feast of Corpus Christi to entertain the community. All the social dances are for couples dancing separately; partners usually do not touch, yet the overriding theme of the dances is courtship. These social dances share a common vocabulary of steps; the most common are the *paseo,* a two-step, and the *seguidillas.* Foot patterns are enhanced by improvised steps and individual styling. Men add lunges, skips, turns, and knee flexions, moving their arms freely about the body and frequently bringing them to a position above the waist. The women make sweeping gestures with their skirts, accentuating a smooth, flowing style. Group formations and floor patterns of these dances are more varied. In Panama's national dance, the *tamborito,* partners alternate dancing in a small area encircled by drummers, a female chorus, and spectators; at any time a single dancer or couple may cut into the dance. The *cumbia* is danced in a large double circle by any number of couples. The *mejorana* employs two parallel lines, men on one side and women on the other. The *punto* is a stately dance for one or two couples who dance opposite each other around a small circle.

Many regional variations are found for each social dance, partly because of the multiethnic composition of the population. Although Panama's people are a mix of Spanish, African, and Native American, there are areas where one ethnic group predominates. The rural farmers of largely Spanish descent have dances laden with foot stamps, a characteristic of Spanish dance. In the coastal towns of the Caribbean and Darien, where there is a higher proportion of African descent, dances are more improvisational, hip movements are emphasized, and African-style drums dominate the musical accompaniment.

Social class has also influenced dance. In rural areas where colonial towns were large enough to support an upper class, variations show a refinement undoubtedly fostered by the nineteenth-century ballroom dances it favored. The lower classes, made up primarily of Africans, developed dances of their own, such as the *cumbia* and *tamborito.* Historical sources are insufficient to determine the evolution of the dances; however, it is clear that dances gradually worked their way from the lower class into the sophisticated balls of the upper class.

The *bunde* and the *congos* are social dances for specific festivals [*see* Congo Dances]. The *bunde* is a Christmas celebration in which couples dance before a cradle representing the Nativity. The *congos* is a Carnival celebration in which participants establish their own kingdom, with a king and queen; dancing is the central activity around which the festival revolves. The choreography is similar to the *tamborito;* the dance has strong sexual overtones and continuous improvisation.

Corpus Christi dances developed from Spanish prototypes. Usually eight to twelve male dancers wearing colorful costumes form a dance troupe. Practice sessions are required to learn the more difficult steps and patterns. All groups use a formation of two parallel lines, from which dancers perform cast-offs, circles, crossovers, and weaving figures. "Los Diablos Limpios" (The Clean Devils) is a folk dance drama in which Saint Michael fights with a band of devils over the possession of a sinner. Foot stamps dominate the choreography of "Los Diablos Sucios" (The Dirty Devils); large animal masks make this a favorite dance. "El Torito" is named for the make-believe bull accompanying the dancers. "Las Pajarillas" (these are small birds) uses costumes made from palm leaves. Dancers in "Saracumbe," completely covered with dried banana leaves, represent field workers who complain of their discomforts.

West Indian dances, such as the maypole dance and quadrilles, are performed by small group-descended from West Indians brought as construction workers for the Panama Canal. Efforts are being made to conserve their dances.

Native American dances include those of the three predominant indigenous populations; Cuna, Choco, and Guaymi. These peoples have remained outside Panama's cultural mainstream and have thus continued and preserved many traditional customs. Dancing is part of communal festivals commemorating birth and puberty, curing sickness, and celebrating harvests.

Contemporary Social Dances. The *pindin* is the most popular social dance in Panama's rural towns and suburban areas. Couples dance mostly in a closed position. The basic foot pattern is a two-step, with many individual variations. Musical accompaniment consists of fast-tempo tunes based on Panamanian-style *cumbias*. The *pindin* appears to be a local adaptation of twentieth-century popular dances originating outside Panama. In the hotels and cabarets of Panama City, salsa rhythms are favored, along with rock, disco, Caribbean rhythms, and whatever dance is the latest fad from the United States.

Theatrical Dance. Performances of theatrical dance, except for folk dance programs, are centered in Panama City, the capital. Interest in ballet is of long standing, and the professional standard is high. The government-sponsored National Ballet Company sometimes invites dancers from other countries to work with the company, but there is a cadre of local artists prepared to assume complete responsibility for classes and productions. Approximately four concerts are performed each year, presenting a repertory of classical and modern works.

Modern dance has a lower profile than ballet. The University of Panama sponsors a student group, and private dance studios provide classes in jazz and modern dance. Interest seems to be greatest among university students. Attempts to create an ongoing performing dance troupe have not been successful; however, one group presents concerts and is working to create greater audience interest.

Professional folk dance performances are popular with Panamanians. Public and private programs are provided by well-trained dance troupes sponsored by a school or government agency. Their repertories favor the couple dances. Although theatrical license alters floor patterns and dance sequences, the troupes' dances conform to traditional step patterns and styles.

[*For related discussion, see* Caribbean Region.]

BIBLIOGRAPHY

Arosemena Moreno, Julio. *Danzas folklóricas de la villa de Los Santos*. Panama, 1994.

Cheville, Lila, and Richard A. Cheville. *Festivals and Dances of Panama*. Panama, 1977.

Garay, Narciso. *Tradiciones y cantares de Panamá* (1930). 2d ed. Panama, 1982.

Schara, Julio César. *Arte y sociedad: Un estudio sobre el pindín*. Panama, 1985.

Smith, Ronald R. "The Society of Los Congos of Panama: An Ethnomusicological Study of the Music and Dance-Theater of an Afro-Panamanian Group." Ph.D. diss., Indiana University, 1976.

Torres de Araúz, Reina. *Estudio etnológico e histórico la cultura Chocó*. Panama, 1966.

Zárate, Manuel F., and Dora P. de Zárate. *Tambor y socavón*. Panama, 1962.

LILA CHEVILLE

PANIGRAHI, SANJUKTA (born c.1932 in Orissa, India, died 24 June 1997 in Bhubaneswar), Indian dancer and choreographer. The daughter of an orthodox brahman family of Orissa, Sanjukta was trained in Oḍissi dance from the age of five under Guru Kelucharan Mahapatra. At that time dance was considered an unacceptable profession for a brahman woman in Orissa, but perceiving her natural talent, her parents encouraged her. They later sent her to Kalakshetra in Madras to study *bharata nāṭyam* under Rukmini Devi. She achieved proficiency in this classical genre and took part in dance dramas there.

Returning to Orissa, however, Sanjukta decided to concentrate on Oḍissi and contributed greatly to its revival. She married the vocalist Raghunath Panigrahi and choreographed dances to the lyrics of Suradas, Tulasidas, Rabindranath Tagore, and Vidyapati, as well as to Oriya songs. She and her husband, whose melodious voice added an extra dimension to Oḍissi performances, appeared throughout India and abroad. Their concerts popularized Oḍissi all over India, especially in their home state of Orissa. More young dancers took up the genre, inspired by Sanjukta as a role model. Her collaboration with Guru Kelucharan Mahapatra resulted in several new compositions; she herself choreographed such innovative works as *Yugmadwandwa* and *Sītā Harāṇa*, about the abduction of Sītā by the demon king Rāvaṇa, based upon the *Rāmcaritmānas* (Holy Lake of the Deeds of Rāma; c.1574) by the poet Tulsīdās.

Working abroad, Sanjukta collaborated with the theater director Eugenio Barba at his International School of Theater Anthropology in Denmark. She participated in major national and international dance festivals. She also performed in dance dramas choreographed by Mahapatra for the Odissi Research Centre in Bhubaneswar.

Sanjukta was an outstanding performer, with excep-

PANIGRAHI. Kneeling before an idol of Jaganath, Sanjukta is seen here in an innovative, nonclassical preperformance ritual. (Photograph by Gay Bodick; used by permission of The Asia Society, New York.)

tional gifts, whose name became synonymous with Oḍissi. In both *nṛtta* (pure dance) and *nṛtya* (expressive dance) she performed with equal felicity. She was honored by the government of India with the Padamshri award; the Central Sangeet Natak Akademi gave her and her husband Raghunath a joint award for their combined work. They had two sons, one of whom is a singer. A documentary film of Sanjukta's dances was produced by the Government of India's Films Division.

BIBLIOGRAPHY

Kothari, Sunil, ed. *Bharata Natyam: Indian Classical Dance Art.* Bombay, 1979.

Kothari, Sunil, and Avinash Pasricha. *Odissi: Indian Classical Dance Art.* Bombay, 1990.

Martin, Carol J. "Feminist Analysis Across Cultures." *Women and Performance* 3.2 (1987–1988): 32–40.

Meisner, Nadine. "Festival of India." *Dance and Dancers* (June 1982): 31–32.

Misra, Susheela. *Some Dancers of India.* New Delhi, 1992.

Pavis, Patrice. "Dancing with Faust." *Drama Review* 33 (Fall 1989): 37–57.

Schechner, Richard. "Collaborating on Odissi." *Drama Review* 32 (Spring 1988): 128–138.

SUNIL KOTHARI

PANTOMIME. [*This entry is limited to discussion of English pantomime. For related discussion, see* Commedia dell'Arte; Mime; *and* Pantomimus.]

From its inception, the entertainment known in England as pantomime was inextricably connected with dance. Indeed, the very use of the term to describe a sort of prose ballet preceded by a few years its meaning as a mixture of allegorical dance and grotesque comedy. Theater scholar Virginia Scott has suggested that the origin of English pantomime is connected to French *forains,* specifically their night scenes, comic episodes whose abundance of mime was due to legal restrictions on dialogue. A night scene shown in London around 1702 contained farcical business with a guitar and a bladder, leaps over tables and stools, ridiculous postures and grimaces, and a comedian in drag giving birth to Harlequin and Scaramouche.

John Weaver, a Shrewsbury dancing master, claimed to have produced "an Entertainment of Dancing, Action and Motion only" called *The Tavern Bilkers* in 1702, but no independent evidence of it has been found. However, in 1717, by which time French mimic scenes were well known, Weaver did produce a "New Dramatick Entertainment of Dancing, after the manner of the Ancient Pantomime, called *The Loves of Mars and Venus.*" This, the earliest entertainment to be termed a pantomime, was intended as competition for the Italian opera by linking the dances of ballet by a story line, in Colley Cibber's words, "to give even dancing . . . some improvement, and to make it something more than motion without meaning."

PANTOMIME. An 1812 etching by William Heath of a comic dance from the popular pantomime *The White Cat,* performed by Messieurs Kirby and Chatterly to the tune of "The Bold Dragoon." (Courtesy of Madison U. Sowell and Debra H. Sowell, Brigham Young University, Provo, Utah.)

In *Mars and Venus,* according to Cibber, "the passions were so happily expressed, and the whole story so intelligibly told, by a mute narration of gesture only, that even thinking spectators allow it both a pleasing and a rational amusement." There were no *commedia dell'arte* figures in this ballet-mime, but later that season, in Weaver's "New Dramatick Entertainment of Dancing in Grotesque Characters," called *The Shipwreck; or, Perseus and Andromeda,* the mythological protagonists were portrayed by *commedia* masks, which lent a tone of parody and overwhelmed the entertainment's serious component. [*See the entry on Weaver.*]

This emphasis was abetted by John Rich, the manager of Lincoln's Inn Fields, who parodied *Mars and Venus* in *The Mousetrap,* with Harlequin as Vulcan, Weaver's role; and in his *Harlequin Executed,* "a new Italian Mimick Scene" featuring "a Scaramouch, a Harlequin, a Country Farmer, his Wife and others" (both in 1717). Under the name Lun, Rich, a performer better suited to gesture than to words, raised the role of Harlequin to star status and instigated what was to become the pattern for pantomime:

> two parts, one serious, the other comic; by the help of gay scenes, fine habits, grand dances, appropriate music and other decorations, he exhibited a story from Ovid's *Metamorphoses* or some other fabulous history. Between the pauses of the acts, he interwove a comic fable, consisting chiefly of the courtship of Harlequin and Columbine, with a variety of surprising adventures and tricks, which were produced by the magic wand of Harlequin; such as the sudden transformation of palaces and temples to huts and cottages; of men and women into wheelbarrows and joint stools, of trees turned to houses; colonades to beds of tulips, and mechanics' shops into serpents and ostriches. (Thomas Davies, *Life of Garrick,* 1784)

According to English novelist and playwright Henry Fielding, the dullness of the mythological part set off Harlequin's tricks to greater advantage.

Disdainful of literature, Rich emphasized spectacular effects and machinery. In *Jupiter and Europa, or The Intrigues of Harlequin* (1723), a Greek god was shot onto the stage from sixty-five feet (twenty-one meters) above it and flown back the same way. In 1739, at his new Covent Garden Theatre, Rich produced the opera *Orpheus and Eurydice* with Harlequin interludes and a mechanical serpent that thrashed its tail, opened and closed its jaws, and flashed sulphurous flames from its eyes. In contrast to the new genres of insipid sentimental comedy and sententious bourgeois tragedy, this was "total" theater; widely popular, it made Rich a comfortable fortune and compelled other theaters to follow suit. The appeal was to all levels of society: the mime was readily accessible to even the illiterate, and as David Garrick, another successful Harlequin, quipped, "when a dance is on my bill / Nobility my boxes fill."

Rich's Harlequin had been acrobatic, famed for his eloquent mime. His successors favored dance; among them were his heir apparent, Henry Woodward, occasionally known as Lun, Jr., who is said to have hired Georgius Lupino as his ballet master. John Hippisley, Francis Nivelon, John Laguerre, John Arthur, and Charles Lalauze are all believed to have benefited from Rich's example. [*See the entry on Rich*] In the late eighteenth century the leading Harlequin was James Byrn, a dancer and choreographer whose first extensive composition was a ballet-pantomime called *The Provocation* (Covent Garden, 1790). Byrn, styled a "vamper-up of the dance" by the *Dramatic Censor,* is credited with inventing the tightly fitting spangled costume that set the panto Harlequin apart from Arlecchino and Arlequin; he danced burlesques such as the *pas de Russe* in *Harlequin's Museum* in 1792 and transferred these specialties to the Royal Circus (1800–1803). Marian Hannah Winter has pointed out that the dance in this kind of pantomime "often resembled the acrobatic *ballet de cour entrées* recorded by [Henry] Gissey and his followers," and even so notable a dancing master as Nicolini (John Baptiste ["Iron Legs"] Grimaldi) lent a hand to supplying pantomime with satyrs and witches "who might have stepped out of [Gregorio] Lambranzi's pages" (*The Pre-Romantic Ballet,* 1974, p. 40).

By the Regency period, the pantomime had assumed its characteristic format: first an opening story, often told in rhyme and often based on some familiar nursery tale, in which the forces of evil oppress or persecute the good characters; then, at a critical moment, the appearance of a good genius who transforms the characters into the personnel of the revised *commedia:* Harlequin, Columbine, Pantaloon, and Clown; and finally, the harlequinade, a loosely knit sequence of dance, slapstick, and comicalities. Clown became the paramount figure, owing to the brilliance of Joseph Grimaldi; grandson of the Italian acrobatic dancer Nicolini and son of ballet master Giuseppi Grimaldi, "Joey" Grimaldi was said to "tread the air" in his performances. As he gained in prominence, the role of Harlequin was reduced to that of a dancing romantic interest.

Although the harlequinade can be viewed as a crude *ballet d'action,* the dance elements relegated to Harlequin and Columbine were relatively insignificant during the reign of Grimaldi. Columbine never spoke, rarely sang, and performed no acrobatics; her primary function was to perform "trips," the technical term for the pas de deux with Harlequin. He was always a skilled acrobat, expert at "cascades and valleys," technical terms for gymnastic exploits; he might accompany the pas de deux on a flageolet, the moment, in the words of David Mayer, having "the benefit of briefly recalling the sentimental tone of the opening." If Clown danced, it was simply as parody. The most famous example occurred in *Harlequin and Mother Goose, or The Golden Egg* (Covent Garden, 1806), when Joseph Grimaldi as Clown and Joe Bologna, Jr., as Harlequin in drag satirized André Deshayes and James Harvey D'Egville's pas de deux from *Achille et Déidamie* (1804–1805). In the parody, Ulysses's hamper became a market girl's basket.

The Times (London) commented in 1840 that the trips of Harlequin and Columbine were "merely to fill up the time while the carpenter is preparing some elaborate piece of mechanism." The interaction between Harlequin and Columbine assumed greater emphasis after James Robinson Planché extended the fairy opening and the transformation scene, thus calling for balletic choruses of fairies to provide spectacle. His reform coincided with the rise of the Romantic ballerina, personified by Marie Taglioni and Fanny Elssler. Columbine, whose role was now meted out to star dancers such as Madame Vestris (Lucia Elizabeth Bartolozzi), adopted the *coryphée*'s short skirts; all of the younger members of the panto clans, the Lupinos, Lauris, Majiltons, and Conquests, were trained as dancers, and they increased the importance of the trips of Harlequin and Columbine. Even Clown was taken over by dancers and posturers; in 1859 *The Era* cited dancing ability as the first requirement for a pantomime clown. Most remarkable of this new breed of clowns were George Wieland, who executed a "flight" (or parody) of Taglioni, and Richard Flexmore, who won popularity at Princess's Theatre for his imitation of opera dancers. Flexmore married the daughter of the French acrobatic clown Auriol, from whom he learned more skills, and he refashioned Joseph Grimaldi's traditional dress so that the tights and the short, frilled trunks showed off his legs during his feats. That a variety of dance had by this time entered pantomime is evident in the program of a Manchester performance given in 1852, in which George Lupino and

Mademoiselle Rosina danced a *pas écossais,* a waltz, a *polka gymnastique,* a sailor's hornpipe, a *manola,* and a pas de deux. Lupino, who excelled at pirouettes, received a gold medal in 1868 for turning 207 single and double pirouettes on a pocket handkerchief.

The importance of ballet increased in 1857, when Mark Lemon styled his *Harlequin à la Watteau,* starring Madame Celeste, on the French *féerie.* Thirty to sixty dancers became standard for pantomime, by this time performed exclusively during the Christmas holidays. The performers were specialists who, in the off-season, worked in penny gaffs, concert rooms, pleasure gardens, and *poses plastiques* and made, in good times, a pound to thirty-five shillings a week. In 1878 George Conquest pioneered flying ballets in pantomime at the Grecian Theatre for the debut of Mademoiselle Enea. These performances, in which dancers were suspended above the stage on wires, became annual presentations, with Madame Grigolati and her troupe appearing at Drury Lane and Kirby's Flying Ballet featured at the Coliseum. Each wire, run along a traveler, was controlled by a single stagehand in the wings; the chorines were often in agonies, imprisoned in iron trusses that dangled near the hot gaslights planted near the border pieces.

From 1863 to 1880 the pantomimes of E. L. Blanchard at Drury Lane were dominated by the dancing, acrobatic Vokes family, in particular by Fred Vokes, a rubber-legged trick dancer whose movements were characterized by exceptional elasticity. In *Tom Thumb* (1871), he performed a

PANTOMIME. Fables and fairy tales were often used as pantomime plots. Here, the actors are shown as characters in the play *Jack the Giant Killer* and in their subsequent roles as *commedia dell' arte* characters. This lithograph was published c.1880 in Great Britain by Benjamin Pollock. (Metropolitan Museum of Art, New York; Elisha Whittelsey Fund, 1952 [no. 52.541.1]; photograph used by permission.)

step dance, Lancashire clog dances, Cornish reels, transatlantic walkrounds, cellar flaps and breakdowns, college hornpipes, and Irish jigs. However, by the end of the Vokes dynasty, critics were complaining that their tumbling and acrobatics distracted from the skill and grace of the ballets and from the more dramatic aspects of the dance set pieces. Such criticism was symptomatic of the larger shift in interest from individual dancers to the opulent attractions of mass movement.

By the 1870s pantomimes, which originally had been part of a longer bill, filled an entire evening, padded out with specialty acts. Augustus Harris, the manager of Drury Lane, swelled the number of *figurantes* and supernumeraries: his ballets, directed by the *danseuse* Katti Lanner, featured 150 dancers who often took more than half an hour to carry out the spectacular stairway descents and the elaborate processions that embellished the performances. Harris also recruited music-hall stars who, the reviewers lamented, introduced "dances which are usually vulgar, when they are not inane" (*The Theatre,* 1881). As a result, the opening was lengthened and the harlequinade reduced to a mere vestigial tail. Lottie Collins performed "Ta-ra-ra-boom-de-ay" with its manic can-can in *Dick Whittington* at the Grand, Islington, in 1891 and later transferred it to Drury Lane, where Dan Leno danced the breakdowns and clog steps for which he was renowned.

A reaction to the lavishness of Harris and his successor, Arthur Collins, who relied on the ballet arrangements of Carlo Coppi and John D'Auban, came in the twentieth century with a reversion to simplicity. Pantomimes continued to feature dance acts from variety as well as ballets and processions, but these aspects were downplayed in favor of the comedy and the story line. Richard Rodgers and Oscar Hammerstein's *Cinderella* (Coliseum, 1958) represented a major innovation by presenting a traditional pantomime subject in the format of the musical comedy. Since then the tendency has been to create "integrated" pantomimes in which dance is merely one (and often the least important) element in the synthesis. The harlequinade has become extinct, and the sumptuous marshaling of massed dancers is to be found only in the ice show pantos that have been staged at Wembley since 1950.

BIBLIOGRAPHY

Avery, Emmett L. "Dancing and Pantomime on the English Stage, 1700–1737." *Studies in Philology* 31.3 (1934): 417–452.

Cibber, Colley. *An Apology for the Life of Colley Cibber.* Edited by B. R. S. Fone. Ann Arbor, Mich., 1968.

Fletcher, Ifan Kyrle, et al. *Famed for Dance: Essays on the Theory and Practice of Theatrical Dancing in England.* New York, 1960.

Johns, Eric. "Dancers in Pantomime." *Ballet Annual* 15 (1961): 67–70.

Mayer, David. *Annotated Bibliography of Pantomime and Guide to Study Sources.* London, 1975.

Papetti, Viola. *Arlecchino a Londra: La pantomima inglese, 1700–1728.* Naples, 1977.

Scott, Virginia P. "The Infancy of English Pantomime: 1716–1723." *Educational Theatre Journal* (May 1972).

Wilson, Albert E. *King Panto: The Story of Pantomime.* New York, 1935.

LAURENCE SENELICK

PANTOMIMUS. Pantomimus, or pantomime, comes from the Greek *pantos,* "all or every" and *mimos,* "imitator or actor." Pantomime, however, can refer both to the performer and the performance. Although some form of interpretive dance had long existed in ancient Rome, it was only in 23 BCE, perhaps at the games of Marcellus, or in 22 BCE according to Jerome, during the Principate of Augustus Caesar, that Pylades of Cilicia and Bathyllus of Alexandria came to the city and established schools of dance that presented pantomime as a highly developed and organized performance. Pylades focused on tragic pantomime presented with complex staging, while Bathyllus specialized in simpler performance on comic themes. Pylades's style outlasted that of Bathyllus, and pantomime soon replaced tragedy in the Roman theater. Lucian (115–200 CE), in his comprehensive essay on pantomime, discussed only the tragic variety.

Aspects of Performance. Pantomime was a highly stylized form of interpretive dance that featured a mute dancer who wore a closed-mouth mask and acted out stories by means of expressive, rhythmic body movements and gestures. Pylades was the first to use a full orchestra and chorus in place of the lone flute player and vocalist. The orchestra consisted of lyres and double flutes, cymbals, hand drums, castanets, *citharae, sistra* (rattles), and *scabelli* (percussion instruments consisting of a shoe with a thick, wooden sole in which there was a horizontal gap in the front half with two metal plates that struck each other when the ball of the foot was pressed down). The chorus, accompanied by this orchestra, sang or chanted the words of the story while the pantomimist performed. A single dancer—pantomimists were often referred to as *saltatores* (dancers)—usually played all the roles in the story, changing masks and costumes to represent the different characters. The masks had closed mouths and realistic features. The costumes appear to have been flowing robes that could easily be shifted and redraped to portray a variety of characters.

Pantomime was especially welcomed in Rome because the audience of immigrants and foreign visitors could easily understand the gestures and, therefore, appreciate the performance. In addition, the performer's gift for mimicry and gesticulation and the pantomimic play of actors in Roman dramas made for public acceptance of the new form. The pantomimist strove, through various rhythmic motions of his body, to reproduce every conceivable emotion. Lucian felt that it was the job of the pantomimist to identify himself so closely with the story and the characters he danced that they became a part of him, yet within the same performance a single dancer also had to change characters completely and convincingly. In the story of Bacchus's return to Thebes, the same person had to portray Bacchus, then Cadmus, then Pentheus, then Agave. These fast changes of costume and character meant that the pantomime had to be quick-witted, as well as skillful. Lucian observes that "[o]ther arts call out only one half of a man's powers—the bodily or mental: the pantomime combines the two. His performance is as much an intellectual as a physical exercise: there is meaning in his movements; every gesture has its significance; and therein lies his chief excellence." The pantomimist's movements were guided by the music, which tended to be noisy and unrestrained, judging by the instruments used. Dance, however, was the important part of the performance.

When pantomimes performed in a theater, an announcer appeared and gave a brief synopsis of the story. The chorus then sang the first part of the libretto. The pantomime entered in a costume designed especially for his opening role. On his head he wore a large closed-mouth mask, which he changed offstage whenever he changed roles. An offstage chorus sang a portion of the libretto before each scene, both to smooth the transition and to fill the interlude needed for costume and mask changes. Not all pantomimes included costume changes:

> Sometimes . . . the dancer performed an even more difficult feat: he wore a swirling cloak, and by a slight rearrangement or handling of it managed to portray vividly all the characters of the story. With a twist of the cloak, say our ancient sources, he could portray a swan's tail, the tresses of Venus, or a Fury's scourge. As a sort of encore after the dance proper, the pantomime frequently gave a dazzling display of technical skill; he leaped violently, crouched, twisted and turned, performed breath-taking feats of balance, halted in poses of statuesque beauty." (Lillian B. Lawler, 1964)

The pantomimes draw their stories both from mythology and from Greek tragedy. Lucian, expanding on what a dancer must know, begins with Greek creation myths and goes on to include Athenian, Corinthian, Mycenean, Spartan, Scythian, Elian, Cretan, Thracian, Egyptian, Italian, Phoenician, and Asian myth and history. As a specific example both of what a pantomime might perform and the skill that he might display, Lucian recounts the story that, during the region of Nero when Demetrius the Cynic made some disparaging comments about dance, a pantomime (most likely Paris) performed the sexual encounter between Aphrodite and Ares, Helios's telling Hephaestus about it, Hephaestus's setting his trap, all the gods seeing the captured lovers, and the reactions of Ares and Aphrodite. Demetrius was so impressed that he shouted "I hear the story that you are acting, man, I do not just see it; you seem to me to be talking with your very hands!"

During the Empire, pantomime became so popular that it overshadowed all other forms of dance and drama in the theaters of Rome, with senators, knights, emperors, and empresses among its avid supporters. The fever spread through the higher ranks of society, especially among women. Seneca the Elder (c.55 BCE–37 CE) admits his addiction to pantomime in his *Controversiae*. Pliny the Younger mentions a woman, Ummidia Quadratilla (c.27–107 CE), who owned a troupe of pantomimes who performed both on a stage in her home and in public. Pliny praises Ummidia because, even though her grandson lived with her, she never allowed him to watch the performances. Many other Romans, including the imperial families, counted pantomimes among their freedmen and slaves.

Performers. Pylades and Bathyllus are the names most closely associated with pantomime. The evidence gathered by Marius Bonaria, in fact, shows that later performers who took up pantomime often changed their names to Pylades or Bathyllus. Of these dancers, two Bathylluses and five Pylades are known. Of the latter, one Pylades performed during the reign of Trajan (98–117); one lived during the rule of Lucius Verus (161–169); and another danced for the emperor Commodus (180–192), who sometimes danced as well. Hylas (Pylades's student and rival) and Nomius the Syrian (a rival of both Bathyllus and Pylades) inspired no such tradition. Paris, however, did become a popular name for pantomimes: Lucius Domitius Paris danced for and was executed by Nero; a Paris who danced during the rule of Domitian (81–96) lost his life for sleeping with the emperor's sister; a Maximinius took the name stage name "Paris" under the reign of Lucius Verus (161–169). Memphis Apolaustus, one of six dancers who took the name Apolaustus, was Lucius Verus's favorite. One other pantomime, Mnester, was the lover of Caligula, an emperor who himself danced. Suetonius reports that Caligula "even used to kiss the pantomime Mnester during public celebrations, and if anyone made a noise, even quietly, while he was dancing, Caligula ordered the man to be dragged from his seat and beat him with his own hand."

In addition to these performers noted at Rome, James L. Franklin, Jr. has identified members of a pantomime troupe that seems to have been based in Pompeii. Graffiti saluting Actius Anicetus and his fellow performers suggest that Castrensis, Mysticus, Echio, Iuvenis, Horus, Crestus/Chrastus, Actica, and Chloe were popular figures in Pompeian entertainment. The evidence presented by Bonaria and Franklin also highlights the fact that pantomimes traveled Italy to give performances. At Pompeii, Aulus Clodius Flaccus, according to his epitaph, brought Pylades and other pantomimes to the city as part of the games for Apollo. Paris (Neronian) performed at Pompeii, as well. Two others—Marcus Pileius Pierus and Marcus Amplius Hyla—may also have danced in both Pompeii and Rome.

Pantomimes generally belonged to the lower classes; some were freedmen, others slaves. Their status, however, did not stop them from gaining fame and wealth. They were extremely well paid; many observers contended that they were overpaid, much like modern athletes and actors. Pylades accumulated so much wealth that in his old age he was able to finance spectacles for the Roman public.

Training. Pylades and Bathyllus each established schools to teach their respective forms of pantomime. Pylades, as well, wrote a book on pantomime, but it has not survived. Lucian, therefore, is our source for the training of these dancers. He laid out a demanding set of qualifications for the pantomime, who had to have a wide knowledge of history from Chaos to the reign of Cleopatra, including a detailed knowledge of Greek mythology and tragedy, Homer, and Hesiod. A pantomime also needed a good memory, an ability to form rapid conceptions, and the judgment to distinguish good poetry and song from bad. Physically, a pantomime had to be perfectly proportioned, supple, firm, and agile. He had to keep his body flexible and strong to be able to make the graceful and delicate movements necessary to play a variety of roles. The pantomime needed to be physically suited to his roles. Lucian states that the audience at Antioch was particularly harsh to pantomimes whose physical build made their performances ludicrous: a short dancer who began to play Hector was chided as being more like Astyanax, Hector's son; a very tall man pretending to use a ladder to climb a wall was told to step over it; a heavy dancer who was performing some leaps was asked to spare the stage; and a very thin man was wished good health, as if he were ill.

Popularity and Repercussions. Pantomime was popular with all levels of society. One of the many problems that plagued all forms of theater in Rome was a noisy, restless, rude, boisterous, and volatile audience that was admitted free to all performances during long holiday celebrations. Audiences usually included men, women, children, and slaves. As actors became more important than playwrights during the period from 150 to 50 BCE, actor-managers introduced hired claques, which enabled them to demand higher fees for their work. Later the claques devoted to actors, pantomimes, and mimes became a nuisance; in the case of the pantomimes, claques evolved into factions whose support of their favorites often led to riots in the theaters and bloodshed.

With the advent of permanent theaters in which the best seats were reserved for senators and knights, performances became events in which the divisions in Roman society were also very visible. William J. Slater has suggested that the riots caused by supporters of pantomimes were especially troublesome because the performers were closely associated with the upper levels of Roman society. Augustus had sponsored and supported their performances; Tiberius, however, had no love for the theater. Slater has pointed out that the riots of 14 CE occurred at the games in honor of Augustus, shortly after the emperor's death. Pantomimes, apparently already used to high pay, rioted because Tiberius had restricted the funds for the games. The riots of 15 CE were also directly related to the low pay provided for the dancers and perhaps to Tiberius's seeming rejection of the theater. Tiberius's son Drusus, however, appears to have favored pantomimes, despite his father's disapproval.

Nevertheless, in 15 CE the senate passed measures to restrict the interaction of senators and knights with the pantomimes. In the *Annals*, Tacitus (55 CE–after 115) noted "that no Senator should enter the house of a pantomime player, that Roman knights should not crowd round them in the public streets, that they should exhibit themselves only in the theater, and that the praetors should be empowered to punish with banishment any riotous conduct in the spectators." After more trouble from the pantomimes and their supporters, and after the death of Drusus, Tiberius banished pantomimes from Italy, but they quickly returned to Rome after his death. Later threats of banishment did not stop occasional uproars in the theaters, but after the second century CE, banishment was no longer enforced.

Church Opposition and Decline. Around 200 CE and thereafter, the pantomimes began to reflect the decadence associated with the decay of Roman society in general. Pantomimes began to make their performances more sensational, grossly erotic, and sometimes horrifying and gruesome. Little was left to the spectators' imagination. Condemned prisoners were even pressed into giving performances in which, in the process of the dance, they were consumed in flames as part of the story of Medea. The emperor Elagabalus (218–222), noted for his very degenerate lifestyle, gave performances at his court where he appeared in a pantomime as Venus and indulged in all kinds of sexual acts.

There were increasing attacks from Christian and pagan moralists that eventually, along with the barbarian invasions, chased the pantomimes out of the Western Roman Empire in the late fourth and the fifth century. Many fled to the Eastern Roman Empire, where pantomime continued to be performed until some time in the seventh century.

[*See also* Music for Dance, *article on* Western Music before 1520; Mimus; *and* Roman Empire.]

BIBLIOGRAPHY

Arnott, Peter D. *The Ancient Greek and Roman Theatre.* New York, 1971.

Beacham, R. *Roman Theatre and Its Audience.* London, 1991.

Bellemore, Jane. "Gaius the Pantomime." *Antichthon* 28 (1994): 65–79.

Bieber, Margarete. *The History of the Greek and Roman Theatre.* 2d ed., rev. and enl. Princeton, 1961.

Bonaria, Marius, ed. *Romani mimi.* Poetarum Latinarum Reliquiae, 6.2. Rome, 1965.

Butler, James H. *The Theatre and Drama of Greece and Rome.* New York, 1972.

Csapo, Eric, and W. J. Slater, eds. *The Context of Ancient Drama.* Ann Arbor, Mich., 1995.

Franklin, James L., Jr. "Pantomimists at Pompeii: Actius Anicetus and His Troupe." *American Journal of Philology* 108 (1987): 95–107.

Friedländer, Ludwig. *Roman Life and Manners under the Early Empire.* Vol. 2. Translated by Leonard A. Magnus. 7th ed., rev. and enl. New York, 1965.

Jory, E. J. "The Drama of the Dance. Prolegomena to an Iconography of Imperial Pantomime." In *Roman Theatre and Society;* edited by W. J. Slater. Ann Arbor, Mich., 1996.

Jory, E. J. "The Literary Evidence for the Beginnings of Imperial Pantomime." *Bulletin of the Institute of Classical Studies, University of London* 28 (1981): 147–161.

Kirstein, Lincoln. *Dance: A Short History of Classic Theatrical Dancing.* New York, 1935.

Kokolakis, M. *Pantomimus and the Treatise Peri Orcheseos.* Athens, 1959.

Lawler, Lillian B. *The Dance in Ancient Greece.* Middletown, Conn., 1964.

Lucian. *The Dance.* In *Lucian.* Vol. 5. Translated by A. M. Harmon. Loeb Classical Library. Cambridge, Mass., 1936.

Radice, Betty, trans. *The Letters of Pliny the Younger.* New York, 1963.

Seneca the Elder. *Controversiae.* Vol. 1. Translated by Michael Winterbottom. Loeb Classical Library. Cambridge, Mass., 1974.

Slater, William J. "Three Problems in the History of Drama." *Phoenix* 47.3 (1993): 189–212.

Slater, William J. "Pantomime Riots." *Classical Antiquity* 13.1 (1994): 120–144.

Slater, William, J. "The Pantomime Tiberius Julius Apolaustus." *Greek, Roman and Byzantine Studies* 36.3 (1995): 263–292.

Smith, William. *A Dictionary of Greek and Roman Antiquities,* vol. 2. 3d ed., rev. and enl. London, 1890.

Suetonius. *The Twelve Caesars.* Translated by Robert Graves. New York, 1957.

Tacitus. *Annals.* In *The Complete Works of Tacitus.* Translated by Moses Hadas. New York, 1942.

T. DAVINA MCCLAIN

PAPLIŃSKI, EUGENIEUSZ (born 18 September 1908 in Warsaw, died 31 May 1978 in Warsaw), Polish dancer, choreographer, ballet director, and teacher. Papliński studied at the Warsaw Ballet School with Bonifacy Śliwiński, Aleksander Gillert, and Piotr Zajlich. Upon his graduation in 1926, he joined the Wielki Theater Ballet, where he became a soloist the following year. He remained with this company, also known as the Warsaw Ballet, until 1935, when he moved on to join Feliks Parnell's newly founded Polish Ballet. Later, Papliński and his wife, Miła Kołpikówna, danced as partners in his own concert dance miniatures in theaters and reviews in Warsaw, Lwów (1935–1939), and Kraków (1945–1949). From 1949 to 1950, he danced as a soloist in the Poznań Opera Ballet.

During his years with the Wielki Theater Ballet in Warsaw, Papliński became known as a talented character dancer, performing with notable success in a number of ballets by Piotr Zajlich, among them *Petrouchka* (1926), *Pulcinella* (1928), *Schéhérazade* (1929), and *Pan Twardowski* (1933). Later in his career, he was ballet director and choreographer for the Poznań Opera (1949–1950), the Mazowsze Song and Dance Ensemble (1950–1954), the Polish Dance Company (1954–1961), the Warsaw Opera (1962), and several other companies. As a choreographer, he preferred simple forms inspired by Polish folk festivals and dances. He was a lover of Polish folklore and an expert in folk dances, particularly those of the Kraków and highland regions. He staged *Harnasie* (The Highlanders), a ballet based on dances of the peoples of the Tatra Mountains in southern Poland, five times: in Berlin (1957), Kraków (1964), Warsaw (1966), Wrocław (1969), and Poznań (also 1969).

Papliński's other works included three productions of *Cracow Wedding* (1947, 1956, and 1969), two versions of *A Peacock and a Girl* (1950 and 1961), *The Warsaw Rhapsody* (1955), *Podhale* (1955), *Polish Devils* (1958), *The Nymph of Świteź Lake* (1960), *Cagliostro in Warsaw* and *Balladyna* (both 1961), and *Peaks* and *The Mermaid* (both 1962). He also produced his own version of *La Fille Mal Gardée* in 1973. As an expert in Polish traditional dances, he choreographed dances for many productions of the national opera, *Halka,* by Stanisław Moniuszko: in Poznań, Prague, Budapest, Helsinki, Berlin, Warsaw, Dresden, Vienna, Kraków, Havana, and Tokyo. From 1968 to 1972 he taught Slavic folk and national dances in the Legat School in England.

BIBLIOGRAPHY

Chynowski, Paweł, and Janina Pudełek. *Almanach baletu warszawskiego, 1785–1985 / Le ballet de Varsovie, 1785–1985.* Warsaw, 1987.

Mamontowicz-Łojek, Bożena. *Terpsychora i lekkie muzy.* Kraków, 1972.

Neuer, Adam, ed. *Polish Opera and Ballet of the Twentieth Century: Operas, Ballets, Pantomimes, Miscellaneous Works.* Translated by Jerzy Zawadzki. Kraków, 1986.

Pudełek, Janina. *Two Hundred Years of Polish Ballet, 1785–1985.* Warsaw, 1985.

Śmielowski, Teodor. "Eugeniusz Papliński." *Taniec* (1978).

Turska, Irena. *Almanach baletu polskiego, 1945–1974.* Kraków, 1983.

Wysocka, Tacjanna. *Dzieje baletu.* Warsaw, 1970.

ARCHIVE. Wielki Theater Museum, Warsaw.

PAWEŁ CHYNOWSKI

PAPUA NEW GUINEA. [*To survey the dance traditions of Papua New Guinea, this entry comprises six articles:*

An Overview
Binandere Dance
Gizra Dance
Kaluli Dance
Maring Dance
Melpa Dance

The first article explores occasions for dance, costumes, and music; the companion articles focus on practices among various peoples. For further general discussion in a broader context, see Oceanic Dance Traditions.]

An Overview

The southwestern Pacific island nation of Papua New Guinea includes the eastern half of the island of New Guinea, islands of the Bismarck Archipelago, and the northern Solomon Islands. It has been an independent country since 1975, with about 180,000 square miles (467,000 square kilometers) and a population of some 4 million. The peoples are Melanesian. Although the great linguistic diversity of the area is often remarked (there are more than seven hundred languages), one should not conclude that groups remained totally isolated and could not communicate with their neighbors. For thousands of years, neighboring languages were learned to meet social, economic, and cultural needs.

Almost all observations of Papua New Guinea traditional dance have been written by anthropologists, missionaries, or travelers rather than by dance researchers. Dance was often noted in passing, but the descriptions usually concentrated on when dancing was performed within a particular ceremony rather than on the meaning of the dance or the formations involved. This has led to a number of erroneous assumptions about Papua New Guinea dance. Few studies of particular dance cultures have been attempted; even fewer attempts have been made to talk generally about dance in Papua New Guinea.

PAPUA NEW GUINEA. Mekeo men, from the Central Province and Southern Lowlands, performing a line dance in characteristic face-paint and ceremonial costumes. (Photograph from the Department of Library Services, American Museum of Natural History, New York [no. 338005]; used by permission.)

Occasions for dance vary from area to area, but dances may be performed for initiation, courting, exchange of valuables, the end of mourning, welcoming, farewell, cults, before and after fighting, and for general celebrations of various kinds. Decorations for dances are often elaborate, including plumes, paint (particularly on the face), ornamental and scented leaves, and oil on the skin. These decorations emphasize an important aspect of Papua New Guinea dance—display.

Dancers are on display in two ways. First, they display themselves to ancestral spirits. In many areas, these spirits may be potentially disruptive to the smooth running of daily life; therefore, dances are often performed to appease them. If the dance, decorations, and accompanying feast are successful, the spirits may join the dancing. The pleasing of ancestral spirits is also a way of assuring the growth of children, crops, and pigs. Dance is a means of communication with these spirits. In areas where elaborate masks are worn in dance, the masked figures may represent various spirits, or the spirits may animate the masked dancers. Masks may also be worn merely to attract spirits. For example, among the Olo (West Sepik), fish spirits enter the masks, but the fact that men are dancing beneath those masks is not hidden: the masks may be removed in public while the dancer rests. Second, dancers are on display to spectators, especially to the opposite sex. Consequently, love magic is frequently performed before the dance. Decorations make the dancer beautiful, and the opposite sex is attracted by this beauty as well as by the singing and movements of the dancer. A woman's joining a man in dance is an indication of her interest in him.

In addition to appeasing ancestral spirits, dance also demonstrates social cohesiveness and the importance of kinship ties. Dance festivals bring together large groups of people, strengthening the relations that already exist and easing tensions.

Throughout many parts of Papua New Guinea, the dancer also performs as singer and instrumentalist, usually playing a hand drum. In parts of New Britain, New Ireland, Manus, and Milne Bay, however, these functions may be performed by separate groups. For example, in the Trobriand Islands, drummers form one group and singers another, while dancers move counterclockwise around them. Instrumentalists also form a separate group when the instruments are large and nonportable, such as wooden slit-drums.

Men and women may dance together, or there may be separate dances for each sex. This sexual dichotomy of dance types is especially apparent in New Britain, New Ireland, and parts of the Highlands of New Guinea.

Dance formations are also variable. Circle dances are very widespread, with the dancers usually moving in a counterclockwise direction. In the northern Solomon Islands, dancers playing large wooden trumpets move clockwise, while singers and men playing panpipes move in a mass, counterclockwise around them. Formations of dancers in two rows facing inward are common in the coastal Central Province and in parts of the Southern Highlands Province. Two lines of dancers are also found in the Northern and the Milne Bay provinces, but here they are in double-file formation. Dancers forming a single line facing out toward the spectators are found in West New Britain, Enga, and Western Highlands provinces.

The dance movements themselves usually involve bending the knees or bouncing in place, with the torso used as one vertical unit. Arm movements may be limited to those necessary for playing instruments, or they may be more intricate, especially when the dance requires only a small number of dancers. Dancers may be either stationary or moving.

Specific dances may be restricted to nighttime or daytime performance. In parts of Southern Highlands and Western provinces, dances take place in men's or communal longhouses. Another indoor dance is the seated courting dance found in Western Highlands Province and among adjacent groups.

Contrary to what has been suggested by some authors, Papua New Guinea dances are not just spontaneous displays of rhythmic movement; they must be learned. In dances that have particularly complicated choreography, the movements may be taught by a dance master.

Mimetic dances are found in a number of areas, for example, Milne Bay, Northern, Western, Morobe, Madang, and West New Britain provinces. Animals, supernatural beings, or daily activities are imitated. Dance dramas or mimes are performed by groups in Northern Province.

Some groups are particularly well known for their dancing. Along the northern coast of Papua New Guinea (Sepik, Madang, and Morobe) and the adjacent part of West New Britain, dances are commonly traded and sold. Consequently, dance songs in this area may not be in the performing group's language. In this area, as well as in most other parts of the country, dance is not just mass participation (another erroneous assumption) but performance as presentation before spectators.

Early Christian missionaries (from the sixteenth to nineteenth centuries) occasionally reacted violently to traditional dances, both because the dances were directed toward ancestral spirits and because they felt that sexual license was encouraged by such displays. All forms of traditional dance were prohibited in areas along the southern coast, which became a British protectorate in 1884. Polynesian missionaries in these areas introduced modified versions of traditional Polynesian dance and song genres, which they felt were more appropriate for Christian converts, such as *taibubu* in Western Province and *peroveta anedia* in Central Province.

PAPUA NEW GUINEA. Kamula dancers, from the south side of Mount Bosavi in the Western Province, at the 1980 Pacific Festival of the Arts in Papua New Guinea. (Photograph © by Adrienne L. Kaeppler; used by permission.)

Today, aside from the traditional occasions for dance at a village level, dancers also perform for events in contemporary society, such as Christmas, government holidays, the opening of stores, or graduations. Large groups from certain areas living in urban centers may dance on a regular basis, thereby lessening their alienation from village life. Traditional dances are also performed at regional shows in which groups from widely separated areas compete against each other for cash prizes. A number of national and regional theater companies incorporate traditional dance into their productions for local and overseas audiences.

String-band music, a development of pan-Pacific pop, has become highly developed musically, but it is more to be heard than danced to. On the rare occasions when dancing accompanies it, the movements are variations on stereotypical Polynesian dance, with swaying hips and undulating hand movements. Live music is most often performed by electric bands playing Western rock. In towns such music is usually heard at hotels by a seated male audience, drinking. Outside the towns, electric bands play at "six to six" parties, which to some extent may be a social substitute for traditional all-night dancing. The generic term *disco* is used for dancing to the prerecorded music of foreign rock, reggae, and disco bands. The movements are imitative of Western counterparts.

BIBLIOGRAPHY

Fitz-Patrick, David G., and John Kimbuna. *Bundi.* Nerang, 1983.

McGregor, Donald E. *The Fish and the Cross.* 2d ed. Papua, 1982.

McLean, Mervyn. *An Annotated Bibliography of Oceanic Music and Dance* and *Supplement.* Auckland, 1977–1981.

Schwimmer, Erik. "Aesthetics of the Aika." In *Exploring the Visual Art of Oceania,* edited by Sidney M. Mead. Honolulu, 1979.

Tuzin, Donald F. *The Voice of the Tambaran.* Berkeley, 1980.

Zelenietz, Martin, and Jill Grant. "Kilenge *Narogo:* Ceremonies, Resources, and Prestige in a West New Britain Society." *Oceania* 51 (December 1980).

DON NILES

Binandere Dance

The Binandere people, numbering about four thousand, live in Oro Province of Papua New Guinea. Of their dance dramas, the *ario* is perhaps the most important genre. The plot of each *ario* is based on a legend or real-life experience. At the same time, there is a convention of formal sequences for performance. The sequences are derived from nature, imitating and abstracting the actions of human beings, animals, birds, and insects. The name of each sequence is derived from the movement of a particular bird or insect; the art itself originates in the Binandere perception of the dance of the bird of paradise or of the hornbill.

Choreographers rehearse the dancers before the *ario* is performed for public view. A minimum of five pairs of

PAPUA NEW GUINEA. Among the Fly River and Papuan Gulf tribes, women are traditionally forbidden from participating in or observing male initiation rites. *(below)* Masked dancers perform a male initiation rite on Urama Island, Papuan Gulf, in the early 1920s. *(opposite page)* Another men's ceremonial dance, probably photographed in the same village. (Photograph by Captain Frank Hurley; from the Department of Library Services, American Museum of Natural History, New York [nos. 125285 and 125289]; used by permission.)

dancers is needed: the first pair is the represented creature's head, the second pair the neck, one to six pairs form the middle, one pair forms the "neck of the tail," and the last pair is the tail itself.

There are twelve sequences in the *ario*. In the *gugu gaiari* (the noise produced when water boils over), the head pair of dancers emerges from an enclosure in the center of the village or the bush, mimicking a butterfly about to alight on a flower. The other pairs follow, beating their drums and turning face to face, then back to back. After reaching the center of the performance area, the dancers pause for several minutes.

In the *bebeku yaungari* ("to split in the middle"), while the main column of dancers beat their drums, the head pair dances around the others, then splits the column to return to the front. In the *deoga,* the dancers swoop like hawks catching rats; the head pair crosses through each other pair of dancers until it reaches the tail. The *biama giri* ("hornbill's tapping"), features the tapping of a drum with the fingertips in imitation of the bird's call. The dancers hop to and fro or move forward in time to the drum.

During *batari* (the sound of a drum), one member of the head pair beats the drum in a different rhythm from the others; the head and tail pairs perform complex motions. In *dabibiro* the head pair slips out and dances backward, outside the group; upon reaching the tail, the pair dances back to the original position, moving between the other pairs.

The next segment is *warawa gatari,* which means "to crack wood and collect grubs from the *warawa* tree"; the action can also be known as *ambe atoro,* "to beat sago from wood pith." *Otara doratugari* means "to brush ants off one's hands or body": the dancers approach one another, bend down to place their drums on the ground, and move backward, rubbing their hands. (Coastal dwellers call this segment of the dance *ewa bedari,* "the breaking of waves.")

The *woiwa,* a red parrot, is often attracted to the sago palm and to the flowering coconut palm. In *woiwa tembari,* each dancer holds up one leg and crosses over to exchange places with his partner. The head pair and the others next perform the beating of pandanus (screw pine) fruit *(gagi).* The head pair pushes the others backward and then chases the head forward. During *woduwa,* one

member of the head pair takes the lead, and the rest of the dancers follow in a single file until the leader joins the tail pair.

Finally comes the *tugata.* From the center, one dancer leads a song that tells the story that formed the basis for the performance. As the song fades away, the dancers disperse.

BIBLIOGRAPHY

Waiko, John Dademo. *A Short History of Papua New Guinea.* Melbourne, 1992.

Williams, Francis E. *Orokaiva Society.* London, 1930.

FILM. John Dademo Waiko et al., *Man without Pigs* (Port Moresby, 1990).

JOHN DADEMO WAIKO

Gizra Dance

The Gizra people are lowland savanna cultivators of Western Province in Papua New Guinea. Approximately one thousand Gizra live in the three villages of Waidor (also called Ziborr), Kupere (Kupiru), and Kulalae (Togo-Tog).

Two major ceremonial dances of the Gizra were traditionally performed at night, from dusk to dawn. Although no longer danced, the *morlbo pipi* dance was exclusively performed to promote the fertility of the coconut palm. The dancers, assembled in two rows, were decorated with young coconut leaves. Most carried drums and a flute. The two leading dancers, a pair of dancers in the center of the group, and another in the rear all wore hornbill bird *(lom)* headdresses.

The flute player chose what to perform and would spit a layer of herbs into the flute to represent each song he performed. By dawn the flute was filled and ready to be broken open in a ceremony performed before all the inhabitants of the village.

The other main dance type included songs representing the distinct features of the Gizra environment. Although rarely performed today, these included the *zil-badu* (river dance), *zil-paza* (savanna dance), and *zil-kerlam* (coastal dance). Many elements, including the hornbill headdresses, were the same as in the *morlbo pipi.*

The dancers in the *zil-badu* assembled in two lines. Most male dancers had female partners. Participants carried live tortoises, file snakes, and the leaves and branches of aquatic plants. Painted with clay from the river, they also might carry lobster-claw rattles. The dance emphasized rhythmic, forward and backward swaying movements.

The dancers of the *zil-paza* carried the leaves of savanna plants and bunches of taro tuber and suckers. They were decorated with white clay from the waterhole. The leader carried the tail of a savanna gonnah *(pazaiam-paiaiam).* The performers of the *zil-kerlam* carried mangrove leaves, coastal flowers, and baskets of seashells.

The leaders of these dances were usually from clans associated with the particular geographical feature being honored. The dancers wearing hornbill headdresses were important figures in the ceremony. They were given large portions of food, especially pork, which would later be distributed to their kinsmen.

Parle was a stylistic element peculiar to this second type of Gizra dance. Performed by the men and characterized by very fast, flexible leg and body work, *parle* was regarded as the dance of the spirits of the ancestors *(abaal markai).* The flexibility of the limbs and body signified the boneless spirit's movements; the slippery motion of the feet imitated the invisible walk of the spirit.

In the late eighteenth century the Gizra people of Waidoro learned the *rotuma* dance, introduced by the Polynesian Pacific Islanders of Fiji, Samoa, and Nauru to the Torres Strait Islanders and Kiwai. The *rotuma* was danced only by men and was characterized by constant repetition of movement.

In the early nineteenth century, the *taibubu,* probably a modernized version of the *rotuma,* was learned by Gizra tribesmen working in coconut plantations on Dirimu (Thursday Island). The dancers are dressed in white singlets and red skirts *(labalaba)* made of shredded young coconut palm leaves. A kerchief or towel is worn around the head, along with wristbands and white anklebands. Sometimes a headdress *(dori)* is worn. The dancers carry items mentioned in the *taibubu* songs, such as bows and arrows, knives, paddles, and toy canoes or airplanes.

Taibubu songs tend to be highly emotional and may be sad or insulting. Very strong, loud singing stirs up the dancers; shouts during the dance indicate the dancer's feelings of prestige.

According to Bamaga Imari, a contemporary composer and choreographer from Waidoro, a *taibubu* song composer must be talented in both music and memorization. Composing is not a hereditary talent. The songs are about events or experiences within the lifetime of a composer. Most Gizra composers are men; Gizra women dance but usually do not compose.

The major times for dancing are during feasts such as church and funeral ceremonies, Christmas, and the New Year. However, the songs can be sung at any time.

BILLAI LABA

Kaluli Dance

The Kaluli people live in twenty longhouse communities scattered in isolated spots in the tropical forest north of Mount Bosavi in Southern Highlands Province of Papua New Guinea. Six kinds of ceremonial dance utilize the same basic movement but differ according to the number of performers, spatial arrangement of dancers in the long-

PAPUA NEW GUINEA: Kaluli Dance. A performer of *gisalo,* about to have his back singed by members of the audience. (Photographs © by Steven Feld; used by permission.)

house, costume, accompanying instruments, and type of song.

As a result of government and Christian missionary pressure, Kaluli ceremonialism began to decline by the 1970s. *Gisalo* was performed for the last time in 1984. *Ilib kuwo:* and fragments of *ko:luba, heyalo,* or *gisalo* are now performed only for local celebrations of Papua New Guinea's Independence Day (16 September).

The basic Kaluli dance motion, an up-and-down bobbing, from the balls of the feet with knees slightly bent, was modeled on the motion of the *wo:kwele* bird (giant cuckoodove, *Reinwardtoena reinwardtsi*) which nests in rock gorges by waterfalls. According to myth this bird taught the Kaluli to dance. The dancer's movements, accentuated by the arching and bouncing flow of feathers, streamers, and rattles in the costume, represent him as a bird singing and dancing at a waterfall. The shimmering sound of the costume, particularly the rear streamers flowing from shoulders to floor, creates the auditory impression of the waterfall, and the dancer's voice becomes that of the bird singing. The usual pulse is sixty motions per minute (120 M.M.).

Three major ceremonial dances *(gisalo, ko:luba,* and *heyalo)* were always performed at night in the main hall of the longhouse, to last until dawn. They were performed by guests for the benefit of their hosts. Depending on the ceremony, the dancers move up and down the center hall of the longhouse alone, in pairs, or in lines. Light is provided by resin torches held by bystanders. The dancers sing songs that evoke nostalgic images of the past and the dead whom the audience knew. Members of the audience become deeply moved by these songs, and some burst into tears. Then, angered by the anguish they have been made to feel, they jump up, grab a torch and burn the dancers on the shoulder. The dancers give no sign of pain and dance unperturbed until the end of the song. The ceremony ends at dawn, when the dancers give compensation payments in the form of small valuable objects to the people they made weep.

Gisalo is the only ceremonial dance the Kaluli claim to have invented. Four dancers with cassowary-feather headdresses take turns singing long, elaborate songs, accompanied by groups of men who sit at each end of the longhouse. Each dancer proceeds alone down the hallway

PAPUA NEW GUINEA: Kaluli Dance. *Ilib kuwo:,* Kaluli ceremonial drumming. The performers' elaborate costumes feature bark belts from which bundles of crayfish-claw rattles are suspended, shoulder-to-ground palm streamers, cross-chest woven bands, and woven, arched headdresses decorated with white cockatoo feathers. (Photographs © by Steven Feld; used by permission.)

and back, singing with the personal accompaniment of a mussel-shell rattle tapped lightly on the floor by his side.

Ko:luba, like *ilib kuwo:,* was introduced from the southeast of Mount Bosavi, and the dancers wear the same type of costume. Twelve to twenty dancers participate. They take turns, two at a time dancing facing each other and singing a song. They sing in overlapping sung parts while dancing in place and skip to a new position in the hall after five repetitions of the song. After every ten songs, the whole group dances and sings in a processional up and down the hallway.

Heyalo was introduced from the region to the west of Bosavi several generations ago. Male dancers costumed as in *ilib kuwo:* and *ko:luba* hop sideways around the edges of the longhouse hall all night, singing in a group and beating on drums. They are accompanied by celebrating women who cheer them on.

In *ilib kuwo:,* dancers wear an elaborate costume with a white cockatoo headdress and palmleaf streamers. They lead arrival processions or, as in *sabio,* dance in the house as a prelude to major ceremonies. One to six dancers beating hand drums and wearing crayfish-claw rattles in the rear of their costumes dance up and down in place at either end of the longhouse hall, then proceed up and down the entire corridor with a skipping step.

Iwo: was introduced from the southwest of Mount Bosavi and is danced only the night before killing pigs. It involves a fixed group of forty-five songs. Each song is begun by two men bursting into the longhouse and banging axes on the floor. They are followed by a line of as many as twenty costumed dancers who accompany a lead singer. There is no weeping or burning as there is in *heyalo, ko:luba,* and *gisalo.*

Sabio is a minor dance introduced in the 1950s to Kaluli from the Foi and Fasu area to the east. Two lines of young men face each other across the longhouse hall and sing alternating lines while bouncing up and down in place, tapping a stick or ax handle on the floor. No special regalia are worn.

[*See also* Music for Dance, *article on* Oceanic Music.]

BIBLIOGRAPHY

Feld, Steven. "Aesthetics and Synaesthesia in Kaluli Ceremonial Dance." *UCLA Journal of Dance Ethnology* 14 (1990): 1–16.

Feld, Steven. *Sound and Sentiment: Birds, Weeping, Poetics, and Song in Kaluli Expression.* 2d ed. Philadelphia, 1990.

Schieffelin, Edward L. *The Sorrow of the Lonely and the Burning of the Dancers.* New York, 1976.

Schieffelin, Edward L. "The End of Traditional Music, Dance, and Body Decoration in Bosavi, Papua New Guinea." In *The Plight of Peripheral People in Papua New Guinea,* vol. 1, *The Inland Situation,* by Robert Gordon et al. Cambridge, Mass., 1981.

RECORDINGS. *Music of the Kaluli* (1982). *Kaluli Weeping and Song* (1985). *Voices of the Rainforest* (1991).

VIDEOTAPE. "Gisaro: The Sorrow and the Burning," produced by Yasuko Ichioka (NAV, 1986).

STEVEN FELD and EDWARD L. SCHIEFFELIN

Maring Dance

The Maring people live in the Madang and Western Highlands provinces of Papua New Guinea. This discussion is based on observations of Maring traditional dances by Western scholars in the 1960s, when the Maring numbered about 5,300 people. Traditional Maring dances consist of two major types, *kaiko* and *kanant.* These differ from each other formally and fulfill diverse social functions.

The *kaiko* dance is traditionally part of the ritual cycle that articulates the intricate network of amity and enmity among the approximately twenty Maring clans. Over a period of up to two decades, each clan progresses through stages of war, truce, and peace. *Kaiko* dancing takes place during the final stages of truce, at which time a celebrating clan repays and thanks its allied clans and ancestor spirits with gifts of pork. The host clan clears and levels a large dance ground on its heavily forested, sloping territory and invites its allies one clan at a time for dancing. These two-clan gatherings take place every two to three weeks over a period of a year and a half, until the concluding ceremony, at which all allied clans are present simultaneously. This is the largest gathering in traditional Maring life, with as many as a thousand people congregating on the dance ground. In a society without written documents, this gathering serves to communicate by direct observation information on the size and vitality of the various clans.

The *kaiko* dance is performed by men of all ages (though unmarried women have been observed to dance on occasion). Its basic movement is an up-and-down bounce, either in place or walking forward, accompanied by the singing and drumming of the dancers themselves. Special clothing and decorations amplify the sound and movement: an unusually long loincloth with a fringe of shells or heavy beads clatters with each forward step; a bustle of pleated leaves affixed to the back of the belt rustles with the vertical bounce; and a feather headdress topped by a long flexible plume sways back and forth with sagittal movement of the whole trunk and head.

Dancers perform in clan groups, alternating their formations between rough clumps and rough columns. The paths of the groups intertwine in endless variations. Men tune their drums individually, one group member starts the song, and the others join in. Drumming is added gradually. Because other groups may be at other stages in their song, there is rarely a complete pause in the music. An additional strand of sound is provided by the high-pitched shouting and yodeling of the women on the sidelines.

The principal dance phrases of the *kaiko* begin with the group stooping in a clump, facing inward, drumming and singing. The group then rises and sets off in a rough column formation (two to four abreast) to a new location, where the pattern begins again. A further elaboration occurs when a dance group first enters the dance ground: two or three men dance in front, wielding ceremonial axes instead of drumming, their paths tracing complex curves on the ground. Dancing customarily begins in the late afternoon and continues throughout the night.

PAPUA NEW GUINEA: Maring Dance. Male dancers from Madang characteristically attired, with plumed headdresses and shell-decorated costumes, for a Maring *kaiko,* c.1929. The accompaniment for this dance included a singing sound the men produced by blowing through the cowrie shells held in their mouths. (Photograph by R. H. Beck; from the Department of Library Services, American Museum of Natural History, New York [no. 115654]; used by permission.)

The *kanant* dance is a courtship dance. Since among the Maring, marriage does not take place within the clan, such dances are especially organized when visitors from other clans or men on trading expeditions come to a village. The *kanant* dance is usually held at night in a married woman's house. Male and female participants sit alternately, touching adjacent thighs and arms. All sing in falsetto voices, swaying gently. Eventually the swaying becomes a full trunk rotation, the couples touching cheeks and, finally, turning their heads side to side so that their noses brush by each other with each phrase. Each individual has his or her own timing. *Kanant* dancing lasts for four to five hours. Partners are changed occasionally.

The *kanant* dance style contrasts markedly with the *kaiko:* unaccompanied falsetto singing versus full-throated singing accompanied by drums; stationary, seated dancing in a confined area versus mobile, standing or stooping dancing through a large open space; and gentle movements in a horizontal plane versus forceful movement through vertical and sagittal planes.

Nevertheless, a core characteristic of Maring movement style is present in both *kanant* and *kaiko:* neither head-turning, drumbeats, nor footsteps are performed by all participants simultaneously, but are instead clustered around a rhythmic pulse. This pattern of loose synchrony is congruent with the individualism characteristic of Maring life, in which joint action is achieved through individual cooperation rather than through rigid frameworks of organization or authoritarian discipline.

BIBLIOGRAPHY

Jablonko, Allison. "Dance and Daily Activities among the Maring People of New Guinea: A Cinematographic Analysis of Body Movement Style." Ph.D. diss., Columbia University, 1968.

Jablonko, Allison, and Elizabeth Kagan. "An Experiment in Looking: Reexamining the Process of Observation." *Drama Review* 32 (1988): 148–163.

Jablonko, Allison. "Patterns of Daily Life in the Dance of the Maring of New Guinea." *Visual Anthropology* 4 (1991): 367–377.

Rappaport, Roy A. *Pigs for the Ancestors.* New ed. New Haven, 1984.

FILM. Allison Jablonko, *Maring in Motion* (1968). Allison and Marek Jablonko, *1968 Jablonko–Maring Archival Collection,* Reels 35 and 51, Human Studies Film Archives, Smithsonian Institution, Washington, D.C., 1989.

ALLISON JABLONKO

Melpa Dance

The Melpa live in Western Highlands Province around Mount Hagen township; they number more than seventy thousand and form one of the largest linguistic groups in Papua New Guinea. The Melpa are well known for their competitive exchanges of wealth, called *moka,* and for their style of "big-man" leadership exercised in these exchanges. *Moka* festivals are also the main occasions for a number of dances, including *mørl, kenan, yap, werl,* and *mølya.*

Mørl and *kenan* are the main formal men's dances performed at *moka. Mørl* is performed by men in full costume with blackened faces, dancing in a row, facing outward to the large crowd of onlookers. Many men play drums; others carry spears or bows and arrows. Dancers beat drums in unison while dancing in place. The movement consists of rising to the toes, then bending the knees in a downward movement so that the front apron of the dancer sweeps outward. The dancers must hold their shoulders and backs straight while bending the knees, and their aprons and plumes should move together gracefully. To achieve this synchrony, dancers touch elbows or interlock little fingers with those on either side. Although this is a men's dance, occasionally an unmarried girl dances with a male relative or with a man she finds attractive. Song texts deal with serious subjects, such as pigs, competitiveness, and exchange relationships.

Although *mørl* is usually practiced for several days before the *moka, kenan* is not. For *kenan,* men line up in a number of rows of four or more and stamp around the entire oblong ceremonial ground, especially encircling the raised tub of cordyline plants in front of the communal men's house. Magical substances are buried in the tub to draw in wealth goods, and ancestral spirits are believed to cluster around the plants. The full name for *kenan* is *nde mbo kenan, "kenan* for the tree shrubs," which reflects the significance of this encirclement. Again, girls may join the men in *kenan.*

As *mørl* is the serious dance for men, *werl* is its female counterpart, dominated by married women. Males are never inducted into it. The women dance separately from the men. They are very heavily decorated, and their faces are painted red. In *werl,* the women beat drums or stand with a stick as a support, slightly bending each knee in alternation. Occasionally they may turn around to display their decorated backs to the spectators. As with *mørl,* the texts of *werl* songs are of a serious nature.

In contrast to this seriousness, *yap* and *mølya,* generally for unmarried males and females, respectively, are frequently sexually provocative. In both *yap* and *mølya,* dancers hold hands in a tight circle, surrounding a number of others standing in the center. When the song begins, the dancers remain in place, but as it accelerates in tempo, the singers begin vigorously jumping sideways in a counterclockwise direction. A boy may join a girl in *mølya* if he is particularly attracted to her. Girls may do likewise in *yap,* or they may dance with a relative, as may married women. At the end of a *moka,* after the seriousness of the main dances and the exchanges and speeches are over, the circles of *yap* and *mølya* dancers engulf the whole ceremonial ground.

Often following *moka* festivals are *amb kenan,* the courting dances, commonly known as "turning head." In the evening, unmarried and married men go to a girl's house. The men sit by the fire and sing until the girl, who usually has some female companions, emerges from a back compartment. The girl kneels, and a boy sits by her side at a right angle. He begins swaying his head back and forth in invitation, which she imitates. Then they make contact with their noses and foreheads, perhaps pivoting twice, after which, with their cheeks touching, they bob down once or twice, bending from the waist, and then begin again. They continue until one breaks away. A different boy then sits next to the girl to dance again. Although there is singing throughout the dance, the movements do not seem to be exactly coordinated to the song.

Exchange festivals are demonstrations of the strength and prosperity of the donors. The Melpa also have religious cults with events similar to *moka* festivals, but they explicitly aim to promote prosperity and fertility by ritual action.

Kor kondi, "to finish the spirit (cult)," refers to the distinctive dance movements at the end of the Female Spirit Cult. Men in the cult line up in pairs, carrying pearl shells, and stomp out of the cult area, circle three times, and return to distribute pork. *Kng kui* and *ware* are special dances at pig killings, very rarely performed today. In decorations and dance movements they seem to resemble those of the mid-Wahgi area to the east (Luzbetak, 1954) and among the Maring to the northeast.

BIBLIOGRAPHY

Luzbetak, Louis J. "The Socio-Religious Significance of a New Guinea Pig Festival." *Anthropological Quarterly* 2 (1954).

Strathern, Andrew, and Marilyn Strathern. *Self-Decoration in Mount Hagen.* Toronto, 1971.

Strathern, Andrew. "'A Line of Boys': Melpa Dance as a Symbol of Maturation." In *Society and the Dance,* edited by Paul Spencer. Cambridge, 1985.

Vicedom, Georg F., and Herbert Tischner. *Die Mbowamb.* 3 vols. Hamburg, 1943–1948.

ANDREW STRATHERN and DON NILES

PAQUITA. Ballet in two acts and three scenes. Choreography: Joseph Mazilier. Music: Édouard Deldevez. Libretto: Paul Foucher and Joseph Mazilier. Scenery: Humanité Philastre, Charles Cambon, Jules Diéterle, Charles Séchan, and Édouard Despléchin. First performance: 1 April 1846, Théâtre de l'Académie Royale de Musique, Paris. Principals: Carlotta Grisi (Paquita), Lucien Petipa (Lucien d'Hervilly).

The plot of *Paquita* was rather contrived: a Gypsy girl saves a French officer from a plot to murder him, then discovers her own noble birth and marries him. The ballet was distinguished by the dancing of Carlotta Grisi, whose role contained an unusual amount of pointe work, possibly in emulation of the rumored abilities of the Milanese ballerina Sofia Fuoco, who arrived shortly after to dance at the Paris Opera.

The Spanish setting of the ballet offered many opportunities for the ever-popular Spanish and Gypsy character dances, including a much praised *pas de manteaux* performed by the female ensemble in the style of Les Danseuses Viennoises, a children's dance troupe famed for its precision.

Marius Petipa revived *Paquita* in Saint Petersburg in 1847 and again in 1881, when he added a pas de trois and a *grand pas* to interpolated music by Léon Minkus. Later revivals of *Paquita* have been based almost exclusively on the Petipa-Minkus *grand pas* rather than the full ballet by Mazilier and Deldevez.

BIBLIOGRAPHY

Beaumont, Cyril W. *Complete Book of Ballets.* London, 1937.

Guest, Ivor. *The Romantic Ballet in Paris.* 2d rev. ed. London, 1980.

Roslavleva, Natalia. *Era of the Russian Ballet* (1966). New York, 1979.

Wiley, Roland John, trans. and ed. *A Century of Russian Ballet: Documents and Accounts, 1810–1910.* Oxford, 1990.

SUSAN AU

PARADE. Ballet in one act. Choreography: Léonide Massine. Music: Erik Satie. Libretto: Jean Cocteau. Scenery and costumes: Pablo Picasso. First performance: 18 May 1917, Théâtre du Châtelet, Paris, Ballets Russes de Serge Diaghilev. Principals: Léonide Massine (The Chinese Conjuror), Lydia Lopokova and Nicolas Zvereff (Acrobats), Maria Chabelska (The Little American Girl), Leon Woizikowski (The French Manager), M. Statkewicz (The New York Manager).

Parade, in which, as the versatile Jean Cocteau (1917) once put it, "four modernist artists had a hand," has with justice been regarded as a landmark in the history of art, theater, and, of course, dance. It brilliantly initiated Serge Diaghilev's efforts to stay in the vanguard by giving his productions a more Western, avant-garde look. Gertrude Stein (1959) said that *Parade* put "cubism . . . on the stage." It was not just Picasso's cubism that was belatedly put onstage, but a subtle and humorous confrontation between cubism and futurism and their respective ideals.

Cocteau, who shaped the production of *Parade* with more freedom than is usually granted the librettist, provided its traditional theme—on a Paris street, a traveling theater company vainly performs three music-hall turns to lure the populace outside into the theater. In the ballet, each of the participating media deviously or overtly juxtaposes and intermingles the classical values of the Mediterranean past and their cubist revitalization with a motif dear to the futurists: the blatant, noisy opportunism of the modern urban world, which telescopes and overthrows distances in time and space as well as values. Picasso's quasi-representational drop curtain and set thus mixed allusions to the course of Western civilization with events in his own life; at the same time, Satie's score shifted wittily from references to contrapuntal church music to that of the variety theater, to which Cocteau added novel machine-age noises.

The staging of the ballet, with its vaudeville-like qualities, incorporated many of the artistic and performance ideals of the futurists. The four collaborators had encountered their work and representatives in Rome, where much of the ballet was created. The two Managers, who represent the vulgar modern purveyors of art, were perhaps the most remarkable contribution of the production. Those ominously towering constructions, which dwarfed the other dancers, were a wondrous blend of Picasso's cubist assemblages and futurist sculpture. As a result, the Managers became moving scenery, rhythmically activated inanimate objects, challenging the static, quasi-perspectival sets. This idea formed the heart of the decor for another Diaghilev production, the futurist artist Giacomo Balla's "dancerless ballet" *Feu d'Artifice,* which was being prepared at the same time in Rome.

In principle and practice *Parade* extended as well as threatened the theatrical ballet. Obviously, the threat resided principally in the Managers, who suggested the potential elimination of the dancers as practitioners of their traditional skills and as necessary artistic presences on the stage. *Parade* was very successful as an integral multimedia spectacle. It set the standard for succeeding modernist collaborations; for Diaghilev's enterprise it represented a frequently decried shift of emphasis away from the ballet and toward the personality of the visual artist—who, to many spectators, seemed to dominate its effect. Picasso's nontheatrical work was deeply affected by this first as well as his later intense contacts with dance.

[*For discussion of scenery for this work, see* Scenic Design. *See also entries on the principal figures mentioned herein.*]

BIBLIOGRAPHY

Axsom, Richard H. *"Parade": Cubism as Theatre.* New York, 1979.

Cocteau, Jean. "La collaboration de 'Parade.'" *Nord-Sud* 4.5 (June–July 1917).

Cocteau, Jean. "A Season of the Ballets Russes." Translated by Frank W. D. Ries. *Dance Scope* 13.4 (1979): 7–11.

Cooper, Douglas. *Picasso Theatre.* New York, 1968.

Garafola, Lynn. *Diaghilev's Ballets Russes.* New York, 1989.

LoMonaco, Martha Schmoyer. "The Giant Jigsaw Puzzle: Robert Joffrey Reconstructs *Parade.*" *Drama Review* 28 (Fall 1984): 31–45.

Martin, Marianne W. "The Ballet *Parade:* A Dialogue between Cubism and Futurism." *Art Quarterly* (Spring 1978).

Rothschild, Deborah M. *Picasso's "Parade."* London, 1991.

Steegmuller, Francis. *Cocteau: A Biography.* Boston, 1970.

Stein, Gertrude. *Picasso* (1938). Boston, 1959.

MARIANNE W. MARTIN

PARIS OPERA BALLET. Many of the leading European and international ballet companies owe their origins, directly or indirectly, to the fame and influence of the world's oldest ballet company, that of the Paris Opera.

Early History. In 1661 King Louis XIV of France founded the Académie Royale de Danse to improve the quality of dance instruction for court entertainments. Eight years later, on 28 June 1669, he granted the poet Pierre Perrin a license to open a French academy of opera. This institution needed dance to attract the public and fill the place of the court ballet, which had fallen into decline after the king's retirement from dance performances. The Jeu de Paume de la Bouteille, formerly a tennis court, was the first home of the Opera. There, in 1671, Robert Cambert presented *Pomone,* a musical pastorale with choreography by Pierre Beauchamps.

The era of French theatrical dance began with lyric entertainments embellished with elaborate stage machinery. Jean-Baptiste Lully purchased Perrin's royal performance license and, in 1673, obtained letters of patent limiting the use of dancers and musicians by other French theaters (a constraint that seriously handicapped Molière's work). Joining forces with Beauchamps, the designer Carlo Vigarani, and the leading dancers of the period, Lully inaugurated the second of the Paris Opera's thirteen homes, in the Jeu de Paume Becquet, with *Les Fêtes de l'Amour et de Bacchus;* this consisted of excerpts from court ballets linked by new *entrées* staged by Beauchamps. Although the king and his noblemen had customarily danced in the court ballets, the dancers in this production were all professionals.

Under Lully's direction, the Paris Opera flourished. Louis XIV was enraptured by *Cadmus et Hermione* (1673), the first *tragédie lyrique,* given by Lully in the theater of the Palais-Royal, which had formerly housed Molière's troupe. Thanks to the libretti of Philippe Quinault and to Lully's staging, dance interludes became an important

PARIS OPERA BALLET. Maximilien Gardel served the Paris Opera Ballet as a dancer, as a choreographer, and, eventually, as a ballet master. Among his most successful works was *Ninette à la Cour,* a pantomime-ballet mounted in 1778. This engraving by J. Thornthwaite, after a drawing by James Roberts, shows Adélaïde Simonet as the Princess in a 1781 performance in London. (Courtesy of Madison U. Sowell and Debra H. Sowell, Brigham Young University, Provo, Utah.)

part of musical drama, which became popular with people of all social classes and with foreign visitors to Paris. Spectators returned again and again to admire the battles in *Thésée,* the magical scenes in *Bellérophon,* and the pastoral scenes in *Armide* or *Acis et Galathée.* Madame de Sévigné wrote to a friend that the dream ballets of *Atys* (1676) included "five or six new young men who dance like Faure, which alone would draw me to see it." Male dancers such as Louis Lestang, Des Airs, and Nicolas de Lorges, all trained in the court ballet, played both male and female roles; for a long time men in female dress performed character roles such as Winds and Furies.

Lully invented expressive steps and required singers to have some familiarity with dance. Beauchamps, an expert dancer and choreographer, freely developed his aesthetic at the Paris Opera, emphasizing elevation, defining the five basic positions of the feet (he reserved the *en dedans* position, which was not turned out, for character roles), requiring rigorous symmetry in groupings, and training a new generation of dancers. His most famous disciple and successor was Guillaume-Louis Pecour, who, according to Pierre Rameau, filled all kinds of roles with grace, precision, and lightness.

In *Le Triomphe de l'Amour* (1681), professional female dancers first entered the troupe. The most famous of them, Mademoiselle de La Fontaine, choreographed her own variations. Her successor, Marie-Thérèse Subligny, danced in *Ballet des Saisons* (1695), the first *opéra-ballet.*

Lully died in 1687, but his works remained in the repertory for nearly a century. Beauchamps retired after Lully's death, and Pecour assumed the post of ballet master, which he retained until 1729. [*See the entries on Beauchamps, Lully, and Pecour.*]

In the early eighteenth century male dancers retained primacy. As in the Comédie Française, dancers were categorized as *noble, demi-caractère,* or *caractère.* A notable dancer of the time was Claude Ballon, who combined lightness with "a gentle air" which he imparted "to his attitudes, especially in pas de deux" (Rameau, 1725). Michel Blondy, a nephew and disciple of Beauchamps, was regarded by the Parfaict brothers (1741) as "the greatest dancer of Europe for *la danse haute* and character and Furies' *entrées.*" [*See the entries on Ballon and Blondy.*]

Opéra-ballets such as André Campra's *L'Europe Galante* (1697) and Jean-Joseph Mouret's *Le Carnaval et la Folie* (1704) included much dance to please the public. Dramatic continuity was neglected in favor of exotic and mythological tableaux that provided occasions for dance *divertissements* accompanied by singing. The best acts of different *opéra-ballets* were often presented together under the title *Fragments.*

The vivid personality of Françoise Prévost, a female dancer who was inimitable in *passepieds,* won the public's favor. Rameau wrote that every one of her dances demonstrated the rules she practiced, "with such grace, accuracy, lightness, and precision that she can be regarded as a prodigy in this genre." Despite the period's emphasis on technical brilliance rather than expressiveness, she attempted to convey emotions in dance. [*See the entry on Prévost.*]

PARIS OPERA BALLET. A lithograph from the late 1820s depicting Lise Noblet as Edile in *Astolphe et Joconde,* performed at the Académie Royale de Musique in Paris in 1827. (Courtesy of Madison U. Sowell and Debra H. Sowell, Brigham Young University, Provo, Utah.)

Of the four Dumoulin brothers who were active at about the same time, Henri, François, and Pierre were character dancers, while David excelled in pas de deux; Jean-Georges Noverre (1807) wrote that David was "always tender, always graceful; sometimes a butterfly, sometimes a zephyr; fickle one moment, faithful the next, always moved by a new feeling." Facial expressions were concealed by the masks that male dancers wore, so body movement had to be very expressive. [*See the entry on the Dumoulin brothers.*]

Poor financial management and an increasing lack of discipline in the company led Louis XIV to promulgate a ruling on 11 January 1713 that penalized tardiness, refusal of roles, and unjustified absences; he ordained that the troupe be composed of fourteen singers and twenty-four dancers. A scale of salaries was set, and, for example, each of the two male principals was paid one thousand livres annually, while the two female principals each received nine hundred livres. A dancing master received five hundred livres, and a choreographer fifteen hundred. The dancers were also given bonuses and were entitled to a pension after fifteen years of service, with an exemption for performers injured while working. The number of dancers and the size of salaries continued to increase throughout the century.

Four performances a week were given throughout a season, which began in mid-October and ended at Easter. Friday was the most popular day for performances. The most coveted seats were the side loges located on the stage, and guards had to be posted to prevent the public from going backstage. The company also performed at the court—at Versailles, Fontainebleau, and Choisy—in works directed by the king's ballet master and paid for by the king. Dancers often appeared at court even after their official retirement from the Paris Opera.

One of the most brilliant dancers of the period was Marie Camargo, a pupil of Prévost. She made her debut at the Opera in 1726, shortly before Marie Sallé, another of his students. Their complementary technical and aesthetic qualities helped increase the prestige of female dance. Antoine Bandieri de Laval, who partnered both, demonstrated a "majestic and noble taste." The three Maltaire (also spelled Malter) brothers excelled in character *entrées* such as Demons and Winds, which allowed them to perform daring acrobatic feats. Louis Dupré perfected the French noble style, dominating his era with his incomparable elegance. Like other contemporary dancers and choreographers, he performed as a guest artist at the principal European theaters, which were eager to emulate the style of the Paris Opera. [*See the entries on Camargo, Dupré, Laval, and Sallé.*]

The *tragédies lyriques* and *opéra-ballets* of Lully, Campra, Mouret, and André-Cardinal Destouches had always included pieces based on court dances—*passepieds,* courantes, rigaudons, minuets, chaconnes, and so on—interpreted by conventional figures such as warriors, priestesses, nymphs, demons, and furies. Around 1720, dance suites were introduced into the repertory, including the famous *Les Caractères de la Danse* and *Les Plaisirs Champêtres.* A suite comprised a series of playlets in dance, performed by two to six soloists; this innovation, however, failed to supplant the splendors of elaborate settings and choreographic virtuosity.

Blondy, who was ballet master from 1729 to 1739, was praised by the journal *Le Mercure* for his inventiveness and his teaching. Despite administrative vicissitudes, the Paris Opera astounded Europe with its diversity, its sumptuous costumes, and the quality of its dances, which according to Luigi Riccoboni (1738) had a brilliance unmatched elsewhere.

In Jean-Philippe Rameau the Paris Opera found a composer whose personality dominated his era. With the accelerated rhythms of *Hippolyte et Aricie* (1733), Rameau renewed the art of ballet, giving a symphonic dimension to the dances. Following a traditional mythological prologue, his *opéra-ballet Les Indes Galantes* (1735) transported the dazzled spectator from Turkey to Peru to Persia. "Les Sauvages," an *entrée* set in North America, was added in 1736. The Persian scene, "Fleurs," is the first example of a *ballet d'action:* as the Rose, Sallé struggled against Boreas and was revived by Zephyr. On several occasions Rameau gave dance a substantive role in the plot, notably in *Les Fêtes d'Hébé* (1739), in which the "Entrée de la Danse" allowed Mademoiselle Mariette to sing and dance the role of Eglé. [*See the entry on* Rameau.]

The ballet fascinated the public. Although Rémond de Saint-Mard criticized the monotony of the *entrées,* he noted that dance was so popular that audiences would yearn for the end of the most beautiful song in the world if they believed that a ballet would follow. Some critics, however, called for more expression in the Paris Opera's dancers.

PARIS OPERA BALLET. The hierarchy of ranks of dancers in the Paris Opera Ballet is one of the most complex in the world. Most major ballet companies distinguish no more than four ranks: principal dancer, soloist, corps de ballet, and apprentice. This chart gives approximate equivalents in English of the French terms used to name the ranks of the Paris Opera Ballet. (Courtesy of Barbara Palfy.)

Structure of the Paris Opera Ballet

Official rank	Approximate Equivalent in English
étoile	star
première danseuse étoile	principal (female) dancer, star
premier danseur étoile	principal (male) dancer, star
première danseuse	principal (female) dancer
premier danseur	principal (male) dancer
grand sujet	first-rank soloist
petit sujet	second-rank soloist
mime	mime (performs nondancing roles)
coryphée	demisoloist (performs in groups of 6–8)
premier quadrille	first-rank corps de ballet[1]
second quadrille	second rank corps de ballet
stagiaire, surnumeraire	extra, supernumerary
élève, "rat"	apprentice, student

1. In France, the term *corps de ballet* is used for the company as a whole.

Soloists often arranged their own *entrées* to display their special talents, while the ballet master choreographed the ensemble dances and coordinated the staging. The result was a certain discontinuity and lack of balance, as well as a monotony that was much criticized: Francesco Algarotti declared, "While the opera is serious, the ballet is farce." According to Louis de Cahusac, each soloist wanted to appear twice, adapting his *entrées* "to his personal style, and without any direct or indirect relationship with the general plan, of which he was ignorant." The dancer, plumed and richly garbed, reigned supreme.

Not surprisingly, dancers became celebrities. The Italian dancer Barbarina Campanini (La Barberina) and her partner Fossano (Antonio Rinaldi) enjoyed only ephemeral success; their acrobatic virtuosity did not appeal to French tastes. Gaëtan Vestris, Dupré's disciple and successor, triumphed under the direction of Laval. Jean-Barthélemy Lany, noted for his *demi-caractère* roles, was master from 1748 to 1767. He possessed both precision and musicality but lacked inspiration except in his own dancing. Marie Allard shone in *demi-caractère entrées* such as *Sylvie;* she bequeathed her lighthearted mastery to her son Auguste Vestris. [*See the entries on Allard, Barberina, Lany, and Vestris.*]

In 1763 the outmoded theater burned down, and the Paris Opera moved to the Salle des Machines in the Tuileries. It returned in 1770 to the Palais-Royal, which had been renovated by Moreau, and performed there Christoph Willibald Gluck's operas *Orphée et Euridice* (1774) and *Alceste* (1776). Gaëtan Vestris, ballet master from 1770 to 1776, restaged Noverre's *Médée et Jason,* which he had danced in Stuttgart; he again played the role of Jason, with Marie-Madeleine Guimard as Medea and Anna Friedrike Heinel as Creusa. Vestris daringly discarded the mask in this production; his example was followed by Maximilien Gardel in *Castor et Pollux* in 1772.

An era of reform was at hand. Noverre, a protégé of Queen Marie Antoinette, followed Vestris in the post of ballet master. His appointment broke with the tradition of selecting ballet masters from among the company and thus aroused hostility. The attitudes and groupings of Noverre's tragic masterpiece *Les Horaces* inspired Jacques-Louis David's painting *The Oath of the Horatii,* a seminal neoclassical work. The public, however, preferred *Les Petits Riens,* his *divertissement* with its score by Mozart, although it accepted the new autonomy of the *ballet d'action,* already established in secondary theaters. [*See the entry on Noverre.*]

In 1780, to remedy its mismanagement by the city government, Louis XVI placed the Paris Opera under the administration of his master of revels, Denis Papillon de la Ferté. Lacking the support of the new masters, Noverre relinquished his post to Maximilien Gardel and Jean

PARIS OPERA BALLET. *The Three Graces,* a lithograph by James Baillie depicting three great ballerinas of the Romantic era in roles they first performed on the Paris Opera stage. At center is Fanny Elssler, in costume for her famous solo "La Cachucha" in Jean Coralli's *Le Diable Boiteaux* (1836). She joins hands with Fanny Cerrito (at left), in costume for the *pas de Diane* in Albert's *La Jolie Fille de Gand* (1842), and Marie Taglioni (at right) as the title character in Filippo Taglioni's *La Sylphide* (1832), the first full-scale ballet on a Romantic theme. (Dance Collection, New York Public Library for the Performing Arts.)

Dauberval. The theater was damaged by fire, and the company was temporarily installed in the rue Bergère while the architect Alexandre Lenoir constructed its new home. Dauberval resigned and left for Bordeaux, leaving Gardel in charge. Although Gardel was an unremarkable choreographer, he succeeded in keeping the peace among a disputatious troupe dominated by the virtuoso Auguste Vestris and the capricious Guimard. An intelligent actress, Guimard discarded the cumbersome panniers of the period's costume; she infused her dancing with a sensuous and affecting freshness that went beyond technique.

Gardel skillfully satisfied the audience's demand for pastorals, adapting Noverre's *ballet d'action* to the con-

PARIS OPERA BALLET. Serge Lifar was the director and *premier danseur étoile* of the Paris Opera Ballet from 1929 to 1945. Among the many ballets he created, usually with himself in the leading male role, was the innovative *Icare* (1935). To illustrate the primacy of dance over music, Lifar choreographed it without accompaniment. Georges Szyfer then composed a percussion score to fit the rhythms of the choreography. (Photograph by Studio Lipnitzki, Paris, © Lipnitzki-Viollet; used by permission.)

temporary style and transforming the comic operas of Charles-Simon Favart and Pierre-Alexandre Monsigny into pantomime ballets, among them *Ninette à la Cour* and *Le Premier Navigateur.* In *Le Déserteur* (1788), audiences were struck by the authority of his brother Pierre Gardel, a noble and expressive dancer.

Pierre Gardel began to assist Maximilien in 1784 and became ballet master after his brother's death in 1787. He reigned alone until 1820 and continued to work until 1829, a tenure comparable to that of Pecour. Under his firm direction, the company, led by Louis Nivelon, Victoire Saulnier, and Geneviève Chevigny, successfully weathered the turbulent period that led to and followed the French Revolution of 1789. The monopoly of the Paris Opera and the Comédie Française was broken in a ruling of 1791; in 1792 the Paris Opera's repertory was subjected to the censorship of the Revolutionary Commune. The Opera moved in 1793 to the Théâtre des Arts in the rue de la Loi, opposite the Bibliothèque Nationale.

Ignoring the themes of the Revolution, Pierre Gardel continued to stage heroic and mythological ballets celebrating the cult of antiquity—*Télémaque, Bacchus et Ariane,* and *Le Jugement de Pâris.* Marie Miller, whom he married, danced the leading role in *Psyché,* which became one of the most frequently seen ballets, with a total of 564 performances. Cold but energetic and devoted solely to the company, Gardel contrived to gain the goodwill of successive political regimes and kept his post as director, although he was occasionally obliged to participate in Revolutionary festivities. A courteous but inflexible teacher, he imposed an iron discipline on the school and the corps de ballet, training many important artists of the early nineteenth century, among them Carlo Blasis, who dedicated his *Elementary Treatrise* (1820) to Gardel.

Gardel's wife Marie Miller, wrote Noverre, "was to dance what the Venus de Medici [at the Uffizi] is to sculpture"; she possessed aplomb, effortlessness, an impeccable ear, and a dazzling presence. In her husband's ballet *La Dansomanie* (1800), a popular parody of social dances that introduced the waltz to the Paris Opera, her wit and humor matched that of Auguste Vestris, who partnered her.

After the Revolution, the Opera faced new challenges. The government's budgets for 1804 to 1830 included provisions for the newly renamed Imperial Academy of Music, which was for a time under the personal protection of Napoleon. It alone could present historical and noble ballets, although in 1806 it was ordered to share pastorals and comedies with other theaters. Gardel excelled in choreographing grand *ballets d'action* that showed off virtuosic performers, such as Louis-Antoine Duport, who played a warrior disguised as a woman in *Achille à Scyros* (1804) and surprised Noverre with his "daring and vivacity." Not satisfied with rivaling Vestris, whom he brilliantly replaced in *Le Retour de Zéphire,* Duport pitted his choreographic talents against those of Gardel; however, his ballets, which included *Acis et Galathée* and *Figaro,* were not well received. He secretly left for Moscow, breaking his contract.

Louis Henry staged the banal *L'Amour à Cythère* (1805) before leaving for Italy, where he was able to use his gifts more freely. Dauberval's pupil Jean-Louis Aumer, who simultaneously danced at the Paris Opera and choreographed ballets at the Théâtre de la Porte-Saint-Martin, obtained permission to mount *Les Amours d'Antoine et de Cléopâtre* (1808), an imposing work that featured the statuesque Clotilde Malfleuroy, one of the most remarkable soloists of the day, partnered by the aging Auguste Vestris.

Gardel presented the moving *Paul et Virginie,* based on a novel by Bernardin de Saint-Pierre, and *La Fête de Mars,* a homage to Napoleon's victories. He gave Vestris the pathetic title role in *L'Enfant Prodigue.* An autocratic man, he nevertheless allowed his assistant Louis-Jacques Milon to mount twelve ballets, the most popular of which were *Nina, ou La Folle par Amour* and *Clari.* Milon's favorite interpreter of female roles was Émilie Bigottini, known for her sensitivity and pathos. [*See the entries on the Gardel family and Milon.*]

Charles-Louis Didelot, who had danced at the Paris Opera from 1791 to 1794, applied for the post of ballet master in 1815, with the support of his Russian admirers. He restaged his masterpiece *Flore et Zéphire,* which was highly acclaimed for its effects of flight (the dancers were suspended on invisible wires) and for the performances of the *danseur noble* Monsieur Albert (François Decombe) and of Geneviève Gosselin, who became one of the first ballerinas to rise on pointe.

Along with Gardel, the teachers Jacques-François Deshayes and Jean-François Coulon gradually came to favor the athletic style foreshadowed by Auguste Vestris. Rapid pirouettes, vigorous leaps, and *degagés à la seconde* increased, especially in the dancing of Duport, Henry, and Antoine Paul. Lighter costumes and more flexible shoes encouraged female dancers to rise on *demi-pointe* and even on pointe, as did Gosselin and Fanny Bias, revealing a feminine grace that was soon to lift the female dancer to sovereignty. The school of dancing that evolved at the Paris Opera was emulated by Filippo Taglioni and Blasis, who gave it international prestige.

With the fall of the Napoleonic Empire a brilliant period came to an end. Milon and Gardel tried diplomatically to engage the reinstated Bourbon monarchy with specially created works such as *Le Retour des Lys* (The Return of the Lily—the royal symbol; 1814), and, after the One Hundred Days, *L'Heureux Retour* (1815). But the protection of Louis XVIII, who continued to subsidize the Paris Opera, turned it into a bastion of conservatism, exacerbated by the prudishness of managers such as Sosthène de La Rochefoucauld, who was more interested in lengthening skirts than in encouraging innovations. The murder of the duc de Berry in 1820 at the Paris Opera led to the demolition of the building at the demand of the archbishop of Paris, who had administered the last rites to the royal heir in the theater. The company was temporarily housed in the Salle Favart, then moved to the rue le Pelletier. This theater became a center of social and artistic life in the age of Balzac, Baudelaire, Daumier, and Degas.

Nineteenth Century. Under the Restoration, the designer Pierre Ciceri promoted the use of gas lighting and created highly original sets, often in the "troubadour" style. Official disapproval of the revealing costumes and sometimes promiscuous subculture of the ballet hindered its development. The school, however, maintained its high standards. Notable pupils included August Bournonville and Jules Perrot; among the female dancers were the sprightly Lise Noblet, who created the role of Fenella in Daniel Auber's opera *La Muette de Portici,* and Amélie Legallois.

For a time male dancing retained its prestige, thanks to the virtuosic Paul and the majestic Albert, who staged a notable *Cendrillon* (1823), based on Charles Perrault's fairy tale. The public, however, complained of a dearth of elegance and taste, and of dreadful pirouettes and too much acrobatic virtuosity, in place of the musicality, grace, and effortlessness of the old French style.

PARIS OPERA BALLET. Lifar's *Blanche-Niege* (Snow White) was mounted in 1951 to showcase the talents of Liane Daydé, who at eighteen was among the youngest *étoiles* of the company in many years. She is seen here being protected from the Queen and her attendants by two good spirits, the Dragonfly and the Firefly. From left to right the dancers are Max Bozzoni, Nina Vyroubova as the Queen, Serge Lifar, Claude Bessy as the Dragonfly, Daydé as Snow White, and Josette Clavier as the Firefly. (Photograph by Baron; used by permission of Camera Press, Ltd., London.)

PARIS OPERA BALLET. The famous *opéra-ballet Les Indes Galantes* (1735), with music by Jean-Philippe Rameau and a libretto by Louis Fuzelier, was revived at the Paris Opera in 1952 by Harald Lander and Maurice Lehmann. Choreography was done by Albert Aveline, Lander, and Serge Lifar, who is pictured here in the second *entrée, Les Incas de Pérou*. The design for this scene was done by Carzou. (Photograph by Roger-Viollet © Lipnitzki-Viollet; used by permission.)

Gardel and Milon were occupied with the school and with opera *divertissements*, so the post of ballet master fell to Aumer, who served from 1820 to 1831. He was content to restage the best of his earlier works, among them *Les Pages du Duc de Vendôme*—a pretext for women to dance in male attire—and *Alfred le Grand*, applauded for its spectacular combats. He also added Dauberval's masterpiece *La Fille Mal Gardée* to the repertory. Aumer's last works, among them *La Somnambule*, benefited from the ingeniously constructed libretti of the playwright Eugène Scribe. Ciceri's painted panorama in *La Belle au Bois Dormant* (The Sleeping Beauty) unfolded laterally to suggest that the dancers were moving through a vast landscape. Pauline Montessu played the title role in *Manon Lescaut*, in which Fromental Halévy used musical leitmotifs for the first time. Other ballets of the period were André Deshayes's *Zémire et Azor*, based on the fairy tale "Beauty and the Beast," and Jean-Baptiste Blache's *Mars et Vénus*.

The mythological stories popular in the preceding century fell out of favor as romanticism began to dominate the arts. Marie Taglioni, who became the symbol of the Romantic-era ballet, made her debut at the Paris Opera in 1827 and immediately demonstrated in secondary roles a fluid grace unequaled by the company's other ballerinas—Julia (de Varennes), Montessu, and Madame Alexis Dupont.

When Louis Philippe became king, the Paris Opera ceased to depend on the royal household and became a subsidized private enterprise. A new director, Louis Véron, set out to attract the newly powerful upper-middle class. According to the poet Heinrich Heine, the Opera "became the paradise of the hard of hearing," for Véron stressed the visual aspects of ballet: staging, complicated scenery, and picturesque or poetic costumes by Paul Lormier or Eugène Lami, which transformed the ballerinas into figures of fantasy. Realizing that foreign stars were an attraction, Véron promoted the meteoric rise of the Italian Taglioni. He offered her a six-year contract at an annual salary of thirty thousand francs, an exceptional amount for that time, and engaged her father Filippo to choreograph ballets for her. These actions overturned the old hierarchy for good and altered the course of the institution. [*See the entry on the Taglioni family*.]

Jean Coralli, whose experience and technical skill exceeded his innovation, served as ballet master from 1831 to 1850. Joseph Mazilier, an excellent mime, was hired, as

PARIS OPERA BALLET. Yvette Chauviré, France's favorite ballerina, as Leucothéa, goddess of the sea, in Lifar's *Nautéos*, revised for the Paris Opera Ballet in 1954. (Photograph by Roger-Viollet © Lipnitzki-Viollet; used by permission.)

was the fabulous virtuoso Jules Perrot, who had earlier appeared in the boulevard theaters. The traditional categorization of dancers (noble, *demi-caractère,* and character) was abolished, along with the practice of dancers' retaining exclusive rights to roles. The school, still free of charge, maintained its international prestige. Patrons had free access to the Foyer de la Danse, an elegant salon frequently described by writers and painters, who contributed to the prevailing view of the female dancers as frivolous. [*See the entries on Coralli, Perrot, and Mazilier.*]

Romanticism at the Paris Opera began with the Ballet of the Nuns, staged by Filippo Taglioni for Giacomo Meyerbeer's opera *Robert le Diable* (1831); according to Fanny Appleton (later Mrs. Henry Wadsworth Longfellow), it was "magnificent and terrific and diabolical and enchanting." The style flowered in Taglioni's *La Sylphide* (1832), which celebrated the irreducible dualism of reality and the supernatural ideal.

Marie Taglioni, who became identified with the role of the Sylphide, was jealous of Perrot, the "male sylph," and her animosity may have provoked his departure from the Paris Opera. She herself had to contend with the seductive Fanny Elssler, who made her Opera debut in 1834 and triumphed in the *cachucha* in Coralli's *Le Diable Boiteux* (1836). A rivalry arose between the two ballerinas despite the difference in their styles, and riots broke out in the auditorium between their admirers. Taglioni left the Opera in 1837 when her contract was not renewed by the new director, Henri Duponchel. Elssler, who displayed her gift for character dancing performing the *cracovienne*—one of her great solos—in Mazilier's *La Gipsy* (1839) and the tarantella in Coralli's *La Tarentule,* was vexed by the hostility of certain critics; in 1840 she broke her contract and left for the United States. [*See the entry on the Elssler sisters.*]

Elssler's abrupt departure set a precedent for other French dancers, many of whom, such as Pauline Duvernay, went on to triumph in London. At the Paris Opera, foreign stars were preferred to French dancers, who were poorly paid and officially subordinated to the foreigners. Perrot, the most gifted French male dancer of the day, attempted to return to the Paris Opera by introducing the Italian ballerina Carlotta Grisi, for whom he and Coralli staged *Giselle* (1841). One of the masterworks of the Romantic era, this ballet was nevertheless dropped from the Opera's repertory between 1868 and 1924.

The elegant Lucien Petipa, the last representative of the noble school of male dancing, eclipsed his contemporaries Eugène Coralli and Auguste Mabille. He continued to uphold male dancing in the face of critical condemnation by Théophile Gautier and Jules Janin.

Gautier's scenario for *La Péri,* choreographed by Coralli in 1843, was dedicated to Grisi, who played the title role. Mazilier also exploited Grisi's technique and comedic skill in *Le Diable à Quatre* and *Paquita.* Pointe work, developed in Milan, gradually came to dominate the fluid French style, with *tours de force* displacing poetic grace. The Opera lost Perrot after *La Filleule des Fées* (1849), in which, as Gautier noted, "everything between the footlights and the backdrop dances." After Perrot's departure, the Opera failed to attract gifted choreographers.

PARIS OPERA BALLET. Claude Bessy and George Skibine in the title roles of Skibine's version of *Daphnis et Chloë,* given its premiere in May 1959. Sets and costumes were designed by Marc Chagall for an earlier production by Lifar. (Photograph by Roger-Viollet © Lipnitzki-Viollet; used by permission.)

Nevertheless, during the Second Empire the Paris Opera remained the heart of European ballet, owing largely to its school and to the ingenuity and dynamism of Arthur Saint-Léon, ballet master from 1850 to 1853, who combined the talents of dancer, choreographer, violinist, and impresario. He introduced the Neapolitan ballerina Fanny Cerrito, whose performances in *La Vivandière* and other ballets adroitly exploited the rage for national social dances such as the *redowa.* Cerrito herself choreographed *Gemma* (1854), with a libretto by Gautier. [*See the entries on Cerrito and Saint-Léon.*]

Mazilier, a competent craftsman, served as ballet master from 1853 to 1859. He preferred melodramatic subjects with surprising plot turns and elaborate decor and machinery. He showed off Carolina Rosati's fiery temperament in *Le Corsaire,* inspired by Byron's poem; the production included a spectacular shipwreck. In *Marco Spada,* Mazilier contrasted Rosati's sensuality with the lightness of Amalia Ferraris.

PARIS OPERA BALLET. In January 1972, Pierre Lacotte presented his reconstruction of Filippo Taglioni's 1832 masterpiece *La Sylphide* on French television, with Ghislaine Thesmar in the title role. So great was her personal success that she was invited to join *les étoiles* of the Paris Opera Ballet. She is seen here in a subsequent performance with Rudolf Nureyev as James. (Photograph by Colette Masson; used by permission of Agence Enguerand/Iliade, Paris.)

Ferraris also danced in *Sacountala* (1858), choreographed by Lucien Petipa, who lifted his ethereal partner with only one arm. He was, however, somewhat sterile as ballet master, a post he held between 1860 and 1868. In *Le Marché des Innocents* (1862) he collaborated with his brother Marius, who, like Saint-Léon and Perrot, chose to work in Saint Petersburg.

With the debut of the young Emma Livry in *La Sylphide* (1858), the romantic lyricism of the French school took on new life. Despite an unprepossessing appearance, Livry proved to be the heir of Marie Taglioni, who choreographed *Le Papillon* (1860) for her. Livry, however, was severely burned when her costume caught fire during a rehearsal, and her premature death signaled the end of Romantic ballet at the Opera. [*See the entry on* Livry.]

The director Émile Perrin regularly called upon the talents of Saint-Léon, who choreographed works for ballerinas from all over Europe. Although these included the Italian virtuosos Amina Boschetti and Guglielmina Salvioni, Parisian audiences preferred the Russian Marfa Muravieva, who created the title roles of Saint-Léon's *Diavolina* and *Néméa* and danced in Lucien Petipa's revival of *Giselle. Néméa* also called attention to the statuesque beauty of Eugénie Fiocre, who modeled for Degas and Jean-Baptiste Carpeaux. The German dancer Adèle Grantzow ensured the triumph of the French style in Saint-Léon's *La Source.* His *Coppélia* (1870) was the last international masterpiece of the nineteenth century to premiere at the Opera; symbolically, the role of Franz was danced in male costume by Fiocre. The conscientious Louis Mérante, after a long career as a dancer, served as ballet master from 1869 to 1887, representing a transitional figure.

The defeat of France in the Franco-Prussian War of 1870–1871 marked the end of an era, and the company then stagnated for more than fifty years. The Salle le Pelletier burned down in 1873, and the Opera moved first to the Salle Ventadour and then in 1875 to the Palais Garnier, its thirteenth and present home.

Although there were fine French dancers, such as Léontine Beaugrand and Laure Fonta, the director Olivier Halanzier preferred the acrobatic virtuosity of the Milanese Rita Sangalli, who created the title role in Mérante's *Sylvia.* Opera *divertissements* increasingly crowded out ballet. The troupe continued to be trained by French teachers and was little influenced by the showy brilliance of such Italian guest stars as Antonietta Dell'Era and Virginia Zucchi. Rosita Mauri, whose mastery and brilliance were noticed by Charles Gounod in Milan, triumphed in Mérante's ballet *La Korrigane,* in which she played a peasant in wooden shoes. André Messager composed the score for *Les Deux Pigeons* (1886), Mérante's last work for Mauri.

The austere *régisseur* Édouard Pluque had only female dancers to direct, some of whom danced male roles; the only remaining male soloist of note was Michel Vasquez. A deputy even proposed to parlement that male dancers be banned. The director Pedro Gailhard, a former singer, preferred opera to ballet; the latter was entrusted to the Belgian Joseph Hansen, ballet master between 1887 and 1907 and choreographer of the mediocre *La Maladetta.*

Mauri was succeeded by Carlotta Zambelli, who quickly developed into a dazzling star. She dominated the company; in 1901 she refused to leave it for the Maryinsky. In 1908 the new administrators, Messager and André Broussan, appointed as ballet master Léo Staats, who created *Javotte* and *Espana.* The guest stars Matilda Kshessinska, Olga Preobrajenska, and Nikolai Legat were eclipsed by

Madame Stichel's *La Fête chez Thérèse,* created for Zambelli and the Milanese ballerina Aïda Boni.

Twentieth Century. The triumph of Serge Diaghilev's Ballets Russes on the Paris Opera's stage in 1910 led to the hiring of the Moscow ballet master Ivan Clustine, whose *Suite de Danses* (1913) remained in the repertory for a long time. Clustine began to bring back notable male dancers, particularly Gustave Ricaux and the classical Albert Aveline, who regularly partnered Zambelli. In 1912 the dancers' union threatened a strike and received new contracts that provided for higher salaries. [*See the entry on Clustine.*]

The 1914 summer season began with another appearance by the Ballets Russes, the only foreign company to dance at the Paris Opera at this time. Jacques Rouché, a patron of the arts, inaugurated an exemplary management system that survived two world wars. In thirty years he reformed French ballet and gradually restored it to international importance. He entrusted to Staats Stravinsky's *Les Abeilles,* and to Nicola Guerra *Castor et Pollux,* a brilliant homage to Rameau. Guerra also created *La Tragédie de Salomé,* with Boni and Anna Johansson in leading roles.

Anxious to open the ballet to new ideas, Rouché introduced Dalcrozian eurythmics in a short-lived experiment illustrated by *La Petite Suite* (1922). Under the firm guidance of Mauri, Zambelli, and Staats, the company again submitted to Italian influence, despite the appearances of the Russian guest artists Michel and Vera Fokine and Anna Pavlova. Maurice Brillant wrote that Zambelli excelled in the "exquisite embroidery" of the "Pizzicato Polka" in *Sylvia* and in Staats's *Cydalise et le Chèvrepied.* Staats also staged the Cambodian-inspired *Siang-Sin* for Camille Bos and Serge Peretti. The poetic Olga Spessivtseva danced in Nicholas Sergeyev's revival of *Giselle* (1924) and in Bronislava Nijinska's *Les Rencontres.* Nijinska also conceived the comical *Impressions de Music-hall* (1927), the last role originated by Zambelli. Despite great efforts and such prestigious guest stars as Ida Rubinstein and Carina Ari, the Paris Opera Ballet was unable to compete with its brilliant Russian and Swedish rivals. It remained a prisoner of bureaucracy, trying to find its identity between a monotonous routine and intermittent experimentalism.

The death of Diaghilev was a signal for renewal, beginning with the gripping *Les Créatures de Prométhée* (1929), choreographed by Serge Lifar, who also danced its principal role. Hired and supported by Rouché despite the reservations of such traditionalists as Zambelli, Aveline, and Ricaux, Lifar (whom André Levinson called a "sublime troublemaker") galvanized the stagnant troupe. As a choreographic apprentice, he defended the classical masterpieces, which he danced with Spessivtseva. He initiated reforms such as turning out the lights in the auditorium during performances and banning patrons from rehearsals in the Foyer de la Danse. He also began to devote entire evenings to dance, presenting new works such as *La Vie de Polichinelle, Salade,* and the innovative *Icare.* [*See* Icare *and the entry on* Lifar.]

Giselle was danced by the Soviet guest artist Marina Semenova. She was followed in the role by the French dancer Lycette Darsonval, who achieved the rank of *étoile (prima ballerina)* with her performance in Lifar's *Oriane et le Prince d'Amour* (1938). Aveline's *Le Festin de l'Araignée* was dominated by the maleficent presence of Suzanne Lorcia. Solange Schwarz (a lively Swanilda in *Coppélia*), Lorcia, Ari, and the talented young Yvette Chauviré found appealing roles in Lifar's great heroic ballets, such as *David Triomphant* and *Alexandre le Grand.* Lifar's *Entre Deux Rondes,* the only creation of the 1939/40 season, won the rank of *étoile* for the scintillating Schwarz.

PARIS OPERA BALLET. Nanon Thibon in a 1977 revival of Lifar's *Phèdre,* first performed at the Paris Opera in 1950. A perennial favorite with French audiences, *Phèdre* was set to the music of Georges Auric and a libretto by Jean Cocteau, who also designed the scenery and costumes. (Photograph by Colette Masson; used by permission of Agence Enguerand/Iliade, Paris.)

Under the German occupation of World War II, Rouché and Lifar defended the independence and prestige of French ballet, for which nationalist pride lent some of its most brilliant hours. Chauviré—a powerful Istar in the ballet of the same title—and Peretti were raised to the rank of *étoile.* The company triumphed in Lifar's sharply contrasting works, which included the medieval fresco *Joan de Zarissa;* the witty *Animaux Modèles,* based on the fables of Jean de La Fontaine; and the plotless display piece *Suite en Blanc.* Among the dancers were the promising newcomers Roland Petit, Roger Fenonjois, and Michel Renault.

After World War II, the dazzling reign of Rouché ended when he was dismissed, along with Lifar, because of accusations of collaboration with the Nazis. The truncated troupe and repertory survived the administrations of Maurice Lehmann and Georges Hirsch, but one member after another resigned. As a remedy, George Balanchine was invited to be guest choreographer, with Tamara Toumanova and Maria Tallchief as guest artists. His ballet *Palais de Cristal* (1947), created for the company, revealed the talents of Renault and Alexandre Kalioujny.

Recalled by public and company demand, Lifar returned as ballet master from 1947 to 1958. Chauviré, Renault, Madeleine Lafon, and Micheline Bardin created leading roles in his masterpiece *Les Mirages.* The repertory was enriched with revivals of Fokine's ballets, notably *Schéhérazade,* which displayed Kalioujny's feline quality. Aveline staged *La Grande Jatte* for Darsonval and Renault, while Lifar's ballets showed off the talents of Pierre Lacotte, Claude Bessy, and Jean-Paul Andréani. Toumanova danced the title role in *Phèdre,* one of Lifar's most impressive works. The lyrical Nina Vyroubova, who danced both the classics and Lifar's works with superb mastery, led Lifar's *Dramma per Musica* to music by Bach. The fairy tale *Blanche-neige* (Snow White), danced by the delicate Liane Daydé, was surpassed by Lifar's lively *Fourberies,* inspired by Molière. Partnered by the romantic Youly Algaroff, Vyroubova danced the title role in Lifar's version of *The Firebird* and the role of the fiancée in *Les Noces Fantastiques,* in which she stole Peter van Dyk, as the captain, from Bessy's sensual Oceanides.

Harald Lander, engaged as a choreographer in 1952, contributed to the brilliant revival of *Les Indes Galantes;* he also created the perennially popular showpiece *Études* and *Qaartsiluni,* inspired by an Inuit (Eskimo) ritual. The choreographer John Cranko gave Chauviré the seductive title role of *La Belle Hélène;* she later played the nereid Leucothéa in Lifar's *Nautéos.* Lifar's *Variations* and *Grand Pas* displayed the talents of Andréani and Christiane Vaussard, who danced with Algaroff in a revival of Léonide Massine's *Symphonie Fantastique.* Van Dyk, Josette Amiel, and Claire Motte lent fervor and conviction to Lifar's *Chemin de Lumière.*

After Lifar resigned, the company suffered from a lack of firm direction, and several principal dancers departed. Lifar was replaced by George Skibine, who in turn was followed by a series of administrators, including A.-M. Julien, Georges Auric, and Rolf Liebermann. Despite frequent union disputes, plans for reform produced no results. No choreographers of great ability were engaged. Although the dancers achieved some stability and perma-

PARIS OPERA BALLET. Louis Mérante's *Sylvia* was a staple of the repertory of the Paris Opera Ballet for many years after its debut in June 1876. Although it was eventually dropped from the repertory, it was revived in 1919 by Léo Staats. A new version was choreographed in 1941 by Serge Lifar. Lycette Darsonval revived Lifar's version in 1979, with Noëlla Pontois in the title role and Jean-Yves Lormeau as Aminta. (Photograph by Daniel Cande; from the Dance Collection, New York Public Library for the Performing Arts.)

PARIS OPERA BALLET. Rudolf Nureyev, who served as artistic director of the company from 1983 until 1989, staged a full-length version of *Raymonda* in 1983. Florence Clerc as Raymonda and Charles Jude as Jean de Brienne are pictured here in a 1988 performance. (Photograph by Colette Masson; used by permission of Agence Enguerand/Iliade, Paris.)

nence, they had to deal with profound differences in choreographic styles. Guest choreographers demanded docility and flexibility, sometimes impeding the Paris Opera's efforts to develop its own style.

In 1960 Gene Kelly staged *Pas des Dieux,* to music by George Gershwin, for Claude Bessy and Attilio Labis; Tatjana Gsovsky created *La Dame aux Camélias* for Chauviré; and Vladimir Burmeister mounted *Swan Lake* for Amiel and van Dyk, who were succeeded by numerous other stars. Michel Descombey, ballet master from 1962 to 1969, staged his version of *Symphonie Concertante,* but he was unable to compete with such prestigious guest choreographers as Balanchine, who staged *The Four Temperaments* and *Concerto Barocco.* Maurice Béjart's works, among them *Le Sacre du Printemps, Les Noces,* and *Webern Opus V,* featured attractive performers such as Cyril Atanassoff, Jacqueline Rayet, Jean-Pierre Bonnefous, and Wilfride Piollet. Petit staged *Notre-Dame de Paris* for Motte, and *Paradis Perdu* for guest artists Margot Fonteyn and Rudolf Nureyev. In 1968 he choreographed *Turangalîla* for the promising young male dancer Georges Piletta.

Although Béjart and Petit were both logical choices for the position of ballet master, neither would accept the post, which was entrusted in turn to John Taras, Claude Bessy, Raymond Franchetti, Violette Verdy, Rosella Hightower, and Rudolf Nureyev. Although the policy of stylistic diversity continued, the troupe made spectacular progress, achieving a high technical level and producing international stars such as Noëlla Pontois, Ghislaine Thesmar, Dominique Khalfouni, Michaël Denard, Jean Guizerix, Charles Jude, and Patrick Dupond. Guest performers in recent decades have included Ekaterina Maximova, Alicia Alonso, Natalia Makarova, Suzanne Farrell, Jorge Donn, Maya Plisetskaya, Vladimir Vasiliev, Mikhail Baryshnikov, Peter Martins, and Peter Schaufuss.

Despite two programs mounted in homage to Lifar, most of his ballets have now disappeared from the repertory, replaced by works by Lacotte, Béjart, Petit, Balanchine, Robbins, Yuri Grigorovich, John Neumeier, Glen Tetley, Oscar Araiz, John Butler, Merce Cunningham, Alwin Nikolais, and Alvin Ailey. In 1983 the troupe numbered 159 dancers, including seventeen *étoiles*—a promising foundation for the future, especially since the distribution of roles is no longer determined by hierarchy.

PARIS OPERA BALLET. Patrick Dupond succeeded Nureyev as artistic director of the Paris Opera Ballet. At a Gala de l'Opéra de Paris in October 1990, he appeared with Dominique Khalfouni in Roland Petit's *L'Arlésienne.* (Photograph by Colette Masson; used by permission of Agence Enguerand/Iliade, Paris.)

Occasionally the troupe was now divided, part of it dancing in Paris while the other danced abroad or in other French cities.

Within the orbit of the Paris Opera, the Salle Favart or Opéra-Comique has often served as a testing ground for new ballets. Among the choreographers who have worked there are Robert Quinault, Constantin Tcherkas, Jean-Jacques Etchévery, and Janine Charrat. The Opéra-Comique first produced Flemming Flindt's *La Leçon,* a frequently revived ballet based on Eugene Ionesco's play about a professor who murders his pupil. In recent years it has presented innovative works by Milko Šparemblek, Joseph Lazzini, Carolyn Carlson, and Moses Pendleton.

Since 1970 the Paris Opera Ballet has opened itself to modern dance by founding two groups in which principals and soloists voluntarily participated. Carolyn Carlson impressed her visionary personality on the Groupe de Recherche Théâtrale de l'Opéra (GRTOP), which was active from 1974 to 1980, producing works such as *Densité 21,5* and *Wind, Water, Sand.* In 1981 Jacques Garnier, a product of the Opera, founded the Groupe de Recherche de l'Opéra de Paris (GRCOP), which has presented works by Garnier, Maguy Marin, Merce Cunningham, Douglas Dunn, Dominique Bagouet, Ulysses Dove, William Forsythe, Karole Armitage, and Louis Falco. The GRCOP was suspended in 1989; some of its dancers remained in the Opera Ballet, but other members of the company worked in contemporary style as well as the classical repertory. For some years the Palais Garnier was reserved almost exclusively for dance, with *Swan Lake* given for the first time in July 1992 at the new Opera Bastille. They stayed there during the Palais Garnier's renovation (1994–1996). The company now appears most often at Garnier, but from time to time at the Bastille Opera. Dance director Patrick Dupond (1989–1994) and then Brigitte Lefèvre (1995) were assisted by Patrice Bart and Eugène Polyakov. Company stars included Monique Loudières, Elisabeth Platel, Isabelle Guérin, Marie-Claude Piétragalla, Elisabeth Maurin, Fanny Gaïda, Laurent Hilaire, Patrick Dupond, Charles Jude, Kader Belarbi, Manuel Legris, Jean-Yves Lormeau, Nicolas Le Riche; departed

PARIS OPERA BALLET. The female ensemble in the Kingdom of the Shades scene in *La Bayadère,* staged in three acts for the company by Rudolf Nureyev and Ninel Kurgapkina in 1992. This work was Nureyev's last artistic endeavor before his death. (Photograph by Colette Masson; used by permission of Agence Enguerand/ Iliade, Paris.)

members Sylvie Guillem and Eric Vu-An were invited back as guests. The soloists of the corps de ballet had skills varied enough to suit such disparate works as those of Balanchine, Petipa-Nureyev, Jerome Robbins, Béjart, Roland Petit, Massine, Lifar, Neumeier, Forsythe, Jiří Kylián, Mats Ek, Twyla Tharp, Kenneth MacMillan, Anthony Tudor, Nijinsky, Nijinska, Lar Lubovitch, Paul Taylor, Martha Graham, Louis Falco, Preljocaj, and Maguy Marin. Never had the choreographic activity been more intense nor the standard of technique and artistry higher than the 1990s.

This vitality owed much to the preparatory work of the company school, almost three hundred years old. In October 1987 it moved to a new building designed for it in Nanterre. Only ten minutes from the Opera, it contains eleven studios, an auditorium seating three hundred, a video room, and a discothèque. At the time of the move, ninety-seven children were lodged at the school during the week. Instruction is free. The pupils attend academic classes in an adjoining building for half the day. In the afternoons, the six divisions study classical dance, music, dance history, folklore, and other relevant subjects. Upon completion of the course some enter the corps de ballet of the Opera; others are engaged by French and foreign companies.

Its long existence and its diversity have given the Paris Opera Ballet an incomparably rich history. It has experienced glory and eclipse, discipline and turmoil. As an official institution, it receives financial support from the government but is also subject to political interference. The company has once again achieved mastery of its art and now ranks among the leading companies of the world. It still seeks an identity that will reflect its origin and the historical brilliance of the French school.

[*For related discussion, see* Ballet Technique, History of, *article on* French Court Dance; *and* France, *articles on theatrical dance.*]

BIBLIOGRAPHY

Algarotti, Francesco. *Saggio sopra l'opera in musica.* N.p., 1755.

Amelot. *Mémoires pour servir à l'histoire de l'Académie Royale de Musique depuis 1663 jusqu'à 1778.* N.p.,n.d. Paris Opéra, Library.

Baron, Auguste A. F. *Lettres à Sophie sur la danse.* Paris, 1825.

Beauchamps, Pierre. *Recherches sur les théâtres de France.* 3 vols. Paris, 1735.

Berchoux, Joseph de. *La danse, ou, La guerre des dieux de l'opéra.* 2d ed. Paris, 1808.

Boccadoro, Patricia. "From Lifar to Nureyev." *The Dancing Times* (September 1995): 1155–1159.

Boccadoro, Patricia. "Nureyev: The Story of the Paris Opéra Ballet, Part 3, 1983–1991." *The Dancing Times* (October 1995): 42–47.

Bonet de Treiches. *De l'Opéra en l'an XII.* Paris, 1803.

Bonnet, Jacques. *Histoire générale de la danse, sacrée et profane.* Paris, 1723.

Bourgade, Yves. "Fifty Years of Opera Ballet and Its Audiences." *Choreography and Dance* 2.1 (1992): 29–34.

Brillant, Maurice. *Problèmes de la danse.* Paris, 1952.

Cahusac, Louis de. *La danse ancienne et moderne, ou, Traité historique de la danse.* 3 vols. La Haye, 1754.

Campardon, Émile. *L'Académie Royale de Musique au XVIIIe siècle.* 2 vols. Paris, 1884.

Castil-Blaze. *L'Académie Impériale de Musique.* 2 vols. Paris, 1855.

Chapman, John V. "The Paris Opéra Ballet School, 1798–1827." *Dance Chronicle* 12.2 (1989): 196–220.

Chazin-Bennahum, Judith. *Dance in the Shadow of the Guillotine.* Carbondale, Ill., 1988.

Christout, Marie-Françoise. "Le ballet en France." In *Encyclopédie du théâtre contemporain.* Paris, 1957.

Christout, Marie-Françoise. "Lifar et le ballet." In *Encyclopédie du théâtre contemporain.* Paris, 1957.

Christout, Marie-Françoise. *Le merveilleux et le théâtre du silence.* Paris, 1965.

Christout, Marie-Françoise. *Histoire du ballet.* 2d ed., rev. Paris, 1975.

Christout, Marie-Françoise. "The Paris Opéra Ballet." *Dance Chronicle* 2.2 (1978): 131–142.

Christout, Marie-Françoise. *Le ballet occidental, XVIe–XXe siècle.* Paris, 1995.

Cochin, C. N. *Lettres sur l'Opéra.* Paris, 1781.

Coeyman, Barbara. "Theatres for Opera and Ballet during the Reigns of Louis XIV and Louis XV." *Early Music* 18 (February 1990): 22–37.

Des Essarts, Nicolas T. L. *Les trois théâtres de Paris.* Paris, 1777.

Deshayes, André. *Idées générales sur l'Académie Royale de Musique.* Paris, 1822.

Despois, Eugène. *La théâtre français sous Louis XIV.* 2d ed. Paris, 1882.

Dorat, Claude Joseph. *Collection complètes des oeuvres,* vol. 5, *Théâtre.* Neuchatel, 1775–.

Du Fayl, Ezvar. *Académie Nationale de Musique, 1671–1877.* Paris, 1878.

Fay, Anthony. "The Paris Opéra Ballet: New York, 1948." *Ballet Review* 21 (Summer 1993): 88–92.

Garafola, Lynn. "Forgotten Interlude: Eurythmic Dancers at the Paris Opéra." *Dance Research* 13 (Summer 1995): 59–83.

Gautier, Théophile. *Histoire de l'art dramatique en France depuis vingt-cinq ans.* 6 vols. Leipzig, 1858–1859.

Guest, Ivor. *The Ballet of the Second Empire, 1858–1870.* London, 1953.

Guest, Ivor. *The Ballet of the Second Empire, 1847–1858.* London, 1955.

Guest, Ivor. *Le ballet de l'Opéra de Paris.* Paris, 1976.

Guest, Ivor. *The Romantic Ballet in Paris.* 2d rev. ed. London, 1980.

Guest, Ivor. "The Paris Opera Ballet: Its Historical Tradition." *The Dancing Times* (July 1982): 733–736.

Hilton, Wendy. *Dance of Court and Theatre: The French Noble Style, 1690–1725.* Princeton, 1981.

Jullien, Adolphe. *L'opéra secret au XVIIIe siècle.* Paris, 1880.

Jullien, Adolphe. *L'opéra sous l'ancien régime.* Paris, 1880.

La Gorce, Jérôme de. *L'Opéra à Paris au temps de Louis XIV: Histoire d'un théâtre.* Paris, 1992.

Lajarte, Théodore de. *Bibliothèque musicale du Théâtre de l'Opéra.* 2 vols. Paris, 1878.

Laurent, Jean, and Julie Sazonova. *Serge Lifar, rénovateur du ballet français.* Paris, 1960.

Levinson, André. *La danse au théâtre.* Paris, 1924.

Levinson, André. *Les visages de la danse.* Paris, 1933.

Levinson, André. *Serge Lifar, destin d'un danseur.* Paris, 1934.

Lifar, Serge. *La danse.* Paris, 1938.

Lifar, Serge. *Traité de danse académique.* Paris, 1950.

Lifar, Serge. *Traité de chorégraphie.* Paris, 1952.

Longfellow, Fanny. *Selected Letters and Journals.* Edited by Edward Wagenknecht. New York, 1956.

Mason, Francis. "The Paris Opéra: A Conversation with Violette Verdy." *Ballet Review* 14 (Fall 1986): 23–30.

Noverre, Jean-Georges. *Lettres sur les arts imitateurs en général et sur la danse en particulier.* 2 vols. Paris, 1807. Edited by Fernand Divoire as *Lettres sur la danse et les arts imitateurs* (Paris, 1952).

Parfaict, François, and Claude Parfaict. *Histoire de l'Académie Royale de Musique.* N.p., 1741. Manuscript located in Paris, Bibliothèque Nationale, nouv. acq. fr.6532.

Pitou, Spire. *The Paris Opéra: An Encyclopedia of Operas, Ballets, Composers, and Performers.* Westport, Conn., 1983–.

Prod'homme, J. G. *L'Opéra, 1669–1926.* Paris, 1925.

Raguenet, François. *Paralèle des Italiens et des François, en ce qui regarde la musique et les opéra.* Paris, 1702. English translation by J. E. Galliard (1709) published in *Source Readings in Music History,* edited by Oliver Strunk (New York, 1950).

Rémond de Saint-Mard, Toussaint. *Réflexions sur l'opéra.* Le Haye, 1741.

Riccoboni, Luigi. *Réflexions historiques et critiques sur les différens théâtres de l'Europe.* Paris, 1738.

Rouché, Jacques. *De l'art théâtral moderne.* Paris, 1910.

Sadler, Graham. "The Paris Opera Dancers in Rameau's Day." In *Jean-Philippe Rameau: Colloque international, Dijon, 21–24 septembre 1983,* edited by Jérôme de La Gorce. Paris, 1987.

Saint-Léon, Arthur. *De l'état actuel de la danse.* Lisbon, 1856.

Sazonova, Julie. *La vie de la danse.* Paris, 1937.

Vaillat, Léandre. *Ballets de l'Opéra de Paris (ballets dans les opéras—nouveaux ballets).* Paris, 1947.

Winter, Marian Hannah. *The Pre-Romantic Ballet.* London, 1974.

MARIE-FRANÇOISE CHRISTOUT
Translated from French

PARK, MERLE (born 8 October 1937 in Salisbury, Rhodesia), dancer and teacher. Park began her ballet training with Betty Lamb in Rhodesia and in 1951 went to England, where she studied at the Elmhurst School for three years. In 1954, after only six months of study at the Royal Ballet School, she joined the company and made her debut as a mouse in Carabosse's train in *The Sleeping Beauty.* Although still in the corps, from 1955 she danced numerous solo roles, including a carefree Milkmaid in *Façade* and a sparkling Bluebird pas de deux.

PARK. As Princess Aurora in the 1981 Royal Ballet production of *The Sleeping Beauty,* partnered by Wayne Eagling as Prince Florimund. (Photograph © 1981 by Zoë Dominic; used by permission.)

Her small, light frame and fleet, sunny style made her a natural soubrette, as was seen in her first Swanilda in 1958. She was promoted to principal in 1959, becoming ever more confident in *La Fille Mal Gardée, The Sleeping Beauty,* and the sweet romance of *The Two Pigeons.* Ever more accomplished, she textured her vivacity with emotional details to portray Giselle, Cinderella, and Titania in *The Dream* and danced her first *Swan Lake* in 1973. In *Symphonic Variations* and as Nikia in *La Bayadère,* her musicality and classical precision glistened, while her Kate in John Cranko's *The Taming of the Shrew* twinkled with roguish humor.

Inspired to highly dramatic performances by modern dramas such as *Romeo and Juliet* and *Manon* and by dynamic partners such as Rudolf Nureyev, Anthony Dowell, Mikhail Baryshnikov, and David Wall, she also created the unearthly Celestial in Antony Tudor's *Shadowplay* and the child-woman Clara in Nureyev's *The Nutcracker.* Capping her multifaceted career with a theatrical triumph, Park created the Countess Marie Larish in Kenneth MacMillan's *Mayerling* (1978) and the title role in his *Isadora* (1981). She was named a Commander of the Order of the British Empire in 1974, opened her own school in 1977, and in 1983, while still the senior ballerina of the Royal Ballet, became director of the Royal Ballet School. She was honored with the title of Dame Commander of the Order of the British Empire in 1986.

BIBLIOGRAPHY

Crickmay, Anthony, and P. W. Manchester. *Merle Park.* Brooklyn, 1976.

Ferguson, Ian. "A New Role." *Dance and Dancers* (April 1983): 37.

Gruen, John. *The Private World of Ballet.* New York, 1975.

BARBARA NEWMAN

PARLIĆ, DIMITRIJE (born 23 October 1919 in Salonika, Greece, died 21 September 1986 in Belgrade), Yugoslav choreographer and director. Parlić began his career as a dancer and later was a soloist in the ballet of the National Theater in Belgrade. As a student in the Acting and Ballet Department of the Academy of Music in Belgrade, he displayed a talent for directing. He began working as a choreographer after World War II. Until 1972 he was the director of the National Theater Ballet several times and was director of the State Opera Ballet in Vienna (1958–1962) and of the Rome Opera Ballet (1962–1964). He was a guest choreographer in Helsinki, Amsterdam, Brussels, Milan, Nice, Monte Carlo, Trieste, and Birmingham, Alabama, where he staged the ballets he had choreographed in Belgrade. For many years he was a choreographer of the ballets at the festival in Bregenz, Austria.

Parlić staged some forty ballets, performed numerous times in theaters in Yugoslavia by the ballet companies of Zagreb, Ljubljana, Skopje, and Sarajevo and abroad. His choreography for *Romeo and Juliet* has been performed since 1949 at the National Theater in Belgrade, and his *Swan Lake* has been performed since 1970 at the same theater. His *Anna Karenina* has had more than one hundred performances.

Parlić was also interested in Yugoslav musical works, using them with varied success, but always in an interesting way. In addition to staging *The Gingerbread Heart* (1951) and *The Legend of Ochrid* (1966), which were already Yugoslav favorites, he choreographed *The Chinese Story* (1954) to music by Kresimir Baranović in 1955. His choreography ranged from the situation comedy of mistaken identities in *La Reine des Îles* (1956) to the depiction of a destructive passion that leads a woman to commit a series of murders in *Katerina Ismailova 77* (the number marks not only the year of the premiere, but also the ballet's modern approach to a nineteenth-century story). Parlić's works are characterized by exceptional choreographic and directing skill; by the employment of classical, neoclassical, and contemporary ballet vocabularies; by his striving after new forms of expression; and by his ability to draw out a work's hidden potential.

BIBLIOGRAPHY

Maynard, Olga. "The Dance in Yugoslavia." *Dance Magazine* (May 1977): 67–82.

Luijdjens, Adriaan H. "Il balletto del Teatro Nazionale di Belgrado." *Balletto* 1 (November 1955): 55–63.

One Hundred Years of Belgrade's National Theater, 1868–1968 (in Serbo-Croatian). Belgrade, 1968.

Veljkovic, Moran. "*Anna Karenina:* Parlic's Belgrade Version." *Dance Magazine* (September 1973): 64–66.

White Book about Opera. Belgrade, 1970.

MILICA JOVANOVIĆ

PARNELL, FELIKS (Feliks Grzybek; born 13 December 1898 in Warsaw, died 4 April 1980 in Łódź), Polish dancer, choreographer, and ballet director. Parnell trained at the Warsaw Ballet School. From 1915 to 1921 he was a principal dancer in Odessa; he also began choreographing and toured throughout Russia. From 1921 to 1927 and from 1931 to 1934 he danced and choreographed in Warsaw for operettas, revues, and cabaret shows. He was a principal dancer and choreographer for the Warsaw Ballet from 1927 to 1930.

In 1935 Parnell founded his own company, known in Poland as Parnell's Ballet and abroad as the Polish Ballet of Parnell. Until 1939 he toured with it in Poland and the rest of Europe, presenting his own stylized versions of Polish national and folk dances. The company won first prize at the 1936 Olympic Games in Berlin. After World War II, Parnell re-formed the group and toured from 1945 to 1949. He later choreographed for various companies in Warsaw, Wrocław, and Poznań. In 1956 he settled in Łódź, where he led a company until retiring in 1965.

Parnell was an outstanding dancer who defied classification. Early in his career he invented his own technique, based on classical ballet, modern dance, and gymnastics, which he used in all his choreography. His fine physique, acting ability, and spontaneous personality immediately engaged audiences. He always performed in his own choreographies, utilizing his dramatic talent; without his presence, his works tended to lose character and expression.

As a choreographer Parnell displayed inexhaustible imagination in seeking new theatrical forms and creating movements. He had successes with large-scale productions such as *Syrena* (1928, music by Witold Maliszewski), *Boruta* (1930, music by Maliszewski), *Pan Twardowski* (1935), *The Fountain of Bakhchisarai* (1961), and *Coppélia* (1962); his favorite form, however, was the detailed miniature. His choreographic interests were wide, including cabaret, revue, and operetta dances as well as folk, modern, and classical pieces. His most enduring creations were Polish-inspired, including many vivacious, sometimes grotesque miniatures, which were very popular with both Polish and foreign audiences.

BIBLIOGRAPHY

Mamontowicz-Łojek, Bożena. *Terpsychora i lekkie muzy.* Kraków, 1972.

Neuer, Adam, ed. *Polish Opera and Ballet of the Twentieth Century: Operas, Ballets, Pantomimes, Miscellaneous Works.* Translated by Jerzy Zawadzki. Kraków, 1986.

Parnell, Feliks. *Autobiography: Taniec.* Warsaw, 1980.

Pudełek, Janina. "Feliks Parnell." *Teatr,* no. 6 (1980).

Pudełek, Janina. *Two Hundred Years of Polish Ballet, 1785–1985.* Warsaw, 1985.

JANINA PUDEŁEK

PARTNERING is the general dance term used to describe the assistance and support given one dancer (usually female) by another (usually male). Partnering allows the supported dancer greater possibility of movement.

In contemporary usage, the words *adagio* (an Italian word meaning "slowly, softly, smoothly") and *adage* (a companion French and English term) have become shorthand for partnering, which culminates on stage as the art of the pas de deux. Sometimes called "supported adagio," to distinguish them from the solo slow movements that are a traditional part of basic ballet-class center work, partnered moves have become a set part of ballet technique. Dance academies conduct specific classes in which young men and women work together in couples. This is sometimes called "double work"—the coordination of one

PARTNERING. *(top left)* During the 1950s, Soviet ballet productions often featured an acrobatic style of partnering. In *Don Quixote*, Vladimir Vasiliev lifted Ekaterina Maximova overhead, rose to *demi-pointe,* and struck a fully extended arabesque. *(top right)* In Konstantin Boyarsky's *Orpheus,* Valery Panov used brute strength to support Galina Pokryshkina in a graceful position while he remained kneeling. *(bottom left)* In the 1970s in the West, partnering styles were less extravagant. In Rosella Hightower's 1977 staging of *The Sleeping Beauty* for the Stuttgart Ballet, Richard Cragun provided a perfect frame for Marcia Haydée's flowing arabesque. *(directly above)* In a 1976 performance of George Balanchine's *Allegro Brillante* with the New York City Ballet, Peter Martins offered solid security to Suzanne Farrell's flying leap. (Photographs at top left and right from the Dance Collection, New York Public Library for the Performing Arts. Photograph at bottom left © 1977 by Max Waldman; used by permission. Photograph directly above by Martha Swope © Time, Inc.; used by permission; choreography by George Balanchine © The George Balanchine Trust.)

dancer with another through various means of support and manipulation.

Of the coordinated moves that are now traditional, supported pirouettes are among the most basic elements in the vocabulary of partnering. With the added support and centering assistance a partner can give, a dancer can turn more continuously. The coordination usually involves the (male) partner's hands as a steadying and positioning aid to the (female) turning dancer; the cavalier simply keeps his hands lightly on the sides of his ballerina's waist, to give her freedom of movement as well as security of axis. The interplay can involve a slight push by the cavalier to initiate the momentum of the turn. There can also be a further impetus from the cavalier during the turn, whereby he keeps the revolutions continuous by repeatedly pushing the torso around. Because the supported ballerina generally turns on the tiny base of her pointe, well-practiced coordination can yield multiple revolutions far beyond the possibility of unsupported turns.

A standard elaboration of supported turns is a *fouetté*-initiated turn known as a "finger turn." Its name derives from the fact that the ballerina's steadying support comes from grasping one of her partner's fingers held over her head. With only this single point of security, the ballerina is free from contact with her partner. Finger turns are usually given a slight extra impetus when the ballerina uses her free hand to push off from her partner's other hand when the move is initiated. The usual preparation, beyond the unobtrusive push-off of the hand, is a *developpé* into a partial *grand rond de jambe en l'air* for the working leg, which is then whipped into *sur le cou-de-pied* during the turns. Such turns are usually executed *en dehors*. [*See* Ballet Technique, *article on* Turning Movements.]

When a ballerina is turned exclusively by her partner's guidance—that is, without any preparation and momentum of her own—the move is called a promenade. A cavalier can promenade his ballerina using a variety of methods while she maintains a fixed pose. In promenade moves, as in supported pirouettes, the ballerina is usually on pointe, and her cavalier revolves her so the audience can see every angle of the pose she holds. Poses in attitude, arabesque, and *passé* are typical positions the ballerina takes for promenade moves. Revolving a dancer *en promenade* can be stately and calculated: the cavalier stands at arm's length from the ballerina, holding her hand as he walks along the circumference of a circle centered on her pointe. Or, especially for arabesque poses, he can stand close behind her and, with his hands firmly at her waist, revolve her more quickly by inching briskly, but delicately, around in place. The close-in position for such promenades is the standard one with which the cavalier will help secure the ballerina as she descends into a long, deep *arabesque penchée*. Sometimes, the cavalier allows his ballerina greater freedom in such moments by using only one hand to secure her; such one-handed supporting ability lends further drama to the configuration as the *danseur's* nonworking arm can add embellished individuality to his own plastique, as well as complementary designs to those made by the ballerina.

The "fish dive," an acrobatic maneuver ending in a dramatic final pose, is one of the more theatrical routines in the vocabulary of partnering. It is a leap or fall by a ballerina into the position of a *temps de poisson* (fish's movement) in the arms of her partner. Its name is derived from the long, arched position the ballerina holds as she balances horizontally across the thigh of her partner's *demi-plié* leg. With the ballerina's arms and torso usually in a first-arabesque position, the fish is capped by the upthrusting curve she makes by lightly flexing her legs behind her—like a flicked fishtail. Sometimes the *danseur* steadies this pose with one arm around the ballerina's waist, especially when the pose follows multiple *pirouettes en dedans*. The best-known example of the fish is in the diagonal sequence now included in most versions of Marius Petipa's *grand pas de deux* from the last act of *The Sleeping Beauty*. When preceded by a simple lift, the pose can be taken so securely that the *danseur* can extend both arms out and away from his ballerina so that she appears poised mid-dive in front of him. This can be seen as the climactic finish of the same pas de deux.

Whenever a dancer guides another dancer's jump and assists the climax of the trajectory as a held pose, the configuration is called a lift. Like all partnering moves, lifts are a matter of coordination; they do not occur solely from the strength of the cavalier to move the ballerina. Lifts are about timing as much as strength. In a shoulder lift, the ballerina sits on her cavalier's shoulder—usually after preparation with an *assemblé* or other jump.

A lift that might be called a close relative of the fish pose is known as a bird. In this lift, the cavalier holds the ballerina in a horizontal position at arms' length above his head by supporting her at the hip bones. The tail-like image of her lightly flexed, upcurved legs, with her feet together, and the winglike spread of her gently outstretched arms provides the graphic outline that gives the pose its name. In the traditional repertory, this bird-pose lift is usually part of the second act of the Jean Coralli–Jules Perrot *Giselle*. It occurs, usually twice in succession, during the early moments of Albrecht's encounter with Giselle's ghost. The elaboration of this lift, which Coralli put into his 1843 *La Péri* (two years after *Giselle*), gives some indication of how acrobatic partnering developed: Carlotta Grisi dropped from a six-foot platform into the arms of her partner, Lucien Petipa.

The Russian, and especially the Soviet, school of ballet, with its long line of accomplished and very strong male dancers, is greatly responsible for further developing the

PARTNERING. The pas de deux for Nikia and Solor in the Kingdom of the Shades scene in Marius Petipa's *La Bayadère* requires purely classical movements and strictly academic partnering skills. *(above left)* From a kneeling position, Anthony Dowell supports Antoinette Sibley in an *attitude croisé derrière* by placing one hand, out of sight, on her waist. Their arms, heads, and bodies are perfectly positioned in relation to each other. *(above right)* With one hand, Mikhail Baryshnikov supports Natalia Markarova by the tips of her fingers as she balances serenely on pointe and holds her extended leg securely *à la seconde*. *(left)* Donald MacLeary gently supports Svetlana Beriosova at her waist as she executes an *attitude ouvert devant*. His gaze is directed to her face; her arms and her gaze establish a line that leads the viewer's eye to her upraised and turned-out foot, the focal point of the movement. (Photograph above left by Leslie E. Spatt; photograph at left by Zoë Dominic; both used by permission. Photograph directly above from the Dance Collection, New York Public Library for the Performing Arts.)

acrobatic art of the lift. Flying tosses and catches of partners, sometimes after revolving horizontally in the air, and one-armed overhead lifts were among the most astounding features that Soviet ballet troupes, especially from the Bolshoi school in Moscow, displayed to audiences when they first visited the West in the late 1950s.

Although George Balanchine's choreographic work in the West had its roots in an experimental period in the Soviet Union during the early 1920s, his development of partnering did not dwell on lifts but on an exploration of presentation and manipulation. His ballets show extensive variation of the complexities possible in supported adagio work. The andante from his *Divertimento No. 15* (1956), for example, consists of five separate and different duets of elaborate and intricate support. By contrast, in Balanchine's pas de deux in *Agon* (1957), the ballerina is seemingly passive: some of her effects are achieved largely by her partner's manipulation of her limbs.

Jerome Robbins developed a particular interest in the mechanics of the lift and its part in double work. His *Dances at a Gathering* (1969) includes many lifts, as well as a set of varied throws and daring catches. England's Frederick Ashton, in his *Monotones I* (1965) and *Monotones II* (1966), displays his long-standing interest in the art of partnering with two pas de trois: *Monotones I* shows variations for two women supported by one man; *Monotones II* involves designs for two men supporting one woman. One generation after Ashton in Britain, Kenneth MacMillan showed consistent interest in the acrobatic possibilities of partnering, especially through elaborate, convoluted lifts.

Martha Graham, Paul Taylor, and Merce Cunningham each experimented with partnering in the creation of their own personal repertories. All used partnering without fear of exposing its mechanics. Graham made counterbalanced resistance part of her dance drama in duets. Taylor created lyricism out of plainly raw moves. Cunningham developed half-position variables of the full positions of standard partnering. One particular Cunningham work, for eight couples, is simply called *Duets* (1980).

BIBLIOGRAPHY

Clarke, Mary, and Clement Crisp. *The Ballet Goer's Guide.* New York, 1981.

Dolin, Anton. *Pas de Deux: The Art of Partnering.* New York, 1969.

Ellis, Richard, and Christine du Boulay. *Partnering: The Fundamentals of Pas de Deux.* London, 1955. Includes an introduction by Frederic Franklin.

Finkel, Anita. "It Takes Two." *Geo* (June 1983).

Guest, Ivor. *The Romantic Ballet in Paris.* 2d rev. ed. London, 1980.

Hodes, Stuart. "Lust for Lifts." *Ballet Review* (Summer 1984): 67–76.

Migel, Parmenia. *The Ballerinas: From the Court of Louis XIV to Pavlova.* New York, 1972.

Winter, Marian Hannah. *The Pre-Romantic Ballet.* London, 1974.

ROBERT GRESKOVIC

PAS DE DEUX. Literally "a step of two," *pas de deux* traditionally has meant a dance for two people, usually a man and a woman. (A dance for two people of the same sex is more commonly called a duet, and the concept of supported dancing is not necessarily present.) The term *grand pas de deux* refers to a dance with a definite structure devised for a ballerina and her cavalier, usually as the culmination of a nineteenth-century ballet.

In his *Dictionnaire de danse,* Charles Compan defined *pas de deux* as "une entrée dansée par deux . . . acteurs" (Compan, 1787). Early eighteenth-century dance-notation scores for theatrical *entrées* reveal couples usually performing identical movements simultaneously, sometimes holding hands but more often dancing separately and symmetrically. Occasionally, the male dancer would embellish a step with more beats of the legs. A substantial number of notated scores of pas de deux composed by leading dancing masters, such as Louis Pecour, indicate names of performers as well as the operas, ballets, or *opéra-ballets* in which the dances appeared. Thus, partnerships were formed in the eighteenth century, as, for example, Claude Ballon and Marie-Thérèse Subligny. Examples of productions featuring notated pas de deux include *Thésée* and *Persée* (music by Jean-Baptiste Lully) and *L'Europe Galante* and *Les Fêtes Vénitiennes* (music by André Campra).

An early advocate for more dramatic content and expression in pas de deux was John Weaver, whose London ballet-pantomimes, such as *The Loves of Mars and Venus* (1717), developed individual characterization of the dancers. In scene 4 of that work, a Monsieur Dupré, performing as Mars, was instructed to express, by actions, "Gallantry, Respect, Ardent Love, and Adoration," while Hester Santlow, as Venus, depicted "Bashfulness, reciprocal Love, and wishing Looks" (Weaver, 1974).

In 1728, also in London, Marie Sallé adapted a solo *divertissement* of her teacher Françoise Prévost, *Les Caractères de la Danse,* into a pas de deux that allowed more scope for dramatic expression. Performed with Antoine Bandieri de Laval, and occasionally billed as *Les Caractères de l'Amour,* each of the eleven *entrées* of the pas de deux depicted an amorous situation.

Jean-Georges Noverre noted that his pupil Jean Dauberval, "with impeccable taste . . . composed a pas de deux full of dramatic action and interest for the opera *Sylvie* [Paris, 1766] . . . which expressed all the sentiments which love might inspire" (Winter, 1974). An expressive moment from the performance by Dauberval and his partner, Marie Allard, was captured in an engraving by the artist Louis Carrogis, also known as Carmontelle.

Late eighteenth-century drawings of Salvatore Viganò and his wife, Maria Medina, reveal the changes taking place in pas de deux during that transitional period between the Baroque and Romantic eras. Simpler, body-conforming costumes allowed closer contact between partners. Viganò is portrayed holding Medina by the waist as she balances on the ball of her laced, sandaled foot. Soon, ballerinas were perched on the tips of their toes, often aided by the supporting hands of their partners. Pas de deux devised by Armand Vestris, Filippo Taglioni, and Charles-Louis Didelot advanced the new technique. The partnership of Amalia Brugnoli and Jean Rozier has been preserved in lithographs whose images reveal a supported arabesque (in *Die Fée und der Ritter,* Vienna, 1823) and a two-handed lift (in *Der Blaubart,* Vienna, 1824).

Still, the tradition of a couple performing the same steps in symmetrical formations continued well into the nineteenth century, as evidenced by the popular duet "Gavotte de Vestris," described and/or notated in similar versions from 1830 (Léon Michel, also known as Michel St. Léon) to 1895 (G. Desrat). This lively pas de deux, eventually known as *la danse classique* (Zorn, 1887), included brief solo passages but with identical steps performed by the man and the woman. A much more technically challenging example is the pas de deux from the opera *La Vestale,* choreographed by Pierre Gardel. As described by Léon-Michel Saint-Léon (in a notebook containing material dated 1833–1836), the couple performs identical steps at the same time or as an "echo," with the woman repeating what her partner has just executed. Similarly, in many of the ballets of August Bournonville, as Erik Bruhn (1961) has observed, the ballerina dances variations "as strenuous and difficult as those of the leading male dancer, and in the pas de deux as conceived by him they often dance opposite one another, executing the same steps."

Changes were in the air, however, as evidenced by another example from Saint-Léon's notebooks, the pas de deux danced by his son, Arthur, for his second debut in Munich in 1835. Here, solo passages for Arthur are different from those of his partner, who performs some of her steps *sur les orteils,* or on the tips of her toes. A tiny drawing by St. Léon depicts Arthur holding his partner by her waist as she balances on full pointe with one leg extended forward at hip level. Arthur Saint-Léon went on to have a famous partnership with Fanny Cerrito that displayed the virtuosity of both dancers, as did the partnership of Jules Perrot and Carlotta Grisi. However, the growing prominence of the ballerina in nineteenth-century ballet scenarios, and concurrently her developing expertise on pointe, resulted in changes in the concept of the pas de deux: it became a formalized means for displaying the female dancer.

In his multiple-act, evening-length ballets created for the Imperial Theater in Saint Petersburg, Marius Petipa firmly established both the structure and the importance of the *grand pas de deux.* Usually the culminating moment of a party or wedding scene, and thus of the ballet, the duet typically opened with an *entrée* by the couple, followed by the *adage* or adagio section in which the *danseur* gave support to the *danseuse* in sustained poses, varied pirouettes, and high lifts (partnering). Next came a solo variation for the male dancer in which he could display his mastery of multiple beats and pirouettes and soaring leaps. Following this came the ballerina's solo variation highlighting her mastery of pointe technique, usually in steps requiring delicate control and balance or brilliant speed and strength. A coda brought the dancers together again for a dazzling finale of virtuoso steps. Examples of such formalized *grand pas de deux* are found in act 2 of *The Nutcracker* (original choreography by Lev Ivanov in 1892 for Antoinetta Dell'Era and Pavel Gerdt) and in act 3 of *Swan Lake* (Petipa's version first performed in 1895 by Pierina Legnani and Gerdt). Because these and other nineteenth-century pas de deux do little to advance the plot of the ballet, but do develop the relationship between the two leading characters, they have often been performed separately, simply as *divertissements.*

PAS DE DEUX. *(left)* Eva Kloborg and Peter Martins, with soloists from the Royal Danish Ballet, in the pas de deux from August Bournonville's *Flower Festival in Genzano,* in 1979. *(right)* Veronica Tenant and Jeremy Blanton of the National Ballet of Canada in Celia Franca's version of the *grand pas de deux* from *The Nutcracker,* c.1970. (Left photograph © 1979 by Johan Elbers; used by permission. Right photograph from the archives at Jacob's Pillow, Becket, Massachusetts.)

The basic outline for this type of pas de deux was several centuries old by Petipa's time. Some late Renaissance dances for a gentleman and his lady were in the form of four-part suites: a pavane-like *intrada* danced together, a lively *galliard* section featuring solo variations by the man and then by the woman, passages of brisk *saltarello* performed together, and lastly a *canario* finale of foot-stamping intensity performed as a "pedalog"—a dialogue of the feet. Examples are Fabritio Caroso's compositions "Laura Suave" and "Nido d'Amore" (from his book *Nobiltà di dame,* 1600).

Not all nineteenth-century pas de deux adhered to strict formulas. Some, as in *Paquita,* include active participation of other soloists and the corps de ballet. The pas de deux choreographed by Ivanov for act 2 of *Swan Lake* is one long adagio section integrated with passages of balletic mime gestures.

Twentieth-century choreographers from Michel Fokine to Antony Tudor to Michael Smuin have created more flexibility in the concept of pas de deux, often having it serve the development of the story line of the ballet. Others, notably George Balanchine and Jerome Robbins, have elaborated on the mechanical possibilities of double work. Acrobatic elements inherent in lifts, throws, and catches have been daringly exploited by Bolshoi choreographers such as Asaf Messerer in his pas de deux *Spring Waters,* which astounded Western audiences in the late 1950s. Audience interest in both classical and modern ballet pas de deux has been stimulated by dynamic partnerships: Alexandra Danilova and Frederic Franklin, Alicia Markova and Anton Dolin, Margot Fonteyn and Rudolf Nureyev, Erik Bruhn and Carla Fracci, Marcia Haydée and Richard Cragun, to name but a few.

The symbolic aspects of the pas de deux have long fascinated dance writers. John Martin (1980) finds the classical pas de deux to be the "epitome of the ballet," an abstraction that emphasizes the idealized male and female in relation to one another as well as separately in full and free range. In the aesthetic of Stéphane Mallarmé, the pas de deux "has as its basis a mere kiss, but the whole dance is only the 'mysterious sacred interpretation of this act'" (Pridden, 1952). The pas de deux, as a Western dance form in which a man and woman dance together (in contrast to some Eastern dance forms where the woman dances alone for the pleasure of the man), has been seen to have moral and philosophical implications as well. Jules Lemaître believed that it "symbolises the social and intellectual partnership of the sexes and the Christian

PAS DE DEUX. *(left)* Rowena Jackson and Brian Shaw of the Royal Ballet in Marius Petipa's Bluebird pas de deux from *The Sleeping Beauty,* c.1955. *(right)* Natalia Makarova and John Prinz of American Ballet Theatre in her staging, after Petipa, of the pas de deux from *Le Corsaire,* early 1970s. (Both photographs from the Dance Collection, New York Public Library for the Performing Arts.)

conception of love" (quoted in Pridden, 1952). New York dance critic Tobi Tobias (1975) sums up perhaps the essence of pas de deux: "All ballet duets have this in common: they deal, on a multiplicity of levels, with one person's relating to another. And what characterizes a successful partnership is perhaps what marks any fortunate partnership: mutual sympathy and a good sense of timing."

[*See also* Ballet Technique, History of.]

Bibliography

Bruhn, Erik, and Lillian Moore. *Bournonville and Ballet Technique.* London, 1961.

Caroso, Fabritio. *Nobiltà di dame* (1600). Translated and edited by Julia Sutton. Oxford, 1986.

Compan, Charles. *Dictionnaire de danse.* Paris, 1787.

Desrat, G. *Dictionnaire de la danse.* Paris, 1895.

Martin, John. "The Ideal of Ballet Aesthetics." In *The Dance Anthology,* edited by Cobbett Steinberg. New York, 1980.

Priddin, Deidre. *The Art of the Dance in French Literature from Théophile Gautier to Paul Valéry.* London, 1952.

Ralph, Richard. *The Life and Works of John Weaver.* New York, 1985.

St. Léon, Michel. Cahier d'exercices pour LL.AA. Royalles les Princesses de Würtemberg 1830, Untitled manuscript volume containing Exercices de 1833, 1834, and 1836. Manuscripts located in Paris, Bibliothèque de l'Opéra, Res.1137 and 1140.

Swift, Mary Grace. *A Loftier Flight: The Life and Accomplishments of Charles Louis Didelot.* Middletown, Conn., 1974.

Tobias, Tobi. "Ballet Partners: Matches Not Made in Heaven." *New York Times* (17 August 1975).

Weaver, John. "The Loves of Mars and Venus" (1717). In *Dance as a Theatre Art,* edited by Selma Jeanne Cohen. New York, 1974.

Winter, Marian Hannah. *The Pre-Romantic Ballet.* London, 1974.

Zorn, Friedrich Albert. *Grammatik der Tanzkunst, theoretischer und praktischer: Unterricht in der Tanzkunst und Tanzschreibkunst, oder, Choregraphie.* Leipzig, 1887. Translated by Benjamin P. Coates as *Grammar of the Art of Dancing* (Boston, 1905).

Sandra Noll Hammond

PAS DE QUATRE. *Divertissement.* Choreography: Jules Perrot. Music: Cesare Pugni. First performance: 13 July 1845, King's Theatre, London. Dancers: Marie Taglioni, Carlotta Grisi, Lucile Grahn, and Fanny Cerrito.

Pas de Quatre, choreographed by Jules Perrot, caused a considerable stir, for it brought together four brilliant *danseuses*—Marie Taglioni, Carlotta Grisi, Lucile Grahn, and Fanny Cerrito. It started out as a clever publicity stunt by theater manager Benjamin Lumley, who wanted to create a sensation by exploiting the tremendous popularity of star dancers; but it became the definitive statement of a new aesthetic; the neoclassical idea that stories must be the focus of ballets to give the art significance, an idea that had prevailed since the eighteenth century, was weakening. *Pas de Quatre,* a *divertissement* without a story or theme, was the result of a trend among dancers and critics to consider dancing as an art form in itself. The notion that the arts could be appreciated for their abstract aesthetic merits alone had been expressed by the writer/critic Théophile Gautier in the "art for art's sake" doctrine of 1835; the plotless *Pas de Quatre* offered audiences "dance for dance's sake."

Many people were simply overwhelmed by the great personalities in *Pas de Quatre* and appreciated the *divertissement* for this alone. But some recognized a deeper significance. The *Court Journal* observed that Perrot had created

> A succession of novelty and artistical beauty which would stamp him a first-rate artist if he had never done anything else. And the way in which he has adapted the separate *pas* of each dancer to her own peculiar forte and powers, without interfering with the harmony and *ensemble* of the entire composition, is worthy of all admiration.

The idea that someone could be a first-rate artist merely through the creation of dances was new.

London's *Morning Herald* offered a detailed description of the work:

> When the curtain rose (discovering the well-known *divertissement* bower) the four heroines, clad alike, were seen hand in hand—the first time perhaps, they had ever touched each other. . . . They commenced with a series of groupings of picturesque and elegant design, and the effect was exquisite. . . . Taglioni was the centre of these graceful clusterings, and the three younger nymphs, as they surrounded and overhung her with outstretched arms, seemed to pay proper homage to one who first gave the art purpose and intelligence. . . . Lucile Grahn led the way, and pampered the eye with dainty semicircular hops upon one *toe,* to which Carlotta Grisi replied with hops of equal dexterity and number, mingled, however, with a world of little sprightly steps, which multiplied her feet into thousands. Matters now took a romantic turn; there was a slow, expressive movement by Taglioni and Grahn, but only for a moment, for Cerito . . . intercepted the sentimentalism of the pair by one of her *tours de force.* . . . Groupings of gentler and languid character were again resumed, to which Carlotta Grisi and Lucile Grahn gave relief by twinkling solos, leading to a magnificent coda, in which steps of various and dazzling complexity were executed by each, terminating with a grand junction of the four in rapid motion, and fixed sculpturesque tableau.

The original *Pas de Quatre* was performed only four times. An 1847 revival was performed twice with Carolina Rosati taking Lucile Grahn's part. Created as it was toward the end of ballet's heyday in London and Paris, it had little lasting impact. Its value rests on its considerable artistic merits and its place as a symbol of the brilliance of the Romantic ballet. Keith Lester (in 1936) and Anton Dolin (in 1941) created ballets to evoke something of the original *Pas de Quatre.*

[*Many of the figures mentioned herein are the subjects of independent entries.*]

BIBLIOGRAPHY

Cavers, J. K. "The Iconography of the *Pas de Quatre.*" *Dance Research* 5 (Spring 1987): 65–69.

Guest, Ivor. *The Pas de Quatre.* London, 1970.

Guest, Ivor. *The Romantic Ballet in England.* London, 1972.

Guest, Ivor. *Fanny Cerrito.* 2d rev. ed. London, 1974.

Guest, Ivor. *Jules Perrot: Master of the Romantic Ballet.* London, 1984.

Kirstein, Lincoln. *Movement and Metaphor: Four Centuries of Ballet.* New York, 1970.

Maynard, Olga. "The Ballet of *Le Pas de Quatre.*" In Maynard's *The Ballet Companion.* Philadelphia, 1957.

Michel, Artur. *"Pas de Quatre,* 1845–1945." *Dance Magazine* (July 1945): 10–12, 32–36.

Reynolds, Nancy, and Susan Reimer-Torn. *Dance Classics.* Pennington, N.J., 1991.

JOHN V. CHAPMAN

PASO DOBLE. *See* Ballroom Dance Competition.

PASSACAILLE. *See* Chaconne and Passacaille.

PASSEPIED. A French dance dating from the sixteenth century or earlier, the *passepied* was first mentioned in 1548, by Noël de Fail, who describes it as a court dance of Brittany. Thoinot Arbeau, in his *Orchésographie* (1588), also refers to the *trihory,* or *passepied,* as a type of *branle* danced in Brittany. Arbeau's example, in duple meter, uses *branle* step variations that are repeated throughout the dance. Several *passepied* settings, also in duple meter, appear in Michael Praetorius's 1612 collection of dance music, *Terpsichore.*

As is the case with several other dance types (such as the *galliard* and the *courante*), no apparent relationship exists between the Renaissance version and the late seventeenth-century court and theatrical dance of the same name. The Baroque *passepied* is set to music in triple meter, usually with a 3/8 time signature and an eighth-note upbeat. The dance shares the step vocabulary of the *menuet,* one step-unit requiring two bars of music, but has a faster tempo.

There are at least twenty-one extant *passepied* choreographies in Feuillet notation. Twelve are of French provenance, seven are English, and the remaining two are from German and Spanish treatises. Although French operas and ballets from Jean-Baptiste Lully to Jean-Philippe Rameau frequently include *passepied* music, none of the surviving choreographies is theatrical in style, and all but one are for a single couple. The passepied frequently occurs as part of a "dance suite," a set of two or more contrasting dance types performed consecutively without a pause. Because of its lighthearted character, the dance is more often found at the end of such suites.

The six *passepieds* by Guillaume-Louis Pecour share certain characteristics also found to some extent in other dances of this type: floor patterns in which the partners move parallel to each other rather than in the more usual symmetrical shapes, a limited step vocabulary, and the use of hemiola—a shift in rhythmic stress—in the music. The parallel floor patterns are either circular, with the couple holding inside hands, or rectilinear. One or both of these patterns also appear in dances by Raoul-Auger Feuillet and Claude Ballon but in none of the English *passepieds.*

Passepied music is usually in binary form, with strains of eight, twelve, or sixteen bars. However, the French dances are considerably more irregular, with strains of four to twenty-two bars. A hemiola often occurs near the end of the second strain. (See example 1.) Pecour's "La Bretagne" (1704) is typical.

A folk dance called *passepied* is still performed in parts of France today, but any conclusions about the earlier versions of the *passepied* drawn from this dance can only be regarded as speculative.

[*See also* Ballet Technique, History of, *article on* French Court Dance; *and* Social Dance, *article on* Court and Social Dance before 1800.]

BIBLIOGRAPHY

Hilton, Wendy. *Dance of Court and Theatre: The French Noble Style, 1690–1725.* Princeton, 1981.

Little, Meredith Ellis. "Passepied." In *The New Grove Dictionary of Music and Musicians.* London, 1980.

Witherell, Anne L. *Louis Pécour's 1700 Recueil des dances.* Ann Arbor, Mich., 1983.

CAROL G. MARSH

PASSEPIED. Example 1. This is the end of the second strain of music that accompanies Guillaume-Louis Pecour's choreography for "La Bretagne." The hemiola, in bars 4 and 5, creates a counter-rhythm to the dance steps (indicated by square brackets above the music) at the climax of the dance. The music is from André Campra's 1704 opera *Télémaque.*

PASSO E MEZZO (also It., *passamezzo;* Fr., *passemeze, passemezze;* Eng., passamezzo, passymeasure). The *passo e mezzo* was a popular and lively sixteenth- and seventeenth-century duple-meter couple dance. It is difficult to define but apparently is related to both the pavan and the galliard. There were, musically, two well-known *passo e mezzo* chord patterns that formed the basis for innumerable musical works: *antico* (Eng., quadro pavan) and *moderno* (Eng., passing-measures pavan). The four extant choreographies with music all appear in Fabritio Caroso (1581, 1600) and are all based on the *passamezzo antico* bass with its chord pattern and a single tune (see examples 1 and 2). Livio Lupi in his first edition (1600) gives only variations and no music. In his second edition (1607), he provides a full choreography for a "Passo e Mezzo in Gagliarda," again without music; it is closely related choreographically to Caroso's versions, but there are forty-five more variations, and its opening step patterns for each variation are more varied. Lupi states further that the dance may be done by a couple facing each other or by three or four dancers in a circle.

The printed choreographies are at least sixty years later than the dance's first appearance in music (Hans Newsidler's *Ein Newgeordnet künstlich Lautenbuch* of 1563), so it is impossible to determine the original choreography or the step pattern that might have given the dance its name.

PASSO E MEZZO. Example 1 *(above)*. The standard bass melody of the *passamezzo antico.*

PASSO E MEZZO. Example 2 *(right and opposite)*. Fabritio Caroso's "Passo e Mezzo" bass and descant as found in his treatises *Il ballarino* (1581) and *Nobiltà di dame* (1600).

There are no verbal definitions in the Italian manuals. To Arbeau in 1588, it was an enlivened and varied version of the pavan, normally to be followed by a galliard (indeed, in musical collections many suites have a *passo e mezzo* followed by a galliard or unnamed triple after-dance); to John Florio (1598, 1611) and to Michael Praetorius (1619), however, the dance was simply a *cinque pas* (i.e., galliard); while to Thomas Morley (1597), it was a type of Italian "ditty" of little import.

Which contemporary definitions are correct cannot be fully confirmed, leaving only speculation on the available evidence. Arbeau gives just a general description, stating that the dance consists of lively variations on the pavan, using steps from the galliard, suitable to a youthful ballroom dance (in contrast to the solemn processional nature of his pavan). The two dances Caroso titles *passo e mezzo* (one in each book) follow an alternating choreographic pattern and use galliard-like steps, but begin the walking parts with steps related to the pavan. In Caroso's two other dances to identical music (but not titled *passo e mezzo*), the picture is hazier: in "Ardente Sole" *(Il ballarino)* the dance seems a typical one-movement *balletto* of several figures for one couple; "Dolce Amoroso Fuoco" (same source) is for three couples in contradance position, with figures typical to such dances (e.g., heys down each line). In each case, however, a middle figure is galliard-like. In other words, in all settings the dance is a hybrid of the pavan and galliard in duple meter, which includes to a greater or lesser degree pavan-related steps leading immediately or after several figures into galliard-like step patterns and paths. Furthermore, the *passo e mezzo* choreographies in Caroso and Lupi are discrete, not followed by any other dance type as part of a suite. Thus, the extant choreographies agree both with Arbeau's viewpoint that the *passo e mezzo* is based on the pavan and with Florio's and Praetorius's that it is a galliard. [*See* Galliard *and* Pavan.]

Despite the vigor of most of the steps in the dances, their general affect is oddly gentle, if not lyric (Praetorius confirms this), possibly because of the music's slow har-

monic rhythm (one chord change every four bars). The resulting affect differs so sharply from the galliard, with its powerful rhythmic motto, that no observer would confuse the two dances.

The differences between the *pavaniglia* (another apparent hybrid of pavan and galliard) and the *passo e mezzo* appear to have been both choreographic and musical. The *pavaniglia* in both Caroso and Negri is also performed to its own specific music, but with the dancers moving simultaneously and mostly side by side, in contrast to the alternating (and facing) *passo e mezzo* variations. In both dance types, each walking section in the *passo e mezzo* and each variation in the *pavaniglia* begins with pavan-related steps and continues with galliard-like steps—but the *passo e mezzo* also includes galliard-like alternating figures and the *pavaniglia* does not. Both dance types are in duple (there is a distinct possibility, however, that the *pavaniglia* was intended to be resolved to triple). Here again, there would have been no confusion to the contemporary observer, whatever the existing problems of definition may be. [*See* Pavaniglia.]

Aside from the *passo e mezzo's* inclusion in the reissue of Caroso's *Nobiltà di dame* as *Raccolta di varij balli* in 1630, it is mentioned as a dance by Marin Mersenne in 1636, but his reference lacks a precise description. The bass *(antico)* and its chords continued as a ground for musical compositions. The dance itself, however, appears to have died out completely by about 1640.

BIBLIOGRAPHY: SOURCES

Alessandri, Filippo degli. *Discorso sopra il ballo.* Terni, 1620.

Arbeau, Thoinot. *Orchesographie et traicte en forme de dialogve, par leqvel tovtes personnes pevvent facilement apprendre & practiquer l'honneste exercice des dances.* Langres, 1588, 1589. Facsimile reprint, Langres, 1988. Reprinted with expanded title as *Orchesographie, metode, et teorie en forme de discovrs et tablatvre povr apprendre a dancer, battre le Tambour en toute sorte & diuersité de batteries, Iouët du fifre & arigot, tirer des armes & escrimer, auec autres honnestes exercices fort conuenables à la Ieunesse.* Langres, 1596. Facsimile reprint, Geneva, 1972.

Arbeau, Thoinot. *Orchesography.* 1589. Translated into English by Mary Stewart Evans. New York, 1948. Reprint with corrections, a new introduction, and notes by Julia Sutton, and representative steps and dances in Labanotation by Mireille Backer. New York, 1967.

Caroso, Fabritio. *Il ballarino* (1581). Facsimile reprint, New York, 1967.

Caroso, Fabritio. *Nobiltà di dame.* Venice, 1600, 1605. Facsimile reprint, Bologna, 1970. Reissued with order of illustrations changed as *Raccolta di varij balli,* Rome, 1630. Translated into English with eight introductory chapters by Julia Sutton, the music transcribed by F. Marian Walker. Oxford, 1986. Reprint with a step manual in Labanotation by Rachelle Palnick Tsachor and Julia Sutton, New York, 1995.

Florio, John. *A World of Wordes.* London, 1598. Facsimile reprint, Hildesheim, 1972. 2d ed., *Queen Anna's New World of Words.* London, 1611. Facsimile reprint of 1611 ed., Menston, England, 1973.

Lupi, Livio. *Libro di gagliarda, tordiglione, passo e mezzo, canari e passeggi.* Palermo, 1600. Rev. ed., Palermo, 1607.

Mersenne, Marin. *Harmonie universelle* (1636–1637). Facsimile reprint, Paris, 1963. English translation of Book 2 by J. B. Egan. Ph.D.diss., Indiana University, 1962.

Morley, Thomas. *A Plaine and Easie Introduction to Practicall Musicke* (1597). Introduction by Edmund H. Fellowes. Oxford, 1937.

Newsidler, Hans. *Ein Newgeordnet künstlich Lautenbuch* (1536). 2 vols. Facsimile reprint, Neuss, 1974–1976.

Praetorius, Michael. *Syntagma musicum,* vol. 3. Wolfenbüttel, 1619. Edited by W. Gurlitt in *Documenta musicologica,* vol. 1. Kassel, 1958.

BIBLIOGRAPHY: OTHER STUDIES

Esses, Maurice. *Dance and Instrumental Diferencias in Spain during the Seventeenth and Early Eighteenth Centuries.* Stuyvesant, N.Y., 1992.

Hudson, Richard. "Passamezzo." In *The New Grove Dictionary of Music and Musicians.* London, 1980.

Moe, Lawrence H. "Dance Music in Printed Italian Lute Tablatures from 1507 to 1611." Ph.D.diss., Harvard University, 1956.

Spohr, Helga. "Studien zur italienischen Tanzcomposition um 1600." Ph.D.diss., University of Freiburg, 1956.

Tani, Gino. "Passamezzo." In *Enciclopedio dello spettacolo.* 9 vols. Rome, 1954–1968.

Ward, John M. "Passamezzo." In *Die Musik in Geschichte und Gegenwart.* 1st ed., vol. 10, 1962. Kassel, 1949–1979.

JULIA SUTTON

PASTORALE is a mode of artistic expression that depicts an idealized vision of rural life. During some periods of its long history, the pastorale has been a distinct genre (for example, the Italian pastoral drama of the late Renaissance), but its significance for dance history lies primarily in the extensive way that pastoral themes and settings have been incorporated into many forms of musical and dramatic expression that involve dancing.

In ancient Greece, the pastoral song emerged as an important genre in the works of Theocritus (third century BCE). The connections that may then have existed between dance and the pastoral song are imperfectly understood. The *Eclogues* of the Roman poet Virgil (70–19 BCE) further established the convention of the urban poet longing for the idealized simplicity of life in the countryside. In France during the Middle Ages, a type of lyric poem known as the *pastourelle* was cultivated by the trouvères and troubadours. There were two main types of *pastourelle,* one in which a knight encountered a shepherdess and attempted to woo her, with varying degrees of success, and another in which a bucolic scene among shepherds and shepherdesses was depicted. These *pastourelles* often included songs, and a number of *pastourelles* from the twelfth and thirteenth centuries have been preserved with their music. Such *pastourelles* were probably sung, played, and danced by jongleurs. *Le Jeu de Robin et Marion,* a pastoral play by Adam de la Halle (*fl.* late thirteenth century), includes several different dances.

During the Renaissance, the pastorale became a major mode of literary expression in poetry, drama, and fiction. The authors of pastorales drew on classical sources such as the *Eclogues* of Virgil and the *Metamorphoses* of Ovid to create a mythical Arcadia peopled by shepherds, nymphs, satyrs, demigods, and magicians. Early examples of pastorales include the set of twelve eclogues entitled *Arcadia* by Jacopo Sannazaro (1481), and the *Favola d'Orfeo* by Angelo Poliziano (1471), a theatrical entertainment that included music and dance.

In Italy, pastoral drama emerged in the 1550s, its most important representative being Giovanni Battista Guarini's *Il Pastor Fido,* a play that had an enormous influence on all the arts in the seventeenth and eighteenth centuries. The theme of these pastorales was wooing or courtship, and the characters bore such names as Amarilli, Silvio, and Tirsi. These dramas accorded a prominent place to music and dance, including such elements as ballets for satyrs, and choruses sung and danced by nymphs.

During this same period in Italy, many plays of varying types were performed with an *intermedio,* a short entertainment involving music and dance, between each act. The *intermedi* were often built on pastoral themes. Another form that made use of pastoral subjects was the *balletto,* an independent choreographic composition, or a dance within a theatrical work. In England, pastoral elements were to be found in another type of sung-and-danced entertainment, the masque, whose heyday lasted from the sixteenth to the eighteenth century. [*See* Ballo and Balletto; Intermedio.]

The influence of the dramatic pastorale on the development of opera was enormous, and, in fact, the earliest operas, beginning with Ottavio Rinuccini's and Jacopo Peri's *Dafne* of 1594, were all pastorales. One of the earliest subjects for pastoral operas, and one that has continued to attract composers and choreographers into the twentieth century, was the myth of Orpheus and Eurydice. As opera developed, historical subjects gained in importance, but the pastoral element remained strong, and when Italian opera spread throughout Europe, pastorales held a prominent place in the repertory.

In France at the end of the sixteenth century, a native pastoral drama grew out of the combined influence of the Italian dramatic pastorale and the Spanish pastoral prose romance. The plots involved nymphs and shepherds (each sighing in vain for the lover of another), complications brought on by sorcery or magical objects, and the appearance of Cupid at the end to set everything right. Toward the middle of the seventeenth century, some of these pastorales were set to music, either wholly or in part. During the same period, the *ballet de cour* ("court ballet") often either incorporated pastoral elements or was entirely constructed on a pastoral theme. [*See* Ballet de Cour.] These two genres, the dramatic pastorale and the *ballet de cour,* were both important components in the development of French opera, and, as in Italy, the earliest operas were pastorales. Examples include *La Pastorale d'Issy* (1659), by Pierre Perrin and Robert Cambert, and *Les Fêtes de l'Amour et de Bacchus* (1672), by Jean-Baptiste Lully. Even after Lully began composing his series of *tragédies lyriques* (serious operas) with *Cadmus et Hermione* in 1673, pastoral elements retained an important place in French opera. They were most conspicuous in the prologue and in the *divertissement* found in each act, which were also the parts of the opera in which dancing figured most importantly; unlike Italian opera, French opera always gave a prominent role to the dance. Thus the newly emerging art of ballet, much of whose early development took place at the Paris Opera, was intimately associated with pastoral themes.

After Lully, French operatic composers continued to write entire pastorales, such as André-Cardinal Destouches's *Issé* (1697) or Jean-Philippe Rameau's *Zaïs* (1748). More important, however, pastoral elements were a prominent feature of all the musico-dramatic forms of the eighteenth-century French stage, such as *tragédie lyrique, opéra-ballet, opéra comique,* and *ballet héroïque.* Certain dance types, such as the *musette, passepied,* and *rigaudon,* were particularly associated with pastoral settings.

The French Revolution of 1789 put an end to the stage reign of the nymphs and shepherds, and librettists and choreographers sought new forms of expression. Nevertheless, pastoral subjects did not entirely disappear from the stage. In the nineteenth century, pastoral ballets were occasionally staged; some examples are Charles Didelot's *Flore et Zéphire* (1815), the first ballet to make use of a flying machine for the dancers; Filippo Taglioni's *Aglaë* (1841); and Louis Mérante's *Sylvie, ou La Nymphe de Diane* (1876). An important twentieth-century pastoral ballet is *Daphnis et Chloë* (1912), with music by Maurice Ravel and choreography by Michel Fokine.

[*For related discussion, see* Opéra-Ballet and Tragédie Lyrique.]

BIBLIOGRAPHY

Grout, Donald Jay. *A Short History of Opera.* 2d ed. New York, 1965.

Harris, Ellen T. *Handel and the Pastoral Tradition.* London, 1980.

La Laurencie, Lionel de. "Les pastorales en musique au XVIIe siècle en France avant Lully et leur influence sur l'Opéra." In *Report of the Fourth Congress of the International Music Society, London, 29th May–3rd June, 1911.* London, 1912.

Marsan, Jules. *La pastorale dramatique en France.* Paris, 1905.

Winter, Marian Hannah. *The Pre-Romantic Ballet.* London, 1974.

REBECCA HARRIS-WARRICK

PATINEURS, LES. Ballet in one act. Choreography: Frederick Ashton. Music: Giacomo Meyerbeer; arranged by Constant Lambert. Scenery and costumes: William Chappell. First performance: 16 February 1937, Sadler's Wells Theatre, London, Vic-Wells Ballet. Principals: Mary Honer and Elizabeth Miller (*entrée;* Blue Girls), Harold

Turner (solo variations; Blue Boy), Margot Fonteyn and Robert Helpmann (pas de deux; White Couple), June Brae and Pamela May (*pas des patineuses;* Red Girls).

Les Patineurs (The Skaters) is a kind of companion piece to Ashton's *Les Rendezvous* (1933): both are danced to ballet music from nineteenth-century operas, both are *divertissements* set in a public garden, and both challenge and display the technical achievements of their dancers. (For the 1849 premiere of Meyerbeer's opera *Le Prophète* at the Théâtre National de l'Opéra, Paris, the skating ballet was originally choreographed by Auguste Mabille.) The Vic-Wells Ballet production (in which four numbers were added from another Meyerbeer opera, *L'Étoile du Nord*) was first planned with choreography by Ninette de Valois, but when Ashton heard the music he asked if he could take over the project, and she agreed.

In 1849 the dancers had performed part of the *divertissement* on roller skates; in Ashton's ballet, ice skating is suggested by steps taken from the vocabulary of classical ballet. Ashton in fact denied any knowledge of skating beyond what he had seen in newsreels. The subject of the ballet, therefore, is the virtuosity of the dancers as much as that of the skaters they imitate, especially the male soloist and the two women in blue, who perform multiple pirouettes of various kinds. The pas de deux provides a romantic interlude, while the two other female soloists, in dark red, have a more sedate *entrée.* The ballet is given a *demi-caractère* quality by the fact that the choreography portrays the various types that can be seen at an ice rink—experts and beginners, lovers and show-offs.

Chappell's original setting, a semicircle of white trellis-work arches hung with Chinese lanterns, beyond which can be seen the shadowy outlines of leafless trees, has never been improved upon and (unlike that for *Les Rendezvous*) has never been changed, except for the revival designed by Cecil Beaton for Ballet Theatre in 1946.

Les Patineurs has been revived by many other companies, including the Royal Winnipeg Ballet and PACT Ballet (Johannesburg) in 1966, the Australian Ballet in 1970, and the Joffrey Ballet in 1977, and it has remained in the repertories of both companies of the Royal Ballet. In 1957 the Royal Ballet introduced an enlarged version, with double corps de ballet, intended for a tour of Soviet Russia that never took place. This version was soon dropped, though the corps was augmented to six couples for a while. *Les Patineurs* was one of the first ballets to be telecast by the British Broadcasting Corporation, in 1937 and again in 1938.

BIBLIOGRAPHY

Coton, A. V. *A Prejudice for Ballet.* London, 1938.

Reynolds, Nancy, and Susan Reimer-Torn. *Dance Classics.* Pennington, N.J., 1991.

Vaughan, David. *Frederick Ashton and His Ballets.* London, 1977.

DAVID VAUGHAN

PAVAN (It., *pavana, padovana, paduana, padoana;* Fr., *pavane, pavanne;* Ger., *Paduana*). Probably originating in Italy, the pavan was danced both as a solemn processional and as a ballroom dance. The meaning and source of the term are still debated. One theory proposes that it is named for, and hence originated in, the city of Padua (both the words *pavana* and *padoane* refer to the Paduan dialect); another theory claims that the dance imitates the strutting peacock *(pavone).* Although the theories of its origin remain unproven, the dance's basic choreographic elements are documented throughout the sixteenth century: either one couple, or a number of couples in processional formation, move side by side and hand in hand with simple walking step patterns (such as a step and close) forward, backward, or sideways.

As early as 1520, Giovanni Andrea da Prato *(Storia di Milano)* compares his writing style to pavan dancers who, "while following the music, take one step forward, and in the next measure return with one step backward" (Cagnola, 1842, vol. 4, p. 300). The few extant choreographies specifically named pavan belong to the late sixteenth century, and they confirm the same pattern. Thoinot Arbeau, for example, in his *Orchésographie* (1588), says the pavan serves in three ways: for kings, princes, and great noblemen and their ladies to display themselves on solemn feast days in their full finery with mantles or long trains; in grand spectacles for the entries of gods and goddesses in their chariots; and to open a grand ball.

The first known direct mention of the pavan is in book 4 of Joan Ambrosio Dalza's *Intabolatura di lauto,* published in Venice in 1508. A few years later, in 1528, Antonius Arena also refers to it in his macaronic dance manual *Ad suos compagnones studiantes,* in a rhyme that seems to support Italian origins, but he gives no choreography and no music. Numerous other Italian and French literary sources mention the dance throughout the century and attest to its importance. Though it may have sprung from Padua, the normal workings of time and fashion seem to have produced different local versions early on. Dalza gives *padoana diverse* on his title page but subsumes under that title several *pavane alla venetiane* and *pavane alla ferrarese,* each type having its own tune. That there were already different musical pavan types by 1508 indicates that the dance may have existed for some time and that it might also have had differentiated choreographies according to its geographic region. Despite the extended discussions of this issue in much modern writing, the question of origins is truly moot, for the first detailed pavan choreographies do not appear until seventy or eighty years after Dalza.

In fact, in the eruption of large choreographic sources of the last quarter of the sixteenth century there exist just two extant detailed choreographies with music: Battistino's "Pavana Matthei" in Fabritio Caroso's *Il ballarino* (1581), a two-movement suite for one couple in which the first movement is clearly a *pavana* and the second is typically a *gagliarda;* and Arbeau's lovely sung pavan, "Belle Qui Tiens Ma Vie," a purely processional dance. The paths and the step vocabulary of both pavan versions are indeed concordant. The French *simples* and *doubles* parallel the Italian *passi puntati* and *seguiti ordinarii;* they also seem to be simplifications of the basic traveling elements of the fifteenth-century processional *bassedanse* or *bassadanza.* The step descriptions with music in both of these sources make reasonable reconstructions of the dances possible. However, the few other named choreographies from this time—the "pavians" in the so-called Manuscripts of the Inns of Court—do not lend themselves to reconstruction that can be solidly supported by evidence. They consist essentially of step cues without description or music and rarely explain the relationship of the members of a couple to one another or of one couple to other couples (e.g., "Cynthia Pavyan," MS Rawl.Poet.108, c.1570). Thus, much must be assumed for reconstructive purposes.

Despite the agreement between the two specific choreographies cited and the contemporary literary descriptions of the dance, it is unclear whether what is being seen is the original dance or what may have been changed by then. By then, too, the word *pavoneggiare,* from *pavone* ("peacock"), was closely associated with the dance (see Caroso, *Il ballarino,* fol. 5r). This reference to a strutting movement suggests another origin than Padua. John Florio (1611) says it means "like a Peacock proudly to court and wantonize with himself." Indeed, in 1636–1637, more than a century after the dance's first appearance, Marin Mersenne adopts this second view, saying that the pavan is a Spanish dance imitating a peacock.

Besides the processional type of pavan, several sources describe a pavan that was highly varied and lively for ballroom purposes and for a solo couple rather than for a procession of couples. In fact, the second dance of Battistino's suite mentioned above consists of a long and complex *gagliarda* that could only have been performed in a ballroom by a solo couple. In *Orchésographie,* which takes the form of a dialogue between the master, Arbeau, and his disciple, Capriol, there is the following exchange:

> CAPRIOL: This pavan is too solemn and slow to dance alone with a young girl in a room . . . .
>
> ARBEAU: The musicians sometimes play it more quickly to a lighter beat, and in this way . . . it is called the *passamezzo* . . . . Good dancers who are agile and lively can make whatever rearrangements seem desirable to them, provided they come down on the last beat. . . . You will understand these passages and divisions . . . when we describe the . . . galliard.
>
> (Arbeau, [1589] 1967, p. 66)

An elaborated version of the pavan itself is well documented earlier in the century, although there are no choreographies. In 1549, for example, Bishop Lanfranco of Loreto says, "As for the Pavana and Gagliarda, let them be as vivacious as they can so that even the very benches, chairs, and vases start to dance" (Palisca, 1953, p. 95). The importance of the pavan is indicated not only by the custom of making showy "divisions" of the steps, as suggested by Lanfranco and Arbeau, but by the recognition through new names of elaborate and vigorous subtypes of the dance, such as the *passo e mezzo* and the *pavaniglia.* [*See* Passo e Mezzo *and* Pavaniglia.]

The pavan was extremely popular in musical collections, appearing in great numbers in suites apparently intended for dancing (as in Joan Ambrosio Dalza's collection of 1508), but also frequently as discrete, and often abstract pieces—that is, not intended for dancing. Some of the most profound and beautiful abstract pavans of this time evoke the solemnity of the dance but exceed it in musical expression, such as John Dowland's instrumental and vocal "Lachrimae Pavans" (Dowland, 1600, 1604). The pavan was normally but not always in duple meter, and when it was part of a musical suite it was usually the first dance, followed by at least one triple-meter *saltarello* and/or galliard, as well as by other dances on the same musical material (see Dalza for pavan-*saltarello-piva* suites).

There is a huge disparity in numbers between the few choreographic sources of pavans and the plethora of musical pavans or *paduanas*—especially those named at the beginning of dance suites in musical collections. This circumstance leads to questions about the many dances in the manuals that are unnamed as to type, especially the first dances in the dance suites (most such suites were called *balletti*). Here indeed many unspecified duple dances open *balletto* suites in Caroso (1581, 1600) and Cesare Negri (1602) that often begin their figures with walking step patterns like those in the specified pavans (two *passi puntati* and a *seguito* beginning on the left foot).

Most of the unnamed dances that begin this way continue with more elaborate figures varying the paths and changing the relationship between the dancers. Their much more complicated step patterns, after an initially simple opening, divide the basic steps and musical beats with rapid footwork usually associated with fast or "high" dances like the galliard. It seems feasible, then, to envisage a pavan family in which the dances, while not classic pavans, nevertheless are pavan types (as in the opening and closing sections of Negri's "So ben mi chi ha bon tempo"). Furthermore, because the majority of step patterns of the late sixteenth century could be either in duple or triple meters, it is entirely possible that unnamed triple dances with a preponderance of pavan-like steps were also considered pavan types (e.g., Caroso's "Bellezza d'Olimpia" of 1600; see Sutton, 1986).

Postulating a pavan family would enormously enlarge the choreographed pavan repertory and help to explain the disparity between the manuals and the musical collections in numbers of pavans. Thus, the reason the manuals omitted the title from many pavan types may have been that its basic elements and position in a *balletto* suite were simply assumed. In fact, without this theory it would have to be concluded from the manuals that the pavan was rarely danced toward the end of the century, and this would not accord with the circumstantial evidence.

After the sixteenth century, the only choreographic sources to mention the pavan are the later Inns of Court manuscripts (which copy the earlier ones); Mersenne (1636–1637), who speaks only of its origins and style; de Esquivel Navarro (*Discursos sobre el arte del danzado*, 1642), who mentions without detail pavan variations to be done in the dancing master's studio; and a few dances with the title from the early eighteenth century that do not resemble the sixteenth-century sources and are indistinguishable from other eighteenth-century dances, such as Guillaume-Louis Pecour's "Pavane des Saisons" (1700). (For further eighteenth-century references see Hilton, 1981). Twentieth-century dances such as Maurice Ravel's *Pavane pour une Infante Défunte* or José Limón's *The Moor's Pavane* use the title to suggest the color of the old dance, but its living tradition and its affect of pomp and circumstance appear to have persisted in modern processional steps at weddings and graduations.

BIBLIOGRAPHY: SOURCES

Arbeau, Thoinot. *Orchésographie et traicte en forme de dialogve, par leqvel tovtes personnes pevvent facilement apprendre & practiquer l'honneste exercice des dances.* Langres, 1588, 1589. Facsimile reprint, Langres, 1988. Reprinted with expanded title as *Orchesographie, metode, et teorie en forme de discovrs et tablatvre povr apprendre a dancer, battre le Tambour en toute sorte & diuersté de batteries, Iouët du fifre & arigot, tirer des armes & escrimer, auec autres honnestes exercices fort conuenables à la Ieunesse.* Langres, 1596. Facsimile reprint, Geneva, 1972.

Arbeau, Thoinot. *Orchesography.* 1589. Translated into English by Mary Stewart Evans. New York, 1948. Reprint with corrections, a new introduction, and notes by Julia Sutton, and representative steps and dances in Labanotation by Mireille Backer. New York, 1967.

Arena, Antonius. *Ad suos compagnones studiantes.* Lyon, 1528. Translated by John Guthrie and Marino Zorzi in "*Rules of Dancing* by Antonius Arena." *Dance Research* 4 (Autumn 1986): 3–53.

Caroso, Fabritio. *Il ballarino* (1581). Facsimile reprint, New York, 1967.

Caroso, Fabritio. *Nobiltà di dame.* Venice, 1600, 1605. Facsimile reprint, Bologna, 1970. Reissued with order of illustrations changed as *Raccolta di varij balli,* Rome, 1630. Translated into English with eight introductory chapters by Julia Sutton, the music transcribed by F. Marian Walker. Oxford, 1986. Reprint with a step manual in Labanotation by Rachelle Palnick Tsachor and Julia Sutton, New York, 1995.

Dalza, Joan Ambrosio. *Intabulatura de lauto, libro quarto* (1508). Facsimile reprint, Geneva, 1979.

Dowland, John. *Flow My Teares.* London, 1600.

Dowland, John. *Lachrimae for Lute.* London, c.1600.

Dowland, John. *Lachrimae or Seven Teares.* London, 1604. Facsimile reprint, 1974.

Esquivel Navarro, Juan de. *Discursos sobre el arte del dancado* (1642). Facsimile reprint, Madrid, 1947.

Florio, John. *A World of Wordes.* London, 1598. Facsimile reprint, Hildesheim, 1972. 2d ed., *Queen Anna's New World of Words.* London, 1611. Facsimile reprint of 1611 ed., Menston, England, 1973.

Manuscripts of the Inns of Court. Located in Bodleian Library, Rawl.Poet.108, ff.10v-11r; British Library, Harley 367, pp. 178–179; Bodleian Douce 280, ff.66av–66bv (202v–203v); Bodleian, Rawl.D.864, f.199v, ff.203r-204; Royal College of Music, MS 1119, title page and ff.1–2, 23v–24r; Inner Temple, Miscellanea vol. 27.

Mersenne, Marin. *Harmonie universelle* (1636–1637). Facsimile reprint, Paris, 1963. English translation of Book 2 by J. B. Egan. Ph.D. diss., Indiana University, 1962.

Negri, Cesare. *Le gratie d'amore.* Milan, 1602. Reissued as *Nuove invenzione di balli.* Milan, 1604. Translated into Spanish by Don Balthasar Carlos for Señor Condé, Duke of Sanlucar, 1630. Manuscript located in Madrid, Biblioteca Nacional, MS 14085. Facsimile reprint of 1602, New York and Bologna, 1969. Literal translation into English and musical transcription by Yvonne Kendall. D.M.A. diss., Stanford University, 1985.

Pécour, Louis. *Recueil de dances composées par M. Pécour.* Paris, 1700.

Playford, John. *The English Dancing Master.* London, 1651. Facsimile reprint with introduction, concordances, and lists of references by Margaret Dean-Smith, London, 1957.

Prato, Giovanni Andrea da. *Storia di Milano.* Milan, 1520.

BIBLIOGRAPHY: OTHER STUDIES

Brown, Alan. "Pavan." In *The New Grove Dictionary of Music and Musicians.* London, 1980.

Cagnola, Giovan Pietro, ed. *Chronache milanesi.* Florence, 1842. See vol. 4, p. 300.

Heartz, Daniel. "Sources and Forms of the French Instrumental Dance in the Sixteenth Century." Ph.D. diss., Harvard University, 1957.

Hilton, Wendy. *Dance of Court and Theatre: The French Noble Style, 1690–1725.* Princeton, 1981.

Moe, Lawrence H. "Dance Music in Printed Italian Lute Tablatures from 1507 to 1611." Ph.D. diss., Harvard University, 1956.

Moe, Lawrence H. "Pavane." In *Die Musik und Geschichte und Gegenwart.* 1st ed., vol. 10, 1962. Kassel, 1949–1979.

Palisca, Claude V. "The Beginnings of Baroque Music: Its Roots in Sixteenth-Century Theory and Polemics." Ph.D. diss., Harvard University, 1953.

Sutton, Julia. "Triple Pavans: Clues to Some Mysteries in Sixteenth-Century Dance." *Early Music* 14.2 (1986): 174–181.

Sutton, Julia. "Musical Forms and Dance Forms in the Dance Manuals of Sixteenth-Century Italy: Plato and the Varieties of Variation." In *The Marriage of Music and Dance: Papers from a Conference Held at the Guildhall School of Music and Drama, London, 9th–11th August 1991.* Cambridge, 1992.

Sutton, Julia, and Sibylle Dahms. "Ballo, Balletto." In *Die Musik in Geschichte und Gegenwart.* 2d ed., vol. 1, 1994. Kassel, 1994–.

Tani, Gino. "Pavana." In *Enciclopedio dello spettacolo.* 9 vols. Rome, 1954–1968.

JULIA SUTTON
with Carol G. Marsh

PAVANIGLIA. A sixteenth-century dance, the *pavaniglia* is a subtype of the pavan and the galliard. The extant, complete, and named *pavaniglia* choreographies consist of four full sets of vigorous and ornate variations, two by Fabritio Caroso (1581, 1600), and two in Cesare Negri's manual (1602). Negri terms one version *alla Romana* (in Roman style) and the other *all'uso di Milano* (in Milanese style). There are as many as sixteen variations in one set; three sets are specified to be performed by one couple, mostly side by side and simultaneously, whereas the Milanese type is for one or two couples. In all four settings the *pavaniglia* is clearly a hybrid of the two dance types, combining the pavan with the galliard by keeping the pavan's side-by-side formation and opening steps, but then using rapid step patterns with jumps, kicks, and other vigorous movements normally found in galliards.

Each variation begins with a typical pavan opening of one or two *passi puntati* and closes with a codetta that includes a *cadenza in gagliarda* (cadence as in a galliard). Occasionally the lady is instructed to substitute less strenuous steps for the ones done by the gentleman; Negri's *pavaniglia* in Milanese style also gives the partners differing paths in some variations. Of special interest choreographically is the requirement in both of Caroso's dances and in Negri's "Pavaniglia alla Romana" that in some variations the partners be on opposite feet while facing each other. In that stance, as Caroso says, they "may move along" together—a unique situation in sixteenth-century dance, where the general rule is for partners to dance on the same foot.

A related pavan-galliard hybrid whose elaborate variations begin with *passi puntati* and end with a *cadenza in gagliarda* is the *passo e mezzo;* the difference between the *pavaniglia* and the *passo e mezzo* seems to be that in the *pavaniglia* the variations are performed simultaneously (and usually side by side), while in the *passo e mezzo* the partners alternate in dancing the showy variations. Both dance types have their own specific music normally asso-

PAVANIGLIA. Example 1. A transcription of the lute tablature for Fabritio Caroso's *pavaniglia* "Amorosina Grimana," a dance found in both his treatises, *Il ballarino* (1581) and *Nobiltà di dame* (1600).

ciated with them, and both appear to be in duple mensuration, although there is a possibility that they were meant to be resolved into fast triple (see Caroso, 1986). [*See* Passo e Mezzo.]

There are two smaller choreographic sources: Thoinot Arbeau gives two brief variations (1588), which he calls "Pavane d'Espagne" (Spanish Pavan) and that are clearly related to the Italian dances; in one of the Manuscripts of the Inns of Court, a short "Spanish Pavan" (Bodleian, Douce 280, c.1600) gives no music but speaks briefly of bounds and capers (galliard step patterns), saying that the dance "must be learned by practise and demonstration."

The musical settings for Arbeau's, Caroso's, and Negri's "Pavaniglia alla Romana" are all concordant (see example 1), and the tune and bass appear elsewhere often as "The Spanish Pavan" (see Poulton, 1961); whether the music or the dance were of Spanish or Italian origin remains unproven; however, the Spanish composer Antonio de Cabezón (1510–1566) wrote two sets of keyboard variations, each called "Pavana Italiana," on the same music, and in at least one instance a *pavanilla italiana* was reportedly danced in Spain in 1608 (see Tani, 1954–1968). The *pavaniglia* does not appear to have continued as a dance beyond the early seventeenth century, but musical examples occur as late as 1645.

[*See also* Pavan.]

BIBLIOGRAPHY: SOURCES

Alessandri, Filippo degli. *Discorso sopra il ballo.* Terni, 1620.

Arbeau, Thoinot. *Orchésographie et traicte en forme de dialogve, par leqvel tovtes personnes pevvent facilement apprendre & practiquer l'honneste exercice des dances.* Langres, 1588, 1589. Facsimile reprint, Langres, 1988. Reprinted with expanded title as *Orchesographie, metode, et teorie en forme de discovrs et tablatvre povr apprendre a dancer, battre le Tambour en toute sorte & diuersité de batteries, Iouët du fifre & arigot, tirer des armes & escrimer, auec autres honnestes exercices fort conuenables à la Ieunesse.* Langres, 1596. Facsimile reprint, Geneva, 1972.

Arbeau, Thoinot. *Orchesography.* 1589. Translated into English by Mary Stewart Evans. New York, 1948. Reprint with corrections, a new introduction, and notes by Julia Sutton, and representative steps and dances in Labanotation by Mireille Backer. New York, 1967.

Caroso, Fabritio. *Il ballarino* (1581). Facsimile reprint, New York, 1967.

Caroso, Fabritio. *Nobiltà di dame.* Venice, 1600, 1605. Facsimile reprint, Bologna, 1970. Reissued with order of illustrations changed as *Raccolta di varij balli.* Rome, 1630. Translated into English with eight introductory chapters by Julia Sutton, the music transcribed by F. Marian Walker. Oxford, 1986. Reprint with a step manual in Labanotation by Rachelle Palnick Tsachor and Julia Sutton, New York, 1995.

Manuscript of the Inns of Court. Located in Bodleian Library, Bodleian, Douce 280, ff.66av–66bv (202v–203v).

Negri, Cesare. *Le gratie d'amore.* Milan, 1602. Reissued as *Nuove invenzione di balli.* Milan, 1604. Translated into Spanish by Don Balthasar Carlos for Señor Condé, Duke of Sanlucar, 1630. Manuscript located in Madrid, Biblioteca Nacional, MS 14085. Facsimile reprint of 1602, New York and Bologna, 1969. Literal translation into English and musical transcription by Yvonne Kendall. D.M.A. diss., Stanford University, 1985.

BIBLIOGRAPHY: OTHER STUDIES

Collins, Michael B. "The Performance of Coloration, Sesquialtera, and Hemiolia, 1450–1750." Ph.D. diss., Stanford University, 1963.

Collins, Michael B. "The Performance of Sesquialtera and Hemiolia in the Sixteenth Century." *Journal of the American Musicological Society* 17 (Spring 1964): 5–28.

Esses, Maurice. *Dance and Instrumental Diferencias in Spain during the Seventeenth and Early Eighteenth Centuries.* Stuyvesant, N.Y., 1992.

Hudson, Richard. "Pavaniglia." In *The New Grove Dictionary of Music and Musicians.* London, 1980.

Moe, Lawrence H. "Dance Music in Printed Italian Lute Tablatures from 1507 to 1611." Ph.D. diss., Harvard University, 1956.

Poulton, Diana. "Notes on the Spanish Pavan." *Lute Society Journal* 3 (1961): 5–16.

Tani, Gino. "Pavana." In *Enciclopedio dello spettacolo.* 9 vols. Rome, 1954–1968.

JULIA SUTTON

PAVILLON D'ARMIDE, LE. Ballet in one act. Choreography: Michel Fokine. Music: Nikolai Tcherepnin. Libretto, scenery, and costumes: Alexandre Benois, adapted from a story by Théophile Gautier. First performance: 25 November 1907, Maryinsky Theater, Saint Petersburg. Principals: Anna Pavlova (Armida), Pavel Gerdt (Vicomte René de Beaugency; Rinaldo), Nikolai Soliannikov (Marquis; King Hydraot, Armida's father), Vaslav Nijinsky (Armida's Page), Georgi Rosai (The Chief Jester), Serge Grigoriev (The Valet).

Serge Diaghilev's desire to present *Le Pavillon d'Armide* in the West is cited as the foundation of his Ballets Russes enterprise. This, the first ballet he produced in Paris, established the fame of Vaslav Nijinsky, Tamara Karsavina, and Alexandre Benois.

For his first commissioned work for the Imperial Theaters, Michel Fokine was to expand a version of Nikolai Tcherepnin's *The Animated Gobelin* that he had staged for the annual student performance of the Maryinsky school on 15 April 1907, with Nijinsky and Elisaveta Gerdt. This *divertissement* became the second of the three scenes of *Le Pavillon d'Armide.*

The ballet's libretto by Alexandre Benois was based loosely on Théophile Gautier's story "Omphale." The complex plot concerns of a nobleman who is given shelter from a storm by the Marquis, who is a magician, in a room that contains a Gobelin tapestry depicting Armida's sumptuous court. During the night the tapestry comes to life, and the nobleman falls in love with Armida. At sunrise he awakens from his "dream" to find the scarf Armida had given him, and falls senseless, prey to the Marquis's magic.

Diaghilev opened both the Paris dress rehearsal of 18 May 1909 and the official premiere of 19 May with a revised version in which Mikhail Mordkin danced the Vicomte, Vera Karalli was Armida, Aleksei Bulgakov the Marquis, and Nijinsky again the Page. The pas de trois, danced by Karsavina, Alexandra Baldina, and Nijinsky, and the "Danse de Bouffons," led by Georgi Rosai, particularly captivated the Parisian audience. As the Page, Nijinsky created a sensation at the Paris premiere by leaping impetuously into the wings. In the pas de trois and later in the season as Armida, Karsavina established her fame. Fokine regarded the fiendishly intricate dance of the jesters as the most technically demanding dance he had ever created. The period charm of Benois's Louis XIV decor also contributed to the ballet's success.

Nonetheless, the ballet quickly began to appear old-fashioned in the context of the Diaghilev repertory, and it was dropped during the 1916 United States tour. This was the only one of Fokine's ballets in which he did not also have a hand in the libretto. He admitted that it could not be considered a "reform" ballet and later repudiated it as the work of a beginner who was "trying too hard."

BIBLIOGRAPHY

Benois, Alexandre. *Reminiscences of the Russian Ballet.* Translated by Mary Britnieva. London, 1941.

Buckle, Richard. *Diaghilev.* New York, 1979.

Fokine, Michel. *Protiv techeniia: Vospominaniia baletmeistera.* Edited by Yuri Slonimsky. Leningrad, 1962.

Garafola, Lynn. *Diaghilev's Ballets Russes.* New York, 1989.

Krasovskaya, Vera. *Russkii baletnyi teatr nachala dvadtsatogo veka,* vol. 1, *Khoreografy.* Leningrad, 1971.

Scholl, Tim. *From Petipa to Balanchine: Classical Revival and the Modernization of Ballet.* New York, 1994.

Wiley, Roland John, trans. and ed. *A Century of Russian Ballet: Documents and Accounts, 1810–1910.* Oxford, 1990. Includes the libretto for *Le Pavillon d'Armide.*

SUZANNE CARBONNEAU

PAVLOVA, ANNA (Anna Matveevna [later changed to Pavlovna] Pavlova; born 31 January [12 February] 1881 in Saint Petersburg, died 23 January 1931 in The Hague), Russian ballet dancer. Anna Pavlova was born in a military hospital in Saint Petersburg, where the registry of births identifies her parents as Matvey Pavlovich Pavlov, a private soldier from the Vyshnevolotsk district, and his lawful wife, Liubov Fedorovna Pavlova. The latter has been variously described as a laundress and as the linen-keeper at the Imperial Theater School. Some years later it was rumored in the Saint Petersburg press that Anna Pavlova was illegitimate and that her real father was a wealthy Jewish businessman of the Poliakov family. Pavlova herself was reticent on the subject, stating merely that her father had died when she was two years old. There is insufficient documentation to support either story.

PAVLOVA. *The Swan,* created for Pavlova in 1907 by Michel Fokine, became her signature solo. She danced it on stages all over the world for the rest of her life. (Photograph 1908 by Hänse Herrmann; from the Dance Collection, New York Public Library for the Performing Arts.)

Pavlova's early childhood was spent with her grandmother in the tiny village of Ligovo, outside Saint Petersburg, where she attended the local school. In 1890, around the time of her ninth birthday, her mother took her to one of the first performances of *The Sleeping Beauty* at the Maryinsky Theater, and from then onward her only desire was to become a dancer. "It never entered my mind," she later confessed, "that there were easier goals to attain than that of principal dancer in the Imperial Ballet."

In 1891 Pavlova was admitted to the Imperial Theater School, where her early dancing teachers included Ekaterina Vazem, Pavel Gerdt, and Christian Johansson. At the age of eleven, she made her first recorded appearance, in *The Magic Fairy Tale,* especially created for the pupils of the Imperial School by Marius Petipa, renowned choreographer, ballet master, and teacher. In 1895, Vazem evaluated the delicate fourteen-year-old girl as "proficient, but lacking strength" and placed her under the tutelage of Petipa, who took to her immediately, as did she to him. Their friendship lasted until his death in 1910. In March 1898, for the school performance at the Mikhailovsky Theater, Petipa revived his ballet *The Two Stars,* set to music by Cesare Pugni, and gave Pavlova the role of a Star.

PAVLOVA. With Alexandre Volinine in *Gavotte* (1913). Choreographed by Ivan Clustine to the bouncy tune of Paul Lincke's "Glühwürmchen-Idyll" (The Glowworm), *Gavotte* became almost as popular a number in Pavlova's repertory as *The Swan*. Her Directoire-style dress, made of lemon satin and trimmed with black velvet, was designed by Serge Oukrainsky. (Photograph 1916 by Mishkin; from the Dance Collection, New York Public Library for the Performing Arts.)

When, on 21 October [2 November] of the same year, Pavlova appeared at the Maryinsky in a pas de trois in Petipa's *La Fille du Pharaon*, a contemporary critic wrote that "the little Pavlova, with her fragile-looking knees, charmed everybody with her femininity, lightness, and grace." Although this performance occurred some six months ahead of her graduation, it is counted as her official debut.

For her graduation performance on 11 [23] April 1899, Pavlova performed in two ballets, Aleksandr Gorsky's *Clorinda* and Pavel Gerdt's *Imaginary Dryads*, into which Gerdt had interpolated a variation from Petipa's *La Vestale* for her. Valerian Svetlov, the most influential ballet critic in Saint Petersburg, wrote years later that in the variation "one could feel . . . something that . . . made one foresee in this fragile dancer a great artist. I do not know how many marks were awarded to her by the jury of experts, but I gave her the highest mark, twelve. Afterward . . . I added a plus to the mark" (Svetlov, 1931). The jury must have been of like mind, for, bypassing the corps de ballet, Pavlova was accepted into the company as a *coryphée*. (*Coryphées* danced in groups of three or four, and their salary was eight hundred rubles a year.) From the outset Pavlova was championed by Svetlov, who also assumed a paternal attitude toward her, if not a romantic one.

In February 1900, Pavlova danced the first role created especially for her, Hoarfrost in *The Seasons*, choreographed by Petipa to a score by Aleksandr Glazunov. Later that year she also appeared with notable success in several secondary parts, such as Zulme in *Giselle*, the Fairy Candide in *The Sleeping Beauty*, a friend of Fleur de Lys in *Esmeralda*, and Aurora in *The Awakening of Flora*. In September 1900, she was given the leading role in *The Awakening of Flora*, which she danced with only limited success, and the following year, in February 1901, she appeared as Lise in *The Magic Flute*, a lighthearted role that suited her much better. In 1902, Pavlova's poetic and powerful performance as Nikia in *La Bayadère*, one of Petipa's greatest creations, firmly established her reputation with both the critics and the public. In 1903, she gave her first performance in the title role of *Giselle*, in which her outstanding aerial quality and lightness appeared to full advantage. Giselle was to become one of her most celebrated interpretations.

Pavlova's physique, as well as the qualities of her dancing, made her particularly well suited to such roles as Nikia and Giselle. In appearance she was the prototype of the ballerina. Her white, oval face, framed by smooth black hair, was illuminated by magnificent dark eyes—her most outstanding feature. Her small head was delicately poised on a slender neck, and her beautiful shoulders topped a long torso: she had a body perfectly proportioned for dance. Her legs, too, were beautiful and slender, without the slightest trace of muscular development, and her small, strong feet were highly arched.

In 1903 Pavlova was granted a leave of absence from the Imperial Theaters to study under the celebrated teacher Caterina Beretta in Milan. She returned to Saint Petersburg with a considerably improved technique, and in 1904 she triumphed in the demanding ballerina roles in Petipa's productions of *Paquita* and *Le Corsaire*, both originally choreographed by Joseph Mazilier. In the same year she made guest appearances at the Bolshoi Theater in Moscow and at the Wielki Theater in Warsaw, where she was again highly praised for her interpretation of Giselle.

In 1905, soon after her promotion to principal dancer, Pavlova became a ringleader in a protest against the management of the Imperial Theaters, as many dancers went on strike, demanding higher pay, improved working conditions, and an opportunity to participate in artistic decisions. Although the insurrection fizzled out, Pavlova maintained her belief in the justice of the artists' cause.

Despite her militant attitude, she was given the coveted role of Kitri in Aleksandr Gorsky's restaging of Petipa's *Don Quixote,* and in December 1905 she was once again acclaimed for the vivacity and brilliance of her dancing and for the charm of her characterization.

In 1906, Pavlova was officially appointed ballerina. Her progress through the hierarchy of female dancers at the Maryinsky had been meteoric. In 1902, only her third year after graduation, she had been promoted to second soloist, earning an annual salary of twelve hundred rubles; in 1903, she was made first soloist, at fifteen hundred rubles; in 1905, principal dancer, at twenty-five hundred rubles; and in 1906, ballerina, at three thousand rubles, plus a long period of leave. (In 1907 she would be given an extra three hundred rubles for each performance, and in 1908 she would earn a salary of eight thousand rubles and be granted leave to travel abroad.)

By 1906, after several changes of living quarters, Pavlova had settled in an elegant apartment in a fashionable district of Saint Petersburg. There, in a magnificently appointed studio, she received private lessons from Enrico Cecchetti, a leading ballet teacher whom she had persuaded to return to Saint Petersburg especially to work with her. (Conscious of a certain weakness in her back, Pavlova particularly wanted Cecchetti to direct her training to overcome this technical deficiency.) By this time, too, she had formed an alliance with Victor Dandré, a wealthy aristocrat who had become the chief supporter of her way of life. Even on a ballerina's salary, she could not have afforded to maintain herself in such comfort without supplementary funds.

A rising young official on Saint Petersburg's municipal council, Dandré was forwarding his social ambitions by taking an active part in charitable work. He found the perfect slot when he became chairman of the Dance Committee of the Society for the Prevention of Cruelty to Children, for this charity's regular method of raising funds was the organization and presentation of ballet galas. Thus it was at Dandré's invitation that Michel Fokine, a solo dancer then just beginning his choreographic career, devised two ballets for one such event and that Pavlova danced in both. On 10 [23] February 1907, at a special charity performance at the Maryinsky Theater, she appeared as Actea in *Eunice,* a dramatic ballet of only passing interest, and in the waltz section of an episodic work entitled *Chopiniana,* later to be revised and to become world-famous as *Les Sylphides,* universally recognized as a masterpiece. [*See* Sylphides, Les.]

The year 1907 proved to be an eventful one for both Pavlova and Fokine. In the summer, leading a small group of dancers from the Maryinsky, they visited Moscow and gave a number of performances. Included in their repertory was a short work by Fokine entitled *The Animated Gobelin,* which he had mounted for the ballet school's graduation performance the previous April. It was, in fact, one scene from a longer work, *Le Pavillon d'Armide,* that had been proposed by the composer Nikolai Tcherepnin and the designer-librettist Alexandre Benois. The following November, at the Maryinsky premiere of the full-length work, Pavlova assumed the leading role of Armida. Partnered by the eighteen-year-old Vaslav Nijinsky and cast in a relatively static role, she was somewhat overshadowed by the virtuosity of the youthful prodigy. The very next month, however, she made a sensational appearance at another charity performance at the Maryinsky when she danced Fokine's composition to a short piece by Camille Saint-Saëns entitled "The Swan." Later known as *The Dying Swan,* it was to become her most famous solo. [*See* Dying Swan, The.]

On 6 [19] January 1908, Pavlova achieved her childhood ambition when she appeared at the Maryinsky Theater as the Princess Aurora in *The Sleeping Beauty* for the first time. Curiously, however, she found herself not en-

PAVLOVA. *The Dragonfly* (1915), a solo danced to Fritz Kreisler's "Schön Rosmarin," was a brief but brilliant display of Pavlova's remarkable allegro technique. The swiftness and lightness of her movements were enhanced by gossamer wings and a dress of blue, green, and purple net. (Photograph 1916 by Hill Studios, New York; from the Dance Collection, New York Public Library for the Performing Arts.)

tirely in sympathy with the academic demands of the role, and it did not become one of her repertory favorites. In February, Pavlova made a few guest appearances in Riga, Latvia, and then in April she and Adolph Bolm led a group of twenty dancers—billed as "The Imperial Ballet from the Maryinsky Theater"—on a tour to Helsingfors (Helsinki), Stockholm, Prague, and Berlin. Upon her return to Saint Petersburg, she was invited by Serge Diaghilev, an ambitious young impressario, to head a company of dancers from the Imperial Theaters that he planned to take to Paris in 1909. She accepted his invitation, but, having committed herself to a spring tour of Berlin, Leipzig, Prague, and Vienna, partnered by Nikolai Legat, Pavlova was unable to join Diaghilev's company in Paris until the end of May, after their season had already begun.

On 2 June 1909, Pavlova appeared with the Diaghilev company in two quite different ballets, both choreographed by Fokine: *Les Sylphides,* formerly known as *Chopiniana,* and *Cléopâtre,* formerly known as *Une Nuit d'Egypte.* Partnered by Nijinsky in the former and by Fokine himself in the latter, she scored a great success, and Diaghilev thereupon announced that she would appear at every subsequent performance of the company. [*See* Ballets Russes de Serge Diaghilev.] After the so-called Saison Russe was over, Pavlova went on to London and on 19 July danced at the house of Lord and Lady Londesborough before the king and queen of England. Her partner on this occasion, who also arranged the Russian dance in which they appeared, was Mikhail Mordkin. A good-looking man with a robust, imposing physique, Mordkin was to play an important part in her later professional life.

The ability to choose her own roles, freedom from the authority of the directorate of the Imperial Theaters, and the adulation accorded to a visiting artist must have had a profound effect on Pavlova. Upon her return to Saint Petersburg in the fall of 1909, she negotiated a new three-year contract that not only provided her with a handsome salary (fifty-five hundred rubles, with increases to seven thousand and eight thousand rubles in each successive year) but that also permitted her to group her performances at the Maryinsky and allowed her freedom to travel. Touring abroad now began to occupy a major part of her life. She would later say that her life of touring and her desire to dance all over the world were inspired by reading a biography of Marie Taglioni, who enjoyed the acclaim of audiences wherever she traveled.

On her first visit to the United States, Pavlova made a triumphant debut at the Metropolitan Opera House in New York on 28 February 1910. She danced Swanilda in *Coppélia,* once again partnered by the handsome but volatile Mikhail Mordkin. The following evening they again appeared on the Metropolitan stage, dancing at a charity gala in aid of the opera company's pension and endowment fund. They appeared in two dances arranged by Mordkin, *Bacchanale* and a number entitled simply *Pas de*

PAVLOVA. With Hubert Stowitts in *Assyrian Dance,* arranged for them by Clustine and first performed on a tour of South America in 1917. This dance was one of several that reflected Pavlova's interest in oriental themes and in non-Western cultures. As she traveled around the world, her repertory expanded to include dances of many nations. (Photograph 1917 by Franz van Riel; from the Dance Collection, New York Public Library of the Performing Arts.)

Deux. As each of these dances was designed to be an electrifying showpiece, Pavlova and Mordkin more than held their own against the popular appeal of such renowned opera stars as Enrico Caruso and Emmy Destinn.

On 18 April 1910, Pavlova opened her first season at the Palace, a London music hall, still partnered by Mordkin and supported by twelve soloists from the Imperial Theaters. This season, which lasted for more than three months, would establish her as a favorite with London audiences but would prevent her from participating in Diaghilev's Saison Russe in Paris the following summer. The repertory of her troupe included three extraordinary pas de deux—the exquisite *Valse Caprice,* arranged by Nikolai Legat to music by Anton Rubenstein; Fokine's romantic Waltz from *Chopiniana;* and Mordkin's exuberant *Bacchanale,* a "glorious frenzy" set to Glazunov's familiar music from *The Seasons*—as well as solos for each of the principal dancers. Among the most popular of Pavlova's solos were *Night,* arranged by Legat to Rubenstein's music; *La Rose Mourante* (The Dying Rose), her own choreography to music by Riccardo Drigo; *Le Papillon* (The Butterfly), arranged by Legat to music by Léon Minkus; and, of course, *The Swan.* For the rest of her career, more than one delighted critic would remark on her unusual ability to characterize flowers and birds and insects in lively and interesting ways.

Upon her return to Saint Petersburg in August 1910, Pavlova requested a two-year leave of absence to tour abroad. When her request was refused, she paid a huge forfeit to break her contract and in September returned to the United States with Mordkin. They were again supported by twelve soloists, and this time their repertory included two ballets, the romantic tragedy *Giselle,* a perennially popular classic, and the exotic *Legend of Aziade,* a new work choreographed by Mordkin to music by Nikolai Rimsky-Korsakov and others. Both these ballets delighted American audiences. Following appearances in the principal cities of the United States and Canada, the troupe returned to London in April 1911 to start another long engagement at the Palace. During this season a serious disagreement arose between Pavlova and Mordkin, and she slapped his face publicly. After a few days they were reconciled, and once again danced together brilliantly. Mordkin nevertheless left the troupe before the end of the season and was replaced by Laurent Novikoff, who had been a principal dancer at the Bolshoi Ballet in Moscow.

By this time, Pavlova had been joined in London by Victor Dandré. In February 1911 he had been accused of embezzlement of public funds and had been held in custody. Released when his brother stood bail for him, he had slipped the bail, escaped Russia, and fled to London. He was thus in the awkward position of being unable to return to Russia.

PAVLOVA. With Uday Shankar in *Krishna and Radha,* one of the two dances in *Oriental Impressions,* both of which were arranged by Shankar to music by Comolata Banerji in 1923. (Photograph 1923 by Stephenson Studio, Atlanta; from the Dance Collection, New York Public Library for the Performing Arts.)

Pavlova, of course, was under no such constraint. She gave several performances at the Maryinsky in September 1911 and then returned to London to take part in Diaghilev's fall season at Covent Garden. Partnered by Nijinsky, she danced in *Giselle, Le Pavillon d'Armide, Cléopâtre, Le Carnaval,* and a pas de deux billed as *L'Oiseau d'Or,* which was in fact none other than Petipa's famous Bluebird pas de deux from *The Sleeping Beauty.* It is difficult to imagine the impact of this partnership upon the London audiences who attended their performances; surely there was no pair more perfectly suited than Pavlova and Nijinsky to dance Giselle and Albrecht, not to mention Columbine and Harlequin or Princess Florine and the Bluebird. This extraordinary partnership was, however, short-lived, for Pavlova would never again dance with Nijinsky or appear with the Diaghilev company. Immediately after this London season, she undertook her first tour of the English provinces, partnered by Novikoff and supported by a small group of soloists from the Imperial Ballet.

PAVLOVA. A studio portrait in costume for *Au Bal,* set in 1927 by Boris Romanov to the mazurka from the last act of *The Sleeping Beauty.* As a coquette who flirts with six young officers at a ball, Pavlova wore this elaborate blue and silver dress and plumed hat designed by Leon Zack. (Photograph by Ross Verlag, Berlin; from the Dance Collection, New York Public Library for the Performing Arts.)

The year 1912 saw Pavlova setting up a life based in London. Returning from a provincial tour in March, she and Dandré moved into Ivy House, a large estate in Golders Green, which she would eventually purchase in 1914. She began to take pupils, including Muriel Stuart, who was to become an important member of her company, and she started her policy of employing English dancers but camouflaging their names with Russianized spellings. Hilda Boot, known as Butsova, remained with the Pavlova company from 1911 until her marriage in 1925, serving as Pavlova's understudy and then dancing as ballerina in her own right.

After another long season at the Palace in the spring of 1912, Pavlova made a second tour of the English provinces and then in December undertook a tour of Germany. Her repertory for this tour included two new Fokine ballets, created especially for her: *The Seven Daughters of the Mountain King* (1912), set to music by the Armenian composer Alexander Spendiarov (Spendiaryan), and *Les Préludes* (1913), a "futuristic ballet" to music of Franz Liszt. From Germany, Pavlova went to Russia, giving performances in Saint Petersburg and Moscow. On 24 February [8 March] 1913 she danced for the last time at the Maryinsky Theater, appearing as Nikia in *La Bayadère.*

Returning to London, Pavlova began her fourth and last season at the Palace, which ran from April to September 1913. This was also the last time her company was billed as "Dancers from the Imperial Ballet." Now forty members strong, it was reorganized on a permanent basis as the Pavlova Ballet. She now had her own ballet master, Enrico Cecchetti (who would be replaced the next year by Ivan Clustine), her own conductor, Theodore Stier (who had joined her in 1910 and who, except for the war years, would remain with her until 1925), her own costumier, Manya Charchevnikova, and her own small orchestra. Her partners were Petr Zajlich and Laurent Novikoff, and her companion, the apparently imperturbable Victor Dandré, was the mastermind of the entire enterprise. He traveled ahead of the company, making bookings and all other necessary arrangements. A special train was hired to transport the company's dancers and baggage, which amounted to some 400 pieces, including about 40 heavy cases of scenery and 120 costume hampers. In the fall of 1913 the Pavlova Ballet set sail for the United States, where it visited 146 cities in six months, sometimes appearing in six different cities in one week.

In the spring of 1914 the company traveled from the United States to Germany, Austria, Czechoslovakia, and Hungary. Pavlova then went on to Saint Petersburg, where with a small group of soloists she performed in Moscow, in Peterhof, and, on 7 [20] June, in Pavlovsk—her last performance in Russia. After a brief return to London, she again undertook a tour in Germany. Meanwhile, on 28 June the assassination of the Austrian archduke Francis Ferdinand by a Serbian nationalist had set off a chain of events that would soon result in declarations of war among the nations of Europe. In early August, after Germany declared war on Russia, Pavlova managed to book passage on a train for London, which she safely reached. The subsequent outbreak of hostilities, the years of conflict (1914–1918), and the Russian Revolution of 1917 meant that she would never again return to her native land.

Pavlova sailed again to the United States in the fall of 1914. Her partner was now Alexandre Volinine, an elegant Russian dancer who would remain with her until 1925, and the repertory of her company had been expanded to include many one-act ballets and a series of social dances—a gavotte, a waltz, a minuet—in which she was often partnered by the company's ballet master, Ivan Clustine. The tour ended with a season at the Century Opera House, New York, and was followed, in March 1915, by the company's first visit to Cuba. The spring and summer were spent touring the United States, and in September

1915 the Pavlova Ballet joined forces with the Boston Grand Opera Company, giving joint performances of opera and ballet. Their nine-month tour was a financial disaster, but Pavlova's subsequent appearance in *The Dumb Girl of Portici* (1916), a Hollywood film directed by Lois Weber, was highly profitable. Her earnings as a film star enabled her to offset some of her debts as a ballerina.

The need to replenish her purse also undoubtedly led to Pavlova's next venture. In August 1916, she and her company joined the cast of *The Big Show*, produced by Charles Dillingham at the New York Hippodrome. Sharing the bill with spectacular acts featuring acrobats, aerialists, and elephants, they performed an abridged version of *The Sleeping Beauty*, with lavish costumes and sets designed by Léon Bakst. When this production proved too sophisticated for American tastes, Pavlova's part on the program was reduced to a series of brilliant *divertissements*, which were greatly appreciated. The company ended its run at the Hippodrome in January 1917.

After a return season in Cuba in February 1917, the Pavlova Ballet set sail for South America, where it would remain for most of the following two years. Early in 1919 Pavlova made another visit to Cuba, followed by a triumphant season in Mexico, where she danced in a bullring to a capacity crowd. After a visit to Puerto Rico, she returned to the southern continent, dancing in Brazil and Argentina from April to September. On 27 September 1919, in Rio de Janeiro, the company gave the first performance of her own ballet, *Autumn Leaves*, set to the music of Chopin, before returning to Europe. This was to be the only complete ballet that Pavlova herself designed and arranged, although she choreographed a number of her own solos and participated in the creation of other works mounted for her company. Sailing from South America in the fall of 1919, the Pavlova Ballet landed in Lisbon and performed in Portugal and Spain before arriving in Paris for a short season at the beginning of 1920. This was followed by brief visits to Brussels and Liège, after which the company returned to Ivy House in London at the end of March 1920.

Although Pavlova has frequently been criticized for the lack of originality in her repertory and for the banality of her musical taste, it cannot be said that she did not know what her audiences wanted to see. Most of them preferred simple narrative ballets, such as *Coppélia*, *The Fairy Doll*, *The Awakening of Flora*, or *Amarilla* (1912), a dramatic, one-act ballet about a passionate gypsy girl choreographed by Petr Zajlich. Her own work, *Autumn Leaves*, a choreographic drama in which she portrayed a chrysanthemum buffeted by the North Wind, rescued and then cast away by an unfeeling poet, was considered a masterpiece. Most popular of all, however, were such *divertissements* as Clustine's *Gavotte* (1913), her own *Dragonfly* (1915) and *Californian Poppy* (1916), and, of course, Fokine's inspired characterization *The Swan*. She occasionally experimented with more esoteric works, such *La Péri* (1917), a one-act ballet on a Persian theme choreographed by Hubert Stowitts and Ivan Clustine to music by Paul Dukas, but these were not popular with her audiences and were, for the most part, poorly received by the critics as well. However, the ballets inspired by her visits to Japan and India, in particular *Oriental Impressions* and *Ajanta Frescoes* (both, 1923), were usually well received by the public and the critics.

Aside from questioning her musical taste and choice of repertory, some latter-day pundits have gone so far as to dismiss Pavlova as a performing artist, saying, "Pavlova had no technique." The truth is that her technique was so perfect that it concealed technique. Her arabesque and *pas de bourrée* have rarely been equaled, and, although she lacked a natural turnout, her line was always impeccable. It is true that she did not perform feats of acrobatic virtuosity, choosing to leave such spectacular tricks to others, but is it also true that as an interpretive artist Pavlova probably, even today, remains unsurpassed. She was supreme in roles requiring feminine coquetry and

PAVLOVA. As the Chrysanthemum, with Aubrey Hitchins as the North Wind, in *Autumn Leaves*, photographed in Buenos Aires in 1928. This one-act work was created by Pavlova in 1920 to piano pieces by her favorite composer, Frédéric Chopin. (Photograph by Franz van Riel; from the Dance Collection, New York Public Library for the Performing Arts.)

light comedy; she excelled in lyrical and poetic roles, in which her fluid, expressive arms and hands were remarkable; and she could be deeply moving in dramatic and tragic roles such as Nikia and Giselle. What made her performances unique, however, was not so much her technical mastery or even her talent at characterization; it was the emotion she poured into her performances, her incomparable stage presence—in short, the power of her personality.

Throughout the decade of the 1920s, Pavlova and her company were constantly on tour. From April to June 1920 they appeared at Drury Lane, in London, then spent a week in the English provinces before returning to London for a short season at the Prince's Theatre. In October they sailed again for the United States to start a six-month coast-to-coast tour. Returning to Europe, they spent the spring and summer of 1921 in France and England, and in October they undertook another long tour of the United States and Canada, which lasted until the following May. In September 1922, the Pavlova Ballet embarked on its first tour of East Asia, which continued until the spring of 1923. After a short holiday the company again toured the English provinces before giving a season at Covent Garden in September. It then left immediately for yet another coast-to-coast tour of the United States, which ended in May 1924. Returning to Europe, Pavlova gave a short season in Paris and then traveled to Barcelona to take lessons in Spanish dancing. A short holiday and another Covent Garden season in the fall were followed by yet another tour of the United States—her last. She then presented a four-week season in Mexico City in April 1925 before returning to Europe for engagements in France, Germany, and England. In December 1925 the company set sail for South Africa, and thence to Australia and New Zealand, where it continued to tour until August 1926. In the fall of 1926 Pavlova began a European tour that ended in Copenhagen in May 1927. That September she gave her last season at Covent Garden. After another provincial tour of England and an extensive tour of Europe, from December 1927 to May 1928, the company—now augmented by the well-known premier danseur Pierre Vladimiroff—set off for South America, where it performed in the major capitals before returning to London in the fall. In November 1928 Pavlova began her final world tour, which lasted until July 1929, taking in Egypt, India, and Australia. From mid-autumn to December 1929, she made another tour of the English provinces, and from January to May 1930 she once again toured Europe.

PAVLOVA. With Lavrent Novikoff in *Chopiniana.* First performed by the Pavlova company as *Une Soirée de Chopin* in 1913, this work included the well-known Waltz in C-sharp Minor from Michel Fokine's *Chopiniana,* which Pavlova had created in 1907, but all other sections were choreographed by Ivan Clustine. It remained in Pavlova's repertory until the end of her life. (Photograph by Ross Verlag, Berlin; from the Dance Collection, New York Public Library for the Performing Arts.)

In the autumn of 1930, following summer holidays in the South of France and at Ivy House, Pavlova made yet another tour of England, ending with a week at the Golders Green Hippodrome. Her performance there on 13 December 1930—in *Amarilla, Gavotte, The Swan,* and the *grand pas classique* from *Paquita*—proved to be her last. She again took a short holiday in the South of France and, en route from Cannes to Paris, caught a chill, which she ignored. By the time she reached Holland, the starting point of her next tour, she had developed pneumonia. She died in the Hôtel des Indes in The Hague in the early hours of 23 January 1931. A doctor, her maid, and Victor Dandré were at her bedside.

No chronicle of Pavlova's travels can convey her own sense of mission to bring dance to audiences not only in great cities but in small towns all over the world. Nor can it suggest the impression of beauty and wonder she left upon the millions of people who saw her dance, many of whom had never before witnessed a ballet performance. In 1917, in Lima, Peru, a schoolboy named Frederick Ashton saw her perform, and he never forgot the artistry of what he had seen. He later wrote the following tribute:

"Of her epoch she was undoubtedly the most famous name throughout the world. Her name can never die, for such a living and passionate spirit must continue to haunt the world to which she gave so much delight and inspiration."

[*See also entries on major figures and works mentioned herein.*]

BIBLIOGRAPHY

Algeranoff, Harcourt. *My Years with Pavlova.* London, 1957.

Beaumont, Cyril W. *Anna Pavlova.* 3d ed. London, 1945.

Dance Magazine (January 1976). Special issue on Pavlova.

Dandré, Victor. *Anna Pavlova in Art and Life.* London, 1932. Reprint, New York, 1979.

Devine, Maggie Odom. "The Swan Immortalized." *Ballet Review* 21 (Summer 1993): 67–80.

Fokine, Michel. *Memoirs of a Ballet Master.* Translated by Vitale Fokine, edited by Anatole Chujoy. Boston, 1961.

Fonteyn, Margot. *Pavlova: Portrait of a Dancer.* New York, 1984.

Franks, A. H., comp. *Pavlova: A Biography.* London, 1956. Reprint, New York, 1979. Includes a biographical sketch, a collection of memoirs, and Pavlova's own recollection, "Pages of My Life."

Garafola, Lynn. *Diaghilev's Ballets Russes.* New York and Oxford, 1989.

Hyden, Walford. *Pavlova: The Genius of the Dance.* London, 1931.

Kerensky, Oleg. *Anna Pavlova.* London, 1973.

Krasovskaya, Vera. *Anna Pavlova* (in Russian). Leningrad, 1965.

Lazzarini, John and Roberta. *Pavlova: Repertoire of a Legend.* New York, 1980. Includes many photographs, an extensive bibliography, and a reliable chronology of Pavlova's roles.

Levine, Ellen. *Anna Pavlova: Genius of the Dance.* New York, 1995.

Levinson, André. *Anna Pavlova* (in French). Paris, 1928.

Magriel, Paul, ed. *Pavlova: An Illustrated Monograph.* New York, 1947. Reprinted in *Nijinsky, Pavlova, Duncan: Three Lives in Dance* (New York, 1977).

Malvern, Gladys. *Dancing Star: The Story of Anna Pavlova.* New York, 1942.

May, Helen. *The Swan: The Story of Anna Pavlova.* Edinburgh, 1958.

Money, Keith. *Pavlova: Her Art and Life.* New York, 1982.

Olivéroff, André, with John Gill. *Flight of the Swan: A Memory of Anna Pavlova.* New York, 1932. Reprint, New York, 1979.

Oukrainsky, Serge. *My Two Years with Anna Pavlova.* Los Angeles, 1940.

Pavlova, Anna. "Vers un Rêve d'Art." Translated from Russian by Sébastien Voirol. *Lectures pour Tous* (1 June 1913). English translations of this brief memoir, titled either "Pages of My Life" or "Towards a Dream of Art," appear in Svetlov (1922), Dandré (1932), Olivéroff (1932), and Franks (1956).

Pavlova, Anna. *Tazende Füsse: Der Weg meines Lebens.* Dresden, 1928. This "autobiography" was not written by Pavlova and was withdrawn from circulation after she brought suit against the publisher.

Ries, Frank W. D. "Rediscovering Pavlova's Dances." *Ballet Review* 11 (Winter 1984): 71–85.

Stier, Theodore. *With Pavlova Round the World.* London, 1929.

Svetlov, Valerian. *Anna Pavlova.* Translated from the Russian by A. Grey. Paris, 1922. Reprint, New York, 1974.

Svetlov, Valerian. *Anna Pavlova.* London, 1931.

Vaughan, David. "Further Annals of *The Sleeping Beauty:* Anna Pavlova, 1916." *Ballet Review* 3.2 (1969): 3–18.

ROBERTA LAZZARINI

PAXTON, STEVE (born 21 January 1939 in Phoenix, Arizona), dancer, choreographer, and a founding member of Judson Dance Theater. Paxton studied at Connecticut College and with Merce Cunningham and Robert Dunn. He danced with José Limón's company (1959) and, as a founding member of the Judson Dance Theater, he worked with many of its members beginning in the early 1960s. He danced in Cunningham's company from 1961 to 1964. Paxton was also a member of Grand Union and an originator of contact improvisation. He worked with other dancers in the group Freelance Dance in the late 1970s and early 1980s.

Paxton's first dance, *Proxy* (1961), included activities that would preoccupy him for the next two decades: ordinary walking (and other mundane actions such as eating), and the use of dance scores comprising a series of pictures (especially sports photographs) to distance the performer's interpretation from that of the choreographer. Paxton has been fascinated by the body as a physical machine and by the intersection of nature and culture expressed through the body. He has also been committed to discovering how theater and dance work as social structures and working toward democratic methods, including improvisational techniques for composition and a search for appropriate physical techniques.

For Paxton, walking was key for several reasons. It opened up a range of nondance movement and enabled him to adopt a performance presence that was both relaxed and authoritative. It was also a link between performers and spectators, an activity that everyone does, and one that tolerates infinite variations of individual styles. The apotheosis of his concern with walking was *Satisfyin' Lover* (1967), a dance for a large group of people (thirty-four to eighty-four), who walk, stand, or sit, according to a written score.

Besides the plain presentation of the ordinary human body and its handling of commonplace objects, Paxton has delighted in using fantastic objects, animals, and even the body transformed. In *Jag ville gorna telefonera* (1964), there were three chickens, a full-sized overstuffed chair made of cake and yellow frosting, and clothes with zippers in the seams that could be taken apart and put back together in new ways. Several works of the mid-1960s, including *Physical Things* (1966), incorporated the use of huge, transparent, inflatable plastic tunnels. In *Flat* (1964), Paxton hung his clothes on hooks taped to his body. A number of Paxton's works in the late 1960s and early 1970s dealt with themes of war, intervention, and censorship.

In 1972 Paxton began, with the help of other dancers, to evolve contact improvisation, initially a duet form, which explores balance, support, and mutual trust. He has continued to work in the arena of group and solo improvisa-

PAXTON. To a score by percussionist David Moss, a frequent collaborator, Paxton dances his *Back Water: Twosome* at Saint Mark's Church in The Bowery, New York, in 1977. The relaxed posture and casual costuming are typical of his work, counterpointing the complicated stuctures that often underlie it. (Photograph © 1977 by Johan Elbers; used by permission.)

tion as well as making more set choreographies. He has collaborated with musician David Moss (since 1974) and dancer Lisa Nelson. In addition to his participation in contact improvisation and his work with blind and disabled performers, his dances in the 1980s and 1990s have included solo improvisations to Glenn Gould's recordings of Bach *(The Goldberg Variations, Some English Suites No. 1* and *Some English Suites No. 2); Suspect Terrain* (1989; to music by Hans Peter Kuhn), a largely improvised group collaboration with dancer-choreographers Dana Reitz, Laurie Booth, and Polly Motley and lighting designer Jennifer Tipton; and imagistic theatrical pieces such as *Excavations Continued* (1996), a collaboration with dancer-choreographer Lisa Nelson and sculptor Richard Nonas.

Paxton has written often about his work and that of his peers. He observes, "In performance, I meditate on movement. It is familiar but never the same, like known territory in a new season."

BIBLIOGRAPHY

Banes, Sally. *Terpsichore in Sneakers: Post-Modern Dance.* 2d ed. Middletown, Conn., 1987. Includes a bibliography.

Banes, Sally. "Vital Signs: Steve Paxton's *Flat* in Perspective." In *Writing Dancing in the Age of Postmodernism.* Hanover, N.H., 1994.

Kaplan, Peggy Jarrell. *Portraits of Choreographers.* New York, 1988.

McDonagh, Don. *The Rise and Fall and Rise of Modern Dance.* Rev. ed. Pennington, N.J., 1990.

Paxton, Steve. "Contact Improvisation." *Drama Review* 19 (March 1975): 40–42.

Paxton, Steve. "Drafting Interior Techniques." *Contact Quarterly* 18 (Winter/Spring 1993): 61–66.

Paxton, Steve and Anne Kilcoyne. "On the Braille in the Body: An Account of the Touchdown Dance Integrated Workshops with the Visually Impaired and the Sighted." *Dance Research* 11 (Spring 1993): 3–51.

Rubidge, Sarah. "Steve Paxton." *Dance Theatre Journal* 4 (Winter 1986): 2–5, 19.

VIDEOTAPES. "Beyond the Mainstream," *Dance in America* (WNET-TV, New York, 1980). "Chute" (1979).

SALLY BANES

PEABODY. *See* Ballroom Dance Competition.

PEASANT PAS DE DEUX. *See* Giselle.

PECOUR, GUILLAUME-LOUIS (also spelled Pecoor, Pécour, Pécourt; born c. 1653, died 12 April 1729 in Paris), French dancer and choreographer. According to the baptismal certificate of his younger brother Louis-Alexandre, Pecour was the son of Jacques Pecour, a royal courier, and his wife Marie Voisin or Raisin (both names appear in family documents), who lived in the rue des Petits Champs.

The Parfaict brothers, in their history of the Royal Academy of Music, state that Pecour studied under Pierre Beauchamps and succeeded him in 1687 as choreographer of French court ballets and those of the Paris Opera. They add that "he was handsome, well-built, and danced with the noblest air possible." Apparently, he ended his dance career around 1703 but continued to compose ballets at the Opera until his death. With Beauchamps, Pecour shared a second career, as choreographer at the Jesuit college Louis le Grand from 1690 to 1711. For these lavish productions, often attended by Louis XIV and his court, he employed a full cast of dancers and musicians from the Paris Opera (Astier, 1983).

Late seventeenth-century ballet programs indicate that Pecour was already dancing in 1673, but in 1674 he made his debut at the Académie Royale de Musique in Jean-Baptiste Lully's *Cadmus et Hermione.* His name begins to fade from the programs around 1704, and he was given a pension in 1705. He was listed, however, in the casts for *Sémélé* and *Méléâgre* (both 1709) and *Hésione* (1710).

Many testimonies to Pecour's popularity and talent can be found in the gazettes and correspondence of the period. For example, in a letter on the *Ballet des Saisons* (26 October 1695):

> The first and second boxes were redoubled, one could have perished in the pit, and people were on each other's laps in the Paradis, all because of Pécour, who danced a Spanish sarabande. . . . [H]e dances like a master.

In 1704, Le Cerf de la Viéville mentioned the beautiful arms and the majestic steps of the dancer who "even in his decline is almost without peer."

On 28 November 1692, Pecour resigned from his appointment as dance master to the pages of the king's chamber. From 1699 to 1712, he was dance master to Madame la Duchesse de Bourgogne. In 1695, he was listed among the members of the Académie Royale de Danse, then directed by Beauchamps, and again in 1719 when Claude Ballon was director.

Pecour's choreographic output was considerable, and more than one hundred of his dances remain chronicled for study. For several decades, he composed the dances in fashion for the annual winter balls. Recorded in Feuillet notation, many of his dances found their way abroad for performance in foreign courts. He was most likely the first choreographer to have such a wide exposure, the result of which was the promotion of a French dancing style throughout Europe. His transformation of the minuet pattern from an S to the more pleasing Z shape was universally adopted. [*See* Minuet.]

Pecour's stage choreography is known by two collections, one recorded in 1704 by Raoul-Auger Feuillet, the other in 1712 by Michel Gaudrau. From these we can tell that Pecour's outstanding knowledge of kinetic impulses, his mastery of body energy, and his exhilarating use of the body's suspension all mark him as a great master.

Little is known at this point of Pecour's private life beyond the countless little satirical poems that point to amorous affairs with both sexes.

His burial certificate in the Archives de la Seine gives the date of his death as 12 April 1729. He was buried the next day in the church of Saint Roch. The following obituary ran in the *Mercure de France:*

> The famous Pécourt, one of the greatest dancers of his time, who had so brightly shone in all the late King's court-ballets, and on the stage of the Opéra, died in Paris on 11 April, 1729, at seventy-eight years of age. He had succeeded the late Monsieur Beauchamps for the composition of ballets which he produced for a very long time and with an admirable and versatile genius. He stopped dancing over thirty years ago.

BIBLIOGRAPHY

Astier, Régine. "Pierre Beauchamps and the Ballets de Collège." *Dance Chronicle* 6.2 (1983): 154–155.

Astier, Régine. "The Influence of Greek Rhetoric on the Composition and Interpretation of Baroque Stage Dances: Lully's *Chaconne de Phaéton.*" In *Proceedings of the 5th International Conference, Dance and Ancient Greece.* Athens, 1991.

Dangeau, Philippe de Courcillon. *Journal du marquis de Dangeau.* 19 vols. Edited by Eudoxe Soulié. Paris, 1854–1860.

Feuillet, Raoul-Auger. *Chorégraphie, ou L'art de décrire la dance, par caractères, figures et signes démonstratifs, avec lesquels on apprend facilement de soy-même toutes sortes de dances.* Paris, 1700. Translated by John Weaver as *Orchesography, or, The Art of Dancing* (London, 1706).

Daniels, Margaret. "Passacaille d'Armide." In *Proceedings of the Sixth Annual Conference, Society of Dance History Scholars, the Ohio State University, 11–13 February 1983,* compiled by Christena L. Schlundt. Milwaukee, 1983.

Feves, Angene, and Sandra Noll Hammond. "La Bacchante: Alternate Performance Styles." In *Proceedings of the Sixth Annual Conference, Society of Dance History Scholars, the Ohio State University, 11–13 February 1983,* compiled by Christena L. Schlundt. Milwaukee, 1983.

Gaudrau, Michel. *Nouveau recueil de dances de bal et celle de ballet, contenant un très grand nombres des meillieures entrées de ballet de la composition de Mr. Pécour.* Paris, 1713.

Harris-Warrick, Rebecca. "La mariée: The History of a French Court Dance." In *Jean-Baptiste Lully and the Music of the French Baroque,* edited by John Heyer. New York, 1989.

Jal, Auguste. *Dictionnaire critique de biographie et d'histoire.* Paris, 1867.

Ladvocat, Louis. *Lettres sur L'opera à l'abbé Dubos* (annotated by Jerome de La Gorce). Paris, 1993.

La Gorce, Jérôme de. "Guillaume-Louis Pecour: A Biographical Essay." *Dance Research* 8 (Autumn 1990): 3–26.

Le Cerf de la Viéville, Jean-Laurent, seigneur de Freneuse. *Comparaison de la musique italienne et de la musique françoise.* 3 vols. Paris, 1704–1706.

Maurepas, Jean. *Recueil de chansons.* N.p., 1696. Manuscript located in Paris, Bibliothèque Nationale, fr.12621 (p. 25), fr.12619 (p. 179).

Mélèze. *Repertoire analytique des documents contemporains d'information concernant le théâtre à Paris sous Louis XIV.* Paris, 1934.

Mullins, Margaret. "Dance and Society in Seventeenth-Century France." In *Musicological Society of Australia, Fourth National Symposium: Music and Dance.* Perth, 1982.

Parfaict, François, and Claude Parfaict, *Histoire de l'Académie Royale de Musique.* N.p., 1741. Manuscript located in Paris, Bibliothèque Nationale, nouv. acq. fr.6532.

Sévigné, Marie de. *Lettres de madame de Sévigné, de sa famille et de ses amis.* Edited by Louis Monmerqué and Paul Mesnard. Paris, 1866. See the letter of 24 June 1683.

Taubert, Karl Heinz. *Barock-Tänze.* Zurich, 1986.

Witherell, Anne L. *Louis Pécour's 1700 Recueil des dances.* Ann Arbor, Mich., 1983.

RÉGINE ASTIER

PEI YANLING (Pei Xin; born 12 August 1947 in Hebei, China), Chinese opera actress specializing in the *Hebei bangzi* genre. Born into a theatrical family, Pei began formal training at five in Beijing Opera, against her father's will, after successfully substituting for a sick actor. She again surprised her father, who had since given her the very feminine stage name of Yanling, when she chose to specialize in her father's martial and bearded male roles with extraordinary energy and determination; at nine she began performing in starring roles with several companies in Hebei and Shandong provinces.

In 1959, Pei switched to *Hebei bangzi,* her mother's special genre. In 1960 she played Chenxiang in *Bao Lian Deng* (The Precious Lotus Lantern), about a celestial woman punished by her brother for loving a man but eventually rescued by their son Chenxiang who grows up to defeat his uncle. Pei's performance won wide praise in Shanghai and elsewhere, and she repeated that success in the 1976 film version. In 1982 she played the title role in another *Hebei bangzi*-based film, *Nezha,* again about a magic young male warrior.

One of China's few female performers of martial and bearded male roles, Pei surpasses most of her male counterparts in playing these roles. She believes that a woman has a better chance to play an ideal man because of the "women's point of view." She portrays Zhong Kui, her best-known role, with a retracted neck, raised shoulders, and protruding buttocks, making the well-known ugly and ferocious ghost surprisingly charming, because she sees a heart of gold in Zhong's love and sorrow for his sister, who is to be married. Another of Pei's favored roles is Lin Chong, an officer-turned-rebel character from the classic novel *The Water Margin.* Although this character was initially taught by a male master of *kunqu* (Kun Opera), she modified much of his choreography to fit her physique; more importantly, she incorporated some female martial artists' styles into a half-hour solo tour de force, in which Lin, through dance and song, muses on a difficult decision to escape persecution and join the peasant rebels, thus creating a more nimble and splendid warrior than the traditional character.

With a rare reputation, simultaneously, as Zhong Kui Reincarnation and Lin Chong Reincarnation, and as head of Troupe I at the Hebei Bangzi Theater in Shijiazhuang, Pei continues to expand her repertory. She frequently stars in Beijing Opera, *kunqu,* and *Hebei bangzi* plays. Her signature roles include teenage boys, like Chenxiang and Nezha, and elderly ones, like general Huang Zhong and King Liu Bei, both from the novel *Romance of the Three Kingdoms.* In a spectacular piece based on *Romance,* Pei played four characters alternately: Huang, Liu, a short-robed warrior, and a long-robed general with four banners on his back.

In 1985 Pei toured Hong Kong, Denmark, Greece, France, and Japan with great success. The following year Eugenio Barba of the International School of Theatre Anthropology invited her to participate in their workshop with master performers from around the world, so many of her performance photos were featured in Barba's *A Dictionary of Theatre Anthropology* (1991). Her career and life, especially her legendary portrayal of the ghost Zhong Kui, are portrayed in a feature film, *Woman, Demon, Human* (directed by Huang Shuqin), in which she stars. It won first prize at the Rio de Janeiro Film Festival in 1988 and another prize at the Thirteenth International Women's Film Festival in France.

BIBLIOGRAPHY

Barba, Eugenio, and Nicola Savarese. *A Dictionary of Theatre Anthropology: The Secret Art of the Performer.* London, 1991.

Zhou Meihui. "Nü Wusheng Pei Yanling." *World Journal* (23 September 1993).

WILLIAM H. SUN

PENCAK. The movement system *pencak* is the training method for an Indonesian style of self-defense and a stylized art form. More than 150 *pencak* styles are found in Indonesia, most of them in Java, Sumatra, and Bali. The application of this training method is called *silat.* The actual fight, however, is not the only goal of *pencak.* In Sunda (West Java) and Minangkabau (West Sumatra), for example, *pencak* is performed to the accompaniment of traditional local music or song. This accompaniment is meant to make the exercise more effective, but it also enhances its entertaining aspect and attracts an audience. The Sundanese *ibing rampak* is an example of this exercise done in a group, while *si pecut langkah empat* from Jakarta is an example done in solo performance. Both "dances" are composed of systematized basic movements designed to dodge or ward off attacks and to retaliate against an assailant by striking or kicking.

The closest connection between *pencak* and dance is found in Minangkabau, where *pencak* is the basic training for every dancer–actor. In this region, *silat* is an important part of the way of life. Practiced mostly for defense, *silat* must be done elegantly; therefore, it contains basic movements very close to dance and is richly ornamented with additional movements. In the local popular dance drama, *randai,* actors and dancers are trained by two teachers—the *gurutuo silek* (martial arts and dance teacher) and the *gurutuo dendang* (song and music teacher). Between *randai* scenes, a group of dancers performs the "wave dance" in a circle, accompanied by *qurindam* songs. The *silat* proper is usually performed during the intermission.

In West Java the basic *pencak* steps are used widely in many different village performances. An example is the *ketuk tilu* dance. Many *pencak* steps are used by both male and female dancers in this Sundanese social couple dance.

Pencak movement can also be found in some *wireng* and *pethilan* of the Central Javanese court dances. One, based on the *Panji* cycle, is the dance *Panji-Bogis,* which depicts a fight between Prince Panji—holding a spear—against Bogis holding a sword and a shield. The combat scene using the *keris,* the Javanese dagger, found in many Javanese dance dramas, also requires the dancers to master basic *pencak* movements in handling this traditional weapon.

Pencak has a strong tradition in Bali as well. However, no research has been done to examine the relationship between the dance of Bali and its *pencak* counterpart.

[*See also* Asian Martial Arts; *and* Indonesia, *article on* Javanese Dance Traditions.]

BIBLIOGRAPHY

Alexander, Howard, et al. *Pentjak-Silat: The Indonesian Fighting Art.* Tokyo and New York, 1970.

Kayam, Umar. *The Soul of Indonesia: A Cultural Journey.* Baton Rouge, 1985.

Murgiyanto, Sal. "Tari Pencak Silat 4 Daerah." *Sinar Harapan* (22 February 1978).

Murgiyanto, Sal. "Gerak-gerik Ninik Mamak." *Tempo* (25 February 1978).

SAL MURGIYANTO

PENNSYLVANIA BALLET. Based in Philadelphia, the Pennsylvania Ballet was founded in 1963 by Barbara Weisberger. It developed out of a school she started in 1962, now known as the School of the Pennsylvania Ballet. The company gave its first complete performance on 30 October 1964.

The Pennsylvania Ballet is an exemplar of the challenges regional companies face. Its history reflects the dance boom and recession as well as conflicts between classical and modern styles of dance; audience expectation and artistic goals; academic and theatrical approaches to teaching; and administrative and artistic management. Initially, the company derived its shape and impetus from two sources, one financial and one aesthetic.

In December 1963, in a controversial move, the Ford Foundation announced a grant of $295,000 to the still-embryonic Pennsylvania Ballet—$45,000 unconditionally and $250,000 to be matched by $500,000 over a ten-year period. Ford granted the company a further $450,000 in 1966 and $2.9 million (over a five-year period) in 1971. Ford was criticized for giving money to the company before it was actually established, but Weisberger believed the early grants enabled it to grow at its own pace.

The other formative influence was George Balanchine, who encouraged Weisberger and gave the company a number of his ballets. It soon became known for its scrupulous renderings of these works and, although the term *Balanchine satellite* did frequently apply, it was a misnomer. Weisberger defined the company as "second-generation American"; as the critic Deborah Jowitt (1974) observed, its "American" character was formed to a considerable extent by Balanchine: "the company . . . has that alert and eloquent, plainspeaking way of dancing that is Balanchine's gift to America." Structurally, too, the

PENNSYLVANIA BALLET. Magali Messac and Steven Majewicz in the company's 1979 production of *Poems of Love and the Seasons,* choreographed by Benjamin Harkarvy. (Photograph © 1979 by Johan Elbers.)

Pennsylvanians had affinities with the New York City Ballet: in their view of the school as the cornerstone of the company; the excellent quality of their orchestra, directed by Maurice Kaplow; and their policy of promoting young dancers.

Weisberger, however, believed that a regional company should be versatile and eclectic and thus included in the repertory modern ballet works (John Butler was an important early source; Hans van Manen a later one) and full-length classics. Although by 1972 the company was recognized as a leading regional troupe, admired for its freshness and good training, it had experienced one severe financial crisis and its programming seemed poor and unfocused. Critic Clive Barnes urged, "This company looks so fine when it is given something good to dance that finding more things that are good for it to dance must be its most urgent priority" (Barnes, 1972).

In response to the problem, Weisberger appointed Benjamin Harkarvy as artistic director. His ideals of lucent classicism and lyrical decorum molded the company style and repertory for the next ten years. That style was characterized, as critic Tobi Tobias (1980) wrote, "by old-fashioned virtues: correctness, harmony, and calm." Other descriptions were "tasteful," "polished," and "unaffected."

During the 1970s the company consolidated its national image with a series of residency programs, including, from 1973, one at the Brooklyn Academy of Music. In 1976 it appeared in Public Television's first *Dance in America* series.

In 1982 lack of funds forced the company to cancel its spring season. In the ensuing management crisis, its board forced Weisberger's resignation; Harkarvy's departure followed. In September 1982, former New York City Ballet principal Robert Weiss became artistic director.

Following a period of retrenchment, Weiss slowly began to enlarge the company and increase the number of performances. In 1987 he initiated a joint venture with the Milwaukee Ballet, but this twin-city arrangement survived for only two years. Weiss's expansionist visions clashed with the more conservative attitudes of the board, and in 1990 Weiss was fired. He was succeeded in that year by Christopher d'Amboise, also a former principal dancer with the New York City Ballet.

Both Weiss and d'Amboise created their own ballets for the company and acquired many additional Balanchine ballets, thus returning the company to its neoclassical roots. As a result of the recessionary economic climate during early 1990s, d'Amboise cut back the company's activities and reduced its roster as well. In 1985 the company performed *La Sylphide,* staged by Peter Martins, a production that was nationally televised in 1989, and also added Merce Cunningham's *Arcade* to its repertory in 1988. Roy Kaiser became artistic director in 1990.

BIBLIOGRAPHY

Barnes, Clive. "Welcome to the Pennsylvanians." *New York Times* (28 January 1968).

Barnes, Clive. "Dance: 'Reconnaissance.'" *New York Times* (13 April 1972).

Croce, Arlene. "Premises, Premises." *New Yorker* (15 November 1976).

Deitch, Mark. "New York's Fourth Major Troupe Is a Pennsylvania Import." *New York Times* (23 October 1977).

Jowitt, Deborah. "Where the Grandeur Lies: The Pennsylvania Ballet." *Village Voice* (3 December 1974).

Maynard, Olga. "Barbara Weisberger and the Pennsylvania Ballet." *Dance Magazine* (March 1975): 45–60.

Tobias, Tobi. "Philadelphia Story: Pennsylvania Ballet." *Soho News* (21 May 1980).

VIDEOTAPE. Merrill Brockway, "The Pennsylvania Ballet," *Dance in America* (WNET-TV, New York, 1976).

SARAH MONTAGUE

PERETTI, SERGE (born 28 January 1910 in Venice), Italian dancer and ballet master. Peretti studied under Gustave Ricaux at the dance school of the Paris Opera. He was engaged for the corps de ballet and was named *premier danseur* in 1930, then in 1941 *étoile,* a title no one before him had held. Peretti danced in the ballets of Gustave Ricaux and Albert Aveline and appeared in *Les Rencontres* (choreography by Bronislava Nijinska). He and his partner, Olga Spessivtseva, performed as harmonious white figures animated by Titan in Serge Lifar's *Les Créatures de Prométhée* and also danced a brilliant *La Péri* (choreographed Léo Staats) after the interpretation by Anna Pavlova and Stowitz. As an interpreter of Lifar's works, Peretti represented the moderate spirit of the French school rather than the exuberant passion of the Russian. His and Lifar's talents also complemented each other in *La Vie de Polichinelle, Salade, Le Chevalier et la Damoiselle, Boléro,* and *Joan de Zarissa.* Aveline staged for him *La Grisi* and *Elvire,* an evocation of a young man dressed in white satin and admirable for his brilliant lightness.

As a ballet master in 1945, Peretti choreographed *L'Appel de la Montagne,* to music by Arthur Honegger. Just before his departure from the Opera in 1996, he danced act 2 of *Swan Lake* with Yvette Chauviré. After a tour of South America, he returned to Paris and opened a dance school; he also taught occasional courses at the Opera.

Endowed with brilliant technique, Peretti knew how to banish all traces of effort with extreme elegance. Whether depicting a butterfly or a flower, a poet or a prince, he revealed the grace of dance in every role.

BIBLIOGRAPHY

Gruen, John. *The Private World of Ballet.* New York, 1975.

Guest, Ivor. *Le ballet de l'Opéra de Paris.* Paris, 1976.

Livio, Antoine. "Peretti, étoile et maître: Le beau Serge." *Danser* (December 1994): 40–42.

Mason, Francis. "The Paris Opéra: A Conversation with Violette Verdy." *Ballet Review* 14 (Fall 1986): 23–30.

Meyer, Gilbert. "Der klassische Tanz." *Ballett-Journal/Das Tanzarchiv* 39 (October 1991): 32–33.

Steinbrink, Mark. "Interview with Serge Peretti." *Ballet News* (October 1981).

Vaillat, Léandre. *Ballets de l'Opéra de Paris (ballets dans les opéras—nouveaux ballets).* Paris, 1947.

JEANNINE DORVANE
Translated from French

PÉRI, LA. Ballet in two acts and three scenes. Choreography: Jean Coralli. Music: Friedrich Burgmüller. Libretto: Théophile Gautier. Scenery: Charles Séchan, Jules Diéterle, Édouard Despléchin, Humanité Philastre, and Charles Cambon. Costumes: Paul Lormier and Hippolyte d'Orschwiller. First performance: 17 July 1843, Théâtre de l'Académie Royale de Musique, Paris. Principals: Carlotta Grisi (The Péri/Leila), Lucien Petipa (Achmet).

Théophile Gautier's scenario for *La Péri* was inspired by his attraction to the Orient and dedicated to the feet of his beloved Carlotta Grisi, who danced the Péri, a Persian fairy. She appears to the wealthy and satiated Achmet in an opium dream and he falls in love with her. To test his love, she takes the form of a runaway slave, Leila. Achmet is killed for refusing to surrender her to her owner, but in an apotheosis he is seen entering heaven with the Péri.

La Péri redeemed Grisi's reputation at a time when she was receiving bad reviews. Jean Coralli provided her with two striking dances: a *pas du songe* that culminated in her daring leap from a six-foot-high (two-meter) platform into Achmet's arms, and a *pas de l'abeille,* a decorous striptease prompted by the invasion of an imaginary bee.

La Péri was given in London in 1843 with Grisi and Lucien Petipa, and in Saint Petersburg in 1844 with Elena Andreyanova. In 1855 George Washington Smith and his partner Pepita Soto staged in New York the first American production of the ballet. Most twentieth-century ballets of this title, notably that by Frederick Ashton for the Royal Ballet in 1956, have used Paul Dukas's score and a less complex scenario. In 1976 Alberto Mendez created a *La Péri* pas de deux to Friedrich Burgmüller's music, with costumes based on Romantic prints, for the Ballet Nacional de Cuba.

BIBLIOGRAPHY

Au, Susan. "Prints of a Parisian Péri." *Dance Perspectives* 61 (Spring 1975):30–49.

Binney, Edwin, 3rd. *Les ballets de Théophile Gautier.* Paris, 1965.

Guest, Ivor. *The Romantic Ballet in Paris.* 2d rev. ed. London, 1980.

Joffe, Lydia. "La péri 1843, La péri 1912, La péri 1967." *Dance Magazine* (April 1967): 39–44.

Moore, Lillian. "The Origin of Adagio in Ballet: Grisi's Leap in *La Péri.*" *Dancing Times* 26 (April 1936): 16–19.

Sticklor, Susan R. "Angel with a Past." *Dance Perspectives* 61 (Spring 1975): 18–29.

SUSAN AU

PERICET FAMILY, Spanish family of dancers and teachers that for five generations has been regarded as the source of authenticity for the dances of the classical Spanish school of dancing known as *escuela bolera.* Notable members include Angel Pericet Carmona (1844–1944) and his son Angel Pericet Jiménez (born 1899 in Valencia, died 1973 in Buenos Aires). The French-born founder of the dynasty, Antoine Pericet, married an Andalusian woman and settled in Aguilar de la Frontera (Cordoba).

Antoine Pericet's grandson, Angel Pericet Carmona, established an academy in San Juan de la Palma, Seville, having studied primarily with the famous dancer La Campanilla and the teacher Maestra Segura. Angel Pericet set about codifying the terminology for the steps of the *escuela bolera* and established a set of three groups of exercises complementary to the teaching of its various dances. These include boleros—*sevillanas boleras, bolero robado, bolero liso, bolero de la cachucha,* and *bolero de medio paso; jaleos,* such as *jaleo de Jerez; olés,* such as *olé de la curra* and *olé andaluza; seguidillas, manchegas, panaderos de la flamenco, la Maja y el torero,* and the eighteenth-century *peteneras* and *caracoles* (not to be confused with their later flamenco counterparts of the same names). Angel's two brothers were also dancers; José immigrated to South Africa, and Rafael eventually took over his brother's studio in Calle Encomienda, Madrid, which Angel had taken over from the Cansino family when they immigrated to America in 1932.

Angel's children, Angel Pericet Jiménez and the sisters Luisa and Conchita, continued the tradition of teaching and performed as Trio Pericet, with the later addition of Angel Pericet Blanco, Angel Pericet Jiménez's son. Angel Pericet Jiménez established his studio first in Calle Amistad, Seville, and then in Plaza de Zuburban. He moved to Madrid after the Spanish Civil War and established a studio in Puerta de Toledo. Also continuing the tradition, his sisters Luisa and Conchita taught in the Calle Encomienda studio, Madrid, until the 1970s; many of Spain's noted dancers studied there. After the Civil War Angel Pericet Jiménez took his family to South America, where they lived for many years.

The Pericet academies have always been the focal point for the study of the *escuela bolera,* and this tradition is continued today. Angel Pericet Jiménez established his own company, which toured extensively in Latin America and featured his brother Eloy and sisters Amparo and Carmelita. His sister Luisa teaches in Buenos Aires.

Angel, Eloy, and Amparo returned in the late 1970s to Spain, fleeing the political unrest in Argentina, and were immediately sought out by teachers and pupils alike. The *escuela bolera,* which appeared to be a dying art form, has as a result of the Pericets' return reemerged from a period of torpor in Spain. Eloy teaches in Madrid, and Angel is associated with the Ballet Nacional Español, where the company studies the *escuela bolera* under his tuition.

[*See also* Bolero *and* Escuela Bolera.]

BIBLIOGRAPHY

Carrasco Benítez, Marta. "Las academias de baile en Sevilla: Los Pericet." In *Encuentro internacional "La Escuela Bolera."* Madrid, 1992.

Carretero, Concepción. *Origen, evolución y morfología del baile por sevillanas.* Seville, 1985.

Cournand, Gilberte. "La dynastie des Pericet." *Saisons de la danse,* no. 240 (November 1992): 17.

Murías Vila, Carlos. "Grandes figures: La succession Pericet." *Danser* (September 1994): 26–29.

Pericet Blanco, Eloy. "Influencia andaluza en la Escuela Bolera." In *Actas del II congreso de folclore Andaluz: Danza, música e indumentaria tradicional.* Seville, 1988.

Suárez-Pajares, Javier, and Xoán M. Carreira. *The Origins of the Bolero School.* Studies in Dance History, vol. 4.1. Pennington, N.J., 1993.

PHILIPPA HEALE

PERROT, JULES (Jules Joseph Perrot; born 18 August 1810 in Lyon, died 18 August 1892 in Paramé, Ille-et-Vilaine), French ballet dancer, choreographer, and teacher. Jules Perrot, whose work would come to epitomize the Romantic period in ballet, was the son of working-class parents. His father, Jean Perrot, was a cabinetmaker at the time of his birth but later became chief machinist at the Grand Théâtre in Lyon. Having begun to study dancing at an early age, Jules made his first stage appearance as a boy of eight at the Grand Théâtre in 1818. Two years later he saw the great comic dancer Charles-François Mazurier in the role of Polichinelle in Louis Milon's ballet *Le Carnaval de Venise* and became obsessed with mastering Mazurier's style and acrobatic technique. So successful was he that he was engaged by the Théâtre des Celestins in Lyon to appear in a parody of Milon's ballet called *Le Petit Carnaval de Venise.* Perrot's astonishing performance in this work became the talk of the town. News of it must have reached the ears of theater managers in Paris, for in 1823 Perrot arrived in the capital for an engagement at the Théâtre de la Gaîté. He was then thirteen years old.

Perrot's destiny seemed to be linked with that of Mazurier, for in December 1823, only a few months after the latter had triumphed at the Théâtre de la Porte-Saint-Martin in the pantomime *Polichinel Vampire,* Perrot appeared in a similar role at the Gaîté in *Polichinelle Avalé par le Baleine.* The two comic dancers were to be pitted against one another again in 1825. In March of that year Mazurier gave the most inspired interpretation of his career, moving audiences at the Porte-Saint-Martin to tears with his portrayal of the monkey hero in *Jocko, ou Le Singe du Brézil;* a few weeks later, on 9 August 1825, the Gaîté responded with a *"folie,* interspersed with pantomime and dance," entitled *Sapajou,* in which Perrot once again proved he was Mazurier's equal. He had spent many hours before the monkey cages at the Jardin des Plantes, observing the antics of the animals.

Perrot now fixed his ambition on new peaks. He had begun taking class with Auguste Vestris, the most celebrated teacher in Paris, who was transforming him into a polished classical dancer of the *demi-caractère* genre. His acrobatic skill was refined into a technique of "almost phosphorescent" brilliance, as August Bournonville, a fellow pupil of Vestris, recalled. The Gaîté could no longer retain Perrot, who moved, at a higher salary, to the Porte-Saint-Martin, where he danced from 1827 until early in 1830. There, he took part as a dancer in the drama *Faust,* in which the actor Frédérick (Antoine Lemaître) gave an unforgettable portrayal of Mephistopheles that would inspire Perrot's interpretation of the role when he produced his ballet version of *Faust* many years later, in 1848.

On 6 February 1830, Perrot made his first appearance in London at the King's Theatre. During his short engagement, he danced in Milon's *Le Carnaval de Venise* and in Arnaud Léon's *Guillaume Tell* and was much admired for his ability. Returning to Paris, he was coached by Vestris for his debut at the Opera. This took place on 23 June 1830, when he and Pauline Montessu danced a pas de deux arranged by Vestris. His first engagement at the Opera was as a *double* (soloist) at a salary of twenty-five hundred francs.

Soon afterward, Dr. Louis Véron, the Opera's new director, singled out Perrot to be the star male dancer. On 14 March 1831 he was featured in a revival of Charles-Louis Didelot's ballet *Flore et Zéphire,* in which he partnered Marie Taglioni and, from all accounts, took an equal share of the applause. His annual salary was increased fourfold, to ten thousand francs, exclusive of bonuses—an exceptional figure for a male dancer, although it was only a third of what was paid to Taglioni. Unfortunately, however, Perrot suffered from a natural and irremediable disadvantage: while no one equaled him as a virtuoso, his features were ugly. This was no doubt one of the reasons why his colleague, Joseph Mazilier, was chosen in preference to him to çreate the role of James in *La Sylphide* in 1832. Nevertheless, Perrot's supremacy was unassailed, and that same year he was given a new two-year contract at an increased salary of fifteen thousand francs.

Perrot's second London season in 1833 brought him into contact with André Deshayes, an experienced choreographer who was to become both a friend and an exemplar. In the major ballet production of the season, Deshayes's *Faust,* Perrot had only a dancing role; however, he no doubt profited by observing how Goethe's drama was presented in dance and pantomime.

Returning to Paris, Perrot was passed over once again in the casting of Filippo Taglioni's new ballet *La Révolte au Sérail.* Mazilier was again chosen for the leading male role, but Perrot was selected to partner Marie Taglioni in a pas de deux. His reception was so rapturous that Taglioni was said to have taken offense. The two stars were both engaged by the King's Theatre in London in 1834, but they did not dance together. Among the other dancers there were Fanny Elssler and her sister Thérèse, and Perrot partnered Fanny for the first time in her sister's short ballet *Armide.* Now at the height of his powers as a dancer, Perrot returned to Paris confident of renewing his engagement on more favorable terms. However, the Opera held a less exalted notion of his worth than he, and the negotiations collapsed.

After leaving the Paris Opera, Perrot fulfilled a short engagement in Bordeaux, following which he went to London for the 1835 season at the King's Theatre, where he danced the role of James in *La Sylphide* with Marie Taglioni. He also played opposite her in *Mazilia,* a short work by her father, Filippo: further proof that the ballerina harbored no resentment on account of his success alongside her.

Perrot was by now having no difficulty finding engagements, and in the autumn he was engaged by Domenico Barbaja for the Teatro San Carlo in Naples. His appearance was delayed by an accident, but he eventually made his first performance there on 12 January 1836. Among the dancers in the San Carlo company at that time was Carlotta Grisi, then a novice of sixteen. Greatly taken with her, Perrot became a friend of her family and was soon accepted not only as her teacher but also as her fiancé. It was no doubt through him that she was engaged, as well as he, at the King's Theatre in the summer of 1836. There, she endeared herself to the London public by her charm both as a dancer and as a singer. How much they inspired one another was revealed that season in their performance of a fiery tarantella. [*See the entry on Grisi.*]

Perrot hoped to marry Grisi, but she was not to be rushed, although she did go so far as to adopt his name. It was as Madame Perrot that she was first seen in Paris, at a benefit performance at the Théâtre Français on 30 August 1836, dancing with Perrot in a pas de deux of his own composition and in their tarantella.

Vienna was the scene of their next triumph, which marked a new step forward in the progress of Perrot's career. Carlo Baldocchino, the director of the Hofoper, advised him to arrange a ballet for Grisi, and his first serious attempt at choreography was highly successful. *Die Nymphe und der Schmetterling,* a collaborative effort with Pietro Campilli, who arranged the corps de ballet work, was first performed on 29 September 1836. Perrot's contribution was well received, and he was encouraged to produce another ballet, this time on his own. *Das Stelldichein,* presented on 23 November 1836, was so successful that it was revived when Perrot returned to Vienna a year or so later. During this second visit he arranged another light work for Grisi and himself, *Die Neapolitanischen Fischer* (10 January 1838), which he followed by his first major work, *Der Kobold* (The Goblin; 2 March 1838). Dancing the title role, Perrot tailored it to his own personality and style, making the Goblin a sympathetic imp with supernatural agility.

On 29 February 1840, Perrot and Grisi appeared at the Théâtre de la Renaissance in Paris in a two-act *opéra-ballet, Zingaro,* with a libretto by Thomas Sauvage and music by Uranio Fortuna. Grisi's role required her to sing as well as to dance, but Perrot conceived his own part exclusively in terms of dance and mime. His character was a young gypsy who had lost his power of speech in childhood. Théophile Gautier in his review praised the agility and musicality of Perrot's dancing and the supple movements of his pantomime, calling him "the male Taglioni."

Perrot's success aroused regrets that he was no longer a member of the Paris Opera Ballet, and he himself desperately wanted to be reengaged there. However, the Opera had recently engaged Lucien Petipa, a young male dancer of great promise, and Perrot was disappointed in his ambition. He had to console himself with the satisfaction of seeing Grisi engaged there and with being permitted to arrange the *pas* for her debut.

For a short time it seemed that the Opera might be interested in making use of Perrot's choreographic talent. His relationship with Grisi brought him into contact with Théophile Gautier, who worshiped the young ballerina (and who was later to marry her sister, Ernesta). Gautier had presented Grisi with the scenario for *Giselle,* which he had written in collaboration with the dramatist Jules-Henri Vernoy, marquis de Saint-Georges. It came at an opportune moment: Grisi had turned down *La Rosière de Gand* (later to be produced as *La Jolie Fille de Gand*) because of its length and the undanceability of its subject. *Giselle* was seen as the very work that was wanted, and Adolphe Adam composed the music for it in a remarkably short time. The work, in fact, took shape in his salon, with

PERROT. While engaged at the Paris Opera, Perrot appeared in Filippo Taglioni's new version of *Nathalie, ou La Laitière Suisse* in 1832. This engraving was made from a drawing by Alexandre Lacauchie. (Courtesy of Madison U. Sowell and Debra H. Sowell, Brigham Young University, Provo, Utah.)

Perrot already working out the dances for Grisi. Although Jean Coralli was *maître de ballet en chef,* Perrot was given the task of arranging Grisi's role anonymously. [*See* Giselle.] His hopes that the success of *Giselle* would result in his being offered a permanent engagement remained unfulfilled. Coralli probably saw him as a threat, and Perrot lacked the ability for intrigue.

Perrot was to be well compensated for his disappointment, however, when he was engaged by Benjamin Lumley, manager of Her Majesty's Theatre in London, as assistant to the principal ballet master, Deshayes, for the 1842 season. Perrot produced *Giselle* for the opening performance on 12 March 1842. Deshayes's name was coupled with his on the playbill, and Perrot himself danced the role of Albert (Albrecht) opposite Grisi. Soon afterward, on 23 June, he was co-choreographer, with Deshayes and Fanny Cerrito, of *Alma, ou La Fille de Feu,* a fantastic ballet. In it, he played Belfegor, a demon rather like the Goblin of *Der Kobold,* and Cerrito had one of her best roles as Alma, the Daughter of Fire. [*See* Alma.]

PERROT. By creating a role for himself that combined dance and mime, Perrot won high critical praise for his role in the two-act *opéra-ballet Zingaro,* choreographed in 1840. (Dance Collection, New York Public Library for the Performing Arts.)

The highlight of *Alma* was Perrot's *pas de fascination,* a dance that was novel in its structure in that it advanced the dramatic development of the ballet. Inspired perhaps by his recollection of a similar scene in the drama *Faust* at the Porte-Saint-Martin, Perrot's choreography depicted the demon Belfegor and the fire spirit Alma bewitching a group of girls and forcing them to dance against their will. This was to be the precursor of many other *pas d'action,* an innovation of which Perrot was recognized as the inventor.

It was at this time that Perrot and Grisi separated. Her career was now to be centered at the Paris Opera, while he remained in England as the principal ballet master at Her Majesty's Theatre for the next six seasons (Deshayes retired after the 1842 season). During the 1843 season Perrot began his association with Cesare Pugni, who, in the coming years, was to compose the music for most of his ballets. [*See the entry on Pugni.*] Their first work together was *L'Aurore,* a minor work that opened the season on 11 March 1843. In it, Perrot suffered a serious injury while dancing that forced him to abandon virtuoso roles, although he continued to appear on stage until the end of his career. He revived *Giselle* that season for Fanny Elssler, who brought a new dramatic intensity to the title role. He also produced a number of minor works, but the important event of the season, produced on 22 June 1843, was *Ondine, ou La Naïade.*

Although Fanny Cerrito, for whom *Ondine* was created, choreographed some sections, the conception of the ballet was truly Perrot's. It was inspired by the novel by Friedrich de La Motte-Fouqué, but the scenario was in many respects original. The hero, the role Perrot conceived for himself, was a simple fisherman. The ballet combined scenes of real life, palpitating with the *couleur locale* of southern Italy, and the typically Romantic fancy of naiads exerting a supernatural fascination over mortals. Among the highlights were a brilliant tarantella and a ravishing solo for Cerrito, the *pas de l'ombre,* in which the Ondine, who has become a mortal in her infatuation for the hero, discovers that she has acquired a shadow. Perrot received great praise for the construction of the work, particularly for its dramatic flow and the skillful way in which the dances were woven into the narrative.

On 20 July 1843, at the request of Queen Victoria, Perrot staged an isolated pas de deux that was to have great consequences. It was arranged for Elssler and Cerrito, whose rivalry had absorbed the London audiences. The pas de deux was remarkable for the skill with which Perrot brought out the best qualities of each ballerina's style so that neither felt herself to be at a disadvantage. He was later to compose several similar pieces for the great ballerinas of Europe.

Perrot's third season as London's principal ballet master in 1844 featured, on the opening night of 9 March, the ballet that many considered to be his greatest work: *La Esmeralda,* a dramatic ballet based on Victor Hugo's novel *Notre-Dame de Paris.* Perrot, as was usual, worked out the scenario himself, with some assistance from Lumley. In his choreography Perrot involved the corps de ballet as an integral part of the opening scene in the Cour des Miracles, portraying the truands of the Paris underworld of the fifteenth century, and again in the Festival of Fools in the final scene. Hugo's narrative was simplified for the balletic medium, and a happy ending was substituted for the novel's tragic climax. Nevertheless, the ballet made a profound impression, with its convincing portrayal of Hugo's principal characters. Esmeralda was one of Grisi's happiest creations, and Perrot took the part of the poor student Gringoire, once again identifying with a humble person. Arthur Saint-Léon played the high-born Phoebus. [*See* Esmeralda, La.]

At the end of the 1844 season Elssler was seen in the role of Esmeralda, which she played with great dramatic power, giving a very different interpretation from the gentle rendering of Grisi. Another highlight of the 1844 season was *Polka,* a theatrical version of the dance that was the latest rage in ballrooms. It was arranged by Perrot and danced by him and Grisi.

The 1845 London season was to be even more brilliant. It opened on 8 March with the ballet *Éoline, ou La Dryade,* in which the young Danish ballerina Lucile Grahn made her London debut. The germ of this ballet was found in a folk tale by Johann Musäus telling of the fate of a girl who was transformed into a dryad at night. Perrot took the role of Rübezahl, Prince of the Gnomes, whose love for Éoline leads him to destroy her. In the *mazurka d'extase* he gave a brilliant display of interpretive dancing with Grahn, who was herself an expressive mime. This *pas d'action* was in the same class as the *pas de fascination* of *Alma,* but it was more profound in its conception, the theme being Éoline's subjugation to the mesmeric powers of a strange demon who appears at her wedding festivities. Another choreographic highlight was the *grand pas des dryades,* an ensemble scene in the tradition of the last acts of *La Sylphide* and *Giselle.*

In the early weeks of the 1845 season, Perrot devoted himself to presenting Grahn to a public that was noticeably slow in appreciating her. The two collaborated on a short ballet on a Norwegian theme, *Kaya,* on 17 April, but it was not until he had presented her in another *divertissement, La Bacchante* (1 May 1845), that the London public began to take her to their hearts. It was this success that led to her taking part in the work that brought the 1845 season to a dazzling climax, *Pas de Quatre.*

No other opera house engaged such a wealth of talent for a single season as Her Majesty's. The simultaneous presence of four celebrated ballerinas—Taglioni, Cerrito, Grisi, and Grahn—gave Lumley the idea of a *divertissement* in which they would appear together onstage. Thus it was that the now legendary *Pas de Quatre* was born. The task of accommodating the four ballerinas was given to Perrot, and he carried it out with a skill that amounted to genius. Following his achievement in the Elssler-Cerrito pas de deux two years before, he gave equal prominence to twice the number of stars. *Pas de Quatre* was first performed on 12 July 1845, and although only performed six times in all, it epitomized the glory of the Romantic ballet. Short though it was, it was hailed as a masterpiece of choreography. [*See* Pas de Quatre.]

For the opening of the 1846 season on 3 March, Perrot produced a colorful dramatic ballet, *Catarina, ou La Fille du Bandit,* based on the supposed capture by bandits of the artist Salvator Rosa in the Abruzzi mountains. Perrot designed the title role for Grahn, and he played her devoted lieutenant, Diavolino, a striking character study of a hotheaded man of the people. The action was packed with incident, culminating with Catarina's death during the Roman Carnival, and there was a great variety of brilliantly arranged dances. [*See* Catarina.]

Perrot was extraordinarily prolific that season, for three months later, on 11 June, he presented a ballet on a mammoth scale, *Lalla Rookh, or The Rose of Lahore.* Based on the poem of that name by Thomas Moore, the ballet incorporated Félicien David's symphonic ode *Le Désert* to accompany a tableau depicting a caravan carrying the bride-to-be of the king of Bucharia across the desert, as well as two songs by the same composer. Pugni arranged the score and wrote most of the music for the dances. At its first performance the ballet lasted nearly three hours, twice as long as *La Esmeralda* and *Catarina.* Cerrito created the title role, with Saint-Léon in the role of the king who wooed her in disguise, while Perrot himself played the comic role of the fussy, ill-tempered chamberlain. The ballet was too long to be a real success, but it was performed a respectable number of times after being judiciously pruned. It contained a striking solo for Cerrito, the *pas de chibouck,* performed to the melody of one of David's loveliest songs. The pas de neuf at the end was seen as a novel departure in choreography, with all nine parts individually choreographed.

The 1846 season closed on 23 July with another triumph, *Le Jugement de Pâris.* Appropriately, Taglioni, Cerrito, and Grahn played the three goddesses whose beauty was judged by Paris. It was the success of the season: Queen Victoria saw it twice, and the duke of Wellington attended ten performances.

The following winter Perrot was engaged for the Carnival season at La Scala, Milan, where, on 9 January 1847, he produced an elaborate and definitive revival of *Catarina,* with a considerable amount of additional music by Giovanni Bajetti, and with Elssler in the title role. This was followed, on 16 March 1847, by a completely new bal-

PERROT. As Gringoire, a poet, with Carlotta Grisi in the title role of his ballet *La Esmeralda,* which premiered at Her Majesty's Theatre, London, in 1844. (Dance Collection, New York Public Library for the Performing Arts.)

let, *Odetta, o La Demenza di Carlo VI Re di Francia.* The plot was probably based on his reading of Louis Michelet's *Histoire de France,* which tells of a power struggle as a result of the king's insanity. Elssler danced the role of the heroine, the king's mistress (known to history as *la petite reine*), whose gentle ministrations brought comfort to the unfortunate monarch. This role was created for Elssler; Perrot himself played the part of the king's jester. The ballet was spectacularly staged and performed with powerful conviction, the corps de ballet again taking a prominent part in creating the atmosphere of the Paris streets of the period. Because Perrot's usual collaborator, Pugni, was unable to travel to Milan, the score was composed by Giacomo Panizza, Giovanni Bajetti, and Giovanni Battista Croff. Unfortunately, Perrot was ill and unable to put the finishing touches to this ballet. Although its merits were recognized, Perrot did not have the opportunity to revive it; however, several ballet masters restaged it in Italy.

Perrot's engagement at La Scala prevented him from being in London for the opening of the 1847 season, so that Lumley engaged Paul Taglioni as an assistant ballet master. Perrot arrived in London in May, limiting his contribution that season to producing the *divertissement Les Éléments* (26 June 1847), for which he used some of the music Bajetti had composed for *Odetta.* The elements of air, water, and fire were portrayed, respectively, by Cerrito, Carolina Rosati, and Grisi; the spirits of the earth were represented by four soloists.

Lumley hoped to present a ballet during the 1847 season based on the *Faust* theme. He had coaxed the poet Heinrich Heine to write a scenario, but the project was aborted. Perrot had long cherished an ambition to create his own version based on Goethe's poem and produced one at La Scala (12 February 1848) with a score by Panizza, Bajetti, and Michael Costa. Elssler was Marguerite and he was Mephistopheles. He based his characterization on his recollections of Lemaître in the same role. The first performance, delayed on account of Elssler's illness, coincided with the period of political upheaval that preceded the temporary ejection of the Austrians from Milan. Passions were running high, and Elssler, who was Austrian, played the role only once. The ballet was then drastically shortened and presented a few weeks later with the American ballerina Augusta Maywood as Marguerite. It was difficult to judge the work in such a highly charged atmosphere. The ballet's highlight, the ambitious set dance of the Seven Deadly Sins, was omitted when Maywood took over the role but was restored when Elssler danced it during her farewell season in Vienna in 1851 and in Perrot's later revival of the ballet in Russia.

From Milan, Perrot went to London for what was to be his last season at Her Majesty's. As in the previous year, Paul Taglioni was joint ballet master, and Perrot produced only one work, *Les Quatre Saisons* (13 June 1848), his last multistellar *divertissement,* featuring Cerrito, Grisi, Rosati, and the younger Marie Taglioni.

Later that year, after protracted negotiations and at the request of Elssler, Perrot was engaged by the Imperial Theaters in Russia. He arrived in Saint Petersburg in December 1848, in time to put the finishing touches to the production of *La Esmeralda,* which was first given for his benefit. He also staged *Catarina.* Both productions created a strong impression on the Saint Petersburg public, and before leaving Russia in the spring of 1849 he signed a contract for the following season.

Meanwhile, Perrot had entered into a commitment to the Paris Opera, which he then had to alter in order to meet his obligations to the Imperial Theaters. He had once very much wanted to be at the Opera but, after the freedom he had known in London, bowing before the custom of the establishment was frustrating. He did his best with Vernoy de Saint-Georges's scenario for *La Filleule des Fées,* produced, after numerous delays, on 8 October 1849. In spite of his difficulties and the indignity of having his contract terminated as part of the economics introduced by the management, he showed himself a master at handling large numbers of dancers and created a wonderful role for Grisi. He played the part of the heroine's unsuccessful suitor, an awkward rustic who aroused sympathy as well as laughter through his able miming.

His Paris contract ended a few weeks after the first performance of *La Filleule des Fées,* and he returned to Saint Petersburg. His principal contribution to the Bolshoi Theater's 1849–1850 season was a revised version of *La Filleule des Fées,* with Elssler in the principal role. In the summer of 1850 he accompanied Elssler to Moscow, where he staged *Le Délire d'un Peintre, Giselle,* and *Catarina.* At about this time he married a Russian woman, Capitolina Samovskaya, and for the next nine years lived in Russia, paying only occasional visits to France.

The Saint Petersburg season of 1850/51 was preceded by a delightful *divertissement* that Perrot arranged for an imperial fête at the Palace of Peterhof in July 1850. Performed on an outdoor stage at the edge of a lake, it consisted mainly of a reworking of scenes from *Ondine*—first a scene in which the naiad exercises her charms on the fisherman Matteo and then, with a change of mood, the arrival of villagers to dance a tarantella. Grisi was engaged in Elssler's place for the 1850/51 season, which opened in September, and Perrot was joined by another old friend, Pugni. Perrot revived several of his ballets for Grisi, including *Giselle, La Esmeralda,* and *La Filleule des Fées,* and staged a version of Mazilier's ballet *Le Diable à Quatre.* His principal contribution came at the end of the season, on 26 January [6 February] 1851, with *The Naïad and the Fisherman,* a ballet that resembled *Ondine* but was in fact almost entirely new. The main characters in *Ondine* reappeared, but the narrative was altered; at the end, Matteo drowned himself to be united with the naiad.

Perrot was apparently absent from Saint Petersburg for much of the following winter, for Mazilier replaced him as ballet master at the Bolshoi and he resumed his duties, as a performer only, shortly before the end of the 1851/52 season. For the 1852/53 season, however, as ballet master he was soon ready with a new ballet, a remarkable work, *The War of the Women, or The Amazons of the Ninth Century,* first performed on 11 [23] November 1852. Based on a historical event—the revolt of the female bodyguard of a prince of Bohemia—it was censored, requiring changes in the scenario. Not only was it about revolt, which disturbed the censor, but it also presented women as a discontented class in a male-dominated society. Grisi played the heroine, Vlaida, and Elena Andreyanova the women's leader; Perrot appeared, typically, in the part of a jester.

The ballet contained all the ingredients expected in a Perrot ballet: the use of the corps de ballet as an integral part of the action, particularly in the opening act, which brought out the contrasting attitudes of the men and the women of the village to the tyranny under which they suffered; dances that grew naturally out of the action—among them a *pas des arcs* in which the women practice using bows; a dramatic pyrrhic dance; and much brilliant choreography for the ballerina.

Grisi's presence was obviously an inspiration, for that season saw another new work, *Gazelda,* first performed on 12 [24] February 1853. This was modest in scope, being inspired by memories of the *opéra-ballet Zingaro,* although the plot was quite different. Perrot and Grisi played a young couple who had been brought up as children among Gypsies. The narrative required a considerable amount of pantomime, but there were many dance passages, including a *pas scénique* entitled *La Bonnaventura,* in which Gazelda tells fortunes to members of a hunting party; two character dances for Andreyanova; and a long and complex dance for Grisi, *La Cosmopolitana,* that introduced a succession of national dances to convey the nomadic nature of Gypsy life.

Perrot remained at his post in Saint Petersburg throughout the Crimean War. While no outstanding star was engaged for the 1853/54 season, he was able to exploit

PERROT. As Diavolino, with Lucile Grahn in the title role of *Catarina, ou La Fille du Bandit* (1846). This lithograph, printed on a music cover for "The Bavarian Polka," was made by M. & N. Hanhart after John Brandard, London, c.1846. (Courtesy of Madison U. Sowell and Debra H. Sowell, Brigham Young University, Provo, Utah.)

PERROT. *La Filleule des Fées* was the only work of Perrot's produced during the 1849 season of the Paris Opera. In this 1849 lithograph, Perrot poses in the role of Alain. (Dance Collection, New York Public Library for the Performing Arts.)

the interpretive talent of a young Viennese dancer, Gabriele Yella, for whom he revived his *Faust,* playing his original role of Mephistopheles. *Faust* remained in the repertory for many years in Saint Petersburg. The critic A. N. Serov considered that Perrot displayed a greater understanding of Goethe's poem than the librettists of Charles Gounod's opera. The absence of a star ballerina, coupled with a pride in native talent engendered by the war, enabled a number of young Russian ballerinas to emerge. Perrot encouraged and aided them, preparing Zina Richard, Anna Prikhunova, and Maria Surovshchikova in leading roles.

At this time Perrot was beginning to fret about the demands made by the Imperial Theaters directorate, which he considered was stifling his creativity. Nevertheless, he signed a new three-year contract that bound him until the end of the 1857/58 season. He continued working on his new ballet, *Armida,* basing his scenario on Torquato Tasso's *Gerusalemme liberata.* Another source, in all probability, was Jean-Georges Noverre's ballet on the same theme, for there are a number of similarities between the two works. It was first performed on 10 [22] November 1855 with Armida played by Cerrito, who was appearing in her first Russian season at the age of thirty-eight, and Marius Petipa as Rinaldo. Perrot played the role of a minstrel, arranging for himself a highly comic yet dramatic *scène dansante,* The Fountain of Laughter. The ballet also featured a young Russian dancer, Marfa Muravieva, who made such an impression as Cupid that she virtually outshone Cerrito. It was a spectacular production, making full use of the scenic resources of the Bolshoi Theater, but was criticized as being too long and containing too little dancing.

Cerrito's position was affected by the return to Russia of Nadezhda Bogdanova, who had become something of a national heroine by having been engaged at the Paris Opera when the Crimean War broke out. Perrot turned his attention back to *Giselle,* in which Bogdanova evoked an emotional response from the Saint Petersburg public, further stimulating the growing interest in native talent.

During the 1856/57 season, the emphasis remained firmly on the young Russian ballerinas. Perrot's new ballet, *La Débutante,* his principal creation of the season, featured Bogdanova, Prikhunova, and Marie Petipa.

For the main production of the 1857/58 season, the directorate had selected *Le Corsaire,* a ballet that had been a sensational success in Paris when Mazilier first produced it at the Opera in 1856. Perrot's version followed the original scenario exactly but contained additional dances for which Pugni had added the required music to Adam's score. When first performed at the Bolshoi Theater in Saint Petersburg, on 9 [21] January 1858, the program credited Perrot with arranging and staging the dances. Being conscious perhaps that his version incorporated ideas and passages from Mazilier's work, he did not include it in the list of his works found among his papers. The leading role of Medora, created in Paris by Rosati, was played in Russia by a ballerina of secondary rank, Ekaterina Friedberg. Perrot himself played the part of Seyd, the pasha.

Perrot's last years in Russia were clouded by ill health, family worries following the illness and death of his father, and a growing discontent with the conditions of his employment. Matters were not helped by an antipathy between him and the new director, Andrei Saburov. Perrot's contract expired in March 1858, and although a new one was drawn up, he put off signing it, while continuing to perform his duties as ballet master at the opening of the 1858/59 season. The Italian ballerina Amalia Ferraris was engaged as the season's star, and for her debut on 4 [16] November 1858 he produced a new and greatly expanded version of *Éoline.* Théophile Gautier, who was visiting

Russia, wrote a long article that contains a vivid description of the ballet.

Very shortly after the premiere of *Éoline,* Perrot was incapacitated by a badly inflamed foot, which caused him to abandon plans for a new ballet for Ferraris. He went to France for treatment in the summer of 1859 but did not return to Russia in time for the new season. When he did return, the directorate of the Imperial Theaters had already arranged for Saint-Léon to take charge of the ballet in Saint Petersburg as well as in Moscow. Matters dragged on inconclusively in the hope that Perrot might recover sufficiently to resume his duties, but eventually the reality of the situation was recognized, and he was dismissed in December 1860.

Perrot returned to France in 1861 and settled in Paris, which was to be his home until his death. He smarted under his impression that the Opera was ignoring his gifts and clearly resented the opportunity given to Marius and Marie Petipa to perform there in 1862. He refused his consent for Marie Petipa to dance the *pas La Cosmopolitana,* which he had composed for *Gazelda,* and when she danced it in defiance of his wishes, he sued her husband for breach of copyright. Although successful, he was awarded a disappointingly small sum for damages. His feelings were to be somewhat assuaged in 1863 when Muravieva, who was engaged by the Paris Opera for the summer, asked him to coach her in the role of Giselle.

Perrot was engaged by La Scala, Milan, for the Carnival season of 1863/64 to stage *Gazelda.* The revival, first given on 27 January 1864, was a disaster, saved only by the performance of Claudina Cucchi as the gypsy heroine. Perrot returned to Paris a disappointed man. He was to produce no more ballets, although rumors arose from time to time that he was to produce a ballet at the Paris Opera. He maintained his links with the ballet world, becoming very friendly with Louis Mérante. After the Franco-German War of 1870–1871, when Mérante had become ballet master of the Opera, Perrot gave classes there and was the subject of one of Edgar Degas's best-known ballet paintings.

Perrot died at his villa in Paramé, after a brief illness, on 18 August 1892, and was buried in the Cimetière du Père-Lachaise, Paris. He was survived by his wife Capitolina (died 1900) and by two daughters, Marie (died 1926) and Alexandrine (died 1941).

Several of Perrot's ballets survived in Russia for many years after his departure, thanks largely to Marius Petipa, who kept them in the repertory. They were refurbished from time to time to preserve their freshness and incorporate the virtuoso technique that became a prominent feature of ballet in the last quarter of the nineteenth century. During his years in Saint Petersburg, Perrot had made *Giselle* very much his own ballet. Later, Petipa revised it extensively, particularly in 1887. He ensured its survival in 1903, when he prepared Anna Pavlova for the title role. It remains one of the gems of the classical heritage. *La Esmeralda* has also survived, although only in Russia. It is impossible to say how much or what of Perrot's choreography remains. *Le Corsaire* also survives, but today's productions retain little of Perrot's choreography. *The Naïad and the Fisherman* survived until 1905, when it was given for the last time with Pavlova as the naiad. *Catarina* was dropped in 1898, but excerpts from *Faust* were still being danced in the 1890s. Because ballets were not recorded until many decades after Perrot's retirement, the survival of so much of his work for thirty or forty years is testimony to his achievement.

Although little of Perrot's choreography survives, his works form a significant part of the ballet tradition. His innovative work was fully recognized in his day: for the development, if not the invention, of the *pas d'action,* for the employment of the corps de ballet to add life to a crowd scene, and for passages of pure dance, whether variations for individual dancers or *pas* for several dancers.

Perrot was essentially a dramatic author working in movement. He enjoyed the good fortune of being able to select his own subjects for nearly all the ballets he created. This freedom, which he enjoyed particularly in London (and to a considerable extent in Russia, although with an occasional tussle with censorship), enabled him to express in dance the trends and philosophy of the Romantic movement. His imagination was fed directly by the works of many celebrated artists of the time: Théophile Gautier, Victor Hugo, Thomas Moore, Friedrich de La Motte-Fouqué, and Louis Michelet among the writers, and such artists as Moritz Retzsch, Eugène Delacroix, and particularly Léopold Robert. Viewed as an individual artist's life work, Perrot's ballets reveal the duality of his genius—to use a literary analogy, that of poet and dramatist. Considered in their historical context, they can be seen to have extended the horizons of choreographic art farther than any of his contemporaries. Perrot was, in the full sense of the term, the master of the Romantic ballet.

BIBLIOGRAPHY

Beaumont, Cyril W. *The Ballet Called Giselle.* 2d rev. ed. London, 1945.

Gautier, Théophile. *Gautier on Dance.* Translated and edited by Ivor Guest. London, 1986. French edition: *Ecrits sur la danse* (Arles, 1995).

Guest, Ivor. *Fanny Elssler.* London, 1970.

Guest, Ivor. *The Romantic Ballet in England.* London, 1972.

Guest, Ivor. *Fanny Cerrito.* 2d rev. ed. London, 1974.

Guest, Ivor. *The Romantic Ballet in Paris.* 2d rev. ed. London, 1980.

Guest, Ivor. *Jules Perrot: Master of the Romantic Ballet.* London, 1984.

Guest, Ivor. "Perrot and Bournonville." *The Dancing Times* (November 1988): 138–139.

Lifar, Serge. *Giselle: Apothéose du ballet romantique.* Paris, 1942.

Lumley, Benjamin. *Reminiscences of the Opera.* London, 1864.

Moore, Lillian. *Artists of the Dance.* New York, 1938.

Roslavleva, Natalia. *Era of the Russian Ballet.* London, 1966.

Slonimsky, Yuri. "Jules Perrot." Translated by Anatole Chujoy. *Dance Index* 4 (December 1945): 208–247.
Sorley Walker, Kathrine. "Perrot and His Lost Choreography." *Ballet* (April 1946): 29–36.
Vaillat, Léandre. *La Taglioni: La vie d'une danseuse.* Paris, 1942.
Vazem, Ekaterina. "Memoirs of a Ballerina of the St. Petersburg Bolshoi Theatre, Part 1." Translated by Nina Dimitrievich. *Dance Research* 3 (Summer 1985): 3–22.
Wiley, Roland John, trans. and ed. *A Century of Russian Ballet: Documents and Accounts, 1810–1910.* Oxford and New York, 1990.
Winter, Marian Hannah. *Le théâtre du merveilleux.* Paris, 1962.

IVOR GUEST

PERU. Located on the Pacific coast of South America, the Republic of Peru, some 496,000 square miles (1.3 million square kilometers), is bordered by Ecuador and Colombia to the north, Brazil and Bolivia to the east, and Chile to the south. The central part of the Andes Mountains runs through the eastern part of the country, forming the *altiplano;* the western part is a low-lying desert, which is driest in the south. Many small river and stream beds run from the Andes through the desert to the ocean. Along these valleys, Native American peoples settled in fishing and farming villages at least ten thousand years ago. Some were so successful that they eventually formed city-states and civilizations—thousands of years before the Inca Empire expanded from the Cuzco area in the Andes and united most of the other empires along the west coast of South America in the one hundred years before the Spanish conquest of the early 1500s. Lima, now the capital of Peru, was the seat of Spanish rule in colonial South America. Peru declared independence in 1821 but ongoing opposition from Spain continued until 1824. In 1860 Peru adopted a republican constitution; in 1879 Spain formally recognized the Republic of Peru. Today some 17 million people live in Peru, 46 percent of Andean Indian ancestry, 42 percent *mestizos* (of Spanish and Andean Indian ancestry), and 12 percent of European ancestry; most are Spanish-speaking Roman Catholics except for those Andean Indians who remain out of the mainstream of national life, preferring traditional ways in their farming villages; some continue to speak Quechua, the language of the Inca.

PERU. Masked dancers in the Andean village of Tinta, near Cuzco, wearing costumes that mimic Argentine traders and cattle herders *(gauchos)* in the dance "Los Argentinos." (Photograph © by Pierre Verger; used by permission.)

The dance culture of Peru, like that of many other Latin American countries, is syncretic. To some Andean traditional dances (primarily ritual) have been added Spanish religious and social dances as well as some elements from Africa. The diversity of cultures within Peru precludes many generalizations, but a few can be made. Julia Elena Fortún (1967, p. 68) noted that the majority of Andean dances belong to the category called "closed" dances. Another general characteristic is the profusion of dances exclusive to males and a scarcity of those done by females. Musical accompaniment is rich and inventive, often employing native instruments that long predate European influence.

Indigenous Dance. At the time of first contact with Europeans, in the early 1500s, Peru was dominated by the Inca Empire, which had for about a century conquered and incorporated several societies that had been long-established in the Andean region. What we know about dance among the Incas and their predecessors comes from pictorial representations that are primarily on ceramics. In addition, early Spanish chroniclers recorded information about the cultures they encountered.

According to these early accounts, Inca men and women usually danced separately, although in some dances men performed in women's attire. In one dance, the *cashua,* men and women in alternation formed a circle, holding hands, and danced around a central ritual object. Some dances mimed activities such as herding, planting, or war; in others, dancers wore animals skins and zoomorphic masks and might carry a small animal. Movements mentioned include skips, jumps, and other steps; writers remarked on the grave, honest attitude of the performers. A leader directed dancing. Accompaniment was provided by singing and by the musical instruments prescribed for each type of dance. Certain dances were associated with certain of the subject nations.

Dancing was part of the ceremonies of thanksgiving, held in May, and of rituals associated with corn planting. The gods were honored with dance and chants. There were dances performed at marriages and funerals, and at special festivals such as the Inti Rayai. Few of the dance names mentioned by early writers correspond with those used today, but the social and choreographic elements they record continue to be important in Andean folk dance.

Certain dances are identified by Merino (1977) as specific to particular regions. From the Puno region, historians record the *chokelas* or *chukilas,* a mythic hunting dance; the *auqui auqui,* dealing with creator gods; and the *queno-maris,* a war dance. Dances mentioned from Cuzco, the Inca capital, include the *sarge,* in honor of a protective spirit of the mountains, and a war dance called *chapaq ch'unchos.* Ancash is the home of two war dances, *wanca* and *cuadrilla mojiganga.* A dance from Amazonas (on the eastern slope of the Andes) represented relationships between humans and animals. The *chimus* or *chimbos* was a product of the dazzling gold culture of the Chimu people of northern Peru and Ecuador.

In various places, dances done after the Spanish conquest seem to conceal a veneration and nostalgia for the Inca Empire. Among them are "La Maroma de Oro," in Cuzco; "La Vispera," the story of Huayna Cepac, from Huánuco; "La Danza del Inca," commemorating Yahuar Huaca, in Apurimac; "Las Coyas," a dance of Inca nobles, from La Libertad; and "La Coya," a dance of the Inca's wife, from Junin. "Las Pallas," another dance of nobles, is performed all over Peru. In Cuzco, the "Kachampa" celebrates victories in war, while the "Qanchis" presents the Camayoc, the representatives of the Inca. The Inca himself (the emperor) appears in "Las Ingas" of Sierra de Lima. Another Cuzco dance, "Altar Tusoq," depicts the lineage of the rebel leader Tupac Amaru.

A few dances display remnants of pre-Christian religion: totemism in "El Condor"; magic in "La Danza de Tijeres" (Scissors Dance). Pastoral and agricultural dances (discussed below) also reflect aspects of ancient rituals.

Colonial Period. The military conquest of the Inca Empire by Spain in the mid-sixteenth century resulted in the suppression and disappearance of many traditional dances. Some persisted, however, even if in fragmentary form. In particular, they were recast in the context of Roman Catholicism, so that they might continue to be performed even as the conquerors were suppressing many aspects of the civilization from which the dances came.

The Conquest itself is commemorated in a complex of dance dramas performed, with variations, all over Peru. The best known is the dance known as "Apu Inca" in Húanuco and by other names elsewhere; it deals with the death of the last Inca emperor, Atahualpa. Others of this dance complex include "Ayarachis," a funeral dance in Puno and Cuzco; "La Marcha de los Capitanes," in Pasco; "Cahuallu-Danza" or "La Caballito Danzante" (Dancing Horse) in Ancash; and "Huanquilla," depicting a battle during the Conquest, from Ancash.

PERU. Wearing old-fashioned colonial costumes, Andean villagers from Hauncavelica dance "Los Pastorcitos" (The Little Shepherds) in celebration of Epiphany, a Christian holiday. (Photograph © by Pierre Verger; used by permission.)

During the colonial era, many mimetic or narrative dances were created that depicted the Spaniards and the bulls and horses they had introduced. Among these, Puno has the amusing "Waca-waca" and two views of the Spaniards—one respectful, in "Español o Taita," and one satirical, in "Achachi Kumo." "La Chonquinada" of Junin and Pasco and "Los Chapetones" of Ancash are ceremonial and elegant mimicries of Spaniards; Ayacucho's "Los Viejos" is a humorous one. The colonial authorities figure in "Los Caballeros de Huari" in Ancash. "Pailachos o Huichos" of La Libertad has been called "almost an operetta" because of its elaborate depiction of everyday life.

When the Spanish brought slaves from Africa to Peru, the indigenous Peruvians quickly incorporated African characters into their dances. A sympathetic African character appears in a recent Puno choreographic cycle called *Morenada* or *Rey Moreno*, as well as in older dances such as the "La Negreria," "Los Negros," or "Los Negritos," preserved in many towns and villages; "Los Negritos de Huanuco" is especially famous.

The Spanish colonists took advantage of Andean highways (built by the Incas) to link their territories by mule trains carrying trade goods. Trade inspired a complex of dances known variously as "Los Arrieros", "Los Argentinos," "La Mula-Mula," "Los Tucumanos," or "Los Gauchos." It is the source of farcical dances—"Los Arrieros" of Ayacucho and "Las Pausas y el Majeno" of Arequipa. Dancers pretend to be Inca traders in "Los Qollas" of Cuzco.

Llama and alpaca husbandry was long established in Peru when the Spanish added sheep, goats, and cattle. Some dances associated with pastoralism appear to come from precolonial times; "Los Santiagos," ostensibly offerings to the saints for the protection of livestock, conceal rites propitiating ancient gods. These lively branding dances of Junin have counterparts in "Los Ch'ukus" of Cuzco and "Pujllay" of Puno. Dancers in "El Llamerada" of Puno mimic a herd of llamas, while "El Llameritos" of Ayacucho and "Los Llamis" of Junin impersonate herders. "Los Pastores" (The Shepherds) and "Los Pastorcitos" (The Little Shepherds) appear to be entirely Christian dances. Puno's "Los Chokelas" mimes the hunt of the vicuña, the wild form of the domesticated llama.

Old rites also survive in agricultural dances. The cult of Pachamama is manifested in such dances as "Rayhuana" from Ancash. Other dances simulate farm work—the corn harvest in "La Jija," grain reaping in "Los Segadores," potato growing in "Waylash," and the planting of *oca* in "Oqa Tarpuy." The widespread dances of Carnival often link the joy of the Easter season with harvest ceremonialism.

Many other dances portray occupations. Three found in Cuzco are "La Contradanza" (featuring carpenters), "Los Herreros" (blacksmiths), and "Los Barberos" (barbers). "Los Kullawas" or "La Kullawada" of Puno depicts spinners, and "Los Chacranegros or "Los Mineros" miners. There are many dances on military themes, including "Los Capitanes;" "Los Capitanes a Caballo y a Pie" (Captains on Horseback and Foot), which has ritual and divining elements; "Turcos," "Moros y Cristianos," and "Carlomagno y los Doce Pares de Francia" (Charlemagne and the Twelve Nobles of France). A unique genre is that of ritual battles, exemplified by "Las Guerrillas Indigenas de Chiyaraque y Toqto" (The Indian Skirmishers of Chiyaraque and Toqto).

Many of the dances mentioned above employ set characters, music, dances, plots, and recitatives to such a degree that they can be considered dance dramas. A precolonial dance drama called *Ollantay* is reported to have existed; its music is still extant. The pan-Peruvian drama *Apu Inca* is discussed above; certain dances such as "Las Pallas" and "Las Ingas" may be detached segments of it. Many dance dramas employ theatrical comedians called Kusillo and Chuto; these jesters seem to have been part of precolonial ceremonies as well.

The Christian devil is embodied in one of the largest pan-Peruvian complexes. It includes "Son de los Diablos"

PERU. Men from the village of Paucartambo, near Cuzco, performing a *contradanza*. Their ornate costumes, including vests, mid-calf pants, stockings, and hard-soled shoes, indicate the dance's partly Basque origin. (Photograph © by Pierre Verger; used by permission.)

(They Belong to the Devils) in Lambayeque; "Diablicos" (Devilish Ones) in Lima; "Diablitos" (Little Devils) in Ancash and Piura; the beautiful "Diablada" (Devil's Dance) of Puna; and "Sagras" (Holy Rites) in Cuzco.

Most localities now have special dances honoring their patron saints, who may be said to have initiated the performances. For example, it is said that the Virgin of Sapallanga (in Huancayo, Junin Province) originally asked that a dance called "Kalachaquis" (Bare Feet) be done for her.

Imported by the upper-class, European social dances became part of Peru's culture and were adapted by local performers. For example, the folk dance called "La Chonquinada" incorporates steps and figures from the cotillon and the quadrille, and "La Pandilla Punena" shows the influence of the minuet.

New ideas and new creatures entered the creative repertory of Peruvian dance; accepted into the Andean choreographic universe were the Spaniard, his bulls and horses, and his devils and angels. Dramatic dances today often feature such alien beings as protagonists. The arrival of African slaves brought still more new themes, characters, rhythms, and styles to Peruvian dance.

The Nineteenth Century. Peru achieved independence from Spain in 1824. Events of the independence period are recorded in the dances "Emancipación" of Junin and perhaps in "Tupac Amaru" of Cuzco. African slaves were emancipated by presidential decree in 1854, as commemorated in the splendid "Pachauara" (Dawn) from Junin.

The heroes and battles of Peru's ill-fated war with Chile (1879–1883) figure in "Los Avelinos" and "Los Caceristas," performed in the valley of the Mantaro in Junin, and in "Los Maqtas" and "Batallon Femenino de Otongo" in the valley of Yanamarca. The "Auga Chileno" or "Misti Chileno" of Cuzco also belongs to the complex. "La Marinera" celebrates the victory of Admiral Grau and is performed and revered all over the country.

Topical dances from this period also include "Los Soldados de Santa Catalina" (Soldiers of Santa Catalina), from Puno, and "Los Marineros" or "Los Marineros Ingleses" (Sailors; or British Sailors), from Piura and Lambayeque. The "Vijuela," a dance of bachelors and married men in the hills near Lima, portrays factionalism. Junin's "La Pierolista" has a political theme. The issue of ethnic minorities is involved in "Los Serranos" (People of the Hills, from Piura) and in "Los Campas" and "Shapish" (from Junin). The amusing "Chujchu" portrays a malaria patient. "Los Siqllas" of Cuzco and "Los Doctorcitos" of Puno subtly satirize magistrates. An evil of the time is revealed in "El Contrabandista y el Recaudador" (The Smuggler and the Tax Collector) from Ayacucho.

Folk Dance Today. The local ceremonial dances mentioned above continue to be performed to some extent in their regions of origin. In addition, there are several recreational dances known and enjoyed throughout Peru.

PERU. Folk dancers attired in festive costumes. The woman, at right, holds a handkerchief, a prop often used in couple dances such as "La Marinera" and the *wayno.* (Photograph © by Serge Lido; used by permission.)

"La Marinera," named in honor of the Peruvian Navy, has Spanish and African elements and may have originated in the colonial "La Zamba" and "La Zamacueca." It is performed by nontouching male-female couples; flourishing a handkerchief, the man pretends to woo the woman, who dodges and flirts with him. Variations are performed in the northern and high-mountain regions.

The other well-known national dance, the *wayno,* seems to be descended from precolonial Quechua dances mentioned by the chroniclers; both Indian and *mestizo* variants are danced in the mountain regions. Local variants may be known by different names, such as the *chuscada* of Ancash, *relojera* of Junin, or *wayno de chacra* of Huánuco. The *wayno* is also a couple dance involving courting, though without the picaresque humor of "La Marinera." The couple, who also carry handkerchiefs, may dance arm-in-arm or holding hands, depending on local custom.

Other recreational dances are restricted to certain regions. These include the *pandilla, chumayche,* and *chumaychada,* as well as a group of so-called traveling dances, such as the *pasacalle* and *muliza.* The Creole society of the coast features the *vals criollo* (Creole waltz) and *polce* (polka).

The usual practitioners of folk dance are the rural people, mostly of Native American descent and lower socioeconomic class. They are mainly pastoralists and agriculturalists living in villages, and they perpetuate their art

PERU. A woman from the Peruvian *altiplano* performing the *wayno*, a national dance with precolonial origins, which is popular in the Andean region. The man at right plays the Inca *antara*, an indigenous type of panpipe. (Photograph © by Pierre Verger; used by permission.)

according to the styles, times, and places dictated by tradition. When they have migrated to large cities, their dances have tended to lose authenticity.

Festivals in Peru draw hundreds of organized dance groups with thousands of performers to dance on city stages or at rural recreation sites. These amateur performing groups form around a repertory (local, departmental, or national), ethnicity (Andean, Creole, African, or rarely Amazonian), or place of performance. They are led by artistic directors and choreographers who may or may not be professionally trained. Despite their amateur status and separation from authentic village culture, these groups still perform a significant role in the preservation and dissemination of Peru's dance heritage.

Folk dance organizations at universities concentrate on the repertory of national dances. Middle-class and lower-class students from both urban and rural areas are active in promoting the culture of the common people, particularly those of the Andes, within a markedly political context. In the late 1980s there were about twenty-two state and private university folk dance groups in Lima and the provinces; the pioneer was FOLKUNI, the Folklore Group of the National University of Engineering, established in 1963.

Peruvians of African descent have for decades participated in the Black Folklore—more recently called the Afro-Peruvian Folklore—movement in Lima and other cities. In 1956 the Pancho Fierro troupe under José Durand performed a repertory of songs and dances based on African-Peruvian heritage, including *Creole Marinera, Agua e Nieve, Zapateo Criollo, Festejo,* and *Alcatraz*. The noted dancers Porfirio Vasquez and Nicomedes Santa Cruz came from this group. Later, Victoria Santa Cruz formed the Teatro y Danzas Negras del Peru (Black Theater and Dances of Peru), taking inspiration from or reworking popular dances of the nineteenth century, such as *mozamala* and *zamacueca*. Her disciple, Ronaldo Campos, in turn formed the popular Peru Negro (Black Peru), which primarily collects and performs the dances of Chincha. Campos's choreographies are generally collective, involving a large number of couples. The group has inspired a number of imitators.

BIBLIOGRAPHY

Aguilar Luna-Victoria, Carlos. *La marinera: Baile nacional del Perú*. Lima, 1989.

Arguedas, José María. *Música y danzas del Perú*. Lima, 1964.

Alvarez, Félix. *Danzas típicas del Perú*. Lima, 1991.

Cuentas Ormachea, Enrique. "La danza Choqela y su contenido mágico-religioso." *Boletín de Lima* 19 (1982).

Cuentas Ormachea, Enrique. *Presencia de Puno en la cultura popular*. Lima, 1995.

Flores Calderón, Oscar. *Historia y belleza del criollismo, 1713–1990*. Lima, 1991.

Fortún, Julia Elena. "Sistema de clasificación de danzas americanas." *Folklore Americano* 15 (1967–1968).

Gilt Contreras, Mario Alberto. "Las guerrillas indígenas de Chiyaraque y Toqto." *Archivos peruanos de folklore* 1 (1955).

Jiménez Borja, Arturo. "Teatro indio." *El Comercio* (18 May 1941).

Lara, Celso. "En torno al problema de la proyección folklórica." *Folklore americano* 18 (December 1974).

Madalengoitia Aubry, Pablo de. *Panorama de danza*. Lima, 1954.

Mandoza-Walker, Zoila. *"Carnival in Q'eros* and *Dancing with the Incas." Latin American Music Review* 16 (Fall-Winter 1995): 260–264. Review of two films by John Cohen.

Merino de Zela, E. Mildred. "The National School of Peruvian Music and Folkdancing." *Ethnomusicology* 11 (January 1967): 113–115.

Merino de Zela, E. Mildred. "Folklore coreográfico e historia." *Folklore americano* 24 (December 1977).

Morote Best, Efraín. *Elementos de folklore*. Cuzco, 1950.

Morote Best, Efraín. *El drama tradicional en los cuadros de contenido de folklore*. Lima, 1953.

Nuñez, Lucy. "Los danzantes se unen." *El comercio* (9 September 1984).

Otter, Elisabeth den. *Music and Dance of Indians and Mestizos in an Andean Valley of Peru*. Delft, 1985.

Patrón Manrique, José. *La Pandilla Puneña: Danza del carnaval*. Puno, 1984.

Poole, Deborah A. "Accommodation and Resistance in Andean Ritual Dance." *Drama Review* 34 (Summer 1990): 98–126.

Quillama Polo, Elena L., ed. *El Tondero como expresión folklórica y artística del Perú*. Lima, 1990.

Raúl Cortazar, Augusto. "Los ferrómenos folklóricos y su contexto humano y cultural." *Folklore americano* 18 (December 1974).

Roel Pineda, Josafath. *Kashkanirajmi Perú.* Lima, 1974.

Rodríguez Amado, Gustavo. *Música y danzas en las fiestas del Perú.* Arequipa, 1995.

Romero, Fernando. "La evolución de la Marinera." *IPNA* 6–8 (May 1946–April 1947).

Romero, Raúl R., ed. *Música, danzas y máscaras en los Andes.* Lima, 1993.

Ruiz, María Angélica. "Carlomagno y los doce pares de Francia." *Folklore americano* 16 (1969–1970).

Schaedel, Richard. "La representación de la muerte del Inca Atahualpa." *Cultura peruana* 53 (March–April 1952).

Tauro, Alberto. *Diccionario enciclopédico del Perú.* Lima, 1967.

Tompkins, William D. "The Musical Traditions of the Blacks of Coastal Peru." Ph.D. diss., University of California, Los Angeles, 1981.

Valcárcel, Carlos Daniel. *La rebelión de Túpac Amaru.* 3d ed. Lima, 1970.

Valcárcel, Luis Eduardo. *Ruta cultural del Perú.* Mexico City, 1945.

Valcárcel, Luis Eduardo. "Teatro y folklore." *Folklore* 30 (June-July 1953).

Valcárcel, Luis Eduardo. *Historia del Perú antiguo.* Lima, 1964.

Vilcapoma, José Carlos. *Waylarsh: Amor y violencia de carnaval.* Lima, 1995.

Vivanco, Alejandro. "El migrante de provincias como intérprete del folklore andino en Lima." Ph.D. diss., University of San Marco, 1973.

Yori, Alejandro. "La danza en Perú." *Monsalvat* (February 1990): 28–29.

E. MILDRED MERINO DE ZELA
Translated from Spanish

PETIPA, JEAN-ANTOINE (born 16 February 1787 in Paris, died 16 [28] July 1855 in Saint Petersburg), French ballet dancer, choreographer, and teacher. From whom Jean-Antoine Petipa received his early training as a dancer is not known. As an adult, he was probably coached by Jean-Baptiste Blache, ballet master at the Théâtre de la Porte-Saint-Martin in Paris, where he made his debut as a principal dancer in 1815. That same year, two other significant events occurred: Petipa made his first appearances in Brussels, when the company from the Théâtre de la Porte-Saint-Martin gave a series of guest performances there, and he married Victorine Grasseau, described in contemporary records as a "tragedienne." Of their numerous children, two of their sons, Lucien and Marius, became famous as dancers and choreographers. [*See the entries on Lucien Petipa and Marius Petipa.*]

Following his initial engagement in Paris, Jean-Antoine Petipa went south to work in Marseille, remaining there until 1819, when he accepted the post of *premier danseur* at the opera house in Brussels. He made his debut there in Blache's *Almaviva et Rosine* in May. Soon he had an opportunity to present his first choreographic composition, at a gala performance celebrating the opening of the Théâtre de la Monnaie. Not long thereafter he was appointed assistant ballet master to Eugène Hus the younger, founder-director of the ballet company at the new theater.

As the leading male dancer at the Théâtre de la Monnaie, Petipa appeared in all the new productions, most of which were revivals of such popular works as Jean-Louis Aumer's *Les Deux Créoles* (1819), Louis Milon's *Les Noces de Gamache* (1819), *Le Carnaval de Venise* (1820), and *Clari* (1821), and Jean-Baptiste Blache's *Lisbeth and Muller.* In the meantime he choreographed his first complete ballet, *La Kermesse* (1819), based on the Flemish national carnival, which was well received. His next important work was a two-act ballet, *La Naissance de Vénus et l'Amour,* in which his young son Lucien made his first stage appearance.

In 1822, shortly after Petipa had produced an ambitious ballet in three acts, *Monsieur Deschalumeaux,* Eugène Hus died, and Petipa was appointed principal ballet master. In 1823 and 1824 he produced nothing of his own, instead mounting ballets by Pierre Gardel, Blache, and Jean Dauberval. In 1825 he had the opportunity to enlarge his corps de ballet and to organize a regular academy of dancing, where his sons began to train. He then retired from dancing but stayed on as ballet master, reviving old ballets or rearranging his own: *Monsieur de Pourceaugnac* and *Jocko, ou Le Singe du Brésil* (1826), *Les Petites Danaïdes* (1828), and *Le 23, 24, 25 et 26 Septembre,* a commemoration of the battle of Brussels (1831).

Petipa then left Belgium to travel in France, especially in Marseille and Bordeaux. He returned to Brussels, where he served as co-ballet master to Bartholomin from 1833 to 1835, even appearing in mime roles. He then devoted most of his time to his sons. (Marius appeared in a gala at the Comédie Française in 1838 and Lucien made his debut at the Paris Opera in 1839.)

In 1839 Petipa accepted an offer to go with Marius to America in a troupe led by Hippolyte and Eugènie Lecomte. In New York, he mounted *La Tarentule, Jocko,* and *Marco Bomba,* which had just been seen in Paris. Displeased (because they were not paid), father and son decided to return to Europe. Once more back in Brussels, Petipa remained there until 1844, mounting French masterpieces such as *La Tarentule, Giselle, La Sylphide,* and *La Gitana.* He invited Fanny Elssler to appear as guest artist in 1843 and Fanny Cerrito in 1844.

In 1847 Jean-Antoine Petipa followed his son Marius to Russia. Marius had been engaged as a principal dancer of the Imperial Theaters, and Jean-Antoine had been invited to teach at the Imperial Ballet School in Saint Petersburg. Soon after his arrival, he assisted his son in mounting a production of Joseph Mazilier's ballet *Paquita* (1847), with Elena Andreyanova and Marius himself in the leading roles, at Saint Petersburg's Bolshoi Theater. Subsequently, Jean-Antoine also assisted his son in staging *Satanilla* (1848), based on Mazilier's *Le Diable Amoureux,* again starring Andreyanova, and in choreographing an original work, *Lida, or The Swiss Milkmaid* (1849), to music by Cesare Pugni. His last years were enriched by his son's early successes and by the development of dancers under his tutelage. Among his pupils who later achieved fame were Lev Ivanov and Pavel Gerdt.

BIBLIOGRAPHY

Dumas, Alexandre, et al. *Nouvelle galerie des artistes dramatiques.* 2 vols. Paris, 1855.

Guest, Ivor. *The Romantic Ballet in Paris.* 2d rev. ed. London, 1980.

Guest, Ivor. *Jules Perrot: Master of the Romantic Ballet.* London, 1984.

Isnardon, Jacques. *Le Théâtre de la Monnaie.* Brussels, 1890.

Moore, Lillian. "The Petipa Family in Europe and America." *Dance Index* 1 (May 1942): 72–84.

MONIQUE BABSKY
Translated from French

PETIPA, LUCIEN (Joseph-Lucien Petipa; born 22 December 1815 in Marseille, died 7 July 1898 in Versailles), French ballet dancer and choreographer. Born into a theatrical family, Lucien Petipa was reared in Brussels, where his father, Jean-Antoine, was ballet master at the Théâtre de la Monnaie. Trained by his father and allowed to appear on stage at La Monnaie as a child, Lucien made his official debut there in a gala performance arranged by his father in 1835. After engagements as a principal dancer in The Hague and in Bordeaux, he joined the Paris Opera Ballet and made his debut with that company in June 1839 in Jean Coralli's new ballet, *La Tarentule.*

LUCIEN PETIPA. A lithograph depicting Lucien Petipa as Achmet and Carlotta Grisi as Leila in act 2, scene 1, of Jean Coralli's *La Péri* (1843). (Dance Collection, New York Public Library for the Performing Arts.)

Two years later, in June 1841, Petipa created the role of Albrecht in *Giselle,* dancing opposite Carlotta Grisi. [*See* Giselle.] The noted critic Théophile Gautier, who had provided the libretto for the ballet, said that Petipa was "gracious, passionate, and touching" in the role. Admired for his handsome looks, elegant bearing, and talent for mime, Petipa became Grisi's regular partner, creating leading roles in numerous works, including Monsieur Albert's *La Jolie Fille de Gand* (1842), Coralli's *La Péri* (1843), Joseph Mazilier's *Le Diable à Quatre* (1845) and *Paquita* (1846), and Jules Perrot's *La Filleule des Fées* (1849). Between 1841 and 1857, Petipa danced in many other ballets with such famous women as Fanny Cerrito, Adèle Dumilâtre, Sofia Fuoco, Adeline Plunkett, and Carolina Rosati. Although much prized by his partners, he was seldom applauded, as audiences of the time were besotted by ballerinas. He received neither acclaim nor salary equivalent to theirs.

In 1853, Mazilier, then ballet master at the Opera, invited Petipa to stage *divertissements* in several operas, including Charles Gounod's *La Nonne Sanglante* (1854), Giuseppe Verdi's *Les Vêpres Siciliennes* (1855), and Daniel Auber's *Le Cheval de Bronze* (1857). Petipa's first major choreography, however, was for a two-act ballet, *Sacountala,* set to music by Ernest Reyer and a libretto by Gautier, which had its premiere on 14 July 1858. In this exotic work, based on a classic Indian drama, he provided ample scope for displays of virtuosity by Amalia Ferraris and Louis Mérante. To the ballerina he gave numerous pirouettes and leaps, and one spectacular pas de deux featured a high lift in which Petipa himself supported Ferraris with one arm.

Although the Opera named Petipa its principal ballet master in 1860, most major assignments for new ballets were given to foreign choreographers. During the 1860s, Petipa mounted only two ballets for the company: *Graziosa* (1861) and *Le Roi d'Yvetot* (1865), both set to scores by Théodore Labarre. He did, however, create ballets for the first French productions of a number of major operas: Gioacchino Rossini's *Sémiramis* (1860), Richard Wagner's *Tannhäuser* (1861), Verdi's *Don Carlos* (1867), and Ambroise Thomas's *Hamlet* (1868). (The Paris Opera had rigid rules: foreign operas had to be sung in French and there had to be a ballet in act 2.) Petipa's participation in the French production of *Tannhäuser,* which was withdrawn by Wagner after three performances, linked his name forever with one of the most notorious failures in operatic history.) Many years later, Petipa created his last ballet, *Namouna* (1882), to a score by Édouard Lalo, with Rita Sangalli and Louis Mérante in the leading parts.

A hunting accident ended Petipa's dancing career and obliged him to retire as the Opera's ballet master in 1868. In the early 1870s he returned to Brussels to serve as director of the ballet school of the Théâtre de la Monnaie (1872–1873), but he spent his last years in Paris as professor of pantomime at the Opera, a post he took up in 1880. Before his death he was named an officer of the Académie Nationale de Musique.

BIBLIOGRAPHY

Dumas, Alexandre, et al. *Nouvelle galerie des artistes dramatiques.* 2 vols. Paris, 1855.

Beaumont, Cyril W. *Complete Book of Ballets.* London, 1937.

Gautier, Théodore. *Histoire de l'art dramatique en France depuis vingt-cinq ans.* 6 vols. Paris, 1858–1859.

Guest, Ivor. *The Ballet of the Second Empire.* London, 1974.

Guest, Ivor, *The Romantic Ballet in Paris.* 2d rev. ed. London, 1980.

Isnardon, Jacques. *Le Théâtre de la Monnaie.* Brussels, 1890.

Kahane, Martine. "La danza nelle versioni parigine delle operre di Verdi." *La danza italiana* 1 (Autumn 1984): 43–60.

Moore, Lillian. "The Petipa Family in Europe and America." *Dance Index* 1 (May 1942): 72–84.

Monique Babsky
Translated from French

PETIPA, MARIUS (Marius Ivanovich Petipa; Fr., Victor Marius Alphonse Petipa; born 11 March 1818 in Marseille, died 14 July 1910 in Gurzuf, Crimea), choreographer. Comparatively little of the rich heritage of ballet's past has survived to this day, but much of what has survived is available in the legacy of three preeminent choreographers of the nineteenth century: August Bournonville, the Danish ballet master, and Marius Ivanovich Petipa and Lev Ivanovich Ivanov, the two contemporary outstanding Russian choreographers. All three had been brought up on the centuries-old traditions of European ballet. Petipa, a jealous custodian of tradition and a master of unique talent, dominated the ballet scene of his day. The art of Petipa was a harmonious blend of various influences: Jean-Georges Noverre's classical academism; Jean Dauberval's innovations in the field of bourgeois comedy of manners; the structural forms of dance elaborated by Pierre Gardel, master of pre-Romantic ballet; and the wide-ranging searchings of the Romantics. A synthesis of the various schools and styles had formed a solid foundation for the development of Petipa's gift. The favorable climate he found in Russia, even though he arrived at a mature age, stimulated the full flowering of his talent.

Petipa's father, Jean-Antoine Petipa, was a dancer; his mother, Victorine Grasseau, a dramatic actress. According to Petipa, his parents had eighteen children and the father traveled with them across western Europe, giving concerts and setting up his own troupe. Music and dance were Marius's companions from early childhood. He studied the violin at the Brussels conservatory. As he recalled, "At seven I started instruction in the art of dancing in the class of my father, who broke many bows on my hands in order to acquaint me with the mysteries of choreography" (Petipa, 1958, p. 2). At age nine he was given his first role, the Little Savoyard in Gardel's *Dansomanie,* which Jean Petipa was able to restage in Brussels. Generally speaking, he used the works of prominent choreographers, mostly in the comic vein. Marius was later to profit by his early introduction to this repertory. At age twelve he appeared as Gilles in Jean-Baptiste Blache's *Le Ballet des Meuniers,* staged by Jean Petipa in Antwerp. In Blache's ballet this character was known as Niqueuse and had been created for the famous grotesque comic Charles-François Mazurier; there is a parallel between the youthful debuts of Petipa and Jules Perrot, who also appeared in Mazurier's role.

Early Works. From an early age Marius was ambitious, determined, and independent. At age sixteen he signed his first contract with the Nantes Theater, where he composed the ballets *Le Droit du Seigneur, La Petite Bohémienne,* and *La Noce à Nantes.* The latter was an attempt to re-create local color and folklore on the ballet stage. A year later he rejoined his father's troupe, then on tour in France and Belgium. In 1839 he and his father went to the United States as part of Eugénie Lecomte's troupe. There, Marius appeared as Nuñez in the ballet *Marco Bomba, ou Le Sergent Fanfaron.* At the end of the American tour, which lasted from 29 November to 21 December, father and son sailed for Europe.

Marius was now twenty-two years old. In Paris he studied under Auguste Vestris, who had an intimate knowledge of the French school of dance from Noverre's classical rules to the most recent Romantic innovations. Having retained the curiosity of a youth in everything new, Vestris was still a strict custodian of the academic tradition, as was the French ballet stage. As Heinrich Heine commented, "The French ballet is akin in spirit to Racine's tragedies and the gardens of Le Nôtre. The same staid dignified manner, the same forms of etiquette, the same courtly coldness, the same splendid indifference, and the same chastity reign supreme here" (*Lutetia,* 7 February 1842). The austere order, far from preventing the appearance of ballets like *La Sylphide* and *Giselle,* formed the basis for Romantic reforms. Petipa saw this clearly and, although he attended Vestris' class for only two months, learned his lessons well: for the rest of his career he pursued a limpid simplicity of outline and image, however elaborate and exquisite the dance ornamentation might be.

Young Petipa resumed his travels. For a year he worked at Bordeaux's Grand Théâtre. Two of the four ballets he

MARIUS PETIPA. The choreographer as Ta-Hor, the hero of his ballet *La Fille du Pharaon* (Daughter of the Pharaoh), set to a score by Cesare Pugni. Presented at the Bolshoi Theater in Saint Petersburg in 1862, this was Petipa's first successful full-length ballet. (Photograph from the archives of the Maryinsky Theater Museum, Saint Petersburg.)

produced there, *La Jolie Bordelaise* and *La Vendange,* dealt with the everyday life and mores of Bordeaux. Petipa then spent four years at Madrid's Teatro del Circo, where he concentrated on Spanish themes. *Carmen et Son Torero,* which he produced there in 1845—the same year that the Prosper Mérimée novella appeared—shows that in adapting it for the ballet stage Petipa was thirty years ahead of its first adaptation for the opera. At the end of 1846 he was back in Paris to appear in Thérèse Elssler's farewell benefit, for which he and his brother Lucien performed *Pas de Quatre* with Fanny and Thérèse Elssler. This marked a turning point in Petipa's career: he was invited to Russia.

Russia. On 24 May 1847 Petipa landed at Saint Petersburg, and on 26 September he made his debut as ballet master and dancer. The ballet *Paquita* had been mounted in Paris by Joseph Mazilier one-and-a-half years earlier; Petipa merely introduced a few adjustments, and Konstantin Lyadov, the conductor, arranged the music of Edouard-Marie-Ernest Deldevez. The role of Paquita was danced by Elena Andreyanova, and Petipa appeared as Lucien. *Paquita* stayed in Saint Petersburg's repertory for more than seventy years, with Petipa repeatedly renewing and adding new dances to its choreography. The ballet as a whole has since been lost; only the children's mazurka, the pas de trois, and the famous *grand pas de deux classique* (to music by Léon Minkus, added by Petipa in 1881) still remain in the concert repertory. On 10 February 1848 Petipa presented *Satanilla, ou L'Amour et l'Enfer,* another ballet based on Mazilier *(Le Diable Amoureux)* to music by François Benoist and Napoléon Henri Reber, also arranged by Lyadov. His father began to assist him: Jean Petipa had signed a contract with the Imperial Theaters on 12 October 1847 and was appointed dancing master for the senior classes of the Imperial Theater School. After Jean's death on 16 July 1855, Marius took over the job. He held the position until April 1863, when, at his request, Aleksandr Borkh, the director of the Imperial Theaters, appointed Christian Johansson to succeed him.

At the end of 1848 Jules Perrot arrived in Saint Petersburg. Petipa was sent to Moscow, where he produced *Paquita* and *Satanilla* for the guest appearances of Elena Andreyanova. On his return to Saint Petersburg he had to content himself with the position of *premier danseur.* A contemporary critic, Y. I. Grigoriev, wrote, "As a dancer Petipa has met his match in Johansson" (*Peterburgskaia gazeta,* 18 February 1848). The comparison was poor: Johansson had a soaring leap, excellent *ballon,* and a virtuosic pirouette technique; Petipa, by contrast, was essentially a character dancer and a mime. He invariably partnered Andreyanova for the Spanish dances of ballet *divertissements,* and in 1851 he performed a brilliant pas de deux with the visiting Italian ballerina Carlotta Grisi in the fashionable dance *Manola.*

Petipa's mime repertory was dominated by roles of aristocratic youths: Lucien d'Hervilly in *Paquita,* the Three Counts in *Satanilla,* and Phoebus de Chateaupers in Perrot's *La Esmeralda.* According to Denis Leshkov (1922, p. 10), Fanny Elssler considered Petipa the best Phoebus of all male dancers who had partnered her in her long career. Petipa's Conrad in Perrot's production of *Le Corsaire* drew high praise from audiences and critics alike. Ivan and Konstantin Ivanov quoted the ballerina Evgenia Sokolova as saying that in the role of Conrad, Petipa "by his superlative acting took in not only the audience but also members of the cast" (Ivanov, 1922, p. 7). Ekaterina Vazem in her memoirs notes Petipa's "great skill" and concludes her story of Conrad with the words, "One could learn from Petipa's acting but not imitate it slavishly as he put too much of his own artistic 'self' into it." In 1854 Petipa married the young *danseuse* Maria Surovshchikova, who succeeded Andreyanova after her retirement from the stage.

Himself retiring as an actor-dancer in 1869, Petipa danced the role of Conrad in his farewell performance.

For a long time Petipa the choreographer did little more than realize Perrot's intentions. He gained freedom and independence only when Perrot's reputation began to totter on the Saint Petersburg stage. Petipa produced a number of one-act ballets to his own libretti and music by Cesare Pugni, including *Un Mariage au Temps de la Régence* (1858) and *Le Marché des Innocents* (1859), and a two-act ballet, *Le Dahlia Bleu* (1860). Until his death in 1870, Pugni was Petipa's permanent composer. Although their first ballets came under fire for their rather vapid content, the critics praised Petipa's gift of dance composition. One unnamed critic, while grumbling that *Le Dahlia Bleu* sounded to him like a rehash of familiar motifs, praised the *grand pas des dahlias* in which the dancers representing flowers were deployed in delightful semirecumbent attitudes, while the magical Dahlia, watering pot in hand, "kept flitting between them" (*Sankt-Peterburgskie vedomost,* 17 April 1860). Another found that the "dances and groups were notable for imagination, refreshing invention, elegance, exquisiteness and variety" (*Severnaia pchela,* 19 April 1860).

In 1859 Arthur Saint-Léon succeeded Perrot as choreographer of the Bolshoi Theater in Saint Petersburg. Saint-Léon proved more generous than his predecessor and allowed Petipa to compose and stage a number of full-length, multiact ballets, in addition to mini-ballets and his own version of *Le Corsaire* (1863), to music by Adolphe Adam and Pugni. Petipa's ballets of that period included *La Fille du Pharaon* (1862), *La Belle de Liban, ou Le Génie de la Montagne* (1863), *Florida* (1866), and *Le Roi Candaule* (1868). These works launched him on his career as choreographer, which spanned the second half of the nineteenth century. Petipa's aesthetic philosophy reflected the influences of his predecessors. Eclecticism, consciously interpreted as a style, was the hallmark of his art. Petipa's first essays as a choreographer prefigured both the achievements and the failures of the mature artist.

Focus on Choreography. Petipa was talented and highly educated in every department of the choreographer's profession as it was understood at the time, and in everything that had a bearing on it. The libretti of his ballet productions often echoed episodes of current history. Petipa co-authored with the playwright Jules-Henri Vernoy de Saint-Georges the libretto of *La Fille du Pharaon,* after Théophile Gautier's *Le Roman de la Momie.* In the year of its premiere, the world followed the contest of British and French interests over the planned construction of the Suez Canal, which was to provide a short shipping route from Europe to Africa. The allegory on this theme in the ballet was the underwater kingdom scene, in which the god of the Nile welcomed some of the world's largest rivers, such as the Rhine, the Thames, and the Neva. Each soloist representing a river performed that river's national dance. Petipa responded to events on the Balkan Peninsula with his ballet *Roxane, la Belle de Montenegro* (1878), while *La Fille des Neiges* (1876) was his response to Nils Nordenskjöld's Arctic expeditions. Both ballets were set to music by Léon Minkus, who succeeded Pugni as Petipa's regular composer.

Petipa was a practicing musician and knew music well. But, faithful to the classical standards of the past, he relegated music to an auxiliary role in his ballets until the 1890s, when the directors of the Imperial Theaters ordered him to work with major composers. He had a good knowledge of ballet dramaturgy ranging from farce to tragedy. In this area he adhered to rigid formats, seeing to it that mime scenes and dances obeyed the rule of alternation. He regimented sentiment by form and made drama the bedrock of his ballet spectaculars. A brilliant dancer, he was open to new ideas and willingly learned from others. But he also put new elements into seemingly im-

MARIUS PETIPA. *Le Roi Candaule* (1868) was Petipa's second big success, owing largely to the performances of ballerina Henriette d'Or and several soloists. Almost four decades after the premiere, Vaslav Nijinsky appeared in the role of the Mulatto in a 1906 revival. (Photograph from the Dance Collection, New York Public Library for the Performing Arts.)

mutable aesthetic frameworks, as with the technique of Italian virtuosic dance in the 1880s and 1890s. By the standards of today, Petipa was rather unimaginative in the area of decor. The scenery of his ballet productions seems to have become frozen in the form of pretty pictures from a children's book. This was the so-called Victorian style of precious, cozy bad taste that dominated the artistic and everyday life of his time.

Choreographic academicism. The choreographic structure of Petipa's ballet productions rested on mime and dance scenes whose sequence and alternation were carefully delineated. Mime scenes were designed to narrate episodes and situations. In full-scale, developed monologues and dialogues, mime scenes relied on a special code of gestures that suggested certain ideas and individual words. The mime vocabulary had its own nouns, adjectives, and verbs from which phrases and sentences were composed. The silent "speeches" of ballet characters did not always come across to the audience, however graphic and vivid the gestures and the miming, so the libretto was called on to help decipher the mime text. The dance was either classical or character. The former was preeminent and used to express the feelings and thoughts of the protagonists, to embellish and crown the action. The character dance sometimes injected into the mime action genre color, the color of everyday life or a particular period of history. More often it performed the function of a *divertissement* number. Both kinds of ballet could be performed solo, in pas de deux, ensemble, or by the corps de ballet. In the latter half of the nineteenth century the ballerina was established at the center of the stage, pushing the male dancer to the background. Thanks to the combined efforts of leading choreographers and virtuosic ballerinas, classical dance reached a high pitch of perfection in terms of form, especially in solo variations.

MARIUS PETIPA. Anna Sobeshchanskaya was the first ballerina to dance Kitri's exciting solo in the last act of Petipa's *Don Quixote,* mounted in Moscow in 1869 and in Saint Petersburg in 1871. Since its premiere, countless ballerinas in many countries have flirtatiously flicked their fans as they danced the technically demanding steps that Petipa set to the lively measures composed by Léon Minkus. This performer is Noëlla Pontois, an *étoile* of the Paris Opera Ballet, pictured about 1975. (Photograph by Colette Masson; used by permission of Agence Enguerand/Iliade, Paris.)

Jumping technique was constantly being developed and elaborated. Soaring leaps could be either smooth and flowing or dynamic, impetuous, and sharply dramatic. The smaller jumps usually consisted of *batterie* and *entrechats.* The rapid, sparkling technique of such jumps called for a flexible development of the foot, which was achieved through special exercises. The technique of dancing on pointe was further perfected. The design of the ballet shoe was changed accordingly: its soft pointed toe was made harder and square for better stability. A stable support was essential as the rate and number of turns increased, as did the speed of running on pointe. In the new virtuosic school of ballet the noiselessly soaring dancer was increasingly yielding ground to a concert dancer with brilliant bravura and a "clean line." The poetry of "ethereal" dance was surrendering to the "steel toe." Slow solo adagios based on lyrical plastique were becoming a thing of the past as even the maximum stability on pointe did not allow the dancers to sustain the slow tempi. Adapted for the pointe technique, the adagio in the female parts of pas de deux underwent considerable modification.

To a certain extent Russian choreography was influenced by the Italian school, but while assimilating interesting new developments in its solo dance, Russian dance preserved the best elements of the "ethereal" school. This was largely owing to the Russian dancers: the staccato, clipped jumping style was less suitable for them than the "smooth flight" style. Russian dancers softened the pointe-work technique of their Italian counterparts to lend it lyrical coloring. In a more profound sense, this was the result of Petipa's adherence to the academic school of classical dance. George Balanchine, one of Petipa's greatest followers, wrote that "Petipa exported from France the tradition of French elegance just as Rastrelli and Rossi before him had brought to the imperial capital the traditions of the Italian Baroque and Empire style" (quoted in Nekhendzi, 1971). Aleksandr Shiriaev wrote,

> Overall supervision of the teaching of dance for the male half of the Imperial Theater School was in the hands of Marius Petipa, with whom all the other dancing masters made a point of coordinating their work. Ballet teachers followed the strict canons of the French classical school. The dancers were taught soft, flowing and graceful movements, a cold, complete sculpture-like performing style. (Shiriaev, 1941, p. 29)

As complex movements crystallized, dance forms were canonized. The solo variation was now a complete, self-contained number consisting of three parts, normally arranged according to the A-B-A system. If the first and the last were rapid, the middle part was slow, and vice versa. On occasion the number of parts varied, and the whole of a variation could be in slow or fast tempo. But in all cases it was a complete line from the point of entry to the finale. Variations for male dancers followed the same pattern, but their technique declined in the 1860s and 1870s and did not begin to improve until the mid-1880s. The solo variation was the heart of pas de deux or ensemble to the extent that the ballerina was the focal point of a production. The number of variations depended on the number of dancers involved. Pas de deux included variations for the ballerina and her partner; the variations of pas de trois were performed by all the participants. When surrounded by soloists, the ballerina had a right to dance a variation of her own. The forms of pas de deux or ensemble were also canonized. Such numbers consisted of several parts: adagio, variations, and a coda. The ballerina, whom the other participants solemnly presented to the audience, remained the dominant figure.

Toward the end of the nineteenth century, apart from *par terre* supports, the technique of high lifts began to be developed. The position of the male dancer gradually shifted until he found himself, literally and figuratively, behind the ballerina to guide and safeguard her dance. The aesthetic function of high lifts also changed. In Romantic ballets partners danced side by side. Lifting the ballerina, the *porteur* held her aloft, suggesting her own soaring flight over him. In the new ballet the lifts were deliberately fixed. Lifted by her partner, the ballerina changed her position in midair. For example, raising the ballerina to the level of his chest, the male dancer suddenly shifted her from arm to arm so that her head was lower than her upward-stretched legs. After a visit to Saint Petersburg, August Bournonville wrote a letter dated 2 May 1874 to the ballet critic Sergei Khudekov, in which he recognized Petipa's "truly creative gift" but was

MARIUS PETIPA. *La Bayadère* (1877), a dark and complex drama set to a score by Léon Minkus, is one of Petipa's greatest creations. In 1902 Anna Pavlova scored a remarkable success as Nikia, the temple dancer who is betrayed by her lover, Solor, and who is murdered by her rival, Gamzatti, by the bite of a viper hidden in a basket of flowers. The full-length ballet is performed today by major companies in Russia, the United States, France, and South Africa, and the famous Kingdom of the Shades scene is performed by companies in a number of other countries. (Photograph 1902 by Fischer Studio, Saint Petersburg; from the Dance Collection, New York Public Library for the Performing Arts.)

critical of his falling in with the current fashion. In particular, Bournonville was annoyed to see the Princess in *Le Papillon* (1874) "fling herself into the arms of a random dancer who proceeds to twiddle her this way and that, eventually pointing the legs of Her Highness straight into the zenith." Bournonville adhered to the aesthetics of romanticism and believed that a display of technical prowess detracted from and was inimical to the poetry of a ballet. But in due course technical devices became an organic part of the new system of ballet conventions.

The climax of a ballet performance was a *pas d'action*, in which the choreographer generalized the main idea

MARIUS PETIPA. When Petipa revived his production of *Paquita* in 1881, he added a pas de trois and a *grand pas,* using music supplied by Léon Minkus. These, along with a mazurka, are the only surviving sections of the production, but they have been handed down by generations of dancers and are today performed by many companies all over the world. Pictured here are Dianne Finch and Jeremy Coles of PACT Ballet in Pretoria, South Africa, with members of the ensemble, in a 1987 performance of the *grand pas.* (Photograph by Edzard Meyberg; courtesy of PACT Ballet.)

of his ballet. The number of characters engaged in *pas d'action* varied from two protagonists to quite a few members of the cast, including the corps de ballet. In major ballets each act climaxed in its own *pas d'action.* Petipa made full-scale classical ensembles part of the *divertissements* of his major ballets, for example, "Les Amours de Diane" in *Le Roi Candaule,* "Grand Pas des Étoiles" in *L'Ordre du Roi* (1886), and "Pas Astronomique" in *Barbe-Bleue* (1896). A comparison of the names of the leading *premières danseuses* and the dancers who took secondary roles sheds light on why such numbers were inserted. While composing "novelties" for visiting ballerinas, Petipa sought to promote local Russian talent. For example, he gave the role of Ysaure in *Barbe-Bleue* to Pierina Legnani and that of Venus in the "Pas Astronomique" to Matilda Kshessinska. Classical corps de ballet dances loomed large in Petipa's ballet productions. The female part of the corps de ballet appeared as fantastic characters (wilis, naiads, shades). In "realistic" scenes the corps de ballet might consist of both male and female dancers portraying peasants, slaves, or courtiers. Petipa also freely used *travesti.*

Character dances were divided into solo and corps de ballet varieties. The corps observed symmetry, either advancing toward the footlights in regular neat rows or parting, fanning out to either side of the stage. The corps would repeat a movement, forming a geometric figure or an architecturally arranged group. It often provided the background to one or several pairs of soloists repeating in more simple movements the patterns of their dance. The folk plastique was based on stylized classical dance principles, with the movements softer and more rounded, and turnout less pronounced. The "Dance of the Saracen Slaves" and the *panaderos* in *Raymonda* and the "Hindu Dance" in *La Bayadère* were based on classical dance movements. Apart from formal experiments in this area, Petipa provided an example of an organic fusion of folk and classical dance in the *grand pas classique hongrois* from the final act of *Raymonda.* Children's classical, character, solo, and mass dances figure prominently in Petipa's compositions. On their own (the Hungarian dances in *Raymonda,* the mazurka in *Paquita*) or woven into the fabric of adult dances (The "Garland Dance" in *The Sleeping Beauty*), they added a welcome dash of color to his ballets.

Music. The standard structural forms of choreography evolved by Petipa became canonical for Russian ballet of the latter half of the nineteenth century. Petipa himself saw these conventional forms as similar to the structural forms of classical music. Using them, he made the dance highly expressive to match the vivid imagery of the music. Petipa knew how to create a concrete scene of action, character, and setting for a dance, as can be seen in the fairy-tale vignettes he created for *The Sleeping Beauty* or in *Cinderella.* But the key component remained the dances that, like music, exalted the message and sentiment to poetic generalization. These dances could be solo variations, or dances for a small ensemble or corps de ballet. Examples of such dances appeared long before Petipa began to collaborate with major composers. Petipa looked for symphonization of the lyrical dance to music that was still far from being symphonic.

Cesare Pugni and Léon Minkus were not symphonists, but the choreography of the 1860s through 1880s was not yet mature enough for symphonic music, and Petipa staged his initial experiments in collaboration with these composers. They had an intimate knowledge of the contemporary ballet scene and were well versed in the rich variety of dance forms of the time. Their music was impulsive, flexibly tuneful, and eminently danceable. Petipa valued it for its convenient tempi and meter, plasticity, and resilience, all of which stimulated imagination; the naive character of the music matched the naive content of his ballets. The music was not without its own imagery. Usually a musical theme announced the entry of the hero and accompanied him for the rest of the performance, undergoing no change. At times the music conveyed only the changing moods of the characters. One set of musical numbers could easily be replaced by another, which more often than not was the case for the solo variations. Here, the composer was dependent not only on the choreographer, but also on the ballerina, as he had to take into account her penchant for either the ethereal dance *en l'air* or the *terre-à-terre* dance, for elegiac meditations or a bravura virtuosity. The ballerina was free to insert adagios and variations by another composer or even another choreographer. In short, music was not the deciding factor in a ballet; rather, it was auxiliary material. It did not prompt dance imagery but was completely at the service of the choreographer, who remodeled it as he saw fit, to suit his needs.

Decor and props. The decor of ballets was expected to delight, surprise, and even dazzle the audience. Scene designers and painters followed every rule of "magnificent spectacle." In Petipa's *La Fille du Pharaon,* for example, the critics identified three apotheoses. The first closed the Prologue: a beam of light struck the mummy of the Egyptian princess, lending a fantastic transparency to her face and causing the diamond solitaires adorning her neck and breast to spring into dazzling life. The second apotheosis was the finale of the scene "From the Depths of the Nile," when a fountain playing with all the colors of the rainbow

MARIUS PETIPA. *The Sleeping Beauty* (1890) was the first of the three great works Petipa set to music by Tchaikovsky. The 1946 production by Nicholas Sergeyev for the Sadler's Wells Ballet in London was based on notes of Petipa's choreography as it was performed in Russia. This scene is from the prologue, "The Christening." The six fairies who have come to bestow gifts on the infant princess Aurora are seated on the knees of their cavaliers. Behind them stand attendants of the Lilac Fairy; in front of them kneel their pages, bearing symbols of their gifts on pillows. At the rear on the right is the cradle of the newborn babe. The variations for the six fairies are among the purest surviving examples of Petipa's choreography. (Photograph from the Dance Collection, New York Public Library for the Performing Arts.)

lifted the heroine onto the surface of the river. The third apotheosis crowned the ballet: the lovers, the Egyptian deities, and the rest of the cast engaged in the prologue were deployed all over the stage in a sumptuous climax. Andreas Roller, the painter who created the scenery for this ballet, was made a full member of the Imperial Academy of Fine Arts for his inventive perspective of the hall in the pharaoh's palace.

The sets of other Petipa ballets were also remarkable for their huge size, magnificence, and ingenious design. Trees bent from violent gusts of wind, the sky might be colored by the sinister glow of a conflagration or by the shimmering light of a peaceful moon, water cascaded in waterfalls or shot up from playing fountains. Details of the architectural and interior decoration were remarkable for their scrupulously delicate workmanship. Sophisticated stage machinery enabled characters to emerge suddenly from underground or to drop out of sight just as suddenly, to glide on the surface of the stage riding special rails, to swing from the boughs of trees, or to fly at dizzying heights. The properties and trappings were varied and elaborate: the stage could be populated with dummies of elephants, camels, monkeys, and lions, and even with live horses.

Petipa liked props and used them to complement the design of corps de ballet dances. In *La Fille du Pharaon*, seventy-two dancers bore flower baskets on their heads from which small children emerged in the finale. Into *Le Corsaire* Petipa inserted a full-scale number, "Le Jardin Animé," in which the female corps de ballet lengthened the movements of the dance by raising, lowering, and swinging garlands of flowers. In his revival of *La Esmeralda* (1886), Petipa inserted a *pas des corbeilles* ("basket dance") into the ball scene at the palace of Fleur de Lys. The baskets and flower garlands in the "Garland Dance" in the first act of *The Sleeping Beauty* created the form of a flowering garden in the transitions of the lines and groups of the female, male, and children's corps de ballet. In the second act of *La Bayadère* the corps de ballet danced with parrots and fans, while the dancer performing the "Manu Dance" kept a jar of water on her head to tease two girls asking for a drink.

Group dance. Petipa handled dancing groups in much the same way a composer handles solo voices and groups

MARIUS PETIPA. After *The Sleeping Beauty* (1890) and *The Nutcracker* (1892) came *Swan Lake* (1895), the third classic work created by Petipa to music by Tchaikovsky. The Royal Ballet production was restaged in 1968 by Peter Wright and Frederick Ashton after Petipa. In this scene from act 3, Anthony Dowell is pictured as Prince Siegfried, partnering Georgina Parkinson as Odile in the Black Swan pas de deux. (Photograph by Houston Rogers; used by permission of the Board of Trustees of the Theatre Museum, London.)

of instruments in the orchestra. He obtained remarkable plastique from juxtapositions and interaction of homogeneous or contrasting elements. Splitting the stage into several "grounds," or sections, Petipa would fill the space with groups of dancers, sometimes introducing vertical lines of symmetrically arranged figures into the horizontal lines of the overall design, as in the waltz in the opening scene of *Swan Lake* or in the dream scene of *Raymonda,* where the *danseurs* move lightweight stools from place to place for the *danseuses* to step up on. Groups of dancers were either localized or shifted about, merging and then separating. A movement or a phrase might be repeated by one group of dancers, either contrasting with the pattern formed by another group or intruding into it either to break it up or to fuse with it in unison. The dancing of one of the groups could serve as a harmonic pedal point against the measured and dense background of which the melodic patterns of another group bloomed, while soloists could appear against the background of the latter, in echo or in contrast. As interpreted by Petipa the dance approached the structures of carefully elaborated musical images. At the outset Petipa wanted only simple, even primitive, musical texts. Not until he had consolidated his gains in the field of dance orchestration did he attempt choreographic symphonism for the ballet productions that he created in collaboration with great Russian composers. But even in these productions he remained loyal to his aesthetic philosophy by varying his favorite methods and devices.

Petipa had borrowed from his predecessors without camouflaging the borrowings too much. The libretto of his four-act ballet *Don Quixote* (Moscow, 1869; Saint Petersburg, 1871) borrowed some of the comic episodes from Louis Milon's *Les Noces de Gamache* but drowned them in an abundance of dances. In the ballets *Camargo* (1872) and *Barbe-Bleue* Petipa introduced a dancing lesson in front of a mirror, thereby reviving a device first used by eighteenth-century choreographers: dancers standing behind a tulle curtain repeated the movements of the ballerina and the soloists. His retentive memory held a vast body of material, embracing every conceivable classical dance combination; he kept adding to these as he looked for new combinations. He insisted that every movement be given full-bodied sonority and unique coloring so that it would become essential to a given dance phrase. By combining simple and complex movements and continually inventing new elements, Petipa was able to convey various moods, human emotions, and characters. Within the constraints of academic classical dance he attained great choreographic skill. In the pas de trois from his version of *Le Corsaire* Petipa composed three different variations on the same bravura theme. Just as in a virtuosic musical piece rapid tempi are followed by slow ones that are no less difficult to execute, so in that ballet the leaps of one variation are followed by the small movements of another. In *Le Papillon* two dancers perform the variations of the fairies of gold and silver. Their chiseled, sparkling movements, staccato running on pointe, and clipped, minute *batterie* anticipate the ringing, iridescent dances of the gold and silver fairies in *The Sleeping Beauty.*

In the same way, Petipa explored the polyphonic potential of the corps de ballet. The ballet critic Aleksandr Ushakov wrote about the Lydian *ballabile* in *Le Roi Candaule,* "Everyone in the *pas* performs his or her own solo while, taken together, they form a remarkable ensemble with a striking combination of tempi. This is a completely new effect in the ballet à la Meyerbeer, a chef-d'oeuvre that gives new impetus to the art of ballet" (*Golos,* 19 October 1868).

Chief Choreographer. The year 1869 was an important one for Petipa, both in his private life and in his creative career. That year he married Liubov Savitskaya, a Moscow corps de ballet dancer (his first wife had died in 1862), and ended his career as a dancer. He also took over as the sole master of Saint Petersburg's Bolshoi Theater; after its closure in 1886, he took the same post at the Maryinsky Theater. Petipa was given unlimited freedom in the choice and realization of the ballet repertory, and in the selection and casting of performers. He was now in a position to give free rein to his imagination. He produced new ballets, big and small, every season, in addition to the ballets he composed for the Hermitage Theater in the tsar's Winter Palace and for fêtes held in the environs of Saint Petersburg. Petipa tried his hand in every genre: comedy and melodrama, fairy tale and historical anecdote. A succession of ballets in the various genres had a common moral message in the triumph of good over evil and a common theme in the festive perception and glorification of life.

Petipa used his extensive powers wisely. He retained in the repertory the best of the ballets by Mazilier, Perrot, and Saint-Léon, introducing only sensible corrections into their choreography, something he always did to his own ballets. Petipa knew well and appreciated the living and mutable nature of the theater. Without changing either the plot or the progress of the dramatic action of ballets, he modified their dancing. In *Giselle,* which he revived in 1884, Petipa's touch is unmistakable. He composed a pas de deux to music by Friedrich Burgmüller and put on pointe the villagers' corps de ballet in the first act and that of the wilis in the second. He brought the "Romantic chaos" that reigned in the ballet of the day into a balanced harmonious unity. The classical limpidity of the transitions and groups of these ensembles recalls the floor-plan sketches of Petipa's ballets, in which the strictly regimented lines of the dancers come together, separate, and move in circles, forming crosses, stars, and other figures. Living examples of these ensembles are "Le Jardin Animé" in *Le Corsaire,* "La Valse Villageoise" and the nymphs scene in *The Sleeping Beauty,* and the Kingdom of the Shades scene in *La Bayadère,* which remains a supreme achievement.

La Bayadère. Created in 1877 this ballet marked the thirtieth year of Petipa's work in Russia. Its libretto echoed that of his brother Lucien's 1858 ballet *Sacountala,* but Petipa replaced the happy ending with a tragic one. He responded to the creative ideas that dominated Russian theater and music of the mid-1870s, but his response was indirect and, in a sense, naive. However, the image of a heroine dying in the name of love and honor, by its drama and spirituality, provided an example of dramatic and lyrical elements forming an integrated unit.

New elements in this instance arose in an apparent paradoxical conflict with Minkus's music. The composer remained loyal to the canons: the score of *La Bayadère* contains many rather bleak musical conventions that play a purely auxiliary role. Far from depicting definite characters, which in Petipa's choreography are sharply delineated, it describes the various moods: sad, joyous, dreamy, reflective. For example, Minkus built the first part of the "Snake Dance" of the heroine, the climax of the dramatic action, on a protracted anguish and its second part on dashing, flamboyant "Gypsy" tempi and rhythms. Minkus composed the coda, which follows a melancholy and fairly pliant adagio in the Kingdom of the Shades scene, as a bold galop. Petipa moved the "Snake Dance" to the end of the long *divertissement* that was designed to retard the dramatic action. The *divertissement* ended a general coda with the kaleidoscopic iridescence of its dance suite. Such a finale invariably drew a round of applause, followed by a calculated pause that was suddenly invaded by the Bayadère's musical theme. The interrupted dramatic theme was thus dominant again. The first part of the dance is built on slow, long-drawn-out arabesques, now tossing the ballerina into the air, now spreading low on the ground. Arabesques also dominate the second part of the dance, this time in a major, cheerful key and a fitful, furious tempo. The ballerina spins rapidly. When, bitten by the snake, the Bayadère dies, the drama shifts into the sphere of a danced elegy.

In the first review after the ballet's premiere, an unnamed critic complained that "the string of shadows in the ballet appeared in daylight rather than in moonlight" (*Peterburgskaia gazeta,* 25 January 1877). This showed that, by abandoning the theatrical effect, the choreographer made the dance convey, on its own, both the tone of the theme and its emotional and dramatic content. *La Bayadère* marked Petipa's maturity as a choreographer. In the years that followed he also produced *Mlada* (1879), *Zoraya, une Mauresque en Espagne* (1881), *La Nuit et le Jour* (1883), and *La Statue de Chypre* (1883). He carefully restored, in his own interpretation, a series of masterpieces of the classical heritage: *La Vivandière* in 1881, *Pâquerette* in 1882, and *Coppélia* in 1884, by Saint-Léon; *Le Diable à Quatre* in 1885, by Mazilier; and Jean Dauberval's *La Fille Mal Gardée* also in 1885.

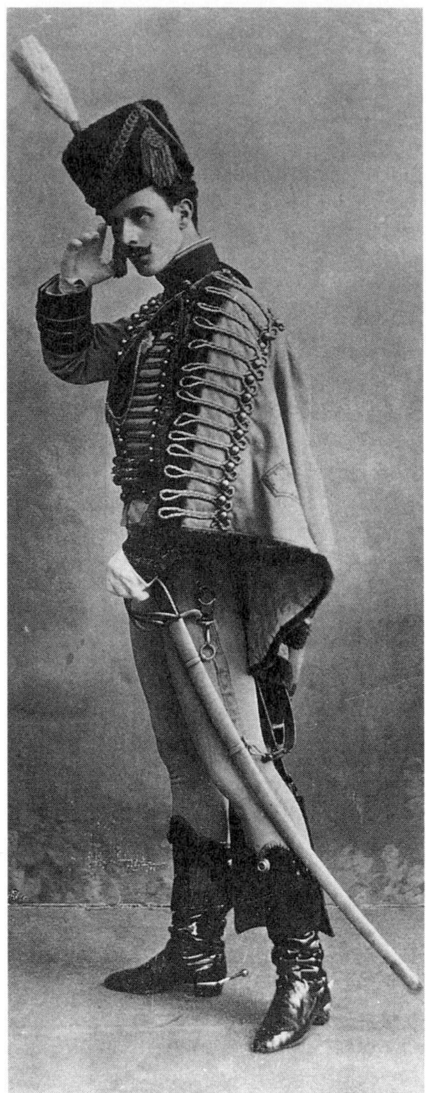

MARIUS PETIPA. *Halte de Cavalerie,* a one-act ballet set to music by Johann Arnsheimer in 1896, starred Pierina Legnani and Pavel Gerdt, leading dancers at the Maryinsky Theater. It remained in the repertory long enough to provide a dashing role as a hussar for Michel Fokine a few years later. (Photograph from the archives of the Maryinsky Theater Museum, Saint Petersburg.)

Petipa realized that Russian ballet was at the time the only custodian of high academic standards and the world's principal center of their further development. He felt responsible for the future of world ballet. Toward the end of the 1880s the ballet theater of western Europe was increasingly on the decline. In Denmark, Bournonville's classical traditions remained firmly established, but his successors did little or nothing to develop them. In Italy, England, and even in France, despite the fact that major French composers had turned their capable hands to the ballet, it was rapidly degenerating into a kind of revue in which the choreographic part was intended merely to entertain. This latest craze reached Russia when the monopoly of the Imperial Theaters was abolished in 1882. By the mid-1880s private enterprise had invaded the field of ballet in Saint Petersburg and Moscow. In various summer parks operettas, other variety programs, and *ballet-féeries* were given alongside serious plays. Private theaters invited Italian guest performers, including the famous dramatic dancer Virginia Zucchi, the virtuosi Carlotta Brianza and Pierina Legnani, and the dancer Enrico Cecchetti. Petipa boldly used their superlative talents to extend and add a valuable dimension to the Russian school of dance. Brianza became the first foreign dancer to appear as Princess Aurora in his *The Sleeping Beauty* (1890); Legnani created Odette-Odile in *Swan Lake* (1895) and the title role in *Raymonda* (1898). Petipa designed the role of Bluebird in *The Sleeping Beauty* especially for Cecchetti's technical brilliance.

While he freely adopted elements of the Italian school, Petipa rejected the Italian type of ballet as a whole and denied the Italian *féerie* the right even to be called ballet. He took the view that in Italian ballet acrobatics replaced art, and told an interviewer, "I consider the Saint Petersburg ballet company the best in the world precisely because it has fully preserved the kind of serious art that the rest of the world has lost" (*Peterburgskaia gazeta,* 2 December 1896). Two years later he made a visit to Milan and on his return demanded that "*féerie*-type choreographic scenes be banished as they have been responsible for the ballet's decline" (*ibid.,* 23 April 1898). Yet on one occasion Petipa did produce a ballet commissioned by the directors of the Imperial Theaters that featured on the same program "dances, singing, and comedy." The *ballet-féerie Les Pilules du Diable* (1886) recalled the stage play of the same name by Fernand Lalou, Auguste Anicet-Bourgeois, and Lorand; the music was by Minkus. The show was in three acts, twelve scenes, and an apotheosis. The principal characters were played by dramatic actors and actresses, with a single dance performed by the entire ballet company in-

MARIUS PETIPA. In 1898, when he was eighty years old, Petipa created *Raymonda* to the melodic score composed by Aleksandr Glazunov. In 1964, Rudolf Nureyev mounted a full-length production for the Royal Ballet Touring Section in England. The ensemble is pictured here in the finale, with Doreen Wells (at left of center) as Raymonda and Nureyev (at right of center) as Jean de Brienne. (Photograph from the Dance Collection, New York Public Library for the Performing Arts.)

cluded in some of the scenes. Varvara Nikitina danced the role of Flamme d'Amour with her partner, Sergei Litavkin, dancing Feu d'Artifice. Dancers in the Amusements scene represented croquet, lotto, checkers, dice, bilboquet, billiards, skittles, and badminton. The "Top Dance," performed by Zinaida Frolova, was based on rapid spins that caused the colored stripes on her costume to merge into an iridescent pattern, and ended with a fall of the top to one side. In the Kingdom of Lace scene the corps de ballet, impersonating gold and silver lace, danced the variations of Venetian, Brussels, English, Spanish, and Russian lace patterns.

The creators of such *féerie*-type performances and their admirers believed that they were saving ballet, without realizing that at the same time they were denying it an independent genre identity. It is very much to his credit that even in this *féerie* ballet Petipa did not abandon the expressive possibilities of mime and dance. Nevertheless, he saw the future of ballet in the development of choreographic forms based on a meaningful, substantive, musical dramaturgy. He carried on his experiments with multiact ballets, such as *La Vestale* (1888), to the music of Mikhail Ivanov, and *Le Talisman* (1889), to music by Riccardo Drigo. Many subsequent versions of Perrot's *La Esmeralda* retained Petipa's added pas de six, set to Drigo's music, an example of the drama dance could convey.

The Sleeping Beauty and last works. Petipa proved that his continuous search for new ideas and fresh approaches was justified by producing *The Sleeping Beauty* (1890), which enabled him to establish his principles of classical dance symphonization on the solid foundation of Tchaikovsky's evocative music. *The Sleeping Beauty* was to remain the high point of Petipa's career; in it his artistic philosophy triumphed and his aesthetic program was reflected most fully. Ill health prevented him from carrying out his intention to produce *The Nutcracker,* for which he had prepared the libretto (it was staged in 1892 in Lev Ivanov's choreography), while in *Swan Lake* (1895) he did not go beyond creating some of the scenes and dances. But even so, Petipa's tally of achievements was quite impressive.

The 1890s were an important period in the history of Russian ballet and in Petipa's career. Increasingly overshadowed by signs of his weariness and exhaustion, the entire system of his views, tastes, and rules was entering a crisis as the aesthetic philosophy of his era, which encompassed the latter half of the nineteenth century, went into a decline. The traditions of that time were handed down from choreographer to choreographer, from dancer to dancer, from teacher to pupil, and they proved more durable and enduring than the traditions of other forms of theater. Petipa's ballets were rooted in the choreography of the eighteenth rather than nineteenth century. Some of his canons and methods were timeless; others inhibited further development. Signs of the conclusion of a major stage in Petipa's illustrious career were clearly discernible in his one-act ballets *Le Nénuphar* (1891), to music by Nikolai Krotkov; Johann Arnsheimer's *Halte de Cavalerie,* and Drigo's *La Perle* (both 1896); and *Thétis et Pelée* (1897), to music by Minkus and Delibes. The plots, situations, characters, and staging effects of earlier ballets were repeated in subsequent works, which also contained valuable examples of a fusion of classical and character dance elements. Aleksandr Pleshcheyev wrote about the 1891 *Kalkabrino,* "Compositionally, the *grand pas d'ensemble* in the third act is refreshingly original, being half-classical and half-*caractère.* A rare combination in ballet" (*Peterburgskaia gazeta,* 15 February 1891).

In *Halte de Cavalerie* the classical dancer Pierina Legnani competed with the character dancer Marie Petipa, the choreographer's daughter. In this instance the classical dance, in keeping with the genre of the ballet, took on the spontaneity and vivaciousness of character dance. Petipa solved the problem of achieving a balanced blend of the two forms of ballet in his brilliant production of Aleksandr Glazunov's *Raymonda* (1898). This ballet was the swan song of the aging choreographer. *The Sleeping Beauty* and *Raymonda* were the culmination of Petipa's dance aesthetics, built with care and taste on Tchaikovsky's and Glazunov's evocative scores with their powerful symphonic imagery.

In 1899 Prince Sergei Volkonsky succeeded Ivan Vsevolozhsky as director-general of the Imperial Theaters. He held the job for three years, during which time he did not commission Petipa to produce a single major ballet, despite his apparent respect for the choreographer. In 1900 Petipa produced Glazunov's one-act ballets *Ruses d'Amour* and *Les Saisons.* The first was little more than a stylish bagatelle à la Watteau, based on a comedy plot popular in the eighteenth century. The second was a plotless suite that recalled even more distant allegorical ballets. Another ballet in the same vein produced by Petipa in 1900 was Drigo's two-act *Les Millions d'Arlequin.* The ballet critic Nikolai Bezobrazov commented, "All the dances have been composed by Marius Petipa with the same impeccable taste and art of which he is the only exponent" (*Peterburgskaia gazeta,* 14 February 1900). Yet, in spite of their undeniable excellence, those ballets were but a repetition of old ideas. Petipa's unique dance did continue to provide fertile soil for the subsequent flowering of Russian ballet and the restoration of the art of ballet in the rest of the world, but his theater was nearing its demise, and this had tragic consequences for a master choreographer who had the misfortune of outliving his fame.

The appointment of Vladimir Teliakovsky as the new director of the Imperial Theaters had disastrous consequences for Petipa. Since 1898 Teliakovsky had had overall charge of the Moscow office of the Imperial Theaters,

MARIUS PETIPA. In 1899, Glazunov's music for *The Seasons* again inspired creativity from Petipa. Under its French title, *Les Saisons,* the ballet was first performed on 7 February 1900 for members of the imperial family and its court on the small stage of the Hermitage Theater, which was linked to the tsar's winter residence by a bridge. Petipa's daughter Marie appeared with the great *danseur noble* Pavel Gerdt as her partner in the autumnal bacchanal. (Photograph from the archives of the Maryinsky Theater Museum, Saint Petersburg.)

and he became their director in 1902. A colonel in the Horse Guards, Teliakovsky had graduated from the General Staff Academy, where he received a typical nobleman's education: he spoke several languages and was a connoisseur of music and painting. He was eager to move with the times, and his first measure was to institute reforms in the academic theater. One of the basic principles of his policy was to graft good painting onto drama, opera, and ballet. He invited some of the leading painters of the day, including Aleksandr Golovin, Konstantin Korovin, Alexandre Benois, and Léon Bakst, to work in government-supported theaters. Teliakovsky, a dedicated advocate of good music, favored opera over ballet. From the beginning he became Petipa's enemy. He dealt him the first blow by commissioning Aleksandr Gorsky to restage *Don Quixote* in 1900. While Gorsky preserved the general outline of the ballet's action, his addition of new dances of his own composition wounded Petipa deeply. Teliakovsky continued to commission other choreographers to stage ballets.

On 9 February 1903 the premiere of Petipa's last ballet, *The Magic Mirror,* to a score by Arseny Koreshchenko, was a resounding failure. Conditions for truly creative work were far from ideal: Koreshchenko had failed to see what Petipa wanted, even though he was assisted by Drigo. Petipa differed with Golovin, the stage designer for *The Magic Mirror,* on the kind of decor he wanted for the ballet: against the background of Golovin's impressionistic, fuzzy scenery the geometric patterns of Petipa's dances and the architectonics of his group compositions were largely lost. But what really ruined the ballet was the fact that the aesthetic standards of Petipa's nineteenth-century ballet had had their day. Refusing to see this, with tragic persistence Petipa stoutly defended the full range of his artistic tastes and methods. The scenes depicting the entry of the royal couple were gaudily glittering and crowded affairs, with their numerous retinue resplendent in gorgeous dress. The Princess and the Prince met in a *pas d'action* surrounded by a retinue of their own, in which the company's best soloists were engaged. The world of everyday life was represented by pages, heralds, lackeys, and gardeners, along with colorful characters of the *divertissement:* Poles, Germans, Swiss, Tyroleans. The fantastic world was even more exotically populated with the soloists, corps de ballet, and children impersonating dryads and gnomes, zephyrs and immortals, shooting stars, sunbeams, gems, precious stones, lace, Bohemian cut glass, and Meissen china. The ballet was a long succession of variations, pas de deux, pas de trois, *pas d'action,* character and grotesque numbers, and corps de ballet *ballabiles.* But for all the splendor of its exterior, the ballet was devoid of soul. No amount of contrivance on the part of the choreographer, any more than the prodigious talents of the company's best soloists, was able to galvanize this ballet. *The Magic Mirror* was dropped from the repertory after the second performance.

On 17 February 1903 Petipa was informed that his contract would be terminated on 1 September but that he could remain in the service of the Imperial Theaters without a contract, retaining for life his current level of pay (nine thousand rubles a year). In 1905 he completed his memoirs, appending a catalog of his ballets. Last on the list was *Le Roman d'un Bouton de Rose,* footnoted "yet to be staged." Apparently the old choreographer hoped until the last to stage a comeback. In the memoirs Petipa (1906) bitterly complained that the creations in which good triumphed over evil had been completely forgotten—and he was right. The new age callously rejected the naive ideals of the past age. It seemed to Petipa that life was cruelly brushing aside his life's work. Embittered, disappointed, and ill, he ended his days with this conviction preying on his mind. But his love for the country that had adopted him remained unshakable. His daughter Vera quoted him, after his death, as saying, "I am indebted to Russia for my fame and I wish to be buried in its soil" (quoted in Nekhendzi, 1971).

Petipa died just when his pupils were conquering Paris with their art. None cared to recall in those days that they owed their success in large part to the coaching they had received from the venerable master. Over time this injustice was rectified. Petipa's best creations are now produced by the world's leading ballet companies, an eloquent tribute to the enduring appeal and vitality of the choreographic heritage of the nineteenth century. Marius Petipa's importance in the annals of world ballet is assured.

[*Many of the figures and works mentioned herein are the subjects of independent entries.*]

BIBLIOGRAPHY

Beaumont, Cyril W. *Complete Book of Ballets.* Rev. ed. London, 1951.

Christout, Marie-Françoise, ed. *Marius Petipa, 1818–1910: Dossier.* Paris, 1994.

Gregory, John. *The Legat Saga.* 2d ed. London, 1993.

Guest, Ivor. *The Divine Virginia: A Biography of Virginia Zucchi.* New York, 1977.

Guest, Ivor. *Jules Perrot: Master of the Romantic Ballet.* London, 1984.

Ivanov, Ivan, and Konstantin Ivanov. *M. I. Petipa.* St. Petersburg, 1922.

Koegler, Horst. "Marius Petipa: A New Perspective." *Dance Magazine* (September 1978): 63–78.

Krasovskaya, Vera. *Russkii baletnyi teatr vtoroi poloviny deviatnadtsatogo veka.* Leningrad, 1963.

Krasovskaya, Vera. *Istoriia russkogo baleta.* Leningrad, 1978.

Legat, Nikolai. "Twenty Years with Marius Petipa and Christian Johansson." *The Dancing Times* (April 1931): 11–14.

Leshkov, Denis I. *Marius Petipa* (1922). Adapted from the Russian. Edited by Cyril W. Beaumont. London, 1971.

Moore, Lillian. "The Petipa Family in Europe and America." *Dance Index* 1 (May 1942): 72–84.

Nekhendzi, Ana, ed. *Marius Petipa: Materialy, vospominaniia, stati.* Leningrad, 1971.

Petipa, Marius. *Memuary Mariusa Petipa.* St. Petersburg, 1906.

Petipa, Marius. *Russian Ballet Master: The Memoirs of Marius Petipa.* Edited by Lillian Moore. Translated by Helen Whittaker. London, 1958.

Petipa, Marius. *The Diaries of Marius Petipa.* Translated and edited by Lynn Garafola. Studies in Dance History, vol. 3.1. Pennington, N.J., 1992.

Roslavleva, Natalia. *Era of the Russian Ballet* (1966). New York, 1979.

Saint-Léon, Arthur. *Letters from a Ballet Master: The Correspondence of Arthur Saint-Léon.* Edited by Ivor Guest. New York, 1981.

Scholl, Tim. *From Petipa to Balanchine: Classical Revival and the Modernization of Ballet.* New York, 1994.

Sergeyev, Nicholas. "Memories of Marius Petipa." *The Dancing Times* (July 1939): 396–397.

Shiriaev, Aleksandr. *St. Petersburg Ballet: Memoirs of a Maryinsky Theater Actor.* Leningrad, 1941.

Slonimsky, Yuri. *Mastera baleta.* Leningrad, 1937.

Slonimsky, Yuri. "Marius Petipa." Translated by Anatole Chujoy. *Dance Index* (May–June 1947): 100–144.

Slonimsky, Yuri. *P. I. Chaikovskii i baletnyi teatr ego vremeni.* Moscow, 1956.

Ushakov, A. "Novy Ballet . . . *Le Roi Candaule.*" *Golos* (19 October 1868).

Vazem, Ekaterina. "Memoirs of a Ballerina of the St. Petersburg Bolshoi Theatre." Translated by Nina Dimitrievich. *Dance Research* 3 (Summer 1985): 3–22; 4 (Spring 1986): 3–28; 5 (Spring 1987): 21–41; 6 (Autumn 1988): 30–47.

Wiley, Roland John. *Tchaikovsky's Ballets: "Swan Lake," "Sleeping Beauty," "Nutcracker."* Oxford, 1985.

Wiley, Roland John, trans. and ed. *A Century of Russian Ballet: Documents and Accounts, 1810–1910.* Oxford, 1990. Includes the libretto for *The Pharaoh's Daughter,* and recollections of its first performance by Sergei Khudekov; the libretto of *The Magic Mirror;* and an essay by Mikhail Ivanov on Petipa.

VERA M. KRASOVSKAYA
Translated from Russian

PETIT, ROLAND (born 13 January 1924 in Villemomble), French dancer and choreographer. The name of Roland Petit, more than any other, evokes the essence of French postwar ballet. A true child of Paris, he grew up in the brasserie owned by his father, Edmond Petit, in Les Halles district. He began his training at the Paris Opera School of Dance at the age of nine, and at sixteen he was hired for the corps de ballet. His first and only major role at the Opera was that of Carmelo in Serge Lifar's *L'Amour Sorcier.* During the years of World War II he daydreamed about the United States, adored jazz, and longed to escape from the routine of the Opera. Tall and thin, with a pale face ringed with brown curls, he was an elegant and expressive dancer but not a finished virtuoso.

The year 1942 marked a turning point in Petit's career. He joined forces with the young dancer Janine Charrat and began his apprenticeship as a choreographer, using as his vehicle recitals the two of them gave in Paris. At first influenced by the neoclassicism of his mentor Serge Lifar, Petit soon developed a livelier, more personal style which can be seen in his first pas de deux ballet, *Paul et Virginie* (1943). After the liberation of Paris, Petit resigned from the Paris Opera Ballet but continued his activity with the Soirées de la Danse (Dance Evenings) organized by Irène Lidova at the Théâtre Sarah-Bernhardt. There he created *Le Rossignol et la Rose,* danced by Nina Vyroubova and Ethéry Pagava to music by Robert Schumann. His talent impressed the stage designer Christian Bérard, the librettist Boris Kochno, and Roger Eudes, director of the Théâtre des Champs-Élysées.

October 1945 saw the birth of the Ballets des Champs-Élysées, with Petit as the star dancer, ballet master, choreographer, and guiding force. His father provided financial support for the company. Between 1945 and 1947 Petit created his most individual works, including *Les Forains* (music by Henri Sanguet), *Les Rendez-vous* (music by Joseph Kosma), *La Fiancée du Diable* (music by Jean Hubeau), *Le Déjeuner sur l'Herbe* (music by Alexander Tcherepnin), and *Le Jeune Homme et la Mort.* The last, created in collaboration with Jean Cocteau, daringly used the majestic music of Bach to accompany the tale of a young painter who, scorned by his beloved, commits suicide in his drab garret. [*See* Jeune Homme et la Mort, Le.]

At the age of twenty-one, Petit was idolized by the art world of Paris and London. In 1947 he broke with the Ballets des Champs-Élysées, where he did not feel in absolute control, and established a new company, Ballets de Paris de Roland Petit, which made its debut in May 1948 at the Théâtre Marigny, with a new repertory and with the participation of Margot Fonteyn, who danced *Les Demoiselles de la Nuit.* [*See* Ballets de Champs-Élysées *and* Ballets de Paris de Roland Petit.]

It was his version of *Carmen,* created in London in 1949, that brought international fame for Petit and his star, Zizi Jeanmaire. Led by Petit as Don José, the featured dancers were all praised for their intensely dramatic performances. At the New York premiere in October, theater critic Walter Terry found that in the then-daring bedroom scene, "the normally elegant and refined movements of the traditional ballet are used with sardonic brilliance." Irving Kolodin saw it a little differently: "This was *Carmen* in the spirit of a vaudeville *apache* turn, with none of its details left to the imagination." The theaters of the United States opened to Petit, with a season in New York and films in Hollywood.

In 1953 he returned to Paris to offer a new ballet season at the Théâtre de l'Empire. His major successes were *Le Loup* (The Wolf), *Deuil en 24 Heures* (Mourning in 24 Hours), and *Ciné Bijou.* His stars were now Colette Marchand, Violette Verdy, Leslie Caron, and Claire Sombert. In 1954 Roland Petit married Jeanmaire, and the couple moved to Hollywood, where Petit choreographed such films as *The Glass Slipper* (1954) and *Daddy Long Legs* (1955) with Leslie Caron and *Anything Goes* with Jeanmaire.

He then returned to Paris to begin a new season of ballets with a new company. His major success at this time was *Cyrano de Bergerac,* set to the music of Marius Constant, at the Théâtre de l'Alhambra; Petit danced the role of Cyrano. He was turning with increasing frequency to the music hall, however, and in 1961 at the Alhambra, he created a revue for Jeanmaire, with the successful *Mon Truc en Plumes.* In 1965 he returned to the Paris Opera with his ballet *Notre-Dame de Paris,* in which he danced Quasimodo. His subsequent creations were all rather sterile: *Eloge à la Folie* (In Praise of Folly), 1966; *Le Paradis*

PETIT. In the film *Les Collants Noirs* (Black Tights; 1960), Zizi Jeanmaire and Roland Petit recreated their famous roles in Petit's *Carmen,* which they had first performed in 1949. The blatant eroticism of the duet between Carmen and Don José, considered shocking at the time, contributed to the ballet's international success. (Photograph from the Dance Collection, New York Public Library for the Performing Arts.)

PETIT. For the Ballets de Paris, Petit created *La Rose des Vents* (1958), with music by Darius Milhaud, in which he appeared as a sailor. (Photograph from the Dance Collection, New York Public Library for the Performing Arts.)

Perdu (Paradise Lost) for Fonteyn and Nureyev in 1967; and *Turangalîla* in 1968. For a short time in 1969 he was the director of the Paris Opera Ballet, but he soon left because of difficulties with collective bargaining agreements and bureaucracy.

In April 1970 Petit assumed the management of the Casino de Paris. *La Revue de Roland Petit* had little originality, but it did have amusing dance sequences. His second revue, *Zizi, Je T'aime,* marked the end of Petit's music-hall career; in 1972 he assumed management of a new company, Le Ballet de Marseille–Roland Petit, supported by the city of Marseille and by the Ministry of Cultural Affairs. The troupe made its debut in May 1972 with *Allumez les Étoiles* (Light Up the Stars), based on the life of the Russian poet Vladimir Mayakovsky.

Ballets, which included *La Rose Malade,* a pas de deux danced by Maya Plisetskaya as guest ballerina (1973) followed; then came *L'Arlésienne* (1974); *Les Intermittences du Coeur,* inspired by the novels of Marcel Proust (1974); an innovative *Coppélia* in which Petit played an elegant, seductive Coppélius; and his *The Nutcracker,* 1976. In 1978 at the Théâtre des Champs-Élysées in Paris, he premiered *La Dame de Pique* (Queen of Spades), to music by Tchaikovsky, danced by Mikhail Baryshnikov.

Other new works were *La Chauve-souris* (The Bat), a comic ballet for Zizi Jeanmaire; *Tales of Hoffmann;* and, in 1982/83, *Les Amours de Franz, La Soirée Debussy,* and *Les Hauts de Hurlevent.* In 1985 Petit created *The Blue Angel,* starring Natalia Makarova; it was presented in New York and in 1986 in Paris, with Ekaterina Maximova and Vladimir Vasiliev as guest artists. In October 1990 in Marseille, Petit staged his own version of *The Sleeping Beauty,* with Zizi Jeanmaire as Carabosse. In 1995 he had another success with *Le Guepard* (The Leopard), based on the 1964 film by Luchino Visconti.

The Ballet de Marseille is now known as the National Ballet de Marseille. The company has made numerous tours, appearing in Japan, the United States, Italy, and other countries. In July 1983 it performed at the Metropolitan Opera House in New York. Outside his company, Petit worked for England's Royal Ballet, La Scala Ballet of Milan, the Royal Danish Ballet, and for companies in Canada. He returned several times to the Paris Opera with such works as *Nana* (1976), *La Nuit Transfigurée* (1976), and *Le Fantôme de l'Opéra* (1980).

Petit's style has consistently been elegant and theatrical, avoiding abstract lines and obscure philosophical meanings. His art is full-bodied, lively, and entertaining.

Petit's youthful style reflected the strict, linear neoclassicism of his Russian mentor, Serge Lifar; however, even his first attempts at choreography were notably individual, with a more theatrical manner of dancing, more sensuality, and gestures borrowed from everyday life. Pure dance or abstract ballet never interested Petit. He always sought out dramatic subjects, full of lyricism or fantasy. From the beginning of his career, he was always the hero of his own ballets: Don José in *Carmen,* Le Loup, Cyrano, and finally Quasimodo. His rich repertory reveals two clear tendencies: nostalgic and poetic ballets based on romantic themes, such as *Les Demoiselles de la Nuit* and *L'Arlésienne;* and ballets in his "champagne style," such as *Deuil en 24 Heures* and *La Chauve-souris,* or his *Coppélia*—all of which sparkle with Parisian elegance.

Petit based his ballets on strict classical technique; pink tights were obligatory. But to this academic grammar he brought eroticism, subtlety, a delectable vitality, and an inventiveness that was often amusing, sometimes moving. The innovations of modern dance did not touch him at all; he remained the inheritor of the grand tradition of the *ballet d'action* for which Jean-Georges Noverre had dictated the rules nearly two centuries before.

Roland Petit is a Chevalier de l'Ordre des Arts et des Lettres (1962) and a Chevalier de la Légion d'Honneur (1974).

BIBLIOGRAPHY

Ballet National de Marseille: Roland Petit. Paris, 1981.

Barnes, Clive. "Roland Petit." *Ballet News* 2 (August 1980): 46.

Cirillo, Silvana, ed. *Corpo, teatro, danza: Béjart, Blaska, Petit.* Brescia, 1981.

Lidova, Irène. *Dix-sept visages de la danse française.* Paris, 1953.

Lidova, Irène. *Roland Petit.* Paris, 1956.

Lidova, Irène. "Roland Petit." *Saisons de la danse,* no. 6 (Summer 1968): 11–14.

Lidova, Irène. "Roland Petit." *danse-Opéra* (April 1969).

Mannoni, Gérard. *Roland Petit.* Paris, 1984.

Mannoni, Gérard. *Roland Petit: Un chorégraphe et ses peintres.* Paris, 1990.

Petit, Roland. *J'ai dansé sur les flôts.* Paris, 1993.

Petit, Roland, and Gérard Mannoni. *Roland Petit: Un chorégraphe et ses danseurs.* Paris, 1992.

Vaughan, David. "Shop Talk with Roland Petit and Zizi." *Dance and Dancers* (May 1958): 42–43, 80–82.

IRÈNE LIDOVA
Translated from French

PETROUCHKA. Also known as *Petrushka.* Ballet in one act and four scenes. Choreography: Michel Fokine. Music: Igor Stravinsky. Libretto: Alexandre Benois and Igor Stravinsky. Scenery and costumes: Alexandre Benois. Lighting: Serge Diaghilev. First performance: 13 June 1911, Théâtre du Châtelet, Paris, Ballets Russes de Serge Diaghilev. Principals: Vaslav Nijinsky (Petrouchka), Tamara Karsavina (The Ballerina), Alexandre Orloff (The Moor), Enrico Cecchetti (The Charlatan).

Petrouchka, a tragicomic work was conceived by Igor Stravinsky in the summer of 1910 in between composing *The Firebird* and *The Rite of Spring* and following completion of his work on the Russian dance and musical episode *The Cry of Petrouchka.* The brilliant contributions of the various original collaborators made *Petrouchka* an important realization of the Diaghilev ideal of the *Gesamtkuntswerk.* Arguably this is the greatest score ever written for ballet; Benois's best achievement in decor and costumes; and choreography that Fokine claimed was possibly the most complete demonstration of his reforms.

The setting is Saint Petersburg's Admiralty Square in the 1830s, during the annual Shrovetide Fair, a festive pre-Lenten event. In the second and third scenes the action shifts, first to Petrouchka's cold, empty, prisonlike room and then to the Moor's well furnished quarters. *Petrouchka* concerns a fairtime puppet show involving three dolls (Petrouchka, the Moor, and the Ballerina) who pantomime a love intrigue for a massive festival crowd. This audience is made up of people from every rung of society—ladies, gentlemen, officers, merchants, coachmen, stableboys, wet nurses, and gypsies—who rush from one diversion to another with gaiety, abandon, and a certain crudeness.

Inside the fair booth, or theater, Petrouchka and the Moor compete for the Ballerina's affections. Petrouchka, who bears a resemblance to Pulcinella, is an awkward and ugly yet pure-spirited rag doll who longs for freedom and love but is held in thrall by the evil Charlatan (also sometimes known as the Puppet Master or Old Showman) and by his public status as no better than a doll. Dancing in loneliness and despair at the Ballerina's rejection, Petrouchka fears both the despotic Charlatan and the smug, bellicose Moor, Petrouchka's rival, who is the very incarnation of stupidity and egotism. After striving for the

PETROUCHKA. Alexander Grant as the Moor, Margot Fonteyn as the Ballerina, and Peter Clegg as Petrouchka, in the Royal Ballet production, mounted by Lubov Tchernicheva in 1957. (Photograph by Marka; reprinted from Horst Koegler, *Ballett International,* Berlin, 1960.)

attentions of the Ballerina, who is attracted instead to the Moor, the bewildered Petrouchka interrupts them in a tryst and is chased onto the fairground and slain by the Moor. The crowd grows alarmed, but the Charlatan convinces bystanders that the victim is "only" a doll and that his "death" is thus insignificant. However, the spirit of Petrouchka then appears on the roof of the booth in defiance of the Charlatan, who is terrified. In a moral sense Petrouchka prevails even though he failed to be recognized as human.

The ballet has often been cited as a metaphorical account of the relationship between Diaghilev (as the Charlatan) and Nijinsky (as Petrouchka). Petrouchka was possibly Nijinsky's most famous role. Benois has written of Nijinsky's complete "metamorphosis" into a half-human. Fokine devised unnatural movements for all three puppets, with their psychological implications speeding the plot. The movement of the Moor was *en dehors,* signifying his extroversion; that for Petrouchka was *en dedans* to indicate his introversion. Nijinsky had padded the tips of his shoes and occasionally rose on pointe in his portrayal. The very simple pointe work for the Ballerina signified her vacuousness. In contrast, the naturalistic, unconnected bits of business for the crowd of more than one hundred was the antithesis of the symmetry of the classical corps de ballet.

Petrouchka has been staged around the world on countless occasions since its Paris premiere in 1911. The ballet took Paris by storm, and the sensation proved to be lasting; *Petrouchka* remained in the repertory of Diaghilev's Ballets Russes until his death in 1929. In that year, during Diaghilev's last season, Richard Capell pronounced *Petrouchka* "the high-water mark of the vast Diaghilev repertory." Fokine staged it for the Royal Danish Ballet in 1925 and for American Ballet Theatre in 1942. Serge Grigoriev and his wife, Lubov Tchernicheva, staged it for Britain's Royal Ballet in 1957. *Petrouchka* was first performed in the United States by Diaghilev's Ballets Russes in 1916. Léonide Massine produced it for the Joffrey Ballet in 1970, while, in the same year, Dmitri Romanoff and Yurek Lazowski revived it for American Ballet Theatre.

Unlike many classics, *Petrouchka* has been little revised over the years. The title role proved to be irresistible to the great male dancers of the twentieth century, with interpreters including Fokine, Adolph Bolm, Massine, Leon Woizikowski, Stanislas Idzikowski, Børge Ralov, Anton Dolin, Rudolf Nureyev, and Mikhail Baryshnikov.

BIBLIOGRAPHY

Barnes, Clive. "The Birth and Death of *Petrouchka.*" *Dance Magazine* (September 1957).

Beaumont, Cyril W. *Complete Book of Ballets.* Rev. ed. London, 1951.

Buckle, Richard. *Diaghilev.* New York, 1979.

Garafola, Lynn. *Diaghilev's Ballets Russes.* New York, 1989.

Fokine, Michel. *Memoirs of a Ballet Master.* Translated by Vitale Fokine. Edited by Anatole Chujoy. London, 1961.

Karsavina, Tamara. "Benois the Magician." *Ballet Annual* 15 (1961): 76–78.

Maynard, Olga. *"Petrouchka." Dance Magazine* (February 1970): 47–62.

Reynolds, Nancy, and Susan Reimer-Torn. *Dance Classics.* Pennington, N.J., 1991.

Taruskin, Richard. "From *Firebird* to *The Rite:* Folk Elements in Stravinsky's Score." *Ballet Review* 10 (Summer 1982): 72–87.

Vaughan, David. "Fokine in the Contemporary Repertory." *Ballet Review* 7.2–3 (1978–1979): 19–27.

White, Eric W. *Stravinsky: The Composer and His Works.* 2d ed. Berkeley, 1979.

MOLLY MCQUADE
Based on materials submitted by
Galina N. Dobrovolskaya and Suzanne Carbonneau

PETROV, ANASTAS (Anastas Dačev Petrov; born 1 September 1899 in Dobric [Tolbuhin], died in Sofia), Bulgarian dancer, teacher, and choreographer. Petrov is recognized as the creator of professional ballet in Bulgaria. He studied classical ballet from 1923 to 1925 at the school of the Russian ballerina Evgenia Eduardova in Berlin; he was exposed to German modern dance from 1925 to 1927, when he worked as a dancer under Max Terpis, a former student of Mary Wigman, at the Berlin State Opera.

In 1927 Petrov was appointed first soloist and ballet master at the Sofia National Opera, where he worked until 1961. His staging of *Coppélia,* first presented on 22 February 1928, is considered to mark the birth of professional Bulgarian ballet. In 1937 he choreographed the first Bulgarian ballet, *The Dragon and Jana,* to music by H. Manolov, taking its theme from Bulgarian legends and folktales. Petrov later used Bulgarian folk dance as a means of enriching his classically based choreography. In addition to his ballets, he choreographed dances for more than ninety operas and for dramatic productions. His original works include the national ballet *Orpheus and Rhodope* (1961), to music by C. Cvetanov; he also staged versions of the classics *Raymonda, Giselle, Swan Lake,* and *Esmeralda.*

Petrov made another important contribution to Bulgarian ballet through his teaching. In 1927 he founded the nation's first professional ballet school in Sofia, teaching many outstanding soloists—among them Nadezda (Nina) Kiradžieva, Liljana (Lili) Beron, L. Kolčakova, Asser Gavrilov, P. Enčeva, and the dancer and ballet master A. Manolov. The internationally known ballerina Sonia Arova was also one of his pupils.

[*See also* Bulgaria, *article on* Theatrical Dance.]

BIBLIOGRAPHY

Konsulova, Violetta. *Anastas Petrov i bulgarskiiat balet.* Sofia, 1976.

Konsulova, Violetta. *Iz istoriiata bulgarskiia balet.* Sofia, 1981.

Popov, Teodor, and Eliana Mitova. *Sreshti s baletni deitsi.* Sofia, 1987.

VIOLETTA KONSULOVA

PHILIPPINES. An archipelago of more than seven thousand mountainous islands, the Republic of the Philippines stretches almost 1,200 miles (3,100 kilometers) from north to south at the eastern perimeter of Southeast Asia, bordered on the west by the South China Sea and on the east by the Pacific Ocean. The Philippines' complex history—including multiple Asian influences and domination during the period of Western colonialism by, first, Spain and, later, the United States—is reflected in the nation's layered cultural traditions. Claimed for Spain by the explorer Ferdinand Magellan in 1521 (and named, fifty years later, for the Spanish monarch Philip II), the islands were under Spanish control until the end of the nineteenth century, after which, largely as a result of the Spanish-American War, they came under U.S. administration. Occupied by the Japanese during World War II, the Philippines achieved independence in 1946.

The Philippines is unique among Asian nations in that the large majority of its population of about 60 million is Christian, and specifically Roman Catholic—the legacy of the centuries of Spanish control of the islands, during which most colonial administration was carried out by Roman Catholic friars. Muslims, who began establishing themselves in the southern Philippines in the mid-fifteenth century and who are still concentrated in the southernmost parts of the archipelago (Mindinao and the Sulu chain), represent the largest religious minority. The lifeways of the Philippines' dozens of indigenous ethnic groups mostly did not survive the repeated onslaughts of foreign cultures, although they do persist in isolated highland regions, especially on the largest islands.

The development of dance in the Philippines parallels the history of Philippine culture. The heterogeneity brought about by geographical barriers, the isolation of various cultural communities, and diverse foreign influences at various periods have resulted in a great variety of dances. This variety exists not only in movements but also in costume, music, spirit, context, and character.

The Philippines does not have a classical tradition in dance, unlike many of its Southeast Asian neighbors. Because its islands are at the crossroads of Asian sea trade and have repeatedly been under foreign domination, foreign influences have long touched its shores and more recently have moved inland. Only in isolated regions, untouched by these waves of cross-cultural influence, have people retained their own identity long enough to establish a tradition in dance; however, no dance genre has become recognized as classical.

Dance in the Philippines today ranges from tribal dancing in isolated regions, still performed in ritual contexts, to the stylized revues of folk dance groups, to theatrical modern dance, ballet, and contemporary social dance.

The repertory of traditional and contemporary Filipino dances reflects progressive and cumulative influences of Hindu, Arabic, Malayan, Spanish, contemporary Western, and other cultures. Changing social mores are similarly reflected in the range of expressions found in Filipino dance, from fire and frenzy, to modesty and grace, to bold, spontaneous, creative movement. Most styles of traditional Filipino dance can still be seen in nearly pristine form in the far-flung mountain regions and island provinces; in the urban areas, however, the dances are highly theatricalized.

PHILIPPINES. Two men performing an indigenous Filipino combat dance. (Photograph from the Dance Collection, New York Public Library for the Performing Arts.)

Dances of the Philippines are divided into two main categories: dances of the non-Christian ethnic communities and dances of the Christianized, Western-influenced population. The former comprise dances of Muslims, mountain province groups, and other ethnic or traditional groups. The latter are dances of the lowland Filipinos.

Non-Christian Ritual and Folk Dances. The dances of the non-Christian Filipinos are of importance in tracing the historical development of dance in the Philippines, because in these dances one can detect the nature of pre-Hispanic dances, of which no record is available. Of great value are the eyewitness accounts of the first Westerners to set foot on Philippine soil, on 16 March 1521 under the leadership of Magellan. Antonio Pigafetta, Magellan's Italian historian, reported early Filipino dancing in his *Primo viaggio interno al mondo* (The First Voyage around the World). The friars Chirino and Colin discussed the role of dancing in magico-religious ceremonies performed by native shamans.

There are more than forty-four non-Christian or traditional groups. For the purpose of this discussion they may be divided into three categories: the highlanders, also known as Igorot; the Islamic groups, also known as *moros* (Muslims); and other indigenous peoples living throughout the islands.

Igorot dance. In the mountain region of northern Luzon live six tribes known generically as Igorots, or Mountain People. While each has its own distinctive cultural patterns, these tribes share enough traits to constitute a loosely homogeneous group. For the most part, they live in villages situated beside their ricefields. They share common religious beliefs, generally animistic, and make propitiatory offerings to household gods called *anitos*. Dancing is part of these ritual offerings. It usually takes place in certain cleared areas in the village, where tribesmen dance around a sacred idol, fire, or animal sacrifice, depending on the purpose of the ritual.

Among these people dance is an expression of community life that animates various rituals. It brings spiritual benefits to the performers and entertains the spectators. It also serves to appease ancestors and gods, cure ailments, ensure success in war, and ward off ill luck and natural calamities. Dance is a vehicle of socialization, contributing to the general welfare and need for recreation, and acting as an outlet for repressed feelings. It is used to ensure bountiful harvests and favorable weather and to mark life milestones such as birth, marriage, and death.

Igorot and other non-Christian dances are less structured and formal than most Christian dances. They employ similar steps and movements but vary in approach, dynamism, emphasis, dramatization, spectacle, and costuming. The dances are characterized by stamping and staccato rhythms and by hands flapping in imitation of the movement of birds. Various tribes have their respective versions of festival, ceremonial, courtship, marriage, war, and social dances. The Bontocs are noted for their war dances, the Kalingas for courtship and wedding dances, the Ifugaos for burial dances, and the Benguets for festival dances.

Moro or Muslim dances. The southern part of the Philippines lies within the periphery of the ancient Southeast Asian trade routes. Arabs, Hindus, Chinese, and Persians, as well as merchants from other parts of Asia, traded there and also brought about social and cultural exchanges. The inhabitants of Mindanao and the Sulu Archipelago particularly were in early and continuous touch with the Hindu, Arabic, and Malayan cultures. Called *moros* by the Spanish (after the Muslim Moors who occupied Spain from 711 to 1492), the Islamized tribes of the southern Philippines evolved well-organized social and political structures that enabled them to resist the Spanish conquest. Thus, to a large degree, their culture—many elements of which antedate Islam—has survived to the present day.

When the Spanish colonizers came ashore in the southern Philippines, the dance culture they found was an amalgam of earlier influences. In their dances the Muslim tribes exhibit traits that link them not only to the Indo-Malayan world but also to other Islamic cultures of the East, including an emphasis on the upper torso, bent knees and upturned toes, and the use of the hands to express nuances of feeling.

Muslim dance styles have absorbed Hindu-Malayan-Arabic influences, combining them in different degrees and evolving dance and music that are unmistakably Filipino, with their own atmosphere and mood. Muslim dances move with a peculiar elasticity and almost serpentine suppleness; curves are emphasized in the apparently jointless, backturned hands, flexible arms, and rounded posture of the body. Leonor Orosa Goquingco (1980), a Filipina dance pioneer, has characterized the "Oriental style" as marked by inner intensity and absorption, mysticism, and languid grace. Much use is made of the upper torso and subtle facial expressions. The arms flow from pose to pose—the fingers now held close and still, now curling in and out, the elbows flexed. The body weight shifts from one bent and turned-out knee to the other; the dancer moves with shuffling steps, creeping on the toes. The use of *singuel* (metal anklets) and the expert manipulation of fans also bespeak the Oriental style. In the dances of Moroland improvisation is allowed, and the dancer performs according to mood. In these dances contrapuntal movements are sometimes used; the feet may follow a vigorous rhythm while head, arm, and hand movements are languid, leisurely, and smooth.

Some popular dances of the Muslim groups are the festival dances called *pangalay* and *pangasik*, the Fish Dance *(tawte-tawte)*, the Orange Harvest Dance *(sua-sua)*, the Wedding Dance *(kandingan)*, the Princess Dance *(dayang-dayang)*, war dances *(bojjak, silat, langka-kuntao,* and *sagayan), a* martial dance *(pagkuntaw)*, the Flirtation Dance *(maglanka)*, a marathon group song and dance *(lunsay)*, the Bird Dance *(linggisan)*, and the Bamboo and Fan Dance *(singkil)*.

Dances of other indigenous tribes. More than twenty cultural communities other than the Igorots live in isolation in hill and mountain areas throughout the Philippine archipelago. Like the hill tribes of Thailand, these groups live in the style of their forebears. Dance for them is a basic part of life, still performed essentially for the gods and generally exhibiting simple, rhythmic movement. These plain, rustic dances are shared by tribes from northern Luzon to southernmost Sulu. Among the well-known dances are the courtship and wedding dances of the Tirurays and the Mansakas; the offering dances of the Bukidnons; the war dances of the Ilongots and Tirurays; the mimetic dances of the Negritos, Manobos, and T'bolis; the *pagdiwata* ritual dances of the Tagbanwas; the trance dances of the Bataks; the ceremonial dances of the Tinggians, such as the *daeng* and *tadek;* and the ritual dances of the Bagobos.

Christian or Western-Influenced Dances. European social dancing has left a strong imprint on the development of folk dances of the lowland Filipinos. So indelible has this influence been, and so thorough its assimilation into the indigenous folk tradition, that it becomes difficult to say precisely where a native dance ends and a foreign one begins.

Dances of the Christian Filipinos are found in the lowland areas of the Philippines, especially where Spain had much contact and influence. The flexibility that Filipinos have shown in their adaptations has been enormous, with foreign dance becoming uniquely filipinized over the years.

When the Spaniards initiated 350 years of colonization, Roman Catholic missionaries had to contend with an ancient religious heritage. To make conversion to Catholicism appealing, the missionaries incorporated some native traditions into church ritual, creating an odd but attractive syncretism. Indigenous dances, for example, were modified and used in the rites celebrating holy days and in religious festivals. The native tradition became a convenient tool shrewdly used by the Spaniards, with dance playing an integral part.

Although the Spanish friars banned non-Christian ceremonies and rituals (just as they burned or destroyed evidence of other aspects of pre-Hispanic culture, such as native writings), they did allow the performance of native dances on important holy days such as the Feast of the Immaculate Conception. In the town of Obando, Bulacan Province, the Feast of the Immaculate Conception (when childless women and men dance their prayer to have children) became something of a fertility rite. The celebrations by the Indio-Filipinos of these Christian feasts were as colorful and spectacular as any in Europe, surpassing those in Spain. The native proclivity for song, dance, and pageantry could also be seen in the inclusion of tourney dances in religious dramas and *zarzuelas* (operettas) and in the processions and shows that were staged with the friars' blessings (because they contributed to the church coffers).

The Spaniards brought to the Philippines not only their religion but also their arts, and the Hispanization of the archipelago inevitably led to the introduction of Spanish dances. On state occasions and at receptions of visiting officials hosted by religious orders, dance by native performers may have been the primary entertainment. The Spanish and other Europeans in the colony had their social dances, too. These were picked up and disseminated among the wealthy Indio-Filipinos, who on occasion mixed socially with the rulers.

With the 250-year galleon trade between Manila and Mexico, and the return of the *illustrados* (Philippine intelligentsia) from Europe in the progressive second half of the nineteenth century, such European dances as the quadrille, waltz, fandango, English contradance, galop, mazurka, *cachucha, jarabe,* and *zapateado* took root in the colony. Inevitably, European dance and music were assimilated and made over into regional dances, with each region adding its own touches. The *polkabal* is a fusion of the polka and the waltz. The *rigodon* (Fr., *rigaudon*)—French, stately, and formal—became a national favorite. Variations of themes and of representations abound in this dance; the complexity of patterns and steps depends on regional interpretation as well as on the skills of the performers.

PHILIPPINES. The Kalinga are one of six indigenous tribes of the Igorot, highlanders from the island of Luzon in the northern Philippines. Balancing pots filled with food on their heads, these women from the Ramón Obusan Folkloric Group perform the Kalinga "Banga" (Pot Dance), from the celebratory *Ragragsakan* (Dance of Happiness). (Photograph courtesy of Ramón Obusan.)

PHILIPPINES. *Singkil* is the popular Bamboo and Fan Dance of Muslim groups in the Philippines. It is here performed by members of the Silayan Philippine Dance Company of Los Angeles. (Photograph from the archives of The Asia Society, New York.)

The music used for such dances as "La Habanera Botolena" (a wedding dance) and "Ilocano a Nasudi" (Lovely Ilocano) comes from Italian airs—the former from Gaetano Donizetti's opera *Lucrezia Borgia* and the latter from the Italian folk song "Marianina." Many of the titles of Philippine folk dances reveal their geographic origins, such as the *habanera* (Havana), *malaguena* (Malaga), and *katalona* (Catalonia). The name of the region that reinterpreted a European dance was often imparted to the stylized creation. The *jota cavitena* originated in Cavite Province, the *jota moncadena* in Moncada, in Tarlac Province.

Some dances derive their names from the principal objects used in the dance. There is the *zapatilla,* so called because the footwear *(zapatillas)* of the women is of focal interest. The *mazurka alcamfor* derives its name from the camphor-scented handkerchief used by the maiden in the dance.

In all these dances a variety of foreign steps and sequences—the *contradansa, abrasete, costados, paseos, engano, brincos,* and *cabeseras*—became regular features. Uniquely Filipino traits can be seen in such courtship dances as "La Carinosa" and "Hele-hele Bago Quiere," where the demure, secretive (but inwardly passionate) traditional Filipina emerges, and in "La Bulakena," where a housewife is shown ministering to her husband just home from work. Some dances, such as "Lulay," "Esperanza," and "Rogelia", were named after the beloved named in their songs. Others have names connoting certain customs, particularly those controlling the relationship between men and women. In the "Sayaw Santa Isabel" the male dancers hold out their handkerchiefs for the women to hold; this reflects the mores of the Spanish era, when suitors were forbidden even to hold the hands of maidens. In a few dances, the roles are reversed: the women hold out their fans to the gentle suitors. While various wedding dances abound throughout the country, most of them share the practical function of gathering gifts for the newlyweds.

Many pre-Hispanic dances were later used to celebrate Christian feasts. On religious and festive occasions dancers are a prime attraction, particularly during the Christmas season. Animals, insects, and birds are central to many Philippine dances; the monkey is a perfect subject for mimetic dance, as are the dove, duck, and other birds. [*For further discussion, see* Tinikling.]

Filipino folk dances are unique among Southeast Asian dances. This may in large part be attributed to the colonization of the country by Spain and later by the United States. Western grafting and Oriental roots, particularly Malay, have produced a cultural heritage in which the combination of East and West is greater than the sum of its parts.

Social Dance, Ballet, and Modern Dance. After the Spanish-American War, the United States took over the Philippines from the Spanish in 1890, American social dancing came to the islands, and its various styles were readily assimilated. American influence can be seen in dances such as the *ba-ingles* (*baile ingles,* or English dances, from the Ilocos region), *lanceros* (from the American square dance, the Lancers), *birginia* (from the Virginia Reel), and *escopitan,* a dance from Negros Occidental that is comparable in general pattern to an American square dance.

The fox trot, swing, Castle Walk, Lindy Hop, Big Apple, and tango, among others, were seen in social gatherings. Incidental dances in local *bodabil* (vaudeville) shows were popular but poor imitations of their American counterparts. Tap dancing found practitioners.

With American colonization, classical ballet and modern dance became known to Filipinos. Classical ballet was first performed in the Philippines in 1915 by Paul Nijinsky (not related to the famous Vaslav Nijinsky) of the Imperial Russian Ballet. Anna Pavlova performed with her company in 1922; and Denishawn in 1925. Luva Adameit, who was said to have been with the Pavlova company, came to Manila in 1927 and started a ballet school, followed by a number of other foreigners who started their own schools. Notable among them were Anita M. Kane and Trudl Dubsky Zipper from Vienna, who blended classical and modern dance (the central European modern dance tradition), emphasizing individual expressionist interpretation.

In the 1950s Ricardo and Roberta Cassell established their own company and produced choreographic pieces that displayed the talents of a new generation of dancers. From their school, Studio Dance Group, emerged the most popular dancers of the day, such as Elizabeth Guasch, Benny Villanueva (Benjamin Reyes), Julie Borromeo, Israel Gabriel, Tony Llacer, Mercy Lauchengco, and Eddie Elejar. However, the Cassells were forced to close their studio and return to the United States when their enrollment dropped, because of the puritanical attitude of religious authorities toward the study of ballet. For a period in the 1950s, Manila's exclusive convent schools prohibited their students from taking ballet, declaring it immoral. This attitude has given way to a more receptive view of the artistic values of ballet. Ballet classes, with their own premises, are considered a socially acceptable pursuit for middle-class children.

In 1962 Leonor Orosa Goquingco established her group Filipinesca, which performed *Philippine Life, Legend, and Lore in Dance.* This was the first attempt at expressionist and interpretive dances based on Philippine folk themes, and the first full-length Philippine dance program of original choreography in Philippine folkloric dance style. Go-

PHILIPPINES. The Ramón Obusan Folkloric Group is one of several dance companies presenting theatrical versions of ethnic and folk genres. *(above)* Women of the company appear in a staged presentation of "Kinakulangan," a Muslim Maranao wedding parade from the island of Mindanao in the southern Philippines. *(right)* Members of the company in "Patlong," a victory dance of the Kalinga. (Photographs courtesy of Ramón Obusan.)

quingco pioneered in integrating the classical and modern ballet idioms with native folk materials. She first attempted before World War II to use Filipino folk dance in the theater, with her *Trend: Return to Native,* and later produced *Noli Dance Suite* (a one-act ballet that includes several episodes from the well-known novel *Noli me tangere,* by the Philippine national hero José P. Rizal).

In the late 1960s, Remedios "Totoy" de Oteyza and her pupil Inday Gaston Manosa formed the Hariraya Dance Company, the predecessors of which were the De Oteyza Ballet and the Manila Ballet Company; both had been very active in the local ballet scene in the late 1940s and early 1950s. Some of Oteyza's outstanding dancers were Maribel Aboitiz, Malot Zialcita, Jamin Alcoriza, Joji Felix, Sony Lopez, Eddie Elejar, Cesar Mendoza, Lulu Puertollano, Vella C. Damian, Effie Nanas, and Maniya Barredo. Hariraya was the first dance group to be subsidized by a large private donation. Hariraya and Dance Theatre Philippines took the first step in elevating dance to the status of a professional career, remunerating their dancers accordingly; however, continuing financial aid failed to materialize.

The idea of professionalizing dance was picked up by a later company, the Cultural Center of the Philippines Dance Workshop Company, later known as CCP Dance Company and presently called Ballet Philippines. Ballet Philippines, one of the resident companies of the Cultural Center of the Philippines, is one of two professional dance companies in the country today. Founded by Eddie Elejar and Alice Reyes in 1970, it has consistently produced regular dance seasons (both classical ballet and modern dance) and has toured extensively in the Philippines and abroad.

From the late 1960s onward, Dance Theater Philippines also contributed significantly to the advancement of dance. The dancer Poul Gnatt was the first producer-choreographer of the company, which was organized by Eddie Elejar, Julie Borromeo, and Felicitas L. Radaic in 1968. It uses a system of examinations based on international syllabi and from 1981 on has sponsored dance seasons at the Meralco Theater. The company conducted the "Ballet at the Park" program for more than a decade until its demise in 1989. Under the direction of Radaic and later of Basilio, it produced dancers of international caliber, such as Irene and Hazel Sabas, Mary Anne Santamaria, Anna Villadolid, Lisa Macuja, Luis Layag, Mitto Castillo, Victor Madrona, and Vinencio Samblaceno.

In the 1950s modern dance was popularized by Manolo Rosado, Carmen Ferrer Adevoso, Corazon Generoso Inigo, and Rosalia Merino Santos; the last founded the Far Eastern University Modern Experimental Dance Group. The formation of the CCP Dance Company of Ballet Philippines gave a new boost to modern dance after the slack period of the 1960s. American and French influences and Filipino choreographic creations added momentum.

In Manila, Dance Concert Company, headed by Eric V. Cruz and Vella C. Damian, was active for fourteen years. Today Cruz directs Ballet Manila, founded by Lisa Macuja, once a member of the Kirov Ballet. In the provinces, the dance scene is enlivened by a number of small ballet groups. Notable were Fe Sala Villarica's Queen City Junior Ballet Company and groups headed by Pancho and Elsie Uytiepo, Rene Dimacale, Mercy Drilon, Rosario Royeca, and others. Lydia Madarang Gaston in Bacolod City, Edwin Duero and Nila Claraval Gonzalez in Iloilo City, and Carmen Locsin in Davao City remain active in the provinces. Younger teachers maintain school groups that are affiliated with the Association of Ballet Academies in the Philippines or with the Royal Academy of Dancing.

Born in 1987, Philippine Ballet Theater integrated the pioneering efforts of the Hariraya Dance Company, Dance Concert, and other groups that merged after cultural policy changed with the fall of the government of Ferdinand Marcos. Now in its tenth year, Philippine Ballet Theater has staged Filipino and foreign works in annual seasons at the Cultural Center of the Philippines and Meralco Theater and has toured internationally.

Although only one professional dance company in the Philippines can match those of the dance capitals of the world, Filipino modern dance and classical ballet groups have been attaining a high level of professionalism. It is left to the emerging, energetic young dancers and choreographers—such as Denisa Reyes, Edna Vida, Nonoy Froilan, Agnes Locsin, Douglas Nierra, Jojo Lucila, Paul Morales, and Raul Alcoseba—to use their drive and training to reach still higher levels.

Philippine Dance Today. Three mainstreams of dance have emerged in the Philippines: the ethnic and traditional dances; stylized and theatricalized forms of these in which ethnic and folk elements are still recognizable; and contemporary choreographies using modern dance and classical ballet to express traditional or other themes.

There is a growing interest in the revival of authentic indigenous dances of the Philippines. Authentic dances are presented by such groups as the Baranggay Dance Group, Darangan Cultural Troupe, Maranao Sining Pananadem, Leyte Kalipayan Dance Company, Tambuli Cultural Dance Troupe of Ligaya Fernando Amilbangsa, Kayaw Group of the Montanosas, and the Ramon Obusan Folkloric Group. Philippine folk festivals are held annually throughout the country, with the ethnic communities of the islands presenting their indigenous dances. Outstanding among these are the Philippine Folk Festival, the Pang-alay, which has been held at the Folk Arts Center every July since 1979, as well as the Kaamulan, Sinulog, and Dinagyang festivals.

PHILIPPINES. Members of Reynaldo Gamboa Alejandro's Philippine Dance Company of New York, with Melinda Acaac and Eddie Sese at center, in "Sayaw sa Bangko" (Bench Dance). (Photograph courtesy of Reynaldo Gamboa Alejandro.)

The Bayanihan Philippine Dance Company and similar folk dance companies keep alive ethnic materials and themes in stylized, theatrical interpretations that vary in their degree of departure from the original movements and costumes. [*See* Bayanihan Philippine Dance Company.] The Filipinescas Dance Company became moribund, but folk dancing as staged by Filipinescas and then by Bayanihan renewed interest in traditional dance. Francisca Reyes Aquino recorded and codified folk dances beginning in the 1920s. Leonor Orosa Goquingco stylized it, and Bayanihan popularized it. Now the cycle has returned to Aquino, as more and more authentic dances are demanded. Some dance repertories now contain many of the movements originally recorded by Aquino or more recently by Ramon Obusan.

The Bayanihan Philippine Dance Company was established in 1957 by Lucrecia Reyes Urtula, who acted as director and choreographer. After its success at the Brussels Exposition in 1958, it became the country's top folkloric company. Today, dance groups abound, most of them affiliated with schools and universities. The Baranggay Folk Dance Group, Far Eastern University Folk Dance Group, University of the Philippines Filipiniana Dance Company, University of the East Dance Company, Leyte Filipiniana Dance Troupe (now known as Kalipayan Dance Company), Fiesta Filipino Dance Troupe, and Ramon Obusan Folkloric Group, have presented works abroad and gained several distinctions and awards. The Philippine Dance Company of New York, founded in 1943 by Bruna P. Seril, and the Filipiniana Dance Company of Hawaii, founded by Ines V. Cayaban, are pioneers in the preservation and presentation of Filipino dance abroad.

A number of companies are encouraging contemporary choreographers in the production of dance pieces combining the modern dance idiom, classical ballet technique, and indigenous dance. Works using ethnic movements and themes include Alice Reyes's *Dugso, Amada, Rama-Hari,* and *Tales of the Manuvu;* Basilio's *Tropical Tapestry, La Lampara,* and *Awit;* Antonio Fabella's *Semana Santa Limang Dipa* and *Ang Kasal;* Eddie Elejar's *Juru-Pakal* and *Kapinangan;* Felicitas L. Radaic's *Tanan;* Julie Borromeo's *Zagala de Manila, Kalingan,* and *Babae at Lalake;* Corazon Generoso Inigo's *Lam-ang, Sisa,* and *Gabriela;* Gener Caringal's *Ang Sultan, Vinta,* and *Filipino Komiks;* Radaic and Borromeo's *Mir-inisa* (the first version); Agnes Locsin's *Igorot, Bagobo,* and *Encantada;* Eric V. Cruz's *Mir-inisa;* Denisa Reyes's *Siete Dolores, For the Gods,* and *Diablos;* and, abroad, Reynaldo Alejandro's *Sayaw Silagan* dance series and the *Bagong Salta* dances, as well as choreographic pieces by Enrico Labayen and Aleluia Panis in San Francisco.

In the classical ballet and modern idioms there are currently five major companies: Ballet Philippines, Philippine Ballet Theater, Ballet Manila, Chameleon Dance Company, and University of the Philippines Dance Company. The most active are Ballet Philippines and Philippine Ballet Theater, which produce classical ballets and contemporary modern dances as well as works with folk themes created by local choreographers. They have mounted such Western classical works as *La Bayadère, Giselle, Swan Lake,* and *The Nutcracker* and have periodically invited foreign guest artists, teachers, and choreographers to their companies.

Research and Development. Dance, above all other arts, has gained international acclaim for the Philippines. This would not have happened were it not for two pioneers, Francisca Reyes Aquino and Leonor Orosa Goquingco. Aquino pioneered in the research and revival of Philippine folk dance and music in the 1920s and is recognized as the foremost authority in this field. A National Artist in Dance, she founded the University of the Philippines Folk Song and Dance Troupe.

Leonor Orosa Goquingco, a former pupil of Francisca Aquino and Luva Adameit, lifted folk dance to artistic and creative levels and made use of Filipino folklore in creating new dances to express the Filipino experience. Founder and choreographer of the Filipinescas Dance Company, she is credited with many innovations in Philippine dance, considered audacious when introduced but now generally followed by Philippine dance troupes, who are often unaware of Goquingco's contributions.

Francisca Reyes Aquino's eight books on the dance of the Philippines, considered by many the "bible" of Philippine dance, stimulated further studies and documentation in the field. The results included Libertad Fajardo's three-volume *Visayan Folk Dances* (1961–1975), the *Bureau of Public Schools' Philippine Folk Dances and Songs* (1966), and Ramon Obusan's unpublished work *Philippine Folkloric Dances* [n.d.] on tribes throughout the country. Related fields are also being researched. Reynaldo Alejandro's *Philippine Dance* (1978) provides a historical survey, a first in Philippine dance literature. *The Dances of the Emerald Isles* (1980) by Leonor Orosa Goquingco looks at the beginnings of Philippine dance in communities, taking a historico-anthropological approach. Jovita Sison Friese's *Philippine Folk Dances from Pangasinan* (1980) touches on the traditional dances of the province of Pangasian, and Juan C. Miel's *Samar Folk Dance* (1979) discusses the development of the Cultural Center of the Philippines Dance Company, now Ballet Philippines. Lucrecia Reyes Urtula's *The First Philippine Folk Festival* (1981) documents indigenous dances throughout the country. Ligaya Fernando Amilbangsa's *Pangalay Traditional Dances and Related Folk Artistic Expressions* (1983) examines the dances of Sulu and Tawi-Tawi in the south.

Master's theses such as Petronilla S. Suarez's "A Collection of Unpublished Folk Dances from the Province of Iloilo" (1971) and Gloria V. Cabahug's "A Study of Fundamental Characteristics of Some Philippine Folk Dances" are being encouraged in universities. Ramon Obusan's as yet unpublished dances, which were documented among ethnic groups throughout the country, are being mounted and performed.

With the advent of video documentation, more dance works are being filmed, with productions ranging from the Cultural Center of the Philippines' *Sayaw: A Documentary and Essay on Philippine Dance* (1989–1993) to local dances by the ethnic communities. The first Filipino certified dance notator, Basilio Esteban Villaruz, is also a noted choreographer, dance critic, and writer, and head of the dance degree program at the College of Music of the University of the Philippines.

Many contemporary dance works in the Philippines have expressed the Filipino soul, but there remains a need for the development and teaching of a technical vocabulary for this expression. Francisca Reyes Aquino's contribution helped tremendously in revealing many aspects of the roots of Phlippine dance. With the publication of the *Cultural Center of the Philippines Encyclopedia of Philippine Arts* (1994), edited by Nicanor Tiongson, many of these materials have been consolidated.

Thanks to the efforts of dedicated dance historians and scholars, research and documentation continue. Conscientious choreographers have read and used these materials as starting points for their works, sometimes in ballet and modern dance; however, these two eloquent means of expression have remained basically Western, not yet adapted to the Filipino physique and temperament. The creation of a national idiom awaits the establishment of a national school with government patronage and the development of a concentrated training program. The beginnings are seen in the dance degree program of the College of Music, University of the Philippines, which has its own active dance company. A similar offering has just begun as a collaboration between La Salle University and Ballet Philippines. One can hope that with joint efforts by choreographers, composers, educators, and researchers, new avenues will be explored.

[*See also* Bayanihan Philippine Dance Company.]

BIBLIOGRAPHY

Alejandro, Reynaldo Gamboa. "Sayaw Silangan: The Dance in the Philippines." *Dance Perspectives,* no. 51 (Autumn 1972).

Alejandro, Reynaldo Gamboa. *Philippine Dance: Mainstream and Crosscurrents.* Quezon City, 1978.

Andin, Carmen T. "State of the Arts in Dance Ethnology Research in the Philippines." In *Manila International Dance Conference.* Manila, 1991.

Blair, E. H., and James Alexander Robertson, eds. *The Philippine Islands, 1493–1803.* 55 vols. Cleveland, 1903–1909.

Bureau of Public Schools' Philippine Folk Dances and Songs. Manila, 1966.

Fajardo, Libertad V. *Visayan Folk Dances.* 3 vols. Rev. ed. Manila, 1964–1975.

Fernandez, Doreen G., and Rudy Vidad. *In Performance.* Quezon City, 1981.

Fernando-Amilbangsa, Ligaya. *Pangalay: Traditional Dances and Related Folk Artistic Expressions.* Manila, 1983.

Forman, Kathleen. "Dancing on the Endangered List." *Dance Connection* 13.3 (1995): 25–30.

Goquingco, Leonor Orosa. *The Dances of the Emerald Isles.* Quezon City, 1980.

Laconico-Buenaventura, Cristina. "The Theaters of Manila, 1846–1946: A Venue for Dance." In *Manila International Dance Conference.* Manila, 1991.

Ness, Sally Ann. "The Tinderas of Opon and Cebu: Exploring Relationships between Dance Style and Social Organization." *Philippine Quarterly of Culture and Society* 13 (1985): 71–84.

Ness, Sally Ann. *Body, Movement, and Culture: Kinesthetic and Visual Symbolism in a Philippine Community.* Philadelphia, 1992.

Reyes Aquino, Francisca. *Philippine Folk Dances.* 6 vols. Quezon City, 1953–1975.

Reyes Tolentino, Francisca. *Philippine National Dances.* New York, 1946.

Reyes Urtula, Lucrecia. *The First Philippine Folk Festival: A Retrospective.* Manila, 1981.

Villaruz, Basilio Esteban S. "Catalabutte's Equivocal Calls to Manille, or, The French-Filipino Connection in the Dance." In *Manila International Dance Conference.* Manila, 1991.

Villaruz, Basilio Esteban S. "Historical Essays." In *Encyclopedia of Philippine Art.* Manila, 1994.

REYNALDO GAMBOA ALEJANDRO

PHOTOGRAPHY. This daguerreotype of Irish-born courtesan and dancer Lola Montez (Eliza Gilbert), one of dance photography's first big stars, conveys something of her beauty, if not her unlimited nerve. With a genius for publicity-generating scandal, Montez became famous as a Spanish dancer, despite an almost total lack of technique, training, or talent. Among her many lovers was King Ludwig I of Bavaria; their affair led to his abdication in 1848. (Photograph 1851 by Meade Brothers, New York.)

PHOTOGRAPHY. Although still photography is powerless to preserve the most important element of dancing—continuity of movement—it can summon up the mood or energy of a dance, or document technique, physique, personality, choreographic figures, and production details. Some photographs attempt to convey this information without even showing dancers. As the photographer-heroine of the 1943 movie *No Time for Love,* Claudette Colbert presents her perplexed editor with prints of shadow patterns and curtain rigging in fulfillment of her assigned photo essay, "Backstage at the Ballet." "Not a sign of a dancer in tights," he moans. "Not a leg, not even a foot." His complaint could be leveled at Barbara Morgan's portrait of the Noguchi set for *Frontier,* a 1935 solo by Martha Graham, in which one sees merely a diagonal of rope angled between two spots of light, like a string on a bow slung over the breast of an Amazon. There is no sign of a dancer, but much is suggested about boundaries, firmness of purpose, the tension between the frontierswoman's exploratory vigor and indwelling maternity—essential themes of that dance.

This article focuses primarily on theatrical dance in Europe and the United States, using photographic material from U.S. repositories, principally the indispensable and wide-ranging holdings in the Dance Collection of the New York Public Library for the Performing Arts. A comprehensive history of dance photography worldwide remains to be written.

The Nineteenth Century. The earliest theatrical dance images on record date from the 1850s, a decade coincident with the origins of fashion photography. (Perhaps owing to a mutual interest in stylization of the body, these two genres have enjoyed an intimate, unbroken relationship to this day.) Since the amount of time then needed to expose photographic plates to record an image was considerable—twenty to forty seconds in 1842 and only a bit less ten years later—the images were invariably portraits. Two half-length daguerreotypes of Lola Montez, owned by the Harvard Theater Collection, show her seated with a shawl (c.1851), but most of the dance images that post-date these portraits frame the dancer's entire figure.

Several photographs of Lucile Grahn from the early 1850s show her in moments from the second act of *Giselle,* costumed as a Wili beside Giselle's grave. In one image, her arms are crossed on her breast and her right foot is pointed in *tendu croisé en avant.* In another image, her left hand gently points to the cross while her left foot stretches backward in an echoing *tendu croisé en arrière.* If these were not actual steps from a stage production, they embody attempts to evoke the appropriate style. (The attempts were more likely Grahn's than the photographer's. During the mid-nineteenth century, it was common for theatrical performers to provide their own costumes at the photographic studio and adopt poses to go with them.) In the first picture, Grahn looks directly at the camera; it is a photograph about a performer. In the second picture she looks in the direction of her gesture; it is a photograph about a role.

PHOTOGRAPHY. Emma Livry, in a studio portrait by Nadar, c.1859, one of several poses he shot in the same session. (Photograph from the archives of the Paris Opera Ballet.)

The first dance photograph by a well-known photographer is among the finest theatrical portraits of the era: a shot by Nadar (Félix Tournachon) of the seventeen-year-old Paris Opera ballerina Emma Livry (c.1859). Livry wears her enormous bacchante tutu from Félicien David's opera *Herculaneum,* with pendant earrings, ropes of pearls, and a small tiger-skin sash. She stands gazing downward meditatively, her long, homely face tilted to one side, hands clasped *en bas,* her right foot crossed over her left. Without partner, props, or surrounding set, Livry's figure seems trapped in psychological as well as spatial isolation. Nadar's lighting has caused shadows to form at her inner eyelids and at one corner of her mouth; her complex features make a dramatic contrast with the brilliant sheen of her satin slippers, whose texture and shape the light clinically delineates. Embedded in this image is the myth of the ballerina as a woman who sacrifices her life for her career. The portrait anticipates the legends of Anna Pavlova, Garbo's dancer in the film *Grand Hotel* (1932), and Victoria Page in the film *The Red Shoes* (1948). The camera angle also reveals much about Livry as a classical dancer. It enunciates the considerable turnout of her crossed leg and the attractive line of her slender calf and ankle; the tip of the crossed foot slightly presses against the floor, showcasing the excellent height and flexibility of the arch. To appreciate the scope of Nadar's achievement here, both in terms of artistry and dance information, one should consult other contemporary images of Livry, especially those of her in her *Herculaneum* costume, such as Disdéri's photographic portrait and the placid lithograph by Marie-Alexandre Alophe. Nadar photographed other dancers, among them Mistinguett (Jenne-Marie Bourgeois), Marie Petipa (Marius's first wife), and La Goulue (Louise Weber) in a split. During the 1850s, Nadar's brother, Adrien Tournachon, also made several exquisite portraits of the mime Charles Deburau, immortalized by Jean-Louis Barrault's role in the film *Les Enfants du Paradis* (Children of Paradise, 1944).

The goal of much nineteenth-century photography was to render the most realistic likeness of a subject possible. Nadar's genius was to illuminate both the corporeal and spiritual aspects of his sitters. Most photographers of dancers, however, settled for representing only the body. The most famous craftsman of this kind was André Adolph-Eugène Disdéri. In 1854 in France, Disdéri patented a format for making small collodion-print portraits, eventually called *cartes de visite,* owing to their similarity in size to visiting cards (4 by 2.5 inches). With the new method, the photographer could fit eight views of a subject seriatim on one negative, reducing the expense of processing the prints.

The *cartes de visite* photographs coincided with techni-

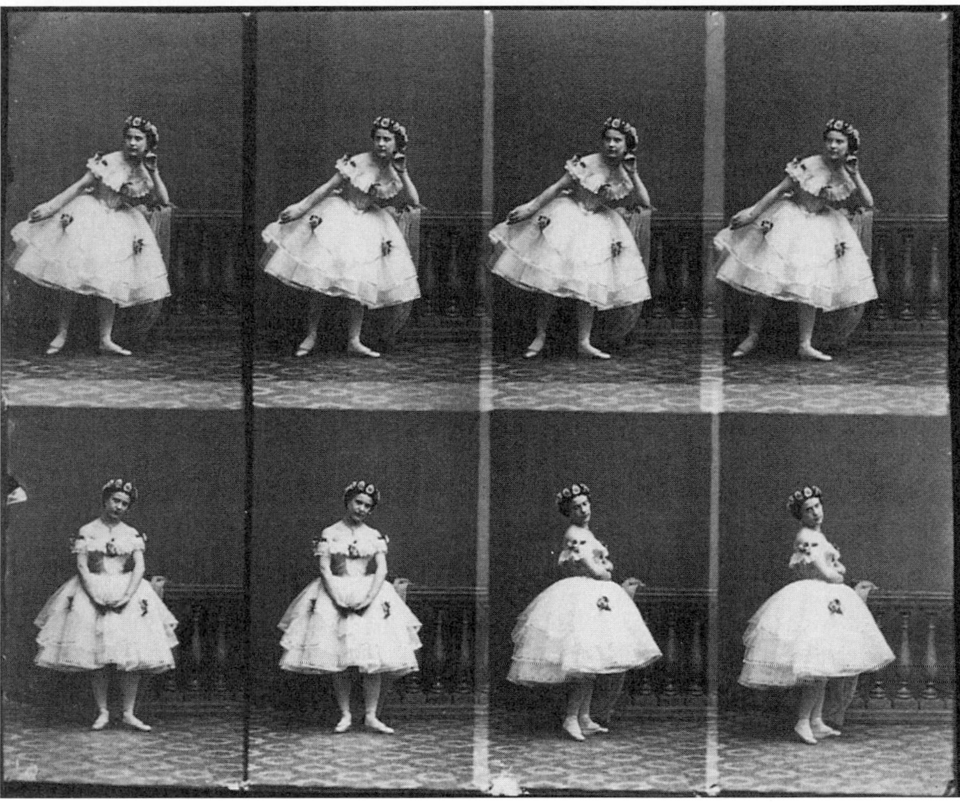

PHOTOGRAPHY. An uncut sheet of *carte de visite* photographs of Fanny Cerrito, by André-Adolphe-Eugène Disdéri, c.1885. (Photograph from the collection of the International Museum of Photography at George Eastman House, Rochester, New York.)

cal progress of another kind. In 1855 the first retouched photographs were exhibited in Paris, and during the 1860s the anastigmatic lens was introduced, capable of unprecedented clarity (which further encouraged the practice of retouching in the cases of most clients). By the early 1860s, Disdéri himself had photographed both the dramatic Russian ballerina Marie Petipa and her Saint Petersburg rival, the virtuoso Marfa Muravieva, who made her debut as Giselle at the Paris Opera in 1863. Among his European clients was Fanny Cerrito, photographed in her mid-forties in a Romantic tutu and pointe shoes, feet planted in what appears to be a moment of mime. He also served many dancers whose names mean little to us now. (During the 1940s, Joseph Cornell resurrected some of Disdéri's dance portraits in the context of his collages, his boxes in homage to the ballet, and his layouts for the magazine *Dance Index.*)

A group of several hundred *cartes de visite* photographs in the Harvard Theater Collection gives an idea of what average nineteenth-century ballet and theater dancers looked like. Notwithstanding their physical imperfections by present-day standards, quite a few of the subjects were obviously proud of their highly arched feet, showing them off in *tendu* or low attitude and, for the stronger dancers, on full pointe. Nearly everyone looks directly at the camera, whether photographed by Disdéri, Sarony in New York, or photographers in Newport, Saint Louis, Pittsburgh, Philadelphia, or Cincinnati. (In Manhattan alone during the 1860s and 1870s, there were at least a dozen theatrical photographers located between 400 and 800 Broadway, a neighborhood still marked by rehearsal studios and costume/novelty shops.)

Performers from the U.S. productions of *The Black Crook* and *The White Fawn* are liberally represented in their often abundant flesh. One finds, too, remarkable individuals: a one-legged dancer, a male transvestite dancer, a dancer identified as "Miss Fitzsimmons" of whom it is noted that she "died on the steps of Harvard Atheneum by freezing." Yet rarely is one struck by any rapport between the subjects and the photographers. By contrast, shots of Danish dancers taken about the same time achieve an unparalleled effect of composure and intimacy. The Danes may have been more talented or simply more comfortable with the circumstances under which the photographs were taken. This grace persists in photographs of Danish dancers taken during the early 1900s, such as those made in England of the ballerina Adeline Genée.

By the 1870s, photography was moving toward an impression of action. Portraits began to look less rigid, and dancers were being placed in more stressful arrangements. A print from 1870, for example, shows Marie Bonfanti in a fish-dive pose with a male partner. In Russian photographs of the period, the dancers look confident and controlled while executing difficult poses. As early as

1865, Vassily Geltser was photographed squatting on one leg in a moment from his role as Ivanushka in *The Little Humpbacked Horse* at the Bolshoi Theater. If he did use a brace to support himself (similar to the ones that Anna Pavlova is known to have used in—and directed to be painted out of—her studio pictures) such an object is nowhere in evidence. One might compare Geltser's camerawise image to the well-known, undated photographic portrait (thought to be from the same period) of America's classic *danseur,* George Washington Smith, in *tendu.* Here, the support that helped Smith to balance for the length of the exposure time is quite visible.

In 1877, the English-born photographer Eadweard Muybridge (who worked in the United States for most of his life) took a series of photographs of a famous California racehorse, named Occident, trotting. Twelve cameras, each two feet apart, were set on a twenty-two-foot section of the track. Silken strands attached to the shutters were triggered by the horse as it rounded the course. Each negative had been exposed for less than one-thousandth of a second, and the prints caught such details of motion as particles of dust flying from the horse's hooves. (It also proved that, at one point in the trot, the horse did have all four hooves in the air, thereby settling an age-old argument of perception.) Over the next few years, Muybridge refined his technique, reducing the exposure time for a single frame to one five-thousandth of a second. He is best known for his photographic series of human and animal actions shot outdoors in broad sunlight—sixteen instants in the act of a sneeze, a run, and so on. The linked images look like filmstrips, and by 1887 Muybridge had invented a device (the zoopraxiscope) to show them in sequence, an antecedent of the motion picture projector. Only a small fraction of Muybridge's series shows dance movements, but the importance of his work for dance photography has been incalculable. He demonstrated that all movement naturally conforms to a narrative of physical action—with beginnings, middles or climaxes, and endings—and he made the uniform illumination of a being in action a major criterion of technical photographic excellence.

Muybridge's influence stretches from his time to ours. In 1882 an admirer of Muybridge's work, the French physiologist Étienne-Jules Marey, invented a camera that could superimpose a series of consecutive exposures on a single plate, so that the viewer saw the entire story of a movement in a single frame. (The American painter Thomas Eakins, a friend of Muybridge, developed a similar process.) During the 1940s, *Life* photographer Gjon Mili produced both Marey-like superimpositions and brilliantly lit individual views of peak dance movements, thanks to a stroboscopic electronic flash with the incredible exposure time of one hundred-thousandth to one-millionth of a second (invented by MIT's world-renowned Harold E. Edgerton).

Both Muybridge and Marey were important forerunners, if not direct influences, on the postimpressionist and futurist painters, whose images of dance have had enormous impact on the way subsequent artists, photographers, and audiences would perceive the art. It is virtually certain that Marey's photographic superimpositions contributed to the manner in which the can-can dancers line up in Seurat's *Le Chahut* (1889/90), and Marey's "chron-

PHOTOGRAPHY. *First Ballet Action,* plate 369 from Eadweard Muybridge's *Animal Locomotion,* 1887, shows a crudely executed *grand rond de jambe* viewed, as it almost never would be in the theater, from behind. Here, as in many of his nude studies, Muybridge drew a line in each frame to emphasize the curve and twist of the spine. (Photograph from the collection of the International Museum of Photography at George Eastman House, Rochester, New York.)

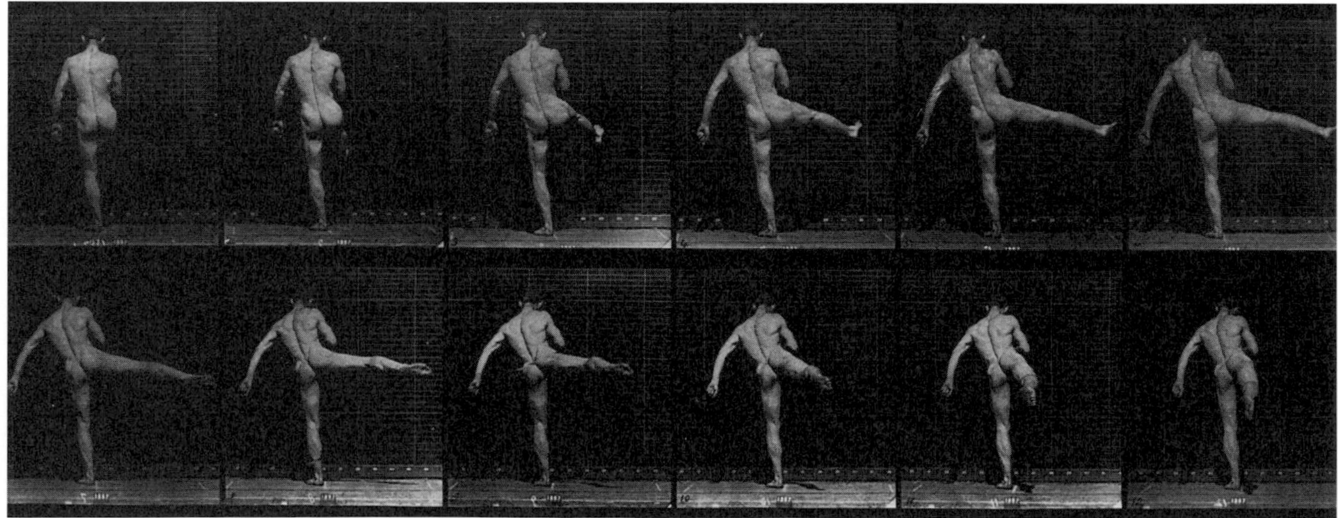

PHOTOGRAPHY. *(above) Measuring the Speed of a Swordthrust by Means of Photochronography,* an image created c.1890 by Étienne-Jules Marey, a pioneer in the use of multiple exposures to record movement. (Photograph from the journal *La nature,* 11 October 1890.)

PHOTOGRAPHY. *(below) Double Jump,* a gelatin-silver print by Thomas Eakins made in 1884, shows another solution to the problem of how to capture motion through still photography, also addressed by Muybridge and Marey. (Photograph from the Franklin Institute, Philadelphia.)

ophotography" seems detectable in Gino Severini's *Dancer at the Bal Tabarin* (1912) and Marcel Duchamp's *Nude Descending a Staircase No. 2.* Muybridge's photographs of racehorses had a profound effect on the paintings of Edgar Degas: the poet Paul Valéry conjectured that Degas's *Scène de Ballet* and *Le Pas Battu*—probably the only canvases in his oeuvre to show *danseuses* in action with both legs off the ground—more than coincidentally date from the time that Muybridge's "instantaneous" photographs were first published in Paris (1879). Degas deliberately overexposed photographs of ballet dancers during the 1890s, but his interest in these quiet, classical studies was mood, tonal range, and sculptural pose—the dancer as ideal—and this was also the focus of his late paintings.

Publicity, souvenir, and amateur photography of dancers also flourished by the century's end. In 1883, Benjamin Falk photographed the entire cast of *A Russian Honeymoon* on the stage of New York's Madison Square Theater, the first time a full setting and cast of a theatrical production was photographed in a scene from an actual performance, as the audience would have observed them.

PHOTOGRAPHY. A partially solarized study of a ballerina, attributed to painter Edgar Degas, c.1895. (Photograph from the collection of the Bibliothèque National, Paris.)

The shot used one long series of electric lights for illumination and an exposure of a half minute; it had required two hours to pose. Soon, the casts of large dance productions, such as *Excelsior* (photographed by Taber in San Francisco), were posing for photocalls. By 1895, printing techniques for halftones had advanced so far that these pictures were appearing alongside stories in newspapers. Dance photographs were also widely used on cigarette cards, covers of sheet music, postcards, and in memento volumes. In Russia, where the postcards were very popular, it was not unusual for fans to be able to secure several views of a favorite dancer in each new role. Cast photographs were also used in the lavish annuals published by Russian imperial theaters. The examples that have survived from the 1892 *Nutcracker* exhibit a sense of fantasy and beauty unmatched by U.S. cast scenes.

The United States, meanwhile, was becoming intoxicated with efficiency and speed. By 1900 more than one hundred thousand of Kodak's Brownie cameras ("You press the button, we do the rest.") were in the hands of amateurs. Weekend anthropologists, adventurers, and explorers, who once had to rely on written accounts or artists' illustrations of the exotic life, could now capture living moments from their travels.

Much of the nineteenth century's photographic record of ethnic dance was compiled from such slivers of time: Native American dances are among the notable subjects. It is ironic in this context that the most famous photographs of tribal dance are those of the idealistic professional, Edward S. Curtis. In his recognition of cultures on the edge of extinction, Curtis carefully staged the facts of a ritual, sometimes going so far as to build deliberate inaccuracies into the movement, if the effect more clearly revealed to the camera his concept of the true spirit in the fleeting gestures of "a vanishing race."

The Twentieth Century. In 1903 Bert Williams and George Walker, the now legendary team of black American vaudevillians, produced a hit show on Broadway called *In Dahomey.* One photograph of a dance scene catches a parade of the leads and their two companions (Walker's wife, Ada Overton Walker, and Williams's wife, Lottie Williams) in various stages of taking a step. The facial expressions are expansive, implying full use of muscles around the cheeks and forehead. The postures, muscle tone, and stress on the fabric portray the instantaneous aspect of motion. One senses how much fun these performers must have conjured, how lively their smiles were, how communicative their mouths and eyes. Seeping through the fuzzy outlines is the chemistry of stardom.

Although this anonymous photograph is technically mediocre—it may have been made from a frame of motion picture film—it has a straightforward, inquiring charm that marks it as a pre–World War I image. From Lewis Hine's tired breaker boys to Jacques Henri-

PHOTOGRAPHY. George Walker, Ada Overton Walker, and Bert Williams in a scene from their Broadway hit *In Dahomey* (1903). In their choreography, Walker and Williams tried to incorporate steps they had seen performed by Dahomean dancers at the San Francisco Winter Fair. Among the most highly paid teams in theater at the peak of their career, they paved the way for many other African-American dancers. (Photograph by Hall, New York; from the Frank Driggs Collection.)

Lartigue's boyish scene of race-car tires, documentary photographs from the Belle Époque (c.1895 to 1914) have a distinctive freshness and an unstudied detachment. In dance photography, one gets remarkably unsentimental views of popular entertainment: vaudeville, cabaret, street performing, cakewalks, can-cans, and "animal dances." The most astonishing sights are casually framed together; conversely, certain natural qualities, especially indications of speed or wind or gravitational force, look almost surreal. Even a century later, the photographs of Théodore Rivére from the 1890s of Loie Fuller rehearsing outdoors, with her frothy bolts of China silk roiling upward into the sunny sky, retain some of the magic that the dancer bestowed on her audiences.

A similar quality also clings to the most important photograph we have of Isadora Duncan's dancing—the mid-motion view of her taken about 1904 by her brother, Raymond, at the Theater of Dionysus on the Acropolis in Athens. Seen in profile against the half-ruined stone bleachers, Duncan is placed high on the ball of her right foot, the left foot having risen into a low, turned-in attitude. Her right arm stretches out before her, and her left arm stretches directly behind, echoing the horizontal line of the raised calf. The momentum of her action seems to carry her body irresistibly forward, yet she is centrally poised thanks to the counterbalance of her head, which falls backward with a free strength. That this dynamic image of motionless motion is unposed makes a good case for the dancer's genius and her successful internalization of the principles of ancient Greek art. To estimate the importance of this picture, one has only to look at the countless photographs taken during the 1910s and 1920s of women flinging their lightly clothed bodies into dance, without any suggestion of Duncan's dynamism or equilibrium. Indeed, the same might be said of other photographs of Duncan and her disciples. In 1921, Duncan and one of her adopted daughters, Maria-Theresa, returned to the Acropolis with Edward Steichen, who recorded them making grand gestures among the columns. The images are glorious, full of formal drama and play of scale. They describe the dramatic plasticity that Rodin recognized in Duncan. But they also intimate much less about her dancing.

The representation of movement transitions, like the one captured by Raymond Duncan, did not become routine in dance photography until the 1950s. Most of the

PHOTOGRAPHY. Isadora Duncan in the Theater of Dionysus on the Acropolis in Athens, photographed by her brother Raymond, c.1904. (Photograph from the Dance Collection, New York Public Library for the Performing Arts.)

widely prized dance photographs from the first half of this century show dancers in poses assumed for the camera. They are great images because the dancers who served as their subjects knew how to make themselves interesting to the eye. They are great photographs because of their technique—their texture, composition, their relationship between subject matter and formal patterns, and their beauty as pictures—rather than their fidelity as records. A case in point is the celebrated album of thirty-three prints devoted to Nijinsky's ballet *L'Après-midi d'un Faune* that Baron Adolf de Meyer made about 1912. Contemporary photographs by Auguste Bert and Waléry of the same ballet show the bodies of all the dancers, most especially Nijinsky, to be tenser, stiffer, more stylized than in de Meyer's work. Not a single image in the de Meyer volume represents that rigorously pulled-in chin and iron neck one finds on Nijinsky in Bert's scene of the Faun's meeting with the chief Nymph. But de Meyer's imagination would not have easily empathized with that particular aspect of Nijinsky's style. Instead, his photographs, masterfully retouched to suggest etchings of bas-reliefs, heighten values one finds in other de Meyer photographs—classic archetypes, idle hours, youth, exquisite illumination, sensuality, and the use of costume as a sign of taste.

Also prized are Arnold Genthe's twenty-four studies of Isadora Duncan, taken during her tours of the United States between 1915 and 1918, and published after her death. Genthe, a San Francisco photographer known for his views of Japan (thanks to an appreciative essay by Sadakichi Hartmann), was accounted a friend by Duncan; he took many photographs of her, both in toga and in street clothes, and of those close to her. Duncan paid Genthe the compliment of saying that one of his photographs—probably a deeply shadowed portrait of her face—had penetrated her "soul." She may have meant that he caught her completely off guard. Genthe (1920) considered it "a principle which I have religiously adhered to: Never to permit the sitter to be conscious of the exact moment when the picture was being taken. Only in this manner, I felt, something of the real personality could be recorded by the camera." Genthe's lighting—soft-focus, like de Meyer's but far less sophisticated in its delineation of the body's surfaces—makes for a rather

PHOTOGRAPHY. Vaslav Nijinsky in *L'Après-midi d'un Faune* in 1914, photographed by Baron Adolf de Meyer. Designer Cecil Beaton called de Meyer "the Debussy of photographers." (Photograph from the collection of the Washburn Gallery, New York.)

murky record on Duncan's physicality while creating a memorable impression of her presence. He took photographs of many other dancers, among them Anna Pavlova, who assumed some poses identical to Duncan's. He did sneak in one true candid photograph of Pavlova moving—a prize, since she always attempted to be in control of her studio shots. This, too, is dark, but it captures the dancer's impassioned energy. Pavlova said she liked it very much.

Both de Meyer and Genthe can be grouped with the pictorial movement in photography, which attempted to impart to the photograph the values and images of nineteenth-century studio art. In contrast, Soichi Sunami, esteemed for his photographs of Ruth St. Denis and Martha Graham, abandoned a career as a modernist painter to pursue photography. There is no soft focus in his images: they are characterized by slashing lines, soaring planes, projected shadows so startling in outline one thinks of Russian futurism or German expressionism. The photographs are also essays in gesture. He shows the dancer not as a moving sculpture but as a silent actor.

PHOTOGRAPHY. Anna Pavlova dancing for Arnold Genthe, c.1915. Genthe was very proud of this shot, claiming it to be the first picture ever taken of Pavlova in motion, rather than in a still pose. (Photograph from the collection of the Gillman Paper Company, New York.)

PHOTOGRAPHY. Agnes de Mille posed for this photograph by Soichi Sunami, entitled *After Degas—Ballet Class,* in 1928. (Photograph from the Dance Collection, New York Public Library for the Performing Arts.)

Trained as a retoucher for the studios of theatrical portrait photographer Nickolas Muray (who photographed dancers such as Fred Astaire), Sunami then pursued a career as a professional studio theatrical photographer. In that capacity, he is properly classed with James Abbe (famous for his backstage portraits of Pavlova), and with Émile Otto Hoppé (Ballets Russes), the White Studios (Denishawn), Maurice Seymour, Max Waldman, Herbert Migdoll, Jack Mitchell, and Kenn Duncan, rather than with innovative society and fashion photographers like de Meyer or portraitists like Genthe. But his style also links him to photographers such as Edward Steichen, George Platt Lynes, and Barbara Morgan, all of whom had unique visions about recording dancers on film.

Sunami's portraits of Martha Graham from the late 1920s are possibly his greatest achievement in the field. They show Graham trying out styles of presentation, lavishing care on the way her costumes show off her lean body, turning herself from an eclectic novice into a modernist choreographer. Between Graham's own sophistication before the camera (she took a class at Denishawn in how to pose for photographs) and Sunami's dramatic range of tones (gauze white to oubliette black), the images are among the most exciting theatrical portraits of the century to that time.

Meanwhile, advances in technology encouraged more documentary photographs of dancing, especially in Europe. In 1924, the German Ermanox camera was introduced to the public, making it possible to take pictures in low-level "available light." In 1925, Leica introduced the "miniature" 35-millimeter camera, permitting thirty-six negatives to be taken in rapid succession on a single loading of film. Was it a prototype of the Ermanox, for example, that allowed the London *Times* to make its famous photographs without flash powder or supplementary lighting during a performance in 1923? In September of that year, a *Times* photographer made twenty exposures (at one-tenth to one-fortieth of a second) of Anna Pavlova's company in *The Fairy Doll* at Covent Garden, a precedent for generations of stop-motion dance photographers.

In 1936, Merlyn Severn published an entire volume of such views, *Ballet in Action,* in which she compared photographing the ballet to going on a safari. Severn, whose collection represents the London ballet seasons of 1936 and 1937, was more concerned with dancers' energy than with their line, and many of the performers she recorded are seen at unflattering moments or from distorting angles. Her photographs do frequently show a pleasing arrangement of light and dark tones, and at least one of her pictures—a view from the wings, of three Nymphs seemingly swallowed up by darkness as they enter the stage during a production of Nijinsky's *L'Après-midi d'un Faune*—can stand comparison with de Meyer's perspective. Severn's importance was primarily as the pioneer of stop-motion dance photographers in England: Baron (Stirling Henry Nahum), the elegant Zoë Dominic (whose distribution of lights and darks recalls Severn's) and Leslie E. Spatt.

In the United States during the 1930s and 1940s, photographers were also working on location in the theater. The most original photographs were by Alexey Brodovitch, (moonlighting from his work as art director for *Harper's Bazaar*) for which his taste and judgment have become legendary standards of excellence. The images, taken backstage at the Ballet Russe de Monte Carlo, were published in 1945 in a book called *Ballet,* with an introductory essay by Edwin Denby. They directly contravened the prevailing standards of sharp focus and overall illumination, as set by Muybridge. Brodovitch's pictures, taken in stage lighting, are blurred, heavily shadowed, often difficult to make sense of at first. They zero in on apparently unimportant details, like the crook of a dancer's knee, or the sweat on a brow, yet the effects are surprisingly sensuous, vivid, and magical. Some of his photographs create very delicate puns on theatrical illusion and photographic reality: a two-page spread of two moments from George Balanchine's *Cotillon* appears as if it is one moment, showing a group of men diving into the arms of a female corps de ballet; in a moment from *Swan Lake,* stage lights rippling above the oceanic darkness of the floor also read as stars in the sky.

PHOTOGRAPHY. Jane Dudley, Sophie Maslow, and Frieda Flier in Martha Graham's *Celebration* (1934), with music by Louis Horst. (Photograph © 1937 by Barbara Morgan; used by permission of the Barbara Morgan Archives, Hastings-on-Hudson, New York.)

By and large, however, the best dance photographs—both posed and stop-motion—that were taken in the United States in this period were products of the studio. During the mid-1930s, the Hungarian-born photographer Martin Munkacsi was applying the rangy, light, joyful style of his *Harper's Bazaar* fashion photography to popular dancing, from Harlem's lindy hoppers to Ray Bolger. Munkacsi loved to see people extending themselves while jumping or running. (His influence has been acknowledged by such masters as Henri Cartier-Bresson and Richard Avedon.) He also seems to have remained unaffected by the 1930s tendency to steep theatrical imagery in chiaroscuro, so marked in the work of his international contemporaries, from the German photographers of Oskar Schlemmer's Bauhaus dances to the Hollywood portraitists who produced the heavily shadowed, highly influential publicity stills of Marlene Dietrich, Greta Garbo, and Joan Crawford. (In England, Gordon Anthony was virtually painting with shadow in his studio portraits of dancers from the Vic-Wells, notably the young Margot Fonteyn, photographed both in motion and posed.)

The other major U.S. photographer of dancers who entirely sidestepped film-noir effects prior to World War II was Thomas Bouchard. Based in New York City, Bouchard made silvery pictures of modern dancers in midmotion; his views of Doris Humphrey and her company are especially sensuous. Bouchard was known for the heroic quality with which he portrayed the moderns—usually arrived at by photographing them from a low angle—and for the finish of his prints, achieved, as one article about him put it, by "doing tricks to his film in the darkroom" so that he could photograph in low-level light without flash. Like Munkacsi and Brodovitch, he made images that remain startling and fresh, although they are rarely reproduced or discussed today.

Barbara Morgan and George Platt Lynes, the two giants of dance photography in the United States between the world wars, pursued chiaroscuro effects so sensitively that lighting, in their hands, became as subtle and expressive as language. Morgan, a painter by training, started taking dance photographs in 1935 "by accident," under the influence of her husband, Willard Morgan, who worked as a writer-photographer for *Life* magazine. She made her subject modern dance, producing individual midmotion studies as well as photomontages that incorporated dance images. The photographs for which she is most celebrated are her dance portraits of Martha Graham, taken in the studio, often using the Harold Edgerton strobe. Morgan knew well the choreography she photographed; before taking pictures, she would have passages in mind that conveyed, in her words, the "essential emotion . . . the intense reality of movement . . . the dance at its visual peak." Sometimes she would ask Graham or her dancers to pose in certain positions, but usually Graham would perform an entire passage preselected by Morgan, so that the image would come out of the dance. By "pre-visioning" the choreography, Morgan could plan her "lighting interpretations." An example of her virtuosity is her signature photograph of Graham as Emily Dickinson, pitched over in a spiral during *Letter to the World.* This stop-motion photograph, illuminated with synchroflash and speedlamps, is lightly but deliberately blurred in certain precisely determined areas, such as the hem of the skirt, to emphasize the sharp focus on hands and head, symbolic centers of the poet's inspiration. Other stop-motion dance photographers active during the 1940s, such as Lotte Jacobi and Gerda Peterich, produced arresting pictures, but their work as a whole missed the precision and visionary focus of Morgan's work.

George Platt Lynes came to photography from literature

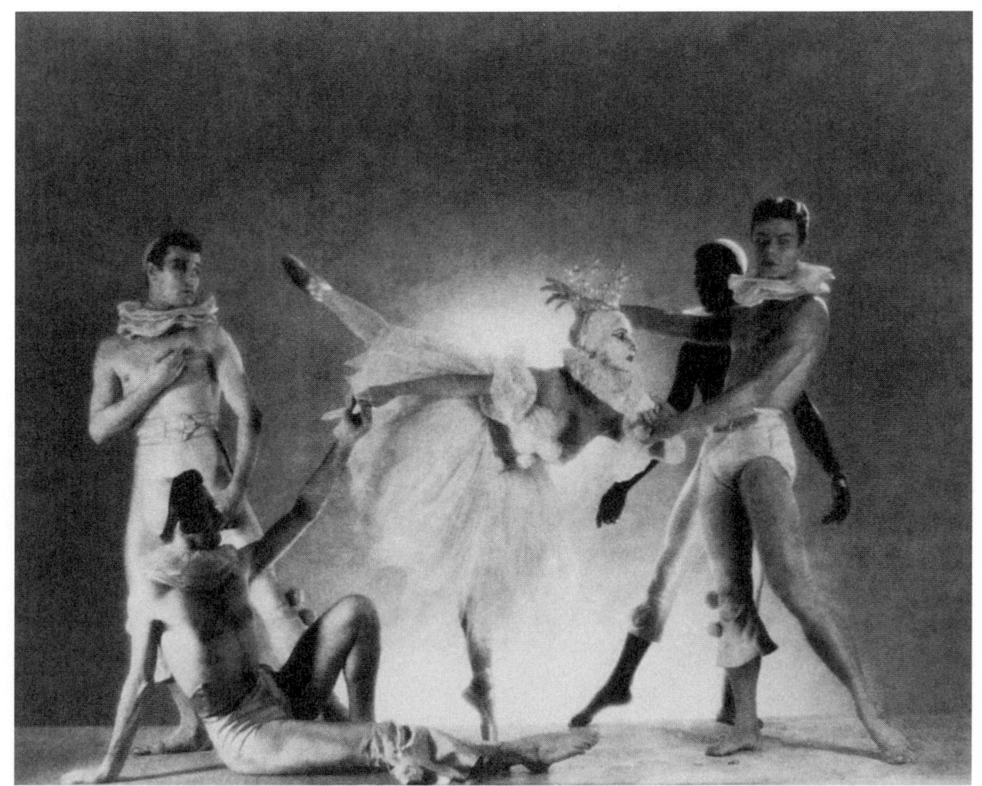

PHOTOGRAPHY. Tanaquil Le Clercq as Sacred Love, with other members of the New York City Ballet, in a study from George Platt Lynes's portfolio of studio photographs of Frederick Ashton's *Illuminations* (1950). The ballet, with costumes and sets by Cecil Beaton, was based on images from the poems of Arthur Rimbaud. (Photograph © by George Platt Lynes; used by permission.)

and art, and he came to dance photography from surrealism and fashion. From the mid-1930s until his death in 1955, he photographed the ballets of George Balanchine, having been invited to do so by his boyhood friend, Lincoln Kirstein. "I consider that George Platt Lynes synthesized better than anyone else the atmosphere of some of my ballets," one reads in a 1956 article signed by Balanchine. "They contain something of the secret and seldom realized intention of choreography; they are pure miniatures." For his part, Lynes treated this assignment with a professional's technique and an amateur's devotion. "I love dancing," he wrote in 1944, "and my idea has been to make prints which will perpetuate what I have seen as an adjunct to my own memory; and for those who have not seen it, a sort of substitute and consolation." Although Lynes's ballet photographs recall themes from elsewhere in his career, many of them were apparently true collaborations, with Balanchine arranging the dancers—and sometimes even clicking the shutter—while Lynes set up the elaborate, dramatic, and glorifying lighting. His most revered work, all posed, records *Orpheus* (in the clothed stage version and a nude studio version), *Errante, Firebird, Concerto Barocco, Renard,* and *Jones Beach.* Lynes's portfolio on Frederick Ashton's Rimbaud ballet, *Les Illuminations,* made for the New York City Ballet, is also considered a masterpiece of theatrical magic and psychological intensity. Lynes's closest rival in style was Britain's Cecil Beaton, also trained by fashion and surrealism, although Beaton's dance images miss both the vividness and the portentous intensity of Lynes's work.

PHOTOGRAPHY. John Travolta was caught in this disco move, soon copied on dance floors around the world, in a publicity still by Martha Swope for the Paramount Pictures film *Saturday Night Fever* in 1977. (Photograph by Martha Swope © Time, Inc.; used by permission.)

The early years of Ballet Theatre were captured by quite a few well-known photographers, including André Kertesz and Fred Fehl. (Fehl amassed a huge and distinguished portfolio of performance photography from many companies over forty years.) During this time, the music critic Carl Van Vechten was making charming studio portraits of Ballet Theatre stars and of dancers from many other companies and techniques.

During the 1950s, photographers from Cartier-Bresson to Garry Winogrand flocked to take stop-motion views of Balanchine and his dancers in class and in rehearsals. An outstanding chronicler of the company to emerge in the late 1950s was Martha Swope, then a young former School of American Ballet student. Her first assignment was to record the creation of *Agon,* with Balanchine and Stravinsky in attendance, and her views of dancers rehearsing and performing over the next two decades are regarded as among the most accurate and appealing documents of the act of dancing. Among her most famous images of popular dance is one of actor John Travolta, frozen in a jutting stance with an index finger outstretched overhead, used in the publicity campaign for the film *Saturday Night Fever* (1977).

Fine photographers of dancing have since emerged, but few of them have shown the combination of technique, personal vision, intensity, and persistence that would lead one to call their work major. In the United States, Paul Kolnik's images of New York City Ballet performing Balanchine works display a startling, almost religious perception of the dancing while conveying a remarkable amount of information about choreography and performance; the views of Balanchine ballets by Kostas are distinguished for their sensual appeal and quality of fantasy. James Klosty's documentary views of the Merce Cunningham company, mostly in rehearsal, are intimate and intellectual, like Cunningham's choreography. Lois Greenfield's studio collaborations with dancers, published regularly in the *Village Voice* and elsewhere, do not attempt to record moments from the stage; instead, they result in unique photographic images of graphic brilliance. During the 1980s, Paula Court became prominent for her anthropological coverage of the downtown New York scene, and Tom Brazil emerged as a trustworthy stop-action reporter of the same subject. During the 1990s, William Boorstein (a photographer trained in molecular biology) has produced vivid color images of modern dance, especially the José Limón company; in the spirit of Rivére, both Annie Liebowitz and Philip Trager have collaborated with postmodern dancers out of doors.

One can identify trends. The group of photographers identified with the Judson Church era—Peter Moore, Al Giese, Terry Schutte—veered between shooting dancers as if they were engaged in pedestrian activities on the street (no stylization of gesture, for example) and showing them impressionistically, with blurring used for a spiritual or hallucinogenic effect. By the early 1970s, however, New York–based photographers like Babette Mangolte and Nathaniel Tileston were giving over large amounts of an image to bare space, as if it were a positive aspect of the dance. Photography itself began to be scrutinized as a medium of signs and symbols. During the late 1970s and early 1980s, shows of dance photography were regularly organized in the United States and Europe. The English photographer Keith Money published books about the skater John Curry and Anna Pavlova that called attention to the way those performers were recorded and represented by the camera. Dancers themselves began to incorporate photography into their work. Photographers provided costume and scenic designs for choreographers, such as Robert Rauschenberg for Trisha Brown and Robert Mapplethorpe for Lucinda Childs, and choreographers like Amy Greenfield have studied such processes as holography.

The stage relationship between photography and dance has become increasingly intimate. Photography has affected the content of choreography and performance style. In Ashton's *Enigma Variations* and Kenneth MacMillan's *Isadora,* both historical ballets, characters have their pictures taken. In Jerome Robbins's *Dances at a Gathering,* the figures momentarily group themselves in such a way that we are meant to think of people posing for a photograph. Rudolph Nureyev's performance of Nijinsky's *L'Après-midi d'un Faune* with the Joffrey Ballet was obviously based on a study of the de Meyer portfolio. David Parsons's entire solo *Caught* is a virtual tribute to stop-action photography and the Edgerton strobe.

Perhaps the strongest onstage meld of dance and photography came in *The Photographer: Far From the Truth,* a 1983 multimedia production about Eadweard Muybridge that was developed by the Brooklyn Academy of Music. The last section, choreographed by David Gordon, plays on differences between the still image and the motion picture, making subtle equations between moments of stillness and action in dancing. Finally, the nationally popular dance form of the 1980s that was developed in New York City by gay black men—Vogueing—combines the walk of runway fashion models with instantaneous changes of pose that are associated with the shooting of fashion photographs for magazines such as *Vogue,* after which the dance was named.

PHOTOGRAPHY. Ashley Roland and Daniel Ezralow hover in undefined space in this shot, typical of the images photographer Lois Greenfield creates in collaboration with dancers in her studio. (Photograph © 1989 by Lois Greenfield; used by permission.)

Even the U.S. Court of Appeals has recognized the amount of information a dance photograph can convey. On 28 April 1986 the Second Circuit Court ruled that "still photographs of a ballet [in this case, Balanchine's *Nutcracker*] can infringe copyright on choreography for such ballet." In a digest of the court's opinion, published in *The United States Law Week,* we read:

> A snapshot of a single moment in a dance sequence may communicate a great deal. Given a photograph of a dancer with two feet off the stage, the viewer understands instinctively that the dancer jumped up from the floor only a moment earlier and came down shortly after the photographed moment. The single instant photographed thus communicates far more than a single chord of a Beethoven symphony—the analogy suggested by the district court.

Far from the truth, no doubt, but also near to the facts.

[*Works by many photographers mentioned herein appear throughout the encyclopedia. To locate these works, see index entries under names of photographers.*]

BIBLIOGRAPHY

Acocella, Joan. "Photo Call with Nijinsky: The Circle and the Center." *Ballet Review* 14 (Winter 1987): 49–71.

Ackerman, Gerald. "Photography and the Dance: Soichi Sunami and Martha Graham." *Ballet Review* 12 (Summer 1984): 32–66.

Anthony, Gordon. *Dancers to Remember.* London, 1980.
Brodovitch, Alexey. *Ballet: 104 Photographs.* Commentary by Edwin Denby. New York, 1945.
de Meyer, Baron Adolf. *L'Après-Midi d'un Faune, Vaslav Nijinsky, 1912: Thirty-Three Photographs.* New York, 1983.
Denby, Edwin. "Notes on Nijinsky Photographs." In *Nijinsky, Pavlova, Duncan,* edited by Paul Magriel. New York, 1977.
Ewing, William A. *Dance and Photography.* New York, 1987.
Fehl, Fred. *Great Stars of the American Ballet Theater.* New York, 1985.
Fehl, Fred. *Stars of the Ballet and Dance.* New York, 1985.
Fonteyn, Margot. *The Magic of Dance.* New York, 1979.
Genthe, Arnold. *The Book of the Dance.* Boston, 1920.
Greskovic, Robert. "Caught in Time." *Ballet News* 1 (October 1979): 28–31; 1 (November 1979): 33–34; 1 (January-February 1980): 30–31; 1 (May 1980): 24–25; 2 (April 1981): 26–28.
Jürgensen, Knud Arne (compiler and annotator). *The Bournonville Ballets: A Photographic Record 1844–1933.* London, 1987.
Kirstein, Lincoln. *The New York City Ballet.* Photographs by Martha Swope and George Platt Lynes. New York, 1973.
Kirstein, Lincoln. *Nijinsky Dancing.* New York, 1975.
Klosty, James. *Merce Cunningham.* New York, 1975.
Lindner, David. "Dance Photography Review: Martha Swope and George Platt Lynes; The International Center of Photography's Exhibit of Masters." *Dance Life* 4 (1979): 1–16.
Lynes, George Platt. *Ballet.* Pasedena, 1985.
Mili, Gjon. *Photographs and Recollections.* Boston, 1980.
Money, Keith. *Anna Pavlova: Her Life and Art.* New York, 1982.
Morgan, Barbara. *Martha Graham: Sixteen Dances in Photographs* (1941). Rev. ed. Dobbs Ferry, N.Y., 1980.
Muybridge, Eadweard. *Muybridge's Complete Human and Animal Locomotion: All 781 Plates from the 1887 Animal Locomotion.* 3 vols. New York, 1979.
Padgette, Paul. *The Dance Photography of Carl Van Vechten.* New York, 1981.
Severn, Merlyn. *Ballet in Action.* New York, 1938.
Tobias, Tobi. "The Photo as Memory." *Dance Magazine* 50 (December 1976): 50–67.
White, Nancy, and John Esten. *Style in Motion: Munkacsi Photographs of the 20s, 30s, and 40s.* New York, 1979.

ARCHIVES. Dance Collection, New York Public Library for the Performing Arts. Harvard University Theater Collection. International Center of Photography, New York. International Museum of Photography at George Eastman House, Rochester, N.Y. Museum of Natural History, New York. Museum of the City of New York. San Francisco Performing Arts Library and Museum. Theater Collection, University of Texas, Austin.

MINDY ALOFF

PHYSICS OF DANCE. Analytical techniques from classical mechanics, a traditional and well-developed area of physics, can be applied to dance movement to understand how the human body moves through space under the influence of forces in its environment. Balance, traveling jumps, rotational motions, and partnered lifts represent four categories of dance movement amenable to such analyses.

An analysis of balance involves techniques and mechanical processes used in maintaining, restoring, or destroying the condition of static balance. Nonrotating motions such as vertical or traveling jumps involve trajectories of bodies moving through space in one, two, or three dimensions under the influence of forces from gravity and the floor. Rotational motions can include turns around a vertical axis (pirouettes), angular oscillations of parts of the body such as the leg in the hip joint, and rotations around other axes as in some leaping turns. In movements carried out with a partner, an additional force—due to contact with the partner—makes the analysis more complex.

In most cases (except when a dancer is working with a barre or partner), earth's gravity and the floor are the only sources of force on the body from outside the dancer. The effects of these forces on the motion of the body follow from Newton's three laws of motion. One of these laws relates the acceleration of an object to the total force acting on it; another equates the force of one object on a second, such as that of a dancer against the floor, with the corresponding reaction force of the second object back on the first—the floor pushing back against the dancer.

These two of Newton's three laws can be applied to an analysis of static balance. A condition of balance exists if the center of gravity of the body, the point where earth's gravity appears to act on the body, lies on a vertical line passing through the area of support at the floor. If the center of gravity is slightly displaced, can the dancer move his or her body in such a way as to restore balance? The only manipulations of the body that are useful are those that result in the appropriate horizontal force between the dancer and the floor that moves the center of gravity back toward the balance condition.

Instincts work in this case. As in walking along a railroad track, if one starts to fall to the right, the instinctive reaction is for the upper body to bend quickly to the right. The resulting force of the feet against the rail (or floor) is also toward the right, a fact made clear if one considers an extreme case of a jackknifing movement to the right, and considers the direction the feet try to move. The corresponding equal and opposite force from the rail (floor) back on the body is directed to the left, and, since it is the only horizontal force acting on the body, it tends to move the body's center of gravity back to the left, toward the balance point. An attempt to restore balance (if falling to the right) by bending the upper body to the left—perhaps an intuitively logical approach—is counterproductive and actually increases the tendency to topple off balance.

Consider now an example of nonrotating motions in two dimensions. An impressive illusion is sometimes created in the performance of a *grand jeté,* a traveling leap from one foot to the other. Some dancers seem to be able to float horizontally for a brief time near the peak of the jump before beginning to descend. Because the center of gravity must follow a parabolic trajectory through space once contact with the floor ceases, how does the dancer create this illusion? The configuration of the body determines the location of its center of gravity. If the legs start low relative to the rest of the body, are then raised into a split near the peak of the jump, and then lowered again when the body descends, the center of gravity will rise and fall relative to the torso during that process. It is therefore possible for the torso and head to move horizontally for a short time while the center of gravity follows a curved rising-and-falling trajectory. Since the eye of an observer tends to follow the head and torso of the moving body, a dancer who achieves that split in the air with the right timing can *appear* to float horizontally briefly, in violation of the expected constraints due to physical laws.

An interesting example of rotational motion is found in the series of *fouetté* turns commonly executed in classical ballet. [*See illustrations on the following page.*] These are successive pirouettes in which the whole body rotates for a half second or so, then most of the body stops rotating while the working leg is extended to the front and moves to the side. When the foot of the working leg is returned to the knee of the supporting leg, the whole body rotates again. This movement can be analyzed using Newton's First Law of motion extended to rotational motion. That is, unless there is a torque acting on a body, its rotational momentum is a constant. The rotational momentum is a product of the rate of turn and the rotational inertia, which is related to the mass but is larger the farther the rotating mass is from the axis of rotation.

During *fouetté* turns, the total rotational momentum of the dancer is approximately constant but is transferred back and forth between the working leg alone and the body as a whole. Thus the body, except for the rotating working leg, can stop rotating for a brief period during each full turn. A competent dancer can perform many uninterrupted *fouetté* turns, using the time when only the working leg is rotating to regain the small amount of rotational momentum lost to friction during the preceding turn and to adjust for slight departures from balance. The movement of the working leg must be timed to ensure that the body is indeed stopped during that brief period, which makes it easier to exert the necessary torque and forces against the floor.

Note that the mechanics of the *fouetté* turn sequence determine the overall shape of the movement, since there must be a torque against the floor to allow the turn sequence to continue at a constant tempo despite some loss of rotational momentum during each turn. But the resulting movement has characteristics compatible with the style of classical ballet, which involves an openness of body position toward the audience. In the *fouetté* turn sequence, the torso and head spend about half of the time facing the audience, the other half spinning quickly around through a full revolution. Perhaps this compatibility between the physical mechanics and the aesthetic style is one reason *fouetté* turns are such a common and impressive part of the classical ballet vocabulary.

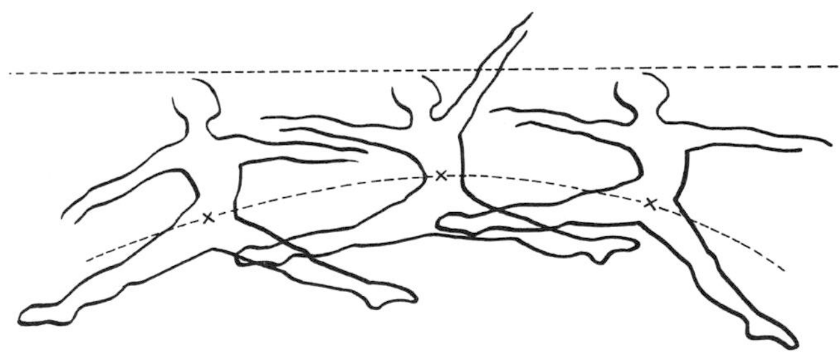

PHYSICS OF DANCE. The *grand jeté* floating illusion, in which the center of gravity follows a parabolic trajectory, yet its position relative to the body moves as the configuration of the body changes. (Courtesy of Kenneth Laws.)

A dancer can jump vertically by exerting a vertical force downward against the floor greater than the body weight for a short time. The resulting acceleration can cause the body to leave the floor, returning due to the downward force of gravity. A partner can contribute to the height of the jump by exerting a lifting force timed to coincide with the jumper's push against the floor. Male dancers are often vulnerable to injury when performing these lifts, and an understanding of the timing of the lift and the corresponding body configurations can minimize the danger. For instance, it is well known that the eccentric forces exerted by the body when cushioning a partner's descent are potentially greater than the concentric forces exerted when lifting the weight. Measurements have shown that the greatest force exerted by the lifting partner on the dancer occurs just before the dancer returns to the floor. The partner must be particularly careful at this moment to avoid body configurations that put excessive strain on the back or shoulders. That is, the lifter should keep the lifted dancer close to his own vertical axis and avoid the lordotic curvature in the lumbar spine that can produce dangerous levels of stress.

Measurements have also shown that about three-fourths of the energy of the lifted dancer comes from the lifting partner's force, and only one-fourth from the vertical jump of the dancer being lifted.

These four examples are indicative of the variety of dance movements that are conducive to analysis. Dancers can benefit by discovering ways in which such understanding contributes to better technique. Dance teachers can develop additional tools with which to approach their students. And observers of dance can gain a deeper appreciation of the art form by understanding the challenges facing the dancer and understanding the role of illusion in dance.

[*For related discussion, see* Kinesiology, *overview article.*]

PHYSICS OF DANCE. Lisa de Ribère performing a *fouetté* turn. The sequence is viewed clockwise from the top left through the six frames, which are then repeated as a continuing movement. Note that the body rotates very little while the leg has most of the rotational momentum in views 2, 3, and 4. Then the body turns rapidly in 5 and 6 while the leg is held in a position close to the body, where it has less rotational momentum. (Photographs © 1993 by Martha Swope; courtesy of Kenneth Laws.)

BIBLIOGRAPHY. There are many resources dealing with medical and physiological aspects of dance. Those listed here deal with a different way of analyzing dance movement—the application of principles of physics to the body moving through space under the influence of various external forces. Kenneth Laws, *The Physics of Dance* (New York, 1984), and Kenneth Laws and Cynthia Harvey, *Physics, Dance, and the Pas de Deux* (New York, 1994), cover a wide variety of movements, including those discussed here. The Laws-Harvey volume also contains a videocassette. Basic principles of physics, discussed briefly in the appendices of these books, are also described in any introductory physics textbook, such as the textbook by David Halliday, Robert Resnick, and Jearl Walker, *Fundamentals of Physics,* 4th ed. (New York, 1993).

Several publications deal specifically with balance. See Kenneth Laws, "Balance," in *Fundamentals of Physics,* by David Halliday and Robert Resnick, 3d ed. (New York, 1988); Kenneth Laws, "The Biomechanics of Barre Use," *Kinesiology for Dance* 7 (June 1985); and Kenneth Laws, "Precarious Aurora: An Example of Physics in Partnering," *Kinesiology for Dance* 12 (August 1990). For vertical jumps and lifts, see Kenneth Laws, "The Physics and Aesthetics of Vertical Movements in Dance," *Medical Problems of Performing Artists* 10 (June 1995); Kenneth Laws et al., "Lifts in Partnered Dance," *Kinesiology and Medicine for Dance* 13 (Spring–Summer 1991); Kenneth Laws, "The Physics and Forces of Partnered Lifts in Dance," *Medical Problems of Performing Artists* 3 (September 1988); and Kenneth Laws, "Physics and the Potential for Dance Injury," *Medical Problems of Performing Artists* 1 (September 1986). Turns are covered in L. T. Daly, "The Application of Laws of Motion to Dance Movement: A Qualitative Analysis of the Pirouette en Dehors," Department of Dance, Mount Holyoke College, 1985; Kenneth Laws and Lisa Fulkerson, "The Slowing of Pirouettes," *Kinesiology and Medicine for Dance* 15 (January 1993); Kenneth Laws, "The Mechanics of Turns in Dance," in *Fundamentals of Physics,* 4th ed., by Halliday, Resnick, and Walker (New York, 1993); Kenneth Laws, "The Biomechanics of the *Fouetté* Turn," in *Proceedings of the April 1986 Arts and Technology Symposium, Connecticut College* (New London, Conn., 1989); Kenneth Laws, "The Mechanics of the Fouetté Turn," *Kinesiology for Dance* 8 (June 1986); Kenneth Laws, "An Analysis of Turns in Dance," *Dance Research Journal* 11.1–2 (1978–1979); and Li Lei et al., "Angular Momentum in Dance Turns: The *Xi Tui Fan Shen,*" *Kinesiology and Medicine for Dance* 14 (Spring–Summer 1992).

The Lei article analyzes movements in Chinese dance. For further discussion of this topic see Li Lei, "The Physical Analysis of *Xie Tan Hai Zhuan,*" *BYU Dance Journal* 5 (Winter 1993); Li Lei and Kenneth Laws, "The Physical Analysis of *Da She Yan Tiao,*" *Kinesiology for Dance* 11 (June 1989); and Li Lei, "The Physical Analysis of *Xi Tui Fan Shen,*" *Kinesiology for Dance* 10 (March 1988).

For the general role of physical analysis in the art form of dance, see the following: Kenneth Laws, "The Physics of Dance: A General Discussion," *Kinesiology and Medicine for Dance* 13 (Spring–Summer 1991); Kenneth Laws and K. Lee, "The *Grand Jeté:* A Physical Analysis," *Kinesiology for Dance* 11 (June 1989); Kenneth Laws, "Application of Physical Principles to Dance," in *The Dancer as Athlete,* edited by Caroline G. Shell, Olympic Scientific Congress Proceedings, vol. 8 (Champaign, Ill., 1986); Kenneth Laws, "Physics and Dance," *American Scientist* 73 (September–October 1985); Kenneth Laws, "The Physics of Dance," *Physics Today* 38 (February 1985); and Kenneth Laws, "Physics and Ballet: A New Pas de Deux," in *New Directions in Dance,* edited by Diana Theodores Taplin (New York, 1979).

KENNETH LAWS

PICASSO, PABLO (Pablo Ruiz Picasso de Blasco; born 25 October 1881 in Málaga, Spain, died 8 April 1973 in Mougins, France), Spanish painter and scenery and costume designer. Picasso's long career as a visual artist of unequaled reputation and influence is well documented and has been the subject of a wide range of critical articles, monographs, exhibitions, and catalogs. That Picasso changed the course of painting forever with his introduction and exploration of a style that became known as cubism is a widely known fact. A less-celebrated aspect of his career, but one that played a significant role in his overall development as an artist, is the impact of his work for the theater, in particular for Ballets Russes de Serge Diaghilev.

Between the years 1917 and 1924 Picasso immersed himself in the world of ballet as one of the School of Paris artists engaged by Diaghilev to design decor and costumes for his productions. Yet long before his first collaboration in theater for the ballet *Parade,* Picasso had shown an interest in spectacle of all sorts, including the theater, cabaret, the circus, and, of course, the drama of the bullring. His early and continued drawings and paintings of Harlequin, clowns, and acrobats attest to his fascination with theater. Between the ages of eighteen and twenty he represented numerous scenes of women dancing the cancan, singing, or taking a bow in cabarets and music halls. He studied the theatrical works of Edgar Degas and Henri de Toulouse-Lautrec, emulating their styles as he was wont to do in his vigorous study of all the masters from the history of Western art. Whereas Degas was the detached observer of primarily classical ballet, Picasso was closer to Toulouse-Lautrec with his active participation as a spectator and his personal involvement in the world of theater and dance. Picasso's early theatrical subjects, be they harlequins, acrobats, singers, or dancers, were treated with sympathy and as symbolic representations of the isolated role of the "artist" in modern, bourgeois society. During his initial years in Paris, Picasso, like Toulouse-Lautrec, found solace in the excited atmosphere and society of the cabarets, where the lights and laughter offered relief from his own impoverished existence.

In 1916 the young poet Jean Cocteau, who was nursing an idea about a ballet spectacle, brought Diaghilev to Picasso's studio. Cocteau and composer Erik Satie had already approached Picasso with the idea of collaborating on a production for the Ballets Russes. Eventually Picasso agreed to participate, primarily on the strength of his friendship with Satie, his respect for Diaghilev, and his voracious appetite for the pursuit of new challenges and experiences. When the company left to rehearse in Rome, Picasso went with them. Picasso's role in the ballet *Parade,* first performed 18 May 1917 at Théâtre du Châtelet, was that of principal collaborator, working closely with librettist Cocteau and choreographer Léonide Massine. Picasso's input into *Parade* shaped the very nature and outcome of the ballet. Not only did he create the visual nature of the piece, but elements of his libretto won out over those of Cocteau. Picasso made suggestions about sound

PICASSO. A stage curtain from *Parade,* Léonide Massine's 1917 one-act ballet with scenery and costumes also designed by Picasso. (Photograph from the Dance Collection, New York Public Library for the Performing Arts.)

effects, and his creation of three cubist costumes for the Manager characters significantly affected the nature of their movements onstage. [*See* Parade.]

Picasso painted curtains and backdrops both with the scene painters and, at times, virtually by himself. On occasion he even did facial makeup. He observed rehearsals, sketching dancers' movements and facial expressions and making portraits of the ballet's many collaborators, supporters, and visitors. He lived, breathed, worked, and played ballet for the many months it took to complete *Parade* as well as some of the later ballets, such as *Le Tricorne* (The Three-Cornered Hat) and *Mercure.*

With *Parade,* Picasso discovered his own ability to adapt to the demands of theatrical spectacle, and he exhibited an instinctive understanding of the dancers' needs. Despite complaints from the dancers who played the Managers that their cubist super-structure costumes were "torture to move about in," Picasso did not self-servingly impose his art on the ballet; rather he considered the ballet as a whole, with his art as but one aspect. In turn, this initial experience in the theater dramatically affected Picasso's art and life. The sense of decorative effect that emerged out of his work on *Parade* was further developed in his synthetic cubist painting and sculpture. With his marriage to Russian ballerina Olga Kokhlova, whom he met while working on *Parade,* and through his travels with the company to such places as Rome, Naples, and London and his various social contacts in Paris, Picasso was introduced to a world of theater and high society, which helped determine the course his career would follow.

After *Parade,* two other Diaghilev ballets also received Picasso's total commitment: *Le Tricorne* in 1919 and *Pulcinella* in 1920, the latter based on the comic character in traditional *commedia dell'arte.* His designs for the former did not fit within the mainstream of his development as did the latter, the subject of which was more in keeping with Picasso's previous range of artistic themes. The designs for *Pulcinella* went through three versions, resulting in a remarkably simple cubist decor with colorful costumes that evoked the original time and place of *commedia dell'arte.* In the next four years Picasso collaborated on four other ballets and one play, all but one for Diaghilev's Ballets Russes: *Cuadro Flamenco,* a suite of Andalusian dances (decor and costumes) in 1921; *L'Après-midi d'un Faune,* a re-creation of a ballet first performed in 1912 (backcloth) in 1922; and *Antigone* (decor), *Mercure,* created by Count Étienne de Beaumont at the Soirées de Paris (curtain, decor, and costumes), and *Le Train Bleu* (curtain), all in 1924. The intense involvement of Picasso's earlier foray into theater was not repeated in these pieces, except perhaps in the case of *Mercure,* a ballet without plot comprising three tableaux for which Picasso created movable scenery that was manipulated by the dancers. His designs for the play *Antigone* were brought in on a crumpled piece of paper two days before the opening, and the curtain for *Le Train Bleu* was adapted from his painting of two years earlier, *Women Running on the Beach* (1922; Musée Picasso, Paris).

By the end of 1924 Picasso was growing restless and impatient with his world of the previous seven years. His marriage was deeply troubled and coming to an end. By June 1925 he had completed the highly expressionist painting *La Danse* (also called *The Dance* and *Three Dancers;* Tate Gallery, London), which was antithetical to the numerous sketches he had been making of dancers in a monumental, neoclassical style. Douglas Cooper (1967) described *La Danse* as "a passionate outburst in which love and hate join hands, in which classical dancing is mockingly contorted into a frenzied jazz idiom."

From 1924 on Picasso worked only sporadically for the theater, and it would be twenty years before he would work for the dance world again. He contributed to seven productions after 1924, making special designs for only three: one play, *Oedipe Rex* in 1947 (decor), and two ballets, *L'Après-midi d'un Faune* in 1960 (curtain) and *Icare* in 1962 (curtain and decor). Picasso's involvement with the theatrical world took on a new form in later years when he began to write plays and star in films.

Although his later work for the dance world did not exhibit the same intensity as in the early 1920s, the dance remained an important subject and influence in his art. Scenes of bacchanalian dancing, inspired by Picasso's interest in the art of Poussin, Titian and the classical world, replaced balletic dancing as expressions of joy and exaltation. Even the artist's nontheatrical subjects reveal the influence of dance and his earlier work for ballet: Picasso's close observations of dancers in the early years led to new groupings of figures in his paintings, and in many of his still-life compositions created from 1930 on, objects are presented against the deep space of a stage seen through a proscenium-like opening with a dramatic play of light and shade. As with the many other subjects that captured his imagination through his long, prolific career, Picasso took the world of dance and made it thoroughly his own.

[*See also* Scenic Design *and* Tricorne, Le.]

BIBLIOGRAPHY

Cooper, Douglas. *Picasso Theatre.* New York, 1967.

Garafola, Lynn. *Diaghilev's Ballets Russes.* New York, 1989.

Genné, Beth Eliot. "Picasso and Ballet." *The Dancing Times* (March 1992): 545–547.

Picasso, Le tricorne: Dessins pour le décor et les costumes du ballet de Manuel de Falla. Lyon, 1992.

Rubin, William, ed. *Pablo Picasso: A Retrospective.* New York, 1980. Includes a comprehensive chronology of Picasso's life and career, with theater works and photo documentation.

Sirvin, René. "Pablo Picasso et la danse: Le grande parade." *Danser,* no. 98 (March 1992): 34–39.

Ellen Breitman

PILLAR OF FIRE. Ballet in one act. Choreography: Antony Tudor. Music: Arnold Schoenberg. Libretto: Antony Tudor. Scenery and costumes: Jo Mielziner. First performance: 8 April 1942, Metropolitan Opera House, New York, Ballet Theatre. Principals: Nora Kaye (Hagar), Lucia Chase (Eldest Sister), Annabelle Lyon (Youngest Sister), Hugh Laing (The Young Man from the House Opposite), Antony Tudor (The Friend).

Pillar of Fire represents a further development of the genre of psychological ballet that Tudor had originated with *Jardin aux Lilas* (1936). It is almost a case history of passion, repression, and forgiveness. The action takes place in a small town, in the early years of the twentieth century, where Hagar, a spinster, lives with her two sisters. She is afraid of becoming like her prudish Eldest Sister, so when the man she loves seems to be attracted to her flirtatious Youngest Sister, Hagar in desperation allows herself to be seduced by a stranger. In the end her beloved helps Hagar overcome her self-hatred and makes her realize that he loves her. The lovers walk together through the forest in the transfigured night.

Tudor had planned a ballet to Schoenberg's *Verklärte Nacht* (Transfigured Night) as early as 1939, for the second season of his London Ballet, but the production was canceled owing to the outbreak of World War II. That September Tudor and Laing left for the United States to join Ballet Theatre (now American Ballet Theatre). During that company's second year he began to work on the ballet again—then called *I Dedicate.* By this time, impresario Sol Hurok had taken over the company's management, and its director was German Sevastianov—the "Russianization" of the company had begun. Hurok and Sevastianov would have been glad to drop Tudor's developing ballet, but at Lucia Chase's insistence it was finally put on, after being in rehearsal for more than a year. An enormous success, it immediately established Tudor as one of the major choreographers of the age and Kaye as its leading dramatic ballerina.

Each of the characters is delineated through gesture and movement: Hagar's smoothing of her hair and pulling at her collar, the Young Man's sensual, swaggering walk, and so on. The role of Hagar demands a great tragic actress but also a dancer of formidable technique; as always in Tudor's ballets the technical difficulties are never obvious—preparations are concealed in the texture of the movement.

Although Hagar is indelibly associated with Kaye, there have been other notable assumptions of the role: by Sallie Wilson, Veronika Mlakar, and (for one performance only) Lynn Seymour. The ballet has been revived at the Teatro Colón, Buenos Aires, in 1958, by the Royal Swedish Ballet in 1962, by the Australian Ballet and the Vienna State Opera Ballet, both in 1969, and by the Birmingham Royal Ballet in 1995 (with Marion Tait as Hagar).

BIBLIOGRAPHY

Balanchine, George, with Francis Mason. *Balanchine's Complete Stories of the Great Ballets.* Rev. and enl. ed. Garden City, N.Y., 1977.

Chazin-Bennahum, Judith. *The Ballets of Antony Tudor: Studies in Psyche and Satire.* New York and Oxford, 1994.

Payne, Charles, et al. *American Ballet Theatre.* New York, 1977.

Perlmutter, Donna. *Shadowplay: Antony Tudor's Life in Dance.* London, 1991.

David Vaughan

PILOBOLUS DANCE THEATRE. Like the fungus after which it was named, Pilobolus was spawned from an unlikely source, three undergraduate students taking their first course in dance at then all-male Dartmouth College. The three—an English major and cross-country skier; a philosophy major, folk dancer, and fencer; and a pre-medical student and pole-vaulter—were Moses Pendleton, Jonathan Wolken, and Steve Johnson. Encouraged by their teacher Alison Chase to perform and to develop choreography based on their movement backgrounds and affinities, the three decided to choreograph a piece for an end-of-year performance. The work was called *Pilobolus* after a sun-loving fungus that frequently grows in barnyards, shooting its spores across enormous distances. First performed early in 1971, the work so impressed Chase that she recommended that it be shown at a New York University–sponsored workshop led by Murray Louis. The outcome was an offer by Louis to organize a New York performance that December.

The company's innovative style rapidly built an audience. Approaching choreography with little training, company members were not confined by the limited conceptions of dance held by many choreographers. Searching for ways to describe Pilobolus, reviewers often called it "acrobatic" or "gymnastic," labels rejected by some company members. As Wolken observed in an article by dance critic Anna Kisselgoff, "Gymnasts are tight. . . . They show you how difficult things can be. A lot of what we do depends upon illusion." The type of illusion created by the group may be seen in Kisselgoff's description:

> [They] have made balancing on each other's backs, necks and hips in interlocking group designs their signature. It isn't footwork or what its members call "dancey dance" that makes Pilobolus what it is. Rather, it is the kinetic and visual impact of the shapes into which the dancers mold themselves. It is, for instance, the sight of one dancer carrying two above him, of one human form cantilevered out from another, of bodies hurtling through space and caught casually, of centipede-like conglomerates of arms and legs, of sculptural chains of bodies and of everchanging forms flowing out from each other with energy and humor.

Much of the company's choreography was supported by American Dance Festival commissions.

The group, based in Washington, Connecticut, has gone through a number of changes since its inception. Johnson left before its first New York performance, and Lee Harris and Robby Barnett, also students of Chase, joined. In 1973, Chase and Martha Clarke became members. Michael Tracy, another former student of Chase, replaced Harris in 1974. From the start members collaborated in all company activities, including choreography, management, and publicity. Only four early members—Barnett, Chase, Tracy, and Wolken—remain with the company, but they have given up dancing and taken on roles as artistic

PILOBOLUS DANCE THEATRE. Robby Barnett, Moses Pendleton, Michael Tracy, and Jonathan Wolken performing *Ocellus,* a staple of the company's early repertory, photographed in performance in the mid-1970s. (Photograph from the Dance Collection, New York Public Library for the Performing Arts.)

directors. Another significant change was the thorough training of the later crop of dancers.

Besides extensive tours of the United States, Pilobolus has toured Europe, South America, Central America, Japan, the Middle East, and Asia. Other companies that have performed its works include the Joffrey Ballet, Feld Ballet, Ohio Ballet, Hartford Ballet, and Italy's Verona Ballet. Pilobolus has been featured on U.S. public television series, *Dance in America* and *Great Performances,* as well as on television networks in Canada, France, Germany, Denmark, Chile, and Bangladesh. In 1990 the Pilobolus Institute was established to promote educational activities, such as workshops, teaching engagements, choreography projects, and tours to schools, further expanding the company's activities. In 1996, Pilobolus celebrated its twenty-fifth anniversary.

BIBLIOGRAPHY

Johnson, Robert. "Pilobolus Evolves to Beat the Recession." *Dance Magazine* (February 1992).

Kisselgoff, Anna. "Not Ballet, Not Acrobatics, but Pilobolus!" *New York Times* (20 November 1977).

Matson, Tim. *Pilobolus.* New York, 1978.

VIDEOTAPE. "Pilobolus Dance Theatre," *Dance in America* (WNET-TV, New York, 1977).

MARA J. PEETS

PION, MAURICE (born 11 September 1801 in Paris, died 14 February 1869 in Warsaw), French dancer, choreographer, and ballet director. Pion trained in Paris and made his debut at the Théâtre de l'Ambigu-Comique. In 1818 he was engaged by Louis Thierry as a principal dancer for the newly founded company at Warsaw's National Theater. Pion remained in Poland for the rest of his life, playing a central role in the development of Romantic ballet there.

Pion adopted Poland as his own through his work and his family connections. He brought his younger sister Eugenia to Poland, and she studied at the Warsaw Ballet School; she performed as a principal with the Warsaw ballet from 1830 to 1842. Pion married a Polish woman, and their two sons studied at the Warsaw Ballet School; they became soloists with his touring company. His daughter sang with the Warsaw Opera, and a grandson was an actor in Polish theater. Pion understood and came to appreciate the national traditions of his adopted country. He cultivated the national style of theatrical dance as in *Cracow Wedding,* and he composed short ballets based on country dances, such as *Maciek i Baśka* (1832) and *Stach i Zośka* (1839).

From 1826 to 1843 Pion directed the ballet at the National Theater, after 1833 known as the Wielki Theater (Great Theater). Initially he received little support from the Russian authorities, but after the unsuccessful Polish insurrection of 1830/31, they supported his work, and he was able to reorganize the ballet school along French lines, even introducing the French repertory of Romantic ballets.

Pion danced the roles of James in *La Sylphide,* Alvarez in *Le Pirate,* and Lutin in *Le Lutin.* He also partnered Marie Taglioni when she appeared in Warsaw in 1838. In addition, Pion invited Marie's father, Filippo, and her brother, Paul, to Warsaw and mounted several of their works for the company. Pion himself also choreographed in their new style.

After retiring from the Wielki Theater, Pion directed a small company that toured eastern Poland and western Russia from 1843 to 1858. He then taught in Warsaw until 1864.

BIBLIOGRAPHY

Chynowski, Pawel, and Janina Pudełek. *Almanach baletu warszawskiego, 1785–1985/Le ballet de Varsovie, 1785–1985.* Warsaw, 1987.

Pudełek, Janina. *Warszawski balet romantyczny, 1802–1866.* Warsaw, 1968.

Pudełek, Janina. *Two Hundred Years of Polish Ballet, 1785–1985.* Warsaw, 1985.

Pudełek, Janina. "The Warsaw Ballet under the Directorships of Maurice Pion and Filippo Taglioni, 1832–1853." *Dance Chronicle* 11.2 (1988): 219–273.

JANINA PUDEŁEK

PIQUÉ TURNS. *See* Ballet Technique, *article on* Turning Movements.

PIROUETTES. *See* Ballet Technique, *article on* Turning Movements.

PISTONI, MARIO (born 11 January 1932 in Rome), Italian ballet dancer and choreographer. Trained at the ballet school of the Teatro dell'Opera in Rome, Mario Pistoni was taken into Rome Opera Ballet upon the completion of his studies. He became a soloist in 1950 and *premier danseur* in 1951. Immediately thereafter, he moved to Milan and joined the ballet company of the Teatro alla Scala, where he danced the entire classical and modern repertory. Gifted with a strong, virile physique, he was the first partner of Carla Fracci, with whom he danced in London's Festival Ballet in 1958.

As a dancer, Pistoni was most successful in intense, dramatic roles such as Romeo in John Cranko's *Romeo and Juliet* (1958). As a choreographer his name is connected particularly with three ballets, all made for La Scala: *Francesca da Rimini,* created for Carla Fracci in 1965, to music by Tchaikovsky; *La Strada,* to music by Nino Rota (1967), also for Fracci; and *The Miraculous Mandarin,* to the music of Béla Bartók (1968). Pistoni's *Mandarin* was coherent, intensely dramatic, and appealing; it also opened the door to success for Luciana Savignano, its leading ballerina (Pistoni himself danced the role of the Mandarin). In the later *Concerto dell'Albatro* (1971), Pistoni recognized Savignano's expressive talent for dancing ambiguous and mysterious roles and using iconoclastic, flexible, and brilliant technique.

La Strada, by contrast, was a challenge for Fracci, considered the personification of noble romantic beauty; here she was forced to assume a pathetic, clumsy, clownish quality of movement and to conceal her long black hair under a red wig. Pistoni succeeded in capturing in short, successive narrative flashes the heartbreaking modern fable created by film director Federico Fellini. *La Strada* was subsequently revived for Italian television.

Pistoni was ballet director at the Teatro San Carlo in Naples from 1977 to 1981. As a choreographer he has been extensively involved in television productions. He is married to Fiorella Cova, formerly *prima ballerina* at La Scala.

BIBLIOGRAPHY

Doglio, Vittoria, and Elisa Vaccarino. *L'Italia in ballo.* Rome, 1993.

Rossi, Luigi. *Il ballo alla Scala, 1778–1970.* Milan, 1972.

"La Strada." Program notes, Teatro alla Scala, Milan, 31 March 1984.

Testa, Alberto, et al. *Il balletto nel novecento.* Turin, 1983.

VITTORIA OTTOLENGHI
Translated from Italian

PITROT, ANTOINE-BONAVENTURE (born in Marseille, *fl.* 1744–1770), French dancer and director. Antoine-Bonaventure Pitrot danced in various cities of Europe before joining the Paris Opera in 1744 as a soloist. He divided his time among Paris, the court of Saxony, and Poland. As first dancer at the Paris Comédie Italienne in 1759, he mounted several ballets, including *Les Amants Introduits dans le Sérail,* a serious work; a pastorale entitled *Les Oiseleurs;* and a comic work, *La Chaconne.* He was admired at the court of Catherine the Great in Russia; he attended the marriage of Archduke Joseph in Vienna, with his student and later wife Louise Rey. Back in Paris in 1764, he was engaged by the Comédiens Italiens, where he directed and danced *Ulysse dans l'Île de Circé* with great success. He presented *The Tempest, Sylvia, The Masked Ball,* and other works at the King's Theatre in London. He spent his later years with the court of Parma. In 1792 he staged several ballets at La Scala in Milan.

The critic Friedrich Melchior von Grimm has left a rather harsh portrait of him as a person with "heavy legs, a great deal of strength, strange stances, no grace whatsoever, nothing soft or easy in his movements." He was, however, well known throughout Europe as a ballet master. His younger brother Dominique was also a talented performer, though less interesting as a choreographer.

BIBLIOGRAPHY

Campardon, Émile. *L'Académie Royale de Musique au XVIIIe siècle.* 2 vols. Paris, 1884.

Grimm, Friedrich Melchior von. *Correspondance littéraire, philosophique et critique.* 17 vols. Paris, 1812–1814.

Hammond, Sandra Noll. "Searching for the Sylph." *Dance Research Journal* 19 (Winter 1987–1988): 27–31.

JEANNINE DORVANE
Translated from French

PITTSBURGH BALLET THEATRE. During the 1970s, several American colleges and universities attempted to support their own resident ballet companies. Point Park College in Pittsburgh was one of these. The Pittsburgh Playhouse, an institution dating back to 1934, had a reputable school of theater and dance. In 1968, the school was made part of Point Park College. That same year, dance faculty member Nicolas Petrov staged *The Nutcracker* using his college students. The success of this production impelled him to approach college president Arthur Blum and arts patron Loti Falk with the idea of forming a ballet company. (Two years previously, Falk had spearheaded a successful fund-raising drive to save the playhouse from closure.) With Falk as chairman and Petrov as artistic director, Pittsburgh Ballet Theatre was founded in 1969. The debut program recalled the Ballets Russes de Monte Carlo. Works by Michel Fokine, Léonide Massine, and Ruth Page were featured.

During the first few years, the company depended on many guest artists and on a nostalgic choice of ballets. In 1974, Frederic Franklin was engaged as co–artistic director with Petrov, but by 1977 the company was without direction and without college backing. Falk guided the orphaned organization until 1978, when John Gilpin, a former artistic director of the London Festival Ballet, was engaged. He departed almost immediately, however, and Patrick Frantz, artistic director of the Tucson Ballet and, before that, principal dancer and resident choreographer of the Pennsylvania Ballet, became Pittsburgh Ballet Theatre's new artistic director. Frantz relied heavily on his own choreography, but it was not enthusiastically received by the press, especially during the company's 1980 New York appearance. By 1982, Frantz had been replaced by Patricia Wilde.

After fifteen years as a principal dancer with the New York City Ballet, Wilde had become director of the Harkness Ballet School and had then occupied the same position with the American Ballet Theatre School. Its demise sent her to Pittsburgh, where she promptly contributed much-needed artistic and organizational stability. Over the ensuing decade, the company grew to thirty-six dancers and a $7 million budget. In 1989, Bruce Wells, a former resident choreographer of the Boston Ballet, joined Pittsburgh Ballet Theatre in the same capacity. His

PITTSBURGH BALLET THEATRE. Willy Shives, Laura Desiree, and Laurie Miller in the company's 1995 production of Bruce Wells's *Pas de Trois Classique*. (Photograph © by Randy Choura; used by permission.)

forte was dramatic works, notably *A Midsummer Night's Dream, Romeo and Juliet,* and *The Great Gatsby* (staged after his departure in 1995).

Wilde's New York City Ballet background gave her easy access to Balanchine ballets, but Pittsburgh Ballet Theatre boasts only a modest number, all dating to before 1970. Her selection of guest choreographers has not often stressed works by experimental choreographers. Instead, she has turned to established artists, such as Agnes de Mille *(Rodeo),* Eugene Loring *(Billy the Kid),* Lynne Taylor-Corbett *(Great Galloping Gottschalk),* Jiří Kylián *(Return to the Strange Land),* John Cranko *(The Taming of the Shrew),* and Ben Stevenson *(Cinderella).* Among more recent works, the 1990 Pittsburgh premiere of Lisa de Ribere's baseball-inspired *Casey at the Bat* was so enthusiastically received that it subsequently was acquired by other regional companies, including the Pacific Northwest Ballet and the Tulsa Ballet Theatre.

BIBLIOGRAPHY

Dacko, Karen. "Dancing on the Wilde Side." *Dance Magazine* (August 1986): 52–54.

Hodgson, Moira. "Pittsburgh Ballet Theatre: Educating the Public." *Dance Magazine* (February 1975): 54–59.

Kline, Elizabeth. "Pittsburgh Ballet Theatre Forges Ahead: The Future Is Now." *Dance Magazine* (October 1989): 36–42.

Maynard, Olga. "Art and Academe: The Pittsburgh Ballet Theatre and Point Park College." *Dance Magazine* (April 1972): 74–81.

Reasner, Pamela. "Satin and Steel." *Ballet News* 6 (October 1984): 10–15.

DORIS HERING

PLACIDE, ALEXANDRE (Alexandre Bussart Placide; born 1750 in Paris, died 26 July 1812 in New York City), French-born dancer, rope dancer, acrobat, and entrepreneur. An internationally celebrated performer when he left Paris in 1788, Placide won further renown as the first entrepreneur in American theatrical history to tour the United States with his own ballet company. He later established or managed theaters in Newport (Rhode Island), Charleston (South Carolina), Richmond (Virginia), and New York City. He also founded one of America's theatrical dynasties, with six children dominating the stage from New York to New Orleans throughout the nineteenth century.

Placide was born into a talented theatrical family. His parents were strolling players, and his sister, Mademoiselle Billioni, was one of the luminaries of the Comédie Italienne. Little is known of Placide's early training, although it is possible that he was the "M. Placide" who danced at the Paris Opera in 1772 and 1773. He made his Paris debut around 1770 at Nicolet's, the most brilliant of the city's popular theaters. He continued to dance at Jean-Baptiste Nicolet's but alternated appearances there with theaters in the Netherlands (1780); London (1780–1785); Bath; Bristol; Norwich; Dublin (1783–1784); and the French provinces (Lille, 1787).

Placide made his London debut at Sadler's Wells Theatre on 6 April 1781 under the name of Signor Placido. It is possible that his parents first used this name at Sadler's

Wells in 1766. Billed as one of "the most capital performers in the known world," he attracted an audience that boasted the presence of the duke of Cumberland, the earl of Chesterfield, Lord Jersey, and others.

Royalty sought Placide out on other occasions. Louis XV granted him the title of *danseur au roi* as reward for a court performance. The count of Artois, brother of the king, learned rope dancing under Placide's guidance. Marie Antoinette and the royal family attended a performance in which he failed to leap over a dozen grenadiers who held upright bayonets. Even though wounded, he added four more soldiers to the row and succeeded on the next attempt.

Contemporaries considered that Placide developed rope dancing into a true art form; however, he should not be considered solely as an acrobat because he was equally famous as the inventor of several successful pantomimes. He composed *Arlequin, Dogue d'Angleterre, Colombine Invisible, Arlequin Péruvien, Le Malade Jaloux,* and *Les Amours du Bucheron et de Nicodeme.* He usually played the role of Pierrot in these harlequinades, all of which he imported to America.

Despite the attractiveness of his stage presence, Placide's violent temper sparked offstage conflicts with fans, police, and even his employers. He was virtually shunned in person, and on the streets of Paris respectable women withdrew into doorways when they spied his approach.

In 1788 Placide sued Nicolet on the grounds that the title "Dancer to the King" had been granted to him personally and therefore should not have been appropriated as the title of Nicolet's company, Les Grands Danseurs du Roi. Placide petitioned the court for the rights to Nicolet's theatrical license, but relief was denied. Around the same time his former wife instigated a police investigation alleging that he had seduced a young girl. Placide took revenge against both his employer and his ex-wife by leaving France forever and taking with him Nicolet's most popular child star, the ballerina Suzanne Taillandet (Douvillier). [*See the entry on Douvillier.*]

For the next four years Placide's Troupe des Danseurs du Roi toured Saint Domingue (Haiti) and perhaps other Caribbean islands. He and the new "Madame Placide" made their debut in Cap-François on 11 October 1788 and performed for the last time on the island on 6 July 1791, shortly before the Haitian revolution erupted. The company's repertory consisted primarily of acrobatic stunts and harlequinades created by Placide. In addition they danced in comical ballets, such as *The Bird Catcher,* which Placide choreographed. Occasionally they enacted Jean-François Arnould-Mussot pantomime-ballets, a melodramatic form that was extremely popular in Paris.

Placide billed himself as "first rope dancer to the King of France" when he came to the United States. The "French Company from Paris" made its debut in Annapolis, Maryland, on 29 October 1791 and soon moved to Baltimore, where it premiered a new ballet each week of the engagement. On 25 January 1792 the Placides were invited to join forces with actors in the Old American Company, a troupe that had dominated American dramatic productions since colonial days. The French dancers' success was such that they contributed to the breakdown of that theatrical monopoly. Placide accompanied the English actors to Philadelphia for the summer season and then joined a different group of English actors headed for Boston to open the New Exhibition Hall—in spite of a stage prohibition of all dramatic entertainments. Only days after the sheriff interrupted a performance to arrest the stage manager, Placide brazenly advertised his own benefit in the *Columbia Centinel* with the disclaimer that, "As Nothing Dramatic will be touched on, the public need not be apprehensive of a Disappointment." He performed in Boston through January 1793 and returned later that spring. In the meantime he was occupied in converting the Newport Market into a theater. He and his troupe appeared there until early fall.

The company's repertory expanded with the addition of professional actors, singers, and dancers who fled from the Haitian slave revolt. The most popular items in the repertory were the Arnould-Mussot pantomime-ballets, including *The Death of Captain Cook, The American Heroine, Old Man and the Two Thieves,* and the first "serious" (as opposed to "comical") pantomime-ballet presented in the United States, *La Belle Dorothée.* The Placide troupe also introduced New England to its first French operas, composed by André-Modeste Gretry and Pierre-Alexandre Monsigny.

Placide opened the Charleston French Theatre on 26 March 1794 with another company of French dancers led by Jean-Baptiste Francisqui. Nine leading dancers and numerous supernumeraries presented an extensive repertory of ballets, pantomimes, acrobatics, and operas as well as French dramas. More than forty ballets or pantomimes and an almost equal number of operas and French plays were produced in 1794 alone.

The prolific Francisqui specialized in heroic pantomimes and *demi-caractère* ballets while Placide choreographed most of the comical ballets, some inspired by Comédie Italienne ballets. He also mounted elaborate spectacles, such as *Jupiter and Europa or, The Jealousy of Juno.* He rarely played Pierrot or young romantic leads any more, and he assigned his most strenuous dancing roles, including the title role in *The Bird Catcher,* to Francisqui. Usually Placide played heroic roles suitable for an older man, such as the Bandit Leader in *La Fôret Noire.* [*See the entry on Francisqui.*]

The company disbanded under scandalous circumstances in 1796. Placide's discovery that his wife was enamored of the company's leading singer, Louis Douvillier, precipitated a duel with his rival in the city streets. Charlestonians gossiped for many years about the duel (of which five contradictory accounts survive). They were further scandalized when Placide married the young actress Charlotte Wrighten only a month after his ballerina eloped with the opera singer. Before the Placides returned from their honeymoon, Charlotte's distraught mother, the well-known English singer Mrs. Pownall, died. So too did Charlotte's twin sister and baby brother. Fairly or otherwise, the Placides were censured for those deaths as well.

Having lost all of his professional dancers, Placide taught his new wife to dance a "much admired allemande." He trained her in pantomime for comical ballets such as *Two Philosophers and the Merry Girl,* a staple of her repertory for many years. Their children were apprenticed to the stage as youngsters and given the kind of training that helped to shape his eldest son into America's leading actor of the legitimate theater.

In 1811 almost the entire family appeared together in *Cendrillon, or The Glass Slipper. L'Oracle* of Charleston described an earlier production as a "glittering exhibition" and complimented Placide for the lavish appointments. It noted, too, the scrupulous attention paid to minor details of stage business. Critics also praised Placide's interpretation of the Prince's role, for which they cited his graceful, noble bearing and stylishly executed pantomime.

Placide continued to demonstrate his suppleness and daring on the tightrope well into his fifties. He was assisted by Laurent Spinacuta, his loyal partner from Nicolet's theater in Paris. Seats at these performances were sought-after prizes, tendered by parents to their children as reward for good behavior.

As proprietor of the Charleston Theatre, which traveled to Richmond, Savannah, and other southern cities, Placide was esteemed for his managerial skills and for his ability to recruit the best actors available in the United States. According to theater historian Charles Durang, Placide's peers regarded him as such a comical actor that he "could make a man under the gallows laugh." That talent was appreciated in private life as well; in sharp contrast to his earlier reputation in Paris, in America acquaintances sought him out as "a man of wit and exceedingly pleasant companion" *(The Clipper).* Placide continued to perform up until his death while on tour to New York City during the summer of 1812. He left his wife as well as five children, all but one of whom became highly respected actors, singers, or theatrical managers in London, Charleston, and New Orleans.

BIBLIOGRAPHY

Brooks, Lynn Matluck. "A Decade of Brilliance: Dance Theatre in Late-Eighteenth-Century Philadelphia." *Dance Chronicle* 12.3 (1989): 333–365.

Columbian Centinel (Boston) (10 December 1792).

Campardon, Émile. *Les spectacles de la foire, 1595–1791.* Paris, 1877.

"Charleston Stage Sixty Years Ago." *The Clipper* (n.d.).

Costonis, Maureen Needham. "The French Connection: Ballet Comes to America." In *Musical Theatre in America,* edited by Glenn Loney. Westport, Conn., 1984.

Costonis, Maureen Needham. *Susanne Douvillier, America's Prima Ballerina.* TK, TK.

Dunlap, William. *History of the American Theatre.* 2 vols. London, 1833.

Durang, Charles. *History of the Philadelphia Stage between the Years 1749 and 1855.* 7 vols. Philadelphia, 1868.

Fouchard, Jean. *Artistes et répertoire des scènes de Saint-Domingue.* Port-au-Prince, 1955.

Fouchard, Jean. *Plaisirs de Saint-Dominigue: Notes sur sa vie sociale, littéraire et artistique.* Port-au-Prince, 1955.

Hoole, W. Stanley. *The Ante-Bellum Charleston Theatre.* University, Ala., 1946.

Ireland, Joseph N. *Records of the New York Stage, from 1750–1860.* 2 vols. New York, 1866–1867.

Manne, Edmond Denis de, and Charles Ménétrier. *Galerie historique des comédiens de la troupe de Nicolet.* Lyon, 1869.

Mayeur de Saint Paul, François-Marie. *Le chroniqueur désoeuvré, ou, L'espion du Boulevard du Temple.* 2d ed. Londres, 1782.

Moore, Lillian. "New York's First Ballet Season, 1792." *Bulletin of the New York Public Library* (September 1960).

L'Oracle (Charleston) (21 and 24 February 1807).

Willis, Eola. *The Charleston Stage in the XVIII Century, with Social Settings of the Time.* New York, 1968.

MAUREEN NEEDHAM

PLAYFORD, JOHN (born 1623 in Norwich, England, died 1687 in London), English publisher of music and dance books. John Playford (the Elder) was one of several children born to John Playford, freeman of the Mercers' Company of Norwich. He probably attended the Cathedral School, also called the Almonry. After the death of his father in 1639, at the age of sixteen Playford moved to London to apprentice himself for seven years to John Benson, a stationer. Shortly after gaining his freedom at the age of twenty-five, he set up a shop near Temple Church; he was to conduct his business there all his life, enjoying a virtual monopoly on music selling and publishing in London.

Playford's publishing is significant for the many books he edited: collections of psalms, songs, and catches and music for viol, lute, and keyboard. When he opened his shop in 1648, however, his first publications were mostly tracts and papers of topical interest, profitable but politically suspect during the uneasy days of the Commonwealth era. Playford decided that this type of publishing was too hazardous, so he turned his attention to other fields. At that time the emerging Puritan ethic condemned public dancing everywhere but in the home, in the belief that it was a matter of private conscience.

During this period Playford began to collect the tunes of country dances, with directions for performing them; as far as we know, directions for the dances had never before been printed. Playford found that "a false and surreptitious" copy of his book was being prepared, so on 7 November 1650, he promptly registered his own at Stationers' Hall. The book was published under the title *The English Dancing Master: or, Plaine and easie Rules for the Dancing of Country Dances, with the Tune to each Dance.* The title page, which gives the place and date of publication as London, 1651, also bears the following information: "printed by Thomas Harper, and are to be sold by John Playford, at his Shop in the Inner Temple neere the Church doore." It is decorated with an engraving by Wenceslaus Hollar, showing a lady and gentleman in Stuart-period dress standing on either side of Cupid playing the lute; below appears the Latin motto "Omnia vincit Amor" (Love conquers all).

In his preface to *The English Dancing Master,* Playford explains his reasons for publishing the book and addresses in particular "the Gentlemen of the Innes of Court, whose sweet and ayry Activity has crowned their Grand Solemnities with Admiration to all Spectators." For the first edition, Playford and a "knowing friend" collected 105 dances, each with its own tune. The book was immediately profitable and popular and went through eighteen editions.

After the first edition, the title was changed to *The Dancing Master.* This title was used in all subsequent editions, albeit modifications were made in the text and plate for the title page. The first seven editions, published by Playford, contain more than 1,030 dances. Many are repeats, but ninety-three new dances appear after the first edition. Henry Playford, John's son, published the eighth through twelfth editions; these include 628 dances, many of them new. In 1706, John Young published the thirteenth edition, containing 364 dances, including eleven new ones. Young then published the fourteenth through eighteenth editions, containing more than 1,400 dances, of which only a few were new. Young subsequently published second and third volumes of *The Dancing Master;* these are distinct from the Playford series, although similar.

In 1686, Henry Purcell composed his *Elegy upon My Friend Mr. John Playford,* who died the following year at the age of sixty-three after turning his business over to his son Henry. His place of burial is unknown; his publications are his true memorial.

[*See also* Country Dance.]

BIBLIOGRAPHY

Dean-Smith, Margaret, and E. J. Nicol. "The Dancing Master, 1651–1728" (parts 1–3). *Journal of the English Folk Dance and Song Society* 4.4–6 (1944–1945).

Grosskreutz, Peter. "John Playford's 'The English Dancing Master.'" *Tanzen* 13.1 (1995): 8–10.

Playford, John. *Playford's English Dancing Master, 1651.* Edited by Margaret Dean-Smith. London, 1957.

Shimer, Genevieve. "English Country Dances: Cecil Sharp (1859–1924): and John Playford (1623–c.1687)." *Country Dance and Song* 13 (November 1983): 24–30.

VanWinkle Keller, Kate, and Genevieve Shimer. *The Playford Ball: 103 Early Country Dances, 1651–1820, as Interpreted by Cecil Sharp and His Followers.* Studies in Dance History, vol. 1.2. Pennington, N.J., 1990.

Worrell, Francis T. "Playford Revisited." *Country Dance and Song* 18 (June 1988): 23–37.

GENEVIEVE SHIMER

PLEBS AND ZOTTO, Argentine tango couple. In 1986, Plebs and Zotto formed a professional partnership and began starring in the Broadway hit *Tango Argentino.* In 1988, they created the show *Tango* × *2,* in which they re-create various styles of the dance pertaining to different historical periods. *Tango* × *2* has been performed to much acclaim in several countries, and because of its success, many young people from diverse social backgrounds have become interested in the tango.

In addition to performing in *Tango* × *2,* Plebs and Zotto have given tango seminars and workshops, primarily in Japan and the United States. In 1991, Plebs and Zotto won the "Premio María Ruanova," the most prestigious prize for Argentine dance; it was the first time that the prize was awarded to tango dancers. In 1992, Plebs and Zotto appeared in the documentary film *Tango,* produced by the National Geographic Society, Washington, D.C.

In contrast to other stage dancers, Plebs and Zotto have not forgotten about their own social dancing. After a performance in the theater they often go to the *milongas* (dance halls), where they do not dance together but with the people of the *milonga.* In this way they continue to incorporate new and popular elements into their repertory, which they learn from *milongueros.*

Milena Plebs (born 5 April 1961 in Buenos Aires), dancer and choreographer. Seven years after beginning ballet classes in 1971, Plebs entered the contemporary dance program of the Teatro Municipal General San Martín, where she studied classical technique, contemporary dance, rhythm, improvisation, and composition. Plebs has also studied jazz and attended workshops given by Pina Bausch, Susanne Linke, Jennifer Muller, and Oscar Aráiz. Plebs joined the Contemporary Dance Company of the Teatro Municipal General San Martín in 1979 and performed in all their productions through 1986. In 1985 she had begun to study with Miguel Zotto, and the following year she became his dance partner in *Tango Argentino*. *Tango* × *2,* the show she created with Zotto in 1988, has continued to be her primary professional commitment.

PLEBS AND ZOTTO. The renowned tango artists in a 1993 studio pose. (Photograph courtesy of María Susanna Azzi.)

Miguel Angel Zotto (born 7 August 1958 in Buenos Aires), dancer and choreographer. As an adolescent, Zotto went to dance in the *milongas* of Buenos Aires, where he learned the techniques and traditions of popular dancers. During his formative years, he studied with the key instructors of the tango. In 1984 he was appointed professor of tango at the Universidad de Belgrano de Buenos Aires. In 1985 he was invited by the director of the Grupo de Danza Contemporánea del Teatro Municipal General San Martín to be instructor of tango and to co-star in the show *Jazmines*. At that time he was also invited to teach tango to dancers of the Inbal Dance Theatre in Israel. He has also given seminars to dancers of the Colón Opera House in Buenos Aires and to those of the Teatro Municipal General San Martín. Zotto represents a synthesis of the traditions of the authentic tango: the embrace of Juan Carlos Copes, the posture of Virulazo (Jorge Orcaizaguirre), and the skillful legs of Antonio Todaro.

[*See also* Tango.]

BIBLIOGRAPHY

Azzi, María Susana. *Antropología del tango: Los protagonistas*. Buenos Aires, 1991.

Hanna, Gabriela. *Así bailaban el tango*. Berlin, 1993.

Meisner, Nadine. "Dancing Differently." *Dance and Dancers* (August–October 1993): 10–11.

Smith-Hampshire, Harry. "Tango Para Dos." *Ballroom Dancing Times* 36 (August 1993): 431–432.

INTERVIEW. Milena Plebs and Miguel Angel Zotto, by María Susana Azzi.

MARÍA SUSANA AZZI
Translated from Spanish

PLIÉ. A bend of the knees, the *plié* is used as an exercise and as a fundamental movement for most ballet steps. The bend may be made to three levels: a small or quarter bend *(plié à quart);* a half bend, with heels remaining on the floor *(demi-plié);* and a full bend, with thighs lowered almost horizontally, and, except in second and open-fourth positions, the heels released from the floor *(grand plié)*. All levels are found in exercises at the *barre*, with combinations of *demi-* and *grand plié* in the five positions of the feet typically being the first *barre* exercise.

Demi-plié precedes and follows all steps of elevation, but *plié à quart* may be sufficient for very small jumps or rapid allegro steps. *Grand plié* is primarily a classroom exercise; however, in the fifth position it can be used as a preparation for adagio pirouettes and in special circumstances for the landing from allegro steps such as *assemblé*. The term *fondu* can refer to a *demi-plié* on one leg, as in *arabesque fondue*, or to the ending of a step when the second foot closes softly and gradually to fifth position *demi-plié*, as in *sissonne fondue*. *Demi-plié*, or *fondu*, combined with *battements*, *ronds de jambe*, and *développés*, are regular exercises at the *barre* and in center-floor work.

The importance of the bending movement of the legs was evident in the *révérence* that characteristically began and ended social dances of the Renaissance and baroque periods. In 1623 François de Lauze described curtsies for women that are not unlike today's *demi-* and *grand plié* in first position. The fundamental nature of the bend of the knees is set forth by Pierre Rameau, who, in 1725, declared that dancing is no more than knowing how to bend and straighten the knees at the proper time. The importance of *plié* in ballet's technical history can be seen from its place in early notation systems. In 1700, Raoul-Auger Feuillet gave *pas plié* as his first step symbol and a *plié* on one and two feet as his first position symbols showing motion. Similarly, in 1831, E. A. Théleur notated the bending movement before all others, as did Arthur Saint-Léon in 1852 and Friedrich Albert Zorn in 1887.

Pliés continued to be standard exercises for social-dance training as well as for ballet in the nineteenth century. In 1820 Carlo Blasis, writing the first description of a ballet lesson, gave *pliés* in all positions of the feet as the first exercise at the *barre*. His contemporary, Giovanni Léopold Adice, recalled Blasis's classes as beginning with three slow *pliés* and three accelerated ones in each position (Adice, 1859). These were done without allowing the heels to leave the floor, a practice echoed by Théleur, who declared that bending "so low as to cause the heels to quit the ground . . . cannot . . . promote the least flexibility or any good in dancing" (Théleur, 1831).

Nevertheless, deep bends of the knees had long been associated with comic and character dances, such as those described by Gregorio Lambranzi in 1716. Gradually, deep *pliés* became standard practice in classes of renowned ballet masters such as August Bournonville and Enrico Cecchetti. Others, however, did not follow the tradition of *pliés* as the first *barre* exercise. According to Berthe Bernay (1890), *pliés* were the fifth *barre* exercise in classes at the Paris Opera, and early in the twentieth century, Stefano Mascagno (1917) preferred *barre* work to begin and end with a series of two *battements dégagés* and two *pliés* in second position. Some contemporary teachers advocate *demi-pliés* for initial exercises at the *barre* and *grand pliés* for later sequences.

The use of *plié* with steps of elevation also has varied over the years. Baroque dance specialist Ken Pierce documents the early eighteenth-century practice of initiating *sauts,* or jumping steps, with a *plié,* and he offers persuasive evidence that many of those steps finished by landing on the balls of the feet with straight knees (Pierce, 1988). The goal was the appearance of lightness, a style valued in the next century as well. Théleur advised that in jumping, "Care should be taken in the descent to arrive on the points of toes . . . permitting the heels to approach the ground gradually. . . . With few exceptions, steps should terminate with the knees straight . . . thus making each step perfect in itself before the commencement of another" (Théleur, 1831). A *plié* would occur when required by the following step.

Later nineteenth-century styles encouraged the use of slower, deeper *pliés,* a continuing practice that some dancers have had to abandon in order to perform the repertory of George Balanchine. In discussing a Balanchine variation, Edward Villella describes the challenge: "The man has to shorten the amount of time he spends in the *plié* as a landing, then take the time he has saved and apply that extra split-second to the push-off for the next propulsion. This is Balanchine dancing" (Villella, 1992). In such instances, the *plié* often is a "no-heels-down" variety—knees bent, heels up, and weight on the balls of the feet for the preparation as well as for the landing from a jump. The rationale is that, if the heels do not press into the floor in *plié,* movements will have more continuity and be smoother and lighter—goals of eighteenth-century dancing as well.

[*See also* Ballet Technique, History of.]

BIBLIOGRAPHY

Adice, G. Léopold. *Théorie de la gymnastique de la danse théâtrale.* Paris, 1859. Excerpts translated by Leonore Loft in *Dance as a Theatre Art,* edited by Selma Jeanne Cohen (New York, 1974).

Beaumont, Cyril W., and Stanislas Idzikowski. *A Manual of the Theory and Practice of Classical Theatrical Dancing* (Méthode Cecchetti). London, 1922. New York, 1975.

Bernay, Berthe. *La danse au théâtre.* Paris, 1890.

Blasis, Carlo. *An Elementary Treatise upon the Theory and Practice of the Art of Dancing* (1820). Translated by Mary Stewart Evans. New York, 1944.

Feuillet, Raoul-Auger. *Chorégraphie, ou L'art de décrire la dance, par caractères, figures et signes démonstratifs, avec lesquels on apprend facilement de soy-même toutes sortes de dances.* Paris, 1700. Translated by John Weaver as *Orchesography, or, The Art of Dancing* (London, 1706).

Grant, Gail. *Technical Manual and Dictionary of Classical Ballet.* Rev. ed. New York, 1982.

Hammond, Sandra Noll. *Ballet: Beyond the Basics.* Palo Alto, Calif., 1982.

Hammond, Sandra Noll. *Ballet Basics.* 3d ed. Mountain View, Calif., 1993.

Kostrovitskaya, Vera, and Alexei Pisarev. *School of Classical Dance.* Translated by John Barker. Moscow, 1978.

Lambranzi, Gregorio. *Neue und curieuse theatralische Tantz-Schul. Deliciae theatrales.* Nuremburg, 1716. Translated by Friderica Derra de Moroda as *New and Curious School of Theatrical Dancing* (London, 1928).

Lauze, François de. *Apologie de la danse, 1623: A Treatise of Instruction in Dancing and Deportment.* Translated by Joan Wildeblood. London, 1952.

Mara, Thalia. *Do's and Don'ts of Basic Ballet Barre.* New York, 1955.

Mascagno, Stefano. *Twenty Exercises in Ballet Technique Embracing Bar Exercises, Port de Bras—Adagio and Allegro.* New York, 1917.

Pierce, Ken. "*Saut* What? (*Sauts* in Early Eighteenth-Century Dance)." Proceedings Society of Dance History Scholars (1988): 68–95.

Prudhommeau, Germaine, and Geneviève Guillot. *Grammaire de la danse classique.* Paris, 1969. Translated by Katherine Carson as *The Book of Ballet* (Englewood Cliffs, N.J., 1976).

Rameau, Pierre. *Le maître à danser.* Paris, 1725. Translated by Cyril W. Beaumont as *The Dancing Master* (London, 1931).

Stuart, Muriel, et al. *The Classic Ballet: Basic Technique and Terminology.* New York, 1952.

Théleur, E. A. *Letters on Dancing, Reducing This Elegant and Healthful Exercise to Easy Scientific Principles.* London, 1831.

Vaganova, Agrippina. *Basic Principles of Classical Ballet: Russian Ballet Technique* (1934). Translated by Anatole Chujoy. Edited by Peggy van Praagh. 2d ed. London, 1953.

Villella, Edward, with Larry Kaplan. *Prodigal Son: Dancing for Balanchine in a World of Pain and Magic.* New York, 1992.

Zorn, Friedrich Albert. *Grammatik der Tanzkunst, theoretischer und praktischer: Unterricht in der Tanzkunst und Tanzschreibkunst, oder, Choregraphie.* Leipzig, 1887. Translated by Benjamin P. Coates as *Grammar of the Art of Dancing* (Boston, 1905).

SANDRA NOLL HAMMOND

PLISETSKAYA, MAYA (Maiia Mikhailovna Plisetskaia; born 20 November 1925 in Moscow), Russian dancer and ballet director. Through her mother, Maya Plisetskaya was born into a famous Russian Jewish theatrical family, the Messerers. Her eldest maternal uncle, Azary Messerer, was an illustrious actor at the Moscow Art Theater and had directed many plays; another uncle, Asaf Messerer, was a matchless Bolshoi Ballet dancer, choreographer, and teacher; and her aunt Sulamith Messerer was for many years a *prima ballerina* of the Bolshoi. At the age of three, Maya was already copying ballet roles she had seen on the stage and performing them in the family home. When she was seven, Sulamith Messerer took her to the Bolshoi Ballet School and asked the director to admit her despite her youth. Maya's elongated proportions did not suggest the grace of a future ballerina, but she performed a folk dance with such energy and spirit and curtsied with such proud grace that the examiners accepted her.

Plisetskaya's first stage appearance occurred not in Moscow but in the far north, where her father the engineer Mikhail Plisetsky directed the coal-mining concession on the Norwegian island of Spitsbergen. She performed before the miners in an amateur opera production, taking the role of the Little Mermaid. On her return to Moscow in 1933 she was readmitted to the Bolshoi school, the youngest pupil in the class of Elisaveta Gerdt. Within two years she was dancing important roles in the school repertory, including the Adagio of the Bread Crumbs in Asaf Messerer's production of *The Sleeping Beauty* and Pussy in the children's ballet *The Little Stork*, choreographed by Aleksandr Radunsky, Nikolai Popko, and Lev Pospekhin.

Plisetskaya's father, mother, and younger brother were imprisoned by Stalin's government, and Mikhail Plisetsky died in 1941 in a labor camp. Her family's tragedy haunted Plisetskaya all her life and certainly contributed to her development into a great tragic ballerina and actress. In most of her roles she portrayed tragic characters whose passion leads them headlong into violent death. Even as a young student she revealed this dramatic feeling; in the *grand pas de deux* from *Paquita*, which she danced in 1941, she amazed the audience with her phenomenally high and dynamic leap. "This was no carefree game, but a desperate leap over the abyss," wrote the veteran Soviet critic Vadim Gayevsky (1981).

Plisetskaya had to interrupt her studies when Germany invaded the Soviet Union in June 1941. As the Germans approached Moscow, the Bolshoi school and the personnel of the Bolshoi Theater were evacuated to the Volga city of Kuibyshev (now Samara). When the Germans had been driven back from Moscow, some schools, including the Bolshoi, resumed, and some professors were invited back. An outbreak of anti-Semitism, however, caused others—mostly Jews—to stay away.

Plisetskaya managed to return to Moscow in 1943. Despite missing a year, she was included in the graduating class and, owing to wartime conditions, performed many soloist roles in the Bolshoi repertory even before graduation; she never danced in the corps de ballet. In her first season she performed more than twenty important roles, rehearsing some of them under the guidance of Agrippina Vaganova. Beginning in 1943, she attended only Asaf Messerer's class for men because it demanded more physical effort and stamina than the women's class.

Plisetskaya's first major role at the Bolshoi was the title role in the 1945 *Raymonda*. The drama director Ruben Simonov was so impressed by her acting talent in it that he tried to persuade her to change her career and join his company. She declined, but she later appeared in dramatic roles in films—*Anna Karenina*, the Soviet-American production *Tchaikovsky*, and the television film *Fantasy*, in which she built the character of the heroine by reserved acting and anguished dancing. Even in her early roles (Masha in *The Nutcracker*, Myrtha in *Giselle*, Aurora in *The Sleeping Beauty*, and Raymonda), Plisetskaya never

PLISETSKAYA. As Odile, with Nikolai Fadeyechev as Prince Siegfried, in the Bolshoi Ballet production of *Swan Lake*, c.1947. Plisetskaya made the dual role of Odette-Odile uniquely her own. As Odette, the White Swan, she was meltingly soft, fluidly smooth, with *port de bras* of amazing liquidity; as Odile, the Black Swan, she was brilliant and hard as jet, with a pulsing energy that set the blood racing. (Photograph from the Dance Collection, New York Public Library for the Performing Arts.)

danced characterless, abstract, classical variations but always acted, introducing a feel of the times, a national flavor, and her own life experience.

This ability to portray character in classical roles prompted many critics and choreographers to compare her talent with that of the nineteenth-century ballerina Fanny Elssler. Plisetskaya was also compared to Elssler in her rivalry with Galina Ulanova, who was likened to Elssler's rival Marie Taglioni for her light, ethereal style. The contrast between the styles of Plisetskaya and Ulanova was especially apparent when they danced together in *The Fountain of Bakhchisarai;* Ulanova, as Maria, embodied purity surrounded by base instincts, while Plisetskaya, as Zarema, acted the tragedy of passion and the torment of jealousy.

In 1947 Plisetskaya appeared for the first time in *Swan Lake* as Odette-Odile and successfully fused the styles of Elssler and Taglioni. By then she had developed her own plastique, featuring broad sweeping movements, great extension, high elevation, and above all fluidity and expressiveness of the arms and hands. Critic Boris Lvov-Anokhin wrote:

> Her arms have a special flexibility. They can twist like snakes, flutter and beat like ribbons in the wind, enthrall one with their slow, wavelike movements. In nearly all Plisetskaya roles there is a special, distinctive pattern of the arms and hands. Her famous exit in act 2 of *Swan Lake* relies for its effect on the remarkable accelerating, wavy movements of the arms on a straight, motionless body. It creates the image of a gliding swan, a proud bird sailing through smooth water. (Lvov-Anokhin, 1976, p. 107)

Plisetskaya herself stresses the special importance of the dancer's arms: "In *Dying Swan* the arms are the swan itself, its fight against death. The arms are its swan song, its melody."

Two notable roles of this period were Kitri in *Don Quixote* in 1950 and the title role in *Laurencia* in 1956. Vakhtang Chabukiani partnered her in both. In *Don Quixote* her character had joy, vigor, and gaiety. In contrast, in *Laurencia* her powerful leaps approached the male elevation technique, and she personified the heroic spirit of a woman like Joan of Arc. These contrasting roles, as well as that of Odette-Odile, revealed Plisetskaya's unique talent for wedding opposite facets of theater: witty character dances and high tragedy. According to Gayevsky, these facets of her style reflect the two traditions of the Bolshoi Ballet, which he calls romantic neobaroque and divertissement.

By the early 1960s Plisetskaya had performed almost all the leading roles in the Bolshoi's classics, with the notable exception of Juliet in *Romeo and Juliet.* She had been preparing mentally for this role for five years, but on the eve of the premiere, she injured her leg and had to put off dancing Juliet until 1961. This role posed a challenge in that it was Ulanova's signature role, and Plisetskaya did not want to imitate her; only a highly original interpretation could satisfy her. When she finally danced Juliet, she succeeded in creating a deep and highly dramatic character, but she herself admitted that it was more drama than ballet.

Plisetskaya realized that traditional classical dance had no future unless some creative elements of modern dance

PLISETSKAYA. The wild revelry of Leonid Lavrovsky's choreography for *Walpurgis Night,* the ballet from Charles Gounod's opera *Faust,* was perfectly suited to Plisetskaya's strong technique and exuberant personality. She is seen here in a 1958 performance as the principal Bacchante, with Vladimir Vasiliev (kneeling before her) as Pan and Maris Liepa as Bacchus. (Photograph by Leonid Zhadnov, reprinted from his *Maya Plisetskaya,* Moscow, 1965.)

could be grafted onto it. She sought a successful blend of classical and modern dance in Yuri Grigorovich's choreography, and she performed successfully in his early ballets *The Stone Flower* (1959) and *Legend of Love* (1965). She also danced two leading roles in three versions of *Spartacus,* by Leonid Yakobson, Igor Moiseyev, and Grigorovich. Yet she could not realize her creative potential in the ballets of Soviet choreographers, whose lack of fresh ideas she found boring and dispiriting.

In 1958 Plisetskaya married Rodion Shchedrin, a leading Russian composer. Shchedrin helped to ease tensions between the authorities and the independent-minded Plisetskaya. He and the American impresario Sol Hurok made possible her first major appearance in the West during the Bolshoi's tour of the United States in 1959. Plisetskaya often mentioned her fondness for the United States, the country in which she had her first triumph abroad. She returned there in 1962, 1968, 1974, and 1977, and each time she proved a great favorite with the American public and critics.

Plisetskaya's next ballet at the Bolshoi was *Carmen Suite* (1967). Playing Carmen had been a long-cherished dream because it was a role that could fully utilize many aspects of her talent and character. Shchedrin adapted the music for the ballet, and Plisetskaya chose the Cuban choreographer Alberto Alonso to stage it. The first production caused an unprecedented scandal when it was condemned by the Soviet cultural authorities, who were displeased with its modernist flavor and apparent sexual overtones. Minister of Culture Ekaterina Furtseva forbade the production, uttering a phrase that became a joke with the Moscow public: "We cannot allow them to make a whore out of Carmen, the heroine of the Spanish people." Plisetskaya's career was jeopardized when she refused to go on a tour to Canada without the role of Carmen and threatened to leave ballet. Her determination and conviction finally prevailed, and *Carmen Suite* is now regarded as a classic. It was staged in most major theaters in Russia and in many other countries. The role of Carmen revealed one of the main themes of Plisetskaya's art: fighting for freedom to love, to be oneself, which inevitably leads to tragedy in a society that scorns freedom and is ruled by a faceless bureaucracy. This theme particularly appealed to the Russian public.

The same theme is obvious in Plisetskaya's own major productions of *Anna Karenina* (1972) and *The Seagull* (1980), both to the music of Shchedrin. Critic Yuri Tyurin wrote, "Plisetskaya gives visual embodiment on the stage to this inevitable perishing of an individual seeking to break out of the whirlpool of hypocritical morality and social deceit." In both ballets Plisetskaya achieved considerable success as a choreographer, finding new plastique to convey the subtle psychological states of characters drawn from the fiction of Leo Tolstoy and Anton Chekhov. Tyurin praised her performance as well.

PLISETSKAYA. The role of Kitri, the coquettish heroine of *Don Quixote,* was first performed by Plisetskaya in 1950. She is pictured here in the early 1960s with Vladimir Tikhonov as Basil the barber, Kitri's sweetheart. (Photograph by Leonid Zhdanov, reprinted from his *Maya Plisetskaya,* Moscow, 1965.)

> Dancing at the ball, Plisetskaya's Anna [Karenina] elegantly and majestically gives her hand to gentlemen around her. Yet the same gesture changes drastically when she meets Vronsky's eye. Now her hands begin to "sing." They convey a whole poem of awakening love. . . . The scene of Anna's despair performed by Plisetskaya resounds with the uncontrollable force of anger, protest, a kind of sombre, tragic indomitability. . . . The choreographic language acquires a sharp and hard graphic quality here. The plastic expressiveness of Plisetskaya's static poses takes on an extreme clarity and simplicity, an immaculate perfection of all lines. (Tyurin, 1976)

In *The Seagull,* as in *Anna Karenina,* Plisetskaya's deep and personal feeling for Shchedrin's music was a key ele-

PLISETSKAYA. As Juliet in Leonid Lavronsky's production of *Romeo and Juliet,* c.1961. The fragility and adolescent innocence of Juliet were not ideally suited to Plisetskaya's grand and buoyant technique or, some were quick to note, to her robust, womanly figure. (Photograph from the Dance Collection, New York Public Library for the Performing Arts.)

ment of her success. Her musicality in all her dancing was almost proverbial; she had the gift of dancing every note, every musical impulse or nuance.

Plisetskaya's choreographic versatility benefited greatly from her work with the most outstanding choreographers of her time, who staged ballets especially for her. They included Kasyan Goleizovsky; Leonid Yakobson; Roland Petit, who dedicated *La Rose Malade* to her; and Jerome Robbins, who staged *Nocturne,* to music by Frédéric Chopin. For her Maurice Béjart revised *Boléro* and choreographed two ballets: *Leda,* never shown on the Soviet stage for fear of a scandal surpassing that of *Carmen;* and *Isadora,* in which Plisetskaya portrayed the legendary American dancer Isadora Duncan, who was so close to her free and daring spirit.

In the late 1970s and into the 1980s there developed an open artistic breach between Plisetskaya and Grigorovich, chief choreographer of the Bolshoi. She would no longer appear with the main company abroad and toured instead at the head of a small ensemble of Bolshoi dancers. Her tours in Latin America, Europe, and Australia continued to bring triumphs. At a 1987 New York gala in honor of Martha Graham, she performed Ruth St. Denis's *Incense,* appearing defiantly on the same stage with the famous defectors Mikhail Baryshnikov and Rudolf Nureyev. For the 1988 Festival of Soviet Art in Boston, she staged and performed *Anna Karenina.*

Plisetskaya was director of the Rome Opera Ballet for the 1983/84 season. She led the Ballet del Teatro Lirico Nacional in Madrid as its artistic director between 1987 and 1990. In a spring 1996 gala in her honor she danced again her signature *The Dying Swan* as well as Béjart's *Kurozuka* and one of thirty Carmens in *Carmen Suite.* Some of the participants had been winners of the international ballet competition in Saint Petersburg, an annual event called "Maya" in her honor. She continues to teach and has been living in Munich.

Plisetskaya received the Soviet Union's most prestigious award, Hero of Socialist Labor, in 1985, and many awards

PLISETSKAYA. With the Ballet du XXe Siècle, Plisetksaya danced the title role of *Isadora,* created for her by Maurice Béjart in 1976. (Photograph by Colette Masson; used by permission of Agence Enguerand/Iliade, Paris.)

from foreign countries, including the 1965 *Dance Magazine* Award. Many books, articles, and movies have been devoted to her both in Russian and in the West. In 1974, *New York Times* critic Clive Barnes wrote of her, "She is one of the greatest dancers of our time simply because everything she does is infused with her own genius."

Béjart, summing up his impressions of their joint work, wrote,

> Maya burns like a flame in the world of dance. Passionate, total, rapturous of movement and temperament, at once classic and modern, she incarnates that fount of choreography that I search for constantly in my creative works.
>
> (Komissarzhevsky and Zhdanov, 1980)

BIBLIOGRAPHY

Barnes, Clive. "Maya Plisetskaya: Original and Totally Free Spirit." *New York Times* (6 October 1974).

Dashicheva, Aleksandra. "Contrasts of Feelings and Colors" (in Russian). *Sovetskaia Kultura* (9 May 1983).

Demidov, Alexander P. *The Russian Ballet: Past and Present*. Translated by Guy Daniels. Garden City, N.Y., 1977.

Feifer, George. "Plisetskaya Portrait" (parts 1–5). *Dance News* (November 1971–March 1972).

Feifer, George. *Russia Close-Up*. London, 1973.

Gayevsky, V. M. *Divertissement: The Fate of the Classical Ballet* (in Russian). N.p., 1981.

Hersin, André-Philippe. "Maia Plissetskaia" (parts 1–5). *Saisons de la danse* (November 1993–March 1994).

Kapterova, Galina, ed. *Maya Plisetskaya*. Translated by Kathleen Cook. Moscow, 1976.

Kisselgoff, Anna. "Success Is What Sustains Her." *New York Times* (16 March 1977).

Koegler, Horst. "A Life between Art and Politics." *Dance Now* 4 (Autumn 1995): 88–93.

Komissarzhevsky, Viktor, and Leonid Zhdanov. *Maiia Plisetskaia*. 2d ed. Moscow, 1980.

Lvov-Anokhin, Boris. "The Magic of an Art." In *Maya Plisetskaya*. Moscow, 1976.

Messerer, Asaf. *Tanets, mysl, vremia*. Moscow, 1979.

Messerer, Azary. "Maya Plisetskaya: Childhood, Youth, and First Triumphs, 1925–59." *Dance Chronicle* 12.1 (1989): 1–47.

Plisetskaya, Maya. *IA. Maiia Plisetskaia*. Moscow, 1994.

Smakov, Gennady. *The Great Russian Dancers*. New York, 1984.

Stevens, Larry. "Interview with Maya Plisetskaya." *Dance Pages* 11 (Fall 1993): 30–34.

Tyurin, Yuri. "Anna Karenina on the Ballet Stage." In *Maya Plisetskaya*. Moscow, 1976.

FILM. *Plisetskaya Dances* (1973).

AZARY MESSERER

POINTE WORK. The French noun *pointe,* referring to the sharp end or tip of something, has become the term in academic dancing that indicates the use of the tips of the toes. No precise documentation now exists to establish the actual origin of this technical feat, but early nineteenth-century dancers such as Maria de Caro, Maria Danilova, Avdotia Istomina, Fanny Bias, Geneviève Gosselin, and Amalia Brugnoli are documented in poses on the tips of their feet.

An illustration and a notation in E. A. Théleur's *Letters on Dancing* (1831) give the first example of pointe work in a dance manual. Describing a position of the feet that he called "tenth half aerial station," the text refers to "the body resting on the balls of the feet, or on the points of the toes." This is illustrated by a lithograph of a female dancer standing in an open position on the extreme tips of her feet. The very next year, in 1832, Marie Taglioni, in her performances in *La Sylphide,* established that pointe work was unquestionably the domain of the ballerina. During the ensuing Romantic era, a vocabulary of movements unique to the female dancer developed from the increased exploitation of pointes.

Eventually, the ballerina's traditional satin slipper became more and more specially constructed to aid the further development of pointe work. Individual detailing, such as darning the toe and the outer edge of the sole, as well as improvisational stuffings and stiffenings, led steadily to the special reinforcing and shaping that became the prototype of footwear manufactured specifically as pointe shoes. [*See* Footwear.]

Virtuosity in pointe work was a distinguishing characteristic of classicism in nineteenth-century Russia. Marius Petipa, in his days as imperial ballet master, increasingly refined pointe work in his choreography, noting that "pointes are the finishing touch to the women's side of classical dance" (Petipa, ed. Moore, 1958). Russian practitioners of pointe work not only assimilated certain technical strengths from touring Italian ballerinas but also adapted the special shoe design that strengthed the Italians' feet. The most distinctive feature of the new slipper specifically designed for pointe work was called blocking. Increasingly common from the 1860s onward, this stiffening of the toe with glue and stronger interfacing created what became known as the box of the slipper and formed a strong, blunt end. This gave the ballerina a broader and firmer base and allowed experimentation in toe techniques to advance beyond the actual strength of the toes themselves.

The basic vocabulary of pointe work was not changed greatly by the aid of the blocked shoe, only the duration of working with the basics. The feat that began around 1820 with an isolated dancer occasionally rising for a moment onto toe tip in traditional soft slippers developed into an entire vocabulary with great expressive and technical range. Turns on pointe could be faster and contain more revolutions. *Piqué* moves could be executed more directly and cleanly.

The accomplishments of Petipa and his dancers, in Russia toward the end of the nineteenth century brought the development of ballet to a new height of technical perfection. The development that continued in the West into the twentieth century was essentially derived from this Russian phase. Michel Fokine, one of the heirs to the Russian school, saw some need to rethink the technical brilliance of his heritage and to guard against its tendency toward mere trickery and dazzling effects. He was especially watchful of pointe work and insisted on its selective use. In *The Firebird* (1911), he reserved pointe work exclusively for the title figure, while in *Schéhérazade* (1910) he used none at all. However, Serge Diaghilev's Ballets Russes, with which Fokine was associated in Europe, developed and displayed pointe work significantly in the works of other choreographers. Its pervasive advancement was strikingly apparent to Alexandra Danilova when she joined the company after leaving Russia in 1924. In an interview with *Ballet Review* in 1973, she said that when she joined Diaghilev's company she "could do a lot on the toes" already but that what she found in the Ballets Russes was "a double portion of toes, more than in Russia."

George Balanchine, a Russian expatriate a generation younger than Fokine, accepted the vocabulary of pointe work comfortably when he began creating ballets for Diaghilev in 1925. In 1928, after experimenting with pointe work to achieve various contemporary aesthetic effects in *Jack-in-the-Box* (1926) and *La Chatte* (1927), Balanchine created *Apollon Musagète,* which unhesitatingly revealed pointe work as an organic element in his renewal of classical dancing. With this work, later revised and better known as *Apollo,* Balanchine continued the Petipa heritage confidently into the twentieth century.

Fokine's followers stressed the very selective use of pointes, amid a whole range of *demi-pointe* work; "artistic" dancers warned that blatant pointe work, especially with the blocked shoe, belonged in the music hall; and concerned pedagogues stressed the potential damage to the feet and legs that could result from short-cut, premature work in pointe shoes. Still, articulate pointe work gradually became accepted as so basic to the vocabulary of the female dancer that the least significant corps de ballet dancer now masters pointe technique once thought to be the distinguishing skill of the star dancer.

Basic pointe technique includes the differentiation between off-pointe positions called *demi-pointes* and full-pointe positions, sometimes referred to as *en pointe* or *sur les pointes.* Of the *demi-pointe* positions, the Italian method of teaching devised by Enrico Cecchetti makes the most precise distinctions. Full foot, flat on the floor, is called *pied à terre;* with the heel slightly lifted, the position is called *pied à quart* (commonly, quarter pointe); more lift is called *pied à demi,* or *demi-pointe* (half pointe); and a fully arched foot resting the weight of the body on the ball of the foot is called *pied à trois quart* (three-quarter pointe). Rising from this last position to the tip of the toes produces *pied à pointe,* or *sur la pointe* (full pointe).

In the Russian school of training, codified by Agrippina Vaganova, there are only two *demi-pointe* distinctions: half-toe (like Cecchetti's *demi-pointe*) and high on half-toe (like Cecchetti's *pied à trois quart*). Muriel Stuart's descriptive text in *The Classic Ballet,* a volume associated with Balanchine's School of American Ballet, specifies only one *demi-pointe* position between flat foot and full pointe. Extensive *demi-pointe* work is a necessity in the training of all dancers. It provides the dance student with a finer base of contact with the floor for turning and balancing.

Each method of teaching has its own theory concerning the degree of lifting the heel off the floor. Most schools concur on the use of the term *relevé* (relifted, or raised) to name the position gained by the climactic lifting of the heel. For the ballerina, *relevé* means a flexing action of the foot that takes the heel high enough off the floor to allow the tips of the toes to become the base of balance. The term refers to the climactic position itself as well as to the act of achieving it. (For the male dancer, the *relevé* move means lifting the heel so that the base of balance is limited to the ball of the foot.) The *relevé* position for the male in sustained balance is today almost exclusively one where the foot and shoe crease clearly at the ball joint, thus bringing the rest of the foot into direct perpendicular alignment out of the ankle of the supporting leg, straight into the floor. The height of the raised heel for men's turning movements, however, can vary according to details of individual technical theory.

Various *relevé* moves are the basis for the female dancer's training in pointe work. After two or three years of study in soft slippers, the female dancer begins simple exercises in pointe shoes at the classroom *barre.* Facing the *barre,* and holding it with two hands for support, she begins by practicing *relevé* moves to full pointe in first and second positions. The mechanics of the transition from full-foot contact with the floor to toe-tip contact differ with individual theory. The French school describes the move from *positions à terre* to *positions sur les pointes* as continuous and steady, rolling up and down. The Italian school, as expounded by Cecchetti and as adapted by Vaganova, recommends that the move be brisk and employ a slight spring. In springing, the toe tips are brought slightly closer together into an adjusted, tightened position on full pointe.

In addition to simple *relevé* exercises in the basic positions of the feet, the dancer learning pointe work also practices *glissade, échappé,* and *assemblé* moves at the *barre,* as well as *relevé* moves from two feet to one foot, with the nonsupporting foot drawn up to *sur le cou-de-pied* back or front. Once the feel and strength of pointe positions have become familiar at the *barre,* the pointe student practices the same *relevé* moves unsupported as center work in her class.

The term *sous-sus* ("under-over") refers to *relevé* moves

from fifth position *à terre* (on the floor) to fifth on pointe. This brisk action can be done to the front, side, or back; the objective is to achieve such a tight position *sur les pointes,* with one foot firmly pressed up against the other, that the impression given is of one foot, not two. *Échappé* ("escaping" or "slipping") moves are *relevés* that go from closed (first or fifth) positions to open ones (second or fourth); in pointe technique, the open positions, with straight knees, are achieved after a slight spring from a *demi-plié* in a closed position. *Échappé sur les pointes* is an elaborate *relevé* move because the aim is not only to rise on the pointes but also to change the position of the feet.

When the *relevé* action of rising to pointe or pointes becomes so practiced as to be nearly automatic, the pointe student can attempt a more direct method of achieving a full-pointe position—the *piqué.* In this "pricking" movement, the dancer steps immediately onto the toe tip, without the roll-up move associated with the *relevé. Piqué* moves are initiated by pushing off from what will be the working leg in the ultimate *piqué* position. Once based in a *piqué* pointe or balance, the move can have various elaborations: the balanced *piqué* pose can be held with the working leg in simple *passé* position (front or back) or with it extended into specific arabesque configuration, or the *piqué* leg can establish the axis of a *piqué* turn.

Successive traveling steps performed on the tips of the toes in a staccato manner are called *taqueté* ("pegged"). The family of these steps is called *taqueterie.* Repeated *pas emboîtés* from fifth to fifth position are one example of *taqueté.* Lighter, more liquid traveling steps on pointe are called *pas de bourrée couru* or *pas de bourrée suivi.* In the case of pointe work, the *couru* ("run") designates a skimming succession of tiny steps usually done in parallel first position. *Suivi* ("followed") is a designation of the Russian school. *Pas de bourrée suivi sur les pointes,* in which one small step quickly follows another, is usually done in fifth position, traveling sideways.

With its late development in the nineteenth century, pointe work qualifies as the newest feature of the vocabulary of academic dancing. Most of its development and sophistication occurred in the twentieth century, alongside the perfecting of pointe shoes, but its advancements have yet to be codified into standard syllabi. Balanchine's fascination with pointe work brought the skill to its present height of virtuosity. To assist in the training of skilled pointe technicians at his company's school, he consulted on the design of a specific pointe shoe for young students with Capezio, the shoe manufacturer. He also insisted that female students at the School of American Ballet, from their intermediate level onward, be required to take complete classes on pointe.

BIBLIOGRAPHY

Beaumont, Cyril W., and Stanislas Idzikowski. *A Manual of the Theory and Practice of Classical Theatrical Dancing: Cecchetti Method* (1922). Rev. ed. London, 1940. Reprints, New York, 1975. Includes a preface by Enrico Cecchetti.

Guest, Ivor. *The Romantic Ballet in Paris.* 2d rev. ed. London, 1980.

Hammond, Sandra Noll. *Ballet: Beyond the Basics.* Palo Alto, Calif., 1982.

Migel, Parmenia. *The Ballerinas: From the Court of Louis XIV to Pavlova.* New York, 1972.

Petipa Marius. *Russian Ballet Master: The Memoirs of Marius Petipa.* Translated by Helen Whittaker. Edited by Lillian Moore. London, 1958.

Schorer, Suki. *Balanchine Pointework.* Studies in Dance History, no. 11. Madison, Wis., 1995.

Sorine, Daniel S., and Stephanie Riva Sorine. *Dancershoes.* New York, 1979.

Stuart, Muriel, et al. *The Classic Ballet.* New York, 1952.

Vaganova, Agrippina. *Basic Principles of Classical Ballet: Russian Ballet Technique.* 2d. ed. Translated from the Russian by Anatole Chujoy. Edited by Peggy van Praagh. London, 1953. Includes an introduction by Ninette de Valois.

Winter, Marian Hannah. *The Pre-Romantic Ballet.* London, 1974.

ROBERT GRESKOVIC

POKOT DANCE. The Pokot (Pökoot or Suk) farmers and herders live in eastern Africa, on the semiarid plains and in the hills of northwestern Kenya and adjoining Uganda. They share many dance forms, such as animal imitation and jumping, with other surrounding pastoralists. Dancing is an important part of many Pokot rituals and may continue for days at initiation feasts (male or female circumcision rites).

The *amumur* dance, for example, celebrates the *sapana* initiation of a boy into manhood, a practice adopted from the Karamojong people of northeastern Uganda. A large group of men, their elaborately painted clay headdresses bedecked with ostrich plumes, approach the initiate's homestead, imitating animals such as elephants—sometimes using their spears as trunks—singing and stamping rhythmically. They are greeted by a group of ululating women standing with uplifted arms and rocking their torsos back and forth while holding their heads high, an action that draws attention to their abundant wire coil–and-bead necklaces. After a period of improvised dance, the men and women proceed in ranks into the corral, forming a semicircle. The men consult alone in a huddle and then begin a new song, filing in and out of a line of women who dance simultaneously in the opposite direction. During such a performance, some of the dancers may collapse in an ecstatic trance.

Women form their own circles at dances, marking time, jumping in place, or clapping and singing. Two or three may also jump as high as they can across the middle of a circle. Sometimes the men join in, each taking one or two women as partners as they jump across the circle.

The culmination of an initiation rite, and of most other Pokot ceremonies, is the *adongo,* a dance in which each man sings the praises of his favorite ox, a symbol of his pride and bravery. While a chorus chants, each man in turn raises his arms in imitation of the ox's horns, then, with two friends, jumps very high while holding his body perfectly rigid. Opposite the three men, three women also jump; then the women sometimes come forward to honor the warriors with slow, shuffling jumps and a final bow. The next warrior then steps forward to sing his own boasting song.

Several dances are performed with men and women facing each other in parallel lines. During one such dance, the women's and men's lines alternate advancing and retreating, at first shuffling but then jumping while raising and lowering one knee. Another dance enacts a legend about a cave that collapsed on a group of dancers. Partners join hands to form an arch and continue bobbing and singing while one couple at a time jumps through the arch.

When young people dance at night during the rainy season, a woman chooses a partner (never a spouse) by pointing a long dancing stick at one of the men. The couples then line up, the women grasping their sticks and the men holding their partners' sides; and they bob to the singing, gracefully rocking their torsos up and down. From time to time, a man bows his head so that the ostrich plumes he wears brush against his partner; she likewise bows so that her plaits of hair brush against him. The men may also wear giraffe tails tied to their arms to swing gently at their partners.

Small children have special game dances of their own. In one, they follow a leader in a serpentine pattern; in another, they join hands in a circle and bob as each dancer individually ducks under the raised arms of the two dancers to his left.

The majority of Pokot dances are accompanied only by singing and clapping, although instruments such as leg bells and wooden horns are sometimes used. Pokot dances are performed not only for recreation and celebration but also for maintaining cohesion in a rural, seminomadic society.

[*See also* Central and East Africa. *For a general discussion, see* Sub-Saharan Africa.]

BIBLIOGRAPHY

Beech, Mervyn W. H. *The Suk: Their Language and Folklore* (1911). New York, 1969.

Docherty, A. J. "The Karamojong and the Suk." *Uganda Journal* 21 (March 1957).

Hennings, R. O. *African Morning*. London, 1951.

Meyerhoff, Elizabeth. "The Threatened Ways of Kenya's Pokot People." *National Geographic* (January 1982).

Peristiany, J. G. "The Age-Set System of the Pastoral Pokot." *Africa* 21 (July 1951).

Robbins, L. H., and Martha E. Robbins. "A Note on Turkana Dancing." *Ethnomusicology* 15 (May 1971): 231–235.

Russell, John. *Kenya, beyond the Marich Pass*. London, 1994.

MARTHA E. ROBBINS

POLAND. [*This entry comprises three articles on dance in Poland. The first article focuses on traditional and social dance; the second explores the history of theatrical dance; the third provides a brief history of scholarship and writing.*]

Traditional and Social Dance

The kingdom of Poland dates to the late tenth century and reached a height of power and prestige in the sixteenth century. It was partitioned by Austria, Prussia, and Russia in the eighteenth century—then reestablished as a republic after World War I. Poland was occupied by Germany in World War II, then liberated by the Allies. From 1945 to 1989, Poland was a member of the Soviet-dominated Eastern bloc.

The primary Polish word for dance, *pląs* or *plęsy* ("capers"), is of Slavic origin. Equivalent terms used in rural areas included *skakanie* ("hopping") and *hulanie* ("cavorting"). Today the most commonly used generic term for dance is *taniec*. Folk dances are traditional dances performed by members of rural communities primarily in native surroundings but secondarily in stage presentations—for the pleasure of dancing, for interpersonal contact, and for the transmission from one generation to another.

Early Sources and Recent Research. The earliest extant dance document is a song in dance rhythm with a folk melody line, "Jesus Sold by Judas," written in 1488 by Blessed Ladislaus of Gielniów. In the 1500s, the *Organ Tablature,* compiled by Jan of Lublin, contained twenty-seven Polish dances, including the *poznanie* (acquaintance dance), *hajducki* (guard's dance), and dances known by the titles "I Pricked Myself on a Blackthorn" and "The Little Cobbler Walks Down the Street." A sixteenth-century poem by Jan Kochanowski mentions girls dancing in a circle, accompanied by singing and rhythmic drumming.

Literary works from the seventeenth and eighteenth centuries name many dances, including the *hajducki, klaskany* ("clapping"), *goniony* ("chase"), and *poduszkowy* ("pillow"). Significantly, the names *krakowiak, mazur,* and *polonez* appear; these dances, performed originally in peasant communities, became popular among the ruling class in the eighteenth century. Descriptions of dances popular among the peasantry also appear, such as "dashing up and off in groups of lads to lasses and of girls to boys."

Zygmunt Gloger's *Old Polish Encyclopedia* (1900) explains many names of earlier dances, and the collected works of Oskar Kolberg contain a wealth of ethnological data on nineteenth-century folk dance. Although ethnological literature from the late nineteenth and early twentieth centuries increasingly made reference to folk dance, it was not until the 1930s that it received serious scholarly study. At that time Zofia Kwaśnicowa recorded and published local dances, and Cezaria Baudouin de Courtenay-Ehrenkreutz-Jędrzejewiczowa initiated the first scholarly studies of folk dance in the Department of Ethnology at the University of Warsaw.

Since World War II, scholars have continued this work. Roderyk Lange investigated the dances of northern Poland, Maria Drabecka those of the Warmia and Mazuria regions, Grażyna Dąbrowska those of central Poland, and Janina Marcinkowa those of Silesia. From 1968 to 1981 the Institute of Art at the Polish Academy of Sciences in Warsaw pursued a project initiated by Dąbrowska to document systematically the dances of various regions. Researchers also collaborate with other ethnochoreologists and members of the International Council for Traditional Music Study Group on Ethnochoreology.

Social Context. Folk dances in Poland have served a number of functions. Dances connected with family rites, especially weddings, fulfilled a ceremonial function in contexts of social and individual change. For example, a bride danced with her bridesmaids before her capping, a folk ceremony consisting of putting a cap on the head of the bride, and with the wedding hostess after the capping. Thus wedding dances marked the bride's transition from one social group to another. These dances followed a strict traditional order; some were performed only at weddings, while others were common dances that assumed a special meaning within the wedding ceremony.

Certain folk dances were reserved for a single gender or social group. For example, on Ash Wednesday married women danced "flaxwise" or "hempwise," jumping as high as they wanted the crops to grow. On Midsummer Night unmarried boys and girls danced around the traditional bonfire. Scholars consider these dances echoes of earlier beliefs in the magical powers of dance to bring good fortune and ward off evil. Such echoes are also found in Carnival dances, in which performers dressed as animals.

Other occasions for dancing included harvest festivals in late summer and early fall, when the community celebrated the fruits of its work. However, dancing was not restricted to special occasions; villagers sometimes held a dance for its own sake, although never during Advent or Lent, when dancing was proscribed by the Roman Catholic church.

Evolution. The evolution of folk dances was influenced by contact between the peasants and the ruling class, the church, and the urban population. For instance, villagers borrowed quadrilles and waltzes from urbanites and adapted the *kontro* from the aristocratic *kontredans,* itself

POLAND: Traditional and Social Dance. An illustration by Jan Lewicki of Polish gentry dancing the *polonez,* with exemplary form, as published in the nineteenth-century Polish periodical *Tygodnik ilustrowany* in 1861. (Photograph courtesy of Grażyna Dąbrowska.)

borrowed from the French *contredanse*. Village musicians were often responsible for importing the latest fashions.

Contacts with neighboring and distant regions also shaped folk dance, as did the reciprocal influence of stage dance ensembles. For example, dances of peasant origin such as the *krakowiak* and *mazur* became popular among the gentry in the nineteenth century, then entered the repertories of professional dance companies, and in this form returned to rural communities. Stage presentations disseminated the *krakowiak,* which originated in the Kraków region, and the *mazur,* which originated in the Mazovia region, throughout the country. As folk dances evolved, new forms were assimilated into older forms, and numerous variations developed. As the result of the many historical contacts and influences, there exists in Poland a rich diversity of regional dances.

Today folk dance has taken on the new function of stage spectacle. Numerous amateur ensembles stage revivals of folk dances, as do the two professional groups subsidized by the state. Mazowsze, known more fully as the Mazowsze Song and Dance Ensemble, was founded in 1948 by Tadeusz Sygietyński and his wife, Mira Zimińska. A second company, Śląsk, was formed in 1954 by Stanisław Hadyńa and Elwira Kamińska. The groups have toured widely abroad, presenting both folk music and folk dances in much transformed stage versions.

Musical Accompaniment. The music accompanying Polish folk dances is most often exclusively instrumental, though at times it may be both instrumental and vocal or exclusively vocal. A cappella singing by the dancers is perhaps the oldest type of accompaniment and is associated with the earliest types of dances. Whereas instrumental accompaniments for older dances are often based on vocal dance songs, those for newer dances appear to have no vocal source.

POLAND: Traditional and Social Dance. A couple from the village of Bukowina Tatrzańska, in the Tatra Mountains, perform the *góralski,* a virtuosic dance in which the man improvises around his partner. (Photograph 1975 by Jaček Chodyna; from the Archiv M. Sobieski, Institute of Arts, Polish Academy of Sciences, Warsaw; courtesy of Grażyna Dąbrowska.)

The violin has long been the most common instrument for dance accompaniment throughout Poland. A tambourine of the Basque type or a big drum hung over the shoulder often aids the violin and beats the rhythm, although in some regions this function is served by a type of double bass, the *basetla* or *maryna,* which is about the size of a cello. Even and uneven rhythms occur through the country, although the former predominate in eastern and southern regions.

Rural bands in some of the southern highland and western regions include various kinds of pipe instruments, such as the *dudy* (bagpipes), called in different regions *gajdy* in the mountains or *kozioł* (the "buck") or *koza* (the "goat") in western Poland. More recently, clarinet and trumpet have been added. In southeastern regions, the cimbalom enriches the sound of the string instruments; in the Kaszuby region, bands include the *diabelskie skrzypce* ("devil's violin"), a string and percussion instrument, and the *burczybas* (droning bass). The accordion and the pedal-accordion are known but rarely used. Instruments are made locally by folk musicians.

In the highlands and the Rzeszów region a dancer introduces the accompaniment by giving the musicians a note upon which they improvise the melody. In other regions a dancer stops in front of the band and sings a short song either before or during the dance to request a change in melody.

Classification. Folk dances can be classified according to the number and arrangement of the dancers. One category comprises group chain dances in which any number of people can participate and any participant can take any place in the group. Individual movements and the patterns covered by the dancers depend on the movement of the entire group, which forms an organic whole. In some dances in this category, dancers do not maintain physical contact with one another; bound only by space and the overall rhythm, they produce a kind of multiple solo performance, such as the Kurpie wedding march.

Chain dances in this category take a variety of forms. Participants may follow a leading dancer who guides the chain, as in the *konik* ("horse"), or form a circle, as in the traditional dance around the bride. The closed circle may give way to an open chain, as in *zbójnicki* (brigands' dance). In some dances, when dancers are ranged in parallel facing rows or in one row facing a central couple, the formations resemble the *contredanse*. The dancers may perform without touching or may form a chain by joining hands or holding one another's shoulders or waists; in the *chodzony,* couples hold hands behind a leading couple.

Within the category of couple dances are those for two women, or, most often, for a man and a woman. Although each couple dances independently of others, multiple couples can join in a dance, as in the highland dance and "Chase around the Table" of the Kurpie region. Sometimes the various pairs change partners, as in the *kowal* ("smith") of Mazovia. Dances for couples may be performed with or without turning and contact. In "Chase around the Table," the dancers never touch—only in the final part of the dance does the couple have any body contact; in the highland dance they touch only fleetingly; and in the *obyrtany* they touch constantly.

Dances performed in couples within a larger group are based on the same principle as dances for one couple, except that all the couples move in a pattern, as in the *oberek, kujawiak,* and polka. The couples move either clockwise or counterclockwise in a circle. When this pattern breaks down, the dance follows the modern ballroom pattern of couples moving independently.

Another category comprises more formalized group dances, usually performed in groups of four facing inward. These dances require a definite number of dancers or couples, and each performer's movement depends absolutely on the movements of others. Each participant in the dance has a set place and moves in a set pattern in relation to other dancers. Examples of this type of folk dance include the *krzyżak* ("cross" dance) and *kaczok.*

Dances for three persons usually group the trio in a line (as in the *trojak* and *dyna*) or a small circle (as in the *koziorajka*). Usually these dances have two parts, but some have more. For instance, in the circle dance, the *okrągły,* a *polski* is followed by a *mazur* and *krakowiak* or *obertas,* much as a musical suite integrates separate parts into a unified whole.

There is also a category of solo dances performed by one man or one woman. Such dances are associated with display in front of an audience. The *zając* ("hare") is a skill dance about two crossed rods on the floor.

Dance Dialects. Within each region of Poland, dances exhibit similarities in such aspects as the amount of contact between participants, floor pattern, technique, rhythm and tempo, and overall performance style. On the basis of these characteristics scholars have differentiated five dance dialects—northwestern, central, eastern, southern, and highland.

Folk dances common throughout Poland take on a number of variations in the different regional dialects. The *chodzony* ("walk"), performed to a 3/4 meter, appears in such variations as the *wolny* ("slow"), *pieszy* ("walker"), and *powolny* ("leisurely"). The polka, performed to a 2/4 meter, appears in the variations *gładka* ("smooth"), *równa* ("straight"), and *trzęsiona* ("shaken"). Each variation is associated with music, dress, and ornamentation characteristic of the region.

POLAND: Traditional and Social Dance. The spirited *krakowiak,* which can be performed as a couple dance or in a group, remains one of Poland's most popular traditional dances. Jan Ptaszek and Krystyna Madej, members of Śląsk, the Polish State Folk Ballet, are pictured here in a whirling step. (Photograph from the Dance Collection, New York Public Library for the Performing Arts.)

Some folk dances are unique to one regional dialect. Dances in the northwestern dialect often have two parts and integrate singing, clapping, gesturing, or manipulating props. Examples include the *klapok* ("clapping"), *kłaniany* ("bowing"), *gołąbek* ("little pigeon"), *szwec* ("cobbler"), and *miotlarz* ("broom maker"). In the central dialect, variations on the double rhythm of the polka or the triple rhythm of the *mazur* are common; dances emphasize the pattern of couples whirling around a circle. Dances in the southern dialect feature duple meters, fast tempos, and the characteristic syncopated rhythm of the *krakowiak.*

While the northwestern dialect has similarities to central European folk dance, the eastern dialect shows influences from Russia as well as from the southern and central dialects. The highland dialect incorporates a variety of dances from the disparate ethnic groups inhabiting the region. Particularly noteworthy are the dances of the Tatra highlanders. The *góralski* (highland dance) features one couple, a man and a woman, dancing for an audience of non-dancers. One man dances with several women in turn, each introduced to him by another dancer. Hence the dance focuses on the man's movements—stamping, clapping, and heel clicks. The dance ends with a short pivot as the partners clasp one another. The *zbójnicki* (brigands' dance) also emphasizes the role of the male dancer. One of the few Polish dances performed only by men, it probably derives from ancient armed dances; it includes steps similar to those of the highland dance, along with squats and high leaps.

Court and National Dances. Medieval chroniclers note the pastime of dancing among the Polish nobility, although they offer little description of performance. Sixteenth-century sources record some contemporary practices: first the ladies danced, carrying garlands and moving in twos, one pair behind another; next young men danced, also grouped in twos; then the men approached the women to partner them in processional dances. One account suggests that the single-sex dances were further divided according to age: "There was a solemn and dignified dance of the matrons, and a more brisk and lively one of the maidens" (Czerniawski, 1858, pp. 62, 104).

It was not until the eighteenth century, when the Polish court established closer relations with the French court, that men and women partnered one another from the beginning of a ball. All the couples formed a circle and followed the leading pair. The oldest of these dances is the *polonez,* followed by the *krakowiak* and *mazur* and later by the *kujawiak* and *obertas.* These five became the national dances of Poland, spreading from the court to townspeople and seen as a manifestation of national identity. They also returned to rural areas and influenced the evolution of folk dance there. In the nineteenth century there spread throughout Europe a fashion of Polish dances, occasionally finding their way into ballets as character dances. Of the five, the *polonez* (polonaise) and *mazur* (mazurka) became the most popular. In many areas these dances spread to rural areas and appeared as folk dances in later collections.

[*See also* Krakowiak; Mazurka; *and* Polonaise.]

BIBLIOGRAPHY

Czerniawski, Karol. *O tańcach narodowych.* Warsaw, 1858.

Dąbrowska, Grażyna. *Tańce Kurpiów Puszczy Zielonej.* Warsaw, 1967.

Dąbrowska, Grażyna. *W kręgu polskich tańców ludowych.* Warsaw, 1979.

Dąbrowska, Grażyna. *Taniec ludowy na Mazowszu.* Kraków, 1980.

Dąbrowska, Grażyna, and Kurt Petermann, eds. *Analyse und Klassifikation von Volkstänzen.* Kraków, 1983.

Dąbrowska, Grażyna, et al. *International Monograph on Folk Dance,* vol. 2, *Poland, Portugal, Sweden.* Budapest, 1987.

Dąbrowska, Grażyna. *Tańcujże dobrze: Tańce polskie.* Warsaw, 1991.

Dahlig, Ewa. "Music and Dance Activities of Polish Folk Tradition." *Dance Studies* 14 (1990): 37–46.

Drabecka, Maria. *Polskie tańce ludowe w dziełach O. Kolberga.* Warsaw, 1960.

Drabecka, Maria. *Tańce i zabawy Warmii i Mazur.* Warsaw, 1960.

Glapa, Adam, and Alfons Kowalski. *Tańce i zabawy wielkopolskie.* Wrocław, 1961.

POLAND: Traditional and Social Dance. Wearing traditional costumes at a wedding, villagers of Kadzidło and Wydrat, in the Kurpie Zielone region, perform the *olender,* a circle dance for couples. (Photograph 1983 by Zygmunt Szargut; from the Archiv PWM, Kraków; courtesy of Grażyna Dąbrowska.)

Grzegorczyk, Piotr. *Teatr ochotniczy i tańce polskie.* Warsaw, 1948.
Kolberg, Oskar. *Dzieła wszystkie.* 68 vols. Wrocław and Poznań, 1961–1990.
Kotoński, Włodzimierz. *Góralski i zbójnicki.* Warsaw, 1956.
Kwaśnicowa, Zofia. *Zbiór pląsów.* Warsaw, 1937.
Lange, Roderyk. "Historia badań nad tańcem ludowym w Polsce." *Lud Folk.* 51 (1967–1968): 415–436.
Lange, Roderyk. "On Differences between the Rural and the Urban: Traditional Polish Peasant Dancing." *Yearbook of the International Folk Music Council* 6 (1974).
Lange, Roderyk. "The Dance Folklore from Cuiavia." *Dance Studies* 12 (1988): 6–223.
Madejski, Zbigniew, and Paweł Szefka. *Kaszubskie pieśni i tańce ludowe.* Wejherowo, 1936.
Marcinkowa, Janina. *Folklor taneczny Beskidu Śląskiego.* Warsaw, 1969.
Marcinkowa, Janina, and Krystyna Sobczyńska. *Folklor Górnego Śląska.* Warsaw, 1973.
Matyka, Henryk. *The Folk Dance and Costume Atlas of Poland.* Rainham, Essex, 1991.
Michalikowa, Lidia. *Folklor Lachów Sądeckich.* Warsaw, 1974.
Moszyński, Kazimierz. "Taniec." In Moszyński's *Kultura ludowa Słowian,* vol. 2, *Kultura duchowa,* pp. 300–395. 2d ed. Warsaw, 1968.
Nartowska, Lidia. *Tańce z okolic Rzeszowa.* Warsaw, 1963.
Piasecki, Eugeniusz. *Zabawy i gry ruchowe dzieci i młodzieży.* Warsaw and Lwów, 1922.
Romowicz, Maria. *Tańce górali od Żywca.* Warsaw, 1969.
Romowicz, Maria, and Jacek Tomasik. *Dances and Folklore of the Zywiec Townspeople.* Irvington, N.Y., 1986.
Sroka, Czesław. *Polskie tańce narodowe.* Warsaw, 1990.
Szefka, Paweł. *Tańce kaszubskie.* 4th ed. Gdańsk, 1982–.

Grażyna Dąbrowska

Theatrical Dance

The first performance of ballet in Poland is believed to have been in 1518 at the royal marriage of Bona Sforza to King Zygmunt I. Presumably Queen Bona brought Italian court dancing, the precursor of ballet, from the Sforza court at Milan, and dancing quickly became the favorite entertainment of Polish kings. Ballet did not immediately develop a national style in Poland as it did in France. King Władysław IV Vasa (reigned 1632–1648) founded a theater in his Warsaw castle and imported fine European companies. Foreign ballet also flourished in the reign of Augustus II, under whose auspices Louis Dupré starred from 1724 to 1726. Augustus III continued his father's patronage, and the ballet appeared not only at the Warsaw palace but also at the public opera house.

In the late eighteenth century, noble families founded their own court ballet companies, relying on foreign ballet masters and peasant dancers. The most important of these companies was founded in 1776 by Count Antoni Tyzenhauz, who established a music and dance school on his Lithuanian estate, hiring the Italian ballet masters Gaetano Pettinati and Cosimo Morelli to train village children. In 1784 Tyzenhauz engaged François Gabriel Le Doux, a student of Gaëtan Vestris and a former dancer with the Paris Opera. The count died the following year, and the company passed in bequest to King Stanisław II Augustus. The king brought the company to Warsaw, christened it His Majesty's Dancers, and personally supervised its artistic development.

Le Doux directed the company jointly with Daniel Curz, a student of Gaspero Angiolini and a former dance soloist in Vienna. During its nine-year existence, His Majesty's Dancers premiered nearly a hundred works. Guest choreographers such as Charles Le Picq mounted both their own works and those by leading European choreographers of the *ballet d'action.* Le Doux and Curz also choreographed ballets for the company, including some on Polish themes. Le Doux adapted *Ritiger et Wenda,* attributed to Jean-Georges Noverre, as *Vanda, Queen of Poland* (1788); it told the medieval legend of a Polish princess who, after refusing to marry a German prince, drowned herself to avert a Polish-German war. Curz also contributed other ballets on Polish themes, albeit with fashionable French names, such as *Les Cracoviens et Cosaques* (1788). [*See the entry on Curz.*]

Performances by His Majesty's Dancers were more popular than dramatic and operatic productions at Warsaw's Teatr Narodowy (National Theater), and the company's reputation spread beyond the city. One foreign visitor wrote, "I have never seen a pantomime ballet that was so close to my ideal of dance art. The ballets in Berlin were more magnificent, but not as well composed. In Berlin they danced with greater mastery, but not with such feeling as in Warsaw." However, the company disbanded at the time of the Kościuszko uprising in 1794. The following year Stanisław II Augustus abdicated, unable to stop the partition of Poland between Prussia, Russia, and Austria-Hungary.

In the early nineteenth century, a number of efforts were made to revive the ballet. In 1802 Le Doux founded a ballet school, and the same year his students began to appear at the National Theater, though both ventures were short-lived. In 1809 a family of French dancers named Volange produced several works at the National Theater, including their own version of *La Fille Mal Gardée.* Louis Duport brought his *Narcissus* in 1812; Madame Ginetti-Guerri performed and taught in 1816; and Fortunato Bernadelli produced several works with a small group of Polish dancers in 1817. It was not until 1818, however, that a group of French dancers headed by Louis Thierry managed to establish a permanent school and company at the National Theater.

Thierry built a repertory that included national works and promoted Polish dancers such as Antonina Palczewska and Mikołaj Grekowski. His most notable achievement was the 1823 premiere of *Kraków Wedding,* choreographed by the Polish ballerina Julia Mierzyńska. The music was adapted from Jan Stefani's opera *Krako-*

POLAND: Theatrical Dance. Lithograph made from Antoni Zaleski's painting *Wesele krakowskie w Ojcowie* (The Wedding in Ojców; 1852), depicting a scene from the first Polish ballet to be based on traditional national dances, *Wesele Krakowskie* (Kraków Wedding). (Teatral Muzeum, Warsaw; photograph courtesy of Grażyna Dąbrowska.)

vians and Highlanders, and the dances were modeled on traditional *mazur*s and *krakowiak*s. High points included a pas de deux for the bride and groom based on the *krakowiak,* a pas de trois for a bridesmaid and two groomsmen based on the *mazur,* and a solo for the first bridesmaid that was also based on the *mazur.* (This solo became a touchstone for young ballerinas, including Marie Taglioni and Carlotta Grisi.) *Kraków Wedding* won immediate success with Polish audiences and unexpected acceptance from the Russian authorities who now monitored all performances.

In 1826 Maurice Pion, a leading dancer in Thierry's company, took over its direction. For the next few years organizational and financial difficulties plagued the company, but following the failure of the Polish revolt in 1830–1831, the Russian authorities took over the management of the Warsaw theater and built a new facility, the Teatr Wielki (Great Theater), which opened in 1833. Pion received much support for his efforts to revive ballet because the Russian authorities considered it a safe entertainment for the rebellious Poles, not to mention a favorite diversion of their own. The Russians made only one restriction: national traditions could not be promoted.

Pion reorganized the school according to French models and introduced the French Romantic repertory, including works by the Taglioni family, whom he invited to Warsaw in 1838. Indeed, Pion nearly singlehandedly brought Romanticism to Polish ballet. Upon his retirement in 1843, Filippo Taglioni took over the direction of the company and over the next decade choreographed such works for the company as *The Isle of the Amazons* (1845) and *Panorama of Naples* (1847), which employed all the spectacular resources and large-scale effects of Romantic ballet. [*See the entry on Pion.*]

In 1853, Roman Turczynowicz, who had been the company's second resident choreographer for seven years, took over its direction. He had already staged his own versions of *Le Diable à Quatre* (1847), *Giselle* (1848), and *Esmeralda* (1851). His choreography sought a balance between mime and pure dance, between classical and character dancing, and, perhaps most importantly, between male and female dancing. Many choreographers elsewhere in Europe created ballets with predominantly female principals. Under Turczynowicz the company included not only skilled ballerinas such as his wife Konstancja, Anna and Karolina Straus, and Maria Frejtag, but also strong male dancers—Aleksander and Antoni Tarnowski, Feliks Krzesiński, Jan Popiel, and Hipolit Meunier. Building on the school curriculum established by Pion, Turczynowicz balanced classical and character training. His stagings of national dances for Stanisław Moniuszko's opera *Halka* (1858) remained in the repertory well into the twentieth century. [*See the entry on Turczynowicz.*]

The failure of the national insurrection of 1863–1864 brought a new wave of Russian restrictions, including the prohibition of Polish directors for the company.

Hence Hipolit Meunier, who would have been Turczynowicz's natural successor, remained second choreographer for almost thirty years while a succession of Italian ballet masters directed the company. Their Italian style came into conflict with the French style that retained a strong hold among teachers at the school. This conflict was not resolved until Enrico Cecchetti (director from 1902 until 1905) established his own standard, which was upheld and adapted through the teaching of Jan Walczak.

The repertory during this period included some of Turczynowicz's works, as well as European successes such as *Coppélia* (1882) and *The Fairy Doll* (1892). The only distinctively Polish work was Virgilio Calori's *Pan Twardowski* (1874), a Polish version of the Faust legend, which remained in the repertory until 1917 and had more than five hundred performances. Cecchetti's predecessor, Raffaele Grassi, had initiated a one-way collaboration with the Maryinsky Theater in Saint Petersburg, so Russian stars appeared with the company (although Polish dancers could not perform at the Maryinsky), and works such as *Swan Lake* (1900) entered the repertory. Turczynowicz's tradition was lost as the Romantic ballets were revived in Maryinsky versions.

After 1905, ballet at the Wielki Theater suffered an artistic decline. Operetta drew away a segment of the ballet audience, the company lacked a strong leading personality, and many of the best dancers left to pursue careers elsewhere, notably with Serge Diaghilev's Ballets Russes and Anna Pavlova's company, both touring companies. When the system established in 1818 for consolidating ballet, opera, and drama under a single management collapsed during World War I, in 1915, it marked the end of the monopoly the Wielki Theater had exercised over Polish ballet for nearly a century.

Although smaller companies had toured the provinces in the nineteenth century, they all traced their origins to the Wielki Theater, because its school was the only Polish institution that offered ballet training. After his retirement Maurice Pion founded a company that toured eastern Poland and western Russia from 1843 to 1856. Between 1882 and 1892 another company, founded by the actor Aleksander Łukowicz, toured the same area, and Tomasz and Eleanor Nijinsky, former dancers at the Wielki Theater and the parents of the great dancers Vaslav Nijinsky and Bronislava Nijinska, led a touring company through the provinces. Polish dancers were forbidden to perform at the Maryinsky and Bolshoi theaters in Russia and rarely journeyed to western Europe, usually to study in Paris and Milan.

Diaghilev's Ballets Russes created new opportunities for Polish dancers, launching the international careers not only of the young Nijinskys, Vaslav and Bronislava, but also of Stanislas Idzikowski, who ultimately settled in England; Tadeo (Tadeusz) Slavinsky, who eventually moved to Australia; and Leon Woizikowski, who later divided his time between Poland and western Europe.

Meanwhile, the dance scene in Poland changed considerably. When Poland regained its national independence in 1918, dance was decentralized and diversified. Although the Warsaw Ballet remained the strongest company, the cities of Poznań and Lwów founded companies and schools as well. In addition, private ballet studios were opened, as well as many private schools for modern dance. Tacjanna Wysocka and Janina Mieczyńska both founded modern dance companies, and Halina Hulanicka

POLAND: Theatrical Dance. Based on a Polish variant of the Faust legend, the three-act ballet *Pan Twardowski*, with music and libretto by Ludomir Różycki, has been mounted in many different versions all over Poland. This scene, from a 1935 production by Feliks Parnell in Warsaw, shows Bogdan Bulder as the young Mister Twardowski marching in front of the dragon bearing Włodzimierz Traczewski as the Devil. (Photograph from the archives of the National Theater, Warsaw.)

POLAND: Theatrical Dance. Śląsk, the Polish State Folk Ballet, specializes in theatrical performances of traditional Polish dances. Here, Maria Kubiesa and Tadeusz Kozielec are seen as one of the twirling couples in *kujawiak* and *oberek*. (Photograph by K. Seko; from the Dance Collection, New York Public Library for the Performing Arts.)

and Ziuta Buczyńska achieved renown as modern dance soloists. Other dancers performed in operettas, revues, and cabarets.

Piotr Zajlich, who had performed with the Ballets Russes and with Anna Pavlova, directed the Warsaw Ballet from 1917 to 1934. His repertory included restagings of both Diaghilev works and national ballets, notably his popular new version of *Pan Twardowski* (1921). Zajlich also reformed the ballet school curriculum by adding rhythmic gymnastics and an academic program. The school produced a host of fine dancers, including the company principals Halina Szmolc, Irena Szymańska, Sylwin Baliszewski, and Zygmunt Dąbowski. Nonetheless, the best students still went abroad, notably Roman Jasiński and Yurek Lazowski, who immigrated to the United States, and Yurek Shabelevsky, who settled in New Zealand. [*See* Warsaw Ballet *and the entry on Zajlich.*]

Maksymilian Statkiewicz, who had performed with the Ballets Russes, built the Poznań repertory with an emphasis on national works, including his own staging and the Polish premiere of Karol Szymanowski's *The Highlanders* (1938), a score based on Tatra folk music. The narrative relates how a peasant girl, betrothed to a young highlander, falls in love with the leader of a band of mountain robbers. The robbers kidnap her during her wedding after a fight with the groom, his companions, and guests. At the end the girl and the robber walk happily through a mountain clearing. The score has been staged by numerous choreographers and has become a staple of the Polish repertory.

In the late 1930s two independent companies were founded with the aim of bringing the national dance tradition to the stage in new ways. In 1935 Feliks Parnell, a ballet-trained revue dancer, founded a company that specialized in gymnastic and often grotesque versions of Polish dance. The company won first prize at the dance competition during the 1936 Olympic Games in Berlin and toured at home and abroad until 1939. [*See the entry on Parnell.*]

In 1937 the Polish Ballet was founded, to propagate Polish dance and ballet abroad. Financed by Poland's Ministry of Foreign Affairs, the company was directed by Arnold Szyfman, who engaged Bronislava Nijinska to stage a selection of her works for the company's first season. Leon Woizikowski, Piotr Zajlich, and Jan Ciepliński were engaged for the second season and created new works for the company, which disbanded in 1939 with the outbreak of World War II.

World War II caused a serious setback in the development of ballet, with Nazi occupation forces in Poland from 1939 to 1945. Training opportunities were limited to private studios, and many theaters were physically destroyed. It took ten years to restore the technical standards of ballet ensembles and twenty years to rebuild the lost theaters. Warsaw's Wielki Theater was not reopened until 1965.

Despite the many obstacles, however, dance activity resumed immediately at the war's end. Small companies toured in the late 1940s, including one led by Woizikowski and another led by Parnell. At the same time, ballet companies were established or reestablished in Warsaw, Poznań, Łódź, Wrocław, Gdańsk, and Bytom. The generally low level of classical training demanded that the repertory focus on character and national dances. Typically, works relied on the abilities of a small group of soloists, and this period produced a number of strong personalities, such as Barbara Bittnerówna, Alicja Boniuszko, Maria Krzyszkowska, Olga Sawicka, Witold Borkowski, Zbigniew Kiliński, Zbigniew Strazatkowski, Stanisław Szymanski, and Henryk Tomaszewski.

In 1950, Poland's Soviet-style government reorganized dance education, founding ballet schools in Warsaw, Poznań, Gdańsk, and Bytom. (A fifth school, in Łódź, was started in 1975.) The 1950s also saw Soviet works enter the repertory: the school in Bytom presented the Polish premiere of *The Fountain of Bakhchisarai* in 1953, and the one in Warsaw presented the Polish premiere of *Romeo and Juliet* in 1954. Premieres of *Cinderella, The Stone Flower, Spartacus, Anna Karenina,* and *Carmen* followed; a number of Russian classics were revived in the 1960s. New works on Polish themes also appeared, including *The King's Jester* (Bytom, 1958) and *Mazepa* (Warsaw, 1958). The traditional choreography of earlier national ballets was dropped and many new versions staged: *Cracow Wedding* was restaged by Janina Jarzynówna-Sobczak (Gdańsk, 1952 and 1959) and Eugeniusz Papliński (Wrocław, 1969); *Pan Twardowski* by Parnell (Poznań, 1955), Stanisław Miszczyk (Warsaw, 1965), and Jerzy Gogół (Bytom, 1970); and *The Highlanders* by Jerzy Kapliński (Poznań, 1947), Miszczyk (Warsaw, 1951), and Jarzynówna-Sobczak (Gdańsk, 1960).

The only choreographer of the postwar generation to derive inspiration from nonclassical sources was Jarzynówna-Sobczak. However, the leading choreographers of the following generation—Witold Gruca, Conrad Drzewiecki, Teresa Kujawa, and Ewa Wycichowska—turned toward the fusion of classical and modern sources. The affiliation with the opera house now seemed more of a hindrance than a help, and in 1973 Drzewiecki founded the Polish Dance Theater in Poznań as a showcase for modern works. Many of these works are set to music by contemporary Polish composers, and few if any make reference to the tradition of national dances.

In the mid-1980s Poland supported eight opera-house ballet ensembles, five government ballet schools, and the independent Polish Dance Theater. Classical theater dance occupied a secure position, yet room existed for modern alternatives. The two-hundredth jubilee of Polish ballet was celebrated in 1985. In 1989, the Soviet-style government was voted out of office.

The historical turning point of 1989 brought, as one of its consequences, the necessity for restructuring Polish ballet. This process is taking more time than originally expected because of a generally underdeveloped economy. Classical ballet companies connected with Poland's opera theaters are still hampered by organizational schemes created around 1950. This is also the case with the former state-supported ballet schools. The most significant development in modern dance activities (this type of theatrical dance was poorly supported under communist rule) is

POLAND: Theatrical Dance. Members of the Polish Dance Theater in Posnań perform *Dziecińistwo Jezusa,* choreographed by Conrad Drzewiecki to *L'Enfance du Christ* by Hector Berlioz. It premiered on 12 December 1980. (Photograph by Andrzej Szozda; from the Dance Collection, New York Public Library for the Performing Arts.)

that new companies can emerge without any problematic relics. The most important dance center is Poznań, especially the Polish Dance Theater; after Drzewiecki's retirement in 1987, it has Ewa Wycichowska as director.

[*For information on other principal figures, see the entries on Cieplinski, Drzewiecki, Gogół Gruca, Lowski, Miszczyk, Papliński, Tomaszewski, and Woizikowski.*]

BIBLIOGRAPHY

Berski, Jan. *Kolokwia baletowe.* Bydgoszcz, 1988.

Chynowski, Paweł. "The Anniversary of Polish Ballet." *Ballett International* 8 (May 1985): 18–21.

Chynowski, Paweł, and Janina Pudełek. *Almanach baletu warszawskiego, 1785–1985/Le ballet de Varsovie, 1785–1985.* Warsaw, 1987.

Dąbrowski, Stanisław, and Zbigniew Raszewski, eds. *Słownik biograficzny teatru polskiego.* 2 vols. Warsaw, 1973–1994.

Drabecka, Maria. *Choreografia baletów warszawskich za Sasów.* Kraków, 1988.

Jasinski, Roman. "Some Recollections of *Swan Lake* in Warsaw." *Dance Chronicle* 14.1 (1991): 102–107.

Karsavina, Tamara. *Theatre Street.* Rev. and enl. ed. London, 1948.

Mamontowicz-Łojek, Bożena. "François Gabriel Le Doux, baletmistrz i choreograf, 1755–1823." *Pamiętnik teatralny* 62.2 (1967).

Mamontowicz-Łojek, Bożena. "Szkoła artystyczno-teatralna Antoniego Tyzenhauza, 1774–1785." *Rozprawy z dziejów oświaty* 11 (1968).

Mamontowicz-Łojek, Bożena. *Terpsychora i lekkie muzy.* Kraków, 1972.

Neuer, Adam, ed. *Polish Opera and Ballet of the Twentieth Century: Operas, Ballets, Pantomimes, Miscellaneous Works.* Translated by Jerzy Zawadzki. Kraków, 1986.

Pudełek, Janina. *Warszawski balet romantyczny, 1802–1866.* Warsaw, 1968.

Pudełek, Janina. *Warszawski balet w latach 1867–1915.* Warsaw, 1981.

Pudełek, Janina. *Z historii baletu.* Warsaw, 1981.

Pudełek, Janina. *Two Hundred Years of Polish Ballet, 1785–1985.* Warsaw, 1985.

Pudełek, Janina, and Jacek Lumiński. "Poland: Anniversary Celebrations of Polish Ballet." *Ballett International* 9 (May 1986): 38–41.

Pudełek, Janina. "The Warsaw Ballet under the Directorships of Maurice Pion and Filippo Taglioni, 1832–1853." *Dance Chronicle* 11.2 (1988): 219–273.

Pudełek, Janina. "The Status of Dance Research in Poland." In *Beyond Performance: Dance Scholarship Today,* edited by Susan Au and Frank-Manuel Peter. Berlin, 1989.

Pudełek, Janina. "*Swan Lake* in Warsaw, 1900." *Dance Chronicle* 13 (Winter 1990–1991): 359–367.

Pudełek, Janina. "Crisis of Polish Dance." *Ballett International* 14 (July–August 1991): 56.

Pudełek, Janina. "Fokine in Warsaw, 1908–1914." *Dance Chronicle* 15.1 (1992): 59–71.

Rambert, Marie. *Quicksilver: The Autobiography of Marie Rambert.* London, 1972.

Turska, Irena. *Krótki zarys historii tańca i baletu.* Kraków, 1961.

JANINA PUDEŁEK

Dance Research and Publication

The first scholarly studies of Polish folk dance were begun in 1935 by the Department of Ethnology of the University of Warsaw under the guidance of Professor Cezaria Baudouin de Courtenay-Ehrenkreutz-Jędrzejewiczowa. The results were published in *Les archives internationales de la danse* in Paris. After World War II, research was resumed, and thirty-nine dances were recorded in the field and published in 1948 by Zofia Kwaśnicowa. Field studies were continued in northern Poland by Roderyk Lange at the Ethnological Museum in Toruń and in the Warmia and Mazuria regions by Maria Drabecka. Among other important ethnochoreologists are Grażyna Dąbrowska, who has studied the dance folklore of central Poland, and Janina Marcinkowa, who has specialized in the folk dances of Silesia. From 1968 to 1981, systematic documentation of the traditional dances of various areas was sponsored by the Institute of Art of the Polish Academy of Sciences in Warsaw. The institute continues to encourage research in the present day. Polish ethnochoreologists are also active members of the International Council for Traditional Music.

The first Polish theatrical dance company was His Majesty's Dancers, established in 1785 by King Stanisław II Augustus. Information about this company comes from various sources: extant playbills and theater records; published libretti; the memoirs of Antoni Magier; the letters of Urszula Mniszchówna; the *Dzieje Teatru Narodowego* (History of the National Theater; 1820), by Wojciech Bogusławski, "the father of Polish theater"; and various contemporary press notices. Descriptions of performances can also be found in eighteenth-century memoirs by foreign visitors, such as Elise von der Recke (*Mein Journal,* 1928) and Friedrich Schultz.

In the nineteenth century, the Warsaw press devoted increasing space to ballet performances. Because of the influence of French criticism, professional Polish dance critics appeared. The first was Antoni Lesznowski, whose work was published in *Gazeta warszawska* (1841–1853); later critics included Władysław Bogusławski of *Kurier warszawski* and Marian Gawalewicz of *Kłosy* and *Tygodnik ilustrowany.* As Polish ballet developed, music and theater critics and other journalists began to concern themselves with dance. These included Stanisław Ciechomski, Antoni Sygietyński, Adam Dobrowolski, Aleksander Poliński, Józef Kotarbiński, Wacław Szymanowski, and Jan Kleczyński.

A great deal of information on ballet in Warsaw at the turn of the twentieth century is contained in the memoirs of the theater historian Paweł Owerło, the singer Janina Korolewicz-Waydowa, the Anglo-Polish ballet director Marie Rambert (née Cyvia Rambam), the Polish-American film actress Pola Negri (née Barbara Appolonia Chalupiec), and the Russian ballerina Tamara Karsavina. The outstanding ballet critics between the world wars were the journalist Henryk Liński and the theoretician Jan Ostrowski-Naumoff. Both contributed criticism to numerous periodicals.

During the interwar period, the first serious Polish attempts at developing a theory of ballet were made. These were Stanisław Idzikowski's *O tańcu* (On the Dance; 1927) and a two-volume anthology, *Taniec* (Dance, 1930), which contains, among other essays, Władysław Witwicki's "O naturze tańca" (On the Nature of Dance), Franciszek Siedlecki's "Taniec religijny i obrzędowy" (Religious and Ritual Dance), and Edward Kuryło's "Taniec ludowy, dworski i towarzyski" (Folk, Court, and Social Dance). The most serious theoretician and historian of the period was Stanisław Głowacki. His more important works were "Balet, taniec sceniczny, szkolnictwo taneczne" (Ballet, Staged Dance, Dance Education; 1936) and "Zarys historii tańca widowiskowego" (Outline of the History of Staged Dance; 1937–1938), both of which were published in the magazine *Scene polska*.

After World War II, the following critics were active: Tacjanna Wysocka, from 1947 in the magazine *Teatr;* Irena Turska, from 1947 in *Ruch muzyczny;* Janina Pudełek, from 1958 in *Pamiętnik teatralny* and *Teatr;* Bożena Mamontowicz-Łojek, from 1967 in *Pamiętnik teatralny;* and Paweł Chynowski, from 1970 in *Ruch muzyczny* and *Życie warszawy. Życie warszawy* was established in 1974 and continues to publish the journal *Taniec.*

Currently the most frequent and important writings on ballet are Chynowski's in the daily *Życie warszawy,* Pudełek's in *Teatr,* and Turska's in *Ruch muzyczny.* These critics also conduct research and publish works on the theory and history of ballet.

Important publications in Polish include Wysocka's *Dzieje baletu* (History of Ballet; 1970) and Turska's *Leon Wójcikowski* (1958), *Pan Twardowski* (1959), *W kręgu tańca* (About the Dance; 1965), *Przewodnik baletowy* (A Guide to the Ballet; 1973), and *Almanach baletu polskiego, 1945–1974* (Almanac of Polish Ballet, 1945–1974; 1983). Especially notable among Pudełek's many publications are *Warszawski balet romantyczny, 1802–1866* (Romantic Ballet in Warsaw, 1802–1866; 1968), "Polskie tańce narodowe na scenie" (Polish National Dances on the Stage) in *Różne formy tańców polskich* (Various Forms of Polish Dances; 1980), and *Warszawski balet w latach 1867–1915* (Warsaw Ballet in the Years 1867–1915; 1981). Mamontowicz-Łojek's works include an important essay, "Szkoła artystyczno-teatralna Antoniego Tyzenhauza, 1774–1785" (The School of Theatrical Arts of Antoni Tyzenhauz, 1774–1785), published in *Rozprawy z dziejów oświaty* (1968), and two books: *Terpsychora i lekkie muzy, 1918–1939* (Terpsichore and the Light Muses, 1918–1939; 1972) and *Polskie szkolnictwo baletowe w okresie międzywojennym* (Polish Ballet Schools during the Interwar Period; 1978). Polish correspondents for foreign magazines have included Chynowski, in *Dance Magazine* and *Monslavatdanza,* and Mamontowicz-Łojek, in *Les saisons de la danse.*

PAWEŁ CHYNOWSKI

POLKA. The precise origin of the polka, a sprightly couple dance in 2/4 time dating from about the 1820s, is obscure, even though much was written about the dance almost from its introduction. Music resembling the polka in rhythm and melodic content has been found in central European manuscripts that predate the ballroom dance by several centuries. Polka music is written in 2/4 time in eight-measure phrases in two parts, each repeated. There follows a two-part trio, also in eight-measure phrases, each repeated. The first part is then played again, ending in a coda. Often an introduction, more or less elaborate, precedes the dance itself. The polka is similar to the galop but is played at a more moderate tempo. The elder and younger Johann Strauss, Frédéric Chopin, Jacques Offenbach, and Bedřich Smetana, among other composers, contributed to the polka repertory.

As for the dance itself, Paul Nettl (1947) gives the Czech word *púlka* ("half," referring to the shift of weight from one foot to the other) as one possible source of the name. Others trace the word *polka* to Slavic words meaning "Polish-like" or "Polish maiden." According to legend, a Bohemian peasant girl from Elbeleinitz called Anna Slezak (or Anna Chadrimova) extemporized the step and melody upon hearing good news of her soldier-lover. The village schoolmaster, Josef Neruda, was present, noted down her steps, and subsequently taught the dance to his pupils. Its popularity spread through village festivals; after reaching Prague, it arrived in Vienna in 1835 and Paris in 1840.

Franatišik Bonus, a Czech dance historian, has offered the theory that early nineteenth-century Bohemian nationalists devised the polka from local folk dance sources, performing it as a patriotic Bohemian statement—much as the czardas was danced at the Habsburg court of Vienna, to draw attention to the cause of Hungarian nationalism. In 1840, a dancing master from Prague named Raab danced the Bohemian polka in Slavic costume at the Odéon Theatre in Paris to much acclaim.

It is generally accepted that the celebrated dancing masters of Paris—Cellarius, Coralli, Laborde, Petipa, and later Markowski—alert to fashionable innovations in dance, took up the polka and refined the steps to accord with the French style, ensuring its immediate acceptance in the fashionable centers of Europe and the New World. The French dancing master Eugène Coulon, who had settled in London, is given credit for introducing the polka to English society in 1844, although Cellarius himself later traveled to England to demonstrate his own version. In the same year the polka was danced on the London stage by Carlotta Grisi, with Jules Perrot as her partner, and later by Fanny Cerrito and Arthur Saint-Léon. It immediately crossed the Atlantic and conquered New York. Captivated, theatergoers in both London and New York could hardly wait to try the polka in the ballroom.

The *Illustrated London News* (23 March 1844 and 11 May 1844) devoted many columns to the polka craze, including a full description of the steps and figures. The dance was said to combine "the intimacy of the waltz with the vivacity of the Irish jig." As originally introduced, the polka was danced only moderately fast, with five specific figures in prescribed sequence: the Bohémienne (or heel-and-toe polka); the Pursuit (partner fleeing from partner, finally succumbing to captivity); the Polka-Promenade; the Polka-Balançant; and the Polka-Waltz (or Turn). The steps were carefully and precisely executed, without stamps or heel clicks (Slavonic characteristics had been suppressed), and dancers were admonished to hold the free foot against the other ankle, toe pointed downward *(sur le cou de pied)*. The sequence of five figures was soon abandoned in favor of the Polka-Turn, the buoyant rotation of couples around the ballroom at ever-increasing speed, which is associated with the polka to this day.

The basic movements of the polka—the *sauté, glissé,* and *chassé* steps—have long been found in dance descriptions. Indeed, the double step of the Renaissance *branle* gives all the weight shifts of the polka, as dancers in the *branle* circle to the left and back to the right, although without the rotation characteristic of the nineteenth-century polka.

The nineteenth-century polka is performed to a count of four. It consists of a hop right, in place; an immediate slide to the left, along the line of direction; a step left, to close the right foot to the left; and a slide or spring with the left foot to the side, with a half turn clockwise. After a pause, the step is repeated on the opposite foot, along the same line of direction, to complete a full turn. The partner performs the counterpart step on the opposite foot.

The original polka step closely resembles the Scottish *strathspey* step, familiar from the Scotch reels of the late eighteenth century. The eminent German dance historian Friedrich Zorn, who saw the introduction of the polka, recounts in his *Grammar of the Art of Dancing* (1887) that he traveled from Odessa to Vienna and Paris in 1844 to learn the new polka step, only to discover that it was nothing but the well-known Scottish waltz in the hands of those "who understood how to advertise it."

Because the fashionable dance world already knew how to *chassé, jeté,* and *sauté,* to galop, waltz, and turn, the polka was easily accepted. Its association with nationalistic sentiments accelerated its rise to fame. "Books, *feuilletons* [pamphlets] novels, poems, plays, music, all dealt with the polka," Vuillier states in *A History of Dancing* (1898). The polka-dot swept the world of fashionable fabrics, and dresses were shortened to reveal the toes for dancing.

The polka relegated the simple galop to an inferior place on the ballroom program. Even the waltz was eclipsed for a time by the polka craze. Only the quadrille held its own, serving as a breathing space between polkas and an opportunity for conversation, not possible during a vigorous polka. Polka steps were soon introduced into quadrille figures, and polka-quadrilles flourished. By the 1850s, the polka step had been adapted to waltz rhythms in triple time, and the popular polka-redowa was born. Polka steps were combined with the galop in the Esmeralda Glide, and later with the mazurka to provide a means of turning in variations known as *polka-mazurka, varsovienne, zingerella, gitana,* and a host of other dances.

POLKA. By 1844 the polka was popular in urban ballrooms of the United States. This illustration appeared in the November 1845 issue of a popular women's magazine, *Godey's Magazine and Lady's Book* and included instructions for dancing the figures. (Courtesy of Elizabeth Aldrich.)

Only after several decades did enthusiasm for the polka give way to a more languid style of dancing. The spring and hop subsided into a glide and barely perceptible rise. With the substitution of a slight dip or pause for the hop, a dance known as the two-step evolved from the polka. This dance became enormously popular toward the beginning of the twentieth century and paved the way for the fox trot. Nonetheless, the polka remained on ballroom programs throughout the nineteenth century. Melvin B. Gilbert, the American dancing master, included no fewer than thirty polka variations in his book *Round Dances* (1890), among them the Glide, Coquette, Rush, Berlin, Wave, Militaire, Duchess, Metropolitan, Antiers, Russe, Baby, and Combination polkas. Polka steps were retained in the one-step and in certain dances of the ragtime era after 1900.

Although generally eclipsed by the tango and other more sophisticated dances of the 1920s and 1930s, the polka was revived during World War II, both in the dance hall and in folk dance societies. The popularity of the polka never waned in rural areas, and it is a mainstay in national dances of most European cultures as well as among their immigrant communities in the United States.

[*See also* Social Dance, *article on* Nineteenth-Century Social Dance.]

BIBLIOGRAPHY

Cellarius, Henri. *The Drawing-Room Dances*. London, 1847.
Gilbert, Melvin B. *Round Dancing*. Portland, Me., 1890.
Grove, Lilly M. *Dancing*. London, 1895.
Illustrated London News (23 March, 11 May 1844).
Michel, Artur. "Polka: The Dance Sensation of 1844" (parts 1–2). *Dance Magazine* (January–February 1944).
Nettl, Paul. *The Story of Dance Music*. New York, 1947.
Richardson, Philip J. S. *The Social Dances of the Nineteenth Century in England*. London, 1960.
Vuillier, Gaston. *A History of Dancing*. 2d ed. New York, 1898.
Zorn, Friedrich Albert. *Grammar of the Art of Dancing* (1887). Translated by Benjamin P. Coates. Boston, 1905.

FILM. *In Heaven There Is No Beer?* (1984), a documentary film on the polka in the United States, by Les Blank, distributed by Flower Films, El Cerrito, California. Features such polka stars as Jimmy Sturr, Eddie Blazonzyck, and Walt Solek.

Desmond F. Strobel

POLONAISE. The *polonez,* a dance with a long history in Poland, was originally known in its folk forms as *taniec wielki* ("great dance"), *pieszy* ("walker"), *wolny* ("slow"), *powolny* ("leisurely"), or *chodzony* ("pacer")—names that indicate its dominant movement qualities. It was mentioned as early as the fifteenth century in a German chronicle that called it *Polnischer Tanz.* The name *polonez,* which came into Poland in the mid-eighteenth century, arrived by way of the French word *polonaise,* meaning "Polish."

In its folk forms the *polonez* was connected with wedding celebrations, with which it remained associated until the 1920s. Foreigners' reports note that it was danced at the Polish court in the seventeenth century. It was adopted as a courtly dance by the nobility and the townspeople, and by the mid-eighteenth century it was danced by all strata of Polish society as well as onstage.

A dignified dance in triple meter (3/4) in a moderate tempo, the *polonez* was often used to open balls. Led by the most distinguished couple present, it was a solemn processional that reaffirmed the importance of rank and provided an occasion for the display of splendid national robes. The male dancer led his female partner on his right side, her hand placed on his palm, which was outstretched in front of him. From time to time he passed the lady in front of him to his other side, then back again. The dance was varied by bows and polite conversation. In the nineteenth century, when the dance reached its highest point of development and popularity, the Poles often saw it as a symbol of their social customs and relationships. The *polonez* also became known as a musical form employed by many Polish composers, notably the pianist Frédéric Chopin; the form called the *polonaise* has undergone changes by non-Polish composers.

Outside Poland, the *polonez,* or *polonaise,* was adopted as a ballroom dance in Russia, Germany, and France. As in Poland, it was often used to open balls, and its processional character, so congenial to the display of fine attire, was retained although it was sometimes concluded with a waltz. The dance achieved a peak of popularity in the mid-nineteenth century, when it was valued for its dignity and regard for social hierarchy. In England its reception was lukewarm, although Queen Victoria and Prince Albert led the *polonaise* that opened their costume ball in 1846; thus it soon appeared at other English costume balls. The popularity of the *polonaise* as a social dance has now waned, even in Poland, although it survives on the stage. In George Balanchine's ballets, for example, it is notable in *Tchaikovsky Suite No. 3* ("Theme and Variations") and in *Diamonds,* set to Tchaikovsky's Symphony no. 3 in D (The Polish, 1875).

BIBLIOGRAPHY

Giordano, Gloria. "La Polonaise." *Chorégraphie* 1 (Autumn 1993): 85–96.
Moreton, Ursula. "National Dances in Ballet" (parts 1–2). *The Dancing Times* (March–April 1935).
Sroka, Czesław. *Polskie tańce narodowe*. Warsaw, 1990.
Szweykowski, Zygmunt. "Tradition and Popular Elements in Polish Music of the Baroque Era." *Musical Quarterly* (January 1970): 99–115.

Susan Au

POLYNESIA. Dance in the central and southern Pacific islands of Polynesia is essentially a visual extension and enhancement of sung poetry, based on complex arm movements performed by dancers either seated or standing in one or more rows facing an audience. The oral literature that dance renders into visual form is an artistic medium used to praise and honor the gods and high-ranking chiefs, to formally recognize national or local events, to praise places and people, and to entertain. Occasionally the poet-choreographer extends his or her net to include satire, ridicule, and social criticism; however, she or he is more likely to uphold the traditional social stratification in which he or she has an honored place. Welcoming visitors and entertaining them, while at the same time honoring one's own group or individuals of it, is an important function of dance. In some parts of Polynesia, ritual performances for the gods were related to dancing and used similar movements, but these were classified as distinct movement activities.

Social prestige is derived from elevated genealogical descent that can be traced to the gods and that is associated with power and authority. Dance performances give allegiance to the rank-based sociopolitical systems and honor and validate social distinctions. Performances are offered as gifts to those with prestige and power. In these societies, where power resides in the office and a regime is long and enduring, specialists compose poetry, add music and movement, and rehearse the performers for these dances of presentation. The audience brings to the performance a critical aesthetic evaluation of poetic composition, musical sound and appropriateness, movement allusion, and choreographic structure, as well as an evaluation of overall performance and appropriateness for the occasion. Sociological information is conveyed by the order of the dances, by the placement of individuals within the group, and by the costumes, which might impart information about the rank of the performers and their genealogical associations.

POLYNESIA. Two female dancers from Takaroa Island, Tuamotu Archipelago, posing for a photograph in the 1920s. Their weighted stance and gentle arm gestures, with wrists bent back, are typical of central Polynesian dancing. (Photograph by R. H. Beck; from the Department of Library Services, American Museum of Natural History, New York [no. 107641]; used by permission.)

Each island group has its own distinctive dance genres and movement traditions, but there have been few studies focusing on dance. Although details of movement, sociocultural context, and local categories or genres differ from area to area, two major groupings or subareas can be delineated, corresponding to the culture areas known as West Polynesia and East Polynesia. West Polynesia includes Tonga, Samoa, 'Uvéa (Wallis), Futuna, Niue, Tuvalu (Ellice), Tokelau, and Fiji. Although Fiji is often included in Melanesia on the grounds of similarity in the people's physical type as well as some sociological and cultural features, Fijian dance is more closely related to West Polynesian dance than to the dances of island Melanesia. Also included in West Polynesia are the dance traditions of certain Polynesian-colonized islands that lie geographically outside Polynesia, including Bellona (Mungiki), Rennell (Mungaba), Anuta, Tikopia, and Ontong Java (Lord Howe). East Polynesia includes the Marquesas Islands, Society Islands (Tahiti), Tuamotu Islands, Austral Islands, Cook Islands, New Zealand, Mangareva, Easter Island, and Hawaii.

In West Polynesia the basic dance distinctions are between formal and informal dances, which are usually terminologically distinguished as *day dances* and *night dances,* respectively. In East Polynesia the basic distinction is between movement used during religious rituals and that used during more secular occasions—often distinguished as movements that express humility and movements that express joy. Today these distinctions have almost disappeared, and information about them must be inferred from the remnants of obsolete dance terms.

Focusing on dance movement itself, the most important distinguishing feature between West and East Polynesia is the use of the hips. Generally speaking, the legs and lower body are used primarily to keep the rhythmic pulse, but in East Polynesia the addition of hip movements has developed lower body movement motifs that are named and judged as aesthetic elements in their own right. In West Polynesia the use of the hips is not significant, and lower-body movements primarily follow from the stepping of the feet; in East Polynesia, by contrast hip sways and tilts as well as circular motions give a very different character to the standing dances. The women's side-to-side or circular hip movements with upper legs parallel often contrast with the movements of the men, who open and close their legs while in a bent-knee position.

A more subtle movement component, which gives each Polynesian dance tradition its distinctive local style, is the use of the hands, wrists, and arms. The placement of the arms in space is a significant element, as are the flexions

POLYNESIA. Iolani Luahine was much admired as a performer of chant-accompanied *hula*. She is seen here performing a Hawaiian *hula pahu*, c.1945. (Photograph by C. R. Fuazien; from the Department of Library Services, American Museum of Natural History, New York [no. 319810]; used by permission.)

and extensions of the wrists and knuckles, the facing of the palms, and the curling of the fingers, as well as the presence or absence of rotation of the lower arm. In Tonga there is a complex interplay among rotation of the lower arm, facing of the palm, flexion and extension of the wrists, and curling of the fingers. Samoan arm movements are based on flexions of the elbows, extension of the wrists, and the curling of the fingers. These motifs can occur only in certain arm positions, which change in characteristic ways within a motif, giving a flowing character to the movement. Also characteristic of Tonga, Samoa, and other West Polynesian areas is the importance of two kinds of hand-clapping—a flat, high-pitched clap (called *pasi* or *pati*) and a cross-clap with cupped hands (called *fu* or *pu*), which emits a lower, hollow sound.

In East Polynesia, arm positions usually do not change within a motif unless they enhance a verse of poetry that conveys movement. In New Zealand, the most characteristic movement is *wiri*, a hand quiver with stiff wrists, with the arms placed in a straight or diagonal position or with the elbow bent at an angle of ninety degrees or more. In Tahiti and other parts of central Polynesia, rather stiff wrists are often flicked outward through pulsed lower arm rotations in bilaterally symmetrical arm positions. In Hawaii, precise hand positions and soft wrist movements without lower-arm rotation are placed in right, left, diagonal, or forward orientations.

Through these movements, the dancers objectify, allude to, interpret, or ornament dance texts, which are often based on traditional stories, legends, or myths, but a story is not "told" in the narrative sense. Instead, information is conveyed in an indirect way, and the poetry is often the vehicle for making inferences relevant to the occasion at which it is presented. Through veiled references and layered meanings in poetry and movement, Polynesian composers and dancers contribute to the artistic and social life of the community.

[*For general discussion, see* Oceanic Dance Traditions. *See also* Bellona; Fiji; Maori Dance; Rapanui; Samoa; Tahiti; Tonga; *in addition see* Hula *and* Music for Dance, *article on* Oceanic Music.]

BIBLIOGRAPHY

Anderson, Johannes A. *Maori Music with Its Polynesian Background.* New Plymouth, N. Z., 1934.

Burrows, Edwin G. "Polynesian Music and Dancing." *Journal of the Polynesian Society* 49 (1940): 331–346.

Kaeppler, Adrienne L. "Polynesian Dance as 'Airport Art.'" In *Asian and Pacific Dance: Selected Papers from the 1974 CORD-SEM Conference,* edited by Adrienne L. Kaeppler Van Zile-Wolz. New York, 1977.

Kaeppler, Adrienne L. "Polynesian Music and Dance." In *Musics of Many Cultures,* edited by Elizabeth May. Berkeley, 1980.

Kaeppler, Adrienne L. *Polynesian Dance: With a Selection for Contemporary Performances.* Honolulu, 1983.

ADRIENNE L. KAEPPLER

POOLE, DAVID (born 17 September 1925 in Cape Town, died 27 August 1991 in Cape Town), South African ballet dancer, choreographer, teacher, and company director. At age eighteen, Poole began his ballet training with Cecily Robinson and Dulcie Howes at the University of Cape Town Ballet School. A few years later, after the war in Europe had ended, he went to London and continued his studies at the Sadler's Wells Ballet School. He was invited to join Sadler's Wells Theatre Ballet in 1947 and was promoted to principal dancer the following year. He remained with this company until 1955, when he joined the Sadler's Wells Ballet at Covent Garden. In 1956 he toured the United States with that company, by then called the Royal Ballet; in 1957 he briefly joined Ballet Rambert and taught for Kurt Jooss at the Folkwang Schule in Essen; and in 1958 he performed with the Edinburgh International Ballet at the Edinburgh Festival.

With the Sadler's Wells Theatre Ballet, Poole danced a large repertory and was particularly admired for his accomplishments as a dancer-actor in character roles, such as the Rake in Ninette de Valois's *The Rake's Progress* and Pierrot in Michel Fokine's *Le Carnaval.* He created roles in several of John Cranko's ballets, notably the Beast in *Beauty and the Beast* (1949) and Jasper in *Pineapple Poll* (1951), in which he was particularly affecting. He also created roles in Alfred Rodrigues's *Blood Wedding* (1953) and in Kenneth MacMillan's *Danses Concertantes* and *House of Birds* (both 1955). With the Edinburgh International Ballet, he created roles in Walter Gore's *The Night and the Silence* and Peter Wright's *The Great Peacock* (both 1958).

During these years Poole returned to South Africa several times, in 1952, 1957, and 1958, to appear as guest artist with the University of Cape Town (UCT) Ballet, for which he also staged works by Cranko and Frederick Ashton. In 1959 he returned once more and joined the staff of the UCT Ballet School. When in 1963 the South African government established the Cape Performing Arts Board (CAPAB) and provided funds for a professional ballet company, the UCT Ballet became CAPAB Ballet, with Dulcie Howes as artistic director and Poole as ballet master. In 1967 Howes retired, and Poole succeeded her as artistic director. He resigned the post for a brief period in 1969 to go overseas but resumed it on his return in 1970. In 1974, he was appointed principal of the UCT Ballet School. He served as professor and principal of the school until 1986 and as director of the company until his retirement at the end of 1990.

During his thirty years' association with CAPAB Ballet, Poole was responsible for producing a large number of works for the company. Under his direction, there is hardly a ballet in the standard classical repertory that failed to find its way to a Cape Town stage. His own original works for the company include *The Snow Queen* (1961), to music by Tchaikovsky; *A Midsummer Night's Dream* (1970), to music by Handel; *Le Cirque* (1973), to music by Bach; and *Variations for Men* (1983), to music by Khachaturian. He also produced two notable works with South African themes: *The Rain Queen* (1973), a reworking of an uncompleted work by Frank Staff, based on an African legend, and *Kami* (1976), based on a story of the Cape Colony. [*For further details, see* CAPAB Ballet.]

Through his work in Cape Town, David Poole had a profound effect on ballet in South Africa. He was a superb teacher, with a special talent for training dancers not only in classical technique but in the subtleties of mime and stagecraft; he was an imaginative and creative producer; and he was a truly visionary company director. He brought the CAPAB company to full professional status, with exceptionally well trained dancers, a widely varied repertory, and productions on a par with those of the best companies elsewhere in the world.

[*See also* South Africa, *article on Ballet.*]

BIBLIOGRAPHY

Beukes, Alec. *David Poole: Tribute.* Cape Town, 1990.

Cooper, Montgomery, and Jane Allyn. *Dance for Life: Ballet in South Africa.* Cape Town, 1980.

Fisher, Hugh, ed. *The Sadler's Wells Theatre Ballet.* London, 1956.

Grut, Marina. *The History of Ballet in South Africa.* Cape Town, 1981.

Woodcock, Sarah C. *The Sadler's Wells Royal Ballet.* London, 1991.

MARINA GRUT

PORT DE BRAS. The balletic term *port de bras* represents the carriage of the arms and their movement from one position to another and a group of exercises for the graceful and harmonious use of the arms. The importance of the placement and carriage of the arms has been summarized as "a basic means of expression for the ballet dancer. They give a finished design to the various poses. Furthermore, the arms must help in the execution of the dance movements, especially turns . . . and the difficult jumps, where they actively aid the body and legs" (Kostrovitskaya and Pisarev, 1978).

In classical ballet, *ports de bras* are performed in smooth, curved designs made slightly in front of the body except when the arms are extended in arabesque positions. Thus, the arms "may be compared to the frame that sets off a picture" (Blasis, 1820). That observation had been made a century earlier, in 1725, by Pierre Rameau. It underscores the long-established importance of the arms as a means of balancing the body visually and physically.

Generally, when the arms are raised from a low to a higher level, they pass in front of the body through the "gateway" position (corresponding to first position in the Russian/Vaganova school, or fifth position *en avant* in the Cecchetti method and Bournonville school). When lowering, the arms generally open outward through second position. In contemporary ballet technique, these movements are made from the shoulders, but earlier styles emphasized movements from the elbows and wrists as well. Writing in 1831, E. A. Théleur advised that a "greater degree of grace" will be achieved if the dancer will "bend the elbows and wrists a little more" when raising the arms before extending them to the final position. Eighteenth-century technique specified three distinct movements of the arms that corresponded and agreed with the three essential movements of the legs. Thus, movement "of the Wrist, has Relation to the Heel; that of the Elbow, to the Knee, and that of the Shoulder, or the whole Arm, to the Thigh" (John Weaver, 1706).

Most writers on dance technique have agreed with Agrippina Vaganova's assessment: "*Port de bras* is the most difficult part of the dance, requiring the greatest amount of work and concentration" (Vaganova, [1934] 1953). According to Théleur, early nineteenth-century technique included "the study of the arms, commencing by placing them in front and lowering them at the sides" and "opposition circles . . . the arms going in contrary directions to each other . . . separately, and in conjunction with the exercises of the legs" (Théleur, 1831). Eighteenth-century dancers were advised by Rameau to practice arm movements in front of a mirror in order to correct any faults (Rameau, 1725).

Although an infinite variety of *ports de bras* may be devised, certain exercises for the arms have become standardized, such as the eight sets of *ports de bras* in the Cecchetti method. Earlier precedents for some of these exercises can be found. For instance, the Cecchetti first *port de bras* (arms move upward from fifth *en bas* to fifth *en avant* and then outward to second position before returning to fifth *en bas*) can be compared with the low *porte de bras* advocated by Gottfried Taubert (1717) for use especially with *courante* and minuet steps (arms fall gently forward, then rise with slightly bent elbows and open directly to both sides, where they gradually stretch and rotate so that the cupped hands are mostly to the front). An earlier hint of this *port de bras* comes from François de Lauze in 1623, also in reference to arm movement to enhance "the grace of the courante." De Lauze writes, "One must, when bending the knee, carry both hands alike toward the busk of the pourpoint, without bending the wrist, and in rising again to make the first step open the arms a little, of which the movements should be gentle and not forced" (Lauze, 1623).

The widespread use of certain arm exercises is apparent, as for example, the Cecchetti second *port de bras* (from an attitude position, the arms open to second position and then extend to arabesque with the downstage arm forward and the torso strongly turned from the waist; the arms then meet in fifth *en avant* and return to the attitude position). This combination is similar to a *port de bras* listed by Vaganova as belonging "to the Italian school, but now widely in use with us." She describes the quality of movement into the arabesque pose as "soft and effortless, like fins" (Vaganova, 1934). This exercise resembles the *double port de bras* contained in one of Arthur Saint-Léon's combinations in *La sténochorégraphie* in 1852.

In 1760 Jean-Georges Noverre, following earlier attempts by John Weaver and others, urged "more variety and expression in the arms," warning that "set rules become almost useless . . . by following them exactly, the *port de bras* will be opposed to the movements of the soul, which cannot be limited to a fixed number of gestures" (Noverre, 1760). Later innovators in broadening the concepts of balletic *port de bras* include Lev Ivanov (e.g., *Swan Lake,* acts 2 and 4) and Michel Fokine (e.g., *The Dying Swan, Petrouchka.*)

The lengthened, more extended silhouette of modern ballet, exemplified in the works of George Balanchine, is reflected in some contemporary classroom *ports de bras.* However, the twisted, angular arm styles introduced in the choreography of Vaslav Nijinsky and many early modern dance pioneers is seldom encountered in the ballet lesson, still a bastion of more traditional forms.

[*See also* Ballet Technique.]

BIBLIOGRAPHY

Beaumont, Cyril W., and Stanislas Idzikowski. *A Manual of the Theory and Practice of Classical Theatrical Dancing* (Méthode Cecchetti). London, 1922.

Blasis, Carlo. *An Elementary Treatise upon the Theory and Practice of the Art of Dancing* (1820). Translated by Mary Stewart Evans. New York, 1944.

Feuillet, Raoul-Auger. *Chorégraphie, ou L'art de décrire la dance, par caractères, figures et signes démonstratifs, avec lesquels on apprend facilement de soy-même toutes sortes de dances.* Paris, 1700. Translated by John Weaver as *Orchesography, or, The Art of Dancing* (London, 1706).

Gerbes, Angelika. "Gottfried Taubert on Social and Theatrical Dance of the Early Eighteenth Century." Ph.D. diss., Ohio State University, 1972.

Gerbes, Angelika. "Eighteenth-Century Dance Instruction: The Course of Study Advocated by Gottfried Taubert." *Dance Research* 10 (Spring 1992): 40–52.

Kostrovitskaya, Vera, and Alexei Pisarev. *School of Classical Dance.* Translated by John Barker. Moscow, 1978.

Lauze, François de. *Apologie de la danse, 1623: A Treatise of Instruction in Dancing and Deportment.* Translated by Joan Wildeblood. London, 1952.

Noverre, Jean-Georges. *Lettres sur la danse et sur les ballets.* Stuttgart and Lyon, 1760. Translated by Cyril W. Beaumont as *Letters on Dancing and Ballets* (London, 1930).

Ralov, Kirsten, ed. *The Bournonville School.* 4 vols. New York, 1979.

Rameau, Pierre. *Le maître à danser.* Paris, 1725. Translated by Cyril W. Beaumont as *The Dancing Master* (London, 1931).

Saint-Léon, Arthur. *La sténochorégraphie.* Paris, 1852. Translated by Raymond Lister. Cambridge, 1992.

Taubert, Gottfried. *Rechtschaffener Tantzmeister, oder Gründliche Erklärung der frantzösischen Tantz-Kunst.* Leipzig, 1717.

Théleur, E. A. *Letters on Dancing, Reducing This Elegant and Healthful Exercise to Easy Scientific Principles.* London, 1831.

Vaganova, Agrippina. *Basic Principles of Classical Ballet: Russian Ballet Technique* (1934). Translated by Anatole Chujoy. Edited by Peggy van Praagh. 2d ed. London, 1953.

SANDRA NOLL HAMMOND

PORTUGAL. [*To survey dance in Portugal, this entry comprises two articles. The first article discusses traditional dance; the second traces the history of theatrical dance.*]

Traditional Dance

Situated on the western coast of the Iberian Peninsula, Portugal is bounded on the north and east by Spain and on the west and south by the Atlantic Ocean. It includes the Azores Islands and Madeira. Although today the country is relatively homogeneous (some 10 million people are Portuguese-speaking Roman Catholics), it has historically been influenced by successive foreign empires, including the Roman and the Arab (North African Moors). Then, between the fifteenth and seventeenth centuries, Portuguese navigators, explorers, traders, and clergy extended its dominion into Africa, Asia, and South America. This era of empire-building resulted in some cultural diversification. Little is known of the dances of the Ibero-Celtic peoples of pre-Roman Portugal. Early documents suggest that from the Middle Ages through the fifteenth or sixteenth century, both courtiers and other Portuguese people appreci-

PORTUGAL: Traditional Dance. A sixteenth-century Flemish tapestry depicting the 1547 triumphal march in honor of Dom João de Castro in Goa (then a Portuguese colony in India). The merry men in the center are dancing to the sounds of drums and tambourines. (Kunsthistorisches Museum, Vienna.)

ated *mouriscas,* dances derived from the Moors, and *judengas,* from the Jews. Some dance dramas depicting battles between Arabs and Christians survive today as religious ceremonial performances.

The social dances mentioned by writers of the sixteenth and seventeenth centuries include the *folia, vilão,* and *tiroliro,* but we have no details of their choreography. Music exists for seventeenth- and eighteenth-century dances, including the *chacota* (probably a *chaconne*) and *xotiça* (probably from the word *Scottish*). In this period, usage distinguished *dança,* in which music was only an accompaniment, from *baile,* in which the music dictated the choreography.

A few archaic ritual dances survived into the early modern period. The "Dança dos Paulitos" (Dance of the Sticks) was a sacred dance, not a martial one. There were dances associated with occupations, such as the "Dança dos Ferreiros" (Dance of the Blacksmiths). Others had biblical themes, including the "Dança do Rei David," the "Dança de Genebres" (the *genebres* was a kind of xylophone), and the *pingacho* and *galandum* of the northeast. From the Middle Ages onward, the Roman Catholic church condemned dancing, but it could not suppress it entirely, and eventually some dances were adapted to religious festivities. The state in general followed the lead of the church, but the Portuguese kings John II and John III (fifteenth and sixteenth centuries) honored some talented dancers.

During the eighteenth and nineteenth centuries, popular dances were adopted in Portugal from the rest of Europe. Two still performed today are the *vira,* derived from the waltz, and the *corridinho,* from the polka. Two nineteenth-century dances of African origin, the *lundum* and *modinha,* are no longer performed.

In the twentieth century, especially under the half-century-long nationalist dictatorship (1925–1974), traditional dance was preserved and encouraged through the creation of *ranchos folclóricos,* groups of dancers and singers established throughout Portugal. Today both the state and the church sponsor these groups through *casas do povo* (popular houses) and *câmaras* (town halls). All the *romarias* (religious festivals in honor of a saint or the Virgin) include performances by *ranchos folclóricos.*

Research and Documentation. There has been little scientific study of traditional Portuguese dance, but a few works have been published. In the 1980s the Faculdade de Motricidade Humana (Faculty of Human Movement), an interdisciplinary group of specialists, undertook the preparation of a choreographic atlas of Portugal. The dances collected were videotaped, transcribed in dance and music notation, and analyzed in various ways. This work included the study of children's dances and games.

Various archives throughout Portugal are maintained by the *ranchos folclóricos* as well as by government institutions. Descriptive notation, rather than Labanotation, is used.

Portugal has no central dance organization. Most of the *ranchos* are affiliated in a federation that exercises both support and control over the authenticity of their choreography, music, and costumes.

Dance Genres. Some well-known traditional dances are ritual in character. The "Dança dos Paulitos," today called the "Dança dos Pauliteiros," is performed by men wearing women's dress of starched white petticoats, flowered hats, scarfs, and ribbons. The "Dança do Rei David" is staged on Midsummer's Day. Lisbon's "Dança do Castelo" (Dance of the Castle) features men who balance on one another's shoulders in a pyramid or "castle." In Madeira, the "Baile da Meia Volta" (Dance of the Half Turn), of Moroccan origin, relates to piracy.

Portuguese traditional social dances are almost all performed in a single or double circle, in pairs. A dance typically begins with a procession, followed by sequences of movements including turns, twirls, jumps, and specific steps. Dances in columns, rows, or quadrilles also exist. There are no solo dances, but some dances involve variations in which one dancer performs a difficult, interesting improvisation, as in the fandango. The structure of the dances is usually repetitive, with the refrain involving the most skillful movements. Some dances, such as the *baile mandado* and *chula,* include group variations directed by a caller, the *mandador.*

The movements of daily life are incorporated into some dances. Along the coast, dancers may raise and swing their arms to imitate the waves of the sea. Feet beating on the soil enact the crushing of grapes in the "Chula do Douro" (a region in the north). The forward-bending posture in some dances reflects work in the field, such as harvesting and olive gathering. Slavery and social domination influenced the bowing in Madeira's *bailinho*. Professions such as shoemaker and barber are mimed in the "Dança dos Pauliteiros."

There are identifiable regional variations in Portugal's dance styles and dynamics. Dances of the central and northern coast have a fast, varied rhythm, grace, fluidity, and harmony, with great beauty of gesture. Those of the mountains are slower but rich in movement variation, with wider, heavier steps. Dances of the plains are slow, with few variations, and they emphasize singing. In the central region, the dances are erotic and demand agility; the steps are emphatic and become faster as the dance progresses, with quick, elaborate footwork. Along the southern coast, the major traits are quickness and lightness, expressing joy.

The most popular traditional dance of the coastal zone is the *vira,* which is also danced throughout Portugal. The singers repeat the last two verses of each quatrain of the song or use vocables. It is a couple dance with steps similar to those of a simple waltz.

In the Douro region, the *chula* has an introduction followed by turns and swirling patterns in which the men pursue the women. The couples in the *malhão* face each other during the introduction, then move forward and back, followed by turns. The *gota* resembles the Spanish *jota* but has more varied figures and a greater number of steps.

The central region has several local specialties. The *verde-gaio* is a quadrille in which couples turn and exchange positions, intermittently beating on the ground and clapping. The *fandango* is the most gallant and flirtatious Portuguese folk dance, done mainly in the Ribatejo area. The *bailarico,* also known as *dança saloia,* has simple movements but is very fast, with a strong rhythm. The *saias* of northern Alentejo are quick dances in 3/4 or 6/8 time, similar to mazurkas or waltzes.

The *corridinho* was developed on the southern coast, from urban dances. Its rhythm is like a polka or galop. It involves turning and swirling movements in which the feet are dragged on the ground, an effect called *escovinha.*

In the Azores, two special dances are the *sapateia,* a refrain dance in 3/4 time, and the *chamarrita,* performed by an even number of couples who hold hands without their bodies touching. In the *bailinho,* indigenous to Madeira, dancers bow repeatedly in 2/4 time.

Music for Dance. The music used is lively, in a major or minor mode, and in 2/4, 3/4, or 6/8 time. Each *rancho* has a *toccata* (orchestra) of instrumentalists and singers; usually the younger people dance while the older ones sing or play. The instruments used are the *gaita de foles* (bagpipe), *bombo* and *zé pereira* (big drums with a deep, powerful sound), and *caixa* (a type of snare drum), all common in the northern and coastal regions. The *adufe* is a square hand-drum with pieces of tin inside, played exclusively by women in the central region. The *pandeiro* and *tamboril* (small drums), *ferrinhos* (triangle), *castanholas* (castanets), and *sarronca* (a resonant instrument made of an earthenware pot with a skin head) are used especially in the northern and central areas. Stringed instruments include the *rabeca* (a fiddle with a short neck, tuned to a very high pitch), several kinds of *viola* (fretted instruments similar to Spanish guitars), and the *cavaquinho* (a four-stringed *viola*). *Flautas* (flutes) are also used. In Madeira, the rhythm is played on the *brinquinho,* seven puppets with castanets arranged on a stick. The imported accordion has become popular, replacing the traditional concertina in the southern and central regions. Certain traditional instrumental combinations exist, such as the *gaiteros,* comprising the *gaita de foles,* the *caixa,* and the *bombo.*

Contexts of Dance. Today's traditional Portuguese dances are performed by the *ranchos folclóricos* in summer, when emigrant workers return home for the holidays, or on special occasions such as harvest, *festas* and *feiras* ("parties" and "fairs"), or *romarias* (religious festivals). Immigrant communities in other countries also hold traditional festivals with dancing. The dancers always have a large, enthusiastic audience, but spectators do not participate in dancing. There are no organized competitions, but some of the dances and songs display virtuoso performances of a competitive nature.

Each *rancho* is very proud of its dances. Anyone can join these groups, and all participants are amateurs; there are special groups for children. They train once or twice a week in a hall, sometimes accompanied by a town orchestra. The *ensaiador* ("rehearsal director") is sometimes older but is not a professional dancer; he may also perform with the group.

BIBLIOGRAPHY

Allenby Jaffe, Nigel, and Margaret Allenby Jaffe. *Ten Dances from Portugal.* Skipton, 1988.

Armstrong, Lucile. *Dances of Portugal.* New York, 1948.

Castelo-Branco, Salwa, and Manuela Toscano. "In Search of a Lost World: An Overview of Documentation and Research on the Traditional Music of Portugal." *Yearbook of the International Council for Traditional Music* 20 (1988).

Caufriez, A. "Introduction à la musique traditionnelle de l'Ile de Porto Santo (Madere)." *Colóquio Artes* 65 (1985).

Dąlabrowska, Grażyna, et al. *International Monograph on Folk Dance,* vol. 2, *Poland, Portugal, Sweden.* Budapest, 1987.

Leça, A. "Danças e cantigas." In *Vida e arte do povo Português,* by António Ferro et al. Lisbon, 1940.

Oliveira, Ernesto Veiga de. *Instrumentos musicais populares portugueses.* Lisbon, 1982.

Ribas, Tomaz. *Danças populares portuguesas.* Lisbon, 1982.

Ribeiro, Mário S. "Música e dança." In *Arte popular em Portugal.* Vol. 2. Lisbon, 1970.

Sasportes, José, and António Pinto Ribeiro. *History of Dance.* Translated by Joan Ennes. Lisbon, 1991.

Sérgio, António. *Breve interpretação da história de Portugal.* 12th ed. Lisbon, 1985.

Viterbo, Sousa. *Arte e artistas em Portugal.* Lisbon, 1892.

FILMS. Faculty of Human Kinetics (FMH), Technical University of Lisbon. National Institute for Workers' Use of Leisure Time (INATEL), Lisbon. RTP (Portuguese Television).

ANA PAULA BATALHA and FERNANDA PRIM

Theatrical Dance

The kingdom of Portugal was established in the Iberian Peninsula in 1142, and the continuity of Portuguese dance history during more than eight centuries illustrates both its geographical isolation and its cultural effort for an integration with the rest of Europe. Economic problems and social conservatism have inhibited artistic life in Portugal over the centuries, so the more expressive moments of dance history tended to occur during periods of sudden affluence—for example, since the 1960s with financial support from the Gulbenkian Foundation, and earlier, in the Renaissance discoveries era and in the 1700s, with the exploitation of Brazil's gold during the colonial period.

In medieval Portuguese song books, in poetry and in illustrations, dance was praised as a noble activity, proper for gentlewomen to engage in to the accompaniment of voice, stringed instruments, or castanets. Dance was related to matters of the heart, such as invitations to tenderness, descriptions of romantic conquest, or expressions of grief at a loved one's departure. Because Portuguese lyrical structure is related to Iberian and Provençal poetic movements, one may surmise that the dance and the court music of the region have similar links. Foreign knights were often welcomed by dancing noblewomen, and by the fourteenth century, visitors were invited to participate. Portuguese royal marriages brought to Lisbon the customs of other European kingdoms, as well as their musicians and dance masters. In 1387, the marriage of King John I to a daughter of the duke of Lancaster enhanced the demand for sophisticated pageantry.

Flemish painter Jan van Eyck, visiting Lisbon in 1428, recorded the spectacular feasts of the Portuguese court. During the same period, King Duarte complained that dance distracted men from martial pursuits. Written accounts refer to all the rulers of Portugal's second dynasty (1385–1580) as good dancers. By 1551, fourteen public dancing schools were operating in Lisbon; in addition, tutors gave private lessons at the homes of the privileged. In the second half of the fifteenth and during the sixteenth century, choreographic masques, organized in the opulent manner of Burgundy, grew in splendor as courtiers amassed wealth from the colonies.

Concurrent with the court's pageantry, a popular religious trend emerged that the Roman Catholic church strove to subdue, because the practices bore similarities to those at ancient pre-Christian feasts. Many of the elements were, however, integrated into the processions that became the large choreographic spectacles referred to by the Jesuit Claude-François Ménéstrier as *ballets ambulatoires.* Despite severe legislation, an erotic element remained and was further developed by contact with exotic dances from the New World. Until the late eighteenth century, both ecclesiastical and royal decrees forbade this sort of dance.

Popular, religious, and aristocratic currents converged and emerged in the theater organized by Gil Vicente (c.1465–1537), the most famous Portuguese playwright. Most of his 50 plays were written for specific festivals, and dance played a large part in them. Some were dance pageants with the participants in fantastic and mythological costumes similar to those of French court ballet. Historians posit that a large number of participants, predominantly courtiers, were required by the choreography of these productions. Consequently, Gil Vicente, in addition to his legacy as writer and producer, can be considered the first Portuguese choreographer. His plays, known as *autos,* were spectacles complete with scenery and machines for producing special effects.

In 1580, Philip II of Spain inherited the crown of Portugal and for sixty years Portugal had no political independence. Lisbon was no longer a court city. Royal receptions were largely arranged by the church, primarily by the Jesuits. The king was treated to a huge procession and a play that showcased the spectacular choreographic elements of earlier court productions: *The Royal Tragicomedy of the Discovery and Conquest of India by the Most Happy Fourteenth King of Portugal, Emmanuel I of Glorious Memory.* The length of the performance was proportional to that of the title. The Jesuits developed this style of theater through sixty years of Spanish rule, and the spectacles were popular despite being written mainly in Latin.

Ballet and Opera. In 1640, Portugal successfully rebelled against Spanish rule and regained independence. The Portuguese court slowly awakened from the shock of Spanish occupation. By the beginning of the eighteenth century, Brazilian gold mines were providing regular revenue, and an influx of new customs came into Portugal with the 1708 marriage of King John V to Marianne of Austria. Portugal was ripe for a blossoming of the arts.

As a patron of the arts, John V commissioned architectural works and religious music, wishing to equal the Vatican's grandeur. He also promoted the expansion of secular music. In 1719 the king invited Italian harpsichordist and composer Domenico Scarlatti to tutor his daughter Maria Barbara, future queen of Spain. Queen Marianne had been educated in the Italian musical tradition, and by 1731 opera had achieved a foothold in Lisbon, where it was first performed in private homes by the Paghettis of Bologna and the composer Gaetano Schiassi. Later opera was performed both at the court and in public theaters. Dance was integral to the performances, and Italian dancers as well as singers traveled to Lisbon to perform.

King Joseph I, son of John V, inherited his father's passion for Italian opera and determined to create a theater equal to the magnificent opera houses being erected throughout Europe. The Casa da Opera, or Opera do Tejo, opened in April 1755 with *Allessandro nelle Indie.* Based on a libretto by Pietro Metastasio, poet and dramatist at the court in Vienna, the music was written by David Perez, a Neapolitan composer. Choreographer Andrea Alberti had accompanied Perez to Lisbon and was to live for many years in Portugal; the dancers came from Genoa. The theater collapsed in the earthquake of 1755, however, and no court theater was immediately planned to replace it. In the years following the earthquake, performances for royalty were mounted on improvised stages.

By 1761 new theaters had opened. Italian opera was still favored, and many dancers came to Lisbon. They produced ballets in the Italian style, presenting them as unrelated entr'actes during operas. François Sauveterre, ballet master in Stuttgart prior to the arrival of Jean-Georges Noverre, lived in Lisbon from 1767 until 1775, during which time he produced *ballets d'action.* Noverre wrote that many of his own ballets were danced in Lisbon. Among the dancers were Giorgio Binetti, Venceslao de Rossi, Alessandro Guglielmi, and Domenico Rossi. Only men performed; until the end of the eighteenth century, Portugal adhered to the papal rule barring women from the stage, so men and castrati played the female roles. The rule was strict in Lisbon but loose in Oporto, where women went onstage.

In 1793 the newly enriched bourgeoisie built the city and crown a theater. Modeled on the former Teatro San Carlo of Naples, it was horseshoe-shaped and named Real Teatro de São Carlos. On its opening night the public applauded an opera by Domenico Cimarosa and two ballets by Gaetano Gioja, *La Felicita Lusitana* and *Gli Dispetti Amorosi.* More than forty productions were mounted in the next seven years by, among others, Pietro Angiolini, Giuseppe Cajiani, Carlo Bencini, Luigi Chiaveri, and Leopoldo Banchelli. Records indicate that in 1794, Cajiani's *Armida e Rinaldo* advertised "a flight of Armida amidst fireworks." This production took place two years before Charles-Louis Didelot's *Flore et Armide,* which is generally accepted as the first ballet in which dancers flew with the assistance of wires. In the following decades, the São Carlos served as the showcase for Italian opera and dance. Little effort was then made to establish a national company with Portuguese dancers. The National Conservatory opened a dance class in 1839 but failed to attract and develop enough worthy dancers.

During the first half of the nineteenth century Portugal suffered three Napoleonic invasions and a civil war, followed by a succession of feuds between conservative and liberal parties. The liberals supported the Romantic movement, and thus history entered the theater. Ballets based on current military events were often performed

PORTUGAL: Theatrical Dance. The interior of the Real Teatro de São Carlos, Lisbon, designed by José Costa e Selva. The theater opened on 30 June 1793 with a production of Domenico Cimarosa's opera *La Balleriñe Amante* and the ballet *A Felicidade Lusitana,* choreographed by Gaetano Gioja to music by Portuguese composer Leal Moreira. (Photograph reprinted from *Dance Perspectives,* Summer 1970, p. 42.)

with the collaboration of actual soldiers, a practice established in the eighteenth century. When brought in to rout the Napoleonic armies, British General Wellington was obliged to forbid his troops to perform in the ballets exalting his victories.

In these early decades of the nineteenth century, the São Carlos strengthened its ties to La Scala of Milan. Carlos Nichili staged some of Salvatore Viganò's ballets and, in 1826, Giuseppe Sorrentino staged *Il Noce di Benevento.* In 1829, Giuseppe Villa mounted a version of *Gli Strelizzi.* Additionally, the French style of ballet had been introduced during Napoleon's incursions; in 1814 Lefebvre had staged *La Fille Mal Gardée.*

The Romantic ferment began with the victory of the liberals. In 1835, Madame Roland was brought in to dance "pas de Sylphide" in the Teatro da Rua dos Condes. In 1838, the São Carlos engaged Claire Lagoutine "to dance all the steps of Mme. Taglioni, as well as all of this kind, on the condition that she will dance only pas de deux with a French dancer." By 1838, Bernard Vestris staged *La Sylphide.* It was not a success; the public, accustomed to the more substantial historical ballets, rejected the airy Taglioni style, and the critics demanded ballets with national themes.

From 1843 to 1845 Gustave Carey produced *La Gipsy* and *Le Diable Amoureux* by Joseph Mazilier, as well as *Giselle,* starring the American ballerina Augusta Maywood. However, *Giselle* fared as poorly as *La Sylphide* and closed after a few performances. The following season, Theodore Martin presented *L'Illusion d'un Peintre,* after Perrot, and *Palmina, ossia La Figlia del Torrente,* which Sofia Fuoco would later dance at La Scala, Milan.

From 1847 to 1851, Maria Luigia Bussola was much applauded; however, the ballets of Lorenzo Vienna in which she appeared were poorly received. In 1851, Turin's Genoveva Monticelli danced *La Fille du Danube* by Luigi Gabrieli, after Filippo Taglioni, and *La Esmeralda* by Nicola Libonati, after Jules Perrot.

The mid-nineteenth century arrival of Arthur Saint-

PORTUGAL: Theatrical Dance. A dramatic scene from Olga Roriz's *Violoncelo não Acompanhado em Suite de Luxo* (Unaccompanied Cello in a Luxury Suite; 1987), set to the music of J. S. Bach. Jasmim de Matos designed the sets and costumes. (Photograph © 1987 by Alice Costa; used by permission.)

PORTUGAL: Theatrical Dance. Members of the Gulbenkian Ballet in Vasco Wellenkamp's *Keep Going* (1988), set to music by Luciano Berio. (Photograph © 1988 by Eduardo Saraiva; used by permission.)

Léon converted Lisbon to Romantic ballet. Ballerinas Julie Lisereux and Elise Fleury engendered Parisian-style adulation. From 1854 to 1856, Saint-Léon staged seventeen ballets, many of them created for the São Carlos. His essay "De l'état actuel de la danse" stated that he improved the São Carlos corps de ballet through his *"traité linéaire du corps de ballet."* His fame worked against his successors, and Carlo Blasis, in charge of the 1857/58 season, was booed repeatedly. From 1862 to 1864, Adrien Gredelue successfully revived some Saint-Léon ballets. In 1869, Luigi Danesi presented *La Fata Nix* and *Gretchen,* ballets that were demanded for years to come in many Italian theaters, where Danesi introduced himself as "choreographer to H.M. Louis I, King of Portugal." The following year, the São Carlos hosted Katti Lanner's company in a repertory that included Perrot's *Giselle, Le Délire d'un Peintre,* and *Esmeralda.*

The decades from 1870 to 1900 saw a general decline of dance in Portugal. Fewer ballets were mounted each year at the São Carlos, until dance appeared only during operas. When the 1910 republican revolution opened the door to social change, the Teatro de São Carlos, symbol of the *ancien régime,* was neglected.

World War I brought the Ballets Russes de Serge Diaghilov to the Iberian Peninsula. The company resided in Lisbon from December 1917 until March 1918. Previous attempts had been made to lure Diaghilev's company to Portugal, but the scarcity of venues caused by the European conflict succeeded where invitations had failed. Neither of Lisbon's theaters offered appropriate decor for the Ballets Russes, but they mounted two series of performances. The public, caught up in war and internal political turmoil, was not very receptive and, though lauded by the press, the Ballets Russes did not meet the expectations of the Portuguese elite, who were familiar with the Paris art world. The company remained in Lisbon for several months without deigning to perform again.

Nonetheless, the Ballets Russes introduced international modernism to the Portuguese public, although Léonide Massine's *Soleil de Nuit* was hooted. The season coincided with a futurist campaign that included the poet Fernando Pessoa and the painter Almada Negreiros, who praised the Ballets Russes for providing "one of the most beautiful seasons of European civilization." The enthusiasm of these young artists led to an attempt to create a Portuguese ballet troupe. Almada Negreiros organized an amateur performance, which he choreographed even though he lacked training in dance. The group performed at the São Carlos shortly after the departure of the Ballets Russes and won general approval.

The momentum created by the Ballets Russes, however, was not sufficient to promote a rebirth of dance at that time. The advent of fascism in Portugal in 1932 led to an appeal for nationalism in the arts. In 1940, the Verde Gaio company was created, with the goal of portraying Portuguese folk and historical themes in ballets. Its founders were António Ferro and Francis Graca. The group's early productions attracted musicians and painters with productions locally lauded as "Portuguese Russian ballet." Lack of solid training was soon evident, so foreign masters were summoned. In 1947 Guglielmo Moresi came from Rome; he was joined the following year by the Swedish dancer Ivo Cramér. Verde Gaio failed to repeat its initial success and ultimately became the corps de ballet at the opera house.

Another group, the Circulo de Iniciaçao Coreográfica, was also active in this period. It was managed from 1946 by Margarida de Abreu, the only dance teacher at the National Conservatory for thirty-two years. The Circulo aimed to be a classical dance company modeled on England's Sadler's Wells. It presented twenty ballets in fourteen years and was well received. In 1960, de Abreu joined forces with Verde Gaio, which was then affiliated with the São Carlos. Margarida de Abreu carried the torch of classical ballet in Portugal, and from the ranks of her students came the dancers who helped to renew Portuguese dance.

Both the Circulo and Verde Gaio were instrumental in stimulating a new audience. In 1945, the São Carlos had been nationalized, and regular seasons commenced with visits by touring European and U.S. companies. Private impresarios also presented short dance seasons with foreign groups. A dance culture grew; American influence slowly replaced the British style—a development exemplified by Merce Cunningham's enthusiastic reception in Lisbon long before he was applauded in Paris.

In 1956, the creation of the Gulbenkian Foundation offered support for artistic growth. The foundation, funded by the legacy of Calouste Gulbenkian, a wealthy Armenian who spent his last years in Lisbon, assisted new artistic ventures in a country closed to international artistic life by a political regime long hostile to the arts. The foundation maintained a museum, choir, orchestra, and a music festival; it became the patron of the small Grupo Experimental de Bailado, then under the choreographic supervision of Norman Dixon, formerly of Ballet Rambert. The Gulbenkian Ballet came into being in 1965; Walter Gore was appointed artistic director, and his wife Paula Hinton with Portuguese dancer Isabel Santa Rosa led the group.

The Gulbenkian Ballet achieved professional status under Milko Šparemblek of Yugoslavia. The company implemented a creative program and constantly expanded its repertory with works by Šparemblek and visiting artists, including John Butler, Birgit Cullberg, Lar Lubovitch, Norman Walker, Paul Sanasardo, Maurice Béjart, and Hans van Manen. Šparemblek encouraged both the use of contemporary music and an original approach to costume and decor primarily created by Portuguese artists. Most of the dancers were not Portuguese, but notable among native choreographers was Carlos Trincheiras, who pursued a career in Brazil after his 1979 departure from the company.

By the mid-1980s, the company had thirty-two dancers, only three of whom were foreign. Jorge Salavisa, formerly a soloist with London's Festival Ballet, was directing the company and Vasco Wellenkamp was resident choreographer. In the early 1990s, the company had thirty-four dancers, only four of whom were foreign. Jorge Salavisa

PORTUGAL: Theatrical Dance. Scene from the Gulbenkian Ballet's 1990 mounting of Nacho Duato's 1983 ballet *Jardi Tancat*, set to the music of Mari del Mar Bonet. (Photograph © 1990 by Eduardo Saraiva; used by permission.)

shaped a style close to those of Hans van Manen and Jiří Kylián, whose works are also represented in the repertory.

On 25 April 1974, a military coup had ended the totalitarian era in Portugal, and a democratic system was adopted. Transitional instability seemed to menace even the Gulbenkian Foundation, however, and in 1976 Šparemblek left the company, returning in 1979 and 1981. When calm prevailed, in addition to the reemergence of the Gulbenkian Ballet, the opportunity arose to create a new ballet group directly linked to the Ministry of Culture and the Teatro de São Carlos. Traditionally oriented, the Companhia Nacional de Bailado has been under the supervision of Armando Jorge, former dancer and choreographer with Les Grands Ballets Canadiens and with the Gulbenkian Ballet. Under his direction the young company established a niche of its own, building a repertory of both nineteenth-century and modern classics, from *La Sylphide* and *Swan Lake* to *Apollo, The Green Table,* and *The Moor's Pavane.* It also forced a definitive change in the guidance of the Gulbenkian Ballet. It has decreased its traditional repertory and now concentrates on two company-trained Portuguese choreographers, Vasco Wellenkamp and Olga Roriz, whose contemporary dance styles have drawn a large audience. The emphasis on expression introduced by Dixon, Gore, and Šparemblek has blossomed in the ballets of Wellenkamp and Roriz.

The two companies stage more than eighty performances annually in Lisbon and tour throughout Portugal as well. They have been well received internationally. The dancers undergo serious training at the Gulbenkian and the National ballet schools and at the National Conservatory, where modern dance is taught and where significant reform has been in progress since 1971. In 1986 the universities opened their gates to dance: a new Escola Superior de Dança was created at Lisbon's Polytechnical Institute and a master's degree program in dance was introduced at Lisbon's Technical University.

A third company was born in 1984, the Companhia de Dança de Lisboa, run by Ruy Horta as an outgrowth of his Grupo Experimental de Jazz. The company emphasizes jazz dance and has a faithful young audience. Ruy Horta left to run a successful group in Frankfurt, S.O.A.P., and the company suffered a crisis from which it has not yet recovered. In 1993, Olga Roriz left the Gulbenkian Ballet to become director of this company but stayed only a year, then formed her own group to perform her works.

In 1996, Jorge Salavisa considered his career as artistic director of the Gulbenkian Ballet at an end, and he was replaced by the Brazilian dancer Iracity Cardoso, formerly with the Geneva Ballet. Salavisa later accepted a position on the board of the Companhia Nacional de Bailado, now under the direction of Isabel Santa Rosa, a former ballerina from the Gulbenkian Ballet, who returned from Brazil where she worked with her late husband Carlos Trincheiras.

PORTUGAL: Theatrical Dance. *(above)* Dancers of the Gulbenkian Ballet in Olga Roriz's *Passagens* (Passages; 1993), set to music by Ravi Shankar, Philip Glass, Piano Circus, and Repercussion Unit. Nuno Carinhas designed the set and costumes. *(below)* Roriz formed her own company in 1993. Here, Ana Caetano and Ludger Lamers of the Olga Roriz Companhia de Dança appear in her *Introdução ao Princípio das Coisas* (1994). (Photograph above © 1993 by Paolo Sabino; used by permission. Photograph below by José Fabião; courtesy of José Sasportes.)

The Gulbenkian Foundation opened a new department in 1984, ACARTE, mostly devoted to the contemporary performing arts. In 1987 it started an annual festival, Encontros ACARTE, that became a showcase for new European dance and was a powerful stimulus for young choreographers and for the creation of a new public for dance. From then on, a "new Portuguese dance" established itself at home and its originality is recognized abroad, in Paris as well as in New York. The struggle of these dancers to impose themselves had public support, but it was also the result of a specific approach from young professionals able to fight for their independence. They benefit from the appearance in Lisbon of new production spaces, such as the Centro Cultural de Belem and Culturgest, a cultural center in the heart of Portugal's largest bank. The main choreographers of this generation are Clara Andermatt, João Fiadeiro, Paulo Ribeiro, and Vera Mantero, but it would be possible to name a dozen more, some of them emerging from the Gulbenkian Ballet—this variety being the sign of the actual vitality of dance in Portugal.

The end of the twentieth century finds Portuguese theatrical dance fully present on the European scene, an accepted and developing part of Portuguese culture.

BIBLIOGRAPHY

Alves, Alfonso Manuel. *Dança.* Lisbon, 1988.

Assis, Maria de. *Movimentos.* Lisbon, 1995.

Ballet Gulbenkian, 1965–1975. Lisbon, 1976. Introduction by Carlos Pontes Leça.

Benevides, Francisco da Fonseca. *O Real Teatro de S. Carlos de Lisboa.* 3 vols. Lisbon, 1883–1902.

Keates, Laurence. *The Court Theatre of Gil Vicente.* Lisbon, 1962.

Koegler, Horst. "The Lisbon Story: Part One." *Dance and Dancers* (August 1972): 40–41.

Langinha, António. "Dance in Portugal: Times of Uncertainty . . . Winds of Change." *Ballett International-Tanz Aktuell* (April 1994): 26–29.

Leça, Carlos Pontes. "Ballet Gulbenkian, 25 anos." *Colóquio/Artes* (July 1991).

Ribeiro, Antonio Pinto. *Dança temporariamente contemporânea.* Lisbon, 1994.

Sasportes, José. "Feasts and Folias: The Dance in Portugal." *Dance Perspectives,* no. 42 (1970).

Sasportes, José. *História da dança em Portugal.* Lisbon, 1970.

Sasportes, José. *Trajectoría da dança teatral em Portugal.* Lisbon, 1979.

Sasportes, José, and António Pinto Ribeiro. *History of Dance.* Translated by Joan Ennes. Lisbon, 1991.

Sasportes, José, Helena Coelho, and Maria de Assis. *Dançaram em Lisboa: 1910–1994.* Lisbon, 1994.

Vasques, Eugénia, ed. *Théâtres et danse au Portugal: D'autres imaginaires.* Alternatives Théâtrales, no. 39. Brussels, 1991.

Williams, Peter. "The Lisbon Story: Part Two." *Dance and Dancers* (September 1972): 38–41.

JOSÉ SASPORTES

POTAPOVA, ELENA MIKHAILOVNA (born 16 February 1930 in Samara [Kuibyshev]), dancer and teacher. Potapova graduated from the school of the Shevchenko Opera and Ballet Theater in Kiev in 1948, having studied with N. V. Verikundova. In 1982 she graduated from the teacher-training section of the choreography department of the Lunacharsky Theater Technicum in Moscow, where she studied under Marina Semenova and Raisa Struchkova. From 1948 to 1978 she was a leading soloist at the Shevchenko Theater, where she taught from 1979 to 1991.

Potapova's main roles were Odette-Odile in *Swan Lake;* Kitri in *Don Quixote;* Giselle, Raymonda, and Esmeralda in those eponymous ballets; Juliet in *Romeo and Juliet;* Shirin in *Legend of Love;* Masha in *The Nutcracker;* and Aurora in *The Sleeping Beauty.* She created vivid characters in several Ukrainian national ballets, among them Mavka in *A Forest Song,* and the title roles in *Lileya* and *Rostislava.* Potapova was instrumental in the creation of the modern Soviet ballet repertory by performing leading roles in heroic ballets on contemporary themes, such as *Youth, Under the Italian Sky,* and *Black Gold.*

Potapova's dancing was noted for its virtuosity, clean line, rhythmic precision, and admirable musicality. She captivated her audiences by her dynamism, *ballon,* and blazing temperament. Possessing a brilliant classical technique, she was able to portray the inner workings of her heroines' characters; at the same time she softened the graphically sharp lines of her dance and plastique with lyricism and innate expressiveness. She conveyed with accuracy the style of the Romantic ballet, but more so the academic classical style of Marius Petipa. Her greatest role was Aurora in *The Sleeping Beauty,* produced by Fedor Lopukhov in 1951 and by Petr Gusev in 1969. Many concert works, including Ukrainian dance miniatures, were also part of Potapova's repertory.

From 1978 to 1983 she was ballet mistress and *répétiteuse* for the Kiev Opera and Ballet Theater, and frequently toured abroad. She held the same positions at the opera and ballet theater in Ankara, Turkey, after 1983, while still teaching in Kiev. Potapova created more than forty vivid characters in the course of her career at the Kiev Theater as well as in her many guest appearances throughout the world. She has made significant contributions to the virtuosic performing style seen on the Ukrainian ballet stage.

Potapova was named People's Artist of the USSR in 1970 and was a prizewinner at the 1951 international ballet competition at the All-World Festival of Youth in Berlin. She has also been a jury member for several international ballet competitions in Moscow.

BIBLIOGRAPHY

Stanishevsky, Yuri. *The Masters of Ukrainian Ballet.* Kiev, 1983.

Stanishevsky, Yuri. *Baletnyi teatr Sovetskoi Ukrainy, 1925–1985.* Kiev, 1986.

Stephanovich, M. *The Shevchenko Theater of Opera and Ballet in Kiev* (in Russian). Kiev, 1968.

YURI A. STANISHEVSKY
Translated from Russian

POULENC, FRANCIS (Francis Jean Marcel Poulenc; born 7 January 1899 in Paris, died 30 January 1963 in Paris), French composer. A pupil of Maurice Ravel's friend Ricardo Vines and later of Charles Koechlin, whose refined Romantic style reflected that of his master Gabriel Fauré, Francis Poulenc was a founding member of Les Six in 1920, along with Georges Auric, Louis Durey, Arthur Honegger, Darius Milhaud, and Germaine Tailleferre. These young musicians, whose styles varied considerably, were for a time given some unity by the subtle influence of Erik Satie, and by the publicizing verve of the imaginative poet and dramatist Jean Cocteau.

Poulenc owed much of his graceful, thoughtful, witty style to the examples of Ravel and Satie, evident in both his instrumental and his vocal music. At the core of his artistic activity were the 146 "mélodies" that he composed over four decades; in these he demonstrated exceptional empathy for the texts he set—works by Guillaume Apollinaire, Max Jacob, Louise de Vilmorin, Georges Bernanos, and more than a score of other poets. The contemporary popular tunes presented by Maurice Chevalier drew praise from Poulenc, but his lucid French attributes were always combined with selected foreign inspirations. Some arrived via his association with Serge Diaghilev; other inspirations came via Claudio Monteverdi, Giuseppe Verdi, Mozart, and Beethoven.

A member of the Diaghilev circle from 1919 on, Poulenc was mobilized by the impresario to prepare Charles Gounod's short opera *La Colombe* for production in a Gounod revival cycle, a project that never was completed. In 1924 Diaghilev produced the playful, sensual *Les Biches,* with music by Poulenc and choreography by Bronislava Nijinska, who also danced in her atmospheric ballet (along with Nemchinova, Danilova, Dubrovska, Vilzak, Woizikowski, and the others). The ambiguity of the production was enhanced by Marie Laurencin's blue-and-rose sets and costumes.

Previously Poulenc had collaborated with Honegger, Milhaud, Auric, and Tailleferre on *Les Mariés de la Tour Eiffel,* a charming, farcical romp that Rolf de Maré's Ballets Suédois produced in 1921. For this Cocteau-Borlin "music-hall tragedy" Poulenc's contributions were the comic polka "La Baigneuse de Trouville" and the satiric "Discours du Général." Poulenc's espousal of neoclassical techniques—a French reaction to the postromanticism of Mahler and Strauss—involved staccato melodies alternating with longer lines, without the percussive thrust of Igor Stravinsky's stabbing rhythms of uneven meter.

Les Biches is a fresh, impertinent, erotic ballet in elegantly sophisticated style, about the busy and trivial pleasures of a house party. The score is divided into Overture, Rondeau, Chanson Dansée, Adagietto, Jeu, Rag-Mazurka, Andantino, Petite Chanson Dansée, and Finale. It updates Fokine's romantic social gathering, *Le Carnaval;* Diaghilev had requested a "modern *Sylphides.*" In addition to a medium-sized orchestra, Poulenc called for soprano, tenor, and bass performing both solos and ensembles—his first vocal ensembles. Duple rhythms, jazz accents, and subtle modulations give the work its profile; the harmonic center is the neutral tonality of C. [*See* Biches, Les.]

In 1927 Poulenc composed the brief "Pastourelle" for *L'Éventail de Jeanne,* a work by Yvonne Franck and Alice Bourgat. This is the ninth movement of a ballet in eleven movements, whose other music was composed by Ravel, Albert Roussel, Jacques Ibert, Milhaud, Auric, Marcel Delannoy, Pierre-Octave Ferroud, Roland-Manuel, and Florent Schmitt.

Drawing on the pastoral theme of Diana the eternally chaste, in 1929 Poulenc created *Aubade,* a ballet for piano and eighteen instruments. At the initial private performance of the work, choreographed by Bronislava Nijinska, the composer himself played the piano, and Ernest Ansermet conducted. Later *Aubade* was presented publicly with new choreography by George Balanchine, sets and costumes by Angeles Ortiz, and a company led by Vera Nemchinova. The sensitive ballet has eight sections: Toccata (a rapid solo for piano), Récitatif I (a lyric larghetto), a charming Rondo, Presto, Récitatif II (with oboe solo), a poetic Andante, a spasmodic Allegro Féroce, and a majestic Conclusion. Once again Poulenc's rhythms are characteristically duple, and the neutral tonality of C is emphasized. *Aubade* has been revived many times since its premiere, by Lifar, Lukas Hoving, and others.

In 1941 Poulenc wrote the last of his five original ballets, *Les Animaux Modèles.* Based on Jean de La Fontaine's seventeenth-century retelling of several of Aesop's fables, this modern ballet, decorated by Maurice Brianchon, helped raise the spirits of French civilian audiences during World War II through its positive humanistic symbolism. Initially Poulenc projected a collaboration with Léonide Massine, but the choreographer turned out to be Serge Lifar. The nine-part score, lasting thirty-five minutes, is orchestrated at the most elaborate level Poulenc ever used: three flutes, three oboes, four clarinets, four bassoons, four horns, three trumpets, three trombones, tuba, timpani, percussion, piano, and strings. Brianchon's refreshing farmyard background transposed the fairy-tale action to eighteenth-century rural Burgundy. Poulenc's limpid music, characteristically emphasizing duple rhythm, accompanies not animals but rather humans who dance and mime. The sections are Overture; "Dawn and Call to Work," andante-moderato; "Hunters," allegro; "The Grasshopper and the Ant," allegretto; "The Lion in Love," serenade-allegro; "A Man between Two Ages, and Two Mistresses," presto; pavane, "Death and the Woodman," adagio; "The Two Roosters," allegro; in the Finale, moderato, the workers return from the fields to a benediction and noon repast. This last tonal, moving section, all of a period and very professional, foreshadows the dignity of Poulenc's multifaceted masterpiece, *Dialogues des Carmélites.*

Early in his career Poulenc established a set of principles on which he worked, combining classical clarity with a contrived satire that still sounds natural. While he was living, his ideas seemed advanced; today they seem more traditional—yet they are uniquely his own. In his comic opera *Les Mamelles de Tirésias,* Poulenc's idiom comes close to musical revue and parody; his film work also reflects this approach. On occasion the composer praised twelve-tone technique, although he did not utilize it. His influence was felt in Europe but not in the United States. Poulenc's sophisticated, entertaining music is ingenious and gay, direct and succinct, although it has a cutting edge, and it always opposes both impressionism and German romanticism. In *Les Biches,* as elsewhere, music-hall flavor is near the surface. A dance-inspired atmosphere is found in many of his works, although not in the deliberately expanded structure of *Dialogues des Carmélites.*

Like many of his contemporary colleagues, Poulenc appreciated burlesque, and when he offers up a major tune, a popular dance, or a march in one of his compositions, the listener may be uncertain whether this is a compliment to the form. Thus, in *Les Mariés de la Tour Eiffel,* Poulenc may be either ridiculing or praising the values of matrimony. In *Les Biches,* he may be censuring the customs of house parties, or he may be encouraging the young to amuse themselves while they can. In *Aubade* he may be approving a classic myth or lamenting the cruelty of destiny.

Poulenc had an innate gift for structuring a composition, and his polished orchestrations are inventive and brilliant without becoming noisy, or Wagnerian. He composed for all media, and his practical style—for the stage, concerts, films, or the church—always served its purpose. He was, according to Colette, "a beloved child of our time."

[*For related discussion, see* Music for Dance, *article on* Western Music since 1900.]

BIBLIOGRAPHY

Bernac, Pierre. *Francis Poulenc.* Translated by Winifred Radford. London, 1977.

Garafola, Lynn. *Diaghilev's Ballets Russes.* New York, 1989.

Hell, Henri. *Francis Poulenc.* Paris, 1958.

Poulenc, Francis. "Francis Poulenc on His Ballets." *Ballet* (September 1946).

Poulenc, Francis. *Correspondence, 1915–1963.* Edited by Hélène de Wendel. Paris, 1967.

BAIRD HASTINGS

POULSEN, ULLA (Ulla Skou; born 5 February 1905 in Copenhagen), Danish dancer. To her generation, dancer Ulla Poulsen became a symbol: between the two world wars, she was the incarnation of Danish romantic spirit to her public. She was unforgettable in her simple poetry as Hilda in August Bournonville's *A Folk Tale* and unequaled in her mournful grace in *La Sylphide.*

Poulsen began her training at the Royal Danish Ballet School in 1913, when she was only eight years old. She danced as Hilda in 1922 and as Sylphide in 1923. In 1924 she was appointed soloist. Svend Kragh-Jacobsen later wrote, "With her tender beauty and sweet youth, she danced with touching effect in the early twenties" (*Royal Danish Ballet,* 1955).

From 1927 to 1930, Poulsen toured with her husband, actor and director Johannes Poulsen (who would later direct her in many plays, including *Hamlet* and *The Tempest*). The time included study with Tamara Karsavina, to whom she was sent by dancer Adeline Genée. When Poulsen returned to the Royal Danish Ballet in 1930, she had gained in both expression and technique.

George Balanchine used Poulsen to her advantage as the Wife of Potiphar in *Die Josephslegende* and as Zobeide in *Shéhérazade* during his stay in Cophenhagen in 1930 and 1931. From that time onward, Poulsen became a truly dramatic dancer and a fine interpreter of character, as in, for example, the title role in Kjeld Abell and Børge Ralov's *The Widow in the Mirror* (1934). The work was a milestone in the Danish ballet's efforts to move from the era of Bournonville into contemporary dance theater.

In all of these modern ballets, Poulsen showed herself to be a graceful mimic and artist while deepening and refining her romantic interpretations. Photographs show her greatest asset as a dancer: her beautiful poses and gestures, which created an almost sculptural sense of spirit.

BIBLIOGRAPHY

Anderson, Jack, and George Dorris. "A Conversation with Svend Kragh-Jacobsen." *Ballet Review* 5.4 (1975–1976): 1–20.

Kragh-Jacobsen, Svend. *Ballettens blomstring ude og hjemme.* Copenhagen, 1945.

HENRIK LUNDGREN

POWELL, ELEANOR (Eleanor Torrey Powell; born 21 November 1912 in Springfield, Massachusetts, died 11 February 1982 in Beverly Hills, California), tap dancer, singer, and actress. Powell, often called the world's greatest female tap dancer, entertained millions with her dazzling syncopated rhythmic style. She was originally enrolled in dancing classes to combat childhood shyness and immediately fell in love with ballet and acrobatics. Powell was first discovered in 1925, on the beach in Atlantic City, New Jersey, by Gus Edwards, who offered her a job in his Ambassador Hotel revue. Powell followed the advice of Jack Benny, Eddie Cantor, and other performers to try her luck in New York City, where she found work in the 1920s nightclubs and vaudeville. She auditioned for Broadway but was rejected once producers learned that she did not tap dance. Although she had had a haughty view of tap dancing, by the age of sixteen she realized that, to have a chance at a Broadway career, she had to learn it.

Powell enrolled in a series of ten lessons at Jack Donahue's dance school. Legend has it that Donahue discovered that her dance training had left her so biased that she was unable to execute the taps. Powell recalled, "The first thing [Donahue] did was sit on the floor in front of me and hold my ankles" (Thomas, 1984). Donahue and Johnny Boyle (a Broadway choreographer who handled many of Donahue's classes) are credited with having Powell wear a war-surplus belt with two sandbags in order to keep her anchored to the floor. The ten lessons she had with them were her only formal tap training.

Powell's first Broadway show was *Follow Thru* (1929). She was then in *Fine and Dandy* (1930), *Hot-Cha!* (1932), *George White's Music Hall Varieties* (1932), *George White's Scandals* (1933), and *Crazy Quilt* (1933). *At Home Abroad* (1935) was Powell's last Broadway musical. Although she had no screen aspirations, the 1935 Hollywood version of *George White's Scandals* was filmed with her reprising her specialty number. Upon seeing the film, Louis B. Mayer, the head of Metro-Goldwyn-Mayer (MGM), cast her in *Broadway Melody of 1936*. Beautiful big-budget black-and-white musicals followed, including *Born to Dance* (1936), *Broadway Melody of 1938* (1937), *Rosalie* (1937), and *Honolulu* (1939), *Lady, Be Good!* (1941), and *Ship Ahoy* (1942). In 1943, Powell married actor Glenn Ford and soon retired from movies after making *Thousands Cheer* (1943), *I Dood It* (1943), and *Sensations of 1945* (1944), where she dances within a pinball machine. In 1950, she returned to films in *Duchess of Idaho*, her last. Her marriage ended in divorce in 1959. With encouragement from other entertainers and her children, she launched a stage comeback, successfully touring the country with her own nightclub act from 1961 to 1964.

POWELL. This rare rehearsal shot shows Eleanor Powell and George Murphy practicing a number from MGM's *Broadway Melody of 1938*. (Photograph from the collection of Rusty E. Frank.)

Despite a storehouse of remarkable tap numbers, undeniably Powell's best was her "Begin the Beguine" duet with Fred Astaire in *Broadway Melody of 1940* (1940). Together they danced across a glistening mirrored floor for one of the most exquisite and exciting tap numbers in cinema history.

[*See also* Tap Dance.]

BIBLIOGRAPHY

Frank, Rusty E. *Tap! The Greatest Tap Dance Stars and Their Stories, 1900–1955*. Rev. ed. New York, 1994.

Schultz, Margie. *Eleanor Powell: A Bio-Bibliography*. Westport, Conn., 1994.

Stearns, Marshall, and Jean Stearns. *Jazz Dance: The Story of American Vernacular Dance*. Rev. ed. New York, 1994.

Thomas, Tony. *That's Dancing*. New York, 1984.

RUSTY E. FRANK

POWWOW. The term *powwow* is derived from *pauau*, which in the Algonquian language family denotes a curing ceremony attended by a large gathering. Europeans erroneously applied the term to any large gathering of American Indians. Since about 1900, *powwow* has referred to tribal or intertribal festivals highlighted by traditional singing, dancing, feasting, gift exchange, and competitions. Once characteristic of Indian events in Oklahoma, since 1955 the powwow has become popular in all parts of the United States and Canada, both on reservations and in urban communities where there are large populations of American Indians.

Although the term is Algonquian, the actual form of the most characteristic dance originated among the Pawnee in present-day Nebraska as a sacred ceremony learned in a vision. From the Pawnee, the dance diffused rapidly throughout the northern and southern Plains. As each tribe adopted it, it assumed different tribal characteristics, producing the subtle variations seen in contemporary powwows.

Modern powwows are held frequently during the summer, and singers, dancers, and spectators may travel from one to the next on what has been called the "powwow circuit." Participants camp around a large circular arbor in the middle of which the dances are held for a weekend or longer. Dancers may perform during the afternoons and evenings and then leave to reach the next powwow hundreds of miles away. During the winter months powwows are held indoors; large and well-known events take place in civic auditoriums in New York City, Denver, Tulsa, and Los Angeles.

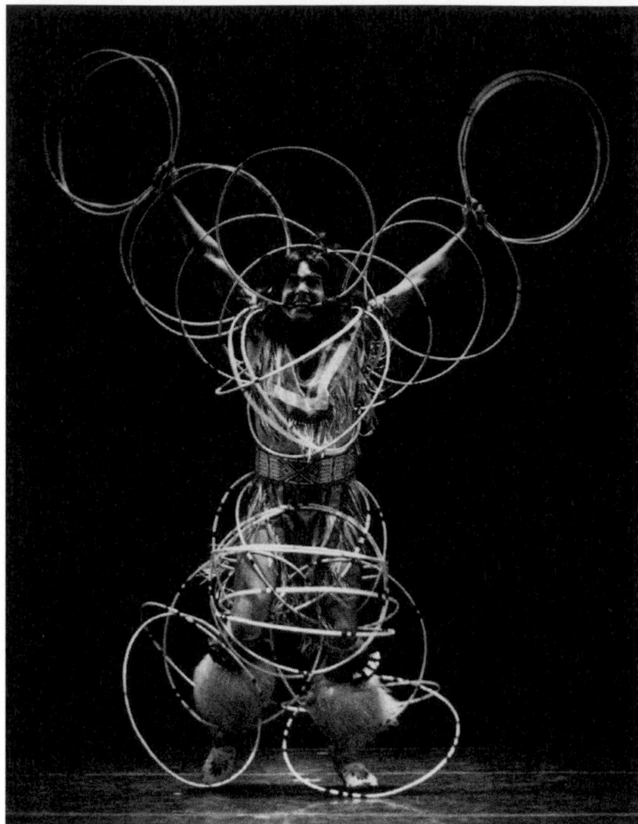

POWWOW. Eddie Swimmer, a member of American Indian Dance Theater, in a Hoop Dance, at the Joyce Theater, New York, in 1989. One of the oldest powwow dances, the Hoop Dance was originally performed for healing or to induce visions of the future. (Photograph © 1989 by Jack Vartoogian; used by permission.)

Most powwows are sponsered by host tribes and follow tribal conventions. They may also be intertribal, attracting participants from many culturally distinct tribes; costumes, songs, and dances have thus tended to become uniform over widely separated groups. Intertribalism allows dancers from one tribe or region to join in the festivities of others with relative ease.

Powwow dances, although organized along the principles of the host tribe, since the mid-1980s have included certain common elements. Traditional men's and women's dances are performed. A free-style dance of reserved character, once called the War Dance and performed primarily by men, now features women prominently; both wear costumes reminiscent of the early reservation period. The Grass Dance for men and Jingle Dress Dance for women are Canadian in origin but enjoy wide popularity throughout North America. Fancy men's dancing, originally from Oklahoma, and the Canadian-derived Shawl Dance for women, are both highly skillful competitive dances. Some dancers may compete in all styles, but usually each specializes in only one.

During the course of a powwow there are regional specializations. In the northern Plains one sees the Rabbit or Owl Dance, performed by male-female couples, and the Crow Hop, a slow, mimetic dance of warriors.

There is more variety in the southern Plains, where dancers also participate in the Stomp Dance, a serpentine follow-the-leader dance originally from the southeast; the Forty-nine, in which dancers form tight concentric circles around the singers; and many specialties in which men and women imitate the movements of animals, as in the Snake, Buffalo, and Eagle dances. The Shield Dance is a mock combat dance done by two men. In the Gourd Dance, men dance in a line holding gourd rattles, intermittently advancing in imitation of an attack on an enemy.

The Round Dance, derived from a women's Scalp Dance, is now a ubiquitous form of welcome dance. Also performed everywhere is the spectacular Hoop Dance, in which the dancer manipulates as many as thirty hoops around his body, forming patterns as he dances.

Powwows are perhaps the most expressive form of modern-day American Indian culture. One of their most outstanding features is the dance contest, in which individuals compete for high stakes. Competitions are held for senior and junior men and women, and for small children. Frequently the purses for major powwows reach tens of thousands of dollars.

[*See also* Native American Dance.]

BIBLIOGRAPHY

Callahan, Alice Anne. *The Osage Ceremonial Dance In-Lon-Schka.* Norman, Okla., 1990.

Nettl, Bruno. *Blackfoot Musical Thought: Comparative Perspective.* Champaign, Ill., 1989.

Powers, William K. *War Dance: Plains Indian Musical Performance.* Tucson, Ariz., 1990.

WILLIAM K. POWERS

PRACTICE CLOTHES are garments worn by dancers for warm-ups, classes, and rehearsals. The primary functions of practice clothes are to allow freedom of movement and to keep the dancer's muscles warm, thus preventing injuries. Practice clothes can be adapted for use onstage. Fashions come and go in practice clothes as in other attire, and some types of practice clothes have been worn as everyday garments by dancers and nondancers alike.

Pre-Nineteenth Century. The earliest professional stage dancers rehearsed in their everyday clothes. In the mid-eighteenth century, when dancers such as Marie Camargo began to expand the range of dance technique, special garments evolved to meet the needs of modesty and freedom of movement. Female dancers adopted the *caleçon de précaution* or "precautionary drawers" to prevent accidental exposure during a jump or turn. Fleshings were worn at the Paris Opera as early as the late seventeenth century, but it was not until around 1810 that Monsieur Maillot, a costumer at the Opera, invented the improved type of knitted tights that are still called by his name in France. These garments, originally intended for use onstage, were the prototypes of later practice clothes.

Nineteenth Century. Carlo Blasis, who became the director of the ballet school of the Teatro alla Scala, Milan, in 1837, designed his dancers' practice clothes. The women wore white muslin bodices and skirts, with black sashes around their waists, and the men wore close-fitting jackets and white trousers, with a black leather belt tightly fitted to give support.

In Paris, female dancers wore a practice costume that eventually developed into what is now known as the Romantic tutu. Although the full skirt and tight bodice became famous in the ballet *La Sylphide* (1832), it was no innovation by then. An earlier drawing of Fanny Elssler at the *barre* depicts her in such a practice costume, with the addition of gloves or mitts on her hands.

Albéric Second left a detailed description of practice clothes of the Romantic period in his 1844 *Les petits mystères de l'Opéra:*

> The girls are bare-headed, their shoulders and arms are uncovered, and their waists confined in a tight bodice. A very short, very bouffant skirt of net or striped muslin reaches to the knees. Their thighs are chastely concealed beneath large calico drawers that are as impregnable as a State Secret. The men are open-necked, and wear short jackets of white piqué and breeches half way down the leg, held at the waist by a leather belt. (Quoted by Guest, 1981)

Pictorial records of practice clothes of this period include Édouard de Beaumont's print series *L'Opéra au XIXe Siècle,* first published in *Le Charivari* in 1844 and 1845, and Albert Smith's *The Natural History of the Ballet-Girl* (1847). Smith includes such curiosities as a child taking class wearing street dress from the waist up and a ballet skirt beneath, and dancers rehearsing in street clothes with handkerchiefs tied over their head. Smith noted that the dancers, like Elssler, kept their gloves on.

Special practice clothes apparently were not worn consistently for rehearsals during the mid-nineteenth century. Dancers who did not have much actual dancing to do often wore their street dresses as well as their bonnets and shawls, as is illustrated in Smith's book. Practice clothes were worn in major theaters, however, such as the Paris Opera and Her Majesty's in London, and the ballet master Jules Perrot instituted a similar rule in Saint Petersburg in 1848. Sometimes dancers wore strange hybrid outfits, for example, removing their skirts to reveal knee-length bloomers, but keeping on their street attire from the waist up.

Female dancers of the late nineteenth century often are thought to have worn the type of practice clothes depicted in the drawings and paintings of Edgar Degas. He, however, omitted the ubiquitous knee-length bloomers. The costume also included a tightly laced corset, cotton stockings, a white batiste bodice, tarlatan skirts, and a white sash around the waist. The brightly colored sashes and black velvet neck ribbons worn by Degas's dancers were an artistic addition rather than actual practice.

Twentieth Century. At the Imperial Russian Ballet School in Saint Petersburg, a system of different colored dresses was instituted among the female students. Tamara Karsavina, who attended the school at the turn of the century, wrote in the December 1927 *Dancing Times,*

> Our dancing dress was meant to make a distinction between the successful and the less successful pupils. The small girls and those who did not show enough progress wore a fawn coloured dress; a dress of white lawn with pink spots was given for application after two or three years of work, and the highest distinction was a white organdi [*sic*] stiffly starched dress. Only very few reached this degree.

The same system was still in effect when Felia Doubrovska and Alexandra Danilova attended the school some years later, although the beginners' color had been changed to gray. After the Soviets came into power the merit system was abolished and all juniors wore pink, all seniors white.

Vaslav Nijinsky and other male students of the Imperial Ballet School wore black trousers and white shirts. Nijinsky continued to wear a similar practice costume throughout his career. Describing his classes with Enrico Cecchetti in London in 1913, his wife Romola wrote in *Nijinsky* (1933), "Nijinsky, as usual, wore his black, close-fitting dancing trousers, blue, green or white beautifully made *crêpe de chine* shirt (like the one in *Sylphides*) and white or cream *chevreau* ballet slippers."

Earlier in the century, Isadora Duncan had discarded the corsets and tutus of the classical ballet dancer and replaced them with the Greek tunic, which enhanced her freer style of movement. This costume was also adopted by ballet dancers such as Anna Pavlova, who wore it both onstage and as practice dress. The female members of Diaghilev's Ballets Russes wore tunics for rehearsals in 1913, as Lydia Sokolova recalled in her autobiography *Dancing for Diaghilev* (1960):

> For class we wore white tutus and pink silk tights, but for the rehearsal which followed immediately, we wore crêpe-de-chine dresses which took three and a half metres of material to make. They were caught in with one bit of elastic under the breast and another around the thigh, and they fell in pretty draperies just below the knee. Although there was a lot of stuff in them, they were easy to move in and as we all had them made in different colours we must have been a wonderful sight.

In later years the tunic grew shorter and simpler in cut. As related in her autobiography *Distant Dances* (1980),

Sono Osato, auditioning for the Ballets Russes de Monte-Carlo in 1934, noted that the female dancers "wore short black tunics to the tops of their thighs and black woolen tights." Dancers at New York's Metropolitan Opera House, however, were required to wear knee-length tunics until 1935. A short tunic was adopted as the uniform of the Sadler's Wells Ballet School in England.

The tunic was not the only garment worn by dancers liberated from the tutu. Photographs of schools and companies in the 1930s and 1940s often show dancers in a motley array of practice clothes, including short play-dresses, rompers, one-piece bathing suits, and combinations of shirts and trunks, often worn with bare legs or fishnet tights. Printed fabrics and ruffled skirts were also worn, although both are now discouraged because they obscure the line of the dancer's body.

The tutu was not completely abandoned as a practice garment. It continues to be worn in partnering classes, so that both partners may get accustomed to its spatial requirements, and in rehearsal by dancers who wish to become accustomed to the feel of moving in costume.

Both tunics and tutus were superseded by the leotard. This garment, originally a suit of knitted jersey extending from wrists to ankles, was invented by a French acrobat, Jules Léotard (1830–1870), who gave it his name. It was first used by circus performers but gained popularity as a dancer's stage costume in the 1920s. Doris Humphrey wore it in her *Sonata Tragica* (1923) and *Hoop Dance* (1924). In 1928 Pavel Tchelitchev designed the "first white unadorned all-over tights or body stockings ever worn on the ballet stage" for Léonide Massine's *Ode* (Buckle, 1981).

American modern dancers were the first to use the leotard as a practice garment. In contrast to the white or pink tutus of the ballet, these leotards were usually black and severe in cut, as if to emphasize their wearers' rejection of ballet's frivolities. They were sleeveless (resembling one-piece bathing suits) or long-sleeved, and were generally worn with black tights or bare legs. The modern

PRACTICE CLOTHES. In a class at the National Ballet of Canada, Karen Kain wears layers of knitted garments. Other variations can be seen in the background. (Photograph © 1978 by Linda Vartoogian; used by permission.)

dancer of Jules Feiffer's cartoon strips in the New York *Village Voice* newspaper exemplifies this look.

Modern dancers also had their own fashions. Photographs and films show that the bare-midriff look was popular in the 1930s. The two parts of this costume consisted of a close-fitting, short-sleeved top and matching trunks or a short skirt. Long jersey skirts, simple in cut yet full enough to allow free movement, were also worn, as were simple knee-length dresses or tunics. The men wore shirts and either shorts or trousers. Alwin Nikolais recalled that in the Bennington period, between 1934 and 1942, men did not wear tights, which they probably did not own, but pants and shirts, while the girls wore skirts.

Trends. As the manufacturers of dance garments began to experiment with both synthetic and natural fibers, leotards and tights became available in an ever-widening array of colors and styles. Some dance teachers find this variety distracting and prescribe uniforms for their students; these usually consist of black leotards and pink tights for the girls and white tops and black tights for the boys. A few schools have adopted the Russian system of assigning different colors to different levels of students. Female ballet students sometimes wear a short wraparound skirt of nylon or chiffon. European schools may require a different sort of uniform: tunics and short socks for the girls, and singlets, shorts, and short socks for the boys.

Drafty, ill-heated classrooms, rehearsal halls, and theaters have often required dancers to add garments for extra warmth. Karsavina recalled how each dancer in Russia's Imperial Ballet School had a shawl to wrap over her practice tutu. With the advent of more form-fitting practice clothes, dancers began to make and wear knitted garments that could be pulled on. Alexandra Danilova claims to have invented leg warmers, which she made from the sleeves of a cast-off sweater. Knitted tights and warm-up suits are also popular. Rubber garments, such as baby pants and harem pants, are sometimes worn in the hope of losing weight through perspiration, although some dancers object to rubber on the grounds that it does not allow the skin to breathe. In recent years parachute cloth, nylon, and other synthetic materials have been used for warm-up clothes.

Dancers also have adopted athletes' garments, such as sweat pants, sweat shirts, heavy socks, and kneepads. With the general vogue for jogging and running, this type of sportswear is sold in an increasing variety of styles and colors. Trisha Brown is credited with being the first to use sweat pants as a stage costume.

The making of practice clothes has grown into a large and lucrative industry. Dancers' practice clothes have generally shared in the dance boom that began in the 1960s, and leotards, tights, and leg warmers have been worn on the street as well as for various types of sports, exercise, and recreation. In a sense, practice clothes have come full circle and are again a part of everyday attire.

PRACTICE CLOTHES. Wearing sweat pants, Merce Cunningham rehearses *Squaregame*. (Photograph © 1978 by Jack Vartoogian; used by permission.)

[*For related discussion, see* Costume in Western Traditions.]

BIBLIOGRAPHY

Buckle, Richard. "Modern Ballet Design, 1909–1980." In *Designing for the Dancer,* by Roy Strong et al. London, 1981.

Guest, Ivor. "Costume and the Nineteenth Century Dancer." In *Designing for the Dancer,* by Roy Strong et al. London, 1981.

Kelly, Deirdre. "Dancewear in the Eighties: Fashion, Function and Form." *Dance in Canada* (Fall 1982).

Kirstein, Lincoln. *Movement and Metaphor: Four Centuries of Ballet.* New York, 1970.

Lawson, Joan, and Peter Revitt. *Dressing for the Ballet.* London, 1958.

Moore, Lillian. "Leotard: Strange Immortality." *Dance News* (January 1945): 7.

Moore, Lillian. "Practice Clothes—Then and Now." *Ballet Annual* 14 (1960): 118–124.

SUSAN AU

PRAETORIUS, MICHAEL (Michael Schultheiss [Schultz, Schulte], born 15 February 1571 in Creuzburg-Werra, Germany, died 15 February 1621 in Wolfenbüttel, Germany), composer, music theorist, and organist. Praetorius was the youngest son of the Lutheran minister Michael Schulteis (the Latinization of the name, according to Forchert, 1949, originated with the Lüneburg branch of the family). He received his early schooling at Torgau in the famous Lateinschule, whose music director Michael Voigt nurtured his obvious musical leanings. In 1582 he matriculated at the University of Frankfurt an der Oder, where he became a full-time student in 1585 and read philosophy and theology. During his student years he served as organist at Sankt Marien Kirche in Frankfurt. By 1595, he had established himself as court organist to Duke Heinrich Julius of Braunschweig-Wolfenbüttel. After an interval of six years during which his activities are unknown, Praetorius appears in Regensburg; here began his friendship with pastor Christoph Donaverus, to whom ten of Praetorius's later works are dedicated. Late in 1602 he had returned to Wolfenbüttel. Although he continued as organist, his principal duty then was to direct the duke's musical establishment, the Hofkapelle. The contract that installed Praetorius officially as Herzoglich Braunschweigischer Kapellmeister was signed on 7 December 1604. His increased salary allowed for the expansion of his household: on 5 September 1603 he had married Anna Lakemaker, with whom he had two sons, Michael (born 1604) and Ernst (born 1606). The happy years between 1605 and 1613 were a time of intense compositional activity and established Praetorius as a major figure in German Protestant music.

On 20 July 1613 Duke Heinrich Julius died unexpectedly in Prague. The elector Johann Georg of Saxony immediately requested that Praetorius be allowed to spend the year of mourning in Dresden. That sojourn lasted from autumn 1613 to spring 1616, during which time Praetorius not only led the Hofkapelle in Dresden but was responsible for the music at several major political and religious events in the state of Saxony. In Dresden he became acquainted with the composer Heinrich Schütz (1585–1672) and, of prime importance for his compositional style and theoretical thinking, with Italian music, which dominated churches and the opera in the capital.

During his absence from Wolfenbüttel the court music there had begun to deteriorate. When Praetorius returned home in 1619 after important engagements elsewhere, he could do little to halt this trend. Because he was in ill health, his contract was not renewed in 1620. He died a year later, a wealthy man and a stout Christian, at his home in Wolfenbüttel.

Of Praetorius's more than one thousand extant musical works, only *Terpsichore* (Wolfenbüttel, 1612; vol. 15 of the composer's collected works), a collection of French dances in four to six parts, is devoted to secular music. The dedication states that these dance pieces are to serve "not only the instrumentalists but first and foremost high-ranking persons of noble blood and others who have practiced these and comparable dances in Gallia [France]," until such time as a projected volume of Italian and English dances might be published. This, unfortunately, never happened, but *Terpsichore* as it stands remains one of our most valuable sources of French dance music for the ballroom and theater from the second half of the sixteenth and the first decade of the seventeenth century.

The book begins with an introduction in twelve chapters that contain, besides some remarks regarding the origins of the collection and a one-page dictionary of French dance terms and proper names (chapter 4), important information about the musical performance of the dances, their notation, and their metrical complexities. A table of contents ("Register") gives an overview of the repertory of the 312 dances contained in *Terpsichore;* then follow the scores. The dances are grouped by genre: first come the *branles,* then the *courantes, voltes,* numbers from French ballets (in part identified by Lesure, 1952), and finally "Passameze & Galliarde," some with "Renprinses." Here and there additional dances—"Spagnoletta," "Canarie," "Bourree," "La Mourisque"—are inserted between the larger groups. In several instances dances of the same genre and in related keys are combined into "suites."

Many of the upper voice parts and some of the basses were known long before *Terpsichore* was published; concordances between *Terpsichore* and the Philidor collections and with dances given in the works of Jean d'Estrées and Thoinot Arbeau are frequent. Praetorius explains that in most cases only the melodies *(die Arien)* were communicated to him through a chain of transmission from the French court and that he "composed the basses and middle parts" himself (chapter 5). While he feels justified in claiming these scores as his own, he is meticulous in giving credit to colleagues such as Pierre-François Caroubel, a former court violinist in Paris who joined the musical establishment at Wolfenbüttel in 1610, many of whose five-part settings of French dances are included in *Terpsichore.*

BIBLIOGRAPHY. The bibliography on Praetorius is extensive. Most of the major studies are cited in three biographical entries: Walter Blankenburg, "Praetorius, Michael," in *The New Grove Dictionary of Music and Musicians* (London, 1980); Arno Forchert, "Praetorius, Michael," in *Die Musik in Geschichte und Gegenwart* (Kassel, 1949–); and Hugo Riemann, "Praetorius, Michael," in *Riemanns Musiklexikon,* 12th ed. (Mainz, 1959–). *Terpsichore* is covered in François Lesure, "Die 'Terpsichore' von Michael Praetorius und die französische Instrumentalmusik unter Heinrich IV," *Die Musikforschung* 5 (1952): 7–17. Questions of meter and rhythm are discussed in Paul Brainard, "Zur Deutung der Diminution in der Tactuslehre des Michael Praetorius," and Carl Dahlhaus, "Zur Taktlehre des Michael Praetorius," both in *Die Musikforschung* 17 (1964).

INGRID BRAINARD

PRAGUE NATIONAL THEATER BALLET. The ballet company of the National Theater in Prague holds a key position in the history of Czech professional dance. Only with its founding in 1883 could the uninterrupted development of ballet begin in Czechoslovakia. The theater's first ballet master was a Czech, Václav Reisinger, who had choreographed the world premiere of Tchaikovsky's *Swan Lake* in Moscow in 1877. At the National Theater Reisinger produced the first Czech ballet of the modern era, *Hashish,* to music by Karel Kovařovic, in 1884. The company then had twenty dancers, three soloists, and only one male dancer, Augustin Berger, who soon thereafter took Reisinger's place and directed the company from 1884 to 1900 and again from 1912 to 1923. [*See the entry on Berger.*]

Berger was a virtuoso Czech dancer of the Italian school, a skillful and effective choreographer, and a good and strict teacher; he enlarged the company and gave it a firm professional base. In addition to staging the classics, he also produced national premieres, among them, *Christmas Eve Dream* (1886, music by Mořic Anger), *The Tale of Found Happiness* (1889, music by Kovařovic), *Rákos Rákoczy* (1891, music by Leoš Janáček), and *Bajaja* (1897, music by Jindřich Kàan). The main repertory, however, was characterized by lavish productions, as exemplified by the 1885 staging of Luigi Manzotti's *Excelsior:* large casts, rich costumes and props, special effects, and outward glitter. Berger's Italian orientation was evident in his selection of exclusively Italian prima ballerinas, such as Giulietta Paltrinieri and Enriquetta Grimaldi. Alongside the mature forms of opera and drama, Czech ballet played an inferior role until the 1920s.

Berger's interim successor, the Italian Achille Viscusi, staged the first fairy-tale ballets of the composer Oskar Nedbal, particularly *Tale about Jack* in 1902 and *From Fable to Fable* in 1908, which formed the foundation of the national repertory. These strengthened the Czech tendency to aim ballet toward child audiences.

During the 1920s and 1930s ballet flourished and the repertory was modernized under the direction of the Polish-born Remislav Remislavsky, who became ballet director in 1923. He staged ballets from the Diaghilev repertory and also choreographed works to the music of Czech composers, such as *Ištar* by Bohuslav Martinů in 1924. A frequent guest at this time who later became ballet director and *prima ballerina* was Jelizaveta Nikolská, who brought about a change in technique from the Italian to the Russian school. Important Czech music premieres were held, such as Martinů's *Songbook* in 1933 and Vítězslav Novák's *Signorina Gioventù* and *Nikotina,* both in 1930. The interest of first-class composers attests to the growing prestige of ballet. The most important choreographic personality during these years was Joe Jenčík, who was the first choreographer of *Songbook* and of *The Pied Piper,* to music by Pavel Bořkovec, in 1942.

The postwar period brought about an unforeseen growth and a full liberation of ballet from opera. The choreographer and director Saša Machov formed a strong and enthusiastic company during his five-year tenure (1946–1951). [*See the entry on Machov.*] The company produced *Romeo and Juliet* in 1950 and original national premieres by the composer Zbyněk Vostřák, including *The Philosophy Lesson* in 1949 and *Viktorka* in 1950. Jiří Němeček directed the company from 1957 until 1970 and again, following Miroslav Kůra, from 1979 to 1989. Němeček, an energetic organizer, was an experienced creator of large realistic dance dramas. The repertory has rested mainly on classical works, both Czech and foreign choreographies. [*See the entries on Kůra and Němeček.*]

Since the midtwentieth century, many fine performers and choreographers have been associated with the National Theater, among them, Jiří Blažek, whose 1958 production of *Doktor Faust* introduced inventive, unconventional choreography that was not burdened by descriptive pantomime. Vlastimil Jílek was a dancer of exuberant energy who excelled in character roles. Marta Drottnerová was known for her interpretations of the great ballet heroines Aurora, Odette-Odile, and Giselle. After the "Velvet Revolution" in 1989, former dancer Vlastimil Harapes was selected as *chef de ballet.*

The National Theater Ballet in Prague is not only the oldest, but also the largest and artistically strongest ensemble in the Czech Republic. It has about seventy-five dancers; the average number of performances is twelve to thirteen a month. Since the early 1990s the repertory has included works by the most renowned choreographers including Juří Kylián, Hans van Manen, George Balanchine, José Limón, and Alvin Ailey.

[*See also* Czech Republic and Slovak Republic, *article on* Theatrical Dance.]

BIBLIOGRAPHY

Brodská, Božena. *Dějiny českého baletu do roku 1918.* Prague, 1983.

Kreuzmannová, Yvona. "Hopes and Prospects." *Ballett International* 16 (April 1993): 35–36.

Schmidová, Lidka. *Československý balet.* Prague, 1962.

Tanec/Dance. Prague, 1991.

Windreich, Leland. "Budapest and Prague." *Ballet Review* 21 (Summer 1993): 10–12.

Windreich, Leland. "Prague." *Ballet Review* 23 (Fall 1995): 9–13.

VLADIMÍR VAŠUT
Translated from Czech

PRATESI, GIOVANNI (born 1863 in Milan, died 1938 in Milan), Italian ballet dancer and choreographer. Son of the renowned choreographer Ferdinando Pratesi, Giovanni, while still a very young man, had many successes in the major Italian theaters in his father's ballets, such as *L'Astro degli Afghan* and *Blanca di Navarre;* in works by Luigi Danesi; and in the balletic spectaculars of Luigi

Manzotti, such as *Excelsior* (1881) and *Amor* (1886). Pratesi was an excellent mime as well as a skillful dancer and choreographer. In the late 1890s he went to London, where he was admired as an interpreter of *L'Histoire d'un Pierrot,* set to the music of Mario Pasquale Costa. While in London, he presented at the Alhambra Theatre in the 1898 and 1899 seasons several works, including *Jack Ashore, A Day Off, Napoli,* and a version of *The Fairy Doll,* set to the score by Josef Hassreiter. Upon his return to Italy, he added to his success as a choreographer with *Bacco e Gambrinus,* presented at the Teatro alla Scala in 1904. This spectacle, splendidly interpreted by prima ballerina Cecilia Cerri, was repeated thirty times and remained in the repertory for several years. Subsequently, Pratesi staged other works at La Scala: *Luce* (1905), set to music by Romauldo Marenco and *Le Porte-bonheur* (1908), to music by Riccardo Drigo.

In 1909, Pratesi went once again to London and staged the children's pantomime *Aladdin* at the Theatre Royal, Drury Lane, after which he remained in England for a number of years. He returned to Italy only after World War I. In the years from 1924 to 1928, Pratesi's name appears in many productions at La Scala, where he regularly choreographed dances for operas, including a revival of Christoph Willibald Gluck's *Orfeo ed Euridice* in 1924, the first production of Franco Alfano's *La Leggenda di Sakuntala,* also in 1924, and the premiere of Giacomo Puccini's *Turandot* in 1928. He also created several choreographies to scores by contemporary composers, including *Il Convento Veneziano* (1925), set to music by Alfredo Casella. In 1927 he staged his own version of *Petrouchka,* reducing the plot to a simple puppet play; the roles of Petrouchka, the Ballerina, and the Old Showman were interpreted by Vincenzo Celli, Cia Fornaroli, and Enrico Cecchetti.

In 1928, Pratesi choreographed three important works at La Scala. Two of them were set to music by Richard Strauss, who also conducted the orchestra for the performances: the ballet *La Leggenda di Giuseppe (Die Josephslegende)* and the dances for the opera *Salome.* That same year Pratesi mounted his last original creation, *Vecchia Milano* (Old Milan), set to a libretto by Giuseppe Adami and music by Franco Vittadini. Critics and historians have emphasized that this work, representing the apex of his career, was Pratesi's nationalistic reaction to the 1927 appearance at La Scala by the Ballets Russes de Serge Diaghilev.

Probably still inspired by nationalistic fervor, Pratesi staged a revival of one of the grandest of all Italian ballets, Manzotti's *Excelsior,* for the Teatro San Carlos in Naples in 1931. It was his final work. The dance historian Gino Tani considered his career exemplary of "the Italian ballet itself at the turn of the century, still modeled on the glorious nineteenth-century tradition of which [he] was the last and most authoritative exponent in our country" (Tani, 1954–).

BIBLIOGRAPHY

Guest, Ivor. *Jules Perrot: Master of the Romantic Ballet.* London, 1984.

Guest, Ivor. *Ballet in Leicester Square.* London, 1992.

Rossi, Luigi. "Pratesi, Giovanni." In *Dizionario del balletto.* Milan, 1994.

Tani, Gino. "Pratesi, Giovanni." In *Enciclopedia dello spettacolo.* Rome, 1954–.

Testa, Alberto. "Pratesi, Giovanni." In *Grande enciclopedia della musica classica Curcio.* Rome, 1982.

ARCHIVE. Walter Toscanini Collection of Research Materials in Dance, New York Public Library for the Performing Arts.

CLAUDIA CELI
Translated from Italian

PRECISION DANCING. Defined as group chorus movement whose main appeal is exactness of performance, precision dancing employs simple steps because the emphasis is on the overall geometric effect of the dancing rather than the individual dancer.

The vogue for precision dancing can be traced directly to John Tiller (c.1851–1925), a prosperous British businessman, who began to produce church pageants in England in the 1890s. By elaborating his drills and marches, Tiller made the transition into dance. As the demand for his work increased, he opened a training school in London. His troupes eventually made their stage debut in 1901. Tiller tried to emphasize ballet in his first theatrical troupes, but before long he returned to the marching routines that had made his earlier pageants so popular. Marching, plus a few can-can kicks and elementary tap dance steps, became the basic routine in the genre and have remained standard.

Tiller's regular troupes were composed of sixteen girls averaging from five feet to five feet, two inches tall. The girls were organized along military lines (as were their American successors). Each line or troupe had a captain who was the lead dancer as well as the social and professional disciplinarian. The strict moral behavior and disciplined talent of Miller's troupes were a revelation to the American public to whom the dubious moral character and negligible ability of the average chorus girl had long been a standard joke.

Many prominent early twentieth-century dance directors were influenced by Tiller. Allan K. Foster, an American director, came under the influence of Tiller in London, married a Tiller line captain, and patterned his dancers after the Tiller troupes, both in organization and technique. Gertrude Hoffman trained many precision troupes, adding acrobatics and circus techniques. Madame Albertina Rasch's interest in precision dancing was prompted by a desire to make ballet dancing acceptable to American tastes. Her troupes became known for their precision work on toes. [*See the entry on Rasch.*] Chester Hale, a veteran of Serge Diaghilev's ballet company, insisted that his female dancers learn basic ballet pointe work before he would put them into a group. Before he was contracted for a specific production, he choreographed and rehearsed his dances.

Precision troupes waned in the late 1930s, but one, perhaps the most famous of all, is still in existence, at Radio City Music Hall in New York City. The troupe, the world-renowned Rockettes, was set up by Russell Markert, who adhered closely to the Tiller style of march and kick. In addition to tap dancing, Markert introduced novelty within the framework. [*See* Radio City Music Hall.]

The vogue that precision dancing enjoyed is easier to understand when it is viewed in the light of its predecessor, musical comedy dance. Precision dancing was not necessarily better dance, but it had a clean pattern and appeared to be totally organized. Because the American audience was essentially untutored in dance, troupe directors did not need to appeal to the artistic perceptions of the public but rather to the audience's admiration of perfection. Thus the essential requirement of precision dance routines in this early period was that they "stop the show." Whether the dance had anything to do with the production or fit the music was not important. Producers and the dance directors judged the dance solely on its ability to elicit applause from the audience. The most widely used formula was to line up the girls and have them perform repeated high kicks until the audience started to clap vehemently.

A basic reason for the rise of precision troupes was that they afforded considerable economic advantage to the producers. By 1925 Chorus Equity, a branch of Actors' Equity, had ruled that rehearsal periods could not exceed five weeks, during which chorus members were to receive half pay. Producers did not consider a five-week rehearsal schedule sufficient to turn out polished dances, however, so they acquired well-trained troupes from various dance schools to augment or provide substitutes for the regular choruses in their musical comedies and revues.

Throughout the history of musical comedy dance, producers have tended to repeat themselves until the Broadway public reaches a saturation point. The same pattern developed in film. Precision tap dancing became the vogue when sound was introduced, most notably in the films of Busby Berkeley in the 1930s, and it continued to be popular in films until after World War II, when the Hollywood musical became too expensive to produce. [*See the entry on Berkeley.*]

Precision dancing, which expanded into precision swimming in *Billy Roses's Aquacades* in 1935, was introduced into the Ice Follies in 1938. Still performed on ice and in water, precision dancing flourishes also as entr'acte entertainment on football fields and basketball courts, where there is as much competition to get in the line as to make the team.

[*For related discussion, see* Music Hall, *article on* British Traditions.]

BIBLIOGRAPHY

Hering, Doris, ed. *Twenty-Five Years of American Dance.* Rev. and enl. ed. New York, 1954.

Levinson, André. "The Girls." *Theatre Arts* 12 (August 1928): 597–605.

McNeill, William. *Keeping Together in Time: Dance and Drill in Human History.* Cambridge, Mass., 1995.

ROBERT D. MOULTON

PREOBRAJENSKA, OLGA (Ol'ga Iosifovna Preobrazhenskaia; born 21 January [2 February] 1871 in Saint Petersburg, died 27 December 1962 in Saint-Mande, France), ballet dancer and teacher. Preobrajenska graduated from the Saint Petersburg theater school in 1889. Her teachers were Lev Ivanov, Marius Petipa, and Christian Johansson. From 1889 onward she danced with the Maryinsky ballet company, becoming a soloist in 1896 and a prima ballerina in 1900. She was a leading dancer of the Maryinsky Theater at the turn of the century, dancing an extremely broad and varied repertory; her leading roles included almost all the ballets of Petipa, Ivanov, the Legats, and many of Michel Fokine. She created a number of important roles on the Russian stage: Anne in Petipa's *Barbe-Bleue* (1896; after 1900 the role of Isaure); Henriette in his *Raymonda* (1898; after 1903, the title role); Pierette in his *Les Millions d'Arlequin* (1900); the title role in Pavel Gerdt's *Javotte* (1902); and Cléopâtra's Slave in Fokine's *Une Nuit d'Égypte* (1908; after 1910, Bérénice). Preobrajenska took part in the 1908 and 1909 productions of Fokine's *Chopiniana,* and Fokine also staged Tchaikovsky's concert piece "Romance" for her in 1915.

Preobrajenska's dance was distinguished by precision and perfection in her *terre-à-terre* technique, soaring leaps, elegance, naturalness, and rare musicality. Describing Preobrajenska as a "poetess of dance," critics invariably pointed out the wealth of semitones and nuances in her interpretations and her penchant for improvisation. She danced variations to encores, invariably modifying the patterns of the dance. The absence of a genuine gift for dramatic acting distinguished Preobrajenska from Matilda Kshessinska and Anna Pavlova; her lyrical talent was fully revealed in the roles of Aurora, Raymonda, Lise, and Javotte. She also successfully danced *demi-caractère* dances, such as "Muzhichok" (Little Muzhik) by Petipa, a Liszt czardas by Ivanov, which was included in *The Little Humpbacked Horse,* and others. Preobrajenska worked constantly to advance her skill. Although she was a well-known ballerina, she took lessons from Enrico Cecchetti (1898–1900) and Nikolai Legat in Russia, Caterina Beretta in Milan, Joseph Hansen in Paris, and Katti Lanner in London. The ballerina also made many successful foreign tours to Western Europe and South America.

Preobrajenska taught at the Saint Petersburg theater school in 1901–1902 and from 1914 to 1921, and at Akim Volynsky's School of Russian Ballet in Petrograd from 1917 to 1921, at the same time directing the dance class of the opera company at the Maryinsky Theater. In 1922 she emigrated and danced at La Scala in Milan, Covent Garden in London, Teatro Colón in Buenos Aires, and in Berlin. From 1923 onward Preobrajenska lived in Paris, where she founded a school of classical ballet at the Studio Wacker. She retired in 1960. Among her students were Irina Baronova, Tamara Toumanova, Nina Vyroubova, George Skibine, and Hugh Laing, to mention but a few. Agrippina Vaganova went through a course of advanced training under her guidance in the early 1900s. She also trained Igor Youskevitch and Margarethe Wallmann.

PREOBRAJENSKA. A studio portrait in the costume she wore to dance the Prelude in Michel Fokine's *Rêverie Romantique: Ballet sur la Musique de Chopin,* the second version of *Chopiniana,* performed at the Maryinsky Theater in March 1908. (Photograph from the Dance Collection, New York Public Library for the Performing Arts.)

BIBLIOGRAPHY

Fay, Maria. "Dancing Begins in the Brain." *The Dancing Times* (December 1993): 281.

Finch, Tamara. "Les Ballets 1933." *The Dancing Times* (March 1988): 532–535.

Gregory, John. *The Legat Saga.* 2d ed. London, 1993.

Karsavina, Tamara. *Theatre Street.* Rev. and enl. ed. London, 1948.

Krasovskaya, Vera. *Russkii baletnyi teatr nachala dvadtsatogo veka,* vol. 2, *Tantsovshchiki.* Leningrad, 1972.

Roné, Elvira. *Olga Preobrazhenskaya: A Portrait.* Translated by Fernau Hall. New York, 1978.

Smakov, Gennady. *The Great Russian Dancers.* New York, 1984.

Svetlov, Valerian. *O. O. Preobrazhenskaia.* Saint Petersburg, 1902.

VALERY A. KULAKOV
Translated from Russian

PRÉVOST, FRANÇOISE (born c.1681, died 13 September 1741 in Paris), French dancer, choreographer, and teacher. Despite the scanty information available about Françoise Prévost, one senses the presence of a personality and talent of exceptional quality and importance. Most surviving testimonies about her come from colleagues, who never tired of paying homage to her mastery as a performer. According to Pierre Rameau (1725), "Any one of her dances contains all the principles which a long reflection upon our art would lead us to lay down. She applies them all so fittingly and with such grace, lightness, and precision that she can be regarded as a prodigy." In 1726, Marie Sallé gratefully acknowledged her debt: "You have taught me which ornament suits a shepherdess's bosom, which gesture pleases, which step conveys the most feeling" (Bibliothèque Nationale, Paris, Ms. fr.25.000).

Long after Prévost's death, leading ballerinas continued to be judged by the standards she had set and maintained throughout an unusually long and distinguished career. In 1745, the *Mercure de France* wrote of the ballerina La Barberina: "In praising you, Barberina, I will not insult Prévost's illustrious memory." Twenty years later, choreographer Jean-Georges Noverre would still flatly assert: "Before Prévost, no other female dancer is worth mentioning" (Noverre, 1760).

The exact date of her debut at the Paris Opera is unknown: early programs do not list casts, and archives began much later. Her teacher was named Thibaud. In October 1695, Mademoiselle Prévost appeared in the program of the *Ballet des Saisons.* Her name did not appear again until 1702 in André Campra's opera *Tancrède.*

In approximately 1705, "La petite Prévost" and another rising star, Marie-Catherine Guyot, were already featured in leading roles. The two dancers were well matched—both had fiery temperaments and solid technique—and they often appeared together in such roles as bacchantes, tambourins, and scaramouchettes. Some of these duets, recorded in Feuillet notation, sparkle with *cabrioles, entrechats,* and *pirouettes à la seconde.* They were bravura pieces that also demanded acting ability.

As a performer, Prévost stood supreme. In *Le maître à danser* (1725), Rameau wrote: "Like Proteus, she can assume all kinds of forms. . . . She uses this talent to captivate her spectators and endear herself to them." Indeed, she was to more fully develop the acting side of her dancing talent. In 1710 she appeared in a *danse du caprice* to music by Jean-Féry Rebel. In 1714, at one of the duchesse du Maine's famous "Nuits" at Sceaux, she reduced her sophisticated audience to tears with her rendering of Camille in *Les Horaces,* a role she danced opposite Claude Ballon. Many historians now see that performance as the beginning of *ballet d'action.*

In 1715, Prévost was to experiment further in *Les Caractères de la Danse,* a piece she choreographed for herself to music by Rebel. Each of the suite's eleven movements was personified, from the giddy gigue of a young girl in love to the stately courante of an elderly gallant. This ballet pantomime was such a success that it became the dancer's favorite encore at the opera and at private parties, where she often received requests for it. Prévost later chose *Les Caractères* for the debut of her pupil Marie Camargo in 1726, and Marie Sallé rechoreographed it as a duet for herself and Antoine Bandieri de Laval in 1729 and exported it to England. Indeed, this brilliant and expressive number was such a perfect vehicle for aspiring ballerinas that it soon became their customary debut piece. [*See* Caractères de la Danse, Les.]

Prévost's work as a choreographer cannot have stopped at *Les Caractères de la Danse.* She must have taken full advantage of the privileges that gave the premier danseurs opportunities to compose their own solos. She also seems to have choreographed for others. At the time of her estrangement from Camargo, according to *Le nécrologe des hommes* (1771), she "refused to go on teaching her and to compose her '*entrées.*'"

Three professional dancers studied with Prévost: Mademoiselle Richalet, who made her debut at the Paris Opera in 1723; Camargo, who made hers in 1726; and Sallé, who appeared in 1727. Each embodied a facet of their teacher's multiple talent, and the spectacular Camargo and the expressive Sallé soon reached a fame comparable to hers.

Much has been written about the pretended rivalry between Prévost and Camargo. Actress Adrienne Lecouvreur recalled in her letters:

> Yesterday, they played Roland, by Quinault and Lully. Mademoiselle Prévost, although she surpassed herself, obtained very meager applause in comparison with a new dancer named Camargo, whom the public idolize, and whose great merit is her youth and vigor. Mademoiselle Prévost at first protected her but Blondy has fallen in love with her, and the lady is piqued. She seemed jealous and discontented at the applause Camargo received from the public.

If Prévost was jealous of Camargo, she seemed not to be jealous of her other pupil, Sallé. In 1731, Voltaire recalled in a letter, "The pit, the loggias, the ladies, the 'Petits maîtres,' Mademoiselle Prévost herself, everyone was ecstatic when she [Sallé] last danced in the new opera."

After more than three decades of dancing leading roles, Prévost retired from the Paris Opera in September 1730. The *Mercure de France,* which recorded the event, noted that the public, "who has always honored her with much applause, will not readily forget her." The "illustrious" Prévost, who, in the pursuit of personal happiness had been as indefatigable offstage as on, was left to spend the last decade of her life in peace and dignity. The gossip chronicles, which had recorded so many of her intrigues and made songs about her amours, stopped mentioning her altogether.

On 1 January 1718, the ballerina had given birth to an illegitimate child, whom she only legally recognized eight years later—at the same time as did the presumed father, Alexandre Maximilien Balthazar de Gand, comte de Middlebourg. This daughter, Anne-Auguste de Valjolly, was to marry composer and violinist François Rebel, the son of Jean-Féry Rebel, both renowned musicians.

In 1740, Prévost made a will, bequeathing to her lawyer her portrait by Raoux portraying her as a bacchante; this is now in the art museum at Tours. On 13 September 1741, the great ballerina died in her home at the age of sixty. She left a comfortable estate to the widow of her brother Jean, a bookbinder. The inventory of her belongings mentions several paintings in their gold frames, several damask hangings, a well-provided cellar, and a lovely garden decorated with crated orange trees, which suggest a well-to-do household that was not nearly so luxurious as Camargo's but far more opulent than Sallé's.

Dances performed by Prévost and recorded in Feuillet notation include the following duets (listed in Gaudrau, *Recueil de danses,* 1713) that were performed with Mademoiselle Guyot: "Canary" from *Le Triomphe de l'Amour,* "Entrée à Deux" from *Issé,* "Entrée de Deux Bacchantes" from *Philomèle,* "Entrée de Deux Femmes" from *Les Fêtes Vénitiennes,* and "Muzette à Deux" from *Callirhoé.*

[*See also the entries on the principal figures mentioned herein.*]

BIBLIOGRAPHY

Astier, Régine. "Françoise Prevost, A Biography." In *Dance History Scholars Conference.* Baltimore, 1984.

Aubry, Pierre, and Émile Dacier. *Les Caractères de la Danse.* Paris, 1905.

Bonnet, J. *Histoire général de la danse sacrée et profane.* Paris, 1724.

Dacier, Émile. *Une danseuse de l'Opéra sous Louis XV: Mlle. Sallé, 1707–1756.* 2d ed. Paris, 1909.

Jullien, Adolphe. *La comédie à la cour: Les théâtres de société royale pendant le siècle dernier.* Paris, 1883.

Lecouvreur, Adrienne. *Lettres.* Edited by Georges Monval. Paris, 1892.

Marais, Mathieu. *Journal et mémoires.* Paris, 1864.

Migel, Parmenia. *The Ballerinas: From the Court of Louis XIV to Pavlova.* New York, 1972.

Noverre, Jean-Georges. *Lettres sur la danse et sur les ballets.* Stuttgart and Lyon, 1760. Translated by Cyril W. Beaumont as *Letters on Dancing and Ballets* (London, 1930).

Poinsinet de Sivry, J., et al. *Le nécrologe des hommes célèbres de France, par une société de gens des lettres.* Paris, 1767–. See the entry for Camargo.

Rameau, Pierre. *Le maître à danser.* Paris, 1725. Translated by John Essex, London, 1728.

Ranum, Patricia. "Les 'Caractères' des danses françaises." *Recherches sur la Musique Française Classique* 23 (1985): 45–70.

Semmens, Richard T. "Terpsichore Reborn: The French Noble Style and Drama." In *Proceedings of the Tenth Annual Conference, Society of Dance History Scholars, University of California, Irvine, 13–15 February 1987,* compiled by Christena L. Schlundt. Riverside, Calif., 1987.

Voltaire. *Le siècle de Louis XIV* (1751). Edited by Adolphe Garnier. Paris, 1857. See chapter 33.

Winter, Marian Hannah. *The Pre-Romantic Ballet.* London, 1974.

RÉGINE ASTIER

PRICE FAMILY, three generations of a Danish family of circus performers, pantomime artists, and dancers. The story of the Price family in Denmark starts with James Price (1761–1805), an English circus rider who gave performances at Dyrehavsbakken—a place of entertainment near Copenhagen—beginning in 1795. With Giuseppe Casorti he presented pantomime performances, first at the old Court Theater in Christiansborg and later in their own building on Vesterbro Morskabsteater. Part of this repertory can still be seen in a certain performance tradition at the Pantomime Theater in Tivoli. The sons of James Price—James (1801–1865) and Adolph (1805–1890)—played Harlequin and Pierrot in the pantomimes. They also fathered a number of prominent dancers.

One son of the younger James Price was Julius (1833–1893), a pupil of August Bournonville. He followed his teacher to Vienna in 1855. By the time Bournonville returned to Vienna in 1874, Julius had become permanent soloist with the opera ballet. He later became ballet master and professor at the conservatory in Vienna. The second son of the younger James was Carl Price (1839–1909), who went from ballet to acting and was the father of the eminent dancer Ellen Price. James's daughter Amalie (1831–1892) became one of the three cousins for whom Bournonville created his *Pas de Trois Cousines.*

Adolph Price was the father of Juliette Price (1831–1906) and Sophie Price (1833–1905), the two other *cousines.* Adolph's son Waldemar (1836–1908) showed himself to be an extremely gifted mime dancer.

PRICE FAMILY. Ellen Price de Plane (1878–1968), daughter of Carl Price, in the title role of Bournonville's ballet *La Sylphide,* in 1903. She was taught the part by her aunt, Juliette Price, who had danced it from 1849 to 1859. (Photograph by Peter Elfelt; from the Royal Library, Copenhagen.)

It was Bournonville who first spotted the talents of the Price children, whose parents had approached him for private lessons. He wrote in *My Theatre Life:* "At first I winced at the thought of undertaking such a task, since, to put it bluntly, I regarded the stepchildren of Terpsichore as completely irrelevant to my endeavors. But my eyes were soon opened to the fine gifts which needed only expert guidance to develop into real talent."

According to Bournonville, "Juliette, Amalie and Sophie created an epoch" with *Pas de Trois Cousines* (1849), and they "were portrayed herein as a modern-day group of the Graces" (Bournonville, 1979). In *Konservatoriet* (1849) he found parts for both Juliette and Sophie, and together they performed the mirror dance in *La Ventana* (1854), still in the repertory of the Royal Theater.

Juliette Price (born 13 August 1831, died 4 April 1906) became Bournonville's favorite dancer and with her father followed Bournonville to Vienna in 1855–1856. Bournonville created the roles of Eleonore in *Kermesse in*

Bruges (1851) and Hilda in *A Folk Tale* (1854) especially for her, to celebrate her chaste and innocent dancing. Her career was short: she was injured during a performance of *Kermesse* in 1865 and never danced again.

Bournonville gave Juliette a worthy memorial in *My Theatre Life:*

> Juliette Price is the one of all the priestesses of Terpsichore who, after Marie Taglioni and Carlotta Grisi, has come closest to *my* ideal of a *danseuse.* Though I by no means wish to place her virtuosity on a par with or above that of those celebrities whose strength lies in *quantity,* . . . I must acknowledge that her dancing possesses not only perfection of training but is inspired by true feminine grace . . . .

Waldemar Price (1836–1908) danced the fisherman Gennaro in Napoli, the title role in *Waldemar,* and Ove in *A Folk Tale* with great feeling according to one critic (Edvard Brandes, 1929). Waldemar was schooled by Bournonville, but the ballet master found the young dancer's technique insufficient. Instead, Waldemar became the great mimic actor in Bournonville's late works: Svend in *The Mountain Hut* (1859), and in two parts created for him, Asathor in *The Lay of Thrym* (1868) and Edouard in *The King's Lifeguards on Amager* (1871). Waldemar performed until 1901 and became a teacher of major importance, particularly to Hans Beck, who was responsible for the Bournonville renaissance during the first two decades of the twentieth century.

BIBLIOGRAPHY

Anderson, Jack, and George Dorris. "A Conversation with Svend Kragh-Jacobsen." *Ballet Review* 5.4 (1975–1976): 1–20.

Bournonville, August. *My Theatre Life* (1848–1878). Translated by Patricia McAndrew. Middletown, Conn., 1979.

Kragh-Jacobsen, Svend, and Torben Krogh, eds. *Den Kongelige Danske Ballet.* Copenhagen, 1952.

Veale, Tom G. "The Dancing Prices of Denmark." *Dance Perspectives,* no. 11 (1961).

HENRIK LUNDGREN

PRIEST, JOSIAH (also known as Josias Preist, possibly Joseph Priest; died January 1735 in Chelsea parish, England), English dancer, dancing master, and choreographer. Members of the Priest family are among the most prominent of the Restoration dancing masters. Josiah was well known for productions of works by composers John Blow and Henry Purcell at his school in Chelsea during the 1680s. A Joseph Priest (also referred to in documentation as John and may or may not be the same person as Josiah), took part in court and theater productions from at least 1667 when he appeared with Moll Davies in the masque for the final act of John Dryden's *Sir Martin Mar-all* at Lincoln's Inn Fields theater.

In 1673 a Joseph Priest collaborated with Luke Channell on the dances for Sir William Davenant's version of *Macbeth* at the Duke's Theatre, Dorset Gardens. He was responsible, with Adrien Merger de Saint-André (described by a contemporary as the king's "master of the compositions for ballet"), for the dances in John Crowne's masque *Calisto, or The Chaste Nymph* (1675), for which he received £100. The professional dancers for the court performance at Whitehall before Charles II included French and English groups: the former led by Saint-André and the latter by Mister Isaac. The princesses Mary and Anne were among the courtly dancers, and the music was by Nicholas Staggins.

In 1680 Josiah Priest moved his boarding school for gentlewomen from Leicester Fields to Chelsea, where it became highly fashionable. Thomas D'Urfey, who spent some time at Priest's school, possibly as a singing master, provided a critical picture of it in his play *Love for Money, or The Boarding School* (1691). Grand balls were held regularly and the school also hosted performances of theatrical works that included Blow's *Venus and Adonis* (1684) and Purcell's *Dido and Aeneas* (1689). John Downes attributed the choreography of three Purcell staged works to "Mr. Priest" (called "Mr. Jo. Priest" only in one of them, but likely Joseph Priest throughout). These works were *The Prophetess, or The History of Diocletian* (Dorset Gardens, 1690), *King Arthur, or The British Worthy* (Dorset Gardens, 1691), and *The Fairy Queen* (Dorset Gardens, 1692). It is likely that "Mr. Priest" also contributed to *The Indian Queen* (Theatre Royal, 1695). [*See the entry on Purcell.*]

As a choreographer, Priest was a man of judgment, culture, and technical expertise who also possessed an excellent musical and theatrical sense; he took care to arrange steps that suited the character of the theatrical moment, which was by no means common. John Weaver regarded him as the greatest master of grotesque dancing to have appeared in London. (Grotesque dancing included the representation of impersonal or preternatural characters and thus encompassed many of the needs of the traditional masque). Weaver wrote,

> A Master or Performer in Grotesque Dancing ought to be a Person bred up to the Profession, and thoroughly skill'd in his Business. As a Master, he ought to be skill'd in Musick, and particularly in that Part relating to Time; well read in History Ancient and Modern, with a Taste to Painting and Poetry. . . . the Master must take peculiar Care to contrive his Steps, and adapt his Actions, and Humour, to the Characters or Sentiments he wou'd represent or express, so as to resemble the Person he wou'd imitate, or Passion he wou'd excite.
>
> (Weaver, *An Essay towards an History of Dancing,* 1712)

Josiah Priest and his wife Franck ran the school at Chelsea until at least 1711/12 when they moved to Saint Lawrence Street. By that time their son Thomas (born

1670/71) was an established dancing master, also living in Chelsea, and both father and son set dances to music by Jeremiah Clarke, Purcell, and others that Thomas Bray published as *Country Dances . . . also the Newest French Dances in Use, Entryes Genteel and Grotesque . . . and other Dancing Tunes* (1699). Another member of the family active as a dancing master at this time was George Priest of Holborn. It is not known who choreographed Mr. Priest's Minuet for twelve ladies and published by Edmund Pemberton in *An Essay for the Further Improvement of Dancing* (1711).

According to the Chelsea parish registers, Mrs. Franck Priest was buried on 20 April 1733, and Mr. Josiah Priest on 3 January 1734/35. If Joseph was indeed a different person from Josiah Priest, his date and place of burial have yet to be established.

BIBLIOGRAPHY

Cohen, Selma Jeanne. "Theory and Practice of Theatrical Dancing: I. Josias Priest." In *Famed for Dance*, by Ifan Kyrle Fletcher et al. New York, 1960.

Falconer, David. "The Two Mr. Priests of Chelsea." *Musical Times* (May 1987): 263.

Goff, Moira, and Jennifer Thorp. "Minuets and Dancing Monkeys." *The Dancing Times* (March 1995): 565–569.

Luckett, Richard. "A New Source for *Venus and Adonis*." *Musical Times* (February 1989): 76–79.

Price, Curtis. *Music in the Restoration Theatre*. Ann Arbor, Mich., 1979.

Walking, Andrew. "Masque and Politics at the Restoration Court: John Crowne's *Calisto*." *Early Music* (February 1996): 27–63.

RICHARD RALPH and JENNIFER THORP

PRIMITIVE DANCE. The word *primitive*, when applied to the graphic arts in the Western world, has several meanings: that the artist is untutored, or that the artist assumes a naive style. It may also refer to a school of painting, to folk art, or to artworks made in a nonliterate society. For dance, however, the word *primitive* has been used to imply a specific style—for which certain movements, rhythms, and dynamics are considered to be generic features that are characteristic of "primitive" dances.

Webster's Ninth New Collegiate Dictionary (1990) defines a primitive culture as "early" or "unsophisticated," but those adjectives are value-loaded, misleading, and inappropriate. In fact, contemporary primitive (nonliterate) peoples comprise the oldest continuous (relatively unchanged) societies in the world. Their sophistication focuses on mentifacts and phenomifacts rather than on artifacts. The last, however, are a visible measure of sophistication for many persons in the Western world, and that measure interferes with objective evaluation.

Many anthropologists characterize a primitive society as one in which the division of labor is only by sex and age, with no economic specializations, one which is totally self-sufficient, with a small population relative to the large amount of available land necessary for economic subsistence. A primitive society is a band of people that depends on hunting and gathering. Today few band societies sustain a traditional lifestyle because of outside pressures. Well-known examples of band societies in the twentieth century are the Bushmen of the Kalahari Desert in southern Africa, the Australian Aborigines, and the Inuit (Eskimo) of the Arctic. The dances of these peoples differ from one another in almost every way, except that characteristically they are performed by one or the other sex, there is not much torso movement, and the rationale for the dance is rooted in metaphysics.

Bushmen dances usually last several hours, are performed by uncostumed groups of from four to eighty dancers, and take place in any convenient location. Dancers often achieve altered states of consciousness, demonstrated by trembling and swooning as a preliminary to their healing rituals. Australian Aborigine dancers spend hours decorating their bodies but only a few minutes or even seconds in dance performances that are performed in secluded outdoor sacred spaces. Typically a soloist or a few men dance in a straight line of direction that represents a totemic ancestor's journey in the mythical Dreamtime. They alternately trot and pause while executing a side-to-side quivering of the knees, called *shake-a-leg*. Inuit dances last only as long as a short song with several stanzas, but the dance event may last many hours, performed in a special "song house." Inuit dancers add costume pieces to their ordinary clothing, such as dance mittens or, in some areas, masks. Solo pantomimic dances are presented in place, with tilting torsos and broad gestures that recount a story or depict an animal. Group ritual dances follow concentric circles, with the women shuffling in one direction and the men in the other.

The so-called primitive dance style portrayed by American concert dancers and included in dance school curricula follows a model that bears no resemblance to the dances of primitive peoples as described above. This theatrical style includes abstractions from the dances of West African or Caribbean societies, which are not primitive. Western choreographers and dance teachers often borrow from non-Western dance cultures. The misnomer *primitive dance* has been applied to the package of exotic movments, rhythms, and dynamics adapted from American dances with West African antecedents. The style fits merely naive assumptions about primitive dance. These ill-chosen stereotypes have blocked a deeper understanding of both African-derived dances and true primitive dances. Today, despite decades of reinforcement of these stereotypes, such terms as *African-American dance*, *Afro-Brazilian dance*, and *Afro-Caribbean dance* are beginning to replace the indiscriminately misused term *primitive dance*.

BIBLIOGRAPHY

Hovey, Walter R. "Primitive Art." In *Encyclopedia of the Arts*. London, 1964.

Grau, Andrée. "Myths of Origin." *Dance Now* 2 (Winter 1993–1994): 38–43.

Katz, Richard. *Boiling Energy: Community Healing among the Kalahari !Kung*. Cambridge, Mass., 1982.

Kealiinohomoku, Joann W. "An Anthropologist Looks at Ballet as a Form of Ethnic Dance" (1969). In *What Is Dance?*, edited by Roger Copeland and Marshall Cohen. New York, 1983.

Palmer, Bruce, and Beth Dean. *South Pacific: Pacific Islands Art and Dance*. Suva, Fiji, 1972.

JOANN W. KEALIINOHOMOKU

PRIMITIVE MYSTERIES. Choreography: Martha Graham. Music: Louis Horst. Libretto: Martha Graham. Costumes: Martha Graham. First performance: 2 February 1931, Craig Theater, New York City, Martha Graham and Dance Group. Principal: Martha Graham.

PRIMITIVE MYSTERIES. Martha Graham and Group in the "Hymn to the Virgin" section in 1935. Agnes de Mille said that "*Primitive Mysteries* was the first successful lay statement in dance of a holy event in the Western Christian church for upward of a thousand years." (Photograph © 1980 by Barbara Morgan; used by permission of the Barbara Morgan Archives, Hastings-on-Hudson, New York.)

Acclaimed at its premiere as a major achievement in American dance, *Primitive Mysteries* is one of only a few group works Graham created prior to 1939 that have survived; it was revived in 1964, 1976, and 1982. Graham's inspiration for the dance is said to have come out of a trip she and Louis Horst made in the summer of 1930 to Native American villages in the American Southwest and from the paintings of José Clemente Orozco. Catholic art and ritual provided the basis for the iconic postures and gestures, but the dance is personal in concept and style and not a re-creation of any actual rite.

A woman in a long, full white dress is attended by a group of women (usually twelve) in long, plain, deep-blue gowns, who respond to her, succor her, and kneel to her. Before and after each of the dance's three sections, all the women enter and leave the stage. The formation alters, but the walk is always the same: arms at their sides, in silence, they stride straight-legged, with a strong thrust of bare heels onto the floor and a slight hesitation after each step. Each dance ends with the women in a circle around the central figure, who seems to be one of them, chosen for this occasion to play the Virgin. Throughout the piece, the dancing shows immense economy, intensity, and strength; a primitive simplicity and boldness of design informs posture, group architecture, and compositional sequence. The music, equally spare, sets flute and oboe against piano chords and occasional light percussion.

The first section, "Hymn to the Virgin," begins as a series of statements and responses: the soloist runs to two groups of women in turn, offering them a gesture or moving with them; some of their answering gestures suggest, in highly abstracted form, rocking a cradle, forming a halo, and other acts associated with Mariology. Throughout almost the entire "Crucifixus" section, the soloist, flanked by two of the women, advances with almost imperceptible steps, while groups of women move forward and backward and into new formations with hushed, weighted steps, hands on shoulders, elbows pointing forward, gazes high. In a moment of silence, the soloist stretches her arms out to the sides and stays like that while the women circle her with big, flying, doubled-over leaps. In the last section, "Hosanna," the women wheel around with quicker, celebratory steps, while one of them joins the soloist in a series of tableaux suggesting such events as the deposition from the cross and the crowning of the Virgin.

No precise cast is given in the program for the first performance, only a listing of the eighteen women then members of Graham's Group. Interviews with some of them have yielded conflicting cast lists, although it seems certain that Mary Rivoire was the Acolyte in the last section. It is not clear either whether there were twelve or more than twelve women besides Graham dancing in the first performance.

BIBLIOGRAPHY

Gardner, Howard. "Martha Graham: Discovering the Dance of America." *Ballet Review* 22 (Spring 1994): 67–93.

Siegel, Marcia B. *The Shapes of Change: Images of American Dance.* New York, 1979.

FILM. *Primitive Mysteries* (1964), Dance Collection, New York Public Library for the Performing Arts.

DEBORAH JOWITT

PRIMUS, PEARL (Pearl Eileene Primus; born 29 November 1919 in Port of Spain, Trinidad, died 29 October 1994 in New Rochelle, New York), dancer, choreographer, anthropologist, instructor, lecturer, and scholar. In the early 1920s Primus's parents brought her from their native Trinidad to New York City, where she attended Hunter College High School and Hunter College, graduating in 1940 with a degree in biology and premedical sciences. Her aspiration to be a physician was thwarted by racial discrimination, which blocked her from being hired by New York's medical laboratories. Turning to the National Youth Administration, she was given a wardrobe position in a dance demonstration unit, despite having no particular interest in dance. She later became a dancer's understudy, and the National Youth Administration assigned her to demonstrate everything from the minuet to the lindy.

Becoming more seriously interested in dance, Primus won a scholarship offered by New York City's New Dance Group in July 1941. She studied and absorbed the techniques of Martha Graham, Doris Humphrey, Hanya Holm, Charles Weidman, and Beryl McCurnie. On 14 February 1943, Primus gave her first professional performance at the Ninety-second Street YMHA (Young Men's Hebrew Association). Wrote John Martin, dance critic of the *New York Times*, of this debut: "If ever a young dancer was entitled to a company of her own and the freedom to do what she chooses with it, she is it."

In April 1943 Primus turned a planned ten-week engagement at the Cafe Society Downtown, a New York City

PRIMUS. In her dance based on Langston Hughes's well-known poem *The Negro Speaks of Rivers,* Primus created dynamic, undulating rhythms and free-flowing torrents of turns. It was presented at her Broadway debut at the Belasco Theatre in 1944. (Photograph © by Barbara Morgan; used by permission of the Barbara Morgan Archives, Hastings-on-Hudson, New York.)

PRIMUS. A scene from Primus's *The Initiation,* a work inspired by her travels in Africa. (Photograph from the Dance Collection, New York Public Library for the Performing Arts.)

nightclub, into a ten-month extended engagement. In December 1943 she performed a solo and two duets with Asadata Dafora at Carnegie Hall in the African Dance Festival, presented by the African Academy of Arts and Research and sponsored by Eleanor Roosevelt, guest of honor along with Mary McLeod Bethune, then president of the National Council of Negro Women. Central to the African Academy's mission were intercultural understanding and appreciation. As though in response to this mission, Primus left the Cafe Society Downtown in February 1944 and went south to study in African-American churches and in cotton fields. She increasingly viewed dance not merely as entertainment but as a broad medium of communication.

By 1944 Primus had developed a repertory of her own creations with a theme she never abandoned: the variety of experiences of peoples of African descent, from traditional African dance to social protest in the United States. Her first creation, *African Ceremonial,* often opened her presentations. In the role of a priestess, she blessed the land and prayed for continued peace. Typically *African Ceremonial* was followed by African and West Indian dances, emphasizing the inherent dignity with which these dances are performed in their natural ceremonial context. Next came dance expressions of the African-American in slavery in the United States, based on spirituals, folk songs, Langston Hughes's poem "The Negro Speaks of Rivers," and works of revival preachers. Audiences were then likely to be treated to the Harlem jitterbug and other social dances set to the beat of contemporary jazz and blues. Social unrest and protest came to life in a group of dances, including *Strange Fruit,* named after Louis Allen's poignant poem about lynching, which is recited during the dance. "Hard Times Blues," the Josh White song for which another dance is named, describes the tragic conditions that lead to social protest. (Josh White accompanied Primus on "Hard Times Blues" for her 4 October 1944 Broadway debut at the Belasco Theater.)

In 1946 Primus toured twenty-three cities with her own company in the second revival of *Showboat.* She choreographed and starred in Broadway's first all-calypso musical review, *Caribbean Carnival,* which opened on 5 December 1947; it also featured Josephine Premice, Claude Marchant, and the Duke of Iron, who were among the day's leading calypsonians.

Following a 1948 performance at Fisk University, Primus was awarded the largest and last Julius Rosenwald Fund grant, which allowed her nine months in Africa to study its dance more formally. She embarked in September 1948 for Africa and remained there more than a year, living among many peoples of Angola, Congo, Cameroon, Ghana, Liberia, Nigeria, Senegal, Tanzania, Rwanda, Burundi, Sierra Leone, Côte d'Ivoire, and Benin.

In Liberia she learned the dance that became *Fanga,* her famous dance of welcome.

In Africa Primus became both observer and practitioner. She learned the language of the drum in order to know when to leap and when to crawl. She participated in dances of welcome, peace, birth, marriage, and death; she learned what she called the "inner conversation of muscles." In some cases she found tradition fading into history, but she often persuaded elders to resurrect dances and don ancient costumes. She documented her findings using motion-picture film, still photography, and dance notation. She gave, as well: as an intercultural communicator, she introduced the peoples of Africa's interior to Mozart, Beethoven, Chopin, Stravinsky, and Gershwin.

On her return to the United States, Primus founded the Pearl Primus School of Primal Dance. On 14 January 1951, eight years after her debut there, Primus returned to the Ninety-second Street YMHA with several pieces based upon her African experiences. Included were *"Excerpts from an African Journey,"* the Senegalese *Blind Beggar Woman,* and *Initiation.* By the spring of 1952 she had developed a full-length program entitled *Dark Rhythms,* which was presented at venues including the American Museum of Natural History (15 May 1952). In September 1958 Primus appeared at the Saint Mark's Playhouse as guest artist and artistic director with the outstanding Trinidadian dancer Percival Borde and his company. The two married; their son, Onwin Borde, later accompanied his mother as percussionist in concerts and workshops on cultural enrichment through dance. Percival Borde died 31 August 1979. The drummer most often associated with Primus was Alphonse Cimber, a Haitian, who worked his superior abilities into Primus's creations from the early 1940s until his death on 16 March 1981. His contributions were mostly Caribbean rhythms; her African rhythms were often the work of Norman Coker of Gambia and Moses Mians of Nigeria.

PRIMUS. This 1940s studio portrait shows the combination of strength and buoyancy that made Primus a celebrated performer. (Photograph by Gerda Peterich; used by permission.)

In March 1961 the African Performing Arts Center, Konama Kende, opened in Monrovia, Liberia, with Primus as its director. In this first arts center of its kind on the African continent, Primus's mission was to document, formalize, and preserve traditional African dance. With Percival Borde as her assistant, she taught aspiring dancers to dance, and accomplished dancers to stage their work. They produced programs for local citizens, royalty, dignitaries, and visitors.

In October 1971, during her tenure as visiting scholar at Brooklyn's Pratt Institute, Primus's company performed *Life Crises,* in which she demonstrated and lectured on the role African dance plays in ceremonies marking critical life phases such as birth, childhood, adolescence, engagement, marriage, and death. The Pratt audience also saw her portray an African storyteller; her brilliance is captured in a three-record album entitled *Pearl Primus' Africa in Story, Legend, Song and Thought.*

In May 1974 the Alvin Ailey American Dance Theater premiered Primus's *Wedding,* which was based on a variety of ceremonies in Zaïre. Principal Ailey dancer Judith Jamison performed Primus's *Fanga* in the same program.

In 1978 Primus established the Pearl Primus Dance Language Institute. Arguing that dance is a language, she was allowed to use dance in fulfillment of her doctoral language requirements at New York University in the same year. She also used these communicative skills to teach dance to the physically impaired.

Primus worked in concert, in opera, on Broadway, and on television. As a choreographer she created the dances for the Broadway play *Mr. Johnson* and the opera *The Emperor Jones* with Lawrence Tibbett. As an anthropologist, she was the first major American dancer to live among the peoples of Africa's interior, various Caribbean islands, and parts of the Southern United States. She recatalogued the entire African art collection of the Newark Museum, was ethnologist for the exhibit "The Dancing Masks of Africa" at New Rochelle's Wildcliff Museum, and served as ethnological consultant for the Ethnic Dance Enrichment Program at Spellman College in Atlanta. As instructor, she taught anthropology, anatomy, and ethnic dance at major universities and colleges. In 1986 Primus was professor of ethnic studies at the Five Colleges of Amherst, Smith, Mount Holyoke, Hampshire, and the University of Massachusetts. She spoke before audiences throughout the United States, Africa, Europe, Israel, the Caribbean, and Mexico on a host of topics, including African dance, African art, African music, dance and society, and dance in education. Beginning in 1948 she published a long list of scholarly and popular articles, focusing primarily on African and African-American dance.

Primus's awards include the Scroll of Honor from the National Council of Negro Women, the Star of Africa from the Republic of Liberia, being named Omowale (Child Returned Home) by the spiritual head of the Yoruba people in Nigeria, the Page One Award by the Newspaper Guild of New York, the Distinguished Service Award from the American Anthropological Association, and the Black National Treasure Award from the Hamilton Hills Community Center of Schenectady.

Asked to summarize her career, Primus said, "I dance not to entertain, but to help people to better understand each other. It is inappropriate to ask when I shall stop dancing. I expect to dance in the courts of the ancestors."

BIBLIOGRAPHY

Barber, Beverly A. "Pearl Primus: In Search of Her Roots, 1943–1970." Ph.D. diss., Florida State University, 1984.

Berryman-Miller, Sherrill. "A Legacy of Pride." *Talking Drums* 5 (January 1995): 4–7.

Dekle, Nicole. "Pearl Primus: Spirit of the People." *Dance Magazine* (December 1990): 62–65.

Emery, Lynne Fauley. *Black Dance from 1619 to Today.* 2d rev. ed. Princeton, 1988.

Estrada, Ric. "Three Leading Negro Artists and How They Feel about Dance in the Community: Eleo Pomare, Arthur Mitchell, and Pearl Primus." *Dance Magazine* (November 1968): 45–60.

Foulkes, Julia. "Pearl in Our Midst: In Memoriam, Pearl Primus, November 29, 1919–October 29, 1994." *Dance Research Journal* 27 (Spring 1995): 80–82.

Glover, Jean R. "Pearl Primus: Cross-Cultural Pioneer of American Dance." Master's thesis, American University, 1989.

Green, Richard C. "Pearl Primus and 'The Negro Problem' in American Modern Dance." *UCLA Journal of Dance Ethnology* 19 (1995): 68–76.

Simmons, Michele. "Experiencing and Performing the Choreography of Mna, Pearl Primus." *Talking Drums* 5 (January 1995): 8–9.

Wenig, Adele R. *Pearl Primus: An Annotated Bibliography of Sources from 1943 to 1975.* Oakland, Calif., 1983.

JAMES BRIGGS MURRAY

PRINTS AND DRAWINGS. Prints and drawings enrich our knowledge and appreciation of dance by showing us not only what it looked like but how it was regarded in various places and periods. Dance images in art may be created for many different purposes: as records of historical events, as symbols or metaphors, as advertisements or publicity, or purely as decoration. Sometimes the image is simply the pretext for a work that stresses artistic values (such as form, color, or line) rather than the accurate depiction of the dance or dancer.

The types of dance images represented in prints and drawings are as diverse as dance itself. They include portraits of real dancers in action or repose, movement studies, scenes from performances, technical illustrations, sketches made by anthropologists in the field, caricatures, and imaginary dancers or scenes.

Prints and Drawings as Representations of Dance. In the study of dance history, prints and drawings can be used for both their informational value and their decorative appeal. The amount of information contained in any visual image depends on variables such as the purpose for which the image was made, the artistic style it is couched in, the special qualities and limitations of the medium or technique, the technical skill and perceptive capacities of the artist, and, last but not least, our own capacity to "read" and interpret the image. Prints and drawings must necessarily reduce dance—a three-dimensional art existing in time and space—to a two-dimensional surface that is usually limited to a single viewpoint and a single moment in time. The artist must decide which of the many fleeting moments of the dance will be portrayed. In looking at a print or drawing, we inevitably see through the artist's eyes: the artist selects what we see and to some extent tells us how to respond.

The purpose for which a print or drawing is made has a significant effect on its content. The portraitist who creates a souvenir for a dancer's adoring fans will depict her differently from a caricaturist who wishes to deflate her vanity. The illustrator of a dance manual must be more meticulous about the fine points of dance technique than the designer of a poster advertising performances. The purpose of the image also affects our response to it: we would not study the poster as we would the manual's illustrations.

Every style of art has its own artistic conventions, although some are more obvious than others. In interpreting an image, it is often necessary to recognize stylistic conventions and understand what they represent. For example, the ancient Egyptians portrayed the human figure in an extremely schematized way: the head, hips, legs, and feet were shown in profile, while the eye and chest were shown in frontal view. This distorted position has become a tongue-in-cheek cliché for "Egyptian" dances, although it was originally used to depict the human figure in a wide range of activities. During the Romantic period in Europe, a readily recognizable stylistic convention arose: the depiction of impossibly small, delicate, pointed feet on the ballerinas of the time.

Like the different dance genres, every medium and technique has its own special qualities and limitations. A pen-and-ink sketch may capture contours but will not preserve the colors of scenery and costumes in the way a watercolor painting can. A copper engraving in which tones are created by patterns of dots and lozenges will probably look less spontaneous than a lithograph, which allows the artist to work in a freer manner.

The capacities and skills of the individual artist also affect the image. An understanding of dance technique may or may not be important in creating a dance image. Artists who are also dancers are not always interested in producing clear technical illustrations, though they may be well qualified to do so. Artists who have never observed dance firsthand also produce dance images. They may work from others' sketches, from still images such as photographs, or from their own imaginations.

Sometimes it is difficult to distinguish a set or a costume design, made before the performance, from an image that shows how these designs were actually realized. Set designers may furnish their sketches with imaginary figures, and costume designers may depict dancers in imaginary poses, surrounded by decorative props or accessories that have little to do with the actual production.

PRINTS AND DRAWINGS. "Expulsion," from Hans Holbein the Younger's series of woodcuts called *Dance of Death,* engraved by Hans Lützelberger and published in 1538. (Metropolitan Museum of Art, New York; Rogers Fund, 1919 [no. 19.57.3]; photograph used by permission.)

Prior to the twentieth century many prints were made by two or more artists: a draughtsman who provided the original sketch, and one or more craftsmen who transferred this image to the woodblock, metal plate, or lithographic stone that was used to make the print. In the nineteenth century, when wood engravings were the primary means of illustrating periodicals, engravers became narrowly specialized: one might execute only figures, another landscape, another architecture, and so on. Therefore, a dance image in a print may be several times removed from reality. Since very few original sketches for prints have survived, it is usually difficult to tell how much an engraver has altered a given image.

Artistic license occurs, of course, in every period of art history. A dancer's facial beauty or physical proportions may be improved, groupings may be made more symmetrical, and the stage picture may be generally arranged to accord with the artist's ideas of good composition. An artist may view the picture as a flat surface (as it is), rather than as a window opening onto three-dimensional space, and may arrange the elements of the picture to create an attractive flat design. Jacques Callot's etching of the first intermezzo of *La Liberazione di Tirreno e d'Arnea* (performed in 1616, published in 1617), made after a drawing by Giulio Parigi, frames the dancers onstage in the center of the chamber with a perfect oval formed by the spectators and the ramps curving down from the stage.

Artistic license may also allow the artist to indulge in flights of fantasy. The Romantic-era ballet particularly encouraged this tendency. The many artists who produced the wood engravings in *Les beautés de l'Opéra* (1845) depicted the heroes and heroines of *Giselle* and *La Sylphide* in densely wooded settings with uneven grassy terrain underfoot rather than the prosaic bare boards of a real stage. In Edward Morton's lithograph after S. M. Joy, the ballerina Lucile Grahn floats above a seemingly limitless lake in *Éoline, ou La Dryade* (1845). This type of art not only preserves but extends theatrical illusion, carrying it further than possible onstage.

On a less exalted level are pictures that depict dancers in costumes more revealing than would have been permissible onstage during the period. Female dancers are sometimes shown with one or both breasts bare when, in fact, they were fully covered by their costumes. Eugénie Lecomte is shown topless in Edward W. Clay's lithograph portraying her as the Abbess in *Robert le Diable* (1837). When legal action was taken against the print, its publisher, Henry R. Robinson, issued it with the subtitle "The Prosecuted Picture."

Images may operate simultaneously on many levels of meaning. The depiction of a group of dancing peasants may convey a sense of gaiety and pleasure, but in the seventeenth century it could also signify more reprehensible qualities, such as frivolity or sensuality. This kind of image, which serves as an emblem or symbol, sometimes places greater emphasis on metaphoric or emotional content than on accuracy of detail. Therefore, in using prints and drawings to study dance of another country or era, the dance historian should compare them with one another and with other kinds of documents, such as reviews, memoirs, field notes, films, photographs, and notated scores. Although it may not be possible to verify every detail of an image, comparisons may result in useful discoveries. Our response to a picture showing a ballerina hovering in midair may be altered by another picture that reveals the wires that kept her aloft.

Cultural conditioning inevitably plays a part in the way we perceive, respond to, and interpret images, and we must be aware of its influence. Although a dance image of the past or another culture may appear humorous to us, it may have been looked upon quite differently by the artist and the audience of its place and time. A historian must also set aside preordained standards of "good" or "bad" art, for images of every quality can contribute to knowledge.

Artists Who Have Portrayed Dance. A list of all the artists who have made dance drawings or prints would run to many pages. Some of the greatest names in Western art are represented: Dürer, Rubens, Watteau, Goya, Manet, Degas, Picasso, and Rodin. Yet the names of many artists of the dance, worldwide, are unknown. Some were considered commercial artists, others mere craftsmen. The following survey is not comprehensive but will serve as an outline of the major types of Western dance drawings and prints and some of their major exponents.

Few examples of drawings have survived from ancient times, but dance was among the subjects depicted. Early examples can be found in Athenian red-figure vase paintings of the sixth to fourth centuries BCE (which may be considered a type of drawing because of their emphasis on line). The type of dance represented varies: dancing maenads and satyrs suggest a religious or perhaps dramatic type of dance, while the dancing men in merrymaking scenes seem more secular and earthy. Dancers who served as professional entertainers also appear in these vase paintings.

Printing developed much later than drawing. In western Europe, the art of making woodcuts appeared in the 1400s. Engraving and etching on metal plates were invented soon after. Wood engraving was invented in the late 1700s. In Europe, printing was first used for the Bible and for sacred (Christian) pictures, so it is not surprising that an early type of dance print—the Dance of Death—had religious connotations. The most famous series of this type, drawn by Hans Holbein and engraved by Hans Lützelberger, was published in 1538; however, few of the figures in this series are shown dancing. Holbein's *Dance of Death* inspired many imitations, and its theme is still used as a powerful allegory with social and political implications. Some versions include representations of the dance forms of their periods. A couple performs a social dance accompanied by a flute-playing skeleton in *Den algemeynen Doodenspiegel* (1730). Thomas Rowlandson depicted dancers in the plates entitled "The Pantomime," "The Waltz," and "The Masquerade" in *The English Dance of Death* (London, 1814–1816).

PRINTS AND DRAWINGS. Marie Taglioni, as the Sylphide, floats barefoot above dense foliage, demonstrating the artistic license often seen in nineteenth-century lithographs. This 1837 print is by Achille Deveria after the bronze by Jean-Auguste Barre. (Private collection.)

Early European prints and drawings of the fifteenth and sixteenth centuries also depicted secular dances. Martin Zatzinger's print *Der Tanzfest* (c.1500) portrays a court dance. Albrecht Dürer drew a sedate, courtly looking dance as a border design for the breviary of Emperor Maximilian (1514); here, a secular dance appears as an ornament in a religious context. Dürer represented a more lively folk dance in the engraving *The Peasant Couple Dancing* (1514). Mythological figures were also shown dancing, as in Andrea Mantegna's study of dancing muses for his painting *Parnassus* (1497). Dancing nymphs, angels, peasants, and nobles often serve decorative or emblematic functions in the art of this period.

More closely linked to the actual dance of the time were the illustrations in dance manuals, which began to appear in Europe in the late fifteenth century. Woodcuts adorn *L'art et instruction de bien dancer* [*sic*], published in Paris around 1490. Fabritio Caroso's *Il ballarino* (1581) was illustrated with etchings by Giacomo Franco. Some notable examples that have appeared over the centuries are Gregorio Lambranzi's *Neue und curieuse theatralische Tantz-Schul* (1716), with engravings of dances as they appeared onstage by Johann Georg Püschner; Pierre Rameau's *Le maître à danser* (1725), with engravings by Rameau himself; and Carlo Blasis's *L'uomo fisico, intellettuale, morale* (first issued 1857, revised 1878), with illustrations "invented" by the author, though drawn and engraved by others. Remy Charlip's *Air Mail Dances* and *Mail Order Dances,* the first of which appeared in 1972, may be considered as a type of technical manual. His drawings depict a series of poses that the dancer(s) may interpret freely in regard to starting point, transitions, and position in space.

In the sixteenth century, illustrated libretti and festival books documented important court ballets and entertainments. The libretto of *Le Balet Comique de la Royne* (performed 1581, published 1582) was illustrated with etchings by Jacques Patin, the painter to the king. Callot, who etched Parigi's drawings for *La Liberazione di Tirreno e d'Arnea,* also illustrated other seventeenth-century festivals in Florence and Lorraine. *Le Nozze degli Dei* (performed 1634, published 1637) was recorded in drawings by Alfonso Parigi the Younger, etched by Stefano della Bella. Many more examples come from France, Italy, and Austria. This type of illustration grew less frequent after the seventeenth century but did not completely die out. In 1822 *Lalla Rûkh, ein Festspiel mit Gesang und Tanz* commemorated a song and dance festival in Berlin in 1821 and contained hand-colored etchings by Heinrich Stürmer after Wilhelm Hensel.

Toward the end of the seventeenth century, identifiable prints were made of professional dancers in action. Many of these were issued by Henry Bonnart and other printers located in the Rue Saint Jacques, Paris. The dancers portrayed include Claude Balon, Pierre Dubreuil, Mademoiselle Desmatins, Marie Thérèse Subligny, and Louis Lestang. This genre of prints and drawings is still very popular today. Sometimes the portrait is actually a caricature; Auguste Vestris was often depicted in this way. In the eighteenth century, prints often reproduced painted portraits. Laurent Cars engraved Nicolas Lancret's portrait of Marie Camargo (c.1740). John Jones engraved Thomas Gainsborough's portrait of Giovanna Baccelli in 1784.

Some artists' names have become closely identified with the dancers they depicted, especially those of the nineteenth century. Johann Gottfried Schadow frequently drew Salvatore Viganò and Maria Medina Viganò. Alfred Edward Chalon's drawings of Marie Taglioni, lithographed by others, are among the most highly esteemed prints of the Romantic-era ballet. Henri de Toulouse-

PRINTS AND DRAWINGS. Reviews of theatrical dance performances and discussions on social occasions were often enhanced in nineteenth-century newspapers by wood engravings. *(left)* The 8 November 1845 edition of *The Illustrated London News* reviewed a Drury Lane performance of *Le Diable à Quatre. (right)* Winslow Homer's engraving, *A Cadet Hop at West Point,* appeared in the 3 September 1859 edition of *Harper's Weekly,* published in New York. (Left: Courtesy of Elizabeth Aldrich. Right: Metropolitan Museum of Art, New York; Harris Brisbane Dick Fund, 1936 [no. 36.13.7 (1)]; photograph used by permission.)

Lautrec portrayed Loïe Fuller, La Goulue (Louise Weber), and Jane Avril. Many artists were inspired by Isadora Duncan, among them Emile-Antoine Bourdelle, André Dunoyer de Segonzac, Auguste Rodin, and Abraham Walkowitz.

In the late eighteenth century, the technique of wood engraving had been pioneered by an Englishman, Thomas Bewick. Lithography had been perfected in the 1790s by Alois Senefelder in Munich. Both techniques were widely used during the nineteenth century. Wood engravings, which could be produced quickly and cheaply, were used to illustrate newspapers until photomechanical processes were introduced toward the end of the century. Reviews in *The Illustrated London News, La vie parisienne,* Vienna's *Theaterzeitung,* and Milan's *Il teatro illustrato* were often accompanied by illustrations of scenes from the ballet or by portraits of the principal dancers.

The lithographs of the Romantic-era ballet are especially prized by dance lovers. Here the artistic medium proved to be perfectly suited to the subject, for the soft textures made possible by lithography enhanced the weightless, insubstantial quality that dancers, costumers, and set designers strove for onstage. Lithography also allowed the artist to draw directly on the stone without using an engraver as intermediary. John Brandard worked in this way; since he was known to be a devoted theatergoer, his mid-nineteenth-century pictures are probably a good reflection of theatrical reality. Other well-known names in the field of Romantic ballet lithography are Chalon, Jules Bouvier, Achille Devéria, Marie-Alexandre Alophe, and Alexandre Lacauchie. Nathaniel Currier issued many American versions of European ballet prints in the 1840s. Later he and his partner, James Merritt Ives, produced numerous prints of different types of American dance, among them country dances, social dances, Shaker, Negro, and Native American dances.

Between 1825 and 1870 illustrated music titles—the cover pages of sheet music—were especially popular. Brandard lithographed many ballet scenes for piano reductions of ballet scores. Although most of the Romantic ballet lithographs were colored by hand, chromolithography, or the process of printing lithographs in color, was already known by the 1830s and well advanced by midcentury. In the late 1860s Jules Chéret used this process to create color posters, many of which advertised dance events. He was a prolific artist whose work advanced poster making both technically and artistically. Toulouse-Lautrec's first poster, depicting La Goulue at the Moulin

Rouge, was created in 1891. Among the many artists who designed dance posters are Paul Colin, Théophile-Alexandre Steinlen, Hans Adolf Albitz, Ruth Albitz, Ben Shahn, Donn Matus, Remy Charlip, and Herbert Migdoll.

Edgar Degas dominates the field of dance images in the late nineteenth century; his drawings and impressionist paintings of ballet dancers are numerous and well known. His contemporary Edouard Manet drew Spanish dancers such as Lola de Valence; some of Manet's work also appeared as prints. Steinlen and Toulouse-Lautrec are also known for their depictions of the music hall, dance hall, and cabaret.

In the early twentieth century, Diaghilev's Ballets Russes inspired a flowering of dance drawings and prints. Some of the artists were set or costume designers attached to the company, such as Léon Bakst, Alexandre Benois, and Mikhail Larionov. Pablo Picasso and Jean Cocteau also produced dance drawings during their association with the company. Other artists inspired by the Ballets Russes included Valentine Gross Hugo, John Singer Sargent, and Laura Knight. These artists have left a treasury of portraits, movement studies, performance and rehearsal scenes, and caricatures.

PRINTS AND DRAWINGS. After seeing Isadora Duncan dance in 1909, Émile-Antoine Bourdelle created a series of drawings, of which this is one. (Reprinted from Gilberte Cournand, *Beauté de la danse,* Tours, 1977, p. 125.)

PRINTS AND DRAWINGS. Edgar Degas was one of many artists who was inspired by dance. This drawing, in chalk and pastel, is entitled *Dancer Tying Her Shoe.* (Reprinted from Gottfried Lindemann, *Prints and Drawings,* New York, 1970, p. 311.)

Although photography has come to be the favored medium for dance representations, dance drawings and prints are still created. Posters, which continue to be an important means of advertising performances, are often sold to the audience as remembrances. Greeting cards and postcards often use original designs, as well as using photographed reproductions of dance images from the past. The image of the dancer continues to be an inspiration to artists.

[*See* Artists and the Dance *and the entries on Bourdelle, Chalon, Degas, Rodin, Toulouse-Lautrec, and Walkowitz.*]

BIBLIOGRAPHY

Amaya, Mario. "The Dance in Art." *Dance and Dancers* 11 (December 1960): 18–23+; 12 (February 1961): 14–18; 12 (April 1961):

18–21+; 12 (May 1961): 20–23; 12 (August 1961): 30–31; 12 (December 1961): 12–14+; 13 (March 1962): 30–31.

Beaumont, Cyril W., and Sacheverell Sitwell. *The Romantic Ballet in Lithographs of the Time.* London, 1938.

Binney, Edwin, 3rd. "A Century of Austro-German Dance Prints, 1790–1890." *Dance Perspectives,* no. 47 (1971).

Binney, Edwin, 3rd. "Sixty Years of Italian Dance Prints, 1815–1875." *Dance Perspectives,* no. 53 (1973).

Binney, Edwin, 3rd. *Glories of the Romantic Ballet.* London, 1985.

Chaffee, George. "A Chart to the American Souvenir Lithographs of the Romantic Ballet, 1825–1870." *Dance Index* 1 (February 1942): 20–35.

Chaffee, George. "American Music Prints of the Romantic Ballet." *Dance Index* 1 (December 1942): 192–212.

Chaffee, George. "The Romantic Ballet in London, 1821–1858." *Dance Index* 2 (September-December 1943): 120–199.

Clarke, Mary, and Clement Crisp. *Ballet Art: From the Renaissance to the Present.* New York, 1978.

Collins, Marcia. *The Dance of Death in Book Illustration.* Columbia, Mo., 1978.

Guest, Ivor. *A Gallery of Romantic Ballet: A Catalogue of the Collection of Dance Prints at the Mercury Theatre.* London, 1965.

Migel, Parmenia. *Great Ballet Prints of the Romantic Era.* New York, 1981.

Moore, Lillian. "Prints on Pushcarts: The Dance Lithographs of Currier and Ives." *Dance Perspectives,* no. 15 (1962).

Moore, Lillian. *Images of the Dance: Historical Treasures of the Dance Collection, 1581–1861.* New York, 1965.

Reade, Brian. *Ballet Designs and Illustrations, 1581–1940.* London, 1967.

Terry, Walter, and Jack Rennert. *100 Years of Dance Posters.* New York, 1975.

Winter, Marian Hannah. *The Pre-Romantic Ballet.* London, 1974.

SUSAN AU

PROCA CIORTEA, VERA (born 30 January 1915 in Sibiu), Romanian dancer, choreographer, and choreologist. Proca Ciortea's work has led her to study a wide range of dance techniques and to use them in her productions. She began her studies in Romania with Floria Capsali, Gabriel Negry, and Ira Lucezarskaya, then went abroad to work with Max Terpis, Mary Wigman, Tatjana Gsovsky, Harald Kreutzberg, Kurt Jooss, and Gret Palucca. She also studied at the Carl Orff Institute of Rhythmics in Berlin. She is a graduate of Bucharest University, where she studied physical education and philology.

Since 1939, Proca Ciortea has worked with "Romanian-educated dance," a personal system she developed by blending various modern techniques with suggestions and rhythms from Romanian folklore. She staged a number of solo and chamber group performances in this style, including a series of recitals in Vienna and other cities in Europe, which brought European recognition to this system. Working with many theaters in Bucharest and in other towns in Romania, she created the stage movement and the choreography for 128 theatrical productions. She created and headed, until 1990, a dance group first called Gymnasion, then The Column; it was made up of former gymnastics champions who were experimenting with the integration of gymnastics and dance. Characterized by poetic joy, vitality, and humor, her works combine modern dance, jazz, rhythmics, gymnastics, and stylized elements of Romanian folk dance.

From 1954 to 1972, Proca Ciortea served as a professor of dance drama at the Bucharest Institute of Theater. She also gave courses abroad, mostly in Germany, Switzerland, and Sweden. In 1963 she became chair of the study group on ethnochoreology of the International Council of Traditional Music, serving until 1982. In 1990, at the International Dance Festival in Kiel, Germany, she was awarded the City of Kiel Prize of Honor.

PROCA CIORTEA. In her solo *Tándáricá,* Bucharest, 1962. (Photograph courtesy of the Romanian Center for the International Theater Institute, Bucharest.)

Vera Proca Ciortea is a very active collaborator and contributor to many Romanian and world publications, with studies and essays on various dance themes. In 1992 she was awarded The Big Prize of the Year by the Romanian Union of Performers and Musical Critics "for the creation of a deeply original style in the Romanian ballet and for the theoretical contribution in the field of dance research and notation." She is an honorary member of the Conseil International de la Dance.

[*For related discussion, see* Romania, *article on* Theatrical Dance.]

BIBLIOGRAPHY

Cursaru, Lucian. *Argonautii marilor iubiri.* Bucharest, 1987.

Peters, Kurt. "Tanz auf allen Wegen: Ein Porträt der rumänischen Professorin Vera Proca Ciortea." *Ballett Journal/Das Tanzarchiv* 37 (February 1989): 64–65.

Proca Ciortea, Vera. *Revista de folclor.* Bucharest, 1956.

Urseanu, Tilde, et al. *Istoria baletului.* Bucharest, 1967.

TEA PREDA

PRODIGAL SON, THE. The biblical story of the prodigal son, told in *Luke* 15.11–24, has attracted a number of choreographers, each of whom reflected some of the artistic ideas of his own time. Particularly notable are versions created by Pierre Gardel in the nineteenth century and by George Balanchine, Kurt Jooss, David Lichine, and Ivo Cramér in the twentieth.

Gardel Version. French title: *L'Enfant Prodigue.* Choreography: Pierre Gardel. Music: Henri-Montan Berton. First performance: 28 April 1812, Théâtre National de l'Opéra, Paris. Principal: Auguste Vestris (The Prodigal Son).

Pierre Gardel, in 1812, aimed to please a post-Revolution audience in France that was unfamiliar with classical ballet but well acquainted with the spectacular productions of the popular boulevard theaters. His libretto states that he deliberately violated the traditional unities in order to include as many scenes as possible. Here the Prodigal Son was seduced by the "riotous living" of Memphis, a city of ancient Egypt, where a grand temple scene featured dances of virgins, priests, and slaves. Banished for deceiving a young girl, he reached his home and family only after an arduous journey through the desert.

Balanchine Version. Original title: *Le Fils Prodigue.* Ballet in one act and three scenes. Choreography: George Balanchine. Music: Sergei Prokofiev. Libretto: Boris Kochno. Scenery and costumes: Georges Rouault. First performance: 21 May 1929, Théâtre Sarah Bernhardt, Paris, Diaghilev's Ballets Russes. Principals: Serge Lifar (The Prodigal Son), Felia Doubrovska (The Siren), Michael Fedorov (The Father), Leon Woizikowski and Anton Dolin (Servants to the Prodigal Son). Revived, as *The Prodigal Son:* 23 February 1950, New York City Center, New York City Ballet. Principals: Jerome Robbins (The Prodigal Son), Maria Tallchief (The Siren), Michael Arshansky (The Father), Herbert Bliss and Frank Hobi (Servants to the Prodigal Son).

Balanchine's work marked a change for the Diaghilev company, which had been producing chic and shocking ballets. According to Boris Kochno (1970), Diaghilev had commissioned the score from Prokofiev in 1927, asking only for something simple, timeless, and poetic. Kochno proposed the theme and prepared the libretto. While the serious tone was practically dictated to Balanchine by the libretto, the groupings used in much of the choreography derived from earlier work in Russia, where he had used devices drawn from the vocabularies of acrobats and clowns; his women dancers were shown in high lifts and splits. Kochno's source for the plot was Aleksandr Pushkin's story "The Postmaster," which describes three

THE PRODIGAL SON. Jerome Robbins in the title role of Balanchine's production, revived for the New York City Ballet in 1950. (Photograph by Ed Carswell; from the Dance Collection, New York Public Library for the Performing Arts Choreography by George Balanchine © The George Balanchine Trust.)

pictures illustrating the parable: the father bidding farewell to his restless son, the son wasting his money with dissolute companions, and his penitent return to the father. The ballet has just these scenes and characters.

The movements of the opening scene are quite simple, with obviously clear gestures but also with some virtuosic stylization as the Son shows his defiance of the Father. In contrast, the movements of the eccentric revelers in the second scene are bizarre and distorted. The Prodigal is victimized by these grotesque creatures and is seduced by the Siren, who winds herself around him like a serpent around her prey. The concluding scene, however, has movements of the utmost simplicity. The Son's final, humble approach to the Father has the moving dignity of biblical language.

Balanchine's Prodigal Son is one of the great dramatic roles for a male dancer in the modern repertory. Outstanding among later interpreters of the role have been Francisco Moncion, Edward Villella, Mikhail Baryshnikov, Robert La Fosse, and Peter Boal. The Siren has been vividly portrayed by Yvonne Mounsey, Diana Adams, Patricia Neary, and Lourdes Lopez. The ballet has been staged for numerous companies, including the Royal Danish Ballet, the Royal Ballet (England), the Paris Opera Ballet, American Ballet Theatre, and Les Grands Ballets Canadiens.

Jooss Version. Original title: *Le Fils Prodigue.* Ballet in two acts and six scenes. Choreography and libretto: Kurt Jooss. Music: Sergei Prokofiev. Scenery and costumes: Hein Heckroth. First performance: 28 May 1931, Folkwang Tanzbühne, Essen, Germany. Principal: Rudolf Pescht (The Prodigal Son). Revised, as *Der Verlorene Sohn:* 6 October 1933, Ballets Jooss, Amsterdam. Revised choreography and libretto: Kurt Jooss. Music: Frederic (Fritz) A. Cohen. Revived, as *The Prodigal Son:* October 1939, Ballets Jooss, Bristol, England. Scenery and costumes: Dimitri Bouchene.

At the time he created his *Prodigal Son,* Jooss, who had been reared in the atmosphere of Rudolf Laban's *Ausdruckstanz,* was still concerned with the social consciousness that motivated many of the expressionists. Here the Prodigal met his downfall not though riotous living but through the pursuit of power. For this, Jooss invented a "Mysterious Companion," who accompanied the Son, sometimes as an outright enemy, sometimes as a false friend. Invested with a robe and crown, the Prodigal became a tyrant. He was presented to the queen of the harlots, but then denounced to the people. At last, seeing that the elements of his destruction were pride and ambition, the Prodigal humbly returned home.

Lichine Version. Original title: *The Prodigal Son.* Ballet in one act and three scenes. Choreography: David Lichine. Music: Sergei Prokofiev. Libretto: Boris Kochno. Scenery and costumes: Georges Rouault. First performance: 30 December 1938, Theatre Royal, Sydney, Covent Garden Russian Ballet (later called Original Ballet Russe). Principals: Anton Dolin (The Son), Tamara Grigorieva (The Siren), Dimitri Rostoff (The Father), Tamara Tchinarova and Kira Abricossova (The Sisters), Boris Belsky and Valery Shaievsky (The Companions), Alberto Alonso (The Beggar).

THE PRODIGAL SON. Robert LaFosse as the Prodigal Son, suffering the abuse of the drinking companions, in a 1986 performance with the New York City Ballet. (Photograph © 1986 by Paul Kolnik; used by permission. Choreography by George Balanchine © The George Balanchine Trust.)

Lichine followed Kochno's libretto, using the same three scenes that Balanchine had used, and employed the same Rouault designs for scenery and costumes. The choreographic merits of this version, according to Edwin Denby (1986), lay in Lichine's exuberance of physical rhythm, his exuberant impulse to dance. The action parts of his *Prodigal Son* were lively, striking dances, but Denby found that the lyric scenes of warning and reconciliation lacked interest. However, the ballet remained in the repertory of the Original Ballet Russe for ten years. Irina Baronova, who frequently performed the Siren, felt that, although some scenes were roughly erotic, they were balanced by the tenderness shown in the final reconciliation.

Cramér Version. Swedish title: *Den Förlorade Sonen.* Ballet in four scenes. Choreography: Ivo Cramér. Music:

Hugo Alfvén. Scenery and costumes: Rune Linstrom. First performance: 27 April 1957, Royal Opera House, Stockholm, Royal Swedish Ballet. Principals: Bjørn Holmgren (The Prodigal Son), Teddy Rhodin (The False Prophet), Elsa-Marianne von Rosen (The Arabian Queen), Julius Mengarelli (The Father), Anne-Marie Lagerborg (The Mother).

In 1945, Cramér had founded his own company, which concentrated on using Scandinavian subjects and musical styles along with folk dance patterns. For his *Prodigal Son,* Cramér told the biblical story as it might have been visualized by the peasants of the region of Dalecarlia, drawing on motifs in traditional wall paintings that were a feature of Swedish peasant architecture.

Here the Son was led by a top-hatted Prophet into a boat bound for Araby. There he met the Arabian Queen who led him in a dance of merry-making. But his pleasures were interrupted by Four Horsemen (Power, War, Pestilence, and Death), who frightened him into returning home. The Son's repentence was short-lived, as the final scene led quickly into folk dances that formed the finale of celebration.

Other Versions. The Prokofiev score and the basic libretto devised by Boris Kochno for the Balanchine version have been used by a number of other choreographers to mount their own productions of *The Prodigal Son.* Senia Gluck-Sandor staged her version as *L'Enfant Prodigue* at the Dance Center in New York in 1932. Aurelio Milloss staged *Il Figliuol Prodigo* at the Teatro Reale dell'Opera in Rome in 1942 and revived it in Perugia in 1957. Ernst Uthoff, a former soloist and assistant ballet master with the Ballets Jooss, staged his version as *El Hijo Pródigo* for the Ballet Nacional Chileno in Santiago and included it in the company's repertory for their first U.S. tour, in 1964.

Other choreographers have turned to other composers for musical inspiration. To the syncopated rhythms of Scott Joplin, the protagonist of Barry Moreland's *Prodigal Son: Ragtime Version,* mounted for London Festival Ballet in 1974, left his family at the turn of the century and tap danced his way through two world wars before returning home. Arriving in a limousine, the Siren had flicked ashes in his face from her long cigarette.

BIBLIOGRAPHY

Beaumont, Cyril W. *Complete Book of Ballets.* Rev. ed. London, 1951.

Cohen, Selma Jeanne. "The Prodigal Son." *Choreography and Dance* 2.3 (1992): 49–56.

Denby, Edwin. *Dance Writings,* edited by Robert Cornfield and William Mackay. New York, 1986.

García-Márquez, Vicente. "The Prodigal Son." In García-Márquez, *The Ballets Russes: Colonel de Basil's Ballets Russes de Monte Carlo, 1932–1952,* pp. 232–239. New York, 1990.

Greskovic, Robert. "*Le Fils Prodigue:* A Ballet Old and New." In *Looking at Ballet: Ashton and Balanchine,* compiled by Jane B. Roberts and David Vaughan. Studies in Dance History, vol. 3.2. Pennington, N.J., 1993.

Hunt, Marilyn. "George Balanchine's *Prodigal Son.*" *Dance Magazine* (May 1981): 128–131.

Hunt, Marilyn. "The Prodigal Son's Russian Roots: Avant-Garde and Icons." *Dance Chronicle* 5.1 (1982): 24–49.

Kochno, Boris. *Diaghilev and the Ballet Russe.* New York, 1970.

LaFosse, Robert, with Andrew Mark Wentick. *Nothing to Hide: A Dancer's Life.* New York, 1989.

Reynolds, Nancy. "Balanchine: An Introduction to the Ballets." *Dance Notation Journal* 6 (Winter–Spring 1988–1989): 15–74.

Slonimsky, Yuri. "Balanchine: The Early Years." *Ballet Review* 5.3 (1975–1976).

Villella, Edward, with Larry Kaplan. *Prodigal Son: Dancing for Balanchine in a World of Pain and Magic.* New York, 1992.

SELMA JEANNE COHEN

PROGRAM NOTES. *See* Libretti for Dance.

PROGRESSES, ELIZABETHAN. *See* Elizabethan Progresses.

PROKOFIEV, SERGEI (Sergei Sergeevich Prokof'ev; born 23 April [5 May] 1891 in Sontsovka, Ukraine, died 5 March 1953 in Moscow), composer, pianist, and conductor. Prokofiev is considered one of the twentieth century's most important composers for the dance. His music is remarkable for its originality, wealth of melodies and rich harmonic language, sharply contrasting musical images, and wide range of themes and genres.

Prokofiev's instinct for the stage was evident early. Precociously talented, he completed *The Giant,* a three-act opera for four voices and piano, not long after his ninth birthday, and another, *Desert Islands,* before he was eleven. The overture to the latter was shown to the composer Sergei Taneyev, who perceived sufficient talent to recommend that Prokofiev undertake full-time musical training. After preliminary studies with Reinhold Glière (during which he wrote another opera), Prokofiev entered the Saint Petersburg Conservatory at thirteen. His style matured early: as his 1914 graduation piece Prokofiev played his First Piano Concerto, written three years earlier and regarded as his earliest fully representative work.

Prokofiev himself (1979), analyzing his style, declared that it was made up of five elements. The first, which he termed the classical, he traced back to early childhood, when he heard his mother playing Beethoven sonatas. The second, innovation, had its origins in Taneyev's good-humored criticism of the "elementary harmonies" of a symphony written during Prokofiev's period with Glière; piqued by Taneyev's reaction, he first sought an individual harmonic language but later channeled his taste for unorthodox exploration into his melodic and orchestral thinking, desiring "to find a medium for the expression of strong emotions." The third Prokofiev described as the toccata or motor element, the use of persistent, machine-like rhythms or ostinatos. Of the fourth element, the lyrical, he wrote wryly that it "for long remained in obscurity" and "has grown but slowly," adding, "At later stages I paid more and more attention to lyrical expression." The important fifth aspect of his style, often termed "grotesqueness," Prokofiev regarded as "merely a variation of the other characteristics." He would have preferred "to replace the word 'grotesque' by 'scherzo-ness,' or by the three words giving its gradations: 'jest,' 'laughter,' 'mockery.'"

"Scherzoness" and innovation, evident in Prokofiev's earliest compositions, soon brought him to the attention of Serge Diaghilev, who intended to use the dissonant and percussive Second Piano Concerto as a ballet score. Prokofiev was more interested in writing an opera, but his attendance at the London rehearsals of Igor Stravinsky's *The Firebird* and *Petrouchka* and of Maurice Ravel's *Daphnis et Chloé* may have influenced him to compose a ballet on a Russian theme, in collaboration with the poet Sergei Gorodetsky. The result was *Ala et Lolli* (1914), with a scenario derived from Scythian legend: the wooden idol Ala is stolen by Chuzbog, the god of evil and darkness, and his seven subterranean monsters but is rescued by the warrior Lolli, inspired by Velyes, the sun god. Diaghilev rejected the ballet; he may have found both plot and music too close to Stravinsky's *Le Sacre du Printemps,* which Prokofiev had heard while writing his own score. *Ala et Lolli,* although dissonant and harshly scored, had little of the innovative rhythmic complexity of *Le Sacre,* but it remains in concert repertory as the *Scythian Suite.*

Diaghilev immediately commissioned another ballet, astutely insisting that this time Prokofiev should "try to write music that truly deserves to be called Russian." A plot from one of Aleksandr Afanasyev's collections of Russian folktales was chosen, and the result was a far richer and stronger score than *Ala et Lolli. Chout* (the full title is *Skazka pro Shuta* [Tale of a Buffoon]) was choreographed by Tadeusz Slavinsky, supervised by Mikhail Larionov, and performed in Paris on 17 May 1921. It was much criticized for brittleness, antilyricism, and aggressive grotesqueness, but it is the masterpiece of Prokofiev's early maturity, scored with brilliant originality; many of the characteristics of his later orchestration may be traced back to *Chout.* It has both a highly personal melody, rooted in the Russian vernacular, and sharp burlesque humor, and it is informed by an already assured sense of the stage.

The completion of *Chout,* drafted as early as 1915, was interrupted by the Russian Revolution and Prokofiev's temporary emigration to America, the consequent necessity of earning his living as a concert pianist, and by a renewal of his operatic ambitions. On his return to Europe in 1922, it once again became possible for him to write music for dance. Prokofiev composed the Quintet, op. 39 (1924), for Boris Romanov's Romantic Ballet. Romanov wanted a chamber score for a ballet evoking circus life, which he choreographed as *Le Trapèze,* probably first presented in Berlin in 1925. Also for Romanov's company, Prokofiev made an arrangement for two pianos of Schubert waltzes, staged by Romanov in Buenos Aires as *Homenaje a Schubert* (1934).

It may have been the first performance, in 1925, of the Second Symphony, the "symphony of iron and steel," that prompted Diaghilev to suggest to Prokofiev a ballet on a Soviet subject. *Le Pas d'Acier* (also called *Age of Steel*), choreographed by Léonide Massine, was performed in Paris on 7 June 1927. It was an almost plotless series of stylized scenes from Russian life; the first part, according to the composer, showed the decay and overthrow of the czarist regime, and the second presented "a picture of socialist reconstruction." It can perhaps best be seen as a homage by Diaghilev and his fellow expatriates to the vigor of the new constructivist art then emerging from the Soviet Union and to the radical style of Soviet theater directors such as Vsevolod Meyerhold and Aleksandr Tairov. Diaghilev chose Tairov's collaborator, the constructivist painter Georgi Yakulov, to design and supervise the ballet. The score owes its remarkable affinity with the aesthetics of the Soviet avant-garde to Yakulov's influence and to Prokofiev's first visit to postrevolutionary Russia early in 1927; he was warmly received and spoke no less warmly of the musical life he encountered there. The score takes up the "mechanism" of the constructivists. Prokofiev may have heard Aleksandr Mossolov's ballet *The Factory* during his visit, but his work's real affinities are with the constructivists' bracing clarity and directness of imagery—for all its insistent percussiveness, the melodic language of *Le Pas d'Acier* is very simple.

Prokofiev dated his return to a Russian style of composing to *Le Pas d'Acier,* explaining that he meant not the fairy-tale Russian qualities of *Chout* but "a Russian language that could describe contemporary life" (Prokofiev, 1979). The work thus marks a biographical turning point, the first sign of Prokofiev's desire to return to Russia, and of his acceptance that it would be a new Russia to which he would return.

Prokofiev did not return again to Russia for some years. Those years were largely devoted to three of his greatest works: the opera *The Fiery Angel* (1919–1927); the symphony closely derived from it, the Third Symphony (1928); and his last ballet for Diaghilev, *Le Fils Prodigue* (The Prodigal Son), choreographed by George Balanchine and presented in Paris on 21 May 1929. Prokofiev's long-obscured lyricism is intermittently apparent in both the opera and the symphony, but it matures fully in the ballet. This lyricism can be heard in the beautiful flute melody after the agitated opening of the first scene, but it is most expressive in the closing pages, where it accompanies the father's blessing of his penitent son. The score is masterly and hard-achieved (according to the conductor Igor Markevitch [1980], Diaghilev's repeated insistence that he rewrite the final scene reduced the composer to tears), and it has a strong physical sense of dance. It seems strange that Prokofiev reportedly did not admire Balanchine's sinewy and vividly inventive choreography, which was closely analogous to the music. [*See* Prodigal Son, The.]

Diaghilev died not long after the premiere of *The Prodigal Son,* and Prokofiev's next ballet score, his last to be written in the West, is dedicated to the great impresario's memory. *Sur le Borysthène* (On the Dnieper) was choreographed by Serge Lifar and presented at the Paris Opera on 16 December 1932. It concerns a Ukrainian peasant girl, in love with a soldier, whose father wishes her to submit to an arranged marriage. The soldier breaks into the betrothal ceremony, fights with the intended bridegroom, and is tied up by the wedding guests; the girl rescues him and they escape together. The score was written hurriedly and rehearsed in the composer's absence (Lifar reportedly rearranged the order of the scenes), and it was not well received. It has seldom been heard since, but although the more energetic parts have little of the purposeful vigor of *The Prodigal Son,* the lyrical passages are interesting as pointers to the future: an important theme in *Romeo and Juliet* and another in *Cinderella* are both prefigured, and there is considerable dramatic thrust in the central scene of the interrupted betrothal ceremony.

Prokofiev left Paris on the evening of the premiere of *Sur le Borysthène* for a tour of the United States before finally returning to Russia. He knew he would be faced there with a difficult task: to write music that would be accessible to the greatest possible number, but without simplification, which he considered "a belittlement both of the maturity of [the audience's] culture and of the evolution of its taste" (Prokofiev, 1979). The difficulty was apparent as early as 1938, when two productions by Meyerhold for the Pushkin centenary, for which Prokofiev had written striking and original scores, were abandoned when Meyerhold's theater was closed by the authorities. Then, an occasional cantata for the twentieth anniversary of the 1917 Revolution was suppressed. As late as 1948 Prokofiev was violently denounced (along with Dmitri Shostakovich, Nikolai Myaskovsky, and Aram Khachaturian) by the Party Central Committee for "formalist and antimelodic modernist tendencies." The music of Prokofiev's Soviet period, the last twenty years of his life, represents to some degree a compromise with political realities, but it also represents the strengthening of his lyrical gifts under the impact of his long-meditated return (spiritual as well as physical) to Russia, past and present.

Soon after Prokofiev's return he received an invitation from the Kirov Theater to compose a full-length ballet (a commission later taken over by the Bolshoi Theater in Moscow), and by the autumn of 1935 he had finished a piano score. But *Romeo and Juliet* did not appear at the Kirov for more than four years, after the music had already become well known in the form of two extensive concert suites and various transcriptions. There were initial difficulties over the scenario because the Kirov wanted both lovers alive and reunited at the end. Sergei Radlov, with whom Prokofiev worked on the dramatic structure, was replaced as choreographer by Leonid Lavrovsky, who irritated the composer by demanding alterations to the score and even inserting earlier music by Prokofiev without informing him. The dancers were unaccustomed to Prokofiev's style (Galina Ulanova, who danced Juliet, at first found the music incomprehensible and impossible to dance to) and continually urged him to orchestrate the score more fully, protesting that it was inaudible from the stage; there is evidence that unauthorized thickenings were later added to the score. The orchestra, too, was perplexed by the music and passed a resolution, two weeks before the opening, demanding that it be canceled in order to avoid a scandal. By this time, a separate production in Brno, Czechoslovakia, choreographed by Ivo Váňa Psota and presented on 30 December 1938, had robbed the Kirov of the prestige of a premiere. However, the ballet opened in Leningrad on 11 January 1940 and was a triumphant success. It has remained in the Russian repertory ever since, and the score is regularly used by choreographers worldwide. [*See* Romeo and Juliet.]

There were fewer difficulties with *Cinderella,* choreographed by Rostislav Zakharov and premiered in Moscow on 21 November 1945, perhaps because Prokofiev was unwell and unable to attend many of the rehearsals. Konstantin Sergeyev, who created the roles of both Romeo and the Prince in *Cinderella* and himself choreographed the Kirov version of the latter, recalled that Prokofiev was very open to suggestions during the composition of the new ballet. The differences between the two scores are dictated by the differences of subject: *Romeo and Juliet* is rich, warm, and consciously Italian, while providing plentiful opportunities for brilliance and athleticism. *Cinderella*'s lines are more angular and its scoring more spare, but in its poised elegance it is closer than its predecessor to an apotheosis of Tchaikovsky.

Prokofiev's last ballet was a less happy collaboration. After a long search for a suitable subject (at one time Don Juan was considered), his choice fell on a folk tale from the Urals concerning a carver of precious stones, his conflict with the Queen of the Mountain (a personification of the obduracy of the materials of his art), and his love for a village girl. *The Stone Flower,* choreographed by Leonid Lavrovsky, premiered in Moscow on 12 February 1954. The story attracted Prokofiev by the opportunities it offered to use folk-derived material in what would be his first Soviet ballet on a Russian subject. The score was completed by early 1949, even though Prokofiev was ill and able to work only an hour a day; finally the project was shelved. When it was eventually revived there were renewed demands for heavier scoring, and critics of the music called it gloomy, heavy, and difficult to dance to. The score is not on the same consistently high level as its predecessors, but Prokofiev clearly enjoyed the opportunity to evoke exotic local color, and there are many pages of elegant lyricism and of characteristically pungent scoring that would well repay the attention of Western choreographers. [*See* Stone Flower, The.]

Prokofiev died while rehearsals for *The Stone Flower* were in progress; he was still working on revisions to the last act. Further alterations were made after his death; the published score even incorporates an interpolated waltz by Khachaturian. The delayed premiere, a year later, was not very successful, but the work has been rechoreographed several times with more satisfactory results and has become part of the Russian repertory.

Ballets have been danced to Prokofiev's music throughout the world. A version of *Chout* choreographed by Gertrud Steinweg was performed in East Berlin in 1957; the ballet was shown on Czech television in 1967, choreographed by Emerich Gabzdyl. *Romeo and Juliet* has been restaged by Frederick Ashton (Copenhagen, 1955), Oscar Araiz (Buenos Aires, 1970), Rudolf Nureyev (London, 1977), and many others. *Cinderella* has been performed in London, Paris, and Washington, and Prokofiev's first and last ballets, *Alla et Lolli* and *The Stone Flower,* have been staged in various countries as well. *Cinderella* and *Romeo and Juliet* continue to be popular with audiences everywhere.

Prokofiev was named Artist of the Russian Federation in 1947. He was awarded the State Prize of the USSR in 1943, 1946, 1947, and 1951, and the Lenin Prize (posthumously) in 1957.

BIBLIOGRAPHY

Blok, Vladimir, ed. *Sergei Prokofev* (in Russian). Moscow, 1978.

Dorris, George. "Prokofiev and the Ballet." *Ballet Review* 4.6 (1974): 80–90.

Garafola, Lynn. *Diaghilev's Ballets Russes.* New York, 1989.

Goodwin, Noël. "Prokofiev and the Ballet." *Dance and Dancers* (January 1983): 13–15.

Guttman, David. *Prokofiev.* London, 1988.

Markevitch, Igor. *Être et avoir été.* Paris, 1980.

Milnes, Rodney. "Prokofiev's Ballet Scores." *Dance Gazette* (July 1984): 10–12.

Prokofiev, Sergei. *Prokofiev by Prokofiev: A Composer's Memoir.* Translated by Guy Daniels. Edited by David H. Appel. Garden City, N.Y., 1979.

Robinson, Harlow. *Prokofiev: A Biography.* New York, 1987.

Savkina, Natalia. *Prokofiev.* Translated by Catherine Young. Neptune City, N.J., 1984.

Schwarz, Boris. *Music and Musical Life in Soviet Russia, 1917–1970.* London, 1972.

Shlifshtein, Semen I., ed. *Sergei Prokofev* (in Russian). Moscow, 1965.

MICHAEL OLIVER

PSOTA, IVO VÁŇA (also known as Vania Psota; born 1 May 1908 in Kiev, Ukraine, died 16 February 1952 in Brno, Czechoslovakia), Czech dancer, choreographer, and pedagogue. Psota, who used the name Vania Psota when performing abroad, inherited his gift for dance from his mother, who had been a solo performer and later opened her own school. In the years 1919–1923 he studied at the Prague ballet school of Augustin Berger. In 1924 Psota was engaged by the Prague National Theater, and after 1926 he became a soloist and from 1928 on the director of the Brno State Ballet. A technically adept, light-footed dancer, he began already at this period to assert himself as a choreographer and pedagogue. He was not satisfied in the provincial atmosphere of Brno, however, as he wished to study with the best available masters.

The turning point of his career came in 1932, when Psota became a member of the Ballets Russes de Monte-Carlo. From a shy dancer in the corps he developed into an interpreter of character and comic roles. Among his roles were the Corregidor in *Le Tricorne,* the Tailor in *La Concurrence,* Rudolf in *La Scuola di Ballo,* and Kastchei in *The Firebird.* The excellent training, the inspiring models of true ballet *étoiles,* and performing in the ballets of Michel Fokine, Léonide Massine, Bronislava Nijinska, George Balanchine, and David Lichine all accelerated Psota's artistic and professional growth. He got to know the European capitals and also took part in a grand American tour, where his performances met with critical acclaim.

In 1936 Psota returned to his directorial post in Brno. In this second Brno period he created a series of successful stagings, for example, Vítěslav Novák's *Signorina Gioventù,* Dvořák's *Slavonic Dances,* and Tchaikovsky's *Swan Lake.* Psota was the first to choreograph Prokofiev's *Romeo and Juliet;* his version, debuting on 30 December 1938, anticipated Lavrovsky's Leningrad version by two seasons. Psota himself danced Romeo; Juliet was portrayed by Zora Šemberová. It was also in this period that his career as a soloist culminated. He was the male protagonist of all the ballets, to which he applied his mature technique and strong acting ability.

At the beginning of 1941, after his country was occupied by the Nazis, Psota left for New York. There, in that same year, he choreographed Dvořák's *Slavonic Dances,* under the title *Slavonica,* for Ballet Theatre. The next year he was engaged by Colonel Wassily de Basil's Original Ballet Russe as a ballet master and choreographer. During World War II the company performed primarily in Central and South America, where Psota produced *Fué Una Vez* in Buenos Aires in 1942, *La Isla de los Ceibos* in Montevideo in 1943, and *Yara* in São Paulo in 1946. In recognition of the choreography of *Yara,* a commemorative plaque dedicated to Psota was placed in the Brazilian theater.

In 1947 Psota returned to Brno, where within a short time he had formed an unusually strong company with many excellent soloists. At the time, technically speaking, the company had no equal in central Europe, and Brno came to be known as a ballet capital. Psota took pains to maintain a high professional polish and refined production. His reputation guaranteed high quality and attracted the best interpreters from throughout the country. His repertory was oriented to classical works, such as *Swan Lake, The Sleeping Beauty,* and the post-Diaghilev repertory.

Psota educated an entire generation of top artists, among them, Miroslav Kůra, Vlastimil Jílek, Viktor Malcev, Rudolf Karhánek, Jiří Nermut, Olga Skálová, Věra Vágnerová, Mirka Figarová, Jiřina Šlezingerová, and Růžena Ellingerová. As a person Psota impressed others with his gentleness, kindness, and well-rounded education (in addition to his native Czech he spoke German, Russian, Polish, French, English, Spanish, Italian, and Portuguese).

Psota's choreographies were built on a firm base of *danse d'école.* He had hoped to establish his Brno company on the international circuit, but his premature death at the age of forty-three, while he was at the peak of his creative powers, kept him from reaching that goal. Nevertheless, together with Prague choreographer Saša Machov, Psota deserves the highest credit for the development of dance in postwar Czechoslovakia.

[*See also* Brno Ballet; Czech Republic and Slovak Republic, *article on* Theatrical Dance; *and* Romeo and Juliet.]

BIBLIOGRAPHY

García-Márquez, Vicente. *The Ballets Russes: Colonel de Basil's Ballets Russes de Monte Carlo, 1932–1952.* New York, 1990.

Matějka, J. S. "Ivo Váňa Psota." *Program of the State Theatre in Brno* 48 (1976–1977).

Rey, Jan. "Change and Growth in Czechoslovakia." *Dance and Dancers* (October 1960): 14–17.

Schmidová, Lidka. *Československý balet.* Prague, 1962.

Telcová, Jiřina. "Pokrokové tradice brněnského baletu." In *Velká pochodeň.* Brno, 1959.

Šemberová, Zora. "Prokofiev's First Juliet." *Ballet Review* 22 (Summer 1994): 20–23.

VLADIMÍR VAŠUT
Translated from Czech

PSYCHÉ ET L'AMOUR. Also known as *Cupid and Psyche.* Ballet in four parts and thirteen scenes. Choreography: Jean-Georges Noverre. Music: Jean-Joseph Rodolphe (Johann Joseph Rudolph). Libretto: Jean-Georges Noverre. Scenery: Innocenzo Colomba. Costumes: Louis Boquet. First performance: 11 February 1762, Grand Ducal Theater, Stuttgart, Germany.

Psyché et l'Amour was choreographed during one of the most productive phases of Jean-Georges Noverre's creative life. His momentous *Lettres sur la danse et sur les ballets* had been published in 1760, the year in which he was appointed ballet master to Karl Eugen, duke of Württemberg, whose generous sponsorship gave him the means to put his ideas into practice. *Psyché,* followed in 1763 by *Médée et Jason,* demonstrated Noverre's thesis that the dance was capable of expressing human actions and emotions according to the dramatic logic of a narrative.

The fable of Cupid and Psyche, which originated sometime after the Augustan age, was so well known in Europe Noverre saw no necessity for providing a program for the ballet. A ballet version of the theme had appeared as early as 1619 in Scipion de Gramont's *Ballet de la Reine;* it was also treated choreographically by Isaac de Benserade, Molière, Franz Hilverding, and others.

In Noverre's ballet, Cupid rescues Psyche, who is chained to a rock, and takes her to his palace, where she is attended by nymphs and the Graces. He alternately delights and disappoints her by being elusive—he appears and disappears. When he falls asleep, she approaches with a lamp to admire him. She inadvertently awakens him and he leaves in a rage, calling down upon her the wrath of his mother, Venus. The Furies bear her off to Hades, where she is tormented until Cupid takes pity on her and rescues her. The two arrive at the court of Venus, but the jealous goddess refuses to forgive Psyche until Cupid induces her to relent. Psyche and Cupid are joined in marriage amid joyous dances.

The ballet was widely performed throughout Europe, doing much to spread Noverre's fame. It achieved a notable success when staged in London in 1788, with Auguste Vestris as Cupid and Charles-Louis Didelot in the minor role of Adonis. Charles Le Picq staged it in Saint Petersburg during his tenure there as ballet master (1786–1796). Other versions of the theme were choreographed by Vincenzo Galeotti, Jean Dauberval, Gasparo Angiolini, Pierre Gardel, Charles-Louis Didelot, and others.

[*See also the entry on Noverre.*]

BIBLIOGRAPHY

Chazin-Bennahum, Judith. "Three Faces of *Psyche.*" In *Proceedings of the Fifth Annual Conference, Society of Dance History Scholars, Harvard University, February 1982,* compiled by Christena L. Schlundt. Riverside, Calif., 1982.

Chazin-Bennahum, Judith. *Dance in the Shadow of the Guillotine.* Carbondale, Ill., 1988.

Nares, Robert. *Remarks on the Favourite Ballet of Cupid and Psyche.* London, 1788.

Noverre, Jean-Georges. *Cupid and Psyche.* London, 1788.

RICHARD RALPH and SUSAN AU

PUEBLO DANCE. The Pueblo peoples of New Mexico dance and sing to celebrate health, fertility, growth, and life. These ritual performances take place within the sacred plazas of the Pueblo villages to honor the gods, influence the weather, and bring the people together. Some of these village events are closed to non-Pueblos, while others are open as long as the guests observe the activities with respect. During the winter the dances tend to have themes of hunting and game animals; performances with farming and agricultural themes dominate the spring, summer, and early fall months. The Pueblo people are committed to their traditional ritual calendar because they believe that as long as they participate in their ancient rituals, they will survive as a culturally distinct group. To become and to remain a member of the Pueblos, one must be active in the communal celebrations.

Archaeological evidence indicates that the ancestors of the Pueblo peoples lived in the Southwest as early as c.500 BCE. The famous sites of Mesa Verde and Chaco Canyon (1100–1300 CE) date from the most expansive period of Pueblo prehistory. Today, these peoples live in a number of villages that can be distinguished according to the location and the language or dialect spoken.

Modern Pueblo language families include Hopi, Zuni, Keresan, and Tanoan. The Hopi-speaking Pueblo people live farthest to the west, in northern Arizona. The Zuni reside near the Arizona–New Mexico border. In the central New Mexico Pueblo villages of Acoma, Cochiti, Laguna, San Felipe, Santa Ana, Santo Domingo, and Zia, they speak Keresan. Tanoan is a Pueblo language with three related dialects, Tiwa, Towa, and Tewa. Tiwa is spoken in the central and northern New Mexico villages of Isleta, Picuris, Sandia, and Taos. The only modern village where Towa is spoken is Jemez. The third Tanoan dialect, Tewa, is spoken in the Pueblo villages of Nambé, Pojoaque, San Ildefonso, San Juan, Santa Clara, and Tesuque. These Tewa villages are all located within a twenty-mile length of land along the Rio Grande and its tributaries north of Santa Fe, New Mexico.

Sixteenth-century Spanish explorers and missionaries (Roman Catholic) were the first Europeans to enter Pueblo lands. These invaders found the Pueblo people to be farmers living in permanent villages. Early records indicate that the Spanish feared Pueblo ritual dance and termed it "idolatrous devil worship." The missionaries were particularly opposed to the Pueblo masked *kachina (katsina)* dances. The Pueblo ceremonial chambers, the *kiva*s, were regularly raided and the *kachina* masks confiscated and publicly destroyed. *Kachina* dances could survive only in secret. Today these sacred masked dances are still closed to outsiders, except among the Hopi, an Arizona Pueblo group, and at Zuni, a New Mexico Pueblo village where the missionaries were unsuccessful in suppressing the masked dancing.

Spanish religious and colonial policies eventually led to the Pueblo Revolt of 1680. Intolerance of Pueblo ritual dance had become a major issue. The Spanish were driven out of the area by the Pueblo people but returned in 1692; however, after that time they took a more accepting view of Pueblo ritual performances.

After more than two hundred years of Spanish rule and twenty-five years of Mexican rule, in 1846 New Mexico became a territory of the United States. Anglo (English-speaking) settlers and Protestant missionaries were attracted to the area. Once again Pueblo ritual dance was criticized as barbaric, pagan, and a hindrance to the assimilation of Native American populations into general American society. New Mexico became the forty-seventh state in 1912. During the 1920s, U.S. Secretary of the Interior Charles H. Burke attempted to ban Pueblo dance. At the same time, Anglo businessmen in the Southwest were encouraging the Pueblo people to perform ritual dance because they saw these activities as potential tourist attractions. Artists and intellectuals also actively supported the Pueblo peoples' right to continue their ritual events. A controversy resulted, and the act of dancing became a potent symbol of the larger issues of religious freedom and Pueblo cultural survival.

Today, the nineteen Pueblo groups in New Mexico freely hold ritual dances throughout the year. In addition, some New Mexico Pueblo individuals and groups perform segments of their dances for tourists in cities. These tourist shows have not replaced the ancient village rituals that survived years of suppression; rather, they have developed as a separate kind of performance event.

Pueblo dance is not technically difficult to perform. Steps and gestures are controlled, repetitive, and relatively small, with the arms and legs remaining fairly close to the body. There are no true dance specialists, and training is informal. As soon as a child can walk, he or she is encouraged to follow a patient sister, brother, or aunt during the dance. Children are gently corrected if they travel in the wrong direction or wander from their positions.

Pueblo dancers usually hold their torsos erect as single units. The arms are usually contracted three degrees (as defined in the Labanotation system) with the elbows positioned four to five inches out from the body. [*See* Labanotation.] For most steps, as the dancers lift their feet, the legs contract only one or two degrees. Men tend to lift their feet slightly higher than do women.

The most basic dance step in Pueblo dance is the foot-lifting step (Tewa, *antege*). The right foot is accented as the weight alternates from the left to right foot with a slight flexing of the knees. This step may be done in place or traveling forward, sideways, or diagonally. Other common Pueblo steps include a stylized deer walk, a buffalo walk, and a shuffle step. The dancers also occasionally employ small jumps, hops, and low short leaps. Knee bends in place with weight on both feet are sometimes used.

Pueblo gestures are usually made through space in a flat arc rather than in a straight line projecting out from the dancer's body. These gestures may symbolize digging, planting, clouds, lightning, or falling rain; they may also involve the manipulation of rattles, evergreen branches, ears of corn, spears, or other ritual paraphernalia held in the hands.

Before a ritual is held, the specific dance and date are selected by the elected village officers. The dance may be requested by a specific village group, such as the unmarried men or a women's society. Once the dance and date are chosen, the officers request one or more song composers to prepare the songs. Some dances require new songs, and others must use traditional ones.

The officers select lead male singers to meet and practice with the composers. Other male participants who have been requested to perform then gather for four or more evenings of practice in the *kiva*. At this time the dance steps are set. Again, for some dances new choreographic combinations are created and for others traditional movement patterns are recalled. Finally, the women participants are formally requested to dance by the officials, who come to their homes. These women and some children join the practices for four more nights in the *kiva*.

Costumes and paraphernalia are prepared throughout the practice period. This includes the gathering of evergreens, the symbol of life, which will be worn or carried by the dancers. The evergreen-gathering expedition is accomplished by young men, usually on the fifth night before the dance. At some Pueblo villages, tradition dictates that these men must walk many miles to the mountains,

PUEBLO DANCE. In New Mexico in 1909, Pueblo ritual dancers were photographed, in antlered headdresses, performing the Deer Dance, a prelude to the fall and winter hunting season. They carried evergreen sprigs, symbol of life. (Photograph by P. E. Goddard; from the Department of Library Services, American Museum of Natural History, New York [no. 14399]; used by permission.)

collect evergreen branches with prayers, and carry them back to the village in the course of one night.

Pueblo dances are usually repeated in several dance areas, following a prescribed spatial circuit around the village. Each dance set usually contains five verses before the group moves on to a new dance area to perform the next set. Sometimes the final set of the circuit is performed within the *kiva*. After a short rest, the dancers return for another circuit through the village. There are rarely fewer than four, and sometimes as many as ten, appearances or circuits completed during the day. In addition, some Pueblo dances involve extra prelude and postlude sections. It is not uncommon for a day of dancing to begin in the early morning and last until sunset.

Dance without song is of little significance for the Pueblo peoples. The words of the songs carry the meaning of the movements. As noted above, only after the songs are learned are the dance patterns practiced. Furthermore, the dancers must become familiar with the songs because musical changes are cues to choreographic changes. This relationship between dance and music is most dramatic in a Pueblo ritual performance in which the dancers are simultaneously the musicians. The dancers accompany themselves with singing; sometimes the male dancer wears a tortoiseshell rattle behind the right knee, sounding with every step.

Pueblo performance costumes vary according to the particular dance, the time of year, and the village; there are, however, some common elements. For example, female dancers generally wear a *manta*, a dress of black or white wool or other heavy fabric, bordered with a combination of red, green, black, and white embroidery. Frequently a cotton shirt or dress trimmed in lace is worn under this heavier garment. A brightly colored shawl may also be pinned at the right shoulder. At the waist, a red embroidered sash is commonly worn. For some dances the women are barefoot and during others they wear moccasins. Women frequently carry evergreens and sometimes ears of corn in each hand. Silver and turquoise necklaces, bracelets, and pins are always part of women's festive attire.

Male dancers wear white kilts with embroidered edges. For some dances the chest is bare except for body paint, and for others white shirts are worn. At the waist the male dancer generally wears bells, an embroidered sash, or a white sash with long fringe called a "rain sash"; a coyote skin hangs down his back. A gourd rattle is carried in the right hand along with evergreen sprigs, which are carried in both hands. The men wear moccasins on their feet and usually a few feathers at the top of their heads.

Some parts of the costume and some paraphernalia have specific symbolic meanings. For example, many of the designs in the embroidery depict clouds or vegetation. The men's rain sash symbolizes falling rain, as does the sound of the gourd rattle. Drums are said to have ritual power, and tortoiseshells promote fertility.

Members of a Pueblo village who are not singing or dancing in a particular ritual performance are still considered important participants. In fact, there are no audiences in the Western theatrical sense. The Pueblo peoples do not simply sit in judgment of the performance or passively watch the action; rather, Pueblo observers consider the role of dance-watching to be one of active listening. The audience members contribute their thoughts to the community prayer being communicated by the song and dance movements.

Many early researchers predicted that the rich ritual life of the Pueblos could not survive the pressures of mainstream American society. Nevertheless, today the Pueblo people are still committed to their religious traditions and the ritual dance central to them. Not only do the elders encourage participation; adolescents actively seek advice from their parents and grandparents regarding ancient Pueblo rituals. One Pueblo man observed that the "dance lines are getting longer and younger each year," and "the people still dance from the heart." Throughout New Mexico there is strong pride in being a Pueblo Indian; and one way to reinforce and express that pride is through participation in traditional village ritual performances.

[*For related discussion, see also* Hopi Dance; Native American Dance, *article on* The Southwest; *and* Tiwa Dance.]

BIBLIOGRAPHY

Dozier, Edward P. *The Pueblo Indians of North America.* Prospect Heights, Ill., 1970.

Frisbie, Charlotte J. *Music and Dance Research of Southwestern United States Indians.* Detroit, 1977.

Frisbie, Charlotte J., ed. *Southwestern Indian Ritual Drama.* Albuquerque, 1980.

Kurath, Gertrude, and Antonio Garcia. *Music and Dance of the Tewa Pueblos.* Santa Fe, 1970.

Ortiz, Alfonso. *The Tewa World: Space, Time, Being, and Becoming in a Pueblo Society.* Chicago, 1969.

Ortiz, Alfonso, ed. *New Perspectives on the Pueblos.* Albuquerque, 1972.

Roediger, Virginia More. *Ceremonial Costumes of the Pueblo Indians.* Berkeley, 1961.

Sweet, Jill D. "Ritual and Theatre in Tewa Ceremonial Performances." *Ethnomusicology* 27 (May 1983): 253–269.

Sweet, Jill D. *Dances of the Tewa Pueblo Indians: Expressions of New Life.* Santa Fe, 1985.

Sweet, Jill D. "The Beauty, Humor, and Power of Tewa Pueblo Dance." In *Native American Dance* ed. by Charlotte Heth. Washington, D.C., 1992.

JILL D. SWEET

PUERTO RICO. The easternmost island of the Greater Antilles, Puerto Rico is about 1,000 miles (1,600 kilometers) southeast of Miami, Florida, a self-governing entity of the United States. Within the population of about four million, the vast majority are descended from Spanish colonists mixed with Africans and the Taino people. The expedition of Christopher Columbus sighted the island in 1493 and that of Ponce de Leon in 1508. Spain began sugar culture there soon after, and Africans were transported as slave laborers to replace the decimated Taino, who fought the Spanish, fled, and died from epidemics. The island was ceded to the United States following the Spanish-American War of 1898, and an independence movement grew; in 1917, Puerto Ricans were granted U.S. citizenship. The sugar industry continued to prosper on the island, using land that had formerly been farmed for subsistence; economic deprivation for the people ensued and was not reversed until the late 1940s. In 1952, the Commonwealth of Puerto Rico was established, which U.S. industrial investments and tax incentives favored; from that time, a movement for statehood grew alongside the independence movement.

Traditional Dance. The earliest documented dance of Puerto Rico, described by the Spanish in the late fifteenth century, was the *areito* or *areyto,* common to several indigenous groups of the Antilles, Mesoamerica, and South America. It was led by a guide, whose steps and chanted recitations were repeated by the participants and was motivated by factors historical-didactic, religious, social, or military. The dancers held on to one another, wore shells on wrists and ankles, and danced until the narration was over, which might take hours or even an entire night.

The dances that arrived in Puerto Rico over the next five centuries were brought in by the Spanish conquistadors, African slaves, English and French immigrants from the Antilles, Latin American refugees from the wars of independence, and U.S. citizens after Puerto Rico was ceded to the United States. These dances developed along the coasts, in the mountains, and in cities. The mountain areas favored dances of European origin, including the waltz, mazurka, and polka, which rapidly acquired Puerto Rican interpretive, rhythmic, and instrumental traits.

The most important dance of Puerto Rican origin was the *seis,* which originally involved six couples who faced each other, crisscrossed, stamped the floor, and finished with a waltz. A sung dialogue concerning love and contempt alternated with the dance, which was disappearing by the end of the nineteenth century.

The most important coastal dance with African influence was the *bomba,* which also had a mountain version. The coastal dance was accompanied by African-Antillean drums and timbrels, and the mountain version by stringed instruments. In the dance couplets were alternated, and the women swirled their wide, long white skirts and stamped on the ground while the men, arms behind their backs, danced around the women; in certain versions the women led the dance by calling out the couplets, which the musicians then interpreted.

The *danza* was the most important upper-class expression of Puerto Rican dance and music. Thought to have originated either from the Dominican *méringue,* the Cuban *upa habanera,* or the European *contradanse* as danced in Venezuela, Colombia, or Peru, it developed its own style, and popular versions appeared. The *danza* is divided into two parts. The first is slow and opens with the couples walking around the room while the women fan themselves; the second, faster part, is danced in the closed position with the couple maintaining a decorous distance between themselves.

The *plena,* dating from the final decades of the nineteenth century, is the last indigenous dance developed before the U.S. invasion. It is a sung "newscast" and the first Puerto Rican dance to become popular on other shores. Latin American dances such as the mambo, cha-cha, rumba, and bolero, and some U.S. dances such as the Charleston, the Twist, and rock-and-roll, have been popular during the twentieth century; rock and salsa became very popular late twentieth-century styles of dance music.

PUERTO RICO. Ballets de San Juan principals Zulma Berrios and Leslie Howard in *Divertimento del Sur,* a pas de deux choreographed by Ana García to music by Hector Campos Parsi. (Photograph © 1995 by Eddy McDonald; used by permission.)

Many folk dance companies exist on the island; most are amateur. Of the professional, Areyto, established in the late 1960s, is the oldest and one of the best known; some specialize in African-Caribbean rhythms, as does the Hermanos Cepeda company. Their dances are now very theatrical and have thus gone through many modifications. Only the African-Antillean dances continued to be practiced uninterruptedly into the twentieth century.

Theatrical Dance. In 1954, with the foundation of the first dance company, Ballets de San Juan, theatrical dance began in Puerto Rico. Before that, only visiting artists and touring opera and *zarzuela* (Spanish popular opera) companies were seen. Anna Pavlova danced in Puerto Rico during the winter season of 1917/18 as part of her South American ballet tour.

Ballets de San Juan began as a ballet and Spanish dance company owing to its founders' training and choreographic preferences: Ana García and Gilda Navarra, sisters who in 1951 founded the Academia de Ballet y Bailes Españoles (now the Ballets de San Juan School), created pieces with Puerto Rican themes, dance styles, and scores. Ballets de San Juan's repertory today includes classical and neoclassical ballets and a few experimental pieces. It performs a number of ballets choreographed by George Balanchine as well as dances by Puerto Rican choreographers. The company has consistently commissioned scores, libretti, costumes, and set designs by Puerto Rican artists; in 1991, it set up the Archive of Puerto Rican Composers, to stimulate the use of local classical and contemporary compositions in dance.

Gilda Navarra left Ballets de San Juan in the early 1960s, retraining to classical pantomime in New York and Paris. In 1971 she founded Taller de Histriones, a mime and dance theater company active until 1985. Its aesthetic project constitutes the only truly original and outstanding movement proposal to have been developed in Puerto Rico. The repertory of Histriones included versions of plays as well as abstract and Puerto Rican–themed pieces called *mime-dramas*, which were not an acting out of the words—the text was only one of the important elements—their movement style was based on the body's capability to convey ideas, feelings, or forms through movement or stillness, with a vocabulary developed for each piece.

García and Navarra, together and separately, have been integral to the dance and theater movement in Puerto Rico since its professionalization. They have trained many of the foremost Puerto Rican dancers, choreographers, and actors, both those on the island and those who have worked abroad.

Two other professional ballet companies were founded in Puerto Rico in the late 1970s—Ballet Concierto de Puerto Rico, headed by Lolita San Miguel, and Ballet Teatro Municipal de San Juan, directed by Juan Anduze and later by Vanessa Ortiz. Their repertories are similar to that of Ballets de San Juan, although Ballet Concierto emphasizes full-length versions of the classics. To develop a strong and recognizable Latino profile, it has also strengthened its repertory of works by Latin American and Caribbean choreographers, such as Alberto Méndez of Cuba, Carlos Veitía of the Dominican Republic, Julio López of Argentina, and José Parés, Jesús Miranda, Oscar Mestey, Ana Sánchez Colberg, Iván Santo, and María Julia Landa of Puerto Rico.

PUERTO RICO. Scene from the Ballet Concierto de Puerto Rico's production of *La Calinda*, with María Teresa Robles in the title role. (Photograph © 1991 by Jack Vartoogian; used by permission.)

Two important but short-lived dance companies were Teatro de la Danza, led by José Parés in the 1950s, and Ballet Puertorriqueño, directed by Ramón Segarra in the 1970s. Parés went on to work in Cuba with Alicia Alonso for many years and later worked in Venezuela; Segarra made his career with the New York City Ballet, in Germany, and in Brazil before returning to Puerto Rico.

Experimental Dance. There is no modern dance tradition in Puerto Rico, but experimental dance has flowered since the late 1970s. Its first generation, composed of Petra Bravo, Viveca Vázquez, Awilda Sterling, and Gloria Llompart, first formed Pisotón, a company directed by Bravo that lasted seven years. They have gone their separate ways, although they often work with and for each

PUERTO RICO. An important figure in experimental dance in Puerto Rico, Viveca Vázquez is seen here crouched over an electric fan in her work *Non-Cordless.* (Photograph © by Tom Brazil; used by permission.)

other; they usually have to produce their own works as well.

Vázquez directs her own group called Taller de Otra Cosa (Something Else Workshop). Bravo prefers to use ballet-trained dancers. Llompart teaches and choreographs; and Sterling, a painter and solo dancer, headed a folk dance company.

All four women trained in the United States, although Bravo comes from Cuba's National Ballet and later also trained in the Graham method. Their styles are different, but they share an interest in everyday movement, breathing patterns as an energy source, and improvisation as a form of composition. Their varied works show an interest in sexual, cultural, and social politics. They incorporate texts, voice, and allegorical titles as well as many forms of humor; and their program notes, props, costumes, and music contribute to a multilayered density that progressively multiplies possible meanings.

Oscar Mestey works parallel to the experimentalists in a modern dance idiom. His choreography is based on a limited number of steps and movements combined into sequences, usually following the compositional canon of dancer-choreographer Merce Cunningham and composer John Cage.

In recent years the University of Puerto Rico has set up a Dance Archive, the first in Latin America or the Caribbean. It will concentrate on this region first but will eventually develop a collection that can serve not only the dance and academic communities but also the general public.

[*For related discussion, see* Caribbean Region.]

BIBLIOGRAPHY

Cadilla de Martínez, María. "La histórica danza de Puerto Rico en el siglo XVI y sus evoluciones." *Revista Musical Chilena* 6 (1950): 43–77.

Concepción, Alma. "U.S. Ballet and Modern Dance in the Caribbean: Cuba and Puerto Rico." In *Proceedings of the Fifteenth Annual Conference, Society of Dance History Scholars, University of California, Riverside, 14–15 February 1992,* compiled by Christena L. Schlundt. Riverside, Calif., 1992.

Davis, Martha Ellen. "The Social Organization of a Musical Event: The Fiesta de Cruz in San Juan, Puerto Rico." *Ethnomusicology* 21 (January 1972): 38-62.

Figueroa-Cruz, Blas Ernesto. "A Historical Documentation, an Instructional Manual, and an Annotated Bibliography of Selected Folk Dances of Puerto Rico." Ph.D. diss., Brigham Young University, 1990.

González, Max. *Trayectoria del ballet en Puerto Rico.* San Juan, 1990.

Homar, Susan. "Rompeforma, or, What Forms Were Broken This Year?" *High Performance* 17 (Spring 1994): 38-41.

Manuel Alum: Danzante. Rio Piedras, 1993.

Pané, Ramón. *Relación acerca de las antiguedades de los Indios* (c. 1495–1498). Edited by José Juan Arrom. 4th ed. Mexico City, 1980.

Teatro puertorriqueño: Noveno festival. San Juan, 1968.

Thompson, Donald, and Annie F. Thompson. *Music and Dance in Puerto Rico from the Age of Columbus to Modern Times: An Annotated Bibliography.* Metuchen, N.J., 1991.

Vega, Hector. "The Bomba and Plena." *Caribe* 7.1–2 (1983): 42–43.

SUSAN HOMAR

PUGNI, CESARE (born 31 May 1802 in Genoa, died 14 [26] January 1870 in Saint Petersburg), Italian composer. Authorities differ in giving the year and place of Pugni's birth, but it is most likely that he was born in 1802 in Genoa. While he was still a child, his parents probably moved to Milan, where his father set up shop as a clockmaker in the vicinity of the Piazza del Duomo, alongside the cathedral. Pugni received his musical education in Milan. He attended the Milan Conservatory from 1814 to 1822, studying with Allessandro Rolla, from whom he learned the violin, and Bonifazio Asioli, who taught him counterpoint and composition. Two other names are mentioned in connection with his musical education, both of operatic composers whose works were produced at the Teatro alla Scala between 1816 and 1818, Peter von Winter and Carlo Soliva.

Pugni is said to have produced his first compositions at the age of seven. He may have been engaged as some sort of musical apprentice at La Scala, probably on the recommendation of Rolla, who was first violin in the orchestra there for many years. Pugni soon showed an unusual facility for composing music for dances quickly. Those early years probably also saw many of the compositions, too inconsequential to be credited to his name, that he later included in the count of his output (he was said to have written music for three hundred ballets, but only about one-third of that number have been identified).

The earliest ballet with which his name is associated was Gaetano Gioja's *Castello di Kenilworth* (1823). The printed scenario merely attributed the music to "various well-known composers," and it may have been Pugni's task to stitch the various pieces together under the choreographer's direction. A few years later he began receiving his first commissions, producing scores for some of the most distinguished choreographers then working in Italy: for Louis Henry, *Elerz e Zulmida* (1826), *L'Assedio di Calais* (1827), *Adelaide di Francia* (1829), and *Macbetto* (*Macbeth,* 1830); for Salvatore Taglioni, *Pellia e Mileto* and *Don Eutichio della Castagna* (both 1827); and for Giovanni Galzerani, *Agamennone* (1828).

At this time, however, his ambitions turned toward opera. There had been occasions when he had produced an aria to order, and such routine assignments encouraged his belief that he was destined for the operatic field. They led him, in the 1830s, to write a series of operas, some of which were listened to with considerable respect. His teacher, Rolla, who supported him in this endeavor, conducted the orchestra when his first opera, *Il Disertore Svizzero,* was produced at the Teatro Canobbiana in Milan, in the summer of 1831. The score was praised for its originality and variety, and the following year Pugni had an opera produced at La Scala, *La Vendetta.* That same year he wrote an opera for the city of Trieste, which was followed by two more works for the Canobbiana, *La Contrabandiera* (1833) and *Un Episodio di San Michele* (1834).

Pugni's efforts to be considered a serious composer are also demonstrated by a number of masses and orchestral pieces, including a brilliant sinfonia for two orchestras, both playing from the same score but one a few bars behind the other. The piece so impressed Giacomo Meyerbeer that he held it up to his friends as a supreme example of virtuosity in composition. It was probably during these years that Pugni gave advice on orchestration to the Russian composer Mikhail Glinka when he visited Italy.

All this creative activity appropriately coincided with Pugni's elevation to the post of director of music and *maestro al cembalo* at La Scala in 1832. At the age of thirty, he was looking forward to a career of distinction, but within two years all his prospects had collapsed. The cause of his downfall was said to be a passion for gambling. He left Milan, apparently in disgrace, and was replaced at La Scala by his two assistants, both of whom were to become distinguished composers of ballet music, Giacomo Panizza and Giovanni Bajetti.

With his wife and family Pugni made his way to Paris, where for some time they lived in extreme poverty while he searched desperately for employment. By a stroke of good fortune his compatriot Vincenzo Bellini was then in Paris. He was preparing for the first production of his opera *I Puritani* at the Théâtre Italien and was simultaneously preparing a special version for Naples. For the Naples production he had to revise the leading soprano role for Maria Malibran, and he found himself under considerable pressure. He engaged Pugni to copy the score for the Naples production, but Pugni surreptitiously made a copy of the complete score, which he tried to sell to La Scala. Bellini was disgusted by this act of dishonesty, which was undoubtedly caused by Pugni's poverty. He also complained of Pugni's laziness, a failing that Marius Petipa was to contend with in later years. Another benefactor was Louis Henry, for whose last ballet *Licaone,* produced in Naples in 1836, Pugni wrote the music.

The appearance of Benjamin Lumley, director of Her Majesty's Theatre in London, was to rescue him from obscurity. The position of composer of ballet music at that theater, then London's principal opera house, gave Pugni a new purpose. In eight successive seasons, from 1843 to 1850, he produced an impressive stream of ballets, *divertissements,* and incidental dances. In 1845 alone he produced six new scores, including the hour-long ballet *Éoline* and *Pas de Quatre.* Gifted with exceptional facility, he needed only a few weeks to produce a complete ballet score—*Ondine* took him three weeks, *Catarina* nineteen days, and *La Esmeralda* a fortnight—and he could put together a score for a *divertissement* such as *Le Délire d'un Peintre* in a single day. Inevitably, his scores suffered from unevenness and occasional negligence, but taken as a whole his music was always eminently danceable and compared well with the work of most of the other ballet composers of his time. Indeed, few of them knew their métier as thoroughly as Pugni. His experience was to be of great value to the choreographers with whom he worked, particularly to Jules Perrot, the most distinguished of them, who, from 1843 onward, produced few ballets that did not have music by Pugni.

The first important score that Pugni wrote for Perrot was *Ondine* (1843). It contains a great variety of dance themes, including a tarantella and a saltarello (used effectively to convey a turning point in the narrative), and some ingeniously descriptive orchestration, particularly in the underwater scenes. Among the other scores he wrote for Perrot in London were *Esmeralda* (1844), *Catarina* (1846), the famous *Pas de Quatre,* and its successor, *Le Jugement de Pâris* (1846).

Pugni made no less an impression on Arthur Saint-Léon, who was himself a skilled musician. In 1847, Saint-Léon needed help in arranging the music for *La Fille de Marbre,* which he was to produce at the Paris Opera. Rather than have a French composer he did not know forced upon him, he came to an arrangement with Pugni. Over the next few years Pugni gave him similar assistance with other ballets. In 1850 he wrote a completely new score for Saint-Léon's *Stella* that was full of infectious Neapolitan melodies.

In 1850, possibly on the recommendation of Perrot, Pugni was offered the position of composer of ballet music to the Imperial Theaters in Saint Petersburg, and he spent the rest of his life in Russia. His contract with the Imperial Theaters was regularly renewed until his retirement in 1869. He received a salary of 3,000 rubles, which was increased to 3,600 rubles in 1857. After his retirement he received a pension, which was all too small for his needs. He supplemented his income by teaching counterpoint at the Saint Petersburg Conservatory.

Many of the ballets that Perrot and Saint-Léon produced in Saint Petersburg were revivals, but they needed to be expanded to meet the conditions of the Russian theater, where it was usual to devote a whole evening to the performance of an important ballet. For nearly twenty years Pugni turned out music to order, as he had done in London. Among the new ballets for which he wrote music were Perrot's *The War of the Women* (1851), *Gazelda* (1853), and *Armida* (1855); Saint-Léon's *The Little Humpbacked Horse* (1864), in which he incorporated Russian folk themes; and Marius Petipa's *Le Dahlia Bleu* (1860), *La Fille du Pharaon* (1862), *La Belle du Liban* (1863), and *Le Roi Candaule* (1868). His last months were darkened by financial difficulties.

Pugni was married twice. His second wife was an Englishwoman, Marian Linton, by whom he had several children, the first two of whom were born in London and the others in Saint Petersburg. Among the descendants of this marriage were the dancer Leontina Pugni, who was in the Imperial Russian Ballet from 1903 to 1913 and who accompanied Anna Pavlova on her Scandinavian and German tour of 1908–1909, and the artists Jean Pougny and Catherine Kobylansky. Pugni's son Nikolai, who danced in the Imperial corps de ballet from 1882 to 1896, was the child of a serf, Daria Petrova.

BIBLIOGRAPHY

Borisoglebskii, Mikhail. *Proshloe baletnogo otdeleniia Peterburgskogo teatral'nogo uchilishcha, nyne Leningradskogo gosudarstvennogo khoreograficheskogo uchilishcha: Materialy po istorii russkogo baleta.* Vol. 1. Leningrad, 1938.

"Cesare Pugni." *Gazzetta musicale di Milano* (9 August 1885).

Guest, Ivor. *Fanny Cerrito.* 2d rev. ed. London, 1974.

Guest, Ivor. *The Ballet of the Second Empire.* London, 1974.

Guest, Ivor. "Cesare Pugni." *Dance Gazette* (February 1979): 22–24.

Guest, Ivor. "Cesare Pugni: A Plea for Justice." *Dance Research* 1 (Spring 1983): 30–38.

Guest, Ivor. *Jules Perrot.* London, 1984.

Saint-Léon, Arthur. *Letters from a Ballet Master: The Correspondence of Arthur Saint-Léon.* Edited by Ivor Guest. New York, 1981.

Weinstock, Herbert. *Vincenzo Bellini.* London, 1971.

Wiley, Roland John, trans. and ed. *A Century of Russian Ballet: Documents and Accounts, 1810–1910.* Oxford, 1990.

IVOR GUEST

PUPPENFEE, DIE. English title: *The Fairy Doll.* Pantomimic *divertissement* in one act, two scenes. Choreography: Josef Hassreiter. Music: Josef Bayer. Libretto: Josef Hassreiter and Franz Gaul. Scenery: Anton Brioschi. Costumes: Franz Gaul. First performance: 4 October 1888, Vienna Opera Ballet. Principals: Camilla Pagliero (Puppenfee, the Fairy Doll), Lucia Balbo (Styrian or Tyrolian Lady Doll), Emma Allesch (Baby Doll), Adolfine Hauffe (Chinese Lady Doll), Wilhelmine Rathner (Spanish Lady Doll), Katharina Abel (Japanese Lady Doll), Marietta Balbo (Moorish Lady Doll), Eduard Voitis van Hamme (Polichinelle Doll), Otto Thieme (Poet Doll), Franziska Well (Drum Majorette Doll), Louis Frappart (Shopowner), Josef Hassreiter (His Assistant), Alfred Caron and Karoline Skofitz (Farmers), Julius Price and Johanna Dulan Telle (Lord and Lady Plumpstershire).

The only old Viennese ballet with a continuous performance tradition, *Die Puppenfee* was the forty-three-year-old Josef Hassreiter's first choreography for the Vienna Opera. He had developed it from a pantomime, *Im Puppenladen,* that he had staged for aristocratic amateurs at a charity benefit planned by Princess Pauline Metternich earlier in that year, in April 1888. The idea was taken from a ballet by Mariquita, which the princess had seen in Paris. So successful was the pantomime that Hassreiter, a first soloist of the Vienna Opera's ballet, was asked to elaborate on it for performance by that company. Some roles were expanded technically, and a huge, final *ballabile* was added, but Hassreiter succeeded in preserving the seeming simplicity of his first version. Into a "naive" story, the librettists packed a variety of themes that erupt easily into mime and dance as well as fit cozily into less than one hour, so that the work could be performed following an opera or with two other dance pieces.

There is genre realism with caricature highlights in the depiction of a doll shop's routine and the arrival of two principal sets of customers: a wealthy, boorish farmer with wife and daughter, and a stiff English lord, his lady, and their peas-in-a-pod children. The mini-dances of the dolls on display are cleverly varied by national, stylistic, or personality traits. The most original are an Alice-in-Wonderland type of nymphet (the Baby Doll) that repeatedly says "Papa! Mama!" and a slightly disheveled stuffed doll (called a bohemian Poet Doll) with floppy movements compared to those of the mechanical dolls. A year after the premiere, Hassreiter and his team added another doll, the Hungarian Doll, a male performed *en travesti* by a female soloist. The individual doll variations in the first scene are capped by a group dance that begins as a pas de deux and multiplies into a pas de cinque. The Farmer has to be convinced that the dolls are not alive; the Lord demands to be shown something finer and is led to the Fairy Doll. He is enchanted. Reluctantly, the Shopowner consents to deliver her the next day. (In an alternate version, the Shopowner refuses to sell to either customer.)

The Fairy Doll is the crucial role, though she dances not one step and even her mime is minimal. In the first scene she must look so magical that she casts her spell while standing perfectly still. In the second scene, after the shop has closed, she conveys the Coppélia-like wonder of waking to life and the Myrtha-like power of her will by but a few visible breaths, turns of the head, and flicks of the wrists. The shop's huge display cases with their legions of dolls begin to glow at the Fairy Doll's command, and the dolls march forth to engage in midnight revels—the *ballabile* with inset variations. Some of the principal dolls of the first scene reappear, each backed by a group of six identical dolls, to dance more expansively than they had for the customers. They are accompanied by other dolls that were only glimpsed in their cases during the daylight scene. The most prominent is the Drum Majorette. She dances the single truly classical variation (drumstick legwork and tattoo steps lyrically phrased), backed by Drum Bunny Girls. The *ballabile*'s maneuvers become complex; there is marching, a galop and a carousel-formation waltz. Moments of pause occur in the midst of the mass action, with sudden emptyings of the stage, reminding one of the dolls' still life during daylight.

The onstage appearance of representatives of the audience is unusual—young dandies performed *en travesti,* who ogle the female dolls through their monocles. With this device, the librettists extend the first scene's social caricature of Vienna's *nouveaux riches* and anglophiles as the shop's customers to the ballet's "customers," and imply that the nineteenth century's fascination with dolls was a form of disguised eroticism.

The work has a horror-story ending. The shopkeeper, awakened by the revels, enters in nightclothes. As the doll horde advances toward him, he sinks to his knees before the Fairy Doll. This pose is held frozen as the final tableau.

Die Puppenfee became the most popular work at the Vienna Opera, accumulating over seven hundred performances by 1944, more than any opera. Over a hundred other theaters, from the Western Hemisphere to Asia, acquired the ballet. Hassreiter's choreography, or a close approximation of it, was given in many cities, including Budapest (1888), Prague (1888), and Milan (1893; Smeraldi after Hassreiter). Other prominent versions were by Flora Jungmann (Munich, 1890), J. Mendez (Bolshoi Theater, Moscow, 1898), Ivan Clustine (Bolshoi Theater, Moscow, 1900) and the Legat brothers (Maryinsky Theater, Saint Petersburg, 1903) with Matilda Kshessinska in the title role, Olga Preobrajenska as Baby Doll, Agrippina Vaganova as Chinese Lady Doll, Anna Pavlova as Spanish Lady Doll, and Vera Trefilova as Japanese Lady Doll. Michel Fokine was also in the cast. A production earlier that year in Saint Petersburg, at the Hermitage, was probably a preview of the Legat version and not staged by the visiting Hassreiter. In London, Katti Lanner choreographed the work at the Empire Theatre in 1905 as *The Dancing Doll,* starring Adeline Genée. New York first saw *Die Puppenfee* in Giovanni Ambroggio's version (Metropolitan Opera, 1890), then in Clustine's (for Pavlova's company, 1914), which was toured widely. Other productions in the United States were Catherine Littlefield's (Philadelphia Ballet, 1935), Peggy Dorsay's (Jordan Ballet, Indianapolis, 1958), Karoly Barta's (Birmingham, 1970), and Andre Eglevsky's (for his Long Island, New York, school in the early 1970s). For years in New York and elsewhere, Vincenzo Celli taught the Hassreiter steps for the Drum Majorette's variation.

Although in Europe during the 1920s and 1930s there were some versions by modern dance choreographers, *Die Puppenfee* was partly eclipsed from the 1920s to the 1940s by Léonide Massine's *La Boutique Fantasque.* The Hassreiter version is, however, gradually regaining its popularity. In Vienna, it was maintained and modified by Anton Birkmeyer and, later, by Willy Fränzl, who revised it considerably in 1958. Hassreiter, in his nineties, attended the fiftieth-anniversary performance in 1938. In 1971, *Die Puppenfee* was transferred from the Vienna Staatsoper (State Opera) to the Volksoper and performed there through 1976, but by the dancers of the former company. Wien Film made a color movie of this ballet in 1971, which has been shown in New York and Washington, D.C., and on television in Europe.

On 20 December 1983, the Vienna State Opera Ballet premiered a restoration of the 1888 production, supervised by Gerlinde Dill in consultation with Riki Raab, *emerita* of the company. The continued popularity of *Die Puppenfee* may be due to the simplicity of the idea, the naturalism of the presentation style, the coordinated detail of the original scenery and costuming with the movement, and a choreographically clever kaleidoscope of charm, irony, seduction, and spookiness.

[*See also the entry on Hassreiter.*]

BIBLIOGRAPHY

Amort, Andrea. "Die Geschichte des Balletts der Wiener Staatsoper, 1918–1942." Ph.D. diss., University of Vienna, 1981.

Jackson, George. "Notes on 'Die Puppenfee.'" *Washington Dance View* 1.1 (1979): 11.

Jackson, George. "Vienna." *Ballet News* 5 (April 1984): 40.

"Josef Hassreiter: Leben und Werk." *Tanz Affiche* 8 (December 1995–January 1996): 18–37.

Knessl, Lothar, ed. *Die Puppenfee* (program). Vienna, December 1983.

Matzinger, Ruth. "Die Geschichte des Balletts der Wiener Hofoper, 1869–1918." Ph.D. diss., University of Vienna, 1982.

Oberzaucher-Schüller, Gunhild, and Alfred Oberzaucher. "Joseph Hassreiter." *Tanzblätter* 27 (June 1980): 11–31.

George Jackson

PUPPETRY. *For discussion of puppetry in Asia, see* Asian Dance Traditions, *article on* Influence of Puppetry. *See also* Bunraku; Khōn; *and* Wayang.

PURCELL, HENRY (born 1659, died 21 November 1695 in London), English composer, organist, and singer. Theatrical dance flourished in Restoration England, and Henry Purcell, the preeminent composer for the London stage between 1690 and 1695, inevitably produced many dance accompaniments. These pieces, unlike those of his fellow composers, are typically sophisticated, intricate works that move the passions. Purcell's career as an opera composer was largely initiated and later nurtured by a prominent dancing master, Josias Priest, and much of Purcell's music, whether for the stage or not, has a distinctive rhythmic vibrance ideally suited to dancing.

Late seventeenth-century English drama, which was influenced by the contemporary French lyrical theater, required two basic kinds of dances, social dances in comedies and grotesque or fantastic dances in tragicomedies and semi-operas. Usually introduced into the dénouement, the former were often executed by members of the speaking cast accompanied by "the fiddles," a small stage band which improvised or drew from the vast repertory of court and country dances. Purcell wrote many songs and duets for comedies, but he is not known to have provided the music for these final dances, though arrangements of his songs and incidental tunes were probably taken over for this purpose. Grotesque dances, which stem directly from the antimasque tradition, were designed by dancing masters and executed by professional performers during scenes of celebration, incantations, serenades, and other entertainments. The accompaniment was usually provided by the full orchestra. From the first decade or so after the Restoration in 1660, little music survives for these kinds of dances, though prominent theatrical composers such as Matthew Locke (one of Purcell's teachers) are known to have provided some. With the emergence of the lavish semi-operas in the mid–1670s, professional theatrical dancing came into its own; such works as the 1674 adaptation of *The Tempest* and Thomas Shadwell's *Psyche* (1675) relied heavily on fantastic dances choreographed and performed by both native and French dancers. Locke and John Banister composed some of the music, but there was a tendency to leave this aspect of production to the foreign musicians. For example, Giovanni Battista Draghi was responsible for all the dances in *Psyche,* but Locke, who wrote the rest of the music (both vocal and instrumental), decided not to include the Italian's efforts in the printed score. By contrast, in Purcell's semi-operas, all of which date from the early 1690s, as much care was taken with the dances as with any other aspect of the production, and Purcell would never have farmed them out to another composer.

Purcell's first major stage work was *Dido and Aeneas,* mounted in 1689 at a girls' boarding school run by the dancing master Josias Priest, who was also a choreographer at the Theatre Royal, Drury Lane. *Dido and Aeneas* is Purcell's only all-sung opera, a fact that has obscured its probable *raison d'être;* to show off the abilities of Priest's young dance pupils. The original libretto calls for seventeen dances, with at least three in each act. The variety of those that survive is remarkable: graceful and noble for the Carthage courtiers; furious and dissonant for the witches; salty and tipsy for the sailors. Many have important narrative function, and nearly every scene ends with a dance which not only rounds off the preceding musical unit but also completes or summarizes the dramatic action. In act 1 the courtiers' unequivocal approval of Dido and Aeneas's illicit love is found only in the "Triumphing Dance" on a ground bass. The witches's scene in act 2 concludes with the "Echo Dance of the Furies" ("fairies" in the original libretto), which, in the absence of a detailed account of Priest's choreography, reiterates the Sorceress's deviousness in a purely musical way. As Edward J. Dent (1928) explains, the echoes "never reproduce the exact harmony of the original phrases; this ingenious device gives them a delightfully fantastic character, as if the human witches on the stage were answered by spirit dancers who strangely distort their movements." The second scene of act 2 was also meant to end with a dance in which Dido's courtiers unknowingly help the witches celebrate Aeneas's imminent departure from Carthage, but the music has not survived; nor, apparently, has that for the last number in the opera, the "Cupids' Dance," though some musicologists maintain that Purcell wanted an instrumental version of the final chorus "With drooping wings" to serve as the accompaniment. One other dance found earlier in act 3 is worthy of special mention. It is described in the 1689 libretto, "Jack *of the* Lanthorn *leads the* Spaniards *out of their way among the Inchanteresses."* With its abrupt changes of tempo and character made for rather obscure choreographic reasons, it closely resembles many antic dances in Stuart masques. *Dido and Aeneas* is so moving a tragedy that one can easily overlook how like a ballet it is. None of the dances is merely decorative or incidental; rather, each shifts the actions of the singing characters onto a higher level, at once more abstract yet more human. The dances are therefore integral, often joined to the pieces preceding them and essential to the overall tonal scheme.

Within a year of the premiere of *Dido and Aeneas,* Purcell was commissioned to write music for the semi-opera *The Prophetess, or The History of Dioclesian,* produced at the theater in Dorset Garden in spring of 1690. This adaptation of Massinger and Fletcher's *The Prophetess,* with musical scenes inserted with little regard for the original drama, was by far the most ambitious stage work an English composer had yet undertaken. One of the main tasks of the adapter, Thomas Betterton, was to devise with Priest some spectacular and novel ballets. In act 1, Delphia the prophetess conjures a "dreadful monster" as an ill omen; in act 3, a tomb explodes for a similar reason; and in act 5, a country dance warns the protagonist that he is about to be murdered. Purcell's deftly mimetic music is richer and more refined than the dances in *Dido and Aeneas.* As the monster creeps in from the dark recesses of the wings into the unflattering footlights, the accompanying prelude grows more chromatic and unstable as the beast becomes visible; when the horrid form separates into a number of furies, the dance is whipped into a tempest of sixteenth and thirty-second notes. Later, in act 4, the same eerie prelude is heard again when a tomb is discovered, raising the audience's expectation of another shock; but the surprise is a pleasant one when the tomb disintegrates into a "Dance of Butterflies," for which Purcell supplies lithe and graceful music, though highly seasoned with dissonance. *Dioclesian* is not the most balletic of semi-operas, but its dances are among Purcell's most ingenious contrapuntal pieces.

In Purcell's next semi-opera, *King Arthur,* or *The British Worthy* (1691), again with Priest as choreographer, dance is less pervasive though no less conspicuous. In the famous Frost Scene in act 3, the inhabitants of a land "cak'd with Ice" sing a shivering chorus "See, see, we assemble" and then perform a grotesque dance, to music appropriately rigid and mechanical. The most impressive dance scene in *King Arthur*—indeed the most extended and elaborate ballet in any English semi-opera—is the G minor Passacaglia in act 4. John Dryden, the librettist, had requested only a minuet to accompany the brief two-verse lyric "How happy the lover," but Purcell, who had by this time obviously studied the *chaconnes* in Jean-Baptiste Lully's *tragédies en musique,* produced a magnificent *tour de force* built on a continually varied four-bar bass pattern. The flawless concatenation of *ritornels* for alternating strings and oboes, solos, duets, trios, and choruses was designed as accompaniment for nymphs and sylvans who dance "with Branches in their Hands" in an attempt to lure a wary King Arthur to destruction. This is one of the few theater compositions in which Purcell borrowed without modification a French convention, though the immediate model may have been the *chaconne* in Louis Grabu and John Dryden's royal English opera of 1685 *Albion and Albanius,* a work which resembles a *tragédie en musique* in all but language.

The Fairy Queen (adapted from *A Midsummer Night's Dream*), the grandest and costliest of all the semi-operas, followed in spring 1692. Its success and expense were owed largely to the dances, which are more abundant here than in any similar work. Priest's diverse designs ("Dance of the Followers of Night," "Dance for the Fairies," "Dance of Four Savages who fright the Fairies away," "Dance of Haymakers," "Monkeys' Dance," "Dance for a Chinese Man and Woman," and others) inspired Purcell to seek unconventional musical forms. While Titania drifts off to sleep during the masque in act 2, the music becomes ever softer and more mysterious, concluding with the "Dance for the Followers of Night," a double canon in which the harmonies are painfully dissonant, perhaps in anticipation of the fairy queen's eventful dream. In the third-act masque, designed as an entertainment for Bottom with the ass's head, a bouquet of rustic dances is presented. According to the libretto, "While a Symphony's playing, the two Swans come Swimming on through the Arches to the bank of the River, as if they would Land; these turn themselves into Fairies, and Dance." To enhance this vignette, Purcell wrote a brisk French overture "while the Swans come forward," in which the fugal *canzona* is truncated, presumably for choreographic reasons. The "Dance of Four Savages" (called "green men" in Purcell's manuscript score) and the "Dance of Haymakers" complete the scene, which is an antimasque to the more courtly and emblematic masque for Oberon in act 4. Despite Purcell's having supervised the copying of a full score of *The Fairy Queen* for a revival in 1693, some of the dances were never written into the volume or were never composed. Blank pages were left for several pieces, including a "Dance for a Clown" in act 3 and a "Dance for the Four Seasons of the Year" in act 4.

Dances have less important roles in the rest of Purcell's stage works and are rarely introduced as independent numbers. "Song and Dance here" is a recurring stage direction in comedies and tragedies of the period, and while the vocal portions of these interpolations survive in abundance, the dances do not. Considering the number of "song-tunes" (instrumental versions of vocal pieces) found in contemporary music publications, one must conclude that the dances following Purcell's songs were often *ad hoc* arrangements of the songs themselves, undertaken by the stage band. There are only a few exceptions. For example, in Dryden's comedy *Amphitryon,* or *The Two Sosias* (1690), for which Purcell wrote all the music, one might assume that the dancers who "come from underground; and others from the sides of the Stage" to entertain Phaedra in act 4 performed to an arrangement of the preceding pastoral dialogue "For Iris I sigh," but in an early manuscript of the complete music there is a piece composed for this purpose; a "Dance for Tinkers," in which hammering on kettles is delightfully suggested by repeated notes in triple meter. The piece is only in two parts, treble and bass, lacking the usual second violin and viola lines, which suggests a rough-and-ready performance by a small stage band.

The vast majority of Purcell's dance movements were not intended for social dancing: the numerous suites of incidental pieces, or "act tunes" as they were called—minuets, sarabands, borrys (bourrées), jigs, roundos, and hornpipes—performed between the acts of plays. It is likely, however, that some of these pieces found their way into dancing schools and court balls, as the title page of the posthumous anthology suggests: *A Collection of Ayres, Compos'd for the Theatre, and upon Other Occasions* (1697). One such act tune, the "Slow air" used in John Crowne's farce *The Married Beau,* or *The Curious Impertinent* (1694), served as a "Magicians' Dance" in an undated revival of Charles Davenant's semi-opera *Circe.*

The dances in the semi-operas and the act tunes for plays fuse contrasting aspects of Purcell's musical style: on the one side, a desire and necessity to be fashionable, emulating French airs and dances by writing elegant melodies; and on the other, an overwhelming need to quench such frivolity with chromatic counterpoint, which is anathema to the French dance style. Herein lies the special character of Purcell's dances, even those designed for specific choreographic effect. The melody and bass played alone sound bold and regular or rough-hewn and folklike as the context requires; but on the addition of the inner parts with their bittersweet dissonances and cross-rhythms, the music acquires a sophistication and depth of expression lacking in the dances of Purcell's French contemporaries.

BIBLIOGRAPHY

Dent, Edward J. *Foundations of English Opera.* Cambridge, 1928.

Goff, Moira, and Jennifer Thorp. "Minuets and Dancing Monkeys." *The Dancing Times* (March 1995): 565–569.

Price, Curtis A. *Henry Purcell and the London Stage.* Cambridge, 1983.

Price, Curtis A., ed. *Purcell Studies.* Cambridge, 1995.

Savage, Roger. "The Shakespeare-Purcell *Fairy Queen:* A Defence and Recommendation." *Early Music* 1 (October 1973).

Savage, Roger. "Producing *Dido and Aeneas.*" *Early Music* 4 (October 1976).

CURTIS A. PRICE

PUSHKIN, ALEKSANDR (Aleksandr Ivanovich Pushkin; born 7 September 1907 in Mikulino, Russia, died 20 March 1970 in Leningrad), dancer and teacher. Pushkin studied at the School of Russian Ballet under Akim Volynsky, Nadezhda Nikolaeva, and Aleksandr Chekrygin; Nikolai Legat occasionally attended lessons. In the summers Pushkin was trained by Agrippina Vaganova. In March 1923 he was admitted to the Leningrad Choreographic Institute, where he studied in Vladimir Ponomarev's class for two years. In 1925 Pushkin and Marina Semenova danced the principal roles in the graduation performance of Achille Coppini's version of *La Source.* As a young dancer Pushkin had neither exceptional professional aptitude nor the impressive looks of a *premier danseur.* But his well-proportioned body, exceptionally soft landing after a leap, and command of pas de deux technique enabled him to dance the most intricate variations impeccably. He joined the ballet company of the Leningrad State Academic Theater for Opera and Ballet in 1925 and was for many of his nearly thirty years as a dancer with the company the best performer of the pas de trois in *Swan Lake* and the pas de deux in the first act of *Giselle.* By dancing all the complex variations in the traditional repertory he trained his body to obey his will.

Pushkin never strayed from classical dance and his loyalty to it finally led to renown, although not as a dancer but as a teacher. In 1932, at the height of his stage career, he started teaching classical dance and partnering at the Institute. His classes were based on historical and logical principles embodied in set combinations, each of which was a product of long reflection on his own experience and the experience of his predecessors. From the first movements at the barre to the classical variations that crowned the class there was a harmonious progression that helped the students to develop perfect command of technique, grow stronger physically, and learn to dance rather than "work" on the stage. Each class encompassed a large variety of steps that Pushkin built into intriguingly complex though logical combinations, forcing the dancers to think fast and to memorize the order of movements. One of his pupils, Nikita Dolgushin, aptly described Pushkin's lessons in the class of perfection by saying that, at first, just enduring a full lesson and meeting at least a minimum of Pushkins' demands was enough to qualify one as a first-rate dancer. Pushkin did not make his pupils train hard because of pressure or vigorous insistence; coercion was alien to his nature. Instead, he used tact and gentleness to encourage improvement, and he himself was an exemplar of hard work and dedication. He also generously shared his expertise with others; written descriptions of thousands of his combinations lie on the desks of dancers and teachers worldwide. Among Pushkin's other notable pupils were Yuri Grigorovich, Rudolf Nureyev, Valery Panov, and Mikhail Baryshnikov.

BIBLIOGRAPHY

"Alexander Pushkin" (obituary). *Dance Magazine* 44 (June 1970): 16.

Alovert, Nina. *Baryshnikov in Russia.* Translated by Irene Huntoon. New York, 1984.

Roslavleva, Natalia. "A Visit to the Leningrad School." *The Dancing Times* (May 1962): 486–490.

Swift, Mary Grace. *The Art of the Dance in the U.S.S.R.* Notre Dame, 1968.

GENNADY G. ALBERT
Translated from Russian

PYRRHIC. The pyrrhic, an armed dance known from Classical Greek writers, is of ancient Greek origin. Its precise steps are not known, but the movement was certainly quick and combatlike—leaping, thrusting, dodging, feinting, and weaving—and was performed to flute accompaniment. The poetic meter called pyrrhic (two unstressed syllables) prevailed in this music and suggests a rhythm for the dance. In more general terms, "pyrrhic dance" or "war dance" might denote any kind of contorted movement, as in Euripides' description in *Andromache* of the death of Achilles' son Pyrrhus. In that legendary event, according to one theory perpetuated by Strabo, lay the origin of the dance and its name. A more persuasive argument places the birthplace of the pyrrhic in Crete, with its associations to the origin myth of the Curetes guarding the infant Zeus with warlike movement and the noisy clashing of swords against shields.

It seems certain that the pyrrhic was ubiquitous in Crete, mainland Greece, and Asia Minor by Homeric times (c.1250 BCE). In the *Iliad,* reference is made to its place in the funeral games honoring fallen heroes, suggesting that the word *pyrrhic* stems from *pyra* ("pyre") or *pyr* ("fire"); it is not related to the phrase "pyrrhic victory," which refers only to the third-century BCE King Pyrrhus of Epirus. In literature the term broadly refers to a dance performed in armor and with weapons, or sometimes also to a victory dance. As the dance evolved, its movements became more selective and codified by its adoption as a military training exercise. In this guise it was cherished in Sparta from as early as the seventh century BCE (and well into the third century CE, according to Athenaeus) and was basic to every youth's education. The dance was also present in Athens, but there, characteristically, greater attention was paid to grace and formality of execution.

Aside from pedagogic application, the importance and popularity of the pyrrhic in the fifth and fourth centuries are everywhere evident. Plato, in the *Laws,* made it one of the two principal divisions of noble dance (the other being the *emmeleia* or "peaceful dance"). It was a major part of the Panathenaea festival and was performed as a votive offering to gods other than Athena, as attested by Xenophon's *Anabasis.* It eventually spread beyond Greece to Rome and throughout the Roman Empire.

With the decline of Classical Greek culture, the original force behind the pyrrhic deteriorated. Still a lively and exciting dance, it was presented by professional dancers as an entertainment at public spectacles and private banquets. Girls as well as youths might perform it, and the weapons were replaced by torches or other props. Even travesties of the dance were sanctioned. Nevertheless, the character of the pyrrhic persisted over the centuries; it can still be found, albeit shorn of direct allusions to battle, in sword and stick dances. It is thought that the modern Cretan *soústa* and *pentozalīs* and the *serra,* a dance of the Pontus region, are linear descendants of the pyrrhic.

[*See also* Greece, *article on* Dance in Ancient Greece; Music for Dance, *article on* Western Music before 1520.]

BIBLIOGRAPHY

Lawler, Lillian B. *The Dance in Ancient Greece.* Middletown, Conn., 1964.

McGowan, Margaret M. "A Renaissance War Dance: The Pyrrhic." *Dance Research* 3 (Spring 1984): 29–38.

BARBARA PALFY

Q–R

QUADRILLE. A ballroom dance for four couples; the quadrille was fashionable throughout the nineteenth century. The term *quadrille* may derive from Italian *squadra,* meaning a troop of armed horsemen formed into a square for military defense and tournament games.

In 1662, the duc de Guise took part in a festival masque, *Le Quadrille des Nations,* at the court of the Louvre, mounted on horseback and dressed in elaborate costume, with other superbly attired mounted performers. By 1743, when Rousseau's court ballet *Les Fêtes de Polymnie* appeared, the term *quadrille* was generally understood to mean a formal entrance of four to twelve dancers dressed alike, performing symmetrical dance patterns as a chorus.

In 1765, Claude-Marc Magny, a French dancing master and choreographer, published directions for six ballroom dances in which two to four couples formed a square and executed a variety of geometric dance patterns. One of these was entitled *le quadrille*—a cotillon especially composed for learning steps and patterns. As late as 1787, however, Charles Compan's *Dictionnaire de Danse* makes no reference to the quadrille as a specific type of square dance; Compan defines the *quadrille au théâtre* not as a dance genre but rather as a theatrical device.

QUADRILLE. *(left)* Le Pantalon (The Trousers) and *(right)* La Poule (The Hen), the first and third figures from the six-figure French Quadrille, shown in caricatures from *Northern Looking-Glass,* 1825. (Reprinted from Lily Grove Frazer, *Dancing,* 1907, p. 281.)

The square-dance form on which the quadrille was based had been in use for several centuries. John Playford includes three squares for eight in the first edition of *The English Dancing Master* (1651).

In eighteenth-century France, the square dance took two forms. In one, two couples stood side by side in one line facing two other couples standing opposite them. In the other form, one couple stood at each side of a four-sided square; each man had his partner at his right. Both of these square formations were called *contredanses françaises* and were distinguished from the *contredanse anglaise,* the English country dance, in which the dancers stood "as many as will" in two long "contrary" lines with gentlemen facing the ladies. In the *contredanse française* (known outside France as a cotillon) the action was across or around the outside of the square and did not progress. It was a kind of *rondeau* in which the theme or figure was alternated with a refrain or change. Ten standard changes were fashionable throughout the century.

After the French Revolution, the cotillon passed out of fashion and a new variety of square dance took its place. In place of the figure and ten different changes, five different figures were combined to form one dance. Thus the nineteenth-century quadrille emerged.

During the first decade of the nineteenth century, many combinations and variations of cotillon figures were strung together and called "sets of quadrilles," while dance manuals, books, and pamphlets on the subject pro-

QUADRILLE. Spectators at a late 1840s formal ball watch dancers executing a quadrille figure known as The Graces. (Courtesy of Elizabeth Aldrich.)

liferated. Thomas Wilson's *Quadrille and Cotillion Panorama* of 1822 offers no fewer than fifty-two configurations. The word *cotillon* (also spelled *cotillion*) was still being applied to the new quadrille. Music publishers often attempted to resolve the confusion by entitling their works "sets of quadrilles or cotillions."

By 1815, when the quadrille was introduced into London society, six popular cotillon figures were regularly being combined into one dance. This combination, known as the French Quadrille, or first set, soon became the most popular set of quadrilles danced. It was found on dance programs throughout the nineteenth century.

Music for the quadrille, adapted from popular operas, ballets, songs, and anthems, was arranged to fit the dance form precisely. Many famous composers contributed to the repertory. A quadrille band was often made up of a string quartet with added flute, harp, piano, and cornet. The tempo varied with each figure, and a pause of approximately twenty-seconds was observed between figures. The tempo was given as 112 beats per minute, although later in the century it was increased. Johann Strauss the younger allowed fifteen to twenty minutes for the quadrille on his court dance programs.

The figures were danced to a specified step pattern, a combination known as three *chassés, jetté,* and *assemblé.* Great skill went into their proper execution. Carlo Blasis in 1828 gave a list of additional ornamental steps for women and men, intended to display grace and agility during solo passages. By the 1840s, however, with the introduction of the waltz, polka, schottische, and other couple dances, the quadrille step was reduced to a simple glide-walk or *marche.* Cellarius in 1847 noted that "our young people no longer dance the quadrille but rather walk the figures with a certain nonchalance." One of the desired attributes of the quadrille was the respite it gave dancers for polite conversation during the pauses, which was not always possible during the more energetic waltzes and polkas.

By 1850, the five-figure Lancers Quadrille rivaled the French Quadrille in popularity. Its last figure, dedicated to the Royal Lancers Regiment, has the dancers marching in single and double files. The Double Lancers, the Caledonians (to Scottish airs), the Saratoga, and the Polo Quadrille followed soon after, and waltz and polka figures were introduced into the quadrille. The *Parisian Variétées* of 1865 includes a waltz, a polka, a mazurka, and a tyrolienne among its five figures. As new quadrilles proliferated, the need for dancing masters to prompt the dancers became unavoidable, and "calling" became necessary.

The quadrille finally fell out of fashion following World War I, when jazz and a new informality made it appear as antiquated as the cotillon. The square dance of today has preserved some of the quadrille's forms but little of its style and elegance.

[*See also* Cotillon *and* Social Dance, *article on* Nineteenth-Century Social Dance. *For related discussion, see* Anglaise; Country Dance; *and* Figure Dances.]

BIBLIOGRAPHY

Blasis, Carlo. "Private Dancing." In Blasis's *The Code of Terpsichore: A Practical and Historical Treatise on the Ballet, Dancing, and Pantomime.* London, 1828.

Cellarius, Henri. *The Drawing-Room Dances.* London, 1847.

Compan, Charles. *Dictionnaire de danse.* Paris, 1787.

Dodworth, Allen. *Dancing and Its Relations to Education and Social Life.* New York, 1885.

Gourdoux-Daux, J. H. *Principes et notions élémentaires sur l'art de la danse.* 2d ed. Paris, 1811. Translated by Victor Guillou as *Elements and Principles of the Art of Dancing.* Philadelphia, 1817.

Grove, Lilly M. *Dancing.* London, 1895.

Magny, Claude-Marc. *Principes de chorégraphie, suivis d'un traité de la cadence.* Paris, 1765.

Richardson, Philip J. S. *The Social Dances of the Nineteenth Century in England.* London, 1960.

Sachs, Curt. *World History of the Dance.* Translated by Bessie Schonberg. New York, 1937.

Wilson, Thomas. *The Quadrille and Cotillion Panorama.* 2d ed. London, 1822.

DESMOND F. STROBEL

QUICKSTEP. *See* Ballroom Dance Competition.

RÁBAI, MIKLÓS (born 18 April 1921 in Békéscsaba, Hungary, died 18 August 1974 in Budapest), Hungarian choreographer. Rábai was one of the most important figures in creating the style of Hungarian theatrical folk dance. His name and activities are allied with the Hungarian State Folk Ensemble, first as its founding choreographer, later its artistic leader, and finally its director.

A self-taught artist and secondary-school teacher in his native town between 1945 and 1948, Rábai began collecting folk dances and choreographing them for his pupils. At the First National Folk Dance Competition in 1949, the centenary of the Hungarian War of Independence, he won first prize, which launched him on his professional career. He was a teacher in the folk dance department of the Budapest School for Physical Education from 1948 to 1950 as well as leader and choreographer of the university's amateur folk dance group and later that of the National Youth League. His success earned him a place as artistic leader and choreographer of the Hungarian State Folk Ensemble.

Rábai's creative activities were most intense in the 1950s; he exerted considerable artistic influence on the first decade of the development of Hungarian theatrical folk dance. This was a most fortunate historic moment when the prevailing opinions encountered a newborn art form and the personal style of a creative artist. Rábai was inherently attracted to the natural, the simple, and the harmonious: his was a childishly open-eyed, naive interest in the world, direct and jocular. This is what brought him close to folk art and enabled him to shape it into theatrical art. His works embody features that are conspicuous in a substantial part of the Hungarian folk dance tradition: intensity and lightness, prowess and martial bearing, naturalness, and a diversity of cheerfulness, forms, and rhythms.

Rábai's best works fall into two major groups. The first comprises short concert dances of a striking structure, relying on some type of folk dance, such as *Bottle Dance, Three Jumps, Pontozó,* and *Lads' Dance from Györgyfalva.* The others are one-act, epic, or lyric dance plays, some of a comic nature and all relying on some folk custom, such as *Wedding at Ecser, Evening in the Spinnery,* or *Evenings at Békés* (in the last the choir and the orchestra also play a creative role).

In a career spanning nearly a quarter of a century, Rábai arranged dances inspired by tragic and comic folk ballads *(Barcsai's Lover, Kata Kádár, Jóka's Devil)* and by dramatic moments in twentieth-century Hungarian history *(Ballad about Latinca, Day Is Breaking, Roads);* he also composed a three-act fairy-tale play. He created several works based on the folklore of Hungary's ethnic minorities. His productions were regularly filmed, beginning in 1954, first for the movies and then for television. A film about Rábai was produced in 1971.

[*See also* Hungarian State Folk Ensemble.]

BIBLIOGRAPHY

Koegler, Horst. "Magyar néptáncművészet" and "Rábai, Miklós." In *Balettlexikon.* Budapest, 1977.

Körtvélyes, Géza. "Korszerű tendenciák a magyar táncművészetben 1957–1977 között." *Tánctudományi tanulmányok* (1978–1979).

Vojnich, Iván, and Gyula Várady. "In Memoriam Miklós Rábai." *Hungarian Dance News,* nos. 5–6 (1984): 3–4.

GÉZA KÖRTVÉLYES

RADHA. Solo dance suite. Choreography, libretto, scenery, and costume: Ruth St. Denis. Music: Léo Delibes. First performance: 28 January 1906, New York Theater, New York. Dancer: Ruth St. Denis.

Radha, subtitled *The Mystic Dance of the Five Senses,* was Ruth St. Denis's first major choreography. She designed her own set and scanty, jeweled costume; the music was excerpts from Léo Delibes's opera *Lakmé.* The dance was set in a Hindu temple where an idol of the goddess Radha (St. Denis) sat in meditation on a pedestal. Temple priests entered to pay homage. Slowly the idol stirred to life, rose from her pedestal, and descended to a semicircular space created by her waiting priests.

There she performed "The Dance of the Five Senses," struggling against the temptation of sensual pleasures. In "The Dance of Sight," to the Persian dance music of *Lakmé,* Radha held a rope of pearls and skimmed the stage in birdlike *bourreés.* She became playful in "The Dance of Hearing." To Delibes's "Rektah" she held tinkling bells and twitched her hips. Crushing a rope of marigolds to her breast, in "The Dance of Smell" she twined the garland around her body as she waltzed and *bourréed* to "Terana." As the music shifted into minor key, she exchanged her flower rope for a clay bowl, which she drained, then flung from her as she whirled in intoxication—"The Dance of Taste." The work culminated in "The Dance of Touch" to "Mallika's Theme." Sitting on the stage, St. Denis began to caress her own body until "The Delirium of the Senses" overcame her. She rose to whirl in a nautch dance that climaxed in her collapse as the stage lights dimmed. With the dawn of a faint light, a chastened Radha rose and drew a lotus blossom from inside her bodice; retreating to her pedestal, she resumed her posture of serene meditation.

Radha received its public premiere on 28 January 1906 at the New York Theater in New York City. It later moved to Proctor's Twenty-third Street Theater, where it languished until a group of art patrons and socialites sponsored it in a society matinee on 22 March 1906 at the Hudson Theater, a performance that made St. Denis famous. A study in sensuality, *Radha* was also a morality tale that extolled self-restraint. Viewers might enjoy its eroticism, secure in the knowledge that virtue would overcome vice. Reviewers noticed its paradoxes. "It is consecrated to the senses, but it is higher," wrote Hugo von Hofmannsthal. "Although her body is that of a woman divinely planned," puzzled a *Boston Herald* reviewer, "there is no atmosphere of sex about her."

St. Denis, aware of the American public's taste for sensuality laced with virtue, mined *Radha* for the remainder of her career. The dance remained in her repertory during the Denishawn era. In 1941 she revived it at Jacob's Pillow in Becket, Massachusetts. John Martin, writing in the *New York Times,* found that *Radha* remained "an extremely well-built piece of theatre art, excellently composed, full of pictorial beauty and variety, and, above all, completely original."

[*See also the entry on St. Denis.*]

BIBLIOGRAPHY

McDonagh, Don, ed. *The Complete Guide to Modern Dance.* New York, 1976.

Shelton, Suzanne. *Divine Dancer: A Biography of Ruth St. Denis.* Garden City, N.Y., 1981.

Sherman, Jane. "Who's St. Denis?" *Attitude* 8 (Fall 1992): 12–17.

SUZANNE SHELTON

RADICE, ATTILIA (born 8 January 1914 in Taranto, died 14 September 1980 in Capranica, Viterbo), Italian dancer, choreographer, and teacher. Radice entered the ballet school of the Teatro alla Scala in Milan at a very early age. She studied with Angelina Gini and later with Enrico Cecchetti, remaining a devoted pupil of the latter until his death in November 1928. She completed her studies in 1932 with Cia Fornaroli.

Radice debuted at La Scala in Léonide Massine's *Belkis* (1932). After her appointment as *prima ballerina* at La Scala, she demonstrated her ability in ballets linked to the tradition of the eighteenth century—Franco Vittadini's *Vecchio Milano,* Romualdo Marenco's *Sieba,* and Riccardo Pick-Mangiagalli's *Carillon Magico.* In 1934 she danced the role of Mugnaia in a revival of Diaghilev's production of *Le Tricorne* rechoreographed by Lizzie Maudrik. In 1935 she danced with Serge Lifar in Michel Fokine's *Le Spectre de la Rose* at the Teatro Argentina in Rome.

Radice was named *prima ballerina assoluta* of the Rome Opera Ballet in 1935 and retained the position until 1957, when she became the director of the Rome Opera Theater's ballet school. She participated with the opera company in a number of foreign tours to Austria, Germany, Yugoslavia, Spain, and South America, as well as in Bologna, Venice, and Turin. Radice's repertory was vast, ranging from the classics (Petipa's *The Sleeping Beauty,* in Boris Romanoff's revival of 1954) to creations by the choreographer Aurelio Milloss, of which she was an intense and expressive interpreter (*Boléro, Petrouchka, The Creatures of Prometheus, The Rites of Spring, The Prodigal Son, Orpheus, Mirandolina, The Miraculous Mandarin,* and many others).

In a period of twenty-five years Radice carved out a place for herself as one of the best Italian classical dancers, with a rare temperament and remarkable expressive qualities. She gave the best of herself with Milloss, and the choreographer showed her special gifts to their best advantage: musicality, expressiveness, strength, and elegance. As a teacher Radice was a treasure house of the

Cecchetti method, which remained the cornerstone of her academic training, particularly the *legato* quality of the adagios and the virtuosity of the allegros. Dancers now prominent in directing ballet in Italy, notably Elisabetta Terabust, have benefited from her mastery.

BIBLIOGRAPHY

Handley-Taylor, Geoffrey. "The Ballet in Italy." *Dance Magazine* (March 1948): 21–23.

"Radice, Attilia." In *Enciclopedia dello spettacolo.* Rome, 1954–.

Testa, Alberto. "Radice, Attila." In *Dizionario gremese della danza e del balletto.* Rome, 1995.

Valerio, Leone. "Le danzatrici." In *L'illustrazione italiana: La donna italiana nel novecento.* Milan, 1946.

ARCHIVE. Walter Toscanini Collection of Research Materials in Dance, New York Public Library for the Performing Arts.

ALBERTO TESTA
Translated from Italian

RADIO CITY MUSIC HALL. Essentially a motion picture theater, Radio City Music Hall, located in the heart of New York's Rockefeller Center, was, in its heyday, famous for its exciting stage spectacles and its world-renowned precision dancers, the Rockettes. The massive theater—the world's largest—attracted tourists from all over the world, packing in five million visitors each year.

The building, designed by Donald Deskey, seats sixty-two hundred. It is a masterpiece of Art Deco architectural style, with clean, geometric lines highlighted by gleaming bronze and steel and a beautifully proportioned vaulted foyer containing a twenty-nine-foot cylindrical chandelier.

The building opened on 27 December 1932 as a super-vaudeville house. Among the opening night acts were Harald Kreutzberg, Patricia Bowman, and Martha Graham. Two weeks later the policy changed; movies were shown followed by forty-minute stage shows, called "presentations," that rivaled Broadway musicals and ranged from modern revues to grand opera pageantry and Hollywood-like extravaganzas. The theater staff included a seventy-five-piece symphonic orchestra conducted by Erno Rapee, a glee club, a corps de ballet, and of course the famous Rockettes.

As produced by Leon Leonidoff, a typical presentation began with the rising of the white and gold Wurlitzer organ from below the stage. The orchestra would then ascend from the orchestra pit to stage level and begin a classical overture, afterward descending back to pit level in order to accompany the rest of the stage presentation, which included a ballet sequence, the chorus, acrobats, knockabout comics, circus-style acts, and the precision dancing line, the Rockettes. The finale would feature each of these components.

Russell Markert, originator of the Rockettes, elaborated on the routines of the British Tiller Girls, the original

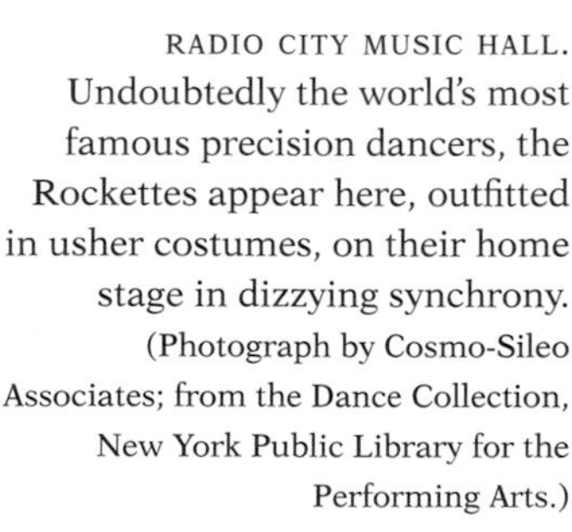

RADIO CITY MUSIC HALL. Undoubtedly the world's most famous precision dancers, the Rockettes appear here, outfitted in usher costumes, on their home stage in dizzying synchrony. (Photograph by Cosmo-Sileo Associates; from the Dance Collection, New York Public Library for the Performing Arts.)

modern precision dance troupe, founded by John Tiller in 1901. Markert formed a line of tall women who could perform multiple high kicks in unison. The Rockettes consisted of forty-seven dancers, although only thirty-six appeared at one time. Each dancer worked three weeks, then had one week off. The corps de ballet numbered forty, with thirty-two in the dancing group. [*See* Precision Dancing.]

The vastness of the Music Hall stage wore out dancers, because sweeping steps and large movements were needed to cover it. Each routine was planned to elicit applause at the climax, when the Rockettes, lined up at the back of the stage, did high kicks on every step. Markert determined that sixteen kicks were sufficient: the applause invariably came between the eighth and twelfth kick.

Ballet presentations ran the gamut of styles from ethnic-inspired spectacles to the purely classical, with an occasional novelty show in which dancers performed as whirling teacups, fireflies, or even imaginative cartoon figures.

Representative of the stage shows was "To the Arts," which ran from 8 February to 19 March 1962. It opened with a Greek ballet extravaganza, followed by six pianists who played Tchaikovsky on pianos that whirled on a revolving stage on top of another revolving stage. The show also included a deadpan juggler and the Music Hall Glee Club with dance illustrations. The finale included the entire company, with dancers performing on several levels, the trademark of unison dances. Spectacular effects through the use of lights, properties, and spaced arrangements were all part of the Music Hall format.

In 1974 soaring costs and changing public tastes led to mounting losses for Radio City Music Hall. The orchestra was reduced from seventy to forty-five, the ballet company was disbanded, and the number of new stage productions was cut to five or six per year. Finding it difficult to book quality movie programs for the family trade, Music Hall management moved toward the presentation of one-shot events, industrial shows, rock concerts, ice shows, boxing matches, and limited-run productions such as George Gershwin's folk opera *Porgy and Bess.*

Besides Russell Markert, Leon Leonidoff, and Erno Rapee, others who have been associated with Radio City Music Hall productions include Florence Rogge, Geoffrey Holder, Gene Snyder, Marc Platt, and Peter Gennaro. Former Rockettes and former ballet corps members include Gloria Steinem, Nora Kaye, Melissa Hayden, Joan MacCracken, Vera-Ellen, and Lucille Bremer.

BIBLIOGRAPHY

Ansen, David. "Radio City Redux." *Newsweek* (11 June 1979).

Como, William. "How High the Corn at Radio City." *Dance Magazine* 40 (August 1966): 36–40.

Kroll, Jack. "Save the Music Hall." *Newsweek* (16 January 1978).

"Marc Platt: Guest from the West." *Dance Magazine* 36 (April 1962): 36–37.

"Radio City Music Hall: World's Largest Theatre." *Life* (26 April 1943).

Ruby, Michael. "Radio City's Last Kick." *Newsweek* (30 August 1976).

"Trouble in Paradise." *Newsweek* (5 October 1971).

"The World's Biggest Playhouse Opens." *Literary Digest* (14 January 1933).

Robert D. Moulton

RADIUS, ALEXANDRA (born 3 July 1942 in Amsterdam), Dutch ballet dancer. Alexandra Radius received her basic ballet training at the Nel Roos academy. In 1957, at the age of fifteen, she joined the Netherlands Ballet. She left in 1959 to follow Benjamin Harkarvy into the Netherlands Dance Theater. There she met her future husband, Han Ebbelaar, who also became her regular dance partner. During the nine seasons she danced with the company, she starred in ten ballets created by Hans van Manen, among them *Metaforen, Symphony in Three Movements,* and *Vijf Schetsen.* The last brought her and her husband to American Ballet Theatre in 1968, first as soloists and later as principals. There she proved her mettle in the full-length classical ballets *Giselle* and *Coppélia.* In 1970 the couple joined the National Ballet in Amsterdam as principals.

Radius was a versatile dancer, shining in parts such as Giselle or Aurora as much as in the contemporary works of van Manen, Rudi van Dantzig, or George Balanchine. The first Dutch ballerina to win international fame, Radius was regularly invited for guest performances abroad and was Rudolf Nureyev's partner in several ballets.

In 1975 she and her husband were given the royal distinction of Knights of the Orde van Oranje-Nassau; in 1980 they were awarded the Silver Medal of the City of Amsterdam. In 1983 Radius received the first Golden Dance Prize instituted by the Veremiging van Schouwburg en Concert Directies (Society of Theater and Concert Directors).

At the celebration of her thirty-year jubilee in 1987, Radius was promoted to Officer of the Orde van Oranje-Nassau, a high royal distinction. Apart from dancing with the National Ballet, Radius and her husband toured the Netherlands with their own program of classical and contemporary pas de deux. In June 1990 Radius retired from dancing. Again she was given a high royal distinction, the seldom-awarded Eremedaille voor Kunst en Wetenschappen in de Huisorde van Oranje.

BIBLIOGRAPHY

Dantzig, Rudi van. *Voorbÿgegaan.* Haarlem, 1980.

Huf, Emmy. *Dancing.* Haarlem, 1979.

Rietstap, Ine. *De Ballerina, een Tÿdsbeeld.* Bloemendaal, 1990.

Utrecht, Luuk. *Het Nationale Ballet 25 jaar: De Geschiedenis van Het Nationale Ballet van 1961 tot 1986.* Amsterdam, 1987.

Ine Rietstap

RĀGA is the generic term in North and South India for tone systems and for melodic theory and practice; in Hindi it is *rāg* and in Tamil *rāgam*. The term first appears in the tenth-century Brhaddesi, though its concepts have roots in ancient Vedic chanting. *Rāga* is derived from the Sanskrit word *rānji*, meaning to color with emotion. This is reflected in extramusical *rāga* characteristics, such as moods and times for use.

Musically, a *rāga* is a scalar-melody form, since it includes aspects of both. Theoretically, a *rāga* is a combination of intervals *(svara)* in two four-note (tetrachord) units that create a scale *(grama)*. There are three smaller, different sized intervals *(śruti)* that are combined to form the actual intervals of the scale. Thousands of combinations are possible but seventeenth-century South Indian theorists grouped tetrachord combinations into seventy-two basic *meḷakarta*. Twentieth-century North Indians created a framework *(thāt)* of thirty-two scales.

Melodic aspects of a *rāga* include various ascending and descending order of scales and possible repeats or playing of pitches in irregular order. *Rāga* have a ground tone *(sa)*. In North India, the terms *vādī* and *samvādī* mean the two tones (one of which may or may not be *sa*) that are most important in a given *rāga*. Ornamentation *(gamaka)* on specific pitches is also essential to a *rāga*. Since *rāga* contain more sonic information than do Western scales, South Asian instruments and musical forms are equally different; they present music that accommodates this greater range of information.

Rāgas were often illustrated in Indian miniature painting, which, influenced by Persian models, spread from Rajputana (modern Rajasthan) throughout North India in the Mughal period, beginning about 1550. Elaborate personified renderings of *rāgas* were a popular theme, drawing on three traditional theories of *rāga:* first, the time theory, which assigns each *rāga* to a time of day, and in many cases, a season as well; second, the idea that each *rāga* embodies one or more of the *rasas*, the essential emotions of Indian esthetics; and third, an ancient, somewhat fanciful scheme for classifying *rāgas* in a patrilineal system, with six principal male *rāgas*, each of which has several wives called *rāginīs* (secondary *rāgas*), and many *putras* (children, or sons—derivative *rāgas*).

RĀGA. In this painting (Rajasthan, c.1610–1620), *rāga* Megh, the quintessential *rāga* of the rainy season—associated with hope, new life, and romance—is imagined as a handsome, virile man dancing outdoors with a female consort in pouring rain, accompanied by a group of female musicians who play *bīn* (stick zither), *kānsya* (hand cymbals), and flute. A flock of cranes flies off before the rolling storm clouds above. (Reprinted from Sir Leigh Ashton, *The Art of India and Pakistan*, New York, 1948, fig. 401.)

BIBLIOGRAPHY

Daniélou, Alain. *The Ragas of Northern Indian Music.* 2d ed. New Delhi, 1991.

Jairazbhoy, N. A. *The Rāgs of North Indian Music.* Middletown, Conn., 1971.

Kaufmann, Walter. *The Ragas of North India.* Bloomington, 1968.

Kaufmann, Walter. *The Ragas of South India.* Bloomington, 1976.

Viswanathan, T. "Rāga Ālāpana in South Indian Music." Ph.D. diss., Wesleyan University, 1974.

Wade, Bonnie C. *Music in India: The Classical Traditions.* Englewood Cliffs, N.J., 1978.

Widdess, Richard. *The Ragas of Early Indian Music.* Oxford, 1995.

WILLIAM P. MALM
Amended by Christopher Caines

RAGINI DEVI (Esther Sherman; born 18 August 1897 in Petroskey, Michigan; died 23 January 1982 in Englewood, New Jersey), American proponent of Indian dance. When Sherman married Ramlal B. Bajpai in 1921, she entered a social circle of young expatriates from India. Enthralled by their culture, she studied music, dance, and Sanskrit and began to perform in informal dance programs, which led to public concerts in 1924. Billed as Ragini, she toured the United States with her "Hindu" dances, accompanied by Indian musicians. Her book *Nritanjali*, published in 1928, was the first book in English on the subject of Indian dance.

Ragini Devi arrived in Madras, India, in 1930. That year she studied classical *bharata nāṭyam* with Mylapore Gauri Amma, gave birth to her only daughter, Indrani, and studied with eminent master teachers in several classical dance genres. She was the first woman to study *kathakaḷi* with Ramunni Nair, at Kerala Kalamandalam, and the first woman to perform it on the professional stage in India and abroad; she was also the first to present lectures about and programs of India's various classical dance styles. Her presentations were appreciated by many important people, including the poet Rabindranath Tagore, who sent a note saying he "experienced a thrill of delight" on seeing a program in his honor at Shantaniketan, his cultural institute.

In 1938 Ragini Devi presented a series of lectures at the University of London and performed with her *kathakaḷi* artists in London and Paris. In 1941 she established the Indian Dance Theatre in New York, where she presented her own repertory and provided a showcase for many ethnic artists. A Rockefeller Foundation grant enabled her to return to India in 1949 to pursue research for her second book, *Dance Dialects of India,* which was finally published there in 1971; her family released a revised edition in 1990. She also gave solo concerts in India until her return to the United States in 1978.

During her retirement at the Actor's Fund Home in New Jersey, Ragini Devi worked on a book devoted to Indian music. This work, as yet unpublished, was funded by the Ford Foundation.

Ragini Devi's last public appearance was at New York University in 1979; joined by her daughter Indrani and her granddaughter Sukanya, she celebrated three generations of the tradition she had begun. That a foreigner was respected by Indians as an authority on the subject of Indian dance demonstrates her effective revival of interest in dance within India as well as her successful introduction of Indian dances to the Western world. Official recognition came posthumously in 1982 when Central Sangeet Natak Akademi of New Delhi presented a Scroll of Honor to Indrani in her mother's memory.

BIBLIOGRAPHY

Meri, La. "Encounters with Dance Immortals: Balasaraswati and Ragini Devi." *Arabesque* 11 (November–December 1985): 12–13.

Misra, Susheela. *Some Dancers of India.* New Delhi, 1992.

Ragini Devi. *Dance Dialects of India.* 2d rev. ed. Delhi, 1990. Includes an appreciation by Rabindranath Tagore.

Sri Ragini. *Nritanjali: An Introduction to Hindu Dancing.* New York, 1928.

LUISE ELCANESS SCRIPPS

RAINER, YVONNE (born 24 November 1934 in San Francisco), dancer, choreographer, and a founding member of Judson Dance Theater and the Grand Union. Yvonne Rainer attended San Francisco City College, studied acting in San Francisco and New York, and studied dance with various teachers, including Anna Halprin, Merce Cunningham, James Waring, and Mia Slavenska. She studied composition with Robert Dunn and danced in the companies of Waring and Edith Stephen. She was one of the founding members of the Judson Dance Theater and the Grand Union.

RAINER. The choreographer in a performance of her *Trio A,* in Portland, Oregon, 1973. (Photograph courtesy of Yvonne Rainer.)

Rainer was one of the most prolific and polemical of the postmodern choreographers in the 1960s and early 1970s, after which she turned from dance to cinema. In her dances of the early 1960s, Rainer's style was eclectic, theatrical, even surrealistic. Her favored method was juxtaposition of radically diverse elements, sometimes by chance. She also experimented with spontaneous determination, a combination of chance and improvisation. She combined movements ranging from dance steps and gestures to quirky motions, like twiddling the fingers in front of the face, to ordinary movements. She also used sounds, from random noise to language, in her dances.

An important turning point in Rainer's choreography came with the 1964 performance of *Room Service*, a collaboration with sculptor Charles Ross, based on a follow-the-leader structure. The task-oriented execution and the manipulation of objects seemed to strip the movements of their expressive qualities. In 1965, continuing her investigation into reductive dance, Rainer wrote her famous manifesto, which began "NO to spectacle, no to virtuosity, no to transformations and magic and make-believe, no to the glamour and transcendency of the star image. . . ."

With *Trio A* (1966), Rainer created a paradigmatic statement of the aesthetic goals of the analytic phase of postmodern dance. The workmanlike style of performance was achieved with pure movement and without props. Sharing the concerns of the minimalist sculptors, Rainer did away with phrasing, development and climax, variation, character, performance, variety, virtuosic feats, and the fully extended body, substituting energy, equality of emphasis, "found" movement, equality of parts, repetition of discrete events, neutral performance, task or tasklike activity, singular action, event, or tone, and human scale. *Trio A* set a dominant style for postmodern dance for the next fifteen years.

Trio A was the nucleus of *The Mind Is a Muscle* (1966), an evening in eight sections and nine interludes of sound (including movie music, a taped conversation, and six minutes of silence). Notes to a 1968 performance of that work read, in part:

> If my rage at the impoverishment of ideas, narcissism and disguised sexual exhibitionism of most dancing can be considered puritan moralizing, it is also true that I love the body—its actual weight, mass, and unenhanced physicality. It is my overall concern to reveal people as they are engaged in various kinds of activities—alone, with each other, with objects—and to weight the quality of the human body toward that of objects and away from the superstylization of the dancer.

Between 1968 and 1970, Rainer made several works that were collages of sections of old works, new choreography, slides, and sound, often incorporating large groups of both professional and nonprofessional performers. In *Continuous Project—Altered Daily* (1970), parts of the performance process, such as rehearsal, invention, learning, and polished performance, took place during the performance itself.

Political concerns surfaced more directly in Rainer's works of the early 1970s, such as WAR and her contribution to the Judson Flag Show, a group protest exhibition. After a study trip to India in 1971, she became more interested in plot and narrative. The result was such dance/performance works as *Grand Union Dreams* (1971) and *Inner Appearances* (1972).

Rainer has made seven feature-length films. *Lives of Performers* (1972) incorporated dance material from previous live performances. With *Film about A Woman Who . . .* (1974), she left the dance arena to become a full-time filmmaker, occasionally returning to reconstruct works from the past. Her other films are *Kristina Talking Pictures* (1976), *Journeys from Berlin/1971* (1980), *The Man Who Envied Women* (1985), *Privilege* (1991), and *Murder and Murder* (1996).

BIBLIOGRAPHY

Banes, Sally. *Terpsichore in Sneakers: Post-Modern Dance.* Boston, 1980. Includes a bibliography.

Banes, Sally. *Democracy's Body: Judson Dance Theater, 1962–64.* Ann Arbor, Mich., 1983.

Carroll, Noël. "Post-Modern Dance and Expression." In *Philosophical Essays on Dance,* edited by Gordon Fancher and Gerald Myers. New York, 1981.

Goldberg, Marianne. "The Body, Discourse, and *The Man Who Envied Women.*" *Women and Performance* 3.2 (1987–1988): 97–102.

Foster, Susan Leigh. *Reading Dancing: Bodies and Subjects in Contemporary American Dance.* Berkeley, 1986.

Rainer, Yvonne. "Some Retrospective Notes on a Dance for 10 People and 12 Mattresses." *Drama Review* 10 (Winter 1965): 168–178.

Rainer, Yvonne. *Work, 1961–1973.* Halifax, N.S., 1974.

Rainer, Yvonne. "Looking Myself in the Mouth." *October,* no. 17 (Summer 1981).

Rainer, Yvonne. "Ages of the Avant-Garde." *Performing Arts Journal* 16 (January 1994): 33–35.

SALLY BANES

RAKE'S PROGRESS, THE. Ballet in six scenes. Choreography: Ninette de Valois. Music: Gavin Gordon. Libretto: Gavin Gordon. Scenery and costumes: Rex Whistler. First performance: 20 May 1935, Sadler's Wells Theatre, London, Vic-Wells Ballet. Principals: Walter Gore (The Rake), Alicia Markova (The Betrayed Girl), Ursula Moreton (The Dancer), Harold Turner (The Dancing Master and The Gentleman with a Rope).

Like de Valois's *Job* (based on illustrations by William Blake), *Bar aux Folies-Bergère* (from Edouard Manet), and *The Prospect before Us* (from Thomas Rowlandson), *The Rake's Progress* was derived from a pictorial source—the series of paintings by William Hogarth (1697–1764) in the Soane Museum in London. Gordon's libretto reduces the eight episodes depicted by Hogarth to six, tracing the young man's "progress" from newly acquired prosperity through dissipation, debauchery, and debt to madness. The pure young woman he has betrayed remains faithful to him and tries in vain to save him. Cyril W. Beaumont wrote (in his *Complete Book of Ballets*) that the piece "is not so much a ballet as a mime play with dances," but in the gambling scene, for example, the pantomime is so formalized and rhythmically structured as to make its effect as dance rather than as drama. *The Rake's Progress* was an early example of the aptitude of British dancers for characterization and ensemble playing.

Gordon's score is a theatrically effective pastiche of eighteenth-century forms. Whistler's drop curtain depicts a street near Covent Garden in the manner of an engraving; the various interiors—brothel, gaming house, and Bedlam—are simple and somber. (For the revival at the Royal Opera House in 1946, Oliver Messel designed a false proscenium to enclose the original sets.)

Both interpreters of the leading roles, Gore and Markova, left the Vic-Wells Ballet soon after the first performance, to be succeeded by Robert Helpmann and Elizabeth Miller. Subsequent interpreters have included, as the Rake, Alan Carter, Harold Turner, Alexander Grant, David Blair, David Poole, David Wall, and Stephen Jefferies; as the Girl, Margot Fonteyn, Julia Farron, Violetta Elvin, Maryon Lane, and Margaret Barbieri. Also notable in the original cast was Turner, in the contrasting dual roles of the elegant Dancing Master and the sinister madman with a rope. The ballet has been frequently revived by both Royal Ballet companies and the Royal Ballet School, and has also been staged by companies in Munich in 1956, Turkey in 1969, and Zurich in 1976.

Another short ballet on the same subject, *The Rake,* with choreography by Léonide Massine (who danced the title role), music by Roger Quilter, and designs by William Nicholson, was included in Charles B. Cochran's revue *On with the Dance,* first performed at the London Pavilion on 30 April 1925.

BIBLIOGRAPHY

Barnes, Clive. "Ballet Perspectives No. 16: *The Rake's Progress." Dance and Dancers* (April 1960): 20–23.

Sorley Walker, Kathrine. *Ninette de Valois: Idealist without Illusions.* London, 1987.

DAVID VAUGHAN

RALOV, BØRGE (Børge Petersen; born 26 July 1908 in Copenhagen, died 17 December 1981 in Copenhagen), Danish dancer, choreographer, and teacher. Ralov entered the Royal Danish Ballet School in Copenhagen in 1918, at age ten, and made his debut with the Royal Danish Ballet in 1927, when he was not yet twenty. In 1933 he was promoted to *solodanser* (soloist, or principal dancer); in 1934 he was appointed ballet instructor; in 1942 he was named *førstesolodanser* (equivalent to *premier danseur*); and in 1945 he became a teacher at the ballet school attached to the Royal Theater. Long before his retirement from the stage in 1957, he was generally recognized as the foremost Danish male ballet dancer of his time, equally skilled in the Bournonville and the international style.

In 1942, Ralov was the first dancer since August Bournonville to receive the title of *førstesolodanser* at the Royal Theater. In 1931, George Balanchine had offered him and Margot Lander an international career, but they remained loyal to the Royal Danish Ballet. Ralov covered a broader spectrum than other Danish male dancers. He adapted his body to the character, giving equally impressive performances in the old Danish repertory and in modern ballets. His sensual quality led the management to consider him less fit for princely roles, but Alexandre Volinine chose him as Albrecht when he staged *Giselle* for the Royal Theater in 1946. Ralov's dramatic interpretation was unforgettable, depicting both the superficial and the complex sides of the character.

In regard to the international repertory, Ralov's interpretation of the title role in *Petrouchka* was perhaps the best in Europe. Harald Lander and Ralov worked on it daily for nine months before the premiere in 1937. Ralov performed the role 182 times.

In the Danish system, the title *ballet instructor* is next to that of ballet master. It involves the responsibility of restaging older works, choreographing *divertissements* for operas and plays, and composing new ballets. The title was given to Ralov for his first ballet, *Enken i Spejlet* (The Widow in the Mirror), premiered 20 November 1934. The book and scenography were created by Kjeld Abell, who had earlier designed for Balanchine's productions in Copenhagen (1930/31). *Enken i Spejlet* is the first successful Danish ballet to depart from the tradition of August Bournonville. It was a satire of *petit-bourgeois* family life and a homage to the working class, but most of all it dealt with the liberation of a woman. The work was performed sixty-four times, the last on 26 May 1952.

In February 1939, Ralov staged Carl Nielsen's symphony *The Four Temperaments,* composed in 1902. His choreographic vocabulary was developing considerably. It was clear that Ralov was able to give movement a personal touch, especially when he worked with contemporary music, as in *The Soldier's Tale* (1946, music by Igor Stravinsky) or *Jeanne d'Arc* (1954, music by Arthur Honegger).

Ralov staged seven ballets for the Royal Theater, including, in addition to those already mentioned, a ballet on a story by Hans Christian Andersen, *Tolv med Posten,* with Knudåge Riisager's music, 21 February 1942; and his last ballet, *Kurtisanen,* which featured the debut of Niels Viggo Bentzon as a ballet composer, on 19 December 1953. Ralov worked during a period when the resources of the theater were very limited. As a result, he created three or four ballets with music by leading Danish composers that never had the opportunity to be staged.

In 1950, Ralov created the first Danish television ballet, *Video,* and became a consultant for Danish state television. He introduced the first successful television ballet in Denmark, Elsa-Marianne von Rosen's *Helios.*

BIBLIOGRAPHY

Anderson, Jack, and George Dorris. "A Conversation with Svend Kragh-Jacobsen." *Ballet Review* 5.4 (1975–1976): 1–20.

Haven, Mogens von. *The Royal Danish Ballet.* Copenhagen, 1964.

Kragh-Jacobsen, Svend. *The Royal Danish Ballet.* Copenhagen and London, 1955.

ALLAN FRIDERICIA

RALOV, KIRSTEN (Kirsten Laura Gnatt; born 26 March 1922 in Baden, Austria), Austrian-born Danish dancer and ballet director. Ralov's career was closely linked to the works of August Bournonville. She entered the ballet school of the Royal Theater in Copenhagen in 1929. Her main teachers there were Harald Lander and Valborg Borchsenius. She had her children's debut as Fanny in Bournonville's *Konservatoriet* (The Dancing School) in 1933, but her professional debut was in the pas de trois in Bournonville's *La Ventana* in 1941; Hans Beck, who was attending the performance, prophesied a great future for her as a Bournonville interpreter. Ralov danced the leading parts of Teresina in *Napoli*, Eleonora in *Kermesse in Bruges*, Birthe in *A Folk Tale*, and a naval cadet and later Rosita in *Far from Denmark, or A Costume Ball on Board*, as well as many interpolated solos.

Ralov and her husband, Fredbjørn Bjørnsson, were among the first to dance the pas de deux from Bournonville's *Flower Festival in Genzano* before an international audience when, in the early 1950s, they traveled abroad with a little group of Danish dancers guided by Inge Sand. In later years Ralov taught and staged Bournonville ballets all over the world, including the Bolshoi Theater in 1989. At the 1979 Bournonville festival in Copenhagen she presented *Napoli* and *A Folk Tale*. Also in 1979, she published in New York—in French terminology as well as Labanotation and Benesh notation—the Bournonville classes, a training system established by his students in the 1890s.

Ralov became a member of the Royal Danish Ballet in 1940 and was principal dancer from 1942 to 1962. The turning point in the early part of her career was her role as Princess Sugarsweet in Harald Lander's *Land of Milk and Honey* in 1942. Her beauty was emphasized in her portrayals of several ingenue roles, such as the Street Dancer in Léonide Massine's *Le Beau Danube*, but she also combined her beauty with an ironic wit, as in her role as the Ballerina in *Petrouchka*, or with a cool eroticism, as in her handling of Myrtha in *Giselle* and of Aurora in *Aurora's Wedding*. Ralov's technique was clean and elegant, her dancing extremely musical. After retiring as a dancer she became ballet mistress in the Royal Theater and from 1978 to 1988 served as vice-director. She retired in 1988.

[*See also* Royal Danish Ballet.]

BIBLIOGRAPHY

Anderson, Jack, and George Dorris. "A Conversation with Svend Kragh-Jacobsen." *Ballet Review* 5.4 (1975–1976): 1–20.

Aschengreen, Erik. "Ralov, Kirsten." In *Dansk biografisk leksikon*. 3d ed. Copenhagen, 1979—.

Fanger, Iris M. "The Royal Danish Ballet's Kirsten Ralov." *Dance Magazine* (November 1979): 71–77.

Ralov, Kirsten, ed. *The Bournonville School*. 4 vols. New York, 1979.

Terry, Walter. "The Bournonville School: An Interview with Kirsten Ralov." In *The Royal Danish Ballet and Bournonville*. Copenhagen, 1979.

Waren, Florence. "Petipa and Bournonville." *Performing Arts Journal* 2 (Winter 1978): 85–93. Report of a seminar with Gusev and Kirsten Ralov.

ERIK ASCHENGREEN

RAMBERT, MARIE (Cyvia Rambam; Myriam Ramberg/Rambach; born 20 February 1888 in Warsaw, died 12 June 1982 in London), Polish-British dancer, teacher, inspiration for choreographers, and company director. The daughter of a Warsaw bookseller, Cyvia Rambam grew up in a book-loving household (her mother, of Russian origin, shared her father's passion for books) and from an early age was encouraged to read voraciously. Warsaw at the time was under Russian domination, and Russian was the language of the household. For various political reasons, members of the family changed their names. Before long, Cyvia Rambam became Myriam Ramberg; later she settled on Marie Rambert. She was always known as Mim to her friends.

Rambert maintained that her mother once said that she burst into the world "kicking her legs and speaking six languages at once"—a delightful exaggeration that was nevertheless to become true as she grew older. She was seldom still and was always talking; her passion for literature spurred her to master languages (for which she had a gift) so she could read favorite authors in their native tongues. Her first enthusiasm was for Russian writers (Aleksandr Pushkin, above all), but by the time she left the High School for Girls in Warsaw she had read most of Racine, Corneille, Victor Hugo, Schiller, and Goethe. When she settled in England and mastered English, she found new joy in Shakespeare and claimed to know no fewer than thirty-one of his sonnets by heart. She was always ready with an apt quotation—one of the joys of her conversation was the breadth of her knowledge of literature, and she attributed her penchant for reading in part to the chronic insomnia she had inherited from her parents.

At school Rambert learned some rudimentary dances from a teacher, named Slowacki, who had been at the Warsaw Opera. She adored dancing and movement but at that time had no interest in classical ballet. She had, however, seen and fervently admired the dancing of Isadora Duncan.

A lively and intelligent girl, Rambert was also interested in student politics, and her enthusiasm for the 1905 uprising in Warsaw alarmed her parents. Fearing that she might become dangerously involved, they sent her to Paris, ostensibly to study medicine—a subject that appealed to her youthful idealism. Once she had arrived in Paris to stay with relations, however, she discovered she was too young to begin medical studies and soon became involved in the artistic life of the city. Above all, she loved to dance and with her companions would go dancing nightly, from café to café, until the early hours. It was at this time that she met Duncan's brother Raymond, who encouraged her to dance professionally.

Rambert began by giving little recitals at fashionable parties, showing a natural gift for movement and taste in presentation but a lack of formal training. In 1910 she went to Geneva to study at the summer school of Émile Jaques-Dalcroze, in whom she found a kindred soul, with a wit and humor to match her own. She also found Dalcroze's eurhythmics—his theory of helping to develop musical sensibility through matching rhythm to movement—fascinating and instructive. During the two-week course she took six lessons a day: she became a devoted pupil and remained with Dalcroze for three years, eventually becoming an assistant teacher at his school in Dresden. It was there that Serge Diaghilev found her when he visited the school with Vaslav Nijinsky, looking for someone to help his young choreographer with the new rhythms created by Igor Stravinsky for *Le Sacre du Printemps*.

On the recommendation of Dalcroze, Rambert joined the Diaghilev troupe. Her principal duty was to help Nijinsky—of whom she was to become very fond—but she was also allowed onstage in the back row of the corps de ballet in works such as *Schéhérazade,* in which no pointe work was required. In 1913, because of a shortage of dancers, she traveled with the Diaghilev company to South America, where her interest in classical ballet was suddenly roused, not least from the experience of watching her adored Tamara Karsavina in class. Karsavina never missed a practice during the tour; working away in the background, Rambert followed her idol's every move, and Karsavina, who became a lifelong friend, was to speak of her affectionately as "my little black shadow" in the classroom.

After the tour Rambert returned to Paris and to her recitals in the houses of the rich. She was helped and encouraged by the elegant Vera Donnet (later, Vera Bowen) and absorbed so quickly the ambience of the city that she was to say later that she "responded to the soul of Russia and the mind of France." Her last engagement in Paris was at the house of Madeleine Lemaire, a friend of Marcel Proust.

Donnet, who had already departed for London, urged Rambert to follow after the outbreak of World War I. Rambert crossed on one of the last channel boats from France, crowded with passengers, including Fedor Chaliapin and his family. In London she taught eurhythmics and then, in collaboration with Vera Donnet, created and danced in a little ballet called *La Pomme d'Or* (1917) for the prestigious Stage Society. It was in this work that she first attracted attention; it made her name. The intelligent and delightful little dancer was greatly in demand for dinner parties, especially to enliven conversation for the benefit of officers on leave, and it was at one of these dinners, later in 1917, that she met her future husband, the dramatist Ashley Dukes. From that first meeting they corresponded daily, and they were married on 3 March 1918. After having signed the register she asked if she was now a British citizen; on receiving the reply in the affirmative she immediately cried, "God Save the King!" Thereafter she was to devote her life's work in ballet to Britain.

Rambert opened her own studio in 1920 while continuing her studies with Serafina Astafieva and Enrico Cecchetti, both of whom were then teaching in London. Rambert's energy and vitality were boundless. Her first daughter, Angela, was born in 1920, and her second, Helena (Lulu), in 1923; she missed class for only a few days each time. At Cecchetti's classes in the early 1920s she had the excitement of working with the Diaghilev dancers when they were in London. Because of Ashley Dukes's position in the London theater world, she now met Diaghilev as an equal, and in addition to her love for ballet she developed an interest in serious and international theater. (This interest never waned; toward the end of her life, the World Theatre seasons presented in London by Peter Daubeny were among her greatest pleasures.)

In 1924, Léonide Massine, who knew Rambert from Diaghilev days, sent her a young pupil—Frederick Ashton. By the mid-1920s she already had many beautiful and gifted young people working in her studio—Diana Gould, Maude Lloyd, Pearl Argyle, Harold Turner, William Chappell, Prudence Hyman, Walter Gore—and by 1926 she had seen the production of the first ballet created as a result of her guidance and encouragement: Ashton's *A Tragedy of Fashion.* The idea had been Dukes's. Rambert had contemplated arranging it, and then one day she saw Ashton demonstrate a step and gesture and immediately cried—she was always a creature of inspired impulse—"*You* must do this ballet." She had known the artist Sophie Fedorovitch from the days when Fedorovitch came to sketch at Cecchetti's classes, and her work for *Tragedy* would be the beginning of a remarkable and long collaboration with Ashton. Rambert's taste in design, cultivated in her Paris days, led her to beautify many of the early productions of her company.

Rambert had found her métier. Her extraordinary flair for finding and encouraging choreographers and for recognizing talent in young artists, dancers, and painters was even more important for the development of British ballet than were her gifts as a teacher. Much as she loved the classical technique, she revered above all the potential creativity of her students. Typically, when Antony Tudor asked to audition for her school—as a late starter—she engaged him because he had "poetic eyes"; she did not even look at his feet.

All the early work of the Rambert company was done for love of and dedication to the art of ballet. There was no money; salaries did little more than cover the expenses of shoes and travel. When Ashton once begged for a new costume he was told not to fret "because the old costume will be disguised by your beautiful movement." If she had no money, Rambert had one priceless asset—a theater of her own. In 1927, Ashley Dukes had acquired a church hall near their house in the west of London, and this was gradually converted into a small theater and ballet studio. Used for rehearsals and performances by the Marie Rambert Dancers, it opened as the Ballet Club on 16 February 1931. It seated only 120 people, and the stage was eighteen feet wide and eighteen feet deep. Renamed the Mercury Theatre in 1933, it was turned into a ballet studio in 1955 (by which time the company had long outgrown it) and was sold in 1987. (The original façade has been retained and adorned with a plaque commemorating Rambert and Dukes and noting the building's historic importance.)

By the end of 1932, the Ballet Club had no fewer than seventeen hundred members, and its Sunday evening performances had become a very select and fashionable meeting place. Dukes believed in civilized foyer space for audiences, and his wine cellar and the collection of prints of the Romantic ballet that he and Rambert had amassed were sources of delight during intermissions.

Because the Mercury was so small, the ballets staged there were known as "chamber ballets"; any flaw would be noticed—not least by Rambert, who was seated in the front at every performance and would be backstage in a flash to reprimand any offender. Her quest for perfection and her volatile temperament resulted in many explosions with high-spirited dancers, and, though she grew calmer as she grew older, she never let standards decline. (During the vicissitudes of wartime touring to small halls and even factories, she would wait in the wings to reprimand some unfortunate dancer who had "ruined, but absolutely *ruined* the choreography of Fokine," regardless of the conditions under which they had to perform.)

It was Rambert's personality, her ever-inquiring mind, breadth of knowledge, and interest in all the arts that fueled her company in its early years and inspired it as long as she lived. She took great interest in her dancers' lives as well as in their performances, always inquiring about their reading, their theatergoing, their visits to art exhibitions, and constantly setting the example herself. Always ready to embrace new enthusiasms, she could be "carried away," a favorite phrase, by dance companies as different as the Bolshoi, the Kirov, and Martha Graham. She was the most faithful of friends and she continued to make new friends until the end of her life. She found great joy in working with Lincoln Kirstein (a new acquaintance) on his book *Nijinsky Dancing* (1975), and she also spent a lot of time with the young sculptor Astrid Zydower, copies of whose portrait head of Rambert are in the Dance Collection of the New York Public Library and the National Portrait Gallery in London.

Marie Rambert died after a stroke at her London home on the night of 12 June 1982. At her cremation on 17 June, the small chapel was filled with family, children, grandchildren, and dancers representing the whole of British ballet. Among her many honors were the Commander of the Order of the British Empire in 1954; chevalier, Légion d'Honneur in 1957; Dame Commander of the Order of the British Empire in 1962; and a D.Litt. from the University of Surrey in 1964.

On her eightieth birthday, at a glittering reception held in the great room of the Arts Council of Great Britain, Rambert received a book of tributes from Karsavina. Then, because she owed to England her husband, her family, and her company, she presented to England her priceless collection of ballet prints. They are now permanently housed in the Victoria and Albert Museum.

[*See also* Rambert Dance Company.]

BIBLIOGRAPHY

Clarke, Mary. *Dancers of Mercury.* London, 1962.

Crisp, Clement, Anya Sainsbury, and Peter Williams, eds. *Ballet Rambert: Fifty Years and On.* London, 1981.

Inglesby, Mona. "From the Cradle of British Ballet." *Dance Now* 4 (Spring 1995): 35–45.

Marshall, Valerie. "A Reminiscence of Rambert." *Dance Now* 1 (Autumn 1992): 70–71.

Pritchard, Jane. *Rambert: A Celebration.* London, 1996.

Rambert, Marie. *Quicksilver: The Autobiography of Marie Rambert.* London, 1972.

Setterfield, Valda. "A Passion for Dance." *Ballet Review* 11 (Summer 1983): 30–34.

Tudor, Antony, et al. "Rambert Remembered." *Ballet Review* 11 (Spring 1983): 62–67.

MARY CLARKE

RAMBERT DANCE COMPANY. Great Britain's oldest existing dance company, formerly known as Ballet Rambert, has been called "the cradle of British ballet." Before the Camargo Society and the Vic-Wells Ballet were established after Serge Diaghilev's death in 1929, Marie Rambert (1888–1982) had, during the 1920s, laid the foundations on which both those groups would build. Unlike Ninette de Valois of the Vic-Wells, however, Rambert was not concerned with giving her company permanence or security; she claimed that she never thought of the future.

Her company's history was therefore one of changes, near-collapses, and fresh initiatives, yet frequently of major creativity. Emphasizing novelty above established repertory, Ballet Rambert perpetuated a policy of Diaghilev. Rambert's record of producing, training, and encouraging choreographers, although she frequently lost them to larger institutions, was exceptional. The company that resulted from her intense coaching is her living memorial today.

Early History. Marie Rambert began teaching ballet in London in 1919. In 1925 her husband, Ashley Dukes, suggested a story from the letters of Madame de Sévigné as material for a satirical ballet. When Frederick Ashton (Rambert's first male student) one day suggested some clever characteristic gestures and movements for his own role, Rambert recognized his choreographic talent. She coaxed the ballet out of him, in the process initiating a collaboration and friendship between Ashton and the designer Sophie Fedorovitch that would be of great value to Ashton's creative work until Fedorovitch's death in 1953.

The ballet was called *A Tragedy of Fashion.* Manager Nigel Playfair took it into a revue, *Riverside Nights,* at the Lyric Theatre, Hammersmith. Its first performance on 15 June 1926 is now generally considered to mark the beginning of Rambert's company and of modern English ballet. Ninette de Valois and Margaret Craske were immediately enthusiastic; Diaghilev saw it twice.

RAMBERT DANCE COMPANY. Frederick Ashton as the *grand couturier* Monsieur Duchic and Marie Rambert as his partner Orchidée in Ashton's first ballet, *A Tragedy of Fashion* (1926), based on a story from the letters of Madame de Sévigné, with costumes by Sophie Fedorovitch. The golden, mannish outfit worn by Orchidée so shocked Duchic's customers that they fled his shop, whereupon he stabbed himself to death with his scissors in despair. (Photograph from the archives of the Rambert Dance Company.)

From 1926 to 1929 Rambert's dancers continued to perform occasional ballets, and Ashton created more works. Susan Salaman, another student, also began to choreograph short, light, popular dances for them. (Rambert herself "arranged dances" on occasion, but she did not consider herself a choreographer.) In 1927, Dukes bought the former Horbury Hall in Notting Hill Gate, and Rambert moved her "Russian School of Dancing (Cecchetti method)" to these larger premises, later to contain the tiny Mercury Theatre. The quality of dance and of Ashton's choreography won increasing admiration. The dancers were a remarkable group. Those who joined up to 1930 included Ashton, Salaman, Diana Gould, Andrée Howard, Maude Lloyd, Pearl Argyle, Harold Turner, William Chappell, Prudence Hyman, Walter Gore, and Antony Tudor. Many of them would play crucial parts in the development of ballet in Britain and elsewhere, and much of their subsequent achievement grew from the passionate coaching of mind as well as body that was Rambert's way of teaching.

In 1930, persuaded by Ashton, Rambert presented her students again at the Lyric, now in a public matinee. One of the ballets created for the occasion, Ashton's *Capriol Suite,* became a popular item of the repertory. This performance, warmly received, led to the next stage in the company's career. In June and July 1930, Tamara Karsavina danced with the company, now called the Marie Rambert Dancers, in a two-week season at the Lyric. Karsavina appeared in dances of her own and taught and performed with the company in *Les Sylphides,* a production Rambert retained until the 1960s. For a three-week season from December to January, Leon Woizikowski and Karsavina were guest artists. Both appeared in Woizikowski's revival of Michel Fokine's *Carnaval,* and Karsavina again led members of the company in *Les Sylphides* and danced in *Le Spectre de la Rose.* The company also appeared in new choreography by Salaman and Ashton and in several works by Marius Petipa.

The 1930s. Late in October 1930, Ashley Dukes and Marie Rambert formed the Ballet Club, with the stated intention "to preserve the art of ballet in England by forming a permanent company of dancers with a theatre of its own." Rambert was already on the committee of the Camargo Society, founded in 1930, which depended on many of her dancers for performances. The Ballet Club, then using a very small theater and unable to present regular performances, would be a vital stimulus to British dance but not its central institution.

The first performance of the Ballet Club took place on 16 February 1931. Ashton's new ballet for the occasion, *La*

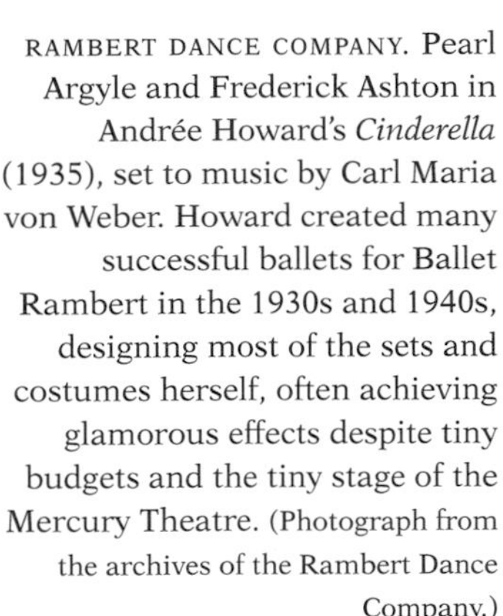

RAMBERT DANCE COMPANY. Pearl Argyle and Frederick Ashton in Andrée Howard's *Cinderella* (1935), set to music by Carl Maria von Weber. Howard created many successful ballets for Ballet Rambert in the 1930s and 1940s, designing most of the sets and costumes herself, often achieving glamorous effects despite tiny budgets and the tiny stage of the Mercury Theatre. (Photograph from the archives of the Rambert Dance Company.)

Péri, presented Alicia Markova in her first created role at the Ballet Club, before she danced for the Camargo Society or the Vic-Wells Ballet. Although paid only the cost of her shoes and travel, she danced regularly with the Club until 1934, creating new roles in Ashton's *La Péri, Foyer de Danse, Les Masques,* and *Mephisto Valse,* de Valois's *Bar aux Folies-Bergère,* and Tudor's *Lysistrata.*

Tamara Karsavina and Leon Woizikowski danced with the Ballet Club in 1931. For Karsavina, Ashton created *Mercure* and partnered her in it as well as in *Les Sylphides.* Woizikowski helped Rambert to produce Vaslav Nijinsky's *L'Après-midi d'un Faune.*

The company's performances soon attracted a fashionable audience. However, to suit both the dancers, often professionally engaged elsewhere, and the audience, which packed premiere performances but not extended seasons, the Club began to perform just twice a week. Music, much of it contemporary, was generally played on one or two pianos. Distinguished musicians often performed. For *Les Masques,* Francis Poulenc's sonata for piano, oboe, and bassoon was played, and there was a singer for Mahler's "Kindertotenlieder," used by Tudor for his *Dark Elegies.*

Beginning in 1931 there were occasional tours outside London, for which the name Ballet Rambert was adopted. Rambert and Dukes drew no fees from the Club. Payments to the dancers could not be high, yet the company presented fine dancers in varied productions generally considered to be in exquisite taste. Several dancers from the pre-Club days, such as Argyle, Gore, Howard, Lloyd, and Tudor, continued into this period. New dancers joining in the 1930s included Hugh Laing, Peggy van Praagh, Elisabeth Schooling, Mary Skeaping, Frank Staff, Celia Franca, and Sally Gilmour. Most of these left to work with larger companies, giving Rambert the frequent obligation of teaching their roles to new artists, but none escaped Rambert's passion for artistry.

Several of these dancers were exceptionally beautiful, in particular Pearl Argyle and Hugh Laing. The attractiveness of the dancers, added to stylish designs by Sophie Fedorovitch, William Chappell, Hugh Stevenson, Susan Salaman, and Andrée Howard, gave the Club's productions a glamour and stylishness achieved on what Karsavina called "blessed poverty." Some designs reflected certain painters' styles: Sandro Botticelli for *A Florentine Picture,* Ludovico Burnacini for *Cross-Garter'd,* Edgar Degas for *Foyer de Danse,* Édouard Manet and Henri de Toulouse-Lautrec for *Bar aux Folies-Bergère.* Painters such as Nadia Benois also created designs for the company. Guest dancers in this period included Kyra Nijinsky, Agnes de Mille (whose book *Dance to the Piper* vividly depicts this era of the company's history), Margot Fonteyn, Robert Helpmann, Bentley Stone, and June Brae.

Most important in the early 1930s was new choreography. Ashton regularly created works for the company as well as elsewhere until he became resident choreographer with the Vic-Wells in 1935. Susan Salaman also presented new works until illness ended her career in 1935. In 1931

Rambert acted as "midwife" to the first ballet by Antony Tudor, *Cross-Garter'd.* (She also encouraged him to teach, at which he quickly became adept.) His third work, the amusing *Lysistrata* (1932), was a great success, remaining in the repertory for several years. He and Ashton, with quite different styles, worked happily together, and Rambert was able to nurture another choreographer in Andrée Howard, whose first work, *Our Lady's Juggler* (a revision of a 1930 piece by Salaman) had its premiere in 1933. With Salaman's assistance, Howard made the touching *Mermaid* (1934), for which, as for many of her other works, she also made the designs, often fitting and making costumes herself. Tudor and Howard, developing in the Rambert climate as rapidly as had Ashton, soon became mature choreographers. In such pieces as Tudor's *Planets* (1934) and Howard's *Cinderella* (1935), they demonstrated distinctive styles and clever use of the little Mercury stage.

In 1935, Ashton, Argyle, Gore, Turner, and others became full-time members of the Vic-Wells Ballet. The contracts de Valois offered, spelling security and regular work, could not be matched by Rambert. However, Lloyd assumed several of Markova's and Argyle's roles; Gore returned after a year, and Laing and van Praagh remained. Tudor now made two works that long remained in the company's repertory: *Jardin aux Lilas* (1936) and *Dark Elegies* (1937). These works brought Tudor's dramatically eloquent style to a new peak, and *Dark Elegies'* combination of ballet with gesture and modern movement, and its passionate humanism, helped to give the company a lasting identity. Four days after its premiere Howard presented a new ballet also "about death," the simple and eloquent *Death and the Maiden* (1937), set to the andante from Franz Schubert's String Quartet in D Minor. The Ballet Club had swiftly achieved a serious choreographic tone different from Ashton's more brilliant or sophisticated styles.

Departures, however, continued to upset the company's work. Tudor, dispirited by the company's irregularity of performance, left in 1937, taking several dancers, including van Praagh and Laing, to set up a new company with Agnes de Mille, Dance Theatre. The achievements of Howard as choreographer helped the company through this crisis, as did the emergence as choreographers of Frank Staff and Walter Gore in 1938. Staff's first work, *The Tartans,* was a witty fulfillment of Rambert's guess that he, only twenty years old, was a choreographer. Gore's first ballet, *Valse Finale,* was his own idea and another promising first work. In 1939 Howard's *Lady into Fox,* based on the David Garnett story, revealed a young dancer hardly noticed before, Sally Gilmour. This sensitive ballet, giving Gilmour's detailed, intense dramatic skill its first and most celebrated vehicle, was preserved on silent film, as were several other Ballet Club stagings of this decade.

The 1940s. With the outbreak of World War II, Rambert evacuated her school to Newbury. In December 1939, after months of inactivity, the company presented a London season. Staff's *Czernyana,* a charming satire of various ballet styles, had its premiere. Rambert then accepted an offer from Harold Rubin to present the company regularly at the Arts Theatre Club, sharing it with the Arts Theatre Ballet and the London Ballet, the company formed by Tudor in 1938. In 1939 Tudor left for New York to join the new Ballet Theatre, and Rubin encouraged van Praagh to reconstitute his former company and repertory. Howard, who had also joined Ballet Theatre but had soon returned to London, created *La Fête Étrange,* a subtle and delicate *ballet d'atmosphère.* In May 1940, Staff (who had also been dancing and choreographing with the London Ballet) made *Peter and the Wolf,* Prokofiev's musical tale skillfully rendered with words and music supporting lively choreography. Ballet Rambert and the London Ballet were so linked by the past, so complementary in styles, and so hard-pressed by scant resources, that in June 1940 they merged to become the Rambert-London Ballet, with a directing committee consisting of Rambert, Howard, Gore, and van Praagh. Ballet Rambert thus inherited the London Ballet's repertory.

In the winter of the "blitz," 1940–1941, daytime performances billed as "lunch ballet," "tea ballet," and even "sherry ballet" helped make Arts Theatre performances popular. Staff created *Enigma Variations* in 1940 and *Czernyana II* in 1941. Also in 1941, Gore demonstrated his matured talent with two dances arranged for the Oxford University Ballet Club and quickly taken up by the Rambert-London Ballet: *Bartlemas Dances* and *Confessional.*

The Arts Theatre arrangement ended in 1941. Consequent legal problems kept the company from performing throughout 1942, a gap in which such dancers as van Praagh and Celia Franca left to join the Sadler's Wells Ballet and the International ballet, respectively, and in which Staff was drafted. Nonetheless, in 1943, the Council for Encouragement of Music and the Arts, later known as the Arts Council, sponsored the first of several major national tours. Howard made *Carnival of Animals* and in 1944 the dramatic *The Fugitive.* Gore's *Simple Symphony* (1944) was a blithe suite of folk dances set on a beach. In 1945 Staff returned to make *Un Songe,* his last work for the company. Throughout this period, Sally Gilmour, whose subtlety and intensity compensated for a lack of technical virtuosity, was the company's leading dancer.

After the war, the Sadler's Wells Ballet moved to the Royal Opera House, Covent Garden, but to Rambert's disappointment its new second branch was now to occupy Sadler's Wells Theatre, and Howard left to become the company's choreographer. Rambert's company was more than ever obliged to become an alternative to the established British ballet institution. However, there were compensations: *Giselle* was staged—act 2 in 1945 and the complete ballet in 1946—with Gilmour in the title role, and Rambert's reproduction of the Romantic idiom was greatly admired. Gore continued to create works for the company, and John Gilpin and Belinda Wright emerged as new leading dancers.

In 1947, the Arts Council, though continuing an annual grant, ceased to manage the company, and a board of directors took over. In 1947 Howard returned to choreograph another David Garnett story, *The Sailor's Return,* the first entirely British two-act ballet, set to a commissioned score for orchestra by Arthur Oldham.

The company's immensely successful tour of Australia in 1947–1948 was extended several times until eighteen months had been spent away from home; however, the proceeds did not cover expenses when most of the scenery and many costumes were ruined on the voyage home. Furthermore, some dancers—Gilmour among them—chose to remain in Australia. On their return, Gilpin and Wright, now experienced and acclaimed dancers, left to work with larger companies. Gore's dramatic choreography reached its climax in *Antonia* (1949), its title role establishing Paula Hinton as a remarkable dance actress. In 1950, however, Gore and Hinton left the company, and Ballet Rambert was for the first time without a choreographer.

The Years 1950–1966. In no other period was the company so unproductive as from 1950 to 1958. In 1950–1951, David Paltenghi, formerly a dancer with the London and Rambert-London Ballets, returned after a period with the Sadler's Wells Ballet and staged five ballets for the company. Rambert and others, however, thought him more adept at coming up with production ideas than at making dances. In 1951, Rambert's daughter Angela and her husband, David Ellis, founded Ballet Workshop at the Mercury Theatre. This independent institution staged programs on Sunday nights; both novices (including Peter Darrell) and experienced choreographers (Celia Franca, Frances James, Michael Holmes, Jack Carter, and Walter Gore among them) produced new work. Between 1951 and 1954 several works first made for the workshop—by Paltenghi, Michael Charnley, and Jack Carter—were taken into Ballet Rambert's repertory. In 1954 Carter and John Cranko made new works for the company, as did Robert Joffrey in 1955, when Kenneth MacMillan's early work, *Laiderette* (made for Sadler's Wells Choreographic Group), was taken into the repertory. In 1955 the workshop ceased activity, and Rambert was joined by David Ellis as associate director of her company. In 1957 there was a new production of *Coppélia,* with designs by Mstislav Dobujinsky. At this time the young Lucette Aldous began to demonstrate remarkable talent and virtuosity.

In 1958, Rambert at last found in her company a choreographer whose work could revive the company's creative reputation—Norman Morrice. His first two ballets, *Two Brothers* (1958) and *Hazana* (1959), showed talent for drama, contemporary in theme and poignant in expression. With his works and others, the company performed at the Jacob's Pillow Dance Festival in the summer of 1959. In 1961–1962 Morrice spent some months in New York studying modern dance forms, especially those of Martha Graham, which influenced his subsequent work.

To satisfy the demands of regional audiences, the company also continued to import more traditional ballets—August Bournonville's *La Sylphide* in 1960, George Balanchine's *Night Shadow* in 1961, the Petipa *Don Quixote* in 1962, and a new *Giselle* in 1965. The obvious dichotomy between older and modern repertory, and the expense of staging and touring such classics, led to a financial and artistic crisis. In 1966 David Ellis resigned; on 2 July 1966, the old Ballet Rambert gave its final performance at the open-air theater in Holland Park, London.

The Years 1966–1980. Morrice, encouraged by the example of the Netherlands Dance Theater, proposed that the company be reconstituted to concentrate on new works, more modern dance than ballet in technique, to restore it to the vanguard of creativity in British dance. The company was to have no stars and no corps de ballet, only soloists. "The idea," Morrice later said, "was to get back to it being a choreographers' company that would make its own repertory." Morrice became associate director and, in 1970, joint artistic director. The company received Arts Council support. Almost no choreography made for the company in the late 1960s and 1970s has survived, and the novelties admired then seem dated today. Nonetheless, Ballet Rambert's metamorphosis—revealed in its first performance in the revised format on 28 November 1966—did much to make contemporary dance forms seem native to Britain. *Faune,* three Tudor works *(Jardin aux lilas, Dark Elegies,* and *The Judgement of Paris),* and MacMillan's *Laiderette* were at first part of the new Rambert repertory, but increasingly the company used its own homemade or recently acquired choreography.

As director until 1974, Morrice made ten works that, along with dances made by guest choreographer Glen Tetley, helped to create a new style for the company. Morrice's works included the dramatic *Blindsight* (1969) and *That Is the Show* (1971); in 1968 his *1-2-3,* made for the Batsheva Dance Company in Israel, entered the repertory. Between 1966 and 1974 John Chesworth made nine works for the company.

Several foreign choreographers made new works or remounted old one; Pierre Lacotte, Rudi van Dantzig, Anna Sokolow, Lar Lubovitch, Louis Falco, Manuel Alum, Cliff Keuter, and above all Tetley. Early in 1967 Tetley's *Pierrot Lunaire* and *Ricercare* were mounted and helped to crystallize the company's new identity. Performances of *Pierrot* and Rambert's own revival of *Faune* established

Christopher Bruce as a major performing talent and one of the company's strongest assets for more than a decade. Later in 1967 Tetley made *Freefall* and *Ziggurat* for the company. Using modern music and serious subject matter, blending ballet and modern dance techniques, Tetley's work had obvious influence both within and beyond Ballet Rambert.

Dancers were encouraged to choreograph, in particular Jonathan Taylor, Christopher Bruce, and Joseph Scoglio. These house choreographers, following Tetley's example, used distinctively modern music by such composers as Witold Lutosławski, Karl-Heinz Stockhausen, Krzysztof Penderecki, Iannis Xenakis, Morton Subotnick, and Carlos Salzedo. The Mercury Ensemble was founded to provide live accompaniment. Design was to be as vital to this new-look Ballet Rambert as it had been to the Ballet Club of the 1930s. Nadine Baylis designed forty works between 1966 and 1979. Often using metallic rods as part of a design and creating an abstract sculptural setting for dance. Baylis made a virtue of minimal resources. Her many atmospheric designs did much to create the Rambert style for that period.

RAMBERT DANCE COMPANY. Norman Morrice (center) in the first dance he choreographed, *Two Brothers* (1958). Morrice was one in a series of choreographers and directors to emerge from the ranks of the company. (Photograph © by John Blomfield; used by permission.)

In 1973, Ballet Rambert appeared, for the first time since changing its style, at Sadler's Well's Theatre, initiating annual seasons there. Also in 1973, Morrice took a six-month sabbatical, and in 1974 he resigned. John Chesworth succeeded him as director, with no radical change of concept. Chesworth himself now ceased to choreograph for the company, but Tetley and Morrice returned to make new works; other British and foreign choreographers also came, including Lindsay Kemp, Robert North, Cliff Keuter, Jaap Flier, Siobhan Davies, and Richard Alston, and company members were still encouraged to create. Bruce, who in 1974 won the first *Evening Standard* award for his contribution to British dance as both performer and creator, became associate director. His *Ancient Voices of Children* (1975) was the first of several works he made for the company to the music of George Crumb. Some of these used texts from Federico García Lorca and in 1977 Bruce used Lorca as the central figure of *Cruel Garden,* a full-evening dance drama conceived by Bruce and Lindsay Kemp; it was not admired by many London critics but was very popular. Bruce took a year's leave in 1979, while Tetley staged *The Tempest* in two acts, with a score commissioned from Arne Nordheim. Although this work was admired in some quarters and was later taken into the repertory of the Norwegian

Ballet, it was generally considered too monotonous and too difficult to decipher. The best of the Tetley years had passed.

The Years 1980–1985. John Chesworth resigned in 1980, and for a year the company ran itself without a director. Richard Alston, after having been invited to make a new work for the company, was appointed the company's resident choreographer. His first works had not been nurtured by Rambert herself, and he was to be the first Rambert choreographer to concentrate on pure dance composition. In his first work, *Bell High,* he demanded a rigor of technique, style, and musicality new to the Rambert dancers of that period.

In the 1980/81 season, *Dark Elegies* and *The Judgment of Paris* were successfully revived, and Alston's modern classicism reached an early climax with *Rainbow Ripples* (1980). In March 1981 his version of *The Rite of Spring,* made to the four-hand piano version of Stravinsky's score, recalled Marie Rambert's own work on the original 1913 Nijinsky version. Alston's *Rite* referred to pictorial documents of Rambert's work and was dedicated to her.

In April 1981, Robert North, who had previously choreographed for the company but who had been principally associated with London Contemporary Dance Theatre as dancer and choreographer, was appointed director. North continued to dance and choreograph, and he revived two works he had made elsewhere. His *Colour Moves* (1983) was a notable collaboration with the painter Bridget Riley.

Bruce, who had returned to the company as associate choreographer in 1980, made five new works under North's directorship. *Sergeant Early's Dream* (1984) was the twenty-second work of his that the company presented. His 1982 *Ghost Dances,* a work "about the innocent people of South America who, from the time of the Spanish Conquests, have been continuously devastated by political oppression," part modern and part folk in style, won exceptional popularity. Alston too made several works for the company in this period, *Java* (July 1985) being the ninth. His collaboration with painters and visual artists, such as Howard Hodgkin for *Night Music* (1981) and Richard Smith for *Wildlife* (1984) and *Dangerous Liaisons* (1985), did much to further the company's record of illustrious stage design. There was also a regular intake of work from American choreographers, including stagings of Paul Taylor's *Airs* (1982), Merce Cunningham's *Fielding Sixes* (1983), and new work created for the company by Tetley (1983) and Dan Wagoner (1985).

Rambert's own interest and involvement in the company continued into her old age. After her death in 1982, the company gave its 1983 spring season as a memorial to her. This season—with a new work by Alston, *Chicago Brass,* in his most austerely classical vein, a revival of his *Rite of Spring,* revivals of Nijinsky's *Faune* and Ashton's

RAMBERT DANCE COMPANY. Christopher Bruce and Julia Blaikie in Glen Tetley's *Pierrot Lunaire,* acquired by the company in 1967. This work, which helped to establish Bruce as a major performer, remained in Rambert's repertory for twenty years. (Photograph by Anthony Crickmay; used by permission of the Board of Trustees of the Theatre Museum, London.)

Capriol Suite, and works by Bruce, North, Cunningham, and Taylor—was a fit evocation of Rambert's career, her eclectic enthusiasm, and her passion for creativity. Ashton also revived *Five Brahms Waltzes in the Manner of Isadora Duncan,* first performed by Lynn Seymour at a Ballet Rambert gala in 1976 and dedicated to Rambert in recognition of the passion for Duncan's dancing she had shared with Ashton. It was now danced by one of the company's most individual dancers, Lucy Burge.

The Years since 1985. As Alston has written, "With North's appointment the company again fell into what seemed to be a repeating pattern of a creative triumvirate. . . . The company remains true to Morrice's idea of a choreographers' company, largely making its own repertoire."

With sixteen dancers in 1985, Ballet Rambert was subsidized by a revenue grant from the Arts Council, important commercial sponsorship, and, for foreign tours, British Council support. Its annual schedule contained approximately fifteen weeks on tour in the United Kingdom, one or more foreign tours, one London season of nearly three weeks at Sadler's Wells, and sometimes a second season at another London venue, supplemented by workshops in which dancers presented their own choreography. Foreign tours had taken the company to both western and eastern Europe and, in 1982, to the United States.

In January 1986, Robert North resigned from the company, and his place as artistic director was taken by Richard Alston. Because the company was preparing to celebrate its sixtieth anniversary that June, Alston at once commissioned new works from several British choreographers, using designs from major British artists and modern scores, effecting a timely revival of the company's tradition of novelty and collaboration. The three-week anniversary season at Sadler's Wells included new works by Alston and Bruce, Mary Evelyn (a company member), Michael Clark (a former member), Ian Spink, and Ashley Page. A remarkable standard of design was reached by John Hoyland for Alston's *Zansa,* Antony Mcdonald for Spink's *Mercure,* and Jack Smith for Page's *Carmen Arcadiae Mechanica Perpetuum.* No less remarkable was the excellence of the dancing. The success of this season, which was seen as a company renaissance, won Ballet Rambert the Society of West End Theatres' Laurence Olivier Award for 1986.

RAMBERT DANCE COMPANY. Amanda Britton and Ian Stewart in Mary Evelyn's *Dipping Wings* (1985), set to music by Simon Waters. (Photograph © by Catherine Ashmore; used by permission.)

RAMBERT DANCE COMPANY. Gary Lambert, Robert Poole, and Ben Craft in Richard Alston's *Java* (1985), to songs by the Ink Spots, with design by Jenny Henry, a substantially reworked version of a piece originally made in 1983 for the Royal Ballet. The new version of *Java* became one of Alston's most popular and admired dances, rich in comic movement invention and joking quotations from other ballets. (Photograph © by Catherine Ashmore; used by permission.)

The company began 1987 with a Stravinsky program shared with Opera North, for which Alston choreographed *Pulcinella,* with vivid new decor and costumes by the painter Howard Hodgkin. The company then toured North America. The year also marked the twenty-first anniversary of the company's change of dance idiom. In a gesture that at last confirmed this revised identity, the company changed its name, and since September 1987 it has performed as the Rambert Dance Company, preserving its founder's name and honoring her policies. Although the company's style is unlike that of its first decades or that of the late 1960s and 1970s, it perpetuates Marie Rambert's desire for creative vitality. No contemporary British company of this or larger size has a comparable record for producing new repertory.

Under Alston's directorship the company's repertory remained eclectic, with an emphasis on abstract works rich

RAMBERT DANCE COMPANY. Amanda Britton and Steven Brett in Laurie Booth's *Completely Birdland* (1991), danced to music by Hans Peter Kuhn, with decor by Graham Snow and costumes by Jeanne Spaziani. (Photograph © by Andrew Cockrill; used by permission.)

in movement invention. Among the nine dances Alston created or revised for the company after *Pulcinella,* the most widely praised was *Strong Language* (1987), to a score by John-Marc Gowans. Between 1987 and 1993 Rambert acquired three works by Cunningham, including *Touchbase* (1992), set simultaneously on Rambert and on the choreographer's own company in his New York studio, and premiered by both companies in the same year. Other American choreographers represented in Rambert's repertory in this period include Trisha Brown (by her quartet *Opal Loop,* danced in silence), David Gordon, and Lucinda Childs. Dominant in the repertory of dances by British artists other than Alston was the work of Siobhan Davies, who contributed five works to Rambert in this period, four of them commissioned by the company. Among the novelties of these years was Laurie Booth's *Completely Birdland* (1991), a structured improvisation greatly enjoyed by the dancers. Major revivals included Tudor's *Dark Elegies* and Tetley's *Embrace Tiger and Return to Mountain.*

In 1993, after a period of waning inspiration, Alston left Rambert over differences in artistic policy with the board of directors. The time was ripe for yet another in Rambert's periodic crises of renewal. After several months during which the dancers continued to tour without a director, and a brief period in which the company was in effect disbanded, the Rambert Dance Company was relaunched on 1 April 1994 with Christopher Bruce returning to be the artistic director, leading a company composed equally of dancers from Alston's vintage, new dancers, and dancers who had worked with Bruce in a variety of previous contexts. Under Bruce the company has built an entirely new repertory, turning away from the abstract, Cunningham-derived aesthetic of Alston's tenure, and restoring an emphasis on dramatic, if not always explicitly narrative, dances, such as American choreographer Martha Clarke's acclaimed dance-theater piece *Garden of Earthly Delights* and Jiří Kylián's *Petite Mort* (both acquired in 1994). Among his many new and revived works for the group, Bruce's *Meeting Point,* to music by Michael Nyman (1995), and *Stream,* with a commissioned score by Philip Chambon (1996), have met with particular success. For many, Bruce has returned Marie Rambert's company to its historical roots; certainly, there has been a profound sense of revitalization, witnessed by the dancers' earning an Olivier Award for their 1996 season at the London Coliseum.

[*See also the entries on the principal figures mentioned herein.*]

BIBLIOGRAPHY

Clarke, Mary. *Dancers of Mercury.* London, 1961.

Crisp, Clement, et al., eds. *Ballet Rambert: Fifty Years and On.* Rev. and enl. ed. [Ilkley, England], 1981.

Haskell, Arnold L. *The National Ballet.* London, 1943.

Kane, Angela. "Rambert Dance Company" (parts 1–3). *Dance Theatre Journal* 8 (Autumn 1990): 34–37; 8 (Spring 1991): 36–39; 10 (Autumn 1992): 36–39.

Macaulay, Alastair. "Sir Fred at Eighty: Frederick Ashton in Conversation with Alastair Macaulay." *Dance Theatre Journal* 2 (Autumn 1984): 2–7.

Mackrell, Judith. "Mission—Impossible?" *Dance Now* 4 (Autumn 1995): 26–31.

Pritchard, Jane. "Rambert Dance Company Archive." In *Dance History,* 2d ed., edited by Janet Adshead-Lansdale and June Layson. New York, 1994.

Rambert, Marie. "Twenty Years After." *Ballet Annual* 1 (1947): 82–89.

Vaughan, David. *Frederick Ashton and His Ballets.* London, 1977.

Vaughan, David. "The Evolution of Ballet Rambert: From Ashton to Alston." *Dance Magazine* (October 1982): 74–77.

ALASTAIR MACAULAY

RAMEAU, JEAN-PHILIPPE (baptized 25 September 1683 in Dijon, died 12 September 1764 in Paris), French composer, organist, and theoretician. Rameau received his musical training from his father, who played the organ at several churches in Dijon. He supplemented his education at the Jesuit Collège des Godrans but did not stay long at the school because he found music more interesting than the study of Latin. In 1701 he left for Italy, where he spent several months. In later years he came to regret that he did not stay longer in that country, where "his taste was improved." In 1702 Rameau began his career as an organist, which for more than twenty years took him to various cities in France. After a period of time as the organist at Notre-Dame des Doms in Avignon, he was appointed to the Cathedral of Clermont-Ferrand. By 1706 he was in Paris, where he occupied posts with the Jesuits in the rue Saint Jacques and with the Pères de la Merci, and where he published his first book of pieces for the harpsichord. Rameau stayed in Paris only a short time, returning to Dijon in 1709 to succeed his father. In 1714 he became the organist for the Dominicans, but the following year returned to the Cathedral of Clermont-Ferrand. He remained there for eight years, composing motets and secular cantatas and writing his *Traité de l'harmonie,* which was published in 1722.

In 1722 or 1723 Rameau settled in Paris, where he became known in intellectual circles and was initially esteemed as a music theoretician. In 1726, the year of his marriage to Marie-Louise Mangot, daughter of a musician in the king's orchestra, he published a new work, entitled *Nouveau système de musique théorique.* His interest in the theater dates from this period of his life. He collaborated with Alexis Piron, another native of Dijon, in *divertissements* for the fair spectacles. He was also interested in the Théâtre Italien, where he saw two Native Americans from the Louisiana territory dancing to the music of their native instruments. It occurred to him to depict them in one of his pieces for the harpsichord, "Les Sauvages," included in the second of two books he published, one in 1724 and one in 1728. Several years later he orchestrated this piece and in 1736 included it in the last act of his *opéra-ballet Les Indes Galantes.* Rameau's dramatic career was also decisively influenced by the performance in 1732 of *Jephté,* a *tragédie lyrique* by Michel Pignolet de Montéclair, which enjoyed great success at the Paris Opera. The first biblical opera to be performed in the secular setting of the lyric theater, it was probably Rameau's inspiration for *Samson,* a work he composed with Voltaire but that was never performed.

His first opera for the public, *Hippolyte et Aricie,* was written with the Abbé Pellegrin, librettist of *Jephté,* whom he had met at the home of Le Riche de la Pouplinière, the tax collector who became his patron. The work was performed at a private concert at the home of this patron before being given at the Paris Opera on 1 October 1733. It was not widely accepted as it baffled some of the spectators, who were accustomed to the simpler music of Jean-Baptiste Lully. Despite the criticisms of the "Lullystes," the fifty-year-old Rameau continued to produce numerous operas for the Paris lyric stage. Most of his best works were created during the next twenty years. In addition to *Hippolyte et Aricie,* these included *Les Indes Galantes* (1735); *Castor et Pollux* (1737); *Les Fêtes d'Hébé* (1739); *Dardanus* (1739); *Platée* (1745); *Zaïs* (1748); *Pygmalion* (1748); and *Zoroastre (Zarathustra,* 1749). During this fruitful period he also composed his *Pièces de clavecin en concerts* (1741) and continued his theoretical studies with *Génération harmonique* (1737) and *Démonstration du principe de l'harmonie* (1750). He became recognized by European experts, and in France he continued to benefit from the protection of La Pouplinière, whose private orchestra he directed from 1744 to 1753. He exploited the instrumental discoveries made during this period, notably by introducing the clarinet to the Paris Opera orchestra when *Zoroastre* was created.

The lyric works that Rameau composed for the festivals at Versailles in honor of the dauphin's first marriage in 1745 brought him to the peak of his career. One of these works, the *comédie-ballet La Princesse de Navarre,* had been written in collaboration with Voltaire, and together with the sets by the Slodtz brothers contributed a prestigious brilliance to these celebrations. In a desire to reward the musician, on 4 May 1745, Louis XV named Rameau *compositeur de la musique de la chambre* ("composer of chamber music"). The artist's reputation soon crossed the borders of France; his *tragédie lyrique Zorastre* was successfully performed (in Italian) in Dresden in February 1752.

In August 1752 a troupe of Italian musicians called the Bouffons put on a series of short comic operas in Paris, including the famous *La Serva Padrona* of Giambattista Pergolesi. These performances triggered one of the most passionate quarrels in the history of the lyric theater. The "war" between the partisans of Italian opera and those of French opera concerned the "old-fashioned" concept of a spectacle as developed by Lully, leader of the French school, and his successors. Mythological subjects, which favored the expression of the fantastic, recitatives, complicated orchestration and choruses, and the importance of the ballets were all violently attacked. A great deal of the criticism, much of it from philosophers such as Jean-Jacques Rousseau, who were partisans of the Italians, was aimed at Rameau, who was rightly considered one of the best representatives of French opera. The fight over the Bouffons had consequences, and in 1755 Rameau began a polemic with Jean le Rond d'Alembert concerning articles on music published in the *Encyclopédie.* During the last ten years of his life Rameau produced theoretical works, such as the *Code de musique pratique* (1760), and also composed several operas, including *La Naissance d'Osiris* and *Anacréon,* ballet acts created for the court at Fontainebleau in 1754, and *Les Paladins,* a *comédie lyrique* ("lyric comedy") performed at the Paris Opera in 1760. Rehearsals were also underway for his new *tragédie lyrique, Les Boréades,* but they were interrupted just before he died.

His twenty-five works for the lyric theater made Rameau one of the most prolific of French opera composers. The complex musical notation of his scores, with the improvements made possible by his knowledge of theory, made him an innovator. He used original rhythmic effects and developed the expressive possibilities of the orchestra through a detailed investigation of the combinations of timbres of the various instruments. However, as a creator he was very respectful of the forms inherited from earlier generations. He made no changes in the French opera structure transmitted to him by Lully and his successors. To the end of his life he composed in genres that had already been used by his predecessors: *tragédies lyriques, opéra-ballets, pastorales héroïauques,* and *comédies lyriques.*

Dance melodies had an important place in Rameau's works, and he composed several for the *divertissements* he introduced into each act or *entrée.* The example of the operas left by Lully and Philippe Quinault showed that ballets could describe an action. Under the influence of Louis de Cahusac, who began collaborating with Rameau in 1745, the *danse d'action* (narrative dance) became a frequent and necessary part of the drama, particularly in the *opéra-ballet.* Cahusac began to put this system into practice in *Les Fêtes de Polymnie* (1745), introducing two *ballets figurés* ("figured ballets") into the first and third *entrées.* His conception came to full fruition with *Les Fêtes de l'Hymen* (1747); the *ballets figurés* became a permanent part of each of the three *entrées* and even of the prologue, sometimes with a detailed program, as with *Canope.*

The term *pantomime* first appears in Rameau's work in the last scene of *Pygmalion* (1748). It appears again in *La Guirlande* (1751), *Acante et Céphise* (1751), *Daphnis et Eglé* (1753), *Les Paladins* (1760), and *Les Boréades.* One of the best examples is found in an *entrée* to the second version of *Les Surprises de l'Amour* (1757), "L'Enlèvement d'Adonis," which ends with a long pantomime ballet depicting the love affair of Diana and Endymion.

In *ballets figurés* and pantomimes Rameau often used conventional dances, such as *gavottes, rigaudons, passepieds, bourrées,* and *menuets,* which he endeavored to vary. He made little use of the *gigue,* but he introduced more *sarabandes* into his operas than did his predecessors. Along with *marches, tambourins,* and *musettes,* the composer also gave *chaconnes* an important role, expanding them particularly in the endings of his early works *Hippolyte et Aricie, Les Indes Galantes,* and *Castor et Pollux.*

Other dances, referred to vaguely as "airs," describe the nature of a character or, more frequently, of a dramatic situation. This places them within the tradition of French opera, according to the examples left by Lully in particular. These dances are sometimes accompanied by descriptive titles that define their role more closely, as in "Gentle Air for the Muses" in the prologue to *Le Temple de la Gloire,* or "Majestic Air" in the apotheosis of *Zoroastre.*

In all his ballet melodies Rameau generally used the *carrure* (from *carrer,* "to square"), that is, the division of the musical phrase into groups of four measures, as he recommended in his *Traité de l'harmonie.* He also sought to adapt his dances to the dramatic situations provided by the libretti. His borrowings from his collections of pieces for the harpsichord are particularly interesting in this regard. In addition to "Les Sauvages," which he reused as the fourth *entrée* in *Les Indes Galantes,* other pieces reappear in several operas: the famous *tambourin* in *Les Fêtes d'Hébé,* "Les Niais de Sologne" in *Dardanus,* and "Les Tendres Plaintes" in *Zoroastre.* The composer also reused some dances from his operas in other later lyric works. The *gavottes* from the prologue to *Hippolyte et Aricie,* for example, were used in *La Princesse de Navarre* in 1745 and for the restaging of *Zaïs* in 1764.

Rameau's attention to the orchestration of his ballet airs promoted the development of instrumental music, and in France he played a role comparable to that of the Italian sonata and concerto composers. His dance music also became widely known and was performed in various European theaters during the second half of the eighteenth century, thereby contributing to the dissemination of the choreographic art.

BIBLIOGRAPHY

Christensen, Thomas S. *Rameau and Musical Thought in the Enlightenment.* Cambridge, 1993.

Foster, Donald H. *Jean-Philippe Rameau: A Guide to Research.* New York, 1989.

Girdlestone, Cuthbert. *Jean-Philippe Rameau: His Life and Work.* Rev. ed. New York, 1969.

Kintzler, Catherine. *Jean-Philippe Rameau.* 2d ed. Paris, 1988.

La Gorce, Jérôme de, ed. *Jean-Philippe Rameau: Colloque international, Dijon, 21–24 septembre 1983.* Paris, 1987.

La Laurencie, Lionel de. *Rameau.* Paris, 1908.

Malignon, Jean. *Rameau.* Paris, 1960.

Masson, Paul-Marie. *L'opéra de Rameau.* Paris, 1930.

JÉRÔME DE LA GORCE
Translated from French

RAMEAU, PIERRE (born 1674 in Cirea, died 26 January 1748 in Nanterre, France), dancing master and writer. Little is known of French dancing master and writer Pierre Rameau's personal life. His parents were Georges Rameau, a wine merchant, and Jeanne Thiersault. Legal documents refer to him as "dancing master in Paris," and by 1745 he had moved to Nanterre, where he died in 1748. His son, Jean-Baptiste, became a dancing master in La Rochelle.

The only evidence of Rameau's life in the theater found thus far is in the opera archives in Lyon. In 1703, along with forty colleagues, he signed a document by which the company resigned the privilege of producing opera in Dijon. How long he remained in Lyon is not known, but his marriage there to Elisabeth La Haye on 23 May 1705 would indicate a period of at least two years. After 1705, however, the opera there functioned only occasionally, owing to financial problems. Another mystery concerns a dancer, "Ramau," active at the Académie Royale de Musique for a few years around 1710. Rameau never mentions this in his writings, but the coincidence is puzzling, considering his knowledge and appreciation of Paris Opera dancers. He is also known to have been involved in the Jesuit ballet production *Le Tableau Allégorique des Moeurs* (1716) where he figured as the Dieu du Temps alongside Paris Opera dancers.

Fortunately for the history of dance, his written work has survived. Two books, written in 1725, represent our major sources of information for the reconstruction and understanding of eighteenth-century dance technique and style. The first book, *Le maître à danser,* reprinted several times, was translated into English by John Essex in 1728 and again in 1732, with new illustrations by George Bickham. A modern English translation by Cyril Beaumont was published in 1931. With its careful verbal description of steps, feet and arm movements, and its very clear, if crude, drawings clarifying the body positions, Rameau's book is an indispensable companion to Feuillet's *Chorégraphie* (1700), to which it provides flesh and blood. Its preface is a mine of information on early eighteenth-century dancers, and its complete description of the minuet is invaluable.

PIERRE RAMEAU. A figure in first position, from Rameau's 1725 treatise *Le maître à danser* (later translated into English as *The Dancing Master*). In his discussion of this classical ballet position, Rameau describes its basic shape—that the dancer's legs are straight, that his heels touch each other, and that his feet turn out at equal angles. (Reprinted from Rameau, 1931.)

Rameau's second book, *Abbrégé de la nouvelle méthode,* is a dance notation manual based on the Feuillet notation system, but with "improved" symbols followed by a collection of twelve dances composed by Guillaume-Louis Pecour, which had already been published elsewhere.

Contrary to what is generally believed and written, Pierre Rameau was never "dancing master to the Queen of Spain"—a position filled by Michel Blondy. In *Le maître à danser,* he calls himself dancing master to the *pages* of the queen of Spain. In *Abbrégé,* he is dancing master *ordinnaire* in "the house of her Catholic Majesty the Queen, second dowager of Spain," which requires clarification. This Spanish queen was Louise Elisabeth Charlotte of Orléans, also called Mademoiselle de Montpensier. She was the daughter of Philippe d'Orléans, regent of France at the death of Louis XIV. On 20 January 1722 she married Louis-Philippe de Bourbon, prince of the Asturias. When Philip V of Spain abdicated in favor of his son in January 1724, Louise Elisabeth became queen of Spain. Unfortunately her husband, Louis I, died a few months later, in August 1724, leaving her with the title of second dowager of Spain (the first being Maria Anna of Bavaria-Neuburg, widow of Charles II of Spain since 1700 and still very much alive in 1724). Louise Elisabeth, former queen of Spain, returned to Paris, where she died in June 1742 at the age of thirty-three. There cannot be any doubt that she is the queen referred to by Rameau.

Pierre Rameau left two wills. One, dated 6 May 1745, does not mention his wife but leaves all his possessions to his son Jean. The other, dated 20 January 1748, makes provision for a maid and specifies a yearly income of one hundred livres to his son for the rest of his life. Rameau seems to have died a poor man in rented premises. Whatever happened to his various inheritances and the dowries of his wives (of which there were three) is not known.

BIBLIOGRAPHY

Hilton, Wendy. *Dance of Court and Theatre: The French Noble Style, 1690–1725.* Princeton, 1981.

Marsh-Rowan, Carol. "P. Rameau: A New Look at an Old Dancing Master." In *Dance History Scholars Conference.* Los Angeles, 1981.

Rameau, Pierre. *Abbrégé de la nouvelle méthode, dans l'art d'écrire ou de traçer toutes sortes de danses de ville.* Paris, 1725.

Rameau, Pierre. *Le maître à danser.* Paris, 1725. Translated by Cyril W. Beaumont as *The Dancing Master* (London, 1931).

Vallas, Léon. *Un siècle de musique et de théâtre à Lyon, 1688–1789.* Lyon, 1932.
Winter, Marian Hannah. *The Pre-Romantic Ballet.* London, 1974.
Witherell, Anne L. "Pierre Rameau's French Menuet." Master's thesis, Stanford University, 1973.

RÉGINE ASTIER

RAND, SALLY. *See* Fan Dancing.

RAO, SHANTA (born 1930 in Mangalore), Indian dancer. Rao began to study dance at an early age at the Kerala Kalamandalam, where she studied *kathakaḷi* with P. Ramunni Menon and *mōhiniyāṭṭam* with Krishnan Panikkar. She later studied *bharata nāṭyam* with Meenakshi Sundaram Pillai, a famous master of the Pandanallur style, and the vigorous Kandyan dance with the renowned Nittawala Guneya of Sri Lanka. Her early training was unusual in that she studied each dance tradition in its own cultural context, living in the rural homeland of each regional genre and following the traditional regimen required by each.

Rao's early concerts were landmarks in setting the direction of the popular revival of traditional dance for educated young urban dancers. Her dynamic intensity and strength of performance were matched by few. Her magnetism and beauty, as well as her prodigious stamina, were crucial assets in her career. Well known for her creative taste in costume design, she made many controversial innovations in her choice of fabrics and jewelry, though always with theatrical success. For example, when performing a *kathakaḷi* dance she wore Orissa fabrics that had no relationship to the tradition of *kathakaḷi,* but, again with consummate taste.

In the early 1950s Shanta Rao was one of the first artists to be presented to the Western world as ambassadors of Indian dance and music. Her second tour of the United States was in 1957, with a *kathakaḷi* troupe. She has also toured in China, Israel, the Middle East, Nepal, England, and Europe; several tours were made as part of a cultural delegation of the Government of India.

Rao's later concert tours in the 1960s revealed a number of juxtapositions and innovations in her treatment of traditional choreography. Her innovations were questioned by some critics. Her individualistic aesthetic approach in interpreting southern India's dance traditions has always sparked controversy.

In 1970 Rao received the prestigious Padma Shri award from the Central Sangeet Natak Akademi in New Delhi. She continues to experiment creatively with traditional southern Indian classical dance forms at her Bangalore headquarters. Her most recent work deals with *bhāma nṛtyam,* a dance genre she evolved after studying the ceremonies of *Bhāma Sūtram* in Andhra.

RAO. A dancer trained in the classical styles of *kathakaḷi, mōhiniāṭṭam,* and *bharata nāṭyam,* Rao has contributed a number of innovations to these forms. Her bold, individual performance style has won her international recognition. She is seen here in a pure-dance pose from *mōhiniāṭṭam.* (Photograph by Herbert Matter; from the archives at Jacob's Pillow, Becket, Massachusetts.)

BIBLIOGRAPHY

Bowers, Faubion. "Shanta Rao." *Vogue* (December 1968): 218–225.
Chatterjee, Ashok. *Dances of the Golden Hall.* New Delhi, 1979.
de Zoete, Beryl. *The Other Mind.* London, 1953.
Hall, Fernau. "Close-Up of Shanta Rao." *Dance Magazine* (June 1955): 26–33, 76–79.
Horst, Louis. "Shanta Rao and Dancers of India." *Dance Observer* (November 1957): 137–138.
Krishna Rao, U. S., and U. K. Chandrabhaga Devi. *A Panorama of Indian Dances.* Delhi, 1993.

CLIFFORD REIS JONES

RAPANUI. Better known as Easter Island in the Western world, Rapanui is an overseas territory of Chile in the eastern Pacific Ocean about 1,250 miles (2,000 kilometers) from its nearest Polynesian neighbor, Pitcairn, and almost 2,000 miles (3,200 kilometers) from the western coast of South America. One of the most isolated land areas on earth, Rapanui was settled by seafaring Polynesians in outrigger canoes. They were decimated by civil wars in pre-European times, and by introduced diseases and slave-taking since Easter Sunday of 1722, when the island was first visited by Europeans. By 1877 only about 110 of the indigenous Rapanui people were alive. The ensuing cultural disintegration included the loss of much of their traditional music and dance. Nevertheless, dance in Rapanui has again become a living tradition, evolving a Polynesian style of its own from the remnants of the past and from other Polynesian introductions.

The remnants of the past comprise reconstructions and recombinations of movement motifs taken from written and pictorial sources, as well as from oral traditions drawn primarily from the knowledge of one old man, Kiko Pate. There are essentially two traditional forms—dances performed with a dance paddle carved or painted in abstract anthropomorphic form, and a dance combining two simultaneous sets of movements performed by men and women. The paddle dances are performed either in a squatting position, with the paddle twirled between the palms while the distal end rests on the floor, or in a standing position, in which the distal end is held between the toes and the head of the paddle is held in the hand. In the standing form the movements consist primarily of hopping on one foot, either in place or moving backward in a circle. The other known old dance form centers on men who are seated and make rowing motions, while standing women perform graceful arm and lower-body movements.

The movements of these early forms derive ultimately from the Polynesian ancestors of the historic Rapanui people, who migrated to this isolated island from central Polynesia. Thus indigenous motifs combine successfully with later importations from that region, especially from Tahiti and the Cook Islands. These later introductions are a combination of side-to-side hip movements in various rhythms and graceful hand and arm movements, characteristic of the central Polynesian *'aparima*. Another dance now considered traditional is based on the Samoan song "Simo Simo" but has hip movements borrowed from central Polynesia.

As elsewhere in Polynesia, dance in Rapanui is based on sung poetic texts. However, because the words of the old songs are no longer completely understood and the new songs are often adapted from various Polynesian languages, the movements have become more ornamental and superficially interpretative, rather than the more allusive enhancement of poetry and ritual movements imbued with religious humility that probably existed in pre-European times.

[*For general discussion, see* Polynesia. *See also* Chile, *article on* Folk and Traditional Dance.]

BIBLIOGRAPHY

Campbell, Ramón. *La herencia musical de Rapanui.* Santiago, 1971.

Métraux, Alfred. *Ethnology of Easter Island.* Honolulu, 1940.

ADRIENNE L. KAEPPLER

RASCH, ALBERTINA (born 1891 in Vienna, died 2 October 1967 in Woodland Hills, California), Austrian-American dancer and choreographer. Trained at the Imperial Ballet School in her native Vienna, Albertina Rasch was performing before the age of fourteen. She left for the United States in 1910 and appeared in Hippodrome and Winter Garden shows before becoming *première danseuse* for the Century Opera Company.

In 1916–1917, Rasch toured with Sarah Bernhardt and then returned as a concert performer with a supporting ballet troupe. This was the beginning of the Albertina Rasch Dancers, a troupe of highly disciplined and balletically trained girls who performed in many revues, musicals, and recitals during the 1920s and 1930s.

Rasch opened her first dance studio in New York City in 1923 and later opened a second studio in Los Angeles. She staged shows in London and Paris and was a prolific choreographer on Broadway from 1924 through 1935. Her Broadway credits include *Rio Rita* (1927), *Show Girl* (1929), *The Band Wagon* (1931), *The Great Waltz* (1934), and *Jubilee* (1935). In 1941 she returned to Broadway for *Lady in the Dark,* and in 1945 she choreographed *Marinka.* Critic John Martin, among others, felt she had raised the level of dancing on Broadway and that her material was of concert caliber.

Rasch worked extensively in Hollywood during two periods, 1929–1931 and 1933–1939, predominantly at Metro-Goldwyn-Mayer (MGM), where she specialized in balletic spectacles and operettas. She supervised and directed almost all of the camera work on her dances and was the only established female dance director in Hollywood. Her credits include nearly thirty films, among them, *Rogue Song* (1930), *The Merry Widow* (1934), *Firefly* and *Rosalie* (both 1937), and *Marie Antoinette, Sweethearts,* and *The Great Waltz* (all 1938).

Rasch gave recitals on both coasts and toured her troupe. Her husband, Dimitri Tiomkin, frequently wrote scores for both her stage and film work. Notable was a series of Lewisohn Stadium concerts in New York City in 1932, revised the next year for the Hollywood Bowl. Rasch also published articles on the need for an American ballet, and she was the first choreographer to stage

RASCH. A scene from *The Great Waltz* (MGM, 1938), the film version of the 1934 operetta about the lives of the Johann Strausses, father and son. Rasch choreographed the dances in the stage production and in the film. (Photograph from the Dance Collection, New York Public Library for the Performing Arts.)

George Gershwin's *Rhapsody in Blue* and *An American in Paris* as ballets. She retired after World War II.

[*See also* Precision Dancing.]

BIBLIOGRAPHY

Ries, Frank W. D. "Albertina Rasch: The Broadway Career." *Dance Chronicle* 6.2 (1983): 95–137.

Ries, Frank W. D. "Albertina Rasch: The Hollywood Career." *Dance Chronicle* 6.4 (1983): 281–362.

Ries, Frank W. D. "Albertina Rasch: The Concert Career and the Concept of the American Ballet." *Dance Chronicle* 7.2 (1984): 159–197.

FRANK W. D. RIES

RĀS LĪLĀ. A genre of Indian festival plays, *rās līlā* features dance segments. The word *rāsa* or *rās* refers to a circular dance, especially the circular dance of Kṛṣṇa (Krishna) and the *gopīs*, or milkmaids. Kṛṣṇa, an *avatāra* (incarnation) of the deity Viṣṇu (Vishnu), is said to have grown up among the cowherd community near the city of Mathura, where he was born. Because his life was threatened by his wicked cousin, King Kaṃsa, he was smuggled away by his foster parents to the area of Vraja (Braj) and then to Vrindavana where his foster parents lived. These areas are thus sacred to his devotees. In Mathura and Vrindavana, *rās līlā* troupes enact, through dance, pantomime, song, and recitation, the plays that commemorate the exploits of Kṛṣṇa as a boy.

The first *rās līlā* play in Mathura is believed to have been presented in the latter part of the sixteenth century, during the period of the *bhakti* religious movements centered about the figure of Kṛṣṇa. Today there are many troupes, called *rāsmaṇḍalīs*, which usually consist of four musicians, four actors who take the parts of *gopīs*, two special actors called *svarūps* who take the parts of Kṛṣṇa and his favorite *gopī*, Rādhā, and a troupe leader called a *rāsdharī* (although all the actors can be called *rāsdharīs*).

The actors or actor-dancers begin their careers as boys of eight or ten years of age; there are no females in the troupes. They begin with the parts of *gopīs*, but some later play the roles of Rādhā and Kṛṣṇa at the age of eleven or twelve. Puberty ends their careers, unless they become musicians or troupe leaders. A remarkable feature is that the boys who take the parts of Rādhā and Kṛṣṇa are offered worship and otherwise treated, for the duration of the play, as if they were indeed these divine figures.

Each troupe has from thirty to forty-five plays in its repertory. There are about 150 plays altogether, some of which have been written by former troupe leaders.

The *Bhāgavata Purāṇa* is the principal source of the plots for the dance dramas. The troupes perform in temples and also at the homes of patrons; many go on tour as well as perform in the area of Mathura and Vrindavana (the two are about six miles apart in southwestern Uttar Pradesh).

Rās līlā is also a dominant element of the dance tradition of Manipur state, where its first performance occurred in 1769. The king of Manipur at the time, instructed by Kṛṣṇa in a vision, conceived the *rās līlā* cycle known in Manipur today, and his daughter danced the role of Rādhā in his composition. There are eight dance dramas in this cycle, each telling a different story. The most elaborate is *mahā rās*, performed on a full-moon night in October; the simplest, *nitya rās*, can be presented on any social or festive occasion. Accompaniment is provided by singers and instrumental music. Like Mathura *rās līlā*, the genre in Manipur features child dancers, but here women too participate. Performances take place in a circular *maṇḍapa*, or pavilion, within the precincts of a Vaiṣṇava temple. The dance dramas are primarily derived from themes in the *Bhāgavata Purāṇa* and the *Gīta Govinda*, a mystical erotic poem about Rādhā and Kṛṣṇa written by Jayadeva in the twelfth century. The Manipuri *rās līlā* tradition became popular throughout India in the

RĀS LĪLĀ. Images of Kṛṣṇa and the *gopīs* dancing hand in hand, in a painting on linen, mounted on a panel, from the Bakura district of Bengal (seventeenth or eighteenth century). The Kṛṣṇa figures are barechested; the rightmost carries his flute. The *gopīs* wear long scarves draped back over their shoulders; pompoms dangle at their wrists. Huge bees and a tiny deer in the foreground seem to join in the dance. *Rās līlā* was a popular theme for illustrations on *pattas* (wooden book covers) such as this one; the style represents the last offshoot of medieval Indian painting untouched by Mughal influence. (Asutosh Museum of Indian Art, Calcutta.)

mid-twentieth century owing to the patronage of nationalist intellectuals.

[*See also* India, *article on* The Rādhā-Kṛṣṇa Theme in Indian Dance; Manipur; *and the entries on the Jhaveri sisters, Sharma, and Singh.*]

BIBLIOGRAPHY

Gargi, Balwant. *Folk Theater of India*. Seattle, 1966.

George, David E. R. *India, Three Ritual Dance Dramas: Raslila, Kathkali, Nagamandala*. Cambridge, 1986.

Hein, Norvin. *The Miracle Plays of Mathurā*. New Haven, 1972.

Massey, Reginald, and Jamila Massey. *The Dances of India: A General Survey and Dancer's Guide*. London, 1989.

Bipinsingh, Guru. "The Rasleela of Manipur." *Quarterly Journal of the National Centre for the Performing Arts* 3 (September 1974): 27–36.

CLIFFORD REIS JONES

RASSINE, ALEXIS (Alexis Raysman; born 26 July 1919 in Kaunas, Lithuania), ballet dancer and teacher. Born in Lithuania to Russian parents, Rassine spent his childhood in Cape Town, South Africa. As a youth of fourteen he began his dance training with Helen Webb in 1933 and also took lessons with Maude Lloyd in 1933 and 1934. Lloyd found him such a promising student that she staged pas de deux for him and Cecily Robinson, another young dancer trained by Webb. In 1937, at age eighteen, Rassine left South Africa to go to Paris, where he continued his studies with Olga Preobrajenska and Alexandre Volinine. That same year he made his professional debut in a revue at the Bal Tabarin.

Having moved on to London, Rassine studied with Vera Volkova and Stanislas Idzikowski. After a brief stint with Ballet Rambert in 1938, he became a member of Ballet Trois Arts (1939–1940), danced with the Anglo-Polish Ballet (1940–1942), and finally in 1942 joined Sadler's Wells Ballet, where he would remain until 1955. During World War II, when many British male dancers were in military service, Rassine made an important contribution to British ballet by participating in the company's performances and carrying on as usual despite the tensions of wartime. He was soon promoted to *premier danseur* and was cast as partner to such ballerinas as Margot Fonteyn and Beryl Gray in such classics as *Giselle, The Sleeping Beauty,* and *Coppélia,* as well as in Fokine's *Le Spectre de la Rose* and Ashton's *Les Patineurs* and *Les Rendezvous.*

During his years with the Sadler's Wells Ballet, and later as a guest artist with the London Ballet and other companies, Rassine created numerous roles in ballets choreographed by Ninette de Valois, Robert Helpmann, Frederick Ashton, and others. For de Valois he danced in the pas de trois in *Promenade* in 1943 and appeared in her *Don Quixote* in 1950. For Helpmann he created the role of the Lover in *Miracle in the Gorbals* (1944) and danced in the original casts of *Hamlet* (1942) and *Adam Zero* (1946). For Ashton he appeared in *The Quest* (1943) and *Les Sirènes* (1946) and created the role of the Spirit of the Earth in *Homage to the Queen* (1953).

Although Rassine's engaging personality made him perfectly suited for lighthearted roles in the classical repertory, such as Franz in *Coppélia,* he was also adept at bringing to life the more complex characters in the dramatic works of Helpmann and de Valois. In addition he was valued both as a solo dancer, where he was admired for his smooth, lithe movement, and as an exceptionally able partner, a role for which he was much in demand throughout his career.

One especially notable performance occurred on 21 February 1946, the second night after the reopening of the Royal Opera House, Covent Garden, when Rassine partnered the exquisitely beautiful Russian ballerina Violetta Elvin in her London debut. They danced the famous Bluebird pas de deux in the third act of *The Sleeping Beauty* to tumultuous acclaim, as Elvin's technical virtuosity and charm were equally matched by Rassine's.

In 1947, Rassine accepted an invitation to return to South Africa to produce and dance in *Giselle,* act 2, for the South African National Ballet in Cape Town, under the direction of his youthful partner Cecily Robinson. He subsequently formed an important partnership with the South African ballerina Nadia Nerina, with whom he toured in South Africa and southern Rhodesia (now Zimbabwe) in 1952 and again in South Africa in 1955, appearing with the University of Cape Town Ballet in *Giselle.* He later performed as partner to the great French ballerina Yvette Chauviré in her guest appearances with the Royal Ballet in 1958. After retiring from the stage, Rassine opened a ballet school in London in 1976.

BIBLIOGRAPHY

Chujoy, Anatole, and P. W. Manchester, eds. *The Dance Encyclopedia.* Rev. and enl. ed. New York, 1967.

Clarke, Mary, and David Vaughan, eds. *The Encyclopedia of Dance and Ballet.* New York, 1977.

Cooper, Montgomery, and Jane Allyn. *Dance for Life: Ballet in South Africa.* Cape Town, 1980.

Grut, Marina. *The History of Ballet in South Africa.* Cape Town, 1981.

Koegler, Horst. *The Concise Oxford Dictionary of Ballet.* 2d ed. New York, 1987.

MARINA GRUT

RAUSCHENBERG, ROBERT (born 22 October 1925 in Port Arthur, Texas), American graphic artist and dance collaborator. Rauschenberg's paintings, constructions, and assemblages have been characterized as situations involving multiplicity. Rauschenberg orchestrates found objects and everyday images in nonhierarchical arrangements—utilizing light, movement, and sound; he conspires with the viewer and the environment, acknowledges time as a compositional device, and embraces the montage of incongruities infusing daily life. Rauschenberg's work also embodies elements and explores modes of experience intrinsic to multimedia, nonnarrative theater.

He has collaborated with many choreographers and dancers, both in designing decor, costumes, and lighting for their work and by engaging them in his own performance pieces. He worked with Paul Taylor on most of his earliest dances, including *4 Epitaphs* (revised as *3 Epitaphs*) and *The Least Flycatcher* (also composing the score), both in 1956, and *The Tower* (with Jasper Johns) and *Resemblances* in 1957. He also worked with several of the dancers of the Judson Dance Theater in the 1960s, including Trisha Brown, Steve Paxton, and Yvonne Rainer; he later created the visual presentation for Brown's *Glacial Decoy* (1979) and *Set and Reset* (1983). His most extensive involvement in dance was as resident designer of costumes, sets, and lighting for the Merce Cunningham Dance Company (c.1954–1964). [*See the entry on Cunningham.*]

In the summer of 1952, at Black Mountain College in North Carolina, Rauschenberg participated, with Cunningham and others, in John Cage's *Theater Piece #1.* Rauschenberg's collection of *White Paintings* (1951) was hung (or was projected) above the audience—just one of the activities taking place simultaneously in the piece. Painted thoroughly white with house paint and devoid of a single subject, the *White Paintings* comprise, through shadow and reflection, the entire environment where they happen to be, and as the space changes, so do the paintings. What Rauschenberg calls their hypersensitivity is thus in some ways analogous to Cage's notion of silence. It is that point in a composition in which (for a duration often determined by chance) all the composer's authority is eliminated: the sounds, all of equal value, evolve circumstantially from the environment. Cunningham also incorporates kinetic silences in his dances, moments where the dancers may hold a position, but where their stillness, like Cage's silence, is filled with activity: the natural movements of the body working.

Cunningham offers his collaborators little, if any, information about a dance he is creating, and encourages the artists to work independently. Hence, both the collaborative process and its realization become situations of interdependence. "Each person, observant of the others, is allowed to act freely" (Cunningham, 1968). The relationship among the elements may simply be that they "coexist" in the same time and space. The unpredictable manner in which often disjunctive objects and images interact and overlap in Rauschenberg's constructions, assemblages, and "combine" paintings (e.g., *Monogram,* 1955–1959—made from, among other items, a rubber tire and a stuffed angora goat—and *Black Market,* 1961) in many ways parallels the Cunningham-Cage liberating sense of coexistence.

As it was initially exhibited, Rauschenberg's combine painting *Black Market* invited the public's participation and in this way was constantly evolving. The viewer was encouraged to exchange his or her own objects for objects in an open valise, joined to the canvas by a rope, and then to draw the object on one of the four clipboards also affixed to the canvas. Rauschenberg's work for Cunningham's controversy-provoking *Winterbranch* (1964) echoed this notion of an ever-changing piece composed of available objects. Rauschenberg invented a different object—affectionately named monster by the company—for each performance from material discovered backstage. He also employed chance to determine a unique lighting design for every concert. The dancers, moving in and out of the lights' random, assaulting paths, plunged from piercing dazzle into an equally blinding darkness. [*See* Winterbranch.]

Other Cunningham dances for which Rauschenberg made combine-style structures include *Minutiae* (1954), *Aeon* (1961), and *Story* (1963). The objects for *Story,* conceived in the same improvisational spirit as *Winterbranch,* also evolved anew in each performance from things (and people) found in the theater. Not all of Rauschenberg's designs employed his combine–found-object technique. For *Summerspace* (1958), he painted the backdrop and costumes in a pointillist manner. Theoretically, the dancers, energized as Seurat-like dots, would both define and explore the painted space, animating it but sometimes camouflaged by it; or they might burst from the backdrop, like animals emerging from nature.

Images of performance pervade Rauschenberg's art works. His 1959 *Trophy I (for Merce Cunningham)* contained Cunningham's photograph, and his 1968 *Autobiography* displayed an image of Rauschenberg performing one of his own works, *Pelican* (1963). He had already appeared in a performance piece in 1961, *Homage to David Tudor,* in Paris, with Tudor, Jasper Johns, Niki de Saint-Phalle, and Jean Tinguely. Cultural writer Calvin Tomkins (1980) reported that Rauschenberg painted onstage *(First Time Painting)* facing the audience yet concealed by the canvas; because he had connected microphones to the easel, his gestures could be heard.

RAUSCHENBERG. Gregory Lara, Lance Gries, Diane Madden, and Carolyn Lucas in Trisha Brown's *Astral Convertible* (1989). (Photograph by Mark Hanauer; used by permission; from the archives of the Trisha Brown Dance Company.)

Pieces by Rauschenberg include *Open Score* (1966), presented in conjunction with "9 Evenings: Theatre & Engineering," which developed into E.A.T. (Experiments in Art and Technology), founded by the artist and Billy Klüver. *Open Score* involved a real tennis game, wired for sound and light, with several hundred people observed by the audience through projections (by infrared television) onto a large screen. Rauschenberg integrated technology and art in his nonperformance work as well, in such pieces as *Soundings* and *Solstice* (both 1968).

In 1976 Rauschenberg collaborated with Viola Farber and David Tudor on the video *Brazos River,* and in 1977 he returned to the Cunningham company to create the set, costumes, and properties for *Travelogue* (a decor he called "Tantric Geography"), which were integral to the choreography. He also collaborated with Trisha Brown in 1983 on *Set and Reset.* Attesting to Brown's interest in articulating the space above the stage, Rauschenberg's design, a montage of images, was projected onto a suspended structure of triangles and rectangles thirty-six feet (ten meters) wide. Although not demanding the audience's participation, this presentation—along with a second collaboration, *Astral Convertible* (1989)—in common with all of Rauschenberg's pieces, offered the viewer visual choices among a bombardment of images. Without a focal point or any apparent hierarchy, unremitting activity was taking place in both time and space. For *Astral Convertible,* Brown asked Rauschenberg for a portable, self-contained system integrating set, music, and lighting. Assisted by engineers Billy Klüver and Per Biorn and lighting designer Ken Tabachnik, he created eight aluminum towers (two to eight feet high) equipped with motion sensors powered by car batteries. The dancers' movements triggered the car headlights and sound equipment installed in each tower, while additional control circuits added an element of randomness. Composer Richard Landry's score included samples of many musics and traffic noise; the result in performance was like changing stations on car radios. Rauschenberg also contributed the costumes (silvery two-toned unitards with, for the women, translucent stretch panels suggesting a skirt) and the work's punning title. Brown called the set "plain as refrigerators"; the artist said he wanted to evoke a "passage through the sky."

BIBLIOGRAPHY

Alloway, Lawrence. *Rauschenberg.* Washington, D.C., 1977.

Cage, John. *Silence.* Middletown, Conn., 1961.

Cunningham, Merce. "Two Questions and Five Dances." *Dance Perspectives* 34 (1968).

Klosty, James, ed. *Merce Cunningham.* New ed. New York, 1986.

Potter, Michelle. "'A License to Do Anything': Robert Rauschenberg and the Merce Cunningham Dance Company." *Dance Chronicle* 16.1 (1993): 1–43.

Tomkins, Calvin. *Off the Wall.* Garden City, N.Y., 1980.

MELISSA HARRIS

RAVEL, MAURICE (Joseph Maurice Ravel; born 7 March 1875 in Ciboure, France, died 28 December 1937 in Paris), French composer. Ravel, whose ballet *Daphnis et Chloé* (1909–1912) is one of the masterworks for dance, enjoyed wide popularity because of his musical imagination and instrumental skill. His father, a Swiss engineer, and his Basque mother moved to Paris when their son was three months old and helped to foster his precocious musical interest. He had the best private teachers before engaging in studies at the Paris Conservatory between 1889 and 1900, but he consistently failed to win academic prizes, usually because he was too innovative.

Although Ravel disliked performing in public, his pianistic skill extended keyboard technique and harmony in a direct line from Franz Liszt and Frédéric Chopin. His reputation became established with the first publication of his works, mostly for piano, around 1900. *Ma Mère l'Oye* (Mother Goose, 1908), a suite of five duets for children's piano, was later extended and orchestrated for the first of three ballets produced with his music in Paris during 1912. *Ma Mère l'Oye* opened at the Théâtre des Arts on 28 January, with choreography by Léo Staats to Maurice Ravel's scenario, based on elements of classic fairy tales, including "Sleeping Beauty" and "Beauty and the Beast." In 1911, *Adélaïde,* in seven scenes, was an epilogue on an orchestration of his *Valses Nobles et Sentimentales* (1911). Choreographed by Ivan Clustine to Ravel's own scenario for Natalia Trouhanova, it premiered at the Théâtre du Châtelet on 22 April. In it, different flowers convey specific symbolic messages between the ballerina and two rivals for her love.

Daphnis et Chloé, a commission for Serge Diaghilev's Ballets Russes, debuted at the Théâtre du Châtelet on 8 June 1912, with choreography by Michel Fokine and designs by Léon Bakst. Ravel took more than two years to compose his "choreographic symphony," as he called it, and it remained his largest-scale work. Unfortunately, Ravel conceived the ballet differently from Fokine, and there were disagreements over Bakst's decor.

In a reminiscence by Ravel that was published posthumously in *La revue musicale* (October 1938), he wrote of *Daphnis:*

> I sought to compose a broad musical fresco, which is less concerned with archaic fidelity than with loyalty to the Greece of my dreams, resembling in many ways what was imagined and depicted by French artists in the latter part of the 18th century. The work is built symphonically, on a strict tonal plan, out of a small number of themes, the development of which ensures its homogeneity. (Ravel, 1938)

The music for *Daphnis et Chloé* involves a large orchestra with an unseen, wordless mixed chorus, and it represents Ravel at his most symphonic. Much of it is pictorial tone painting, not only the celebrated Dawn episode that introduces part 3, but the dances of the nymphs and their invocation to Pan in part 1, the Pirates' dance in part 2, and the symbolic mime of the Pan and Syrinx legend in part 3. A motif expressing the love of Daphnis and Chloé runs throughout the work, and the final General Dance was the most extended use of 5/4 meter for dance at that time (although anticipated by composers Petr Ilich Tchaikovsky and Cesare Pugni).

Ravel's two other ballets of 1912 are musically significant in illustrating aspects of Ravel's personality: his love of childlike matters, classical antiquity, oriental fantasy, and mechanical precision. For him, art was less a matter of subjective truth (as practiced by the Romantics) than a dazzling artifice, paralleled by his fondness for collecting fake works of art and sophisticated knickknacks.

Ravel later composed *La Valse* (1920), calling it a "choreographic poem." Although Diaghilev had asked Ravel to conceive the work in balletic terms, the impresario decided *La Valse* was unsuitable for the purpose, deeply offending the composer. Its first choreographic version was by Bronislava Nijinska for Ida Rubinstein in 1929.

Ravel's other score intended for dance, *Boléro* (1928), also choreographed by Nijinska for Rubinstein, premiered at the Paris Opera. No one was more surprised than Ravel by its instant success and continuing popularity. Essentially a repetition of two sixteen-bar phrases in basic C-major harmonies, varied on each reprise by the addition of fresh instrumental colors and louder dynamics, *Boléro* could be thought a precursor of the minimalist music of the 1970s. The sudden release of accumulated tension by an abrupt change of key to E major near the end remains unsurpassed even by techniques of pop music.

Ravel's other works for the theater were the one-act opera, *L'Heure Espagnole* (1907–1909), which premiered in Paris in 1911, and the "lyric fantasy," *L'Enfant et les Sortilèges* (1925), which involved elements of dance and mime for a story by Colette. He toured the United States from 1927 to 1928 and turned down George Gershwin's request to study with him, with the warning that Gershwin would "stop writing good Gershwin and end up writing bad Ravel." Ravel's own fondness for jazz and swing music soon emerged in some concert works, notably the Violin Sonata (1927) and the two Piano Concertos (1931).

Dance forms occur in much of Ravel's concert music, as in *Pavane pour une Infante Défunte* (1899), *Rapsodie E-spagnole* (1907), and the movements of *Le Tombeau de Couperin* (1917), and choreographers have been continually attracted to his ballet scores and other works. *Daphnis et Chloé* was later choreographed by, among others, Frederick Ashton (1951), Serge Lifar (1958), John Cranko (1962), John Neumeier (1972), Glen Tetley (1975), and John Taras (1975); *Boléro* by Lifar (1941), by Pilar López with La Argentinita (1943), by Maurice Béjart (1961), and by Leonid Lavrovsky (1964); *La Valse* by George Balanchine (1951) and by Ashton (1958); *Valses Nobles et Sentimentales* by Lifar (1938), Ashton (1947), Kenneth MacMillan (1966), and Ronald Hynd (1975); *Ma Mère L'Oye* by Cranko (as *Beauty and the Beast,* 1966) and by Balanchine (1975); *L'Enfant et les Sortilèges* by Balanchine (1946 and 1975), Michel Descombey (1960), Janine Charrat (1964), and Jiří Kylián (1984); the String Quartet by Murray Louis (as *Moment,* 1975); items from *Trois Poèmes de Stéphane Mallarmé, Chansons Madécasses,* and the Violin Sonata (as *Taste,* 1975) by Cliff Keuter; the Piano Concerto in G by Jerome Robbins (1975), by MacMillan (as *La Fin du Jour,* 1979), and by Graeme Murphy (as *Beyond Twelve,* 1980).

Ravel died in 1937 after a five-year bout with a progressive disease of the brain. He provided his own clear-sighted epitaph: "It is lucky that I have been able to write music, because I do not think I could ever have done anything else." For the Ravel centennial in 1975, the New York City Ballet mounted "Hommage à Ravel," with sixteen ballets arranged in three programs to choreography by Balanchine, Robbins, Taras, and Jacques d'Amboise.

BIBLIOGRAPHY

Barnes, Patricia. "Ravelling Ravel." *Dance and Dancers* (November 1975): 21–25.

Dutronc, J. L. "Les musiciens et la danse: Maurice Ravel et le ballet." *Saisons de la Danse,* no. 78 (November 1975): 19–21.

Garafola, Lynn. *Diaghilev's Ballets Russes.* New York, 1989.

James, Burnett. *Ravel: His Life and Times.* New York, 1983.

Kennicott, Philip. "Ravelation." *Dance Magazine* (April 1990): 68–69.

Myers, Rollo H. *Ravel: Life and Works.* London, 1960.

Nichols, Roger. *Ravel Remembered.* London, 1987.

Orenstein, Arbie. *Ravel: Man and Musician.* New York, 1975.

Orenstein, Arbie. *Lettres, ecrits, entretiens.* Paris, 1989.

Ravel, Maurice. *Ravel according to Ravel.* Translated by Frances Tanner. London, 1988.

NOËL GOODWIN

RAVEL FAMILY. For almost one hundred years, from the late eighteenth century into the nineteenth century, at least four generations of the Ravel family devoted themselves to theater. From their generational home in Toulouse, France, the family toured abroad to exhibit a performance that included rope dancing, acrobatics and tumbling, ballet, mime, and illusionistic tricks—the theatrical skills and inheritance of pre-Romantic spectacle theater.

Early in the eighteenth century (approximately 1716 to 1723), the French crown adopted a more liberal attitude toward previously banned performances of *commedia dell'arte.* This shift legitimized popular entertainments and brought attention to the spectacular rope dancing of François Ravel (born c.1755, died 1849). François and his wife, Marie Françoise Colman, had three sons, Gabriel Ravel (born 1781, died 27 October 1859), Pierre Henri Ravel (born 26 October 1785 in Limoges, France, death unknown), and Jean Ravel (born 7 July 1797 at Toulouse, death unknown). Jean Ravel's first wife, Leticia Cotti, who accompanied him on the 1832 tour of the United States, died of cholera in 1833 while the company was on the Mississippi River. His second wife, whom he married 7 March 1835, was Angelica Maddalena. She appears on programs as Pâque Preato and as Mademoiselle Emily. The Ravels' extended family was the basis of their company. The repetition and similarity of family names makes it difficult to establish particular appearances and roles based on printed programs.

Gabriel Ravel married Madame Lonati, a widow older than himself with two sons who subsequently adopted the name Ravel. The oldest child was Dominique; the other was Desiret. Both sons performed with the company. In addition, Gabriel and Madame Lonati had five sons and one daughter: Gabriel (born 1810 in Rouen, died 14 April 1882 at Toulouse), Antoine Rémi (born 14 July 1811 at Marseille or Cuges-Les-Pins, Bouches-du-Rhône, died 26 November 1872 at Toulouse), Angelica Maddalena (Pâque) (born 9 January 1813 in Vicenza, died 10 January 1899 in New York), Jérôme (born 6 August 1812 or 1814 in Vicenza, died 7 August 1890 in Castelmaroun); Louis (born 20 August 1814 or 1815 at Toulouse, death unknown), and François Seraphim (born 19 July 1819 or 1823 in Vienna, died 25 November 1880 at Toulouse).

Tours. The elder François Ravel's sons, Pierre Henri, Jean, and Gabriel (called Gabriel Aîné, "the elder," to distinguish him from his son), began their career by performing together but subsequently formed separate companies. They toured in Italy, Germany, and France but ended in Paris at the Théâtre Montansier, where, on 12 August 1806, the unchallenged champion of rope dancers in France, the Italian Pierre Furioso, called "The Incomparable," attempted to defend this position against Gabriel Aîné, billed as "Le Terrible." The contest, reportedly judged by Auguste Vestris and Paul Duport, was immortalized in a series of separate drawings of Furioso and Gabriel Aîné on the ropes. The results established the Ravel name in Paris.

Like their grandfather, father, and uncles, Gabriel Aîné's children began their profession when they were all under the age of ten in Germany; they later appeared in Italy and France. Their early repertory was *vaudevilles* ("little" spoken pieces, usually comic character sketches involving parody and farce), arranged especially for their talents, and tightrope dancing. The Ravels were all in Paris in 1825 at the Théâtre de l'Ambigu-Comique, where young Gabriel triumphed in a pantomime-ballet, *Cocambo*, in which he appeared as Punch on stilts. Following another tour of the French provinces, in Paris, at the Théâtre de la Porte-Saint-Martin, Gabriel Aîné's children commenced their successful engagements and association with the French pantomime artist, "comic dancer," and scenario writer Charles-François Mazurier (1793–1828).

After Mazurier's untimely death, the young Ravels began to tour their newly inspired repertory on a broad and ambitious scale. After a season at the Théâtre de la Porte-Saint-Martin in early 1832, and under the management of their uncle Jean, on 5 July three of the brothers and six other family and company members arrived in New York City for a tour that was to include New York City, Philadelphia, Boston, and points south to New Orleans. They returned to France in 1833. In the latter part of 1834 and after a series of performances in Paris, the theatrical "family" continued their practice of dividing and traveling several companies at once. On roughly a yearly basis the family would gather in Toulouse to re-form their companies, work on their repertories, and rest.

In 1834, after a farewell engagement in Paris, Gabriel, Antoine, Jérôme, François, and Angelica Ravel went with Eugène Baptiste Fénelon (whom Angelica would marry in 1835) and the Javellis—Martin, Leon, and Emily—to London, where on 5 January 1836 they appeared for the first time at Drury Lane and, subsequently, at the Strand and Adelphi theaters. They undertook a provincial tour in April and ended at Vauxhall Gardens in June. From England they left again for the United States, to which they returned almost yearly thereafter for seasonal tours. After its opening in July 1850 in New York City, Niblo's Gardens was their headquarters in the United States. From their 1834 tour of England, the company adopted a plan of organization that, for the most part, they maintained from that point onward. Jérôme became stage manager, playwright, and general director of performances. Antoine handled financial affairs. Fénelon took the post of musical conductor. Gabriel and François handled staging and did not deal with business matters.

The Ravel brothers returned to the United States through 1868, but the Ravel name remained before the American public until the 1880s. Angelica's daughter Josephine Fénelon-Winther Marietta Ravel (born 4 November 1844 in Rio de Janeiro, died December 1898?), a dancer, mime, and actress, carried the family tradition into the 1870s. The Ravel name was carried on also through its unauthorized use by the Martinetti family who, having been brought in the 1850s to the United States as company members by the Ravel family, remained in the United States and continued to perform much of the Ravel repertory through the mid-1880s and to use the same techniques and rewritten scenarios through the 1920s. When asked by Charlie Chaplin to join him in his film productions, members of the Martinetti family refused; they saw film as a passing fancy.

Theatrical Art. The Ravel family continued and enlarged upon pre-Romantic ballet and *commedia dell'arte* traditions. A mania for pantomime—mute narratives delivered with gestures (both tragic and comic)—swept Paris in the 1740s. Pantomime-ballets developed from movements in which the principals depended on a mimic manner formally codified and stylized in performance. With steps from the *ballet d'école* to provide variety and with displays of physical virtuosity to provide comic alacrity, these pantomime-ballets were more formally structured than the waning *ballets d'action*. Cohesion of the pantomime-ballets was supplied by the kaleidoscopic rhythm of plot events.

The Ravels built upon a traditional structure of pantomime that had evolved between 1806 and 1836, a one-act drama, one to two hours long. Traditionally the act was divided into episodes, varying in number from twelve to eighteen. Two unequal parts divided the action: the shorter first part, "the opening," usually gave the pantomime its title, its subject drawn from legend, classical mythology, literary classics, or exotic locale. Obligatory elements of plot and action conspired to create a crisis that precipitated the second part, or "transformation scene." The Ravels' *The Green Monster* opens with the Sorcerer's Cave, in which witches and sorceresses seek to maintain their power over the Green Monster and Bottle Imp; at the expiration of their power at midnight an explosion occurs and the Green Monster is set free, vanishes into thin air in a transformed scene, and hovers over a pair of lovers whom he is determined to protect. Significant is the fact that the first part is brief (following an earlier model for pantomimes), that major characters are masked, and that the intervention by a friendly agent marks the division between the opening and the second section of the pantomime.

The major characters of *The Green Monster* are transformed into harlequinade figures in the second half of the pantomime. A clown, who usually did not undergo a change from first to second half, dominates the action of the second half of the drama. A traditional knockabout pursuit ensues until the penultimate scene, or "dark scene," which takes place in a gloomy or macabre setting. Here disaster threatens, but the major characters are reconciled, and all are transported (and sometimes changed back into their old shapes) in an apotheosis.

The Green Monster closely followed the formula of the Ravels' *Raoul.* Its supernumeraries included knights, warriors, guards, satyrs, dwarfs, sorcerers, nymphs, and genii. It expanded to ten from an earlier six settings. Passage of time was indicated not by act divisions but by tableaux. Acrobatic feats and specialty dances were performed at the close of the curtains of the tableaux, and the final tableau, termed the "Grand Transformation Scene," received distinction with a kaleidoscopic unfolding of lighting, setting, and cast. Made possible by recent technical theatrical advancements, this layered presentation of spectacular elements culminated the production in a visual whole. This type of scene, by drawing attention totally to embellishments as opposed to acting and plot, influenced the whole development of spectacle theater. Additionally, ballet, previously employed as an integral part of the story in a traditional pantomime, was now used within the play as *divertissements.* However, the scenario informs that in the first scene of *The Green Monster* the unearthly witches continue to move expressively in mystic dance; in the second scene, the heroine Rosalie's soul dances "in aerial flights."

Mazurier's Influence. The Ravels were strongly influenced by Mazurier, whose style depended upon star performers with fantastic magnetism and inviting temperament—a combination of passion and charisma. These two qualities enlivened his scenarios, which combined aspects of melodrama, fairy tales, and fantasy projected by warm humor. Mazurier's pantomime-ballets might never be completely visualized, but we know that they brought new attention to the *commedia dell'arte* masques, especially that of Polichinelle, that they began to unite acrobatic illusionistic tricks (similar to those in Gregorio Lambranzi's *Nuova e curiosa scuola de balli theatrali,* 1716), that they introduced seemingly more spontaneous burlesque sketches, and that they linked dancing and mime choreographically with acrobatics. Lifts, holds, and jumps widened, freed, and vitalized the ballet. The pantomime-ballet *Jocko, ou Le Singe du Brésil* was exemplary of Mazurier's art. Choreography exceeded classical steps. The Monkey somersaulted, grimaced, mimicked human activity, and defied gravity in all sorts of jumps and turns from heights to depths. He also moved his body such as to create the illusion of contortion and swung on ropes; critics deemed Jocko's characterization natural in its perfection. Similarly, in *La Neige* (the Ravels titled their version *Godenski, or The Skaters of Wilna*) the performers maintained the perfect illusion of being on ice: sliding out of control, tripping, flipping, somersaulting, and finally skating (dancing) easily and gracefully.

Unlike the short career of Mazurier, the Ravels' theatrical activities spanned the rapid development of more elaborate stage machinery and spectacular effects, larger theaters, changing and competing tastes and aesthetics in the theatrical presentation of the body, and more efficient and specific physical training. These changes in the physical theater and in the tastes of its audience led to new interpretations of and adaption of Mazurier's formulas. Performances originally developed for more intimate settings were now required to project broadly for larger theaters. Furthermore, the development of the Romantic ballet after 1827 demanded new and different physical skills of spectacle theater performers, necessitating that company dancers be trained solely for the ballet. Notwithstanding the fact that the Ravel brothers did age and lose some of their youthful agility, economic necessity and audiences' desire for ballet dancers seem to have contributed to the prominence of strictly ballet-trained dancers, like Harriet and Henri Wells, Augustine Proche-Guisbilei, Charles Winther (Angelica Ravel's second husband), Emma Doutreville, and Louis Ferin. The 11 November 1855 edition of the *Golden Era,* a San Francisco newspaper, noted that pantomime and ballet had been presented by the Rousset, Montplaisir, and Espinosa troupes at levels that Gabriel Ravel and his touring company could not hope to rival.

Performance Style and Innovations. Changes in the Ravels' style and choreography between their association with Mazurier in the 1820s and the peak of their artistry in the late 1840s and 1850s are difficult to assess and fully understand. In his *History of the Philadelphia Stage* (1860), Charles Durang, who saw the Ravels perform in 1832, wrote that he admired them as "professors of gymnastics." Yet the Ravels preserved the French style of pantomime, which was light hearted, gay, and mischievous, in contrast to the English style, which was characterized by macabre English irony with noise, bombast, and battles. The French style impressed and delighted by quietly representing comical characters studied from nature—a kind of living portraiture. The English style was a personal display, direct and thrusting, formal and heroic, what theater historian Lawrence Senelick has called "ballet of assault." The knit of both spectacular physical feats and dancing distinguished the totally silent French pantomimes from the partially dialogued English pantomimes. Ethnic or fantastic dance action and scenic effects used to display local color and themes related to daily life made the French pantomime; English pantomime was more dependent upon topicality and contemporary locale for its satiric effectiveness. [*See* Pantomime.]

The Ravels, with their superior physical training, took the French pantomime-ballet forward in several ways. They placed more emphasis on visual, especially illusory, tricks in contrast to Mazurier's concern with dumb narrative and sight gags. The Ravels' use of aerial flights, trap-door disappearances, and sudden transformations presented the performers either as passive and unsuspecting victims of a complex and bewildering world or as superhumans with godlike powers. In contrast, English pantomime characters caused their own plight, and survival was a physical and verbal fight against circumstances. The Ravels also enlarged on the grand transformation scene, particularly its musical accompaniment.

Typical Program. Including traditional genres and distinctive innovations, the essential building blocks of Ravel programs were rope dancing, acrobatics and tumbling, classical posing, gymnastic demonstrations, mime, *commedia dell'arte, vaudevilles,* ballets and other exhibition dances, and illusionistic tricks aided by stage machinery. In a typical Ravel program, tightrope acts and/or acrobatic feats consistently preceded a ballet; the major fare of the evening was the pantomime-ballet. In a program that might have had two ballets or portions of pantomime-ballets instead of a full pantomime-ballet, entr'actes of dance, acrobatics, and solo demonstrations of particular virtuosity and skill varied and expanded the design.

However eclectic, even illogical, the assemblage of acts would seem to a modern audience, these shows actually achieved a high degree of unity. For example, separately highlighted acrobatics and popular ballroom and ethnic dances presented in costume ("fancy dances") might later appear in the pantomime-ballets. Gymnastics and ballet were used technically and choreographically to connect pantomimic episodes, to spur on dramatic action, and to accomplish tricks and illusions. Somersaults, improbable escapes facilitated by human pyramids, and walking on stilts provided surprising plot solutions. Dances lent verisimilitude to the locale of the drama, gave evidence that the heroine was graceful and romantic, and led to relationships of characters, most obviously in danced love duets. Stylized scenes of combat and battle were full of choreographed maneuvers, posturings, and formal exhibitions of dueling, wrestling, and boxing.

Repertory. A definitive Ravel repertory is difficult to list because the Ravels, as part of their business acumen and art, constantly repeated and recombined elements of their entire repertory, retitled pieces, and added new materials. The Ravels worked for a critical balance—to surprise their audiences with the unexpected and to satisfy them with the expected. Spectators at the time, who were also entertained by hoaxes, such as those perpetrated by showman P. T. Barnum and his American Museum, delighted in being fooled by the "magic" (transformations and visual illusions) that earmarked the Ravels' pantomime-ballets and in being awed by the gymnastic feats and displays of seemingly superhuman strength and agility. The public knew well the basic materials of the programs, yet they found them alluring, despite their repetition, because of their clever reuse and their means of finding solutions to the difficulties of the characters.

Among the Ravels' pantomime-ballets were *Monsieur Molinet, or A Night of Adventures* (later entitled *Vol-au-Vent* and *Lise and Colin*); *Godenski, or The Skaters of Wilna* (inspired by Mazurier's *La Neige;* Paris, 1827); *Jocko, or The Ape of the Brazils* (inspired by Mazurier's *Jocko, ou Le Singe du Brésil;* Paris, 1825); *Four Lovers, or The Harvest Home (Four Lovers, ou Les Rivales Rendevous); The Robbers, or The Burglary at Night* (later titled *Italian Brigands, or The Midnight Assault*); *La Fête au Village, or The Unfortunate Adventures of Monsieur Deschalumeaux* (inspired by the ballet produced by Jean-Antoine Petipa in 1822 at the Théâtre Royal de la Monnaie in Brussels); *Raoul, or the Magic Star* (c.1849); *Jeannette and Jeanot; Kim Ka, or the Adventures of an Aeronaut* (c.1851); and *Asphodel, or the Magic Pen* (c.1854).

The dances that appeared on Ravel programs included excerpts from pantomime-ballets, theatrical versions of popular social dances, and full ballets. Examples include *Le Carnival de Venise; Danse de Pierrot en Panniers; Pas de Derviche au Tambour; Pas Tartare* from *Lodoiska,* original choreography for the opera by Charles-Louis Didelot in 1818; *Le Diable à Quatre,* original choreography in 1845 in London by Joseph Mazilier, to music by Adolphe Adam, after a 1756 idea from an English comedy and opera; *Grand Tarentella,* based on the 1839 Paris Opera production, choreography by Jean Coralli, to music by Gide; *Le Jugement de Pâris,* original choreography in 1793 by Pierre Gardel; *Gavotte de Vestris; The Hornpipe; La Sylphide,* first act, original choreography in 1832 by Filippo Taglioni, to music by Jean Schneitzhoeffer; *Esmeralda,* original choreography in 1844 by Jules Perrot; and *Flore et Zéphire,* original choreography in 1796 by Didelot, revived at the Paris Opera in 1815.

Comic pieces reminiscent of *commedia dell'arte* included *The Living Flour Sack* and *The Perilous Ladder.* Gymnastic exercises—exhibitions illustrative of classical canons of beauty such as those noted by the first-century Roman rhetorician Quintilian—were *Three Gladiators; Somersaults Aeriens;* "attitudes of the Antique Statues of the Royal Academy of Rome"; *Bedouin Arabs; Le Colonne Horizontale; Herculean Feats* (tableaux); *Vulcan and Cyclops, ou L'Enlèvement de Vénus par Mars; Les Forces d'Alcide, ou Les Positions Académiques* (Academic Positions; tableaux). *Tableaux vivants* included *The Punch Club* and *La Vengeance d'Amour, or The Incendiary.* Among their French *vaudevilles* were *Le Conscrit* by Merle, Simonnin, and Ferdinand; *The Genii without Arms, or The Talisman Recovered* (1841); *The Conjurer's Pills* (later *Magic Pills;* 1841); and *Robert Macaire.*

The Ravels' long appeal can be attributed to their consummate skill as performers, their canny business abilities, and their morally didactic repertory, which, on a less obvious level, portrayed social themes that preoccupied the mid-nineteenth century—for example, domesticity and the idea of sexual spheres of influence, fear of violence and the need for social control, power as embodied in the idea of the superhero, and cultural diversity (exoticism of locale and character types). Responding to their enduring popularity, in 1858 the *Boston Courier* noted that for a quarter century the Ravel family had been a virtual constant before the American public, "with whom their name has become a familiar household word, the synonym for all that is cheerful, joyous and merry."

BIBLIOGRAPHY

Downer, Alan S. "Players and Painted Stage: Nineteenth-Century Acting." *Proceedings of the Modern Language Association* (June 1946): 522–576.

Duchartre, Pierre-Louis. *The Italian Comedy.* Translated by Randolph T. Weaver. London, 1929.

Kirstein, Lincoln. *Movement and Metaphor: Four Centuries of Ballet.* New York, 1970.

Mayer, David. *Harlequin in His Element: The English Pantomime, 1806–1836.* Cambridge, Mass., 1969.

Oliver, George B. "Changing Pattern of Spectacle on the New York Stage, 1850–1890." Ph.D. diss., Pennsylvania State University, 1956.

Schneider, Gretchen. "Gabriel Ravel and the Martinetti Family: The Popularity of Pantomime in 1855." In *American Popular Entertainment: Program and Papers of the Conference on the History of American Popular Entertainment,* edited by Myron Matlaw. Westport, Conn., 1979.

Swift, Mary Grace. *Belles and Beaux on Their Toes: Dancing Stars in Young America.* Washington, D.C., 1980.

Winter, Marian Hannah. *Le théâtre du merveilleux.* Paris, 1962.

Winter, Marian Hannah. *The Pre-Romantic Ballet.* London, 1974.

GRETCHEN SCHNEIDER

RAYET, JACQUELINE (born 26 June 1932 in Paris), French dancer and teacher. Rayet studied at the dance school of the Paris Opera before beginning her climb up the ladder of the corps de ballet. First dancer *(première danseuse)* in 1956 and a star *(étoile)* in 1961, she owes to the Opera her sense of tradition, expanded by the influences of Olga Preobrajenska, Lubov Egorova, and Nora Kiss. She revealed her individuality in Serge Lifar's works, as the Fairy in *Snow White* and the Woman in *Les Mirages,* and in *Suite en Blanc.* She also demonstrated an affinity for George Balanchine's style, dancing in his *Serenade, Le Palais de Cristal, Scotch Symphony,* and *Apollo.* Her incarnation of Giselle in 1961 delicately evoked her illustrious predecessors.

Rayet's perfect line, sensitivity, and intelligence made her an ideal instrument for the choreographers whom she inspired. Roland Petit created the most beautiful moments of his *Turangalîla* for her. Two associations nourished the flowering of her personality: the first with Peter van Dyk, and the second with Maurice Béjart. Van Dyk created *Unfinished Symphony* with her in 1957, in which they expressed an internalized romanticism in the purest language. They danced in Hamburg in *Romeo and Juliet,* (music by Sergei Prokofiev) and *Pelléas et Mélisande,* (music by Arnold Schoenberg), displaying both lyricism and rigor.

In 1965 Rayet danced at the Opera in *Le Sacre du Printemps* (choreography by Maurice Béjart). She was an exceptional interpreter, at once modest and sensual. A year later Béjart staged for her and Jean-Pierre Bonnefous the strictly constructed *Webern Opus V.* Her character and her art were now fully developed.

As the organizer of the Festival de Brantôme and the Cadets de l'Opéra group, teacher, and *répétitrice*—particularly with the Ballet du XXe Siècle—Rayet has faithfully defended a craft she esteems. She was named a Chevalier des Arts et Lettres in 1957 and a Chevalier de la Légion d'Honneur in 1973. In October 1986 she became professor at the Conservatoire National Supérieur de Paris.

BIBLIOGRAPHY

Cournand, Gilberte. "Jacqueline Rayet." *Opéra de Paris* (March 1986): 29.

Hersin, André-Philippe. "Jacqueline Rayet." *Saisons de la danse* (November 1969).

Williams, Peter, and Marie-Françoise Christout. "The Queen of Spades." *Dance and Dancers* (December 1978): 14–18.

JEANNINE DORVANE
Translated from French

RAYMONDA. Ballet in three acts and four scenes. Choreography: Marius Petipa. Music: Aleksandr Glazunov. Libretto: Lydia A. Pashkova and Marius Petipa. Scenery and costumes: Oreste Allegri, Konstantin M. Ivanov, and Petr Lambin. First performance: 7 [19] January 1898, Maryinsky Theater, Saint Petersburg. Principals: Pierina Legnani (Raymonda), Sergei Legat (Jean de Brienne), Pavel Gerdt (Abderrakhman).

Raymonda is in love with the gallant knight Jean de Brienne. On the eve of her wedding to Jean, Raymonda dreams of her fiancé, who is suddenly replaced by an ardent Saracen knight. On the day of the wedding, as Raymonda receives congratulations from the guests, there appears among them the Saracen emir, Abderrakhman, whom she recognizes as the knight of her dream. At the height of the wedding feast Abderrakhman tries to kidnap Raymonda, but Jean de Brienne intervenes and mortally wounds the emir in a duel. Everybody celebrates the happy outcome of the wedding of Raymonda and de Brienne.

The ballet's musical score is built on a sequence of suites: the *demi-caractère* suite of act 1 is followed by a classical suite; in act 2 the classical suite is joined to a character suite, and in act 3 the unity of classical and character suites is completed. Glazunov substantially altered the adagio, the key variations, and also the coda as a conclusion to the suite. He composed the adagio of the first act as a pas de deux of union of the protagonists. The *pas d'action* of the second act is treated as a dueling "dialogue" between Jean de Brienne and Abderrakhman. In a *pas classique hongrois* Glazunov again united the protagonists with great expressiveness. The final variation of each suite belongs to the heroine, who appears also in the final episode and in the coda of each suite. Thereby, Raymonda is the focal point of all the intonational, rhythmic, and timbral innovations introduced by the composer to give musical flesh to the skeleton of the plot.

Raymonda has been staged by many different choreographers, each of whom sought to overcome the flaws of its libretto and to bring out the message implicit in the musical score. Aleksandr Gorsky, in his 1918 version for Moscow's Bolshoi Theater, completely redesigned Jean de Brienne's variation and his pas de deux with Raymonda in act 1, abandoned the symmetrical deployment of the corps de ballet along with the tutu, and converted Abderrakhman from a warrior to a merchant. Fedor Lopukhov, in his 1923 version for the Maryinsky Theater, changed the number of scenes and recomposed several variations, including Raymonda's "Pizzicato" in the first scene.

In 1931 Agrippina Vaganova unveiled a convincing revision of Marius Petipa's version of the ballet, after which successive attempts were made to alter the ballet's libretto radically in order to enhance its dramatic realism. The first attempt along these lines, made by Vasily Vainonen in collaboration with Yuri Slonimsky in 1938 for the Kirov Ballet in Leningrad, failed, principally because the music was at variance with the new ballet's personality. The choreographers also reversed the order of the second and third acts, transferred some of the variations from act 2 to act 1, introduced a new episode from *The Oriental Rhapsody,* and converted Abderrakhman into a positive hero and Jean de Brienne into a villain. Leonid Lavrovsky, in his 1949 version for Moscow's Bolshoi Theater, redesigned the ballet's dramatic action: in act 1 Jean de Brienne parted with Raymonda as he set out on a crusade; Abderrakhman was portrayed as a Moorish chieftain and appeared in the flesh before Raymonda in act 1. This scene anticipated Raymonda's abduction. Drawing on the choreography of Petipa and Gorsky, Lavrovsky recomposed a number of dances in the first and second acts.

Perhaps the most effectual version of *Raymonda* was the one created by Konstantin Sergeyev for the Kirov Ballet in 1948. The scenery and costumes on that occasion were by Simon Virsaladze. Raymonda was danced by Natalia Dudinskaya, Jean de Brienne by Sergeyev, and Abderrakhman by Semyon Kaplan. Jean de Brienne, who is absent from act 1, is represented by a tapestry given to Raymonda as a gift by his father. The duel in Petipa's version and the newlyweds' ceremonial cortege in Gorsky's version were replaced in the apotheosis of Sergeyev's production by a honeymoon scene before a moving panorama. Sergeyev restaged many of the dances of act 1.

Raymonda was reinterpreted by Yuri Grigorovich, chief choreographer of the Bolshoi, in 1984. The scenery and costumes for this production were again by Virsaladze. The role of Raymonda was danced by Natalia Bessmertnova, Jean de Brienne by Aleksandr Bogatyrev, and Abderrakhman by Gedeminas Taranda. The striving for the ideal, the tug-of-war between the sensuous and the spiritual were portrayed by Grigorovich not so much as a clash between the principal characters, but rather as contradictory drives and motivations within the heroine, who attains perfection after resisting all temptations. Victor Vanslov wrote,

> The production retains Petipa's original choreography with some of the numbers (e.g., de Brienne's variations, the adagio of de Brienne and Raymonda in act 1) presented in Gorsky's choreographic treatment. . . . Grigorovich has converted *divertissement* dances and scenes into action dances to lessen their significance as background and enhance their dramatic importance. To this end, Grigorovich on occasion introduces principal characters into them (e.g., Raymonda and de Brienne in the "Grande Valse," Abderrakhman in "Panaderos"), an innovation as compared to the previous version.
>
> (Grigorovich and Vanslov, 1987)

Grigorovich brought in Jean de Brienne from the start by composing an opening scene in which he parts with Raymonda before setting out on a crusade. By cutting some of the mime scenes depicting everyday life in act 1, Grigorovich enhanced the poetry of the dancing. The episode involving Raymonda's dream, which is repeated twice, is treated as a pas de deux representing her parting with Jean de Brienne and later her memory of her fiancé. Having moved the symphonic entr'acte for the second scene of act 1 to the conclusion of act 1, Grigorovich, for the first time, embodied this music choreographically as an adagio of the principals' feeling of complete and triumphant love. Following the musical score, Grigorovich substituted Abderrakhman for Jean de Brienne in the Reverie Scene, much to Raymonda's surprise and dismay. By introducing Abderrakhman at the center of the *panaderos* and bacchanal and as a force of magnetic attraction, Grigorovich treated Raymonda's "Oriental Dance" (previously excluded) as a dance-vision of the spellbound heroine. The male characters were presented as extreme contrasts: Jean de Brienne is a noble knight, ascetic and dour; Abderrakhman is portrayed as a high-minded warrior of bewitching charm. Raymonda dominated the ballet, appearing not only in pas de deux and variations, but also in the coda of every suite.

In the West, complete productions of *Raymonda* have been less successful; short-lived versions were staged by Britain's Royal Ballet and by American Ballet Theatre. George Balanchine and Alexandra Danilova staged a three-act version for the Ballet Russe de Monte Carlo in 1946, and the New York City Ballet has since performed Balanchine's several extractions of *divertissements* from it: *Pas de Dix* (1955), *Raymonda Variations* (1961), and *Cortège Hongrois* (1973). All feature classical ballet style colored with tinges of Hungarian motifs.

BIBLIOGRAPHY

Asafiev, Boris. "Balety Glazunova." In Asafiev's *O balete: Stati, retsenzii, vospominaniia.* Leningrad, 1974.

Beaumont, Cyril W. *Complete Book of Ballets.* Rev. ed. London, 1951.

Grigorovich, Yuri, and Victor V. Vanslov. *The Authorized Bolshoi Ballet Book of Raymonda.* Translated by Alexander Kroll. Neptune City, N.J., 1987.

Guest, Ivor. "*Raymonda*'s History." *The Dancing Times* (December 1965): 121–122.

Krasovskaya, Vera. *Russkii baletnyi teatr vtoroi poloviny deviatnadtsatogo veka.* Leningrad, 1963.

Maynard, Olga. "*Raymonda.*" *Dance Magazine* (July 1975): 53–58.

Molden, Peter L. "Glazunov and the Ballet." *The Dancing Times* (July 1987).

Slonimsky, Yuri. "Raymonda." In *Glazunov: Issledovaniia, materialy, publikatsii, pisma,* vol. 1, edited by M. O. Iankovskii. Leningrad, 1959.

Souritz, Elizabeth. *Soviet Choreographers in the 1920s.* Translated by Lynn Visson. Durham, N.C., 1990.

Wiley, Roland John, trans. and ed. *A Century of Russian Ballet: Documents and Accounts, 1810–1910.* Oxford, 1990. Includes the libretto for *Raymonda.*

KARINA L. MELIK-PASHAYEVA
Translated from Russian

RECONSTRUCTION. [*To discuss the role of reconstruction as a tool in the understanding and re-creation of dance, this entry comprises three articles:*

Use of Historical Notations
Use of Modern Scores
Beyond Notation

The first article examines use of Renaissance and Baroque dance notations; the second focuses on the use of modern notation scores; the third describes the role of reconstruction in understanding authenticity. For related discussion, see Notation.]

Use of Historical Notations

Dance, as movement in space and time, would seem to be ephemeral, unless captured on film or videotape, or depicted by modern notation systems. However, throughout the centuries, numerous attempts have been made to conserve and transmit dances and dance styles. From the fifteenth century on, European dance masters wrote manuscripts, books, and treatises, either for use by aristocratic or upwardly mobile neighbors in the next kingdom or, sometimes, for posterity. Many of these dance masters, though they wrote in different eras and countries, shared a belief that the choreographers, dancers, and dance music of their times brought dance to its highest possible level as an art form; they notated and described dances to preserve and instruct others in this perfected dance style and to point out its improvement over previous styles. As the beneficiaries of their instructions, and through their work, we are able to leap back in time to reconstruct and perform dances of the past. And, through this reconstruction of dances, entire eras are sometimes brought to life. Historical dances are transformed from two-dimensional descriptions in centuries-old books, plays, and manuscripts into three-dimensional movement and energy, expressed in present-day space and time. Steps uncovered from the surviving "how-to" manuscripts and books fit together with myriad other details about courtly life to create an ever-expanding and fascinating jigsaw puzzle of observable Early Dance. Dance reconstructors enjoy time travel, meeting people who choreographed and danced three hundred to five hundred years ago. The words and clues left behind by the old masters, or their publishers, offer introductions to the personalities of otherwise unknown dance teachers as well as the steps they performed and taught. Information on specific movements and dances also serves musicians (by revealing theory, tempi, and articulation of dance suites) and actors (by portraying correct sitting, standing, walking, and bowing for historical costuming in plays by Shakespeare, Molière, and others).

Dance reconstruction from original sources is similar to piecing together a jigsaw puzzle, but that resemblance is only one of the cerebral games dance historians can enjoy. Books and manuscripts from the fifteenth through nineteenth centuries contain mysteries as engrossing and compelling as in any Agatha Christie detective novel. Detection skills must be put to use to answer not only "whodunit?" but also "howdunit?" Like careful detectives, dance historians must keep track of the details of time and place that distinguish eras and styles. From original sources dating back centuries, the descriptions of steps must be disentangled and then fitted with their dance patterns to the accompanying music. In some cases, before the steps can be deciphered, it is necessary to study Renaissance handwriting manuals to learn how to decode Gothic and Italic scripts or to unravel the enigmas of Elizabethan Secretary handwriting. After obvious attention is paid to the original dance source, the real work begins, with an in-depth search for supplemental information. Clues can be gleaned from a variety of sources, including contemporary diaries, etiquette books, letters, biographies, autobiographies, and tailors' clothing-pattern books. If the aim is to reconstruct a dance, and to present it as closely as possible to the way in which it was performed in its own era, this compilation of data is vital. All components help to round out the understanding of an era and a dance.

Perceptions of movement, behavior, and taste vary infinitely, in the present as in the past. Each era, however, reveals different philosophies and theories of movement, which demonstrate and reflect the arts and philosophies of that time. The dances of an era do not exist in isolation. In re-creating old dances, it is necessary to seek to understand the framework of conventional behavior that was then taken for granted and that underlay all daily activities. Social dance forms, for example, arose from and related to many attitudes, beliefs, and myths in polite society. Convictions relating to an individual's place in society, agreement as to what constitutes personal beauty, and the prevailing etiquette and decorum have all helped to shape dances and their movements.

Step descriptions from sixteenth-century books often make little sense until careful research into the clothing of the era reveals how a dancer's range of movement was restricted or enhanced by the bulky and heavy garments worn. And yet, although some garments were heavily boned, and some were expanded by fashionable trains, panniers, or padded sleeves with oversleeves, it cannot be assumed that dances consisted mainly of walking in patterns. Indeed, descriptions in sixteenth- to eighteenth-century books written for gentry and courtiers—not professional dancers—give instructions for elaborate jumps, multiple turns, and intricate footwork. In *Le gratie d'amore* (1602), Cesare Negri described steps to enhance a vigorous *galliard.* These included fourteen types of *tours en l'air,* jumped from one or both feet, and thirteen ways to leap, turn, and then kick a tassle held several feet off the ground. Most eighteenth-century books about *Chorégraphie,* the dance notation system first published by Raoul-Auger Feuillet in 1700, present tables showing a huge step vocabulary, including more than seventy variations of the *pas de bourrée*—far more than in current dance movement vocabulary—to be performed by elaborately garbed and bewigged dancers.

The delicate tracery of dances recorded in Feuillet notation gives the researcher a spatial overview of a dance pattern, not unlike a bird's-eye view of eighteenth-century garden design. The reconstructor has an immediate sense of the shape of a dance as well as its steps and can relate it to other arts of the era.

Concepts of beauty and elegance change from era to era. To the Elizabethan or Renaissance courtier, a substantial, portly look was most attractive—appearing too thin might reveal the poverty of one's income and estates. A padded doublet, a cloak, hat, and sword, or a stiffened bodice, a neck ruff, and a skirt with train gave form and line to the dancers' motions. The actual weight of carefully copied sixteenth-century garments contributes to the style of movement, as do the reconstructed wigs and elaborate headdresses worn by the eighteenth-century dancer. Often the movement of the clothing requires its own musical time; heavy, long skirts and capes need time to unwind and settle down after the many revolutions of a pirouette or a *salto tondo in aria* (a single or double tour in the air).

In the reconstruction of historical dances, therefore, twentieth-century concepts of beauty must be recognized, acknowledged, and then ignored. In order to portray late sixteenth-century dances and dancers and give a close approximation of style, shape, and movement, a twentieth-century dancer often must suffer through drastic changes in mind set. After years of striving to attain and maintain a muscular yet sleek body, and after studying and performing for years in lightweight leotard and tights, a would-be Elizabethan dancer must be willing to move in an outfit weighing twenty to forty pounds and to add pads

RECONSTRUCTION: Use of Historical Notation. Charles Garth and Elizabeth Aldrich, of the Court Dance Company of New York, a company specializing in the reconstruction of French and Italian Renaissance dance, performing a *passo e mezzo.* This duple-meter Italian couple dance, popular in the sixteenth and seventeenth centuries, was described by Fabritio Caroso in his 1581 treatise *Nobiltà di dame.* (Photograph by Pedro Sanchez; courtesy of the Historical Dance Foundation, Inc., New York.)

RECONSTRUCTION: Use of Historical Notation. Jean-Baptiste Lully's 1676 opera *Atys*, originally performed at the court of Louis XIV, was revived for the first time since the eighteenth century in 1988. The reconstruction was produced by the Paris Opera, with choreography by Francine Lancelot, featuring dancers from her Ris et Danceries. The music was conducted by William Christie and played by Les Arts Florissants. Seen here, in an intricate gold costume, is a dancer from the Paris Opera Ballet in the opera's dream scene. (Photograph by Michel Szabo; courtesy of the Brooklyn Academy of Music, New York.)

and stuffing to give the appearance of high cholesterol obesity—and a Renaissance view of wealth.

Rigid rules of decorum and deportment were often as important as dance steps and music. Etiquette and socially accepted rules of behavior, "the usual genteel observances of Polite Society" are outlined in many books, including those by Negri, Fabritio Caroso (*Nobiltà di dame* [1600]) and Giovanni Della Casa (*Galateo* [1559]), and later, those by John Essex (*The Young Ladies Conduct* [1722]), Pierre Rameau (*The Dancing Master* [1725]), Giambatista Dufort (*Trattato del ballo nobile* [1728]), and Kellom Tomlinson (*The Art of Dancing* [1735]). These instructions, which include guidelines on how to sit, stand, bow, and enter and depart a room, influence the patterns of a dance and its shape in space, whereas more specific rules about how to manage a sword, wear a cape, and greet a prince inspire specific arm and torso motions. All rules lead the noble dancer to cut a fine figure in society while also cutting a brilliant caper and performing an elegant *entrechat*.

Carefully thought-out reconstruction of historic dance affords present-day dancers the opportunity to study, move through, and have access to their choreographic heritage. A dance becomes the medium through which cultural roots and influences can be traced through time and nationalities. For example, the *canario* described in sixteenth-century sources as a masking dance, possibly from the Canary Islands, contains stamping foot movements often seen in African dances; unexpectedly, its movement patterns are also recognizable in flamenco footwork, Irish step dances, Appalachian clogging dances, and even American tap steps.

A dance reconstructor must strive to avoid many pitfalls. To fully depict the inventiveness and creativity of past masters, and the disagreements among them, centuries of information cannot be lumped into one catch-all classification. The many conflicting admonitions included in rules about accepted stance, movements, dances, style, and choreography before the late eighteenth century show that no uniform "pre-classic" style existed. For example, between 1550 and 1660, placement and use of the foot changed completely from a preference for flexed feet with uplifted toes to stretched feet with pointed toes, and from little or no foot turnout to acceptance and desire for turned-out feet. In the late sixteenth century Caroso warned gentlemen to avoid turning out their feet, "with one foot toward the Orient, and the other to the Occident, as the feet appear distorted," but by 1728, Giambattista Dufort was disparaging Caroso's style and advice and advocating turned-out foot positions. Dufort scoffed that the parallel feet and lack of turnout made the earlier steps harsh and inflexible. For Dufort, the foot placement, arm positions, well-rounded figures of the dancers, and even the music described by Caroso lacked "the good taste which reigns today." Dufort even asserted that although "the Italians were the first Inventors of Dance according to Rules, it was the French who led dance to the highest perfection."

Dance historians can see, as Dufort could not, that dances do not evolve according to Darwin's theory of evolution; later styles may differ from earlier styles, but they are not necessarily better. Fashions, including fashions in dance, art, and architecture, change but also interact. For example, late twentieth-century taste in dance may have been shaped to some extent by architects, since the economics and design of large performance halls may have influenced that era's preference for high leg extensions and expansive movements. Subtle shadings of movement, expressive mime, and speedy, intricate footwork that were highly regarded in previous centuries have not been totally superseded, but they are best seen and appreciated in more intimate halls.

A cautious dance historian must therefore avoid jumping to conclusions based on only a few facts or on beliefs based on childhood dance training—and must oppose the prevailing philosophies (or biases), however deeply held, to better portray past concepts of fashion and beauty. Otherwise, to cite an example previously mentioned, researchers might not have discovered that bulky and complex garments did not in fact preclude dancers in the sixteenth through eighteenth centuries from doing complicated footwork, difficult leaps, cabrioles, and *tours en l'air.*

Useful character traits for a dance historian working to reconstruct from original sources include (1) curiosity, of course; (2) tenacity, to keep rereading an obscure source so as to decipher the handwriting and foreign languages (often written in obsolete and outmoded styles) or to uncover the unstated assumptions (things taken for granted then but not now); (3) respect for cultural differences as well as viewpoints that differ from modern beliefs; (4) flexibility and a willingness to change one's interpretation in the light of newly discovered old information; (5) humility, to face sudden illumination from an obvious, yet overlooked, insight that forces a reinterpretation of all previous work ("Oh! Why didn't I see *that* before?"); and ultimately, (6) acceptance of frustration: We must face the fact that we may never know for certain if the printed version of a dance or step that has survived to the present day is the version that was preferred by the *maestro* himself.

The study and reconstruction of dances from the past requires one to overcome vast distances across national boundaries and centuries of time. The process of trying to understand the dance movements and the world of past dance masters necessitates decades of one-sided communication with teachers long dead in a patient attempt to understand not only what they said, but also what they omitted saying. For some dance reconstructors, long after they have discovered how to execute a *volta tonda* or a *pas grave,* the fierce quest to *understand* the words and the steps of others—to dance in their shoes—remains. This hard-won empathetic understanding is a lasting gift that dance historians can choose to use in their own time, with their own neighbors, to bridge the cultural differences, the language barriers, and the physical spaces that separate peoples from one another. Perhaps this particular kind of understanding could even ease tensions and help us to communicate better on our small planet in our jointly shared time.

[*See also* Ballet Technique, History of, *article on* French Court Dance; Feuillet Notation; *and* Renaissance Dance Technique.]

BIBLIOGRAPHY

Aldrich, Elizabeth. *From the Ballroom to Hell.* Evanston, Ill., 1991.

Arbeau, Thoinot. *Orchesography* (1589). Translated by Mary Stewart Evans. New York, 1948.

Brinson, Peter, and Joan Wildeblood. *The Polite World.* London, 1965.

Caroso, Fabritio. *Nobiltà di dame* (1600). Translated and edited by Julia Sutton. Oxford, 1986.

Cornazano, Antonio. *The Book of the Art of Dancing* (c.1455–1465). Translated by Madeleine Inglehearn and Peggy Forsyth. London, 1981. Text and English translation by A. William Smith in *Fifteenth-Century Dance and Music.* Stuyvesant, N.Y., 1995.

Della Casa, Giovanni. *Galateo* (1559). Translated and edited by Konrad Eisenbichler and Kenneth R. Bartlett. 2d ed. Ottawa, 1990.

Elias, Norbert. *The History of Manners.* New York, 1978.

Guglielmo Ebreo da Pesaro. *On the Practice or Art of Dancing* (1463). Translated by Barbara Sparti. Oxford, 1993.

Lauze, François de. *Apologie de la danse, 1623: A Treatise of Instruction in Dancing and Deportment.* Translated by Joan Wildeblood. London, 1952.

Magri, Gennaro. *Theoretical and Practical Treatise on Dancing* (1779). Translated by Mary Skeaping. London, 1988.

ARCHIVES. Dance Collection, New York Public Library for the Performing Arts. Bender Collection, Mills College Library, Oakland, California.

ANGENE FEVES

Use of Modern Scores

Restaging a work from a contemporary score requires not only a knowledge of notation, but also an understanding of style. Because most dancers do not read notation, works are generally staged by a professionally trained notation expert able to direct the work for public performance.

The score is first read in sections: the reader senses its movement, finds its structure and phrasing, and seeks its style. In the Laban method of movement notation, for example, the shape, length, and shading of the symbol give a powerful impression of the combined use of space and time. Sparseness or density and continuity, for example, can be seen in the clusters of symbols. The reader must find the movement's intent; separate decoration and embellishment from basic structure; discover the relationship of the movement to the accompanying music; research the choreographer's philosophies; study the period to which the dance is related, as well as the costume and lighting design for the piece; and read the reviews and literature relating to the whole. In this way, the dance director can separate the technique from the aesthetic and the structure from the interpretation and decide how best to stage the work.

Working from the score avoids the inevitable influence of a particular performer's interpretation, which can occur when a revival is based on a film or videotape. As an actor does not copy a former actor's interpretation, neither should a dancer follow this procedure. At some point following the preparatory work the reader must move into the studio to tackle the movement sequences physically, experiencing them in his or her own body.

Armed with perception molded by imagination, but controlled by the definite boundaries established in the score, a director is free to make decisions about how to restage a dance to satisfy the choreographer's intention and capture the original's vitality and excitement. The final result must be accessible to what may be a new generation of dancers and audiences with their own values. Depending on the system of notation and on the individual notator, the latitude for judgment and interpretation varies.

The act of choreographing on the human body is a more personal and emotional experience than writing a play or composing music on a piece of paper. For this reason, choreographers are reluctant to accept the premise that, if well structured, with movement thoughtfully chosen, a dance can lend itself to more than one interpretation and that someone other than the choreographer or an original cast member can restage it.

With increased interest in dance repertory, procedures for mounting works have become varied. The result is a careless use of terms when referring to the way the performance was realized for the stage: for example, reconstructed by, restaged by, staged by, mounted by, directed by, realized by, taught by, rehearsed by, and directed and staged by are often used without giving due consideration to the actual procedure. Responsibilities fall on different shoulders and credit should be properly given:

1. The dance is learned, taught, and directed from the score up to performance level.
2. The dance is learned and taught from the score but rehearsed and/or coached for performance by another person.
3. The dance is learned, taught, and directed by the same person—who is not responsible for costumes, setting, and the like, which may be faithful to the original or designed anew.
4. A dance previously "lost" is pulled together or reconstructed or re-created from various sources, such as fragments of silent film at the wrong speed, photographs, articles, reminiscences and reviews, an audiotape for correct tempo, interviews with original cast members or the audience, scraps of notation, unpublished photographs collected by dancers, or proofsheets from which only one photo may have been published.
5. A known or partly remembered work is used as a basis, an inspiration for a new version—that is, the choreography is intentionally modified.
6. A known work is given special updating in style or presentation.
7. The score is incomplete and the notator-director or an original cast member must complete it.

The general consensus among American dance directors working from the score is to rid the profession of the prefix *re,* as in restage, remount, and reconstruct. *Reconstruct* should be used when the work is indeed reconstructed, from gathered pieces of information.

The incre asing number of dancers directing from a score has created a new profession. These artists not only retrieve a movement from notated symbols but create a work of art from them. By so doing they keep the dance heritage alive in a manner analogous to the challenges faced by an orchestral conductor or a theatrical director. It is the dance director's responsibility to give correct program credit, so that future generations of directors, historians, and critics can separate the original from what is being witnessed on stage, film, or video.

[*See also* Labanotation *and* Notation.]

BIBLIOGRAPHY

Blum, Odette. "Developing Characterizations from the Dance Score." In *The Second International Congress on Movement Notation at the Fifth International Dance Conference.* Hong Kong, 1990.

Cook, Ray. *The Dance Director.* 2d ed. New York, 1978.

Cook, Ray. "Dawn in New York: Researching a Lost Masterpiece." In *The Second International Congress on Movement Notation at the Fifth International Dance Conference.* Hong Kong, 1990.

Copeland, Roger, et al. "Perspectives in Reconstruction." In *Dance Reconstructed,* edited by Barbara Palfy. New Brunswick, N.J., 1993.

Dils, Ann. "Performance Practice and Humphrey Reconstruction." In *Dance Reconstructed,* edited by Barbara Palfy. New Brunswick, N.J., 1993.

Jordan, Stephanie. "The Musical Key to Dance Reconstruction." In *Dance Reconstructed,* edited by Barbara Palfy. New Brunswick, N.J., 1993.

Reynolds, William C. "Film versus Notation for Dance: Basic Perceptual and Epistemological Differences." In *The Second International Congress on Movement Notation at the Fifth International Dance Conference.* Hong Kong, 1990.

RAY COOK

Beyond Notation

Dance reconstruction, in the 1970s, 1980s, and 1990s, in many ways rode the waves of the Early Music movement, that international swell of interest in historically informed performance practice and the use of period instruments. Because historical music performance was intimately linked with accompanying dance materials, the Early Music movement supplied rationales for studying past movement practices through bodily performance. And, importantly, it stimulated contemporary audiences eager to view the danced fruits of this research. The Joffrey Ballet's enduring interest in ballets past has fueled important reconstructions of *Le Sacre du Printemps* and *Cotillon;* ongoing research in dance notation systems, one result of which was *L'Après-midi d'un Faune* reconstructed from Vaslav Nijinsky's score, has supplied another impetus. Millicent Hodson and Kenneth Archer, with Robert Joffrey's encouragement, researched, reconstructed, and staged *Le Sacre du Printemps* and *Cotillon* in 1987 and 1988. Ann Hutchinson Guest with Claudia Jeschke deciphered Nijinsky's *Faune* score and rendered it in Labanotation, from which productions were mounted in Naples, Montreal, and New York in 1989. Like these specialists, numerous independent directors and troupes in North America and Europe have devoted their work, in whole or significant part, to reconstruction. A brief list of these includes directors Régine Astier, Eva Campianu, Mary Skeaping, Barbara Sparti, and Julia Sutton. Notable troupes include the Cambridge (Massachusetts) Court Dancers, the Wendy Hilton Dance Company, the New York Baroque Dance Company, Ris et Danceries, the Historical Dance Foundation/Court Dance Company of New York, Dance Through Time, the Cincinnati [Ohio] Court Dancers, the Ken Pierce Baroque Dance Company, Les Menus Plaisirs, Danse Baroque Toronto, and Opera Atelier. In North American and European dance, performance has come to be viewed as a customary and primary product of reconstruction work.

Academic scrutiny has in recent years put into question efforts to "authentically" reproduce dances of the past. (Early Music initiatives, similarly queried, have frequently reframed their quest as one for "historically valid" performance.) Poststructuralist theory has evaluated quests for "origins" and "originals" as amounting to the search for universal ontological "ground," for *ur-texts*, absolute truths, and courts of appeal to which to turn. Poststructuralist theory proposes instead that stable and unitary meanings do—and did not—exist, whether with regard to personal subjectivity or widely joined social practices. Seen from this perspective, efforts to reconstitute past instances of dancing can result in nothing more than citations of instable, ever-shifting practices. Neither can the intentions of producers past be taken to guarantee the substance and meaning of historical dances. In a related vein, reception theory calls into question whether contemporary audience reception replicates historical apperceptions of dance, those meanings for dancing that were forged by historically and socially situated communities of viewers of "receivers" of dance.

Such theoretical injunctions may be joined with fruits won, for example, from several decades of work in the United States with reconstruction of "Baroque" dance (c.1690–1720). Theoretical insights should impel researchers to give new weight to findings that dance manuals were pitched from the writers' class position to those of their consumers and that manuals prescribed rather than documented ideal performance practice. They prompt fresh consideration as well of evidence that notated dance scores differed as a function of their notator's "hand" but also in the graphic solutions notators achieved while employing a common symbol system (Beauchamps-Feuillet notation). And they urge further attention to the differences manifest in at least one national school (English dance practice) that was based on but not identical to French noble-style dancing. Such theory-promoted considerations focus the class and national tensions operating through dance and disrupt the notion of a seamless, unitary, pan-European Baroque dance genre.

The case for reconstruction need not fade with the critique of origins and authenticity or wane with shifts in the emphases pursued by the Early Music revival. Theoretical issues push dance studies to reconsider longstanding views of staged, public performance as the primary and final product of reconstruction. That is, scholars may now

RECONSTRUCTION: Beyond Notation. Nijinsky's *Le Sacre du Printemps* (1913) was performed only seven times by Diaghilev's Ballets Russes. Relying mainly on annotated scores by Igor Stravinsky and Marie Rambert, historian and choreographer Millicent Hodson spent more than a decade reconstructing the work. The result was the Joffrey Ballet's 1987 production, seen here in act 1, with Nikolai Roerich's designs painstakingly reproduced by Kenneth Archer. (Photograph © 1987 by Herbert Migdoll; used by permission.)

also conceive reconstruction as a methodology, as a means of pursuing answers to still other questions. Rather than frame and fix a stable and unitary bodily phenomenon, reconstruction may illuminate kinetic and kinesthetic ways that dance made meanings in specific historical societies and moments. Reconstruction may thus be rethought as a technology—a physical, investigative method—for comprehending and complicating traditional questions about dance performance. This methodology may be used to weigh dance as a form of representation; to intervene in and disrupt dance's canon; and to test interdisciplinary or additional disciplines' theoretical formulations in terms of particular dance historical practices.

Traditional studies of past dance practices typically ask questions about movement vocabulary, dance's relationship with music, coordination with scenic/visual elements, and dancers' training and careers. Reconstruction as a research methodology (not necessarily directed toward staged performance) facilitates extension and complication of such questions. Extant Baroque dance choreographies, for example, are generally set to music using binary, sometimes rondo form, but bodily investigation of notated dance scores has revealed that choreographies do not render musical repeats by identically iterating previous dance material. Thus, a tune heard twice through sustains two different sets of movement designs. This lack of coincidence in music and dance design constitutes a choreographic strategy characteristic of Baroque dance. Working with notated scores, but without kinetic and auditory realizations, scholars would find it difficult to discern this compositional relationship. In another vein, efforts to bodily comprehend Baroque movement vocabulary and choreographic design position scholars to theorize the kinds of "expression" the form attempts. Reconstructors in the 1980s and 1990s differed on this point, some asserting "affective" expression, some championing "characterization." Period theories and concepts of rhetoric, acting, and human physiology all bear on this point; the bodily investigation of reconstruction is essential to formulating and testing conclusions about it. Still further, reconstruction shows dance to be intimately connected with historical as well as changing views of the body, being, and knowledge. In this it militates against framing purely internal analyses of dance. Deriving from physical, kinetic investigation, and not necessarily intended for public, staged performance, reconstruction and the fruits thereof may be deployed by researchers proceeding from varied disciplines and points of view.

Scrutiny of compositional strategies and expressive models—just two possible investigations facilitated by reconstruction—can only help scholars in the project of assessing dance as representation, as a discursive mode. Bodily explorations of choreographies and scores can illuminate ways in which dance inscribed such things as political values, gender roles and notions of sexuality, and hierarchies of race and power. The relationship between dance and the ideas or structures it inscribes need not be limited to the longstanding but too-simple formulation that dance merely mirrors social and political givens. Rather, danced representations can be assessed as reciprocally related to social and political matters. Constituting and being constituted by them, danced representations are capable of contesting, confirming, resisting, and mediating ideas, practices, and structures at issue in given cultures over time.

Reconstruction offers a potent vehicle for assessing constructions of gender in eighteenth- and nineteenth-century Europe, for example. Historians agree that Romantic ballet foregrounded women as subjects for and executants of theater dance, thus relegating men to largely supporting roles and reducing their number as performers. Representations of femaleness in Romantic ballet correlate with shifting gender-role definitions that theorized male and female as incommensurably different in biological terms, feeding an ideology of "separate spheres" or domains for men's and women's social action. To assess the magnitude, causes, or modalities of this shift, historians can profitably explore the construction of gender roles in and through eighteenth-century dance. Court and theater dances reconstructed from early in that century show that males and females shared a broad movement vocabulary and common aesthetic ideals; physical contact in partnering consisted in joining or releasing hands. The shift from eighteenth- to nineteenth-century danced constructions of gender suggest that the transition proceeded from more equal to radically imbalanced statuses for men and women, and not inversion of a previous ranking.

Issues of political and racial ordination may similarly draw significantly from dance reconstruction findings. The complement of dancers, along with the selection, sequencing, and choreographic patterns of folk dances for girls' after-school athletics in early 1900s' New York, for example, provided means with which to address the era's urgent cultural debates. These included the right relationship between individuals and groups in a laissez-faire, mass-production industrial economy; assimilation of immigrant peoples in a major port city; and women's claim to public sphere activity, which pressed the limits of separate spheres ideology. The meanings societies made through dance for racial and ethnic groups may be exposed by scrutinizing classical ballet, for example, and searching out the gender assignments, researching movement vocabularies, and limning compositional strategies with which "character dance" constructed representations of "others." These choreographic devices and other staging procedures may be scrutinized for the ways in which they pictured foreign peoples in ethnographic exhibitions (that included dance) at Euro-American world's expositions and fairs since the 1840s.

To consider probing classical ballet's character dancing for its choreographic construction of ethnographic and geographic "others" is already to intervene in the canon of topics recognized by dance scholarship. The art dance forms of ballet and modern dance have enjoyed sustained study by dance history academics; dance anthropologists typically have cast the nets that encompass dance practices of geographically distant others or peoples culturally distinct from dominant groups within Euro-American societies. Reconstruction as a methodology, as a procedure for bodily citing and comprehending (oftentimes systematic) movement practices, has the capacity to breach the canon of traditional genres and topoi. Reconstructions can give access (partial though it must be) to movement materials for study; they can make immediate the demand to denaturalize modernist rankings of dancing as "art" or "social" or "popular." In but one example, the dancing of Southern mountain people—long marginalized in American dance historical studies as social or folk dances—may be brought center stage, so to speak, and evaluated for its utility to and interpretive management by diverse groups. These uses and meanings include the notation and theorization of the Kentucky Running Set by Englishman Cecil Sharp in the 1910s to consolidate a construction of English national identity (itself a project propelled by the English folk dance revival movement) and the revivalist interest in Southern folk arts fanned by the founders and workers of rural settlement schools during the first half of the twentieth century. Notably, the choreographic canon for modern or experimental dance already has been disrupted by contemporary choreographers such as Mark Morris, Susan Foster, and Mark Franko when they mobilize past compositional strategies or intended effects for dances as material for new works.

Finally, reconstruction as a body and motion-utilizing research strategy may create conditions for testing theories advanced in other fields and discourses. French philosopher Michel Foucault's theories about "the order of things" have played an important part in shifting historians' attention from absorption with causation to consideration of discourses as networks of power. He mapped the eighteenth century as part of a "classical episteme" consumed with arraying and classifying varieties of knowledge. This eighteenth-century focus on plotting and specifying (apparent, for example, within natural history studies in taxonomies of flora and fauna) may be extended to and tested against early eighteenth-century manuals explaining or employing the newly minted Beauchamp-Feuillet notation system. Foucault saw classifying tables as stipulating not just varieties of matter but also their possible combinations. Scrutiny of Raoul-Auger Feuillet's *Choregraphie* (1700, 1701) confirms that while this compendium charts steps, positions, and gestures for legs and arms, and their myriad variations (more limited for arms), it speaks not at all to combinatory possibilities. The power and limits for representation of sequencing and combining movements is not rendered transparent by this text or by notated scores that trace out dances. Researchers must sort through and query gaps of this kind. Here reconstruction may test theory; the two arguably sustain and reciprocally inform each other. In this and other projects like those mentioned above, then, bodily investigation as research technology, rather than performance as *summum bonum,* promises reconstruction's expanded instrumentality.

BIBLIOGRAPHY. Reconstruction work by Hodson, Archer, Guest, and Jeschke is detailed in Millicent Hodson and Kenneth Archer, "Ballets Lost and Found: Restoring the Twentieth-Century Repertoire," in *Dance History: An Introduction,* edited by Janet Adshead Lansdale and June Layson, 2d ed. (London, 1994); Millicent Hodson, "Ritual Design in the New Dance: Nijinsky's *Le Sacre du Printemps,*" *Dance Research* 3 (Summer 1985): 35–45 and 4 (Spring 1986): 63–77; Mindy Aloff, "On Death and the Maiden and Diligence: *Sacre* Reconstructed for the Joffrey," *Ballet Review* 15 (Summer 1987): 69–74; Kenneth Archer, "The Quest for Cotillon," *Ballet Review* 16 (Summer 1988): 31–46; and the special issue devoted to "A Revival of Nijinsky's Original *L'Après-Midi d'un Faune,*" *Choreography and Dance* 1.3 (1991): 1–90.

A recent symposium on reconstruction is documented in *Dance Reconstructed,* edited by Barbara Palfy (New Brunswick, N.J., 1993). Digests of poststructuralist theory may be found in Terry Eagleton, *Literary Theory: An Introduction* (Minneapolis, 1983), and Chris Weedon, *Feminist Practice and Poststructuralist Theory* (Oxford, 1987). Also important are Mark Franko, "Repeatability, Reconstruction, and Beyond," *Theatre Journal* 41 (March 1989): 56–74, and *The Dancing Body in Renaissance Choreography, c. 1416–1589* (Birmingham, Ala., 1986). Wendy Hilton's *Dance of Court and Theatre: The French Noble Style, 1690–1725* (Princeton, 1981) supplied a periodization for Baroque dance that held through the 1980s; Mark Franko's *Dance as Text: Ideologies of the Baroque Body* (New York, 1993) applies that appellation to Molière's comedie-ballets (dating from the 1660s).

Works useful for weighing the fluidity of Baroque dance practices include Carol G. Marsh, "French Court Dance in England, 1706–1740: A Study of the Sources," Ph.D. diss., City University of New York, 1985; Rebecca Harris-Warrick and Carol G. Marsh, *Musical Theatre at the Court of Louis XIV: Le Mariage de la Grosse Cathos* (Cambridge, 1994); and Elizabeth H. Rebman, "Chorégraphie: An Annotated Bibliography of Eighteenth-Century Printed Instruction Books," Master's thesis, Stanford University, 1981.

On matters of expression and compositional strategy, see suggested works by Joseph R. Roach, *The Player's Passion: Studies in the Science of Acting* (Ann Arbor, Mich., 1983), and Susan Leigh Foster, *Reading Dancing: Bodies and Subjects in Contemporary American Dance* (Berkeley, 1986). On conceptualizing dance as a technology of representation and social ordination, see Teresa De Lauretis, *Technologies of Gender: Essays on Theory, Film, and Fiction* (Bloomington, 1987); Michel Foucault, *The History of Sexuality,* vol. 1, *An Introduction,* translated by Robert Hurley (New York, 1978); Judith Butler, "Performative Acts and Gender Constitution: An Essay in Phenomenology and Feminist Theory," *Theatre Journal* 40 (December 1988): 519–531; Edward W. Said, *Orientalism* (New York, 1978); Linda J. Tomko, "Fete Accompli: Gender, 'Folk Dance,' and Progressive-Era Political Ideals in New York City," in *Corporealities,* edited by Susan Leigh Foster (London, 1995); and Robert W. Rydell, *All the World's a Fair: Visions of Empire at American International Expositions, 1876–1916* (Chicago, 1984).

On uses of southern American mountains (and English traditional) dance, see Maud Karpeles, *Cecil Sharp: His Life and Work* (London, 1967); Dave Harker, *Fakesong: The Manufacture of British "Folksong" 1700 to the Present Day* (Milton Keynes, England, 1985); and David E. Whisnant, *All That Is Native and Fine: The Politics of Culture in an American Region* (Chapel Hill, N.C., 1983). For work on present-day southern dancing that links bodily investigation to theorizing conceptions of community in American culture, see Susan Eike Spalding, "Definition of Community in Old Time Dancing in Rural Southwest Virginia," *Dance Research Journal* 26 (Spring 1994): 1–7.

For Foucault's classical episteme, see *The Order of Things: An Archaeology of the Human Sciences* (New York, 1971). See also Raoul-Auger Feuillet, *Chorégraphie, ou L'art de décrire la dance* (Paris, 1700; 2d ed., Paris, 1701; reprint, New York, 1968).

LINDA J. TOMKO

RED DETACHMENT OF WOMEN, THE Choreography and libretto: Li Chengxiang and Wang Xixian, after Lian Xin's film *Red Detachment of Women*. Music: Wu Zuqiang, Du Minxin, and others. Scenery: Ma Yunhong. Costumes: Ma Yunhong and Li Keyu. First performance: September 1964, Beijing, Central Opera Ballet Troupe (now Central Ballet of China). Principals: Bai Shuxiang, Zhong Runliang (Qiong Hua), Xue Qinghua, Yu Leidi (Detachment Commander), Wang Guo-hua (Hong Changqing), Li Chengxiang (Nanbatian), Wan Qiwu (Laosi).

The Red Detachment of Women (1964) was the first full-length ballet created by Chinese choreographers with a revolutionary theme. It was first performed in Beijing on 1 October 1964 and was filmed in 1970 with the Central Ballet of China. The ballet was choreographed just before China's Cultural Revolution (1966–1976) was launched by Mao Zedong, in response to criticism of the performing arts by his wife, Jiang Qing, and her supporters.

Taken from an opera (a film of which won a prize at the 1961 Moscow Film Festival), the ballet's plot concerns the struggle and victory of an early Red Army detachment, consisting chiefly of women. On the island of Hainan during China's Second Civil War (1927–1937), they fought General Chiang Kai-shek's Kuomintang and the tyrannical local gentry.

Traditional ballet forms and elements of Chinese national and folk dances were combined to create a new type of dance language. The ballet includes a series of portraits of Revolutionary heroes, such as Qionghua, turned from a slave girl into a Revolutionary woman soldier, and Hong Changqing, the Communist party leader in the detachment. The ballet, characterized by a distinctive nationalistic style and a regional flavor, was filmed in color.

The Central Ballet of China toured with *The Red Detachment of Women* to Yugoslavia, Romania, Albania, West Germany, the United States, and Austria. It has acquired a reputation outside China through the tours but also from wide telecasting of the film version in the West. In the 1960s the ballet was also staged by the Tirana Opera Theater of Albania and by the Matsuyama Ballet Troupe of Tokyo.

[*See also* China, *article on* Contemporary Theatrical Dance.]

BIBLIOGRAPHY

Barnes, Clive. "The Ballet Nixon Saw in China." *New York Times* (19 March 1972).

"Documents from China: *The Red Detachment of Women*." *Drama Review* 15 (Spring 1971): 262–267.

Percival, John. "Dancing Their Own Way." *Dance and Dancers* (November 1986): 16–19.

Perris, Arnold. "Music as Propaganda." *Ethnomusicology* 27 (January 1983): 1–28.

The Red Detachment of Women. Beijing, 1972.

Snow, Lois Wheeler. *China on Stage*. New York, 1972.

Strauss, Gloria B. "Dance and Ideology in China, Past and Present: A Study of Ballet in the People's Republic." *CORD Research Annual* 8 (1977): 19–53.

Wan Kung. "How Our Revolutionary Operas and Ballets Were Produced." *Chinese Literature*, no. 5–6 (1977): 66–72.

Wan Kung. "What Chiang Ching Did to Culture." *China Reconstructs* 26 (May 1977): 2–6.

ZHU LIREN

REDDY, RAJA AND RADHA, Indian dancers, husband and wife: Raja Reddy (born 6 October 1943 in Narasapur, Andhra Pradesh); Radha Reddy (born 15 February 1955 in Kotalgaon, Andhra Pradesh). Raja and Radha Reddy, a dynamic dance team, specialize in Kuchipudi dance, the classical school of the Kuchipudi village Andhra Pradesh, South India. Married when Radha was very young, they were one of the first dancing couples in this tradition. They were trained by Prahlad Sarma, brother of the great dancer and teacher Vedantam Satyam, and further by Pasumarti Venugopal Krishna Sarma of Kuchipudi village.

Raja Reddy began his career as a *bharata nāṭyam* soloist in the company of Indrani Rehman, with which he toured abroad. He soon drew the attention of connoisseurs. After teaming with Radha, he devised duets in the Kuchipudi style, introducing innovations in presentation and choreographing works which highlighted the duo's individual but complementary talents. The Reddys soon made Kuchipudi dance popular not only in Delhi but all over India. Later they worked on the international dance circuit, performing in many festivals worldwide and winning acclaim for their spirited, captivating performances.

They enlisted Kaushalya, Radha's younger sister, to produce their programs. She is also a talented Kuchipudi dancer and often performs with the Reddys, but her major contribution is in conducting the performances with dramatic flourish.

The Reddys established Natya Tarangam, a dance academy, in their home city of Delhi. Among their well-known students are Kaushalya, Suman Arcot, and Shanta Rati

Misra. The renowned *bharata nāṭyam* and Oḍissi exponent Indrani Rehman also learned a few Kuchipudi dances from them.

For their contributions to classical dance, the Reddys have received the Padamshri award from the government of India and the Central Sangeet Natak Akademi award, as well as other honors. They have two young daughters who are learning Kuchipudi under them. They continue to teach, choreograph, and perform new works. The Films Division of the government of India has made a documentary film on the Reddys.

BIBLIOGRAPHY

Kothari, Sunil, ed. *Bharata Natyam: Indian Classical Dance Art.* Bombay, 1979.

Najan, Nala. "Procession of Indian Dance" (parts 1–2). *Arabesque* 12.2–3 (1986).

SUNIL KOTHARI

RED POPPY, THE. Russian title: *Krasnyi Mak.* Ballet in three acts and eight scenes with an apotheosis. Choreography: Lev Lashchilin and Vasily Tikhomirov. Music: Reinhold Glière. Libretto: Mikhail Kurilko. Scenery: Mikhail Kurilko. First performance: 14 June 1927, Bolshoi Theater, Moscow, Bolshoi Ballet. Principals: Ekaterina Geltser (Tao-Hoa), Aleksei Bulgakov (Soviet Ship Captain), Ivan Smoltsov (Li Shan-fu), Asaf Messerer (Chinese Conjurer).

As *The Red Poppy* begins, a Soviet ship drops anchor at a Chinese port, where the dancer Tao-Hoa works at a restaurant. She becomes an eyewitness to a noble act by Soviet seamen, who help the tired Chinese unload the ship, and she falls in love with the ship's captain. In her dreams Tao-Hoa sees a wonderful garden, which is the scene of a struggle between monsters that personify the decrepit past and the forces of good, the poppy flower in particular. The port chief, Heeps, and Tao-Hoa's fiancé, Li Shan-fu, organize an attempt on the captain's life: Tao-Hoa is to serve him a cup of poisoned tea. At the last moment she refuses and dies at the hand of Li Shan-fu. Before her death Tao-Hoa hands to Chinese children a red poppy as a symbol of struggle.

The Red Poppy was prepared by a team of creators and produced for the ballerina Ekaterina Geltser. They had chosen a vital topic. Most explanations of the plot literally reproduce newspaper reports detailing attempts on the lives of Soviet citizens or on hijacking. This was at a time when the Bolshoi Ballet was often reproached for ignoring modern problems. At the same time the creators sought to preserve the traditional form of classical ballet. Such a contradiction was representative of many characteristic trends, both positive and negative, in the late 1920s.

Created in the heyday of the NEP (New Economic Policy, when individual capitalism and elements of the bourgeois way of life revived for a time), *The Red Poppy* was oriented to the tastes of rich theatergoers and demonstrated colorful Western social dances, such as fox trot and the Boston, and music hall attractions. At the same time the dance of the Soviet seamen in the first act, choreographed by Lashchilin to the popular tune "Yablochko" (Apple), was one of the first examples of the folk heroic mass dance, which would become firmly established in Soviet ballet in the next decade. The image of the heroine, although tending toward melodrama, in its extended psychological characterization anticipated the images of drama ballets of the 1930s.

The Red Poppy was a great success on the Bolshoi stage. In eighteen months it was shown one hundred times, while the average number of performances of all repertory ballets did not surpass eighty per season as a rule. At the same time it stirred heated debates in the press and invited sharp criticism from avant-garde artists, Vladimir Mayakovsky among them. Before long *The Red Poppy* became the most popular ballet on the Soviet stage; it was in the repertories of all Soviet theaters in the 1930s. In 1949 new versions were produced by Leonid Lavrovsky at the Bolshoi and Rostislav Zakharov at the Kirov. Lavrovsky created an entirely new version, renamed thereafter *The Red Flower,* in 1957. The ballet has been staged abroad, in particular in the United States (abridged version) in 1943 by the Ballet Russe de Monte Carlo, choreographed by Igor Schwezoff.

BIBLIOGRAPHY

Beaumont, Cyril W. *Complete Book of Ballets.* Rev. ed. London, 1951.

Bogdanov-Berezovskii, V. M. *Krasnyi mak.* Leningrad, 1933.

Roslavleva, Natalia. "*Krasnyi mak:* Pervy sovetskii balet." In *Vasilii Dmitrievich Tikhomirov,* edited by P. F. Abolimov. Moscow, 1971.

Schlee, Alfred. "The Dance in Soviet Russia." *The Dancing Times* (July 1932): 339–343.

Shvetzov, Igor. "The Red Poppy." *The Dancing Times* (August 1943): 508.

Souritz, Elizabeth. *Soviet Choreographers in the 1920s.* Translated by Lynn Visson. Durham, N.C., 1990.

Swift, Mary Grace. *The Art of the Dance in the U.S.S.R.* Notre Dame, 1968.

ELIZABETH SOURITZ

RED SHOES, THE. Film. Choreography: Robert Helpmann and Léonide Massine. Script writers and directors: Michael Powell and Emeric Pressburger. Music: Brian Easdale. Scenery and costumes: Hein Heckroth. Premiere: 22 July 1948 at the Gaumont, Haymarket, London. Principals: Moira Shearer (Victoria Page), Marius Goring (Julian Craster), Anton Walbrook (Boris Lermontov), Léonide Massine (Grisha Ljubov).

More than twenty years after its premiere, the film critic Philip Jenkinson characterized *The Red Shoes* as

> perhaps the most valiant attempt in the history of the movies to integrate ballet, fantasy, surrealistic settings, classic and contemporary music, all within a conventional narrative framework.

His assessment still holds true.

As befits a movie about daily life in an international ballet company, this one combines the most vivid elements of a world composed of outsized passions and personalities. It features a budding ballerina and a promising composer who fall in love; a temperamental ballet master; an impresario—part Serge Diaghilev, part Svengali—to whom ballet is a religion; and an original ballet designed expressly for the film camera. The action unfolds on several planes of reality—outside and inside the theater, in the company, and in the characters' imaginations—and simultaneously recounts several versions of one fairy tale.

In Hans Christian Andersen's tale, a girl wants to dance in a pair of red shoes. Once she puts them on and starts dancing, she discovers that she cannot stop; wearing those shoes, she is fated to dance forever, until she dies. As the basis for the new ballet Lermontov's company is preparing, the same story provides both the goal that motivates the film's plot and the ultimate expression of each character's sensibility. It also shapes the story of the young ballerina, whose life mirrors the fiction precisely. Having left the company to marry Craster, the composer, after her triumph in *The Red Shoes,* Vicky is inexorably drawn back to dancing. Craster and Lermontov confront her before a performance, each demanding her complete devotion. Unable to choose between life and art, she lets the red shoes dance her away from both, out of the theater, and to her death.

Even if the sentimental love story and the arbitrary life/art choice seem hackneyed today, the dancing—particularly Shearer's in the title ballet and in excerpts from *Swan Lake, Coppélia,* and *La Boutique Fantasque*—the larger-than-life characterizations, Heckroth's exquisite designs, and Jack Cardiff's inventive cinematography are still vibrant and engaging.

In her first film appearance, Shearer seems to play herself, a modest, charming ballerina of exceptional beauty and delicate grace. Léonide Massine, Robert Helpmann, and Ludmilla Tcherina portray the more experienced dancers with slightly more cunning, gently spoofing their real and fictional status as "stars" by exaggerating both the public glamour and backstage turbulence of dancers' lives. Walbrook makes Lermontov the perfect distillation of the film: daring for its time, colorful, and feverishly dedicated to ballet.

At its best, Helpmann's choreography for the twenty-minute *Red Shoes* ballet recalls his *Miracle in the Gorbals,* but its theatrical effectiveness is irrelevant. Conceived and executed as a cinematic experiment, it succeeds brilliantly

THE RED SHOES. At the end of the ballet within the film, the lifeless body of the Girl (Moira Shearer) is lifted by her partner (Robert Helpmann) as the Shoemaker (Léonide Massine) capers behind them. A spotlight falls on the fatal red shoes. (Photograph from the Dance Collection, New York Public Library for the Performing Arts.)

in blending stage and film conventions, fantasy, dream, and nightmare. Honored in 1948 with one Academy Award for color art direction and set decoration and another for the scoring of a drama or comedy, *The Red Shoes* is now considered a milestone in the imaginative fusing of film and dance.

[*For related discussion, see* Film Musicals, *article on* Hollywood Film Musicals.]

BIBLIOGRAPHY

Cardiff, Jack. "*The Red Shoes* and Ciné-Choreography." *Ballet Annual* 3 (1949): 56–60.

Cardiff, Jack. *Magic Hour.* London, 1996.

Gibbon, Monk. *The Red Shoes Ballet.* London, 1948.

McLean, Adrienne L. "*The Red Shoes* Revisited." *Dance Chronicle* 11.1 (1988): 31–83.

Powell, Michael. *A Life in Movies: An Autobiography.* London, 1986.

FILM. Michael Powell, *The Red Shoes* (1948).

BARBARA NEWMAN

REEL. Though often embellished, a reel is essentially a simple dance that at one time was the most common dance genre in the English- and Gaelic-speaking world. The word *reel* may derive either from the Anglo-Saxon *hreol,* "to make a weaving motion," or the Gaelic *ruidhle.* The reel is supposed to be considerably older than its earliest documentation in the seventeenth century, although its early origins are obscure and may never be understood.

In the eighteenth century, reels were the most popular dances among the common people in Britain, its colonies, and the United States. Reels were not considered the type of dance that needed to be studied, however, so although constantly mentioned there are few notations of reels until the end of the eighteenth century. By then, reels, especially the varieties for three or four dancers, were widely believed to be of Scottish origin, a belief that has persisted to the present day. Whether or not reels do have a Scottish origin, or any single origin, this perception of them has had a significant effect on their performance and survival since the 1800s, both in Scotland and in the rest of the world.

Although reels were rarely included in formal dance instruction, during the 1700s they were often part of even the most formal dance events. They disappeared from ballrooms during the nineteenth century but remained a staple for many rural dancers through most of this time. They had largely died out in the United States by the beginning of the twentieth century, but they continue to be danced in Scotland and in parts of Ireland and England. Reels are also an integral part of the present folk dance revival in Britain and Ireland.

Since the 1700s, one of the standard traditional dance music forms has also been called a reel—indicating a tune in 2/4 time, in which each beat is subdivided into four notes of approximately equal duration. These tunes are used for a wide variety of dances, including reels, but also including country dances (also known as *contredanses* or contradances), quadrilles, and a variety of step dances. A reel dance is not necessarily done to a tune in reel time, although this association is generally the case in today's Irish and Scottish dancing. Tunes in jig time (6/8) are also used for reel dances; twentieth-century traditional examples include the "Hullican Jig" of lowland Scotland and the "Foula Reel" from the Shetland Islands.

Among the earliest types of reels are the straight reels for three or four dancers. Called three- or four-hand reels, they place the participants in a straight line. The figure usually consists of improvised stepping alternating with a single figure, most commonly either swinging or weaving, as in the figure called the Hey. The Hey, in which the dancers move through a figure-eight pattern as they interweave with each other, was so frequently used in reels that it came to be known as a reel itself. [*See* Hey.]

An alternate formation for a four-hand reel is that of one couple facing another; it frequently has a longer and more complicated sequence of figures than the straight four-hand reel. This couple-facing-couple reel may also have been the inspiration for the "visiting couple" type of square dance that evolved in parts of the United States in the nineteenth century. This theory is supported by the fact that some communities in the southeastern states refer to their indigenous form of square dancing as "four-handed reels," even though today they are for eight or more dancers.

Almost as common in the eighteenth century were six-hand reels, which are danced with the participants standing in two lines of three, men on one side and women on the other. This formation had been common in the seventeenth-century form of English country dance, although it is not known whether the six-hand reel was a peasant dance imitated by the ballroom country dances or whether it evolved out of the seventeenth-century country dance. In any event, the six-hand reel was very familiar in the eighteenth and nineteenth centuries and continued to evolve in certain areas of Britain, notably southern England and Shetland. Six-hand reels were also popular in the United States until the mid–nineteenth century; they were sometimes referred to by Americans as "Virginia reels," just as four-hand reels were known as "Scotch reels." (The term *Virginia reel* was appropriated in the second half of the nineteenth century for a very popular and completely different dance.) Six-hand reels in their most basic form consist of alternate stepping and Heys. There were many more elaborate sequences as well, and six-hand reels frequently consisted of figures adapted from country dances.

A special form of six-hand reel, generally known as the "Highland reel," was introduced into ballroom dancing in the early nineteenth century. For this dance, a line of three partners, usually a man and two women, faced another line of three partners. This pattern was repeated by several other groups of six around the ballroom. At the conclusion of one complete sequence of figures, which were not standardized, the groups of three progressed around the room to face other groups of three dancers for the continuation of the dance.

Eight-hand reels, called in Scotland "eightsome reels" and in England "square eights," are still part of the dance repertory in areas of Britain and Ireland where older dance traditions have been maintained. They are a folk adaptation in the late nineteenth century of quadrille and lancer figures; they share with other reels only the feature of being a dance for a specified number of couples.

Yet another dance often considered to be a reel is one in which eight or more dancers face one another in parallel lines of men and women. The top couple moves to the bottom of the set at the completion of one round of the dance figures, and the dance continues until all the couples have had a turn at the top. This type of figure became popular in the late eighteenth century; the method of progression was used in six-hand reels somewhat earlier. In the early nineteenth century a dance of this type called "Sir Roger de Coverly" formed the standard conclusion for a ball in England. Many of these dances are still used, including the Irish "Haymaker's Jig," the Scottish "Strip the Willow," and the American adaptation of "Sir Roger de Coverly," the "Virginia Reel" (not to be confused with the six-hand Virginia reels popular earlier). This last is considered by Americans to be a type of reel, although nineteenth-century writers usually categorized it as a special type of country dance.

The foregoing categories include the vast majority of reels, but there are others, such as the five-hand reels and variants of an eight-hand reel—the "Swedish Dance," popular in the nineteenth century. Another use is made of the word *reel* in Ireland and parts of England where dancers perform "reel steps," that is, step dancing to music in reel time. There are also a large number of country dances with titles such as "Lady Walpole's Reel" or "Miss McLeod's Reel" that are not considered reels—the titles refer to the music to which the dances are performed rather than to the type of dance.

[*See also* Great Britain, *article on* Scottish Folk and Traditional Dance.]

BIBLIOGRAPHY

Breathnach, Breandán. *Folk Music and Dances of Ireland.* Rev. ed. Dublin, 1977.

Emmerson, George S. *A Social History of Scottish Dance.* London, 1972.

Flett, J. F., and T. M. Flett. *Traditional Dancing in Scotland.* London, 1964.

Morrison, James E., ed. *Twenty-Four Early American Country Dances, Cotillions, and Reels.* New York, 1976.

JAMES E. MORRISON

REICH, WILHELM. *See* Body Therapies.

REINHOLM, GERT (Gerhardt Schmidt; born 20 December 1923 in Chemnitz), German ballet dancer, teacher, and company director. Gert Reinholm studied at the ballet school of the Berlin State Opera. He joined the ballet company in 1942 and was appointed soloist in 1946, gradually emerging as Tatjana Gsovsky's principal male dancer, accompanying her to the Teatro Colón in Buenos Aires (1951–1953). He returned with her to West Berlin, joining the Municipal Opera there as principal dancer in 1953; he has stayed with the company ever since (it moved to its rebuilt former premises and became the German Opera Ballet in 1961). Reinholm was also principal dancer and co-director (with Gsovsky) of the Berlin Ballet during the 1950s. He held various positions at the German Opera Ballet before being installed as the company's artistic director in 1972. He has run his Berlin Ballet Academy (with Gsovsky) and has been a teacher at the West Berlin Academy of Music.

Never particularly strong as a technician, Reinholm excelled in roles requiring personal presence and dramatic projection, making him the ideal interpreter of Gsovsky's male protagonists in works such as *Hamlet* (1953), *Othello* (1956), *Joan of Zarissa* (1958), and *Tristan* (1965). He won the German Critics Prize in 1963. Reinholm resigned as artistic director of the ballet company of the German Opera Berlin in 1990 but continued to teach at the Berlin Ballet Academy.

BIBLIOGRAPHY

Geitel, Klaus. "Gert Reinholm." In *Deutsche Oper Berlin: Spielzeit 1989/90.* Beiträge zum Musiktheater, 9. Berlin, 1990.

Kellermann, Heinz. *Gert Reinholm* (in German). Berlin, 1957.

Theobald, Christiane, ed. *Gert Reinholm: Festschrift zur Verleihung der Ehrenmitgliedschaft der Deutschen Oper Berlin am 29. Juni 1990.* Berlin, 1990.

HORST KOEGLER

RELÂCHE. Instantaneous ballet in two acts, cinematographic *entr'acte,* and a *queue de chien.* Choreography: Jean Börlin. Music: Erik Satie. Libretto: Francis Picabia. Scenery and costumes: Francis Picabia. Film: René Clair. First performance: 4 December 1924, Théâtre des

RELÂCHE. A view of Francis Picabia's setting for *Relâche,* which was the final and most famous work presented by Les Ballets Suédois. (Photograph by Isaby, Paris; from the archives of the Dansmuseet, Stockholm.)

Champs-Élysées, Paris, Les Ballets Suédois. Principals: Jean Börlin, Edith Bonsdorff, Kaj Smith.

A collaboration between Les Ballets Suédois and leading Dada artists, *Relâche* means "no performance." The decor consisted of several enormous, receding arches covered with 370 lights housed in reflective disks. The music, based on popular songs, set the audience howling with laughter and insults. Much of the movement was nondance action, such as a fireman emptying one pail of water into another, a woman smoking a cigarette, and dancers changing from evening clothes to leotards. There was also dancing, some of it without music. *Entr'acte,* the intermission film by René Clair, has become a classic of avant-garde cinema. It shows Man Ray and Marcel Duchamp playing chess, a hunter bringing a bird to life, a man dressed as a ballerina, and an antic funeral, to repetitive "furniture music" by Satie. The press found the ballet scandalous. Like the cannon Picabia and Satie fire on the city of Paris in the film, *Relâche* launched a Dadaist attack on bourgeois culture. The work was revived by Moses Pendleton for the Joffrey Ballet in New York in 1980.

[*See also* Artists and the Dance, *article on* Artists and the Dance, 1760–1929; Ballets Suédois; *and* Scenic Design.]

BIBLIOGRAPHY

Banes, Sally. "An Introduction to the Ballets Suédois." *Ballet Review* 7 (1978–1979): 28–59.

Beaumont, Cyril W. *Complete Book of Ballets.* London, 1937.

Camfield, William. "Dada Experiment: Francis Picabia and the Creation of *Relâche.*" In Nancy Van Norman Baer, ed. *Paris Modern: The Swedish Ballet 1920–1925.* San Francisco, 1995.

Carroll, Noël. "Entr'acte, Paris, and Dada." *Millennium Film Journal* 1 (Winter 1977–1978).

Häger, Bengt. *Ballets Suédois.* Translated by Ruth Sharman. New York, 1990.

Shattuck, Roger. *The Banquet Years.* New York, 1958.

SALLY BANES

RENAISSANCE COURT DANCE. *See* Social Dance, *article on* Court and Social Dance before 1800. *For related discussion, see* Music for Dance, *articles on* Western Music before 1520 *and* Western Music, 1520–1650; *and* Renaissance Dance Technique. *For information on important dancing masters and their works, see* Dancing Masters; Technical Manuals, *article on* Publications, 1445–1725; *and the entries on Arbeau, Arena, Caroso, Cornazano, Domenico de Piacenza; Guglielmo Ebreo da Pesaro; and Negri. For historical information on Renaissance dance in the courts of western Europe, see the theatrical dance articles within individual country entries. See also* Balet Comique de la Royne, Le; Ball; Ballet de Cour, *article on* Ballet de Cour, 1560–1670; Banquet; Bergamasque; Dance of Death; Elizabethan Progresses; Figure Dances; Guild Dances; Hey; Intermedio; Libretti for Dance, *article on* Sixteenth- and Seventeenth-Century Libretti; Masque and Antimasque; Masquerades; Matachins, *overview article;* Mommerie; Moresca; Reconstruction, *article on* Historical Notations; Renaissance Fêtes and Triumphs; *and* Revels. *For discussion of Renaissance dance types, see* Allemande; Alta; Ballo and Balletto; Barriera, Torneo, and

Battaglia; Bassedanse; Branle; Canary; Cascarda; Galliard; Passo e Mezzo; Pavan; Pavaniglia; Saltarello; Sarabande; Spagnoletta; Tordion; *and* Volta.

RENAISSANCE DANCE TECHNIQUE. The Renaissance can be divided into two major cultural periods: the early Renaissance, c.1430–1550, which in northern Europe (Burgundy and France) can also be called the late Middle Ages or the late Gothic period, and the high Renaissance, c.1550–1650. Our knowledge of the dance techniques of Renaissance Europe and their development over the centuries comes mainly from the dance instruction manuals of the period, beginning around 1440, and is supplemented by contemporary iconography, by developments in fashion, and by written commentaries, descriptions of dance events in chronicles and correspondence, and references to dance in drama, poetry, and novels.

High Renaissance dance manuals, primarily those by Thoinot Arbeau, Fabritio Caroso, and Cesare Negri, painstakingly describe each step, devote whole chapters to style and the social graces, and give innumerable step combinations for the dances they record. In contrast, technical information about dancing in the early Renaissance is scattered throughout the theoretical introductions of the manuals. Especially in Italian manuals, many steps are named in the choreographic descriptions without being described. Nevertheless, the richness of the techniques and the manner of their execution are sufficiently clear. [*See the entries on Arbeau, Caroso, and Negri.*]

Early Renaissance Dance. The main dance type documented for the northern regions of Burgundy, France, England (and Spanish and German outposts) during the late Gothic period is the *bassedanse.* Only five steps were used in the composition of this elegant stepping dance: single steps, double steps (*ss* and *d* in the choreographic tablature), the *branle (b), reprise* or *démarche (r),* and the *révérence (R).* The descriptions of these steps in various sources are skeletal at best, but they do contain clues regarding the technical execution. Repeatedly emphasized is the calmness and grace of movement, the smallness of the steps, and the raising and lowering of the body while stepping, equivalent to the *ondeggiare,* the undulation or wavelike movement of the contemporary Italian dance technique. Because of the processional nature of the *bassedanse,* the walking steps (singles and doubles) went mainly forward, in the line of direction. The singles involved nothing more than one leg motion and weight transfer each and the lowering and raising of the body; the doubles consisted of three small steps each, the first beginning with the left foot, the next with the right, and so on, and also involved the lowering and raising of the body. *Reprises* went backward; when three occurred as a group they had to be kept small to prevent the lady from becoming entangled in the long, heavy train of her dress. The gently swaying sideways motion of the *branle,* first to the left, then back to the right, posed no such problem even in the full ceremonial attire of the second half of the fifteenth century. Except for a walked half-circle in "La Danse de Cleues" in the source known as the Brussels Manuscript, turns are absent in the *bassesdanses* of France and Burgundy, although they do occur in fifteenth-century Spain, as attested by the several instances of the term *voltat* in the Cervera Manuscript (Crane, 1968). The dancers' feet were, as the iconography shows, slightly turned out (a more pronounced turnout while standing was required of the fifteenth-century gentleman), the body was erect, and the torso flexible (corsets were not worn during this period). The gentleman's free left arm was carried slightly away from the body in an elegant curve, while the lady tucked a fold of her long overgarment into the crook of her right elbow, from which decorative cascades of cloth then descended to the floor. [*See* Bassedanse.]

Despite its elongated shape, the *poulaine* shoe allowed not only comfortable stepping, rises on the toe, and the semicircular leg motion required for the man's *révérence* and the *reprise* (descriptions in the Brussels Manuscript and in Antonius de Arena's *Leges dansadi;* Brainard, 1981, pp. 16ff., 30ff.) but also permitted the restrained skipping or hopping of the *pas de breban* (or *saltarello*) sections of a few Burgundian *bassesdanses* (for example, "Lesperance de Bourbon" and "Roti Boully Ioyeulx" in the Brussels manuscript and in Michel Toulouze's *L'art et instruction de bien dancer* of 1488). Occasional hops and jumps *(sault)* occur in the one-page choreographies of the manuscript Nancy 1445, the so-called "Ballet de la Reine de Cessile."

While the dance technique of Burgundy preserves the Gothic heritage, that of Italy in the same period inaugurates the Renaissance. Domenico da Piacenza was the first to systematize all the steps of the current repertory, subdividing them into "movements given us by nature" *(movimenti naturali)* and others "acquired by accident" *(movimenti accidentali),* such as the ornamental movements. Domenico arranged the natural movements into groups in accordance with their natural manner of execution: forward steps *(sempio, doppio, contrapasso),* steps to the side *(ripresa, continentia),* backward steps *(riverenzi),* turns *(volta tonda, mezza volta),* leaps or jumps *(salto, salteto),* and postures *(positura, possa).* Besides their "normal" direction, nearly all natural steps could go in other ways; the dance descriptions abound in diagonal, backward, and turning *riprese,* sideways *passetti,* and *riverences* of various intensities and durations *(riuerentia piccola, inchino).* The variability of step execution was justified by the theory that all good dancing requires *di-*

versità di cose ("the variety of things"), concerning which Antonio Cornazano wrote in his *Libro dell'arte del danzare* (1455–1465), "When one of [the steps] is done, do not make another immediately like it."

Additional color was given to the dance sequences by the *movimenti accidentali,* none of which is described but whose names suggest stamps *(frapamento, piçighamento),* leg crossings *(trascorsa, stracorsa),* and leg gestures *(squassetto, schosso, schossetto)*—all motions that were possible in Italian garments (which, as a rule, were less voluminous than those of Burgundy) and in the fashionable shoes, which, although still pointed, fit the wearer's foot snugly.

Besides listing the basic steps in the theoretical introductions to their manuals, the fifteenth-century Italian dancing masters included a large number of variants in their choreographies for *balli* and *bassedanze,* which indicate a highly developed, finely shaped dance technique (for examples, see Brainard, 1981). Worthy of note is the first appearance of the *jeté:* the "throwing" *(gettare)* of the moving body from one foot onto the other in a forward direction. A decorative adjunct to the step is the rise and fall of the *ondeggiare,* complemented by the *campeggiare,* probably a sideways "spreading out" and ancestor to the ornamental *pavoneggiare* of the sixteenth century. Both, according to Cornazano, "give breadth and beauty to the movements you make."

Because the dance technique of the early Renaissance is a courtly technique, designed for the nobility and not for commoners ("dignissime madonne et non plebeie," in Cornazano's phrase), excesses in technical brilliance were avoided lest the courtly dancer resemble a professional or a buffoon. Domenico, especially, stresses adherence to the Aristotelian mean—"Avoid the extremes," he cautions—that must govern the steps as well as the gestures of courtly dancers.

Gestures and facial expressions were demanded in *balletti* that told a story, such as Domenico's "La Sobria," in which the lady responded to the approaches of four of her five male companions with surprise, disbelief, anxiety, and other emotions.

The technique for men permitted greater strength of movement, higher jumps, and more elaborate ornamentation than that for women, which called for restraint, gentleness, lightness, and grace. The lady had to hold herself straight and tall, with head erect but eyes modestly lowered (see Guglielmo Ebreo's chapter addressed "to the young and virtuous lady," which appears in all his treatises), and had to avoid the display of power and virility that was the men's prerogative.

Certain dance types were taboo even for men, at least in public settings. One of these was the moresca, which a gentleman might perform "in camera privatamente ma in pubblico on così" ("in a private room but not in public," according to Baldassare Castiglione's dialogue on courtly life, *Il cortegiano*). One of the trademarks of the *moresca,* a performance dance that flourished especially in the fifteenth and sixteenth centuries, was its strong technique, consisting of leaps, high kicks, deep knee-bends, generous arm motions, and a mobile torso. Castiglione's reservations notwithstanding, *morescas* were danced at court by courtiers as frequently as they were in urban or theatrical settings (references to such events occur in the fifteenth-century dance manuals and pictures in the Freydal Manuscript of Emperor Maximilian I). It is impossible to know whether court *morescas* used a refined version of the more extravagant noncourtly technique or achieved their exotic flavor mainly by costuming, masks, and musical accompaniments. The two versions of early Renaissance dance technique existed side by side, and any dancer might make use of either one in accordance with his or her good taste, breeding, and judicious estimation of the performance occasion. [*See* Moresca.]

RENAISSANCE DANCE TECHNIQUE. The first ballet *barre,* as described in Cesare Negri's *Le gratie d'amore,* published in 1602. (Photograph from the Dance Collection, New York Public Library for the Performing Arts.)

High Renaissance Dance. With the sixteenth century came many changes in clothing fashion. Bulk replaced the sculpted, elongated look of Burgundy and the flowing, lithe grace of fifteenth-century Italy. New additions, from the early Tudor period on, were corsets (worn by men and women); ruffs or other stiff collars; padding around the hips; full-cut, swinging cloaks; and—a novelty of the 1570s—heels on the shoes (Brainard, 1983; Squire, 1974). All these innovations helped to shape the dance technique of the high Renaissance.

Because the corset precludes torso motion and the ruff forces the head to remain more or less still, the dance technique of the sixteenth century emphasized footwork, executed with precision and often with great speed. The majority of steps were now described in extensive detail. The Frenchman Thoinot Arbeau, in his *Orchésographie* (1588), makes his step descriptions part of the running dialogue between himself and his disciple, Capriol, and adds small drawings of dancers, which show the placement of feet and legs, the moderate turnout, the relaxed and unpointed toes, and the slightly bent knee of the gesturing leg—all indicative of the French version of high Renaissance dance technique. The Italian dancing masters Fabritio Caroso and Cesare Negri devote entire sections of their instruction books to the steps and their proper execution. Of the fifty-five *regole* ("rules") in the first edition of Caroso's treatise *Il ballarino* (1581), fifty-three are step descriptions, one is devoted to the man's handling of his hat, and one to the lady's ballroom etiquette. In *Della nobiltà di dame* (1600), Caroso expands the repertory to sixty-seven *regole* for steps, but there is still only one rule regarding the man's hat gestures. The technical instructions, which include frequent warnings about what not to do during the execution of a given step, are followed by an extensive dialogue between master and disciple concerning walking, sitting, bowing, and manners both in and outside the ballroom. Great emphasis is placed on what to do with accessories—sword, gloves, fan, kerchiefs, and the like. These discussions of the social graces contain much additional information about dance technique. Negri's treatise *Le gratie d'amore* (1602) contains some of the most difficult steps of the high Renaissance and is packed with an enormous amount of technical detail, including thirty-five separate step descriptions. Both Caroso and Negri use engravings, sometimes repeated, to illustrate their texts.

The repertory of motions included the basic walking steps, quick running steps *(scorsi)*, bows, *riprese*, and *continenze*, all described in several versions and, like their fifteenth-century predecessors, designed to accommodate both the triple and the duple meter. Foot crossings and cut steps *(entretaille; sotto-piede; fioretto)* are frequent, as are leg swings *(ruade; campanella)*, beats *(botta)*, leg raises *(pied en l'air)*, and vigorous stamps. The last were the chief ingredient of the *canario*, on record from the time of Caroso's *Il ballarino* and coincident with the advent of shoes with heels (Brainard, 1983, p. 24), which allowed the Spanish flavor of the dance to become audible. [*See* Canary.] Of particular interest to male dancers in this, the age of the *galliard*, were the leaps and jumps, which ranged from unassuming two-foot *(sault; salteto)* or one-foot *(grève* in *galliards; zoppetto)* hops and small sideways jumps from one foot to the other *(trabuchetto)* to complicated turning jumps involving double *tours en l'air (salto tondo)*, leg changes and vibrations of the gesturing leg at the height of the leap *(triglio*, or *tremolante)*, and high kicks forward and back while in the air (for example, Negri's competition *galliard* for men, "The Kick to the Tassel" in *Le gratie d'amore*). For the first time in history the *entrechat* makes its appearance: the earliest version was the *capriole* or *capriola*, consisting of quick forward and backward motions of the lower legs during the jump. Caroso and Arbeau both describe this manner of execution; Caroso also records the more fashionable version in which the feet cross three, four, or even five times. Because of such jumps' difficulty, the dancing masters suggest practicing by supporting oneself "with the strength of the arms" on the backs of two chairs or by holding on to a tightly stretched rope (Negri). This is the prototype of the ballet *barre*. [*See* Galliard.]

As in the previous century, individual steps could be combined to form larger units; examples are the many *galliard* five-steps, eleven-steps, and seventeen-steps (Arbeau) and the *canario* stamping sequences. Some step-units were shaped after classical verse meters such as the *dattile, spondeo, saffice, destice*, and *corinto* (Caroso, *Della nobiltà di dame*).

Turns are frequent everywhere in the manuals. Arbeau's preference is for revolutions executed in three small jumps with alternating leg-raises (for example, in the "Branle de Malte," among others) or in *galliard* steps, ending in a *cadence*. Caroso's "Molinello" (*Il ballarino*, rule 40; *Della nobiltà di dame*, rule 46) is a full turn in *galliard* five-steps, first to the left, then to the right. Genuine *pirouettes* are described by Negri: the free foot is placed near the ankle, halfway up the calf of the supporting leg, or near the knee, extended in a gesture or executing beats during the turn. In this difficult feat may be seen the beginnings of the *fouetté*. Arm motions are seldom mentioned, but a plate in Negri's *Le gratie d'amore* shows a *pirouette* preparation that illustrates the arm position described in the accompanying text (rule 44).

In the Middle Ages, lifts were relegated to peasant dances, but in the sixteenth century they reappeared in social dances. The lift or leap executed by the lady with the assistance of her partner is the characteristic figure of the *volta* (Arbeau); it also occurs in Negri's "Balletto . . . La Nizzarda" in *Le gratie d'amore* and in Arbeau's "Branle de l'Official" in *Orchésographie*. [*See* Volta.]

Caroso and Negri stress the turnout, which, although required, was not to be extreme (*un poco* is the operative term in the relevant passages). They likewise emphasize the ornamental *pavoneggiare,* a sideways motion involving knees and hip that had to be incorporated into all steps, including jumps. They lay stress, too, on the raising and lowering of the body while stepping, which added grace to the prevailing vigor, and especially on the straightness of the knees *(le ginocchie ben distese)* whenever a leg gesture occurred. This emphasis on straight legs is one of the few recognizable differences between French and Italian dance technique of the high Renaissance.

All steps of the repertory could be executed by men and women. The choreographies, however, show that the sexes' different styles as advocated by the dancing masters of the fifteenth century were maintained with equal strictness in the sixteenth century, especially in *galliard* passages, where the men were given the complicated jumps and fast beats while women moved with a more leisurely grace.

A large variety of steps and step combinations not dealt with by Caroso and Negri are mentioned by name in the books of Lutio Compasso (1560), Prospero Luti di Sulmona (1589), and Livio Lupi da Caravaggio (1607); unfortunately, only a very few of these are described, leaving one with images of a rich and demanding dance technique that will perhaps never be totally recovered.

[*See also* Ballo and Balletto. *For discussion of Renaissance dance types, see* Cascarda; Passo e Mezzo; Pavan; Pavaniglia; Saltarello; Spagnoletta; *and* Tordion.]

BIBLIOGRAPHY

Brainard, Ingrid. "Die Choreographie der Hoftänze in Burgund, Frankreich und Italien im 15. Jahrhundert." Ph.D.diss., University of Göttingen, 1956.

Brainard, Ingrid. "Bassedanse, Bassadanza, and Ballo in the Fifteenth Century." In *Dance History Research: Perspectives from Related Arts and Disciplines,* edited by Joann W. Kealiinohomoku. New York, 1970.

Brainard, Ingrid. "Fifteenth and Early Sixteenth Century Court Dances." In *Institute of Court Dances of the Renaissance and Baroque Periods,* edited by Juana de Laban. New York, 1972.

Brainard, Ingrid. *The Art of Courtly Dancing in the Early Renaissance.* West Newton, Mass., 1981.

Brainard, Ingrid. "Modes, Manners, Movement: The Interaction of Dance and Dress from the Late Middle Ages to the Renaissance." In *Proceedings of the Sixth Annual Conference, Society of Dance History Scholars, the Ohio State University, 11–13 February 1983,* compiled by Christena L. Schlundt. Milwaukee, 1983.

Brainard, Ingrid. "The Art of Courtly Dancing in Transition: Nürnberg, Germ.Nat.Mus.Hs.8842, a Hitherto Unknown German Dance Source." In *Crossroads of Medieval Civilization: The City of Regensburg and Its Intellectual Milieu,* edited by Edelgard E. DuBruck and Karl Heinz Göller. Detroit, 1984.

Celi, Claudia. "Talhor tacere un tempo e starlo morto: Il moto in potenza e in atto." In *Guglielmo Ebreo da Pesaro e la danza nelle corti italiane del XV secolo,* edited by Maurizio Padovan. Pisa, 1990.

Crane, Frederick. *Materials for the Study of the Fifteenth-Century Basse Danse.* Brooklyn, 1968.

Cruickshank, Diana. "'E poi se piglieno per mano': A Brief Study of Hand Holds in Fifteenth- and Sixteenth-Century Portraits." *Historical Dance* 2.5 (1986–1987): 17–20.

Cruickshank, Diana. "'In due a la fila'—'E la donna vadia innanzi.'" In *Guglielmo Ebreo da Pesaro e la danza nelle corti italiane del XV secolo,* edited by Maurizio Padovan. Pisa, 1990.

Cruickshank, Diana. "Doppii suxo uno piede, or, Contrapassi in Quadernaria Misura." *Historical Dance* 3.1 (1992): 11–13.

Daye, Anne. "From Word to Movement." *Historical Dance* 2.4 (1984–1985): 14–23.

Daye, Anne. "The Problem of Negri's Term *fioretto spezzato.*" *Historical Dance* 2.5 (1986–1987): 36.

Daye, Anne. "Skill and Invention in the Renaissance Ballroom." *Historical Dance* 2.6 (1988–1991): 12–15.

Dixon, Peggy. "Reflections on Basse Dance Source Material: A Dancer's Review." *Historical Dance* 2.4 (1984–1985): 24–27.

Dolmetsch, Mabel. *Dances of England and France from 1450 to 1600.* London, 1949.

Dolmetsch, Mabel. *Dances of Spain and Italy from 1400 to 1600.* London, 1954.

Francalanci, Andrea. "L'importance de la 'mezza volta' dans les danses au XVe siècle en Italie." In *Les goûts réunis: "La danse," Actes du Ier colloque international sur la danse ancienne.* Besançon, 1982.

Francalanci, Andrea. "Le ricostruzione delle danze del '400 italiano attraverso in metodo di studio comparato delle fonti." *La danza italiana* 3 (Autumn 1985): 55–76.

Garth, Charles. "Sixteenth-Century Social Court Dances." In *Institute of Court Dances of the Renaissance and Baroque Periods,* edited by Juana de Laban. New York, 1972.

Jones, Pamela. "Spectacle in Milan: Cesare Negri's Torch Dances." *Early Music* 14.2 (1986): 182–198.

Kendall, Yvonne. "*Le gratie d'amore* (1602) by Cesare Negri: Translation and Commentary." Ph.D.diss., Stanford University, 1985.

Lo Monaco, Mauro, and Sergio Vinciguerra. "Il passo doppio in Guglielmo e Domenico: Problemi di mensurazione." In *Guglielmo Ebreo da Pesaro e la danza nelle corti italiane del XV secolo,* edited by Maurizio Padovan. Pisa, 1990.

Merritt, Meredith. "Dance Terms in Renaissance Dictionaries." In *The Myriad Faces of Dance: Proceedings of the Eighth Annual Conference, Society of Dance History Scholars, University of New Mexico, 15–17 February 1985,* compiled by Christena L. Schlundt. Riverside, Calif., 1985.

Pontremoli, Alessandro, and Patrizia La Rocca. *Il ballare lombardo: Teoria e prassi coreutica nella festa di corte del XV secolo.* Milan, 1987.

Pontremoli, Alessandro. "Estetica dell'ondeggiare ed estetica dell'aeroso: Da Domenico a Guglielmo, evoluzione di uno stile coreutico." In *Guglielmo Ebreo da Pesaro e la danza nelle corti italiane del XV secolo,* edited by Maurizio Padovan. Pisa, 1990.

Pugliese, Patri J., and Joseph Casazza. *Practise for Dauncinge: Some Almans and a Pavan, England, 1570–1650.* Cambridge, Mass., 1980.

Smith, A. William, trans. and ed. *Fifteenth-Century Dance and Music: The Complete Transcribed Italian Treatises and Collections in the Tradition of Domenico da Piacenza.* 2 vols. Stuyvesant, N.Y., 1995.

Smith, Judy. "The Art of Good Dancing: Noble Birth and Skilled Nonchalance, England, 1580–1630." *Historical Dance* 2.5 (1986–1987): 30–32.

Sparti, Barbara. "Stile, espressione e senso teatrale nella danza italiana del '400." *La danza italiana* 3 (Autumn 1985): 39–53.

Sparti, Barbara. "Style and Performance in the Social Dances of the Italian Renaissance: Ornamentation, Improvisation, Variation, and Virtuosity." In *Proceedings of the Ninth Annual Conference, Society of Dance History Scholars, City College, City University of New York, 14–17 February 1986,* compiled by Christena L. Schlundt. Riverside, Calif., 1986.

Sparti, Barbara. "How Fast Do You Want the Quadernaria? Or *Verçepe* and *Gelosia* Revisited: The Tale of the Three *Contrapassi in Quadernaria.*" In *The Marriage of Music and Dance: Papers from a Conference Held at the Guildhall School of Music and Drama, London, 9th–11th August 1991.* Cambridge, 1992.

Sparti, Barbara. "Rôti bouilli, Take Two: 'El Gioioso Fiorito.'" In *Studi musicali* 24.2 (1995): 231–261.

Squire, Geoffrey. *Dress and Society, 1560–1970.* New York, 1974.

Stark, Alan. "What Steps Did the Spaniards Take in the Dance?" In *Dance in Hispanic Cultures: Proceedings of the Fourteenth Annual Conference, Society of Dance History Scholars, New World School of the Arts, Miami, Florida, 8–10 February 1991,* compiled by Christena L. Schlundt. Riverside, Calif., 1991.

Sutton, Julia. "Reconstruction of Sixteenth-Century Dance." In *Dance History Research: Perspectives from Related Arts and Disciplines,* edited by Joann W. Kealiinohomoku. New York, 1970.

Sutton, Julia. "Dance IV: Late Renaissance, before 1630." In *The New Grove Dictionary of Music and Musicians.* London, 1980.

Thomas, Emma Lewis. "Music and Dance in Boccaccio's Time." *Dance Research Journal* 10.2 (1978): 19–42.

Via, Claudia Cieri. "Note sull'iconografia della danza nel quattrocento fra movimento ed espressione." In *Guglielmo Ebreo da Pesaro e la danza nelle corti italiane del XV secolo,* edited by Maurizio Padovan. Pisa, 1990.

Wilson, David R. *The Steps Used in Court Dance in Fifteenth-Century Italy.* Cambridge, 1992.

Wilson, David R. "'Finita: Et larifaccino unaltra volta dachapo.'" *Historical Dance* 3.2 (1993): 21–26.

Wilson, David R. "A Further Look at the Nancy Basse Dances." *Historical Dance* 3.3 (1994): 24–28.

Wood, Melusine. *Some Historical Dances, Twelfth to Nineteenth Century.* London, 1952.

Wood, Melusine. *More Historical Dances.* London, 1956.

INGRID BRAINARD

RENAISSANCE FÊTES AND TRIUMPHS, elaborate festivals organized by or for royalty, incorporated many forms of entertainment, including dance. The triumphs, named for the triumphal arches erected for the occasion by townspeople, welcomed the monarch to their city as the royal entourage traveled the realm to assert the monarch's authority; the festivities were organized at court to demonstrate royal power, some were directed at impressing both rebellious lords and foreign rivals.

Court festivals comprised many entertainments for several days: tournaments, banquets—often enlivened by masquerades, some of which presented the challenge for the joust; plays, with or without interludes; and the social dancing with which each evening ended—often introduced by a masquerade (or morisco, disguising, maskers—all terms for essentially the same type of entertainment). Many of the entertainments had common characteristics: the joust and the masquerade shared a processional element, a romantic framework, and a contest with knights battling in dance or with weapons for their ladies' favors or to overcome the vile wretches who held their ladies prisoners. Participants in both were brought into the playing area, often on stages, disguised as mountains, elephants, castles, or globes, or on triumphal carts. Developments in one form, therefore, might spread quickly to another and from country to country, since princes were feted in foreign, often conquered, territories (e.g., Spaniards in the Low Countries and Italy, the French in Italy, Henry VIII of England in France).

Some types of festivity were more popular in one place than another; France developed a dance genre, ballet (though it was not the only entertainment favored), while Italy developed a fascination for singing and spectacular stage effects, which when combined resulted in the rise of opera. The evolution of these forms was gradual and related as ballet became a feature of opera for many years. In England, masking faded away around 1530 only to reappear in the reign of Elizabeth I, when it was referred to as *masque.* Spectacle replaced military prowess in tourneys, transforming them into horse ballets in Italy and France, where water spectacles were also popular. The steadiest development was in the visual arts.

As the easily constructed wood-and-canvas Roman triumphal arches replaced Gothic architecture for royal entries, medieval allegories gave way to classical figures in the entertainments. Festival halls and temporary theaters (stages on wheeled platforms) were transformed into Roman interiors, castles, and mountains that brought maskers into the hall, and these became the triumphal carts of Venus and other deities, suitably costumed. In Italy, these characters were made to descend from the skies amid swirling clouds onto temporary stages graced with mechanically movable scenery—a sight to astonish spectators. These multimedia events developed along with the other arts, as princes called upon architects, poets, musicians, singers, and choreographers to collaborate in making their festivals truly magnificent.

For these events, and in contrast to other forms of art and literature, no rules yet existed; there was extreme flexibility; the entertainment might be performed indoors or out and in any order. The presence of a river might suggest marine gods or naval warfare, as in Rouen in 1550. That city's trade with the New World also inspired the construction of a Brazilian village complete with fifty South American Indians who went about their daily lives and even conducted a tribal war while Henri II of France watched. In Italy, dramatic interludes (literally, "between the games" or "the play") rarely had any connection with one another or with the play and could even be performed with several different plays, as was the set performed in Florence in 1589. They could be, and usually were, however, related to the occasion being celebrated.

Most festivals celebrated coronations, weddings, or the visits of other rulers, and the flexibility of the entertainments made them ideal for the expression of political views: praises were sung for the ruler or the bridal pair, while their illustrious ancestors were compared with the glorious heroes or divinities of antiquity. One ruler who used eulogy for specific political aims was Catherine de Médicis. She encouraged the warring Catholic and Protestant nobility to dance out their differences in the presence of a king—as depicted in the famous *Balet Comique de la Royne*—who was determined to drive discord from his realm. She used the 1565 festival at Bayonne for her daughter, the queen of Spain, to express similar goals. As guests journeyed to a banquet on an island in the river they were entertained by Triton, Neptune in his chariot, Arion on his dolphin, and three Sirens, all of whose songs were of peace and of praise for the two royal families. Charles IX of France headed the champions of Virtue as they fought those of Love in one tournament. In another, he was the courageous knight, as fortunate in peace as in war, who would fulfill Merlin's prophecy by overcoming innumerable enemies and storming the castle of Bellona, thus rescuing the prisoner, Peace, and restoring the Golden Age. As it happened, the king's brother was the first to conquer the final defender of the castle, a giant, but the organizers were prepared—a huge cloud descended and deftly whisked him away. The growing elaboration of such entertainments and their evolution into new forms (*ballet de cour,* opera, masque), coupled with the political aspect, would also be characteristic of baroque fêtes.

Little outdoor dancing occurred at these festivals. In one of the *tableaux vivants* for the entry of Charles V of the Holy Roman Empire into Bruges in 1515, Pan may have danced a few measures of a *branle* with his nymphs and satyrs, but this is not certain. During the outdoor banquet at Bayonne, however, the dance of the peasants from various provinces and the ballet that followed it were performed outside.

Most of the dancing at fêtes and triumphs occurred indoors and was based on social dancing. Unfortunately, although there are plot descriptions for the dances, there is no mention of steps or figures. We know that social dances of the time were of two types: (1) the basic dances (including the *branle, canarie, courante, galliard, pavan,* and *volta*) and (2) those invented by dancing masters for one or several couples, consisting of some ten figures with several changes of step and rhythm for variety. These masquerades probably consisted of a mixture of dance forms and figures, with unity provided by the plot. For a solemn entrance of ladies or downcast lovers, the processional pavane could be used; for the more lively characters, various branles or even galliards might be used. The semidramatic element usually comprised a love theme and a battle, with knights wooing their ladies and being scorned, fighting their rivals for the ladies' favors, or rescuing their ladies from giants. The love theme was present in embryo in the various dances for one woman and two men (and vice versa), expressed by the continual turning away from the one toward the other. Thoinot Arbeau mentioned a *courante* for three couples in which the men cajole their partners. This basic material could be expanded and developed for a masquerade. Fighting could be represented by a battle *moresca* (a dance originally symbolizing battling Moors and Christians, not the masquerade-like entertainment), by a Morris, or by sword dances such as *buffins.* In Fabritio Caroso's "Battaglia," the dancers' steps and postures symbolize attacks with various weapons.

"Battaglia" introduces the genre of mime dancing. The moves in the battle dances are highly stylized and strictly choreographed; even the Maltese *branle,* which according to Arbeau was invented for a masquerade, had stylized mime gestures, as did a 1576 French ballet. Yet to judge by later *ballet de cour* entries, the theme would be conveyed more by the costumes and the *livret* than by the way of dancing. It may be that mime played a part in some sections of an entertainment but not in most. It would be absent from the final dances of rejoicing, which would be figured, sometimes including geometric forms. These might lead to spelling out the prince's name as a fitting conclusion to the festivities.

[*For general discussion, see historical articles under European country entries. For related entertainments, see* Balet Comique de la Royne, Le; Ballet de Cour; Banquet; Barriera, Torneo, and Battaglia; Horse Ballet; Intermedio; Masque and Antimasque; Moresca; *and* Wirtschaft.]

BIBLIOGRAPHY

Anglo, Sydney. "The Evolution of the Early Tudor Disguising, Pageant, and the Mask." *Renaissance Drama* 1 (1968).

Arbeau, Thoinot. *Orchesography* (1589). Translated by Mary Stewart Evans. New York, 1948.

Caroso, Fabritio. *Il ballarino* (1581). New York, 1967.

Caroso, Fabritio. *Nobiltà di dame* (1600). Translated and edited by Julia Sutton. Oxford, 1986.

Jacquot, Jean. "La fête princière." In *Histoire des spectacles,* edited by Guy Dumur. Paris, 1965.

Jacquot, Jean, ed. *Les fêtes de la Renaissance.* 3 vols. Paris, 1956–1973.

Jacquot, Jean, ed. *Le lieu théâtral à la Renaissance.* Paris, 1964.

Kernodle, George R. *From Art to Theatre.* Chicago, 1944.

McGowan, Margaret M. *L'art du ballet de cour en France, 1581–1643.* Paris, 1963.

McGowan, Margaret M., et al., eds. *Renaissance Triumphs and Magnificences.* Amsterdam, 1976–.

Nagler, A. M. *Theatre Festivals of the Medici, 1539–1637.* New Haven, 1964.

Reyher, Paul. *Les masques anglais.* Paris, 1909.

Welsford, Enid. *The Court Masque.* Cambridge, 1927.

Yates, Frances A. *The Valois Tapestries.* London, 1959.

HELEN M. C. PURKIS

RENDEZVOUS, LES. Choreography: Frederick Ashton. Music: Daniel Auber. Scenery and costumes: William Chappell. First performance: 5 December 1933, Sadler's Wells Theatre, London, Vic-Wells Ballet. Principals: Alicia

Markova and Stanislas Idzikowski (The Lovers), Ninette de Valois, Robert Helpmann, Stanley Judson (pas de trois).

Les Rendezvous is a *demi-caractère divertissement* danced to the ballet music from Auber's opera *L'Enfant Prodigue,* originally choreographed at the Théâtre National de l'Opéra, Paris, in 1850 by Arthur Saint-Léon. Its pretext is the meetings of lovers in a public garden (in later productions; photographs of the 1933 original suggest an interior setting). Ashton said that his purpose was to provide a showcase for both Idzikowski, the virtuosic dancer of Diaghilev's Ballets Russes, who appeared as a guest artist with the Vic-Wells Ballet, and Markova. The ballet presented a technical challenge as well to the dancers who appeared in support of these two stars, and, whether by accident or design, the work was an early statement of Ashton's own personal classicism, both in the Petipa-like figures he devised for the corps de ballet and in the writing for the solo dancers, with the sometimes extreme use of *épaulement* and the brilliant *petit allegro.*

Both of the principal Lovers have solo variations; the man's features jumping *pas ciseaux,* the woman's a variety of pirouettes punctuated by a characteristic gesture, a twist of the wrists as she opens her arms to the side. There is a pas de deux in which they are backed by the corps de ballet. A woman and two men from the corps dance a sprightly pas de trois in which they sweep around the stage with a little prancing step. In 1934 Ashton added a pas de quatre of four small women who end the ballet with a typically Ashtonian quizzical gesture.

The ballet has undergone many additional revisions over the years. It was redesigned in 1937, at which time further changes were made in the choreography. The revival by Sadler's Wells Theatre Ballet in 1947 introduced still further modifications. When the ballet was revived by the Royal Ballet at the Royal Opera House, Covent Garden, in 1959, the corps de ballet was enlarged to ten couples from the original six; this version has been performed by both companies of the Royal Ballet, but the touring section (later Sadler's Wells Royal Ballet) also sometimes performed the smaller 1947 version, which since 1971 has become definitive. The nomenclature of the characters also has changed, the original designations having been translated into French in 1947 (the Lovers became Amoureux; the Walkers Out, Promeneurs).

In the Vic-Wells Ballet production Markova and Idzikowski were succeeded by Margot Fonteyn and Harold Turner, and the roles have since been danced by many others. *Les Rendezvous* has been revived by many companies, notably the National Ballet of Canada in 1956, the Australian Ballet in 1962, and American Ballet Theatre in 1980.

BIBLIOGRAPHY

Macaulay, Alastair. "Ashton's Classicism and *Les Rendezvous.*" In *Looking at Ballet: Ashton and Balanchine, 1926–1936,* compiled by Jane B. Roberts and David Vaughan. Studies in Dance History, vol. 3.2. Pennington, N.J., 1993.

Vaughan, David. *Frederick Ashton and His Ballets.* London, 1977.

DAVID VAUGHAN

REVELATIONS. Choreography: Alvin Ailey. Music: traditional religious songs. Scenery and costumes: Ves Harper. First Performance: 31 January 1960, Ninety-second Street YM-YWHA, New York.

At the premiere of *Revelations* the score was performed by singers Nancy Redi and Gene Hobgood, with the Music Masters Chorus of the Harlem Branch YMCA. The cast consisted of seven dancers and the choreographer. The work was greatly revised after its premiere; some numbers were replaced and others deleted. A performance at Clark Center, New York, on 10 December 1961, showed the piece in very nearly its permanent form. The ensemble grew along with Alvin Ailey's company until it numbered eighteen dancers.

Revelations has become the Ailey company's signature piece and is the choreographer's most respected and successful work. The clear rhythms and sweet melodies of the music are echoed by strong shapes and decisive movements, and the piece exuberantly displays Ailey's interest in theatrical values. The dance is a vision of the history of black people in America.

Revelations is divided into three sections. The first section deals with deprivation and longing; the second with redemption; and the third with salvation. The dance begins with the ensemble grouped in the center of the stage in drab costumes: deep *pliés,* arching torsos, and reaching hands suggest intense suffering. The second section is based in large part on the riverside baptisms Ailey saw when he was a boy in Texas: the costumes are white; colored streamers represent the river; the music is joyous and the movements are fluid. The final episode, with its bright costumes and its ensemble spread over the stage space, suggests an urban setting: the dancers stand erect and move in long, straight lines with sharp, brisk steps. The attack is vigorous, the accents are stressed, and the spirit is one of unrestrained joy.

BIBLIOGRAPHY

Mazo, Joseph H. *Prime Movers: The Makers of Modern Dance in America.* New York, 1977.

Mazo, Joseph H., and Susan Cook. *The Alvin Ailey American Dance Theater.* New York, 1978.

Reynolds, Nancy, and Susan Reimer-Torn. *Dance Classics.* Pennington, N.J., 1991.

JOSEPH H. MAZO

REVELS. In Tudor and Jacobean courts of the sixteenth and early seventeenth century in England, the participatory dancing that followed a masque proper but that preceded its concluding speeches, songs, or final mask dances was called a revel. In France, revels known as *le grand ballet* marked the formal finale of the masque rather than the interval of dancing within the more drama-oriented English masque. Characterized by performers and spectators dancing together, reveling began when maskers entered the hall and "took out" the hosts and principal guests to perform social dances of the period.

In England, revels belonged to the ballroom rather than to the theater. In form, they progressed from solemn figure dances of "measures" to lighter, livelier court dances, especially *galliards, corantos, voltas,* and less frequently, *branles, durettos,* and *morescas.*

Revels occurred in royal palaces and manor houses on holidays and state occasions. The season of high revels came at Christmas, culminating in the year's most important court function, Twelfth Night (6 January). Later in the year, revels were revived at Candlemas (2 February) and at Shrovetide, preceding Ash Wednesday and Lent.

The object of Elizabethan court revels was the queen's entertainment. Appointed to an office (established in 1545) with an annual salary of ten pounds, the master of the revels organized masques, accounted for production expenses, and kept custody of all masking paraphernalia. The masques financed by the queen were essentially dances, in contrast to the pageants staged and paid for by the nobility during her progresses. [*See* Elizabethan Progresses.]

Under King James I, masques and revels continued to enjoy an important place in court life but were produced more for diplomatic purposes than for pure entertainment. "Taking out" was still practiced, with Queen Anne often doing the honors with foreign ambassadors and other visiting dignitaries. King James's master of the horse supervised the revels, reflecting the king's preoccupation with the hunt. King James trimmed the responsibilities of the revels office and made it answerable to the lord chamberlain.

Revels seem to have died out with the end of court masques under Charles I (James's son), by the time of the Civil War in 1642, although the post of master of revels was revived in 1660, following the restoration of the monarchy.

[*See also* Great Britain, *articles on* Theatrical Dance, 1460–1660 *and* Masque and Antimasque. *For discussion of dances, see* Renaissance Dance Technique.]

BIBLIOGRAPHY

Chambers, E. K. *The Elizabethan Stage.* 4 vols. Oxford, 1923.

Feuillerat, Albert, ed. *Documents Relating to the Office of the Revels in the Time of Queen Elizabeth.* Louvain, 1908.

Reyher, Paul. *Les masques anglais.* Paris, 1909.

Sullivan, Mary. *The Court Masques of James I.* New York, 1913.

Welsford, Enid. *The Court Masque.* Cambridge, 1927.

ROBIN WOODARD WEENING

RÉVÉRENCE. [*This entry comprises three articles that discuss the importance of deportment and bows and curtseys in relation to social dance:*

Origins of Modes and Manners
Early Eighteenth-Century Modes
Nineteenth-Century Modes

For related discussion, see Medieval Dance; Social Dance, *articles on* Court and Social Dance before 1800 *and* Nineteenth-Century Social Dance.]

Origins of Modes and Manners

A *révérence* (also Fr., *honneur;* It., *riverenza;* Sp., *reverencia;* Ger., *Reverenz*) is a gesture of respect and courtesy, especially as performed on social occasions or as a part of a dance. Bows and other gestures of respect have been common to all polite societies, but their forms have changed as these societies have changed. They have been fully documented only since the fifteenth century. But before they are ever described in a dance manual, *révérences* appear in iconography. Medieval squires presented tournament prizes, gifts, and food platters to their superiors on bended knee; the suggestion of a similar movement is recognizable in some fourteenth- and fifteenth-century dance pictures. However, a distinction must be made from the start between the ceremonial bow, which often seems to have gone all the way to the floor, and the dance bow, in which the knees were bent a little, the body inclined toward the person honored, and the hat or bonnet removed and replaced while the bowing gentleman reassumed his upright posture.

Through the Mid-Sixteenth Century. The *bassedanse* sources are the first to give skeletal directions for the man's bow: "One makes reverence to the woman inclining oneself towards her and this inclination must be made with the left foot" (in the Brussels Manuscript and likewise in Michel Toulouze's manual of 1488 and Robert Coplande's treatise of 1521). When the bow is choreographed into the step sequence of a *bassedanse,* it requires one note of the tenor melody; the invitational bow prior to dancing has no time value. Nothing is said about the lady's *révérence* in these sources.

It is not until we get to Antonius de Arena's *Leges dansandi* (c.1519 and later editions) that the *révérence* receives the same attention as the steps of the then-current repertory. Arena, the university dancing master of Avignon, describes both the man's and the lady's bows in a chapter entitled "Modus de choreando bené." Characteristic of the man's *révérence* is the semicircular gesture of the working leg, compared by Arena to the swing of a scythe (details in Brainard, 1981, pp. 16ff.) while "the lady keeps her feet together," bends her knees, and rises again. After having stated that the man's bow is always done with the left foot, Arena concedes that the dancer can decide "which leg it is better to use."

The Italian dancing masters of the fifteenth century do not describe the *riverenza* but use it frequently in their choreographies. Full reverences with the time value of *un tempo di musica* (as in Domenico da Piacenza's manual of c.1450) occur on the left and on the right foot; the smaller and presumably faster bows, *riuerentia picola, un poco di riuerentia,* and *inchino,* are without musical time value. Yet hints regarding the execution of at least some of these bows can be found especially in Guglielmo Ebreo's dance descriptions. Formulas such as "then they make a reverence that ends on the floor" or "this reverence does not end on the floor" seem to indicate that Guglielmo's preference was the ceremonial bow mentioned above and not the Arena *révérence,* which cannot be taken all the way to the floor. In the dance iconography of the period, only men are shown executing *révérences* of the ceremonial type. Guglielmo's wordings, however, suggest that women at times also honored their partners with a bow on one bent knee. Whether this was common practice or happened only in isolated instances is unknown.

Neither in Italy nor in Burgundy is any mention made of the removal of the hat (for reasons, see Brainard, 1981 and 1983). Only Arena directs the gentleman to take his hat off with the left hand while bowing to his lady.

Late Sixteenth Century. All dance steps, including *révérences,* are described in minute detail in the dance manuals of the late sixteenth century. Fabritio Caroso in his *Il ballarino* (1581) distinguishes three kinds of bow: *riuerenza graue, riuerenza minima,* and *riuerenza semiminima in balzetto* (rules 2–4). According to Caroso, the preferred leg is the left one "because . . . one honours a person from the heart" but also because for most people it is easier to maintain balance on the stronger right leg. The emphasis is on firmness and clarity of execution: the left foot is pulled straight back without raising the heel, while head and body are inclined somewhat; then both knees are bent *con bella gratia* ("with beautiful grace"); to end, body and head return to their upright position and the left foot is brought back next to the right foot (first position).

An intricate procedure of removal and replacement of the hat, described in Caroso's *Della nobiltà di dame* (1600), must be synchronized with the leg and body motions: the gentleman takes his hat off with the right hand and transfers it to the left; the right hand is then kissed and offered to the lady while the left replaces the hat securely on the head. The lady only kisses her fingertips lightly before extending her left hand to her partner.

The jumped *riuerenza in balzetto,* a trademark of Caroso's early dances, is not mentioned in *Nobiltà* anymore.

Cesare Negri's *riuerenza graue* and *riuerenza minima*

RÉVÉRENCE: Origins of Modes and Manners. This engraving, c.1500 by Martin Zatzinger, depicting a ball given by Albrecht IV, grand duke of Bavaria, shows a gentleman (at right) making a half *révérence,* or the beginning of one, to a lady who sits in front of the window. (Reprinted from Lilly Grove, *Dancing,* London, 1895, p. 291.)

(*Le gratie d'amore,* 1602, p. 104–5) are not substantially different from those described by Caroso.

While the Italians give preference to the left-foot *révérence,* the Frenchman Thoinot Arbeau insists that one should bow "with the right foot" (*Orchésographie,* 1589). He distinguishes between the gentleman's "*révérence* of salutation," with a musical value of four bars or *quaternions;* the *galliard révérence,* which is identical with the salutation except for the faster tempo; and the *reuerence passagiere,* which "is done in almost the same manner" as the other two but can be executed with either the right or the left foot *(reuerence passagiere droicte* and *gaulche).* The hat, which is removed in the stationary formal bows, is kept on the head in the *reuerence passagiere. Révérences* of salutation, explains Arbeau, can occur at the beginning, at the end, and sometimes in the middle of the dances, a practice that is documented in choreographic sources as early as the fifteenth century.

Stylistically, Arbeau emphasizes that the man's *révérences* be done by bringing the working leg smartly to the rear: "A man must avoid effeminate attitudes." The lady, on the other hand, must move with gentleness. Her bow consists of an easy bending and straightening of the knees ("Et les Damoiselles plient les deux genoulx doulcement & se releuent de mesme").

Seventeenth Century. François de Lauze in his *Apologie de la danse* (1623) describes with great care the execution of *révérences* for both men and women at different social occasions and at the beginning of different dances, such as *courante, branle,* and *galliard.* While the man's hat gesture is not unlike that described by Caroso in *Della nobiltà di dame,* the footwork with its emphasis on the initial sideways motion as well as the doubling of the bow—first to the "Presence" (that is, to the king, queen, or ranking personage presiding), then to the partner—bears all the signs of the approaching Baroque; in fact, the lady's bow is almost the same as that described by Pierre Rameau (1725), including the well turned-out legs and feet, the lowering and raising of the glance, and the lifting of the heels in a profound curtsy.

De Lauze places great emphasis on facial expression and the eyes: a gentleman looks at the assembly with a face that is "gay, open, smiling," and "if he finds . . . several assemblies in the same place," he will make his bows "without any gesture or posture of the body; because in this the direction of the glance is sufficient." A lady is advised on rising from her bows not to stare fixedly at the person opposite her because that is considered an affront. When a man salutes a woman, he not only kisses his own hand before offering it to her but also embraces the lady before completing the leg motions of his *révérence.* De Lauze recommends that the various *révérences* be practiced diligently in order to achieve the required "assured grace and dignity."

Possibly because of its geographical isolation from the rest of Europe, Spain developed its own dance technique and style at its own pace. As the fifteenth-century Cervera Manuscript and the Spanish Caroso translation show, Renaissance Spaniards moved in ways similar to those of central Europe. In the seventeenth century, however, differences became more pronounced as demonstrated by the *reuerencias* and other steps described by Juan Esquivel de Navarro's *Discvrsos sobre el arte del dancado* (Seville, 1642). Esquivel distinguishes between the *reuerencia cortada* ("cut" or brief reverence) containing a jump; the *reuerencia cierta y comun* (ordinary *révérence*); the more elaborate *reuerencia galana* (genteel *révérence*); and the *reuerencia del villano* (peasant *révérence*) in which the working leg is lifted higher than usual and the hat taken off with both hands. The *reuerencia in gallarda* is mentioned only in passing and is not described in detail except for the statement that "it is done with the left foot."

English seventeenth-century dance sources such as the Inns of Court Manuscripts (Cunningham, 1965) and John Playford's book of 1651 do not describe the "Honours" at all. More than other nations, the "dancing English" cultivated the embrace as part of their bow ceremonial, a practice often referred to in the literature and correspondence of the period and much to the liking of Erasmus and other visitors from abroad.

BIBLIOGRAPHY

Brainard, Ingrid. *The Art of Courtly Dancing in the Early Renaissance.* West Newton, Mass., 1981.

Brainard, Ingrid. "Modes, Manners, Movement: The Interaction of Dance and Dress from the Late Middle Ages to the Renaissance." In *Proceedings of the Sixth Annual Conference, Society of Dance History Scholars, the Ohio State University, 11–13 February 1983,* compiled by Christena L. Schlundt. Milwaukee, 1983.

Cunningham, James P. *Dancing in the Inns of Court.* London, 1965.

Franko, Mark. *The Dancing Body in Renaissance Choreography.* Birmingham, Alabama, 1986.

Hilton, Wendy. *Dance of Court and Theatre: The French Noble Style, 1690–1725.* Princeton, 1981.

Wilson, David R. "Dancing in the Inns of Court." *Historical Dance: The Journal of the Dolmetsch Historical Dance Society* 2.5 (1986–1987): 3–16.

Wilson, David R. *The Steps Used in Court Dancing in Fifteenth-Century Italy.* Cambridge, 1992.

INGRID BRAINARD

Early Eighteenth-Century Modes

A *révérence* (called in English an Honour), was a bow or curtsy, an act of politeness and respect that expressed the social status of the recipient and the giver; its depth acknowledged the social rank of the recipient and the quality of its execution revealed the breeding and education of the giver.

A person of upper-class birth was trained by a dancing master from early childhood to make Honours with a culti-

RÉVÉRENCE: Eighteenth-Century Modes. A bow forward was used when presenting a gift or handing an object. Engraving by L. P. Boitard from Francis Nivelon's *The Rudiments of Genteel Behaviour* (1737). (Dance Collection, New York Public Library for the Performing Arts.)

vated ease and simplicity entirely devoid of affectation. Awkward exaggerations and a self-conscious stiffness revealed a lack of breeding, as in a would-be gentleman, while the extreme wavings about of hats and handkerchiefs were affected gestures employed by those of a foppish disposition. Honours constantly punctuated everyday life and were, within their discipline, imbued with personality and often with innuendo. In a status-conscious society, where no motion in everyday social life was left to chance, and when "an air of ease will more distinguish a man from the crowd than the richest clothes that money may purchase," the ability to perform a beautiful and distinguished Honour was of paramount importance.

The Honours are most comprehensibly described in the treatises of Pierre Rameau (*Le maître à danser,* 1725), Kellom Tomlinson (*The Art of Dancing,* 1735), and F. Nivelon, (*The Rudiments of Genteel Behaviour,* 1737). Differing only in detail, these writers describe three different Honours: the bow and the Courtesy (curtsy)—forward, backward, and in passing. The Honour forward was usually preceded by forward steps; the Honour backward by a retreating motion; the passing bow was used in passing. Although Honours were not performed in exactly the same way throughout Europe, these descriptions provide the basic structural principles.

The gentleman's bows required extremely good coordination, for a removing and replacing of the hat had to be combined with an inclination and straightening of the torso, an action usually combined with a bending and straightening of one knee, yet all to be executed smoothly, with punctuation and articulation. The hat and its management played a vital role in a gentleman's social life. It was generally worn indoors as well as out, unless in the presence of the king when a gentleman should remain "uncovered." When removed, the hat might have been carried beneath the left arm against the body. By the turn of the seventeenth century, the three-cornered hat was in general use. According to Rameau, to have a fashionable angle, it was necessary for "the Fore-part to be lower a small matter than the Back-part. The Button ought to be on the left Side, and the Corner or Point of the Hat over the left Eye, which disengages the Face." Before bowing, a gentleman removed his hat with a broad, simple gesture and directed his bow by looking at the person to be honoured. At the conclusion, the hat was replaced with the same unembellished motion unless another bow followed. Children spent many hours practicing the art of replacing the hat at the fashionable angle by a simple arm motion, concluding with only one firm pull to secure the hat upon the head.

Of the three Honours, the bow backward was the most ceremonious and formal. In this, the gentleman removed his hat, directed his bow while moving his front foot to the side, the weight still on one foot, or transferred to both. He then bowed from the waist, lowering his gaze, returned to an upright position looking once more at the person honoured, and closed the other foot. (If this bow followed another, the back foot could be the one to be moved to the side.) The bow forward was generally made at the end of steps forward, the foot moving ahead as though to take another step, but coming to rest with the knee extended, the ball of the foot resting upon the floor. Toward the end of the forward progression and the leg gesture, the hat was removed and the bow directed. The gentleman inclined the torso as in the bow backward, simultaneously bending and straightening the back knee. To conclude, the weight was transferred to the front foot and the back foot closed to it. The passing bow interrupted a walk forward when passing and greeting someone. It was executed like the bow forward, with the body turned to incline diagonally across the front leg. As the body resumed an upright posture, the weight was transferred to the front foot and the walk resumed.

The lady's Courtesies (curtsies) were simpler. With the weight supported equally on both feet, the legs rotated outward, she had only to bend, then straighten her knees while lowering and raising the gaze, her head remaining absolutely upright. A profound Courtesy, however, required the heels of the shoes to be raised from the floor. In a Courtesy backward, the lady moved her front foot to the side and closed the other foot to it, making her Honour with the feet together. In the Courtesy forward, and in passing, her feet were apart, one in front of the other. Her arms may have been disposed downward, the hands resting one on top of the other against the bottom of her bodice, perhaps holding a fan or, if out-of-doors, being enclosed in a muff.

In the central dances at a ball, the *danses à deux* (couple dances), only one couple danced at a time. Following the first dance by the persons of highest social rank, men and women alternated in leading the dancers out in strict order of social precedence. The Honours of invitation and the exact procedure depended upon the presence or absence of the king. Immediately before and after dancing, two Honours backward were made, one to the Presence, the person or persons of highest social rank, the second by partners to each other. These Honours were not accompanied by music, except in the *menuet ordinaire* (the only *danse à deux* not choreographed to a particular air or a set number of measures).

[*For related discussion in a broader context, see* Social Dance, *article on* Court and Social Dance before 1800.]

BIBLIOGRAPHY

Annas, Alicia M. "The Elegant Art of Movement." In Annas's *An Elegant Art*. Los Angeles, 1983.

Brinson, Peter, and Joan Wildeblood. *The Polite World*. London, 1965.

Hilton, Wendy. *Dance of Court and Theatre: The French Noble Style, 1690–1725*. Princeton, 1981.

Nivelon, Francis *The Rudiments of Genteel Behavior*. London, 1737.

Rameau, Pierre. *Le maître à danser*. Paris, 1725. Translated by Cyril W. Beaumont as *The Dancing Master*. London, 1931.

Sol, C. *Méthode très facile et fort nécessaire pour montrer à la jeunesse de l'un et l'autre sexe la manière de bien danser*. The Hague, 1725.

Tomlinson, Kellom. *The Art of Dancing Explained by Reading and Figures . . . Being the Original Work First Design'd in the Year 1724, and Now Published by Kellom Tomlinson, Dancing-Master*. 2 vols. London, 1735.

WENDY HILTON

RÉVÉRENCE: Eighteenth-Century Modes. A lady's Courtesy (i.e., curtsy) from Nivelon's *The Rudiments of Genteel Behaviour*. (Dance Collection, New York Public Library for the Performing Arts.)

Nineteenth-Century Modes

By the beginning of the nineteenth century, a person of good breeding, having been trained by a dancing master, was expected to present himself or herself with ease, grace, assurance, and "a mind fixed and determined in itself to do nothing repugnant to the rules [of] honor and decency" (Saltator, 1802, p. 67). Bows and curtsies were used in all aspects of daily life and had special applications for use while dancing, when passing in the street, and upon entering and leaving social gatherings. Even in the waning years of the nineteenth century, when shaking hands became acceptable as a means of greeting, etiquette authors admonished ladies and gentlemen to utilize bows and curtsies in the ballroom. "The hostess at a ball does not usually shake hands with her guests, but makes them a sweeping courtsey instead" (Hall, 1887, p. 136). Throughout the nineteenth century, a gentleman was expected to bow before taking his partner out to the dance floor and, again, when he returned her to her seat.

In early nineteenth-century dance and etiquette manuals, the movements of the feet, torso, head and eyes, arms, and hands and fingers as well as the removal of the gentleman's hat were explained in elaborate detail. A gentleman did not bow his head but kept it in line with the body, and a lady was instructed to keep her body as well as her head perpendicular. The eyes for both were directed toward the person honored, for "what looks worse, when respect is meant to be conveyed, than to present the hair of the head" (Saltator, 1802, p. 69). The arms were to hang down naturally and without stiffness, the hands somewhat bent, and the fingers positioned "rather as if one held a pinch of snuff" (Mädel, 1805). The gentleman's hat was brought down from the head in a straight line with the brim turned toward the back or toward the leg.

By mid-century, the Industrial Revolution had changed the nature of society, but the bow and the curtsy remained important for all social classes. The upper classes learned the art of dancing and appropriate behavior from early and long-lasting instruction. Then, too, the growing middle class was expected to demonstrate similar knowledge of dance and etiquette, although many were introduced to such refinements much later in life and often without benefit of professional instruction. As a result, many facets of mid-century social life—bows and curtsies included—became less complex. Less importance was attached to the fine points of torso and hand and finger placement, and both sexes were encouraged to be as unaffected and natural as possible. Bows and curtsies, as in other matters of etiquette, differed slightly from place to place.

The Bow. During the first quarter of the nineteenth century, all social dancers were acquainted with the five foot positions of classical ballet. The gentleman's bow consisted of stepping to the side into second position and, while inclining the torso forward, drawing the other foot into first or third position. The torso was then straightened after the feet were brought together. The arms hung down in a relaxed manner, and the hat was removed as the bow commenced. The actual step sequence remained the same throughout the century but, as the century went on, the tilt of the torso began as soon as the bow commenced. Throughout the nineteenth century, less and less attention was paid to the exactness of the foot positions, so that by mid-century, the normal turnout of the feet was less than ninety degrees. By century's end, an inclination of the head (a nod) or the touching of the hat brim (although when addressing ladies, men were expected to lift the hat), was considered sufficient. Inclination of the torso was discouraged.

RÉVÉRENCE: Nineteenth-Century Modes. A gentleman pays his respects to a lady. This print by Gavarni is in dancing master Henri Cellarius's manual, *La danse des salons,* published in Paris in 1847. (Courtesy of Elizabeth Aldrich.)

The Curtsy. The early nineteenth-century lady's curtsy consisted of stepping one foot into second position, placing the other foot behind in third or fifth position, bending the knees, then rising slowly. Although covered by an ankle-length skirt, the knees were to be well turned out and the torso erect. There were many variations. One was to step one foot into second position, place the opposite foot into fourth position behind, and bend the knees. The weight was then shifted to either the front or back foot, and the curtsy was concluded by drawing the opposite foot to first or third position as the knees were straightened. As with gentlemen, the exactness of the classical ballet positions became less important throughout the century and, by the end of the nineteenth century, an acceptable curtsy for ladies was simply to step to the side, bend the standing leg, while at the same time bringing the opposite foot behind the standing leg and lightly touching the floor with the toe. The arms were relaxed or might hold the front of the skirt.

History. During the first quarter of the century, great attention was paid to the differences between bows and curtsies appropriate for public as opposed to private gatherings. Later, it became acceptable to use one form of bow or curtsy for all occasions. Althought variously described in dance manuals and etiquette books, bows and curtsies were an expected part of the etiquette and performance of dance. While it was expected that partners would exchange bows prior to stepping onto the dance floor, it became rare to find bows and curtsies employed at the beginning or conclusion of each dance, as had frequently been choreographed into the dances of earlier centuries. One exception to this was the early nineteenth-century quadrille, in which dancers would bow to their partners and to their corners during the first eight bars preceding each figure of the quadrille. By mid-century, this practice was abandoned, much to the dismay of one dance master:

> In the figures of which there is an exchange of Salutations, many persons, through an ignorance of the form and manner of performing them, were subjected to ridicule and remark, which might have been avoided had they paid some regard to the first principles of dancing. (Ferrero, 1859, p. 119)

In the dance manuals that were published during the last quarter of the nineteenth century, it becomes increasingly rare to find instructions for the bow and curtsy. In contrast, etiquette manuals continued to stress the importance of proper salutations, which by this time included not only bows and curtsies but also the handshake, instilling in their readers a concern and fear of making a social faux pas.

> The bow is the touchstone of good breeding, and to neglect it, even to one with whom you may have a trifling difference, shows deficiency in cultivation and in the instincts of refinement. . . . Its entire neglect reveals the character and training of the person; the manner of its observance reveals the very shades of breeding that exist between the ill-bred and the well-bred. (Young, 1883, p. 46)

By the end of the nineteenth century, the handshake began to replace the bow outside the ballroom. In a ballroom, however, where "the introduction is to dancing, not to friendship," a handshake was considered inappropriate, and ladies and gentlemen were expected to honor each other with bows and curtsies, no matter how unceremonious such honors might be. Stressing the importance, one writer suggested, "A gentleman should always make a bow to a lady when asking her to dance, and both of them should bow and say 'Thank you' when the dance is over" (Hall, 1887, p. 139). Knowing the appropriate circumstances for bowing or handshaking and the subtle varients were important benchmarks for middle-class society. However vague the directions may have been for the actual performance of bows and curtsies, nevertheless they were considered a cornerstone of polite society and remained important components of ballroom etiquette throughout the nineteenth century and into the twentieth.

BIBLIOGRAPHY. During the nineteenth century, book publishing was a major and profitable business. Owing in part to lax international copyright laws, many books published during this time were simply pirated. Others were compilations, based on one or more previously published books and put together by a publisher. Still others were reprinted over and over, often given different titles. Among the most popular titles were books on entertainment, including dance. Many books, especially in the United States, were also aimed at the nineteenth-century preoccupation with self-help and the need to improve social status. Written as *aide-mémoires* (some small enough to fit into a pocket), etiquette and dance manuals were published to instruct readers about how to present themselves properly. Diatribes included instructions on appropriate clothes to wear for any occasion, which fork to use for luncheon or at the dinner table, suggested topics for conversation, introductions, bows and curtsies, and how to dance the latest and most fashionable dances. Although it is not certain how much impact these handy manuals had, they do illuminate one facet of the forces that shaped the multiple levels of nineteenth-century society.

For a detailed analysis and annotated bibliography of dance and etiquette manuals as well as a discussion of the importance of social dance in middle-class society, see Elizabeth Aldrich's *From the Ballroom to Hell: Grace and Folly in Nineteenth-Century Dance* (Evanston, Ill., 1991).

Virtually all etiquette manuals published during the nineteenth century contain information on bows and curtsies as well as general ballroom demeanor. A chronological listing of the most illuminating manuals includes *The Mirror of the Graces, or, The English Lady's Costume, by a Lady of Distinction* (London, 1810); *Exercises for Ladies* by Donald Walker (London, 1836); *The Laws of Etiquette, or Short Rules and Reflections for Conduct in Society, by a Gentleman* (Philadelphia, 1836); *Hints on Etiquette and the Usages of Society* by Charles William Day (London, c.1834); *The Ladies Pocket Book of Etiquette* by A. F. (London, 1838); *Morals and Manners, or, Hints for Our Young People* by Catherine Maria Sedgwick (New York, 1846); *The Behaviour Book: A Manual for Ladies* by Eliza Leslie (Philadelphia, 1853); *The Hand-Book of Etiquette: Being a Complete Guide to the Usages of Polite Society* (London, 1860); *Sensible Etiquette for the Best Society, Customs, Manners, Morals, and Home Culture, Compiled from the Best Authorities by Mrs. H. O. Ward*, 16th rev. ed. (Philadelphia, 1878); *Social Etiquette of New York* by Abby Buchanan Longstreet (New York, 1879); *Our Deportment* by John H. Young (Detroit, 1883); *The P. G., or Perfect Gentleman* by Ingersoll Lockwood (New York and London, 1887); and *Social Customs* by Florency Howe Hall (Boston, 1887).

Early to mid-nineteenth-century dance manuals are also a source for bows and curtsies and a chronological selection includes *A Treatise on Dancing and on Various Other Matters* by Saltator [pseud.] (Boston, 1802); *Die Tanzkunst für die Elegant Welt* by E. C. Mädel (Erfurt, 1805); *Principes et notions élémentaires sur l'art de la danse*. 2d. ed. by J. H. Gourdoux-Daux (Paris, 1811), translated by Victor Guillou as *Elements and Principles of the Art of Dancing* (Philadelphia, 1817); *De l'art de la danse* by H. Honoré (Geneva, 1833); *The Drawing-Room Dances* by Henri Cellarius (London, 1847); and *The Art of Dancing, Historically Illustrated* by Edward Ferrero (New York, 1859).

ELIZABETH ALDRICH

RIABOUCHINSKA, TATIANA (Tat'iana Riabushinskaia; born 17 May 1917 in Moscow), dancer. Riabouchinska's parents moved to Paris at the time of the Russian Revolution, and Tatiana studied ballet from an early age with Matilda Kshessinska and Alexandre Volinine. She made her debut with the Chauve-Souris company of Nikita Baliev. In 1931 George Balanchine, as ballet master, invited her to join the Ballets Russes de Monte Carlo, the newly formed company directed by René Blum and Colonel Wassily de Basil. At its debut performance on 12 April 1932, Riabouchinska, then fifteen, was one of the three "baby ballerinas" of the company (along with Tamara Toumanova and Irina Baronova, both thirteen). In 1935 she married the dancer and choreographer David Lichine; they had one daughter.

Riabouchinska remained with de Basil until 1941. She then appeared with Ballet Theatre during the 1944/45 season, returning to de Basil's company, now named Original Ballet Russe, for the 1946/47 season. In 1947 she danced with the company of the Teatro Colón in Buenos Aires, then with the Ballets des Champs-Élysées in 1948, Le Grand Ballet de Monte Carlo (directed by the marquis de Cuevas) for the 1949/50 season, and London's Festival Ballet in 1951, before moving to the United States and opening a studio with Lichine in Hollywood. Before Lichine's death in 1972 they also ran a small company there, the Ballet de la Ville des Anges.

Riabouchinska's particular qualities were a strong technique coupled with speed, lightness, musicality, and a fine *port de bras* (a special feature of Kshessinska's training). She created many important roles for de Basil, including the Child in Léonide Massine's *Jeux d'Enfants* and Frivolity in his *Les Présages,* the title roles in Michel Fokine's *Le Coq d'Or* and *Cendrillon,* the Florentine Beauty in his *Paganini,* and the Mistress of Ceremonies in Lichine's *Graduation Ball.* Additionally, she was widely praised for her Prelude in *Les Sylphides.*

BIBLIOGRAPHY

Barnes, Clive. "Legendary Baby Ballerinas." *Ballet News* 3 (January 1982): 46.

Finch, Tamara. "The First Baby Ballerinas." *The Dancing Times* (August 1985): 952–954.

García-Márquez, Vicente. *The Ballets Russes: Colonel de Basil's Ballets Russes de Monte Carlo, 1932–1952.* New York, 1990.

Lidova, Irène. "Tatiana Riabouchinska." *La Danse,* no. 3 (1949): 80.

Sorley Walker, Kathrine. *De Basil's Ballets Russes.* New York, 1983.

Swisher, Viola Hegyi. "The Real Mirror: A Portrait of Tatiana Riabouchinska." *Dance Magazine* (April 1972): 30–35.

FILM. The Barzel Collection, Newberry Library, Chicago, contains a film of Riabouchinska as Frivolity in Léonide Massine's *Les Présages*.

KATHRINE SORLEY WALKER

RICH, JOHN (born 1691 or 1692, died 26 November 1761 in London), English actor-manager and pantomimist. Rich is the individual singly most responsible for instituting pantomime as a British theatrical form. On inheriting the patent of Lincoln's Inn Fields from his father, Christopher Rich, in 1714, he imposed his tastes on that playhouse. Inimical to literary drama and tragedy in particular, as early as 1716 he staged his first pantomime *Harlequin Executed, or The Farmer Disappointed,* followed the next year by *The Cheats, or The Tavern Bilkers.* In both of these, Rich, under the stagename Lun, portrayed Harlequin.

The success of these performances led to *A New Dramatick Opera in Serious and Grotesque Characters, Call'd Amadis, or The Loves of Harlequin and Columbine* (1718), which established the standard format for what came to be known as pantomime: a serious plot drawn from chivalric romance or classical mythology intermingled with comic episodes involving Harlequin and Columbine and punctuated with magical tricks and transformations. The most important of Rich's endeavors in this line were *Jupiter and Europa, or The Intrigues of Harlequin* (1723); *The Necromancer, or Harlequin Dr Faustus* (1723), in which Harlequin loses a leg and chooses a new one from an assortment flying about the room; and *The Sorcerer, or The Loves of Pluto and Proserpine* (1725). *Harlequin Dr Faustus* drew twenty full houses, a remarkable run for the time, and proved to be more successful than such rival legitimate attractions as Barton Booth as Othello and Colley Cibber as Lord Foppington.

The fortune that Rich made from John Gay's *The Beggar's Opera* (1728) enabled him to build Covent Garden Theatre, to which he transferred the pantomime. Between 1716 and 1760 Rich staged at least one pantomime a year, the most successful running from forty to fifty nights consecutively. This popularity of the genre compelled Drury Lane to follow suit.

Rich's favorite pantomime author was Shakespearean scholar Lewis Theobald. His favorite composer was Johann Ernst Galliard, who graced the action with music that was suitable, if unimaginative. The prime ingredients, however, were always acrobatics, animal acts such as Swartz's dancing dogs, processions, ingenious machines, and lavish costumes to embellish works that, according to author Horace Walpole, were full of "wit and coherence."

Rich had learned to play Harlequin from the French fairground dancer Francisque Moylin (Molin). Owing to his own scanty literacy and poor memory, Rich played it as a character who never spoke, but, as one anonymous reviewer put it, his "mute Harlequin was eloquent in every gesture." Rich's basic poses can be conjectured from F. Le Roussau's *Chacoon for Harlequin* (1733), but he was essentially an energetic, dynamic actor best appreciated in motion. He was famed for his affecting farewell to Columbine, his doglike trick of scratching his ear with his foot, and his ability to dance three hundred steps in a rapid advance of only three yards. His vaulting Lion's Leap, his scenes of Catching the Butterfly and The Statue, and especially his hatching from an egg in *Harlequin Sorcerer* (1752) were classic *lazzi,* or stunts. As theater historian John Jackson observed,

> From the first chipping of the egg, his receiving of motion, his feeling of the ground, his standing upright, to his quick harlequin trip round the empty shell, through the whole progression every limb had its tongue and every motion a voice which spoke with most miraculous organ to the understandings and sensations of the observer. (Jackson, 1793)

Rich lived up to his name, and his theatrical enterprises earned him a handsome fortune. His 1746/47 season alone netted nearly £9,000. He bequeathed Covent Garden to his son-in-law, the singer John Beard, but his greater legacy was the training he gave and the example he set for a generation of mimes and dancers.

[*See also* Pantomime.]

BIBLIOGRAPHY

Cibber, Colley. *An Apology for the Life of Colley Cibber.* Edited by B. R. S. Fone. Ann Arbor, Mich., 1968.

Davies, Thomas. *The Life of David Garrick.* London, 1784.

Green, E.M. "John Rich's Art of Pantomime." *Restoration and Eighteenth-Century Theatre Research* 4 (1965).

Jackson, John. *History of the Scottish Stage.* Edinburgh, 1793.

Sawyer, Paul. "John Rich's Contribution to the Eighteenth-Century London Stage." In *Essays on the Eighteenth-Century English Stage,* edited by Kenneth Richards and Peter Thomson. London, 1972.

LAURENCE SENELICK

RICHARDSON, PHILIP (Philip John Sampey Richardson; born 17 March 1875 in Nottinghamshire, England, died 17 February 1963 in London), British editor, author, and dance critic. P. J. S. Richardson, as he signed his work, was one of the most important promoters and participants in the development of British ballet and ballroom dance during the first half of the twentieth century. In 1910 he and the publisher T. M. Middleton bought the small house magazine of the Cavendish Rooms in London and transformed it into the first national British dance journal of the twentieth century, *The Dancing Times.* As its editor and critic from 1910 to 1957 (writing under a *nom de plume,* The Sitter Out), he ardently championed the cause of British ballet and its dancers at a time when there was little other support for them. Richardson's journal was a forum for expert opinion about dance, a clearinghouse for information about teachers and students, and a rallying point for those concerned with promoting British dance in all its manifestations.

In 1916, in *The Dancing Times,* Richardson and Édouard Espinosa launched a campaign for the much-needed reform of ballet training in Britain. This resulted, in December 1920, in the formation of the Association of Operatic Dancing, which became the Royal Academy of Dancing. Richardson headed the list of founding members and served as secretary-treasurer. He also promoted the cause of dance history, publishing historical articles by Cyril Beaumont and Lillian Moore, among others. He regularly commissioned serious articles on all forms of dance, including ballroom dance and non-Western dance.

Richardson was also co-founder, with Arnold Haskell, of the Camargo Society (1930–1933), which commissioned a number of important ballets (by Frederick Ashton and Ninette de Valois, among others). In a series of historic performances it convincingly demonstrated that British artists could, if given the chance, fill the gap left by the death of Serge Diaghilev in 1929.

An ardent ballroom dancer, Richardson was the founder and chairman (1929–1959) of the Official Board of Ballroom Dancing and president of the International Council of Ballroom Dancing. As well as his writings in *The Dancing Times,* he wrote *Who's Who in Dancing* (with Haskell, 1932), *The Art of the Ballroom* (with Victor Silvester, 1936), *History of English Ballroom Dancing 1910–1945* (1946), and *Social Dances of the Nineteenth Century* (1960).

Richardson received the prize of the French Ministry of Arts in 1931, was awarded an O.B.E. (Order of the British Empire) in 1951, and was made a Knight of the Order of Dannebrog in 1952. He appeared on stage as a performer only once, when, accompanying a troupe of British dancers on a tour of Denmark in 1932, he was commandeered to fill the role of the Godhead ("Job's Spiritual Self") in de Valois's *Job.* He later said, with typical good humor, that after he had appeared as the Godhead, anything else would be a comedown.

BIBLIOGRAPHY

Genné, Beth Eliot. "P. J. S. Richardson and the Birth of British Ballet." In *Proceedings of the Fifth Annual Conference, Society of Dance History Scholars, Harvard University, 13–15 February 1982,* compiled by Christena L. Schlundt. Riverside, Calif., 1982.

Kane, Angela, and Jane Pritchard. "The Camargo Society" (parts 1–2). *Dance Research* 12 (Autumn 1994): 21–65.

BETH ELIOT GENNÉ

RIGAUDON. The lively *rigaudon,* spelled *rigadon* or *rigadoon* in English usage, was popular at the French court of Louis XIV from about the 1670s. From there it spread to other European courts and cities, especially in England and Germany. The *rigaudon* is mentioned by French writers of dictionaries (Ozanam, 1691; Furetière, 1701; Compan, 1787) as a dance from Provence. Artists working under Louis XIV probably transformed it to suit aristocratic taste, and it became one of the favorite dance types associated with the French court (others included the *menuet, courante, passepied, gavotte, sarabande, loure,* and *bourrée*). It was mentioned as early as 1673 in a letter from Madame de Sevigné to her daughter: "Madame Santa Cruz triumphs in the Rigadon." The *rigaudon* was enjoyed both as a social dance and as a ballet *entrée,* and in the form of both instrumental and vocal music, reflecting the elegance of the court in a lively though controlled manner.

The musical accompaniment is duple on all metric levels and has a quarter-note upbeat, with almost all phrases four or eight measures in length. Although it seems to be virtually identical to the *bourrée,* the melodies tend to have larger leaps, greater range, and more movement in a single direction without turning; in addition, the tempo is slightly faster (possibly 88–100 M.M. to the half note in a time signature of 2 or ¢). This was considered a fast tempo at the time, though it would seem rather moderate to the twentieth-century listener. The music usually consists of a bipartite piece with repeats, sometimes followed by a second rigaudon, also bipartite with repeats.

The steps of the *rigaudon* are the usual ones of French court dancing—*pas de bourrée, contretemps, glissade, jeté,* and *sissonne*—but most rigaudons also contain at least one *pas de rigaudon.* This unusual step-unit, occasionally used in other dance types as well, comprises several springs in place, along with leg gestures to the side (see Hilton, 1981, for performance details). It is usually seen only once or twice in a dance and marks a particularly important moment or climax. Charles Compan (*Dictionnaire de danse,* 1787) remarked that the courtly *pas de rigaudon* was more graceful and actually quite different from the one done in Provence; the leg, instead of extending to the side, was extended to the front in Provence, as if the dancers were kicking each other.

The figures of the *rigaudon* follow the geometric patterns common to French court dancing, with both performers of a pair usually doing the same steps but on opposite feet to create a mirror image.

Many *rigaudons* survive in choreographic notation. In addition to numerous *contredanses* (for example, "La Frêne," published by Raoul-Auger Feuillet in 1707) there are at least twenty-nine theatrical and social dances, composed by choreographers residing in France (Louis Pecour, Feuillet, Claude Ballon, and Jacques Dezais), in England (Mister Isaac, Anthony L'Abbé, Kellom Tomlinson, and Jean Jacques Rousseau), and in Germany (the French dancing master Jean Dubreuil). Although most of the pieces are ballroom dances for mixed couples, we have two theatrical *rigaudons* for two men, by Feuillet (*Recüeil de dances,* 1700). No solos are extant. Some of the most popular ballroom *rigaudons* were "Le Rigaudon de la Paix" (Feuillet), "Le Rigaudon des Vaisseaux" (Pecour), and, in England, Isaac's "The Rigadoone."

In ballet, *rigaudons* were often used in pastoral scenes or as a sailor's dance. None occurs in the works of Jean-Baptiste Lully (died 1687), but later French theatrical composers such as André Campra, Henry Desmarets, André Cardinal Destouches, and Jean-Philippe Rameau used it frequently. It was also popular in England, as the stage works of Henry Purcell and George Frideric Handel show. Johann Georg Sulzer (*Allgemeine Theorie der schönen Künste,* 1794) remarked that the *rigaudon* in ballets was not a noble dance but was used for flighty and low-born characters.

The characteristic melodies and phrase structure of *rigaudon* music were exploited by Baroque composers of many countries. Keyboard *rigaudons* may be found in the works of Purcell, François Couperin, Rameau, Elisabeth-Claude Jacquet de la Guerre, Louis-Claude Daquin, Gottlieb Muffat, Johann Pachelbel, and Johann Kirnberger. Composers of orchestral or chamber music with *rigaudons* include Couperin (IV *Concert Royal*), Joseph Bodin de Boismortier, Hendelinne, Michel-Richard de Lalande, Michel Monteclair, Johann Casper Ferdinand Fischer, Handel ("Water Music"), though not Johann Sebastian Bach. The *rigaudon's* popularity in the theater died out after the 1750s, but it continued to be enjoyed in stylish ballrooms well into the nineteenth century.

Rigaudon folk dances of various types have been mentioned by European writers from the Renaissance to modern times, but no systematic research has been done. Violet Alford (1944) reported on numerous traditional *rigaudons* performed by local people in the south of France in the late 1930s.

[*For related discussion, see* Ballet Technique, History of, *article on* French Court Dance.]

BIBLIOGRAPHY

Alford, Violet. "The Rigaudon." *Musical Quarterly* 30 (1944): 277–296.

Hilton, Wendy. *Dance of Court and Theatre: The French Noble Style, 1690–1725.* Princeton, 1981.

Witherell, Anne L. *Louis Pécour's 1700 Recueil des dances.* Ann Arbor, Mich., 1983.

MEREDITH ELLIS LITTLE

RIISAGER, KNUDÅGE (born 6 March 1897 in Port Kunda, Estonia; died 26 December 1974 in Copenhagen), Danish composer. Riisager studied political science at the University of Copenhagen, graduating in 1921. In addition to his musical activities he worked in the civil service until 1950; from 1939 on he was head of a department in the Ministry of Finance.

While studying in Copenhagen, Riisager was taught theory and composition by Otto Malling and Peder Gram, and violin by Peder Møller. In Paris from 1921 to 1923 he studied with Albert Roussel and Paul Le Flem, and there he came in contact with Les Six, French neoclassicism, and the music of Igor Stravinsky. In 1932 he studied with Hermann Grabner in Leipzig.

At a very early stage in his career Riisager showed an interest in the newest musical trends in Europe. He went on to become the most internationally oriented Danish composer of his generation. As an anti-Romantic and anti-impressionist, he remained throughout his life true to a French-flavored, neoclassical tonal language. His work in this respect contrasts with the Nordic tradition of Danish music exemplified by Carl Nielsen and popular during the period between the two world wars.

Riisager's international reputation rests particularly on the music he wrote for the ballet. The ballet captivated Riisager; he worked with the leading choreographers at the Royal Danish Theater, contributing to the renewal of the Royal Ballet's repertory.

Although his ballet *Benzin* (Gasoline; 1930, choreography by Elna Jørgen Jensen) was judged by critics as episodic and bizarre, Riisager went on to compose the music for the critically successful ballets *Tolv med Posten* (Twelve for the Mail Coach), with choreography by Børge Ralov, and *Slaraffenland* and *Qarrtsiluni,* both choreographed by Harald Lander. All of these ballets premiered in 1942. Even though its music was not originally written for the ballet, *Qaartsiluni* marked the beginning of a successful collaboration with Lander that culminated in the brilliant *Études* in 1948, built upon Karl Czerny's *études* for piano. Riisager continued composing ballet music, producing scores for Birgit Cullberg's *Månerenen* (Moon Reindeer) in 1957 and *Fruen fra Havet* (The Lady from the Sea) in 1960. He also composed for Flemming Flindt's *Gala Variations* in 1967 and *Le Porcher* in 1969.

Riisager based his ballet music on pronounced rhythm and clearly demarcated structures suited to rhythmic movement. A close collaboration between the composer and his choreographer was of great importance. The most noticeable characteristics of his work are a contraction and clarity of form, polytonal structures, energetic rhythms, and illustrative, exciting orchestrations. The music ranges in mood from the burlesque and humorous to the passionate. A whole composition often stems from very short melodic themes and small rhythmic cells, well suited to choreographic elaboration.

BIBLIOGRAPHY

Balzer, Jürgen. "Knudåge Riisagers *Qarrtsiluni*." *Levende musik* 1 (1942).

Berg, Sigurd, and Svend Bruhns. *Knudåge Riisagers kompositioner.* Copenhagen, 1967.

Cockshott, Gerald. "Knudåge Riisager." *Music in Education* 30 (1966).

Debièvre, P. "Un grand compositeur danois." *La vie musicale* (December 1959).

Johnsson, Bengt. "Knudåge Riisagers klavermusik." *Dansk musiktidsskrift* 5 (April 1981).

Riisager, Knudåge. "Balletmusik." In *Den Kongelige Danske Ballet,* edited by Svend Kragh-Jacobsen and Torben Krogh. Copenhagen, 1952.

Riisager, Knudåge. *Tanker i tiden.* Copenhagen, 1952.

Riisager, Knudåge. *Det usynlige mønster.* TK, 1957.

Schiørring, Nils. "De tre Riisager-balletter." *Dansk musiktidsskrift* 17 (1942).

Ole Nørlyng

RINALDI, ANTONIO (also known as Il Fossano or Fusano; *fl.* 1733–1759), Italian dancer, choreographer, and teacher. Nothing is known of Rinaldi's early life. In 1733 he was a *premier danseur* and composer of comic ballets at the Teatro San Samuele of Venice, where he composed the dances for Giuseppe Sellitto's opera *Ginevra.* From 1736 to 1738 he was at Saint Petersburg with Francesco Araia's opera and ballet company. Rinaldi, better known as Il Fossano, choreographed and danced in intermezzi of the first opera performance in Russia, Araia's *La Forza dell'Amore et dell'Odio,* performed in 1736. From 1738 to 1741 he danced in Paris and London with his pupil Barbara Campanini, known as La Barberina. In 1742 he was again in Russia, where he created comic ballets and the choreography for intermezzi in works performed at the Imperial Theater, including *Scipione* (1745), *Eudossia Incoronata* (1751), and *Alessandro in India* (1755), all by Araia. In 1748, following the death of Jean-Baptiste Landé, he became the director of Russia's court corps de ballet, and in 1755 he composed ballets for the Oranjebaum Theater. Il Fossano ended his choreographic activity in 1757 or 1759 and is believed to have returned to Italy, where he died toward the end of the 1750s.

Il Fossano is not a widely known figure in the panorama of eighteenth-century dance. Jean-Georges Noverre regarded him as a model of Italian technique, particularly in the leap. This is evidenced by the fame of his pupil La Barberina, who was said to be able to perform an *entrechat huit.* In addition to Il Fossano's technical gifts, Noverre acknowledged his spiritual gifts. "Il Fossano, the most pleasant and most spiritual of all the comic dancers, charmed the students of Terpsichore: even those who had not seen him wanted to copy him" (Noverre, 1760, Letter VII).

Il Fossano introduced Western theatrical dance into Russia and began a dance tradition that has become one of the most famous and celebrated of all.

[*See also the entry on* La Barberina.]

BIBLIOGRAPHY

Ciofi degli Atti, Fabio. "La danza in Russia." *La Danza* 5.1 (1985).

Lifar, Serge. *A History of Russian Ballet* (1950). Translated by Arnold L. Haskell. New York, 1954.

Maynard, Olga. "The Forgotten Empress." *Dance Magazine* (February 1975): 26.

Noverre, Jean-Georges. *Lettres sur la danse et sur les ballets* (1760). Paris, 1978. Translated by Cyril W. Beaumont as *Letters on Dancing and Ballets* (London, 1930).

Moore, Lillian. "The Adventures of La Barberina." *Dance Magazine* (December 1958): 68–69, 116–117.

Elena Grillo

RIOJA, PILAR (María del Pilar Rioja del Olmo; born 13 September 1932 in Torreón, Coahuila), Mexican dancer. Rioja's Spanish parents taught her the first steps of the Aragonese *jota* and other Spanish dances. She studied ballet in Torreón and in 1950 took Spanish dance lessons in Mexico City with Oscar Tarriba. In Spain she later studied Basque dances with Snaola, flamenco with Juan Sánchez ("El Estampío"), bolero with Angel Pericet, and folk dances with Elvira Real. Between 1960 and 1970 she alternately studied in Mexico with José Domingo Samperio (Spanish Baroque music) and Manolo Vargas (flamenco) and in Spain with Regla Ortega.

In 1947 Rioja appeared on the stage and in Spanish taverns in the north of Mexico. She made her debut in Spain in 1950 and then returned to Mexico City, where she achieved success dancing at recitals, cultural events, nightclubs, and theaters. In 1960 she danced in New York at El Chico, and later at Carnegie Hall, the Gramercy Arts Theatre, and the Spanish Repertoire Theatre. From 1964 onward, Rioja offered recitals accompanied by actors, guitar players, and flamenco singers. She has performed in the United States, the Soviet Union, Spain, Canada, and many Latin American countries.

An expert in classical Spanish dances, flamenco, and castanets, Pilar Rioja is one of the world's foremost Spanish dancers. She has taught for professional dance companies in Cuba, Spain, Mexico, and the Soviet Union. Awards have been presented to her in Mexico, the Soviet Union, and the United States. She has succeeded in restoring authenticity to flamenco, doing away with triviality in castanet-playing, and incorporating classical music into Spanish dance.

[*See also* Flamenco Dance.]

BIBLIOGRAPHY

Aloff, Mindy. "Women Off Pointe." *Dance Magazine* (September 1983): 38–42.

Dallal, Alberto. *La mujer en la danza.* Mexico City, 1990.

Dallal, Alberto. *La danza contra la muerte.* 3d ed. Mexico City, 1993.

"Dance Ink Celebrates Five Years." *Dance Ink* 6.4 (1995): 1–29.

Garafola, Lynn. "Pilar Rioja." *Dance Magazine* (December 1992): 102–103.

Rosen, Lillie F. "Pilar Rioja." *Attitude* 9 (Winter 1993): 55.

Rothman, Faustino. "Pilar Rioja." *Attitude* 2 (August 1984): 27–28.

Shaw, Alan J. "The Undoing of What Comes Naturally." *Dance Magazine* (February 1975): 73–75.

ALBERTO DALLAL

RITE OF SPRING. *See* Sacre du Printemps, Le.

RITHA DEVI (born 12 June 1934 in Baroda), Indian dancer. A great-grandniece of the poet Rabindranath Tagore and the granddaughter of Lakshminath Bezbaroa, a leading figure in modern Assamese literature, Ritha Devi graduated with honors from Bombay University, where she majored in Sanskrit and English. Although she did not begin her career in Indian dance until after her marriage, since about 1958 she has performed to critical acclaim all over the world.

Ritha Devi is esteemed both for her command of orthodox dance forms and for her creative versatility. She thrives on sharing her knowledge of all forms of Indian dance, including the exclusively male *kamalabari satra* style, which she learned from her grandfather. Her articulate lecture-demonstrations enlarge viewers' understanding of the technical and symbolic content of the classical Indian dance styles, which Ritha Devi continues to study under distinguished masters. She was the first to bring *satriya nṛtya,* an Assamese classical style used in worship by Buddhist monks in island monasteries, from its cloistered home to the international stage.

Ritha Devi's temperament, style, and petite stature are well suited to her favorite dance genre, Oḍissi. Her large repertory of solos is enriched by her own creations. Sanskrit literature provided the inspiration for her *māhārī* (temple dancer) solos, dance dramas about heroines whose deeds defy social conventions. Later in her career she turned to the Bible as a source of inspiration for dances such as *Mary Magdalene, David and Bathsheba,* and *Song of Solomon.* Ritha Devi now resides and works in New York City.

BIBLIOGRAPHY

Anderson, Jack. "Ritha Devi in 'Dances of India.'" *Dance Magazine* (August 1970): 80–81.

Jowitt, Deborah. "The Dancer as Divinity." In Jowitt's *Dance Beat.* New York, 1977.

Misra, Susheela. *Some Dancers of India.* New Delhi, 1992.

Najan, Nala. "Festival of India, 1985–86." *Arabesque* 11.2 (1985): 8–12.

PATRICIA A. ROWE

RITUAL AND DANCE. Dance historians, anthropologists, artists, and audiences have often drawn associations between ritual and dance. Both terms can refer to a great variety of activities in diverse cultural settings.

Ritual. The word *ritual* denotes a standardized, structured, and social action or series of actions, often with religious or mystical significance. Dance may be an accompaniment to or an integral part of these actions.

Cultural biases have clouded the scholarly understanding of ritual dance. European and American scholars have tended to view all dance performed by nonliterate peoples outside theatrical settings as ritual, while viewing dance performed by literate peoples in theatrical settings as art. Furthermore, they conceived of theatrical dance in Western society as having "evolved" from primitive ritual. This idea originated in the eighteenth century and was elaborated by nineteenth-century anthropologists and dance and theater historians. In their desire to discover human origins and cultural evolution, such scholars believed that culture evolved from the simple to the complex, from what they viewed as primitive to their notion of civilized and progressive.

While we will never know how people danced four thousand years ago, let alone forty thousand years ago, we do know from what early ethnographers reported about the many societies they studied that people dance not only in ritual, but also in play, in dramatic enactment, in social exchange, and in individual artistic activity. Moreover, as the anthropologist Clifford Geertz (1973) points out, these contexts of social activity are not perfectly distinct but rather they overlap and coincide.

We also know that in the West, dance and ritual have been part of the religious traditions of Judaism, Christianity, and Islam. People worshiped with dance in biblical times, in the early Christian church, and in the still vigorous Islamic Sufi tradition. Today, after centuries of proscription among some sects, liturgical dance is enjoying a resurgence in Judaism and in Christianity.

Thus, the ethnographic and historical evidence now collected over the centuries invalidates attempts to generalize about the attributes of ritual dance in different cultures. Misconceptions that "primitive" dance is either ecstatic and disorganized, or, alternatively, rigid and controlled with no individual variation or improvisation, or that civilized people worship without ritual dance, all stem from the earlier tendency to classify cultures as either primitive or civilized. A corollary of this tendency is the popular belief, pervasive throughout the twentieth century, that ritual can connect the participants with a preindustrial way of life that has great spiritual meaning and close harmony with nature.

Throughout the world, rituals are observed for many reasons. They may mark changes in social status (these are often called *rites of passage*), such as birth, marriage, or death; or they may aim at curing illness (called *rites of affliction*), activities which in many cultures are carried out by a religious person with special training (often called a *shaman*). They also mark dates and seasons that are important in the subsistence, religion, or history of a culture.

Ritual activity often includes unusual behavior, such as extreme formality or informality, the breaking of social taboos, or the reversing of gender or other roles. It may include distorted chronology: people are born again; the past or the future occurs in the present; or time stands still. Rituals often contain repetitive action, a set order of events, and a characteristic sequence. This sequence typically includes moving participants into the ritual space and establishing the ritual atmosphere, carrying out the ritual events in a state of consciousness and a form of social organization that are exceptional (sometimes called *liminal*), and bringing the participants back into everyday life.

Examples of Ritual Dance. Dance frequently plays an important role in ritual events by providing a means of connection or communication with the spiritual realm. Relationships with the spiritual are established in many ways: supernatural beings or spirits may possess the dancer; the dance may fill the dancer with special power; the dancer may become a character from a sacred story or text, often performed as a tribute to a deity; and the dancer's performance may embody a spirituality that infuses the audience. The following four examples of ritual dance, in which dancers are believed to interact with the spiritual realm, suggest the diversity of ritual dancing in different cultures.

!Kung San. These egalitarian hunters and gatherers, who live in the Kalahari Desert of southern Africa, perform an all-night curing ritual, the Giraffe Dance, that allows powerful forces to enter the participants. During the night, men and women trained in the observance receive the potent healing force called *n/um chi.* The possessed individuals, in a controlled trance, then perform *!kia,* an activity in which the power in their bodies draws sickness from afflicted individuals. *!Kia* affects not only the possessed and those whom they treat but also the rest of the community. [*See* !Kung San Dance.]

Everyone participates in some way in the !Kung curing dance, and the group judges success on the basis of the enthusiasm of the participants and the extent of possession and healing. Some ethnographers have seen the curing dance as an essential part of the political and social egalitarianism of !Kung life: the dancing unites everyone by allowing all to partake of the spiritual powers.

Kaluli. In New Guinea, the Kaluli perform an all-night ceremony known as *gisaro,* in which the key figures are dancers. In this ritual, the dancers provoke feelings of grief and loss in the audience; as a consequence, the spectators become overwhelmed with anger and sorrow. Through this complicated ritual dance, participants are said to unite in experiencing the central spiritual principles of the community.

The ethnographer Edward Scheiffelin (1976) interpreted this ritual as a part of a cultural scenario by which the Kaluli understand and organize their lives. According to Scheiffelin, the Kaluli stress interdependence and reciprocity in their dealings with one another. He interprets the symbolism of the dancer and the ceremony as unifying Kaluli social structure with healing and life-restoring forces. [*See* Papua New Guinea, *article on* Kaluli Dance.]

Haitain Vodun. An extensive series of ritual dances form an essential part of Haitian Vodun, a complex, syncretic religion that combines West African sacred traditions with Roman Catholicism. Vodun dances exemplify several ways of connecting everyday life with the spiritual realm. The religion has a pantheon of spirits, the *loa,* who communicate directly with human beings during the ritual. Dancing and drum rhythms, along with prayer and song, produce the power that attracts the *loa.* Each important *loa* is associated with a particular set of dances and rhythms.

Initiates to Vodun learn dancing as part of their education and strive to develop their endurance, agility, and improvisational ability. During the dance, the *loa* possesses or "mounts" the dancer, his "horse," who, after initial convulsive movements, in a trance state, becomes the god incarnate and dances like that spirit.

The possession dance is perhaps the most extreme example of a ritual dance involving an extraordinary state, but it is not the only dance in Vodun ritual. After his extensive ethnographic study of Haitian Vodun in 1948 and 1949, Alfred Métraux (1959) commented on the difficulty of applying the classical distinctions between sacred and profane to Vodun dances because of the complexity of the ceremonies:

> Some [dances], which are merely entertainments, can work their way into a ceremony simply because they are regarded as pleasing to the god or because the god particularly asked for them through the mouth of his 'horse.' Similarly at certain public jollifications dances are done which differ little or not at all from ritual dances. . . . Finally there are some dances such as the *gabienne* and the *mascort* which are not addressed to the spirits but merely fitting into services to fill in blank periods and provide a certain relief.

Métraux's comments illustrate the distinctiveness of Haitian Vodun as well as the complexities of the dance–ritual relationship. Vodun is a popular, flexible religion that people have shaped and adapted to situations of slavery, poverty, and repression. Its rituals are dance dramas, rich in spectacle, that entertain and astonish while calling forth the sacred. Some of its ritual dances can be performed on a theater stage for audiences of outsiders; in such performances, dancers may still become possessed while the audience views the performance as an aesthetic experience. [*See* Vodun.]

Bali. Ritual dances on Indonesia's island of Bali also exhibit such characteristics as possession, attempts to please the spirit world, and demonstrations of spiritual principles, in a style formed by Bali's cultural and social history. The religious tradition syncretizes Balinese practices with Hinduism. The most sacred of the dances are performed in connection with regular religious rituals, usually in the inner space of the village temple. In such dances, only sanctified objects and masks may be used, and certain roles can be played only by priests. Many of these dances involve trance and possession by spirits; particular spirits move the possessed to dance in culturally prescribed ways.

Some observers claim that Balinese dance can be divided into sacred and secular; others disagree. No one, however, disputes the idea that aesthetic factors are important in every performance, as they are in virtually all other aspects of Balinese life. For example, dances presented in a temple's outer space for the explicit entertainment of an audience are also a part of temple festivals; they thereby assume a religious meaning. With the growth of tourism in Bali, ritual dances have been enacted for visitors ("Rangda and Barong" and the *kécak* are probably the most famous), and these do not involve sanctified objects or genuine trances. Thus, the sacred or secular "meaning" of a dance cannot always be discerned by its appearance alone; its context must be considered as well. [*See* Indonesia, *articles on Balinese dance*.]

Ritual and Theater Dance. Many works in modern American dance have been based on some conception of ritual; qualities, themes, and structures associated with ritual dance have provided models for many choreographers, among them Ruth St. Denis, Ted Shawn, Martha Graham, Doris Humphrey, Katherine Dunham, Erick Hawkins, and Anna Halprin. If dances by these and other choreographers have ritual qualities, it is because they are modeled after known or imagined ceremonies and because they aim to connect the participants and the audience to universal or fundamental spiritual principles. Just as rituals have an aesthetic dimension, art dances may join the dancer with the spiritual realm.

Ritual and dance display similarities in both structure and process. It is no accident that casual observers may view ritual as art, that artists may use ritual as a model, that audiences may interpret art as ritual, and that people in many cultures make no distinction between dance and ritual. Comparing dance and ritual may provide scholars with insights into how and why both attain special cultural significance throughout the world.

First, ritual and dance are almost always distinguished from ordinary everyday activity. They are made conspicuous by their unusual nature. In other words, both are types of specialized performance. They have been framed, in some ways, by the mutual understanding of the participants and often by the setting for the event.

Second, the forms and the effects of ritual and dance are often similar. As the anthropologist Gilbert Lewis (1980) has suggested, both have performers (makers and doers), performances (action, objects, and media), and beholders and interpreters. In many cases, we allow and expect latitude, variety, and complexity from participants' interpretations of ritual, just as we do from audiences' reactions to dance. In fact, if we limit either ritual or dance to literal or obvious meanings, we diminish and falsify any significance. The complexity and the ambiguity of both ritual and dance, and the ensuing difficulties of interpreting them, are not shortcomings; they can evoke power, evocative strength, resistance, and changeability (Lewis, 1980).

Third, the meanings of both ritual and dance always depend on context. In some sense, all rituals and dances have a sociopolitical element in the form and content of what they present, and open-endedness in the ability of participants and audience to experience and interpret that presentation. By evoking emotions in the audience and the participants, dance and ritual both exercise enormous persuasive power, even if the event may not have an explicit message. For example, belief and participation in Vodun and ritual dance played an important role in the successful slave rebellion against colonialism in Haiti (1791–1804). Another example would be the rituals of Nazi Germany, where the marches, rallies, and public ceremonies that included dance were tools for stirring nationalist fervor and maintaining the dominance of the regime.

Anthropological Views. At the end of the nineteenth century Émile Durkheim (1961) proposed that the religious or sacred realm provided the basis for social solidarity by integrating the belief of the individual with the values of the society. According to Durkheim, through ritual the social structure achieved a reality and magnitude for its members that perpetuated the social system. Durkheim's association of ritual with the structure and function of social life has influenced most subsequent analyses.

The American anthropologist Margaret Mead, in contrast, argued that ritual and dance in Bali had psychological origins and functions for participants. Gregory Bateson, in a pioneering symbolic study, tried to demonstrate that the structural relationships of roles and symbols in Iatmul (New Guinea) dance revealed kinship relations.

Analyses that try to locate the function or usefulness of ritual dance, in order to explain its existence, have their limitations. They run into difficulty when they try to distinguish firmly between the secular and the sacred, or between the practical and impractical. The apparently utilitarian or practical actions that occur in ritual dance, and indeed in all forms of social life, are inextricably intertwined with the beliefs of the participants. Critical to developing new ways of describing and interpreting ritual and ritual dance has been a conception of ritual that sees symbols and forms as irreducible—that is, not as a function or the result of social structure but as integral parts of it.

Many other anthropological discussions could be cited. One of the most influential theorists of ritual, Victor Turner, carried out an extensive investigation of ritual symbols, including those of dance, among the Ndembu of Africa. Turner suggested that ritual symbols embody multiple meanings and associations, a property Turner called *multivocalic* or *polysemic*. Turner also speculated that the power of ritual derives from the symbolic unification and condensation of normally disparate actions or objects—an observation that has also been made with regard to symbolism.

Finally, theorists including Clifford Geertz and James Peacock have advocated an actor-centered, interpretive study of ritual that treats social life as a text to be "read" both by the participants and by the outside observer. For example, Geertz analyzed the nineteenth-century Balinese political state, the *negara*, as being based on its ritual events. Geertz therefore called the *negara* a *theater-state*, because political processes and symbols were fused with ritual enactments and meanings, all of which were interpreted by the Balinese "actors." Peacock saw the subtle transformation of character relationships and plots within the Javanese theater of the 1960s as part of a process of change in Indonesia; through the plays, participants could transform old values and associations to give meaning to changes in their lives.

BIBLIOGRAPHY

Bateson, Gregory. *Naven*. Cambridge, 1936.

Bateson, Gregory, and Margaret Mead. *Balinese Character*. New York, 1942.

Bandem, I Madé, and Fredrik Eugene DeBoer. *Balinese Dance in Transition: Kaja and Kelod*. 2d ed. New York, 1995.

Belo, Jane, ed. *Traditional Balinese Culture*. New York, 1970.

Bloch, Maurice. "Symbols, Song, Dance, and Features of Articulation: Is Religion an Extreme Form of Traditional Authority?" *European Journal of Sociology* 15.1 (1974).

Durkheim, Émile. *The Elementary Forms of the Religious Life*. Translated by Joseph Ward Swain. New York, 1961.

Geertz, Clifford. *The Interpretation of Cultures*. New York, 1973.

Geertz, Clifford. *Negara: The Theatre State in Nineteenth-Century Bali*. Princeton, 1980.

Gennep, Arnold van. *The Rites of Passage*. Translated by Monika B. Vizedom and Gabrielle L. Caffe. Chicago, 1960.

Katz, Richard. *Boiling Energy: Community Healing among the Kalahari Kung*. Cambridge, Mass., 1982.

Leach, Edmund. *Rethinking Anthropology*. London, 1961.

Leach, Edmund. "Ritual." In *International Encyclopedia of the Social Sciences*. New York, 1968–.

Lewis, Gilbert. *Day of Shining Red*. Cambridge, 1980.

Métraux, Alfred. *Voodoo in Haiti*. Translated by Hugo Charteris. New York, 1959.

Munn, Nancy D. "Symbolism in a Ritual Context: Aspects of Symbolic Action." In *Handbook of Social and Cultural Anthropology*, edited by John J. Honigmann. Chicago, 1973.

Novack, Cynthia J. *Sharing the Dance: Contact Improvisation and American Culture*. Madison, Wis., 1990.

Peacock, James L. *Rites of Modernization: Symbolic and Social Aspects of Indonesian Proletarian Drama*. Chicago, 1968.

Radcliffe-Brown, A. R. *The Andaman Islanders*. Cambridge, 1922.

Schieffelin, Edward L. *The Sorrow of the Lonely and the Burning of the Dancers*. New York, 1976.

Turner, Victor. *The Forest of Symbols*. Ithaca, N. Y., 1967.

Turner, Victor. *The Ritual Process*. Ithaca, N. Y., 1969.

Wolf, Eric R. *Europe and the People without History*. Berkeley, 1982.

CYNTHIA J. NOVACK

RIVERA, CHITA (Dolores Conchita Figueroa del Rivero; born 23 January 1933 in Washington, D.C.), American dancer, singer, and actress. Broadway's last genuine dancing star, Rivera began performing with her siblings by "putting on a show" in their Washington, D.C., basement. She was the third of five Puerto Rican children who were inspired and nurtured by their father's musicianship and their mother's love of dance. Rivera began formal dance training at seven with ballet classes at the Jones-Haywood School in Washington. At fourteen, she won a scholarship to the School of American Ballet in New York and moved there to live with relatives.

She accompanied a friend to an audition at the age of seventeen, later saying, "The audition didn't mean anything to me, so I was just out there, dancing away" (Sandla, 1994), but she got the job, making her professional stage debut in the touring company of *Call Me Madam* in 1950. She appeared on Broadway in the choruses of *Guys and Dolls* (1951) and *Can-Can* (1953), in which she remembers observing its dance star, Gwen Verdon, and being inspired by her seamless blend of song, dance, and acting skills. Cast in an industrial show choreographed by Peter Gennaro, she began taking his jazz class, broadening her dance scope. With her unique alto singing voice, precise dance skills, and acting expertise, she received her first critical notices doing a parody of Marilyn Monroe in off-Broadway's *Shoe-String Revue* (1955), which led to featured roles on Broadway in *Seventh Heaven* (1955) and *Mr. Wonderful* (1956).

When Gennaro and Jerome Robbins co-created Leonard Bernstein's *West Side Story* (1957), Chita was cast in the role of Anita. Nightly, her Gennaro-staged number "America" stopped the show. It won her Broadway stardom. During the run of the show, she married her *West Side Story* colleague Tony Mordente and they had a daughter. With Rivera's new fame, director-choreographer Gower Champion cast her in *Bye Bye, Birdie* (1960), in which she adroitly spoofed her fiery Latin image and caused *Daily Mirror* reviewer Robert Coleman to proclaim, "Chita Rivera explodes like a bomb over West 45th Street."

After *Zenda* on the West Coast (1963), she returned to Broadway in *Bajour* in 1965. A 1967 tour of *Sweet Charity* finally led to Hollywood. Although two of her best-known stage roles had been filmed with other actresses (Rita Moreno in *West Side Story* and Janet Leigh in *Bye Bye, Birdie*), Rivera repeated her role in *Sweet Charity* (1969) and was later captured on film in *Pippin* in 1982. She remained on the West Coast for several years, performing her cabaret act and appearing in *1491* (1969). An opportunity to co-star with Verdon, her early inspiration, brought her back to Broadway in *Chicago* (1975). *Bring Back Birdie* (1981), *Merlin* (1983), and cabaret engagements *(Chita Plus Two)* kept her on the East Coast. After five Tony award nominations, she finally received one for *The Rink* (1984).

While appearing in *Jerry's Girls* in 1985, Rivera was in an automobile accident, in which her left leg was broken in twelve places, disabling her for eleven months. "There's no doubt about it—without the School of American Ballet and my training with Doris Jones in Washington, I could not have recovered from the accident" (Sandla, 1994), she said after rehabilitation returned her to nightclubs and touring in *Can-Can* (1988). Back on Broadway in *Kiss of the Spider Woman* (1993), she won her second Tony award. In 1994, she was given a lifetime achievement award from her alma mater, the School of American Ballet.

In a 1991 interview with *Dance Magazine*'s Marian Horosko, Rivera said, "I don't want to be considered a jazz dancer because that's a limited description. To be called a dancer indicates that you have studied several techniques and mastered some to a degree." Not a dancer who personifies one particular style, Rivera has successfully interpreted the diverse styles of Jerome Robbins, Peter Gennaro, Michael Kidd, Gower Champion, Ron Field, Bob Fosse, Vincent Paterson, and Rob Marshall, creating a theater-dance magic of her own.

BIBLIOGRAPHY

Bordman, Gerald. *The Concise Oxford Companion to American Theatre.* New York, 1987.

Palatsky, Eugene. "She Dances with Marvelous Joy." *Dance Magazine* (January 1965): 32–35.

Sandla, Robert. "Chita Rivera: Now Is the Gleam in the Eye." *Dance Magazine* (February 1994): 76–81.

Suskin, Steven. *Opening Night on Broadway.* New York, 1990.

LARRY BILLMAN

ROBBINS, JEROME (Jerome Wilson Rabinowitz; born 11 October 1918 in New York City), American dancer and choreographer. Called the greatest of American-born ballet choreographers and the best choreographer on Broadway, Jerome Robbins fits both descriptions. And his contribution to twentieth-century American dance extends far beyond them.

Unlike most choreographers, Robbins is a superb humorist. In *The Concert* (1956), in *The Pied Piper* (1956), and, occasionally, in *The Four Seasons* (1979), there is a sense of the unexpected, all the more unusual because its roots are not mimetic but kinetic. Best known is the Mistake Waltz section of *The Concert,* in which a group of sylphs performs earnestly to Chopin, with someone always out of sync. These flawed moments are so brilliantly timed that they assume a life of their own, as though there were such a thing as a perfect mistake. This acute sense of timing has often enabled Robbins's dances to enliven less-than-brilliant Broadway musicals. For example, his Mack Sennett ballet in *High Button Shoes* (1947) inspired the *New Yorker's* critic to write, "The . . . ballet is probably the funniest thing in the musical."

Also typical of the Robbins style are a deep musical sensitivity and a meticulous pursuit of choreographic detail. The latter makes him a difficult taskmaster in rehearsal. His secondary works are models of structure, whereas his seminal ballets, such as *Fancy Free* (1944), *The Cage* (1951), *Afternoon of a Faun* (1953), *Les Noces* (1965), *Dances at a Gathering* (1969), *The Goldberg Variations* (1971), and *Watermill* (1972), offer a harmony of creative spontaneity and intellectual discipline.

Robbins's prolific output has always contained conscious points of contrast: pure dance versus theater dance; a twentieth-century metabolism versus a respect for the past; solemnity versus brashness. Through a career of searching and questioning, he has compensated for a relatively limited early classical background to become a distinguished classical choreographer.

Robbins was born in New York City. His parents, Harry Rabinowitz and Lena Rips Rabinowitz, were Russian Jews who immigrated to the United States to escape religious persecution. His father owned a delicatessen. His mother was a housewife and, like most middle-class Jewish women, made sure her children were exposed to the arts. For Jerome this meant violin and piano lessons. He also painted and had an interest in marionettes. During his early years, the family moved to Weehawken, New Jersey, where Harry Robbins became a corset manufacturer. (The family name was formally changed when Jerome began his theatrical career.)

As a boy, Jerome sometimes accompanied his older sister, Sonya, to her interpretive dance classes with Alys Bentley. He took the classes now and then, but it was his sister who really became his first teacher. In 1935 he enrolled in New York University, but in 1936 family business reverses forced him to withdraw. Sonya had been studying with Senia Glück-Sandor and Felicia Sorel, New York teachers of what they called the "German technique" of modern dance. They also ran The Dance Center, a performance workshop. Robbins began studying with them in earnest and has since claimed Glück-Sandor as a major influence in his development.

This was during the heyday of early modern dance, but Glück-Sandor wisely urged Robbins to study ballet. He began with Ella Daganova, a former member of the Pavlova company. At the same time he studied Spanish dance with Helen Veola and Asian dance with Yeichi Nimura. By the end of his first year with Glück-Sandor, Robbins was appearing in Dance Center productions, and he was selected for a small role in her choreography for the Yiddish Art Theater's *Brothers Ashkenazi.* Robbins also began five summers at Camp Tamiment, an adult resort in Pennsylvania known for hiring gifted young artists to create and perform in its revues. Jobs as a dancer in Broadway shows also enlarged his range: *Great Lady,* choreographed by George Balanchine and William Dollar, in 1938; *The Straw Hat Revue,* by Jerome Andrews and Ruthanna Boris, in 1939; and *Keep Off the Grass,* by Balanchine, in 1940. Robbins then joined the corps of the recently formed Ballet Theatre.

Robbins's penchant for comedy was quickly discovered when he made his solo debut as the Youth in Agnes de Mille's *Three Virgins and a Devil* (1941). And as Hermes in David Lichine's *Helen of Troy* (1942), his impudent munching on an apple during one of the boudoir scenes

ROBBINS. With his very first ballet, *Fancy Free* (1944), Robbins scored a major hit. The original cast included Janet Reed, Muriel Bentley, Robbins, John Kriza, and Michael Kidd. More than fifty years after its creation, the work still seems fresh. It is in the repertory of both American Ballet Theatre and the New York City Ballet. (Photograph from the Dance Collection, New York Public Library for the Performing Arts.)

elicited outright laughter. A very different facet emerged in Michel Fokine's *Petrouchka* (1941). The humanity of Robbins's portrayal of the title role placed him in the history-making ranks of Vaslav Nijinsky and Yurek Lazowski.

Robbins was beginning to formulate an artistic viewpoint. He was becoming impatient with the Russian character works that occupied so much of the repertory. As a dancer he did not identify with the Gypsies and peasants he often was required to perform. He began to think about creating a ballet that would reflect his New York environment and his own era.

The Metropolitan Opera House in which Ballet Theatre performed was then near Times Square, where Robbins could watch the strutting of sailors on shore leave. These observations, plus a keen knowledge of the social dances of the time, were absorbed into *Fancy Free* (1944), his first work for Ballet Theatre. The plot is simple. It concerns three sailors on shore leave and their eager search for girls. Outside a bar, they meet two girls and invite them inside, where the sailors engage in a hilarious dance competition—and eventually in a fistfight—because there are not enough girls to go around. The girls flounce off. Chastened, the sailors leave the bar. A third girl pauses under a streetlight. She departs, and they careen after her. Within this slim framework Robbins wove supremely clever horseplay and formal jazz solos, each of which set forth the individuality of its performer. [*See* Fancy Free.]

ROBBINS. *Age of Anxiety,* a dramatic ballet in six scenes set to Leonard Bernstein's Second Symphony, was created for the New York City Ballet in 1950. Pictured here in the four principal roles are Todd Bolender, Tanaquil Le Clercq, Robbins, and Roy Tobias. (Photograph from the Dance Collection, New York Public Library for the Performing Arts.)

ROBBINS. *The Concert* (1956), subtitled *The Perils of Everybody,* is a series of humorous sketches based on the behavior and the fantasies of a group of concertgoers at a recital of piano pieces by Chopin. The "Butterfly Prelude" causes the characters to imagine themselves as butterflies, endowed with gauzy wings. In this performance photograph, Sara Leland seems to be floating gently across the floor, oblivious to the recumbent male in the background. (Photograph by Martha Swope © Time, Inc.; used by permission.)

By the end of 1944, Oliver Smith, in association with Paul Feigay, had become the producer as well as designer for *On the Town,* a Broadway musical that expanded upon the theme of *Fancy Free.* The clever young team of Betty Comden and Adolph Green provided the book and lyrics. Jerome Robbins and Leonard Bernstein collaborated daily on the score and choreography. Sono Osato had the principal acting-dancing-singing role.

In 1945 Robbins worked under director George Abbott on *Billion Dollar Baby.* Its 1920s subject matter, although deftly handled by Robbins, was termed merely "lively" and "amusing." Nonetheless, Robbins was fast becoming the most sought-after choreographer on Broadway, and his progress within the ballet world was being watched with equal interest. Also in 1945, between *On the Town* and *Billion Dollar Baby,* he created *Interplay* (1945), a spirited yet lyrical jazz ballet set to Morton Gould's *American Concertette.*

But Robbins was eager to prove himself capable of serious themes. Toward that end he and Leonard Bernstein created *Facsimile* (1946) for Nora Kaye, Hugh Laing, and himself. Its most memorable moment comes when the woman, tired of being pursued by two indecisive men, cries out, "Stop! Stop!" Critic John Martin summed up Robbins's work on *Facsimile* as follows: "he had to show that he could get along without gags and double takes. Now he can drop the matter and get along with his creative work."

Jerome Robbins has managed his career instinctively, knowing when to change and how. Fortunately, Broadway has provided him with a substantial income, so that he has been free of financial pressure. Between 1947 and 1949 he created two minor ballets, but on Broadway he turned out *High Button Shoes* (1947), *Look, Ma, I'm Dancin'* (1948), and *Miss Liberty* (1949). It was a tribute to his growing stature that in addition to doing the choreography, he co-directed *Look, Ma, I'm Dancin'* with George Abbott, the most respected director in American musical theater. Nancy Walker was featured as the heiress who paid to dance in a ballet company. Some likened the character to Lucia Chase, director of Ballet Theatre.

Miss Liberty had the advantage of an Irving Berlin score and of dancer Allyn Ann McLerie as star. Opinions of the choreography were mixed. But the *Philadelphia Inquirer* rang forth with, "Mr. Robbins has emerged this time as a near-genius at handling a period piece with imagination, invention, and taste."

With his Broadway career cresting, Robbins wrote a note to George Balanchine asking if he might become involved with the New York City Ballet. Balanchine cordially invited him to dance and to choreograph. By 1950 Robbins had been named associate artistic director. His first ballet for the company was *The Guests* (1949), to a score by Marc Blitzstein, with Maria Tallchief, Francisco Moncion, and Robbins in the principal roles. It was a touching commentary about a couple from differing social groups who fall in love and are subsequently ostracized by both groups. In 1950 Robbins and Balanchine collaborated on a trifle called *Jones Beach*. They subsequently were to join forces on *The Firebird* (1970), *Pulcinella* (1972), and *Le Bourgeois Gentilhomme* (1979). Later in 1950 Robbins undertook a major work, *Age of Anxiety*, based upon the W. H. Auden poem and Leonard Bernstein's symphony, which the poem had inspired.

The two ballerinas who were to prove most stimulating to Robbins were Nora Kaye and Tanaquil Le Clercq. In *Age of Anxiety*, Le Clercq joined Robbins, Todd Bolender, and Francisco Moncion as the principals in this choreographic search for identity in which the dancers came together as strangers and struggled through a nightmare world that eventually led to self-acceptance. The difference between Robbins and Auden was that Auden's solution was religious and Robbins's viewpoint, consonant with the era, was psychoanalytical. Although *Age of Anxiety* did not long remain in the New York City Ballet's repertory, its impact was undeniable. It also marked a new level of maturity for the choreographer.

A similar maturity was exhibited in Robbins's dramatic and moving performance in the title role of Balanchine's *The Prodigal Son* in 1950. It was the apex of his dancing career, although his comic talents were brilliantly demonstrated in Balanchine's *Bourrée Fantasque* (1949) and as the resilient hero of Balanchine's *Tyl Ulenspiegel* (1951).

With *The Guests* and *Age of Anxiety*, Robbins had been making strides toward the fluid realm where only movement speaks. In *The Cage* (1951) his concept of dramatic dance, as opposed to dance drama, burst powerfully onto the stage. Using Igor Stravinsky's lean and rhythmically insistent Concerto in D for String Orchestra, Robbins created a rite of initiation for a coven of predatory females. Above them loomed a huge web of rope designed by Jean Rosenthal, who was also responsible for the lighting.

These insect-women exuded menace as they thrust their

ROBBINS. *(left)* The fight scene between the Jets and the Sharks in the Broadway production of *West Side Story* (1957), with Thomas Hasson and George Marcy as the principle combatants. *(right)* The Jets watch female dancers in a parking lot, in a scene from the Hollywood film (1960). (Left photograph by Fred Fehl; used by permission. Right photograph from the Dance Collection, New York Public Library for the Performing Arts.)

ROBBINS. *Dances at a Gathering* (1969) is arguably the most popular ballet ever set to the music of Chopin, exceeding even Fokine's *Les Sylphides.* Pictured here are Kay Mazzo and John Prinz. The shadowy figures in the background are Patricia McBride and Robert Maiorano. All were in the original cast. (Photograph by Martha Swope © Time, Inc.; used by permission.)

arms forward and opened their mouths in silent screams. A novice was helped from her cocoon. It was Nora Kaye, her hair slicked into a dark cap, a quizzical, newborn look on her face. The creatures, with their hair matted in nests and with serpentine patterns on their leotards (designed by Ruth Sobotka), left the novice alone to encounter her first male. With savage dispatch she crushed him between her legs and flipped him aside. A second male brought fulfillment. The group materialized from the shadows and goaded her to destroy him. *The Cage* welled up from deep feeling within Robbins, and so it was as poetic as it was honest. It has not lost its impact with time.

There was another intriguing aspect to *The Cage.* It mirrored the second act of *Giselle,* in which the wilis condemn Hilarion to death and intend the same fate for Albrecht. The two principal women in *The Cage* were also versions of Giselle and Myrtha.

In the same year as *The Cage,* Robbins also staged the enchanting "Small House of Uncle Thomas" ballet for *The King and I,* his first Rodgers and Hammerstein musical. Then, with characteristic daring, he turned to a familiar piece of music, Claude Debussy's *Prélude à l'Après-midi d'un Faune,* and to a ballet title, *Afternoon of a Faun,* closely associated with Vaslav Nijinsky. Like Nijinsky, Robbins commented upon narcissism, but here the resemblance ended. Whereas the Nijinsky ballet was deliberately archaic, Robbins's was totally contemporary.

In the sun-drenched ambience of a dance studio, a male dancer lies stretched on the floor. He rises and begins to flex languidly, all the while watching himself in an imaginary downstage mirror. A female dancer plucks her way on pointe along an imaginary corridor leading to the studio entrance. She enters and also becomes transfixed by her mirror image. The two dance together, half absorbed by each other and half by their combined image. She kneels. He gently kisses her on the cheek. She touches the spot, rises, and leaves. He stretches out again on the floor. Within the chaste atmosphere of a dance studio, a knowing comment has been made about the life and nature of dancers. [*See* Afternoon of a Faun.]

The year 1953 brought the exuberant *Fanfare,* with its introduction to the instruments of the orchestra. It also brought an incident of considerable seriousness in Robbins's nontheatrical life. Summoned to testify before the House Un-American Activities Committee, he admitted that he had been a member of the Communist party between 1944 and 1947, a not unusual practice among idealistic young intellectuals at that time. Robbins also gave the committee the names of eight other party members.

In 1957 Robbins was again deeply engrossed in a Broadway show—*West Side Story,* which he conceived, directed, and choreographed. If Agnes de Mille's choreography for *Oklahoma!* can be said to have integrated dance into the continuity of a musical, Robbins's handling of *West Side Story* can be said to have integrated the play into the dancing. And because virtually the entire cast had dance training, the production had incredible vitality.

For *West Side Story* Leonard Bernstein and Oliver Smith were again Robbins's collaborators. Stephen Sondheim was entrusted with the lyrics, Arthur Laurents with the book, and Irene Sharaff with the costumes. Perhaps *West Side Story* had its early germination in Robbins's *The Guests,* but its story was directly inspired by Shakespeare's *Romeo and Juliet.* It dealt with two young people who fall in love even though they come from warring social strata on the streets of New York. Like *Romeo and Juliet,* it had a tragic ending unusual in musical comedy. Robbins's viewpoint about the New York City street gangs was sympathetic without being sentimental. As gang members crouched and darted through their rumbles or described the frustrations of their impoverished lives, their dance patterns were tough and athletic but genuinely human.

Robbins also co-directed and choreographed the screen

version of *West Side Story* (1961). That and *The King and I* (1956) were by choice his only Hollywood productions.

Early in 1958 the composer Gian-Carlo Menotti, director of the Festival of Two Worlds in Spoleto, Italy, invited Robbins to assemble a small company for the following summer, and the sixteen-member Ballets: USA was born. They returned to Spoleto the next summer and then embarked on a State Department–sponsored tour of Europe. A Broadway season and an American tour ensued. The company was subsequently disbanded until it was reassembled to appear in 1962 at a White House gala for the shah of Iran.

Ballets: USA's all-Robbins repertory consisted of *N.Y. Export: Opus Jazz, 3 × 3, The Concert,* and *Afternoon of a Faun.* Influences of *West Side Story* and of the cityscape works of Anna Sokolow could be found in *N.Y. Export: Opus Jazz.* In fact, it was the first of Robbins's works that seemed derivative. And in *3 × 3* he drew upon sentimental material to be found especially in his own *Ballade.* The only ballet to remain from this experiment was *Moves* (1959), a challenging work danced in silence. It subsequently became an important part of the repertories of six other companies, notably the Joffrey Ballet and the New York City Ballet. Some works in silence seem to frame the involuntary sounds made by members of the audience. Others use silence for its ominous effect. Robbins used silence the way sculptor Henry Moore used space—as a unifying force. It enabled the dancers to establish a mutually aware group rhythm.

When Ballets: USA opened on Broadway in 1958, Robbins was simultaneously represented in five theaters. He had three works active in the New York City Ballet's repertory and one in American Ballet Theatre's. *West Side Story* was flourishing, and *Bells Are Ringing* (1956), which he directed himself and choreographed with Bob Fosse, was still running. Robbins also had just established the Lena Robbins Foundation (later to become the Jerome Robbins Foundation) to assist choreographers. He soon directed and choreographed *Gypsy* (1959), based upon the autobiography of noted stripper Gypsy Rose Lee.

For a brief time Robbins successfully tried his hand at directing nonmusical productions, principally off-Broadway. Notable were *Oh, Dad, Poor Dad, Mama's Hung You in the Closet, and I'm Feelin' So Sad* (1962) and *Mother Courage and Her Children* (1963). He was production supervisor for *Funny Girl* (1964), a Barbra Streisand vehicle with Carol Haney as choreographer. And then came *Fiddler on the Roof* (1964). Like *West Side Story,* it would be a satisfying artistic experience as well as a major source of future income. In 1970, part of the gross income enabled him to establish the Jerome Robbins Film and Videotape Archive at the Dance Collection of the New York Public Library for the Performing Arts at Lincoln Center. In 1987 the project was formally dedicated as the Jerome Robbins Archive of the Recorded Moving Image.

Robbins has always been a slow, meticulous worker, and the brief rehearsal span of a Broadway production had given him little or no time for experimentation. Again he made an important career decision. In 1966 he asked the recently founded National Endowment for the Arts for a two-year grant amounting to $300,000; with it he formed the American Theater Laboratory, whose stated purpose was "to provide a place for performing and creative artists to join together on ideas, create new works, extend and develop the musical theater into an art capable of poetically expressing the events, deep hopes and

ROBBINS. Set to music by Teijo Ito and strongly influenced by Japanese *nō* drama, *Watermill* (1979) has been called a "ritual of remembering." Edward Villella starred as the man reflecting upon the passage of his life, symbolized by the ever-changing phases of the moon and the inexorable cycle of the seasons. Here he is seen at a contemplative moment, set against the vigorous action of others. Settings were designed by Robbins in association with David Reppa. (Photograph by Martha Swope © Time, Inc.; used by permission.)

ROBBINS. Natalia Makarova and Mikhail Baryshnikov in *Other Dances* (1976). These dances are so named because they are other dances (i.e., still more dances) to the piano music of Chopin. (Photograph by Beverly Gallegos; used by permission.)

needs of our lives." It was thought that out of this unhurried, even contemplative, process works-in-progress or rehearsals would emerge for the general public to see. The participating dancers, actors, and musicians were selected by audition and were sworn not to discuss what went on.

Before embarking upon the American Theater Laboratory project, which he has termed the hardest work he has ever done, Robbins returned to American Ballet Theatre to stage a magnificently theatrical version of Stravinsky's *Les Noces.* In *Fiddler on the Roof* he had drawn upon his Russian Jewish heritage as filtered through the reminiscences of his father, who could only too clearly recall *shtetl* life and the religious pogroms. *Les Noces,* on the other hand, required extensive research into the Christian and pagan sources of its theme. With Erin Martin as the bride and William Glassman as the groom, Robbins depicted an arranged Russian peasant wedding with all its trepidations and its rigidly preordained rituals. The stage was dominated by two huge icon figures designed by Oliver Smith and by Stravinsky's driving score, which included two onstage pianos as well as four tympanists and thirty-six singers. But throughout, it was Robbins's choreography—by turns humble, earth-aware, and sublimely atavistic—that united all these elements into a resounding sociological, as well as emotional, statement.

With the applause for *Les Noces* ringing in his ears, Robbins withdrew from the scene to re-explore the elements of his art at the American Theater Laboratory. As required by the grant, he did so in silence and in secrecy, and when he emerged two years later he returned like a triumphant, albeit respectful, prodigal son to New York City Ballet, where he was given the title of ballet master. (Balanchine used the same title for himself, preferring it to artistic director.) In a way, Robbins's 1968 return took courage. The New York City Ballet was an environment in which George Balanchine not only dominated but was deeply venerated. Even so, the relationship between the two choreographers remained harmonious and mutually supportive. In 1984, after Balanchine's death, Robbins became co–ballet master in chief with Peter Martins.

Upon his return, Robbins produced four of his most significant works in rapid succession. They were *Dances at a Gathering* (1969), *In the Night* (1970), *The Goldberg Varia-*

ROBBINS. Peter Martins and Suzanne Farrell in *The Four Seasons* (1979), danced to music by Giuseppe Verdi. (Photograph from the Dance Collection, New York Public Library for the Performing Arts.)

ROBBINS. *Opus 19 / The Dreamer* was choreographed in 1979 to Sergei Prokofiev's Violin Concerto no. 1 in D (op. 19). Peter Boal, flanked by Jerome Kippper and Todd Williams, is pictured here in a 1991 performance. (Photograph © 1991 by Paul Kolnik; used by permission.)

tions (1971), and *Watermill* (1972). He seemed to be constantly challenging himself, as if choreography had become a huge intellectual landscape for him to explore, not always with the spontaneity of his earlier years but with a deeper flow of creative energy. It was sometimes unalloyed, as in *Dances at a Gathering* and *In the Night,* but more often it was combined with a strong component of formal discipline, as in *The Goldberg Variations* and *Watermill.*

For *Dances at a Gathering* Robbins returned to the piano music of Chopin, which he had used to entirely different effect in *The Concert.* As critic Edwin Denby wrote, "The music and dance seem to be inventing each other" (Denby, 1986). The hour-long ballet begins and ends pensively. At the outset a lone man walks serenely through what might be a field. He has space and spaciousness around him as he lets the opening mazurka seep into his body and evoke dancelike memories. He circles the area in a glorious run and then departs. At the end of *Dances at a Gathering,* its participants, who have strolled and flirted and taken flight in a deep and unspoken closeness, gaze upward as if sharing a vision.

Although the ballet, with its skylike drop, designed by Thomas Skelton, seems to take place outdoors, there are overtones of Robbins's most cherished locale, the dance studio. And *Dances at a Gathering* can easily be taken as a statement about the nature of dancers. [*See* Dances at a Gathering.]

The music of Chopin continued to course through Robbins's blood, and he combined four nocturnes, played onstage by pianist Gordon Boelzner, who had performed the same task in *Dances at a Gathering.* It seemed the mysterious cloud that had hovered unseen over the final moments of *Dances at a Gathering* now motivated *In the Night.* Here three couples each dance separately from the others before a star-pricked night sky, also designed by Thomas Skelton. One couple succumbs to mindless giddiness; another is torn by a conflict between passion and propriety; and the third shifts from an impasse of egos to a tender balance of dominion and submission. All of these people seem older and more worldly than those in *Dances at a Gathering.* And they seem to grow in depth and understanding with each step they take. *In the Night* concludes with all of the couples coming together for a brief dusting of social amenity and then going off, yielding to the pull of their individual relationships.

In *The Goldberg Variations* Robbins confronted J. S. Bach at his most architectural. He also confronted himself with an hour and twenty minutes of music, thirty variations in the same key, and forty-nine dancers. With all of this at hand, he proceeded to leaf through the classical lexicon with logic and humor juxtaposed. Here was Robbins loving his craft; reveling in its breadth, variety, and subtlety; and expansively sharing all of this with dancers and audience.

Whereas *The Goldberg Variations* was a veritable maze of steps, *Watermill* was deliberately understated. With its clean, strong gestures and its use of time as an important structural as well as dramatic element, *Watermill* might be called a Western choreographer's tribute to the Japanese *nō* drama. In it Robbins used Edward Villella as a mature man contemplating his past and gradually being made aware of his mortality. The casting was imaginative, for Villella was known for his energetic virtuosity, and in *Watermill* his principal resource was stillness.

As the ballet unfolds, the man watches adolescent boys at play, a young girl inviting sex, a crone crossing his path. Such incidents are interlaced with the rhythms of nature. The moon slips through its phases; rice is gathered; seeds are sown; snow falls. Eventually all comes to rest and to the promise of renewal. For some viewers, the apparent simplicity of *Watermill* and its use of many props (designed by Robbins and David Reppa) seemed antidance. For others it was bold in its deliberateness and in the choreographer's self-revelation.

The New York City Ballet has conducted three spring festivals devoted to the music of a single composer. The Stravinsky Festival (1972) consisted of twenty-three works, five of them by Robbins. The Ravel Festival (1975) had fifteen works, again five by Robbins. The Tchaikovsky Festival (1981) contained eighteen works; three were by Robbins. He did not participate in the American Music Festival (1988) because he was at work on *Jerome Robbins' Broadway,* a brilliantly conceived retrospective of his choreography for nine musicals extending back forty-five years. Grover Dale was co-director, and the show, which had a twenty-week rehearsal period (a length of time unheard of on Broadway) employed sixty-two performers.

Each New York City Ballet festival inevitably produced its share of *pièces d'occasion,* but in each a single work seemed to absorb the core of Robbins's attention. At the Stravinsky Festival it was *Requiem Canticles,* with its stark depiction of grief and loss. Of the five Ravel pieces, it was *In G Major* (originally called *Concerto in G*). Here, fourteen dancers stroll and gambol before a stylized impression of the sea (designed by Erté), each of them gradually taking on its characteristics. Less enduring but equally intriguing was *Chansons Madécasses,* which contrasted two couples in the sultry atmosphere suggested by the music. The Tchaikovsky Festival yielded *Piano Pieces,* a sweet-natured blend of Russian folk gestures and pure dance set to fifteen piano works.

In 1976 Robbins returned again to Chopin (one waltz and four mazurkas) for *Other Dances,* a pas de deux created especially for Natalia Makarova and Mikhail Baryshnikov. It was performed at a benefit for the New York Public Library for the Performing Arts at Lincoln Center and was subsequently taken into the repertories of American Ballet Theatre and the New York City Ballet.

Jerome Robbins did not need festivals, with their urgent deadlines, to stimulate his productivity. Between the close of the Stravinsky Festival and his 1988 hiatus, he created eighteen ballets and four collaborations. Of these, *Dybbuk* (1974), later named *Dybbuk Variations* and, ultimately, *Suite of Dances* (1980), probably meant the most to him. He kept reworking it. This ballet had a commissioned score by Robbins's early collaborator, Leonard Bernstein. But whereas Bernstein took a dramatic approach, Robbins remained on a purely abstract level. The resulting dichotomy between music and choreography may be one reason why the work never reached its full potential.

The mysticism of *Dybbuk* and the contemplativeness of *Watermill* made their presence felt in *Opus 19 / The Dreamer* (1979), set to Prokofiev's Violin Concerto no. 1 in D Major. Even though the solo male in *Opus 19* is paired with a partner, each is more like a mirror image of the other. The man is as elusive to the audience as he is to himself as he sits and watches the women dance or as he nervously pierces through the fluidity of their action. The

ROBBINS. (*below*) Women of the New York City Ballet in *Antique Epigraphs* (1984), set to music by Claude Debussy. (*opposite page*) Men of the New York City Ballet in *Ives, Songs* (1988), set to music by Charles Ives. (Photographs © 1991 and 1989 by Paul Kolnik; used by permission.)

ballet concludes in a sort of apotheosis, with the principal couple assuming the shape but not the impulse of an embrace.

In keeping with the *Zeitgeist,* Robbins selected scores by the two then most widely known minimalist composers, Steve Reich and Philip Glass. The latter fusion was especially felicitous. The ballet *Glass Pieces* (1983) had a look of Euclidean purity, both in its setting and in the choreography, which contrasted walking, bouncing, and running for the corps against more subtle statements for the principals. The result opened a window through the music.

In *Antique Epigraphs* (1984) Robbins set balletic classicism within a Greco-Roman atmosphere. The corps, performing in long, diaphanous garments, combined the limpidity of the Debussy accompaniment *(Six Épigraphes Antiques* and *Syrinx)* and the contained outlines of figures on archaic friezes. The result was again a commentary on the power of simplicity in art.

Undoubtedly the death of George Balanchine deeply affected Jerome Robbins. Balanchine had not assumed the role of teacher, but he had remained a deeply respected presence in Robbins's artistic life. Although Robbins did not say so, it might be that his *In Memory of . . .* (1985), set to Alban Berg's Violin Concerto, had Balanchine in mind. Perhaps, on the other hand, its inference is broader. Robbins may well have been contemplating his own mortality. Either way, he used Balanchine's most cherished ballerina, Suzanne Farrell, in a role that enabled her to traverse the lonely territory suggested by Berg's program note. It was that of young love, death, and transfiguration.

All through his career Robbins has accumulated professional awards. Included among them are the City of Paris Award (1971), New York's Handel Medallion (1976), the Capezio Dance Award (1976), a Kennedy Center Honor (1981), and Denmark's Hans Christian Andersen Award (1988). He has also received thirteen theater awards, five film awards, three television awards, five media awards, and two honorary doctorates.

In a 1981 interview, Robbins made a statement that in time has amounted to a credo:

> One thing I have absolutely no patience with in the theater is anyone who works in it without being a completely dedicated artist and professional in all senses of the word, bringing to the theater not only the talent, but also coming equipped with technique and craft. I feel that if someone doesn't have an insane love for the theater, he shouldn't be in it.

In June 1990, the New York City Ballet devoted two weeks to a festival of Jerome Robbins ballets. It consisted of twenty-seven works. In addition, an excerpt from his *Les Noces* was performed by members of American Ballet Theatre, the company on which the ballet had originally been set. Five decades of Robbins's creative life were spanned by the festival, which ended on 17 June with an onstage tribute to Robbins. Although he resigned as co–ballet master in chief of the company, he has continued to supervise rehearsals of his works that remain in the repertory.

[*See also* Jazz Dance; New York City Ballet; *and* United States of America, *article on* Musical Theater.]

BIBLIOGRAPHY

Ballet Review 16 (Summer 1988): 12–30. Special section entitled "A Fanfare for Jerome Robbins."

Boultenhouse, Charles. "The 'Poetics' of Jerome Robbins." *Ballet Review* 23 (Summer 1995): 59–65.

Challender, James W. "The Function of the Choreographer in the Development of the Conceptual Musical: An Examination of the Work of Jerome Robbins, Bob Fosse, and Michael Bennett on Broadway between 1944 and 1981." Ph.D. diss., Florida State University, 1986.

Chujoy, Anatole. *The New York City Ballet.* New York, 1953.

Croce, Arlene. *Going to the Dance.* New York, 1982.

Denby, Edwin. *Dance Writings.* Edited by Robert Cornfield and William MacKay. New York, 1986.

Hering, Doris. "Jerry's Legacy." *Dance Magazine* (April 1989): 44–51.

Payne, Charles, et al. *American Ballet Theatre.* New York, 1977.

Schlundt, Christena L., et al. *Dance in the Musical Theater: Jerome Robbins and His Peers, 1934–1965.* New York, 1989.

ARCHIVE. Jerome Robbins Foundation, which among other items contains a complete chronology of Robbins's work (1944–1997). Dance Collection, New York Public Library for the Performing Arts.

DORIS HERING

ROBINSON, BILL (Luther Robinson; born 28 May 1878 in Richmond, Virginia, died 25 November 1949 in New York City), American tap dancer, vaudeville performer, and actor. As a child, Luther Robinson, nicknamed "Snowbird," changed his name to Bill and began to dance in the local taverns and on street corners of Richmond for small change. It was at about age eleven that he was hired by vaudeville headliner Mamye Remington and joined the touring show *The South before the War.* Despite his lack of a formal education, and even though Robinson never learned to read, he was able to memorize lengthy film scripts, and he negotiated his way through an enormously successful professional career, testaments to both his intelligence and perseverance.

ROBINSON. A scene from the film *The Little Colonel* (Fox, 1935), whose success marked the beginning of a popular screen partnership between Robinson and Shirley Temple, the first interracial duo to appear in the movies. (Photograph from the Film Stills Library, Museum of Modern Art, New York; used by permission.)

Robinson went to New York in 1898 and by 1900 was working in variety houses at Coney Island, elsewhere in New York, and in Connecticut. He earned the nickname "Bojangles," according to his friend, musician Tom Fletcher, because of his reputation as a squabbler and a "jangler." Robinson earned his reputation as the finest tap dancer in the country when champion white tap dancer Harry Swinton declined to compete against him in the infamous tap contests that were a regular feature of the show *In Old Kentucky,* when it played at the Bijou Theater in Brooklyn.

Bojangles sharpened his style by successfully defending his title, and as champion he was known for his strict tempos and smooth, even shifts from one foot to the other. Before 1908 he worked with various partners, but he then decided to become a solo act. Billed as "the Dark Cloud of Joy," and guided by his agent Morty Forkins, who worked for him for forty years, Robinson quickly became a star, earning at his peak $3,500 per week in vaudeville and $6,500 in films.

By the early 1920s Robinson had perfected his "Stair Dance." Although Robinson was not the first, nor the only, tap dancer to perform a stair dance, he brought it to a level of unparalleled excellence. Perhaps his most famous routine, it became known all over the United States in 1935 when he made the film *The Little Colonel* with Shirley Temple. Between 1928 and 1945 he appeared in six Broadway shows and fourteen movies while performing regularly at the best variety houses and appearing in memorable editions of the Cotton Club Revues. In 1934, as the tap dancer who had become a hero to his people, he was named honorary mayor of Harlem.

Robinson's living habits were peculiar yet fastidious: he neither smoked nor drank, he consumed at least a quart of ice cream daily, and he perfected the knack of running backward as fast as some men could run forward. Bojangles celebrated his sixtieth birthday by tap dancing sixty blocks, from Harlem to the Broadhurst Theater, where he was starring in *The Hot Mikado.*

Robinson tapped up on his toes, infrequently dropping the heels. This was a major shift in tap technique, which, before him, had been more flat-footed. In tap dance history Robinson, called the Father of Tapology, is renowned for his delicate, crisp tap percussions (he always wore split-soled wooden shoes that were handmade by a Chicago craftsman), his simple, clean rhythms, and his charming trick of talking to the audience and to his feet, acting as if he were surprised by the rapid chattering below.

Of all the tap dancers of the twentieth century, Robinson remains the best known. His generosity and fierce competitive spirit have become legendary, and the high standards of excellence that he set are still honored. The tap dancers guild, the Copasetics, was formed in 1949, the year Bojangles died. The guild's name comes from the word *copasetic,* which Robinson coined to signify that everything is fine.

BIBLIOGRAPHY

Emery, Lynne Fauley. *Black Dance from 1619 to Today.* 2d rev. ed. Princeton, 1988.

Fletcher, Tom. *One Hundred Years of the Negro in Show Business.* New York, 1954.

Haskins, James. *The Cotton Club: A Pictorial and Social History of the Most Famous Symbol of the Jazz Era.* New York, 1977.

Haskins, James, and N. R. Mitgang. *Mr. Bojangles.* New York, 1988.

Johnson, James Weldon. *Black Manhattan.* New York, 1930.

Stearns, Marshall, and Jean Stearns. *Jazz Dance.* Rev. ed. New York, 1994.

FILMS. *From Harlem to Heaven* (Independent, 1929). *Dixiana* (RKO, 1930). *The Big Broadcast of 1936* (Paramount, 1935). *In Old Kentucky* (Fox Film Corp., 1935). *The Little Colonel* (Fox Film Corp., 1935). *Stormy Weather* (Twentieth-Century Fox, 1943). Stephan Chodorov, *Honi Coles: The Class Act of Tap* (1993).

SALLY R. SOMMER

RODEO. Agnes de Mille as the Cowgirl, in a characteristic display of high spirits and energy. (Photograph © by Maurice Seymour; used by permission.)

ROCKETTES. *See* Radio City Music Hall.

RODEO. Original title: *Rodeo, or The Courting at Burnt Ranch.* Ballet in one act, three scenes. Choreography: Agnes de Mille. Music: Aaron Copland. Scenery: Oliver Smith. Costumes: Kermit Love. First performance: 16 October 1942, Metropolitan Opera House, New York. Principals: Agnes de Mille (The Cowgirl), Casimir Kokitch (The Head Wrangler), Frederic Franklin (The Champion Roper), Milada Mladova (The Rancher's Daughter), Anton Vlassoff (The Caller).

Rodeo is a ballet that deals with an issue of great concern to some women in the American West: how to get a suitable man. It makes use of riding movements that Agnes de Mille devised in London in 1938, for a recital dance with Hugh Laing and Peggy van Praagh, and it includes such vernacular forms as a square dance and a cadenza for a tap dancer.

Commissioned for Sergei Denham's Ballet Russe de Monte Carlo, *Rodeo* had enormous success on its first American tour, which de Mille joined as guest dancer. Lubov Roudenko and Dorothy Etheridge succeeded her as the Cowgirl, and *Rodeo* remained in the company's repertory until 1950. Produced by Ballet Theatre that year, it has had remarkable performances over the years by Allyn McLerie, Jenny Workman, and Christine Sarry.

Rodeo was not the first all-American ballet collaboration, but like the Copland-Loring *Billy the Kid,* it has proved to be one of the most enduring. Its initial success offered de Mille entrée to the field of Broadway musicals, inspiring the dances she composed for the 1943 musical by Rodgers and Hammerstein, *Oklahoma!*

Rodeo has been restaged for various companies by de Mille and her assistants, including the Royal Winnipeg Ballet (1973), Boston Ballet (1973), Wuppertal Ballet (1974), Joffrey Ballet (1976), Cleveland Ballet (1980), Royal Ballet van Vlaanderen (1983), and the San Francisco Ballet (1989). The first two scenes of the ballet, featuring Christine Sarry as the Cowgirl with dancers of American Ballet Theatre, are featured in the public television documentary *American Ballet Theatre: A Close-Up in Time* (1973).

[*See also the entry on de Mille.*]

BIBLIOGRAPHY

Anderson, Jack. *The One and Only: The Ballet Russe de Monte Carlo.* New York, 1981.

Barker, Barbara M. "Agnes de Mille's Heroines of the Forties." In *Proceedings of the Twelfth Annual Conference, Society of Dance History Scholars, Arizona State University, 17–19 February 1989,* compiled by Christena L. Schlundt. Riverside, Calif., 1989.

Copland, Aaron, and Vivian Perlis. *Copland: 1900 through 1942.* New York, 1984.

Easton, Carol. *No Intermissions: The Life of Agnes de Mille.* Boston, 1996.

Goodwin, Noël. "Copland Musical Americana." *Dance and Dancers* (November 1990): 21–23.

de Mille, Agnes. *Dance to the Piper.* Boston, 1952.

Maynard, Olga. *The American Ballet.* Philadelphia, 1959.

Reynolds, Nancy, and Susan Reimer-Torn. *Dance Classics.* Pennington, N.J., 1991.

Rosen, Lillie F. "Talking with Agnes de Mille." *Attitude* 8.3 (1992): 20–24.

Windreich, Leland. "Agnes." *Dance International* 21.4 (Winter 1993–1994): 10–13.

LELAND WINDREICH

RODIN, AUGUSTE (François-Auguste-René Rodin; born 12 November 1840 in Paris, died 17 November 1917 in Meudon, France), French artist. Rodin's instinctive comprehension of the dance is evident in numerous sculptures and drawings. His desire to capture the human figure in motion and his belief in the absolute and expressive power of movement and gesture attracted him to dance.

Born in Paris in 1840, Rodin lived half his life unrecognized and impoverished before he achieved artistic prominence. Although he was drawing avidly by the age of nine, his family could not afford tutors or training. He studied instead at the École Impériale Spécialede de Dessin et de Mathématiques (1854–1857) where he won medals for his draftsmanship and modeling.

Rodin failed in his three attempts to enter the prestigious École des Beaux-Arts. Lacking influence and connections, he supported himself with various art-related jobs in Paris and in Belgium from 1857 to the early 1880s. In Brussels he began to exhibit his sculpture and to support himself by making portraits. A trip to Italy in 1875 reinforced Rodin's determination to succeed as a sculptor. He returned to Paris in 1877, the same year that his first life-size work, *The Age of Bronze,* was accepted for the Paris Salon. Within a short time the French government began to purchase the sculptor's works, and his reputation grew quickly. By the 1890s he had been awarded several coveted commissions, including the monuments to the burghers of Calais (1884), to Victor Hugo and Claude Lorrain (1889), and to Honoré de Balzac (1891).

In 1894, Rodin moved from Paris to the nearby village of Meudon where he maintained a studio and residence for the rest of his life. The artist's interest in depicting the dance seems to have begun about this time. Prior to the 1890s, he had associated dance with the conventional, classical style of the Paris Opera Ballet, which bored him. He responded intuitively, however, to the acrobatic movements of the can-can dancers in the French music halls and, later, to the expressive, natural movement style of the American dancer Isadora Duncan. Rodin met Duncan at the Paris Exposition of 1900, where the first major retrospective of the sculptor's work was exhibited in a specially built pavilion. Both artists viewed the human body as an expressive instrument, and on this basis their friendship and mutual admiration developed.

In his drawings and sculpture of the dance, Rodin sought to give the impression of movement by depicting more than one pose simultaneously. He used multiple outlines in his watercolors to indicate the successive positions of a dancer's arms and legs and the progression from one attitude, or pose, to another. A thin color wash was brushed over the drawn outline both to unify the figure and to create an additional shape, and to give the impression of two distinct movements melting into one. When modeling clay, Rodin also sought to fuse two movements into one by representing different parts of the figure at successive instants. In this way he felt he could truly represent the figure in movement, instead of the movement of the figure. Rodin worked quickly as he sketched and modeled, often without removing his eyes from his subject.

Another innovator in the dance who influenced Rodin was the American artist Loie Fuller. Fuller captivated Parisian audiences with her performances incorporating light, color, and costume, which she kept in perpetual motion. Rodin was fascinated with her work and they became good friends, although he apparently never made a drawing or sculpture of her. Fuller became Rodin's self-appointed agent in 1903 when she brought the first large collection of his work to New York for exhibition. Between 1914 and 1920 she encouraged Alma de Bretteville Spreckels in San Francisco and Samuel Hill in Seattle to establish museums with extensive Rodin holdings that were purchased through her.

Loie Fuller also introduced Rodin to the Javanese ballet company in 1896 and the Cambodian ballet company in 1906 during their Paris appearances. The artist was enchanted with the infinite grace, perfect proportions, and fluidity of the Asian dancers. An inspired series of watercolors distinguished by the use of additional color and drapery was the result.

Rodin's interest in the dance was not confined to the figures of women. In his small plaster statue of Vaslav Nijinsky, created in 1912 after the controversial premiere of *L'Après-midi d'un Faune,* Rodin came closest to achieving his goal of representing the abstracted essence of a figure in movement. The sculpture, modeled from life in the artist's studio, contains tremendous vitality. Its rough surface augments the overall impression of action, while its form illustrates Rodin's understanding of movement as the "transition from one attitude to another."

Rodin died in 1917. One of his last acts was to bequeath his collection of sculpture, drawings, and photographs to the nation of France as a permanent museum.

[*See also* Artists and Dance, *article on* Artists and Dance, 1760–1929.]

BIBLIOGRAPHY

Elsen, Albert E. *Rodin.* New York, 1963.

Elsen, Albert, and Kirk Varnedoe. *The Drawings of Rodin.* New York, 1971.

Rodin, Auguste. *Art.* Translated by Mrs. Romilly Fedden. Boston, 1912.

NANCY VAN NORMAN BAER

RODOLPHE, JEAN-JOSEPH (Johann Joseph Rudolph; born 14 October 1730 in Strassbourg, died 18 August 1812 in Paris), Alsatian musician and composer. Rodolphe first studied music with his father, a musician. Later, around 1745, he studied violin with Jean-Marie Leclair in Paris. He was an orchestra violinist in Bordeaux and Montpellier. In 1754 he was in the chapel of Don Philipp, duke of Parma, where he studied harmony and counterpoint with Tommaso Traetta and developed into an exceptionally fine horn player. He played a very important role in the evolution of the concertante horn and its virtuoso technique.

In 1760 Rodolphe left Parma and went to the court orchestra in Stuttgart. Here he met the Italian opera composer Niccolò Jommelli, who served as *Kapellmeister,* and the ballet master Jean-Georges Noverre. In Stuttgart Rodolphe composed at least three scores for Noverre's ballets—*Renaud et Armide* (1761), *Psyché et l'Amour* (1762), and *Médée et Jason* (1763). In 1764 Rodolphe played horn at the Concerts Spirituels in Paris; his opera *Le Mariage per Capitulation* was produced in the same year at the Comédie Italienne. Possibly owing to Noverre's dismissal and a reduction in the ballet budget, Rodolphe left Stuttgart around the end of 1766 and settled in Paris. His most successful opera, *L'Aveugle de Palmire,* was produced at the Comédie Italienne in 1767. During the same year he played in Prince Conti's orchestra. He was a member of the orchestras of the Paris Opera and of the King's Chapel. For the wedding of the count of Artois (later Charles X) and Marie Thérèse of Savoy he composed an *opéra-ballet, Isménor,* performed in Versailles in 1773. Rodolphe and Noverre met again and collaborated in 1776 in *Apelles et Campaspe* for the Opera. Two years later he met Mozart, who was visiting Paris; they became friends and Rodolphe tried to find a position for the young composer. In 1780 Noverre restaged *Médée et Jason* at the Opera to a revised score by Rodolphe.

From this time until his death, Rodolphe concentrated on pedagogical activities. He took part in the creation of the École Royale de Chant, where he became *maître de composition* in 1784; later he was appointed *professeur de solfège.* He was dismissed during the Revolution but was accepted as professor again in 1798 at the newly renamed Conservatoire de Musique. He was pensioned in 1802 but worked as a private teacher until 1812.

Rodolphe composed a considerable amount of instrumental music and published several important pedagogical works. His career as a composer of ballet music is closely linked to that of Noverre. Noverre collaborated with many composers—for example, Niccolò Piccinni, Christoph Willibald Gluck, and W. A. Mozart—but from the point of view of ballet history, his collaborations with such minor composers as Florian Deller and Joseph Starzer were of greater importance. Noverre wanted the music to be totally subordinated to the dramatic ideas of his *ballet d'action,* and Deller, Rodolphe, and Starzer were willing to model their music accordingly. Rodolphe's scores consist of a long series of numbers determined by Noverre's pantomime and choreography. The music is programmatic and illustrative, both in dramatic setting and emotional conflict. From early on, Rodolphe was strongly influenced by Jean-Philippe Rameau's music, especially the melodies and rhythms of Rameau's character dances; Rodolphe, however, allows the story content of the ballet to characterize the individual dance pieces. Elements of Italian style figure in the melodramatic orchestra recitatives in his grand pantomime scenes. The orchestra consists of a standard string section with cembalo, flutes, oboes, horns, trumpets, and kettledrums. The solo oboe is used pronouncedly in the passionate passages, while the trumpets and drums represent the militant elements. Homophony and upper-part melodies dominate, side by side with melodramatic figuration. The *gavotte* and long *chaconne* are frequently used dance forms, with the *chaconne* often used as the finale. Single sections are completely individual, with varied tempi and tonality. Within the preclassicist musical framework, the music for *Médée et Jason* is, in concord with Noverre's concept, total music dramatization, ranging from melodramatic exaltation to lyrical lingering.

[*See also* Médée et Jason *and* Psyché et l'Amour.]

BIBLIOGRAPHY

Abert, Hermann. Foreword to *Medée et Jason.* 1913.

Fétis, François-Joseph. *Biographie universelle des musiciens.* Paris, 1875.

Krauss, Rudolf. *Das Stuttgarter Hoftheater von den ältesten Zeiten bis zur Gegenwart.* Stuttgart, 1908.

Lynham, Deryck. *The Chevalier Noverre: Father of Modern Ballet.* London, 1950.

Sittard, Josef. *Zur Geschichte der Musik und des Theaters am württembergischen Hofe, 1458–1793, nach Original-Quellen.* 2 vols. in 1. Stuttgart, 1890–1891.

Uriot, Joseph. *Description des fêtes données.* Stuttgart, 1763.

OLE NØRLYNG

ROERICH, NIKOLAI (Nikolai Konstantinovich Roerich; born 27 September 1874 in Saint Petersburg, died 13 September 1947 in Kulu, India), Russian painter and scenery designer. As a young man, Roerich—who studied both law and art—displayed a keen interest in archaeology, taking part in a number of expeditions devoted to the art and rituals of the ancient Slavs. He then collaborated with the patron and collector Maria Tenisheva, an enthusiast for preserving and fostering Russian craft traditions, on the interior of the church at her artists' retreat at Talashkino (near Smolensk).

Early in the 1900s Roerich came into contact with the *Mir iskusstva* (World of Art) group, and he contributed to their exhibitions. In 1909 he designed Serge Diaghilev's production of the *Polovtsian Dances* from *Prince Igor,* which Paris considered one of the most sensational presentations of the Ballets Russes. Roerich was a close adviser to Diaghilev during the company's first season, and in 1913 he became involved in another "sensation," as designer for Vaslav Nijinsky's controversial *Le Sacre du Printemps.* [*See* Sacre du Printemps, Le.]

Although of uneven talent, Roerich applied his extensive knowledge of what were then referred to as primitive cultures to his many paintings and designs, sometimes with great success, as in the case of the *Polovtsian Dances* and *Le Sacre du Printemps.* Igor Stravinsky, the composer of *Le Sacre du Printemps,* recognized Roerich's artistic and archaeological expertise and considered him the perfect visual interpreter of his "lapidary rhythms." Nijinsky also reacted with enthusiasm to the design for *Le Sacre du Printemps,* exclaiming, according to Bronislava Nijinska, "Roerich's art inspires me as much as does Stravinsky's powerful music. . . . Roerich has talked to me at length about his paintings, . . . [which] he describes as the awakening of the spirit of primeval man. In *Sacre* I want to emulate this spirit of the prehistoric Slavs."

Like Léon Bakst and, to a lesser extent, Alexandre Benois, Roerich provided the element of Russian "barbarity" that so captivated the early audiences of the Ballets Russes. Even so, Roerich's reputation as a leading stage designer was short-lived because he was too academic and rooted in the past to score a permanent success as an artistic innovator.

In 1920 Roerich arrived in the United States. Three years later he founded the Nicholas Roerich Museum in New York City, where work from his far-flung world travels is displayed.

[*For related discussion, see* Scenic Design.]

BIBLIOGRAPHY

Archer, Kenneth. "Nicholas Roerich and His Theatrical Designs." *Dance Research Journal* 18 (Winter 1986–1987): 3–6.

Decter, Jacqueline. *Nicholas Roerich: The Life and Art of a Russian Master.* Rochester, Vt., 1989.

Garafola, Lynn. *Diaghilev's Ballets Russes.* New York, 1989.

Garafola, Lynn. "The Enigma of Nicholas Roerich." *Dance Chronicle* 13 (Winter 1990–1991): 401–412.

Hodson, Millicent. "Nijinsky's Choreographic Method: Visual Sources from Roerich for *Le Sacre du Printemps.*" *Dance Research Journal* 18 (Winter 1986–1987): 7–15.

Kiseleva, Ekaterina. *Katalog eskizov dekoratsii i kostiumov N. K. Rerikha k muzykalnym postanovkam.* Alma-Ata, Kazakh S. S. R., 1984.

Korotkina, Liudmila, ed. *Nikolai Roerich* (in Russian). Leningrad, 1985.

Kuzmina, Marina, et al. *N. K. Rerikh: Zhizn i tvorchestvo.* Moscow, 1978.

ARCHIVES. Cordier and Ekstrom Gallery, New York. Nicholas Roerich Museum, New York.

JOHN E. BOWLT

ROGERS, GINGER (Virginia Katherine McMath; born 16 July 1911 in Independence, Missouri; died 25 April 1995 in Rancho Mirage, California), dancer and actress. A quintessential star of the golden age of Broadway and Hollywood musicals, Ginger Rogers (a childhood nickname paired with the surname of a onetime stepfather) studied singing, dancing, and acting from an early age, predestined for show business by her mother, Lela, who managed Rogers's career until her death in 1977. In 1925 Rogers won a Charleston contest in Fort Worth, Texas, and subsequently toured in vaudeville. Lured by the promise of work as a band singer, Rogers moved to New York in 1929, making her musical comedy debut, in *Top Speed,* in the same year. Producer Walter Wanger, who saw her in the show, arranged for a screen test; the following year she made her first appearance on film, as a smart-alecky flapper in *Young Man of Manhattan,* whose line "Cigarette me, big boy" entered the popular lexicon of the 1930s. The role prefigured the characters most vividly associated with Rogers throughout her film career: smart, wisecracking women, just this side of cynical, an alluring blend of glamour and earthiness.

Rogers met Fred Astaire in 1930, when he was hired to doctor the choreography in the Broadway musical *Girl Crazy,* in which she played the ingenue lead. Their rapport as dancers was kindled instantly. With the show's close, Rogers moved to Hollywood and was soon under contract to RKO. She had nineteen films to her credit when the

ROGERS. With Fred Astaire in a tap dance number from *The Story of Vernon and Irene Castle* (RKO, 1939). (Photograph from the Dance Collection, New York Public Library for the Performing Arts.)

studio teamed her with Astaire as the second leads in 1933's *Flying Down to Rio* (his second film): they stole the picture, and were an immediate success. Although their off-screen relationship was always cool, and though she lacked the skill and training of some of Astaire's later partners (her tapping was often dubbed by choreographer Hermes Pan), Rogers is universally celebrated as Astaire's greatest partner. Rogers's rejoinder to critics of her dancing—"I did everything Fred did, only backwards and in high heels"—is often quoted, as is Katharine Hepburn's assessment of the reason for the team's chemistry: "He gives her class, and she gives him sex." They went on to make eight more films for RKO in six years. The plots were slight, even absurd (in one, Astaire plays a dancing psychotherapist who cures Rogers of amnesia), but the song-and-dance numbers are among the most renowned film sequences ever shot, rhapsodic idylls of urbane romance.

After *The Story of Irene and Vernon Castle* (1939) the pair separated, reuniting only for MGM's *The Barkleys of Broadway* in 1949, their sole color film. When she retired in the late 1960s, Rogers had appeared in more than twenty major stage productions (including an acclaimed two-year Broadway run and national tour of *Hello, Dolly!* in 1965 and London's first production of *Mame,* in 1969) and seventy-three films, winning a best actress Academy Award for *Kitty Foyle* in 1941 (by which time she had also become the most highly paid woman in the United States). In 1992 Rogers was one of the recipients of the fifteenth annual Kennedy Center Honors for lifetime achievement.

[*See also* Film Musicals, *article on* Hollywood Film Musicals *and the entry on Astaire.*]

BIBLIOGRAPHY

Astaire, Fred. *Steps in Time.* New York, 1959.

Bordman, Gerald. *American Musical Theater: A Chronicle.* 2d ed. New York, 1992.

Croce, Arlene. *The Fred Astaire and Ginger Rogers Book.* New York, 1972.

Dickens, Homer C. *The Films of Ginger Rogers.* Secaucus, N.J., 1975.

Faris, Jocelyn. *Ginger Rogers: A Bio-Bibliography.* Westport, Conn., 1994.

Rogers, Ginger. *Ginger: My Story.* New York, 1991.

CHRISTOPHER CAINES

ROLF, IDA. *See* Body Therapies, *overview article.*

ROMAN EMPIRE. According to tradition, Romulus founded Rome in 753 BCE and increased the original population by offering a home to anyone who chose to settle within this small group of hills near the Tiber River in central Italy, by conquering the neighboring towns and relocating some of their inhabitants to Rome, and by forging alliances with others. This willingness to create a unified community from a variety of peoples was characteristic of the native population of Latium (the region around the city of Rome), which developed its culture by incorporating and adapting the practices and beliefs of the surrounding peoples. Sabine and Alban elements dominated Rome's population until the Etruscans, who occupied the land to the north of Rome in the region between the Tiber and Arno rivers, arrived in Latium during Rome's monarchic period (753–509 BCE). Members of this highly developed civilization ruled Rome during the last part of the monarchy, until the Romans ejected them from the city (between 500 and 450 BCE). Etruscan influence on Roman practices was wide ranging. They first introduced stage dancing to the Romans, as well as a new form of improvised drama that included dance. In addition to the Sabine, Alban, and Etruscan elements in Rome, Greeks who had previously settled in Magna Graecia (Sicily, Campania [the area around Naples], and extreme southern Italy) during the ninth and eighth centuries BCE also moved north. The customs and practices brought by these arrivals were eventually responsible for the greater part of theatrical entertainment that evolved in Italy under Roman rule. Rome's acceptance of other peoples and customs continued as Rome's power spread throughout the Mediterranean during the Republic (509–27 BCE) and the Empire (27 BC–476 CE).

Etruscan Influence. Tradition also has it that in 364 BCE the Roman consuls invited a group of Etruscan dancers and musicians to perform in Rome in an attempt to appease the wrath of the gods and end the epidemic that was then ravaging the city. The Roman historian Livy

ROMAN EMPIRE. An Etruscan fresco from the Tomb of the Triclinium (c.470 BCE) depicting a dancing youth. (Museo Nazionale Tarquiniense, Tarquinia.)

notes that this introduction of Etruscan scenic entertainment and dancing to flute music was new for the Romans, who had previously found their entertainment primarily in the races of the circus. In the absence of any written records for Etruscan choral dancing, Mary Johnstone has based her speculations about the nature of their dance on a detailed examination of the painted tombs, frescoes, and sculptured representations made by Etruscans in the sixth and fifth centuries BCE. Johnstone argues for the following characteristics of Etruscan dance: The dancers never joined hands or touched each other, allowing the dance to be individualistic, spontaneous, unhampered by rules. The musicians danced as well. The whole body took part in the dance, and there was a great amount of gesticulation. The music was furnished by the double pipe *(tibia)* and lyre, supplemented at times by castanets. As for the dancers' costumes, the women were fully clothed, and the men wore draped mantels. The dancers always wore shoes of some sort. All the dancers appear to have been professionals.

Just why the Romans invited the Etruscan dancers to perform is very much a puzzle. Johnstone has found no evidence to support the claim that the Etruscans ever danced to win favor from the gods. Livy states that young Romans were attracted to Etruscan dancing and began to imitate and add elements (like bantering remarks and matching gestures) to create a form of entertainment so popular that it was soon taken over by native professional actors who took the name *histriones,* from *ister,* the Etruscan word for players. Their performances progressed to the point where they included a mixture of dances, improvised songs, and farcical sketches without plots. The name applied to this branch of theater was *satura* ("medley"). Again, the lack of written evidence has led scholars to speculate about the form and performances of *saturae.* Some authorities contend that it was similar to, or may have been blended with, the Fescennine verses—apotropaic verses recited at rural festivals and weddings.

Greek Influence. Even though Greeks had migrated to Italy as early as the ninth century BCE, their direct influence on Roman practices came much later. After the Second Punic War (218–202 BCE), Greek customs, including dancing, made their way into Rome and became popular very quickly. Greeks and Etruscans taught private classes and established dancing schools for the children of the patricians, but dance was never an integral part of Roman education, as it had been in Greece.

Not everyone was delighted by the popularity of dancing. Scipio Aemilianus (185–129 BCE), who was consul from in 147 and in 134 BCE, believed that dancing was harmful to Roman citizens because it softened their moral fiber. He claimed that degenerates were mixing with the sons and daughters of noble birth. He had closed the dance schools about 150 BCE, but they soon reopened. In response to Cato the Younger's accusations about the moral character of Lucius Murena, the orator Marcus Tullius Cicero (106–43 BCE) declared, "Perhaps you ought not refer so ill-advisedly to the consul of the Roman people as a dancer and ought to look into the problem of what other vicious habits are usually said to characterize a man who goes by that name. No one, unless he were drunk, would be caught dancing or kicking up his heels—except, of course, if he were quite mad—either at a quiet friendly dinner party or in private." Although this passage from the *In Defense of Murena* shows Cicero's disdain for dancing at parties by upper-class citizens, in his *In Defense of the Poet Archias,* Cicero admiringly remarks on the power of one of Rome's most famous performers, Quintus Roscius: "If we cannot become accomplished ourselves in the practice of the arts or participate directly in them we should all the more admire seeing others do so. Who of us was so uncouth and stony-hearted as to be untouched by the recent death of Roscius? Although he died at a ripe old age, it still seemed as though because of his supreme talent and grace he ought not to have died, really. Here was a man who had won all hearts by the motion of his body."

Not only did Cicero admire Roscius, but he counted him and Lucius Pomponius, another skilled dancer, among his friends.

Roman Literary Drama. Roman literary drama began primarily as copies and adaptations of Greek plays, although a few plays did deal with Roman history. From the beginning, music and dance played an important part in the staging of Roman literary plays. The composers of the lyrical parts of the tragedies often had as large a share as the playwrights in crafting the finished productions. The texts of Terence's plays not only included the name of the actor-directors Lucius Ambivius Turpio and Lucius Hatilius of Praeneste, but also the name of the choreographer Flaccus, a freedman of Claudius. In the dialogue portions of a play the actor brought together speech and gesture. In the lyrical monologues, however, gesture and movement became dance accompanied by flute music and a soloist.

Livius Andronicus, a Romanized Greek (c.284–204 BCE) who is traditionally credited with translating, adapting, and producing the first Greek plays in Latin, was responsible for introducing the practice of having a singer sing portions of a play while an actor illustrated the action by means of appropriate gestures and movements. According to Livy, when Andronicus's voice became weak from performing and singing he asked to have a boy stand with the flautist and sing the part while he acted; This allowed him to focus on and improve his gestures. Other actors followed suit by using separate performers for the singing parts, reserving the dialogue for themselves. This practice of dividing a stage role between a singer and actor was, according to Friedländer carried even further by some tragedians, who sometimes performed their parts in a silent pantomime while another performer sang and spoke their parts. By the end of the Republic, however, tragedy began to lose popularity. The building of large permanent theaters (Theater of Pompey, 55 BCE; Theater of Balbus, 13 BCE; Theater of Marcellus, 11 BCE—each accommodating more than ten thousand spectators) changed the dynamics of performance. The size of these magnificent buildings made it difficult for actors to be heard and made it necessary for performances to be more visual than verbal. Actors donned large masks, padding that emphasized body parts, and costumes. The dramatic aspect of tragedy gave way to lyrical chanting, singing, and dancing, all accompanied by music and elaborate scenic decoration. Eventually tragedies were replaced by pantomimes that retained only vestiges of

ROMAN EMPIRE. A Pompeiian mosaic shows a Greek satyr play in rehearsal, accompanied by a double-pipe player. (Museo Archeologico Nazionale, Naples.)

the dramatic. For their part, tragedians turned their attention to solo performances in masks and full costume, possibly changing costumes to represent the various characters.

Atellan Farce. Improvised forms of drama—Atellan farce, mime, and pantomime—originated in Magna Graecia before being introduced to Rome. Of the three, pantomime gave the most prominent role to dance. The earliest native form of Italian theater, however, was the *fabula Atellana* (the Atellan farce). Said to have originated in the town of Atella in Campania (the area around modern Naples) sometime in the fourth century BCE, the early Atellan farces were influenced by Greek farces performed in Magna Graecia. The first performers spoke Oscan, the language of Campania; when the Atellan farces moved to Rome, they began to be performed in Latin. Later, around the first century BCE, Atellan farces assumed a written form.

The chief characteristics of these farces were improvised dialogue, a liberal use of music, dance, and a set of stock characters who wore masks. Their dances consisted of exaggerated gestures and body movements choreographed to make their speech more vivid. These movements were similar to those used later by masked tragedians when they mimed the action while other performers delivered the lines.

Atellan farces dealt with intrigues, buffoonery, topical allusions, and often with subjects that bordered on the erotic. The principal characters were Maccus (The Stupid), Bucco (The Fool), Pappus (The Grandfather), and Manducus (The Chewer), a humpbacked character, and possibly one or two others. Titles such as *The Fullers, The Transalpine Gauls, Young Friends, The Pimp,* and *The Brothel* give an idea of some of the subjects treated in the farces. The crudity and coarseness of some of the racier titles had an especially great appeal for imperial audiences. The Atellan farces were used as afterpieces following tragedies and comedies and retained their popularity down to the end of the Empire, although by then they progressively lost ground to the Roman mime.

Roman Festivals. Roman festivals or funeral games provided the occasion for most performances. The Saturnalia was a yearly festival celebrated for one week starting on 17 December, during the season of winter planting. A holiday atmosphere prevailed much like Mardi Gras: the Romans chose a mock king and crowds danced in the streets. Business activity, as well as work, was suspended; citizens and slaves alike enjoyed a great deal of freedom during the week. People exchanged gifts and lit candles throughout the festivities, practices similar to those now observed at Christmas and Ḥanukkah.

On 15 February Rome celebrated the Lupercalia. It was administered by two colleges whose members were chosen from the Fabian and Quintilian families. A third college, the Luperci Iulii, was added in 44 BCE in honor of Julius Caesar. The Lupercalia was a festival of expiation, purification, and of fertility for flocks, fields, and people. The ceremony was as follows: Two young men were smeared on the forehead with the blood from the knife used to sacrifice he-goats. The blood was then wiped off with pieces of wool dipped in milk, at which point two youths laughed. A sacrificial feast followed at which the youths (Luperci) were crowned and anointed; naked except for goatskin loin cloths, they ran or possibly danced around the walls of the ancient city on the Palatine, striking women with thongs made from the skins of the sacrificial goats (supposedly to ensure the women's fertility). The Lupercalia fell into disuse during the civil wars (82–31 BCE) but was revived by Augustus Caesar (ruled 27 BCE–14 CE), under whose rule members of the priesthood were selected from the equestrian rank. The festival continued without further interruption until 494 CE, when it was changed by Pope Gelasius I to the Feast of Purification.

In 173 BCE the Romans established the Floralia, an annual festival in honor of Flora, the Italian goddess of flowering plants. The existence of a *flamen Floralis,* a priest of Flora, suggests that worship of this goddess occurred in some form previous to the annual festival. A central feature of this women's celebration was the performance of mimes by female actresses *(mimae)* who reputedly stripped as they danced.

Pyrrhic Dances. Greek pyrrhic dances made their way to Rome during the latter part of the Republic. Ariadne's dance, or the Troy game, was one of the oldest examples. The Troy game was introduced by the Roman general and dictator Sulla (138–75 BCE) and was later fully developed during the Principate of Augustus Caesar, who sponsored frequent performances. Suetonius records that Augustus thought it "a time-honored and worthy custom for the flower of nobility to become known in this way." While still a boy, Nero appeared in one of the Troy games and reportedly won great favor and applause from the audience. In the *Aeneid* Vergil includes a vivid description of one of these early dances, in which three squadrons of boys on horseback moved in interweaving patterns and pretended to fight in stylized battles as part of the funeral games for Anchises, Aeneas's father.

The imperial Romans were fascinated by Greek pyrrhic dances. Several new species were soon developed in which horses were no longer used. Many foreign troupes of boys were summoned to give performances in Rome. Slaves, along with professional dancers, were trained in the techniques of the dance, and performed pyrrhics that featured not only boys alone but boys and girls together. Costumes for the dancers consisted of beautiful gold-embroidered tunics, over which they wore scarlet or purple cloaks; on their heads were wreaths. The dancers moved in intricate patterns, grouping and separating, in lines and as individuals.

In Book 10 of *The Golden Ass,* Apuleius has left a vivid account of one of the dramatic, mythological pyrrhics featuring Paris and the story of the golden apple. First, a simple Greek pyrrhic was performed by young boys and girls gorgeously attired; then boys and girls in costumes representing Mercury, Paris, Juno, Venus, and Minerva performed the story in front of a stage decorated to suggest the fields near Mount Ida.

Water Shows. During the empire the Romans also became fond of staging *naumachiae* (ship battles) in specially constructed water basins in and about Rome in which they reenacted famous historic sea battles. Closely related to these were water ballets or aquacades held in specially converted theaters, with oval water basins built into the orchestra area. These two forms of water dancing seem to have originated in Rome. Evidence of the facilities for water shows has been found in the remains of Roman theaters in Sicily, Greece, and North Africa. Mosaics in Sicily show a group of young women in bikini-type bathing suits either preparing for or just completing a water ballet. Martial (c.40–102 CE), in *Libellus spectaculorum* 28–29, mentions of a water ballet in which Leander swam to Hero. He also describes a water ballet in which the performers were so enchanting that the audience seemed to see the boat and oar depicted in their skillful dance.

Dancing Priests. According to Livy, the earliest known Roman ritual dance was performed by a college of priests of Mars, the Salii ("leapers," "jumpers"), established by Rome's second king, Numa Pompilius, around 710 BCE. Numa set the number of Salii at twelve, but his successor, Tullus Hostilius, doubled the number to fulfill a vow made during battle. The major festival involving the Salian priests began on the first of March—the day on which the *ancile* (sacred shield) fell from the sky—and lasted until the twenty-fourth of the month. During this period the Salii made a daily solemn procession through the public sections of the Capitol. Each member of the college was dressed in an embroidered tunic, bronze breastplate, and a tall, cone-shaped helmet and carried a sword, shield, and staff. According to Livy, "[T]heir special duty was to

ROMAN EMPIRE. *(left)* Detail of a Roman mosaic, showing a female dancer with hand clappers. *(right)* A fresco from the Villa of Mysteries in Pompeii depicting a scene of flagellation, at left, and a dancer, at right. (Mosaic: Museo Pio Clementino, Vatican City State. Fresco: Museo Archeologico Nazionale, Naples.)

carry the *ancilia,* or sacred shields, one of which was fabled to have fallen from heaven, as they moved through the city chanting their hymns to the triple beat of their ritual dance." During this same time, the Salii also participated in a number of festivals. On 11 March a chariot race honored Mars Equiria and a feast was held to honor Marurius Venturis, the artisan who supposedly made copies of the original sacred shield. On 19 March the shields were cleansed. On 23 March (the Tubilustrum) the sacred horns were also cleansed and put away. Finally, on 24 March, the sacred shields were put away and not brought out again until 19 October, when they were cleansed in the Campus Martius (Field of Mars).

In addition to the Salian priests of Mars, there were also *salii* of Saturn. The *salii* of Saturn were involved in fertility or purification dances held each year in connection with spring planting. In these festivals, Saturn (the sower) figured prominently in his original role as an Italian agricultural deity. Little is known about the form of the dance other than that the priests jumped high in the air as a magical means of encouraging the crops to grow tall.

In his monograph on the Catilinarian Conspiracy, the historian Sallust includes a description of one of the female conspirators, Sempronia: "She could sing, dance, and play with more skill than necessary for a respectable woman and do many other things which were trappings of decadence." Even though Romans liked to watch dancing, they did not approve of amateurs or upper class women performing public dances with professional skill. Otto Kiefer suggests that the Romans associated such private displays of dancing with sexual stimulation, whereas military and religious performances—dancing sanctioned by the state and the gods—received criticism only when associated with nudity in the Floralia.

Several Roman writers did, however, comment on the sensuality of foreign dancing girls. The satirist Juvenal (60–140 CE) was highly critical of the dances performed by girls from Cadiz, who quivered and shook all over as they sank to the floor to the sound of applause from the spectators. These dancers, he felt, were stimulating to both men and women, and helped to rejuvenate rich men sexually. Juvenal's contemporary Martial tended to agree with him, for he criticized their endless wiggling, shaking, and quivering. In the empire, nonetheless philosophers, orators, and tutors were replaced in many wealthy homes by dancers, dance teachers, and musicians, and the mimes and pantomimes flourished as never before.

[*See also* Music for Dance, *article on* Music for Dance before 1520; Mimus; *and* Pantomimus. *For related discussion, see* Greece, *article on* Dance in Ancient Greece.]

BIBLIOGRAPHY

Apuleius. *The Golden Ass.* Translated by P. G. Walsh. Oxford, 1995.

Beare, William. *The Roman Stage: A Short History of Latin Drama in the Time of the Republic.* 3d ed. New York, 1963.

Bieber, Margarete. *The History of the Greek and Roman Theatre.* 2d ed., rev. and enl. Princeton, 1961.

Butler, James H. *The Theatre and Drama of Greece and Rome.* New York, 1972.

Cicero. *In Defense of the Poet Archias* and *In Defense of Murena.* In *Cicero: Nine Orations and The Dream of Scipio.* Translated by Palmer Bovie. New York, 1967.

Conte, Gian Biagio. *Latin Literature: A History.* Translated by J. B. Solodow. Baltimore, 1994.

The Context of Ancient Drama. Ed. by Eric Csapo and W. J. Slater. Ann Arbor, Mich., 1995.

Dumézil, Georges. *Archaic Roman Religion.* Vols. 1–2. Translated by Philip Krapp. Chicago, 1966.

Friedländer, Ludwig. *Roman Life and Manners under the Early Empire.* Vol. 2. Translated by Leonard A. Magnus. 7th ed., rev. and enl. New York, 1965.

Jones, Michael R. "Roscius and The Power of Performance." *Classical Outlook* 73.4 (1996): 123–128.

Johnstone, Mary A. *The Dance in Etruria: A Comparative Study.* Florence, 1956.

Jory, E. J. "Continuity and Change in the Roman Theatre." In *Studies in Honor of T. B. L. Webster,* vol. 1, edited by J. H. Betts et al. Bristol, 1986.

Jory, E. J. "The Drama of the Dance: Prolegomena to an Iconography of Imperial Pantomime." In *Roman Theater and Society: E. Togo Salmon Papers I.* Ann Arbor, Mich., 1996.

Juvenal. *The Sixteen Satires.* Translated by Peter Green. New York, 1967.

Kiefer, Otto. *Sexual Life in Ancient Rome.* London. 1956: 166–177.

Kirstein, Lincoln. *Dance: A Short History of Classic Theatrical Dancing.* New York, 1935.

Knox, Bernard. *Word and Action: Essays on the Ancient Theater.* Baltimore, 1979.

Konstan, David. *Roman Comedy.* Ithaca, N.Y., 1983.

Livy. *The Early History of Rome.* Translated by Aubrey de Sélincourt. New York, 1960.

Livy. *Rome and Italy.* Translated by Betty Radice. New York, 1982.

Lucian. *The Dance.* In *Lucian.* Vol. 5. Translated by A. M. Harmon. Loeb Classical Library. Cambridge, Mass., 1936.

Martial. *Libellus Spectaculorum.* In *Martial: Epigrams.* Vols. 1 and 3. Translated by D. R. Shackleton Bailey. Loeb Classical Library. Cambridge, Mass., 1993.

Martínez-Pinna, N. J. "La danza de los salios, rito de integración en la curia." *Archivo Español de Arqueologia* 53 (1980): 15–20.

Rose, H. J. *A Handbook of Latin Literature.* New York, 1960.

Sallust. *The Jurgurthine War and The Conspiracy of Catiline.* Translated by S. A. Hanford. New York, 1964.

Scullard, H. H. *Festivals and Ceremonies of the Roman Republic.* London, 1981.

Suetonius. *The Twelve Caesars.* Translated by Robert Graves. New York, 1957.

Virgil. *The Aeneid.* Translated by Robert Fitzgerald. New York, 1981.

Wright, John. *Dancing in Chains: The Stylistic Unity of the Comoedia Palliata.* Rome, 1974.

T. Davina McClain

ROMANIA. [*This entry comprises three articles on dance in Romania. The first article focuses on folk dance; the second explores the history of theatrical dance; the third provides a brief history of folk dance scholarship and writing.*]

Folk Dance

Folk dance in Romania varies according to region. The folkloric zones partially correspond to the historical provinces of Wallachia, Oltenia, Transylvania, Moldavia, the Banat, and Dobrudja. There are three large dialect zones: the Sub-Carpathian zone, on both sides of the eastern and southern Carpathian mountains; the Danubian Plain; and Transylvania. Within these areas lie choreographic zones with strong specific traits; these are subordinated, however, to a general national style, and the choreographic zones have influenced one another. Very old dances such as the *hora, brîul, învârtita,* lads' dances, and *căluş* make up the classical repertory of Romanian folk dance.

Performance style also varies according to the age of the participants. Older people dance in a moderate, subtle style that preserves the traditional forms, while young people tend to emphasize the dynamics and amplitude of the movements, sometimes generating qualitative changes in the dance structure.

Twentieth-century socioeconomic developments have helped to increase contacts among groups. Schools, military service, the Houses of Culture, and regional and national folk festivals have encouraged the circulation of dances. The modern media enhance people's receptivity to new forms. Musicians frequently travel, facilitating the circulation of tunes and dances.

The range of the repertory varies with each region, reaching thirty-five to fifty variants in some villages in Wallachia, Oltenia, the Banat, and Moldavia, and being limited to three to five variants in some in Transylvania. Quality, however, is not determined by quantity; the small number of dances in Transylvania is compensated for by intricate technique and rich choreographic substance.

The fundamental characteristics of the Romanian dancing style are swift, virtuosic, rhythmic leg movements, vitality, inventiveness, and high technical complexity in the combination of movements. Men's and women's group dances are similar. Movement combinations may include walking, leaping, hopping, crossed steps, heel claps (on the ground or in the air), and numerous syncopated and counterpoint steps. The arms perform small movements while bent vertically, or ample swinging movements from the shoulder joint. In couple dances there is a marked differentiation between the dancing of the two sexes: the men often execute *ponts* (leaps accompanied by slaps on various parts of the leg, requiring excellent coordination between arms and legs), while the women perform pirouettes with virtuosity and elegance.

Romanian folk dance favors simple, divided, or syncopated binary rhythm transcribed as 2/4 meter, and asymmetric rhythm. Ternary rhythm, notated in 3/4 or 3/8 measure, seldom occurs in Romanian repertories. Out of the eleven hundred dances that have been investigated, fifty-six rhythmic formulas of movement have been identified and classified.

The instrumental accompaniment is specific to Romanian dance folklore. Older *jocs* (rural dances) were accompanied by pipes, bagpipes, and long shepherd's pipes. More recently a complex accompaniment for dance has been provided by bands called *taraf,* which vary from one region to another. Their current form generally includes first and second violin, double bass, drums, *kobza* (a stringed instrument with a bulging resonance box), guitar, big and small *ţambal* (cembalo), brass instruments, clarinet, saxophone, and *taragot* (intermediate between the last two). In recent years the accordion has spread to many areas, enjoying ever-greater popularity.

In Romanian folk dance the lyrics and the music are organically linked with the dance. The *strigături,* or interjections and dancers' shouts, are kinetically connected with the movement in specific ways. The texts are short commands guiding the sequence of movements, lyrical verses, or satirical and sarcastic allusions to certain persons or comic situations.

From a structural point of view, Romanian folk dances fall into the categories of group dances, dances in pairs, gang dances, and solo dances. Each category includes certain groups, types, subtypes, and variants, which altogether make up a total of fifty-five types.

Group Dances. In the group dances, dancers are linked by armholds. The *hora* group (round dances) occupies a very important place in Romanian folk dance. The *hora* is most frequently danced in the Danubian Plain and in the Sub-Carpathian and Dobrudjean zones, with several ceremonial, ritual, or recreational functions. It has a wide range of variants. Some are mixed-group dances with an unlimited number of dancers forming a chain with bent arms and moving in a circle in a moderate tempo and a binary rhythm. Some have symmetrical rhythm in 2/4 time; others have various asymmetrical rhythms.

Dances in the *sîrba* group, which is found throughout the country, have a recreational function and are performed on all dance occasions. The *sîrba* is a dynamic dance in which the participants move in a semicircle with their arms laid on one another's shoulders. There are virtuosic variations in marked time, alternating with extensive passages of leaping and running steps. A characteristic feature is the lack of concordance between the ternary choreographic motifs and the binary musical motifs.

Initially a men's virtuosic dance, the *brîul* group is widespread on both sides of the southern Carpathians and in the Danubian Plain. It may also have a mixed form and a semicircular or linear orientation, the arms being laid on the adjacent dancers' shoulders or crossed at waist level to hold hands. Three types may be distinguished within the group: the Carpathian, Transylvanian, and Moldavian

ROMANIA: Folk Dance. Men and women performing an *învârtita*-type couple dance in Braşov, 1986. (Photograph courtesy of the Romanian Center for the International Theater Institute, Bucharest.)

brîu, in which virtuosic movements in marked time alternate with more moderate syncopated walks; the Oltenian *brâulet,* assimilated into the swift Oltenian style, with tripping movements on tiptoe, swinging, and small bilateral and frontal shifts; and the Banatian *brîu,* which took over the local characteristics and can be further subdivided into the old *brîu* and the new swift *brîu,* which is performed in phrases grouped in a binary dactylic rhythm in accordance with the musical rhythm.

Women's *jocs* accompanied by melody are called *purtatas.* They may be derived from old ritual dances spread over a large area of southeastern Europe. In Romania they are danced by groups of girls who link arms with an elbow hold, with hands folded at the back. The dance is performed with syncopated steps in a spiral path, to songs with lyrical texts. The vocal accompaniment is interrupted at intervals, and the dance is continued in the rhythm of the steps. The time may be symmetrical 2/4 or asymmetrical 10/16.

Dances in Pairs. The *învârtita* group of pair dances is found in Transylvania. Their form is bipartite, made up of a walk in which dancers, strung in single and double connection, perform bilateral movements, and a spinning *(învârtire),* in which partners facing each other are freely spread over the dancing area. Four types can be distinguished: the syncopated *învârtita,* found in southern Transylvania; the slow, straight, nonsyncopated *învârtita;* the swift, straight *învârtita,* which displays very complex forms, the men introducing many *ponts* (leaps accompanied by slaps) characteristic of the boys' *jocs,* while the girls perform graceful pirouettes; and *învârtita bătută,* found in the Sub-Carpathian zone and distinguished by dynamic spinning with counterpoint steps, sometimes performed by small groups of four to eight dancers.

The *ardeleana* group is found in the western part of the country. The partners dance face to face, the pairs making up a compact line that moves alternately on the same spot and bilaterally. Its types include the syncopated *ardeleana,* in which the men periodically detach themselves from their partners in order to execute *ponts* to the same melody; the slow (or moderate), straight *ardeleana;* the straight *ardeleana* with spinning movements and counterpoint steps; and the swift, straight *ardeleana* danced in a rapid, trampling manner. The "Banatian for Two" displays the characteristic varied arm play of the partners, connected by one arm or by both, with many under-arm passes of the female who spins around the male. The subtype *sorocul,* found in the Banat, is the most virtuosic dance in the local repertory.

Purtatas in pairs are very old dances, mentioned in documents dating back to the sixteenth century. They have been influenced by seventeenth- and eighteenth-century ballroom dances, from which they borrowed movement in a column or a circle as well as a solemn, slow style. The step structure is similar to that of the *învârtita,* consisting of walks and spinning. The *purtatas* open the cycle of dances at a Sunday *hora;* a *purtata* may be followed by a *fecioreasca* (boys' dance *învârtita*) and *învârtita.* In the wedding ceremonial they acquire a ritual function. Types include the asymmetrical *purtata* and the symmetrical straight *purtata.* The most complex type is *de-a lungul* ("all along"), in which the steps have a ternary organization (10/16); it displays spectacular arm variations and connections between partners, under-arm passes, and men's *ponts.*

The *de doi schimbat* ("change the partner") group is found throughout the country. Couples move around in a circle while changing partners. The woman passes from one partner to another at the man's request; the partners may also alternate, while the couples spin around and advance in the same direction.

The *breaza* group, found in the Sub-Carpathian zone in Wallachia and southern Transylvania, is frequently performed at the Sunday *hora.* The partners, linked by varied armholds, move bilaterally, frontally, or by spinning around, in a syncopated rhythm. The tempo is lively and the form a varied concatenation of phrases. All the variants have their own names and tunes.

Gang Dances. These are young people's dances. Together with the *învârtita* and *purtata,* they make up the basic repertory in Transylvania. The dancers perform identical steps simultaneously but without being linked. These virtuosic *jocs* are characterized by athletic, acrobatic movements such as big bounds, scissors steps, slaps on various parts of the legs, and turns in the air, while the dancer is supported by his partner or a club. Types include *haidăul* (a suite including *sărita, purtata, de băt,* and *învârtita*), *căluşerul,* and *fecioreasca rară* ("young men's slow dance"). Their tempo is moderate and the movements large and elegant. The form is ternary, with an introduction, a *pont,* and a conclusion making up the final motif. *Fecioreasca deasă* ("young men's swift dance") is characterized by the speed and technical difficulty of the movements. The subtype *bărbuncul,* from the German *Werbung,* used to be danced at recruiting parties; it has a dynamic military character. *Fecioreasca fetelor* (girls' dance) is the female counterpart to the boys' dances and is danced occasionally in the region of Braşov-Rupea.

Solo Dances. Men perform solo dances for display or in contests, on occasions such as the Monday morning after a wedding, at the Sunday *hora,* and at rural festivals *(nedeas),* always in a context of entertainment. They are based either on dances of the group repertory or on leaps over objects.

Ritual Dance. On ceremonial and ritual occasions (except those in which the dance itself functions as a ritual), dance is a secondary factor, but it is occasionally practiced. One example is Surăţia ("brotherhood" or "sisterhood"), a puberty ritual that involves an oath of friendship between boys who are sworn brothers and girls who are sworn sisters. It is practiced in Moldavia and Transylvania on the Monday following Easter Sunday, when the young people may join the Sunday *hora.* Vergelul is a prophecy ritual followed by dancing, held on New Year's night. Şezătoarea ("evening sitting") can be considered a social occasion meant for collective work or a courtship ritual. Groups of girls or women spin and sew together in the evenings from December until March, during the intervals when the *joc* is prohibited. The men and boys come later and the dance begins. This event provides an opportunity to meet a marriage partner and allows children to learn to dance.

Weddings are complex ceremonials lasting three days. Their many rituals include dance, music, drama, and metaphorical texts. Dance opens and closes the ceremony and marks the most important moments of the ritual. On Saturday, decorating the standard at the bridegroom's house and adorning the fir and the bride's wreath are occasions for the tinsel *hora* and the fir tree *hora.* On Sunday there are many occasions for dance: shaving the bridegroom and dressing the bride, with parting rituals accompanied by specific dances; the bridal procession from the bridegroom's house to the bride's house; the bride's parting with her parents, an impressive dramatic moment with singing, weeping, pardon-begging, and dancing; and the procession to the church, the holy service, and the

ROMANIA: Folk Dance. A group of men and women performing an *ardeleana*-type couple dance. Three of the pictured couples, at left, face their respective partners, link hands, and create a characteristic line formation. (Photograph courtesy of the Romanian Center for the International Theater Institute, Bucharest.)

dance in front of the church. In welcoming the bride and bridegroom, the mother-in-law dances with the bride, passing her thrice under her arm in a ritual of welcome and taking possession. A feast with ritual dishes takes place simultaneously at the bride's and the bridegroom's places. The cook dances with a hen on a tray, destined for the godparents, while singing verses. Money is at stake in the dance of the bride; the last to dance is the bridegroom, in a ritual of integration and taking possession. The adornment of the bride, the climactic moment, serves as an integration ritual and is accompanied by a dance around her. The *periniţ a* is danced by everybody on Monday morning, along with obscene, imitative solo dances such as "The Cowbell" and "The Hedgehog." The *hora* of young wives is performed six months after the wedding.

One of the most ancient, authentic, and interesting Romanian ritual customs is the *căluş*. A similar custom is found under different names and variants on the right bank of the Danube, in Bulgaria, Macedonia, and Yugoslavia as well as in some countries of central Europe and in England. The frenzy and rapture of the dance and its phallic imagery suggest an origin in the Dionysiac dances of the northern Thracians.

In its traditional form, the *căluş* was an intricate ritual performance including dance, music, pantomime, imitative gestures, and drama. The *căluşari* wore the national costume with specific properties for each part of the ritual, such as a flag, stick, or herbs.

The team of *căluşari* is composed of seven, nine, or eleven dancers; these numbers were formerly believed to have magical significance. Within the team, a few characters with specific functions and properties stand out: the chief, who has absolute command over the group; the mute, a masked character who appears with a ritual object in his hand and performs as a kind of soloist, a mime who acts out the comical, theatrical part of the program, thus balancing the dance displays of the ensemble; and the flagbearer.

The *căluş* has three well-defined parts. In the first the *căluşari* team is confirmed as an official group. They take an oath called the "promise" or "binding of the *căluş*," which is followed by the raising of the flag, a long pole topped by a towel and as many cloves of garlic and pieces of wormwood as there are dancers on the team. The second part consists of the *căluş* dance, the so-called feast, which lasts from two to three days, moving to different houses in the village. In the third part, the *căluş* is dissolved with the burying of the flag, which signifies the breaking up of the magic guild and the dancers' return to the community.

The musician, who belongs to the *căluşari* team, is bound by their oath and obeys their rules. In the past the dance was accompanied by bagpipe and shepherd's pipe. Later the bagpipe was replaced by the violin in almost all regions.

The dance is in a three-part form composed of an introduction, generally known as the walk, followed by a central part, the movement, and a never-changing, compulsory end, the *hora căluşului.* The dances form a cycle that is found in all the regions where the custom is kept alive, and the whole community participates in it.

Dance in Nonritual Contexts. The terms *hora* and *joc* define certain categories or individual dances such as the straight *hora,* bride's *hora,* young maiden's *hora,* and *un joc* (a *joc;* in Transylvania and Banat, a fixed set of *jocs*). These terms may also indicate the place where the com-

ROMANIA: Folk Dance. Forming a circle, male dancers execute a turned-in jump characteristic of the virtuosic *fecioreasca deasă* ("young men's swift dance"), in a 1986 performance in Braşov. (Photograph courtesy of the Romanian Center for the International Theater Institute, Bucharest.)

ROMANIA: Folk Dance. The *căluş* is one of the oldest extant forms of ritual performance in Romania. Here, a team of *căluşari* execute a pushup-like movement, accompanied by a violinist, during a performance at the International Folklore Festival in Bucharest, 1995. (Photograph courtesy of the Romanian Center for the International Theater Institute, Bucharest.)

munity gathers for entertainment (at the *hora* or at the *joc*).

The Sunday *hora,* in which the whole community participates, is an occasion for social communication. Dance is the main element. The dancers and the audience have precise relationships, the parents and old people representing social control. The order of joining the *hora* and the place of each group is determined by an etiquette that varies from one region to another. For young people the *hora* is an occasion of transition to adult social status. Girls are admitted at fourteen and boys at sixteen, from among those belonging to the *ceata flăcăilor* or boys' club, a social organization of young boys headed by a manager who is responsible for discipline during the various dance occasions. The Sunday *hora* is danced throughout the year, with interruptions during Christian fasting periods.

The draft dance was formerly an opportunity to see young recruits off with songs and dances. The *claca,* or bee, was an old custom of mutual help in the community. In the evening, after the work was done, the host offered the participants a dinner with music and dancing.

In the past, fairs of two to three days' duration brought together people from remote villages. These provided opportunities for making new acquaintances and organizing dancing parties, which played an important role in courtship. In Transylvania families went to the Mount Găina Fair with their daughters' dowries, with a view to marrying them off.

Balls, which first appeared in Romanian villages after World War I, involved all social classes. They included both ballroom dances such as the tango, waltz, and fox trot, and suites from the local traditional repertory.

The selection of dances in the course of the Sunday *hora* observes certain rules established by tradition. Three to five favorite dances are usually performed in a suite without any change of partner, and these suites recur cyclically throughout the festival. In southern Transylvania, for example, the *haidău* suite *(sărita, purtata, de bâtă,* and *învârtita)* is often performed cyclically. In the areas where ballroom dances have penetrated, they have come to form suites that are part of the local cycles. The peasants call such suites *dances,* whereas traditional suites are called *jocs;* for example, in Wallachia a *joc* suite might include a *hora,* a *sârba,* and a *ţigăneasca,* while a *dances* suite might comprise a tango, a waltz, and a fox trot.

BIBLIOGRAPHY

Bucsan, Andrei. *Specificul dansului popular românesc.* Bucharest, 1971.

Costea, Constantin. *Jocuri fecioreşti din Ardeal.* Bucharest, 1961.

Giurchescu, Anca. "Le Calus: Procès de transformation d'un rituel roumain." In *Tradition et histoire dans la culture populaire,* edited by Jean-Michel Guilcher. Grenoble, 1990.

Giurchescu, Anca, and Sunni Bloland. *Romanian Traditional Dance: A Contextual and Structural Approach.* Mill Valley, Calif., 1995.

Kligman, Gail. *Calus: Symbolic Transformation in Romanian Ritual.* Chicago, 1981.

Kürtz, László. "The Bachelor's Dance of Transylvania." *Arabesque* 8 (March–April 1983): 8–14.

Louis, Maurice L.-A. *Folklore et la danse.* Paris, 1963.

Martin, György. "Considerations sur l'analyse des relations entre la danse et la musique des danses populaires." *Studia Musicologica* 7 (1963).

Massoff, Ioan. *Teatrul românesc.* Bucharest, 1961–.

Niculescu, Varone. *Folclor românesc coregrafic.* Bucharest, 1932.

Nistor, Viorel. *Folclor coregrafic.* 2 vols. Bucharest, 1991.

Popescu-Judetz, Eugenia. *Sixty Folk Dances of Romania.* Pittsburgh, 1979.

Preda, Tea. "Du ballet contemporain roumain." *Revue Roumaine,* no. 3 (1980).

Proca Ciortea, Vera. "On Rhythm in Rumanian Folk Dance." *Yearbook of the International Folk Music Council* 1 (1969).

Proca Ciortea, Vera. "The 'Calus Custom' in Rumania: Tradition, Change, Creativity." *Dance Studies* 3 (1978–1979): 1–43.

Sachs, Curt. *World History of the Dance.* Translated by Bessie Schönberg. New York, 1937.

Sulzer, Franz Joseph. *Geschichte des transalpinischen Daciens.* 3 vols. Vienna, 1781–1782.

Wilson, Tink, and Eva Kiss. "An Interview with László Dioszegi." *Viltis* 48 (January–February 1990): 12–13.

Wolfram, Richard. "Der Volkstanz als kulturelle Ausdrucksform des südost europäischen Völker." *Südosteuropa Jahrbuch* 5 (1962).

VERA PROCA CIORTEA

Theatrical Dance

Romania's long struggle to maintain its ethnic and territorial integrity has inevitably affected the development of its theatrical dance. Folk dancing has generally dominated Romanian dance because of its central and vibrant role in the life of the people and because it provided a means of asserting ethnic and national identity. An example is the *romana,* a folk-inspired dance created in 1850 by Iacob Mureşianu and Ştefan Emilian, which was performed in the parlors and meeting places of the democraticly minded intelligentsia. In the early nineteenth century, folk dance was an integral part of the nascent Romanian professional theater, which presented musical comedies, operettas, farces, vaudevilles, and pastorals—all with songs and dances. The folk tradition remains a potent influence and source of inspiration in Romanian theatrical dance.

The Eighteenth and Nineteenth Centuries. Theatrical dance was introduced to Romania in the eighteenth century by visiting troupes of actors, singers, and dancers, primarily from Italy, Germany, and France. By the nineteenth century, some of these foreign companies had begun to create works based on Romanian history, legends, and folk dances; for example, in 1822 a German troupe visiting Bucharest presented the ballet *Horea and Cloşca,* named after two leaders of a late eighteenth-century peasants' uprising in Transylvania.

The first dancing schools in Romania were established in the nineteenth century. The School of Music and Declamation, founded in 1833 in Bucharest, offered dance instruction under a French ballet master named Duport. Private dancing schools were opened in Bucharest and Jassy, and Romanian dancers began to take part in foreign opera productions.

The ballet *Doamna de Aur* (The Golden Lady), presented in 1870 with music by Ludwig Anton Wiest and libretto by Petre Grădişteanu, utilized a mixture of classical ballet and indigenous folk dances. It was choreographed by the Romanian Gheorghe Moceanu and the American ballerina Augusta Maywood. Moceanu also created the ballet *O Sărbătoare la Ţară* (Feast in the Countryside) for the Chicago World's Fair of 1893. The characters in this full-length ballet are Romanian peasants dressed in festive garb, and the action takes place in a Carpathian mountain village.

Romania's oldest opera company, founded in 1877, was the Lyrical Company of the Bucharest National Theater. The company's corps de ballet was created in 1898 under the leadership of the choreographer Thomasso Paris.

The Twentieth Century. The Romanian Opera, as the company was known, became a state-supported institution in 1921, with ensembles in both Bucharest and Cluj. This marked the beginning of an important stage in Romanian ballet history, and since that time ballet has developed as an independent art. In the early years of Romanian ballet, the choreographer Roman Romanov created works such as *Faunul şi Nimfa* (The Faun and the Nymph) and *Arlechiniada* (Harlequinade). Maria Bălănescu, the first prominent Romanian prima ballerina, began to train a native corps de ballet at the Bucharest Opera.

During these early years, however, the lack of a permanent corps de ballet in Romania forced some Romanian composers to take their ballet scores abroad for production. *Ioana d'Arc* (Joan of Arc), composed by Alexis Catargi, was produced in London in 1906. The Paris Opera Ballet mounted *Ileana Cosînzeana,* composed by Ion Nonna Ottescu, in 1918; it was based on a Romanian legend, with verses for chorus written by the Romanian poet Elena Vacarescu.

The ballet master Anton Romanowski played a decisive role in shaping Romanian ballet. A pupil of Sergei Legat and Graci Rafael, Romanowski had danced with the Russian ballerinas Anna Pavlova, Tamara Karsavina, and Ekaterina Geltser. After settling in Romania in 1925, he began to restage major works from both the Russian repertory and from Diaghilev's Ballets Russes, among them *Schéhérazade, Petrouchka,* and *The Fountain of Bakhchisarai;* he also staged original ballets to music by Romanian composers, notably *Iris* by Constantin C. Hottara and *Fata Căpitanului* (The Captain's Daughter). He was also responsible for training the ballet ensemble of the Bucharest Romanian Opera, which included the outstanding dancers Elena Penescu Liciu, Oleg Danovschi, and Tilde Urseanu.

Vera Karalli, who was formerly a *prima ballerina* at the Bolshoi Theater in Moscow and a soloist in Diaghilev's company, served as ballet mistress of the Bucharest Opera from 1930 to 1937. By 1932, the ballet company had achieved enough technical proficiency to present *Swan Lake.* Under the leadership of ballet masters such as Fulda Dacia, Iosif Lighetti, Elena Penescu Liciu, and Roman Moravski, the Cluj Romanian Opera House presented *The*

Fairy Doll, Coppélia, Schéhérazade, and *The Four Seasons of Love,* the last to the music of Schubert.

Folk dance had always been a pervasive influence on Romanian theatrical dance, but with the work of Floria Capsali its elements were genuinely integrated into the classical vocabulary. The most outstanding personality in Romanian ballet in the first half of the twentieth century, Capsali studied with Enrico Cecchetti, Nikolai Legat, Leo Staats, and others; her training also included rhythmical movement with Raymond Duncan and acrobatics with Saulnier. Upon settling in Romania in 1913 she developed a system called "Romanian educated dance," which obeyed the canons of classical ballet yet displayed the stylistic and spiritual marks of Romanian folk dance. She produced many ballets in this style at the Bucharest Opera, often to music by renowned Romanian composers; a few examples are *Wedding in the Carpathians,* with music by Paul Constantinescu; *Demoazela Măriutza,* (Miss Măriutza); *When the Grapes Grow Ripe,* with music by Mihail Jora; *The Elf,* with music by Zeno Vancea; and *The Ciuleandra.* From 1938 to 1950 Capsali headed the ballet school of the Bucharest Opera, and she also founded ballet schools for the Ministry of Home Affairs and Central House of Trade Unions.

Other choreographers adopted and enriched Capsali's system. Vera Proca Ciortea gave it a note of poetry and exuberance, while Petre Bodeuţ and Gabriel Negry laconically expressed the symbolic meanings of age-old dances and rituals. Negry, the founder of the National Committee of Dance in 1990, a branch of the International Dance Council in Bucharest, was awarded a prize of honor at the Dance and Folk Costumes Exhibition sponsored by the Archives Internationales de la Danse in Paris in 1937.

After World War II, a new phase in the history of Romanian ballet began. Romania became a satellite state of the Soviet Union and state-subsidized ballet schools were founded in Bucharest and Cluj. These schools offered a nine-year course of general education as well as ballet instruction. New opera companies were also established, among them the State Opera of Timişoara, the Magyar Opera House of Cluj-Napoca, and the State Opera of Jassy, all of which soon acquired professional ballet ensembles. New ballet groups were also organized at the Musical Theater of Braşov, the Lyric Theater of Constantza, and the N. Leonard Musical Theater of Galaţi. Amateur groups were fostered by a complex network of People's Art Schools, as well as by various urban and rural enterprises.

Interchange with Soviet dancers and ballet masters also helped enrich Romanian ballet. Soviet guest artists periodically appeared in Romania, while young Romanian dancers went to study in Leningrad (now Saint Peters-

ROMANIA: Theatrical Dance. *(left)* Floria Capsali in her *Chopin Waltz,* Bucharest, 1937. *(right)* Gabriel Negry in his *Japanese Dance,* 1937. (Photographs courtesy of the Romanian Center for the International Theater Institute, Bucharest.)

burg) or Moscow. As Romanian ballet developed, it began to incorporate into its repertory major classics, such as *Giselle, Swan Lake,* and *The Sleeping Beauty.* Romanian choreographers also began to stage their own versions of well-known Western and Russian ballets, such as *Romeo and Juliet, Don Quixote, The Stone Flower,* and *La Fille Mal Gardée.* Many of these were produced as grand spectacles that exploited the full resources of the company and the theater.

Romanian choreographers soon created original works, varied in theme and style, to scores by Romanian composers. Oleg Danovschi's *Domnişoara Nastasia* (Miss Nastasia), set to music by Cornel Trăilescu, premiered in December 1965; it takes place in Bucharest in the 1940s and tells the tragic story of a girl who kills herself on her wedding day to punish her bridegroom, who had killed her beloved in order to win her. Vasile Marcu choreographed *Omagiu lui Brâncuşi* (Homage to Brancusi), a tribute to the famous Romanian sculptor. *Romanian Rhapsody,* composed by George Enescu, has inspired many choreographers. The range of subjects treated by Romanian choreographers included vast historical panoramas, social commentaries, and poetic excursions into Romanian fairy tales and mythology. Many of these ballets are characterized by an indigenous tone and an emphasis on folklore, manifested in choreographic style as well as in themes.

A number of Romanian dancers have gained renown during the twentieth century. Irinel Liciu studied in Moscow and with Maurice Béjart in Brussels, as well as in Romania. From 1950 to 1968, as *prima ballerina* of the Bucharest Opera, she displayed remarkable insight, expressiveness, and vividness, and she excelled in both lyrical and dramatic ballet roles in *Romeo and Juliet, The Red Poppy,* and *The Bronze Horseman.* She also danced in Romanian works, such as Danovschi's *The Return from the Deep,* to music by Mihail Jora, Urseanu's *Călin,* to music by Alfred Mendelsohn, and Marcu's *Homage to Brancusi.*

The dynamic and brilliant Ileana Iliescu was a product of the Choreography School in Bucharest, where she studied under Danovschi, Urseanu, and Marcu. She danced the role of Odette-Odile in *Swan Lake* at the age of nineteen and went on to become a *prima ballerina* of the Bucharest Opera. She has been called one of the best Odettes of her time. Her many and varied roles included Swanilda in *Coppélia,* Zarema in *The Fountain of Bakhchisarai,* Kitri in *Don Quixote,* Aurora in *The Sleeping Beauty,* and the Girl in *The Miraculous Mandarin.*

Elena Dacian began her training at the Choreography School in Bucharest, then studied at the Vaganova Choreography School in Leningrad. She was a *prima ballerina* at the Bucharest Opera from 1960 to 1988 and danced roles in the international classical repertory—notably *Giselle, The Sleeping Beauty,* and *Coppélia*—as well as in Romanian ballets such as *Return from the Deep* and *Homage to Brancusi.* She excelled in romantic roles, in which she created an impression of candor and ingenuousness. Her many tours abroad included frequent guest appearances in the Ballet Evenings of Herbert von Karajan and the Berlin Philarmonic.

Alexa Mezincescu, a choreographer as well as a dancer, trained at the Bucharest Choreography School, in Leningrad, and at the Royal Academic Institute of Choreography in Stockholm. She won prizes in ballet competitions in Romania, Moscow, and Vienna. A soloist of the Bucharest Opera from 1953 to 1988, she has danced leading roles in *Swan Lake, Romeo and Juliet,* and *The Fountain of Bakhchisarai.* She has worked with Natalia Dudinskaya, Konstantin Sergeyev, Birgit Cullberg, Anton Dolin, and Agnes de Mille. Her musicality and expressiveness brought her particular success in lyrical roles, and she was commended for her delicate and convincing interpretation of the Giselle role. She has choreographed a number of ballets to both Western and Romanian music, among them *Cinderella* to music by Gioachino Rossini;

ROMANIA: Theatrical Dance. Alexa Mezincescu, a soloist with the Bucharest Opera from 1953 to 1988, won admiration for her interpretation of the title role in *Giselle.* (Photograph courtesy of the Romanian Center for the International Theater Institute, Bucharest.)

Tristan and Iseult, Season of the Stags, Byzantine Poem, and *Ancient Courts* to music by Mihail Jora; *The Four Seasons* to Antonio Vivaldi's set of violin concertos; a version of Carl Orff's *Carmina Burana;* and a version of Igor Stravinsky's *Le Sacre du Printemps.*

Magdalena Popa, hailed as the epitome of the Romantic ballerina, studied at the Bucharest Choreography High School and the Vaganova Choreography School in Leningrad. She made her debut at the age of seventeen at the Kirov Theater, dancing as a first soloist in *Swan Lake* and *The Nutcracker.* As a *prima ballerina* of the Bucharest Opera from 1961 to 1982, when she chose to live in Canada, she danced all the classics and the Romanian works, such as Danovschi's *Iancu Jianu;* she also appeared in Danovshi's versions of *Carmen* (one of her greatest achievements), *The Miraculous Mandarin,* and *Petrouchka.* Frequently she danced abroad as a guest star with Ballet Théâtre Contemporain, Le Grand Ballet Classique de France, London Festival Ballet, and Ballets de Monte Carlo. Since 1982, she has been with Les Grands Ballets Canadiens, as ballet mistress.

Before 1990, the Romanian Opera of Bucharest's ballet company repertory with emphasis on national themes came from Romanian choreographers. They staged their own highly personal versions of the classics *Swan Lake, Coppélia,* and *Giselle* but also modern works, such as *Le Tricorne, The Stoneflower,* and *Carmen.* Major contributors to the company's repertory included Danovschi, Marcu, Urseanu, Mezincescu, and Ion Tugearu. These choreographers also produced a number of Romanian works, among them Marcu's *Miss Măriuţze,* Tugearu's *At the Market,* and Mezincescu's *Season of the Stags.* The company's ballet section had been headed for many years by Doina Andronache, with Marcu as master choreographer. After a brief period, in 1992 and 1993, when Ion Tugearu was the leader of the opera's ballet ensemble, it has been headed by the former *prima ballerina* Ileana Iliescu and Mihai Babuşka, a younger dancer.

The company toured mainly in the former Soviet Union, Spain, Portugal, Germany, the Netherlands, Italy, Poland, the former Czechoslovakia, Hungary, Bulgaria, Greece, France, Cuba, Mexico, Great Britain, and South Korea. It was highly praised for its performances at the Third International Festival of Dance in Paris in 1965, when the modern ballet *Le Marteau sans Maître,* to music by Pierre Boulez and choreography by Stere Popescu, one of the Romania's great dancers of that time, was a success.

As a choreographer, Ioan Tugearu—a very expressive dancer—has staged many ballets throughout Romania: *The Seagull,* to music by Roman Vlad, at the Iaşi Opera House; *Mass for the Young,* to Maurice Ravel's *Boléro,* at the Lyric Theater in Constantza; *Mediterranean Legends,* for Danovschi's company; and *Manfred,* to the Tchaikovsky symphony, for the Bucharest National Opera. His ballet version of *The Taming of the Shrew* successfully toured in Europe.

In 1968, the Experimental Studios of Dance was founded within traditional institutions such as opera and operetta houses. It has provided an outlet for innovative works ranging from classical ballets to expressionistic or abstract works. A wide variety of music was used, from Antonio Vivaldi to Alban Berg, Edgar Varese, Paul Hindemith, and contemporary Romanian composers. Among the new works presented by the Experimental Studios were *Izvoare şi Rădăcini* (Springs and Roots), which also displayed Tugearu's gifts as a dancer, and *Nunta Însângerată* (Blood Wedding), choreographed by Tugearu from Federico García Lorca's play.

Following a series of successful productions at the opera house in Iaşi (Jassy), the choreographer Mihaela Atanasiu organized a contemporary ballet ensemble at the operetta house in Bucharest. She created there *Viaţa, Dragostea Omului* (Life, Man's Love), *Nesfârşit Zborul Măiastrei* (Infinite, the Flight of the Magic Bird), and *Drumul Sângelui* (The Way of Blood), works that displayed her metaphorical vision, a keen sense of theater, and an ability to combine classical and modern movement with songs and words in highly expressive performances. The ensemble was much acclaimed abroad. With the Bucharest Opera House ballet ensemble, Atanasiu created *Peer Gynt* and *A Midsummer Night's Dream.* These were mounted again in the 1990s shortly before she died.

The Classical and Contemporary Ballet Ensemble, created and headed by Oleg Danovschi, was founded in 1979 in Constantza. It was originally called the Fantasio Theater (for the musical theater that hosted it); after more than a decade, it took the name of its founder. Its members, graduates of Romanian ballet schools, perform full-length classical ballets such as *The Nutcracker;* Romanian ballets such as Danovschi's *Vox Maris,* to music by George Enescu; and modern works such as *Study,* to rock music by Pink Floyd, or to symphonic works of folkloric inspiration such as those by George Enescu. Their repertory includes the world classics—*Swan Lake, The Sleeping Beauty, Carmen, Giselle, Romeo and Juliet, Coppélia, Cinderella*—all choreographed by Danovschi (1917–1996). They also present short works, such as *The Miraculous Mandarin* and *Schéhérazade,* as well as works created by guest choreographers, such as Adina Cezar and Ion Tugearu. The ensemble tours abroad regularly. The exactness of its corps de ballet, the prominence of its soloists, and the beauty of its stage direction have resulted in this company's reputation as one of the best in Romania. Among its soloists are Betty Manolache-Lux (until 1991, when she left for Germany), Călin and Delia Hanţiu, Felicia Şerbănescu, Traian Vlaş, Aliss Popescu, and Monica Bârlea.

In addition to ballet companies connected to large institutions, some smaller groups existed, such as Miriam Răducanu's. During her long career she presented, among other theatrical events, programs such as *Nocturnal 9½*. These intimate, humorous dialogues of music, verse, and movement—modern dance, jazz, and stylized Romanian folk dance—used fantasy to explore the varied experiences of human life. Gigi Căciuleanu, a member of Răducanu's early ensemble and a dancer with a classical background, after 1973 became one of France's most important choreographers. In 1984, Răducanu organized a series of multimedia shows, including acting, pantomime, dance, stage movement, lighting, and music. The performers were usually actors, as in *A World on Stage,* which was presented at the Bulandra Theater in Bucharest. Another of her creations, *On Jazz Themes,* was performed in 1991 by the professional dancers of the Orion Ballet company.

The Columna ensemble was founded and headed by Vera Proca Ciortea and featured former champions in gymnastics in her effort to integrate gymnastics and dance. The company had a tormented existence. It was called Gymnasion from 1974 to 1982, when most of its members defected to the West. Reborn and baptized Columna, from 1982 to 1990 it had all new members. This special genre—a blending of acrobatics, folklore, rhythm, and body expression—has not yet inspired similar companies in Romania.

The Contemp, a modern dance group, was started by Adina Cezar and Sergiu Anghel; it utilized European, Asian, and African styles of physical expression. Cezar, who studied ballet in Bucharest and modern dance with Yuriko, Glen Tetley, Donald McKayle, and Karin Waehner, has choreographed works characterized by a nervous, un-

ROMANIA: Theatrical Dance. Miriam Răducanu in *Scherzo,* a solo section, set to Mozart's music, from her larger work *Nocturnal 9½,* Bucharest, 1970. (Photograph courtesy of the Romanian Center for the International Theater Institute, Bucharest.)

ROMANIA: Theatrical Dance. Members of the Group Gymnasion, a dance company composed of former gymnastic champions, in a 1982 performance of *Intrecerea* (Contest), choreographed by Vera Proca-Ciortea to jazz music by Ramon Tavernier. (Photograph courtesy of the Romanian Center for the International Theater Institute, Bucharest.)

predictable rhythm with burlesque notes. Anghel trained at the ballet schools in Bucharest and Cluj, then studied university-level philology. His works tend to be symbolic and existential. The company has made many foreign tours, and both choreographers frequently serve as consultants in stage movement. After 1990 they parted, with Cezar remaining the leader of the Contemp company (functioning within the frame of the Ion Dacian operetta theater in Bucharest), for which she created most of the choreographies, such as *Fereastra Roz* (The Pink Window) and *Viaţa, O Călătoria I şi II* (Life, A Journey I and II). Her main dancer and closest collaborator is Liliana Iorgulescu, who is also a choreographer.

Sergiu Anghel took the lead of the Orion Ballet company in 1992. This was the first modern dance ensemble, founded by Ion Tugearu, after the 1989 anticommunist revolutions. Since then, he has styled personal features into his work and he has tried various experiences, such as dance theater *(Barococo Party)*, video-dance (*The Four Seasons* to Vivaldi's concertos), or stage movement *(Richard III)*.

In 1990, a department of choreography was created within the Academy of Theater and Film in Bucharest, offering a four-year course at university level to both ballet teachers and choreographers. Cormeliu Cezar, Sergiu Anghel, Raluca Ianegic, and Liliana Iorgulescu are staff members.

Raluca Ianegic, a graduate of the ballet school in Bucharest, was a former member of Răducanu's group. In 1980, she became a solo recitalist. Her choreographies displayed a very personal style, with simple yet dramatic self-oriented movements. In 1982, she was granted a U.S. International Communications Agency (USICA) scholarship to study modern dance in the United States. During that year she performed in Los Angeles, New York, and other American cities. From 1992 to 1995, she headed the Center of Artistic Expression, which she had founded within the Odeon Theater in Bucharest. At this multimedia laboratory she held workshops and was host to several important foreign choreographers.

Francisc Valkay, working mostly in Timişoara, has distinguished his choreography by a personal blend of neoclassical and modern styles. His ballet productions include *The Miraculous Mandarin, Daphnis and Chloe, Boléro, Andante-Allegro,* and *Les Petits Riens.* At the Magyar Opera in Cluj-Napoca he produced, among others, *Romantic Waltzes* to music by Chopin, and he toured in France with *A Strauss Waltz Evening.* He toured Europe with *The Nutcracker.*

Before the 1989 political changes, several festivals offered performing opportunities and prizes to Romanian dancers. Founded in 1979, the National Festival of Art and Creation's Cântarea României (Song to Romania) was a large-scale annual venue for amateur and professional creators in all the art forms. Prizes were given to the most successful ballet works in Romania, based on socialist standards. The Panorama of Contemporary Ballet was held in Focşani from 1981 to 1985 and in Bucharest in 1986, a spectacle coordinated by the Association of the Artists in the Theater and Music Institutions in Romania (ATM). Its aim was to promote and encourage new elements in Romanian ballet.

Since 1990 many things have changed, mostly for the better. In classical dance, the ensembles of both opera houses and lyrical theaters were largely rejuvenated by the lowering of the retirement age. The place of the renowned *prima ballerinas* of the 1970s was taken by a multitude of younger dancers, such as Simona

ROMANIA: Theatrical Dance. A scene from Sergiu Anghel's dance theater work *Barococo Party,* set to music by Royou y Le Mée, at the Odeon Theater in Bucharest, 1996. (Photograph courtesy of the Romanian Center for the International Theater Institute, Bucharest.)

ROMANIA: Theatrical Dance. Mihai Mihalcea in his and Florin Fieroiu's *Suspinul* (The Sigh), in a 1996 performance in Bucharest. Mihalcea and Fieroiu are two of the founders of Marginalii (Outsiders), an experimental dance company based at the National Opera. (Photograph courtesy of the Romanian Center for the International Theater Institute, Bucharest.)

Şomăcescu, Anne-Marie Vretos, Doina Axinte, Corina Dumitrescu, Cristina Crăciun, Mihai Babuşka and others.

Unfortunately, many dancers left the country, this time on a legal contract basis. Some of the older ones became teachers in various European countries; some of the younger ones are gaining fame for the theaters and countries in which they dance. At this writing (1996), Simona Noja and Laurenţiu Guinea are in Düsseldorf, Alma Munteanu is in Berlin. Gheorghe Iancu has for a long time been one of Italy's soloists and a partner of the renowned Carla Fracci.

From 1991 to 1993 in Romania, a cultural project involved some twelve French touring companies of contemporary dance. Most also held workshops. Called *La Danse en Voyage* (Dance on a Journey), this project was important for the further development of modern dance in Romania, especially for younger dancers. At the same time, the New Wave creators emerged, most of whom are graduates of the choreography department of the Artists in the Theater and Music Institutions. Florin Fieroiu, Cosmin Manolescu, Mihai Mihalcea, and Irina Costea founded the Marginalii group (The Outsiders), to give performances in which each was both a dancer and an author. In 1996, Cosmin Manolescu also proposed a more restrained formula (himself and a female dancer) called Studio DCM. One of the most promising young choreographers and directors, Răzvan Mazilu, an outstanding dancer himself, creates most dance-theater events, working mainly with professional actors and amateur dancers.

Since 1990, the Union of Performers, Choreographers, and Musical Critics (UICCM), has awarded prizes to the best performers, choreographers, and ballet critics. Also since 1990, an annual Festival of Contemporary Dance has been held in Jassy, gathering the most interesting achievements of the genre and hosting foreign companies touring in Romania. In Constantza, the Opera and Ballet Festival has been held annually for over two decades. Since 1994, the National Competition for Young Dancers (both classical and modern) has taken place; founded by the late Oleg Danovschi, it was given his name as a token of gratitude for this "Patriarch of Romanian dance."

More state-subsidized ballet schools have been founded in some of the main towns, yet among the younger generation there is an ever-expanding taste for contemporary dance. There is also a trend toward theatrical experiments, dance workshops, and movement creativity.

[*See also the entries on Danovschi and Proca Ciortea.*]

BIBLIOGRAPHY

Balcar, J. Alexander. *Knaurs Ballet Lexikon.* Zurich, 1958.

Baril, Jacques. *Dictionnaire de danse.* Paris, 1964.

Cantemir, Dimitrie. *Descriptio Moldaviae* (1716). Bucharest, 1956.

Cosma, Octavian L. *Opera românescă.* 2 vols. Bucharest, 1962.

Cosma, Viorel. *Exegeze muzicologice: File din istoria baletului autohton.* Bucharest, 1984.

Curasru, Lucian. *Argonautii marilor iubiri.* Bucharest, 1987.

Gheorghe, Aglaia. "A Romanian Ballerina Speaks of Revolution." *Dance Magazine* (April 1990): 18–19.

Goritz, Helmut. "Das Ballett in Rumänian." *Das Tanzarchiv* 17 (October 1969): 129–133.

Massoff, Ioan. *Teatrul românesc.* 8 vols. Bucharest, 1961–1981.

Negry, Gabriel. *Memoria dansului.* Bucharest, 1986.

Preda, Tea. "Du ballet contemporain roumain." *Revue Roumaine,* no. 3 (1980).

Siegfried, W. *Theatre, Opera, Ballet in Romania* (in English). Bucharest, 1957.

Urseanu, Tilde, et al. *Istoria baletului.* Bucharest, 1967.

TEA PREDA and VIVIA SĂNDULESCU

Folk Dance Research and Publication

Research on Romanian folk dances began prior to World War II but the scientific basis was later established by the musicologist and folklorist, Constantin Brăiloiu (1893–1958). His most important works on music for Romanian folk dances were *Le rhythme akasak* (1951) and *Le giusto syllabique: Un système rhythmique roumain* (1952).

The Folklore Institute was established in Bucharest in 1949 during a time when the study of folk dance was a focus throughout much of Europe. Following the principles of Brăiloiu, the Institute studied folk dance as a complex phenomenon deeply involved in the traditional life of Romanian villages. A disciple of Brailoiu, Vera Proca Ciortea joined the Institute in 1951, where she defined and developed Romanian ethnochoreology. During this initial period, four goals were formulated: to organize a professional organization; to create working tools that would be specific to research in the field of folk dance; to build a corpus of documented research; and to collect and anaylze folk dances.

In 1963 the Folklore Institute was renamed the Ethnography and Folklore Institute and the Institute went under the aegis of Academia Română (Romanian Academy). This began a new stage of development in Romanin ethnochoreology as a distinct and consolidated discipline. The goals included analysis of the choreographical structure of Romanian folk dances, evaluation of historical documents, and determination of specific regional and national manifestations and typological classification of folk dance. In 1974 the Institute became the Ethnology and Dialectology Research Institute and, in 1990, two separate institutions were created, the Ethnography and Folklore Institute "Constantin Brăiloiu" and the National Center for the Conservation and Promotion of Folk Creation. The former continues its scientific research and the latter promotes folklore.

After forty-five years of research, conservation, and promotion of folklore, Romanian ethnochoreology has made important contributions. More than 580 investigations have been made in 462 villages throughout Romania; 11,000 choreographical variants have been recorded and notated after Vera Proca Ciortea's system or in Labanotation as well as recorded on film. Thousands of photographs have been set up as the Arhiva Natională de Folclor (National Folklore Archives) and eleven printed volumes or works of collections or monographs and more than 250 studies and articles found in scientific or cultural publications in Romania and abroad are available. Important researchers in this fileld are Vera Proca Ciortea, Anca Giurchescu, Emanuela Balaci, Andrei Bucșan, and Constantin Costea.

CONSTANTIN COSTEA

ROMANOFF, DIMITRI (born 1907 in Tsaritsin, Russia, died 6 February 1994 in Saint Helena, California), dancer, ballet master, and *régisseur.* The Romanoff family left Russia after the 1917 Revolution, fleeing the country through Siberia and Mongolia. They settled in Yokohama, Japan, where Dimitri was placed in a French school. In Japan, he saw Anna Pavlova perform, and this experience ignited his early interest in dance. He went to the San Francisco area in 1924 and studied engineering at Stanford University while simultaneously taking ballet classes with Theodore Koslov. Among his other teachers was Michel Fokine.

In the early 1930s, Romanoff performed with the San Francisco Opera Ballet under Adolph Bolm and with the Pavley-Oukrainsky Company. In 1935, he appeared in Max Reinhardt's film *A Midsummer Night's Dream* opposite the French ballerina Nini Theilade and subsequently went on a concert tour with her. In 1937, Romanoff joined the Mordkin Ballet as a soloist. His roles included Prince Desiré in *The Sleeping Beauty,* Colin in *Naughty Lisette,* Hilarion in *Giselle,* and the Poet in *Les Sylphides.* In 1940 he joined Ballet Theatre as a charter member, becoming *régisseur* in 1946 and remaining with the company until 1959. He created the role of Friar Laurence in Antony Tudor's *Romeo and Juliet* (1943), among others, and also danced in *Dark Elegies, Bluebeard, Helen of Troy,* and *Petrouchka.*

Responsible for the staging of many ballets, Romanoff was also a valued coach who encouraged individuality and expressiveness in his dancers. John Martin once wrote in the *New York Times* that Romanoff should be brought onstage for a bow after performances he had supervised so well. Among his major successes was his lively staging of *La Fille Mal Gardée,* modeled closely on the Maryinsky version he himself had learned from Mikhail Mordkin.

BIBLIOGRAPHY

Hering, Doris. "'Violette Lunaire.'" *Dance Magazine* (April 1962): 38–42.

Ostlere, Hilary B. "Keepers of the Flame: Ballet Masters and/or Regisseurs." *Dance Magazine* (October 1975): 72–73.

Obituary. *The Dancing Times* (July 1994): 999.

PATRICIA BARNES

ROMANOV, BORIS (Boris Georgievich Romanov; born 10 [22] March 1891 in Saint Petersburg, died 30 January 1957 in New York City), Russian-American dancer, choreographer, and ballet master. A graduate of the Imperial Ballet School, where he studied with Mikhail Obukhov and Michel Fokine, Boris Romanov entered the Maryinsky corps de ballet in 1909. He revealed great brilliance as a character dancer, both in the traditional repertory (where his roles included the Jester in *The Nutcracker* and the Negro in *La Fille du Pharaon*) and in Michel Fokine's works, above all as the Polovtsian Chief in *Prince Igor.* His choreographic career began in Saint Petersburg with the mime drama *The Hand* (1911) and the pantomime *Nocturne for a Blind Pierrot* (1912), both created for the Litny Miniature Theater troupe.

Without relinquishing his connection with the Maryinsky, where he received the title of *premier danseur* in 1914, Romanov performed with Serge Diaghilev's Ballets Russes from 1910 to 1914, appearing in the major Fokine ballets and choreographing *La Tragédie de Salomé* (1913) and *Le Rossignol* (1914). Appointed ballet master by the

Maryinsky at the beginning of World War I, he staged numerous opera *divertissements* while also choreographing experimental works for the Litny Miniature Theater. Settling in Berlin in 1921, he founded the Russian Romantic Theater, which had as its principal dancers his wife Elena Smirnova, Alice Nikitina, Claudia Pavlova, Anatole Oboukhoff, and Elsa Kruger. Between 1922 and 1926 the company presented several of his works, in addition to a much-admired *Giselle* (Paris, 1924).

After the demise of the Russian Romantic Theater, Romanov became one of the most accomplished and sought-after opera ballet choreographers of his generation, serving as ballet master at Teatro alla Scala in Milan (1926, 1934), the Teatro Colón in Buenos Aires (1928–1934), the Teatro Reale dell'Opera di Roma (1934–1938), and the Metropolitan Opera in New York City (1938–1942, 1945–1950). He was also associated with various ballet companies, including the Ballet de l'Opéra Russe à Paris, the Anna Pavlova company, the Marquis de Cuevas's Ballet International, and Sergei Denham's Ballet Russe de Monte Carlo.

A disciple of Fokine, whose ballets in the 1910s and 1920s bore the imprint of modernism, Romanov brought to his later work few of the innovative qualities that had distinguished his earlier compositions. Nevertheless, in productions such as the *Orfeo* he staged during his first Metropolitan season, he often achieved, as Lillian Moore wrote, "a rare and memorable harmony between movement and music."

BIBLIOGRAPHY

Garafola, Lynn. *Diaghilev's Ballets Russes.* New York and Oxford, 1989.

Krasovskaya, Vera. *Russkii baletnyi teatr nachala dvadtatogo veka,* vol. 1, *Khoreografy.* Leningrad, 1971.

Levinson, André. "Les ballets romantiques russes." *La danse* (April 1924).

Mara, Thalia. "Boris Romanoff: In Memoriam." *Dance Magazine* (March 1957): 21.

Moore, Lillian. "The Metropolitan Opera Ballet Story." *Dance Magazine* (January 1951): 20–29.

Nikitina, Alice. *Nikitina, by Herself.* Translated by Baroness Budberg. London, 1959.

Shaïkevitch, André. "Le 'théâtre romantique russe.'" *Archives internationales de la danse* (October 1934): 136–138.

LYNN GARAFOLA

ROMEO AND JULIET. The story of Romeo Montague and Juliet Capulet, "a pair of star-cross'd lovers" whose fate is sealed by the enmity of their respective families, is told in one of the best-loved plays of William Shakespeare. Written in the late sixteenth century (1594–1595), Shakespeare's romantic tragedy has proved irresistible to twentieth-century choreographers. Right behind *The Nutcracker* in popularity, *Romeo and Juliet* is in the repertory of almost every established ballet company, earning it the nickname of "a warm-weather *Nutcracker*" by *Los Angeles Times* critic Lewis Segal.

Because *Romeo and Juliet,* unlike most other full-length ballets, is based on a well-known literary masterpiece, choreographers can go back to a renewable source for artistic inspiration quite independent from previous choreographies. The shifting focus of the literary narrative from the public world of Verona to the private, increasingly restricted world of the lovers presents any number of interpretive challenges to choreographers. Shakespeare's play also provides a number of supporting characters (The Nurse, Tybalt, Mercutio, Lady Capulet) who flesh out the narrative and illuminate the background of its protagonists.

The first ballet about the star-crossed lovers—at least, the first one of historical significance—was *Romeo og Julie,* created in 1811 for the Royal Danish Ballet by August Bournonville's predecessor Vincenzo Galleotti. Possibly inspired by the same sixteenth-century Italian novella that served as a model to Shakespeare and other writers—Luigi da Porto's *Ritrovata di Due Nobili Amante Jiulietta i Roméo*—Galleotti created his five-act, largely mimed tragedy to a score for chorus and orchestra composed by Claus Schall.

In the twentieth century, *Romeo and Juliet* has most often been choreographed to the 1935 score by Sergei Prokofiev, although some productions have used music by other composers, notably Petr Ilich Tchaikovsky, Hector Berlioz, and Frederick Delius. Prokofiev's score is a powerful work of vibrant musical imagery, clashing tonalities, and narrative pull. Written shortly after his return from Paris to the Soviet Union, the music synthesizes the sophistication of the Parisian Saisons Russes mounted by Serge Diaghilev with the melodic lyricism and realism favored by the Soviet regime. While this score offers choreographers bold characterizations and dramatic emotions, it can be something of a straitjacket because of its strongly suggestive visual imagery—a skill Prokofiev acquired writing music for films—and the tightness of its programmatic structure.

The idea for a new ballet on *Romeo and Juliet* was conceived by Sergei Radlov, a Russian theatrical director, who arranged for a commission in early 1935 for Prokofiev from the Bolshoi Theater. Prokofiev and Radlov began work on the libretto together and were eventually joined by the choreographer Leonid Lavrovsky and the playwright Adrien Piotrovsky. The original scenario, later changed, had included a happy ending, partly because, as Prokofiev said, "the dead cannot dance" but also because socialist realism demanded uplifting final messages. The latter requirement was to be fulfilled by having the two clans, the Montagues and the Capulets, reconcile over the bodies of their children.

Problems in the scenario were not, however, the only ones encountered. When Prokofiev delivered his score, it was rejected by the artistic direction of the Bolshoi Theater as "undanceable." Consequently, the first production to use his music took place not in Russia but in Czechoslovakia, with choreography not by Lavrovsky but by Ivo Váňa Psota. [*See the entry on Prokofiev.*]

Psota Version. Czech title: *Romeo a Julie: Devet Tanechnich Scen o Velike Lasce* (Dance Pictures on a Great Love). Ballet in nine scenes with a prologue and an epilogue. Choreography: Váňa Psota. Music: Sergei Prokofiev; Suites 1 and 2 from a score for an unrealized ballet, *Romeo and Juliet.* Scenery and costumes: Václav Skrušny. First performance: 30 December 1938, Brno State Theater for Opera and Ballet. Principals: Váňa Psota (Romeo), Zora Šemberová (Juliet), Jan Sokol (Mercutio), Arnost Krap (Tybalt), Olrich Nápravil (Benvolio), Marie Zavadiková (Nurse), Mirka Figarová (Chorus), Mimi Mitysková and Vera Olsovská (Angels).

After the Bolshoi's rejection of Prokofiev's score in 1935 as "undanceable," the composer made two suites from it that were broadcast on Czech radio in 1938. It is possible that Prokofiev met Ivo Váňa Psota at that time; they may have also met at some time earlier, while Psota was performing with Colonel W. de Basil's Ballets Russes (1932–1936). For his choreography to the Prokofiev suites, Psota worked in a strongly modernist tradition, emphasizing two-dimensional, stylized ballet combinations and expressionistic mime. He dispensed with large crowd scenes but included a female figure as the Chorus, who commented on the action, and two Angels in the prologue and the epilogue. Šemberová, who had studied modern dance with Rosalia Chladek, convinced Psota to let her choreograph her own solos and to let her dance Juliet in soft slippers to underline the youthfulness of the role.

Lavrovsky Version. Russian title: *Romeo i Dzhulietta.* Choreography: Leonid Lavrovsky. Music: Sergei Prokofiev. Libretto: Leonid Lavrovsky, Sergei Prokofiev, Sergei Radlov, and Adrien Piotrovsky, after Shakespeare. Scenery and costumes: Petr Williams. First performance: 11 January 1940, Kirov Theater for Opera and Ballet, Leningrad. Principals: Konstantin Sergeyev (Romeo), Galina Ulanova (Juliet), Andrei Lopukhov (Mercutio), Robert Gerbek (Tybalt). Restaged: 28 December 1946,

ROMEO AND JULIET. Act 2, scene 3, of the Lavrovsky version, produced at Moscow's Bolshoi Theater in 1946. Aleksei Yermolayev as Tybalt and Mikhail Gabovich as Romeo struggle at center stage. (Photograph from the A. A. Bakrushin Central State Theatrical Museum, Moscow.)

ROMEO AND JULIET. Galina Ulanova as Juliet in the Lavrovsky version, at the Bolshoi Theater, 1946. Ulanova first danced Juliet in 1940, when Lavrovsky created the work for the Kirov Ballet in Leningrad. Many balletomanes believe that her interpretation of the role has never been surpassed. (Photograph from the Dance Collection, New York Public Library for the Performing Arts.)

Bolshoi Theater, Moscow. Principals: Mikhail Gabovich (Romeo), Galina Ulanova (Juliet), Sergei Koren (Mercutio), Aleksei Yermolayev (Tybalt).

For his production, Lavrovsky chose to emphasize romanticized spectacle, setting the Shakespearean tale in broad strokes, with huge crowds and realistic street and fighting scenes. His Verona is one of coarse brutality and feudal repression, which have fatally infected even personal and family relationships, one example of which is the incestuous relationship between Lady Capulet and Tybalt. Against these forces of corruption, the lovers cannot prevail. With the exception of some lively folk dances and a few ballet sequences given to Juliet, this version relied heavily on pantomime and cinematic sweep to sustain its dramatic narrative.

Even though Lavrovsky and Prokofiev agreed on the basic realism of the ballet, its creation had been fraught with conflict. Prokofiev was initially resistant to requests that he expand the score, but he eventually agreed to add more music and to enlarge the orchestration. The dancers, on their part, reluctantly realized that the music was not so "undanceable" as at first they had thought. Galina Ulanova, especially, developed an acute sensitivity to the music, and her interpretation of Juliet became a sublime model against which all subsequent performers would be measured.

It was the Lavrovsky version of *Romeo and Juliet*, created in the middle of the gathering storm of World War II, that stunned western European audiences when the Bolshoi Ballet performed it in London on its first engagement there in 1956. Preceded by a much-praised 1955 film version, the London performances assured it permanent recognition as an archetypal representative of Soviet-style ballet. The Lavrovsky production also started a fascination with Romeo and his bride, Juliet, and with the Prokofiev score, by choreographers working in western Europe, resulting in major productions by John Cranko (1962), Kenneth MacMillan (1965), John Neumeier (1971), and Rudolf Nureyev (1977). A remarkable exception to the influence of the Lavrovsky version was a production mounted to an excerpted Prokofiev score by Frederick Ashton for the Royal Danish Ballet in 1955.

Ashton Version. Danish title: *Romeo og Julie*. Choreography: Frederick Ashton. Music: Sergei Prokofiev. Libretto: Frederick Ashton, after Shakespeare. Ten scenes and an epilogue. Scenery and costumes: Peter Rice. First performance: 19 May 1955, Royal Theater, Copenhagen, Royal Danish Ballet. Principals: Henning Kronstam (Romeo), Mona Vangsaae (Juliet), Frank Schaufuss (Mercutio), Flemming Flindt (Benvolio), Niels Bjørn Larsen (Tybalt), Britta Cornlius-Knudsen (Nurse), Kjeld Noack (Paris), Kirsten Ralov (Rosaline), Lillian Jensen (Lady Capulet). Restaged, as *Romeo and Juliet*, by Niels Bjørn Larsen, supervised by Frederick Ashton: 23 July 1985, Coliseum, London, London Festival Ballet. New scenery and costumes: Peter Rice. Lighting: Jennifer Tipton. Principals: Peter Schaufuss (Romeo), Katherine Healey (Juliet), Raffaele Paganini (Mercutio), Nicholas Johnson (Tybalt), Kirsten Ralov (Lady Capulet), Niels Bjørn Larsen (Lord Capulet), Patrick Armand (Paris), Frank Schaufuss (Prince of Verona).

In 1955, as the Lavrovsky production of *Romeo* had yet to be seen in the West, Frederick Ashton's eyes were unencumbered when he approached Prokofiev's music. He cut and rearranged the score—down to ten scenes and an epilogue—and set it as a classical ballet. Taking his cue from the lyricism of Shakespeare's text, Ashton refocused the story on the growing relationship between the high-spirited young lovers. Central to the ballet are three lyrical pas de deux for Romeo and Juliet that trace their maturing love. Far from a heroic setting, Ashton conceived of his Verona as inhabited by recognizable human beings whose misfortune is to get caught up in events beyond their control.

Although Ashton took advantage of the Danes' excellence in mime to advance his narrative, in his *Romeo* people express themselves primarily through movement, often flavored by the modesty and feathery footwork of the Bournonville tradition. Harkening back to Petipa, Ashton's work abounds with formal ensemble numbers: for the townspeople, for Juliet and her friends, for Paris and his kinsmen, for Romeo and his friends, for the Capulets and their guests at the ball. Even the fight scenes are carefully choreographed. Since an excess of passion, not clan hostility, precipitated the tragedy, Ashton deemed a reconciliation at the tomb unnecessary, and the ballet ends with the deaths of the lovers.

Cranko Version. Original Italian title: *Romeo e Giulietta.* Choreography: John Cranko. Music: Sergei Prokofiev. Libretto: John Cranko, after Shakespeare. Scenery and costumes: Nicola Benois. First performance: 26 July 1958, Teatro Verde, Venice, La Scala Ballet. Principals: Mario Pistoni (Romeo), Carla Fracci (Juliet). Restaged and revised by John Cranko as *Romeo und Julia:* 2 December 1962, Württemberg State Theater, Stuttgart Ballet. Scenery and costumes: Jürgen Rose. Principals: Ray Barra (Romeo), Marcia Haydée (Juliet), Egon Madsen (Paris), Ken Barlow (Tybalt), Hugo Delavalle (Mercutio).

Aided by a simple, flexible set, Cranko's version moves as a series of action-packed encounters in which the lovers are part of the social whirl in a fast-paced Verona. In portraying a vivid picture of a specific society Cranko leaned heavily on Lavrovsky, although without the latter's sense of oppressiveness. Some of his choreography, such as the Cushion Dance, for example, closely imitates that of Lavrovsky. Still, there are significant differences. Cranko's Lord Capulet is no tyrant; he is a civilized host and an understanding though puzzled husband and father. Juliet undergoes less of a maturing than in other versions, nor do these lovers immediately seem destined for each other. Borrowing from Shakespeare, Cranko introduced Rosaline as an object of flirtation for Romeo, and Juliet at first is quite flattered by Paris's attention. Cranko introduced a new ending: Romeo does not die by poison but stabs himself to death. Juliet then uses the dead Paris's sword to kill herself.

ROMEO AND JULIET. In 1963, Anna Lærkesen and Ole Fatum appeared in the title roles of the Ashton version, staged for the Royal Danish Ballet in 1955. Standing on the steps behind Lærkesen are Lillian Jensen and Svend Erik Jensen as Lady and Lord Capulet. (Photograph © by Rigmor Mydtskov; used by permission.)

Cranko's version is notable for its spirited and detailed crowd scenes, realistic fights, and the interplay between the main characters and the members of the ensemble. It has been restaged for numerous companies all over the world, including the National Ballet of Canada (1964), the Bavarian National Ballet of the Munich Opera (1968), the Australian Ballet (1974), the Frankfurt Ballet, with revisions by Egon Madsen (1981), the Scottish Ballet (1982), and the Paris Opera Ballet (1983), where the opening-night cast was headed by Michaël Denard as Romeo and Noëlla Pontois as Juliet. The first performance by an American company was given by the Joffrey Ballet in New York on 12 December 1978.

MacMillan Version. Choreography: Kenneth MacMillan. Music: Sergei Prokofiev. Libretto: Kenneth MacMillan, after Shakespeare. Scenery and costumes: Nicholas Georgiadis. Lighting: William Bundy. First performance: 9 February 1965, Royal Opera House, Covent Garden, London, Royal Ballet. Principals: Rudolf Nureyev (Romeo), Margot Fonteyn (Juliet), David Blair (Mercutio), Desmond Doyle (Tybalt), Anthony Dowell (Benvolio), Gerd Larsen (Nurse), Ronald Hynd (Friar Laurence), Julia Farron (Lady Capulet), Michael Somes (Lord Capulet), Derek Rencher (Paris).

ROMEO AND JULIET. Lynn Seymour and Christopher Gable in the title roles of the MacMillan version, created for the Royal Ballet in 1965. (Photograph from the Dance Collection, New York Public Library for the Performing Arts.)

When Kenneth MacMillan decided to choreograph *Romeo and Juliet,* his first full-length ballet, he had to do so against the background of the Lavrovsky, Ashton, and Cranko versions. Not surprisingly, traces of all three of them can be found in his interpretation. Nevertheless, he did give the ballet his own personal stamp. Taking a cue from Shakespeare, MacMillan shaped his ballet so that everything is focused on the maturing relationship between Romeo and Juliet. A dreamlike quietness envelops them, and is often expressed in stillness: Juliet playing Romeo's lute during the ballroom scene; watching each other at the beginning of the balcony scene; Romeo observing a MacMillan-inserted wedding celebration and dreaming of his own wedding; Juliet overwhelmed, sitting on her bed after Romeo leaves.

While there is plenty of rambunctiousness and pagentry in this Verona, the public dances and the fight scenes are controlled and formalized into ensemble numbers. There is a restraint to this production that some have called characteristic of British dance. Yet at its core beats a palpitating heart with an expansive lyricism that soars even as it remains achingly intimate. That is why the tragedy of this *Romeo and Juliet* is, ultimately, a private affair.

After the opening night, the roles of Juliet and Romeo were danced by Lynn Seymour and Christopher Gable, for whom MacMillan created them, Merle Park and Donald MacLeary, and Antoinette Sibley and Anthony Dowell. Other notable couples to dance these roles were Georgina Parkinson and Jonas Kåge, in the 1969 production by the Royal Swedish Ballet, and Leslie Browne and Robert La Fosse in the 1985 production by American Ballet Theatre.

Neumeier Version. German title: *Romeo und Julia.* Choreography: John Neumeier. Music: Sergei Prokofiev. Libretto: John Neumeier, after Shakespeare. Scenery: Filippo Sanjust. First performance: 14 February 1971, Städtische Bühnen, Frankfurt am Main. Principals: Lloyd Riggins (Romeo), Henriette Muus (Juliet).

Taking his inspiration from the "Don't trust anyone over thirty" movement of the 1960s, Neumeier made his *Romeo and Juliet* with a strong focus on the protagonists' youth and budding sexuality. We first see Juliet rushing out wrapped in a bath towel; Romeo is discovered sleeping on the steps of the Capulet's house. These are young people in the middle of a rebellious adolescence; they and their companions are as likable in their impetuousness as they are awkward in their lack of experience. This is a sexually charged production that enlarges on the Lavrovsky-inspired incestuous relationship between Lady Capulet and Tybalt.

ROMEO AND JULIET. Nora Kaye (at left of center) and Hugh Laing in a scene from Tudor's version, created for Ballet Theatre in 1943. (Photograph from the Dance Collection, New York Public Library for the Performing Arts.)

Borrowing the play-within-the play device from *Hamlet,* Neumeier introduced a troupe of wandering actors who pantomime the narrative for the audience. He also employed the innovative idea of giving Juliet a drug-induced vision of Romeo and Tybalt after she swallows the sleeping potion. For his production, Neumeier used a simple set that can be transformed by means of moving panels. As much a response to Shakespeare's text as to Prokofiev's score, his version relies less on pure dance than on dramatic gesture and everyday movement.

Tudor Version. Full title: *The Tragedy of Romeo and Juliet.* Choreography: Antony Tudor. Music: Frederick Delius, arranged by Antal Dorati; "Eventyr," "Over the Hills and Far Away," "Brigg Fair," "The Walk to the Paradise Garden," "Prelude to Irmelin." Libretto: Antony Tudor, after Shakespeare. Scenery and costumes: Eugene Berman. First performance: 6 April 1943 (incomplete); 10 April 1943 (complete), Metropolitan Opera House, New York, Ballet Theatre. Principals: Hugh Laing (Romeo), Alicia Markova (Juliet), Nicholas Orloff (Mercutio), Jerome Robbins (Benvolio), Antony Tudor (Tybalt), Sono Osato (Rosaline), Lucia Chase (Nurse). Restaged: 30 December 1962, Royal Theater, Stockholm, Royal Swedish Ballet. Principals: Conny Borg (Romeo), Berit Sköld (Juliet). Revived: 22 July 1971, New York State Theater, American Ballet Theatre. Scenery and costumes: Eugene Berman. Lighting: Nananne Porcher. Principals: Hugh Laing (Romeo), Alicia Markova (Juliet).

Ballet Theatre had been interested in mounting a production of *Romeo and Juliet* to Prokofiev's score with choreography by Michel Fokine. When this work did not materialize, the subject was given to Antony Tudor, who rejected the Prokofiev score in favor of a selection of orchestral works by Delius. Tudor also rejected designs that had been commissioned from Salvador Dali, insisting instead that the ballet be designed by Eugene Berman, who created a set and costumes inspired by Renaissance paintings. As always, Tudor worked slowly on the ballet, so slowly that it was not finished on the first night; the complete work was danced four nights later.

Berman's designs perfectly melded with Tudor's stylized choreography, which he had based on Renaissance postures and dancing patterns. Tudor compressed the story and drew out its essence with small but telling details. By allowing for simultaneity of action, he was able to create a rich and densely moving tapestry out of which characters emerged and receded very much in the Elizabethan spirit of Shakespeare's play. Tudor also tailored the action to the music in masterly fashion. Edwin Denby described the ballet as a "reverie" or meditation on the play, and the music enhanced this quality in the choreography, the sense that all is suspended in a timeless trance.

Unique among choreographers, Tudor kept the lovers apart during the balcony scene. They never touched but mimed to each other, oblivious to the swirling nighttime adventures of Verona's citizens around them. Tudor also changed the ending by having Juliet revive before Romeo dies. Like the symbols of love they have become, they address the audience before he collapses and she then kills herself.

Béjart Version. French title: *Roméo et Juliette.* Choreography: Maurice Béjart. Music: Hector Berlioz, op. 17, and sound collages. Scenery: Germinal Casado. First performance: 17 November 1966, Cirque Royal, Brussels, Ballet du XXe Siècle.

Created in the middle of the Vietnam War era, Béjart's *Romeo and Juliet* is a reflection of the popular "Make love, not war" slogan of the period. Set to the powerful *symphonie dramatique* for chorus and orchestra composed by Berlioz in 1839, supplemented by an electronic sound score, the work was designed as a visually impressive spectacle to be performed in large public spaces and popular venues, such as a circus, a sports arena, or the Boboli Gardens in Florence, where it was also filmed.

ROMEO AND JULIET. Sean Lavery and Suzanne Farrell in the production mounted by Paul Mejia for the Chicago Lyric Ballet in 1979. Using the Tchaikovsky score, Mejia had created his work for Ballet Guatemala in 1978. (Photograph © 1979 by Max Waldman; used by permission.)

Béjart staged this *Romeo and Juliet* as an "us"-against-"them" parable in which competing power blocs, as represented by the feuding families, manage to kill off everyone. Shakespeare's Mab is used here not as a mischievous fairy queen but as a virago who inflames the passions of conflict and war. The choreography, which has been described as "like a frieze in constant motion," is severely symmetrical and geometric. Béjart framed the work as a rehearsal with himself as the ballet master. In the end he resurrects the lovers who unite for the first time in the middle of the crashing sounds of war.

Other Versions. Countless other choreographic versions of the story of Romeo and Juliet have been presented by dance companies worldwide. Among the more notable are the following. (1) Bronislava Nijinska's 1926 version, set to a score by Constant Lambert, for the Ballets Russes de Serge Diaghilev, featured an entr'acte by George Balanchine in which only the legs of the dancers were visible from a half-lowered curtain. (2) Balanchine also designed a happy-ending *Romeo and Juliet Ballet,* with tap-dancing Capulets and toe-dancing Montagues, for the 1938 Hollywood film *The Goldwyn Follies.* The ballet music was by Vernon Duke; William Dollar and Vera Zorina were Romeo and Juliet; and the Ritz Brothers were notable standouts among the Capulets. (3) Also in 1938 Willam Christensen, using Tchaikovsky's Fantasy Overture, choreographed the first American *Romeo and Juliet,* a one-act version for the San Francisco Opera Ballet, with Janet Reed dancing Juliet.

(4) About twenty years later, in 1957, Jerome Robbins electrified Broadway audiences with his choreography for *West Side Story,* a modern version of the tragedy of Romeo and Juliet set to the music of Leonard Bernstein. Among the dancers were Chita Rivera, George Chakiris, and Eliot Feld; Chakiris and Feld repeated their roles in the 1961 Hollywood film. (5) The first American production to Prokofiev's ballet score was by Nicholas Petrov for Pittsburgh Ballet Theatre in 1971. (6) But it was Michael Smuin's rollicking 1976 version, mounted for the San Francisco Ballet and subsequently translated for the television series *Dance in America,* that started a flood of *Romeo*s in the United States. In Smuin's production, Evelyn Cisneros created the role of Juliet.

(7) The following year, in 1977, Rudolf Nureyev created a fate-ridden, gloom-filled version for the London Festival Ballet in which dream figures interact with the protagonists. Scenery and costumes were designed by Ezio Frigerio. Patricia Ruanne danced Juliet to Nureyev's Romeo. (8) In 1978, Oscar Araiz mounted a new version of his earlier (1970) choreographic interpretation of *Romeo and Juliet* for the Joffrey Ballet, featuring three Juliets to indi-

ROMEO AND JULIET. Elizabeth Olds as Juliet, c.1992, in the production mounted by Rudi van Dantzig for the Royal Winnipeg Ballet in 1981. (Photograph by David Cooper; used by permission.)

cate the heroine's maturing process. (9) In 1979, in Moscow, Yuri Grigorovich replaced the mime-laden, realistic Lavrovsky version for the Bolshoi Ballet with one that brims with dance steps but whose characters lack emotional motivation. The lackluster roles of Romeo and Juliet were danced by Viacheslav Gordeyev and Natalia Bessmertnova.

(10) Using a collage of Tchaikovsky pieces, Kent Stowell in 1991 replaced the ballet's social and political context with a religious framework in his version for Pacific Northwest Ballet. (11) The Ballet de Lyon's 1990 fierce, deconstructed *Roméo et Juliette* by Angelin Preljocaj is a savage take on the modern police state. (12) In New York City in 1992, Francis Patrelle proved that even chamber ensembles can create an effective *Romeo*. In his production for Dances . . . Patrelle, he filled his Verona with street urchins (students from his school) to emphasize that in social clashes and family feuds children are the real victims.

BIBLIOGRAPHY

Acocella, Joan. "Ashton's *Romeo:* A Wise Virgin." *Ballet Review* 13.3 (Fall 1985): 60–67.

Anderson, Jack. "The View from the House Opposite." *Ballet Review* 4.6 (1974): 14–23.

Anderson, Jack. "Complex Edifices/Edifices Complexes." *Dance Magazine* 49.8 (August 1975): 31.

Archer, Kenneth, and Millicent Hodson. "Three Romeos." *Dance Now* 1.3 (Autumn 1992): 10–19, 21.

Balanchine, George, with Francis Mason. *Balanchine's Festival of Ballet.* Vol. 2. London, 1978.

Chazin-Bennahum, Judith. "The Tragedy of Romeo and Juliet." In *The Ballets of Antony Tudor: Studies in Psyche and Satire,* pp. 120–129. New York and Oxford, 1994.

Croce, Arlene. "The Bolshoi's Pathetic Fallacy." In *Going to the Dance,* pp. 215–221. New York, 1982.

Croce, Arlene. "*Romeo* Revisited." In *Sight Lines,* pp. 256–260. New York, 1987.

Denby, Edwin. "Markova's Dance Rhythm: Tudor's *Romeo and Juliet*" and "Tudor's *Romeo and Juliet* Revisited." In *Dance Writings,* edited by Robert Cornfield and William MacKay, pp. 106–110, 393–398. New York, 1986.

Felciano, Rita, and Eric Hellman, eds. *Crossed Stars: Artistic Sources and Social Conflict in the Ballet "Romeo and Juliet."* San Francisco, 1994. Includes a filmography/videography compiled by Virginia Brooks and a selected bibliography by Leslie Getz.

Finkel, Anita. "Not Necessarily Alike in Dignity." *The New Dance Review* 3.4 (April–June 1991): 10–15.

Genêt. "Letter from Paris." *The New Yorker* (14 January 1976), pp. 109–114.

Ostlere, Hilary. "Endless Love." *Ballet News* 6.9 (March 1985): 14–17.

Howard, Camille Cole. *The Staging of Shakespeare's "Romeo and Juliet" as a Ballet.* San Francisco, 1992.

Royce, Anya Peterson. "*Romeo and Juliet:* Choreography and Contexts." In *Movement and Meaning: Creativity and Interpretation in Ballet and Mime,* pp. 181–201. Bloomington, 1984.

Siegel, Marcia. "*Romeo and Juliet*" and "*Romeo and Juliet* (II)." In *At the Vanishing Point: A Critic Looks at Dance,* pp. 43–45, 45–46. New York, 1972.

Tobias, Tobi. "Bournonville and the Royal Danish Ballet." *Dance Magazine* 50.8 (August 1976): 58–62.

Tobias, Tobi. "Rival Romeos." *Dance Magazine* 59.3 (March 1985): 58–60.

Vaughan, David. *Frederick Ashton and His Ballets.* New York, 1977.

Vaughan, David. "Ashton's *Romeo and Juliet* Restored." *Dance Magazine* 60.1 (January 1986): 72–75.

RITA FELCIANO

ROME OPERA BALLET. The Rome Opera Theater was originally known as the Teatro Costanzi, named in honor of its architect, Domenico Costanzi (1819–1898). In the 1880s the theater was used frequently, mostly for lyric operas and seasons of drama, as well as for occasional dance performances. The most heavily attended dance performances were those of such major ballets as Luigi Manzotti's *Sieba* (1878), *Excelsior* (1881), and *Amor* (1886). The most memorable seasons after the turn of the century were those of the Ballets Russes de Serge Diaghilev in 1911 and 1917, featuring the premieres of *Les Feux d'Artifices,* with sets and lighting by Giacomo Balla and music by Igor Stravinsky, and *Les Femmes de Bonne Humeur* by Léonide Massine.

In 1926–1928 the theater was renovated architecturally by Marcello Piacentini and, as the Teatro Reale dell' Opera, became the headquarters of a "lyric institution," that is, a public institution with autonomous management but presided over by the mayor of Rome and subsidized by state and local funds. At the end of 1928 the theater, now called simply the Teatro dell'Opera, opened a ballet school that was directed first by Ileana Leonidoff and Dimitri Rostoff, followed by Nicola Guerra (1931) and thereafter by his pupil Ettore Caorsi (1932–1938). From 1938 to 1957 the school was directed by Teresa Battaggi, followed by Attilia Radice and then by Walter Zappolini.

The permanent ballet company, also established in 1928, made its debut with the creation of *La Giara,* choreographed by Ileana Leonidoff to music by Alfredo Casella. The most interesting performances of the early years included a 1933 revival of Michel Fokine's *Petrouchka* in which Fokine himself played the protagonist, and Ettore Caorsi and Bianca Gallizia danced supporting roles. In 1934 Boris Romanov, an outstanding Russian choreographer, was named choreographic director of the theater. This was the start of richer and more consistent ballet activity that included creations by Romanov, such as *Gli Uccelli* (The Birds; 1937), to music by Ottorino Respighi, and revivals of nineteenth-century classics, including *Swan Lake,* starring Attilia Radice.

From 1938 to 1945 the company was directed by Aurelio Milloss, who contributed greatly to increasing the prestige of dance in Rome with a series of structural reforms and additions of contemporary ballets to the repertory. He involved major Italian musicians and painters, such as Goffredo Petrassi and Renato Guttuso, in the life of the ballet. Amid charges that he did not sufficiently resist the fascist regime and the German occupation of Rome in 1944–1945, Milloss resigned his post to Romanov, who held it from 1945 to 1954. Romanov devoted himself to rebuilding the classical repertory, in addition to instituting a new policy of opening the doors to major foreign companies (Paris Opera Ballet, 1949; American Ballet Theatre, 1950; and the New York City Ballet, 1953 and 1955).

The management of the post-Milloss era intended to turn the Rome Opera Ballet toward the classicism of British ballet. After the Milloss decades, which were devoted to the central European style centered around the teaching of Laban, the company's technical level—which in Milloss's ballets was secondary to expressive values—

ROME OPERA BALLET. A scene from *Marsyas,* staged by Aurelio Milloss for the company in 1948, with music by Luigi Dallapiccola and decor and costumes by Toti Scialoja. At the center of the group in the foreground is Teofilo Giglio as Marsyas; Walter Zappolini as Apollo stands on the upstage platform. (Photograph by Giacomelli; from the archives of the Teatro dell'Opera, Rome.)

had declined. This was the age of the maximum expansion of English ballet, when thanks to the creative activity of Frederick Ashton and the artistic organization and direction of Ninette de Valois, the Royal Ballet was conquering the world. It is not surprising, therefore, that the revival of Roman ballet, beginning with the second Romanov administration, was entrusted to several major English teachers.

In particular, Anton Dolin, who during the 1961/62 season was ballet director of the Rome Opera, influenced the rejuvenation of the company with his elegance and wealth of experience. He began with a revival of *Giselle,* starring Nina Vyroubova and André Prokovsky, and his *Variations for Four* was a stimulus for a new generation of Roman dancers, among them Walter Zappolini and Gianni Notari.

Thereafter a series of chiefly foreign teachers tried to promote Dolin's ideology, with varying success. The Yugoslav Dmitrije Parlič enriched the repertory with an outstanding production of *The Miraculous Mandarin* (1963/64 season). The Yugoslav Zarko Prebil, who served with the theater several times between 1967 and 1979, concentrated on rebuilding the classics—including *Cinderella* (1971), *The Nutcracker* (1973), and *Don Quixote* (1979)—along Soviet lines. The Anglo-French-Russian André Prokovsky produced a new version of *The Sleeping Beauty* (1977/78 season), with splendid sets by Beni Montresor. There is no doubt, however, that a high point of quality and charm in the history of the Rome Opera Ballet was reached under the artistic management of Massimo Bogianckino (1963–1969). Bogianckino was perhaps the only artistic director on the Italian scene at that time who truly knew and esteemed dance. To him was owed perhaps the most exciting performance of 1966, on 24 March, in which Erik Bruhn, Rudolf Nureyev, and Carla Fracci, all then at the peak of their form and charm, danced together in a mixed program that included scenes from August Bournonville's *La Sylphide;* Bruhn and Fracci also danced the balcony scene from *Romeo and Juliet,* recreated by Bruhn to the music of Sergei Prokofiev. Bogianckino also made the decision to appoint the very young Elisabetta Terabust as *prima ballerina* in 1966.

In the 1980s the company was disheartened by inadequate programming (three performances a year, plus one at the outdoor Baths of Caracalla), inadequate rehearsal buildings, and a chronic shortage of good long-term teachers. It tried to find new enthusiasm under the guidance of Maya Plisetskaya and two Soviet teachers, Inna Zubrovskaya and Anatoly Nisnevich. The beginning of this artistic management, with Plisetskaya's *Raymonda,* staged at the Baths of Caracalla in 1984, was controversial. Dmitri Briantzev's *The Little Humpbacked Horse,* in January 1985, showed a company undergoing renewal, and the suite from *Paquita,* presented in March 1985, aroused hope for the future.

Notwithstanding the difficulties of life in a theater that is unenthusiastic about ballet, the Rome Opera Ballet continued to produce a number of excellent dancers, including Terabust, Lucic Truglia, and Raffaele Paganini. Some of them, discouraged by the scant programming, chose to work abroad for at least a few years.

A new era seemed to have begun after the nomination of Terabust as director of the Rome Opera Ballet School (1989) and then of the ballet company (1990). Having studied at the school and having been a leading dancer in the company for several years, she knew the theater's problems and all the difficulties of promoting dance in Rome, one of opera's strongest strongholds. Undaunted, she made great improvements both at the school and in the company, which for the 1990/91 season included Lucia Colognato, Stefania Minardo, Mario Marozzi, and Luigi Martelletta as principal dancers. In April 1991 the company presented a revival of *La Sylphide* in a production mounted by Peter Schaufuss, and in 1992 the school's annual performances included a work by ballet master Derek Deane and Matz Skoog's staging of act 3 of *Napoli,* all of which were encouraging signs.

Despite such evidence of progress, however, Terabust was ultimately defeated by public indifference and lack of official support. She resigned the directorship of the company in 1993 and abandoned Rome in favor of Milan, where she took charge of the ballet company at the Teatro alla Scala. In the wake of her departure, the Rome Opera Ballet virtually fell apart. Under its current director, Mario Pistoni, the company is now being rebuilt.

BIBLIOGRAPHY

Fagiolo, Marcello, et al. *Cinquant'ranni del Teatro dell'Opera.* Rome, 1978.

Pitt, Freda. "Italy." In *World Ballet and Dance, 1993–1994: An International Yearbook,* edited by Bent Schoenberg, pp. 87–91. Oxford and New York, 1994.

VITTORIA OTTOLENGHI
Translated from Italian

RÓNA, VIKTOR (born 17 August 1936 in Budapest; died 22 January 1994 in Budapest), Hungarian dancer and ballet master. Róna studied at the Budapest Opera School from 1945 to 1950, at the State Ballet Institute from 1950 to 1954 with Ferenc Nádasi, and in Leningrad with Aleksandr Pushkin in 1959. He was engaged in 1950 as a dancer with the Budapest Opera and became a soloist there in 1957.

He was a *danseur noble* of excellent technique, mastering all leading roles and many *demi-caractère* parts. Some of his outstanding renderings were the Prince in Vasily Vainonen's *The Nutcracker* (1955), Albrecht in Leonid Lavrovsky's *Giselle* (1958), Mercutio in Lavrovsky's *Romeo and Juliet* (1962), Désiré in Petr Gusev's *The Sleeping Beauty* (1967), the title role in László Seregi's *Spartacus* (1968), and the Prince in versions of *The Wooden Prince* by Gyula Harangozó (1958) and by Seregi (1970).

In addition to dancing in guest performances with his company abroad, Róna toured the world from the late 1950s to the late 1960s, often with his partner Adél Orosz. He also performed with Margot Fonteyn and Janine Charrat at their home stages and toured the United States with Liane Daydé.

Róna danced in a documentary film with Orosz (1967), and appeared in Fonteyn's biographical film (1968). He featured in the film of Seregi's *The Wooden Prince* (1969) as the Prince, and in that of Harangozó's *Mischievous Students* as Adam.

Róna was *premier danseur,* choreographer, and ballet master of the Oslo Opera between 1974 and 1980. He worked as ballet master in Paris at the Opera Ballet with Rosella Hightower between 1980 and 1983 and at the Teatro alla Scala, Milan, between 1983 and 1988. He was guest choreographer in cities such as Berlin, Bonn, Stockholm, and Tokyo and choreographed *The Nutcracker* for the Norwegian National Ballet and *The Sleeping Beauty* for the Budapest Opera Ballet (1991). His awards include the Liszt Prize (1961); the Kossuth Prize (1965); the White Rose, a Finnish order of knighthood (1968); and Hungarian designations as Merited Artist (1972) and Eminent Artist (1976).

BIBLIOGRAPHY

Kun, Zsuzsa. "Maître de Ballet: Viktor Róna." *Hungarian Dance News,* no. 5 (1980): 4.

Körtvélyes, Géza, and György Lőrinc. *The Budapest Ballet: The Ballet Ensemble of the Hungarian State Opera House.* Vol. 1. Translated by Gedeon P. Dienes and Éva Rácz. Budapest, 1971.

"Róna, Viktor (1936–1994)." *Táncművészet* 1–12 (1994): 88 (obituary).

"Viktor Róna." *Ballet Today* (August–September 1963): 18–20.

GEDEON P. DIENES

ROND DE JAMBE. The ballet step *rond de jambe* ("circle of the leg") can be executed in four basic ways. In *rond de jambe à terre* the working leg, turned out from thigh to pointed toe, describes a semicircle on the floor in one continuous movement and then passes through first position. The leg may move in an outward, clockwise direction *(en dehors)* or inward and counterclockwise *(en dedans).* The movement is generally accented just after the foot passes through first position, imparting a whiplike quality to the rotation, which loosens the hip joint and increases the flexibility of the entire leg.

In *grand rond de jambe,* the working leg sweeps off the ground in a semicircle. When the whipping motion is stressed, or when the body itself turns as the leg is rotating *(grand rond de jambe en tournant),* the step contains the essential motions of the *fouetté.*

In *rond de jambe en l'air,* the leg is straightened to the side at forty-five to ninety degrees (usually either by brushing it from the floor or from a *fondu* or other movement in which the working leg is already off the ground). The lower part of the leg then traces an oval in the air, with the pointed toe grazing alternate sides of the knee or calf—back and then front *(en dehors)* or front and then back *(en dedans).* The leg is then extended to the side again. Quickness may be attained only if the oval is described solely by the lower leg; the thigh remains motionless. Speed is essential in the *rond de jambe en l'air sauté,* in which the rotation of the leg is executed while the body is in the air.

Rond de jambe à terre is primarily a classroom exercise, whereas the others are commonly incorporated into choreography. *Grand rond de jambe* is often found in supported adagio. Double *rond de jambe en l'air,* with the supporting leg on pointe, is a feature of Odette's solo in act 2 of *Swan Lake.* Perhaps the most characteristic and brilliant example is the double *rond de jambe en l'air sauté* as used by choreographer August Bournonville. Almost all of his variations for men include this step; consequently, Bournonville recommended that it be part of daily practice and devised classroom combinations that developed a truly circular path of the lower leg in the air. The double *rond de jambe en l'air* is also a highlight of the male variation in George Balanchine's *Theme and Variations* (1947); thus, this jumping *rond de jambe* continues to be a test of male technical virtuosity.

The *rond de jambe à terre* as it is now practiced at the *barre* was codified by Carlo Blasis in 1820, although "ronds ou tours de jambe en dedans ou en dehors" are already mentioned in Jean-Georges Noverre's *Lettres sur la danse* in 1760. Pierre Rameau cites a possible antecedent, the *ouverture de jambe,* in *Le maître à danser* (1725). As described in this guide to social dance, the leg is taken in the air slowly from front to side, its stately tempo contrasting with the proceeding quick step. The *gargouillade,* a variation of the *rond de jambe en l'air* in which both legs successively describe circles, appears as early as 1704 in a dance by Guillaume-Louis Pecour. A 1714 collection of his choreography contains numerous versions of the *rond de jambe en l'air* as performed by the professional dancers Michel Blondy, François Marcel, and Michel Gaudrau (who also notated the dances). Variants of the basic steps are found in many folk dances as well as in the Spanish dance of Andalusia, which has been incorporated into the *escuela bolera.*

[*See also* Ballet Technique.]

BIBLIOGRAPHY

Blasis, Carlo. *An Elementary Treatise upon the Theory and Practice of the Art of Dancing* (1820). Translated by Mary Stewart Evans. New York, 1944.

Bournonville, August. *Études chorégraphiques.* Copenhagen, 1861.

Feuillet, Raoul Auger. *Recueil de danses contenant un très grand nombres des meilleures entrées de M. Pécour.* Paris, 1704.
Gaudrau, Michel. *Nouveau recueil de danse de bal et celle de ballet, contenant un très grand nombres des meillieures entrées de ballet de la composition de Mr. Pécour.* Paris, 1714.
Noverre, Jean-Georges. *Lettres sur la danse et sur les ballets.* Lyon and Stuttgart, 1760.
Rameau, Pierre. *Le maître à danser.* Paris, 1725. Translated by Cyril W. Beaumont as *The Dancing Master* (London, 1931).
Stuart, Muriel, et al. *The Classic Ballet.* New York, 1952.
Vaganova, Agrippina. *Basic Principles of Classical Ballet: Russian Ballet Technique* (1934). Translated by Anatole Chujoy. Edited by Peggy van Praagh. 2d ed. London, 1953.

NANCY GOLDNER

RONZANI, DOMENICO (born 1800 in Italy, died 13 February 1868 in New York City), dancer, mime, choreographer, and reconstructor. Ronzani began his career performing in provincial Italian theaters and ended it in the United States, the first impresario to have taken a ballet company of significant size to the New World. As a young performer he was recognized as an exceptionally talented mime, cited for his strength, grace, and precision. His progress to leading roles was rapid. In 1825 he was one of eight *ballerini di mezzo carattere* (*demi-caractère* dancers) at the Teatro La Fenice in Venice. The following year he was engaged as a mime at the Teatro alla Scala, Milan, a theater known for its large, well-trained contingent of mime artists and its repertory of spectacular, dramatic ballets. By 1829 Ronzani was appointed *primo ballerino mimico assoluto* at La Scala and remained intermittently associated with that opera house for more than thirty years. During that time he worked with many of the most noted artists of Romantic-era ballet, including Fanny Elssler, Fanny Cerrito, Carlo Blasis, Jules Perrot, and Salvatore Taglioni.

Although Ronzani was a choreographer in his own right, he was better known for his faithful reproductions of the ballets of Monticini, Antonio Cortesi, and, most important, Jules Perrot. Perrot originally choreographed *Esmeralda* for Carlotta Grisi and himself at Her Majesty's Theatre, London, in 1844. That year Perrot remounted the production at La Scala with Fanny Elssler in the title role and Ronzani portraying Frollo. One year later he revived this production for Elssler in Bologna and Venice, and for her once again in Vienna in 1846. Ronzani revived *Esmeralda* in 1854 at La Scala, and in 1857 at Her Majesty's Theatre, London. Other Perrot ballets frequently revived by Ronzani were *Faust; Odetta; Catarina, ou La Fille du Bandit;* and *Uriella.*

Of Ronzani's original ballets produced at La Scala, none achieved the remarkable success that greeted his revivals. In 1840 at the Teatro Carignano in Turin, he made his choreographic debut with the ballet *La Morte di Procotieff.* He created two ballets featuring Elssler: *La Zingara* in

RONZANI. Lithograph of Ronzani and Francesca Pezzoli, *primi ballerini mimici,* in an unidentified ballet at the Teatro di Apollo in Rome during Carnival season in 1835. (Photograph from the Dance Collection, New York Public Library for the Performing Arts.)

Bologna in 1845, and *Caterina Howard* in Padua in 1847. Several of his ballets were performed in the United States as well as in Europe. *The Golden Horse,* for example, first created in Vienna in 1854, was subsequently performed by his company in New York. In addition to his talents as a choreographer and performer, Ronzani proved himself an able administrator. From 1850 to 1852 he managed, choreographed, and performed in the company at the Teatro Grande in Trieste.

In 1856 Ronzani interrupted his usual schedule of choreographing, remounting ballets, and administering in Italy and Germany to travel to London, where he became, for the summers of 1856 and 1857, the ballet master of Her Majesty's Theatre. There, too, he performed the leading role in Joseph Mazilier's newly choreographed, elaborate three-act ballet *Le Corsaire* in 1856. This was quite a remarkable accomplishment, considering that, at the time, Ronzani was fifty-six years old.

While in London the choreographer was contacted by Max Maretzek, an opera impresario. Maretzek had been asked by the manager of the new Philadelphia Academy of Music (today one of America's most important surviving nineteenth-century theaters) to find an attraction suitable for the 1857 opening performance. Maretzek contacted Ronzani and sent him back to Italy to engage a first-rate company.

On 3 September 1857, Ronzani's troupe of twenty-four dancers arrived in New York on the steamship *Asia.* The company included Filippo Baratti, leading male dancer; Louise Lamoureux, *prima ballerina*; and leading mimes Cesare and Pia Cecchetti and their seven-year-old son, Enrico. Principal dancers and pantomimists included the Pratesi family, father, mother, two daughters, and two sons; Emma Santolini; and the male dancers Heckman, Dalton, and Mancy. It opened at the Academy of Music in Philadelphia on 15 September 1857 with Perrot's full-length ballet *Faust*. Difficulties plagued its opening performance, and the audience response was poor. Far more serious, a financial panic began less than a month after their arrival in America; banks closed in Boston and New York. The La Scala dancers thus performed to nearly empty houses.

At the conclusion of their two-week engagement in Philadelphia, the company moved to New York City. It opened at the Broadway Theatre on 5 October 1857 in *Faust*, and followed this a week later with *Il Biricchino di Parigi;* the young Enrico Cecchetti was featured in the title role. On 22 October the bill changed to *The Golden Horse*, and the engagement ended 7 November 1857. For these performances Ronzani augmented his Italian company with American supernumeraries. Playbills boast of the *Faust* cast, for example, of eighty *coryphées* and *figurantes* and nearly one hundred males.

Shortly after the New York season ended, Ronzani returned to La Scala, where he produced *Il Birrichino di Parigi* and *Le Corsaire*. The following year he returned to the United States with a new ballerina, Annetta Galletti, and two new ballets, *The Village Apothecary* and Monticini's *Theresa, the Orphan of Geneva*. Enrico Cecchetti in his autobiography describes Ronzani's sensational performance in *Theresa*, in which he fell backward, head first, down a flight of stairs.

In its second American season, 1858, Ronzani's company performed not only in New York but also toured as far west as New Orleans, traveling on the Mississippi River on a steamboat. Unfortunately, the reception was disappointing. Although Americans had enthusiastically flocked to ballet during the 1840s, interest had since waned and was not to revive until 1866, with the production of the spectacle *The Black Crook*. At the end of the second year's winter tour the Cecchetti family and most of the other dancers returned to Europe, but Ronzani remained to form a new company, of largely resident or American dancers. In 1859 his newly founded company, featuring George Washington Smith and Annetta Galletti, joined forces with the Escott Opera Company. It performed *La Bayadère* and Perrot's *Esmeralda* in Philadelphia in June 1859, and then moved to the Boston Museum, where it presented programs of ballet and opera. Once again Ronzani's company met with a poor reception, so in August the company closed its engagement and disbanded.

Although Ronzani made occasional attempts to revive the company, he was not successful. After having been so honored in Italy, he was now reduced to performing in cheap beer halls, such as the New York Melodian. Occasionally he was engaged to choreograph and to direct the ballet for a musical spectacle or for various opera companies. For example, in June 1863 he choreographed the incidental dances for *The Duke's Motto* at Niblo's Garden Theatre in New York. Four years later he was again in New York, choreographing the dances for *The Devil's Auction*, which opened at Banvard's Theatre and Opera House on 3 October 1867. This company featured a number of excellent European ballerinas, including former La Scala associate Giuseppina Morlacchi. Critics deemed the dances in the production better than those in the competing *Black Crook*. The production had technical and managerial problems, however, and closed in New York after only three months. It moved in December 1867 to Boston's Theatre Comique. While in Boston, Ronzani grew ill and had to return to New York, where he died.

BIBLIOGRAPHY

Brown, T. Allston. *A History of the New York Stage*. 3 vols. New York, 1930.

Guest, Ivor. *Jules Perrot: Master of the Romantic Ballet*. London, 1984.

Moore, Lillian. "George Washington Smith." *Dance Index* 4 (June–August 1945): 88–135.

Odell, George C. D. *Annals of the New York Stage*. 15 vols. New York, 1927–1949.

BARBARA BARKER

ROPE DANCING. *See* Circus.

ROSARIO. *See* Antonio and Rosario.

ROSATI, CAROLINA (Carolina Galletti; born 13 December 1826 in Bologna, died May 1905 in Cannes), Italian dancer. A student of Antonia Torelli and Carlo Blasis, Rosati became *prima ballerina assoluta* at the Teatro di Apollo of Rome in 1841. In 1843 she married Francesco Rosati, also a dancer. In 1846 she danced at Teatro alla Scala in Milan, and in 1847 at Her Majesty's Theatre in London, replacing Lucile Grahn in Jules Perrot's *Pas de Quatre*. In 1848 she performed with Fanny Cerrito, Carlotta Grisi, and Marie Taglioni in Perrot's *Les Quatre Saisons*. In the 1847/48 season in London she also danced in Paul Taglioni's *Coralia; Théa, ou La Fée aux Fleurs;* and *Fiorita et la Reine des Elfrides;* and in 1849 in Taglioni's *La Prima Ballerina* and *Les Plaisirs de l'Hiver*. In 1851 she made her debut in Paris as Ariele in Fromental Halévy's opera *La Tempesta,* and in 1853 she danced at the Opera in Joseph Mazilier's *Jovita, ou Les Boucaniers.*

In 1856 Rosati enjoyed her first real success in Paris, in Mazilier's *Le Corsaire.* The following year, Mazilier's *Marco Spada* provided the occasion for a comparison of her vivacious, earthy style with the more ethereal and spiritual style of her rival Amalia Ferraris. The admirers of Rosati and Ferraris agreed in acknowledging the grace, interpretive intelligence, and poetic style of Rosati. In subsequent years, however, Ferraris became a more imposing presence on the opera stage and Rosati chose to leave Paris for Saint Petersburg. There, in 1859, she danced in Mazilier's *Le Corsaire* and enjoyed flattering acclaim. Her performances in his *Jovita,* in Jules Perrot's *Gazelda,* and in Arthur Saint-Léon's *Pâquerette* and *The Pearl of Seville* were less successful.

In 1862 Rosati was extremely successful in Marius Petipa's *La Fille du Pharaon,* in which her gifts as a mime and a ballerina shone brightly. No subsequent ballerina achieved such memorable success in this ballet. In 1862 she left Saint Petersburg and retired to Cannes, where she lived quietly until her death.

ROSATI. Engraving of Rosati in the role of Amalia, the heroine of Joseph Mazilier's ballet *La Fonti,* which Rosati created at the Paris Opera in 1855. (Dance Collection, New York Public Library for the Performing Arts.)

BIBLIOGRAPHY

Beamont, Cyril W. *Complete Book of Ballets.* Rev. ed. London, 1951.
Guest, Ivor. *The Romantic Ballet in England.* London, 1972.
Guest, Ivor. *The Ballet of the Second Empire.* London, 1974.
Guest, Ivor. *The Romantic Ballet in Paris.* 2d rev. ed. London, 1980.
Guest, Ivor. *Jules Perrot: Master of the Romantic Ballet.* London, 1984.
Migel, Parmenia. *The Ballerinas: From the Court of Louis XIV to Pavlova.* New York, 1972.
Roslavleva, Natalia. *Era of the Russian Ballet* (1966). New York, 1979.
Wiley, Roland John, trans. and ed. *A Century of Russian Ballet: Documents and Accounts, 1810–1910.* Oxford, 1990.

ELENA GRILLO

ROSE, JÜRGEN (born 25 August 1937 in Bernberg), German costume and stage designer. Jürgen Rose is known primarily for his many collaborations with choreographer John Cranko, who brought the young designer to prominence with his Stuttgart production of *Romeo and Juliet* in 1962. Rose's opulent spectacle, framed by a two-storied piazza and Renaissance façades, was somewhat eclipsed by Nicholas Georgiadis's designs for the Kenneth MacMillan version a few years later, but Rose had proven his gift for designing a richly detailed historical setting. He brought this gift to fruition with Cranko's *Onegin* (1965), in which the sets and costumes evoked the provincial charm and romantic domesticity of much of the story while still providing grandeur on an opera-house scale.

The narrative tradition in which Rose worked with Cranko during the 1960s gave way in the 1970s to more abstract situations. For *Poème de l'Extase* (1970), Cranko's tribute to Margot Fonteyn in the role of the Beauty, an older woman reliving her amorous past, Rose's designs were derived from Gustav Klimt's distinctive mode of Art Nouveau: every surface was covered with swirling forms, highly colored and richly ornamented. In the ornate drawing room of the first scene, a trail of rising smoke suggesting incense made the lavishly sensual surroundings seem almost to impinge on the sense of smell. The lovers of the woman's vision appeared in flesh-colored tights embellished with decorative curlicues, and they exited under billowing colored capes. These flamboyant designs achieved much acclaim and some notoriety in the annals of ballet decor.

Rose has worked with other choreographers, such as John Neumeier and Celia Franca, primarily on traditional full-length ballets. Although he dressed Neumeier's *Lady of the Camelias* (Stuttgart, 1978) in opulent period costume, not all of his design elements are traditional. His *Sleeping Beauty* for Neumeier (Hamburg, 1978), for example, featured a prince in blue jeans among the tutus, and for Neumeier's *Midsummer Night's Dream* (Hamburg, 1977), in keeping with the choreographer's concept, the fairies were transformed into twenty-first-century creatures in Lurex unitards and flesh-colored helmets.

BIBLIOGRAPHY

Kilian, Gundel. *Stuttgarter Ballett.* New ed. Weingarten, 1991.

Percival, John, and Noël Goodwin. "Poème de l'extase." *Dance and Dancers* (May 1970): 30–34.

Schneiders, Heinze L. "Jürgen-Rose-Ausstellung in Stuttgart." *Das Tanzarchiv* 26 (December 1978): 522.

CLAUDIA ROTH PIERPONT

ROSEN, ELSA-MARIANNE VON (born 21 March 1924 in Stockholm), Swedish dancer, choreographer, and ballet director. Von Rosen began her dance studies as a child with Vera Alexandrova and continued with Otto Thoresen, Valborg Franchi, Albert and Nina Kozlovsky, and Jenny Hasselquist. She had two important years as a guest pupil at the Royal Danish Ballet School under the tutorship of Harald Lander. After making her professional debut in 1941 in an independent dance concert, von Rosen performed in various recitals, was a soloist at Oscarsteatern, Stockholm (1947–1949), and became a member of the Metropolitan Ballet (1947) and the Original Ballet Russe (1948–1949). She had a breakthrough in 1950 as Miss Julie in Birgit Cullberg's ballet of the same name under the auspices of the Swedish Riksteatern. Owing to this success, she was engaged by the Royal Opera House in Stockholm as a guest artist to dance Miss Julie.

ROSEN. A studio portrait in costume for the title role of Birgit Cullberg's *Miss Julie* (1950). (Photograph © by Merkel Rydberg; used by permission.)

Von Rosen's career as a ballerina was set from 1951. She was the first ballerina ever to be taken into the Royal Swedish Ballet from outside its school. She danced leading parts in both classical and modern ballets: Odette-Odile with partner Björn Holmgren in Mary Skeaping's version of *Swan Lake;* Aurora in *The Sleeping Beauty;* the title role in *Giselle;* and leading roles in ballets by Cullberg, Ivo Cramér, and Léonide Massine.

Von Rosen left the Royal Swedish Ballet in 1959, and together with her husband, Danish writer and stage-designer Allan Fridericia, she founded a touring company, the Skandinaviska Baletten. The company operated under the auspices of the Swedish Riksteatern and the Danish Andelsteatret. She staged and danced in a repertory consisting of *La Sylphide* as well as several of her own ballets.

Beginning in 1961, von Rosen danced in revivals of August Bournonville ballets to international acclaim. The first was *La Sylphide* for Ballet Rambert. Fridericia contributed to these revivals with thorough research on Bournonville. In 1970 von Rosen accepted a post as ballet director at Stora Teatern, Göteborg. Her first production for this theater was a full-length *Napoli* (choreography by Bournonville). She then staged *La Sylphide* and her own versions of *Swan Lake* and *Romeo and Juliet.* She choreographed *Pictures at an Exhibition* (music by Modest Mussorgsky, adapted by Emerson, Lake, and Palmer). After leaving Göteborg in 1976, von Rosen worked as a freelance choreographer. In 1980 she accepted a post as ballet director of the Malmö Stadsteater, Malmö. There she choreographed *Johannesnatten* (music by G. de Frumerie; libretto by Rune Lindström) and produced full-length versions of *Napoli* and *The Sleeping Beauty* in cooperation with Mary Skeaping.

Von Rosen is the only Western choreographer to have been invited to stage Bournonville ballets in the Soviet Union. *La Sylphide* was given with great success at the Maly Theater, Leningrad (1975); it later moved to the Kirov Theater and then to Kiev (1982). She staged her version of *Jenny from Westphalen* for the Cuban National Ballet in 1978. *Napoli* was also produced at the Kirov Theater (1982).

Von Rosen developed outside the traditional ballet institutions. After a period as *prima ballerina* she decided to strike out on her own as a choreographer, director, and *régisseuse.* She was awarded the Ingrid Jespersens and Thagea Brandt prizes and was chosen as "Most Honored

Artist" by Danish critics. In 1982 she was given the Thalia Award in Malmö.

BIBLIOGRAPHY

Fridericia, Allan. *Elsa Marianne von Rosen: En Svensk ballerina.* Stockholm, 1953.

Lidova, Irène. "Une heure avec Elsa Marianne von Rosen." *Saisons de la Danse,* no. 89 (December 1976): 19–20.

Näslund, Erik. "Elsa Marianne von Rosen och Göteborgbaletten." *Dans,* no. 5 (November 1974): 7–41.

Näslund, Erik. *Birgit Cullbergs Fröken Julie en svensk balettklassiker.* Stockholm, 1995.

Percival, John. "Danish Tarantella in Sweden." *Dance and Dancers* (April 1971): 20–22.

Percival, John. "A Question of Repertory: The Malmö Ballet." *Dance and Dancers* (December 1983): 35–36.

Williams, Peter, and John Percival. "Regional Ballet Comes to London." *Dance and Dancers* (July 1975): 27–31.

LULLI SVEDIN

ROSENTHAL, JEAN (born 16 March 1912 in New York, died 1 May 1969 in New York), American lighting and stage designer. Stage lighting was still a new profession when Jean Rosenthal turned it into an art form. In American dance from the 1930s on, her lighting designs provided not only clarity of vision but often the ambient and dramatic effects of absent scenery and costumes.

Beginning her theatrical education at the Neighborhood Playhouse School in New York, Rosenthal studied lighting at Yale University's Drama School and went on to work as production supervisor for the WPA's Federal Theater Project and the Mercury Theater group from 1937 to 1939. At the same time she worked on Broadway and began the professional collaboration with Martha Graham that was to last all her life.

Lincoln Kirstein invited Rosenthal to work for Ballet Caravan in 1939, and her relationship with him, and later with George Balanchine, lasted until 1957. She was technical supervisor for their joint venture, Ballet Society (1946–1948), and a vital component of their subsequent company, the New York City Ballet, during its early seasons at the City Center in New York, beginning in 1948. The spectral and ominous atmosphere of Balanchine's *La Valse* (1951) owes much to the looming shadows produced by streaming shafts of side lighting. She also occasionally designed decor, always with simplicity and elegance. For Jerome Robbins she created the spiderweb of ropes of *The Cage* (1951) and the rippling china silk tent of *Afternoon of a Faun* (1953), a shimmer of summer heat and breeze made visible.

In 1954 Rosenthal devised both the magically growing Christmas tree in Balanchine's production of *The Nutcracker* and the decor for his bizarre *Opus 34,* a hospital nightmare set to music by Arnold Schoenberg, in which the final effect was a battery of lights turned directly and blindingly on the audience. Balanchine seemed to be exploring Rosenthal's technical and dramatic gifts as he would those of a dancer. In the majority of works, however, her lighting was neutral and unobtrusive, showing off choreography with an all-exposed brightness that suited and expressed the company's style.

[*See also* Lighting for Dance, *overview article.*]

BIBLIOGRAPHY

Goodman, Saul. "Meet Jean Rosenthal." *Dance Magazine* (February 1962): 19–23.

Rosenthal, Jean. "The Dance: Pattern of Light." *New York Times* (29 July 1951).

Rosenthal, Jean. "Lighting the Dance." *New York Times* (21 July 1963).

Rosenthal, Jean, and Lael Wertenbaker. *The Magic of Light: The Craft and Career of Jean Rosenthal, Pioneer in Lighting for the Modern Stage.* Boston, 1972.

CLAUDIA ROTH PIERPONT

ROSS, BERTRAM (born 14 November 1920 in Brooklyn, New York), American dancer and choreographer. Ross was Martha Graham's leading male dancer from 1953 to 1973, noted for vigorous roles that lent dramatic contrast to Graham's interpretations of mythical and tragic women. Described by one critic as "tall, impassioned, [and] granite visaged," Ross created the roles of Saint Michael in *Seraphic Dialogue* (1955), Adam in *Embattled Garden* (1958), Agamemnon and Orestes in *Clytemnestra* (1958), Holofernes in *Legend of Judith* (1962), Ulysses in *Circe* (1963), and Abelard in *Time of Snow* (1968), among others.

Ross joined Graham's company in 1949, several years after seeing a performance of her *Letter to the World* in Washington, D.C., while stationed there in the army. A graduate of Erasmus Hall High School in Brooklyn, he had attended the Art Students League with the aim of becoming a painter but instead turned to dance. He first partnered Graham in 1953 as Oedipus in *Night Journey.* Ross has been described as Graham's alter ego during his years with her company. On the creation of *Clytemnestra* he said, "I was there at every rehearsal, working with [Martha], feeling every nuance"; according to Ross, Graham often incorporated his suggestions and ways of moving into her work.

Beginning in 1966, Ross served as co-director of the Graham company, first with Robert Cohan and later with Mary Hinkson. In 1973, while Graham was severely ill, the company faltered and slowly disbanded, but Ross and Hinkson were able to keep the Graham studio together and to present student performances at the school. When Graham returned to take charge, she began a new company with young dancers; both Ross and Hinkson left, apparently unwanted by the new regime.

Ross, who has choreographed since 1965, has from time to time had his own company, for which he created, among other works, *Cases,* to music by Walter Caldeon (1970), and *Threads,* to music by John Wallowitch (1983). In addition he has presented a solo work incorporating dialogue, acting, and singing, called "An Evening with Bertram Ross," and performed song programs in supper clubs and nightclubs and, with Wallowitch, in cabarets in New York and other U.S. cities as well as in London. Ross also has taught dance at several schools, including New York University and Juilliard as well as at the Mary Anthony Studio in New York City. In July 1993 he worked in Berne, Switzerland, teaching and choreographing for Anne Marie Parekh. His memoirs, tentatively titled "My Life with Martha Graham," have yet to be completed, but a chapter was excerpted in the summer 1991 issue of *Dance Pages.*

BIBLIOGRAPHY

Nuchtern, Jean. "Bertram Ross, Person and Performer." *Eddy: About Dance,* no. 5 (Winter 1974): 10–14.

Ross, Bertram. "My Life with Martha Graham." *Dance Pages* 9 (Summer 1991): 22–27.

Stein, Betty Jane. "Bertram Ross: The Emergence of a Man." *Dance Magazine* (August 1976): 38–43.

KITTY CUNNINGHAM

ROSS, HERBERT (born 13 May 1925 in Brooklyn, New York), American dancer, choreographer, and film director. After 1969 Ross became known principally as a film director, but he began his professional career as a dancer and choreographer in theater and ballet. Although film replaced dance as Ross's primary interest, his most innovative and personal films, *The Turning Point* (1977), *Nijinsky* (1980), *Pennies from Heaven* (1982), *Footloose* (1984), and *Dancers* (1987), combined dance and film.

Raised in Florida after his mother's death, Ross did not start dance training until his midteens, but once committed he studied ballet and modern dance and worked as a chorus dancer on Broadway. His first choreographic attempt, *Caprichos* (1950), set to music of Béla Bartók and inspired by etchings by Goya, was done for a choreographers' workshop but soon was added to the repertory of American Ballet Theatre. A somber dramatic ballet, it presaged his work as a ballet choreographer. He contributed several works for Ballet Theatre, including *Paean* and *The Maids,* both in 1957; *Concerto* and *Ovid Metamorphoses,* both in 1958; and *Dialogues* in 1960. *The Maids,* revived by Eliot Feld in 1969, and *Caprichos* are the only ballets remaining in repertory.

Ross also became an active dance director in theater and television. He worked with Milton Berle and Martha Raye and did the choreography for, among others, *A Tree Grows in Brooklyn* (1951), *House of Flowers* (1954), *I Can Get It for You Wholesale* (1962), *Do I Hear a Waltz?* (1965), and *On a Clear Day You Can See Forever* (1965). In addition, with his wife, Nora Kaye, he assayed a short-lived company, the Ballet of Two Worlds, that toured Europe for several months in 1960 and for which he created a full-length dramatic ballet, *The Dybbuk.*

Ross's first assignment in Hollywood was *Carmen Jones* in 1954, but his film career did not reach fruition until 1969 when, after a time as a choreographer (*Doctor Doolittle* in 1967, *Funny Girl* in 1968), he directed the musical version of *Goodbye, Mr. Chips.* Subsequently he directed a wide variety of films, including comedies written by Neil Simon (*The Sunshine Boys,* 1975; *The Goodbye Girl,* 1977; *California Suite,* 1978; *I Ought to Be in Pictures,* 1982), musicals (*Funny Lady,* 1975; *Pennies from Heaven,* 1982), mystery-dramas (*The Last of Sheila,* 1973; *The Seven Percent Solution,* 1976), and others (*The Secret of My Success,* 1987; *Steel Magnolias,* 1989; *My Blue Heaven,* 1990; *True Colors,* 1991; *Undercover Blues,* 1993; and *Boys on the Side,* 1995).

The generally bleak and pessimistic atmosphere of Ross's choreography generally gave way to a more optimistic spirit in his films, particularly his work with Neil Simon. Yet an underlying tension between hope and despair remained in many of the films, and those most imbued with dance, especially the deeply cynical *Pennies from Heaven,* reflected some of the attitude of his early dance creations.

[*See also* Film Musicals, *article on* Hollywood Film Musicals.]

BIBLIOGRAPHY

Joel, Lydia. "Dancer—Choreographer—Show Doctor: Now Film Director Herb Ross Talks Shop." *Dance Magazine* (December 1967): 42–49.

Pally, Marcia. "'Giselle' Goes to Hollywood." Film Comment (October 1987): 80–82.

Zito, Stephen. "The Rise of Herbert Ross." *American Film* (November 1978).

JEROME DELAMATER

ROTA, GIUSEPPE (born 1823 in Venice, died 23 May 1865 in Turin), Italian ballet dancer, mime, and choreographer. Rota received his dance training at the school of the Teatro La Fenice in Venice and became a member of the company while he was still in his teens. Records of productions at La Fenice show that he performed numerous times between 1838 and 1843. In 1838 he was a *ballerino di mezzo carattere* in Giovanni Briol's *Giaffar;* in 1839 he danced in Emanuele Viotti's *Adelaide, Regina de' Longobardi;* and in 1842 his name appears in the cast of Viotti's *Li Bravi.*

In 1844 Rota presented his ballet *Josè* at the Teatro San Samuele in Venice, and after 1853 his creations appeared regularly in most of the major Italian theaters. In 1853 he presented in Milan at the Teatro alla Scala *Un Fallo* (The Mistake), based on the sentimental play *Il Fornaretto di Venezia* by Francesco Dall'Ongaro, and *Bianchi e Negri* (Whites and Blacks), based on Harriet Beecher Stowe's famous novel *Uncle Tom's Cabin* (1851–1852). Both were widely reproduced with success, as also were *Il Giuocatore* (The Gambler), presented in Florence at the Teatro La Canobbiana in 1853, and *Il Conte di Montecristo,* after Alexandre Dumas's novel, given at La Fenice in 1856.

In these ballets, based on subjects taken from the popular literature of the period, the main action was enlivened by the addition of skillful ensemble scenes and brilliant pas de deux performed by such famous dancers as Carolina Pochini and Pasquale Borri. Rota, notwithstanding his declared purpose to revive the Italian tradition of dramatic pantomime, did not exclude virtuosity from his ballets, and he often availed himself of the acclaimed dancers trained at the Milanese school by Carlo Blasis or Auguste Hus. The music for *Il Conte di Montecristo* was composed by Paolo Giorza, whose style was marked by a popular vein "full of spirit and of a lively dancing quality" (Monaldi, 1910). The collaboration between Rota and Giorza, both fervent Italian patriots, continued regularly until Rota's death.

With *Cleopatra,* presented at La Scala in 1859, Rota expressed his admiration for the style of the Italian choreographers of the beginning of the century, and particularly for Gaetano Gioja's *Cesare in Egitto.* In Rota's ballet, however, the role of the seductive Egyptian queen who brings Antony to perdition, performed by Assunta Razzanelli alternating with Raffaella Santalicante, is more reminiscent of the adventuresses and "vamps" from popular fiction than of Gioja's noble characters. The legacy of Gioja and Salvatore Viganò is more apparent in the spectacular mass scenes, such as the orgy in the first act or the elaborate rite during Cleopatra's funeral. Rota reproduced *Cleopatra* at the Teatro Regio in Turin in 1860, and in the subsequent years several choreographers staged it in many Italian theaters until 1887.

Other successful ballets by Rota presented at La Scala were *Il Vampiro* (1860) and *La Contessa di Egmont* (1861). In Venice, at La Fenice, he mounted *Tutti Coreografi* (1857) and in Rome, at the Teatro di Apollo, *Il Genio Anarak* (1860), both of which satirized the capriciousness of dancers and the practice of plagiarism among choreographers. Rota also presented his ballets at the Hofoper in Vienna in 1861 and 1862. In 1863 he was ballet master at Her Majesty's Theatre in London, and in 1864 he created his last ballet, *La Maschera, o Le Notti di Venezia* (The Mask, or Venetian Nights), performed by Amina Boschetti, for the Paris Opera.

Rota's evaluation by his contemporaries was not unanimous. Regli (1860), while conceding the commercial success of Rota's ballets, expressed a negative opinion of him, especially in comparison with Salvatore Viganò. For others, however, he was a fertile innovator and was preferred to his contemporaries Hippolyte Monplaisir, Antonio Pallerini, and Pasquale Borri.

BIBLIOGRAPHY

Celi, Claudia. "Il balletto in Italia: Il Ottocento." In *Musica in scena: Storia dello spettacolo musicale,* edited by Alberto Basso, vol. 5, pp. 89–138. Turin, 1995.

Cohen, Selma Jeanne. "Freme di Gelosia! Italian Ballet Librettos, 1766–1865." *Bulletin of the New York Public Library* 67.9 (November 1963): 555–564.

Cohen, Selma Jeanne. "Virtue (Almost) Triumphant." *The Dancing Times* (March 1964): 297–301.

Girardi, Michele, and Franco Rossi. *Il Teatro La Fenice: Cronologia degli spettacoli 1792–1936.* Venice, 1989.

Guest, Ivor. *The Ballet of the Second Empire.* London, 1974.

Monaldi, Gino. *Le regine della danza nel secolo XIX.* Turin, 1910.

Pasi, Mario, ed. *Il balletto: Repertorio del teatro di danza dal 1581.* Milan, 1979.

Reyna, Ferdinando. "Tre grandi italiani del balletto." *La Scala* (November 1958): 35–41.

Ruffin, Elena, and Giovanna Trentin. "Catalogo generale cronologico dei balli teatrali a Venezia dal 1746 al 1859." In *Balli teatrali a Venezia (1746–1859).* Milan, 1994.

Spinelli, Alessandro G. *Memorie del celebre coreografo veneziano Giuseppe Rota.* Venice, 1866.

Zambon, Rita. "1832–1862: La breve storia della Scuola di Ballo del Gran Teatro la Fenice di Venezia nell'Ottocento." *Chorégraphie* (Spring 1997).

CLAUDIA CELI
Translated from Italian

ROUND DANCING. A form of Western couple dancing, round dancing shares the recreational and communal aspects of square dancing while including some types of music and steps found in ballroom dancing. A "cuer" directs the dancers in much the same way that a square-dance caller announces steps. Round dances are written to specific arrangements of given tunes. All the dancers do the same dance at the same time.

Emerging in the United States during the 1940s and 1950s alongside modern western square dancing, this genre is still considered part of the square dancing context. Because its immediate ancestors are couple dances of the nineteenth and early twentieth centuries, early modern round dances included polkas and schottisches; with a gradual slowing in both tempo and energy levels, waltzes and two-steps in a moderate tempo became typical. At first, sequences were short, repetitive, and fairly simple; dancers learned by imitation. As travel and communications improved among round dancers, the desire for standardization arose along with an increase in the number and complexity of dances and the introduction of cueing to take the place of memorizing routines.

There are an estimated eighty thousand participants in

round dancing in the United States, and it is also popular in Canada. Round dancing groups now exist as well in Europe, Japan, Australia, and in other countries. Dances are taught by demonstrating to the group rather than by individual coaching. Leaders are frequently self-taught, although increased standardization and organization are evident in a trend toward accreditation, teaching aids, and workshops for leaders. Teachers familiar with English ballroom dancing are the most recent substantial influence.

The easier squares and rounds will be maintained as both figures develop subgroups of followers who specialize in the more complex areas of their respective forms—including additions from the quickstep and the Latin social dances. This will make it possible for many people with varying interests to participate.

BIBLIOGRAPHY. Literature on round dancing may be found in *Qtr Trn* and *Round Dancer Magazine*.

VERONICA ANN MCCLURE

ROUSELLES, CÉLESTE DES. *See* Céleste, Madame.

ROWE, MARILYN (also known as Marilyn Rowe Maver; born 20 August 1946 in Sydney, Australia), dancer and director. After studying privately, Rowe was taken into the Australian Ballet School when it was founded in 1964. A year later she joined the company and by 1969 was a principal. Her attributes were many: a fine technique, natural grace of movement, exceptional beauty, musicality, and intelligence.

In 1973 she and Kelvin Coe took part in the Second International Ballet Competition in Moscow and were awarded silver medals. In 1978 they were invited back and danced the leading roles in the Bolshoi Ballet's version of *Don Quixote*.

Rowe's roles included the classics (she was particularly fine in *Swan Lake*), Frederick Ashton's *La Fille Mal Gardée*, Rudolf Nureyev's *Don Quixote*, John Cranko's *Onegin* and *Romeo and Juliet*, Jerome Robbins's *The Concert*, Lázló Seregi's version of *Spartacus*, and Glen Tetley's *Le Sacre du Printemps*. Works created for her include Tetley's *Gemini*, André Prokovsky's *Anna Karenina*, and Ronald Hynd's *The Merry Widow*.

Rowe retired temporarily in 1980 to have a child. When her husband was killed in an airplane crash, she took his last name and performed for a number of years as Marilyn Rowe Maver. Following an industrial dispute between the dancers and the administration in 1981, she was invited by the dancers to return to the Australian Ballet,

ROWE. A studio portrait in costume for the title role of *Anna Karenina*, created for her by André Prokovsky in 1979. (Photograph courtesy of the Australian Ballet.)

which she did with the title of special adviser. She made a triumphant return to the stage in November 1981 as the Merry Widow and continued to make guest appearances in that role for a number of years.

From May to December 1982 Rowe held a caretaker role as ballet director of the company, until the appointment of Maina Gielgud, at whose request she became deputy during 1983. Between 1984 and 1986, and again in 1990, Rowe was artistic director of the Dancers Company, a touring company composed of final-year students of the Australian Ballet School. In a dancing career that lasted twenty years, Rowe danced leading roles in more than thirty countries. She is currently a consultant and coach to the Australian Ballet School and a director of the Australian Ballet.

[*See also* Australian Ballet.]

BIBLIOGRAPHY

Pask, Edward H. *Ballet in Australia: The Second Act, 1940–1980*. Melbourne, 1982.

Potter, Michelle. "Dance Greats: Marilyn Rowe." *Dance Australia* 85 (August–September 1996): 34.

Thornton, Elaine, et al. *Marilyn Rowe and the Technology of Dance.* Carlton, Vic., 1991.

Williams, Peter, and Noël Goodwin. "The Merry Widow." *Dance and Dancers* (September 1976): 14–19.

GEOFFREY WILLIAM HUTTON
Amended by Michelle Potter

ROYAL BALLET. In 1926, Ninette de Valois, a former pupil of Édouard Espinosa and a former member of the Ballets Russes de Serge Diaghilev, opened the Academy of Choreographic Art in Kensington, London. She also approached Lilian Baylis, who had started a drama and opera company at the Old Victoria (Old Vic) Theatre on Waterloo Road, South London, and suggested adding a ballet company. Baylis engaged de Valois as both a teacher of movement for actors and a choreographer for dancers in operas and plays. Thus de Valois began the building of Britain's national ballet. [*See the entry on de Valois.*]

History of the Royal Ballet. The roots of Britain's Royal Ballet are not in the royal courts, where almost every other European national ballet evolved, but in British popular theater. As a result, ballet in Britain has had a strong base of public support, the extent of which became clear during the company's years at Sadler's Wells Theatre in Islington (north of the Thames River). The theater's history goes back to its establishment in 1684 as an inn, which was transformed into a spa for the drinking of waters from two wells found in the garden of a Mr. Sadler. In the nineteenth century it became an important theater and music hall. By the early twentieth century, however, the concentration of theater in London's West End had left the Sadler's Wells isolated. Baylis saw it as a twin to her Old Vic Theatre south of the Thames. It would house "the operatic side" and thus also her fast-growing dance venture. Money was raised in sixpence, shillings, and some larger sums so that on the Twelfth Night after Christmas 1930, 6 January 1931, the theater was reopened to the public. Its trust deed, like that of the Old Vic, obliged it "to provide seats at prices within the means of laborers and artisans, and financial gain is strictly debarred." The first performance was Shakespeare's *Twelfth Night.*

On 5 May 1931, a date now considered the birthday of the Royal Ballet, de Valois and her small troupe of women dancers presented their first full program of ballets (single ballets had been presented with short operas since 1928). On 15 May the company, called the Vic-Wells Opera Ballet, gave the first full-evening ballet program in the theater that was to become its home. Among the dancers were Ursula Moreton, Molly Lake, and Joy Newton—all of whom later played important roles in the development of the new company.

For the ballet programs on 5 and 15 May, the troupe was reinforced by the Diaghilev dancer Anton Dolin, the actor

ROYAL BALLET. *Job,* a "masque for dancing" choreographed by Ninette de Valois for the Camargo Society in 1931, is considered to be the first truly English ballet. With a libretto by Geoffrey Keynes, based on William Blake's illustrations for the biblical *Book of Job,* it was set to music by Ralph Vaughan Williams. The unidentified dancers in this photograph appeared in the 1948 production by the Sadler's Wells Ballet, for which new scenery was designed by John Piper. Gwendolen Raverat's costume designs were derived from Blake's illustrations. (Photograph from the Dance Collection, New York Public Library for the Performing Arts.)

Leslie French, two men, and eight women—nineteen in all. The death of Diaghilev on 19 August 1929 led to the dissolution of his company, forcing his dancers, including Dolin, to seek work wherever they could. This caused a diaspora that significantly aided the development of ballet throughout western Europe and the United States.

De Valois's new venture needed more than famous dancers; it needed to develop a repertory that could extend and strengthen the troupe at Sadler's Wells Theatre. For a time, new repertory was created by a separate organization, the Camargo Society, founded in 1930 to fill the gap left by Diaghilev's death. Supported by intellectuals and dance lovers, the Camargo Society commissioned *Job,* to music by Ralph Vaughan Williams that was orchestrated by Constant Lambert in 1931 and choreographed by de Valois with Dolin in the starring role of Satan, and *Façade,* choreographed by Frederick Ashton. Each epitomized an aspect of the English dancer's theatrical talent. "The English dancer," remarked de Valois in a paper to London's Royal Society of Arts on 29 May 1968, "shows himself to possess neatness, speed and precision in his technical feats. In his most expressive moments we are aware that he has a marked lyrical quality. In his dramatization of narrative scenes, he can show talent for detailed characterization."

The team that guided the creative work at Sadler's Wells began to form as early as 1931. It consisted of de Valois as ballerina, artistic director, and choreographer; Frederick Ashton was also choreographing, bringing experience from Paris and from working with Marie Rambert; and Constant Lambert, a composer of striking talent, was musical director, who conducted all the Camargo Society

ROYAL BALLET. Frederick Ashton's *Apparitions,* danced to the music of Franz Liszt, was created for the Vic-Wells Ballet in 1936. Decor and costumes were designed by Cecil Beaton. The original cast included Margot Fonteyn (standing, upstage left) as the Woman in the Ball Dress and Robert Helpmann (standing, at right) as the Poet. (Photograph © by Roger Wood; used by permission.)

ROYAL BALLET. *The Sleeping Beauty,* produced by Nicholas Sergeyev after the original choreography of Marius Petipa, was the work with which the Sadler's Wells Ballet reopened the Royal Opera House, Covent Garden, after World War II. First performed on 20 February 1946, it featured Margot Fonteyn as Princess Aurora, Robert Helpmann as Prince Florimund, and Beryl Grey as the Lilac Fairy. They are seen here, with members of the female ensemble, in act 2, "The Vision." Costumes and scenery for this production were designed by Oliver Messel. (Photograph by Edward Mandinian; used by permission of the Picture Library, Victoria and Albert Museum, London.)

performances. Although Ashton worked only part-time at Sadler's Wells until 1935, the company's artistic philosophy was already evident by 1932, when fortnightly programs of ballet were first given. [*See the entries on Ashton and Lambert.*]

Productions of the great classical ballets, made possible by the presence of Dolin, Alicia Markova, and occasionally other Diaghilev dancers, were cornerstones of the new company. This classical repertory was to be balanced with new works by Ashton and de Valois. In 1932 there were productions of *Les Sylphides* and the second act of *Le Lac des Cygnes* (renamed *Swan Lake* in 1963), both with Markova and Dolin, followed in 1933 by a two-act version of *Coppélia* by the Russian *régisseur* Nicholas Sergeyev. The presence of Sergeyev, who brought with him details of the original Saint Petersburg productions, made possible performances of many of the great classics at Sadler's Wells during the 1930s. Only when the Bolshoi and Kirov companies first appeared outside Russia in the late 1950s was it possible to compare Sergeyev's versions with theirs. The differences were of detail or emphasis, showing Sergeyev's fundamental accuracy. In 1934 he produced full-length versions of *Giselle, The Nutcracker,* and *Le Lac des Cygnes.* This classical repertory was strengthened by Michel Fokine's *Le Carnaval* and *Le Spectre de la Rose* and, more importantly, by new works from de Valois and Ashton. The most significant of these between 1933 and 1939 were Ashton's *Les Rendezvous* (1933); de Valois's *The Haunted Ballroom* (1934), *The Rake's Progress* (1935), and

ROYAL BALLET. The premiere of Ashton's *Symphonic Variations,* set to the music of César Franck, took place at Covent Garden in April 1946. The four principal dancers, pictured here, were Moira Shearer, Michael Somes, Pamela May, and (bending backward) Margot Fonteyn. (Photograph from the Dance Collection, New York Public Library for the Performing Arts.)

Checkmate (1937); and Ashton's *Apparitions* (1936), paid for in part with money from the Camargo Society as it dissolved itself, its work accomplished; *Les Patineurs* and *A Wedding Bouquet* (both 1937), and *Horoscope* (1938).

Evolution. It is striking that the classical works were produced mostly in the first half of the 1930s and the original choreography mostly in the second half. This evolution is due partly to chance and partly to changes within the company. It was obviously wise to engage Sergeyev as soon as he became available in the early 1930s, but his productions left few opportunities to perform new works from de Valois or Ashton. There was also competition throughout the 1930s from successors to Diaghilev's Ballets Russes, usually appearing at London's Covent Garden. Of these the most important was the Ballets Russes de Monte-Carlo, later called the Ballets Russes du Colonel W. de Basil (1934–1937), the Covent Garden Russian Ballet (1939), and the Original Ballet Russe (1939–1952). Markova, around whom the classical repertory was built, left the company in 1935, making it imperative to create works tailored to the new, younger dancers rising in the ranks.

The company soon grew in strength and technique so that it was ready for important new challenges. These came in various ways, especially for the men, who included Stanley Judson, William Chappell, Walter Gore, Claude Newman, and Harold Turner. Revivals of *Les Rendezvous* and *Les Patineurs,* for example, show that as early as 1933 the company had a very strong reservoir of male talent. The strongly dramatic *The Haunted Ballroom, The Rake's Progress, Checkmate, Apparitions,* and *A Wedding Bouquet* debunked notions that ballet was mostly an undramatic composition of pretty pictures and pretty people, neither amusing nor seriously theatrical. The repertory of the 1930s demonstrated the technical precision and expressive qualities that in 1957 de Valois was to identify as distinctively British.

From the mid-1930s onward, as the choreographic direction and technical qualities of British ballet evolved, so did the dance talent that would inspire and be inspired by that choreography. The very young Margot Fonteyn began to attract public notice with featured roles in *The Haunted Ballroom, Apparitions, Le Baiser de la Fée,* and *A Wedding Bouquet,* as well as in *Giselle* and *Le Lac des Cygnes.* Robert Helpmann, newly arrived from Australia, was partnered with Fonteyn and brought forward in *Giselle* and *Le Lac des Cygnes;* his comic genius was exploited in *A Wedding Bouquet* and his dramatic ability in *Checkmate.* Pamela May, Elizabeth Miller, Mary Honer, and others soon built their own public followings. The climax of this period was marked by Baylis's most ambitious project, a production of *The Sleeping Princess* (later renamed *The Sleeping Beauty*), staged on 2 February 1939 with Fonteyn as Aurora and Helpmann as the Prince. Baylis never saw it—she died in November 1937. The production became her memorial, and money was raised to extend the Sadler's Wells stage to make the elaborate production possible.

By 1939 the company had built up a base of support, an artistic policy, and a reputation that would sustain it through the difficult years of World War II. From its beginnings with six dancers, it now numbered between thirty and forty. Through the box office and public appeals, the company was self-sufficient; the idea of a British national ballet was well established, and de Valois could count on the support of the royal family and influential members of the cultural establishment. The company had appeared in Copenhagen and Paris and was acquiring a certain patriotic significance. The creative achievements of the early years proved important enough to survive the war. Ashton's choreography showed an emerging English classical style that molded and challenged company dancers. De Valois's ballets developed the company's dramatic talent for characterization, particularly through *Job, The Rake's Progress,* and *Checkmate.*

Surviving the War. During World War II, the company was sustained largely by extensive provincial tours, backed by the government in a scheme to sustain morale through the arts. Ballet Rambert and other dance groups also participated, so that these tours developed a national audience for classical ballet that proved to be just as faithful as the London audience. The London seasons continued at the New Theatre. The company changed, not only because its male members, including Ashton, were called into military service but also because of its new status as a national institution. Without Ashton, Helpmann had the opportunity to develop into a useful, if not major, dramatic choreographer. The most significant change was the increasing influence exerted by the cultural establishment.

The Council for the Encouragement of Music and the Arts had been established at the beginning of the war. Through this channel, and the public subsidy it commanded, the Sadler's Wells Ballet moved into the Royal Opera House in 1946 as the permanent resident company. The opening production on 20 February was *The Sleeping Beauty,* redesigned by Oliver Messel, with Fonteyn in the leading role. It became the company's signature at home and its passport to international recognition. During the postwar years, the company struggled to expand to the dimensions of the Royal Opera House and to rebuild its male element. Creatively, after his return, Ashton continued his process of molding and challenging English physiques and temperaments. In particular, *Symphonic Variations* in 1946 and *Scènes de Ballet* in 1948 advanced the qualities of an English classical style for both men and women. For Christmas 1948 Ashton took the next great step for British choreography with *Cinderella,* the company's first evening-length ballet. The production was both a response to the larger opportunities and demands of the Opera House and a natural development of Ashton's talent.

The Opera House began to exert its influence in other ways, too. Its board of directors appointed a ballet subcommittee to discuss and oversee artistic policy. Partly as a result of their nervous response to foreign visitors (in 1946 both American Ballet Theatre and the Ballets des Champs-Élysées from Paris showed London triumphantly new conceptions of ballet), the repertory was expanded. Léonide Massine, choreographer and star of the Diaghilev company, mounted three of his works at the Opera House during 1947: *Le Tricorne, La Boutique Fantasque,* and *Mam'zelle Angot.* Roland Petit of the Ballets des Champs-Élysées created *Ballabile* for the company in 1950 and, in the same year, came Britain's first work by George Balanchine, *Ballet Imperial.* The ballet school grew to include a full academic curriculum, and a second company was founded at Sadler's Wells Theatre.

The company's growth at Covent Garden was recognized in official tours abroad—to six countries in eastern and western Europe in 1947 and 1948—and at the new Edinburgh International Festival. In 1949, the Sadler's Wells Ballet made a triumphant visit to the United States and Canada through the American impresario Sol Hurok. American audiences applauded not only the quality of the company's dancing—decisively English and lyrical (and almost the direct opposite of Balanchine's spare, lean idioms)—but also the decision to present mostly three-act ballets, *The Sleeping Beauty, Le Lac des Cygnes,* and Ashton's *Cinderella.* This approach, wrote the British dance critic Alexander Bland in 1981, "was a gamble which paid off so resoundingly that it was to shape the image of the company for many years in the American mind and to influence its whole future development at home."

The first-night reception in New York on 9 October 1949, and the equally enthusiastic receptions that followed in other cities on the tour, significantly enhanced

ROYAL BALLET. Moira Shearer created the title role of Ashton's *Cinderella* in 1948. She is seen here in act 1, with Franklin White as the Father. (Photograph © 1948 by Roger Wood; used by permission.)

the company's national and international status. It affirmed the company's stylistic and technical values and gave the dancers new self-confidence. It transformed Fonteyn overnight into an international star, giving her an influence on the company and on Ashton that she retained for two decades. It reinforced the company's cultural and political standing in Britain and therefore increased its support from public and private sources; this new status helped the company gain a royal charter seven years later. Finally, it began a gradual and probably inevitable move away from the working-class traditions of the company's Islington audience and toward an image of conservative tradition and philosophy, a rich man's entertainment far from the vision of Lilian Baylis.

The most immediate effect upon the company, however, was a call for further exhausting tours of the United States (which ultimately replaced the provincial tours) and a reaction amounting almost to a creative standstill at home. Over the next five years, apart from Ashton's *Daphnis and Chloe* in 1951, his second three-act ballet *Sylvia* in 1952, and a production of *The Firebird* in 1954 that gave Fonteyn a brilliant role in a new style, nothing emerged of particular distinction. Yet the company had sufficient strength to withstand this period of difficulty and public criticism. The company was now sixty-seven dancers strong and led by artists of great experience. Among the ballerinas were Violetta Elvin, Beryl Grey, Nadia Nerina, Moira Shearer, and Pamela May; among the men, Michael Somes, John Field, Brian Shaw, and Alexander Grant. Coming forward was a new generation, including Svetlana Beriosova and David Blair. The company had two immensely experienced choreographers and two very promising new ones.

ROYAL BALLET. Ashton's production of *Sylvia,* mounted for the Sadler's Wells Ballet in 1952, retold the complicated tale of the nymph Sylvia, a votaress of the goddess Diana, and the shepherd Aminta, whom she wounds when he surprises her during her dance celebrating the glories of the chase. David Blair and Nadia Nerina were among those who performed the roles of Aminta and Sylvia. (Photograph © by Zoë Dominic; used by permission.)

These strengths became more apparent in the late 1950s. Kenneth MacMillan created *Noctambules,* his first ballet at London's Covent Garden, introducing a modern dance influence into the company's choreography. In the summer of 1956, the first visit by the Soviet Union's Bolshoi Ballet initiated a profound and enduring Russian influence upon the company's teaching and dancing, especially for the men; at the end of 1956, the company received its royal charter. The organization, including its school and touring company, became the Royal Ballet.

The Russian connection flourished in spite of international tensions. The Kirov Ballet exchanged seasons with the Royal Ballet in 1961, and the Bolshoi returned in the summer of 1963. Rudolf Nureyev's defection to France in 1961 at first appeared to threaten Anglo-Russian dance relations; but he soon appeared in London at a gala that November and began his ten-year partnership with Fonteyn in February 1962 in *Giselle.* In fact, his presence helped to consolidate the influence of Soviet teaching and style upon the Royal Ballet. Nureyev's frequent appearances significantly raised the standard of British male dancing and introduced additional works from the Petipa tradition (notably *La Bayadère*). Equally important, Nureyev probably extended Fonteyn's career by ten years. The first performance of Ashton's *Marguerite and Armand* in March 1963 established a signature work for the famous partnership.

The Royal Charter. The royal charter helped to give the company and its associated organizations the kind of permanence and security enjoyed by the Paris Opera Ballet, the Royal Danish Ballet, and the Soviet Union's Bolshoi and Kirov ballets. The charter arose from a curious legacy of the move to Covent Garden in 1945/46 and the development since then of the practice of public subsidy. The subsidy on which the company depended was given to the two theaters where it appeared, not to the company itself. This decision raised important questions about its control and the guarantees for its continuation. The relationship between the school and the two companies was unresolved, and the ballet needed an identity separate from the opera with which it shared, somewhat uneasily, the limited space at the Royal Opera House. The royal charter, which "hereby created one body corporate with the name of 'The Royal Ballet' with perpetual succession and a common seal," went a long way toward solving these problems.

This guarantee of security and existence seemed to be confirmed by a series of significant events. Both MacMillan and John Cranko produced works that confirmed their standing as classical choreographers. From MacMillan came *Agon* in 1958, *Le Baiser de la Fée* in 1960, *The Rite of Spring* in 1962, and *Symphony* in 1963. In January 1960 Ashton created his masterpiece, *La Fille Mal Gardeé,* now regarded as the clearest distillation of the English capacity for technical dexterity, lyricism, and characterization. With the company's future provided for, de Valois could consider her own retirement. In March 1963 she announced that she would hand over direction of the company to Ashton at the end of the season, when she was sixty-five.

The transfer to Ashton, wrote Bland, seemed like "the deft passing of a baton in a relay race." Ashton maintained the organization he had inherited and the creative policy he had done so much to shape. Nevertheless, the atmosphere changed. Ashton's taste inclined always to French culture, to the achievements of Diaghilev's company, and to the classical tradition. His personal style was a gentle, sophisticated romanticism. All these traits were evident in Ashton's seven years as director, which included Nureyev's production of part of Petipa's *La Bayadère* in 1963; *The Dream* (1964), Ashton's own interpretation of Shakespeare; the purely classical *Monotones* (1965–1966); and *Enigma Variations* (1968), nostalgia for the Victorian past. Ashton brought Bronislava Nijinska to recreate with outstanding success her *Les Biches* and *Les Noces* from the Diaghilev period, and he introduced Balanchine's *Apollo* from the same period. At the same time he encouraged MacMillan to explore a style of classical choreography that acknowledged modern influences. Ashton himself drew on jazz vocabulary for *Jazz Calendar* in 1968 and persuaded Antony Tudor to try new departures in *Shadowplay* (1967), with Anthony Dowell in the leading role.

By the end of the 1960s, however, it was clear that the company needed to change direction to survive both artistically and financially. The policy and artistic initiatives of the 1930s were exhausted. Ashton's departure in the summer of 1970 marked the end of the first phase of Royal Ballet history and provided an opportunity for change. The touring company was merged with the Covent Garden company; a small experimental company was established to perform in London and in other towns; and MacMillan was persuaded to become director of the company, working with John Field, director of the touring company. [*See the entries on Field and MacMillan.*]

Some of these changes were misguided. Field and MacMillan, as many people within the companies knew, were temperamentally incompatible, and Field resigned at the end of 1970. It was also clear that provincial theaters were not suited to the presentation of experimental works, so the plan for an experimental group was abandoned almost before it began. These reversals created tension and a lack of confidence in the board's leadership at the Royal Opera House. While no one denied the need for change, especially in the company's financial affairs, an administrative leadership that offered convincing answers was missing. Continuing financial difficulties were created, as increasingly the Royal Opera House depends on private or business sponsors to fund not only new projects but even essential development.

Artistically, nevertheless, the seven years of MacMillan's direction continued to strengthen the Russian connection—Mikhail Baryshnikov and Natalia Makarova both danced with the Royal, as had Nureyev, introducing new directions in choreography. Works of the American choreographers Jerome Robbins and Glen Tetley were also brought into the repertory, including *Dances at a Gathering, Afternoon of a Faun,* and *The Concert* from Robbins and *Field Figures* and *Laborintus* from Tetley. These works blended classical choreography with modern dance and linked the Royal Ballet with new thinking across the Atlantic. Meanwhile, MacMillan continued to choreograph new three-act ballets, *Anastasia* (1971),

ROYAL BALLET. *La Fille Mal Gardée,* mounted by Ashton in 1960 to John Lanchbery's radical rearrangement of Ferdinand Hérold's score, is one of the jewels of the Royal Ballet repertory. It was the first British ballet to use English folk dance as source material: a Maypole dance, a Morris dance, a sword dance, and Lancashire clogging. Graham Usher and Merle Park are pictured here as Colas and Lise, the principal characters. (Photograph by Houston Rogers; used by permission of the Board of Trustees of the Theatre Museum, London.)

Manon (1974), *Mayerling* (1978), and *Isadora* (1981). All show a gradual reworking of the three-act ballet form to introduce modern dance influences and to align it more closely with British dramatic traditions and narrative strengths. This reshaping of the full-length ballet in the twentieth century has been Britain's unique achievement in choreography.

MacMillan's creative effort seemed, however, to bring to the surface the inevitable conflict in one person who serves as both choreographer and artistic director, a conflict between the need to create and the time consumed in administration. MacMillan resigned as director in June 1977 but retained his choreographic post. A measure of artistic continuity was thus maintained through the nine years of the next director, Norman Morrice, who concentrated on bringing forward new talent among his dancers and encouraging new choreographers like David Bintley, then of the Royal Ballet, afterward resident choreographer of Sadler's Wells Royal Ballet. The developments of this period were undermined by some internal conflicts and administrative problems; Morrice's tenure became a period of stasis and indecision, of waiting, it might seem, for Anthony Dowell, the next director, in 1986. [*See the entry on Dowell.*] Morrice had danced with Ballet Rambert during its evolution into a modern company and was imbued with the modern dance philosophy of Martha Graham; he, like MacMillan, stressed modern choreography. Observers noted a distinct diminution in the time and attention given to the Ashton legacy. Many critics hoped that the appointment of Dowell, trained as a classical dancer and nurtured by Ashton, would redress the balance.

ROYAL BALLET. In November 1963, the Royal Ballet presented the Kingdom of the Shades scene from Petipa's famous ballet *La Bayadère,* staged for the company by Rudolf Nureyev. With Margot Fonteyn as Nikia, he is seen here as Solor, surrounded by members of the female ensemble as the Shades. (Photograph © by Zoë Dominic; used by permission.)

ROYAL BALLET. Kenneth MacMillan's *Mayerling,* first performed in February 1978, featured Lynn Seymour as the teenage Baroness Mary Vetsera and David Wall as Crown Prince Rudolf of Austria-Hungary. The romantic story of their illicit love affair, ending in a double suicide in the hunting lodge called Mayerling, was set to the music of Franz Liszt. (Photograph © by Leslie E. Spatt; used by permission.)

By the time Dowell took the helm, however, the Royal had made a decision to replace its traditional stylistic model, based on the Cecchetti training method, with a Russian one. All of Ashton's choreography was designed with the square, precisely directional Cecchetti technique as its frame, and in many ways the Royal's drift away from its traditions into the Russian camp proved irreversible. The company was left with a sleek, but not especially strong or distinctive, Anglo-Russian look and approach that were not truly hospitable to Ashton's choreography.

Combined with the shift in schooling was the adoption of an American, Balanchinean look for the dancers, especially the ballerinas. Fonteyn, the original model, had been petite, and, while ideally proportioned, not especially loose in the hip joint, with a conservative extension and demure line. Her retirement left a vacuum of close to twenty years in which the company lacked a persuasive ballerina, though many candidates emerged, some relatively accepted and successful, like Lesley Collier, and some utterly rejected and condemned, like Marguerite Porter. During this period, the model shifted to prefer long-legged, loose-hipped women who resembled New York City Ballet's leading female dancers; Bryony Brind, Karen Paisey, and Deirdre Eyden were the partly successful incarnations of the mold that was fully realized only with the emergence of Darcey Bussell in the 1990s—the first Englishwoman since Fonteyn recognized on the world stage as a true ballerina. Also during the 1990s, Sylvie Guillem, the French ballerina, became associated with the Royal as a guest artist often invited and featured by Dowell. During the 1980s the Royal ended its policy of admitting only British or Commonwealth citizens as dancers. Italian Alessandra Ferri, a MacMillan protégée, was acclaimed in the early 1980s but left to carve out an international career.

There was a corresponding lack of top-level male dancing. AIDS, departures for other companies and countries, and retirement all took a toll. By the 1990s the Royal was depending on guest stars and foreign-born danseurs, such as Laurent Hilaire, Irek Mukhamedov, and Zoltán Solymosi, to lead its ranks.

In terms of repertory, the Royal, which shared the Opera House with the opera company and could give only a limited number of programs in its home theater annually, failed to find a persuasive post-Ashton voice. MacMillan continued as resident choreographer until his death in 1992; his last gift to the company was his discovery of Bussell, for whom he made the three-act *Prince of the Pagodas* in 1989, and *Winter Dreams,* based on Anton Chekhov's play *Three Sisters,* in 1991. He was succeeded by David Bintley, whose works, Ashtonian in style, received restrained admiration. As director, Dowell commissioned relative newcomers such as Ashley Page and Christopher Wheeldon to choreograph new works. He also turned to the repertory of the American Twyla Tharp, importing many pieces and commissioning *Mr. Worldly Wise,* a full-evening ballet, in 1995.

Dowell's own stagings of *Swan Lake* (1987) and especially *The Sleeping Beauty* (1994), were universally condemned for their expensive, hideous sets and costumes. Dowell was also criticized for jettisoning still more of Ashton's choreography than MacMillan had found necessary. In the area of ballerinas, however, Dowell was luckier; three strong women emerged during his tenure—in addition to Bussell, the public and the critics embraced Sarah Wildor and a second Italian-born dancer, Viviana Durante.

Sadler's Wells Royal Ballet. Sadler's Wells Royal Ballet (SWRB), originally the second company of the Royal Ballet, became an important company in its own right. It has been located in Birmingham under the name the Birmingham Royal Ballet, since 1990. After 1976, when the company returned from the Royal Opera House to Sadler's Wells Theatre, it developed its own artistic policy and style, commissioned more than forty original works, and mounted productions of *Swan Lake* and *The Sleeping Beauty.*

Historically, however, Sadler's Wells Royal Ballet is very much part of the Royal Ballet tradition, fulfilling specific purposes within the Royal Ballet structure. It began in 1946 as Sadler's Wells Theatre Ballet, occupying Sadler's Wells Theatre when the parent company moved to the Opera House. Its original function was to provide dancers for the Sadler's Wells Opera and give performances of its own that could develop young dancers and choreographic talent. Working under the guidance of Peggy van Praagh between 1946 and 1955, the company gave scaled-down productions of the classics, such as *Coppélia, The Nutcracker,* and act 2 of *Swan Lake,* and works by Ashton. These productions demonstrated the potential of dancers such as Svetlana Beriosova, David Blair, Anne Heaton, Elaine Fifield, Patricia Miller, David Poole, and Stanley Holden. The period was also notable for the development of John Cranko as a major choreographer and the beginning of the choreographic career of MacMillan—both fostered by van Praagh.

The growth of Sadler's Wells Ballet in size and commitment at Covent Garden brought about a change of function for the second company. It withdrew from touring the country; the Sadler's Wells Theatre Ballet was instead enlarged to become the touring section of the Royal Ballet, based on Covent Garden, then replicating much of the Covent Garden repertory, especially the classics. At the same time, it continued to provide opportunities for the choreographic development of MacMillan.

From 1955 to 1970, the company's standards and reputation rose. It toured extensively abroad and in Britain, providing a Royal Ballet presence outside London. It de-

ROYAL BALLET. Using music by Michael Tippet, Richard Alston created *Midsummer* for the Royal Ballet in 1983. The leaping dancers pictured here are (from left to right) Phillip Broomhead, Bruce Sansom, Jonathan Cope, and Ashley Page. (Photograph © 1983 by Bill Cooper; used by permission.)

veloped its own talent with such prominent dancers as Lynn Seymour, Doreen Wells, Jane Landon, Brenda Last, Elizabeth Anderton, Donald MacLeary, Christopher Gable, David Wall, and Paul Clarke.

In 1964, the company became home to a new venture called Ballet for All, an educational group that drew its dancers in rotation from the company to perform special ballet plays combining dancers, actors, and musicians in presentations about the history and practice of classical ballet and the experience of dancing professionally. The first venture of its kind in Britain, it enjoyed marked success in reaching new audiences until it was disbanded in 1979.

The size and effort of the Sadler's Wells Royal Ballet's touring venture, however, created immense financial problems. On Ashton's retirement, responsibility for Ballet for All was transferred to Covent Garden, and the touring company was reduced to twenty-two soloists under the direction of Peter Wright. The reorganized company was dedicated to new works and the performance of small-cast master works. This formula was doomed to fail on tour because regional audiences demanded to see at least some of the classical repertory. To respond to this demand, the group was gradually enlarged to a maximum of fifty dancers. In this form, it has developed its own style. Dancers who have become well known as members of this particular company include Galina Samsova, Margaret Barbieri, Marion Tate, Nicola Katrak, Alain Dubreuil, and Roland Price. Sadler's Wells Royal Ballet has also provided important opportunities for new choreographers like David Bintley, Michael Corder, Jonathan Burrows, and Jennifer Jackson. Above all, it has won a large and loyal audience for the changing image of classical ballet that it represents. This fresh approach, reflected in both the repertory and the performance approach of its dancers, has done a great deal to educate audiences and is perhaps the company's most significant achievement. The achievement is symbolized by the success of the move to the Hippodrome Theatre in Birmingham and the honors heaped upon Peter Wright, recognized now as a leading classical producer and director. The company works in custom-built facilities on one of the largest stages in Britain. It has increased to more than sixty dancers and hopes to open its own branch of the Royal Ballet School. It maintains, still, its regional and international touring commitments.

ROYAL BALLET. Principal dancers Darcey Bussell and Irek Mukhamedov in MacMillan's *Winter Dreams* (1991), set to music by Tchaikovsky. (Photograph © by Catherine Ashmore; used by permission.)

ROYAL BALLET. One of Frederick Ashton's last works was *Varii Capricci*, created in 1983 for Anthony Dowell (Lo Straniero) and Antoinette Sibley (La Capricciosa). It was danced to music composed by William Walton. (Photograph © 1983 by Jack Vartoogian; used by permission.)

Royal Ballet School. Founded by Ninette de Valois at Sadler's Wells Theatre in 1931 and preceded by her own Academy of Choreographic Art, which opened in 1926, today's Royal Ballet School is the oldest of the several Royal Ballet organizations. In keeping with de Valois's assertion that a school must precede a company, most of the dancers who have entered the company have been trained at the school or have spent at least one or two years there. Housed at the theater during the 1930s and for much of World War II, the school was able to draw from the beginning on the traditions of French, Italian, Danish, and Russian teaching—the four great schools of European classical ballet—as represented by experienced teachers then escaping Nazi domination and working in London.

When the Sadler's Wells Ballet moved into the Royal Opera House, the school was expanded to meet new responsibilities. In 1947 it moved to its present site in Baron's Court, West London. An academic curriculum was added, students and staff were increased, and the distinguished critic and writer Arnold Haskell became its director. In 1955 a lower school, offering ballet training and a grammar-school education to boys and girls between eleven and sixteen was established, with boarding facilities at White Lodge, Richmond Park. The senior school, for students over sixteen, remained at Baron's Court. Students from both schools were able to take part, when needed, in performances at Covent Garden. Later, a teacher-training course was added, so that the school's organization compared with its great counterparts in Leningrad, Moscow, and Paris. Students are admitted to both schools from all over the United Kingdom through regional auditions; students from abroad are accepted into the senior school only. Training includes classical ballet and contemporary dance; folk, national, and character dance; dance composition; Benesh notation; and a continuing program of academic studies. The staff includes the school's permanent teachers, members of the Royal Ballet, and visiting teachers from abroad, who help to maintain liaisons with the principal classical ballet training centers in Russia, Europe, China, and the United States.

BIBLIOGRAPHY

Anglin, Werdon. "The Royal Ballet and Sadler's Wells Royal Ballet." In *Twentieth-Century Dance in Britain,* edited by Joan W. White. London, 1985.

Bland, Alexander. *The Royal Ballet: The First Fifty Years.* London, 1981.

Brinson, Peter, ed. *The Ballet in Britain.* London, 1962.

Clarke, Mary. *The Sadler's Wells Ballet.* New York, 1955.

Greskovic, Robert. "The Royal Ballet in 1994, or, Goodbye to All That." *Ballet Review* 22 (Winter 1994): 76–95.

Sorley Walker, Kathrine, and Sarah C. Woodcock. *The Royal Ballet: A Picture History.* Rev. ed. London, 1986.

Vaughan, David. "Royal Ballet at Fifty: Entering a Golden Era." *Dance Magazine* (June 1981): 80–87.

PETER BRINSON and ANITA FINKEL

ROYAL BALLET OF FLANDERS. Called Ballet van Vlaanderen in Flemish, the Royal Ballet of Flanders is one of the three ballet companies in Belgium; the others are the Ballet du XXe Siècle and Charleroi/Danses (formerly the Ballet Royale de Wallonie). It was founded in 1969 under the auspices of the Belgian Ministry of Dutch Culture. The board of directors includes representatives from the Flemish provincial governments, from different towns and communes throughout Flanders, and from the ministry. Jeanne Brabants was appointed artistic director and André Leclair, a former dancer of the Ballet du XXe Siècle, was named principal choreographer. The company was formed of dancers from the Municipal School for Ballet in Antwerp and the opera houses of Ghent and Antwerp. Because there were not enough dancers in Belgium, foreign dancers were also engaged. Rehearsals began in 1970, and the first ballet, Leclair's *Prometheus* (1970), to music by Beethoven, was broadcast by the Belgian Television Network. [*See the entries on Brabants and Leclair.*]

It is the directors' policy to include in the repertory ballets by internationally known choreographers, encompassing a wide range of styles. The company also encourages the creative efforts of Belgian choreographers, as well as music by Belgian composers. Thus the repertory includes works by such Belgian choreographers as Aimé de Lignière, Jeanne Brabants, and André Leclair to music by Belgian composers George Delerue, François Glorieux, Elias Gistelinck, Raymond Baervoets, Frederik Devreese, and Daan Sterneveld. In 1976 King Boudoin of Belgium bestowed the epithet "Royal" on the Flanders and Wallonie ballet companies.

The Royal Ballet of Flanders comprises four groups. One is the touring company, performing in Belgium and abroad. A second group performs the *divertissements* at the Flemish Royal Opera. The remaining two groups travel from school to school, teaching children to view dance as an art form and thus building an audience for dance. This is a task of great importance because Flanders has no ballet tradition. Dancers who have contributed to the fame of the company include Rita Poelvoorde, Jan Nuyts, Tom van Cauwenbergh, Winni Jacobs, Frieda Brijs, Aimé de Lignière, Andrée Marlière, and Marie-Louise Wilderijckx.

In 1984 Valery Panov took over the directorship. This changed the nature of the company; it was only the choreographic work of Panov that stayed on the bill. Besides revivals of his older works, he created new choreographic pieces such as *Panoveriana* (1985, an overview of all Panov's works), *Moves* (1986, music by François Glorieux), *Till Eulenspiegel* (1987, music by Pierre Bartholomé), and a new choreographed version of Prokofiev's *Romeo and Juliet* (1984). Panov's choreography is filled with the virtuosic features of traditional Russian classical ballet, but the dancing is colored with a more natural expressiveness. The coming of Panov and his wife, Galina Panova, to the Royal Ballet of Flanders attracted such outstanding dancers as Andria Hall, Vivien Loeber, Mehmet Balkan, Koen Onzia, and Tom and Ben van

Cauwenbergh. The daily classes of the company were taught according to the Russian method. The company has toured in Belgium and in various countries, including the United States and China.

In January 1987, Robert Denvers was named artistic director. A former dancer with the Ballet du XXe Siècle and the National Ballet of Canada, Denvers also founded his own school in New York City, the West Side School of Ballet. With Denvers, Danny Rosseel was named choreographer, and the company changed to a repertory company including the works of George Balanchine, Jiří Kylián, Antony Tudor, Maurice Béjart, Flemming Flindt, Ib Andersen, Mauricio Wanrot, Thierry Maladain, Christopher d'Ambroise, Stuart Sebastian, Peter Anastos, and Marc Bogaerts.

In 1985 an offspring company was formed to produce musicals, and Linda Lepomme was appointed director. From 1985 to 1995, eighteen hundred performances were restaged and included *Jesus Christ Superstar, My Fair Lady,* and *Evita.* In 1986 the company premiered *Sacco and Vanzetti* (music by Dirk Brossé; libretto by Frank van Laecke and Paul Berkenman; and directed by Stijn Coninx).

[*See also* Belgium, *article on* Theatrical Dance.]

BIBLIOGRAPHY

Barbier, Rina. *Het Koninklijk Ballet van Vlaanderen: creaties en realisaties.* Antwerp, 1980.

Barbier, Rina. *The Royal Ballet of Flanders, 1970–1980.* Brussels, 1980.

Brabants, Jeanne. "Trees in the Desert." *Ballett International* 7 (June–July 1984): 20–23.

Koninklijk Ballet van Vlaanderen: Souvenir Program, U.S. Tour, 1978. New York, 1978.

Peters, Kurt. "Koninklijk Ballet van Vlaanderen immer jubiläumsreif." *Das Tanzarchiv* 28 (July 1980): 409–412.

Uytterhoeven, Michel. "Quatorze moments de danse en Flandre: Politique de la danse, 1982–1995." *Nouvelles de danse* (Winter 1995): 5–16.

Luc Vervaeke

ROYAL DANISH BALLET. During the twentieth century, the Royal Danish Ballet (Danish, Den Kongelige Danske Ballet) achieved enormous international prestige. The company has long been identified with the work of August Bournonville, one of the premiere choreographers of the nineteenth century, who was the company's ballet master for nearly five decades.

Historical Background. When the first native Danish theater opened in Copenhagen in 1722, dance was a significant aspect of the theater system, both as a part of various plays as well as an independent entertainment that attracted people to the theater. The first theater was located in Grønnegade, and Ludvig Holberg wrote his comedies for production there. Molière's plays and comedy ballets also were presented in Grønnegade, and Holberg's plays often included dancing. In 1726 French ballet master Jean-Baptiste Landé came to work at the theater. He later went to Saint Petersburg, where, in 1738, he participated in founding the Imperial Theater School, which became the basis for the Imperial Ballet Company.

Dance activities in Grønnegade were modest, but Landé's productions, featuring characters from the Italian *commedia dell'arte,* became the forerunners of the pantomimes that continue to be performed at the Tivoli Theater in Copenhagen. When the theater at Grønnegade closed because of financial difficulties and fire swept Copenhagen in 1728, theatrical art came to a halt in Denmark for nearly two decades, mainly because of the puritanical beliefs held by the royal family at that time.

In 1747 the theater reorganized, and in 1748 the actors moved to a theater housed at Kongens Nytorv, where the Royal Theater was formed in 1772. Until then, the theater had been part of the city of Copenhagen. The ballet was connected to the theater from its inception, but very few of the dancers were Danish. Most of the ballet masters as well as the dancers were international artists who came from Germany, Italy, and France. Changes took place quite frequently, but from the theater leadership's point of view, there was always great interest in dance, which often was the best means of attracting and entertaining audiences still not accustomed to theatrical art.

The first ballet master was a Frenchman, called Des Larches, who remained until 1753. For 1755/56, he was succeeded by another Frenchman, Neudin. The next ballet master was an Italian, Antonio Como, who with his temperamental, beautiful, and complex wife, Anna Como, was active at the theater until 1763. Because in addition to being a dancer Anna Como had a beautiful voice, singing was included in most of the ballets, a not uncommon practice at that time; it was quite customary in the harlequinades that were then blossoming at the theater. Antonio Como's contribution was significant because he was the first person employed to teach dance to the actors who figured in the ballets, and he thereby gradually created the basis for the Danish Corps de Ballet (The Danish Ballet Company.)

In Como's ballets dance was most important and was often supported by pantomime. The subjects were all taken from mythology, a foreign country, or famous professions. After Como came another Italian, Antonio Sacco, who remained in charge of the ballet from 1763 to 1767. Sacco was influenced by the European ballet reforms instituted by Jean-Georges Noverre and Gaspero Angiolini, and he did not hesitate to copy their works. In so doing he introduced the new dramatic-action ballet, *ballet d'action,* to Denmark.

Sacco broke with the Royal Ballet but continued to work in Copenhagen at the new Hof (or Court) Theater, built in 1767 by King Christian VII, a theater lover, to allow himself to perform in a comedy; it now houses a theater museum. The economic resources were greater at the Hof, and Sacco and several supporters provided significant competition for the ballet at the comedy house (Komediehuset) at Kongens Nytorv. It was not uncommon to see the best artists defect to the Hof Theater; for example, French dancer Jean-Baptiste Martin, who became Sacco's successor as ballet master at Kongens Nytorv in 1767, transferred the following year to the Hof.

The most important event that occurred during this period was the establishment of the first Danish ballet school in 1771. Its founder and leader was the French dancer Pierre Laurent, who in 1752 had come to Copenhagen, where he functioned as a ballet master with various Italian opera troupes and later was appointed as royal ballet master. At the school Laurent taught both children and *figurantes,* and these classes constituted the origins of the school from which the Royal Danish Ballet developed.

After Martin's brief tenure, a rapid succession of Italian ballet masters served at Kongens Nytorv: Innocente Gambruzzi (1768), Martini (1769–1770), Vincenzo Piattoli (1770–1772 and 1773–1775), and Domenico Andreani (1772–1773). When Piattoli left for the second time in 1775, the first chapter of the history of the Royal Danish Ballet came to an end. Ballet had been established as an art form, and its position at the Danish theater had been confirmed, but a significant Danish ballet art had yet to be created, and the company lacked national influence. Continuity had been lacking for many years, during which the ballet masters had turned over quickly, and the company had yet to produce a significant Danish artist.

ROYAL DANISH BALLET. Vincenzo Galleotti staged *The Whims of Cupid and the Ballet Master* for the Royal Danish Ballet in October 1786. It is the oldest ballet to survive with its original choreography intact. In a performance during the 1972/73 season, Lillian Jensen and Niels Bjørn Larsen appeared as the Elderly Couple. (Photograph © by John R. Johnsen; used by permission.)

Vincenzo Galeotti oversaw the first flourishing period for the Royal Danish Ballet. Born in Florence in 1733, he had an international career as a dancer and a ballet master before settling in Copenhagen in 1775. Galeotti was a student of Gaspero Angiolini, and as was often done at that time, he produced two of Angiolini's ballets in Copenhagen and claimed them as his own: *Zigeunernes Lejr* (The Gypsies' Camp) in 1776, after Angiolini's *Les Cosaques,* and *Den Forladte Dido* (The Abandoned Dido) in 1777, from *Didone Abbandonata.* Galeotti had danced and had been a ballet master in Venice. His wife, Antonia Guidi, had danced in Noverre's large reform ballet in Stuttgart, and it is possible that Galeotti himself had participated. In any event, in Galeotti the Royal Danish Ballet now had a ballet master who was a ballet artist with great international awareness and experience. He had spent a few years in London around 1770 and then returned to Venice before moving to Copenhagen, where he remained, took up Danish residence, and continued as ballet master at the Royal Theater until his death in 1816.

Galeotti led the ballet for more than forty years and produced forty-nine ballets onstage. Naturally it was very beneficial for the Danish ballet to have the same leader for such a long period, but equally important was the fact that Galeotti was a man who knew what he wanted. He introduced Denmark to an international repertory; he made the *ballet d'action,* in which events were expressed in dance and pantomime, the outstanding genre; and he produced great dramatic works that often had a literary inspiration. He started with Voltaire's tragedies, staging the ballets *L'Orphelin* in 1780 and *Semiramis* in 1787, and he concluded his career with Shakespeare, creating *Romeo and Juliet* in 1811 and *Macbeth,* his last ballet in 1816. Galeotti worked in different modes, from deep, mythological ballets to small, light productions. His only surviving ballet belongs to the latter group; called *Amors og Balletmesterens Luner* (The Whims of Cupid and the Ballet Master), it has been produced as an ongoing tradition since 1786.

In all his great works, Galeotti, like Noverre and Angiolini, tried to show that ballet could reflect strong emotions. To him, ballet was more than entertainment, and his vivid imagination and firm grasp of the scenic instruments—he worked most effectively with large mass scenes—enabled him to create impressive ballets that Copenhagen audiences had never seen. He also kept up with the times. *Rolf Blaaskæq* (Bluebeard) was inspired by André-Ernest-Modeste Grétry's opera *Raoul Barbe-bleue,* and in 1801 Galeotti created the first Nordic ballet, *Lagertha,* and thus participated in bringing romanticism to the Danish theater. Claus Schall created the music for this ballet, as he did for many other Galeotti works, but

Galeotti used Jens Lolle as well. In developing native composers, Galeotti began a tradition that August Bournonville, Harald Lander, and Flemming Flindt would continue. Galeotti's impact on the Danish ballet in this initial phase should not be underestimated. His school, which replaced Laurent's as the official school, became the base for the Royal Danish Ballet, the third oldest company in the world (only the Paris Opera Ballet and the Maryinsky Ballet in Saint Petersburg are older). [*See the entry on Galeotti.*]

The Danish Ballet Company now had a regular company corps and soloists. Among the women was Anine Frohlich, who made her debut in 1773 and who became the first Danish ballerina; later Margrethe Schall became particularly well known in the title role of Galeotti's production of *Nina, eller den Vanvittige of Kærlighed (Nina, ou La Folle par Amour)* in 1802. Although Galeotti was in his forties when he came to Denmark, he was the company's leading male dancer and continued onstage until 1812.

During Galeotti's later years, Jean-Pierre Laurent, the son of Pierre Laurent, returned to his native Copenhagen. Laurent had been educated at Noverre in Paris and had been the solo dancer at the Paris Opera. After the French Revolution he was a ballet master in Marseille before returning in 1800 as the solo dancer at the Royal Theater, where he took over his father's position at court.

In 1792 another French dancer, Antoine Bournonville, came to the Royal Danish Ballet from Stockholm. Born in Lyon, he had danced throughout Europe and with Noverre in London in 1781. He also had spent ten years at the Swedish court, where he became one of King Gustav III's favorite artists. Bournonville was a great asset to the ballet in Copenhagen. He was handsome and from a dance perspective provided international elegance to Copenhagen. Moreover, he was an outstanding mime, though not a particularly good choreographer. [*See the entry on Antoine Bournonville.*]

This characterization applied as well to the Swedish dancer Caro Dahlen, who came to Copenhagen from Stockholm. In the history of Danish ballet Dahlen is remembered only for his flop *Armida* in 1821, when Hans Christian Andersen's name was printed on the theater's billboard. At that time Andersen was a ballet student at the theater, and he danced the part of a troll in Dahlen's ballet.

The beginning of the nineteenth century were lean years for the ballet. Galeotti had stayed too long and grown too old to manage the Royal Danish Ballet with authority. Antoine Bournonville, who became his successor as ballet master, had neither the ability nor the ambition to advance the ballet or to keep up to date with international developments in dance. When Bournonville retired in 1823, dancer Pierre Larcher began to lead the ballet, although he was not officially appointed ballet master. Over the next few years the art, which had been so much admired under Galeotti, was met with growing public indifference. It would take the talents of another Bournonville to bring the ballet back to its feet.

The Influence of August Bournonville. From his years of study in Paris, August Bournonville had become aware of the standards of the international world of ballet. He became ballet master at the Royal Danish Ballet in 1830 and retained this position with few interruptions until 1877. Under his leadership the ballet flourished as never before. The art regained the respect of the audience, and, earlier than in any other country, the dancers obtained social equality with other artists of the theater and with the citizens of the city.

During Bournonville's tenure, the Royal Danish Ballet obtained several truly significant dancers whom Bournonville encouraged, cared for, and often fought with, especially the ballerinas. The most important women dancers were Andrea Kraetzmer, for whom he created the part of Gretchen in *Faust* in 1832; Lucile Grahn, who danced the part of Astrid in Bournonville's historical ballet *Waldemar* in 1835 and who the next year became the first Danish Sylphide; Augusta Nielsen, who was Celeste in *Toreadoren* (The Toreador) in 1840; Caroline Fjeldsted, who created Teresina in *Napoli* in 1842; Juliette Price, who made her debut in *Konservatoriet* in 1849 and who was the first Hilda in *Et Folkesagn* (A Folk Tale) in 1854, Rosita in *Fjernt fra Denmark* (Far from Denmark) in 1860, and Svava in *Valkyrien* (The Valkyrie) in 1861. Of all his dancers, Price was the closest to Bournonville's ideal. She was succeeded by Betty Schnell, who later became an actress and under the name of Betty Hennings was the first Nora in Henrik Ibsen's *A Doll's House.* Marie Westberg of Sweden danced the leading part in Bournonville's last ballet, *Fra Sibirien til Moskva* (From Siberia to Moscow), in 1876.

For his first eighteen years with the Royal Danish Ballet, Bournonville was also the leading male dancer. He made room for other dancers, however, and in particular promoted a number of excellent mimes who were necessary for his repertory. The continuing Royal Danish Ballet tradition of featuring outstanding mime artists was founded during the time of Galeotti and was extended through this period with performers such as Andreas Füssel, Edvard and Johan Stramboe, Frederik Ferdinand Hoppensach, and Carl Fredstrup, who was the first Witch in *Sylfiden (La Sylphide)* in 1836. This rich mime tradition flourished in part because the Danish ballet coexisted with the Royal Theater, which also housed the opera and today keeps the three arts together. Furthermore, Bournonville at times used actors for the mime parts in his ballets, a common practice at the Royal Theater until the 1930s.

ROYAL DANISH BALLET. Under the Danish title *Sylfiden,* August Bournonville mounted his version of *La Sylphide* for the company in 1836, using music by Hermann Løvenskjold. It has since only rarely been absent from the repertory. In September 1903, Gustav Uhlendorff appeared as James, with Ellen Price de Plane in the title role. (Photograph by Georg Lindström; from the Theater Museum, Copenhagen.)

Bournonville's own performances and the prominence of male dancers in his ballets also established a tradition of excellent male dancing, which, more than in other European countries, has been maintained into the present. After Bournonville stopped performing the Danish ballet's most significant male dancer was Waldemar Price, who made his debut in 1857 and until his retirement in 1901 was the incarnation of the Lover in Bournonville's Danish Romantic ballets.

August Bournonville became the personification of the Royal Danish Ballet. He not only produced significant dancers trained in the French style, but he also created an enormously rich repertory and about fifty ballets in addition to a number of other forms of entertainment as well as introductions to operas and plays. With the exception of *The Whims of Cupid and the Ballet Master,* Galeotti's ballets disappeared from the repertory during Bournonville's tenure; the repertory was totally dominated by Bournonville ballets, and other talents could not compete: in 1841, when Bournonville was in Italy, Paul Taglioni produced his father, Filippo Taglioni's *The Swiss Milkmaid,* which was not successful; in 1862, while Bournonville was working at the opera in Stockholm, the Frenchman Gustave Carey was employed to renew the repertory with *Giselle,* which also quickly disappeared, not to reappear in the Royal Danish Ballet repertory until 1946, with Margot Lander.

Not only in terms of style but also through production activity and ballet themes Bournonville was influenced by what he had seen and learned in Paris. Throughout his entire tenure he kept up with developments in the French capital such that, under him, the Danish ballet simultaneously exhibited an international flair and the specific characteristics that have distinguished it and continue to make it interesting: mime, male dancing, and a light, graceful style.

Bournonville created ballets of many styles. He fashioned straightforward, uncomplicated, and entertaining idyllic ballets, such as *Fjernt fra Danmark* (Far from Denmark) in 1860 and *Livjægerne på Amager* (The King's Volunteers on Amager) in 1871. He created sensitive pictures of the merry Flemish in *Kermessen i Brügge* (Kermesse in Bruges, or The Three Gifts) and of Norwegian peasants in *Brudefærden i Hardanger* (A Wedding Festival in Hardanger) in 1853 and *Fjeldstuen* (The Mountain Hut, or Twenty Years) in 1859. Inspired by the poet Adam Oehlenschläeger, who had brought Romanticism to Denmark, Bournonville created ballets to the Nordic stories of *The Valkyrie* in 1861 and *The Lay of Thrym* in 1868. His main works, though, were *La Sylphide, Napoli,* and *A Folk Tale,* the three great Romantic ballets that became the treasures of the Royal Danish Ballet repertory, representing the core of Bournonville's artistic vision.

Despite strong influence from France and French Romanticism, Bournonville was very Danish in his art. The attitude toward life represented by his works is as distant as possible from French and English Romanticism. With a very strong Christian ethic and attitude, Bournonville entered into the Danish Biedermeier tradition with its idealistic superstructure: art should elevate and bring harmony. Bournonville agreed with other Danish authors and artists of his time who believed that art is a means of establishing connections between this world and a higher world of order, beauty, balance, and pleasure; with regard to Bournonville's ballets, it is where the highly erotic, the passionate, and the dramatic are eliminated or conquered.

Bournonville's influence on the Danish ballet has endured over time. The Danish ballet's world reputation has represented an enormous challenge to Danish ballet artists for more than a century, and the Royal Danish Ballet has felt an obligation to protect this outstanding tradition, however much it has at times hindered the company's development. [*See the entry on August Bournonville.*]

Post-Bournonville. For many years after August Bournonville's retirement in 1877, great changes did not take place at the Royal Danish Ballet, and perhaps that was the best that could have happened. In the late nineteenth century in Europe ballet entered a period of naturalism—and despite this, audiences in Denmark still loved Bournonville, whose ballets are not naturalistic at all. At the Royal Theater in Copenhagen, where Ibsen's realistic plays were being presented for the first time, audiences and the theater leadership retained a warm love for Bournonville's work, which was regarded with reverence.

Ludvig Gade headed the company from 1877 to 1890, and Emil Hansen headed it from 1890 to 1894. There was little change in the repertory, however, until Hans Beck became responsible for the company, leading it from 1894 to 1915. The most popular of Beck's own ballets was *Den Lille Havfrue* (The Little Mermaid), which premiered in 1909 with Ellen Price in the title role. Beck also distinguished himself with a production of *Coppélia,* which German choreographer Max Glasemann produced in 1896 at the Royal Theater; the dominance of national and character dances (in the Bournonville tradition) distinguished this production from the international version. Beck himself danced the part of Franz, and as a dancer he upheld the high level of male dancing established by Bournonville. Beck's partner was Valborg Borchsenius, who during the next half century played a significant role as an expert on Bournonville.

His other roles notwithstanding, Beck's main contribution to the ballet was as Bournonville's conservator. His artistic ideas were similar to Bournonville's, and he protected the master's ballets with great care. He was responsible for the form and third act of *Napoli,* and in 1890 he organized the Bournonville school's ballet curriculum, which became the company's daily training program for the next thirty to forty years.

The Royal Danish Ballet presented a number of popular works during Beck's period: Emilie Walbom choreographed *Les Millions d'Arlequin* (Harlequin's Millions) in 1906 in the style of Petipa and *Drommebilleder* (Dream Pictures) in 1915; in the latter Walbom transferred Michel

ROYAL DANISH BALLET. Bournonville's *Flower Festival in Genzano* (1858) was his third work with an Italian setting. At the center of this group from the 1919 production stand Elna Jørgen-Jensen and Karl Merrild as Rosa and Paolo, the principal characters. (Photograph by Sophus Juncker-Jensen; from the collection of Erik Merrild, Copenhagen.)

Fokine's *Le Carnaval* to Biedermeier-style Danish surroundings with music by Hans Christian Lumbye, a Danish composer of popular dance melodies.

Beck retired as ballet master in 1915. He felt out of touch with the modern impulses of Diaghilev's Ballets Russes, which was rejuvenating ballet in Europe. Beck could not contribute to this renewal, and he had no desire to do so. In Denmark, therefore, ballet remained synonymous with Bournonville, even though performances of his works were becoming tiresome because they were often produced so routinely. [*See the entry on Beck.*]

The Ballet after 1915. Gustav Uhlendorff managed the Royal Danish Ballet from 1915 through 1928. He, too, helped preserve the Bournonville tradition, but he did not significantly influence the ballet, and he failed to take artistic advantage of the presence of the Russian choreographer Michel Fokine and his wife, Vera Fokina, who resided in Copenhagen in 1918 and 1919. The two artists were invited to perform for a couple of evenings in 1918, but they were not asked to work with the Danish dancers; neither was Fokine asked to produce his ballets. Some of the dancers, however, did take private classes from him. In 1925, Fokine was finally invited to the Royal Danish Ballet, where he produced *Les Sylphides* (known in Denmark as *Chopiniana*), *Petrouchka,* and the dances from *Prince Igor.* These evenings were very successful and inspired the dancers enormously. For the first time the ballet's talented young dancers, including Elna Jorgen-Jensen, Elan Lassen, Ulla Poulsen, Karl Merrild, John Andersen, and Sven Aage Larsen, as well as the audience, realized that the ballet had something to offer other than Bournonville's work. For the young Harald Lander, Fokine's productions were very significant; in 1927 he went to the United States to continue to study with the renowned choreographer.

Kaj Smith, who replaced Uhlendorff in 1928, attempted two productions of *Rosendrommen (Le Spectre de la Rose)*

ROYAL DANISH BALLET. George Balanchine's *Symphony in C* was staged for the company by Vida Brown in 1952. The principal dancers pictured here are (from left to right) Margrethe Schanne and Frank Schaufuss, Mona Vangsaae and Børge Ralov, Inge Sand and Erik Bruhn, and Kirsten Ralov and Stanley Williams. (Photograph by H. J. Mydtskov; from the Dance Collection, New York Public Library for the Performing Arts. Choreography by George Balanchine © by John Taras.)

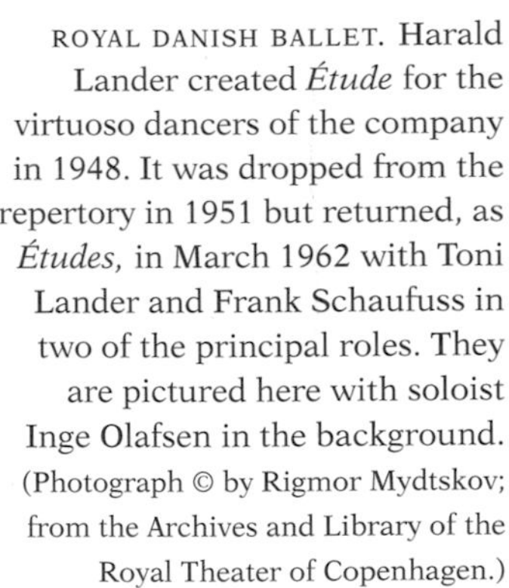

ROYAL DANISH BALLET. Harald Lander created *Étude* for the virtuoso dancers of the company in 1948. It was dropped from the repertory in 1951 but returned, as *Études,* in March 1962 with Toni Lander and Frank Schaufuss in two of the principal roles. They are pictured here with soloist Inge Olafsen in the background. (Photograph © by Rigmor Mydtskov; from the Archives and Library of the Royal Theater of Copenhagen.)

and *The Firebird,* but nothing significant happened until George Balanchine produced six ballets as a guest ballet master in 1930/31: Fokine's *Schéhérazade* and *Die Josephslegende,* Léonide Massine's *Le Tricorne* and *La Boutique Fantasque,* and Balanchine's own *Barabau* and *Apollon Musagète.* Dancers in the Balanchine guest performance included Ulla Poulsen, Else Højgaard, Leif Ørnberg, Børge Ralov, Margot Lander, and *prima ballerina* Elna Larsen, who died in 1930, just as she was beginning an international career. Max Reinhardt had become interested in her during the spring of 1930 with the production of *Die Fledermaus* at the Royal Theater and had taken her to the German Theater in Berlin. The Royal Danish Ballet was about to enter a new and significant phase that would alter the entire status of the ballet in Denmark.

The Modernizing Influence of Harald Lander. In 1931 Harald Lander created his first ballet, *Gaucho,* a colorful ballet with an Argentine theme, and he became ballet master in 1932. Like Bournonville a century before, Lander was in charge of rebuilding the company and creating new dances, a new repertory, and new interest for the audience. He also revised the training school and very slowly strengthened the technique of the Danish dancers. In 1938 Lander presented a one-act version of *Swan Lake,* and in 1948 his presentation of *Études* demonstrated that his nearly twenty years of work with the dancers had produced excellent results in the Danish technique. In 1951, however, he came into conflict with many sections of the company and left Denmark to become ballet master and choreographer at the Paris Opera Ballet.

As ballet master of the Royal Danish Ballet, Lander modernized the company without sacrificing its distinctive characteristics. Lander created a number of ballets that made the art extremely popular. During World War II he used the ballet as a symbol of unity in his choice of works, such as *Troldmandens Laerling* (The Sorcerer's Apprentice) in 1940 and *Festpolonaise (Polonaise de Fête), Våren,* and *Qaartsiluni,* all in 1942. Lander had successful working relationships with the composer Knudåge Riisager and with the author Kjeld Abell, who was Lander's idea man and scriptwriter. One of the most significant Danish writers of the twentieth century, Abell got his start at the ballet. He created the sets and costumes for five of the six ballets that Balanchine started in 1930/31 and, in 1934, his own ballet *Enken i Spejlet* (The Widow in the Mirror), with choreography by Børge Ralov set to the music of Bernard Christensen. The first modern ballet in Denmark, *Enken* introduced dancers in overalls, dealt with current social problems, and featured jazz music.

In 1936 Lander choreographed Bertolt Brecht and Kurt Weill's *The Seven Deadly Sins.* Although it was a big success, the ballet was shown only twice. Rumor had it that production was halted by request of the German embassy.

The wealth of dancing talent brought out by Lander contributed significantly to the success of the ballet in Denmark in the 1930s and 1940s. At the center were Margot Lander and Børge Ralov. Among the young people who would influence the Danish ballet during the next forty years were Mona Vangsaae, Margrethe Schanne, Kirsten Ralov, Inge Sand, Toni Lander, Hans Brenaa,

Svend Erik Jensen, Niels Bjørn Larsen, Poul Gnatt, Frank Schaufuss, Stanley Williams, Fredbjørn Bjørnsson, Erik Bruhn, Henning Kronstam, and Flemming Flindt. When the Royal Danish Ballet went abroad in 1950 and became world famous, Lander's dancers had the main roles in the ballets.

As ballet master, Lander directed the Danish ballet to take international challenges. Alexandre Volinine produced *Giselle* in 1946, and in 1948 Léonide Massine staged two guest productions, *Le Beau Danube* and *Symphonie Fantastique.* The latter was an example of a symphonic ballet, which Danish native Nini Theilade had introduced in Denmark in the 1930s. In 1936 she produced *Psyché,* with music by César Franck, at the Royal Theater and in 1938 *Cirklen* (The Circle), set to Petr Ilich Tchaikovsky's Sixth Symphony. Finally, in 1950 Lander founded the annual ballet festivals that contributed substantially to the Royal Danish Ballet's reputation for the next twenty-three years.

The 1930s were meager years for Bournonville ballets. Lander was initially quite busy with his own choreography, and in a number of everyday ballets he slowly tested the strength of the company; in addition, he believed that the audience needed something besides Bournonville. In the 1940s, however, Lander, with the help of Valborg Borchsenius, started seriously to work on the Bournonville repetory. Together they produced eight Bournonville ballets, which subsequently were saved for the future. Lander often emphasized dancing and entertainment and tightened up the mime passages. In order to strengthen the mime tradition, in 1941 Lander had Borchsenius instruct the dancers in mime, and over the next decade she trained outstanding mimes such as Gerda Karstens, Lillian Jensen, and Niels Bjørn Larsen. The form that the Bournonville ballet achieved under Borchsenius and Lander, with the assistance also of Hans Beck, defined such productions at the Royal Theater until the Bournonville Festival in 1979. Lander's productions were restaged in more or less revised forms but according to the same basic structures that Lander had created. [*See the entries on Borchsenius and Harald Lander.*]

ROYAL DANISH BALLET. Flemming Flindt choreographed his ballet *The Lesson,* inspired by Eugene Ionesco's play, for Danish television in 1963. He mounted it for the stage the following year. During the 1964/65 season, the principal roles were danced by Henning Kronstam (The Teacher) and Mette Hønningen (The Student). (Photograph © by Rigmor Mydtskov; from the Archives and Library of the Royal Theatre of Copenhagen.)

The Company after 1951. When Lander left in 1951, Niels Bjørn Larsen became ballet master and served until 1965, except for the years 1956 to 1958, when Frank Schaufuss was in charge. These were golden years for the Royal Danish Ballet, when the company reached full technical and artistic maturity, aided greatly by Vera Volkova, who served as a ballet teacher from 1951 until her death in 1975. [*See the entries on Larsen and the Schaufuss family.*]

Volkova gave the Royal Danish Ballet its last international polishing. Under her guidance the dancers were able to dance the great Russian classics, which had not been fully produced until this time: *The Sleeping Beauty* in 1957, *Swan Lake* in 1964, and *The Nutcracker* in 1971. Volkova influenced many generations of dancers, including Kirsten Simone, Mette Hønningen, Annemarie Dybdal, Henning Kronstam, Flemming Flindt, Niels Kehlet, Flemming Ryberg, Peter Martins, Peter Schaufuss, and Adam Lüders; in the 1980s, Linda Hindberg, Mette-Ida Kirk, Lis Jeppesen, Arne Villumsen, and Frank Andersen. Ib Andersen was one of the last dancers influenced by Vera Volkova; he, as had Martins, Schaufuss, and Luders before him, left in 1980 for a career at New York City Ballet. [*See the entry on Volkova.*]

After Lander's departure and until 1980, the Bournonville repertory was maintained by Hans Brenaa and Kirsten Ralov, who made modest alterations but introduced no new concepts; they saw their main task as mounting productions in line with the tradition of Lander's time. [*See the entries on Brenaa and Kirsten Ralov.*]

During the 1950s and the early 1960s, the Royal Danish Ballet hosted guest productions by many foreign choreographers, whose works updated the company and gave it an international perspective: David Lichine with *Graduation Ball* in 1952; George Balanchine with *Symphony in C* in 1952, *Concerto Barocco* and *Night Shadow* in 1955, *Serenade* and *Apollo* in 1957, *The Four Temperaments* and *Bourrée Fantasque* in 1963; Frederick Ashton with *Romeo and Juliet,* created especially for the Royal Danish Ballet in 1955 with Henning Kronstam and Mona Vangsaae in the leading roles, and *La Fille Mal Gardée* in 1964; Anton Dolin with *Pas de Quatre* in 1955; Birgit Cullberg with *Moon Reindeer* in 1957 (created especially for the Danish Ballet), *Miss Julie* in 1958, *Medea* in 1959, and *The Lady from the Sea* in 1961; Roland Petit with *Carmen* in 1960 and *Cyrano de Bergerac* in 1961; and Kenneth MacMillan with *Danses Concertantes, Solitaire,* and *Under Jorden* in 1961. With this repertory of both modern and classical works, the company began large tours abroad: London in 1953, Edinburgh in 1955, and the United States in 1956. The tours would continue for the next twenty-five years.

A significant break with tradition came in the late 1950s, when the Royal Danish Ballet opened the company to dancers—Danish and foreign—who had trained or danced elsewhere. Dancers such as Anna Lærkesen and Dinna Bjørn were privately educated by the Latvian dancer and teacher Edite Feifere Frandsen. (In 1961 Frandsen was hired as an instructor at the theater.) This new openness also allowed Flemming Flindt to bring Danish dancer Palle Jacobsen back to the Royal Danish Ballet, where he had his first training. At the beginning of her career Eva Evdokimova danced for the Royal Danish Ballet, and Finnish dancer Sorella Englund was the first foreign dancer to become a principal soloist of the ballet.

ROYAL DANISH BALLET. In modern times, the Danes have never shied away from eroticism on the ballet stage. Flemming Flindt's *Caroline Mathilde* (1991), set to the music of Peter Maxwell Davies, depicts the torrid love affair of Queen Caroline Mathilde of Denmark (1751–1775) with the court physician, Count Johann Friedrich Struensee, who had seized political power. Caroline was divorced by King Christian VII after Struensee was beheaded in 1772. Seen here are Rose Gad and Nikolaj Hübbe as the hapless lovers. (Photograph © 1991 by David Amzallag; used by permission.)

ROYAL DANISH BALLET. A playful moment from John Cranko's *Jeu de Cartes* (Card Game), staged for the company in 1968: Niels Kehlet as the Joker dives through the legs of a five-card "hand." The cheerful score composed by Igor Stravinsky was his way of having musical fun with his favorite card game, poker. (Photograph © by Rigmor Mydtskov; used by permission.)

Flemming Flindt Brings Modern Dance to Copenhagen. By the mid-1960s the Royal Danish Ballet was a classical company with a very strong tradition, a new repertory, and dancers of high technical skill whose presence radiated onstage. These elements gave the Danish ballet its particular profile among international dance companies. It was a cultured, classical profile that over the next ten years would be greatly overshadowed by the totally new challenges placed before the company by Flemming Flindt, ballet master from 1966 to 1978.

Established choreographers returned: Jerome Robbins with *Afternoon of a Faun* in 1966; Roland Petit with *Le Loup* in 1967 and *L'Arlesienne* in 1970; Balanchine with *Donizetti Variations* and *The Prodigal Son* in 1968; and Birgit Cullberg with *The War Hero* in 1975. New choreographers also appeared: John Cranko with *Jeu de Cartes* in 1966 and *The Lady and the Fool, Opus 1,* and *Quatre Images* in 1971; Antony Tudor with *Gala Performance* and *Jardin aux Lilas* in 1970; Rudi van Dantzig with *Monument for a Dead Boy* in 1973; and John Neumeier with

Romeo and Juliet in 1974. But the most significant event during the Flindt period was the introduction of modern dance at the Royal Danish Ballet, by Paul Taylor with *Aureole* in 1968, by Glen Tetley with *Pierrot Lunaire* in 1968, by José Limón with *The Moor's Pavane* in 1971, and by the works of Murray Louis and Lar Lubovitch, among others. Simultaneously a new type of dancer appeared who could master the new style: Vivi Flindt, Johnny Eliasen, and Bruce Marks. During the 1970s, Marks, together with Toni Lander, also choreographed several ballets for the company.

With Flindt the Royal Danish Ballet once again had a resident choreographer. Since Harald Lander a number of Danish dancers had attempted to be choreographers, but none had created anything of remaining value. Flindt, however, introduced forceful and dramatic new productions, often inspired by the Romanian-French dramatist of the absurd, Eugène Ionesco: *The Lesson,* televised in 1963 and staged at the Royal Theater in 1964; and *The Young Man Must Marry* in 1965. Flindt's *The Triumph of Death,* televised in 1971 and staged in 1972 at the Royal Theater, became the Danish theater's biggest ballet success since 1900. Flindt collaborated with Danish composers, such as Per Nørgård and the beat group Savage Rose, and he gave other Danish choreographers opportunities to work. The strongest of these were Elsa-Marianne von Rosen and Eske Holm. Von Rosen's works included *Irene Holm,* presented by the Scandinavian Ballet in 1960 and the Royal Danish Ballet in 1963, *Jomfrukilden* (Virgin Spring) in 1964, *Don Juan* in 1967, and *Helios* in 1970. Holm choreographed *Orestes* in 1968, *Cicacriticis* in 1969, and *The Firebird* in 1972. [*See the entry on Flindt.*]

In 1978 Henning Kronstam became ballet master, with Kirsten Ralov as associate ballet master. Together they managed a highly versatile ballet repertory, with works ranging from Glen Tetley's *Le Sacre du Printemps* in 1978 and his *The Firebird,* created for the Royal Danish Ballet in 1981, to John Neumeier's *A Midsummer Night's Dream* in 1980, to Alvin Ailey's *Memoria* in 1981. [*See the entry on Kronstam.*]

ROYAL DANISH BALLET. The ballets of August Bournonville remain the foundation of the company's repertory. His masterpiece, *Napoli, or The Fisherman and His Bride,* was first performed in 1842. One hundred and fifty years later, in 1992, the triumphal procession in the final scene looked much the same as in the original production. In the cart stand Lloyd Riggins as Gennaro, Heidi Ryom as Teresina, and Eva Kloborg as Veronica. (Photograph © 1992 by David Amzallag; used by permission.)

In 1979 and again in 1992 the Royal Danish Ballet held two internationally acclaimed Bournonville festivals where all the Bournonville ballets that have survived in an unbroken tradition were performed. In 1985 Kronstam left the post of artistic director and was succeeded by Frank Andersen, with Lise La Cour as associate artistic director. Andersen and La Cour have stressed the Bournonville tradition but also with an interest in reconstructions of his works, for example, *Abdallah* (by Toni Lander, Bruce Marks, and Flemming Ryberg) in 1986 and *The Lay of Thrym* (by Allan Fridericia and Elsa-Marianne von Rosen) in 1990. The company showed its strong talent for dramatic ballets with John Cranko's *Onegin* in 1989 and Flemming Flindt's *Caroline Mathilde,* with an original score by Peter Maxwell Davies, in 1991. In 1985 John Neumeier created a Hamlet ballet, *Amleth,* for the company. A new generation of dancers has emerged, including Heidi Ryom, Rose Gad, Silja Schandorff, Nikolaj Hübbe, Alexander Kølpin, and Lloyd Riggins. As a choreographer, former principal dancer Anna Lærkesen has been impressive with her lyrical-dramatic talent. Another young Danish choreographer who should be mentioned is Kim Brandstrup. Educated in London as a modern dancer, he has made several ballets for the Royal Danish. A new generation of Bournonville producers has emerged as well: Frank Andersen, Dinna Bjørn, Henning Kronstam, and Anne Marie Vessel. Vessel, who heads the children's school, produced with Andersen *A Folk Tale,* for which the Danish queen, Margrete II, designed the sets and costumes.

In 1994 Peter Schaufuss took over after Frank Andersen as artistic director. He introduced himself with his world-acclaimed version of Bournonville's *La Sylphide.* Schaufuss stayed as ballet director for only a year. In the summer of 1995, Johnny Eliasen was appointed temporary artistic director until Maina Gielgud took over in March 1997. She is the first woman to be artistic director in Copenhagen and the first foreigner since August Bournonville's father Antoine Bournonville in 1816. Responsible for the Bournonville tradition and the Bournonville policy, Dinna Bjørn was appointed consultant; she is also artistic director for the Norwegian National Ballet. Peter Schaufuss went on working with the Danes. In 1996 he brought Ashton's *Romeo and Juliet* back to the company and, in the summer of the same year, created a full-length *Hamlet* for the company's new male star, Johan Kobborg.

[*See also* Folk Tale, A; Kermesse in Bruges; *and* Konservatoriet.]

BIBLIOGRAPHY

Acocella, Joan. "Danish Minister Threatens RDB." *Dance Magazine* (August 1990): 20–21.

Aschengreen, Erik. "Tradition og kamp for fornyelse." In *Dansk teater i 60'erne og 70'erne,* edited by Stig J. Jensen et al. Teatervidenskabelige Studier, 8. Copenhagen, 1982.

Aschengreen, Erik. "The Royal Danish Ballet Season of 1954–1955." *Dance Chronicle* 18.3 (1995): 419–426.

Croce, Arlene. "Is There a Cure for Moon Reindeer?" *Ballet Review* 1.3 (1966): 2–12.

Fog, Dan. *The Royal Danish Ballet, 1760–1958, and August Bournonville: A Chronological Catalogue.* Copenhagen, 1961.

Fridericia, Allan. "Working Conditions for Dancers in Denmark." In *World Ballet and Dance, 1989–90,* edited by Bent Schønberg. London, 1989.

Georg, Anders, and Søren Dyssegaard, eds. *The Royal Danish Ballet and Bournonville: Centenary in Honour of August Bournonville.* Copenhagen, 1979.

Guy, John. "Spotlight on Frank Andersen: Ballet Master to the Queen." *The Dancing Times* (August 1991): 1030–1031.

Hunt, Marilyn. "Bournonville Pas de Six." *Dance Magazine* (June 1988): 37–43.

Jackson, George. "The Bournonville Caper." *Dance View* 9 (June 1992): 146–154.

Kanter, Katharine. "A Conversation with Flemming Ryberg." *Dance Now* 3 (Winter 1994): 58–62.

Kragh-Jacobsen, Svend. *Ballettens blomstring ude og hjemme.* Copenhagen, 1945.

Kragh-Jacobsen, Svend, and Torben Krogh, eds. *Den Kongelige Danske Ballet.* Copenhagen, 1952.

Kragh-Jacobsen, Svend. *Ballet bogen.* Copenhagen, 1954.

Kragh-Jacobsen, Svend. *The Royal Danish Ballet.* Copenhagen, 1955.

Murray, Jane Ward. "The Theatre School." *Dance View* 9 (June 1992): 71–83.

Siegel, Marcia B. "Hoping for Eternal Spring." *Hudson Review* (Autumn 1992): 467–472.

Tomalonis, Alexandra. "Bournonville's Gifts." *Dance View* 9 (June 1992): 42–54.

Windreich, Leland. "The Bournonville Legacy." *Vandance* 20 (Spring 1992): 4–9.

ERIK ASCHENGREEN

ROYAL WINNIPEG BALLET. The Royal Winnipeg Ballet is the oldest ballet company in Canada and the second oldest (after the San Francisco Ballet) in North America. In 1954 it was the first ballet company in the British Commonwealth to receive permission from Queen Elizabeth II to use the word *Royal* in its name, and its extreme portability (its complement of performers has rarely exceeded twenty-seven) has enabled it to act as a dancing ambassador for Canada in more than five hundred cities and towns in forty-one countries. Its repertory has always been eclectic, although until the late 1970s the work of neoclassical and contemporary ballet choreographers of the middle and late twentieth century was given the greatest prominence.

Winnipeg, a lonely city of about 500,000 people, situated almost at the center of the North American continent, is an unlikely base for an international ballet company. Neither its harsh climate nor its conservative audience would seem to offer much encouragement for the development of the arts. What assured the growth of the Royal Winnipeg Ballet was the foresight and determination of a small band of dedicated individuals.

The company had its origins in the Winnipeg Ballet Club, founded in 1938 by two immigrant English dance teachers, Gweneth Lloyd and her associate and former pupil Betty Farrally. To attract the city's better dancers they offered free concentrated training and opportunities for performance. One of the club's first members was a nine-year-old boy, David Adams, later to become a principal dancer with the National Ballet of Canada and Britain's Royal Ballet. Another was Paddy Stone, then a sixteen-year-old tap specialist, later to become a distinguished choreographer of variety shows on British television. Stone's original partner was Jean McKenzie, the Winnipeg company's first ballerina and in 1962 the founding principal of the company school.

The club gave its inaugural performance in June 1939, as part of a pageant to celebrate a visit to Winnipeg by King George VI and Queen Elizabeth. Two short works were presented: *Grain,* depicting the history of the grain cycle; and *Kilowatt Magic,* celebrating the arrival of hydroelectric power to the prairie. Both were choreographed by Lloyd, and both were aimed directly at the hearts and interests of the Winnipeg audience.

Lloyd stated from the first days of the club's operations that she believed ballet was "no longer a champagne-and-caviar treat but a beer-and-skittles entertainment." This emphasis on the importance of popular appeal was enthusiastically embraced and endorsed by succeeding artistic and administrative leaders, and it was the motivating force behind the company's national and international successes in the late 1960s.

ROYAL WINNIPEG BALLET. The 1952 production of *Swan Lake,* act 2, with Eva von Gencsy as Odette, Arnold Spohr (standing, far right) as Siegfried, an unidentified dancer as Benno, and members of the ensemble. The choreographic credit, "after Petipa," should have read "after Ivanov." But note the unorthodox presence of male dancers among the swans. (Photograph by Phillips-Gutkin; from the archives of the Royal Winnipeg Ballet.)

The Winnipeg Ballet Club became the Winnipeg Ballet in 1941. In 1945 it was the first Canadian dance company to tour (to Ottawa and across western Canada), and in 1948 it co-sponsored the first Canadian Ballet Festival, an important step toward self-understanding for the fledgling Canadian dance community. Throughout its initial decade, the Winnipeg Ballet's repertory was dominated by Lloyd's choreography, much influenced by her memories of performances she had seen in London (among them the 1918 visit of the Ballets Russes de Serge Diaghilev) and by the work of the touring international companies of the time. However, once the company established its professional status, with its incorporation in 1949, the repertory began to be diversified, with the choreographic debuts of David Adams that year and of principal dancer Arnold Spohr in 1950.

In 1951, Lloyd moved to Toronto, leaving Farrally in charge of the company. She continued to create ballets for the company, and her last work, *Shadow on the Prairie,* is considered by many to be her best. Its subject is the inability of a young immigrant woman to deal with the challenges of life on the prairie, and it is popularly, albeit inaccurately, regarded as the first all-Canadian ballet.

Touring activity steadily increased for the Winnipeg company, and in January 1954 it made a lengthy tour of the central United States with Alicia Markova as guest artist. Progress came to an abrupt halt the following June, however, when a fire destroyed the company's headquarters and its entire stock of costumes, sets, original scores, and choreographic notes. The company was reconstituted in 1955, with Farrally as artistic director. There followed several confused seasons of hirings and firings. Artistic direction passed first to Ruthanna Boris (1956–1957) and then to Benjamin Harkarvy (1957–1958) before Arnold Spohr stepped in when Harkarvy departed abruptly in midseason. Initially, Spohr was reluctant to accept the post; he took it because of his loyalty to the company's founders and his desire to see their principles maintained. The company he built was founded firmly in precepts important to Lloyd and Farrally: the provision of diversified entertainment designed for a broad audience range, with the emphasis on contemporary ballet blending classical and modern styles and themes.

Spohr searched Canada and much of the rest of the world for choreographers and dancers who might give his company definable character. The first choreographer to do this was the Canadian Brian Macdonald, whose production of *The Darkling* in 1959 marked the beginning of a company-choreographer relationship that lasted more than a decade. Through such works as *Les Whoops-de-Doo, Pas d'Action,* and *Aimez-vous Bach?* he gave the company a bright, clever, and socially concerned image. [*See the entry on Macdonald.*]

ROYAL WINNIPEG BALLET. Jacques Lemay choreographed *The Big Top, a Circus Ballet* to lively music by Victor Davies in 1986. Set and costume designs by Mary Kerr contributed to the work's success. (Photograph © by David Cooper; used by permission.)

The early 1960s were years of consolidation and expansion for the Royal Winnipeg Ballet. In 1962 Spohr persuaded Agnes de Mille to revive *Bitter Weird,* to music from *Brigadoon.* Another important image maker for the company, de Mille was to create or revive five ballets (including *Rodeo* and *Fall River Legend*) for the Royal Winnipeg Ballet in the next decade. At the same time, Spohr went out of his way to introduce his audiences to prominent dancers from other countries. In 1961, Olga Moiseyeva and Askold Makarov, from the Kirov Ballet in Leningrad, became the first Soviet stars to appear with a Canadian company. The following year two members of the Bolshoi Ballet, Rimma Karelskaya and Boris Khoklov, danced in Winnipeg.

In terms of touring, these were groundbreaking years for the company. In 1964, a performance of *Aimez-vous Bach?* persuaded Ted Shawn to book the Royal Winnipeg Ballet for that year's Jacob's Pillow festival, and in 1965 the company danced in London and New York (the U.S. appearances were part of the first tour by a Canadian company ever booked by impresario Sol Hurok). In 1966, at the Stratford International Festival in Ontario, the company offered the first full-evening ballet on a Canadian theme, Macdonald's *Rose Latulippe,* based on a French-Canadian legend about a girl who danced with the devil to her doom. (The following year the ballet became the first to be filmed in color for broadcast on national television.) Christine Hennessy, Sheila Mackinnon,

Alexandra Nadal, Richard Rutherford, and David Moroni became established as principal dancers in this period.

The company's rise to international success began in the fall of 1968, with the introduction of four new works by U.S. choreographers (including the world premieres of Eliot Feld's *Meadowlark* and John Butler's *Labyrinth*), and an extensive European tour. In competition with companies from the United States, Argentina, Austria, and France, the Royal Winnipeg Ballet took two of five prizes at that year's Paris International Festival of Dance: the award for best company and, for Christine Hennessy, the gold medal for best female interpretation. The Paris successes were followed by an equally successful tour (the first by a Western ballet company) of the Soviet Union and Czechoslovakia.

The company now began to cash in on the youth movement of the late 1960s, again with works by Macdonald, notably *The Shining People of Leonard Cohen* and *A Ballet High,* which featured music by a live rock band. However, this youth-oriented image increasingly militated against the company's acceptance as a serious contributor to the art of ballet, and Spohr began to seek a cooler, more sophisticated look. Macdonald's association with the company came to an end, and other choreographers made works that began to forge a new company image—first the Canadian Norbert Vesak, then the American John Neumeier.

Vesak's first work for the company was *The Ecstasy of Rita Joe* (1971), about the plight of Native Americans trapped between white culture and their own. This and his second work, *What to Do till the Messiah Comes* (1973), were to prove two of the most successful ticket sellers in the company's history, and it is from *Messiah* that Vesak's medal-winning pas de deux, *Belong,* is taken.

It was Neumeier, however, who most effectively cooled down the company look. His *Rondo,* drawn from his 1970 triptych, *Invisible Frontiers,* and presented by the Royal Winnipeg Ballet in 1971, was followed in 1971 by his controversial production of *The Nutcracker,* set in a dance milieu and offering a psychological study of a child on the brink of maturity. *Twilight,* created in 1972 as *Dämmern,* was added to the repertory in 1973, and *The Game,* a 1972 work that sees life as a giant pinball game, was added in 1974.

Neumeier's contribution of a more serious image for the company was soon reinforced by the Argentine choreographer Oscar Araiz, who gave the company eight works over a period of three years, including its first *Rite of Spring* (1966; mounted for the company in 1975) and one of his finest works, *Mahler 4: Eternity Is Now* (created for the Royal Winnipeg Ballet in 1976). The work of Araiz formed the principal component of the company's repertory on its visit to New York in 1978.

Roughly coinciding with this period of change in the company's artistic profile was a major turnover in management and performing personnel. The group of dancers who had succeeded the Rutherford-Moroni-Hennessy group as company principals—among them Ana Maria de Gorriz, Louise Naughton, and Craig Serling—were themselves replaced by a team headed by Salvatore Aiello, Marina Eglevsky, and Bonnie Wyckoff. Rutherford became production coordinator (he left the company in 1977, becoming a dance officer with the Canada Council the same year), and in 1970 Moroni became founder-director of the professional training program in the company school.

Throughout the early 1970s the company toured extensively—to Australia in 1972, to Cuba and Central and South America in 1974, to Israel in 1975—and continued to work with guest performers. However, by the middle of the decade the impetus that had carried the Royal Winnipeg Ballet to its international successes of the late 1960s and early 1970s began to falter. Financial problems that had begun in the 1973/74 season intensified. The gradual shift in programming emphasis led to an identity crisis for the company; hometown subscription sales fell as Spohr threw much of his resources behind the talents of a solitary choreographer, Araiz. Meanwhile, uncertainty over the ailing Spohr's future with the company led to a series of damaging power struggles. The problems came to a head in 1979, with the departure from the company of eleven of its twenty-five dancers and five members of the administration and staff. In the end Spohr retained overall artistic direction; management was effectively restructured; a new performing team was put together (with Bonnie Wyckoff, Evelyn Hart, Joost Pelt, and Michael Bjerkenes as principals); and the company rapidly regained its equilibrium.

Spohr began to exploit what he termed the company's Dutch connection, with new acquisitions from Hans van Manen *(Songs without Words, Five Tangos)* and Rudi van Dantzig *(Four Last Songs).*

In the fall of 1981, van Dantzig's *Romeo and Juliet* (the company's first full-evening ballet in almost a decade) was introduced to showcase the talents of Evelyn Hart, and a year later she danced the lead in a new mounting of Peter Wright's *Giselle.* [*See the entry on Hart.*] Spohr also introduced a number of works by the Venezuelan choreographer Vicente Nebrada *(Our Waltzes, The Firebird),* and in 1982 the company followed a triumphant return to New York with sold-out performances in Cyprus, Greece, Britain, West Germany, and Egypt.

To accommodate works of the size of *Romeo and Juliet, Giselle,* and *The Firebird,* the Royal Winnipeg Ballet found it necessary to expand its ranks with students from the professional division of the company school, a full-time professional establishment. By the late 1970s, under the direction of David Moroni, the school was producing between 80 and 90 percent of the company membership.

ROYAL WINNIPEG BALLET. Elizabeth Olds as Titania with members of the ensemble in Frederick Ashton's *The Dream,* mounted for the company's 1991/92 season. (Photograph © by David Cooper; used by permission.)

The school had done much to improve the often erratic quality of the company's performance in earlier years, when it was a struggle to persuade dancers in large centers to join a company located so far from the dance mainstream.

Spohr's achievements in building a company of international reputation in Winnipeg, and in constructing a repertory that successfully blends elements of European classicism with the more modern movement influences of North America, have been widely recognized. He was awarded Canada's Centennial Medal in 1967, was made Doctor of Law *honoris causa* at the University of Manitoba in 1970, was enrolled in the Order of Canada, and won the $15,000 Molson Prize for outstanding contributions to the arts the same year. In 1981, he became the first Canadian to receive a *Dance Magazine* Award. [*See the entry on Spohr.*]

Spohr stepped down as artistic director in 1988 and was succeeded by Henny Jurriens, a former principal of the Dutch National Ballet who had been a guest in Winnipeg for several seasons. However, Jurriens died in an auto accident less than a year later, and early in 1990 the Australian dancer John Meehan, formerly a principal with American Ballet Theatre, became artistic director. During his tenure, Meehan enriched the repertory with works by choreographers such as Antony Tudor *(Jardin aux Lilas),* Frederick Ashton *(The Dream),* Jiří Kylián *(Stoolgame),* and Jerome Robbins *(Other Dances).* He was succeeded in 1993 by William Whitener, formerly of the Joffrey Ballet and Montreal's Les Ballets Jazz. Whitener, in turn, increased the repertory with works by, among others, Robert Joffrey *(Pas des Déesses),* Twyla Tharp *(Deuce Coupe),* and Ashton *(Five Brahms Waltzes in the Manner of Isadora Duncan).* After two years in the post, he was succeeded in 1995 as artistic director by André Lewis, formerly a principal dancer with the company.

In 1990, company soloist Mark Godden was appointed the first resident choreographer in the history of the Royal Winnipeg Ballet. He took the top choreographic award at the 1991 International Ballet Competition in Varna, Bulgaria, with his work entitled *Myth.* International acclaim was also garnered as the company continued its practice of making extensive tours abroad: to Asia in 1988, to eastern Europe and the Soviet Union in 1990, and to Japan in 1995.

BIBLIOGRAPHY

Dafoe, Christopher. *Dancing through Time: The First Fifty Years of Canada's Royal Winnipeg Ballet.* Winnipeg, 1990.

Wyman, Max. *The Royal Winnipeg Ballet: The First Forty Years.* Toronto, 1978.

Wyman, Max. *Dance Canada: An Illustrated History.* Vancouver, 1989.

Wyman, Max. *Evelyn Hart: An Intimate Biography.* Toronto, 1991.

MAX WYMAN

RUBINSTEIN, IDA (Lidiia L'vovna Rubinstein; born 5 October 1883 in Kharkov, Russia, died October 1960 in Vence, France), Russian dancer, producer, and impresario. Rubinstein was the director of her own company. Little is known about her early life; after study with the Moscow actor and producer Alexander K. Lenskii and with a certain Ozarovsky of the Imperial Theaters (possi-

RUBINSTEIN. A studio portrait in costume for the role of Zobéïde, the Shah's favorite, in Fokine's *Schéhérazade* (1910). This photograph was taken in the studio of the painter Jacques-Émile Blanche, in front of the same coromandel screen he used as a backdrop for his portraits of Karsavina in *The Firebird* and Nijinsky in "La Danse Siamoise" from *Les Orientales*. (Photograph by Druet; from the Dance Collection, New York Public Library for the Performing Arts.)

bly Yuri Erastovich Ozarovskii), Rubinstein made her professional dramatic debut in the title role of Sophocles' *Antigone* on 16 April 1904 at the Aleksandrinsky Theater in Saint Petersburg. Her association with Léon Bakst, who designed the costumes for the play, resulted in an introduction to Michel Fokine, with whom she studied in 1908. Fokine also choreographed dances that Rubinstein planned to use in her first independent production, Oscar Wilde's *Salomé*. This project, however, was canceled by Russian censors, although she did perform the "Dance of the Seven Veils" during an evening of art dances at the Grand Hall of the Petersburg Conservatory on 20 December 1908.

After Serge Diaghilev saw this performance, he decided to use Rubinstein in the title role of *Cléopâtre* for his Ballets Russes premiere season in Paris; the ballet was first presented in June 1909. Rubinstein again performed with the Ballets Russes in 1910, portraying the enchantress Zobéïde in *Schéhérazade*. Diaghilev, however, refrained from using her in other ballets.

Although Rubinstein liked to think of herself as a dancer, she was not a great one, and Léonide Massine, who choreographed works for her in the 1920s, later wrote that it was difficult to get her to move gracefully when she danced traditional variations. She also envisioned herself as an actress, and after her rift with Diaghilev, she began her own productions. Her first independent work in the West was *The Martyrdom of Saint Sebastian*, which Gabriele d'Annunzio wrote for her. Claude Debussy was commissioned to write incidental music for this play, which had its premiere at the Théâtre du Châtelet in Paris on 22 May 1911. The following year Rubinstein presented *Helen of Sparta* by the Belgian writer Emile Verhaeren, with incidental music by Déodat de Sévèrac and direction by A. Sanine; it opened at the Théâtre du Châtelet on 4 May 1912. This was followed in 1913 by another play by d'Annunzio, *La Pisanella, ou La Mort Parfumée*, directed by Vsevolod Meyerhold, first performed at the same theater on 11 June 1913; like *Saint Sebastian*, it was written expressly for Rubinstein.

During World War I (1914–1918), Rubinstein produced none of her own works, instead devoting her energies to the care of the wounded. Toward the end of the war she began to appear again on the stage in diverse roles. She continued this practice during the first half of the 1920s, frequently appearing in plays produced by others: in 1917 as Phaedra in Racine's play; in 1918 at the Théâtre Sarah-Bernhardt, in Paris, she recited Robert de Montesquiou's poem "Sabliers et lacrymatoires"; in 1919, in a new version of *Salomé* by Robert d'Humiere at the Paris Opera, 1 April, with choreography by Nicola Guerra; and also in 1919, in the Italian director Giulio Aristide Sartorio's film about Saint George. (Her only other known film role was as the personification of Venice in a version of d'Annunzio's *La Nave*.)

Rubinstein produced her first post–World War I production, André Gide's translation of Shakespeare's *Antony and Cleopatra*, in June 1920. She returned to dance in Guerra's ballet *Artemis Troublée* in April 1922, to music by Paul Paray. In June 1923 she produced a version of Gabriele d'Annunzio's *Phaedra* to music by Ildebrando Pizzetti, and in November she performed the title role in *The Lady of the Camellias*, by Alexandre Dumas *fils*. In mid-1924 Rubinstein presented two ballets in Paris—*Orphée*, with choreography by Léo Staats and music by Jean-Roger Ducasse, and *Ishtar*, with choreography by Staats and music by Vincent d'Indy. In March of the same year she appeared in a production of Maurice Rostrand's dramatic poem *Le Secret du Sphinx*, originally written for Sarah Bernhardt. In March 1925 Rubinstein appeared as Nastasia Filipovna in a dramatic adaptation by Noziere (Fernand Weyl) of Dostoevsky's novel *The Idiot*. In 1926 she performed yet another work by d'Annunzio, *Francesca da Rimini*, in Paris. She was instrumental in mounting a production of *L'Imperatrice aux Roches* by Saint-Georges de Bouhelier, which was presented at the Paris Opera in February 1927, with choreography by Bronislava Nijinska and music by Arthur Honegger.

None of Ida Rubinstein's dramatic presentations was critically praised, although she felt herself to be the successor to Sarah Bernhardt. In the late 1920s she therefore shifted her attention back to dance, organizing her own company with some of the best dancers available, with Bronislava Nijinska as the main choreographer and

Alexandre Benois as artistic director. For her first season at the Théâtre National de l'Opéra in Paris in late 1928, she presented seven new ballets, all but one choreographed by Nijinska: *Les Noces de Psyche et de l'Amour* to music by Bach as orchestrated by Arthur Honneger, *La Bien-aimée* to music by Franz Schubert and Franz Liszt as orchestrated by Darius Milhaud, *Le Baiser de la Fée* to music by Igor Stravinsky, *Nocturne* to music by Aleksandr Borodin as orchestrated by Nikolai Tcherepnin, *La Princess Cygne* (to music by Nikolai Rimsky-Korsakov from the opera *Tsar Sultan*), *Boléro* to music by Maurice Ravel, and *David and Goliath* with choreography by Léonide Massine to music by Henri Sauguet. The second season of Les Ballets d'Ida Rubinstein began at the Paris Opera in March 1929. Two new works were added to the repertory—Massine's *Les Enchantements d'Alcine* to music by Georges Auric and Nijinska's *La Valse* to music by Ravel.

Rubinstein did not produce a 1930 season. In 1931 she took her troupe to London, where she performed her repertory as well as a revival of d'Annunzio's *The Martyrdom of Saint Sebastian* and the ballet *Amphion,* which she had originally presented at the Paris Opera in June 1929, with choreography by Massine and music by Honneger. She did not present her third season of ballets and melodrama until May 1934. For this she mounted three new pieces: *Perséphone,* with choreography by Kurt Jooss and music by Stravinsky, and two Fokine ballets, *Diane de Poitiers* to music by Jacques Ibert and *Semiramis* to music by Honneger.

Although 1934 was the last of Rubinstein's official seasons, she continued to commission new works for future productions. Darius Milhaud and Paul Claudel collaborated on a biblical story to be called *Le Festin de la Sagesse,* a work that Rubinstein never produced. Darius Milhaud and Paul Claudel began work on a version of the story of Joan of Arc, which in its completed form was a collaboration between Claudel and Honneger. As *Jeanne au Bûcher,* it was performed once in Basel in 1938 and in a concert version in June 1939 at the Palais de Chaillot, Paris. This was Ida Rubinstein's last public performance. But it seems unlikely that she intended to end her career with this work, as she was then working on three other projects (*Orienne la Sans Egale* by F. Schmitts, *Le Chevalier Errant* by Jacques Ibert, and *L'Histoire de Tobie et de Sara,* commissioned by Claudel). With the outbreak of World War II in 1939, these were never to be realized.

Rubinstein spent the last years of her life in isolation in southern France. Although Rubinstein's entire career was an exercise in self-glorification, it is noteworthy that the dancers, musicians, composers, poets, dramatists, and designers she employed were among the most influential and important in their professions in the twentieth century.

BIBLIOGRAPHY

Alberobello, Peppino d'. "Una visita a Mlle. Ida Rubinstein." *La Scene Illustrata* TK (1912).

Bragaglia, Anton Giulio. "Commento a Ida Rubinstein." *Lavoro Fascista* (26 February 1933).

Ciampelli, Giulio M. "Una parentesi coreografica: I balletti di Ida Rubinstein." *Musica d'Oggi* (April 1920).

"The Dancer of the Perfumed Death." *Bystander* (28 May 1913).

De Cossart, Michael. "Ida Rubinstein and Diaghilev: A One-Sided Rivalry." *Dance Research* 1 (Autumn 1983): 3–20.

De Cossart, Michael. *Ida Rubinstein, 1885–1960: A Theatrical Life.* Liverpool, 1987.

"The 'Divine Sarah' Yields Her Mantle to the 'Divine Ida.'" *Current Opinion* 69 (September 1920).

Dumesnil, René. "Rubinstein." *Journal Musical Français* (15 November 1960).

Garafola, Lynn. "Circles of Meaning: The Cultural Contexts of Ida Rubinstein's *Le Martyre de Saint Sébastien.*" In *Proceedings of the Seventeenth Annual Conference, Society of Dance History Scholars, Brigham Young University, 10–13 February 1994,* compiled by Linda J. Tomko. Riverside, Calif., 1994.

Lester, Keith. "Rubinstein Revisited." *Dance Research* 1 (Autumn 1983): 21–31.

Levinson, André. "Mecene ou danseuse." In Levinson's *Visages de la danse.* Paris, 1933.

Mayer, Charles S. "Ida Rubinstein: A Twentieth-Century Cleopatra." *Dance Research Journal* 20–22 (Winter 1989): 24–51.

Moon, Michael. "Flaming Closets." *October,* no. 51 (Winter 1989): 19–54.

Nozière, Fernand. *Ida Rubinstein.* Paris, 1926.

Rubinstein, Ida. "D'Annunzio: A Woman's Version." *The Living Age* (7 January 1931).

Rubinstein, Ida. "O Sebe." *Solntse Rossii,* no. 25 (1913).

Severn, Margaret. "Dancing with Bronislava Nijinska and Ida Rubinstein." *Dance Chronicle* 11.3 (1988): 333–364.

Thomas, Louis. "Le peintre Bakst parle de Mme. Ida Rubinstein." *Revue critique des idées et des livres* 26 (1924): 87–104.

Turner, W. J. "The Rubinstein Ballets." *New Statesman and Nation* (23 July 1931).

Wollen, Peter. "Fashion/Orientalism/The Body." *New Formations,* no. 1 (Spring 1987): 5–33.

CHARLES S. MAYER

RUDNER, SARA (born 16 February 1944 in Brooklyn, New York), American dancer and choreographer. The career of Sara Rudner is closely linked with that of Twyla Tharp. Widely regarded as one of the consummate performers of her generation, Rudner was the quintessential Tharp dancer. Her immaculate technical facility was combined with musical fluidity and an expansive, highly personal sense of ease.

A 1964 graduate of Barnard College in New York (in Russian studies), Rudner made her professional debut with the Paul Sanasardo Dance Company (1964–1966). She studied with Sanasardo and Mia Slavenska, and with Merce Cunningham, Carolyn Brown, Richard Thomas, and Barbara Fallis (1965–1970). She first performed with Tharp in *Re-Moves* (1966) and continued with her company, Twyla Tharp and Dancers, until 1974, creating ma-

RUDNER. Vicky Shick (right) with Rudner in a 1978 performance of Rudner's *Dancing Part Time* at Saint Mark's Church, New York. (Photograph © 1978 by Johan Elbers; used by permission.)

jor roles in such works as *The Fugue* (1970), *Eight Jelly Rolls* and *The Bix Pieces* (both 1971), and *Deuce Coupe* (1973).

Rudner began choreographing in 1972 and formed the Sara Rudner Performance Ensemble in 1976. Her work, which focuses on the process of dancing itself as both the content and context of a performance, includes the five-hour *Dancing-on-View* (1975), *One Good Turn* (for the Lar Lubovitch Dance Company, 1975), *33 Dances* (1977), *As Is* (1977)—a three-hour event danced simultaneously in two adjoining rooms—*Dancing: "For an Hour or So"* (1981), and *As the Audience Enters* (1982).

During her 1975–1978 absence from Tharp's company, Rudner was a guest artist with Lubovitch and later with Pilobolus, where she danced her own work as well as appearing in company pieces. She performed in Carolyn Brown's film *Dune Dance* (1975). She rejoined Tharp in 1978, creating roles in *Short Stories* (1980), *The Catherine Wheel* (1981), *Nine Sinatra Songs* (1982), and *Fait Accompli* (1983).

A hip injury caused Rudner to leave Tharp's company again at the end of 1984. For the next five years she devoted herself to teaching, both on her own and in workshops for Tharp. In January 1990 she performed a collaborative duet with Wendy Rogers, *Conversations*, at Danspace/Saint Mark's Church, New York; in February she performed a new version of *As the Audience Enters* in a program called "Talking Dance" at Theatre Artaud in San Francisco. In April she again worked with Rogers, in an improvised, untitled performance, with the painter Deborah Freedman, at P.S. 122 in New York.

In September 1990 Rudner began working with a group of women for whom she choreographed *Eight Solos*, first performed at Danspace in May 1991. Rudner choreographed and danced a solo, *Today*, in a program directed by Patricia Hoffbauer at Wave Hill in the Bronx in July 1991, and she performed in a work by Hoffbauer, *Big Judy*, at Dance Theater Workshop in November 1991. At the University Settlement House in New York in January 1992, she performed her own solo, *Happy Birthday Kirk—Yours, Lifetimes, Tina;* in February she returned as a guest artist to Tharp's company, at New York's City Center, to perform her original role in the revival of *Deuce Coupe*.

Since 1992 Rudner has continued to teach (at Barnard College among other places), choreograph, and perform. In 1993 she began collaborating on an investigation of light and movement with dancer-choreographer Dana Reitz and lighting designer Jennifer Tipton that resulted in an intricately structured evening-length improvisational work entitled *Necessary Weather*, developed partly at The Kitchen in New York City, and performed in the 1993/94 season in London, at The Kitchen, and at the Avignon Festival. In 1995 she created choreography for Caryl Churchill's play *The Skriker* at the Public Theater. She fur-

RUDNER. In a 1980 performance of Twyla Tharp's *Deuce Coupe*. (Photograph © 1980 by Jack Vartoogian; used by permission.)

thered her interest in unusual collaborations in *MINE,* a forty-five-minute work with choreography by Rudner in an installation created by visual artist Rona Pondick with artist Robert Feintuch, produced in the Brooklyn Academy of Music's Artists in Action series at the Brooklyn Museum.

Rudner is featured in *Making Dances,* Michael Blackwood's 1980 documentary on postmodern dance, and she appeared as a performer in the American public television *Dance in America* segment "Beyond the Mainstream." She also appeared as a performer in several of Tharp's video broadcasts. Rudner received a Guggenheim Fellowship in 1982 and was a recipient of one of the first New York Dance and Performance Awards (Bessies) in 1984.

BIBLIOGRAPHY

Croce, Arlene. "Rudner's Turn." In Croce's *Going to the Dance.* New York, 1982.

Dalva, Nancy. "Light Matters." *Dance Ink* 5 (Summer 1994): 46–48.

Gopnik, Adam. "Climate of Thought." *Dance Ink* 5 (Summer 1994): 40–46.

FILM. *Making Dances* (Blackwood Productions, 1979).

ALLEN ROBERTSON

RUMBA. *See* Ballroom Dance Competition; Social Dance, *article on* Twentieth-Century Social Dance to 1960.

RUSKAJA, JIA (Evgenia Borisenko; born 1902 in Kerch, Russia, died 19 April 1970 in Rome), Russian-Italian dancer, choreographer, and teacher. Jia Ruskaja was without doubt the most controversial personality in the history of Italian dance between 1930 and 1970. She arrived in Italy at the height of the new, free-dance style of central Europe. She was beautiful, tall, and full-figured, and she enjoyed a certain personal success at the Teatro degli Indipendenti in Rome, where she made her debut in 1923 in a series of short pantomimes directed by Anton Giulio Bragaglia. He was an open-minded exponent of the avant-garde in a period that was extremely nationalistic and conservative.

After a short and not particularly happy period in the administration of the ballet of the Teatro alla Scala in Milan, Ruskaja was appointed by the Fascist government to direct the Royal School of Dance, attached to the National Academy of Dramatic Art in Rome. It later became an autonomous entity and in 1948 was transformed into the National Academy of Dance, located in a splendid building on the Aventine Hill. Here Ruskaja established a commanding position in the field of dance teaching in Italy. Legislation was passed providing that only the new National Academy of Dance and its director Ruskaja could grant licenses to dance teachers in Italy, after an examination or, in exceptional cases, on the basis of reputation. (This law was later overturned by the Constitutional Court.)

Ruskaja's supporters long maintained that this law was a sound safeguard of quality and professional dignity and that the work of Ruskaja and her female students (she was not in favor of opening the academy to male students) was characterized by seriousness, excellence, and rigor. Along with instruction in classical technique Ruskaja introduced instruction in "orchestic" dance, her personal version of central European free dance, performed in long tunics and gold sandals. She explained her mystical concept of dance in a book, *Danza come modo di essere* (Dance as a Way of Being), published in 1928. For decades the National Academy of Dance under Ruskaja's direction produced almost exclusively dance teachers, not dancers. These teachers taught an art they had never, or hardly ever, practiced professionally. Ruskaja's enemies condemned both this divorce and the technical level of the academy's instruction, alleviated sporadically by the presence of prestigious outsiders. The unquestionable merit of Ruskaja, however, is that she left a strong and well-articulated scholastic structure, an enthusiastic teaching staff, and a tradition of discipline and order.

BIBLIOGRAPHY

Monna, Marialisa, and Giuliana Penzi. *Giuliana dai capelli di fuoco.* Turin, 1990.

Ruskaja, Jia. *La danza come un modo di essere.* Milan, 1928.

"Ruskaja, Jia." *Enciclopedia dello spettccolo.* Rome, 1954–.

VITTORIA OTTOLENGHI
Translated from Italian

RUSSIA. [*To survey the dance traditions of Russia, this entry comprises nine articles:*

Traditional Dance
Siberian Dance Traditions
Theatrical Dance before 1917
Theatrical Dance since 1917
Secondary and Provincial Dance Companies
Twentieth-Century Plastique
Dance Education
Folk Dance Research and Publication
Theatrical Dance Research and Publication

The first article explores Russian national dances; the second focuses on the dances of northern and southeastern Siberia; the third and fourth articles discuss the history of theatrical dance; the fifth considers secondary dance companies in Moscow and Saint Petersburg as well as provincial companies; the sixth examines modern dance; the concluding articles address dance education and the history of scholarship and writing. For further discussion of theatrical dance, see entries on individual companies, choreographers, and dancers.]

Traditional Dance

The territory of Russia extends across northern Eurasia. The Arctic Ocean is to its north, Central Asia and China to its south and southeast, and Europe to its southwest. Russia traditionally began in the ninth century CE, when Rurik, a Scandinavian invader, sailed up the Volkhov River and established a kingdom at Novgorod, near the Baltic Sea. During the ninth and tenth centuries, the Varangians—Scandinavian conquerors—invaded. Eastern Slavs had long occupied this northwestern region, while Khazars, a Turkic people, controlled the south-central region. In about 988, Vladimir I established Christianity (Eastern Orthodoxy) as the state religion. About 1147, Moscow was founded, and in the fourteenth century the duchy of Moscow began its rise as the center of the modern Russian state. In the mid-sixteenth century, Ivan IV (the Terrible) was the first to call himself *tsar.* Russian expansionism then pushed the borders southwestward into Poland and the Baltic countries, eastward into Siberia, and southward into the Persian and Ottoman domains.

By the nineteenth century, the Russian Empire had become a major European power, but oppressive conditions for the peasantry and serfs and the minority nations continued. A radical reaction occurred while the military was engaged in World War I—the Russian (October) Revolution of 1917. It brought the Bolsheviks to power and created the first Communist state, named in 1922 the Union of Soviet Socialist Republics (Soviet Union or USSR). After World War II, the Soviet Union was considered a world power. It engaged the Western powers in the Cold War until 1991, when the Soviet leader was deposed, and it soon divided into independent republics. Russia is the largest of the newly independent, now capitalist-oriented, republics.

RUSSIA: Traditional Dance. Dmitri Rovinsky's *Russkiia narodnyia kartinki* (1881) included this print showing a village youth dancing for his friends. The musician accompanying him plays a balalaika, a three-stringed instrument commonly played in rural Russia. (Reprinted from Mary Grace Swift, *The Art of the Dance in the U.S.S.R,* Notre Dame, Indiana, 1968, p. 24.)

In Russia there are two terms for "dance": *tanets* came to the Russian language from the German *Tanz;* in early times, however, the Russian word was *pliaska.* Currently both are used but, despite their seeming similarity, there is a difference in their professional usage. *Tanets* in Russian dance is a composition consisting of fixed choreographic patterns; *pliaska* designates a spontaneous, expressive improvisation, an individual form of danced self-expression done by a particular person. When "folklore" is applied to Russian dance, it is used to mean "authentic." Today, Russian dancing is done not only in its authentic form but also in a theatrical form in which the performer creates a personalized version. Some performers "stylize" folk dances; others try to keep their own rendition of a folk dance as close as possible to the original.

Russian national dances were historically linked to specific religious rites. Within these rites, dancing was not just an embellishment; it served a functional purpose for the life of the people. These dances occupied a special place in wedding rituals. Most weddings took place in the fall, after the crop harvest. There was dancing throughout these happy occasions, in which the entire village, and sometimes several neighboring villages, participated. The wedding, which lasted three days, was similar to a full-length production consisting of many acts, in all of which dancing occupied a special place. For example, in the dance called *devishnik* (from *deva,* "maiden") the friends of the bride prepared her for the wedding and loosened her "maiden braid." They then performed a round dance. There were also dances that had both a traditional, ritualistic aspect and a spontaneous one. Among these were the handing over of the bride to friends of the bridegroom, the meeting of the young people coming back from the church, the guests' congratulations, and the old people's dance. The bride and groom also danced at the request of the guests. Other dances took place before a wedding, such as those performed during the meetings among the young people that often played a part in the selection of a bride.

Depending on the season, the games and dances of young people took place under different circumstances. There were winter events, such as *posidelki* (from the verb *sidet,* "to sit [together]") and *vechorki* (from *vecher,* "evening"). The latter often occurred in a village home with only a few participants. At some of the small evening gatherings *(vecherinki)* there was acting, with elements of song and dance. Even now, in some Russian villages people use the expression "to act a dance." In the old days, village people separated the year into the winter *kolyada* (Christmas carols) and the summer *kupala* (from the verb

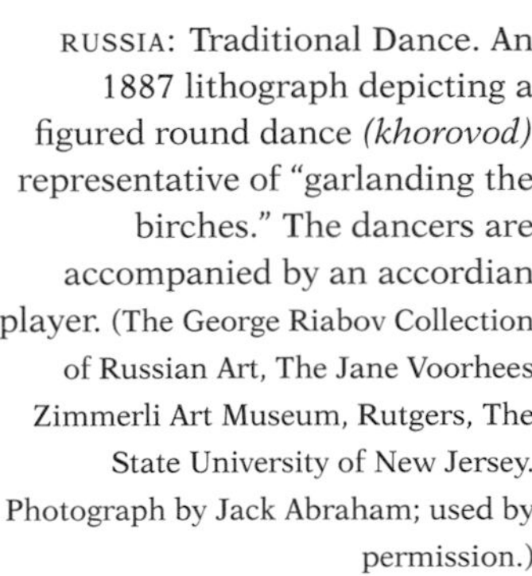

RUSSIA: Traditional Dance. An 1887 lithograph depicting a figured round dance *(khorovod)* representative of "garlanding the birches." The dancers are accompanied by an accordian player. (The George Riabov Collection of Russian Art, The Jane Voorhees Zimmerli Art Museum, Rutgers, The State University of New Jersey. Photograph by Jack Abraham; used by permission.)

kupat, "to bathe" or "to swim"). The winter festivities began when the harvest had been completed. Young people gathered in a house to sing and dance. One line of girls, in a softly rhythmic motion accompanied by singing, stepped up toward the other group of girls and then returned to its original place in a slow tempo. This was repeated by the other line. The song "We Have Sown Millet" was used in this type of dance. Sometimes the lines of girls alternated in a vocal call and response, while stepping toward one another, bowing, and stepping back. At other times the group formed a snake figure *(zmeyka)* and came to a stop in a circle. One of the girls then enacted the queenly role of *tsarevna,* circling and finally stopping in front of another girl and bringing her forth while praising her with words. The action then resumed; the serpent figure was formed again and moved spirally throughout the entire space of the room.

Each region and sometimes each village had its own version of games and songs. The same "bride and groom" scenes were acted out in a variety of ways. Mummers or maskers wearing animal masks of bears, goats, or cranes often took part in these events. The most poetic and beautiful festivities took place in the spring. There were bonfires, plaiting garlands made from spring flowers for the maidens' hair, and guessing or foretelling of one's future husband. There were many forms of such games. One was called "Zavivat Berezku" (to curl or intertwine the branches of the birch tree), done in order to attract a boyfriend. All these activities led to dancing. Many of the festivities were linked to water or fire. There were also occasions when the maidens, wearing long white dresses and with garlands in their hair, would bathe in the river. During the bathing festivities *(kupalski),* maidens and youths danced around a bonfire and jumped over the flames. Costume parties were also held in the spring. People walked on stilts while representing animals, such as pigs and horses, or they burned scarecrows in the bonfires. These activities, too, led to dancing. The autumn harvest feast called The First Haystack included songs, dances, and games. Having gathered the hay, boys and girls wearing peasant costumes put clothes on the haystacks and danced around them. In regions where cabbages *(kapusti)* were gathered, festivities *(kapustiki)* were held to the accompaniment of flutes and balalaikas (three-stringed triangular guitars).

When Christianity was adopted, many of these celebrations were perceived as being pagan, full of superstition, leading to sin—and thus were prohibited. The old dances, considered immoral, were replaced by so-called saintly *(sviatye)* dances, which were celebrated in villages during the time of sowing. The priests participated in these events, marching in front of the groups of dancers with censors swaying before them. They blessed the ground, praying to the south, east, and west, and sowed the seed. This was followed with more prayers and bows. Thereafter, however, many permissible occasions for dancing were observed throughout the country, with an important part of the festivity devoted to the *khorovod,* a round dance. Several definitions of this dance have been offered: a gathering of village youths in the open air to dance *pliaski* and to sing; acting out scenes of everyday life, accompanied by songs; a collectively danced and sung event, with performers holding hands in a circle in the center of which a few dancers act out the content of the songs. Usually, the women danced in majestic long gowns *(sarafany)* with wide overblouses *(shugai).* They wore high headdresses embroidered with river pearls.

RUSSIA: Traditional Dance. A solo moment in a "Cossack's Dance," performed by the Red Star Army Chorus and Dance Ensemble. Until the late ninteenth century, Cossacks, peasants of chiefly Russian and Polish descent, lived in autonomous communes, principally in Ukraine; in return for special privileges they served in the cavalry under the tsars. Their dances, performed today in theatricalized versions, are those of military horsemen. (Photograph © 1992 by Jack Vartoogian; used by permission.)

Sometimes, after work, youths gathered at the outskirts of town and proceeded to a predetermined setting for a gathering. This was then a *sborny khorovod* (from the word *sbor,* "to gather"), also called *tsepochechny* (from *tsepochka,* "a small chain"). Another type of *sborny khorovod* included the invitation to take part in the *khorovod.* The older women, one after another, approached the girls who were gathered there. Bowing, they asked a girl to step out and then placed her in the circle to participate in the *khorovod.* This aroused the excitement and nervousness of the girls because the order in which they were called out showed their rank, as determined by moral character, conduct, and ability to work. To find oneself at the end of such a "chain" was an embarrassment, especially since the action took place in front of all the young men and their parents, who were present to choose suitable brides. The most important part of the festivity was taken up by the *igrovie khorovody* (from *igrat,* "to play").

The *khorovod* was danced throughout Russia but assumed different styles in different regions, as many specific traits of Russian dances were determined by their locales. In northern Russia, the dances were distinguished by a slow and severe style. A whole group of dances called *khoduchi* comes from the word *khodit,* "to walk" or "step": the performers take simple steps; their gait is wide and secure, as if stepping on level ground. In central Russia, the dances were reserved; in the south, they were lively and openly joyful. A characteristic of the southern *khorovod* was the intertwining of figures, for example, by the performers' linked hands raised above their heads to form arches for the others to pass through. Many other figures could be formed in a *khorovod.* The performers held each other by the hands, by the waist, or by each holding the end of a handkerchief. By intertwining arms, a circle, star, cross, or other shape could be formed. The richness and complexity of the figures depended on the imagination and mastery of the leader of the *khorovod.* Leaders, either men or women, were honored in Russian villages. They knew many traditional dances and figures, which they used as a basis for creating their own compositions. Much Russian choreography has drawn inspiration from such dances.

Another type of Russian dance was the *pereplias* ("to outdo in dance"), a competition dance. Two men, surrounded by their male companions, alternated in performing increasingly difficult step combinations (*kolentsa,* literally "knee joints," meaning "tricks") until one of the dancers emerged victorious. Then someone else challenged the winner with new combinations, and the competition continued. Each generation of dancers repeated, expanded, and passed on the tradition, creating a multitude of versions for the next generation.

Lyrical dances for couples were also common throughout Russia. In the *posidelki* and other open-air festivities, "wedding scenes" were played out. A young man and woman performed the roles in the dance called "Golubets" (from *golub,* "dove," also an endearment). In this dance the young man courted the girl while she acted coquettish and demanded respectful behavior from him. "She glides like a young swan; he moves like a fine falcon," says the song. The movements of the performers evoked the characteristics of these images. These young people represented the prototypes of the Russian people: she must be modest, hard-working, tender, and soft-spoken; he must be brave, daring, and courteous. This dance did not have specific rules; all the movements were guided by the deep feelings of the performers. A female *pliaska* improvisation was another traditional Russian dance. "Among all the dances of Europe, it is impossible to find one that could surpass the Russian village *pliaska,* if this one is performed by a beautiful adolescent girl or a young woman. No other national dance in the world can compare to the charm of this one," wrote Jakob von Staehlin (1935). The dancer improvisationally acted out the words of the song, with her movements often repeated by those standing in the *khorovod* circle.

Of the social form of folk dance, quadrilles were common in Russia at the end of the seventeenth and the beginning of the eighteenth century. There were several versions. Unlike the early popular folk dances, which had their own individual characteristics, the quadrilles showed the influence of European contradances. The *écossaise* from Scotland made its appearance, through the presence of itinerant French dancing masters, at the end of the eighteenth and the beginning of the nineteenth century. The idea of creating a dance based on specific figures was handed down from the aristocratic salon to the village. At that point the dances acquired a typically Russian style of performance. The figures were invented by local performers. Another version of the contradance was linked to the seafaring trade. Northern Russia, being maritime, danced the Lancers—a set of quadrilles danced in sequence for eight or sixteen couples. The structure of this English dance is a square, with four pairs of dancers placing themselves in each corner. In Russia, however, all the movements derived from Russian dances, which gave birth to a new form of Russian quadrille.

The quantity of versions of *pliaska* steps is practically endless. The following walking steps *(khodi)* are the most common.

1. Simple. Slow, measured, rhythmic steps with alternating right and left feet.
2. A small stamping step. Before stepping forward, the heel brushes the floor from back to front.
3. Changing step. Three steps are performed on the first three eighth notes of 2/4 music. The fourth eighth note is a pause that prepares for the next combination of three steps. The basic three-step has a multitude of versions, such as putting the legs together before moving out, stepping on *demi-pointe,* adding a small jump, stamping on the floor.

There are also many specialty steps, some of which were choreographed. The well-known step that consists of small steps on *demi-pointe* is called *voronezhsky* (after the Voronezh region). It is also called the *berezka* ("birch") step because the choreographer Nadezhda Nadezhdina used it in the creation of her dance "Berezka." In turn, the name was taken by the folk dance company. The step called *verevochka* ("string") is unique. The feet are alternately brought forward. One foot is raised and brought from front to back as the supporting foot slides a bit forward. This gives the impression that the feet are twining a string. In *kovyrialochka* (from *kovyriat,* "to pick or dig into") the legs alternately open to the side and the foot taps the floor, first toe then heel. At the same time, the supporting leg makes a low, light jump. In *motalochka* (from *motat,* "to wind"), the feet alternately strike one another, first to the front, then to the back. *Kontsovka* (from *konets,* "the end"), the culmination of the dance, is an important element in Russian folk dance. It can be a stamping of one foot on the floor, simultaneously opening the arms or placing them vigorously at the waist, or a combination of stamps and jumps, called *kliuch* ("key"). Movements of the arms are important, especially in dances for women. All gestures should be soft and flowing. The play of the arms, neck, and shoulders is a key to the mood of the dance. The dance becomes a conversation, its meaning expressed through the body.

The art of solo folk dance performing is largely lost in Russia. It exists only rarely under the transforming guise given it by choreographers for the stage. An important published resource is Kasyan Goleizovsky's *Images of Russian Folk Choreography* (1964). The poetic Russian couple dance "And I Walk in the Meadow" was performed for many years by its creator, Tatiana Ustinova. There has been a resurgence of interest, with professional as well as amateur companies incorporating solo folk dances into their repertories.

BIBLIOGRAPHY

Bachinskaya, N. M. *Russkie khorovody i khorovodnye pesni.* Moscow, 1951.

Goleizovsky, Kasyan. *Obrazy russkoi narodnoi khoreografii.* Moscow, 1964.

Klimov, Andrei. *Osnovy russkogo narodnogo tantsa.* Moscow, 1994.

Lebedeva, Anna, ed. *Krestianskaia odezhda naseleniia evropeiskoi Rossii.* Moscow, 1971.

Staehlin, Jakob von. *Muzyka i balet v Rossii XVIII veka.* Leningrad, 1935.

Uralskaya, Valeria. *Poiski i resheniia; Tanets v russkom khore.* Moscow, 1973.

Uralskaya, Valeria. *Priroda tantsa.* Moscow, 1981.

Ustinova, Tatiana. *Berech krasotu russkogo tantsa.* Moscow, 1959.

Ustinova, Tatiana. *Russkie tantsy.* Moscow, 1955.

Valeria I. Uralskaya
Translated from Russian

Siberian Dance Traditions

The region of Siberia extends between the Ural Mountains in the west and the Pacific Ocean in the east; it extends south from the Arctic Ocean through the tundra

RUSSIA: Siberian Dance Traditions. A group of northern Siberian Koriak women in ceremonial dress. All Koriak songs and dances are performed to appease animal spirits and to ask for a successful hunt. (Photograph from the archives of The Asia Society, New York.)

and the great taiga forests to the steppes and deserts of Central Asia and Mongolia, and east along the Amur River valley. Most of Siberia is sparsely populated by some thirty indigenous ethnic groups, both coastal and inland, as well as by Russians and Ukrainians who began to migrate northeast in the thirteenth century. Russian conquest of the region ended in 1598, and since the early 1600s, Siberia has been notorious for its political penal colonies. The Trans-Siberian Railroad was completed in 1905, and in 1922, after the Russian Revolution, the entire northeast was incorporated into the Soviet Union as the Soviet Far East. Since the demise of the Soviet Union in 1991, it has become part of the Russian Federation and is known as the Russian Far East, especially to the business community interested in its mineral deposits.

The cultures of the Arctic peoples of northern Siberia, whose roots go back to deep antiquity, are varied and rich. Among them, culture traits were formed that permitted them to function in cold, harsh surroundings as well as to express themselves as societies. For ceremonial occasions and during the long, dark winters (of six to nine months), Siberian dance traditions, music, ritual lore, and other aspects of sociocultural life have been transmitted from generation to generation. The performance of similar dances throughout this ecologically varied region indicates contact, diffusion, and a reciprocity of cultural influences. Among the indigenous peoples of Siberia, dance was not an independent art form but a component either of ceremonial ritual or of games.

Dance was integral to the ceremonies and traditions associated with hunting. Special animals were revered, especially the whale, the bear, the wolf, and the raven. Northern Siberians offered festivals to them—and the dances associated with them—as statements of gratitude for successful hunting; they were also offered as inducements for continued success in the future. Most Siberian ceremonial dances imitate the birds and animals of the region and present different stages of the hunt. Sometimes, a dance section expresses pity for the hunted animals—and the dancer wipes away tears. In some regions the most elaborate festivals were for the bear. Bear dances were strictly divided into categories—for men, women, solo, duet, and group dancing. The accompaniment was singing, recitation, and music played on a stringed instrument, the *sengultap*.

Northern Siberia. Among the Siberian Eskimo, the Koriak, and the shore Chukchi of northeastern Siberia, the primary occupation was sea mammel hunting and the majority of ceremonial dances were performed to celebrate the festival of the whale. At this festival, in their dances, Eskimo hunters reproduced the entire process, starting with movements that depicted the launching of the *umiak* (a boat) into the sea and concluding with the hauling ashore of the killed whale and the division of the carcass. Ordinarily these dances were performed to the accompaniment of singers with special songs.

Among the Koriak, who live along the coast of Penzhina Bay (between the Kamchatka Peninsula and the mainland), festivals were timed to coincide with the catching of the white whale. Some dances were performed on the shore; others, those dedicated to seeing-off the spirits of the killed seals, took place indoors. The meaning of these dances among all groups of the Koriak was the same—the attempt to cajole the spirits of the animals into allowing the hunt to be successful.

The Siberian Chukchi, Koriak, Evenki, and Eveny ceremonial dances usually mime the elements of their economic base—reindeer breeding and herding. The dances also imitate the habits of the reindeer, and they are usually accompanied by sounds and song imitative of deer, ducks, cranes, seagulls, and other birds and animals of the region.

Among the inland reindeer-herding Chukchi, one of the most significant festivals was the celebration of the herds' return from the summer grazing grounds. The turning point of the several-day-long festival was the ritual act of banishing the spirits, or "ghosts." It was believed that men were possessed by wicked spirits, and that women needed to banish them; this ritual dance was performed in a variety of positions—sitting, standing, with facial expressions of disgust, grimacing, spitting, and such. According to anthropologist Tan Bogoraz, it is possible that originally special masks worn to scare the ghosts were replaced with grimaces.

The dances of the Koriak differ from those of other Siberian groups in that they are mostly improvised. Their movements are dynamic, rhythmical, and emotional. The position of the upper body of the dancer is very straight, while the head, arms, shoulders and hips are very mobile. The musical component usually consists of tambourine beating and rhythmic shouts of "O-cha! Eht-cha! It-cha!"

The original Itelmeny dances have been lost, but according to the nineteenth-century scholars who saw them, the fall festival at the end of the hunting season included ritual dances that imitated animals, especially the bear.

Ritual dances existed among all the Samody groups—the Nentsy, Entsy, and Nganasany. These were devoted to the spirits of the water, soil, and sky. There was a special ceremonial dance for the spirit of thunder, which was performed inside the habitation *(chuma)*, around the sacrificial sledge. Children and adults, holding hands, danced for the spirit of thunder, asking it to spare their habitations and their lives. Another ritual dance was performed during the marriage ceremony. A bride danced in front of her bridegroom, asking for fertility and posterity.

The ceremonial dances of the Yakuts include some rhythmical elements and movements that repeat themselves from dance to dance, like dancing around the trees. Some dance elements can be traced to the shaman dances that were performed during the trading festivals in Siberia. The term *shaman* is derived from the Tungusic word for a magician, medium, or healer whose powers are based on mystical communion with the spirits; he or she has much power and prestige. As a rule, the shaman dances were improvised, but the vocabulary of movements was restricted. One reason was that shaman dances were usually performed in a very small space, inside a structure. The shaman dances may be categorized as three types: (1) simple, consisting mainly of rhythmical movements; (2) mime, imitations and pantomimes; and (3) ecstatic dances, often culminating in trances.

Siberian Game-Dancing. Game-dancing occurred in Siberia during holidays, at gatherings, feasts, and parties, with no ritual purpose or special reason other than for having fun. Very popular were the competitions among the dancers and singers. Sometimes the movements and melodies for the dance competitions were predetermined (we might say choreographed), as they were, for example, among the Eskimo. Sometimes the movements were improvised, as was more typical for other regions. The contests included categories for men, women, and mixed game-dances.

In the regions of the Evenki, Eveny, and Dolgany, game-dances had a circular form. The number of performers was unrestricted, and the dance was performed to the improvised singing of a special group of men. The singing started first and signaled the dancers to begin. At first, a few dancers began, and then gradually more and more would join the circle. They moved with growing speed, in the same direction as sun moves, clockwise, repeating its daily circle. In the northeastern region of Siberia, traditional game-dances have a linear form. They are usually performed as solo or duet dances.

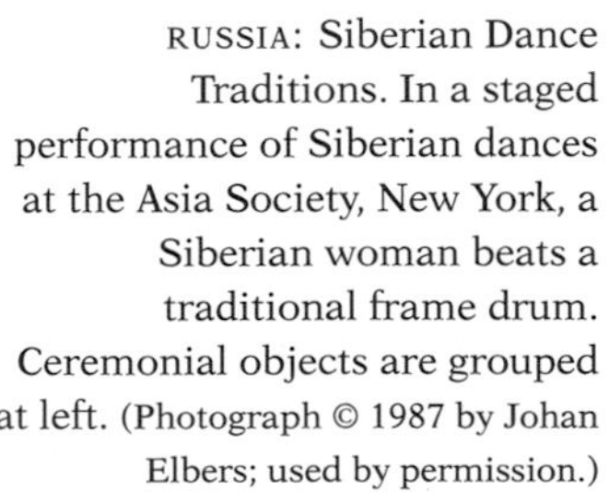

RUSSIA: Siberian Dance Traditions. In a staged performance of Siberian dances at the Asia Society, New York, a Siberian woman beats a traditional frame drum. Ceremonial objects are grouped at left. (Photograph © 1987 by Johan Elbers; used by permission.)

In summary, Siberian dance traditions are of two types: ceremonial dances and game-dances. In northeastern Siberia, mime dances are typical, with tambourines, singing, shouting, and the imitation of animal sounds and postures. Similarities in movement, structure, and the composition of dances exist in the different Siberian regions—elastic movements on bent knees; the formation of an open circle in ritual dances; and a linear structure in game-dances. In the inland tundra region, most ritual dance imitates aspects of the economic base—bear hunting or reindeer herding—with accompaniment on various kinds of local stringed instruments, singing, and reciting. The restricted space may have dictated the special musical rhythm (beat): 2/4 for most of the dances, but sometimes 2/4 for the first part and 3/4 or 5/8 for the second part.

Theatrical forms of dance started to develop in Siberia only at the end of the 1950s but they are still based on Siberia's traditional dances. Several amateur dance ensembles exist in the region, as well as a few professional companies: Ehrygon (The Dawn), formed by the Chukchi in 1965, and Mehnga, formed by the Koriak in 1965 (in 1992, Mehnga became The Yakut Dance Theatre).

Southern Siberia: The Amur Region. The earliest information we have about the folk dances of the indigenous peoples of southeastern Siberia, those near the Amur River, dates from the mid-nineteenth century. The Amur flows generally southeast, forming for more than 1,000 miles (1,610 kilometers), the border between Siberia and China. It enters the Tartar Strait opposite Sakhalin Island. Researchers then noted that the dances and individual rhythmic movements of these groups were connected primarily with the bear festivals and the shaman. Even later, at one such festival in 1930, according to E. A. Kreinovich, a Nivkhsky women's dance, *t'ig'ynd,* was performed with the dancers depicting various habits of the bear: how it gambols, pacing on its hind paws; how it rushes about in a cage. Only women dressed in robes made from the skin of the carp (the freshwater fish *Cyprinus* spp) could perform this dance. The women put wreaths on their heads and held *k'org-or* ("rattles") made from hollow pieces of wood.

Information about the songs and dances of the Ul'chi has been collected by A. V. Smoliak. Illustrating the journey of a killed bear in the world of "taiga people," each melody—those for "Stop by a Lake," "A Rest by the Crossing," or "The Bear Eats"—has its own rhythm. As the Ul'chi reason, the bear belongs to the world of "taiga people"; the Nivkhi regard the bear as a full member of the "hill people." The dances are religious in character and are assumed to have been developed in prehistoric times. The musical accompaniment—rhythmic blows on a log—provide an argument in favor of such ancient origins.

Siberian shamans have traditionally used various means to influence not only natural, but supernatural, existence. The imitative character of their movements vividly depicts the behavior of birds and animals. Lev I. Shternberg has noted that a shaman sometimes attained such perfection that many eyewitnesses and participants in the ritual fell into trances, hallucinating. Dance steps with a slight swinging of the hips are the basic movements of a shaman's dance. Usually, during such dances, the

RUSSIA: Siberian Dance Traditions. A staged performance of jumping rope *(tyakh krt'),* a game dance of the Nivkh people from the Amur region. The three rope jumpers are Cheu Nam, Alexander Sangi, and Yevgeni Si. (Photograph © 1990 by Jack Vartoogian; used by permission.)

RUSSIA: Siberian Dance Traditions. A group of people from Sakhalin Island prepare for a ceremony. Festivals in this area usually center around bear hunting and sacrifice. (Photograph from the archives of The Asia Society, New York.)

movements are repeated and performed by all who are present at the ceremony. The shaman's dance consists of three parts: an introduction, a middle section, and a culmination. In the final ecstatic section, the shaman may either jump or rotate while gesticulating and beating forcefully on a tambourine.

The Udegeitsy of the Amur region regularly used to perform a ceremonial dance tied to a rite of initiation for boys attaining puberty. The initate stood in the center, holding a satchel filled with cooked meat. His older sisters, moving in a circle, jumped one after the other and sang. During this dance, a sister depicted the motions of a wild boar and, with shrieks, begged the hunter for refreshments. Meanwhile, the brother fed his sisters with meat. Here, various games also started with dancing, like the "Game of the Bear" and the "Game of the God of the Manchurian Deer."

Today, the dance arts of the Amur region are presented mainly by folk dance and song companies and amateur folk groups. The most popular among them are Giva (The Dawn), from the Bulava township of the Ul'cha region; Mangbo (Amur), of the Niznie Khalby township; and Mehngumeh Ilga (The Silver Patterns), from South Sakhalin. The Dawn was founded by the P. L. Dechuli, its longtime artistic director, a great student of the Amur dance traditions and the creator of many dance compositions, including *Kaur's Love, Ulcha Suite,* and *Nine Amur Daughters.*

The theatrical dances of the Amur region are based on the ceremonial dances, and the most typical musical instruments used at performances are the tambourine, the musical log, and the rattle. The most popular reproduce the various activities of the native population—bear hunting, fishing, wrestling, fencing with sticks, and so on. For example, *Ducklings, Fishermen,* and *Nanaitsy Boys Wrestling* are offered by the Nanaitsy folk dance companies. *Rattle Dance* and *Holiday Dance with Twigs* are presented by the Nivkha folk dance companies; and from the *Nehlehngu* comes the woman's dance imitating boating, nesting, and the dressing of animal skins.

BIBLIOGRAPHY

Karabanova, S. F. *Tantsy malykh narodov iuga Dal'nego Vostoka SSSR.* Moscow, 1979.

Kreinovich, E. A. *Nivkhgu: Zagadochnye obitateli Sakhalina i Amura.* Moscow, 1973.

Shternberg, Lev I. *Pervobytnai a religiia v svete etnografii: Issledovaniia, stat'i, lektsii.* Leningrad, 1936.

Uralskaya, Valeria. "Research Aspects of the Choreographic Culture of the U.S.S.R." In *Beyond Performance: Dance Scholarship Today,* edited by Susan Au and Frank-Manuel Peter. Berlin, 1989.

Zhornitskaya, M. I. *Narodnye tantsy Iakutii.* Moscow, 1966.

Zhornitskaya, M. I. "The Study of Folk Dancing in the Soviet Union: Its State and Tasks." In *The Performing Arts,* edited by John Blacking. The Hague, 1979.

Zhornitskaya, M. I. *Narodnoe khoreograficheskoe iskusstvo korennogo naseleniia Severo-Vostoka Sibiri.* Moscow, 1983.

MARIA I. ZHORNITSKAYA
Translated from Russian

Theatrical Dance before 1917

What is distinctive about Russian dance may be traced in its evolution from the slow round dances performed at wedding feasts to the round dance of the swans in *Swan Lake* and the waltz of the snowflakes in *The Nutcracker.* In early Russia the worship of the pagan god Yaru (Yarilo) often took the form of ritual dances. In medieval Russia contact between paganism and Christianity affected every aspect of life. The history of folk art is a record of its own struggle for survival. In the ninth and tenth centuries all forms of entertainment were banned as sinful by the church; songs and dances were considered pagan. Later the indigenous population stoutly resisted the influence of the conquering Tatar-Mongol hordes and still later defied the European influences promoted by the upper class. Russian folk art preserved its identity partly through its dances, including the merry *pletni, trepak,* and *kamarinskaya.*

Origins to 1600. Under feudalism the culture of the ruling elite—the boyars, princes, and landed gentry—was influenced by folk art. At splendid gatherings in stately mansions the nobility danced the same round dances that the peasants did in their huts. Russian folk art celebrated the beauty of the countryside, the oneness of humankind

RUSSIA: Theatrical Dance before 1917. *The Little Humpbacked Horse* was choreographed for the Bolshoi Theater in Saint Petersburg in 1864 by Arthur Saint-Léon. In this early photograph, c.1870, Liubov Roslavleva is pictured in the role of the Tsar-Maiden, surrounded by her entourage. (Photograph from the Dance Collection, New York Public Library for the Performing Arts.)

with nature, and the benevolence of the sun. The patriotic defense of the Russian homeland was another dominant theme. While many group dances reflected scenes from life in the countryside, the accompanying songs were sometimes of a lyrical nature, sometimes concerned with family themes. The heroes of such songs embodied the ideals of the common people: the young men were always brave and dashing, but also polite and gallant; the maidens were always hardworking, gentle, and dutiful, "a dainty stepper and soft-spoken." They were fair-faced, rosy-cheeked, bright-eyed, tall, slender, and alluring. Such images called for dances that were stately, serene, and full of dignity and beauty. Among the typical folk dances the *khorovod,* a circle or chain dance, was most important. A group of girls linked hands to form a circle, singing as they moved slowly clockwise or counterclockwise, while one or several women inside the circle acted out the words of the song.

The first professional exponents of Russian folk dance were the medieval performers known as *skomorokhs.* These wandering minstrels and buffoons are first mentioned in chronicles of the eleventh century. Custodians of Russian tradition, the *skomorokhs* came from peasant and artisan families. They improvised jokes, trained animals, played many musical instruments, and, of course, sang and danced. Most of their lives were spent traveling from village to village, performing on makeshift stages and joining in whatever festivities they encountered. Often the *skomorokhs* were the heralds of popular rebellion; their art carried the message of protest against evil, violence, lies, and injustice. Various forms of folk theater survived until the end of the nineteenth century. Such entertainments often featured characters portrayed entirely through pantomime or dance. In puppet comedies a particular dance was often associated with Petrouchka, the archetypal character of the puppet, who was expected to dance the whole time he was on the stage.

Seventeenth Century. In the seventeenth century, rich noblemen and landed gentry used their increased wealth to satisfy their newly refined tastes, and their palatial country residences became home to the emerging art of choreography. But alongside the new repertory, Russian folk songs and dances were still performed with gusto. During the reign of Peter the Great (1689–1725), expanding intellectual horizons, increased interest in learning and science, and the subsequent erosion of the traditional puritanical way of life *(domostroi)* facilitated the introduction of western European customs. The first ballet performed by Russians, *Orpheus,* had been given in Moscow in 1673; others followed. In tearing down traditional ways, Tsar Peter cleared the path for economic, political, and cultural development. In 1718 he instituted social assemblies where ballroom dancing took place, and Russian society began to study drawing-room dances imported from the West. Foreign dancing masters were imported to teach the nobles in their homes and schools. The assemblies helped to develop an appreciation of cultivated dance techniques and forms, but they also insulated upper-class society from folk dance. Enthusiasm for the new dances prepared the ground for the introduction of the more sophisticated forms of choreography that emerged in the eighteenth century. The new culture was expected to strengthen the upper class. Yet folk art was also developing from features rooted in national tradition, and this trend ran counter to the upper-class taste for western European styles.

Advent of ballet. In 1736 an Italian opera and ballet troupe arrived in Russia. Engaged for its performances were Russian noblemen, cadets of the Noblemen's Corps who had been taught by the Frenchman Jean-Baptiste Landé. The arrival of the ballet company prompted the establishment of a national school to train Russian dancers, which was opened in 1738. Its graduates were the first generation of Russian professionals: Aksinia Sergeeva, Elizaveta Zorina, Avdotia Timofeeva, Afanasy Toporkov, and Andrei Nesterov. When Landé retired, Nesterov took his place. Regular musical performances began in Saint Petersburg in the 1730s. Dances for operas and comic ballets were staged by the Italian choreographer Antonio Rinaldi. Landé and his pupils staged serious ballets on pastoral and mythological themes. Another Italian troupe, led by Giovanni Locatelli, arrived in 1756, giving public performances of both serious and comic ballets in the Summer Garden Theater at Tsarskoye Selo.

In the second half of the century many other Western choreographers worked in Russia. They brought Russian dancers up to the standards of European ballet and introduced the choreographic reforms of Jean-Georges Noverre. Yet despite their various backgrounds, their creative work reflected Russian life. Among Franz Hilverding's ballets the most significant was *The Refuge of Virtue* (1759), in which Russia gave sanctuary to Virtue after it had been banished from other countries. Gaspero Angiolini created ballets that would find favor at court, among them the allegorical pantomime *Prejudice Conquered* (1768), which celebrated vaccination against smallpox, a crusade of the royal family. Noverre's *ballet d'action* was congenial to the principles of Russian culture. Charles Le Picq staged Noverre's *Médée et Jason* in Saint Petersburg in 1789. He also produced spectacular ballets that dazzled the court, including new works for state occasions, such as *Prince Oleg's Reign* (1791). Although this ballet celebrated

RUSSIA: Theatrical Dance before 1917. Marius Petipa's *La Bayadère* was first performed in 1877 at the Bolshoi Theater, Saint Petersburg. The ballet's most spectacular scenic effect, depicted in this contemporary engraving, was the destruction of the temple in the last act. (Photograph from the Dance Collection, New York Public Library for the Performing Arts.)

tsarism and was of a semi-official, even antipopular, character, it was full of Russian folk music and dances.

Serf theater and comic opera. Serf theaters, owned and run by wealthy landowners who wanted to imitate the court, were a unique Russian phenomenon. They enjoyed great popularity in the 1780s and 1790s, particularly in Moscow and is environs. The serf performers were handpicked by their highborn owners from every rung of the peasant population. Original dances staged by these companies were often also included in operas and comedies on Russian themes, in which folk dances were performed in traditional costume. Unlike the court and private theaters in Moscow and Saint Petersburg, the serf performers introduced theater to the public of the various provinces of the Russian empire. Some of the serf dancers later appeared on the stages of the imperial theaters after being bought from their owners by the tsar. The serf theaters began to disintegrate early in the nineteenth century. In spite of all the cruelty and the willful ways of their despotic owners, these theaters played an important role in shaping the Russian school of classical dance.

In the late 1700s national characteristics were at their most graphic in the dance scenes of comic operas, which satisfied the democratic public and were geared to its interests. Typical was a form of folk entertainment that made use of little songs, dance rhythms, and folk rituals. Mikhail Matinsky's opera *Saint Petersburg Arcade* (1779) presented a theatricalized engagement ceremony, complete with traditional paraphernalia: women's parties with songs and choral dances, a wedding feast, and so on. Various dances were used to characterize the protagonists and establish the atmosphere of Evstigney Fomin's *The Post-Chaise Driver* (1787). Outstanding dancers of this period included Timofei Bublikov, Gavrila Ivanov-Raikov, Varvara Mikhailova, and Arina Sobakina.

Ballet in Moscow. The Moscow ballet dancers maintained their folk dance tradition with loving care. Unlike the court theater in Saint Petersburg, the Moscow Theater developed as a public theater. The first dancers were trained at the city's orphanage, where ballet classes were started in 1773 for fifty-four boys and girls aged ten to twelve. The first teachers were Filippo Beccari and his wife. Leopold Paradisi, who succeeded Beccari in 1779, staged the first two ballets for the pupils, *The Fisherman* and *The Dutch Ballet*. In 1784 the orphanage ballet school became a part of the English entrepreneur Michael Maddox's Petrovsky Theater, which was inaugurated with Paradisi's ballet *The Magic Shop*. Later ballets were created by Francesco and Cosimo Morelli. The repertory consisted of comic ballets and dance scenes from rural life, such as *The Simple-Hearted Villager* (1783) and *The Outwitted Miller* (1793). The Italian choreographer Pietro Pinucci carried on the repertory traditions of the Moscow theater until the end of the eighteenth century with comic ballets like *The Deceived Village Doctor*.

Nineteenth Century. Eighteenth-century Russian choreography had favored the tastes of the court and the nobility, who liked lavish decor, brilliant staging, and scenic effects. The court theater seemed isolated from the world of the common people, and this isolation was encouraged by the desire of the upper classes to transplant French and Italian ballet and ignore their Russian roots.

RUSSIA: Theatrical Dance before 1917. Sofia Fedorova as Mercedes in Aleksandr Gorsky's version of *Don Quixote* (1900), produced for the Bolshoi Theater, Moscow. (Photograph from the Central A. A. Bakrushin State Theatrical Museum, Moscow.)

RUSSIA: Theatrical Dance before 1917. The Russian taste for the grand scale is evident in this scene from Aleksandr Gorsky's revival of Marius Petipa's *La Fille du Pharaon,* staged for the Bolshoi Theater, Moscow, in 1905. (Photograph from the Central A. A. Bakrushin State Theatrical Museum, Moscow.)

Valberkh, Glushkovsky, and Didelot. At the beginning of the nineteenth century the ballet scene was dominated by the first Russian-trained choreographer, Ivan Valberkh. While recognizing the achievements of European ballet, Valberkh introduced a new style that drew on the traditions of sentimentalism in Russian art. The trials and vicissitudes of ordinary people, and the morals to be drawn from their behavior, constituted the main theme of his choreography. Auguste Poireau and Charles-Louis Didelot also created ballets that showed their interest in Russian life. Outstanding dancers of this period included Evgenia Kolosova, Avdotia Istomina, Anastasia Novitskaya, Marie Danilova, Maria Ikonina, Ekaterina Teleshova, Constance Pletin, and Agrafina Makhayeva.

The war of 1812 against Napoleon had far-reaching implications for cultural life in Russia, as did the movement against autocracy that culminated in the Decembrists' revolt of 1825. Understandably, Russian choreographers tried to reflect the exploits of the people in the war against the French invaders. Valberkh was the first to produce a series of patriotic ballets. In August 1812, together with Poireau, he presented *The Home Guard, or Love of the Homeland.* Other nationalist works followed, concluding with *The Triumph of Russia, or Russians in Paris* (1813). Although many of these ballets were tributes to the royal family, they also celebrated the Russian soldier.

Divertissements were now gaining in popularity. Kolosova and Danilova were acclaimed as the best performers of Russian folk dances in this genre. Folk *divertissements* had a flexible dramatic structure, with plots taken from everyday life. Choreographers presented colorful panoramas of folk amusements that were easy to understand and consequently appealing to even the most unsophisticated audiences. In Moscow, Isaac Ablets was the leading exponent of this form. His best-known folk *divertissement, The Seventh Thursday after Easter, or Popular Festivities at Maryina Roshcha* (a woodland on the edge of town), was staged in 1815. Abletz depicted an old ritual of festooning birch trees with brightly colored ribbons and flower garlands before dancing in a ring around the trees. This popular work remained in the repertory until the 1870s. Valberkh and Adam Glushkovsky also produced works in this genre, as did Ivan Lobanov, whose *The Masked Ball at the Cracow Redoubt* and *The Hungarian Festival in Kissberg Forest* incorporated elements of Polish and Hungarian dances. In these works, choreographers began to portray ordinary people on the stage, describing faithfully how they lived and worked. These *divertissements* combined academic and folk dance and also carried a stirring message of patriotism.

The ballets of Didelot measured up to the requirements of dramatic works defined by Aleksandr Pushkin: "Truthful passions and plausible emotions in the circumstances described." Didelot was strongly influenced by his observations of Russian life, and his works therefore depicted heroes, rebels, and romantic freedom fighters. His *The Prisoner of the Caucasus* (1823), based on the poem of

RUSSIA: Theatrical Dance before 1917. Mikhail Mordkin and Viktorina Kriger in Gorsky's *Salammbô*, choreographed for the Bolshoi Theater, Moscow, in 1910. (Photograph reprinted from Mary Grace Swift, *The Art of the Dance in the U.S.S.R.*, Notre Dame, Indiana, 1968, p. 51.)

Pushkin who was in exile at the time, shows that the choreographer had the courage of his convictions. In addition to producing more than forty ballets in Saint Petersburg, Didelot also groomed a galaxy of dancers and choreographers who shared his philosophy and later implemented his ideas in their own works. After the brutal suppression of the Decembrists' revolt, Didelot, who had a reputation as a free thinker, had to leave Saint Petersburg. Didelot's work was continued by Glushkovsky.

It was Glushkovsky who introduced Moscow audiences to the works of Noverre, Valberkh, and Didelot. He was also a prolific creator of original ballets. An admirer of Russian literature, he had been the first to base a ballet on the work of Pushkin, staging *Ruslan and Ludmila* in 1821. In 1826 his spectacular *The Three Girdles, or The Russian Cinderella* used the poems of Vasily Zhukovsky. Glushkovsky also brought the Moscow company to a high level of professionalism, exemplified in particular by the ballerinas Tatiana Ivanova-Glushkovskaya and Aleksandra Voronina-Ivanova. He established for the Moscow ballet its tradition of dance with a significant message, a democratic spirit, and expressive acting. Yuri Slonimsky (1937) wrote that "the birth of the Moscow ballet was inseparable from the life and work of the renowned Adam Glushkovsy."

Romanticism. Following the suppression of the Decembrists' revolt, all manifestations of nationalism and ideological independence were discouraged. The consequences for the ballet were dramatic. The repertory of the previous period was eroded. A new spirit took over: from 1830 until the 1850s many exponents of the Romantic ballet worked in Russia, including Marie and Filippo Taglioni, Fanny Elssler, Jules Perrot, and Carlotta Grisi. Antoine Titus produced *La Sylphide* in Saint Petersburg in 1832 and *Giselle* ten years later. Although the Russian choreographers carefully studied the themes and style of the Romantic ballets and sincerely admired the skill of visiting dancers, they were no passive imitators. Within the framework of romanticism, Russian dancers responded to the contemporary social scene, emphasizing those issues and moral problems raised by the Romantic ballets and highlighting those facets of human character that were most important to Russian audiences. For example, in 1837 two fundamentally different interpretations of *La Sylphide* were presented: in Saint Petersburg, Taglioni's Sylphide was a beautiful and unattainable dream who died upon contact with crude reality; in Moscow, Ekaterina Sankovskaya's Sylph reached out to people to understand their feelings but died because she could not live without freedom. In 1848 Jules Perrot arrived in Russia; in the ten years of his stay, he produced eighteen of his own ballets. His works, with their well-constructed plots and their rebel and outcast heroes, were popular with Russian audiences. Connoisseurs, too, acclaimed his attempts to re-create in ballet the popular literary characters created by Hugo, Goethe, and Byron. Many of his ballets are still in the repertories of Russian companies.

By the end of the 1830s, the provinces had a number of private theaters, many of which had dance groups. Saint Petersburg companies helped to popularize ballet during their guest performances in the provinces. That effort was pioneered by Elena Andreyanova, who appeared with a small company in a number of cities. In 1854 in Voronezh she premiered her ballet based on Pushkin's *The Fountain of Bakhchisarai*, the first choreography based on that work. This period also saw the rise of Russian nationalism in music, exemplified by Mikhail Glinka. Russian ballet music probably traces its origins to choreographic scenes in the operas of Glinka. For the first time, dances in opera were not mere inserts to liven up the action but essential components of that action. In *Ivan Susanin* (1836) Glinka drew a portrait of the Polish gentry by using a symphonic presentation of traditional Polish folk dances, and in *Ruslan and Ludmila* (1842) the very characters were defined symphonically.

Saint-Léon and Blasis. In 1859, the French choreographer Arthur Saint-Léon became the head of the Saint Petersburg company and staged some of his works in Moscow as well. His major ballet in Russia was *The Little Humpbacked Horse* (1864), which, despite its oversimplified message, stayed in the repertory until the end of the century, thanks to its folk theme and vivid theatricality. Although Saint-Léon's ballets were criticized for being light in meaning, he enriched both classical and character dance as well as ballet composition. Along with Carlo Blasis, who worked in Moscow, Saint-Léon emphasized the improvement of dance technique. Ballets were now divided into classical and character dances. Pantomime and dance scenes were alternated, and the structure of solo and ensemble numbers was formalized. With the development of pointe technique, the female dancer dominated the stage.

In the 1860s there were still many foreign ballerinas on the Russian stage, among them Carolina Rosati, Claudina Cucchi, Adèle Grantzow, and Guglielmina Salvioni. However, audiences began to display a growing interest in native talent as the Crimean War generated patriotic feelings and as the skills of Russian dancers improved. Among the Russian dancers who rose to prominence were Nadezhda Bogdanova, who specialized in lyrical themes; Praskovia Lebedeva, who excelled in dramatic roles; Maria Surovshchikova (wife of Marius Petipa), who was particularly expressive in pantomime; and the romantic Marfa Muravieva, who became one of the first Russian ballerinas to dance at the Paris Opera.

During the later 1800s, the Moscow ballet went into a prolonged decline because of the frequent replacement of choreographers and some ill-conceived administrative and financial reforms. In 1861 Blasis was appointed chief choreographer and teacher. While his productions did not make an appreciable impact, his teaching did; his pupils had remarkable musicality, fine technique, and an assured stage manner. After Blasis left, however, the Bolshoi Theater had no permanent choreographer for almost ten years. The contributions of Julius Reisinger and Joseph Hansen did not significantly alter the situation. Matters improved in the 1890s with performances by some fine dancers, including Ivan Yermolov, Dmitri Kuznetsov, Gustav Legat, Alfred Bekefi, and Vasily Geltser. Among the ballerinas were Olga Nikolaeva, Anna Sobeshchanskaya, and Polina Karpakova. Rising stars in this period were Lydia Geiten, Liubov Roslavleva, Adelina Giuri, Ivan Clustine, Fedor Manokhin, Maria Stanislavska, and Nikolai Domashov. All of them strove for dramatic fervor and vivid individualization of their roles, thus advancing realist tendencies in the art of ballet.

Petipa and Ivanov. In Saint Petersburg, the progress of ballet in the second half of the nineteenth century is associated with Marius Petipa, who headed the Maryinsky company from 1869 to 1903. In addition to creating some fifty ballets, he revised virtually the entire repertory. Ensemble dances polyphonically intertwined with the solos and pas de deux, refined forms, and rich folk colors in his first productions heralded the symphonic integrity of his

RUSSIA: Theatrical Dance before 1917. Matilda Kshessinska, *grande dame* of the Imperial Ballet and a favorite of the tsar, was partnered by Pierre Vladimiroff in Michel Fokine's *Eros* (1915), performed at the Maryinsky Theater, Petrograd. (Photograph from the archives of the Maryinsky Theater, Saint Petersburg.)

later ballets. The culmination of the first phase of Petipa's work was *La Bayadère* (1877), in which the principles of symphonic dance were consummated in the Kingdom of the Shades scene. In 1890 *The Sleeping Beauty* firmly established symphonism as a principle of ballet structure. Every act included mime, *demi-caractère,* and classical dances. His last great production was *Raymonda* (1898). Vera Krasovskaya (1963) has noted that the ballet is based on three types of suite—character, *demi-caractère,* and classical—that form an original succession through which the action unfolds. Lev Ivanov also contributed to the development of choreographic symphonism. His choreography for the second and fourth acts of *Swan Lake* achieves the ultimate unity of dance imagery, plastique expressiveness, and musical development.

The compositions of Petipa and Ivanov could be executed only by a major company, and in the late nineteenth century the Maryinsky troupe, trained by Christian Johansson and Enrico Cecchetti, was equal to the task. Among its dancers were the virtuoso ballerina Ekaterina Vazem, the lyrical Evgenia Sokolova, the fiery Aleksandra Vergina, and the fluid Maria Gorshenkova; the leading classical male dancer was Pavel Gerdt. In the 1880s Virginia Zucchi, Carlotta Brianza, and Pierina Legnani performed at private theaters in Saint Petersburg as well as at the Maryinsky, exhibiting their Italian virtuosity. The flowing manner of the native tradition was now enriched with the technique of the school of Milan, which lent a touch of brilliance to the poetry of the Russian tradition.

At the end of the nineteenth century artistic innovations arose from the contest between realist and antirealist tendencies in Russian art. Developments included the emergence of the Moscow Art Theater of Konstantin Stanislavsky and Vladimir Nemirovich-Danchenko, the new drama of Maxim Gorky and Anton Chekhov, and the provocative productions of Savva Mamontov's opera house. The ballet also produced innovators, and the collision of ideas split the dance community. The innovators rejected the canonized forms of academic ballet painstakingly preserved by Nikolai Legat, Klavdia Kulichevskaya, and Samuil Andreonov. The intricate forms of classical choreography in the new ballet clashed with their simple content. The custodians of tradition, however, looked askance at Aleksandr Gorsky and Michel Fokine, who sought historical and national veracity in ballet. The new generation rejected the possibilities offered by symphonic dance, substituting for it choreodramatic ideas. This attitude brought the reformers closer to contemporary visual artists.

1900 to 1917. In the early twentieth century, the ballet began to collaborate with the World of Art group, which included Alexandre Benois, Aleksandr Golovin, Konstantin Korovin, and Léon Bakst. Their collaboration resulted in a stylistic unity of sets, costumes, and choreography. Painting also influenced the dance as choreographers introduced new plastique forms that they interpreted as "natural."

Gorsky. The revival of the Moscow ballet is associated with Gorsky, who joined the Bolshoi in 1901. He advocated the integrity of ballet presentation, historical and national veracity of style, and natural movement. Many scenes in his ballets were danced barefoot, bearing the imprint of Isadora Duncan's free dance. Gorsky repeatedly turned to past productions, trying to strip them of stereotyped movements and poses learned by rote. In *Gudule's Daughter* (1902), expressive mime was the dominating element. By borrowing techniques from the dramatic theater; balancing dance, sets, music, and elements of literature; and transplanting character dances onto the ballet stage Gorsky contributed to the rise of the Moscow company. He also groomed a galaxy of dancers, including Vasily Tikhomirov, Mikhail Mordkin, and Alexandre Volinine.

Fokine. The same period saw the rise at the Maryinsky of Nikolai and Sergei Legat, Olga Preobrajenska, Matilda Kshessinska, Julie Sedova, Vera Trefilova, and Agrippina Vaganova. Their mission was to preserve the purity of classical dance. But Fokine considered precise classicism hopelessly outdated. Like Gorsky, he instilled in his pupils an ability to dance expressively and to master free dance. His one-act ballets *Eunice* and *Le Pavillon d'Armide* (1907) fused mime and dance into plastique drama. The main traits of Fokine's innovations were his close cooperation with stage designers, his use of symphonic music, and his enrichment of the expressive means of choreography. The names of Anna Pavlova, Tamara Karsavina, Vaslav Nijinsky, and Pierre Vladimiroff are closely associated with Fokine's.

[*See also the entries on the principal figures and works mentioned herein.*]

BIBLIOGRAPHY

Asafiev, Boris. *Glinka.* Moscow, 1947.

Bakhrushin, Yuri. *Aleksandr Alekseevich Gorskii.* Moscow, 1946.

Bakhrushin, Yuri. "Balet Russkoi provintsii nachala XIX veka." *Sovetskii balet,* no. 1 (1982).

Benois, Alexandre. *Reminiscences of the Russian Ballet.* Translated by Mary Britnieva. London, 1941.

Benois, Alexandre. *Memoirs.* 2 vols. Translated by Moura Budberg. London, 1960–1964.

Chujoy, Anatole. "Russian Balletomania." *Dance Index* (March 1948): 43–71.

Degen, Arsen. "Then and Now at the Maryinsky Theater." *Ballet Review* 20 (Summer 1992): 40–48.

Demidov, Alexander P. *The Russian Ballet: Past and Present.* Translated by Guy Daniels. Garden City, N.Y., 1977.

Elyash, Nikolai. *Pushkin i baletnyi teatr.* Moscow, 1970.

Fokine, Michel. *Memoirs of a Ballet Master.* Translated by Vitale Fokine. Edited by Anatole Chujoy. London, 1961.

Fokine, Michel. *Protiv techeniia: Vospominaniia baletmeistera.* Edited by Yuri Slonimsky. 2d ed. Leningrad, 1981.

Garafola, Lynn. *Diaghilev's Ballets Russes.* New York, 1989.

Glushkovsky, Adam. *Vospominaniia baletmeistera.* Leningrad, 1940.
Goldman, Debra. "Background to Diaghilev." *Ballet Review* 6.3 (1977–1978): 1–56.
Gozenpud, A. A. *Muzykalnyi teatr v Rossii: Ot istokov do Glinki.* Leningrad, 1959.
Guest, Ivor. *The Romantic Ballet in Paris.* 2d rev. ed. London, 1980.
Guest, Ivor. *Jules Perrot: Master of the Romantic Ballet.* London, 1984.
Kamensky, Alexander, ed. *The World of Art Movement in Early Twentieth-Century Russia.* Translated by Arthur Shkarovsky-Raffe. Leningrad, 1991.
Karsavina, Tamara. *Theatre Street.* Rev. and enl. ed. London, 1948.
Koni, Fedor, ed. *Panteon russkago i vsiekh evropeiskikh teatrov.* Saint Petersburg, 1840–.
Krasovskaya, Vera. *Russkii baletnyi teatr: Ot vozniknoveniia do serediny XIX veka.* Leningrad, 1958.
Krasovskaya, Vera. *Russkii baletnyi teatr vtoroi poloviny deviatnadtsatogo veka.* Leningrad, 1963.
Krasovskaya, Vera. *Russkii baletnyi teatr nachala dvadtsatogo veka,* vol. 1, *Khoreografy;* vol. 2, *Tantsovshchiki.* Leningrad, 1971–1972.
Krasovskaya, Vera. *Istoriia russkogo baleta.* Leningrad, 1978.
Kshessinska, Matilda. *Dancing in Petersburg: The Memoirs of Kschessinska.* Translated by Arnold L. Haskell. London, 1960.
Kyasht, Lydia. *Romantic Recollections.* Edited by Erica Beale. New York, 1929.
Lawson, Joan. "Masters of the Ballet of the Nineteenth Century" (parts 1–6). *The Dancing Times* (November 1939–April 1940).
Lawson, Joan. "Pages from the History of Russian Ballet" (parts 1–6). *The Dancing Times* (December 1940–May 1941).
Legat, Nikolai. *Ballet Russe: Memoirs of Nicolas Legat.* Translated by Paul Dukes. London, 1932.
Lifar, Serge. *A History of Russian Ballet* (1950). Translated by Arnold L. Haskell. New York, 1954.
Lunacharskii, A. V., and I. V. Ekskuzovich, eds. *Moskovskii Bolshoi Teatr, 1825–1925.* Moscow, 1925.
Nekhendzi, Ana, ed. *Marius Petipa: Materialy, vospominaniia, stati.* Leningrad, 1971.
Petipa, Marius. *Russian Ballet Master: The Memoirs of Marius Petipa.* Edited by Lillian Moore. Translated by Helen Whittaker. London, 1958.
Petipa, Marius. *The Diaries of Marius Petipa.* Translated and edited by Lynn Garafola. Studies in Dance History, vol. 3.1. Pennington, N.J., 1992.
Petrov, Oleg. *Russkaia baletnaia kritika kontsa XVIII pervoi poloviny XIX veka.* Moscow, 1982.
Petrov, Oleg. "Russian Ballet and Its Place in Russian Artistic Culture of the Second Half of the Nineteenth Century." Translated by Tim Scholl. *Dance Chronicle* 15.1 (1992): 40–58.
Propert, W. A. *The Russian Ballet in Western Europe, 1909–1920.* London, 1921.
Racster, Olga. *The Master of the Russian Ballet: The Memoirs of Cav. Enrico Cecchetti.* New York, 1923.
Roslavleva, Natalia. *Era of the Russian Ballet, 1770–1965* (1966). New York, 1979.
Scholl, Tim. "From Apollon to Apollo." *Ballet Review* 21 (Winter 1993): 82–96.
Scholl, Tim. *From Petipa to Balanchine: Classical Revival and the Modernization of Ballet.* New York, 1994.
Slonim, Marc. *Russian Theatre from the Empire to the Soviets.* Cleveland, 1961.
Slonimsky, Yuri. *Mastera baleta.* Leningrad, 1937.
Slonimsky, Yuri. *P. I. Chaikovskii i baletnyi teatr ego vremeni.* Moscow, 1956.
Souritz, Elizabeth. *Carlo Blasis in Russia, 1861–1864.* Studies in Dance History, vol. 4.2. Pennington, N.J., 1993.
Staehlin, Jakob von. *Muzyka i balet v Rossii XVIII veka.* Leningrad, 1935.
Svetlov, Valerian. *Sovremennyi balet.* St. Petersburg, 1911.
Swift, Mary Grace. *A Loftier Flight: The Life and Accomplishments of Charles Louis Didelot.* Middletown, Conn., 1974.
Teliakovsky, Vladimir. "Memoirs: St. Petersburg Ballet." Translated by Nina Dimitrievich. *Dance Research* 9 (Spring 1991): 26–39.
Teliakovsky, Vladimir. "Memoirs: The Balletomanes." Translated by Nina Dimitrievich. *Dance Research* 12 (Spring 1994): 41–47.
Valberkh, Ivan. *Iz arkhiva baletmeistera.* Moscow, 1948.
Vazem, Ekaterina. "Memoirs of a Ballerina of the St. Petersburg Bolshoi Theatre." Translated by Nina Dimitrievich. *Dance Research* 3 (Summer 1985): 3–22; 4 (Spring 1986): 3–28; 5 (Spring 1987): 21–41; 6 (Autumn 1988): 30–47.
Vladykina-Bachinskaia, N. M. *Ruskie khorovody in khorovodnye pesni.* Moscow, 1951.
Volkonsky, Sergei. *My Reminiscences.* 2 vols. Translated by A. E. Chamot. London, 1925.
Wiley, Roland John. "Three Historians of the Russian Imperial Ballet." *Dance Research Journal* 13 (Fall 1980): 3–16.
Wiley, Roland John. *Tchaikovsky's Ballets.* Oxford, 1985.
Wiley, Roland John, trans. and ed. *A Century of Russian Ballet: Documents and Accounts, 1810–1910.* Oxford, 1990.
Zhitomirskii, Daniel. *Balety P. Chaikovskogo.* Moscow, 1950.

Valeria I. Uralskaya, Galina V. Inozemtseva,
and Elena G. Fedorenko
Translated from Russian

Theatrical Dance since 1917

After the Socialist Revolution of 1917 all the imperial theaters were nationalized. Despite the many difficulties resulting from the civil war, the government took care to retain theatrical companies, although some performers continued their careers abroad, where they spread the influence of Russian ballet. From the outset the Soviet ballet was faced with two important tasks: to preserve the classical heritage, and to create new works that adhered to the requirements of the day. Some classical ballets were carefully retained; others were given new stagings. Choreographers who strove to preserve the classical heritage had to fight tendencies toward plebeian simplification, which was gaining popularity at the time. There was even debate as to whether the new audience needed ballet at all. Fortunately, the preservationists won and the ballet was saved for its enthusiastic new audience. While all agreed that new ballets were needed to reflect the changing times, there was little agreement about the precise form innovations should take. These were days of eager experiments and intense competition between various methods and trends.

In Petrograd/Leningrad in the 1920s a truly innovative choreographer, Fedor Lopukhov, experimented by creating a ballet symphony, *The Magnificence of the Universe* (1923); a ballet depicting the October Revolution, *The Red Whirlwind* (1924); and Stravinsky's *Pulcinella* (1926) and *Le Renard* (1927). His *The Ice Maiden* (1927) approximated traditional nineteenth-century "grand ballet" in structure, but its choreography was modern. In Moscow at the Bolshoi Theater an ambitious ballet was created by Kasyan Goleizovsky, *Joseph the Beautiful* (1925). Goleizovsky also choreographed for his own company, the Chamber Ballet (1922–1927), many other works in his individual style, which was based on renovated classical dance. Other groups and studios sprang up during the 1920s: founded in Moscow were Isadora Duncan's school and Nikolai Foregger's Workshop, popular for its "mechanical dances," both opened in 1922; Nina Gremina's Drambalet (dramatic ballet) company in 1924; and studios headed by Inna Chernetskaia, Ludmila Alekseeva, Vera Maya, and others; and in Petrograd in 1922 George Balanchine began his choreographing career with the Young Ballet. All of these groups were doing interesting experimental work, but by the beginning of the 1930s most of them were defunct, owing to official disapproval of whatever was not traditional ballet or folk dance. This new mentality, which excluded experiment and a search for new styles in dance, was embodied in a work that was enormously successful at the Bolshoi Theater and soon throughout the country—*The Red Poppy* (1927). It treated a story about revolution in China, using classical movement vocabulary, character dance, and forceful dramatic pantomime. Among the principal dancers of the time were Elena Lukom, Olga Mungalova, Boris Shavrov, and Petr Gusev in Leningrad, and Ekaterina Geltser, Viktorina Kriger, Vasily Tikhomirov, Nikolai Tarasov, and Leonid Zhukov in Moscow.

In the 1930s this turn toward drama in ballet gave rise to a new style of staging, generally known as drama ballet *(drambalet)*. The drama ballet soon became the only acceptable form and prevailed throughout the 1930s and 1940s. Some successes were achieved in this story ballet genre, which was generally based on a well-known literary work by Shakespeare, Pushkin, Lope de Vega, or the like, and sometimes on revolutionary themes, for example, Vasily Vainonen created *The Flames of Paris* (1932), Rostislav Zakharov *The Fountain of Bakhchisarai* (1934), Vakhtang Chabukiani *Laurencia* (1938), and Leonid Lavrovsky *Romeo and Juliet* (1940). All too many of these ballets were plays, with much pantomime and little dance. In such productions dance was used mostly as background or was introduced for a ball or festival scene. The choreographers had no use for abstract ensemble structures that, in the ballets of the nineteenth century like *Giselle* or *Swan Lake,* depict the atmosphere and the emotions of the heroes. A whole generation of dancers was molded on these drama ballet productions, along with the standard repertory of traditional ballets. Already in the second half of the 1920s a new style of performing was emerging. Marina Semenova and Aleksei Yermolayev were the first to give classical dance a new, bolder, more virtuosic look. By the 1930s dancers were more inclined toward drama and translating emotions into dance. The greatest of the dramatic dancers were Galina Ulanova and her partner Konstantin Sergeyev, while Natalia Dudinskaya, Olga Lepeshinskaya, Vakhtang Chabukiani, and Asaf Messerer were distinguished by their strong technique.

Another feature of the 1930s and 1940s was the creation of new ballet companies throughout the country. Theaters

RUSSIA: Theatrical Dance since 1917. *The Red Poppy,* mounted at Moscow's Bolshoi Theater in 1927, was the first major Soviet ballet with a revolutionary theme. With a libretto by Mikhail Kurilko and music by Reinhold Glière, it was choreographed by Lev Laschilin and Vasily Tikhomirov. When Fedor Lopukhov staged it in Leningrad in 1929, he revised the choreography. The dance for the Soviet sailors in act 1, the most popular number in the ballet, was set to the tune of the folk song "Yablochko" (Little Apple). The monumental set, designed by Boris Erbstein, reflected the style that would become known as Soviet realism. (Photograph from the archives of the Maryinsky Theater, Saint Petersburg.)

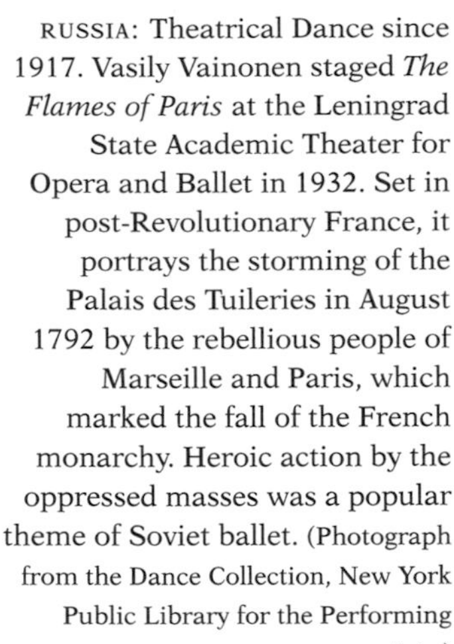

RUSSIA: Theatrical Dance since 1917. Vasily Vainonen staged *The Flames of Paris* at the Leningrad State Academic Theater for Opera and Ballet in 1932. Set in post-Revolutionary France, it portrays the storming of the Palais des Tuileries in August 1792 by the rebellious people of Marseille and Paris, which marked the fall of the French monarchy. Heroic action by the oppressed masses was a popular theme of Soviet ballet. (Photograph from the Dance Collection, New York Public Library for the Performing Arts.)

of opera and ballet were now in existence in all fifteen capitals of the national republics and many Russian and some Ukrainian towns—Ekaterinburg (then Sverdlovsk, 1924), Saratov (1928), Samara (then Kuibyshev, 1931), Nizhniy Novgorod (then Gorky, 1935)—as well as capitals of the Russian autonomous republics, such as Bashkiria, Buryatia, and Tataria. From the republics where ballet had never been cultivated, such as those in Central Asia, children were sent to Leningrad and Moscow to study and some very good dancers evolved. At festivals of the national art of these republics, held in Moscow, ballets using local themes were presented, generally choreographed with music and choreography by Russians. But all of the works that used local legends or stories of local life were made on the same model of full-length drama ballets, usually with indifferent music and primitive choreography that was partly ballet technique, partly folk dance. The important element was the story, which had to be told as comprehensibly as possible. An example of the type of ballet created in the autonomous republics is the Buryat choreographer Mikhail Zaslavsky's *The Angara*, which, although created in 1959, is representative of the style. It relates the legend of the Angara River that flows through Buryat: when imperious Baikal cannot overtake his fleeing daughter Angara and her lover, he transforms them into two rivers, which nevertheless unite in the final underwater scene that culminates in a festival of folk dances. Also typical is *Song of the Crane* (1944), which combined classical vocabulary and the folk dance of Bashkir to lyrical effect. [*See the entry on Anisimova.*]

World War II and the Aftermath. There is an old saying, "When the cannons speak, the Muses are silent." As it happens the Soviet muses were not silent during the war. The Bolshoi Theater was evacuated to Samara and the Kirov Theater to Perm, where they continued to function. Other companies played to audiences of frontline troops who went directly from the theater into battle. New ballets were created: *Gayané* (1942) by Nina Anisimova, *Crimson Sails* (1942) by Aleksandr Radunsky, Nikolai Popko, and Lev Pospekhin, and *Lola* (1943) by Vladimir Burmeister. In the postwar period Rostislav Zakharov created the first Soviet *Cinderella* in 1945 for the Bolshoi Ballet and *The Bronze Horseman* (1949) for the Kirov Ballet, and Boris Fenster produced *Youth* (1949) for the Maly Ballet in Leningrad. While celebratory of the end of war, these works tended to subvert the principles of drama ballet with gratuitous spectacular effects. A new generation of technically superb, dramatically powerful dancers was emerging—Maya Plisetskaya, Raisa Struchkova, Marina Kondratieva, Rimma Karelskaya, Nina Timofeyeva, Violetta Bovt, Yuri Zhdanov, Georgi Farmaniants, Vladimir Levashev, Nikolai Fadeyechev, Yaroslav Sekh, Alla Shelest, Irina Kolpakova, Alla Osipenko, Aleksandr Gribov, Anatoly Gridin—and in the provinces theaters were multiplying. In 1945 an opera and ballet theater was inaugurated in Novosibirsk that became so popular it was called the Bolshoi of Siberia.

The most significant productions by the major companies in the late 1940s and early 1950s were *Spring Tale* (1947) by Fedor Lopukhov, *Seven Beauties* (1953) by Petr

RUSSIA: Theatrical Dance since 1917. Nina Anisimova created *Gayané* to a score by Aram Khachaturian in 1942. The tale of two young Armenian lovers, Armen and Gayané, ends happily at a wedding feast where guests perform traditional dances of many peoples of the Soviet Union: Russians, Armenians, Georgians, Kurds, Ukrainians, and others. Here, Esfandiar Kashani is pictured in a 1962 performance with the Bolshoi Ballet. (Photograph from a Bolshoi Ballet souvenir program, 1962.)

Gusev, and *Shurale* (1955) and *Spartacus* (1956) by Leonid Yakobson. But it was only in the late 1950s, during the so-called "thaw" after Stalin's death, that Soviet ballet began to change as new influences impinged. Many of these came from the West, after the first tours of foreign companies and especially that of Balanchine's New York City Ballet. In the 1960s the drama ballet approach met with increasingly sharp criticism by choreographers and dancers, who wanted ballets in which not only the story, but also the dancing was important. The breakthrough came after Yuri Grigorovich staged *The Stone Flower* (1957) and *Legend of Love* (1961), and Igor Belsky produced *The Coast of Hope* (1959) and *Leningrad Symphony* (1961). The ballets of Grigorovich met modern requirements because they were permeated with moral and philosophical ideas, raising issues rooted in contemporary life. While retaining the dramatic achievements of the preceding era, he brought abstract ensemble dancing back to ballet. Belsky's characters were heroic Soviet people, and he demonstrated that a modern theme could be expressed through both symbolic images and the long-forgotten idioms of symphonically structured dance. Other choreographers extended the range of characters and ideological issues raised by Grigorovich and Belsky. In addition, the role of dancing and the use of contemporary themes was increasing. Influenced by the work of foreign choreographers such as George Balanchine, Jerome Robbins, and Frederick Ashton, the Russian predilection for full-length ballets gave way to shorter, one-act ballets. Some of Michel Fokine's ballets were revived and Soviet choreographers produced one-act ballets. These new trends were evident in *Vanina Vanini* (1962), *Heroic Poem* (1964), and *Le Sacre du Printemps* (1965), staged by Natalia Kasatkina and Vladimir Vasiliov for the Bolshoi Ballet. Additional interesting work was done by Olga Tarasova, Aleksandr Lapauri, Oleg Vinogradov, and Konstantin Boyarsky.

Ballet masters of the older generation joined in the process of renovating the ballet. Kasyan Goleizovsky created the poetic *Leili and Medzhnun* (1964), while Leonid Lavrovsky produced the romantic *Paganini* (1960), and Leonid Yakobson made daring experiments in his *Choreographic Miniatures* (1958), *The Bedbug* (1962) after Vladimir Mayakovsky's play, and *The Twelve* (1964), based on the poems of Aleksandr Blok. Throughout this period two opposing points of view were in contention: the official line that eschewed plotless ballet as worthless, and the forward-looking assertion that progress would be made only by shedding reliance on plot or story in favor of the dancing itself. New dancers who came to the fore were Ekaterina Maximova, Natalia Bessmertnova, Nina Sorokina, Gabriella Komleva, Vladimir Vasiliev, Mikhail Lavrovsky, Maris Liepa, Yuri Vladimirov, Yuri Soloviev, and Nikita Dolgushin. These performers managed to act without sacrificing the importance and quality of the dancing. Also notable during that period of Soviet ballet was the diversity of generations and national cultures represented by its choreographers. Coming to prominence in the 1960s and 1970s were Georgi Aleksidze, Bulat Ayukhanov, Nikolai Boyarchikov, Dmitri Briantzev, Ülo Vilimaa, Vladimir Vasiliev, the Dementev brothers Anatoly and Aleksandr, Vilen Galstian, Valentin Elizariev, Henrik Mayorov, Maxim Martirosian, Mai-Ester Murdmaa, Nela Nazirova, Andrei Petrov, Aleksandr Polubentsev, Uran Sarbagishev, Igor Chernyshev, Anatoly Shekera, Boris Eifman, Viktor Smirnov-Golovanov, and Natalia Ryzhenko.

The 1970s to Mid-1980s. Movies and television were making ballet accessible to millions in the remotest parts of the Soviet Union. Many ballets were filmed, but television ballet was an entirely new genre. Most popular of the latter were Dmitri Briantzev's *Galatea* (1977) and Vladimir Vasiliev's *Aniuta* (1982; expanded for the stage in 1986). Meanwhile, many new opera and ballet theaters opened in various republics. Dramatic and musical comedy theaters also often maintained permanent ballet companies. Folk dance companies existed in all the autonomous republics of the Russian Federation. The difference between the center and outlying districts of the country was being gradually erased. Amateur ballet became popular. Workers and office employees danced in numerous peoples' theaters that had begun to appear in the 1930s, for example, the Island of Dance in Moscow's Gorky Park and the

People's Theater of the Gorky Palace of Culture in Leningrad, both organized in 1934. It was in the Palace of Culture that Yuri Grigorovich staged his first ballet. But many more such theaters sprang up beginning in the 1960s; among the largest were the one attached to the Hammer and Sickle Works in Moscow, which opened in 1962, and the amateur ballet theater at the Kirov Palace of Culture in Leningrad, which dates from 1963. Such theaters were most important in areas where no professional company existed. Amateurs were also studying in numerous ballroom studios.

Beginning in the 1970s internal touring companies that staged both classical and modern ballets, most often miniatures or one-act works, also grew in popularity. Still in existence and best known among them are Choreographic Miniatures, headed by Leonid Yakobson from 1969 to 1975 and thereafter by Askold Makarov; Saint Petersburg State Theater of Ballet, headed by Boris Eifman from 1977 onward; and Moscow Classical Ballet, directed by Yuri Zhdanov from 1971 to 1977 and then by Natalia Kasatkina and Vladimir Vasiliov. International understanding was being fostered by major Soviet companies' tours abroad.

Soviet choreographers were again turning to symbolic subjects, but now they were full-blooded and lifelike, serving to convey a philosophical message. Most remarkable among these were *Till Eulenspiegel* in 1978 and *Carmina Burana,* choreographed by Valentin Elizariev in 1983. The genre range of Soviet ballets became wider and the language changed. Although still based on classical dance, they were more daringly enriched by elements from other vocabularies. Folklore and dramatic pantomime continued to be used but were often combined with sport, labor, and everyday gestures as well as with free plastique and jazz movements. Russian history was a growing concern to artists of the 1970s. Writers began to pay closer attention to the traditional features of people's lives, ancient folk songs began to be included in the repertories of choirs, architectural monuments were being restored, and there was intense interest in medieval Russian painting. Among ballets with subjects drawn from Russian history were Oleg Vinogradov's *Yaroslavna* (1974), Nikolai Boyarchikov's *Tsar Boris* (1978), Yuri Grigorovich's *Ivan the Terrible* (1975), and Aleksei Chichinadze's *Stepan Razin* (1977).

New ballets were also based on prehistory or myth. In *The Creation of the World* the birth of Adam and Eve with the contest between God and the Devil was staged by Natalia Kasatkina and Vladimir Vasiliov as a grotesque comedy in 1971 and by Elizariev as a lyrical drama in 1976. Vladimir Vasiliev's *Icarus* of 1971 told of human hopes and striving and heroic feats. There was also a kind of

RUSSIA: Theatrical Dance since 1917. *The Bronze Horseman,* choreographed by Rostislav Zakharov for the Bolshoi Ballet in 1949, was based on a poem by Aleksandr Pushkin telling the tragic love story of Yevgeny and Parasha who was drowned in the great Saint Petersburg flood of 1824. This scene from act 1, depicting Evgenia Farmaniants dancing as Columbine, is dominated by the statue of the "bronze horseman" (i.e., Peter the Great). (Photograph from the A. A. Bakrushin Central State Theatrical Museum, Moscow.)

Shakespearian renaissance in ballet, with six productions of *Hamlet* appearing between 1969 and 1981. The 1960s and 1970s brought six new versions of *Romeo and Juliet,* all attempting to compensate for the inadequate dance idiom of the original production. Vasiliev's *Macbeth* (1980) showed the spiritual bankruptcy of the principal character and was also interesting for having the three witches performed by men on pointe. Other literary classics were also adapted for ballet, among them, Maya Plisetskaya's staging of *Anna Karenina* (1972), *The Seagull* (1980), and *Lady with a Lapdog* (1985), as well as Boris Eifman's *The Idiot* (1980) and Oleg Vinogradov's *The Inspector-General* (1980). Formerly these novels had seemed totally unbaletic; although their adaptation stirred much controversy, they added to the potential dramatic range of ballet as theater. Most significant, however, were the ballets on contemporary subjects. Many works focused on moral problems. The theme of war was treated in Uran Sarbagishev's *Mother's Field* (1975) and Dina Aripova's *The Eternal Song* (1976). Ballets devoted to the struggle for peace and human dignity were Igor Chernyshev's *Remember!* (1981) and Eifman's *The Interrupted Song* (1977). The best of the ballets on modern themes were Yuri Grigorovich's *The Angara* (1976) and *The Golden Age* (1982), for they demonstrated that the full range of ballet forms could be used to portray an up-to-date story. Among the prominent new dancers to emerge in this period were Nadezhda Pavlova, Ludmila Semenyaka, Margarita Drozdova, Natalia Bolshakova, Galına Mezentseva, Alla Mikhalchenko, Viacheslav Gordeyev, Aleksandr Bogatyrev, Boris Akimov, Vadim Gulyaev, and Sergei Berezhnoi.

RUSSIA: Theatrical Dance since 1917. The first production of Khachaturian's *Spartacus* was mounted by Leonid Yakobson for the Kirov Ballet in 1956, with Askold Makarov (at center, with arm upraised) in the title role. This work was a radical departure from the conventions of classical ballet, as turnout and pointe work were abandoned in favor of a naturalistic style of movement. Moreover, it had no strictly developed plot; the emphasis of the production was on the heroism and courage of Spartacus, who incites his fellow slaves to revolt against their Roman oppressors. (Photograph from the archives of the Maryinsky Theater, Saint Petersburg.)

RUSSIA: Theatrical Dance since 1917. Based on a novel by the South African writer Peter Abraham, *Path of Thunder* was created by Konstantin Sergeyev for the Kirov Ballet in 1957. Sergeyev created the role of Lenny, a black man in love with Sari, a white girl, performed at the premiere by Natalia Dudinskaya. This work was subsequently mounted by various choreographers at many theaters in the Soviet Union. (Photograph from the archives of the Maryinsky Theater, Saint Petersburg.)

Throughout the Soviet era classical ballets continued to be revived and restaged. In the course of this work all manner of extremes in interpretation were exposed as insipid, sterile restoration of the obsolete on the one hand, artificially stilted modernization on the other. The best results were obtained by those who treated the heritage with respect, preserving what was of merit and rejecting what was hopelessly passé. Especially successful were Leonid Lavrovsky's *Giselle* in 1944, Vakhtang Chabukiani's *La Bayadère* in 1947, Konstantin Sergeyev's *Raymonda* in 1948 and *The Sleeping Beauty* in 1952, Vladimir Burmeister's *Swan Lake* in 1953, and Yuri Grigorovich's *The Sleeping Beauty* in 1963, *The Nutcracker* in 1966, *Swan Lake* in 1969, and *Raymonda* in 1984.

The Mid-1980s Onward. A new era in Russian ballet and dance began with great political and economic reforms that soon brought changes in cultural life. Between 1985 and 1987, when Mikhail Gorbachev, still general secretary of the Communist Party, announced a "new course" and "renovation of the ideology," the changes were not instantly apparent. The life of the ballet companies in Russia and the republics that were still part of the Soviet Union continued as before. The typical ballet company was still attached to a theater of opera and ballet, of which there were then forty-seven in the capitals of national and autonomous republics and important provincial towns. There were also theaters of musical comedy and operetta with ballet companies and numerous folk dance ensembles both large and small. Professional ballet dancers were trained in sixteen ballet schools throughout the Soviet Union. The repertory of all of these ballet companies did not change either; it was almost identical in all of them. Statistics show that, for example, in 1987 there were one hundred premieres throughout the country, of which only twenty were newly choreographed ballets. The remainder were revivals of the nineteenth-century classics (especially *Swan Lake*), which received the greatest number of performances. Next in popularity were ballets by well-known Russian choreographers: *Spartacus, Romeo and Juliet, Cinderella, The Fountain of Bakhchisarai,* and the like. Provincial choreographers sometimes produced their own versions, but more often the ballets were copies of those given in Moscow and Leningrad.

In 1987 a "theater experiment" was announced, giving theater companies, including those of ballet, more financial liberty and less supervision by administrative and party officials. Nevertheless, ballet was little affected except for increased contact with the West and the chance to include works by Western choreographers in the repertory.

Gradually through the second half of the 1980s the Soviet system crumbled. In 1991 the Soviet Union was replaced by the Commonwealth of Independent States (CIS), and some of these states began to change their cultural policy as they grew more independent of Russia. In some states, especially in Asia, Russian ballet was no longer so welcome, and financial help was no longer offered. The turn toward a free market was dramatic and painful. Ballet companies that had been completely supported by the state now found expenses so high that for many of them new works became impossible; profit did not cover expenses, so that premieres became scarce. The biggest companies were losing their best dancers to the West and survived largely through fund-raising foreign tours that brought in hard currency. The Saint Petersburg companies were the first to open their doors to Western choreographers. Kirov Ballet director Oleg Vinogradov's policy was to give the company access to works by Mau-

RUSSIA: Theatrical Dance since 1917. The classic works of Marius Petipa remained basic to the repertories of most ballet companies in the Soviet Union. In 1945, Leonid Lavrovsky mounted a new production of *Raymonda* at Moscow's Bolshoi Theater, to replace an earlier version by Aleksandr Gorsky. The title role was one of the first important parts danced by Maya Plisetskaya, who achieved international fame during the 1950s and who succeeded Galina Ulanova as *prima ballerina* of the Bolshoi Ballet in 1962. (Photograph from a Bolshoi Ballet souvenir program, 1966.)

rice Béjart, George Balanchine, August Bournonville, Roland Petit, Antony Tudor, and Jerome Robbins. The Bolshoi Ballet in Moscow was more conservative. Its director, Yuri Grigorovich, had built a repertory of old classics that he had reworked and his own ballets. But his last premiere had been *The Golden Age* in 1982, so that the dancers had reason to be unhappy about the poverty of the repertory and the confinement to only one style of dancing. As a result Grigorovich had to leave in 1995, and Vladimir Vasiliev was appointed director of the Bolshoi Theater.

The Stanislavsky and Nemirovich-Danchenko Musical Theater Ballet, under Dmitri Briantzev's direction since 1985, has fought financial problems by performing not only Briantzev's new works—*Optimistic Tragedy* (1985), *Othello* (1994)—but also the classics. At the Modest Mussorgsky (formerly Maly) Theater of Opera and Ballet in Saint Petersburg Nikolai Boyarchikov has worked on ballets with literary subjects, such as Pushkin's *Tsar Boris* (1978), Schiller's *The Robbers* (1982), Shakespeare's *Macbeth* (1984), and Andrei Bely's *Petersburg* (1992). These are essentially narrative ballets, but Boyarchikov uses movement and *mise-en-scène* to layer metaphors that allow one to penetrate the inner life of the characters or understand the events. For example, after every murder in *Macbeth*, whether or not seen onstage, a tree grows from the floor, large for the adult victims and tiny for the children.

Classical ballet is still the most important form of dance in Russia, so that the smaller independent companies now emerging are largely ballet companies. The Moscow State Theater of Classical Ballet under Natalia Kasatkina and Vladimir Vasiliov is a touring company that has existed since the 1970s, dancing classics and new works, some of the latter built around the dancer Vladimir Malakhov. The Saint Petersburg State Theater of Ballet is one of the most popular companies; Boris Eifman's vigorous, dynamic style appeals to audiences. He sometimes uses acrobatic movement filled with drama that depicts strong emotions verging on pathology in ballets such as *The Idiot* (1980) and *The Brothers Karamazov* (1995), after

RUSSIA: Theatrical Dance since 1917. The female ensemble of the Maryinsky Ballet in a 1992 performance of *Swan Lake*. (Photograph © 1992 by Johan Elbers; used by permission.)

Dostoyevsky; *The Murderers* (1991), after Zola's *Thérèse Raquin;* and *Tchaikovsky* (1993), based on the composer's biography. The Kremlin Ballet began in 1990 under the direction of Andrei Petrov, whose aim has been to produce shows for large audiences in the huge Kremlin Palace of Congresses. Still other companies are working in Moscow, among them Russian Ballet directed by Viacheslav Gordeyev until 1995, Russian Chamber Ballet "Moscow" under Edvald Smirnov, and Renaissance Ballet under German Pribylov; in Saint Petersburg there are the Lebedev Modern Ballet and an all-male company directed by Valery Mikhailovsky; in Ekaterinburg there is Ballet-Plus under Oleg Petrov. All of these companies work mostly under one choreographer and the company reflects that artist's ideas and style. There are in addition small ballet companies with purely commercial aims: dancers come together to rehearse well-known classics, such as *Giselle* or *Swan Lake,* generally abridged, and perform them abroad to earn money. Among new dancers in classical ballet who emerged in Moscow are Nina Ananiashvili, Nadezhda Gracheva, Galina Stepanenko, Andris Liepa, Irek Mukhamedov, Aleksei Fadeyechev, and Vladimir Malakhov, and in Saint Petersburg Altynai Asylmuratova, Yulia Makhalina, Uliana Lopatkina, Konstantin Zaklinsky, and Farukh Ruzimatov. Several of these dancers have appeared as guest artists with Western companies, and some have left Russia to join English and American companies.

Companies that dance ballet are not the only ones in Russia since the 1980s. The return to the "free dance" style, forbidden from the 1930s through the 1970s, is a new and important phenomenon. Russian dancers began to be aware of how much narrower the choreographic range was since the 1930s, while Russia was separated from the West by the iron curtain and all the experimental trends that had flowered in the 1920s were rejected or banned. Nowadays there is a great interest in everything hitherto unknown or prohibited. The younger generation of dancers and choreographers is drawn toward American modern dance; quite a few foreign companies have traveled in Russia, teachers (including Merce Cunningham) have taught, and Russian students have gone abroad to study. There is also an interest in the German dance theater and the French modern companies. At the same time Russian choreographers are looking back to what was done in the country before the 1930s. The tradition of the Isadora Duncan school has been revived by several dance groups; pupils of Ludmila Alekseeva are teaching and choreographing in Moscow.

On the whole Russian ballet is in crisis, if one considers that the major established companies have not recently produced any outstanding works and have lost many dancers to contracts abroad. On the other hand there is a flowering of new dance groups, a variety of styles, much experimental work going on all over the country, many festivals of modern dance, and a general atmosphere of independence and creativity, which did not exist before the political and economic reforms begun in the 1980s.

[*For further information, see also entries on the principal figures, works, and companies mentioned herein.*]

BIBLIOGRAPHY

Avaliani, Noi, and Leonid Zhdanov, comps. *Bolshoi's Young Dancers.* Translated by Natalie Ward. Moscow, 1975.

Balet, no. 3 (1995): 8–24, 32–36.

Brinson, Peter, ed. *Ulanova, Moiseyev, and Zakharov on Soviet Ballet.* Translated by E. Fox and D. Fry. London, 1954.

Chernova, Natalia, guest ed. "Moto-Bio—The Russian Art of Movement: Dance, Gesture, and Gymnastics, 1910–1930." Special issue of *Experiment: A Journal of Russian Culture* 2 (1996).

Degen, Arsen, and Igor Vasilievich Stupnikov. *Leningradskii balet, 1917–1987.* Leningrad, 1988.

Degen, Arsen. "Then and Now at the Maryinsky Theater." *Ballet Review* 20 (Summer 1992): 40–48.

Demidov, Alexander P. *The Russian Ballet: Past and Present.* Translated by Guy Daniels. Garden City, N.Y., 1977.

Krasovskaya, Vera. *Stati o balete.* Leningrad, 1967.

Krasovskaya, Vera, ed. *Sovetskii baletnyi teatr, 1917–1967.* Moscow, 1976.

Lawson, Joan. "A Short History of the Soviet Ballet, 1917–1943." *Dance Index* 2 (June–July 1943): 77–96.

Lifar, Serge. *A History of Russian Ballet* (1950). Translated by Arnold L. Haskell. New York, 1954.

Lvov-Anokhin, Boris. *Novoye v sovetskom balete.* Moscow, 1966.

Propert, W. A. *The Russian Ballet, 1921–1929.* London, 1931.

Roslavleva, Natalia. *Era of the Russian Ballet, 1770–1965* (1966). New York, 1979.

Slonim, Marc. *Russian Theatre from the Empire to the Soviets.* Cleveland, 1961.

Slonimsky, Yuri, et al. *The Soviet Ballet.* New York, 1947.

Slonimsky, Yuri. *V chest tantsa.* Moscow, 1968.

Souritz, Elizabeth. *Soviet Choreographers in the 1920s.* Translated by Lynn Visson. Durham, N.C., 1990.

Swift, Mary Grace. *The Art of the Dance in the U.S.S.R.* Notre Dame, 1968.

Vanslov, Victor V. *Balety Grigorovicha i problemy khoreografii.* 2d ed. Moscow, 1971.

Vanslov, Victor V. *Stati o balete: Muzykalno-esteticheskie problemy baleta.* Leningrad, 1980.

VICTOR V. VANSLOV
Translated from Russian
Amended by Elizabeth Souritz

Secondary and Provincial Dance Companies

The two principal dance companies in Russia, the Maryinsky Ballet in Saint Petersburg and the Bolshoi Ballet in Moscow, are, inevitably, the primary focus of attention in any historical survey of theatrical dance in Russia. Still, a number of other dance companies in Moscow and Saint Petersburg and in other cities throughout Russia have played important parts in the cultural life of the country. That they are sometimes identified as "secondary" or "provincial" companies is in no way a judgment on the artistic quality of their productions.

RUSSIA: Secondary and Provincial Companies. The Ballet of the Stanislavsky and Nemirovich-Danchenko Musical Theater is known for its presentation of light, comic ballets such as Nikolai Kholfin's *Doctor Aibolit* (Doctor Oh-It-Hurts; 1948). In a 1975 performance, Yuri Trepykhalin (center) appeared as Doctor Oh-It-Hurts, with members of the ensemble in various human and animal guises. (Photograph courtesy of Elizabeth Souritz.)

Moscow. After the Bolshoi Ballet, there are two major ballet companies in Moscow. The company of the Stanislavsky and Nemirovich-Danchenko Musical Theater was formed to provide popular entertainment, and it has maintained a repertory of full-length classics made accessible for general consumption along with light, short ballets. The Moscow State Theater of Classical Ballet, aimed at widespread audiences, presents full-length modern ballets, revivals of the classics, and works of renowned non-Russian choreographers.

The Ballet of the Stanislavsky and Nemirovich-Danchenko Musical Theater. The second largest company in Moscow, the Ballet of the Stanislavsky and Nemirovich-Danchenko Musical Theater evolved from an eighteen-member troupe formed in 1927 by Dmitri Golubin, which catered to the workers of Moscow and environs. During its first ten years the company toured to many towns, introducing classical ballet to audiences of workers and thus arousing their interest in it. In 1928 the company revived *The Red Poppy* in a version produced for a small stage by Nikolai Gerber, and then went on to adapt other works from the standard repertory. From this beginning as a group that copied Bolshoi ballets it grew into a company of experimenters, searching for a repertory that would meet the needs of the time. Its direct association with worker audiences determined the course of its development.

In 1930 Viktorina Kriger was appointed director, and the next year Kasyan Goleizovsky staged several of his ballets for the company, but these were not successful. Heated debates on the art of ballet and individual productions revealed the most important principle for the company: a ballet must be based on dance that is comprehensible to a large audience. Kriger wrote in her 1930 autobiography, "A dancing actor is an actor, rather than a dancer."

In 1932 the company was joined by a group from the Drambalet company, which had first formulated the principle of the "dancing actor." Among them was Nikolai Kholfin, who sought to portray real life on the ballet stage, ignoring classical dance in favor of plastique and pantomime. In collaboration with associates of Konstantin Stanislavsky, Kholfin devised clear plot structures and guided the work of his dancing actors in accordance with the Stanislavsky method. By the late 1930s the company had gained a reputation as an original troupe that rejected conventional ballet gesture and technique for its own sake. In 1939 Vladimir Nemirovich-Danchenko invited the group to join his musical theater, and two years later the ballet company was amalgamated with the Stanislavsky Theater; hence its present name. Except for short intervals Vladimir Burmeister led the company from 1941 to 1971. By a special government exemption the company was allowed to stay in Moscow during the war, when Burmeister produced several assuaging lyrical-romantic and comedy ballets. However, his *Lola* of 1943 did take a heroic theme borrowed from history: the Spanish resistance to Napoleon's invasion. Burmeister later turned to contemporary themes, as in *The Coast of Happiness* (1948), which dealt with the Soviet heroes of World War II. This was also a period of revised versions of the classics, notably his 1953 production of *Swan Lake*, in which he followed the original sequence of Tchaikovsky's score, but rechoreographed all but the second act to endow the work with greater dramatic motivation and coherence. In addition to creating original realistic and drama ballets Burmeister also produced plotless works. Ballets by guest choreographers were also performed in the 1960s and 1970s.

In 1971 Aleksei Chichinadze was appointed chief choreographer. His style tended toward technically sophisticated dance, lyrical adagios, and virtuosic variations. He staged new ballets to works of Soviet composers and also produced traditional stagings of the classics. From 1983 to 1985 the chief choreographer was Henrik Mayorov. Since then Dmitri Briantzev has led the company. His most important ballets are *Bravo, Figaro!* and *Optimistic Tragedy* (both 1985), several one-act works in 1987 and 1988, and *Othello* (1994). Among the leading dancers from the 1980s onward are Margarita Drozdova, Galina Krapivina, Svetlana Smirnova, Svetlana Tsoi, Tatiana Chernobrovkina, Vadim Tedeev, Vladimir Kirillov, Mikhail Krapivin, and Yuri Grigoriev.

Moscow State Theater of Classical Ballet. Founded in 1966 as the Choreographic Concert Ensemble "Young Ballet," it has undergone several changes of name—Concert Ensemble "Classical Ballet" of the USSR, State Concert Ensemble "Moscow Classical Ballet" of the USSR, State Theater of Ballet of the USSR—before arriving at its current designation in 1992. Formed as a touring company to introduce audiences to Russian classical dance and the various trends in modern ballet, it was first directed by Igor Moiseyev and presented a repertory of works by several Soviet choreographers. In 1971 Yuri Zhdanov was appointed director. Since 1977 the company has been led by Vladimir Vasiliov, with his wife, Natalia Kasatkina, as chief choreographer. Together they have changed the character of the company from a concert troupe to a touring ensemble that concentrates on full-length spectacles. Their own works are *The Creation of the World* (1978), *Le Sacre du Printemps* (1979), *The Geologists* (1981), *The Tale of Romeo and Juliet* (1981, to the Prokofiev score), *The Magic Frock Coat* (1982), *Terpsichore's Pranks* (1984, a divertissement), *Pushkin* (1986), *Faces of Love* (1987), *Le Baiser de la Fée* (1989, staged for Vladimir Malakhov), *The Crystal Shoe* (*Cinderella*, 1993), *The Nutcracker* (1994, after Vasily Vainonen), and *The Lady of the Camellias* (1995, to Verdi arranged by P. Salnikov). In addition to restagings of the classics—*Swan Lake* in 1988, *Don Quixote* in 1990, *Giselle* in 1991—they have brought to Russia works from the international repertory, among them August Bournonville's *Kermesse in Bruges*, the Pierre Lacotte revival of Filippo Taglioni's *La Sylphide*, Michel Fokine's *Le Spectre de la Rose*, and George Balanchine's *Theme and Variations* as well as contemporary works that include Maurice Béjart's *Bhakti* and Roland Petit's *L'Arlésienne*. Given so broad a repertory the dancers must be versatile enough to perform not only the traditional classical vocabulary, but also folk, grotesque, eccentric, and free styles. The company has toured more than two hundred cities in the commonwealth and more than twenty foreign countries.

Saint Petersburg. In addition to the Maryinsky Ballet, Saint Petersburg is home to one major company and two smaller troupes. The Modest Mussorgsky (Maly) company throughout its long history has mirrored the fluctuations in aesthetics and the development of Russian ballet by presenting the full-length ballets of diverse choreographers, most recently those based on well-known works of literature. The Choreographic Miniatures company exemplifies the work and the principles of its founding choreographer, Leonid Yakobson, who perfected the mixed program of brief, integral ballets. The Theater of Contemporary Ballet is a youthful, largely touring small company that presents a mixture of dramatic and comic one-act ballets.

The Modest Mussorgsky Theater of Opera and Ballet (Maly). The company was established in 1918 as an affiliate of the Maryinsky Opera under the name Leningrad Maly Academic Theater of Opera and Ballet. Familiarly called "Maly" (small), in its early years it principally presented operettas that featured a small group of dancers. After the Revolution some classical ballets were produced, but the dancers displayed a preference for light comedy. In time it became clear that the theater needed to maintain a ballet troupe of its own, and Fedor Lopukhov was invited to assemble a company, with the expectation

RUSSIA: Secondary and Provincial Companies. Ekaterina Maximova and Stanislav Isaev in a 1980 photograph of the Moscow Classical Ballet's production of *Natalie, or The Swiss Milkmaid*, choreographed by Pierre Lacotte, after Filippo Taglioni. (Photograph courtesy of Elizabeth Souritz.)

that comic ballets would predominate. In the 1930s a new style of comedy was emerging to cater to the tastes of the working public; episodes had to center on a distinct plot that often involved social conflict. Thus, in 1933 Lopukhov turned his *Harlequinade* into the love story of a poor student and the daughter of a rich burgher. With its full range of ballet technique and clear message *Harlequinade* set the tone of the Maly repertory. Lopukhov also staged a new version of *Coppélia* and in 1935 choreographed to music by Shostakovich *The Bright Stream,* which depicted a romantic triangle on a collective farm.

In the mid-1930s Leonid Lavrovsky staged several ballets at the Maly. Replacing the comedy genre with lyrical and psychological drama Lavrovsky asserted that he had relinquished the most superficial principle of theater while adhering strictly to the basic: clear-cut dramatic action. Meanwhile a new breed of dancers was developing: lyrical heroines with supporting male partners who looked handsome but did very little dancing.

Over the next two decades the company expanded its repertory but the focus shifted to the literary merits of its productions. Boris Fenster stimulated the creative imagination of the dancers by reviving the idea of improvisation. He gave much thought to the psychological basis of action and to its organization. In the early 1950s Fenster challenged the performing potential of his dancers by inviting Leonid Yakobson and Petr Gusev, whose views differed considerably from his own, to join the theater. Their choreography marked the return of traditional ballet imagery and sophisticated dance forms. At the same time the company added several previously neglected classical ballets to its repertory. Lopukhov with Konstantin Boyarsky attempted to revive the original choreography of *Swan Lake* in 1959, and Lopukhov's concept of symphonic form in dance was expanded by Igor Belsky. This period also saw a wide range of young choreographers making their debuts at the Maly. Conventional ballet pantomime was being replaced with the creation of character through dance.

In 1973 Oleg Vinogradov became director of the company. In addition to staging new versions of the classics he created the drama ballet *Yaroslavna* (1974), based on the twelfth-century exploits of Prince Igor against the Polovtsians and set to a score composed by Boris Tishchenko. His choreography continued to combine free dance forms with folklore idioms. Vinogradov also resumed contact with drama-theater producers. In 1977 Nikolai Boyarchikov became principal choreographer. Alert to a revived interest in literary classics he staged *Tsar Boris* (1978), based on Pushkin's *Boris Godunov,* followed by Schiller's *The Robbers* (1982), Shakespeare's *Macbeth* (1984), Gogol's *The Marriage* (1986), Sholokhov's *Quiet Flows the*

RUSSIA: Secondary and Provincial Companies. Konstantin Boyarsky mounted his production of *Orpheus* in 1962 for the Maly Theater Ballet, known more formally as the Modest Mussorgsky Theater Ballet. Boyarsky's work, pictured here with Valery Panov in the title role, was influenced by the ballets of George Balanchine, presented in Moscow by the New York City Ballet during its 1962 Russian tour. (Photograph from the Dance Collection, New York Public Library for the Performing Arts.)

Don (1988), and Andrei Bely's *Petersburg* (1992). At the same time Leonid Lebedev was creating ballets on modern themes and young graduates of the Choreographic Department of the Leningrad Conservatory were staging some of their works at the Maly. Among the leading dancers under Boyarchikov's direction have been Margarita Kurshakova, Yuri Petukhov, Gennady Sudakov, and Yuri Vasikov.

Choreographic Miniatures, Saint Petersburg. Leonid Yakobson founded the company in 1969 and directed it until his death in 1975. Its name and program policy derive from a 1959 production at the Kirov Theater that demonstrated the breadth of short ballets and their potential for programming. Most of the repertory reflects Yakobson's development as a choreographer, for example, his interest in "natural" choreography as expressed in the cycle based on Rodin sculptures (1970–1971), and the evolution of his attitude toward classical dance as in suites such as *Mozartiana* (1974). Some of his works were critical and satirical; in various pas de deux love scenes are transformed into satire that ridicules middle-class vanity or affectation. Still other works were strongly dramatic. Yakobson expected his dancers to be pliable and submissive to his will. In his late years his productions were extremely complex, emphasizing new movements and postures.

In 1976 Askold Makarov took over the company. He has sought to carry on the tradition established by Yakobson and to keep the best of the original works in the repertory. New programs also feature the work of young choreographers who are in accord with Yakobson's principles, among them Konstantin Rassadin, Georgi Aleksidze, Aleksandr Polubentsev, Vadim Budarin, Leonard Lebedev, Natalia Volkova, the Hungarian László Seregi, and the Czech Pavel Šmok. The company presents on average four new productions a year and goes on regular concert tours throughout the commonwealth and abroad.

Saint Petersburg Theater of Contemporary Ballet. Formed in 1977 under the name Leningrad Ballet Ensemble (later Leningrad Theater of Contemporary Ballet and Leningrad State Theater of Ballet) to tour programs of chamber-sized and one-act ballets, the company defined the principal themes of its repertory from the outset: young people entering the adult world and the travails of personality development. Boris Eifman has been artistic director of the company from its inception and has provided most of the choreography. His treatment of Dostoyevsky's *The Idiot* (1980), set to Tchaikovsky's Sixth Symphony, revealed the psychological texture of the conflict between the characters and brought into focus a cruel indifference on the part of society to the fate of the individual. Antithetically, only two years later Eifman created a comedy set to music of Rossini, *A Day of Madness,* based on Beaumarchais's *The Marriage of Figaro,* which was full of buffoonery and sparkling fantasy. Chamber compositions as well as further dramatic and comic ballets followed: *Twelfth Night* to Donizetti (1984); *The Master and Margarita,* based on Bulgakov's novel and set to music by Andrei Petrov (1987); *The Murderers,* to Bach, Mahler, and Schnitke (1991); *Tchaikovsky,* based on the composer's life (1993); and *Don Quixote* (1994). Today the company has a distinctive repertory and a corps of young dancers who have mastered Eifman's style, and has toured abroad.

RUSSIA: Secondary and Provincial Companies. Choreographic Minatures dancers E. Selivanova and I. Khokhlov in Leonid Yakobson's *The Bedbug* (1974), based on a play by Vladim Mayakovsky. (Photograph by Vladimir Zenzinov; courtesy of Elizabeth Souritz.)

Provincial Ballet Companies. In addition to Moscow and Saint Petersburg, there are repertory theaters in twenty-two other cities that have opera and ballet companies and give regular ballet performances. Their official names vary: opera and ballet theaters, musical theaters, theaters of music and drama. In comparison with the Bolshoi and Maryinsky, these companies are rather young.

The nineteenth century was the period of decline for serf theaters: many were closed, but the most professional were bought by the State, and the performers—dancers among them—became the first employees of public companies. For example, in Nizhniy Novgorod, Prince Nikolai

Shakhovskoy's theater was turned into a public company in 1798. Its repertory consisted mainly of opera productions, but according to the playbills at least two ballets were performed, *Blue Beard* and *La Fille Mal Gardée*. The lack of professionally trained resources (there were only two schools: one in Moscow and one in Saint Petersburg) was one of the reasons why in provincial Russian cities ballet dancers were used only for divertissements or interludes in operas and vaudevilles or drama performances, but never in full-length productions. Especially in the second half of the century, dancers from the Bolshoi and Maryinsky Theaters were regularly going on tours throughout Russia, introducing the novelties of the capitals' stages to provincial audiences.

Ekaterinburg. The real making of the provincial ballet companies started only after the October Revolution. Among the first in that process was the Ekaterinburg Opera Theater. In 1914 its ballet company emerged with a production of *The Magic Flute;* unfortunately, it was not successful. Still, the company was able to stage two more productions, *The Mystery of the Temple of Izida* in 1919 and *Coppélia* in 1922. Only by 1924 did the company establish itself as professionally stabilized. Choreographers Pavel Yorkin and Mikhail Moiseyev staged *Don Quixote, Giselle, Le Corsaire,* and *Swan Lake* in 1928. Just a year after its Moscow premiere *The Red Poppy,* with choreography by Moiseyev, was performed at the newly named Sverdlovsk Opera and Ballet Theater. From that time onward, works of modern choreographers were produced and they remain part of the company's repertory. Two original dramatic productions were prepared for the company: *The Stone Flower,* based on Pavel Bazhov stories choreographed by Konstantin Muller, and *Without Dowry,* based on Aleksandr Ostrovsky's play choreographed by Georgi Yazvinsky, both to music by Aleksandr Friedland, a local composer; later, *The Left-handed Craftsman,* based on Nikolai Leskov's story choreographed by Yakov Romanovsky, and *First Love,* based on the Ruvim Fraerman novel choreographed by Sofia Tulubieva were produced. In the 1960s and 1970s choreographers from Moscow and Leningrad—Igor Belsky, Aleksei Chichinadze, Evgeny Changa, Natalia Kasatkina and Vladimir Vasiliov, and Nikolai Boyarchikov—were working actively in Ekaterinburg. The results of this cooperation were *Leningrad Symphony, Francesca da Rimini, Spartacus, The Creation of the World, Pushkin,* and *Romeo and Juliet.* At the same time the company continued to work actively on masterpieces of the classical heritage. As a rule, well-known artists were invited to stage these productions, for example, Petr Gusev in 1984 reconstructed the 1877 version of *La Bayadère,* and in 1994 Boris Blankov reconstructed Konstantin Sergeyev's version of *Le Corsaire.*

Perm. The ballet company of the Perm Opera and Ballet Theater is often called the factory for future Maryinsky and Bolshoi ballet stars. In fact, many of the dancers who had graduated from the Perm ballet school and had distinguished themselves at the beginning of their career on the stage of the Perm theater were later invited to join

RUSSIA: Secondary and Provincial Companies. *Don Quixote* has a long history in Russia: first staged in Moscow by Marius Petipa in 1869, it was subsequently revived and revised by Aleksandr Gorsky (1900, 1906), Rostislav Zakharov (1940), and Kasyan Goleizovsky (1942). During the Soviet era, it was staged by virtually every ballet company in the USSR. At the Perm Opera and Ballet Theater, c.1950, the roles of Basil and Kitri were danced by A. Borovik and N. Akhmarova. (Photograph by Petr Agafonov; courtesy of Elizabeth Souritz.)

those companies. Nevertheless, the Perm Ballet continues to work actively, giving interesting premieres and offering a number of so-called old ballets. Evidence of the company's high professional level was the invitation to be part of the cultural program at the 1980 Olympic Games in Moscow.

It is thought that the Perm theater opened in 1870, but it took almost a half century for the first ballet production to be performed on its stage. In 1926, Boris Shcherbinin, the Bolshoi Ballet dancer, staged *Giselle* for the Perm ballet company. Then, in 1927 there was *Coppélia,* in 1931 *Swan Lake,* in 1933 *La Fille Mal Gardée,* and *Esmeralda* in 1936. Of great importance for the company was the Leningrad Kirov Theater's evacuation to Perm during World War II. From 1941 to 1944 the Kirov Ballet performed various classics on the Perm stage, prepared a premiere of *Gayané,* and started working on *Cinderella.* Perm audiences had a chance to see the great stars of the Kirov. For the comparatively young Perm ballet, the significance of watching Kirov performances, classes, and rehearsals could not be overestimated; it gave the young company a new impetus. Even more, the arrival of the Kirov ballet coincided with the opening of the Perm Ballet School under the directorship of the former Kirov ballerina and Vaganova student, Ekaterina Geidenreikh. Since 1950 the ballet company in Perm has been replenished with students from the school, which is now a major source of dancers for ballet companies all over Russia. Many well-known choreographers worked with the company for a number of years, helping it to create its individual image. Along with the classical repertory, the company has also performed commissioned works, among them, *Doctor Aibolit* (Doctor Oh-It-Hurts) and *The Nutcracker* by Ksenia Esaulova; *Chess-Game* and *The Shore of Hope* by Marat Gaziev; *Tsar Boris, Orpheus and Eurydice,* and *Romeo and Juliet* by Nikolai Boyarchikov; and *Seven Beauties, Spartacus,* and *The Stone Idol* by Vladimir Salimbaev. Since 1986 Perm Ballet Theater has been the host of the ballet competition named Arabesque.

Nizhniy Novgorod. For some years there was no ballet company in Nizhniy Novgorod (formerly Gorky), but Moscow and Saint Petersburg companies toured the region on a regular basis, introducing novelties of the ballet repertory. Among them were Savva Mamontov's and Sergei Zimin's private ballet and opera companies of Moscow. The first repertory company in Nizhniy Novgorod opened its doors in the fall of 1935 with a classical repertory. The company also produced ballets based on works by contemporary authors as well as on poems by Aleksandr Pushkin. (The poet's estate is located nearby in the Nizhniy Novgorod region, and the theater itself was named after him.) Boris Asafiev's *The Fountain of Bakhchisarai* and Sergei Vasilenko's *Tsygany* (Gysies), both choreographed by Pavel Yorkin, were among the first; Valery Kikta's *Dubrovsky* and Georgi Sviridov's *Blizzard,* both choreographed by Aleksei Badrak, were later added. Other works to music by Soviet composers were commissioned by the theater, including Arkady Nesterov's *Timur and His Team* choreographed by Georgi Yazvinsky and Otar Dadishkiliani, Evgeny Glebov's *Little Prince,* choreographed by Dadishkiliani, and Valery Gavrilin's *Letters from the Front,* choreographed by Aleksei Badrak. There is no ballet school in Nizhniy Novgorod; the company members are Moscow, Saint Petersburg, and Perm school graduates along with students from the theater's own workshop.

RUSSIA: Secondary and Provincial Companies. Svetlana Kuznetsova and members of the female ensemble of the Novosibirsk Ballet in *Don Quixote,* act 3, scene 2, "Dulcinea's Garden." (Photograph courtesy of Elizabeth Souritz.)

Novosibirsk. The Novosibirsk Opera and Ballet Theater opened in May 1945 with Mikhail Glinka's opera *Ivan Susanin.* All eighty-five dancers of the new ballet company gave their first performance that day in the dance scenes of the opera, and sixty-five of them had graduated from the local school. The choreographer and ballet master of the company, Mikhail Moiseyev, was a Moscow ballet school graduate. In 1946 the company presented its first full-length production, Moiseyev's version of *Le Corsaire.* In the following years many other works from the classical heritage as well as by Soviet composers and choreographers were presented, among them *The Scarlet Flower, The Red Poppy, The Bronze Horseman, Masquerade, The Fountain of Bakhchisarai, Leningrad Poem, Yaroslavna,* and *The Three Musketeers.* Novosibirsk Opera and Ballet Theater was the only one in Russia to stage the Chinese composer Jiang Zuhui's ballet *The Precious Lotus Lantern,* in a joint production by the Russian choreographer Elena Macheret and Chinese choreographers Li Gepia and Wang Xixian. Also in Novosibirsk Oleg Vinogradov made his debut as a choreographer with Prokofiev's *Romeo and*

Juliet and *Cinderella.* Yuri Grigorovich created new versions of his own *The Stone Flower, Legend of Love,* and *Spartacus,* and the young Natalia Kasatkina and Vladimir Vasiliov choreographed their own version of Prokofiev's *Romeo and Juliet.* In the 1980s the Leningrad choreographer Vadim Budarin was appointed the company's artistic director. Among the most successful works of the Novosibirsk Ballet were his *Coppélia, Peer Gynt, Stepan Razin,* and *Répétez.* In 1957 the Novosibirsk Ballet School was opened and in a few years the company was reinforcing itself with the graduates from the school.

Other cities. There are other cities in Russia with the same kind of repertory companies. In 1928 a theater was opened in Saratov, in 1931 in Samara (formerly Kuibyshev), in 1966 in Voronezh, in 1977 in Krasnoiarsk, and in 1981 in Omsk. One can see a certain regularity in their development. They usually started with the classics, which were needed to polish their technique and artistry, and only when they acquired a high level of professionalism did they move on to creating their own repertories. Thus, the Saratov Ballet Company started in 1928 with the classics and after seven years of work commissioned *Ferendzhi,* with music by Boris Yanovsky and choreography by Sergei Kevorkov. Then, there were several more years of the various classics before the company was ready for another contemporary work—in 1956 *The Kerchief,* with music by the Hungarian composer Jen"o Kenessey and staged by Zsuzsa Kun and Viktor Fülöp, followed in 1961 by *The Young Girl and Death,* with music by Vladimir Kovalev and choreography by Valentin Adashevsky. In 1977 the company commissioned the ballet-oratorio *Mother's Field,* with music by the Kirgiz composer Kalyi Moldobasanov and choreography by Anatoly Dementev. The Voronezh Ballet Company at first performed various classics. In 1971 the company created *The Song of Triumphant Love,* with music by Mikhail Nosyrev and choreography by Dina Aripova, and in 1982 *The Tale of the Russian Land,* with music by Gennady Stavonin and choreography by Yakov Livshits. In 1931 the ballet company of the Samara Opera and Ballet Theater also opened with classics, but in a few years the company was performing *Chitra,* based on Rabindranath Tagore's plays with choreography by Natalia Danilova, and the unique rhythmical compositions choreographed by Igor Chernyshev: *The Angara, Antony and Cleopatra,* and *The Execution of Stepan Razin.*

RUSSIA: Secondary and Provincial Companies. Leonid Lavrovsky created *The Prisoner of the Caucasus,* based on a poem by Aleksandr Pushkin and set to music by Boris Asafiev, for the Maly Theater Ballet in Leningrad in 1938. That same year it was mounted by the Kiev Ballet, with N. I. Tregubov as the Prisoner and A. I. Vasileva as Nina. (Photograph from the Dance Collection, New York Public Library for the Performing Arts.)

Russian provincial companies maintain regular connections with the Bolshoi and Maryinsky Theaters. Dancers go to Moscow and Saint Petersburg for classes and workshops, while teachers and choreographers from Moscow and Saint Petersburg travel to other cities to organize workshops and sometimes create works for the companies. Guest appearances with provincial companies by Moscow and Saint Petersburg ballet stars are a long-time tradition.

Besides the ballet companies in Russian cities there are a number of them in former Soviet autonomous republics in Russia, where they began to emerge in the 1930s and are still developing. The majority of these companies follow the same pattern: a combination of classical repertory and the works of local composers and choreographers. In Kazan, capital of Tataria, the ballet *Shurale,* about a wood demon of Tatar folklore, was staged in 1945. The music was commissioned from the Tatar composer Farid Yarullin, and the original choreography, created in 1941 but preempted by World War II, was by Gay Tagirov and Leonid Zhukov. *Shurale,* in Leonid Yakobson's revised version, was later performed in many Russian theaters, including the Bolshoi and the Maryinsky. After the war, the

Kazan Opera and Ballet Theater repertory included classics as well as the works of contemporary Russian and Tatar composers. The same is true for Bashkiria and Karelia. The Bashkir Opera and Ballet Theater in Ufa opened in 1944 with the premiere of *Song of the Crane,* with music by Les Stepanov from Moscow and choreography by Nina Anisimova from Leningrad. Yuri Grigorovich created for the company his version of *Don Quixote,* and his student Andrei Melanin staged *La Fille Mal Gardée.* In 1959 the Karelian Ballet of the Musical Theater of Karelia in Petrozavodsk brought to Moscow its production of *Sampo,* with music by the Karelian composer Ilmer Sinisalo and choreography by Igor Smirnov from Moscow; Smirnov was connected with the company for more than twenty years. The Yakutsk Ballet, similarly slow to develop, was founded in the 1930s but only in 1947 was able to commission an original work, *The Wild Flower,* based on local folklore, with music by Mark Zhirkov and Georgi Litvinsky, choreographed by S. Vladimirov-Klimov. Having developed into a mature company, it is now able to house the continuing international ballet festival called The Northern Divertissement. The Buriat Ballet was founded in Ulan-Ude in 1943. Its first production was *The Fountain of Bakhchisarai,* newly choreographed by Mikhail Arseniev, the company's ballet master. For a number of years thereafter the mainstay of the repertory was classics until Lev Knipper and Buadorzhi Yampilov's *The Angara* was staged in 1959, choreographed by Mikhail Zaslavsky and Igor Moiseyev, which became the company's signature piece. In 1961 the Buriat Ballet School was opened in Ulan-Ude.

RUSSIA: Secondary and Provincial Companies. Larisa Sakhianova and Petr Abasheev in an undated photograph of the Buriat Theater of Opera and Ballet's production of *The Angara.* (Photograph by O. Shadanova; courtesy of Elizabeth Souritz.)

Folk Dance Ensembles. Ensembles of folk dance and song have been popular in Russia from the beginning of the twentieth century onward. In the 1920s the art historian Vsevolod Vsevolodsky-Gerngross established in Petrograd a company that gave performances of Russian wedding dances and songs, and in 1928 an Army company of song and dance was founded in Moscow that presented a repertory of sailors' and soldiers' songs and dances, for example, the "iablochko" (Little Apple) dance, which combined characteristics such as intricate footwork and contests of virtuosity from sailors' dances of different countries. After the Olympiad of folk art in 1936 there was a growth of interest in folk dance, and in 1937 the folk dance company under the direction of Igor Moiseyev came into being. From the outset Moiseyev insisted that the company must be more than just a custodian of tradition; it had to evolve constantly, building on folk idioms and developing new forms. Traditional activities like weddings and games readily lent themselves to choreographic treatment. Modern themes, such as the exploits of wartime partisans, a May Day gathering, or present-day village life, have been more difficult to depict, but even on these subjects Moiseyev created effective dance dramas. Acting ability is expected of the dancers, who were originally amateurs but are now graduates of the company-affiliated school. The company has toured throughout the world.

In 1948 another popular ensemble, Berezka, was founded by Nadezhda Nadezhdina in Moscow. Begun as a women's choir with a repertory based on Voronezh folk traditions of round dancing with singing, the company later expanded its repertory, and added men dancers after 1960. The company's name means "young birch tree" and refers to a round dance from the Kalinin region, in which women glide along carrying branches of birch, that is the company's signature piece. In the early 1980s a former soloist of the company, Mirra Koltsova, succeeded Nadezhdina as artistic director. Berezka has toured internationally.

In 1988 the Gzhel ensemble was founded in Moscow by Vladimir Zakharov. The name was borrowed from that of a company dealing in various artifacts. The ensemble thus recreates in its round dances and quadrilles the images and colors of lacquer boxes of Palekh, silver jewelry of Krasnaia Gorka, shawls of Pavlov Posad, and nesting dolls and toys of Viatka.

Regional folk choirs are the major outlet for the presentation of theatrical folk dance. The State Choir of the Urals in Ekaterinburg recreates traditional holiday dances and songs of the region. A number of dances are based on the Russian quadrille, which the director Olga Kniazeva discovered during folklore-collecting expeditions. There are a number of Russian choirs in the Voronezh region, among them the well-known State Academic Piatnitsky Folk Choir. Formed in 1911 by Mitrofan Piatnitsky with the local peasants of Voronezh, the company was the first professional folk choir in Russia. In Russian folk tradition singing was always accompanied by dancing, but it was not until 1938 that a group of professional dancers joined the Piatnitsky Choir. The first choreographer for the ensemble was Tatiana Ustinova, who later became a well-known teacher of theatrical folk dancing in Russia. The dances she created for the ensemble were varied in form: placid round dances, quadrilles, spirited scenes of village merrymaking, and epics like *A Tale of the Russian Land.* Other such choirs that have introduced new elements to the staging of folk dance are M. Chernyshov's Voronezh Russian Choir, Ivan Merkulov's Northern Folk Choir, and V. Modzalevsky's Volzhsky Folk Choir.

New Classical and Modern Dance Companies. In the 1980s the Theater of Chamber Dance of Olga Bavdilovich in Vladivostok became very popular. Her choreography is full of symbolic images of human life, of nature, of the universe itself. The source of Bavdilovich's inspiration is the legends of the ancient East, in particular Tibet. Choreographed primarily to the music of modern Russian composers, the ballets present an interesting juxtaposition of the contemporary and the ancient. In 1990 the Kremlin Ballet, founded and directed by Andrei Petrov, opened its first season at the Palace of Congresses. The repertory includes various classics; one of the most interesting is Vladimir Vasiliev's 1991 version of *Cinderella,* in which he himself performed the role of the Stepmother. The production was also notable for the collaboration with the Italian couture house of Nina Ricci. In 1992, in Cheliabinsk, Vladimir Pona formed a new company called The Russian Version. Its repertory is dominated by miniatures to music of Beethoven, Debussy, and Schnitke. The company also offers workshops and lecture-demonstrations for professionals and amateurs. At the 1994 Vitebsk International Dance Competition, The Russian Version was awarded first prize for its miniatures *March of Single Women* and *Stikhira.* In 1993 the Moscow Renaissance Ballet was founded to present the most authentic reconstructions possible of the old classical repertory. Within two years the company prepared productions of *Paquita,*

RUSSIA: Secondary and Provincial Companies. Folk dance ensembles make an important contribution to Russian dance. *(above)* Soloists with the Moiseyev Dance Company perform a vigorous Ukrainian dance, "Gopak" from *The Ukrainian Suite,* choreographed by Igor Moiseyev. *(left)* The Berezka Dance Company performing "Beriozka," a traditional round dance staged by Nadezhda Nadezhdina. (Photograph above reprinted from a Moiseyev Dance Company souvenir program. Photograph at left by A. Stepanov; courtesy of Elizabeth Souritz.)

Chopiniana, and *Pas de Quatre*, arranged by its artistic director German Pribylov. Also in 1993 The Saint Petersburg Chamber Ballet, under the artistic direction of Andrei Kuznetsov, was founded. In March 1995 at the Hermitage Theater the company performed *The Real Story of Little Red Riding Hood*, a humorous experimental work with an outlandish movement vocabulary. Among the newest ballet ensembles are Fouetté of Saint Petersburg, artistic director Aleksandr Polubentsev; Moscow Art Ballet, artistic director Yuri Puzakov; and in Ekaterinburg Ballet-Plus, artistic director Oleg Petrov. Some companies—Alla Chernova Theater of Plastique Arts, Ballet of the XXIst Century led by Svetlana Voskresenskaia, and Moscow's Russian Chamber Ballet under Edvald Smirnov—use a mixture of styles.

Of the new modern dance ensembles there is Provincial Dances in Ekaterinburg, which performs dance theater–like works by its director, Tatiana Baganova. In 1990 The Theater of Modern Dance opened in Perm; the company changed its name several times and has come to be known as Experiment. The company's repertory consists of unusual and often controversial ballets choreographed by its director Evgeny Panfilov, including *The Chase*, *Five Impromptus with a Table in the Background*, *Waltzes for Lunatics*, and *The Second and the Last Part*. Among recent premieres is *Lolita*, which the company performed at the 1994 American Dance Festival. Panfilov's style is a mixture of classical and modern dance techniques of different styles and times. The modern dance company Independent of Alla Sigalova also began in 1990. Its first production, *Hide and Seek with Solitude*, remains one of its most popular works. Since the company's inception Sigalova has created a number of productions that combine acting and singing with dance, such as her *Game*, her *Queen of Spades*, and *La Divina*.

At no time during the Soviet era did the number of ballet companies grow as rapidly as since its demise. In general, the art of choreography in Russia nowadays is represented by the diverse approaches taken by the many ballet ensembles and theaters. There are a number of traditional companies with classical repertory, which are modernizing the classical vocabulary and including works of foreign choreographers; companies that base their repertory on folk dance traditions, in both authentic and theatrical forms; and companies devoted to jazz, tap, and modern dance as well as experimental groups whose choreographic orientation is not easy to define.

[*For further information, see also the entries on the principal figures and works mentioned herein.*]

BIBLIOGRAPHY

Acocella, Joan. "Moiseyev Dance Company." *Dance Magazine* (December 1986): 35–36.

Alovert, Nina. "Jacobson Foundation Helps Establish New Company." *Dance Magazine* (November 1991): 24.

Balet musikalnogo teatraimeni K. S. Stanislavskogo i Vl. I. Nemirovicha-Danchenko. Moscow, 1975.

Barnes, Clive. "It's Folk Dance, But Different." *New York Times* (30 June 1974).

Belova, Ekaterina. "Geroini baletov Dmitriia Briantseva." In *Voprosy teatra*, no. 13. Moscow (1993): 54–81.

Chernova, Natalia. "Chiuso 'per lavori.'" *Balletto Oggi* (June 1991): 36.

Chizhova, A. E. *Beryozka Dance Company: Russian Folk Dance Company Directed by Nadezhda Nadezhdina*. Translated by R. Flaxman. Moscow, 1968.

Christout, Marie-Françoise, and John Percival. "Leningrad's Other Company." *Dance and Dancers* (October 1976): 23–26.

Chudnovsky, Mikhail. *Ansambl' Moiseyeva*. Moscow, 1959.

Clarke, Mary. "State Ballet Theatre of Perm." *The Dancing Times* (January 1994): 358.

Coton, A. V., et al. "A Symposium: The Russian Dancers in London." *Ballet Annual* 9 (1955):75–82.

Dance Magazine (May 1972): 50–77.

La danse en révolution. Paris, 1989.

Deery, Rachel W. "International News." *Dance Magazine* (October 1993): 32–33.

Degen, Arsen. *Balet Molodikh: O Baletnoi Trupe Leningradskogo Akademicheskogo Malogo Teatra Opery i Baleta*. Leningrad, 1979.

Degen, Arsen. "St. Petersburg Journal." *Dance International* 22 (Summer 1994): 36–37.

Dobrovolskaya, Galina N. *Baletmeister Leonid Iakobson*. Leningrad, 1968.

Festivali iskusstv. Moscow, 1964.

Horosko, Marian, and Richard Philp. "The Presence of Russian Dance." *Dance Magazine* (November 1971): 42–69.

Horwitz, Dawn Lille. "St. Petersburg." *Ballet Review* 23 (Winter 1995): 6–9.

Ilicheva, Marina. "Boyarchikov." *Teatralnia zhizn*, no. 5 (1988).

Jones, Betty, and Carla Maxwell. "Changing Times." *Ballet Review* 19 (Summer 1991): 46–50.

Keller, I., ed. *Permskii gosudarstvennyi ordena trudovogo krasnogo znameni akademicheskii teatr opery i baleta im. P. I. Chaikovskogo: 100 let*. Moscow, 1970.

Koegler, Horst. "The Perm Ballet." *Dance and Dancers* (December 1973): 49–51.

Koegler, Horst. "Guests from Leningrad: Leonid Jakobson and His 'Choreographic Miniatures.'" *Ballett International* 12 (December 1989): 56–58.

Konrad, Bertram. "Sankt Petersburg: Tradition und Fortschritt." *Ballett-Journal / Das Tanzarchiv* 43 (June 1995): 8–11.

McDonagh, Don. "To Russia with TSU." *Ballet Review* 18 (Summer 1990): 82–92.

Moiseyev's Dance Company (in English and Russian). Moscow, 1966.

Orloff, Alexander, and Margaret E. Willis. *Russian Ballet on Tour*. London, 1989.

Percival, John. "Ballet for All?" *Dance and Dancers* (July 1984): 10–13.

Pitt, Freda. "Reports." *Ballet News* 1.5 (October 1979): 37–38.

Poliakov, A. I., ed. *Sverdlovskii gosudarstvennyi ordena trudovogo krasnogo znameni teatr opery i baleta im. A. V. Lunacharskogo: 50 let*. Sverdlovsk, 1963.

Quraishi, Ibrahim. "Russia and Ukraine: A 1993 Impression." *Ballet Review* 21 (Fall 1993): 79–84.

Romm, Valerii. *Bolshoi Teatr Sibiri*. Novosibirsk, 1990.

Roslavleva, Natalia. "Ballet in Soviet Russia." *The Dancing Times* (December 1962): 165–171.

Roslavleva, Natalia. "How Large Is Soviet Ballet?" *Dance Magazine* (November 1963): 35–37, 58–61.

Roslavleva, Natalia. "Siberian Thaw." *Dance and Dancers* (November 1963): 24–26.

Rubina, Marina, and I. I. Vershinina. *Novosibirskii akademicheskii: Teatr opery i baleta.* Novosibirsk, 1979.

Scheidl, Sylvia. "Alla Sigalowa." *Tanz Affiche* 6 (April–May 1993): 35.

Sheremetyevskaya, Natalia. "Molodyie baletnyie teatry." In *Sovetskii baletny teatr.* Edited by Vera Krasovskaya. Moscow (1976): 155–217.

Sokolov-Kaminsky, Arkady. "O mastere-masterski." *Balet,* no. 1 (1994): 37–38.

Souritz, Elizabeth. "Moscow." *Ballet Review* 19 (Summer 1991): 11–14; 19 (Winter 1991): 6–9; 20 (Fall 1992): 6–13.

Sutton, James. "At the Maly." *Ballet Review* 19 (Spring 1991): 63–67.

Swift, Mary Grace. *The Art of the Dance in the U.S.S.R.* Notre Dame, 1968.

Uralskaya, Valeria, and V. Maranzman. "Boris Eifman." *Balet,* no. 3 (1995).

Vaccarino, Elisa. "Balletto del Teatro Stanislavsky-Nemirovich Danchenko." *Balletto oggi* (August 1991): 25–26.

Vedekhina, O. "Tanzuiushcy *Tchaikovsky,*" *Balet* no. 1 (1994): 38–39.

Vikhreva, N. "Po osobomu rasporiazheniiu." *Sovetskii balet,* no. 3 (1985).

Verrièle, Philippe. "Le théâtre de la révolte danse." *Saisons de la danse,* no. 255 (March 1994): 18–19.

Windreich, Leland. "Moscow." *Dance International* 21 (Fall 1993): 48.

ARCHIVES. The Dance Collection of the New York Public Library for the Performing Arts contains files for the Maly Opera Theater, Leningrad, the Moscow Classical Ballet, the Novosibirsk Opera and Ballet Theater, the Perm Opera Ballet School, and the Pianitsky Folk Choir.

ELIZABETH SOURITZ
Based on materials submitted by Natalia Shereemetyevskaya, Natalia Chernova, Valeria Uralskaya, Galina V. Inozemtseva, Nadezhda Vikhreva, and Yelena Yerofeyeva

Twentieth-Century Plastique

From the end of the eighteenth through the nineteenth century, ballet and academic dance were paramount in Russia, with ballet companies and schools under the protection of the tsar's court. But in the twentieth century another kind of professional dance emerged, a form that, if not similar, at least bears a certain likeness to German *Ausdruckstanz* and American modern dance. In Russia it is called "free" or "plastique" (sometimes "rhythmoplastique") dance.

It began with Isadora Duncan coming to Russia for the first time in December 1904. Her performances were a great success and soon attracted Russian followers and imitators, generally named "barefoot dancers." Some had lessons with Isadora's sister, Elizabeth; many improvised their own dances after studying Greek art in museums. Another growing source of inspiration was Émile Jaques-Dalcroze's eurhythmics, as Russians went to his school in Hellerau and in 1911 Dalcroze courses opened in Saint Petersburg and Moscow. Among the studios and schools of Duncan dance two in Moscow were particularly important for the future: the Francesca Beata school (opened c.1909) and the Rabenek studio. Ellen Rabenek was a dancer who under the name of her first husband, Knipper, taught dance and choreographed at the Moscow Art Theater from 1907 to 1910; in 1911 opened her own studio under the name of her second husband, Rabenek; and as Ellen Tels toured Europe with her students in 1912 and 1913. She choreographed plastique dances to classical music, in which free movement and pantomime merged. After Duncan's 1907 Russian tour a group of her followers in Saint Petersburg, calling themselves Heptachor (after the Greek *hepta,* "seven," because initially they were seven girls), began to study Greek art, to dance, and later to perform and teach. They started as amateurs but became a professional group in the 1920s.

However, it was not in Saint Petersburg but in Moscow, more inclined toward experimentation beyond classical ballet, that most plastique dance studios worked. From Rabenek's studio came Ludmila Alekseeva (1890–1964), who, dissatisfied with Duncan dance, began in 1913 to work on a technique of her own, later called "harmonious gymnastics." After the 1917 revolution she had a studio and also choreographed for amateurs in the Proletcult (Proletarian Culture Association), where her most impor-

RUSSIA: Twentieth-Century Plastique. Dancers from Isadora Duncan's Moscow school in "Labor" from *Impressions of Modern Russia,* with Maria Toropchenova, Aleksandra Aksenova, Valentina Boye, and Elena Terentieva. (Photograph by Frank Derbas; reprinted from *Dance Perspectives* 64 [Winter 1975], p. 36.)

tant production was *Gloom, Passion, Marseillaise* (1918). From Beata's school came Vera Maya. She, too, did not want to continue as a Duncan dancer and so began to enrich her vocabulary by introducing other techniques: Dalcroze, acrobatics, calisthenics, even ballet. In her so-called studio of expressive movement she choreographed plastique compositions based on classical music, acrobatic studies, pseudo-oriental dances, and the like. Inna Chernetskaia (1895–1965?) called her style "synthetic dance." She had studied not only with Elizabeth Duncan and Dalcroze students, but also with drama teachers in Russia and was influenced by *Ausdruckstanz,* having been to Germany in the 1920s. Her productions—*Pan,* to music by Dohnányi, and *M.F.,* using Liszt's "Mephisto Waltz" (both c.1924)—were dramatic dances strongly reminiscent of German expressionism.

Other dancers working in plastique and rhythmoplastique dance in the 1920s were Valeria Tsvetaeva, Inna Bystrenina, Natalia Tian (also a pupil of Beata), and Nikolai Posniakov in Moscow; Zinaida Verbova and Tamara Glebova in Leningrad. Sometimes, as in the case of Aleksandr Rumnev or Lev Lukin, it is difficult to say if they were using a form of free dance (plastique or rhythmoplastique), had invented a style of their own, or had even turned to pantomime (especially in the case of Rumnev). Like German or American modern dancers the Russians also looked at each for its individual style of movement. They generally considered pure Duncan dance old fashioned and obsolete. This point of view prevailed among free dance dancers even when in 1921 Isadora Duncan herself (with Irma Duncan) opened a school in Moscow. While the students were trying to preserve Isadora's heritage, they were also obliged to meet Soviet society's requirements by staging dances of social protest and using Russian folk songs. By then, the early Duncan followers had already gone their own ways.

The diverse dancers and groups of free dance interpreters in the 1920s had different interests and aims. Some stressed the importance of music and interpreted it by means of dance: the Heptachor dancers always had musicians to work with them; Nikolai Posniakov was a professional musician, so that the relation between sound and movement was his prime interest as a choreographer and a researcher. For others it was the story told by dance that was important and they were attracted toward theater. As early as 1912 a group of Rabenek students staged a dance play in three acts, *Chrysis,* to a libretto after Pierre Louÿs and music by Reinhold Glière. It reflected the need for telling a story, then typical of many kinds of dance and movement art in Russia. Along with plastique dance groups there were in the 1920s others, such as the Drambalet studio, where ballet movements were used in a strictly narrative way. But whether interested in music visualization or storytelling, most free dancers were in search of new ways of moving, combining and developing all known styles to create a style of their own.

RUSSIA: Twentieth-Century Plastique. Members of Nikolai Foregger's troupe in his *Dance of Machines,* which premiered on 13 February 1923. In this work, which caused a sensation throughout the Soviet avant-garde, dancers imitated the motions of linchpins, pistons, flywheels, and other mechanical devices. (Photograph reprinted from Swift, 1968, p. 44.)

In the beginning of the 1920s all dance groups had the freedom to experiment and perform; some even got financial help from the state. There was also at the State Academy of Art Science (GAKhN) a Choreological Laboratory that answered the free dancers' need for study in the theory of artistic movement and for research, a freedom in which they indulged, contrary to ballet dancers who were content with a traditional system. GAKhN in the period 1923–1929 attracted theorists, dancers, and choreographers for practice, research, conferences, and discussions. Beginning in 1924, when many private studios were closed by government decree, GAKhN had let them work under its aegis. The 1924 decree was the first attack on

RUSSIA: Twentieth-Century Plastique. Members of Olga Bavdilovich's Theater of Chamber Dance in her *Requiem,* c.1994. (Photograph by Vladimir Lupovsky; courtesy of Elizabeth Souritz.)

free dance. By the end of the 1920s the difficulties multiplied. It became clear that Soviet ideology did not approve of that kind of art, which was too individualistic and too much based on foreign ("alien") traditions, in contrast to the national heritage of ballet and folk dance. GAKhN was closed in 1930. What served for a while as a refuge to free dance in the beginning of the 1930s was the Section of Artistic Movement of the Moscow's Gorky Central Park of Culture and Recreation. Many dance groups worked there, and the school and Island of Dance theater situated in the Park had from 1933 to 1936 a section of rhythmoplastique dance under the leadership of Nikolai Posniakov, who had been a researcher at GAKhN.

But in the middle of the 1930s most free dance groups had either to stop working or change the direction of their activities. Alekseeva turned to sports and beginning with 1934 taught "harmonious gymnastics" to amateurs in the House of Scientists in Moscow. Maya's group, now called Theater of Dance, performed dances and small ballets that gradually became more and more like the style of folk dance ensembles, a new type of dance company that began to appear in the second half of the 1930s. The Duncan studio had a longer life than many others (it closed in 1949), owing either to the fame of Isadora or to the fact that during the war many patriotic dances were choreographed there. But most free dancers had to leave the stage to work in drama or opera theaters, teach in schools and kindergartens, or train athletes. The same was the plight of rhythmiciens, as Institutes of Rhythm in Moscow and Leningrad were closed and rhythmicians worked in drama schools and hospitals.

During the decades 1940 through 1960 it looked as if the tradition of free dance in Russia were completely destroyed, and even the names of the pioneer plastique dancers were unknown to specialists, having never been mentioned in any study on ballet or dance in Russia. This situation was aggravated by ballet dancers' attitude toward free dance, which they considered unprofessional and of no value. Even in the 1960s, when the first modern dance companies from abroad began to tour the Soviet Union, the Russian dance world still clung to the idea that only ballet training produced real art and dancers who were "able to perform all this nonsense just as well and even better." It took another generation to destroy the prejudice, but during this time the tradition was not completely lost; there were still underground forces that could be revived. The students of Ludmila Alekseeva, still teaching at the House of Scientists, remembered her dances and exercises; in 1990 there was a gala performance to commemorate her birth centennial, at which her works were shown. Duncan students Elena Terentieva and Lydia Gicheva were still alive as was Stefanida Rudneva (1890–1989) from the original Heptachor, so that Duncan dance studios could be revived: Natalia Fedorova's New Heptachor, the Moscow Center of Musical Movement under Vera Beloscrovich, and others.

But there were also dancers who did not want to revive styles of the past but rather to invent their own ways of moving. Many companies emerged during the 1980s and 1990s, after Russian dancers had had the opportunity to get acquainted with touring modern dance companies from other countries, after modern dance teachers (especially from the United States) had given classes, and after films and videotapes had become available. Several influential festivals of American modern dance and German *Ausdruckstanz* and dance theater were organized; avant-garde companies from France and Holland came to Russia and also influenced contemporary Russian dance.

Companies were formed in a number of cities in the provinces. In 1987, Evgeny Panfilov (born 1956) began to stage dance works in Perm for his company, which changed names several times before becoming Experiment. He prefers storytelling in a strong, often grotesque, style, staging works like *Cage for Parrots, Metamorphoses, Lolita,* and *Duets the Color of Fog.* The subjects vary considerably, but there has always been a strong sense of theater and the style is energetic, provocative, even sexy. In Ekaterinberg, Provincial Dances began in the 1990s to perform works by Tatiana Baganova. Somewhat similar to German dance theater, her dances are strong and aggressive, using scores by Luigi Nono and Sofia Gubaidulina as well as jazz and music from Japan. There have been an ambitious eveninglong work, *Zoar,* and short dances like "The cage should be open for the bird to return" and "When time will come for the one to come, who. . . ." There is the Theater of Chamber Dance of Olga Bavdilovich (born 1953), who began to choreograph in Vladivostok in the mid-1970s. She describes her work as "dances of emptiness" and says that she uses flowing movements like a "live stream," often combined horizontally. All of these dances are plotless, but Bavdilovich uses ideas based on Asian concepts of time, space, and the significance of numbers. She choreographs to scores by Bach, Shostakovich, and Gennady Artemov as well as music from India and Tibet.

In Saint Petersburg in 1988 Anton Adassinsky formed a movement-drama company called Derevo ("tree"). Working to various genres of up-to-date music as well as in silence, the company iconoclastically rejects all principles of classical dance in performances that appear improvisational and are often shocking. To avoid any connotation of ballet Adassinsky calls his company members performers, rather than dancers. Several groups have developed within Moscow. In the Graphic Ballet, several students of the late Gennady Pescanny perform his choreography, strongly influenced by calisthenics; Gennady Abramov works with his students on improvising expressive movements; Alla Chernova leads the Theater of Plastique Arts; Elena Bogdanovich stages acrobatic solos.

In many companies, genres have been merged. Some use acting, singing, and the spoken word as well as movement. The Independent of Alla Sigalova (born 1959) is one of these. Among her works for the company are *Othello* and *Salome.* Others use classical dance along with other styles, like Ballet of the XXIst Century under Svetlana Voskresenskaiya or Moscow's Russian Chamber Ballet under Edvald Smirnov. Still others concentrate on pantomime and plastique. What has been excitingly new for Russia is the diversity of styles after a long period of monopoly by ballet and folk dance groups.

BIBLIOGRAPHY

Balet, no. 1–2 (1993); no. 3 (1995): 8–24, 32–36.

Belova, Ekaterina. "Drambalet. Studiia-masterskaia-teatr-ansambl'." *Balet,* no. 5–6 (1993); no. 2–3 (1994).

Chernova, Natalia, guest ed. "Moto-Bio—The Russian Art of Movement: Dance, Gesture, and Gymnastics, 1910–1930." Special issue of *Experiment: A Journal of Russian Culture* 2 (1996).

Gayevsky, Vadim. "O svoystvakh strasti." *Moskovsky nabliudatel',* no. 3 (1991).

Ivanov, V. "'Eksperiment' Panfilova." *Sovietsky balet,* no. 2 (1990).

Misler, Nicoletta. "Designing Gestures in the Laboratory of Dance." In *Theatre in Revolution,* edited by Nancy Van Norman Baer. San Francisco, 1992.

Naborshchikova, S. "Lider. O khoreografe E. Panfilove i yego teatre." *Moskovsky nabliudatel',* no. 11 (1991).

Roslavleva, Natalia. "Prechistenka 20: The Isadora Duncan School in Moscow." *Dance Perspectives,* no. 64 (1975).

Sheremetyevskaya, Natalia. *Tanets na estrade.* Moscow, 1985.

Sidorov, Aleksandr. *Sovremenny tanets.* Moscow, 1922.

Souritz, Elizabeth. "Der 'plastische' und 'rhythmoplastische Tanz' in Russland der zehner und zwanziger Jahre." In *Ausdruckstanz,* edited by Gunhild Oberzaucher-Schüller. Wilhelmshaven, 1992.

Souritz, Eliabeth. "Moscow's Island of Dance, 1934–1941." *Dance Chronicle* 17.1 (1994): 1–92.

"Tri mneniia ob odnoy truppe." *Sovietsky balet,* no. 3 (1991).

Voskresenskaya, N. "Eksperimenty L. Lukina." *Balet,* no. 4 (1993).

ELIZABETH SOURITZ

Dance Education

In the eighteenth century, when ballet instruction was first introduced in Russia, the only technique considered was that of the French; the Italian school later dominated. In time, however, the Russians evolved their own technique, teaching system, and style of performance.

Dance training in Russia has been maintained by the state since its inception. Before the Revolution, there were schools only in Moscow and Leningrad. Some small schools had been attached to the serf theaters, and some private studios had sprung up in various towns, but these had no substantial influence on dance training. By the 1990s there were nine ballet schools in Russia. Current practice for all of them sets the minimum age for enrollment at ten years, and the course of study lasts eight years. All the schools work under a common curriculum that includes classical dance, theatrical folk dance, historical and vernacular dance, pas de deux, acting, rhythmic exercises, gymnastics, breathing, and stage practice. In the former constituent republics, national dance was also part of the compulsory curriculum. In addition, students learn piano-playing and the history of the arts. All receive a secondary education. Semiannual concerts attest to the students' progress, and each year concludes with a graduation performance. Some schools specialize also in training professional folk dancers.

The Saint Petersburg school is recognized as the cradle of Russian ballet. It was opened in 1738. Founded by Jean-Baptiste Landé, it offered classes in ballet, drama, music, and painting. The government decree that established it called it the Dance School; at the turn of the century it was renamed the Saint Petersburg Theatrical School. In the eighteenth century the chief teachers were Franz Hilverding and Giuseppe Canziani. In 1794 the classes were placed under the direction of Ivan Valberkh, who introduced a distinctively national style. For twenty years in the early nineteenth century the principal ballet master was Charles Didelot. Leading dancers and choreographers of the Romantic ballet later taught in Saint Petersburg. Eventually, both the company and the school were closely linked to the work of Marius Petipa, who was assisted by Christian Johannson and Pavel Gerdt. In the early 1900s Michel Fokine revised the teaching methods and took the school in the direction of modern art.

A new curriculum was introduced in 1918. Three years later Agrippina Vaganova began to teach and later became principal of the school. She systematized the instruction and reorganized the curriculum. The first edition of her manual, *Fundamentals of the Classic Dance,* was published in 1934. Five years later *Fundamentals of Character Dance* was compiled by Aleksandr Shiriaev, Mikhail Bocharov, Andrei Lopukhov, and Nikolai Ivanovsky. By this time a teacher training department and a department for training dancers from the constituent republics had been added. In 1957 the school was named after Vaganova.

Konstantin Sergeyev took over the school in 1973. Among the leading teachers during his tenure were Aleksandr Pushkin, Natalia Dudinskaya, Elena Shiripina, Inna Zubkovskaya, and Boris Bregvadze. The current director is Leonid Nadirov.

The founding of the Moscow ballet school was preceded by classes at the Moscow Orphanage in 1773. The first teacher was Filippo Beccari, who was followed by Leopold Paradisi. On this foundation the Moscow Imperial Theatrical School was opened in 1806. The first teacher was Jean Lamiral, who was followed by Dominique Lefebre. From 1812 to 1839 the school was led by Adam Glushkovsky, who strictly applied the methods of his own teacher, Charles Didelot. During the Napoleonic Wars, the school was evacuated to the town of Ples; lessons were never suspended. As the Romantic ballet blossomed, new methods were introduced by Félicité Hullin-Sor and especially by Carlo Blasis who taught there from 1861 to 1864.

From 1896 to 1931 Vasily Tikhomirov taught at the school, developing a system of instruction that aimed at a harmonious development of dance technique and acting skills. As ballet master for the school between 1902 and 1924 Aleksandr Gorsky made bold experiments in building dramatic skills; he was also the first to replace the violin with piano accompaniment for classes. The style of the school was also influenced by the acting method developed by Konstantin Stanislavsky. In 1920 the school was attached to the Bolshoi Theater, enabling it to offer more stage experience to the students.

Leading Moscow teachers in the Soviet period were Tikhomirov, Nikolai Tarasov, Aleksandr Chekrygin, Maria Kozhukhova, Margarita Vasilieva-Rozhdestvenskaya, Maria Leontieva, Elisaveta Gerdt, Asaf Messerer, Galina Petrova, and Tamara Tkachenko. Sofia Golovkina has been principal since 1960.

In 1946 the Lunacharsky Institute of Theatrical Art opened a department to train choreographers for opera and ballet theaters, musical comedy theaters, and dance companies. Only graduates of ballet schools with a record of practical work may enroll for the five-year course, which was founded and led for forty years by Rostislav Zakharov. The curriculum includes courses in composition of classical dance, theatrical folk dance, and historical dance. The history and theory of dance, theater, and music are also taught. Publications that developed from this program have included Zakharov's *A Choreographer's Notes* and Tarasov's *Classical Dance.*

In 1958 a department was opened to train teachers for ballet schools and ballet coaches for theatrical companies. Choreographers are also trained in a department of the Rimsky-Korsakov Conservatory of Music in Leningrad, a course that was inaugurated in 1962 by Fedor Lopukhov. Ballet schools are also maintained in many other Russian cities and in all the former autonomous republics of the Russian Federation, working under the same programs as the academies in Moscow and Saint Petersburg.

One of the trends of the 1990s has been to give dancers a higher education after they graduate from a ballet school. The schools in Moscow and Saint Petersburg actually have the status of academies, and "institutes" that give college diplomas are attached to them. The Moscow Institute, headed by Sofia Golovkina, opened in 1988 and gives diplomas to teachers, choreographers, coaches, and accompanists. A similar institute, founded in 1991, is attached to the Saint Petersburg Academy. Here, however, choreographers are trained only in the music conservatory, while in Moscow they are also trained in RAKIS, the Russian Academy of Theater Art.

Some private schools with the title of *lycée,* or college, have also been opened. There are several in Moscow, Saint Petersburg, and other large cities, some of which have highly professional ballet dancers as directors. Some theaters also have their own ballet studios.

BIBLIOGRAPHY

Bocharnikova, Ella, and Olga M. Martynova. *Moskovskoe Khoreograficheskoe Uchilishche.* Moscow, 1954.

Borisoglebskii, Mikhail. *Proshloe baletnogo otdeleniia peterburgskogo teatral'nogo uchilishcha, nyne Leningradskogo gosudarstvennogo khoreograficheskogo uchilishcha.* 2 vols. Leningrad, 1938–1939.

Elyash, Nikolai. *Russkaia Terpsikhora.* Moscow, 1965.

NIKOLAI I. ELYASH
Translated from Russian

Folk Dance Research and Publication

Descriptions of dances are found in ancient Russian chronicles beginning in the tenth century and are depicted in oral folk art, drawings, and frescoes. Information on the character, style, types, and form of Russian folk dances is contained in works by ethnographers and historians and in memoirs of seventeenth- and eighteenth-century travelers; but ethnographical literature and memoirs rarely contain detailed descriptions. Researchers assume that round dances were such common and popular events that it was considered unnecessary to describe them in detail. Even without detailed description, the authors provided enough information about the national features to form a basis for the methodology of studying Russian folk choreography. Pictures of people dancing serve as original documents: dances are portrayed in ninth- to nineteenth-century works of art, such as paintings, engravings, and popular prints, and in seventeenth- to nineteenth-century lithographs of individual episodes of Russian dance folklore, such as round dances, dances, and play scenes.

In the nineteenth century several organizations demonstrated an interest in Russian folk dance, among them the Russian Imperial Geographic Society (a society composed of natural science amateurs, anthropologists, and ethnographers), its Musical and Ethnographic Committee, the Society of Ancient Russian History, and various regional organizations like the Archangelsk Society, dedicated to studying the Russian north. Scientists and researchers from these organizations found and recorded ethnographic material, songs, ceremonies, games, and round dances. Descriptions were kept in scientific archives, and some of them were published in collections of articles and in the scientific notes of the societies. These descriptions are, however, unsatisfactory for the modern researcher, as they are often incomplete and schematic.

Serious research on Russian folk choreography became possible only after the 1917 October Revolution, because of the rapid increase of interest in and explosive growth of folk art. The earliest research based on specialized expeditions was conducted in the 1920s and 1930s by Vsevolod Vsevolodsky-Gerngross. In his book *Peasant Dance,* he classifies Russian folk dance art by dividing it into dance and round dance, and he discusses the classification system on the basis of content, purpose, and the character of the action. He also provides descriptions of Russian folk dances along the Mezen River in northern Russia. According to the author, researchers on the expeditions not only recorded the dances in writing with the help of the literary-graphic method but also filmed many of them. In his two-volume *History of the Russian Theater,* Vsevolodsky-Gerngross has traced the development of Russian dance art as it parallels the development of theatrical art from the origins to the Soviet period. He also organized the so-called ethnographic theater (1923–1933), where, along with the games and customs of the peoples of the Soviet Union, folk dances were also demonstrated. He makes an attempt to bring together what was done earlier in his book *Games of the Peoples of the USSR* (1933).

Important work in gathering dance folklore was carried out by folk art clubs in all regions of the USSR. These clubs collect materials and publish collections of works that include descriptions of Russian folk dances. In 1936 an All-Union Festival of Folk Dance took place in the USSR. As a result of this, the first professional group of folk choreographers in the world—the State Ensemble of Folk Dance, headed by Igor Moiseyev—was created. Digests by A. Zelenko, V. Okuneva, V. Iving, T. Ustinova, and A. Rudneva appeared at that time. They contained descriptions of authentic Russian folk dances, variations on their themes, and a short theoretical section dedicated to Russian folk choreography. Among the materials written in the 1940s and 1950s, these are the most interesting: *Russian Folk Dance,* by V. Iving (1945); *Russian Folk Round Dances and Dances,* by V. Okuneva (1948); and *Russian Round Dances and Round Dance Songs,* by N. Bachinskaya (1951). In these works one finds authentic ethnographic versions of the dances as well as attempts to provide a scientific classification of Russian folk choreography.

Among major works in this field, foremost is *Images of Russian Folk Choreography* (1964), written by a prominent Russian choreographer and researcher, Kasyan Goleizovsky. Goleizovsky was the first to describe the elements of Russian dance movements and to arrange them in a system: (1) games, ceremonies, festivities, and celebrations; (2) round dances and games, and (3) dances and figures. The materials gathered in the book, if studied seriously, can be of considerable assistance to the practitioner who wants examples of Russian folk choreography and to the theoretician continuing research in the field of folk choreography.

The extent of knowledge about Russian folk choreography varies in the country's different regions. Although there is no central facility to unite research processes in this narrow field, certain aspects of folk choreography research are included in general fundamental works on national folklore, history, culture, theater, and music. In the Soviet era the pragmatics of managing the development of folk choreography was handled by the All-Union Scientific and Methodological Center on Folk Art and by the cultural work of the Ministry of Culture, which had branch offices in all the national republics. Festivals and folk dance performances were regularly held at different sites. Examples of dances were recorded using the descriptive method. Based on these descriptions, collected editions of folk dances were published in the republics, as well as the series Dances of the Peoples of the USSR published by the Arts Publishing House and the editing board of the Ministry of Culture. Collections of Russian, Ukrainian, Lithuanian, Azerbaijani, Armenian, Moldavian, Kirghiz, and Belarussian dances have been published.

Because of the peculiarities of the choreography among the various peoples of the country and the distinct issues raised by specialist-researchers and practitioners, a variety of methods is used for conducting studies. Nevertheless, a regional approach to the material prevails, incorporating methods of classification, detailed analysis (revealing features of construction such as general composition, structure, and pattern), and rhythmical and movement formulas. Lack of a universally accepted general system of description results in a variety of ways for presenting the material. Most frequently, dances are recorded using a literary and graphic method that describes the movements and patterns of the dance in the language of its people, and it includes schematic sketches, drawings, and photographs of the phases of performance. Some researchers use a kinetographic method devised by Professor S. Lisitsian for his studies of Armenian, Kalmuck, Bashkir, and Yakut dances. Researchers have also begun to use Labanotation. There are a number of unique systems having local significance that are used only by particular researchers, for example, the system of H. Sune, who studies Latvian dances. Videotape and filmed recordings are now also made.

Among the peoples of the country, some still possess the knowledge of live, functioning folklore, although they do not practice it in everyday life. There are others who have lost the link with tradition; the dancing they now do can be classified as reconstructed folk dance. This, in turn, has affected the extent and form of research. The creation of an extremely rich professional art based on folk choreography by both ensembles of folk dance and ballet theaters has influenced, and continues to influence, the ongoing processes of folk dance development and the character of research.

Quite a number of books containing folk and scenic choreographic examples have been published in the former Soviet republics. In Ukraine, research in the theory and history of choreography is being conducted by U. Stanishevsky and K. Vasilenko; in Belarus, U. Churko is the author of a number of research studies embracing all aspects of choreography—folklore, folk scenic dances, and the problems of development of ballet theaters, among others. Books dedicated to Lithuanian folk choreography have been written by Lingis; Latvian, by H. Sune. Serious works on the history of Georgian choreography have been written by L. Gvaramadze; Armenian dance and folklore culture is a long-standing subject of research for Lisitsian. In Central Asia, research work is being conducted by L. Avdeeva (Uzbekistan) and R. Urazgildeev (Kyrgyzstan).

Practice shows that the development of any type of choreography, including the creation of new forms and new schools, is directly linked to the traditional choreographic fund of all people. This is why research in the field of choreographic art is impossible without an understanding of the interplay between traditional and professional practices.

VALERIA I. URALSKAYA
Translated from Russian

Theatrical Dance Research and Publication

The first reviews of dance performances were published in Russia in the second half of the eighteenth century. A collection of them was published in 1982 in Oleg Petrov's *Russkaia baletnaia kritika kontsa XVIII–pervoy poloviny XIX veka* (Russian Ballet Criticism at the End of the Eighteenth–First Half of the Nineteenth Century). Jean-Georges Noverre's *Lettres sur la danse* was published in French in Saint Petersburg in 1803–1804. During the nineteenth century many eminent writers, including poets such as Aleksandr Pushkin, wrote about ballet and described dances in their works. Important magazines and newspapers in the second half of the century published articles on current events in and the history and theory of dance.

The first historical books on ballet were written at the end of the nineteenth century by enlightened balletomanes. Aleksandr Pleshcheyev in *Nash balet* (Our Ballet; 1896) compiled a year-by-year chronicle of the Saint Petersburg ballet. Valerian Svetlov's *Sovremenny balet* (Modern Ballet; 1911) is dedicated to the problems of the "new" ballet, represented by Isadora Duncan's influence and the work of Michel Fokine, against the "old" ballet of Marius Petipa, with emphasis on Diaghilev's Ballets Russes Saisons Russes. The four-volume *Istoriia tantsev* (History of the Dance; 1913–1918) by Sergei Khudekov gives an overview of ballet in all countries and a survey of Russian ballet in the last volume. Of particular interest were the books of André Levinson, based on serious historical research and analysis: *Mastera baleta* (Masters of the Ballet; 1914), *Stary i novy balet* (Ballet Old and New; 1918), and others that he published after emigrating to France in 1921. Of great importance for the theory of classical dance was Akim Volynsky's *Kniga likovany* (Book of Exultation; 1925), in which Volynsky analyzed its principles, asserting that they conformed to the laws ruling both other arts and life itself.

In the 1920s the Institute of the History of the Arts nurtured the so-called Leningrad school of theater studies, which played an important part in the evolution of ballet research. Working here were the musicologist and composer Boris Asafiev and the theater historian Aleksei Gvozdev, who introduced a sociological dimension to theater studies. Under their tutelage in the 1930s Yuri Slonimsky elaborated his sociohistorical approach to ballet. Wishing to elevate the accomplishments of Russian choreographers of the nineteenth century, he looked for democratic trends in their works. He also favored strong dramatic lines in ballet. In addition, he encouraged the publication of classics like Noverre's book and of historical documents, such as the memoirs of the pioneer Russian choreographers Ivan Valberkh and Adam Glushkovsky. In 1938–1939 Mikhail Borisoglebsky published two volumes of his *Materialy po istorii russkogo baleta* (Materials on the History of Russian Ballet), a history of the Saint Petersburg school. Lubov Blok did important research on the history of ballet technique and on the choreographers Charles Didelot and Filippo Taglioni. Less intensive historical study was done in Moscow, but important work was accomplished there by Yuri Bakhrushin on Moscow ballet in the first half of the nineteenth century.

Most researchers who began to work after World War II were pupils of Slonimsky or of Slonimsky and Bakhrushin. In Leningrad the center was the Institute of Theater, Music, and Cinema, first under Slonimsky and then Vera Krasovskaya followed by Galina Dobrovolskaya. In Moscow the centers were the Institute of Theater Arts (GITIS) under Nikolai Elyash, and since the 1960s the Institute of Research in the Arts, under Elizabeth Souritz and Natalia Chernova.

Before 1917 research had been concentrated on the study of Russian ballet, and gradually material was collected for a systematic history. Krasovskaya assumed the task of writing the four-volume *Russkii baletnyi teatr* (Russian Ballet Theater; 1958–1972). This work, embracing both the Saint Petersburg and Moscow companies, was based not only on material from newspaper accounts but also on archival material, most of it published for the first time. In the meantime Natalia Roslavleva wrote in English *Era of the Russian Ballet* (1966). The publication of Krasovskaya's work prompted further research because Moscow specialists, Mikhail Gabovich among them, were not satisfied with her Leningrad-slanted approach to Moscow ballet, especially her view of the Moscow choreographer Aleksandr Gorsky. Some of Gabovich's collected research appeared in *Mikhail Gabovich* (1977). Earlier Russian ballet was also reconsidered at this time because Krasovskaya's first volume was the weakest. The first productions of *Swan Lake* and *The Sleeping Beauty,* by Alexander Demidov and Marina Konstantinova respectively, appeared in the series "Ballet Chefs-d'oeuvre." Another series, "Russian Thought about Ballet," included Petrov's study of Russian ballet criticism and a collection of Lubov Blok's writings from the 1930s to the 1980s.

Some Russian ballet personalities have been treated differently at various times. This is especially true of those who, after having brought fame to Russian ballet after World War I, continued to work abroad or left Russia after the October Revolution. These include Serge Diaghilev, Michel Fokine, and those who worked with them. Many were never mentioned, being considered deserters. Anna Pavlova and Vaslav Nijinsky were more or less exonerated, having left Russia before 1917. The attitude toward Fokine was rather negative. He was criticized for his adherence to one-act ballets, breaking the Russian tradition that favored large-scale productions with elaborate plots. Some called Fokine antirealistic and decadent, as did Slonimsky in his *Sovetskii balet* (Soviet Ballet; 1950). By 1962 the situation had changed and, when publishing Fokine's memoir *Protiv techeniia* (Against the Current), Slonimsky reconsidered his views. In 1981 a second edition of the memoir appeared with a forward by Galina Dobrovolskaya that reflected the modern attitude. A detailed analysis of Fokine's ballets before 1917 is given in Krasovskaya's *Russkii baletnyi teatr.* The attitude toward Diaghilev had been still worse. He was called a representative of the "emigrant arts," having lost his connections with the Motherland, renounced national traditions, and encouraged modernism which was alien to the spirit of Russian art. Krasovskaya was the first to pay him due tribute. Changing attitudes were also reflected in the two-volume *Sergei Diaghilev i russkoe iskusstvo* (Serge Diaghilev and Russian Art; 1982), published by Ilya Silberstein and Vladimir Samkov, although this dealt more with painting than ballet. In 1987, 1989, and 1991 in Perm there were exhibitions and symposiums devoted to Diaghilev. Then 1994 saw the publication of Aleksandr Laskin's *Neisvestne Diaghilevy ili konets tsitaty* (The Unknown Diaghilevs, or The End of a Quotation), dealing with the family and their descendants in Russia.

Much still remains to be done. There is no book on Petipa except the collection *Marius Petipa: Materialy, vospominaniia, stati* (Memoirs, Reminiscences, Articles; 1971), a chapter in Vadim Gaevsky's *Divertissement* (1981), and some magazine articles resulting from a conference in 1993. There is also no book on Lev Ivanov.

Soviet Era. There are more books on Soviet ballet than on the prerevolutionary period. Readers are most interested in dancers they have seen on the stage. During the 1970s and 1980s Iskusstvo publishers launched several series; one, called "Ballet Soloists," accounted for nine books on contemporary dancers, and there have been many others devoted to individual personalities. Researchers have been especially attracted to the period of the 1920s. For several decades there had been a strong bias against this period. Everything done by 1920s choreographers was proclaimed erroneous, as it was not in accord with the principles of the 1930s, which favored full-length drama ballets. The work done by all "free dance" interpreters beginning with Isadora Duncan, studios and groups (like that of Nikolai Foregger), the experiments of Kasyan Goleizovsky, Fedor Lopukhov, and the early works of Leonid Yakobson were negated. But beginning in the 1960s historians felt an urgent need to review this attitude. One of the first books to do this was the collection *Sovetskii baletnyi teatr, 1917–1967* (Soviet Ballet; 1976), edited by Vera Krasovskaya. Later books devoted to this period were *Khoreograficheskoe iskusstvo dvatsatych godov* (1979; translated into English as *Soviet Choreographers in the 1920s* [1990]), by Elizabeth Souritz, *Fedor Lopukhov* (1972) by Galina Dobrovolskaya, which she based on his reminiscenes and a collection of articles "Choreograficheskoe otkrovennosti" (Choreographic Revelations), and a collection *Kasyan Goleizovsky* (1985), compiled by his widow, Vera Vasilieva, and Natalia Chernova.

At this time also came the realization that there were in Russia many interesting dance events outside the large state ballet companies. In the 1920s many groups and studios worked on experimental dance, some of them followers of Isadora Duncan or Émile Jaques-Dalcroze, others working in their own style of movement. In *Tanets na estrade* (Dance Upon the Concert Stage; 1985) Natalia Sheremetyevskaya described some of the "free dance" studios of the 1920s. She and Souritz also contributed to the collection based on a symposium held in Schloss Thurnau, Austria, *Ausdruckstanz* (1992), and the magazine *Balet* published several articles. There has also been special interest in Duncan. In 1975 Natalia Roslavleva's study "The Isadora Duncan School in Moscow" could be published only abroad (in the American journal *Dance Perspectives*, no. 64), but since then articles have appeared in Russia. An important example is the collection of writings *Isadora. Gastroli v Rossiyi* (Isadora: Tours in Russia; 1992).

The 1930s in Soviet ballet have been less studied. Of the choreographers of this period only Yakobson has received attention, in a book by Dobrovolskaya published in 1968. Thorough books on Vasily Vainonen, Rostislav Zakharov, and Leonid Lavrovsky have not appeared. The cause of this situation is not hard to find. A serious, objective book that would consider both the achievements and the failures of this time (generally called the *drambalet* period) could be written only by a researcher at some distance from it. In the 1930s the above-mentioned choreographers monopolized Soviet ballet; an objective evaluation of their work was impossible. All of their productions received prizes; the critics always praised them. But a new period in Soviet ballet history began in the late 1950s when young choreographers started to seek new directions for their art. Refusing to consider ballet as merely a drama devoid of words and decorated with dances, they encouraged the existence of different genres, including symphonic and one-act, plotless ballets. Both Zakharov and Lavrovsky began a frenzied campaign against the innovators, accusing them of "formalism" and obsequiousness to Western ideas incompatible with Soviet ideology. Progressive ballet critics naturally denounced the works of the 1930s and 1940s.

Only in the 1970s did the conflict subside, making it possible for writers to assess this period as historians, rather than as publicists involved in the struggle of ideas. Attempts to analyze this period began in 1976 with the publication of the collection *Sovetskii baletnyi theatr*, containing an article on this period by Natalia Chernova. A collection on Lavrovsky was also compiled in 1983 by Valeria Uralskaya. Victor Vanslov, in his *Yuri Grigorovich i problemy khoreografii* (Yuri Grigorovich and Problems of Choreography; 1969, 1971), tried to define this *drambalet* period. In succeeding years numerous books about individuals have been published. Grigorovich has most attracted researchers, but in time he became as much a monopolist as Zakharov and Lavrovsky had been in the 1930s and 1940s; his attitude toward all trends different from his own was just as negative. This was recognized in Gaevsky's *Divertissement*, which Grigorovich succeeded in having banned. Not until the 1990s was it possible for writers to express personal views on what was happening at the Bolshoi. As yet there are neither books nor substantive articles on promising choreographers of the younger generation.

Foreign Ballet. The study of foreign ballet by Soviet researchers began in the 1920s when sections on ballet were included in textbooks on Western European theater and excerpts from historical works were translated and published with explanatory articles. In the 1930s Lubov Blok wrote on the evolution of classical dance from ancient Greece onward, but it was not published until 1987. From the 1940s to the 1960s, however, Soviet scholars had no access to primary sources outside Russia and had to rely on books already published. Natalia Roslavleva used Mary Clarke's *Sadler's Wells Ballet* for her *Anglisky balet* (English Ballet; 1959), but criticized productions when their form or orientation did not correspond to what was acceptable in Russia at the time. Valeria Chistiakova based her 1977 book on Roland Petit on foreign publications and films.

Nevertheless, the need for a comprehensive history of ballet in Western Europe was acutely felt. The gap is being filled by Vera Krasovskaya, who published four volumes on the subject between 1979 and 1996. Using world ballet studies, she interprets her material according to principles developed in Russia. The history of ballet in each country is considered in relation to its development in other countries. Ballet is seen as a cultural phenonmenon, closely connected to music, literature, drama, visual arts, and social life. Broad knowledge combined with the ability to see various phenomena in their complexity and to identify important trends are the main merits of Krasovskaya's work.

The study of contemporary foreign ballet has fared less well. Foreign companies, such as the Paris Opera Ballet and some American troupes, began to tour Russia in the 1950s, producing reviews from talented critics such as Moissey Iofiev, and articles on individual choreographers such as George Balanchine and Maurice Béjart by Vadim Gaevsky. Booklets published for the tours and sold in the theaters helped to familiarize Soviet readers with contemporary foreign dance. One such, issued for the tour of the José Limón company in 1973, supplied for the first time some objective information on American modern dance, which had previously been spoken of only in derogatory terms. A most ardent opponent of contemporary foreign dance was Rostislav Zakharov, who published books in the 1950s that declared that "realistic" dramatic ballets (like his own) were the only acceptable kind of dance production and classical technique was the only legitimate dance system.

Russian Ballet Abroad. Only recently has it become possible to write of Russian émigrés not as traitors to their country but as representatives of Russian culture abroad. Even in 1975 Slonimsky was able to publish his research on Balanchine's early years only in the American periodical *Ballet Review.* As to the defectors of the 1970s (such as Rudolf Nureyev, Mikhail Baryshnikov, and Natalia Makarova), their names are not even mentioned in the encyclopedia *Ballet* (1980). Not only are their biographies omitted, but also their names are deleted from the cast listings of premieres in which they created roles. This situation changed in the 1990s. A collection, *Natalia Makarova,* was compiled in 1993 and memoirs of others, like Matilda Kshessinska and Serge Lifar, have been published in Russian.

Theory and Aesthetics. Theoretical problems of dance have interested Russian writers since the beginning of the nineteenth century, many magazine articles being not simply reviews but discourses on the essence of dance. In the beginning of the twentieth century Alexandre Benois, Akim Volynsky, André Levinson, and Aleksandr Cherepnin each had his own theoretical platform. In the 1920s and early 1930s studies of even remote historical periods revealed the writer's bias in relation to contemporary issues. In the 1930s, when *drambalet* came to the fore, researchers pointed to similar situations in the past. Nevertheless, in the 1920s there had been strong interest in "free dance" that led to an attraction to theoretical analysis of dance and artistic movement, and a special interest in dance notation. In 1922 Aleksei Sidorov published *Sovremenny tanets* (Modern Dance). Most of the theoretical work was done by scholars (Aleksandr Larionov, Aleksei Sidorov, Nikolai Posniakov, Evgeny Yavorsky) and choreographers at the Choreological Laboratory of the Moscow State Academy of Art Sciences (GAKhN).

In the 1930s and 1940s there was a heated debate over what dance can and cannot express. Vladimir Golubov and Yuri Slonimsky defined ballet as better at expressing emotions than depicting events and pointed out the shortcomings of the lifelike ballets that dominated the Soviet stage. The creators of such productions, headed by Rostislav Zakharov, accused their attackers of idealism, departing from the official materialistic worldview. Those who supported the position that dance itself should prevail had to prove that they did not adhere to principles alien to Marxism-Leninism. Nevertheless, Golubov, Slonimsky, and later Vera Krasovskaya firmly stood their ground, and they were joined in the 1950s and 1960s by young choreographers (like Yuri Grigorovich and Igor Belsky) who, as soon as the political climate began to change, choreographed ballets relying on music and dance, not only on drama. Krasovskaya's collection *Stati o balete* (Articles about Ballet; 1967) contains a number of important ideas. Occasionally she anticipated in theory what later became obvious in practice; an understanding of the historical development of the art allows an attentive researcher to foresee its future.

By the late 1960s researchers began to analyze the new trend. In his book on Grigorovich, Victor Vanslov considered the choreographer's productions in connection with theoretical problems. Simultaneously, theoretical books were being written for a wide audience: Valeria Chistiakova's *V mire tantza* (In the World of Dance; 1964), Poel Karp's *O balet* (On Ballet; 1967), and Galina Dobrovolskaya's *Tanets, pantomima, balet* (Dance, Pantomime, Ballet; 1975). Karp also wrote a book for specialists, *Balet i drama* (Ballet and Drama, 1980), which compares the laws of the two and analyzes different genres of ballet. But many ideas and arguments of the 1960s and 1970s now seem obsolete. With new research, historical facts have taken on a different meaning.

Numerous musicologists write on music for ballet, but they rarely consider its balletic specificity. Among the few exceptions is Irina Vershinina. In *Ranniye balety Stravinskogo* (Stravinsky's Early Ballets; 1967) and in many articles she was the first to formulate a number of important postulates for ballet music. Other works on this topic include *O musyke zarubezhnogo baleta* (About Ballet Music Abroad; 1984) by Rimma Kosacheva, *Sovetskaia baletnaia musyka* (Soviet Ballet Music; 1980) by Svetlana Katonova, and articles by Elena Kurilenko.

Reference Books. The first ballet dictionary published in Russia was a translation of Charles Compan's *Dictionnaire de danse* (1787). Beginning at the end of the nineteenth century lists of ballets were published in *Ezhegodnik Imperatorskikh Teatrov* (Annals of the Imperial Theaters). Collections of libretti and summaries of ballets were published in the 1960s and 1970s. The first Russian ballet dictionary was *Vse o balete* (All about Ballet; 1966) by Souritz and Slonimsky. *Mastera tantsa: Materialy k istorii Leningradskogo baleta, 1917–1973* (Masters of Dance: Material on the History of the Leningrad Ballet, 1917–1973) by Arsen Degen and Igor Stupnikov was published in 1974, with a revised and updated edition in 1988. The comprehensive encyclopedia *Ballet* was published in 1980 under the title *Leningradsky balet* (Leningrad Ballet).

Publishing Facilities. Beginning in the 1930s most ballet books were published by the state publisher, Iskusstvo (Art), and some by Musyka (Music). But since the end of the 1980s these no longer have the necessary funds. Some ballet books, mostly translations, have been published by private companies. There is one magazine, *Balet* (Ballet), known from 1981 to 1992 as *Sovetskii balet* (Soviet Ballet). One periodical, *Musyka i khoreografiia sovremennogo baleta* (Music and Choreography of Modern Ballet), published five issues between 1974 and 1978. By the mid-1990s the difficulty of publishing a scholarly book had become insurmountable.

ELIZABETH SOURITZ

RWANDA. *See* Central and East Africa.

S

SABIROVA, MALIKA (Malika Abdurakhmanovna Sabirova; born 22 May 1942 in Dushanbe, Tajik Soviet Socialist Republic, died 27 February 1982 in Dushanbe), dancer. After graduating in 1961 from the Leningrad ballet school, where she studied with Elena Shiripina, Vera Kostzovitskaya, and Boris Shavrov, Sabirova made her debut at the Aini Tajik Opera and Ballet Theater in Dushanbe. Among her leading roles in ballets staged by local choreographers between 1962 and 1982 were the title role in *Giselle,* Odette-Odile in *Swan Lake,* Sari in *Path of Thunder,* Juliet in *Romeo and Juliet,* Kitri in *Don Quixote,* Leili in *Leili and Medzhnun,* Nikia in *La Bayadère,* the lead ballerina in *Ballet Class,* and Aurora in *The Sleeping Beauty.* Moscow audiences applauded Sabirova during her numerous appearances with the Bolshoi Ballet in *Don Quixote* and *Giselle,* as well as in her concert classical and modern ballet programs. She danced many roles during concert tours in the Soviet Union and abroad.

Sabirova owed much of her success to her collaboration with the choreographer Natalia Konyus of the Moscow ballet school, who staged two productions in Dushanbe, *Path of Thunder,* to music by Kara Karayev, and *Leili and Medzhnun,* to music by Sergei Balasanian. While in Moscow Sabirova studied with Galina Ulanova and Asaf Messerer. Messerer noted the classical purity and beauty of her dancing, and her musicality and virtuosity. Her dancing was distinguished by verve, a subtle feeling for style, a culturally Eastern plasticity of the body and arms, and emotionalism. Ulanova praised Sabirova's high professional level and the exacting standards she set for herself.

Malika Sabirova won prizes at the international ballet competitions in Varna (1964) and Moscow (1969), the Rudaki Prize of the Tajik Republic (1967), the Leninist Komsomol Prize of the Tajik Republic (1968), and the Leninist Komsomol Prize (1970). The title of People's Artist of the USSR was conferred on her in 1974.

BIBLIOGRAPHY

Bocharnikova, Ella. "A Leninist Komsomol Prize Laureate" (in Russian). *Teatralnaia Zhizn* 19 (1972).

Nurdzhanov, N. K. *Tadzhikskii teatr: Ocherki istorii.* Moscow, 1968.

Obituary. *Dance News* (April 1982): 4.

Yamauchi, Emi. "World Ballet Festival." *Dance News* (June 1976): 10–11.

ARCHIVE. Dance Collection, New York Public Library for the Performing Arts.

Ella V. Bocharnikova
Translated from Russian

SACRE DU PRINTEMPS, LE. English title: *The Rite of Spring.* Scenes of pagan Russia in two parts. Choreography: Vaslav Nijinsky. Music: Igor Stravinsky. Libretto: Igor Stravinsky and Nikolai Roerich. Scenery and costumes: Nikolai Roerich. First performance: 29 May 1913, Théâtre des Champs-Élysées, Paris, Ballets Russes de Serge Diaghilev. Principal: Maria Piltz (The Chosen Victim).

Igor Stravinsky apparently conceived the idea for *Le Sacre du Printemps* in 1910. Together with the painter Nikolai Roerich, he devised a final scenario in 1911. Roerich designed the two backdrops—the first a lakeside scene, the second a rocky hill in twilight—on the basis of his archaeological studies of ancient Russia, reinterpreted through a quasi-symbolist pictorial style. The costumes, stenciled smocks, were based on actual Russian folk costumes. The music was composed between the summer of 1911 and March 1913, and the choreography between November 1912 and May 1913, when the ballet was at last produced by Diaghilev's Ballets Russes.

Le Sacre du Printemps concerns the rituals performed by a prehistoric Slavic tribe at the coming of spring. Part 1 includes a lesson in augury given by an old woman to the tribe's youths; a mock abduction, a *khorovod,* and a scene called "Games of the Rival Clans," all performed by the young men and women of the tribe; a procession of the tribe's elders, leading forth their sage, who prostrates himself on the earth, kissing it; and the "Dance of the Earth," in which the whole tribe dances frenetically to pounding drums. In part 2 the tribe's maidens do a circle dance. One among them is singled out as the Chosen Victim, and the others dance around her, glorifying her. The elders enter, in bearskins, and dance in invocation of their ancestors. Finally, the Chosen Victim, sacrificing herself to renew the fertility of the earth, dances herself to death as the tribe watches.

In keeping with the primitivism of the theme, and with Stravinsky's violent music, Vaslav Nijinsky devised a heavy, jagged, antiballetic choreography. Most of the ballet consisted of ensemble work, but with the corps arranged asymmetrically and moving like "ecstatic spastics" (Kirstein, 1975), stamping, shuffling, pounding, and trembling, their bodies rugged and earthbound, their feet turned in. In accordance with his understanding of Émile Jaques-Dalcroze's eurhythmics, which influenced his work at this time, Nijinsky designed the movements to correspond closely with the score. (Marie Rambert, a Dalcroze student, served as Nijinsky's assistant during the company rehearsals.) According to Robert Craft (1988), however, the dancing was often in counterpoint to the music.

Aggressively unorthodox in its music and choreography (less so in decor), *Sacre,* at its premiere, caused a riot in the theater. The French reviews were generally harsh, an important exception being two essays by Jacques Rivière in *La nouvelle revue française,* the first of which declared that *Le Sacre du Printemps* marked a turning point in the history of Western art, and the second of which (1 November 1913) described the ballet as a descent to the very springs of life, a portrayal of "the terrifying labor of the cells."

Rivière's judgment is now the accepted view: that Nijinsky's choreography was as boldly modernist as the score, a culmination of the experiments he had begun in *L'Après-midi d'un Faune* the year before. There is also a minority view. In 1921 T. S. Eliot wrote that the choreography, unlike the music, had lacked "the sense of the present"—that it had looked like "primitive ceremony." The issue cannot be settled, for while Stravinsky's composition has become a classic, Nijinsky's ballet was lost, having been dropped from the Ballets Russes repertory after only nine performances. In 1987 Millicent Hodson created for the Joffrey Ballet a version of Nijinsky's *Sacre* based primarily on scores annotated by Stravinsky and Rambert, but the choreographic information on the scores was apparently too sparse to permit a reconstruction in any strict sense of the term.

The score has since been used by many other choreographers, including Léonide Massine (1920), Lester Horton (1937), Mary Wigman (1957), Maurice Béjart (1959), Kenneth MacMillan (1962), Natalia Kasatkina and Vladimir Vasiliov (1965), John Neumeier (1972), Hans van Manen (1974), Glen Tetley (1974), Pina Bausch (1975), Valery Panov (1977), Paul Taylor (1980), Richard Alston (1981), and Martha Graham (1984).

[*See also the entry on Nijinsky.*]

BIBLIOGRAPHY

Acocella, Joan, Lynn Garafola, and Jonnie Greene. "*The Rite of Spring* Considered as a Nineteenth-Century Ballet." *Ballet Review* 20 (Summer 1992): 68–71.

Acocella, Joan, Lynn Garafola, and Jonnie Greene. "Rites of Spring." *Ballet Review* 20 (Summer 1992): 68–98. Includes a catalog of *Rite of Spring* ballets, plus extensive bibliographies.

Berg, Shelley C. *"Le Sacre du Printemps": Seven Productions from Nijinsky to Martha Graham.* Ann Arbor, Mich., 1988.

Bullard, Truman Campbell. "The First Performance of Igor Stravinsky's *Sacre du Printemps.*" Ph.D. diss., University of Rochester, 1971. Includes a collection of the French reviews, in French and in translation.

Craft, Robert. "The Rite: Counterpoint and Choreography." *Musical Times* 129 (April 1988): 171–176.

Garafola, Lynn. *Diaghilev's Ballets Russes.* New York, 1989.

Hodson, Millicent. "Ritual Design in the New Dance: Nijinsky's *Le Sacre du Printemps.*" *Dance Research* 3 (Autumn 1985): 34–45.

Hodson, Millicent. *Nijinsky's Crime against Grace: Reconstruction Score of the Original Choreography for "Le Sacre du Printemps."* Stuyvesant, N.Y., 1996.

Kirstein, Lincoln, et al. *Nijinsky Dancing.* New York, 1975.

Macdonald, Nesta. *Diaghilev Observed by Critics in England and the United States, 1911–1929.* New York and London, 1975.

Nijinska, Bronislava. *Early Memoirs.* Translated and edited by Irina Nijinska and Jean Rawlinson. New York, 1981.

Rivière, Jacques. "Le Sacre du Printemps." *Nouvelle Revue Française* (1 November 1913). Excerpt translated by Miriam Lassman and published in *What Is Dance?*, edited by Roger Copeland and Marshall Cohen (New York, 1983).

Stravinsky, Igor. *The Rite of Spring, Le Sacre du Printemps: Sketches, 1911–1913.* London, 1969.

Stravinsky, Vera, and Robert Craft. *Stravinsky in Pictures and Documents.* New York, 1978.

Taruskin, Richard. *Stravinsky and the Russian Traditions: A Biography of the Works through "Mavra."* Berkeley, 1996.

ARCHIVES. The Rambert Dance Company Archive, London, contains a photocopy of Marie Rambert's annotated score of *Sacre.* The Dance Collection of the New York Public Library for the Performing Arts has a photocopy of Stravinsky's annotated score; the original is at the Paul Sacher Foundation (Basel). A slightly less detailed version of his annotations can be found in Stravinsky's *The Rite of Spring, Le Sacre du Printemps: Sketches, 1911–1913.*

JOAN ACOCELLA

SADDLER, DONALD (born 24 January 1920 in Van Nuys, California), American dancer, choreographer, and director. A choreographer and director of unusual versatility, Donald Saddler is especially noted for his work in musical theater and gala performances. He has roots both in ballet and—from performing since age nine—in theater. Rather than starting with a personal style or a technical vocabulary, he prefers working with the period, style, and feeling of a particular subject.

Saddler grew up in California, steeped in American popular music, dance, and films. There he studied ballroom dance with Nico Charisse and ballet with Theodore Koslov and Carmelita Maracci, while attending Los Angeles City College and dancing in films to support himself.

Moving to New York, Saddler joined Ballet Theatre (1939–1943 and 1946–1947, interrupted by military service), becoming a soloist with varied roles, including the Antony Tudor repertory, Alias in *Billy the Kid,* and the Friend in *Swan Lake.* He danced in the musical *High Button Shoes* (1948), among other shows, partnering Valerie

Bettis in *Bless You All* (1950). He established his own company in 1958 and appeared as guest artist with Bettis's Dance Theatre in 1960. Saddler attended classes in modern dance with Doris Humphrey and Hanya Holm, and others in acting, all at the American Theatre Wing, as well as Katherine Dunham's technique at her school.

Saddler choreographed for numerous musicals, receiving two Tony awards for *Wonderful Town* and the 1971 revival of *No, No, Nanette,* for which he also received a New York Drama Desk Award. Of the letter Hubert Saal wrote that Saddler "staged the musical numbers with high style, flawless taste and real love. Authenticity was Saddler's goal." This 1930s-vintage show, in which Ruby Keeler returned to the stage, was instrumental in reviving interest in tap dance. Saddler was also nominated for Tony awards for choreography for the 1972 *Much Ado about Nothing* and the 1982 revival of *On Your Toes.* More recent work has included the 1993 revival of *My Fair Lady.*

His work as choreographer, director, and producer has extended to ballet companies (Joffrey and Harkness), drama (New York Shakespeare Festival), opera (New York City Opera, Metropolitan Opera, Los Angeles Civic Light Opera, and Washington Opera), ice ballet (*Palais de Glace* for John Curry's Ice Dancing, 1978), films (including several for Doris Day, and Woody Allen's *Radio Days,* 1987), and television (Bell Telephone Hour, Tony awards shows, and others) in the United States, Italy, and England. His stagings of tributes and galas for the performing arts have been marked by graceful presentation of artists, sure pacing, and warm atmosphere.

Saddler served as assistant to the director of the Harkness Ballet (1964–1967), becoming associate director (1967–1969) and executive vice president of the Rebekah Harkness Foundation (1967–1969), overseeing the Harkness School. He also produced the New York Dance Festival at the Delacorte Theater in Central Park for five seasons. He received a *Dance Magazine* Award in 1984.

BIBLIOGRAPHY

Current Biography (January 1963).

Gale, Joseph. "The Broadway Musical: Sweet? Or Turned Sour?" *Dance Magazine* (October 1971): 51–66.

Gruen, John. "Reviving *On Your Toes.*" *Dance Magazine* (March 1983): 60–67.

McDonagh, Don. "The 'Nanette' Log." *Ballet Review* 3.5 (1971): 34–45.

Michaels, Paul. "Whoever Heard of Dancing in the Dark?" *After Dark* (July 1970): 34–41.

Saal, Hubert. "The Dance: Broadway Rhythm." *Newsweek* (13 December 1971).

INTERVIEW. Donald Saddler, by Marilyn Hunt (1978–1979), Dance Collection, New York Public Library for the Performing Arts.

VIDEOTAPES. "American Dance Machine" (1978) and "Gala Performance in Barcelona" (1966), both in the Dance Collection, New York Public Library for the Performing Arts.

MARILYN HUNT

SADLER'S WELLS BALLET. *See* Royal Ballet.

SAINT-ANDRÉ, ADRIEN MERGER DE (born 1635 in Paris, died July 1716 in Paris), French dancer and choreographer. Adrien was the third child of Charlotte Mesnager and Gilles Merger, called Saint-André, a violinist in the service of Louis XIV. Nothing is known of Adrien's training, but his name appears on programs of French court ballets as early as *Les Dérèglements des Passions* in January 1648. He continued to appear in ballets, plays, and operas, including *L'Amour Malade* (1657), *Royal D'alcidiane* (1658), *Des Saisons* (1661), Des Arts (1663), and *Les Noces du Village* (1663), *Des Plaisirs de l'Isle Enchantée* (1664), *Royal de la Naissance de Vénus* (1665), *Des Muses* (1666), *Royal de Flore* (1669), *Divertissement Royal* (1670), and *Ballet des Ballets* (1671). He was also in several of the collaborations of Jean-Baptiste Lully with Molière: *Le Mariage Forcé* (1664), *Georges Dandin* (1668), *Les Amants Magnifiques* (1670) (in which Louis XIV made his last appearance as a dancer), *Le Bourgeois Gentilhomme* (1670), the lyrical tragedy *Psyché* (written with Pierre Corneille and Philippe Quinault, 1671), and *Les Festes de l'Amour et de Bacchus* (1672). Many of these works were staged by Lully himself with his close collaborator, choreographer Pierre Beauchamps. One of Saint-André's younger brothers (referred to in the livrets as Saint-André *cadet*) was also a dancer at the French court. Saint-André was occasionally hired to choreograph ballets at the Jesuit Collège de Clermont in Paris (later called Louis-le-Grand). For the college he composed and danced in *Les Tartares Convertis* in 1657 and the *Ballet de la Vérité* in 1663. His collaborator and partner in both was the dancer Desbrosses.

When Louis XIV visited the Académie Royale de Musique in 1672 for *Les Fêtes de l'Amour et de Bacchus,* one *entrée* was danced by four noblemen and four professionals, including Saint-André. James Crofts, duke of Monmouth, the illegitimate son of Charles II of England, was among these nobles who had a passion for dancing. Monmouth shortly afterward arranged for Saint-André to come to the Duke's Theatre in London (probably in 1674) to choreograph a new version of *Psyche,* written by Thomas Shadwell (vocal music by John Locke, dance music and interludes by Giovanni Battista Draghi, and elaborate new sets by "Mr. Stephenson"). Saint-André apparently brought French dancers to join him in this successful production, which opened 24 February 1675. Saint-André also danced at court that same month in John Crowne's masque *Calisto,* choreographed by Josiah Priest. The dances in *Psyche* seem to have been in the style of the *ballet de cour,* such as the act 1 "Entry for Four Sylvans and Four Dryads to Rustick Music" and the act 4 "Cyclops Dance."

How long Saint-André remained in London is unknown, but he taught dancing to fashionable society and a reference in Sir George Etherege's comedy *The Man of Mode* seems to establish him there at least until 1676. A reference in John Dryden's satire *MacFlecknoe* (1682) suggests his continuing fame, but he probably had returned to Paris by then. According to biographer Régine Astier, his name appears on the list of members of the Académie Royale de Danse in 1682, showing that he was recently elected. In 1695 his name came second, following Pierre Beauchamps, suggesting that he may have replaced Louis Hilaire d'Olivet as secretary of the Académie. His son-in-law, Louis Germain, also became one of the Académie's thirteen members. Saint-André continued to teach dancing in Paris (as a reference in the London *Post-Boy* for 4–6 February 1696 makes clear); he died there in 1716 and was buried in the parish of Saint André-des-Arts.

Although there are few specific accounts of Saint-André as a dancer or choreographer, he had worked closely with Beauchamps and Lully during the early years of their important collaboration. He seems to have been a strong performer who also helped reinforce the British taste for the French style in dance, setting a high standard for British dancers. As a teacher, his position in the Académie Royale de Danse attests to Beauchamps's high regard for him.

[*See also* Académie Royale de Danse *and the entries on the principal figures mentioned herein.*]

BIBLIOGRAPHY

Christout, Marie-Françoise. *Le ballet de cour de Louis XIV, 1643–1672.* Paris, 1967.

Fletcher, Ifan Kyrle. "Ballet in England, 1660–1740." In *Famed for Dance: Essays on the Theory and Practice of Theatrical Dancing in England,* by Ifan Kyrle Fletcher et al. New York, 1960.

Highfill, Philip H., Jr., et al. "St. Andreé." In *A Biographical Dictionary of Actors, Actresses, Musicians, Dancers, Managers, and Other Stage Personnel in London, 1660–1800.* Carbondale, Ill., 1973–.

ARCHIVE. Bibliothèque Nationale, Paris: Fichier Laborde 117, CXVII, nos. 47928 and 47937.

RÉGINE ASTIER and GEORGE DORRIS

ST. DENIS, RUTH (Ruth Dennis; born 27 January 1879 in New Jersey, died 21 July 1968 in Hollywood, California), American dancer and choreographer. Ruth Dennis was the eldest child of Thomas Laban Dennis and Ruth Emma Hull, who were natives of England. Her father had immigrated with his family to Boonton, New Jersey, before the Civil War and had later enlisted in the New Jersey Cavalry. Her mother's family had settled in Canandaigua, New York, the heart of what was called the "burned-over district" because of its association with intense religious revivalism; there, her mother had been exposed to the diverse cultural influences of Methodism, utopian socialism, Swedenborgianism, phrenology, and mesmerism—she became a freethinker and a feminist, a legacy passed on to her daughter. In 1872 her mother had been the second female graduate of the University of Michigan Medical School. A nervous ailment had prevented her from practicing medicine, so she had sought treatment for her neurasthenia at the Jackson Sanitarium in Dansville, New York, where she had been introduced to the principles of dress reform and the use of dancing as therapy. She had later drifted into an artists' colony near Perth Amboy, New Jersey, where she had met Tom Dennis, who divorced his first wife in 1878 to marry her. In December of 1878, in a hasty ceremony in the studio of the artist William Page, a marriage by contract had agreed that the parties were wed, without clergy or license. One month later, their daughter Ruth was born.

The circumstances of St. Denis's birth helped shape her character. Bohemianism and conservatism mingled in her personality. She became extraordinarily sensitive to social ostracism, fearful of sexuality and of pregnancy. When the Dennis family moved to Pin Oaks Farm near Somerville, New Jersey, they were considered odd by their neighbors. Mrs. Dennis refused to wear corsets or bustles; Tom Dennis drank heavily and was unable to hold a steady job. The family was joined by Tom's son from his previous marriage and by a baby boy, whose only given name was Brother. Ruth escaped family and social pressures by romping in the countryside and indulging her talent for mimicry and acrobatics. Her father, a machinist by trade, preferred to spend his time designing bicycles, dynamos, and other inventions that he patented but never managed to manufacture. To supplement the family income, Mrs. Dennis converted the family home into a boardinghouse that catered to a bohemian clientele. The boarders, an assortment of Christian Scientists, Theosophists, and vacationing artists and actors from New York City, regularly gathered on the farmhouse veranda to watch the antics of the talented Dennis daughter, Ruth.

To channel this talent, Mrs. Dennis arranged dancing lessons for her daughter at the Maud Davenport school in Somerville, where Ruth studied ballroom and skirt dancing. Mrs. Dennis also drilled her daughter in Delsarte theory and technique, using a manual acquired from a visiting Delsarte teacher, Aurilla Colcord Poté. With her agile body and quick mind, Ruth mastered a blend of Delsarte poses, dancing steps, and acrobatics, which she demonstrated in a series of performances arranged by her mother under the rubric of the Pin Oaks Dramatic Club. The entire Dennis family appeared in the club's plays, but the undisputed star was the fourteen-year-old Ruth. As a reviewer for the *Somerset Unionist Gazette* wrote in 1893, "For so young a person she displayed really remarkable talent."

Determined to promote this talent, Mrs. Dennis wrote to the New York dancing master Karl Marwig and requested an audition. In the spring of 1891 Ruth peddled watercress to her neighbors to earn money for the New York trip. After she performed an improvised Spanish dance for Marwig, the teacher encouraged her to pursue a professional stage career.

These plans were interrupted, however, when relatives anxious to prevent a stage career financed a term for Ruth at Dwight Moody's Northfield Seminary in Massachusetts. Ruth remained at the school through most of one term, until she argued with the famed evangelist over the merits of a stage career. She fled home in time to appear in the Pin Oaks Dramatic Club production of *The Old Homestead.* Stagestruck, she accompanied her mother on frequent trips to New York, where on one occasion they attended a concert by Genevieve Stebbins, a leading exponent of the Delsarte system. Stebbins's concert of statue poses ignited St. Denis's imagination and became, as she wrote in her autobiography, "the real birth of my art life."

Another deep impression on her budding artistic sensibility was made by an outdoor spectacle at the Eldorado resort on the Jersey Palisades. St. Denis attended *Egypt through Centuries* with a family friend and watched "110 centuries of Egyptian culture" unfold in a series of colorful tableaux. Most exciting was the "Grand Ballet of the Virgins," with hundreds of young dancers moving in synchrony as a sacrificial virgin ascended temple steps and flung herself from them into the River Nile. Years later, in her own Egyptian ballet, St. Denis borrowed the themes of *Egypt through Centuries* and wed them to the form of Genevieve Stebbins's statue poses.

During a trip to New York in January 1894 St. Denis obtained her first professional job at Worth's Family Theatre and Museum. During the week of 29 January she performed as a skirt dancer on a variety bill that included a juggler and Lillie the Trick Dog. Worth's Museum typified the uneasy American attitude toward the performing arts. Advertising itself as an "instructive, moral, and entertaining" museum, Worth's disguised its popular entertainment as education and moral instruction. St. Denis, whose career began in this environment, reflected this ambivalence in her own art.

From these humble beginnings at Worth's, the fifteen-year-old dancer gradually obtained more remunerative employment, appearing in such posh establishments as the Metropolitan Opera Vaudeville Club and in variety houses such as the Casino Theatre. Throughout the 1890s, with a year out for schooling at the Packer Collegiate Institute in Brooklyn, St. Denis built a solid career in the variety theater, performing variously as "Ruth" and "The Only Ruth."

Variety dancing at the turn of the twentieth century was the incubator for American modern dance. St. Denis and other variety dancers explored ways to motivate and regenerate the static posing that dance had become. The progress of dance during this period might be likened to the evolution of photography into film. The task for early modern dancers was to connect movement to an ongoing motivational and motional impulse. St. Denis's primary tools were the Delsarte exercises that had developed her naturally flexible spine and taught her such "successional" movements as a jointless arm ripple that she added to her routines. She also used the swirl of draperies, which had been popularized by Loie Fuller, to extend her movements into space and to provide a frame for her moving body. Using her natural gifts, she exploited her flexible arms and torso, creating a sculptural movement that edged her toward modern dance. By the time she discovered Indian dancing and borrowed its polyrhythms and its triple-torsional and flexional contours of the body, she had added a philosophical and emotional motivation to her dances that earned for her the right to be regarded as a mother of American modern dance.

As St. Denis's variety career developed, her mother became her manager, a tireless promoter and rigorous critic of her daughter's dancing. In time the entire Dennis family relocated to Brooklyn, though St. Denis's parents soon separated, leaving her as her mother's sole means of support.

After an appearance in an Augustin Daly play in 1899, St. Denis successfully made the transition from variety to the legitimate theater. In 1900 she was hired for the road company of a David Belasco play and spent the next five years as a Belasco player, appearing in *Zaza, Madame DuBarry,* and *The Auctioneer.* Trained by Belasco as a dancer, singer, and actress, St. Denis learned the intricacies of stage lighting, authentic costuming, and set design. She also absorbed the craft of acting by watching Mrs. Leslie Carter, the Belasco protégée and stage star.

In 1900, while touring abroad with the Belasco company, St. Denis visited the Paris World's Exhibition, where she sampled the orientalism celebrated in that landmark fair. She saw Egyptian belly dancers, Turkish dervishes, Cambodian and Spanish dancers, the Art Nouveau–suffused dances of Loie Fuller, and the Japanese pantomimes of Yakko (known in Europe as Sada Yakko). Inspired by these influences, St. Denis devised her own first oriental dance, a Japanese solo that she hoped to perform in Belasco's 1900 production of *Madama Butterfly* (from a story by J. L. Long).

During this first trip abroad, St. Denis eagerly collected books on Buddhism and varieties of Eastern thought and, as was her habit, read voraciously. She also loved to scribble essays and mystical poetry, an avocation that earned for her the nickname "Miss Montgomery, the Mystic Girl." By 1903 her reading had led her to the serious study of Christian Science, a new religion scarcely twenty-five years old that she had first discovered through the boarders at Pin Oaks Farm. Christian Science stressed the spiritual nature of reality, the illusory nature of matter, and the essential harmony of existence, which manifests itself in the natural healing process. These themes echoed the interests of Mrs. Dennis, who herself had studied Christian Science. St. Denis, in turn, adopted the faith, though the official church twice rejected her for membership on the grounds that she occasionally indulged in medicines. While she advocated Christian Science, she also read widely in Buddhism, Vedanta, and Christian theology.

Her spiritual search led her to question the direction of her career. By now in her mid-twenties, she remained a minor player in the Belasco company, with only an occasional speaking role to supplement her chorus work and

ST. DENIS. A studio portrait in costume for *Radha,* taken in Paris, 1908. Upon examination, trick photography is revealed: strings were attached to the hem of St. Denis's skirt to raise folds and create the illusion of spinning. *Radha* culminated in a solo called "The Mystic Dance of the Five Senses," a whirling dance meant to symbolize a total delirium of the senses. (Photograph from the Dance Collection, New York Public Library for the Performing Arts.)

dances. She longed to create a spiritually significant art and spent her spare time in libraries along the tour route, studying books on oriental religions and varieties of mysticism. During a Belasco tour in 1904 she spied in a drugstore window in Buffalo, New York, a poster advertising Egyptian Deities cigarettes. Gazing at the poster with its depiction of the goddess Isis meditating on the virtues of Turkish cigarettes, St. Denis suddenly envisioned an artistic form for her spiritual quest. She resigned from the Belasco company, returned to New York, and gathered a group of East Indian university students, clerks, and Coney Island performers. With the help of her mother and her library notes, she began rehearsals for her first major dance.

The dance that emerged, *Radha,* launched her solo career. A blend of exotic spectacle and morality tale, the dance depicts an Indian goddess who wrestles with, but overcomes, the temptations of the flesh. The dance established the basic structure and theme of the dances that St. Denis performed over the next fifty years. She first presented *Radha* at the New York Theatre in January 1906; the dance was then sponsored by a group of art patrons and socialites in a matinee concert at the Hudson Theatre in New York. For that 22 March 1906 performance she changed her name to Ruth St. Denis, the "saint" nickname having been supplied by her mentor Belasco. She also added two new Indian dances to her program, *The Incense,* a ceremony of worship in which her undulating arms emulated the wafting of incense smoke, and *The Cobras,* a snake-charmer dance set in a noisy bazaar. One source of these dances was the Streets of Delhi exhibition at Coney Island, where St. Denis had seen snake charmers and dancing girls. [*See* Radha.]

The Hudson Theater matinee made St. Denis a theatrical sensation. After a brief American tour she departed for Europe in the time-honored tradition of young American artists who sought the cachet of international success. She began her tour in London, where she danced for King Edward VII, then traveled to Paris, where she encountered the first of many imitators who tried to capitalize on her success.

In the winter of 1906 St. Denis traveled to Berlin in the company of her mother, who served as stage manager, chaperon, and deterrent to any offstage romance. For the next three years St. Denis made Berlin her base, touring German opera houses with her triple bill of *Radha, The Incense,* and *The Cobras.* In 1908 she added two new dances to her program, *The Nautch,* a saucy Indian street dance with *kathak* foot rhythms, and *The Yogi,* a pantomimic study of an Indian ascetic meditating in a forest.

During her stay in Germany, St. Denis was lionized by a group of artists and intellectuals who helped her achieve her own artistic and intellectual maturity. Chief among them were Hugo von Hofmannsthal, the Viennese poet, librettist, and critic, and the arts patron Count Harry Kessler. Hofmannsthal wrote in the journal *Die Zeit* one of the finest notices of St. Denis's career; a perceptive essay, it identified the paradox at the heart of her art:

> In this extraordinarily hieratic art—strange combination of a strangely alive being with primeval tradition—every trace of sentimentality has vanished. It is the same with her smile, and this it is that from the first moment estranges the hearts of women and the sensual curiosity of men on seeing Ruth St. Denis. And it is just this that makes her dancing incomparable. It borders on voluptuousness but it is chaste. It is consecrated to the senses, but it is a symbol of something higher. It is wild, but bound by external laws. It could not be other than it is.

Enchanted by her dancing, Hofmannsthal and Kessler introduced St. Denis to the artistic and intellectual elite of Vienna and Berlin.

In Berlin, Count Kessler arranged a meeting between St. Denis and Max Reinhardt, who invited the dancer to appear in a forthcoming production of Oscar Wilde's *Salomé* at his Kammerspielhaus. The project apparently never materialized, but a full description of St. Denis's ideas for *Salomé* is included in the Kessler-Hofmannsthal correspondence. For the first time in her career St. Denis found her art taken seriously. The German experience strengthened her resolve to leave behind the variety theater, to make her way onto the legitimate concert stage.

Returning to New York City in the summer of 1909, she found a cultural climate primed for her art. As a Boston journalist explained, the United States had become infected with "the somewhat prevalent microbe of Orientalism." Ernest Fenollosa's Chautauqua lectures, Lafcadio Hearn's oriental tales, and John LaFarge's Japanese-inspired art fed the American appetite for exotica. Japanese, Chinese, Filipino, and Korean spectacles crowded the American theater, while advertisements for Chinese porcelains, Japanese kimonos, and Turkish cigarettes filled American periodicals. A popular song of the pre–World War I era, "The Egypt in Your Smile," summarized the appeal of St. Denis's dancing:

All the Orient is in your smile,
Mysterious as the River Nile,
And you stole my heart
With your cunning heart
And the Egypt in your smile.

Famous and fashionable during the years between 1909 and 1914, St. Denis performed both on the concert stage and on the society circuit. In 1913 she was the featured attraction at an Egyptian costume fête hosted by Louis Tiffany. As the New York Philharmonic Orchestra played a pseudo-oriental tune by Theodore Steinway, four "Nubian slaves" carried aloft a rolled oriental rug, which spilled forth St. Denis, who performed an Egyptian dance.

ST. DENIS. In *Legend of the Peacock* (1914), first performed in Chicago's Ravinia Park, St. Denis portrayed the favorite dancing girl of a rajah whose jealous wife dooms her to inhabit a peacock's body. This work, which epitomized Denishawn's Orientalia, was a staple in the company's repertory for several years. (Photograph from the Dance Collection, New York Public Library for the Performing Arts.)

Her more serious work, inspired by her German experience, took the form of evening-length dance dramas that included dialogue. *Egypta,* which had its premiere 12 December 1910 at the New Amsterdam Theatre in New York, was the fruition of St. Denis's earliest dance idea. She combined elements of Genevieve Stebbins's statue poses, effects from the spectacle *Egypt through Centuries,* and the image of the goddess from the Egyptian Deities cigarette poster. The four-act ballet, which featured a score by Walter Meyrowitz, was carefully researched and authentic in its historical detail. The enormous cost of this spectacle was borne by St. Denis's new manager, Henry B. Harris, who perished tragically with the sinking of the ocean liner *Titanic* in the midst of rehearsals for St. Denis's second dance drama. She managed to complete her program of *Bakawali,* a Hindu ballet, and *O-Mika,* a Japanese dance drama, in 1913, but Harris's death effectively ended this experimental phase of her career.

To recoup the losses incurred by her dance dramas, St. Denis toured American cities and small towns performing

ST. DENIS. In addition to Oriental-theme ballets, St. Denis created a number of lyrical, Duncanesque dances. Most famous was her pair of solos *Brahams Waltz* and *Liebestraum,* set to Liszt's music. This portrait, c.1931, shows her in a flowing chiffon costume typical of this genre of dances. (Photograph from the Dance Collection, New York Public Library for the Performing Arts.)

solo dances excerpted from her longer productions. She also began choreographing lyrical solos inspired by Isadora Duncan's dancing. The finest of these solos, *Liebestraum* (1922), was a free-form waltz to Liszt's piano composition that allowed St. Denis to use her expressive arms to suggest a story of unrequited love. Her repertory of oriental and lyrical solos waned in popularity, however, as American audiences discovered ballroom dancing, a fad ignited by Irene and Vernon Castle. St. Denis decided to expand her act and in 1914 auditioned a young male dancer, Ted Shawn, who became her partner and, in short time, her husband.

Shawn, a divinity student turned dancer, was twelve years St. Denis's junior. Trained in ballet and ballroom dance, he was the perfect complement to St. Denis's high-minded moralism. When she confided to him her vision of a great temple of the dance, where purity of body, mind, and soul might fuse in artistic expression, Shawn promised to build her one. After a brief struggle with Mrs. Dennis, who opposed the match, Shawn overcame St. Denis's own reluctance, and they were married on 13 August 1914. With a small company they continued touring the United States until they settled in Los Angeles, where they established a school.

The Ruth St. Denis School of the Dance and Its Related Arts, or Denishawn as it became known, opened in the summer of 1915 to a clientele that included silent film actresses eager to polish their gestural skills, aspiring dancers, and young ladies who attended Denishawn as a finishing school. Among those students were Martha Graham, who came to Denishawn in the summer of 1916, and Doris Humphrey, who arrived the following year. Louis Horst joined Denishawn as music director and offered courses in counterpoint, harmony, and the theory and history of music. Other courses in the curriculum included classes in Delsarte gesture, classical ballet, character dancing, Dalcrozian music analysis, fabric manipulation and plastique, Greek and oriental dancing, and dance history and philosophy. Shawn was the organizational genius behind Denishawn and taught most of the classes, while "Miss Ruth" contributed demonstrations of her solo dances and gave lofty philosophical monologues.

During the winter months St. Denis and Shawn toured with their first Denishawn company, which included among its dancers Margaret Loomis and Carol Dempster, both of whom later made film careers. The company performed a few dates in concert halls, but their bread and butter was the vaudeville circuit. A staple of this earliest Denishawn repertory was *Radha,* and St. Denis expanded some of her other solos to include a moving backdrop for company dancers.

The most prestigious concert date for the first Denishawn company was an invitation from the Greek Theatre of the University of California at Berkeley; it was the first time that dancers had been invited to appear in the theater's summer festival. Denishawn's *Dance Pageant of Egypt, Greece, and India,* which opened 29 July 1916, featured the entire student body of the Denishawn school as well as dancers recruited from the summer school classes of the university. Essentially a reworking of *Egypta* and St. Denis's East Indian dances, the pageant was a three-part depiction of the daily life and spiritual beliefs of three ancient civilizations. One of the most enduring dances from the pageant was *Tillers of the Soil,* a moving duet choreographed by St. Denis and Shawn that portrayed them as Egyptian peasants in their cycle of daily work. The dance remained in the Denishawn repertory for years and is the only St. Denis–Shawn duet preserved on film.

While the Denishawn company was on tour in 1917, the directors learned that the United States had declared war on Germany. Shawn resisted joining the armed forces for as long as was practical so that he might keep the Denishawn school and company functioning. But in 1918 he received a draft notice and immediately enlisted in the Army Ambulance Corps. St. Denis took this opportunity to confront a recurring tension in her career, an issue that threatened her marriage. She thought of herself as a serious, highbrow concert dancer even though the root of her art was the lowbrow variety stage. She prized experimentation but found that financial necessity forced her to create a popular art that was palatable to vaudeville audiences. In Denishawn she felt trapped in an institutional environment that siphoned her creative energies and ideas even as it paid her bills. This tension between popular and fine art became a persistent leitmotif in St. Denis's career and a constant source of friction between her and Shawn. While he was in the army, she decided to retire from vaudeville and concentrate her energies on her own artistic goals.

She formed a small company, the Ruth St. Denis Concert Dancers, which included Doris Humphrey, who served as her assistant; Pearl Wheeler doubled as dancer and costume designer. Inspired by Isadora Duncan's dancing and by the Dalcroze system of rhythmic exercises, St. Denis devised a repertory of "music visualizations," which she defined as "the scientific translation into bodily action of the rhythmic, melodic, and harmonic structure of a musical composition." To piano compositions by Debussy, Beethoven, Chopin, Brahms, and Schumann, St. Denis and Humphrey choreographed dances characterized by wafting silk scarves and lyrical movement.

One of these music visualizations, which has survived, is *Soaring,* a visualization of Schumann's *Aufschwung: Fantasiestücke.* Four girls grasp a heavy silken square at each of its four corners, hoist it high, then let its ballooning form collapse in an approximation of the dynamics and pitch of the piano composition. In St. Denis's music visualizations, the dancers' movements echoed, sometimes slavishly, the architectural structure of the musical score. On each musical rest, the dancers paused. They repeated phrases on musical repeats, sank to the stage when the musical scale descended, and rose on tiptoe with each rise to treble clef. Intermittently they grouped themselves into Delsarte poses of Greek inspiration. The standard costume design for these music visualizations was a silk chiffon shift worn over a flesh-tone leotard, bare feet, and a curly blond wig.

After the war ended and Shawn was released from the army, he begged St. Denis to rejoin him in a revived Denishawn. Their marriage was troubled, plagued by fleeting infidelities and artistic rivalry, but professionally they depended on each other for support. Although St. Denis believed that Denishawn was death to her creativity, she needed the company for financial survival. Her cherished concert company had proved to be an artistic success but a commercial failure. Reluctantly she rejoined Denishawn.

From 1922 to 1925, the vintage years for Denishawn, the company brought dance to American cities and small towns under the management of Daniel Mayer. The company included Charles Weidman, Martha Graham, who left after the first season to join the Greenwich Village Follies, and Doris Humphrey, who became the troupe's principal dancer. The repertory consisted of Shawn's ballets, colorful and sometimes comic productions with ethnic or American themes, and St. Denis's more mystical morality plays built around oriental heroines. She represented a broad range of exotic goddesses and royalty, from the Byzantine empress Theodora to the Chinese goddess Guanyin (Kuan Yin). These dances often followed the *Radha* formula, beginning and ending in tranquillity, with a moral struggle in between. Typical of her Denishawn ballets was *Ishtar of the Seven Gates,* choreographed for the second Mayer tour. A retelling of the Babylonian myth of the goddess of fertility, the dance follows Ishtar (St. Denis) as she descends into Hades in search of her lover (Shawn), whom she rescues after a struggle with the Queen of the Underworld (Humphrey).

ST. DENIS. As the Naga Queen in *Angkor Vat,* St. Denis sported seven cobra heads in her fan-shaped headdress. Costumed by Pearl Wheeler and set to music by Sol Cohen, this work was first performed in 1930 at Lewisohn Stadium, New York. (Photograph from the archives at Jacob's Pillow, Becket, Massachusetts.)

The Mayer tours represented Denishawn at its zenith. As a touring company it educated a generation of Americans about dancing. As a franchise operation it conducted the main Denishawn schools in California and New York as well as authorized branch schools in a dozen American cities. The Ampico piano roll company distributed rolls of Denishawn technique classes, recital dances, and music visualizations. An entire course of study was available by mail order from Denishawn. Americans in the 1920s may have missed seeing Anna Pavlova or the Russian Ballet, but they almost certainly knew of Denishawn.

St. Denis was in her midforties during the Mayer tours. She was tired of a life of one-night stands, unhappy in her marriage, and artistically stifled. She considered retirement but was dissuaded by a lucrative offer of a company tour to Asia. After building her career on pseudo-oriental dances, St. Denis finally had the opportunity to examine the mother lode. Wary of taking her own oriental dances there, she prepared a repertory of her lyrical solos and music visualizations, with only a few samples of her more famous exotic solos.

In the summer of 1925, at the close of the third Mayer tour, the Denishawn company, with St. Denis's brother Buzz as stage manager, sailed for Japan. Among the twelve dancers who made the trip were Humphrey, Weidman, and Jane Sherman, who later recalled that no matter how early the Denishawn dancers arose to visit some oriental tourist site, invariably St. Denis would already be there, posing for publicity photographs. The company spent fifteen months touring Japan, China, Malaya, Burma, India, Ceylon, Indonesia, Indochina, and the Philippines, acquiring authentic costumes, properties, and sets along the way. They also studied briefly with prominent performers, including Matsumoto Koshiro, leading actor of the Imperial Theater in Tokyo, and Mei Lanfang in Beijing.

The Denishawn repertory gained new material from this tour; among the new works were *Momiji Gari,* based on Matsumoto's ballet drama of the same title, and *General Wu Says Farewell to His Wife,* a replica of a dance performed in Beijing by Mei Lanfang. St. Denis was inspired to create one of her most famous solos during a visit to the Altar of Heaven in Beijing. While standing at the center of that magnificent marble structure, she felt the "Sun of Life, pouring into my spirit" and conceived *White Jade,* one of her masterpieces. In the dance a porcelain figurine comes to life, manipulating white draperies in a languid plastique. St. Denis also found that her Indian solos were received enthusiastically by Asian audiences. Her *Dance of the Black and Gold Sari,* a clever display of the art of wrapping a sari, and her *Nautch* were enormously popular on tour. In India, where the British colonialists had suppressed native Indian dancing, St. Denis was credited with helping to revive the native art.

As the Denishawn company traveled through Asia, St. Denis and Shawn conducted a mobile argument that subsided each evening as the stage curtain rose and resumed immediately after it fell. The argument, which was central to their marital and artistic incompatibility, was never resolved. Shawn, a shrewd businessman and essentially an entertainer, favored the institutionalization of their art. St. Denis, who had no financial or managerial capabilities and minimal interest in the Denishawn school and company, was interested primarily in her own creative abilities. As Shawn argued for an expansion of their Denishawn empire, with a permanent New York facility, St. Denis contended that institutions only benefit already formed ideas. "As soon as they become crystallized they have already shed themselves from the creative spirit," she said.

Shawn won the argument, at least temporarily. When the Denishawn company returned from Asia, they began the construction of Denishawn House in New York City. A Moorish mansion with airy studios and a costume workshop, the Denishawn compound adjoined Jerome Reservoir near Van Cortlandt Park in the Bronx. It was a handsome structure, home to hundreds of students who came to Denishawn to study. To finance it, the Denishawn company undertook an arduous and unrewarding tour with the Ziegfeld Follies. Inaugurated with high hopes in 1927, Denishawn House survived but five years.

The stock market crash of October 1929 and the ensuing Great Depression hastened the demise of Denishawn and its directors' marriage. Disaffected students began to break away; Doris Humphrey and Charles Weidman, who disagreed with Denishawn policies, had left the company in 1928. Although dancers from the school and company performed summer concerts at City College's Lewisohn Stadium in New York until 1931, Denishawn was becoming passé. Martha Graham's radical experiments in dance were attracting a small but devoted following in New York, as were the Humphrey-Weidman concerts. John Martin, critic for the *New York Times,* championed this newly emerging modern dance and suggested that Denishawn dancing had become weak and artificial.

> How one would rejoice to see her bid a happy adieu to the old aestheticism; to watch her lay away in camphor balls all the veils and scarfs and garlands, and pack in chests the lyres and spears and torches, along with the pleasant tunes of Liszt and Chopin and Moskowski, which have for so long been the trimmings of Denishawn dancing. (Martin, 1928)

For St. Denis, Martin's advice came too late. She was forty-nine years old, with overdue bills and a broken marriage. Virtually overnight she became an out-of-work, middle-aged dancer. In 1934 the loan company foreclosed on the Denishawn mortgage, and she lost the school. Shawn, still young at thirty-seven, had left to pursue his own career and, ultimately, to direct the Jacob's Pillow Dance Festival in Becket, Massachusetts. The couple never divorced, but they never again lived together. St. Denis applied for welfare benefits in New York and settled into a small apartment-studio provided by a friend.

The decade of the 1930s was a bitter time for St. Denis, but with characteristic pluck she resurrected her life and career. She founded the Society of Spiritual Arts, which began as a philosophical discussion group and evolved into a performing ensemble. With the help of loyal dancers such as Anna Austin and Jack Cole, she directed her Rhythmic Choir in a series of church performances. These dances, exclusively on Christian themes, combined Delsarte poses and rhythmic postures with music visualization. One of her finest compositions, *The Masque of Mary,* was a ritual pageant that began with an organ prelude and readings from the Gospels and then introduced the Madonna (St. Denis), who posed on an altar while around her danced the Angels of the Heavenly Host. Sol Cohen, who frequently collaborated with St. Denis on her church dances, provided the score. The premiere of *The Masque of Mary,* at Riverside Church in New York City in 1934, inaugurated a new phase in St. Denis's career.

An important influence on St. Denis during this decade was the Chinese poet and diplomat Sum Nung Au-Young, who became her lover and mentor. Au-Young encouraged her to choreograph and write. In 1932 St. Denis published a collection of poems, *Lotus Light,* and in 1938 she found work as director of dance at Adelphi College (University) in Garden City, New York; the affiliation lasted into the 1960s. She also joined the ethnic dancer La Meri in establishing the School of Natya in New York City. St. Denis lent her presence, while La Meri did most of the teaching.

The most important event of the Depression decade for St. Denis, however, was the publication in 1939 of her autobiography, *An Unfinished Life,* ghostwritten by Henrietta Buckmaster. The translation of her life into art signaled a transformation of St. Denis's image and career: she graduated into the pantheon of dance pioneers. Transformed from an outmoded, middle-aged dancer into the esteemed mother of American modern dance, she found herself again in demand as a performer. Invited by Shawn to revive her earliest dances at Jacob's Pillow in 1941, St. Denis began a new phase of her career as a dancer of historical interest. The mythical St. Denis began to take shape. As Miss Ruth, the beloved First Lady of American Dance, St. Denis prolonged her performing career by another two decades. Tirelessly promoted by her devoted friend, the young critic Walter Terry, St. Denis created a new historic image, part *grande dame,* part theater gypsy still batting her eyelashes and spinning backstage yarns.

With the onset of World War II, St. Denis moved to Hollywood, California, to be near her brother, who built her a studio of her own. She briefly worked at the Douglas Aircraft Factory in Santa Monica, where another American dance pioneer, Maud Allan, also joined the wartime work. In Hollywood St. Denis opened her own dancing school, where she occasionally performed for her friends. In April 1945 she traveled east again for her first joint concert with Shawn in fifteen years. At Carnegie Hall in New York they performed *Tillers of the Soil* and other Denishawn dances as part of a benefit concert for Shawn's Jacob's Pillow Dance Festival. Edwin Denby, reviewing that concert, described the sixty-six-year-old St. Denis as still having "a wonderfully touching mildness and a striking clarity of movement. The tilt of the head, the turn of the wrists are in every way lovely and delicate."

ST. DENIS. Manipulating fans and cocking her head, St. Denis is pictured here in one of her Balinese-style solos, 1930. (Photograph from the archives at Jacob's Pillow, Becket, Massachusetts.)

During the 1950s and 1960s, St. Denis occasionally traveled back to the East Coast for appearances at Jacob's Pillow, where, in a culmination of the myth-making process, she celebrated her golden wedding anniversary with Shawn, with great fanfare, in 1964. She had received the Capezio Award in 1960 and was honored each year by a Ruth St. Denis Day at Adelphi University.

In May 1966, at the age of eighty-seven, she performed her *Incense* dance at Orange Coast College in Costa Mesa, California. It was her last public dance appearance. She suffered a bad fall but recovered sufficiently to give a lecture-demonstration later that year at the University of California at Los Angeles, the eventual recipient of many of the St. Denis papers. She died two years later in Hollywood of a heart attack and was cremated and interred at Forest Lawn Cemetery, in Los Angeles. On her vault are the lines of a St. Denis poem that begins, "The Gods have meant / That I should dance / And by the Gods / I will!"

[*See also* Denishawn *and the entry on Shawn. For related discussion, see* Costume in Western Traditions, *article on* Modern Dance.]

BIBLIOGRAPHY

Brady, Susan, ed. *After the Dance: Documents of Ruth St. Denis and Ted Shawn.* Performing Arts Resources, vol. 20. New York, 1997.

Coorlawala, Uttara Asha. "Ruth St. Denis and India's Dance Renaissance." *Dance Chronicle* 15.2 (1992): 123–152.

St. Denis, Ruth. *Lotus Light.* Boston, 1932.

St. Denis, Ruth. *An Unfinished Life.* 2d ed. New York, 1939.

Schlundt, Christena L. "An Account of Ruth St. Denis in Europe, 1906–1909." *Research Quarterly* 31 (March 1960): 82–91.

Schlundt, Christena L. *The Professional Appearances of Ruth St. Denis and Ted Shawn: A Chronology and Index of Dances, 1906–1932.* New York, 1962.

Schlundt, Christena L. "Into the Mystic with Miss Ruth." *Dance Perspectives,* no. 46 (1971).

Schlundt, Christena L. "The Choreographer of *Soaring.*" *Dance Chronicle* 6.4 (1983): 363–373.

Shawn, Ted. *Ruth St. Denis: Pioneer and Prophet.* San Francisco, 1920.

Shelton, Suzanne. "The Influence of Genevieve Stebbins on the Early Career of Ruth St. Denis." *CORD Dance Research Annual* 9 (1978): 33–49.

Shelton, Suzanne. "Ruth St. Denis: Dance Popularizer with 'High Art' Pretensions." In *American Popular Entertainment: Program and Papers of the Conference on the History of American Popular Entertainment,* edited by Myron Matlaw. Westport, Conn., 1979.

Shelton, Suzanne. *Divine Dancer: A Biography of Ruth St. Denis.* Garden City, N.Y., 1981.

Shelton, Suzanne, and Christena L. Schlundt. "Who's St. Denis? What Is She?" *Dance Chronicle* 10.3 (1987): 305–329.

Sherman, Jane. *Soaring: The Diary and Letters of a Denishawn Dancer in the Far East, 1925–1926.* Middletown, Conn., 1976.

Sherman, Jane. *The Drama of Denishawn Dance.* Middletown, Conn., 1979.

Terry, Walter. "The Legacy of Isadora Duncan and Ruth St. Denis." *Dance Perspectives,* no. 5 (1960).

Terry, Walter. *Miss Ruth: The "More Living Life" of Ruth St. Denis.* New York, 1969.

ARCHIVES. Denishawn Collection and Ted Shawn Collection, New York Public Library for the Performing Arts. Ruth St. Denis Collection, Special Collections of the University Research Library, University of California at Los Angeles.

SUZANNE SHELTON

SAINT FRANCIS. *See* Nobilissima Visione.

SAINT-LÉON, ARTHUR (Charles-Victor-Arthur-Michel Saint-Léon; born 17 September 1821 in Paris, died 2 September 1870 in Paris), French ballet dancer, violinist, composer, and choreographer. Arthur Saint-Léon was the son of Léon-Michel Saint-Léon, a dancer at the Paris Opera who was responsible for directing fight scenes. During his boyhood, his father encouraged him to develop his talents as a musician and dancer. He studied the violin with Joseph Mayseder and Niccolò Paganini and made his debut as a violinist at the age of thirteen in Stuttgart, where his father was employed as dancing master at the royal court. His dancing debut took place a year later in Munich, where he performed in a pas de deux in Joseph Schneider's *Die Reisende Ballett-Gesellschaft.*

The year 1837 found the sixteen-year-old Saint-Léon in Paris, where he gave two violin recitals and studied dancing with Monsieur Albert (François Decombe). He made his debut as a principal dancer in 1838 at the Théâtre Royal de la Monnaie in Brussels, in a *demi-caractère* dance arranged by Albert for a production of Giacomo Meyerbeer's opera *Robert le Diable.* In 1839 Saint-Léon appeared again at La Monnaie, in a revival of Albert's version of *Le Corsaire.* Subsequently, he went to Anvers and Vienna, performing as a violinist as well as a dancer. In 1841, at the Kärntnertor Theater in Vienna, he danced with Fanny Cerrito in Pierre-Jean Aniel's production of Jean Coralli's *Le Diable Boiteaux.* This was the first time that Cerrito and Saint-Léon danced together.

After appearing in Turin and Milan, Saint-Léon made his London debut in 1843 at Her Majesty's Theatre, where his youthful talent was recognized by both the public and the critics. A critic for *The Times* declared that

> his dancing is the sport of a young Hercules . . . . So amazing were his tours de force that he at once won the acclaim of a public which in general abhorred the presence of male dancers . . . . We cannot surmise how many times he goes round in a single spin. (*The Times,* 28 April 1843)

While in London, Saint-Léon again encountered Cerrito, whom he partnered at Her Majesty's Theatre in a *divertissement* called *Pas Styrien* and in the premiere of Jules Perrot's *Ondine, ou La Naïade* (1843). He also danced in a pas de quatre in Antonio Guerra's *Le Lac de Fées,* in which Cerrito appeared in the starring role. During this engagement, Saint-Léon fell in love with Cerrito and became her regular partner. [*See the entry on Cerrito.*] He followed her to Rome, where he danced with her in her ballet *L'Allieva d'Amore* and in *La Vivandiera ed il Postiglione,* which they had jointly choreographed. After their season in Rome, they performed in Parma and Florence.

Upon returning with Cerrito to London in April 1844, Saint-Léon presented a revised version of *La Vivandière,* set to new music by Cesare Pugni and including a new pas de deux danced to a redowa, a type of polka; this dance was described by one critic as "a capital thing of its kind . . . full of character, life and fun" (*The Times,* 24 May 1844). The ballet was also praised for Cerrito's *pas de la vi-*

vandière, the *pas de l'inconstance,* and the pas de six. Saint-Léon and Cerrito then toured the English cities of Bath, Brighton, and Bristol before embarking once more for Italy, where they danced in Bologna, Rome, and Venice. In Paris, they paused in their travels long enough to be married, on 17 April 1845, at the Église des Batignolles.

Saint-Léon and Cerrito then returned to Her Majesty's Theatre in London, where he resumed his role of Phoebus in Perrot's *La Esmeralda,* which he had created in 1844 opposite Carlotta Grisi. In May 1845, he created the leading role of Alman, opposite Cerrito, in the ballet *Rosida, ou Les Mines de Syracuse.* This ballet, although attributed solely to Cerrito, had been jointly choreographed by them both to a score by Pugni. Saint-Léon later inserted the ballet's popular *pas sicilienne* (Sicilian dance) into other ballets.

During the winter of 1845–1846, Saint-Léon and Cerrito went to Florence and Turin, where they created the leading roles in Luigi Astolfi's ballet *La Encatadora de Madrid.* In March 1846, Saint-Léon made his debut in Berlin as Albrecht in *Giselle.* Back in London in May, he created roles in two new ballets by Perrot: *Lalla Rookh, or The Rose of Lahore,* dancing opposite Cerrito in the title role, and *Le Jugement de Pâris,* dancing with Marie Taglioni, Lucile Grahn, and Cerrito. In January 1847, he restaged *Esmeralda* at the Königstheater in Berlin for his wife, while he himself danced opposite her in Perrot's former role of Gringoire. While in Berlin, Saint-Léon also made his debut as James in a production of Filippo Taglioni's *La Sylphide,* collaborated with Cerrito in choreographing and dancing a *divertissement* called *Der Maskenball,* and produced on his own a comic ballet, *Das Blümenmädchen im Elsass,* using music by August Conradi.

The year 1847 would prove to be even more eventful, and an important one for Saint-Léon's career, for he was commissioned by the Paris Opera to stage a new ballet, in which he and Cerrito were engaged to perform. He wrote voluminously to Henri Duponchel, the director of the Opera, as much to discuss his contract as to arrange various details of the ballet before his arrival. *La Fille de Marbre* was created in October. Essentially a revision of *Alma, ou La Fille de Feu,* a work created in 1842 by Cerrito, Perrot, and André Deshayes, it won favor with the king, Louis Philippe, and with critics. In *La presse* (28 October 1847), Théophile Gautier wrote,

> Saint-Léon caused astonishment by the taut boldness of his dancing and the strength of his jump. He succeeded in winning applause for himself, not an easy thing at a time when male dancing is out of favor. (Gautier, ed. Guest, 1986, p. 188)

Pier-Angelo Fiorentino, music critic for *Le moniteur,* called Saint-Léon "the most amazing, most extraordinary, the most aerial dancer that has ever been seen."

Delighted with their success in Paris, Saint-Léon and Cerrito departed for Venice, where, during the first part of 1848, he created no fewer than three ballets at the Teatro La Fenice. *Giovanna Maillote,* for which he wrote part of the music, was a revised version of *La Vivandière* that included the acclaimed *pas sicilienne* from *Rosida.* He both danced and played the violin in *Tartini il Violanista,* and in *L'Anti-Polkista ed i Polkamani* he exploited the possibili-

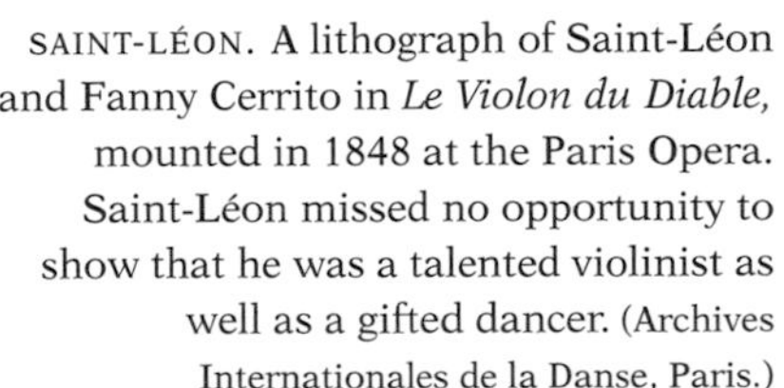

SAINT-LÉON. A lithograph of Saint-Léon and Fanny Cerrito in *Le Violon du Diable,* mounted in 1848 at the Paris Opera. Saint-Léon missed no opportunity to show that he was a talented violinist as well as a gifted dancer. (Archives Internationales de la Danse, Paris.)

ties of popular dances in ballet. The populace of Venice, which had just experienced a political revolution, much appreciated this kind of light entertainment.

After their customary season in London, Saint-Léon and Cerrito returned to Paris, where the Revolution of 1848 had also left its mark. After the bloody revolt of the June Days (23–26 June), Parisian audiences eagerly sought diversion. At the Opera, Saint-Léon revived *La Vivandière,* which remained in his repertory until 1872. In *La presse* (2 October 1848), Gautier observed,

> Saint-Léon was also much applauded. Not for a long time has a genuine male dancer been seen in France . . . . Since Perrot retired, Saint-Léon is the only man who has dared to dance at the Opera for the sake of dancing, and his success has been a surprise to everyone. (Gautier, ed. Guest, 1986, pp. 205–206)

His second creation, *Le Violon du Diable,* was a revision of *Tartini il Violanista,* set to a score of tunes written by himself, Stefano Felis, and one of his favorite composers, Cesare Pugni. As usual, he and Cerrito danced the leading roles. The ballet was praised by both Gautier and Jules Janin, theater critic of the *Journal des débats,* who declared,

> This M. Saint-Léon is a real demon. He dances a hundred times better than the famous zephyr of 1820 called Paul l'Aerien [Antoine Paul, nicknamed Paul the Aerial]; he plays the violin like Mlle Milanollo; he prepares a ballet as well as Théophile Gautier himself.

The indefatigable couple then left for a northern tour. Saint-Léon restaged a number of ballets, among them *Le Violon du Diable, La Vivandière,* and *Giselle,* in Königsberg (Prussia), where the couple's original two-week engagement was extended to six.

In February 1850, Saint-Léon staged *Stella, ou Les Contrebandiers* at the Paris Opera, again using music by Pugni. Set in Naples, the ballet included a number of character dances, among them the popular *pas sicilienne.* A critic for the *Journal des théâtres* (27 February 1850) stated, "Saint-Léon creates a style and seems to blend all that the dances of Europe possess in the way of piquant originality and dainty coquetry, while conforming to the traditions of the French school." In a later review, the same critic praised his performance as a dancer: "He has never ascended so high. He soars to the 'flies' like a rocket, he twirls like a leaf in a whirlwind—the stage might be made of India rubber."

Saint-Léon's next major production at the Opera was *Pâquerette* (1851), set to music of François Benoist, in which he and Cerrito danced the leading roles. In March 1851 the couple went to Madrid, where they danced at the Teatro Real. In June, after a period of heated quarrels, Saint-Léon returned alone to the Paris Opera, where he had accepted the post of principal ballet master. He and Cerrito had decided to separate, and they subsequently danced together only once more, at a gala in October 1851. When she came back to the Opera in December 1852, he gallantly gave way to her and left his post before his contract had expired.

During his eighteen months at the Paris Opera, from June 1851 to December 1852, Saint-Léon served not only as ballet master but as a leading dancer and the teacher of the *classe de perfectionnement.* During this time he put the finishing touches on his book on dance notation, *La sténochorégraphie, ou L'art d'écrire promptement la danse* (1852). He remained in Paris in 1853 to compose the music and devise the choreography for two new works at the Théâtre-Lyrique: *Le Danseur du Roi,* a *divertissement* featuring Spanish, Tyrolean, Neapolitan, Indian, and English dances, and *Le Lutin de la Vallée,* an *opéra-ballet* starring Marie Guy-Stéphan in which she performed two Spanish dances and he played a violin solo. After leaving Paris, he performed for a short season in London, at the Theatre Royal, Drury Lane, and then left for Portugal.

In Lisbon, where he worked for three years at the Teatro de São Carlos, Saint-Léon presented a repertory of old and new ballets. Among them were *Saltarello, ou O Maniaco po la Dança* (1854), a revision of *Le Danseur du Roi,* and *O Ensaio Geral, ou As Afflicçoés de Zefferini* (1855), for which he arranged the music. Among other works, he also presented *Os Saltimbancos, ou Os Processo do Fandango* (1856), to music orchestrated by Francisco Pinto, and *Météora, ou As Estrellas Cadentes* (1856), also set to a score by Pinto. His pamphlet *De l'état actuel de la danse,* published in Lisbon in 1856, criticized the contemporary dominance of the ballerina and proposed an improved system of training a corps de ballet.

Although Saint-Léon had been named a professor of the Lisbon Conservatory and awarded the Cross of the Order of Christ by the king of Portugal, the financial difficulties of the Teatro São Carlos prompted him to leave Lisbon in 1856. For eighteen months he toured Vienna, Turin, Dresden, Stuttgart, Munich, and other cities. In 1859 he was engaged as ballet master of the Imperial Theaters in Russia, a post that he held until his death. Because his duties occupied only six months of the year, he was able to accept other offers, and he divided his time between Paris and Saint Petersburg.

Saint-Léon's first ballet for the company of the Maryinsky Theater in Saint Petersburg was a revival of Joseph Mazilier's *Jovita, ou Les Boucaniers Mexicains,* staged for Carolina Rosati in 1859. He then restaged *Pâquerette,* in which Marie Petipa danced an important role, and created *Graziella, ou Les Dépits Amoureux* (1860), set to music by Pugni, for Rosati. *Météora* was restaged for Nadezhda Bogdanova, and *Théolinde l'Orpheline,* a revision of *Le Lutin de Vallée,* was mounted in 1862 for Marfa Muravieva, who triumphed in a dance before a mirror. During the following season in Paris, Saint-Léon staged *Diavolina* (1863) for Muravieva. Based largely on *Graziella,* this work was set in Italy and included a number of *demi-caractère* dances, such as La Scarpetta (The Dancing Pump), in which a young woman attempts to put on a shoe while dancing in order to discern if a certain youth is her future husband. He also mounted a work in Moscow entitled *Plamya Lyubvi* (Love's Flame; 1863), set to music of Léon Minkus, and soon to be revised as *Fiammetta.*

The next year in Saint Petersburg, Muravieva's performance in *Fiammetta, ou L'Amour du Diable* (1864) earned her a return engagement at the Paris Opera, where Saint-Léon again revised and restaged the ballet as *Néméa, ou L'Amour Vengé.* His last ballet for Muravieva, who had decided to leave the stage, was *Konek Gorbunok* (The Little Humpbacked Horse), presented in Saint Petersburg in December 1864, in which he included Russian folk dancing. [*See* Little Humpbacked Horse, The.] André Levinson (in Beaumont, 1930) contrasted the "three worlds" juxtaposed in this ballet: the world of the Russian peasant, an Oriental world, and "the ideal kingdom of the Russian dance," complete with a ballerina dressed in tutu, satin shoes, and diadem.

While in Paris in 1865, Saint-Léon accepted an offer from Émile Gredelue to stage three ballets at the Théâtre Italien: *Il Basilico* (1865); *Don Zeffiro* (1865), a revision of *Saltarello* (1854); and *La Fidanzata Valacca* (1866). He also staged the dances in two new operas: Meyerbeer's *L'Africaine* (1865) and Mozart's *Don Juan* (1866). During his time in Paris, Saint-Léon again encountered the young German dancer Adèle Grantzow, whom he had first seen in Hanover in 1858. He was so impressed with her dancing that he recommended her for the post of prima ballerina at the Bolshoi Theater in Moscow. She would, in a way, become his muse in Russia. [*See the entry on Grantzow.*]

The librettist Charles Nuitter had earlier introduced Saint-Léon to the composer Léo Delibes, with whom he collaborated in the creation of *La Source.* After a number of delays, this ballet was finally presented at the Paris Opera on 12 November 1866. Grantzow, who was to have created the leading role, had been unable to get an extension of her leave from the Bolshoi management. She was replaced by Guglielmina Salvioni, who danced the role of Naïla, the Spirit of the Spring, in a cast that included Eugènie Fiocre and Louis Mérante. Salvioni again came to Saint-Léon's rescue when she replaced Praskovia Lebedeva in the Saint Petersburg production of *Zolotaya Rybka* (The Little Goldfish; 1867), set to the music of Minkus. Although Lebedeva had taken Muravieva's place as reigning ballerina at the Maryinsky, she lacked Muravieva's technical proficiency and musicality, and her relationship with Saint-Léon was stormy.

SAINT-LÉON. A contemporary rendering of Saint-Léon in *Le Lutin de la Vallée* (The Sprite of the Valley), an *opéra-ballet* staged in 1853 at the Théâtre-Lyrique in Paris. (Courtesy of Madison U. Sowell and Debra H. Sowell, Brigham Young University, Provo, Utah.)

In 1869, Saint-Léon staged three ballets in Saint Petersburg, all of which were failures. Although Grantzow received an ovation for her role in *Liliya* (The Lily), the ballet was quickly dropped from the repertory because of a lack of inventiveness in the ensembles. The other two ballets were so poorly received that the disappointed Saint-Léon challenged one critic to a duel.

All of Saint-Léon's energy was now channeled toward completing *Coppélia,* which he had been preparing for the Paris Opera since 1868. It was finally presented before the emperor Napoleon III on 25 May 1870. As Saint-Léon's letters to Nuitter attest, *Coppélia* was carefully worked out with Delibes, to whom he sent folkloric airs for inclusion in the score. The ballet owed its success partly to their collaboration and partly to the fact that it had taken three years to complete, giving Saint-Léon time to tighten up the plot and to work with the young Giuseppina Bozzacchi, who triumphed in the leading role. [*See* Coppélia.]

Suffering from poor health since 1866, Saint-Léon went to Wiesbaden in June 1870 to take the cure. He returned to Paris shortly before the Franco-Prussian War broke out and died there of a heart attack on 2 September. Most of his ballets soon disappeared from the Opera's repertory. *Coppélia,* however, survives to this day, and, thanks to his book *La sténochorégraphie,* the pas de six from *La Vivandière* has been reconstructed by Ann Hutchinson Guest and Pierre Lacotte.

Saint-Léon was first of all an exceptional male dancer at a time when only women were truly appreciated on the stage. In London he quickly assimilated Perrot's method of putting together variations, and he surpassed his master in flattering directors of theaters from Portugal to Russia, for he was something of an *arriviste.* His great flair for music enabled him to recall and mix classical variations and folk dances with success. He was also fortunate in having the composer Delibes as a collaborator and friend. Circumstances decreed that he would become the last great European choreographer of the nineteenth century, for the ballets of Marius Petipa were not seen in France for many decades. As a perennial reminder of his genius, his masterpiece, *Coppélia,* has rarely been absent from the repertory of the Paris Opera Ballet for more than one hundred and twenty-five years.

[*For further discussion of* La Source *and* Coppélia, *see the entry on Delibes.*]

BIBLIOGRAPHY

Beaumont, Cyril W. *A History of Ballet in Russia, 1613–1881.* London, 1930.

Beaumont, Cyril W. *Complete Book of Ballets.* Rev. ed. London, 1951.

Binney, Edwin, 3rd. *Les ballets de Théophile Gautier.* Paris, 1965.

Christout, Marie-Françoise. "Revelations of the Choreographer of *Coppélia.*" *Dance Chronicle* 5.3 (1983): 349–353.

Duarte, José Antonio. "Em busca da dança perdida." *Adagio* (May–June 1991): 23–31.

Gautier, Théophile. *Histoire de l'art dramatique en France depuis vingt-cinq ans* (1858–1859). 6 vols. Geneva, 1968.

Gautier, Théophile. *Gautier on Dance.* Translated and edited by Ivor Guest. London, 1986.

Guest, Ann Hutchinson. "Saint-Léon Revived." *The Dancing Times* (November 1976): 81–82.

Guest, Ann Hutchinson. *La Vivandière Pas de Six: Text and Labanotation.* Amsterdam, 1996. Choreography transcribed by Guest from Saint-Léon's own notation score. Also includes music score by Cesare Pugni and Jean-Baptiste Nadaud.

Guest, Ivor. *The Romantic Ballet in England.* London, 1972.

Guest, Ivor. *The Ballet of the Second Empire.* London, 1974.

Guest, Ivor. *Fanny Cerrito.* 2d rev. ed. London, 1974.

Guest, Ivor. *Jules Perrot: Master of the Romantic Ballet.* London, 1984.

Hammond, Sandra Noll. "*La Sténochorégraphie* by Saint-Léon: A Link in Ballet's Technical History." In *Proceedings of the Fifth Annual Conference, Society of Dance History Scholars, Harvard University, 13–15 February 1982,* compiled by Christena L. Schlundt. Riverside, Calif., 1982.

Kahane, Martine. "La danza nelle versioni parigine delle opere di Verdi." *La danza italiana* 1 (Autumn 1984): 43–60.

Krasovskaya, Vera. *Russkii baletnyi teatr vtoroi poloviny deviatnadtsatogo veka.* Leningrad, 1963.

Moore, Lillian. "Fanny Cerrito and Arthur Saint-Léon." In Moore's *Artists of the Dance.* New York, 1938.

Saint-Léon, Arthur. *Letters from a Ballet Master: The Correspondence of Arthur Saint-Léon.* Edited by Ivor Guest. New York, 1981.

Slonimsky, Yuri. *Mastera baleta.* Leningrad, 1937.

Sveshnikova, A. "Teatral'naia atmosfera Peterburga i Moskvy vremen Sen-Leona, 1859–1869." In *Permskii ezhegodnik–95: Khoreographiia.* Perm, 1995.

Wiley, Roland John, trans. and ed. *A Century of Russian Ballet: Documents and Accounts, 1810–1910.* Oxford and New York, 1990.

MONIQUE BABSKY
Translated from French

SAINT-LÉON NOTATION. To his remarkable achievements, the French dancer and choreographer Arthur Saint-Léon added that of inventing a system of dance notation. *La sténochorégraphie, ou L'art d'écrire promptement la danse,* published in Paris in 1852, explains the system and contains the complete score of the pas de six from his ballet *La Vivandière.* The pas de six has been reconstructed by Ann Hutchinson Guest for numerous companies.

Saint-Léon's was the first published system to be based on the visual device of a modified stick figure. Although it has been alleged that he took the idea from the renowned ballet teacher Monsieur Albert (François Decombe), no evidence supports this.

Saint-Léon used a horizontal five-line staff for stylized leg indications and a single line above this staff to notate arm and head positions. The figure drawings are written as seen by the audience, right and left thus being reversed on the page. A thick line indicates the supporting leg and a thin line the leg that is in the air or only touching the floor. He solved the missing third dimension by using music notation: sharps and flats. Turn signs and additional information are placed below the staff.

The dance staff is placed above the music staff, the movements being correlated with the melody line of the music. When such a general indication of timing was inadequate, as a musician-dancer Saint-Léon added the appropriate music-note head and tail to step- and leg-gesture indications. Small floor plans indicate the location of the dancers on stage; a black pin was used to represent a male dancer and a white pin a female dancer.

Guest's transcription of the pas de six score revealed Saint-Léon's careful analysis of movement—sometimes too careful because the details given could not be achieved at performance tempo. It is evident that the score was not proofread, and it is doubtful that either Saint-Léon or anyone else achieved speed and fluency with his system. Saint-Léon's performing and choreographic activities left him no time to record his works. Only a few other scattered notations written above the music score have so far come to light.

[*See also* Notation.]

BIBLIOGRAPHY

Guest, Ann Hutchinson. *Choreo-Graphics: A Comparison of Dance Notation Systems from the Fifteenth Century to the Present.* New York, 1989.

Guest, Ann Hutchinson. *La Vivandière Pas de Six: Text and Labanotation.* Amsterdam, 1996.

Hammond, Sandra Noll. "*La Sténochorégraphie* by Saint-Léon: A Link in Ballet's Technical History." In *Proceedings of the Fifth Annual Conference, Society of Dance History Scholars, Harvard University, 13–15 February 1982,* compiled by Christena L. Schlundt. Riverside, Calif., 1982.

Saint-Léon, Arthur. *La sténochorégraphie, ou L'art d'écrire promptement la danse.* Paris, 1852.

ANN HUTCHINSON GUEST

SAKHAROFF, ALEXANDER (Alexander Zuckermann; born 25 May 1886 in Mariupol, Russia, died 26 September 1963 in Siena, Italy), Russian dancer and teacher. Influenced by German interpretive dance, Sakharoff held a special position in the world of dance in the 1920s and 1930s. He studied art in Paris and acrobatics in Munich. His first appearance as a dancer was in Munich in 1910. Gifted with a keen aesthetic sense and a feeling for plastic depiction and expressive coloring, he worked with his wife, the German dancer Clothilde von Derp, to develop abstract pantomime as a modern dance form.

Sakharoff's dances were often inspired by painting and sculpture, particularly that of the Renaissance. Both as a solo dancer and with von Derp, he tried to empathize with the gestures and visual compositions of Neoclassicism and, in the manner of Isadora Duncan, to embody them in dance. He portrayed Orpheus, Narcissus, Bacchus, and other mythic figures; one of his most famous dances was called *Der Florentinische Frühling* (The Florentine Spring). He took the Greek's sensitivity to the body as his model. His representations had nothing of male brutality; they were marked by a nearly feminine suppleness and courtly elegance. His choreographies consisted of dignified and measured movements with many flowing combinations of arm and torso movements and steps, and few powerful, dynamic leaps. He aimed for abstract, androgynous bodily representation. Classical music served him as a stimulus; it had a evocative but always subordinate function. His tendency was toward pure dance without music, obeying only the rhythms of the body.

The German writer Hans Brandenburg described Sakharoff's art in the following terms:

> To Sakharoff's credit, he was the first fully conscious seeker of form to research every question about dance in relation to music and to the laws of his own being, who strove to construct movement architectonically without, however, abandoning the elements and descriptive colors as they exist above all in historical links and in the background, costumes, and makeup, but rather maintaining them with refined taste.
>
> (Brandenburg, 1921).

In 1953 Sakharoff and his wife moved to Rome, having become famous through numerous tours in many countries. In 1954 they gave their farewell performance in Siena, where they settled and taught dance.

BIBLIOGRAPHY

Brandenburg, Hans. *Der moderne Tanz.* 3d ed. Munich, 1921. See pages 139–155.

HEDWIG MÜLLER
Translated from German

SALLÉ, MARIE (born 1707?, died 27 July 1756 in Paris), French dancer, teacher, and choreographer. Marie Sallé was born to itinerant artists, probably during their travels in 1707. According to the Parfaict brothers (1743), her father was an actor and a tumbler and her uncle was the famous Arlequin Francisque Moylin or Molin (both spellings are found), who had gathered the various members of their large family together into a company. The Molins and their in-laws, the Sallés and Cochoises, had made a name on the Parisian fair circuit, where they presented their pantomimes and tumbling acts.

Marie Sallé learned all the tricks of her trade early and was especially well grounded in the art of dramatization, so essential to fair entertainments. With her older brother (named Francis by contemporary historians although no official records are available to confirm this), Sallé made her first recorded appearance in London, not Paris, at John Rich's Lincoln's Inn Fields theater on 18 October 1716. The pair were advertised as "the children, scholars of M. Ballon, lately arrived from the Opéra at Paris." This advance publicity suggests that the young performers, whose teacher was the most celebrated star of the Paris Opera, were possibly already groomed for a career there. In London, the little Sallés (aged ten and twelve) kept a grueling schedule of three to four performances a week with featured duets both comic and serious, which included Kellom Tomlinson's "The Submission" (later published in Feuillet notation), several then-fashionable "Night Scenes" (in the Italian manner), and a most intriguing "French Andromache burlesqued with Marie Sallé as Hermione and her brother as Oreste," perhaps a take-off of the celebrated Claude Ballon/Françoise Prévost innovative duet from Pierre Corneille's *Les Horaces* danced at Sceaux in 1714.

The young dancers were immensely successful in London and saw their engagement extended from January until 10 June 1717 with appearances at the King's Theatre and two lucrative benefit performances, the last one of which on 11 May included their father. Sallé was to work again in London for three separate periods: with her brother from October 1725 to September 1727 and from October 1730 to March 1731, both times for John Rich at Lincoln's Inn Fields; and from October 1733 to June 1735 at the Covent Garden Theatre. The young artists made their first recorded Paris debut at the Saint Laurent fair in 1718 in Alain-René Lesage's *La Princesse de Carisme,* and from 1718 to 1725, at which time they returned to England, it must be assumed that they continued to tour the provinces with their family in between appearances at the regular Parisian fairs. They must have also continued to study with other luminaries from the Paris Opera, notably Françoise Prévost and Michel Blondy.

It is most certainly Prévost who taught Sallé her own famous masterpiece, *Les Caractères de la Danse,* which she danced during her second London season in 1725, two years before performing the piece in Paris and one year before Marie Camargo made her own debut in the same work at the Paris Opera. Indeed, Sallé repeatedly chose to dance *Les Caractères* for her 1726 and 1727 London benefits, and she choreographed it again as a duet for Antoine Bandieri de Laval and herself in 1729 and danced it once more with her brother in London in 1731. On 17 February 1729, the *Mercure* had reported that "la Delle Sallé and le Sieur Laval danced 'Les Caractères de la danse' (at the end of the Opera Alceste) in their street clothes and without a mask." The dramatic qualities of *Les Caractères* that Prévost had emphasized in her own performance appealed to Sallé, who had always been exploring self-expression in dance. Her English programs for this second season, for example, *Apollo and Daphne* (1726) and *L'Enlèvement de Proserpine* (1727), attest to repeated integrations of dance and drama.

In late 1727, Sallé left her brother in England to return to France where she made her official debut at the Paris Opera in Jean-Joseph Mouret's *Les Amours des Dieux* and soon appeared in prominent roles alongside Prévost and Camargo. Sallé never felt at ease at the Académie Royale de Musique, which rigidly produced lavish and meaningless formula pieces and was a quagmire of intrigues. She left three times after conflicts with the administration. Nevertheless, she left her mark there, especially during her collaboration with Jean-Philippe Rameau.

During her fourth and fifth London seasons, Sallé came into her own as a mature artist, creating her most daring and original productions. On 14 February 1734 at Covent Garden, she presented *Pygmalion,* a ballet pantomime entirely of her own composition. The *Mercure* reported that "she dared to appear without paniers, or corps, disheveled and with no ornament in her hair . . . just draped in chiffons on the model of a Greek statue." Her next new ballet, presented 26 March, astounded the *Mercure* even more:

> The dancer expressed the deepest sorrow, despair, anger, and dejection . . . through gestures, attitudes, and steps depicting a woman abandoned by her lover. She becomes here the rival of . . . Lecouvreur.

While in England, Sallé also collaborated with George Frideric Handel on several of his "Italian" operas, for which she pioneered dance interludes, as for example *Ariodante* and *Alcina.*

SALLÉ. This engraving, by Nicolas IV de Larmessin after a 1733 painting by Nicolas Lancret, depicts Sallé in an idealized setting, with her arms extended and her thumbs and forefingers touching, in a delicate gesture. (Courtesy of Madison U. Sowell and Debra H. Sowell, Brigham Young University, Provo, Utah.)

Sallé also created the major roles for individual *divertissements* in three *ballets d'action—Les Fêtes Grecques et Romaines* (1733), *Les Indes Galantes* (1735), and *Les Fêtes d'Hébé* (1739), the latter two by Rameau—and according to Louis de Cahusac, all of the *divertissements* in André Campra's *L'Europe Galante* (1736). Despite the immense success of these operas, Sallé left the Royal Académie Royale de Musique for the last time in 1740 because of clashes with the directors.

Sallé continued to dance, however. Jean-Georges Noverre was a frequent visitor to her home and reported in 1745 that she practiced daily. She appeared in many court *divertissements* and ballets. In 1745, she danced in Rameau's *La Princesse de Navarre, Platée,* and *Le Temple de la Gloire,* as well as "Vainqueur des Titans" in *Les Fêtes de Ramire, Thésée,* and *Zélindor.* In 1746, she appeared in *Armide, Zelisca,* and *La Félicité;* in 1747, *L'Année Galante, Persée,* and *Les Fêtes de l'Hymen et de l'Amour.* She appeared in 1752 in *Le Sicilien, L'Inconnu,* and *Tyrcis et Doristée.* Finally, in 1753, she danced in *Phaëton.*

Sallé's name has remained inextricably associated with that of her more flamboyant colleague, Marie Camargo, because both dancers exemplified two major aspects of classical ballet: elevation and expression. Voltaire compared the two in a madrigal published in the *Mercure* (January 1732) in which he summed up the public's fanatical but divided opinion: "Ah! Camargo, how brilliant you are, but, great Gods, how ravishing is Sallé. . . . [Y]ou leap like the nymphs, but she dances like the graces."

In fact, nothing could be more unfair to Sallé's greater achievement; she was more than an outstanding dancer. She was an innovator with a vision that went beyond her times. Hers was a lonely revolution, the fruits of which were reaped by others. She was the true inventor of the *ballet d'action* that was to sweep the late eighteenth-century stage under Noverre's more outspoken personality. Her reforms were multiple, because she consciously developed the themes of her ballets through the logical and sensitive blend of music, gesture, and quality of dancing, as well as by appropriate costumes and scenery. When her innovations were finally accepted, ballet ceased to be a purely decorative entertainment and was regarded as a valid form of human expression that was as eloquent as theater.

A few portraits were made of Sallé, among them one by Nicolas Lancret that was conceived as a pendant for Camargo but which no longer exists. Another was a pastel by Georges de La Tour that captured her in a quiet and reflective mood.

Marie Sallé died on 27 July 1756 in a rented house on rue Saint-Honoré where she lived with her faithful friend, Rebecca Wick, and a servant. The home was comfortable but modest and could not compare with Camargo's far more luxurious accommodations.

[*See* Caractères de la Danse, Les, *and the entries on the principal figures mentioned herein.*]

BIBLIOGRAPHY

Avery, Emmett L. "Two French Children on the English Stage." *Philological Quarterly* 13 (January 1934): 78–82.

Avery, Emmett L. *The London Stage, 1660–1800,* part 2, *1700–1729.* Carbondale, Ill., 1960.

Beaumont, Cyril W. *Three French Dancers of the Eighteenth Century: Camargo, Sallé, Guimard.* London, 1934.

Cahusac, Louis de. *La danse ancienne et moderne, ou, Traité historique de la danse.* 3 vols. La Haye, 1754.

Dacier, Émile. *Une danseuse de l'opéra sous Louis XV: Mlle. Sallé, 1707–1756.* 2d ed. Paris, 1909.

Deutsch, Otto Erich. *Handel: A Documentary Biography.* London, 1955.

McCleave, Sarah. "Marie Sallé: A Comparison of English and French Sources. In *Dance to Honour Kings Conference, Sources for Court and Theatrical Dramatic Entertainments 1690–1740. Kings' College, London, 22–24 August 1996.*

Migel, Parmenia. *The Ballerinas: From the Court of Louis XIV to Pavlova.* New York, 1972.

Moore, Lillian. "Marie Sallé." In Moore's *Artists of the Dance.* New York, 1938.

Murphy, Anne. "Rebel with a Cause." *Ballet News* 6 (June 1985): 14–19.

Noverre, Jean-Georges. *Lettres sur la danse, sur les ballets et les arts.* 4 vols. St. Petersburg, 1803–1804.

Parfaict, François, and Claude Parfaict. *Mémoires pour servir à l'histoire des spectacles de la foire.* Paris, 1743.

Prudhommeau, Germaine. "Camargo-Sallé: Duel au pied levé." *Danser* (March 1986): 78–81.

Ranum, Patricia. "Les 'Caractères' des danses françaises." *Recherches sur la Musique Française Classique* 23 (1985): 45–70.

Schneider, Marcel. "Camargo-Sallé: L'art d'être rivales." *Danser* (May 1993): 44–46.

Semmens, Richard T. "Terpsichore Reborn: The French Noble Style and Drama." In *Proceedings of the Tenth Annual Conference, Society of Dance History Scholars, University of California, Irvine, 13–15 February 1987,* compiled by Christena L. Schlundt. Riverside, Calif., 1987.

Vince, Stanley W. E. "Marie Sallé, 1707–56." *Theatre Notebook* 12.1 (1957): 7–14.

Voltaire. *Le temple du goût.* Rouen, 1733. See chapter 8.

RÉGINE ASTIER

SALTARELLO. Nothing is known of the *saltarello*'s early choreographic character, but from its first written appearance in a fourteenth-century music manuscript until today it has apparently existed in many guises: as an independent fifteenth-century dance type or one of the sections of a multipart *ballo;* as a step type in fifteenth-century *balli* and *bassedanze* that could be used either in a whole *saltarello* section or in other dance types within a *ballo,* adapted to their mensurations; as one of the fast triple after-dances of many of the sixteenth-century *balletto* suites in both books by Fabritio Caroso (1581, 1600); as a term for a few lively dances in the eighteenth-century collections in Feuillet notation; and as a traditional dance type throughout much of contemporary rural Italy, possibly handed down through the nineteenth century. [*See* Ballo and Balletto.]

The etymology of *saltarello* derives from the Latin *saltare* ("to dance"), but the earliest written evidence for the *saltarello* as a special dance type appears in four monophonic tunes, each called a *saltarello* and given without choreography, in a fourteenth-century Italian manuscript (McGee, 1989). The tunes vary in mensuration, and their connection to the fifteenth-century dance type is unknown, as is their performance.

Although evidence of both the dance and the step type is ample in the dance manuals from fifteenth-century Italy and in poetry and other texts, there is no extant choreography for the *saltarello* as an independent dance (as opposed to being a step or part of another dance). It clearly was performed in this manner, however. In these sources, the *saltarello* is a court dance, and literary references assume knowledge of it by the aristocracy. Some writers, such as Antonio Cornazano (1465) and Domenico da Piacenza (1455) relate it to the lively French *pas de Brabant* and the Spanish *alta,* which often followed the quieter *bassedanse* and *bassadanza* in those countries (Cornazano, 1981; Domenico da Piacenza, 1995). Cornazano refers to the *saltarello* as "the most merry dance of all" and cites it as one of the favorites in distinguished ballrooms, next to the *ballo* and *bassadanza.* Other references confirm this and indicate that it could be lengthy and highly varied.

With respect to the standard tempos of the four dance types within a fifteenth-century *ballo,* the *saltarello* is two-thirds faster than the *bassadanza.* It seems to have been usually in fast triple or compound duple mensurations (e.g., in modern meters 3/8, 6/8, 12/8, 6/4).

Most fifteenth-century *balli* begin with a *saltarello* section that seems planned to bring the dancers to the center of the hall. It usually consists of several *saltarello* step patterns repeated two or three times, possibly more as space demands. The rhythm is predominantly [3] ♩♪♩♪. For repeated *balli,* a longer intervening *saltarello* section appears, perhaps to allow the dancers to cover ground between repetitions of the main figures. There are also *saltarello* sections within the different main figures of a *ballo,* in which the male dancers demonstrate their gallantry, often with dramatic innuendos, as in Domenico's "Verçeppe," "La Mercantia," and "La Sobria." The *saltarello* may also have been employed occasionally for the final withdrawal of the dancers.

The fifteenth-century *saltarello* step pattern is somewhat ambiguously described in Domenico and Cornazano as a double with a hop, initiated—musically and in movement—on the upbeat, with the first step coinciding with the downbeat and the entrance of the tenor. The placement and mode of performance of the hop, or rise, are both debatable; Cornazano even forbids the lady to leave the ground. More significant, however, is that, as with other step patterns, the *saltarello* step pattern could be adapted to different mensurations for use in other dance types, such as the *bassadanza, quadernaria* (considered the Germanic duple version of the *saltarello*), and *piva.*

Throughout the sixteenth century, musical sources continue to label pieces *saltarello* that are frequently triple after-dances to the pavan. Some have the predominant rhythmic motto of the *galliarde,* but many are clearly not *galliardes.* Some modern writers identify the *saltarello* with the *galliarde;* others identify it with the *tordion,* a low, quick *galliarde.* However, the only written *saltarello* choreographies and the only references to the *saltarello* as a dance type in the sixteenth-century manuals are by Caroso, and his *saltarelli* differ significantly from his *galliardes* or *tordiglione.*

The *saltarelli* identified as such in Fabritio Caroso's manual are never independent but are one of the several types of triple after-dances common to *balletto* suites (e.g., *galliarde, canario*). In Caroso's suites the *saltarello* is always a *sciolta*—that is, a fast, triple-meter dance whose music is based on the same musical material as the first movement and either follows a *sciolta in galliarda* movement or is the only *sciolta* in a simple two-movement suite. His *saltarelli* are always distinguished from his galliards and tordions by having a different preponderance of step types, never using the *galliarde's* characteristic step pattern, the *cinque passi,* in full; different paths (none call for the typical *galliarde/tordion* alternation between partners); and a different affect (less showy), rhythmic character (the *galliarde's* rhythmic motto is missing), and tempo (the *galliarde* is in a more moderate tempo, to allow for virtuosic leaps). Instead, Caroso's *saltarelli* have the one-chord-per-bar harmonic rhythm that signals rapidity. They are in two-bar musical and step patterns, and they have a preponderance of light-footed and charming step patterns (such as *brève révérences, seguiti spezzati, fioretti,* or paired, one-bar *passi minimi*). Indeed, there seems to be no unique *saltarello* step pattern but rather a group of step types that characterize it when they occur together. It is this combination of step types that makes it possible to recognize untitled *saltarelli.* The paths also frequently consist of typical inner figures of a standard *balletto* (e.g., traversing the floor side by side). Most important, Caroso's *saltarello* movements are shorter than, but otherwise choreographically and musically indistinguishable from, the discrete triple dances he terms *cascarde.*

After Caroso, the *saltarello*'s existence as a seventeenth-century dance cannot be proved. It next appears early in the eighteenth century in a few examples in Feuillet notation by Guillaume-Louis Pecour and Mister Isaac. All in compound duple, they do not seem distinctive from other lively couple dances of the time and contain typical air steps—*jetés, contretemps,* and *assemblés.* Sébastien de Brossard (*Dictionnaire de musique,* 1703) says that the dance has jumping movements in dotted triple meter and compares its music to other gay dances, such as the English jig. Much later, Charles Compan (*Dictionnaire de danse,* 1787) echoes Brossard's definition so closely that it raises the question whether he ever saw the dance.

In the nineteenth century, a number of sources demonstrate that the *saltarello* is considered Italian in origin, a courting folk dance that grows in frenzy until the dancers kick off their shoes and dance barefoot with sliding steps and leaps, accompanied by voice and tambourine.

In the twentieth century, the dance enjoys tremendous popularity in central and southern Italy. Every region and village has its *saltarelli,* with varied character and formations: some have step patterns peculiar only to them and some have pantomimic elements, such as two females vying for one man. All are wooing dances, but the affects vary from dignified to lightly flirtatious to intensely passionate. Sung to a rhythm provided by a percussion instrument (a large or small, round frame drum), some have their own distinctive tunes, while others (especially near Sicily) have melodies identical to *tarantella* tunes but differentiated from them by a continuous triplet drum rhythm. It is impossible to know the age of these dances, for they are part of a living but unwritten tradition that has only periodically surfaced in written sources; what is clear is that the dance in its myriad varieties is firmly rooted in current Italian culture and that all observers and accompanists are deeply involved in it, egging on the performers and showing pleasure at every move. Thus, despite the gaps in its known history, the *saltarello* demonstrates both remarkable continuity and vitality.

BIBLIOGRAPHY: SOURCES

Caroso, Fabritio. *Il ballarino* (1581). Facsimile reprint, New York, 1967.

Caroso, Fabritio. *Nobiltà di dame.* Venice, 1600, 1605. Facsimile reprint, Bologna, 1970. Reissued with order of illustrations changed as *Raccolta di varij balli.* Rome, 1630. Translated into English with eight introductory chapters by Julia Sutton, the music transcribed by F. Marian Walker. Oxford, 1986. Reprint with a step manual in Labanotation by Rachelle Palnick Tsachor and Julia Sutton, New York, 1995.

Cornazano, Antonio. *The Book on the Art of Dancing* (c.1455–1465). Translated by Madeleine Inglehearn and Peggy Forsyth. London, 1981.

Domenico da Piacenza. *De arte saltandi et choreas ducendi* (c.1455). Manuscript located in Paris, Bibliothèque Nationale, f.ital.972. English translation by D.R. Wilson in *Domenico of Piacenza,* corr. ed. Cambridge, 1995.

Guglielmo Ebreo da Pesaro (also known as Giovanni Ambrosio). *De pratica seu arte tripudii.* Milan and Naples(?), 1463, 1471–1474. In Paris, Bibliothèque Nationale, f.ital.973 and f.ital.476. Transcribed and translated by Barbara Sparti as *On the Practice or Art of Dancing.* Oxford, 1993. Other MS copies or versions under the same title c.1461–1510.

BIBLIOGRAPHY: OTHER STUDIES

Commune di Roma Assessorato all Cultura. *La danza tradizionale in Italia, mostra documentaria.* Rome, 1981.

Galanti, Bianca Maria. *La danza della spada in Italia.* Rome, 1942.

Little, Meredith Ellis. "Saltarello." In *The New Grove Dictionary of Music and Musicians.* London, 1980.

Little, Meredith Ellis, and Carol G. Marsh. *La Danse Noble: An Inventory of Dances and Sources.* Williamstown, Mass., 1992.

McGee, Timothy. *Medieval and Renaissance Music: A Performer's Guide.* Toronto, 1985.

McGee, Timothy. *Medieval Instrumental Dances.* Bloomington, Ind., 1989.

Smith, A. William. "References to Dance in Fifteenth-Century Italian *Sacre rappresentazioni.*" *CORD Dance Research Annual* 23 (1991): 17–24.

Tani, Gino. "Saltarello." In *Enciclopedio dello spettacolo.* 9 vols. Rome, 1954–1968.

JULIA SUTTON
with Barbara Sparti

SAMBA. The most popular genre of dance and song in Brazil, the samba assumes a great variety of configurations, performed by groups singing and dancing together, by couples in a ballroom context, or as a solo. Its essential characteristics are a binary compass (one-two, one-two beat) and a syncopated accompaniment.

The samba's origins are West African, mainly Yoruba. It was introduced to Brazil with slavery, when Africans from Angola and Congo were captured, brought to Brazil, and forced to work primarily on sugarcane and coffee plantations. This practice lasted from the second half of the sixteenth century until the end of the nineteenth. Their ritual celebrations, which included vibrant dances and martial arts similar to today's *capoeira,* also provided them a way to express their identity on alien cultural ground and to rebel against their suffering.

The word *samba* is derived from a word used in Congo and Angola to designate a traditional dance that was also called *umbigada.* In the original *umbigada,* which was adapted to create the samba, the performers form a circle, singing and clapping their hands in time with drums and other percussion instruments. One or several soloists dance in the middle of the circle, swinging their hips and stamping their feet. At a certain point, the person in the middle chooses a performer to alternate with him or her by touching that person on the navel.

Shaped from the African *umbigada* tradition, the samba as known in Brazil originated in the country's northeastern state of Bahia. There, in the seventeenth century, it developed on the *ranchos* ("farms"). Around the end of the nineteenth century, the samba gained popularity in Rio de Janeiro, at that time the capital of Brazil. In the early twentieth century, the samba was brought from Bahia to Rio by soldiers returning from the Canudos Revolution, an unsuccessful revolt by Bahian blacks.

The samba in Bahia is closely attached to its African roots. Nowadays, one of its strongest manifestions is *axé* music, an adaptation of African rhythms to popular bal-

SAMBA. Members of two samba schools (groups of dancers) performing *samba-enredo* during Carnival in Rio de Janeiro. (Photographs © 1980 by Johan Elbers; used by permission.)

lads. In Rio, the samba acquired polyphonic sounds produced by bands playing *batuques* (various percussion instruments).

Although the samba always remains a rhythmic unit composed of a 2/4 beat, it can vary according to the particular styles developed at different times and places. There are several important types of samba.

The *samba de breque* was developed in the 1930s in Rio de Janeiro. Here the singer makes sudden stops (breaks) to talk to the audience, usually making funny remarks.

The *samba-enredo* is a narrative samba, created for the samba schools (performing groups) during Carnival, particularly in Rio de Janeiro. It includes a theme song with historic and patriotic lyrics, which becomes a background for the dance spectacle in the streets.

The *samba de partido alto* is a genre related to the African *batuque,* cultivated in Rio de Janeiro since the end of the nineteenth century among urban blacks. Its name reflects the high quality and dignity of the black people who created and still practice this kind of samba. Also called the *umbigada* dance, it is accompanied with clapping hands; it be accompanied by percussion—with knives, kitchen plates, *cavaquinho,* or other instruments.

The *samba-canção* is a very sentimental and syncopated samba, danced by couples. In fact, it is a romantic ballad played to the samba beat.

[*See also* Brazil, *article on* Ritual and Popular Dance.]

BIBLIOGRAPHY

Alencar, Edigar de. *Nosso sinhô do samba.* 2d ed. Rio de Janeiro, 1981.

Browning, Barbara. *Samba: Resistance in Motion.* Bloomington, 1995.

Carneiro, Edison. *Folguedos tradicionais.* 2d ed. Rio de Janeiro, 1982.

Ferretti, Sérgio, et al. *Tambor de crioula.* Rio de Janeiro, 1981.

Guillermoprieto, Alma. *Samba.* New York, 1990.

Guimarães, Francisco. *Na roda do samba.* 2d ed. Rio de Janeiro, 1978.

Leopoldi, José Sávio. *Escola de samba, ritual e sociedade.* Petrópolis, 1978.

Meireles, Cecília. *Batuque, samba e macumba: Estudos de gesto e ritmo, 1926–1934* (1935). Rio de Janeiro, 1983.

Oliveira, Valdemar de. *Frevo, capoeira e "passo."* 2d ed. Recife, 1985.

Valença, Suetônio Soares. *Trá-lá-lá.* Rio de Janeiro, 1981.

Vianna, Hermano. *O misterio do samba.* Rio de Janeiro, 1995.

KATIA CANTON

SAMBURU DANCE. The Samburu are a branch of the pastoral Masai in northern Kenya. The most popular spectacle at many social gatherings, such as weddings, is the dancing of their *moran* ("warriors"), who display both horizontal and vertical rhythmic movements. The first are characterized by a forward thrust of the head as they raise their heels, twirl their spears, and utter assertive bull-like grunts. In the earlier phases of a dance, there is an undertone of competition in the accompanying singing, and the dance itself may on occasion disintegrate into fighting between individuals or rival groups; however, the urge to fight may be dissipated in a fit of shaking, a seizure that follows the pattern of head-thrusting and grunting. Those who begin to shake assume a trancelike state and are led to one side and held to prevent them from hurting themselves or others. When they recover, they may resume dancing. Typically, a successful dance leads to a climax in which shaking spreads among the dancers, followed by more relaxed phases when further shaking is unlikely to occur.

Vertical rhythmic movements in the *moran* dancers are exemplified by their leaping. They jump without holding their spears, their bodies held straight and their long hair flowing freely behind them. The ideal in this movement is not only to attain height, but also to synchronize with the other dancers. Whereas the horizontal thrusting movement expresses and even precipitates competition among individuals, the vertical leaping emphasizes group unity. In the course of a dance, as the aggressiveness of the early phases wanes, there is increasing emphasis on sequences that contain more vertical movement, more compulsive rhythms, and less grunting.

In the early stages of these *moran* dances, girls are spectators. They join the men only after the competitive aspects of the performance have subsided. Gentle vying, taunting, and thrusting movements between the sexes then follow; these lead to the wordless leaping dances characteristic of Samburu childhood. In the final phase, when dancing at night, formal dancing breaks down into unstructured and uninhibited play. In this way, dancing among the Samburu *moran* and girls reverses the pattern of their upbringing, which starts in play as small children, and then leads to the formation of self-conscious peer groups, and then to the fierce rivalries of the warriors. Their dancing can thus be viewed as a process of social as well as emotional regression, with the various phases successively loosening bonds of conditioning and leading ultimately to children's play. In fact, "play" *(enkiguran)* is an alternative term for "dance" in the Masai language.

[*For related discussion, see* Central and East Africa.]

BIBLIOGRAPHY

Spencer, Paul. "Dance as Antithesis in the Samburu Discourse." In *Society and the Dance: The Social Anthropology of Process and Performance*, edited by Paul Spencer. Cambridge, 1985.

PAUL SPENCER

SAMOA. The archipelago of Samoa, in the southern Pacific Ocean, comprising the independent nation of Western Samoa and the territory of American Samoa, stands at the center of Polynesian culture. From it emigrated by outrigger canoe the ancestors of most populations in Polynesia (including the peoples of Hawaii, Tahiti, New Zealand, and various isolated islands). Samoa came under European influence in the 1830s, with the arrival of Christian missionaries; the character of indigenous dancing then began to change because of ecclesiastical restrictions on traditional social events and the introduction of foreign ritual and music. Many Samoan dance genres have therefore disappeared since their first description by outsiders. Most of the extinct genres involved sequences

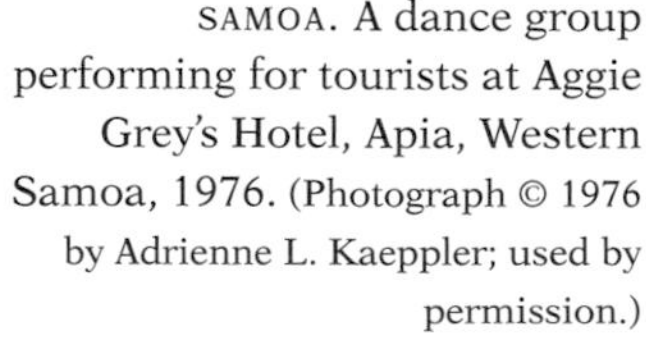

SAMOA. A dance group performing for tourists at Aggie Grey's Hotel, Apia, Western Samoa, 1976. (Photograph © 1976 by Adrienne L. Kaeppler; used by permission.)

of movement choreographed for presentation in synchrony.

The Samoan word *siva* denotes dance in general, especially improvised dancing. (The corresponding formal term, *sa'a,* is cognate with the Maori word *haka,* which denotes a genre of dance in New Zealand.) In the past, dancing occurred either by day *(aoula, aosiva)* or night *(pōula);* performance in darkness encouraged greater freedom of expression. Most modern dances are held at night.

Several sitting dances—the *talalo, fiti, vila,* and *mamaū*—are no longer performed; these genres involved motion of the hands and upper limbs. The old standing dances included the *soa, sa'ē,* and *ula.* The first, a dance performed by one hundred or more people, took place in the open air at great ceremonies, such as the funeral of an important chief. The participants slowly moved their outstretched arms up and down. The *sa'ē,* was held at night, a dance of old women who performed naked. An infrequently performed standing dance is the *'ailao,* or *siva satē,* during which men display clubs (or special knives) while posturing in parallel rows. Today, Samoan men sometimes present a rehearsed standing dance, the *fa'ataupati* (slap dance), during which they rhythmically slap various parts of the body; women sometimes perform an apparently new genre of sitting dance, the *sāsā.*

The *ula* has become the typical dance occasion, when Samoans perform for Samoans. The participants usually divide into two groups, guests at one end of a house and hosts at the other; the sides feel a sense of rivalry and competition. Representatives of one group take turns at solo dancing, and representatives of the other respond similarly. Children often dance at the beginning; the event continues with dances of teenagers and adults. While not dancing, the members of a side participate by singing. At the close of an evening's entertainment, the final dance, *taualuga,* is performed by a high-ranking person (often a ceremonial hostess), who moves in a stately, dignified manner, surrounded by persons exhibiting the *'aiuli* clowning—wild and crude behavior including improvised body slapping, jumping, groveling, shrieking, and shaking of house posts—which honors the soloist through contrast of style.

Dancers may attempt to convey in their gestures the subjects of songs. Gesture matches text most closely in mimetic dancing, such as the dance accompanying the song that, translated, says "do eat the bitter plaintain," or the one that says "water-rat steals food." A song having a short, simple text can continue for several minutes, with the mimetic movements becoming more and more grotesque, while the dancers try harder and harder to amuse the spectators, even through self-abasement. Mimetic dancing often occurs after athletic competitions, when the losers must entertain the winners.

Performances for tourists include the *sāsā* and the *fa'ataupati;* a man may twirl one or two *nifo'oti* (special dance-machetes) or one or two lighted torches; sitting dances may utilize plaited palm-leaf fans waved in various ways and coconut shells struck together and against the floor. Samoan groups also present their versions of foreign Polynesian styles, particularly the New Zealand Maori's *haka* and *poi* dances and the Hawaiian *hula.*

[*See also* Oceanic Dance Traditions *and* Polynesia.]

BIBLIOGRAPHY

Krämer, Augustin. *De Samoa-inseln,* vol. 2, *Ethnographie.* Stuttgart, 1903. See especially pages 314–328.

Mead, Margaret. *Coming of Age in Samoa: A Psychological Study of Primitive Youth, for Western Civilization.* New York, 1928. See especially chapter 8, "The Role of the Dance."

FILM. Robert Flaherty, *Moana: A Romance of the Golden Age* (Paramount, 1926).

JACOB WAINWRIGHT LOVE

SAMSON, LEELA (born 6 May 1951 in India), Indian dancer, choreographer, and teacher. Born into an Indian Jewish family, the daughter of an admiral, Leela Samson was sent to Kalakshetra, an academy of classical dance in Madras, to train in *bharata nāṭyam* under the famed dancer Rukmini Devi. There she also studied Sanskrit, Tamil, and other languages, and classical Karnatic music. During her stay at Kalakshetra she participated in several dance dramas choreographed by Rukmini Devi, as well as assisting the troupe in technical areas such as lighting and sound recording, thus acquiring first-hand knowledge of stage presentation and choreography.

Samson moved to Delhi and joined Sri Ram Bharatiya Kala Kendra, training young dancers in the Kalakshetra technique and giving solo performances both in India and abroad. In her understated delineation and deceptively relaxed approach, one discerns her adherence to the basic Kalakshetra technique as well as her own aesthetic excellence. While evolving an individual style, she maintained a sound understanding of the forms and principles of Indian classical dance theory.

In addition to performing and teaching, Samson collaborated with the Oḍissi and *kathak* dancer Madhavi Mughal to choreograph dances that explore the similarities between those genres and *bharata nāṭyam* in both pure *(nṛtta)* and expressive *(nṛtya)* dance. These attempts, which both underline similarities and reveal complexities, have been well received by both connoisseurs and general audiences. Her recent group work in *bharata nāṭyam* style, *Spanda* (1995), has been noteworthy.

Samson is a keen observer of dance genres and styles and succeeds in communicating their essences meaningfully in writing. *Rhythm in Joy,* her book on the major Indian classical dance genres, drew favorable critical response; she also authored the biography *Rukmini Devi.* She is a member of the governing body of Kalakshetra, assisting in continuing its tradition of *bharata nāṭyam,* its training method, and its way of life. Samson now lives and teaches privately in Delhi and pursues an active performing career both at home and abroad. She has been honored by the government of India with the Padamshri award (1990) and by Sanskriti Pratishthan of New Delhi with the Sanskriti award (1982).

BIBLIOGRAPHY

Jones, Betty True. "Traditional Dance-Drama Forms of South India and the Kalakshetra Presentations." In *Sixth Festival of Asian Arts.* Hong Kong, 1981.

Kothari, Sunil, ed. *Bharata Natyam: Indian Classical Dance Art.* Bombay, 1979.

Samson, Leela. *Rhythm in Joy: Classical Indian Dance Traditions.* New Delhi, 1987.

Sarada, S. *Kalakshetra-Rukmini Devi: Reminiscences.* Madras, 1985.

Tegeder, Ulrich. "'. . . because they have no shadows!'" *Ballett International* 8 (August 1985): 18–23.

SUNIL KOTHARI

SAND. As Swanilda, in *Coppélia,* with Fredbjørn Bjørnsson as Franz, c.1955. This was one of Sand's most successful roles. (Photograph from the archives at Jacob's Pillow, Becket, Massachusetts.)

SAND, INGE (Inge Sand Sørensen; born 6 July 1928 in Copenhagen, died 9 February 1974 in Copenhagen), Danish dancer, ballet master, and producer. Known as a witty and skillful dancer with a flawless allegro technique, Sand was also a clever organizer of the Royal Danish Ballet's international tours. Svend Kragh-Jacobsen (1965) writes, "Before anyone else in this country, she realized the enormous potential asset represented by the youth, skill, and tradition of our ballet, ready for immediate presentation to a foreign audience."

Harald Lander was Sand's teacher, and she made her debut in his *Spring* (3 October 1945). He made her a soloist in the Royal Danish Ballet in 1950. Her agility and grace had at that point been shown in Léonide Massine's *Le Beau Danube* and in the Bluebird pas de deux. In 1951 Lander entrusted her with the part of her lifetime: Swanilda in *Coppélia,* a ballet that has found its own form in the Danish tradition; it has been staged by many, from Lander to Hans Beck. Sand took the opportunity to show all her qualities as a *demi-caractère* dancer in the typical Danish tradition: her Swanilda had lightheartedness, sweet humor, and unforced charm. Her seemingly effortless jumps and allegro dance made her the ideal interpreter of many of George Balanchine's ballets: the first movement of *Bourrée Fantasque,* the third movement of *Symphony in C,* and *Serenade.* In 1973 Sand retired as a dancer (among her later character parts were the Headmistress in David Lichine's *Graduation Ball* and the Old Woman in Flemming Flindt's *The Triumph of Death.*)

From 1966 to 1971, Sand was assistant ballet master to Flindt. However, her most important contribution as an organizer were her tours to the United States with the Inge Sand Group in 1955, 1957, 1960, 1961, 1963, and 1964, tours that paved the way for the guest performances of the Royal Danish Ballet in America in 1956, 1960, and 1965. Sand retired as a dancer in 1973.

BIBLIOGRAPHY

Hering, Doris. "Ten Young Danes from the Royal Danish Ballet." *Dance Magazine* (October 1961): 12.

Hollander, Michael. "Walter Terry with Inge Sand and Fredbjørn Bjørnsson." *Dance Observer* (December 1956): 152.

Kragh-Jacobsen, Svend. *Twenty Solodancers of the Royal Danish Ballet.* Copenhagen, 1965.

HENRIK LUNDGREN

SAN FRANCISCO BALLET. For its tenth anniversary and its second season in the War Memorial Opera House, in 1933 the San Francisco Opera engaged Adolph Bolm to restage and perform in his ballet-opera version of *Le Coq d'Or.* The San Francisco Opera Ballet was thus established, with Bolm as director, choreographer, and founder of the essential school. Nina Verchinina, Julieta Mendez, and Stefano Mascagno were among its early teachers, and Bolm engaged West Coast dancers to appear in both operas and recital performances of his own ballets.

Serge Oukrainsky replaced Bolm in 1936, and William Christensen, a Portland teacher, and Janet Reed, his promising pupil, were brought in as principal dancers.

They made their debut in the dances for *La Traviata* that year. Christensen succeeded Oukrainsky as director in 1938 and increased the ballet's spheres of operation with extensive tours in the western and midwestern states. In 1942 the ballet separated from the opera's management, becoming the San Francisco Ballet, but Christensen continued to serve its requisites for incidental dances, culminating his affiliation in 1953 with a production of Beethoven's *The Creatures of Prometheus* on a program shared with Richard Strauss's *Elektra*.

Christensen's early ballets were inspired by popular revues of the era and the fare of the itinerant Ballets Russes. In 1939 he mounted a full-length *Coppélia* for himself and Janet Reed, assisted by local dancers and students from the growing school. His brother Harold Christensen joined the organization in 1940 to take over the school's operation, thus freeing Willam to mount America's first production of the four-act *Swan Lake*. Lew Christensen danced Siegfried at the premiere, with Jacqueline Martin as Odette and Janet Reed as Odile. A full-length version of *The Nutcracker* followed in 1944, informally advised by George Balanchine and Alexandra Danilova.

In 1947 a new fifty-two-member board of directors secured municipal funding for the company, which for two years became known as the San Francisco Civic Ballet. The critic and author Irving Deakin was appointed general manager, and performances were given under the sponsorship of the San Francisco Arts Commission. Ballets were commissioned from Adolph Bolm and John Taras, and a production of *Giselle* was mounted for guest stars Alicia Markova and Anton Dolin. Tamara Toumanova appeared the following year in works from the classic repertory. In 1948 poor financial management brought bankruptcy to the company and dispersed many promising dancers.

Activities were curtailed until 1951 when Lew Christensen permanently settled in San Francisco, bringing his wife, the Cecchetti-trained Gisella Caccialanza. Lew's popular ballets, *Jinx* and *Filling Station*, became the cornerstones of a new repertory when Willam left to head the dance department at the University of Utah. Lew's prolific

SAN FRANCISCO BALLET. Emily Hagenmaier as Clara and Yuri Zhukov as Drosselmeyer in *The Nutcracker*, act 1. "Original choreography" for the current production is credited to Lew Christensen, with additional choreography by Willam Christensen and Helgi Tomasson; scenery and costumes are by Jose Varona. (Photograph by Marty Sohl; used by permission of the San Francisco Ballet.)

output of bright, topical ballets brought a new vitality and encouraged the collaboration of many local designers and painters. Frequent appearances by guest dancers from the major companies helped raise public consciousness. In initiating an exchange program with the New York City Ballet, Lew Christensen thereby developed for his company the second major repository of the works of George Balanchine. [*See the entry on the Christensen brothers.*]

In 1957, company manager Leon Kalimos organized a ten-week tour of Asia for the company. Subsequent junkets under U.S. State Department auspices to Africa, Latin America, and the Middle East afforded the San Francisco Ballet significant status abroad.

The chronic problem of economic insecurity and limited employment opportunity for its dancers drained the company of its native talent over the years, depriving it of such remarkable performers as Janet Reed, James Starbuck, Harold Lang, Onna White, Jocelyn Vollmar, Conrad Ludlow, Cynthia Gregory, Terry Orr, and Michael Smuin. In 1973 the tides finally turned when Smuin came back from American Ballet Theatre to serve as co-director, bringing with him several of that company's soloists.

In 1974, bankruptcy and imminent dissolution were circumvented when loyal dancers personally initiated a massive fund-raising program. Solvency came with the appointment of Richard LeBlond as president. Richard Cammack assumed directorship of the school, freeing Lew Christensen and Michael Smuin to concentrate on artistic goals.

The company, which operated with about forty-five dancers, was unique for its democratic policies in assignment of roles, its nurturing of choreographers in the ranks, and a firm artistic loyalty to the popular theater. Frequently remounted, *The Nutcracker* became a local institution for the winter season. Both Smuin and Christensen contributed full-length ballets and continued to devise shorter pieces reflecting their personal heritages. Works by Frederick Ashton and Jerome Robbins were acquired, and many Balanchine ballets were performed with a style deeply rooted in the era of their origin. Tomm Ruud, Robert Gladstein, John McFall, Betsy Erikson, and Val Caniparoli were among the resident choreographers.

Smuin's success in developing a solid local patronage and his insistence on achieving world status for the company guided the organization to impressive debuts at major dance centers and international festivals. Television productions of his *Romeo and Juliet* (1978) and *The Tempest* (1981) for the Dance in America series reached vast audiences at home and abroad.

In 1983 the company moved into new headquarters, a $10 million structure adjacent to the War Memorial buildings in San Francisco's growing Performing Arts Center. A vast complex of studios, rehearsal halls, offices, and a library serve the needs of the dance community, the six

SAN FRANCISCO BALLET. Evelyn Cisneros and Anthony Randazzo in James Kudelka's *The Comfort Zone* (1989). (Photograph © 1991 by Jack Vartoogian; used by permission.)

hundred fifty students at the school, and the company's administrative personnel.

Lew Christensen died in 1984, and Smuin, whose artistic vision displeased many on the board who preferred a more traditional aesthetic, was fired. Iceland-born Helgi Tomasson replaced him in 1985. Most of Smuin's young choreographers and several of his dancers left. Tomasson preferred to recruit from a broader international pool. Richard LeBlond, who weathered the turbulent transitional years, ended his tenure with the company in 1987. W. McNeil Lowry assumed the position of president of the San Francisco Ballet Association, and Willam Christensen was reinstated as artistic director emeritus.

Tomasson established a traditional hierarchy with his dancers and initiated an objective of strengthening the company's technical skills. A number of his own neoclassical ballets were introduced, and new creations and restorations were commissioned from Glen Tetley,

William Forsythe, James Kudelka, David Bintley, and Lisa de Ribere. In 1988 Tomasson, in collaboration with the designer Jens-Jacob Worsaae, staged a new production of *Swan Lake,* which received international attention. It was followed in 1990 with a new staging of *The Sleeping Beauty* by the same team, with ballet mistress Irina Jacobson's assistance as coach. At its premiere the company boasted a roster of bright young dancers from six continents.

Tomasson's artistic policy strikes a balance between the classics and the innovative. His own production of the Prokofiev *Romeo and Juliet* was introduced in 1994, and he continues to create new works, both in the Romantic and contemporary modes for his dancers each season. Mark Morris, William Forsythe, James Kudelka, and David Bintley, frequent guests as choreographers, have also mounted significant original ballets. The Balanchine repository is frequently supplemented.

In May 1995, the company celebrated the fiftieth anniversary of the signing of the United Nations Charter, which had taken place in its home theater in 1945. Ballet troupes from five continents sent dancers to perform original works created especially for the ambitious festival. UNited We Dance offered three programs over a week of performances, and the dancers of the San Francisco Ballet shared each evening with a characteristic work from its popular repertory.

In 1996 the San Francisco Opera House was closed for seismic upgrading, for two years. This necessitated the use of several new venues throughout the San Francisco Bay Area and adjustments in repertory to fit the conditions of smaller stages.

[*See also* United States of America, *article on* Regional Dance Companies; *and the entry on Tomasson.*]

BIBLIOGRAPHY

Amberg, George. *Ballet in America.* New York, 1949.

Barnes, Clive. "San Francisco Ballet Is on Point." *Performing Arts Magazine* (February 1992).

Bloomfield, Arthur. *The San Francisco Opera, 1922–1978.* Sausolito, Calif., 1978.

Doeser, Linda. *Ballet and Dance.* New York, 1977.

Dorris, George. "Willam Christensen Reminisces." In *Proceedings of the Twelfth Annual Conference, Society of Dance History Scholars, Arizona State University, 17–19 February 1989,* compiled by Christena L. Schlundt. Riverside, Calif., 1989.

Frankenstein, Alfred. "The San Francisco Ballet." *Dance Magazine* (April 1955): 16–21.

Graham-Lujan, James. "The San Francisco Ballet." *Dance News Annual* (1953): 145–157.

LeBlond, Richard E., Jr. *From Chaos to Fragility.* Dubuque, Iowa, 1988.

Maynard, Olga. *The American Ballet.* Philadelphia, 1959.

Maynard, Olga. "The Christensens: An American Dance Dynasty." *Dance Magazine* (June 1973): 44–58.

Maynard, Olga. "San Francisco Ballet's Michael Smuin: Young Man in a Hurry." *Dance Magazine* (May 1976): 42–51.

Parish, Paul. "Swan's New Way." *Ballet Review* 16 (Spring 1988): 18–27.

Ross, Janice. "Back to Basics." *Dance Magazine* (August 1987): 38–43.

Ross, Janice. "The California Dream at Sixty." *Dance Magazine* (February 1993): 56–61.

Steinberg, Cobbett. *San Francisco Ballet: The First Fifty Years.* San Francisco, 1983.

Stoop, Norma McLain. "Michael Smuin and the San Francisco Ballet: Hands across the Continent." *Dance Magazine* (November 1978): 67–72.

Von Buchau, Stephanie. "A Bold New Face: San Francisco Ballet." *Dance Magazine* (September 1977): 38–41.

Von Buchau, Stephanie. "San Francisco." *Ballet News* 2 (October 1980): 40.

LELAND WINDREICH

SANGALLI, RITA (born 20 August 1849 in Antegnate, Italy, died 3 November 1909 in Carpesino d'Arcellasco, Italy), dancer and writer. Having studied ballet at the Teatro alla Scala, Milan, under Auguste Hus, Sangalli made her debut in 1864 in Paul Taglioni's *Flik e Flok.* She performed in Italy until April 1866, when she was hired at Her Majesty's Theatre, London. There she was seen by the American impresarios Henry Jarrett and A. M. Palmer, who engaged her as one of the principal dancers for a musical spectacle. On 12 September 1866 Sangalli made her New York debut in the enormously popular, long-running musical spectacle *The Black Crook* at Niblo's Garden Theatre. Her bravura technique—precise, strong, and voluptuous—won a crowd of admirers and divided the audience at Niblo's between those who favored Sangalli and the champions of her rival from La Scala, Maria Bonfanti. Jarrett and Palmer exploited the rivalry for publicity purposes, angering Sangalli and causing her to leave *The Black Crook* in September 1867. She accepted an engagement with B. F. Whitman, manager of the Continental Theatre in Boston, for a tour of Boston, Buffalo, Detroit, and Philadelphia, performing incidental dances in the musical spectacles *Cinderella, Bluebeard, A Midsummer Night's Dream,* and *The Black Crook.*

On 10 March 1868 Sangalli returned to New York to appear in George L. Fox's extremely successful burlesque-pantomime *Humpty Dumpty.* She performed several *divertissements* in Fox's production, including a shortened version of *La Sylphide* and a "Dance of Deportment," in which she and Fox satirized the ballroom conventions of the day. On 18 May 1869, two days after the close of *Humpty Dumpty,* Fox opened a new production, *Hiccory Diccory Dock,* in which Sangalli was featured, and in October, Jim Fisk, manager of the Grand Opera House, engaged Sangalli to perform a can-can in his production of Shakespeare's *The Tempest.* Later that same month Sangalli organized her own company, and on 23 October they opened at Wood's Museum in the so-called pantomime burlesque fairy extravaganza *Flick [and] Flock,* Sangalli's adaptation of the ballet in which she had made her debut at La Scala. The ballerina danced five roles and sang a suite of waltzes called "La Sangalli," composed by the theater's music director, Signor Aberle. Sangalli made her last New York appearance in December 1869, with the Riching's Opera Company at the Grand Opera House in *The Bohemian Girl* and *Les Huguenots.*

On 3 January 1870 Sangalli embarked on a transcontinental train journey to San Francisco for a season of ballet. She toured a circuit of theaters in California—Stockton, Sacramento, and San Francisco—and Virginia City, Nevada. In interviews given many years later in Europe, Sangalli reminisced about this tour. She recalled performing for miners who threw gold dust and nuggets at the dancers instead of the usual bouquets of flowers, and she claimed that she traveled "armed with a knife to ward off Indians and desperadoes." Traveling on the same circuit was her *Black Crook* rival, Maria Bonfanti. Although the tour was arranged to capitalize on their competition, they did not perform together. In April 1870 Sangalli returned to New York, stopping along the way to appear in Omaha, Saint Louis, and Chicago.

SANGALLI. A portrait of Sangalli, poised on pointe, c.1868. (Photograph by Otto Sarony; from the Dance Collection, New York Public Library for the Performing Arts.)

On 9 July 1870 Sangalli sailed for Europe. Her ambition was to dance at the Paris Opera, but she arrived in Paris the day the Franco-Prussian War began. Sangalli therefore immediately left for England, where she performed at the Prince's Theatre in Manchester. She returned to Paris in 1872, making her debut at the Paris Opera in *La Source.* She remained there for the rest of her career, creating the ballerina roles in Louis Mérante's *Sylvia* (1876) and *Yedda* (1879) and in Lucien Petipa's *Namouna* (1882). Sometime during this period she married the baron Marc de Saint-Pierre.

At the height of her power at the Paris Opera, Sangalli wrote the preface to *Terpsichore,* a book on ballet technique designed for the balletomanes who frequented the Foyer de la Danse and the dressing rooms of the Opera. Her words reflected her La Scala training and the ideals of Carlo Blasis. She spoke out against technique for technique's sake and urged a return to the simplicity of classical composition. Although rooted in tradition, Sangalli was an intrepid dancer. During her twenty-year career she amazed audiences in America and Europe with her feats of strength and set high technical standards for dancers to follow.

[*See also* Black Crook, The.]

BIBLIOGRAPHY

Barker, Barbara. *Ballet or Ballyhoo: The American Careers of Maria Bonfanti, Rita Sangalli, and Giuseppina Morlacchi.* New York, 1984.

Beaumont, Cyril W. *Supplement to Complete Book of Ballets.* London, 1942.

Freedley, George. *"The Black Crook* and *The White Fawn." Dance Index* 4 (January 1945): 4–16.

Guest, Ivor. "Sylvia, from Mérante to Ashton." *Ballet Annual* 8 (1954): 67–72.

Guest, Ivor. *Le ballet de l'Opéra de Paris.* Paris, 1976.

Odell, George C. D. *Annals of the New York Stage.* Vol. 8. New York, 1936.

Terpsichore: Petit guide à l'usage des amateurs de ballet par un abonné de l'opéra. Preface by Rita Sangalli. Paris, 1875.

ARCHIVE. Dance Collection, New York Public Library for the Performing Arts.

BARBARA BARKER

SAN JOSE BALLET. *See* Cleveland–San Jose Ballet.

SANKOVSKAYA, EKATERINA (Ekaterina Aleksandrovna Sankovskaia; born c.1816, died 16 [28] August 1878), Russian dancer. Sankovskaya graduated from the Moscow Theater School in 1836, having studied ballet under Félicité Hullin-Sor. While she was still a student her acting talent attracted the attention of the great actor of the Maly Theater, Mikhail Shchepkin, and she successfully performed in drama as well as ballet productions on the stages of the Maly and Bolshoi Theaters.

In 1836, Hullin-Sor took Sankovskaya with her to Paris. While in Paris the young teacher and dancer became acquainted with the new Romantic repertory of western European ballet. In 1837 Sankovskaya danced the title role in the ballet *La Sylphide*, choreographed by Hullin-Sor after Filippo Taglioni. Sankovskaya became the first Romantic ballerina of Moscow's Bolshoi Theater. The new technique in ballet, its plots and characters, attracted the attention of Moscow's intelligentsia to Sankovskaya's art. Performing in the lyrical Romantic repertory, Sankovskaya added a new flavor to the style of ballet and to the treatment of various characters, all in accordance with her natural talents and with the traditions of the Moscow school.

Delicate and slightly built, Sankovskaya displayed in her performing style not breadth and boundlessness of line, but lightness, elegance, and weightlessness. Her Sylphide was not an abstract dream of the hero but a live and loving creature. The ballerina concretized and added a psychological dimension to some of ballet's imaginary characters. The student youth of Moscow perceived her as the embodiment of poetry, the female ideal. The art of Sankovskaya was praised by the leading literati of the 1830s and 1840s, including Sergei Aksakov, Mikhail Saltykov-Shchedrin, and Aleksandr Hertzen. Saltykov-Shchedrin called her the "plastique elucidator of the new word," the "spirit of the Moscow ballet."

After *La Sylphide* Sankovskaya appeared in the major ballets of Marie Taglioni's repertory. Vissarion Belinsky, the literary critic, wrote favorably about her performances in *La Fille du Danube*. In 1843, after the performance in Moscow of the first Russian *Giselle* with the Saint Petersburg ballerina Elena Andreyanova in the title role, Sankovskaya began to appear in that role, too, on the stage of the Bolshoi Theater. During Fanny Elssler's guest performances in Moscow (1848–1850), the ballets of Jules Perrot became a part of the repertory of the Bolshoi Theater. Realism, the forces of emotions, and the down-to-earth acting of Elssler's art harmonized well with both the traditions of the Moscow ballet and the individuality of Sankovskaya. After Elssler's departure Sankovskaya began to perform what had been Elssler's roles, dancing the main roles in Perrot's ballet *Catarina, ou La Fille du Bandit* and Arthur Saint-Léon's *Le Violon du Diable*.

When Hullin-Sor abandoned the theater, Sankovskaya independently produced in 1849 *Le Diable à Quatre*, after Joseph Mazilier, on the Moscow stages. Her last role was that of Esmeralda in Perrot's *La Esmeralda* in 1853. Sankovskaya left the stage in 1854 and began to train young dancers, including Maria Manokhina, and to teach ballroom dancing to the family of the great reformer of Russian drama theater, Konstantin Stanislavsky.

BIBLIOGRAPHY

Bakhrushin, Yuri. *Istoriia russkogo baleta*. 3d ed. Moscow, 1977.

Chaffee, George. "The Ballettophile." *Dance Magazine* (April 1945): 18, 30.

Guest, Ivor. *Fanny Elssler*. London, 1970.

Krasovskaya, Vera. *Russkii baletnyi teatr: Ot vozniknoveniia do serediny XIX veka*. Leningrad, 1958.

Lunacharskii, A. V., and I. V. Ekskuzovich, eds. *Moskovskii Bolshoi Teatr, 1825–1925*. Moscow, 1925.

Wiley, Roland John, trans. and ed. *A Century of Russian Ballet: Documents and Accounts, 1810–1910*. Oxford, 1990.

NATALIA Y. CHERNOVA
Translated from Russian

SANO, KEMOKO (Siaka Sano; also known as Mohamed Kemoko Sano, or Sanoh; born 1942 in Macenta, Forest Region of Guinea, French West Africa), ensemble director, choreographer, percussionist, and teacher. Kemoko Sano is recognized in Francophone West Africa as one of the foremost exponents of traditional music and dance. He has directed large music and dance ensembles in Guinea in regional, national, and international venues, beginning with the Prefectural Troupe of Macenta in 1960, the Ballet National Djoliba from 1973 to 1986, and Les Merveilles d'Afrique, which he founded in 1986 with the sanction of Guinean authorities but without their material support. Since 1986 he has also been choreographer for Les Ballets Africains of the Republic of Guinea. A consummate teacher, he has trained some of the finest dancers and musicians of the generation that came of age after Guinean independence in 1958.

Named Siaka Sano at birth, he had a traditional upbringing in a village near Macenta. His father died while he was a child, after which he was called Kemoko, which means "the boy." As a teenager he was considered to be particularly observant in his religious devotions, and was called "Mohamed." Early in his career Sano's mentors were a Roman Catholic priest named Father Mauricel whom he knew in Boy Scouts in Macenta, Sékou-Oulen Condé at the Lycée Technique in Conakry, and Soumah Mangué, a founding member of Les Ballets Africains who later had his own troupe, Le Ballet Noir d'Art Dramatique, in Guinea in the years before independence in 1958.

Sano was recruited by Fodéba Kéita to rehearse Les Ballets Africains in 1964 after the Macenta troupe won first prize in the National Performing Arts Festival. He was paralyzed in a fall during a performance by Les Ballets Africains at the Théâtre l'Alhambra in Paris later the same year and returned home in a wheelchair. His mother cured him with traditional healing practices, beginning by throwing away the wheelchair and finally having a pestle rolled over his back by two strong men as he crouched over a mortar. He took up his former position as director of the local troupe and in 1968 became artistic director of Le Ballet National Djoliba, the second major Guinean national dance troupe, which won the gold medal at the Pan-African Festival in Algiers the following year. He was director general of this troupe from 1973 until 1986 when, following his return with the troupe from an American tour during which they had been abandoned by their impresario, he was removed from this position.

After becoming choreographer of Les Ballets Africains, Sano made *La Cloche de Hamana* (The Bell of Hamana), which was presented by Les Ballets Africains in a performance at the national theater, attended by President Lansana Conté, his cabinet, and the then-ruling Military Committee for National Recovery (CMRN) on 2 October 1988, the thirtieth anniversary of Guinean independence.

Although Kemoko Sano lives in Conakry, the capital of Guinea, and considers the African milieu essential to his creativity, in recent years he has been involved in a variety of projects outside Guinea. He was the director of percussion for a French-funded production, *Waramba: L'Opéra Mandingue,* by the Guinean-born director Souleymane Koly in 1991. He taught a performance workshop in the Dance Department of San Francisco State University as Fulbright Artist in Residence in the spring semester of 1994. During this period he spent one day in Los Angeles assisting Debbie Allen in integrating two of his male dancers into her choreography for sixteen dancers from eight international dance companies for the 1994 Academy Awards broadcast.

The basic components of the genre in which Sano works are traditional rhythm patterns, from which he creates evermore complex rhythmic structures. He creates and directs both the music and dance and is considered to have a rare talent for "marrying" steps. However, as of this writing, he, like his Guinean colleagues, does not have title to the many works he has created for Guinean troupes. He describes his work as "harmonizing traditional rhythms to the present time for the pleasure of a worldwide public." A piece called *Stop Violence against Women!* for a student performance at San Francisco State University responded to an incident on campus in 1994 that affected his students. He says of his society, "We do not believe in art for art's sake." New work may reflect new influences. In 1992 he made *A Tempest of Rhythms* for Les Merveilles, a piece that incorporates African, European, American, and Asian rhythms. He likes to say, "A culture does not develop in a box; it develops in relation to other cultures."

[*See also* Ballets Africains, Les.]

BIBLIOGRAPHY

Dunning, Jennifer. *New York Times* (7 October 1991, 6 December 1993, 15 April 1996).

Zomou, Roger Goto. "Kemoko Sano, grand sculpteur de danses et de rythmes." *Horoya,* no. 3588 (22–24 August 1991).

VIDEOTAPE. *Kemoko Sano Teaches African Dance from the Republic of Guinea,* vol. 1. (Sano Videos, Scarsdale, N.Y., 1991). Excerpts from *La Cloche de Hamana* are included in *Les Ballets Africains* (*After-Image,* Channel 4, London, 1990).

LOUISE BEDICHEK

SANQUIRICO, ALESSANDRO (born 27 July 1777 in Milan, died 12 March 1849 in Milan), Italian painter and set designer. Sanquirico first worked for the Teatro alla Scala in Milan in 1805, and between 1817 and 1832 he was that theater's sole scenic artist. His tenure coincided with one of the richest periods in Italian opera and ballet: choreographers Salvatore Viganò and Salvatore Taglioni (uncle of Marie) were active at La Scala at the time, and several operas by Gioacchino Rossini, Gaetano Donizetti, and Vincenzo Bellini had their world premieres there.

Astonishingly prolific, Sanquirico designed more than three hundred productions, alone or in collaboration, most of them for La Scala. He also redecorated the theater in 1829–1830. Among the important ballets for which he provided sets were *Gli Strelizzi* and *Il Noce di Benevento* (both, 1812), *I Titani* (1819), and *Alessandro nelle Indie* (1820) by Viganò; *Amleto* (1817) and *La Silfide* (1828) by Louis Henry; and *Sesostri* (1824) and *Il Patria* (1828) by Taglioni.

Although essentially a neoclassical designer, Sanquirico was also called on to supply Gothic fantasies for the emerging Romantic-era productions. Informed by the same spirit of inquiry that had motivated Johann Joachim Winckelmann a generation before, he had a passion for historical accuracy that sometimes worked to the detriment of spontaneity. Sanquirico's immense repertory ran the gamut from Rome in flames to triumphal halls to mystical landscapes. The *coreodrammas* of the day generally required architectural backgrounds from classical antiquity, or perhaps from ancient Egypt or from the Napoleonic era, and Gothic buildings—often in ruins—to suit the Romantic imagination. Although many of his designs seem static, in others he achieved dramatic effects by radical foreshortening of the architectural elements, and he heightened some of his designs by creating luminous central areas. His drops for *I Titani,* for example, are reminiscent of the paintings of Claude Lorrain and Nicolas Poussin, both in the tonality of their palettes and in their lighting effects.

Sanquirico left two albums of aquatint engravings of his theatrical designs. (Many of the engravings are in the Dance Collection of the New York Public Library for the Performing Arts at Lincoln Center.) The largest collection of his work is preserved at the Museo Teatrale of La Scala. Although his fame rests on his hundreds of scenic designs, material uncovered by Mercedes Viale Ferrero and published in 1984 suggested for the first time that Sanquirico designed costumes as well.

BIBLIOGRAPHY

Carrieri, Raffaele. *La danza in Italia, 1500–1900.* Milan, 1945.

Mazzocca, Fernando. *Neoclassicism and Troubadour in the Miniatures of Giambattista Gigola.* Exhibition catalog, Poldi-Pezzoli Museum. Milan, 1978.

Raccolta di scene teatrali eseguite o disegnate dai più celebri pittori scenici di Milano. 2 vols. Milan, 1819–1824.

Rossi, Luigi. *Storia del balletto.* Rev. ed. Milan, 1967.

Sanquirico, Alessandro. *Raccolta di varie decorazioni sceniche: Inventate ed eseguite per il R. Teatro alla Scala di Milano.* N.p., c.1812–1827.

Viale Ferrero, Mercedes. "Costume Designs by Alessandro Sanquirico and Others for Ballets Performed at the Teatro alla Scala, Milan, 1820–24." *Dance Research* 2 (Summer 1984): 24–40.

NANCY REYNOLDS

SANTLOW, HESTER (Hester Booth; born c.1690, died 15, 21, or 31 January 1773), English dancer and actress. The date and place of Santlow's birth are unknown, but she was probably born about 1690, for in 1704 she was apprenticed to the French dancing master René Cherrier, who was then working in the London theaters. She made her debut as a dancer at the Theatre Royal, Drury Lane, on 28 February 1706 and very quickly established herself on the London stage, alongside the leading French and English dancers. On 3 December 1709, she added to her status by making her debut as an actress at Drury Lane. In the 1709/10 season she enjoyed notable success, particularly for her Harlequin dance and her appearance in the title role of *The Fair Quaker of Deal* by Charles Shadwell, which helped to revive the flagging fortunes of the Drury Lane theater and which made her a leading member of the company. She remained at Drury Lane as a dancer and an actress for most of her career.

As an actress, Santlow excelled in comedy and specialized in witty heroines; among her most popular roles were Harriet in *The Man of Mode,* by George Etherege, and Hellena in *The Rover,* by Aphra Behn. She also played tragic roles, including Ophelia in *Hamlet* and Desdemona in *Othello.* Her dance repertory was broad, encompassing John Weaver's genres of "serious," "grotesque," and "scenical" dancing. Leading choreographers, such as Mr. Isaac and Anthony L'Abbé, created dances for her. Among her serious dances were solo and duet minuets and *passacailles;* her grotesque and character dances included the Harlequin dance (a duet as well as a solo, with which she was particularly associated) and the duet called *Hussars.* She danced the leading female part in many of the group dances given in the entr'actes at Drury Lane, including *Lads and Lasses* and *Myrtillo.* Santlow also appeared in a number of very successful pantomimes: she played Daphne in John Thurmond's *Apollo and Daphne* (1725) and Andromeda in Roger and Weaver's *Perseus and Andromeda* (1728), and she danced as Diana in the "Masque of the Deities," which came at the end of Thurmond's phenomenally successful *Harlequin Doctor Faustus* (1724).

Santlow's greatest achievements were in the innovative experiments by John Weaver, now called the first *ballets d'action.* She played Venus in *The Loves of Mars and Venus* (1717), Eurydice in *Orpheus and Eurydice* (1718), and Helen of Troy in *The Judgement of Paris* (1733). In all these works she was required to express a series of "passions" or "affections," through formal mime, and was to perform the more conventional dances that were also part of the action. Her success in these roles is indicated by Weaver's repeated choice of her as his leading dancer.

Santlow's dancing partners during her career included Weaver himself; Dupré (who may have been Louis "Le Grand" Dupré, then at an early stage of his career); the leading English dancer John Shaw; and Desnoyer (who during the 1731/32 season created the *Grand Ballet d'Amour* and *Le Chasseur Royal,* in which they danced together). Both John Weaver and the dancing master John Essex payed tribute to her. Weaver referred to her in the preface to his *Anatomical and Mechanical Lectures upon Dancing,* in which he wrote,

> we may value our selves, that we have a Dancer in the Person of Mrs. Booth, where Art and Nature have combin'd to produce a beautiful Figure, allow'd by all Judges in our Art to be the most graceful, most agreeable, and most correct Performer in the World. (John Weaver, 1721)

In his preface to *The Dancing-Master* Essex described her as "the incomparable Mrs. Booth," adding that

> the many different Characters she represents is the Wonder and Admiration of the present Age, and will scarce be credited by the Succeeding. I shall beg leave to mention the Chaconne, Saraband, Menuet, in all which she appears with that Grace, Softness and Address none can look on but with Attention, Pleasure, and Surprise. She far excels all that went before her, and must be the just Subject of Imitation to all that dare attempt to copy after her. (John Essex, 1728)

Santlow's beauty attracted many admirers. Early in her career she became the mistress of the politician (later secretary of state) James Craggs, by whom she had her daughter Harriot in 1713. On 3 August 1719, Santlow married the actor-manager Barton Booth. His poem "Ode on Mira Dancing," printed in his Memoirs of the Life of Barton Booth (London, 1733), is said to describe his wife's performances. When Booth died in 1733, she retired from the stage almost immediately. Shortly before her death in January 1773, she had erected a monument to him in Westminster Abbey.

Hester Santlow has been described as "the first British ballerina." In her own time, her fame and popularity were greater than those of the many French dancers who came to dance in the London theaters. Her expressive abilities as a dancer-actress were motivational in Weaver's creation of his *ballets d'action,* and her influence on her contemporaries and her successors, both in London and elsewhere, was considerable. Several portraits of her survive: a full-length portrait in Harlequin dress, probably by John Ellys; a head-and-shoulders portrait, said to show her in the title role of *The Fair Quaker of Deal,* of which there is a mezzotint by the nineteenth-century artist R. B. Parkes; and a three-quarter-length portrait, showing her in mourning for Barton Booth, also by Ellys.

Seven dances from her repertory survive in notation. There are the three ball dances for a man and a woman, which were also given in the theater: "The Union" (1707) and "The Saltarella" (1708), both by Mister Isaac, and "The Prince of Wales's Saraband" (1731) by Anthony L'Abbé. There are also the four theatrical dances from *A New Collection of Dances* (London, c.1725) by Anthony L'Abbé: "Passacaille of Armide" (a duet for two women), "Menuet" (a solo), "Chacone of Galathée" (a duet for a man and a woman), and "Passagalia of Venus & Adonis" (a solo).

BIBLIOGRAPHY

Cohen, Selma Jeanne. "Theory and Practice of Theatrical Dancing: III. Hester Santlow." In *Famed for Dance,* by Ifan Kyrle Fletcher et al. New York, 1960.

Essex, John. *The Dancing-Master.* London, 1728.

Goff, Moira. "Dancing, by Miss Santlow: The Recorded Eighteenth-Century Dances of the Time of Hester Santlow." *The Dancing Times* (April 1992): 646–648.

Highfill, Philip H., Jr., et al., eds. *A Biographical Dictionary of Actors, Actresses, Musicians, Dancers, Managers, and Other Stage Personnel in London, 1660–1800.* Carbondale, Ill., 1973–.

Macaulay, Alastair. "The First British Ballerina." *The Dancing Times* (December 1990): 248–250.

Rader, Patricia Weeks. "Harlequin and Hussar: Hester Santlow's Dancing Career in London, 1706–1733." Master's thesis, City University of New York, 1992.

Weaver, John. *Anatomical and Mechanical Lectures upon Dancing.* London, 1721.

MOIRA GOFF

SARABANDE. The *sarabande* (Sp., *zarabanda;* Eng., *saraband*) was a dance in triple meter that was popular from the sixteenth to the second half of the eighteenth century. The term also refers to a Spanish poetic form associated with early versions of the dance and to an instrumental dance piece that was one of the standard movements of the Baroque suite. The saraband has both fast and slow versions.

The name has been variously explained as coming from the Arabic *ser-band* ("turban") or Persian *sar-band* (the wreath that holds a woman's headdress in place), from the word *zaranda* (from *zanandar,* meaning "to move nimbly"), or from the name of a Spanish dancer and actress who first performed the dance. Musicologist Daniel Devoto believes that the dance and its poetry are Andalusian in origin; Robert Stevenson asserts that the saraband originated in Latin America.

The earliest literary references to the *zarabanda* come from the New World. The *zarabanda* is first mentioned in 1539, in a poem by Fernando Guzmán Mexía in a manuscript from Panama. In 1569 a *carauanda a lo divino,* a sacred processional, was danced in Pátzcuaro (Michoacán, Mexico) on the feast of Corpus Christi. Ten years later the form is mentioned in Diego Durán's *Historia de las Indias de Nueva España.*

The first Spanish mention is a strongly worded prohibition, issued in Madrid in August 1583, of all singing, reciting, and dancing of *zarabandas* either in private residences or in the streets. Citizens who disobeyed the official decree were liable to a fine and, if they were men, to six years of servitude on a galley, or, if they were women, to exile.

The roots of the dance reach back into the days of Roman colonization and into folk traditions of Catalonia. Women were involved in the performances from the beginning, and the use of traditionally feminine instruments such as castanets and the *tambour de basque* is documented early. The sexual explicitness of early group sarabandes, which may have had ritual origins, appears to have been maintained through the sixteenth century. It gave the dance a reputation as licentious and even obscene: Juan de Mariana (1536–1624) calls it "a national disgrace" and describes the sarabande as "a dance and song so lascivious in its words, so ugly in its movements, that it is enough to inflame even very honest people" (*Tratado contra los juegos publicos,* first published under the title *De spectaculis,* Cologne, 1607).

The Swiss physician Thomas Platter saw a saraband in Barcelona in 1599 performed by "fifty men and women, playing castagnettes, moving mostly backwards with ridiculous contortions of the body, the hands, the feet." The chorus of irate voices of moralists and authorities condemning the saraband as "a creation of the devil" (Devoto, 1960) serves, however, as testimony to the popularity of the dance. It even gave its name to a fashionable hairstyle in the early seventeenth century.

Spanish *zarabanda* texts have a fairly strictly maintained poetic form consisting of six rhyming verses, the last two of which constitute a refrain. All known verse saraband date from the second half of the sixteenth and the early years of the seventeenth century.

Mentioned repeatedly in Spanish literature of the Golden Age, the dance in its early form had a number of choreographic shapes. It is documented as a processional through the streets at sacred and secular festivals in Seville in 1593 and in Barcelona in 1599. It was also performed in enclosed spaces, city squares, dance halls, and ballrooms as a circle dance by women alone or by men

SARABANDE. The starting position for a saraband for two gentleman as described by the English dancing master Kellom Tomlinson. One of a series of plates published as the second part of his 1735 treatise, *The Art of Dancing.* Descriptions of some of the steps in Feuillet notation can be seen on the floor. Commenting on these plates, Tomlinson noted that the prints not only aided understanding of the dance but that they could be framed and used as "agreeable and informative furniture." (Photograph from the Dance Collection, New York Public Library for the Performing Arts.)

and women together. It also occurred as a couple dance or as a solo. It could be either lively and licentious or grave and mannered.

From Spain, the *zarabanda* traveled to France and became part of the *ballet de cour* (as in the "Sarabande des Espagnols" in *La Douairière de Billebahaut,* 1625). Around 1635 the lovesick Cardinal Richelieu reportedly (Gédéon Tallemant des Réaux, *Historiettes,* written c.1657–1659) danced a *sarabande* with castanets and silver bells at the knees for his lady.

In England the dance is mentioned as early as 1616 in Ben Jonson's play *The Devil Is an Ass.* John Playford includes two sarabands in the first edition of his *English Dancing Master* (1651), but both are traditional English longways, one for six, the other for "as many as will," and show no trace of Spanish origins.

Most surviving examples of early saraband music occur in Italian tablatures for the Spanish guitar. Michael Praetorius gives music for two types of sarabands in his *Terpsichore* (1612), "La Sarabande" in even four-measure phrases without upbeat, and "Courrant Sarabande" with upbeat. As late as 1676 Thomas Mace still describes the saraband as a fast dance: "Sarabands, are of the Shortest Triple-Time; but are more Toyish, and Light, than Corantoes; and Commonly of Two Strains" *(Musick's Monument).* The repeated strains and the predominant harmonic pattern are common to all early sarabands.

Meanwhile, in France as well as in England, the famous rhythm patterns of the later *sarabandes* were beginning to emerge. By 1670, the slow triple meter was favored everywhere, giving rise to the notion of the *sarabande* as slow and stately, but faster types remained common.

When the guitar *zarabanda* was joined with other dances, the suite was born (earliest examples in Angelo Michele Bartolott's book of guitar music *Libro primo di chitarra spagnola,* Florence, 1640). Nearly all Baroque composers wrote suites for various instruments, including keyboard and instrumental ensembles. The *sarabande* reached its highest stage of artistic idealization in the works of Johann Sebastian Bach. In music after the end of the eighteenth century, the *sarabande* occurs mainly as a nostalgic look backward in compositions by Daniel Auber, Claude Debussy, Camille Saint-Saëns, and others (Hudson, 1980b).

As a dance, the Baroque *sarabande* was a favorite ingredient of French operas and ballets (sometimes called *entrée espagnole,* as in, for instance, the third *entrée* of *Le Ballet des Nations,* 1670) and became one of the most popular ballroom dances at the court of Louis XIV. Less "solemn and grave" than the *courante, sarabandes* for the ballroom nevertheless vary in speed from "very slow" and "slow" to a quicker, lighter pace equivalent to Jean-Philippe Rameau's "gracieusement" and Michel-Richard de Lalande's "légèrement." The steps, usually one step-unit per measure, go across the accentuated second beat and the hemiola at the end of each couplet, resulting in an intricate relationship of music and dance.

Writers of the period compare the *sarabande* to a slow *menuet.* Johann Mattheson speaks of the *grandezza,* the "haughty condition" of the *sarabande* for dancing.

In keeping with the Spanish associations of the dance, theatrical *sarabandes* in the seventeenth and early eighteenth centuries seem always to have been danced with castanets. In 1700 Raoul-Auger Feuillet gives a castanet score for the "Folies d'Espagne," which Gottfried Taubert calls "the most famous of all sarabande melodies." This practice can probably be applied to other fully notated *sarabande* choreographies. Jean-Jacques Rousseau refers in his *Dictionnaire de musique* (1777) to the use of castanets in *sarabandes.* By then, it appears, the *sarabande* was on the wane; Rousseau also refers to the dance as a thing of the past.

[*See also* Ballet Technique, History of, *article on* French Court Dance.]

BIBLIOGRAPHY

Applegate, Joan S. "English Cavalier Dance-Songs: Henry Lawes and Robert Herrick." In *Proceedings of the Sixth Annual Conference, Society of Dance History Scholars, the Ohio State University, 11–13 February 1983,* compiled by Christena L. Schlundt. Milwaukee, 1983.

Chadima, Helen Gower. "The Use of Castanets in Baroque Dance." In *Proceedings of the Sixth Annual Conference, Society of Dance History Scholars, the Ohio State University, 11–13 February 1983,* compiled by Christena L. Schlundt. Milwaukee, 1983.

Cotarelo y Mori, Emilio. *Bibliografía de las controversias sobre la licitud del teatro en España.* Madrid, 1904.

Cotarelo y Mori, Emilio. *Colección de entremeses, loas, bailes, jácaras, y mojigangas.* Madrid, 1911.

Devoto, Daniel. "La folle sarabande." *Revue de musicologie* 45 (1960); 46 (1961).

Devoto, Daniel. "Encore sur la sarabande." *Revue de musicologie* 50 (1964).

Devoto, Daniel. "Qué es la zarabanda?" *Boletin interamericano de música,* no. 45 (1965); no. 51 (1966).

Devoto, Daniel. "De la zarabanda à la sarabande." *Recherches sur la musique française classiques* 6 (1966): 27–72.

Herrmann-Bengen, Irmgard. *Tempobezeichnungen: Ursprung. Wandel im 17. und 18. Jahrhundert.* Tutzing, 1959.

Hilton, Wendy. *Dance of Court and Theatre: The French Noble Style, 1690–1725.* Princeton, 1981.

Hilton, Wendy. "Dances to Music by Jean-Baptiste Lully." *Early Music* 14.1 (1986): 51–63.

Hudson, Richard. "The *Zarabanda* and *Zarabanda Francese* in Italian Guitar Music of the Early Seventeenth Century." *Musica Disciplina* 24 (1970).

Hudson, Richard. "Folia." In *The New Grove Dictionary of Music and Musicians.* London, 1980a.

Hudson, Richard. "Sarabande." In *The New Grove Dictionary of Music and Musicians.* London, 1980b.

Little, Meredith Ellis, and Natalie Jenne. *Dance and the Music of J.S. Bach.* Bloomington, 1991.

Little, Meredith Ellis, and Carol G. Marsh. *La Danse Noble: An Inventory of Dances and Sources.* Williamstown, Mass., 1992.

Mather, Betty Bang, with Dean M. Karns. *Dance Rhythms of the French Baroque: A Handbook for Performance.* Bloomington, 1987.

Querol Gavaldá, Miguel. *La música en las obras de Cervantes.* Barcelona, 1948.

Ramos Smith, Maya. *La danza en México durante la época colonial.* Mexico City, 1979.

Ranum, Patricia. "Audible Rhetoric and Mute Rhetoric: The Seventeenth-Century French Sarabande." *Early Music* 14.1 (1986): 22–39.

Sachs, Curt. *World History of the Dance.* Translated by Bessie Schönberg. New York, 1937.

Seefrid, Gisela. *Die Airs de danse in den Bühnenwerken von Jean-Philippe Rameau.* Wiesbaden, 1969.

Stevenson, Robert. "Sarabande." In *Die Musik in Geschichte und Gegenwart.* Kassel, 1949–.

Stevenson, Robert. "The First Dated Mention of the Sarabande." *Journal of the American Musicological Society* 5 (1952).

Stevenson, Robert. "The Sarabande: A Dance of American Descent." *Interamerican Music Bulletin* 30 (1962).

Stevenson, Robert. "Communication." *Journal of the American Musicological Society* 16 (1963).

Stevenson, Robert. "The Mexican Origins of the Sarabande." *Interamerican Music Bulletin* 33 (1963).

Taubert, Karl Heinz. *Höfische Tänze: Ihre Geschichte und Choreographie.* Mainz, 1968.

INGRID BRAINARD

SARABHAI, MALLIKA (born 9 May 1954 in Ahmedabad), Indian dancer, actress, choreographer, and film director. Mallika Sarabhai is the daughter of the renowned dancer Mrinalini Sarabhai and Vikram Sarabhai, a scientist. She studied classical *bharata nāṭyam* with her mother and traditional Kuchipudi dance with C. R. Acharyulu. In addition, she holds a master's degree in business administration and a doctorate in psychology from Gujarat University.

Sarabhai combined a career as a classical and modern dancer with film and stage acting for nearly two decades. She played Draupadi in Peter Brooks' play *The Mahabharata,* in both the English and the French versions (1984–1988). Her international performances have included appearances at the Avignon Festival, the Brooklyn Academy of Music, Australia's Perth and Adelaide festivals, and at venues in Los Angeles, Tokyo, and Glasgow.

Sarabhai returned to India in the late 1980s and launched a series of experimental works. *Shakti* (Power of Women) concerns the image of Indian women and was written with English actor and director John Martin. *Sita's Daughters,* a performance piece in Hindi and English, developed with women activists, addressed such women's issues as rape and the abortion of female fetuses. *Itan Kahanai,* directed by John Martin, was the first collaboration between an Indian classical dancer and a Nigerian dancer, exploring the hidden agenda of folktales. These sociopolitical works invited audiences to think about issues and to explore innovation in dance, drama, music, and related performing arts. Sarabhai's experimental works also include *Mothers, Daughters, and Other Women* (1991); *Germinations, Structures,* and *Mean Street on Earth* (1993); and *Jazz Tillana, Changing Planes, Transposed Heads, Thattukazhi* (1994) and *V for . . .* (1996).

Sarabhai has directed a series of educational films, using traditional performance techniques to create awareness of environmental issues, female literacy, and health education, under the aegis of Darpana for Development, a program of the Darpana Dance Academy, established by her mother. Her film *Mena Gujarati* won an award. She has authored a book, *Understanding Kuchipudi,* with C. R. Acharyulu, and has edited several volumes on the performing arts of India.

Honors awarded to Sarabhai include the Gold Star for best young dance soloist (Paris, 1977), the Gold Medal for her folk dance company Janvak (Dijon, 1984), and the Gaurav Purashkar for her outstanding contribution to the arts (Gujarat, 1992). She lives in Ahmedabad; her young son Revanta performs with her, and her daughter Anahita is also interested in performing arts.

BIBLIOGRAPHY

Acharyulu, C. R., and Mallika Sarabhai. *Understanding Kuchipudi.* New Delhi, 1992.

Kolmes, Jacqueline. "Sarabhai Speaks to India's Downtrodden Women." *Dance Magazine* (January 1995): 55–58.
Kothari, Sunil, ed. *Bharata Natyam: Indian Classical Dance Art.* Bombay, 1979.
Massey, Reginald. "Mallika Sarabhai." *The Dancing Times* (January 1991): 354.
Misra, Susheela. *Some Dancers of India.* New Delhi, 1992.
Sloat, Susanna. "Mallika Sarabhai and Darpana Troupe." *Attitude* 10.4 (1994–1995): 30–31.

SUNIL KOTHARI

SARABHAI, MRINALINI (born 11 May 1928 in Madras), Indian dancer, choreographer, and educator. Sarabhai performed as a soloist and also with her company of dancers. She has toured throughout India and other parts of Asia, Europe, and North, South, and Central America.

In 1949 Sarabhai founded the Darpana Academy of the Performing Arts in Ahmedabad. She subsequently developed Darpana into one of India's foremost institutions for training in the traditional theater arts, maintaining a staff of artists teaching *kathakaḷi, bharata nāṭyam, mōhiniyāṭṭam,* and Kuchipudi dance drama techniques, as well as music and puppetry.

Sarabhai's own background includes training with such master teachers of *bharata nāṭyam* as Muthukumaran Pillai of Mannarkoil and Meenakshi Sundaram Pillai of Pandanallur, and the famous *kathakaḷi* actor Kunju Kurup. She also studied Javanese dance with Prince Tedjoekoesoemo. In addition to Indian classical dance and dance drama, Sarabhai also studied acting and stage technique at the American Academy of Dramatic Arts in New York.

Sarabhai's awards include the Vira Srinkhala for her contributions to *kathakaḷi,* and the coveted Vishwa Gurjari award. She is one of the few dance artists in India who write and publish significantly in the field of Indian dance. In 1986 she wrote a book, *Creations,* centered on her many original dance compositions over the years.

Although Sarabhai is still the Director of Darpana, her daughter Mallika is now Joint Director. Mallika continues to perform, touring and presenting original compositions on significant social themes such as the women's movement, non-violence, and other timely subjects. Some of her concerts have been sponsored by UNESCO.

BIBLIOGRAPHY

Barnes, Clive. "A New Approach to Ancient Dances." *New York Times* (17 December 1972).
Kothari, Sunil, ed. *Bharata Natyam: Indian Classical Dance Art.* Bombay, 1979.
Lynton, H. Ronken. *Born to Dance.* London, 1995.
Misra, Susheela. *Some Dancers of India.* New Delhi, 1992.
Mortimer, Chapman. "Mrinalini Sarabhai's Hindu Ballet." *Ballet* 11 (December 1951): 22–26.
"Mrinalini Sarabhai." *The Dancing Times* (May 1949): 428–430.
Sarabhai, Mrinalini. "Dance Is My Beloved." *Dance Magazine* (January 1964): 54–57.
Sarabhai, Mrinalini. "The Eight Nayikas." *Dance Perspectives,* no. 24 (1965).
Sarabhai, Mrinalini. "Darpana: A Mirror for India." *Dance and Dancers* (September 1971): 38–40.
Sarabhai, Mrinalini. *The Sacred Dance of India.* Bombay, 1979.
Sarabhai, Mrinalini. *Understanding Bharata Natyam.* 3d ed. Ahmedabad, 1981.
Sarabhai, Mrinalini. *Creations.* New York, 1986.
Venkataraman, Leela. "Sangeet Natak Akademi." *Sruti* (Madras), no. 35 (August 1987): 16–21.

CLIFFORD REIS JONES

SARDANA. Catalonia, the province of Spain bordering France and the Mediterranean Sea, celebrates the *sardana* as its national dance. It has been a unifying force, together with the Catalan language, of Catalonia's regional identity, particularly at times of political conflict with Spain's central government.

The *sardana* is a circle dance, moving alternately left and right. Individuals are free to break into or out of the circle at any point during the performance, provided their intrusion or exit does not disrupt the rhythmic flow of the steps or the raising or lowering of the arms. There is no restriction on the number of performers taking part nor on their sex or age.

The accompanying *cobla* (band) consists of the *flaviol* (the tabor pipe that introduces the dance), *tambor* (drum), *cornamusa* (bagpipe), *tiple* (a variety of oboe), and other brass instruments; in all, there are eleven musicians. The *sardana's* musical structure is divided into two sections known as *llargs* (long steps) and *curts* or *corts* (short steps). The dancers must be alert in order to complete each musical cycle in the correct direction and to end a sequence on the correct foot. At the beginning of the dance, during the first play-through of the music, the dancers listen carefully in order to count the measures so they can complete the dance satisfactorily on the repeat of the music.

The *sardana* is performed throughout the province of Catalonia on festival occasions, and regularly on Wednesdays or Sundays in Barcelona's central Plaza de Catalunya, where circles within circles performing the dance can be witnessed. Specialist clubs also exist for the regular weekly performance and enjoyment of this dance; newspapers print details of their dates and venues.

[*See also* Basque Dance.]

BIBLIOGRAPHY

Brandes, Stanley. "The Sardana: Catalan Dance and Catalan National Identity." *Journal of American Folklore* 103 (1990): 23–41.
Capmany, Aurelio. *El ball i la dansa popular a Catalunya.* Barcelona, 1948.
Mainar, Joseph. *La sardana: Dansa nacional, dansa viva.* Barcelona, 1986.
Martí i Pérez, Josep. "The Sardana as a Socio-Cultural Phenomenon in Contemporary Catalonia." *Yearbook for Traditional Music* 26 (1994): 39–46.

Mas i Solench, Josep M. *La sardana, dansa nacional de Catalunya.* Barcelona, 1993.

Zynda, Shirley. "Catalans and the Sardana." *Viltis* 48 (January–February 1990): 10–11.

PHILIPPA HEALE

SARDONO (Sardono Waluyo Kusumo; born 6 March 1945 in Surakarta [Solo], Central Java), Indonesian dancer, choreographer, director, filmmaker, teacher, and theoretician. Sardono W. Kusumo has had a significant influence on Indonesian arts and culture since the 1970s. As an instigator of research expeditions across the diverse cultures of the Indonesian archipelago and as director of collaborative artistic experiments, he has helped to establish continuities between Indonesian identity and traditions and the contemporary world community. His work has always been controversial for social and aesthetic reasons because he challenges fixed ideas of dance, theater, and performance context. Although Sardono does create new choreography and guide his company members in the composition of movement, his work is more concerned with bringing traditional dance forms and their psychospiritual roots into a new conceptual and dramatic vision reflecting contemporary concerns.

Sardono began studying the traditional martial art of *silat* at age eight and classical Javanese dance at age ten, learning from R. M. Djoko Suhardjo. His mother had various businesses involving catering, restaurants, and batik fabrics. Sardono's father, Raden Tumenggung Sarwono Waluyo Kusumo, was an officer in the royal court in Surakarta until 1945, when he opened a pharmacy. He exposed young Sardono to European literature as well as Tarzan comic books and the *Rāmāyaṇa* and *Mahābhārata*. Sardono attended a high school affiliated with the *kraton* or royal court of Surakarta, where he studied dance with R. T. Kusumokesowo, concentrating on refined *alus* male roles such as Arjuna.

In 1961 Kusumokesowo was creating a new dance drama form, *Sendratari,* intended as tourist entertainment at the Hindu temple of Prambanan. When he chose Sardono to develop the role of Hanoman, the white monkey general, the young dancer referred to his old Tarzan comic books and Javanese martial arts movements. Two years later his role was changed to that of the strong, *gagah*-style King Rahwono, principal antagonist in the *Rāmāyaṇa.* On graduating from high school, Sardono entered Gadjah Mada University to study economics.

He performed with the Indonesian cultural mission at the 1963–1964 World's Fair in New York. Before returning home he spent some months taking classes with modern dancer–choreographer Jean Erdman, from whom he acquired insights into combining the processes of improvisation and choreographic composition. From 1966 to 1968, just after the fall of President Achmad Sukarno and the bloody purge that followed, Sardono gave in to family concerns and entered the economics department at the University of Indonesia. By 1968 he was back in the arts as a member of the Jakarta Arts Council and a leading force in the newly established Jakarta Arts Center, Taman Ismail Marzuki (TIM). There he led experimental movement workshops exploring spiritual and cultural depths in various Indonesian dance forms. Joining him were other accomplished dancers, such as Sentot Sudiharto, Wayan Diya, Huriah Adam, Farida Feisol, S. Kardjono, and Yulianti Parani. Sardono formed an ensemble including Maruti, S. Kardjono, Sal Murgiyanto, Sentot, and Martati. Much of the process of creative exploration involved meditation at Java's Hindu and Buddhist temples, and experiences in the natural environment of mountains and seacoast. His interest was in each dancer's personal inner exploration, cultivating energies at the core of the

SARDONO. A controversial Javanese dancer-choreographer who takes an innovative approach to traditional forms, Sardono is seen here balancing at Borobudur. (Photograph © 1989 by Jack Vartoogian; used by permission.)

human spirit, drawing from Javanese mysticism, Indian *haṭhayoga,* and Buddhist meditation. Rather than repeating formal structures of Indonesian dance or discarding altogether the traditional and embracing a foreign form, Sardono chose to bring new meaning to Indonesian choreography by rediscovering the roots of psychospiritual processes underlying the forms. With his group he choreographed a scene from the *Rāmāyaṇa* in which the monkey kings Subali and Sugriwa do battle over the goddess Tara. His departure from standard artistic forms prompted the throwing of eggs by some audience members.

In 1969 he participated in a U.S. tour of the Budaya Dance Company, which included artists from various regions of Indonesia. Since 1971 Sardono has explored cultural and artistic traditions in Bali. Two of his major works emerged from his collaboration with various individual Balinese artists, but primarily the dancers and musicians of the Balinese rice-farming village of Teges Kanginan. *Kecak Rina* (1973) grew out of improvisations involving Sardono, fifty-five adults and children of Teges, Javanese dancers including Sal Murgiyanto, and the young Balinese innovators Madé Netra, Tapa Sudana, and Wayan Diya. New choreography and dramatic interactions emerged alongside the standard aspects of *kecak* dance and chorus. The final production, however, was deemed by the government's Balinese Arts Board to undermine traditional Balinese religious and aesthetic values, and it was not allowed to leave the island for a festival in Jakarta. It was not until 1976 that Sardono was allowed to bring *Kecak Rina* out of Bali, when they performed in Iran and several years later in Japan. The work is now performed regularly in Bali by the village of Teges.

In 1973 Sardono and Sentot performed alone at the Festival Mondial du Théâtre in Nancy, France. They were invited back for the next year with a full-scale production. During this trip Sardono also met his future wife, Amna Shahab, an Indonesian studying in Paris, who soon became manager of his company. He brought *The Sorceress of Dirah,* another innovative reinterpretation of Balinese and Javanese performance traditions, incorporating the Balinese dance and music masters Wayan Pugra, Madé Gerindem, Madé Pasek Tempo, and shadow-puppeteer Ida Bagus Madé Geria. In 1992 he directed a film based on this production.

Beginning in 1978, Sardono has been involved with ecological and cultural survival issues of Dayak groups in the rain forests of Kalimantan (Borneo) as well as the Dani and Asmat people of Irian Jaya. Research and collaboration with Kenyah and Modang Dayaks led to various performance projects, including *The Plastic Jungle* (1983) and *Lamenting Forest* (1987) in Jakarta.

Over the years Sardono has not maintained an ongoing company and has continually changed each of his productions as his creative impulse pursues new possibilities. Both factors have frustrated some of his dancers and Indonesian audiences alike. Since 1974, the Sardono Dance Theater has performed a variety of innovative works in Japan, India, Australia, Canada, Southeast Asia, and Europe, including festivals in Nancy, Avignon, Amsterdam, Rome, and Berlin. He is on the faculty of Jakarta Institute of the Arts (IKJ) and has also taught at the American Dance Festival. In 1990–1991 he was chairman of the Performing Arts Board of the Festival of Indonesia, which presented performances throughout the United States. In *Meta Ecology* (1979) Sardono's dancers were immersed in mud, performing in a rice paddy he had moved to the Jakarta Arts Center. *Maha Buta* (1988), combining Balinese and Javanese contemplative elements, was performed in Geneva and Mexico. *Passage through the Gong,* a reexploration of his Solonese roots, toured the United States in 1993, and *Detik . . . Detik . . . Tempo . . .* (1994) dealt with the decline of journalistic freedom in his homeland.

BIBLIOGRAPHY

Anderson, Benedict R. O'G. *Mythology and the Tolerance of the Javanese.* Ithaca, N.Y., 1965.

Brakel-Papenhuijzen, Clara. *The Bedhaya Court Dances of Central Java.* Leiden, 1992.

Brandon, James R. *On Thrones of Gold: Three Javanese Shadow Plays.* Cambridge, Mass., 1970.

Holt, Claire. *Art in Indonesia: Continuities and Change.* Ithaca, N.Y., 1967.

Murgiyanto, Sal. "Four Indonesian Choreographers: Dance in a Changing Perspective." Ph.D. diss., New York University, 1990.

Olsin-Windecker, Hilary. "Characterization in Classical Yogyanese Dance." In *Dance as Cultural Heritage,* vol. 1, edited by Betty True Jones. New York, 1983.

EDWARD HERBST

SARUKKAI, MALAVIKA (born 15 June 1959 in Bombay), Indian dancer. Malavika Sarukkai received her initial training in classical *bharata nāṭyam* as a young child from Guru Kalyansundaram at Shri Rajaraje Bharata Natya Kala Mandir in Bombay. Gifted with a resilient body and a quick grasp of the essentials of dance, as well as keen observation and an intellectual approach to performance, she drew critical attention by the age of twenty. She then moved on to the school of guru Swamimalai Rajaratnam Pillai in Madras to study the *vazhuvoor* style of *bharata nāṭyam.*

Sarukkai explored the architectonic qualities of *bharata nāṭyam,* revealing its exquisite lines, geometric forms and alignments, sculptural quality, and inherent dignity and grandeur. Her performances won the acclaim of connoisseurs. She pursued dance with singleminded devotion, rising to the top rank. She is regarded as this genre's leading exponent among the younger generation.

Sarukkai also studied Oḍissi dance under Guru Ramanj Ranjan Jena and Guru Kelucharan Mahapatra, acquiring equal proficiency in this genre and becoming one of its most admired performers. Her Oḍissi presentations at the Festival of India in the United Kingdom won excellent notices. After a few years, however, she gave up Oḍissi to concentrate on *bharata nāṭyam.*

As a choreographer, Sarukkai created *Fireflies,* set to poems by her younger sister Priya Sarukkai Chhabaria and to traditional Tamil and Sanskrit lyrics; it explores the manifold aspects of love through the responses of the *nāyikā,* or heroine, in Sanskrit drama. The production used back projections of traditional miniature paintings, drawing attention to the unity of the graphic and performing arts.

Sarukkai has also appeared in Festivals of India in the United States and Japan and in most major international dance festivals. She lives in Madras, choreographing traditionalist works which reflect the structural and formal beauty of *bharata nāṭyam,* based on her firm belief in its eternal appeal and ability to transcend mere technique. She strives to achieve that perfection in which dancer and dance become one. Her work has brought her several honors and awards.

BIBLIOGRAPHY

Kothari, Sunil, ed. *Bharata Natyam: Indian Classical Dance Art.* Bombay, 1979.

Meisner, Nadine. "Festival of India." *Dance and Dancers* (June 1982): 31–32.

Najan, Nala. "Procession of Indian Dance" (parts 1–2). *Arabesque* 12.2–3 (1986).

Sloat, Susanna. "Malavika Sarukkai." *Attitude* 10.4 (1994–1995): 62–63.

SUNIL KOTHARI

SATIE, ERIK (Eric-Alfred-Leslie Satie; born 17 May 1866 in Honfleur, died 1 July 1925 in Paris), French composer and pianist. The eccentric, cabaret-classical French musician Erik Satie left Normandy at the age of twelve to join his father in Paris and lived there for the rest of his life. His undistinguished studies at the Paris Conservatory led to jobs as a piano-player in Montmartre cabarets and to occasional composing for the Rosicrucians, a mystical society. Two of his earliest works, *Trois Gymnopédies* (1888) and *Trois Gnossiennes* (1890), remain among his most popular. While still in his twenties and utterly unknown, Satie made three unsuccessful rounds of protocol visits as an apparently serious candidate for the French Academy. His music became increasingly humorous in its titles, instructions, and style. Around 1900 he moved to an obscure suburb and dropped out of sight, except for seeing his old friends, the composers Claude Debussy and Maurice Ravel. He also went back to school at the age of forty, studying counterpoint with his junior, Albert Roussel, at the Schola Cantorum.

It was Debussy and Ravel who, around 1910, helped bring Satie out of hibernation for concerts of his music, new commissions, and after World War I, considerable success in Parisian artistic and social circles. His intransigent independence from all foreign influences, especially from Richard Wagner, won him musical followers, including the loose group of composers whom the critic Henri Collet named "Les Six." In 1920, after he had created the "symphonic drama" *Socrate* (1919), Satie invented "furniture music," a kind of background sound not to be listened to consciously. *Cinéma,* composed for the René Clair film *Entr'acte,* which was projected during the intermission of the ballet *Relâche* (1924), is a strikingly effective example of early film music based on a similar principle. During his last illness, Satie was cared for by the composer Darius Milhaud and his wife, the Catholic philosopher Jacques Maritain, and the sculptor Constantin Brancusi.

From the beginning Satie had his eye on the stage. His earliest works are dance pieces and incidental music for plays. In 1895 he composed a "Christian ballet" called *Uspud,* now lost. Satie's early ballet *Jack-in-the-Box* (1899) was staged after his death by Serge Diaghilev, and his marionette opera *Geneviève de Brabant,* composed the same year, was also performed only after his death, conducted by Roger Desormière. After *Geneviève,* Satie composed mostly piano pieces until Diaghilev asked him to collaborate with Jean Cocteau, Pablo Picasso, and Léonide Massine on *Parade* (1917). Rehearsed in Monte Carlo, this cubist or realist ballet had a turbulent premiere in Paris. Typewriters, a propeller, and sirens were added to the orchestra, and ten-foot (3 meter)-high costumes intended to be "moving scenery" scandalized the audience and the critics. Satie responded to one critic with an obscene and insulting postcard, landing himself in court, and almost in jail, on a damage suit. For all its modernist frills, *Parade* remains an effective and moving spectacle about carnival performers, a little American girl, and a Chinese prestidigitator.

The *succès de scandale* of *Parade* was followed by two more ballets. In *Mercure* (1924), again with Picasso's sets and costumes and Massine's choreography, Satie's music went further than ever toward a stripping down to essentials. Also in 1924, Satie collaborated with the painter-poet Francis Picabia on *Relâche,* a Dadaist ballet produced by Les Ballets Suédois and choreographed and danced by Jean Börlin. The dancers smoked, the fire inspector wandered on stage, and all the principal collaborators as well as Marcel Duchamp appeared in René Clair's uproarious intermission movie. Satie drove a midget car for the curtain calls. The audience howled. The self-effacing score for *Relâche* was Satie's last work.

The musical score for *Jack-in-the-Box* was discovered shortly after Satie's death and was presented by Diaghilev on 3 July 1926, with one of George Balanchine's earliest choreographies, and designs by André Derain. Orchestrated by Milhaud, the three parts of the piece have a childlike charm suited to Derain's toy-box decor.

The simplified, repetitive, unassertive music Satie composed for ballet and film approaches what is today called minimalist style. He also wrote some wonderfully entertaining lectures and musical spoofs, such as "A Musician's Day." Satie's renewed popularity since the 1960s and the clarity of his scores have led to a number of revivals. Massine restaged *Parade* for Le Ballet du XXe Siècle (1964), City Center Joffrey Ballet (1973), and London Festival Ballet (1974); the Joffrey Ballet production was especially important in establishing the work as a modern classic in its juxtaposition of music, design, and choreography. The Joffrey Ballet also staged a new version of *Relâche* by Moses Pendleton in 1980, closely modeled on the original version.

Frederick Ashton's *Monotones* for the Royal Ballet makes particularly effective use of Satie's music for a timeless, genderless effect, using the *Trois Gymnopédies,* orchestrated by Debussy and Roland-Manuel (1965); in 1966 Ashton added *Trois Gnossiennes,* orchestrated by John Lanchbery. John Cage long had a particular affinity for Satie's music and ideas, so it is not surprising that Cage's collaborator Merce Cunningham used Satie's scores for a number of dance works, adding yet another generation of artists influenced by Satie.

[*See also* Monotones; Parade; *and* Relâche.]

BIBLIOGRAPHY

Garafola, Lynn. *Diaghilev's Ballets Russes.* New York, 1989.
Gillmor, Alan. *Erik Satie.* Boston, 1988.
Myers, Rollo H. *Erik Satie.* London, 1948.
Rey, Anne. *Erik Satie.* Paris, 1974.
Satie, Erik. *Écrits.* Edited by Ornella Volta. Paris, 1977.
Satie, Erik. *The Writings of Erik Satie.* Translated and edited by Nigel Wilkins. London, 1980.
Satie, Erik. *Satie Seen through His Letters.* Translated by Michael Bullock. London, 1989.
Schmitt, Florent. "Erik Satie." *Montjoie!* (14 March 1913).
Shattuck, Roger. *The Banquet Years.* New York, 1958.
Templier, Pierre-Daniel. *Erik Satie* (1932). Translated by Elena L. French and David S. French. Cambridge, Mass., 1969.
Volta, Ornella. *Satie et la danse.* Paris, 1992.

ROGER SHATTUCK

SAUGUET, HENRI (Jean-Pierre Poupard; born 18 May 1901 in Bordeaux, died 22 June 1989 in Paris), French composer. After studying piano and organ with Paul Combes, for training in composition Henri Sauguet turned to Joseph Cateloube and then to Charles Koechlin, who were both influenced by late Romanticism. Darius Milhaud introduced Sauguet to fellow-composer Erik Satie, and Sauguet soon joined Satie's École d'Arcueil, a group of composers that also included Roger Desormière (1898–1963), Henri Cliquet-Pleyel (1893–1963), and Maxime Jacob (1906–1977); the last should not be confused with the distinguished French poet Max Jacob (1876–1944), with whom Sauguet often collaborated. In the 1930s Sauguet was a member of another group, La Sérénade. Sauguet's other lasting artistic attachments were his collaborations with choreographers Léonide Massine and George Balanchine, as well as Serge Lifar, Janine Charrat, and John Taras; he also had a lifelong association with librettist Boris Kochno and stage designer Christian Bérard.

Sauguet's prolific career of ballet composition began in the 1920s with a work for Etienne de Beaumont's soirées, *Les Roses,* choreographed by Massine but since lost. An important success came in 1927 with his score for Boris Kochno's ballet *La Chatte,* produced by Serge Diaghilev. This modernized Aesop's fable about a man's beloved cat metamorphosed into a woman but then tempted back into her original feline state, to the despair of the man, was choreographed by George Balanchine, with sets and costumes by Naum Gabo and Nicolas Pevsner; the first cast featured Olga Spessiva (also known as Olga Spessivtseva) and Serge Lifar, with subsequent performances by Alice Nikitina and finally Alicia Markova.

Honest warmth and engaging spontaneity abound in the poetic music of Sauguet, along with a craft that is unobtrusive and impeccable. Sauguet's typical, refreshing French approach, at times seeming to draw on Emmanuel Chabrier and Georges Bizet, is to do what the subject calls for. In his attitude he is an iconoclast: sociable and friendly, he stands alone but not apart. His music is in the mainstream in that it can be enjoyed by any listener. (Deeply religious, he composed relatively rarely for the church.) Although many of his mature works combine chromaticism with the witty, no-nonsense approach of Satie, his vocal works continue the tradition of Gabriel Fauré (at times extending back to Charles Gounod and Léo Delibes) and present a simple tenderness and tragedy all their own. It takes no special preparation, beyond knowing French, to appreciate Sauguet's 150 songs composed to the poems of various early twentieth-century poets. Another of his particular interests was the "composing of tonal portraits" to immortalize members of his Parisian entourage (analagous to the "portraits" of his friend Virgil Thomson).

As he employed idiomatically the musical forms appropriate to ballet, Sauguet's rhythmic and tonal surprises are infrequent. He achieves diverting character and emotional distinctions without wounding or violence. Although rhythmic and harmonic contrasts and effective oppositions enliven his music, the various elements and procedures form a lively balance rather than distracting the listener with vainglorious and noisy tensions. As Virgil Thomson pointed out, "Sauguet does not purge the emotions; he feeds them and makes them flower, give off perfume." His works for the stage are of human dimension, just as his chamber works are kaleidoscopic in the personal sphere.

Both imaginative and effective as a neo-Romantic, Sauguet often collaborated with one of the finest neo-Romantic painters, Christian Bérard (1902–1947). They and Boris Kochno collaborated on three touching ballets—*La Nuit, Les Forains,* and *La Rencontre.* In his neo-Romantic ballets, which have occasional neoclassical features, Sauguet's extended melodies are purged of the exotic excesses found in some earlier compositions for French lyric theater.

Sauguet's music for *Les Forains* (dedicated to Erik Satie) is one of the artistic revelations from the period of World War II. The twenty-five-minute score is a worthy successor to Satie's seventeen-minute *Parade,* in which Satie, Léonide Massine, Pablo Picasso, and Jean Cocteau presented vignettes of succinct brilliance built around a melancholy group of entertainers. Two decades later, *Les Forains* evoked a similar troupe—the Girl Acrobat, the Artistes, the Clown, the Siamese Sisters, the Magician, the Sleeping Beauty. Sauguet's score has twelve sections, with several unifying repeats, emphasizing duple rhythm; the tonality centers around the neutral key of C, with occasional wide swings between flats and sharps. There are differences between the two ballets: between Satie's tersely improbable score for *Parade* and Sauguet's music for *Les Forains,* which is touched with a shade more sugar; between Pablo Picasso's remarkable range of fantasticized characters and Bérard's brilliantly unpretentious emphasis on the very *saltimbanques* of Picasso's early Rose Period; and perhaps above all between Massine's early, concisely incredible mastery of variety in character as opposed to Roland Petit's discursive gift for filling space with diverting movement telling a nostalgic story but underplaying a more determined spirit. As a result one might pair *Parade* with Alban Berg's *Wozzeck,* and *Les Forains* with Kurt Weil's *Mahoganny*—all works of artistic commentary.

In addition to his ballets, Sauguet composed six operas and various vocal works, chamber music, four symphonies, concertos, and music for stage plays of Jean Giraudoux, which were filmed by Louis Jouvet. Experimenting throughout his long life, despite his admiration for Igor Stravinsky, Arnold Schoenberg, and Béla Bartók, Sauguet remained French to the core—witty, rational, humane, and true to his neo-Romantic center.

BIBLIOGRAPHY

Les Ballets 1933. Brighton, 1987. Exhibition catalog, Royal Pavilion.

Bril, France-Yvonne. *Henri Sauguet.* Paris, 1967.

De Cossart, Michael. *Ida Rubinstein, 1885–1960: A Theatrical Life.* Liverpool, 1987.

Sauguet, Henri. *La musique, ma vie.* Paris, 1990.

BAIRD HASTINGS

SAUTS. *See* Ballet Technique, *article on* Jumping Movements.

SAVIGNANO, LUCIANA (born 30 November 1943 in Milan), Italian dancer. Luciana Savignano received her dance training at the ballet school of the Teatro alla Scala in Milan. She also attended, along with her contemporaries Liliana Cosi and Anna Maria Prina, the class of perfection at the Bolshoi Ballet School in Moscow, under a special arrangement between the Bolshoi Theater and the Teatro alla Scala. Upon completion of her studies, Savignano joined La Scala Ballet in 1961 and for a number of years remained in the shadow cast by the triumphant rise of Carla Fracci and then of Liliana Cosi. Savignano's unusually long, slender body and exotic face seemed to preclude her success in the predominantly classical ballet repertory of La Scala.

Thanks to the choreographer and dancer Mario Pistoni, however, Savignano gained a foothold on success with works he conceived especially for her and her sinuous beauty. These included *Concerto dell'Albatro* (The Concert of the Albatross; 1971) and, above all, *The Miraculous Mandarin* (1968), which introduced the audience of La Scala to a new type of dancer and a new type of femininity: free, decisive, and secret. These special qualities of Savignano—lunar, nocturnal, and mysterious—were taken to their extreme by Maurice Béjart, who created for her *Ce que l'Amour Me Dit* (What Love Tells Me; 1975) and the solo "La Luna" (The Moon) in the ballet *Héliogabale, ou L'Anarchiste Couronné* (1976). The solo, especially, seemed to sum up Savignano's way of dancing and being.

In 1980 Savignano performed her first recital at the Piccola Scala theater, incorporating small pieces created for her by Pistoni, Béjart, and Roland Petit. Her second recital in 1983 was made up exclusively of pieces by Petit, among them *La Voce Umana,* based on a text by Jean Cocteau recited by the actress Mariangela Melato. In 1982, after a long run of Nicholas Beriozoff's *Swan Lake,* Savignano and her group of solo dancers from La Scala toured the whole of Italy and several French cities with a program that culminated in Béjart's *Boléro,* of which she was one of the best interpreters.

Savignano is the third in a great trio of Italian ballerinas, together with Carla Fracci and Elisabetta Terabust. Among the many ballets in which she gave notable performances are *L'Histoire du Soldat* by Amedeo Amadio (1973); *Omaggio a Picasso* (1977), *Cinderella* (1977), *Incontro* (1978), and *Nuits d'Été* (1978), all by Paolo Bortoluzzi; *Bhakti III* and *Romeo and Juliet* by Béjart (both, 1978); *After Eden* by John Butler with Dennis Wayne (1979); *Les Vainqueurs,* by Béjart (1980); *Schéhérazade,* by Bortoluzzi (1980); *Eagle's Nest,* by Louis Falco (1980); *The Taming of the Shrew* by John Cranko (1980); *The Rite of Spring* by Glen Tetley (1981); *Die Josephslegende* by Joseph Russillo (1982); *La Chatte* by Misha von Hoecke (1982); *Lieb und Lied* by Joseph Russillo (1983); and *La Stanza di Leonardo* by Falco (1983). During the later 1980s Savignano was guest star with La Scala Ballet and resident principal with Compagnia di Balletto del Teatro Nuovo di Torino.

BIBLIOGRAPHY

Doglio, Vittoria, and Elisa Vaccarino. *L'Italia in ballo.* Rome, 1993.

"Luciana Savignano." Program notes, Teatro alla Scala, Milan, 6 May 1980.

Pasi, Mario. "Luciana Savignano: La Scala o il mondo?" *Balletto oggi* 3 (June–August 1981).

Rossi, Luigi. *Il ballo alla Scala, 1778–1970.* Milan, 1972.

"Savignano, Luciana." In *Enciclopedia dello spettacolo.* Rome, 1954–.

Testa, Alberto, et al. *Il balletto nel novecento.* Turin, 1983.

VITTORIA OTTOLENGHI
Translated from Italian

SCALA BALLET. From the opening of the Teatro alla Scala in Milan, ballet, along with lyric opera, has played an integral part in the theater's musical productions. The first important choreographer appearing in the playbills was Gaspero Angiolini (1731–1803), who, during the decade beginning in 1779, composed three ballets for La Scala. This great reformer (along with Jean-Georges Noverre) of eighteenth-century dance did not rely on the masterpieces that had already made his name, such as *Don Juan* and *Semiramis,* but on new works such as *Solimano* (1781), composed to its own music.

The transition from the neoclassical to the Romantic period at La Scala had two main protagonists, both born in Naples, Gaetano Gioja and Salvatore Viganò (1769–1821). The most memorable performance of the period was the staging of Gioja's *Cesare in Egitto* (1809), which Napoleon Bonaparte enthusiastically supported. Viganò's ten years of activity at La Scala ushered in perhaps the most important creative period in the entire history of the theater, with the presentation of several masterpieces that earned universal admiration, beginning with the French author Stendahl, who considered Viganò, the inventor of the "choreodrama," to be one of the greatest living geniuses next to the composer Gioachino Rossini. Among Viganò's masterpieces presented at La Scala was an expanded version in 1813 of *Prometheus,* based on *Die Geschöpfe des Prometheus* (The Creatures of Prometheus), created in Vienna in 1801 to the score by Ludwig van Beethoven, which retained some parts of the original production. Another important opera, presented in 1817, was *Mirra,* based on the tragedy of the same name by Vittorio Alfieri. During the following year, Viganò presented *Otello,* based on Shakespeare's play, and *La Vestale* (The Vestal Virgin), inspired by Spentini's work of the same name. His last important opera was *I Titani* performed in 1820, the year before his death.

Carlo Blasis (1795–1878) made his debut at La Scala as a dancer in a ballet choreographed by Viganò in 1818; in the following year he made his debut as a choreographer in *Finto Feudatorio* with music by his father, a production that was regarded as a genuine failure. His true vocation, however, was that of theorist and teacher. In 1837 he was named the director of the academy of dance at La Scala, which had been founded in 1813. He held this position until 1850, and trained some of the most important dancers of the period, such as Carlotta Grisi, Fanny Cerrito, Amalia Ferraris, Carolina Rosati, Amina Boschetti, Claudina Cucchi, and Giuseppe Lepri. Lepri became, in his turn, the instructor of another great teacher, Enrico Cecchetti. [*See the entry on Blasis.*]

The Romantic period was an especially rich one in the Milanese theater. The first star to captivate ballet lovers was the beautiful Neapolitan Fanny Cerrito, who, a few months after the debut of Marie Taglioni at La Scala, appeared in a version of *La Sylphide,* choreographed by Antonio Cortesi on the same theme as Filippo Taglioni's production. Another star to appear at La Scala during this period was Fanny Elssler, who starred in a number of productions, including *Giselle, Esmeralda,* and *Catarina,* all by Jules Perrot. Her success continued through 1848 when, in the tumultuous atmosphere of insurrection against the Austrians in Milan, she was vehemently booed for having opposed a patriotic manifesto by the ballerinas of La Scala Ballet.

The rather late appearance of Marie Taglioni at La Scala occurred in 1841 when she performed in *La Gitana,* created for her by her father three years earlier at St. Petersburg. A few days later she triumphed in an outstanding performance as the lead in *La Sylphide,* her most accomplished role. Afterward, the entire orchestra of La Scala fêted her with a serenade under the window of her hotel. Taglioni's last performance for the Milanese audience was in *L'Ombra* (The Shadow) in 1846, also by Filippo Taglioni, a performance coolly received by a public that had become aware of the decadence of the star's personal life.

The second half of the nineteenth century began a period of large-scale emigration of the stars of La Scala to France and England, and, above all, to the tsarist theaters of Saint Petersburg and Moscow. These performers included Amalia Ferraris, Claudina Cucchi, and Caterina Beretta, who would later become a teacher at La Scala for an extensive period of time. But the major sensations were Carlotta Brianza, Pierina Legnani, and, above all,

Virginia Zucchi, who had a profound influence on the Russian theater, directly inspired by the famous "method" of Konstantin Stanislavski.

Late in their careers at La Scala, both Zucchi and Brianza repeated the performances that had brought each of them such triumph in Russia, but without their previous success. Meanwhile, a new star, Luigi Manzotti, who was destined to dominate the last decades of the century, appeared. The stupendous debut of this Milanese choreographer and mime took place at La Scala in 1881 with the production of *Excelsior,* a dance that celebrated the march of progress by glorifying such inventions as electricity and the telegraph, as well as the construction of a tunnel through Mont Censis connecting Italy with France. The triumph of civilization over obscurantism, personified respectively by the prima ballerina and by a mime disguised as an evil devil, was underscored by the brilliant music of Romualdo Marenco. After the highly successful European production of *Excelsior,* the team of Manzotti and Marenco staged a production in 1866 at La Scala of *Amor* that traced the history of its subject from the beginning of the world through the present. Finally in 1897, the tryptich of the team's successes was completed by *Sport,* an anthology of popular sports of the day, from horse racing to rowing.

LA SCALA BALLET. *Cinderella,* set to the Prokofiev score, was staged at La Scala in 1960 by Alfred Rodriguez. Scenery and costumes were designed by André Beaurepaire. The title role was danced by Italy's *prima ballerina assoluta,* Carla Fracci, pictured here in act 2, at center stage. (Photograph by Erio Piccagliani; used by permission of the Teatro alla Scala, Milan.)

The formulaically exaggerated spectacle of what was called the *ballo grande* ("grand dance") in time became decadent and sterile. Nonetheless, in the early years of the twentieth century La Scala continued to repeat Manzetti's weary formula, and La Scala artists greeted the appearance of the Ballets Russes in the 1920s with apprehension and a sense of crisis. Only in the forties was the theater reinvigorated with the arrival of Aurelio Milloss. In 1942 he staged at La Scala his production of *The Miraculous Mandarin* by Béla Bartók in its first production as a ballet. In 1946 Milloss was asked by Arturo Toscanini to direct the ballet company at La Scala, where he created other compositions such as *La Follia di Orlando* (The Madness of Orlando) with music by Gofredo Petrassi (1947). [*See the entry on Milloss.*]

Even in its darker moments, however, La Scala continued to be an important center for teaching. In 1925 Toscanini had asked the great teacher Enrico Cecchetti to refound the school, which went on to produce such figures as Cia Fornaroli (who would succeed Cecchetti when he died in 1928), Attilia Rodice, Gisella Caccialanza, and Vincenzo Celli. Cecchetti and Fornaroli were followed by other important teachers such as Ettorina Mazzucchelli, Esmée Bulnese, Vera Volkova, John Field, and Anna Maria Prina, La Scala's current director.

Since World War II, La Scala has produced other well-known figures, such as Olga Amati, Luciana Novaro, Ugo dell'Ara, and Mario Pistoni. The next generation saw the emergence at La Scala Ballet of a true international star, Carla Fracci, who was followed by Liliana Cosi, Luciana

Savignano, Oriella Dorella, Alessandra Ferri, and Amedeo Amodio.

[*For related discussion, see* Italy, *articles on theatrical dance.*]

BIBLIOGRAPHY

Arruga, Lorenzo. *La Scala.* New York, 1975.

Doglio, Vittoria, and Elisa Vaccarino. *L'Italia in ballo.* Rome, 1993.

Pitt, Freda. "Capriccio italien: A Look at the Chequered History of Dance at Teatro alla Scala." *Ballet News* 3 (July 1981): 14–18.

Rossi, Luigi. *Enrico Cecchetti il maestro dei maestri.* Vercelli, 1978.

Rossi, Luigi. *Il ballo alla Scala, 1778–1970.* Milan, 1972.

Testa, Alberto, ed. *Due secoli di ballo alla Scala. 1778–1975.* Milan, 1975. Exhibition catalogue, Museo Teatrale alla Scala.

LUIGI ROSSI
Translated from Italian

SCAPINO ROTTERDAM. Established in 1945 by Hans Snoek and Abraham van der Vies, Scapino Rotterdam (Scapino Ballet) was, until 1990, the only professional dance company in the world performing exclusively for children. Now the oldest ballet company in the Netherlands, the Scapino aimed to introduce children to the art of dance through performances, demonstrations, lectures, and classes. The company is fully subsidized by the Dutch government and provincial and town councils.

The name *Scapino* is that of a well-known *commedia dell'arte* figure; until 1970, the company had a Scapino character who introduced the ballets and often took part in them. He was a popular link between children and the events onstage. Letters, drawings, and questions were sent to him by children from all over the Netherlands.

Story ballets were the backbone of the company's repertory, especially during its first twenty years, when ballet was still an unknown art form in many parts of the Netherlands. During Snoek's time as director, she attracted many Dutch composers, writers, painters, and choreographers, and several now well-known artists made their debuts with the Scapino. The most important choreographer during Snoek's directorship was Jan Rebel, whose uncomplicated movements, theatrical effects, and feeling for what appealed to children found their best expression in ballets such as *De Prinses op de Erwt* (The Princess and the Pea; 1952), *Het Vrouwtje van Stavoren* (The Lady of Stavoren; 1954), *De Verjaardag van de Infante* (Birthday of the Infanta; 1958), *Jantje's Eerste Schooldag* (Johnny's First Day at School; 1959), and *Het Meisje met de Zwavelstokjes* (The Little Match Girl; 1963). Other choreographers during that period were Snoek, Karel Poons, Richard Glasstone, and Walter Gore.

After Snoek's retirement in 1970 the company was directed by Armando Navarro and Aart Verstegen; the latter departed in 1977, leaving Navarro as sole director. The course of the company was changed, the Scapino figure was abandoned, and the repertory was enlarged with more abstract ballets and Navarro's adaptations of such classics as *The Nutcracker* (1974), *Coppélia* (1970), and *Cinderella* (1978). Of the abstract ballets, those of Hans van Manen, Charles Czarny, and Nils Christe were well received because of their contemporary approach to dance

SCAPINO ROTTERDAM. A scene from the company's 1992 production of *Pulcinella,* choreographed by Nils Christe to Igor Stravinsky's 1920 score. The central figure in this photograph is Andreas Jüstrich, who portrayed the title character. Behind him, in a white cap and half-mask, is Mariëtte Redel as Pimpinella, Pulcinella's lover. (Photograph © 1992 by Jack Vartoogian; used by permission.)

in general and their ability to touch the imagination of children. In Czarny's ballets, for example, many props are used to great effect.

Special difficulties confronted the dancers who performed in this company. The repertory seldom called for technical brilliance; the audiences were often quite noisy (performances were given during school hours, so attendance was compulsory); and the normal two performances each day were often given at early hours. It is no surprise, then, that many of the company's members considered the Scapino to be a stepping-stone to an "adult" company. Its most important performers have included Lizzy Demmenie, Greetje Donker, Jennifer Roders, Aart Verstegen, Jan Rebel, Bob Verbrugge, Marianne Sarstadt, Käthy Gosschalk, Toos Waldman, Willy Roemers, Wim Bender, Ine Rietstap, Mary Siegel, Robin Woolmer, and Tom de Graaf (as the Scapino figure).

From the twelve dancers who assembled in 1945, the Scapino Ballet grew to approximately forty members in the 1980s. Since 1968 a special demonstration group has been attached to the company. It initially consisted of only three dancers, but their demonstrations were so popular that more were added. The group had its own repertory but also appeared in the larger company's programs. Apart from the special group, an educational department provided creative dance classes and school projects. The company also has frequently traveled abroad; in 1963, it performed at the White House in Washington, D.C.

In 1986 Christe became the company's co–artistic director with Navarro; in 1991, he succeeded Navarro as director. In 1988 the company moved from Amsterdam to become one of the major companies to perform at the newly built theater in Rotterdam.

In 1990 the company changed its course completely. Performing for children was abandoned, as were the educational activities. The name was changed to Scapino Ballet Rotterdam, which became a regular company dancing ballets by contemporary choreographers. In the same year Ed Wubbe was appointed choreographer in residence. When Christe left the company in 1992, Wubbe became temporary artistic director. In 1992 Wubbe was named artistic director, and the name was changed to Scapino Rotterdam. Wubbe's most successful works have included *Rameau* (1990); *Perfect Skin* (1991); *Kathleen* (1992); a full-length *Romeo and Juliet* (1995); and *Le Sacre du Printemps* (1996).

[*See also* Netherlands, *article on* Theatrical Dance; *and the entry on Snoek.*]

BIBLIOGRAPHY

Scapino Nieuws. Information bulletin of the Scapino Ballet.

Schaik, Eva van. *Op gespannen voet: Geschiedenis van de Nederlandse theaterdans vanaf 1900.* Haarlem, 1981.

Voeten, Jessica. *Scapino.* Amsterdam, 1985.

INE RIETSTAP

SCÈNES DE BALLET. Ballet in one act. Choreography: Frederick Ashton. Music: Igor Stravinsky. Scenery and costumes: André Beaurepaire. First Performance: 11 February 1948, Royal Opera House, Covent Garden, London, Sadler's Wells Ballet. Principals: Margot Fonteyn, Michael Somes.

Ashton believed that a ballet should have, as distinct from subject matter, a basic idea, not necessarily discernible to an audience. In *Scènes de Ballet* he had three such ideas: the Stravinsky music, an unusually complex score for Ashton, which he was obliged to analyze in greater detail than had been his custom; the example of Marius Petipa's choreography, which was his conscious model for the first time in his career; and theorems from Euclidian geometry. The last helped him to organize new floor patterns, making the ballet equally satisfying, yet quite different, to watch from any angle. André Beaurepaire provided an architectural decor and costumes—tunics for men and tutus for women—decorated with geometrical designs. (Both costumes and scenery were revised in subsequent stagings.)

Ashton's choreography was a dense array of the ranks, devices, and forms of classical ballet, such as a dance by the female corps, a male pas de quatre, a ballerina's *entrée,* her supported adagio, solo variation, and pas de deux—all given a new complexity of organization. The ballet also used intricate embellishments from the *danse d'école,* such as leanings of the torso, wrist flicks, head nods, pointe taps, and other details. The ballet builds all these parts together into an increasingly elaborate structure, with a powerful ensemble climax.

Ashton was particularly proud of this *Scènes de Ballet.* Moira Shearer was greatly admired as the second-cast ballerina; Nadia Nerina and Antoinette Sibley were also especially successful in the role, as were David Blair and Michael Coleman as the leading *danseur.* In 1968, twenty years after its premiere, the ballet was successfully staged for the German Opera Ballet in Berlin, without decor and in practice dress, and in 1990, when it was more than forty years old, it was revived for the Dutch National Ballet in Amsterdam.

Ashton's was not the first choreographic treatment of Stravinsky's score, nor the last. The first was done by Anton Dolin for a number featuring himself and Alicia Markova in Billy Rose's revue *The Seven Lively Arts,* which, after previews in Philadelphia, opened on Broadway at the Ziegfeld Theater on 7 December 1944. Later, post-Ashton productions using the Stravinsky score were choreographed by Gustav Blank (Berlin, 1952), Robert Mayer (Stuttgart, 1952), Peter van Dyk (Hamburg, 1962), John Cranko (Stuttgart, 1962), Nicholas Petrov (Pittsburgh, 1972), and John Taras (New York, 1972). The production by Taras was done for the New York City Ballet's Stravinsky Festival and was planned by the choreographer as a digest of Romantic ballet. It featured Patricia McBride and Jean-Pierre Bonnefous in the leading roles, six female demi-soloists, and a corps de ballet of twelve women.

BIBLIOGRAPHY

Clarke, Mary, and Clement Crisp. *The Ballet Goer's Guide.* New York, 1981.

Macaulay, Alastair. "To Stravinsky." *The Dancing Times* (August 1984): 921–922.

Vaughan, David. *Frederick Ashton and His Ballets.* London, 1977.

ALASTAIR MACAULAY

SCENIC DESIGN. The history of design for dance is essentially the history of design for all Western performing arts. From the earliest times in Europe, dance has been an integral part of the theater. There is, however, a major difference in focus between Western dance and theater, which is reflected in design: dance is concerned primarily with movement in space; theater tends to use movement merely as a tool to emphasize other aspects such as language, theme, or imagery. Design for theater may be seen as creating an environment or locale in which actors perform, and design for dance is concerned with the organization of space. Yet dance design also may help tell a story, create an appropriate mood, or make political or thematic statements through the use of emblematic imagery; its primary purpose, however, is to provide adequate and appropriate space in which the performers may move.

Dance Design Classifications. Since the Renaissance, most Western dance has been performed on either a thrust stage, with the audience on three sides, or a proscenium-style stage, a raised stage at one end of a room, usually framed; these arrangements have necessitated a certain approach to design. The dancer moves on the horizontal plane of the stage floor, but the audience is most aware of the vertical planes of the back and sides of the stage. Thus, design for dance is basically design of the background, leaving the main stage space empty for the dancer's movement; the dancer becomes a force connecting design with dance space. Because of this, costume has been a crucial element in design and, in the twentieth century, decor and costume have literally merged in several instances.

Designer Rouben Ter-Arutunian classified dance design as classic, romantic, sculptural, or decorative. Theater design has been classified as architectural, sculptural, or painterly. If design for dance is perceived as the organization of space, a logical classification of dance design might break down into open-space, sculptural, and environmental.

Open-space design. In the open-space arrangement, the stage floor is kept free and design concerns the treatment of the vertical planes, the walls, of the stage. There are several approaches to this style. One approach—the neutral design, very common in modern dance—encloses the stage space with black drapes, a cyclorama bathed in light, or some other nonexpressive, background (Ter-Arutunian's classic). The stage becomes a closed space with the emphasis on the stage as a stage. Focus clearly is on the dancer.

In the decorative approach to open-space design, the background becomes a canvas for the designer. There are two aesthetic approaches basic to this method—representational (illusionistic) or presentational (abstract). Representational design tries to create the illusion of reality by representing something in the real world. This is the approach of the Renaissance and of the narrative ballets of the Romantic era. The implication of illusionistic scenery is that the stage world continues beyond the wings. Presentational scenery makes no attempt at illusion. It may range from the purely decorative to the thematic. The stage may be painted with emblematic images, broad swatches of color, or abstract designs intended to enhance the theme or aesthetics of the dance. There are designs that fall between these two—fragmentary or suggestive designs that create an image of a real place without creating an illusion of reality.

Sculptural design. Sculptural design treats the stage as a three-dimensional space *through* which the dancers move. The design consists of one or more three-dimensional objects that serve as focal or anchor points for the dance. (This is not the same as open-space design, which simply placing a rock or tree onstage is merely an extension of the two-dimensional approach.)

Environmental design. Environmental design eliminates a central focal point and incorporates all the natural or found elements of the environment into the spectator's perception of the space. Design in the conventional sense is eliminated in favor of using the real world.

Western Dance Design from Antiquity to the Renaissance. The earliest dance design was probably the ancient Mediterranean dancing circle (Greek, *orchēstra*), a space in which the dancers performed while the spectators stood around the perimeter—a true example of design as the organization of space. When individual actors began to dominate Greek tragedies and comedies, a raised stage was added to the orchestra. By the fourth century BCE—the Classical era of ancient Greece—the orchestra was truncated and diminished in size as the chorus lost its importance and, ultimately its very existence. With the emergence of the raised stage came a form of painted scenery. Theater architecture during the Classical era consisted of either permanent architectural stages (in which all the features are permanent architectural elements) or movable booth stages. The permanent stages consisted of three parts: an audience area, the orchestra, and a raised stage in front of an architectural facade. Booth stages consisted of a small raised stage (a platform on trestles or a rolling cart) with a curtain at the back. The booth stage was portable, or at least temporary, and could be set up wherever there was a potential audience, usually in a city's market square. Unlike performances in formal architectural theaters that controlled the spectator's focus, performances on booth stages often incorporated the natural features of the surrounding environment into the mise-en-scènes.

After the invasions of the Goths and the fall of the Roman Empire, this approach became a significant element in the reemergence of Western theater—first in the medieval Christian church and, subsequently, in the development of early Renaissance dance design.

Mansion, platea, and simultaneous staging. Early Roman Catholic liturgical drama, beginning about the tenth century, used the space and features of the churches themselves, with specific locations suggested by *mansions,* emblematic booths or scenic units. As with the booth stages, performers incorporated the space in front of or around the mansion into the performance. This neutral or transformable space was known as the *platea,* and it was often shared with the audience. Later medieval performances moved out of churches and into towns and cities, usually the market squares, still keeping the basic mansion and platea principles. In some cities presentation of the so-called mystery plays utilized simultaneous staging, in which several mansions were presented simultaneously, either on a long raised stage facing the audience or within or around a given space. In either arrangement the mansions in simultaneous staging shared a single platea.

The mansion and platea concept allowed an emblematic piece of scenery to represent a place, and a neutral playing area to be defined by the performers and the scenery, lessening the need for illusionism. Also, the use of simultaneous staging allowed a flow from one location to the next, unencumbered by the logic of the external world or cumbersome illusionistic scenery. Scenery in the Middle Ages was suggestive, in that it helped the spectator locate an action in time and space, suggested the important attributes of the place, and even created a sense of wonder with its beauty and technological trickery—but it rarely tried to convince the spectator that it was real. Most importantly, it was an allegorical statement.

The medieval approach to stage design and the use of simultaneous staging clearly was exemplified in the early Renaissance *ballet de cour* (court ballet) and was documented in the engravings of *Le Ballet des Polonais* in the Palace of the Tuileries in Paris in 1573 and *Le Balet Comique de la Royne,* designed by Jacques Patin in 1581, in the Salle du Petit Bourbon. Engravings of the 1581 production illustrate the royal party seated at floor level at one end of the hall while the other spectators stood in tiers along both long walls. Most of the floor space is empty—a platea—but against the back wall is a fairly elaborate scenic unit: the garden of Circe with flowers, fountains, animals, and a perspective view of a city. On either side of the space are two islands of scenery: the grove of Pan and a cloud-shrouded cave containing singers. At least three locales were represented simultaneously, yet the entire space could represent, at any given moment, an extension of any one of the scenes. The design of the *ballet de cour* was medieval in concept, using simultaneous

SCENIC DESIGN. Jacques Patin's designs for *Le Balet Comique de la Royne* (1581), in the Great Hall of the Palais Bourbon in Paris, simultaneously represented several different settings. This contemporary lithograph of the event shows, at right, the grove of Pan; at left, a clouded archway covering seated singers; at the rear, a tree-lined grotto filled with animals; and in the distance, Circe's Palace. The central floor space represented, at given times, extensions of these locales. Seen here at center, in the opening of the court spectacle, is a nobleman who has escaped from Circe's garden, telling the audience of his adventures. Seated in the foreground are Henri III, the Queen Mother, and attendant nobles and guards. Other spectators line the tiers. (Dance Collection, New York Public Library for the Performing Arts.)

SCENIC DESIGN. An etching depicting Giacomo Torrelli's design for act 1, scene 1, of *Les Noces de Pélée et de Thétis* (1654), performed at the Palais Bourbon, Paris. A flying machine, a popular stagecraft device at the time, carries the figure of Peleus in his chariot across the heavens. Below, in Chiron's cave, Torrelli's series of painted flats created a vanishing-point perspective. (Dance Collection, New York Public Library for the Performing Arts.)

scenes, mansion and platea, and emblematic imagery that carried a specific message for the principal spectator.

Spectacles at court—such as royal entries, mummings and masquerades, and tournaments and carrousels (mock tournaments on horseback; equestrian ballets)—also influenced design significantly. These elaborate displays were usually given in conjunction with a court event, such as a wedding or a royal visit. Although each form had its own specific characteristics, they all involved lavish costumes, music, singing, dance, processions, and spectacular, often technically complex, scenography. The Garden of Circe in *Le Balet Comique de la Royne* is reminiscent of a tableau stage from a royal entry.

On a confined scale, the spirit and style of court spectacles found their way into the theater in the form of intermezzi—allegorical scenes presented by dancer-performers between the acts of a play or between the courses of a banquet. By the Renaissance, audience sensibility was not content with the relatively simple spectacle of the *ballet de cour*—it demanded the marvelous. Thus, transformation scenes and the rapid change from one scene to another became staples of the intermezzi. Changeable scenery replaced the simultaneous stage and became one of the two keystones of Renaissance scenography. The other was the discovery of perspective painting.

Perspective painting and changeable scenery. Perspective painting was first used in the theater in Ferrara, Italy, in 1508 in a production of Ariosto's *La Cassaria*. Through the sixteenth and seventeenth centuries, various methods were developed to create an ever more illusionistic perspective scene. The intent of the decor was to represent on the stage a real time and place that existed separately from the world of the audience (although the places depicted were more often than not mythical and fantastic). The perspective, however, worked only from a limited viewing point—the center of the auditorium—because it was intended only for a principal spectator.

The simplest way to create a perspective setting was with a two-dimensional, painted backcloth behind the performers. A more effective perspective scene could be created with the use of a symmetrical arrangement of painted flats along either side of the stage in combination with a painted backcloth. This method was described by Sebastiano Serlio in 1545. Increasingly deep stages and improved techniques of perspective painting continued to enhance the illusion of the scene over the next century. But performers had to act in front of, not in, the scenery in order to preserve the illusion. Furthermore, this one scene would have to function for the whole performance. Over the next century Serlio, Nicola Sabbatini, and Joseph Furttenbach suggested methods for creating changeable scenery. The methods were awkward, however, and since there was no front curtain to mask scene shifts, crude devices were suggested to divert the audience's attention during the change, such as blowing a horn at the rear of the auditorium.

One of the first uses of changeable scenery was probably in the *intermedio* staged by Bernardo Buontalenti in

1585, in the new theater he designed within the Uffizi Palace in Florence.

Stage Machines. Changeable scenery fed the growing Renaissance appetite for wonder and spectacle, since it allowed the audience to be magically transported to several locales over the course of a several-hour performance. The sense of wonder was further enhanced by stage machines that created spectacular effects. The most awe-inspiring and frequently employed were the cloud machines—moving structures that flew in on counterweight or winch-controlled wires from above or behind the stage and opened up to reveal gods, allegorical figures in horse-drawn chariots, or choruses several dozen strong. Other effects included individual performers flying around, ships sailing across storm-tossed seas, huge conflagrations, and the sudden appearance or disappearance of monsters, mountains, or caves.

Buontalenti was also a major designer of theater machines and served as court designer for the ruling family in Florence (the Medici) for some fifty years. Upon his death in 1608, he was succeeded by his pupil Giulio Parigi and, afterwards, by Parigi's son Alfonso. These three were the first great practicing stage designers of the Renaissance. They not only established Italy as a leader in theatrical production, but created the style of design that was to dominate much of Europe for more than two centuries, referred to simply as *Italianate design.*

Flat Wing and Groove. In 1606 in Ferrara, Giovanni Battista Aleotti developed the first practical method of scene changing: the *scaena ductilis,* or flat wing and groove. In this system a series of perspective-painted flats were set on tracks in the stage floor. At the scene change, stagehands slid the flats offstage simultaneously, revealing a new scene behind. At the back of the stage a sliding shutter operated in the same way. By 1640 this method was common throughout Europe and was introduced in England in the court masques by designer Inigo Jones.

Although the system was more effective than its predecessors it was still subject to erratic movement and human error. These problems were solved by Giacomo Torelli, who worked in Venice and Paris in the 1640s and 1650s. Torelli essentially mechanized the *scaena ductilis.* The wings and backshutters were attached through slits in the floor to rolling carriages attached by cables to a central winch beneath the stage. Overhead masking pieces such as cloud borders were similarly controlled. A single person operating the winch could smoothly change an entire scene. (This method may actually have been in use in Parma in the Teatro Farnese by 1628, but Torelli certainly perfected it.) The effect was something like a cinematic dissolve and apparently aroused in the audience a great sense of admiration and wonder. The results were so spectacular that productions began to introduce changes in the midst of scenes for no apparent purpose other than the visual delight they provoked.

Proscenium Arch. With the development of stage machinery and changeable scenes came the need to mask the sides of the stage. This was fundamental in the development of the proscenium arch, the architectural framing device still used today in conventional staging. Whatever its practical value, the proscenium had the perceptual effect of separating the spectators from the performance. The stage became a world separate from that of the auditorium. Until the mid-seventeenth century, however, most of the dancing and performance occurred in front of the proscenium, in an orchestra-like space surrounded on three sides by the audience. There is speculation about

SCENIC DESIGN. A famous etching, by Jacques Callot after Giulio Parigi, depicting the setting for the first *intermedio* of *The Liberation of Tirreno and Arnea* (1616), a *veglia* (court entertainment) at the Teatro Ducale of the Palazzo Uffizi, Florence. This stage arrangement represents a transitional phase in the development of the proscenium theater. Here, dancers perform on several levels in relation to the audience: in a cleared space in front of the stage; on curved ramps leading to the stage; on the elevated stage proper; and, at far back, suspended in cloud machines. (Courtesy of Madison U. Sowell and Debra H. Sowell, Brigham Young University, Provo, Utah.)

the theoretical and physical origins of the proscenium, but the first known example was in Parma's Teatro Farnese, built in 1618.

The perspective wonders of the stage remained visible in full only to the selected audience directly facing the stage—a reminder that ballets and other court performances originally were intended as political statements for a royal audience and were directed only to that presence.

Italian influence. The Italian approach to scenic design made inroads in the French court as early as the 1540s when Catherine de Medici became queen to Henri II. It reached its height after the 1640s when Cardinal Mazarin imported Torelli to stage the ballets and spectacles of the French court. Under Louis XIV of France, both ballet and scenic design flourished. Succeeding designers of note at the court of Louis XIV included Gasparo Vigarani and his sons Carlo and Lodovico, Henry Gissey, and Jean-Louis Berain. One of the highlights of this period was a three-day presentation designed by Carlo Vigarani, entitled *Les Plaisirs de l'Île Enchantée;* it consisted of ballets, banquets, plays (including Molière's comedy-ballet *La Princesse d'Elide*), fireworks, and mock combat.

The splendor of the French court at Versailles was rivaled in Vienna by productions designed by Giovanni Burnacini and subsequently by his son Lodovico. An example of the important advances in scenery design is apparent in Lodovico's staging of *Il Pomo d'Oro* in 1667. The scenes magically shifted from Hades to Olympus, Mount Ida, the palace of Paris, the sea with a fleet of ships, the fortress of Mars, Athena's temple, and the heavens.

In general, the scenery of this period was formal and architectural and illusion was enhanced by the lighting, consisting of oil and candles. The relative dimness and the inevitable flickering hid techniques that would appear glaringly obvious in a modern theater. The scenic techniques virtually demanded a symmetrical design, which the best artists, such as Burnacini, could transform into a

SCENIC DESIGN. This design by Giuseppe Galli da Bibiena is a fine example of angled perspective *(scena per angolo),* which replaced Renaissance single-point perspective in the seventeenth and eighteenth centuries. Note the characteristic symmetry and the sophisticated use of light, which appears to stream through the portals. (Reprinted from Beaumont, 1946, p. 18.)

dynamic visual rhythm through contrasts of light and shadow and a flowing sense of line. Design and architecture allowed the performance to exist on three planes: the orchestra, the stage, and the clouds or other flying machines. Since the performers had to remain almost entirely in front of the scenery, the dancers in the orchestra space became a connective bridge between the spectators and the scenic spectacle. Because it was created in vanishing perspective from a central viewpoint, the scenery could be seen as an extension of the auditorium.

The crowning glory of Baroque design came with the Bibiena family. Beginning in the early seventeenth century with Giovanni Maria Galli, three generations of Bibienas designed for most of the court theaters and opera houses of Europe until well into the late eighteenth century. Aside from the unequaled grandeur of their settings, their most important contribution was the development, around the beginning of the eighteenth century, of the *scena per angolo,* or angled perspective. This is generally attributed to Ferdinando Bibiena.

Angled perspective replaced the single-point, central perspective of the sixteenth and seventeenth centuries with multipoint perspective, in which the scene could appear to vanish at several points. Not only did this improve the overall quality of perspective scenery, but it allowed for settings that no longer appeared to be mere extensions of the auditorium. Although the proscenium had enhanced a psychological separation between stage and spectator, the new technique created the visual illusion of a completely separate world.

In 1723, Giuseppe Bibiena was the first designer to use back-lit transparent scenery. This, combined with his skillful use of foliage and masses of light and shade worked to soften the formality of earlier design while maintaining the inevitable symmetry. [*See the entry on the Bibiena family.*]

Changes in the Eighteenth and Nineteenth Centuries. Early in the eighteenth century this symmetry was broken by the work of Filippo Juvarra, who developed a method for placing flats anywhere he wished onstage—but always parallel to the proscenium. As methods like these deepened the illusion of perspective, they allowed the performers to retreat farther and farther into the scenery, hastening the day when the forestage would disappear and performers would be totally contained within the confines of the proscenium stage. Among other designers of note is the eighteenth-century French artist Jean-Nicolas Servandoni. In an attempt to enhance perspective illusion, he was not content with scene painting; he also arranged dancers according to height and used children dressed like the adults, in the background, their smaller proportions and shorter height enhancing the illusion.

The basic technology of stage design in place by the mid-seventeenth century remained in use in some places into the twentieth century. The style of design did however continue to change. In the eighteenth century, there began a slow movement toward a greater naturalism on the stage, fueled by an interest in antiquarianism as well as a fascination with the exotic: Jean-George Noverre's first ballet, *The Chinese Festival,* is an example. Naturalism must be seen as a relative term, since the realistic style and detail of eighteenth-century settings still seem false or idealized by our standards.

In the eighteenth century the opera houses, rather than the courts, became the home of ballet, and the changing tastes and sensibilities of public audiences altered the style of design. The Italian influence continued throughout the century, in large part because of the prolific Bibienas, but its formalism was softened by a predominant rococco style. Images of edifices from the Classical era were often replaced with carefully arranged ruins or else surrounded by lush foliage backed by exotic, mysterious landscapes.

The Alsatian designer Philippe Jacques de Loutherbourg, brought to England by actor-manager David Garrick in 1771, was instrumental in developing new approaches to design that suited eighteenth-century tastes. By breaking up the symmetry of the wings with ground rows (low, freestanding scenic pieces representing hedges, horizon lines, etc.), cutouts, and transparent scenery, and by the most sophisticated use of lighting to date, de Loutherbourg created exotic country scenes as well as highly acclaimed illusions of fire, volcanoes, sunlight, moonlight, and rain.

Thus, by the late eighteenth century, stage settings were no longer always symmetrical or formal. Idyllic and exotic landscapes filled with realistic detail and local color predominated, but the interiors of average homes were increasingly common. In response to this emerging realism, a resurgence of neoclassicism manifested itself in opera and ballet design. Ordered settings, now employing the diagonal perspective of the Bibienas—the vanishing point off to one side—depicted heroic scenes.

In ballet, this style was best exemplified by Alessandro Sanquirico working in the early nineteenth century at the Teatro alla Scala in Milan. Other notable designers of this period were Paolo Landriani and Pasquale Canna. Working with choreographer Salvatore Viganò, Sanquirico created monumental, magnificent settings that might best be described as fantasies based on realistic images. His dozens of designs depicting such settings as a greenhouse, an Egyptian harbor, mountain ravines, and gothic cellars are fantastic, idealized, larger-than-life versions of their real-world models. As a result, the dance was often overwhelmed by the design.

The Romantic era and Romanticism. By the 1820s most of Europe was in the throes of the Romantic era. Romanticism was a response to the formality and rules of neoclassicism; instead of relying on observable phenomena and the rational mind, it was felt that truth could be found in spirituality and nature. They idolized the genius-artist and felt art could unite the dichotomous worlds of body and soul.

In design, Romanticism resulted in a diminution of formal perspective and order; sets depicted nature rather than human creations. The innovations of Servandoni, de Loutherbourg, and others of the eighteenth and early nineteenth centuries allowed the final elimination of the symmetrical setting. Through the use of ground rows, cutouts, transparencies, and freestanding scenery, a sense of three-dimensionality and depth could be created without considerable reliance on forced perspective, and performers were able to retreat farther into the setting. Although scenic methods were purely illusionistic (virtually all images, including furniture, were created with painting and two-dimensional scenery), the intent was to create a representation of reality, however idealized. The style became known as Romantic realism.

In ballet design, Romanticism was first seen in the work of Lorenzo Sacchetti, who did much of his early work in Venice and then spent the remainder of his life in Vienna. His designs were dominated by curves and irregular lines, soft edges, and groupings of scenic elements around the stage.

Atmosphere and Flying. The greatest designer of the Romantic era was Pierre Ciceri, whose work at the Paris Opera included *La Sylphide* (1832) and *Giselle* (1841). His imagery shifted to the rustic and supernatural. The combination of de Loutherbourg's transparent scenery and the introduction of gas lighting in the theater (1816 in Philadelphia, 1817 in London, and 1822 at the Paris Opera) allowed for the beautiful effects of moonlight so

SCENIC DESIGN. Alessandro Sanquirico, who worked at the Teatro alla Scala in the early nineteenth century, is noted for his diagonal one-point perspective designs. This etching and aquatint, c.1827, by Carolina Lose after Sanquirico, depicts a scene inside a greenhouse, from Louis Henry's ballet *Elerz e Zulmida* (1826). (Dance Collection, New York Public Library for the Performing Arts.)

SCENIC DESIGN. A quintessentially Romantic design by Pierre Ciceri for the forest glade in *La Sylphide* (1832). Dwarfed by enormous trees, James and the Sylphide appear here overwhelmed by the atmospheric setting. Ciceri's use of light is especially inspired, giving the impression of a combination of deep, wooded shade and filtered sunlight. (Dance Collection, New York Public Library for the Performing Arts.)

essential to Romantic ballets. The key word for Romantic design was *atmospheric*.

Another aspect of Romantic dance scenography was the inclusion of flying—not the cloud machines of the Renaissance, but the attachment of dancers to wires, creating the illusion of flight. The reliance upon machines that had been so much a part of the Renaissance and Baroque eras was over, but special effects created through the manipulation of light and transparent scenery, were still an essential ingredient of ballet.

Curtain. As Romantic realism came to dominate, the method of scene shifting changed. The constantly evolving stage picture was replaced by a series of discrete, realistic scenes. Largely under the influence of Ciceri, a curtain or drop cloth was lowered between acts or scenes to allow unseen scene shifts. Although the actual mechanics of scene shifting had never been visible to the audience, the seemingly magical transformation of scenes in full view had the effect of emphasizing the theatricality of the decor rather than the reality of it. With the masking of the scene shift, the audience, theoretically, would have a greater belief in the illusion of each individual scene—what English essayist William Hazlitt (1778–1830) referred to as "the suspension of disbelief." As scene changing no longer necessarily relied on a central system, scenery became more cumbersome and the changeover became increasingly lengthy, sometimes taking as much as half an hour.

By the end of the nineteenth century, Romantic ballet design had been debased by antiquarian detail and often ludicrous spectacle. The new naturalism that had supplanted romanticism in theater, led by the dramatic theo-

SCENIC DESIGN. The Indian temple set for act 1, scene 1, of the original production of Marius Petipa's *La Bayadère* (1877) at the Bolshoi Theater in Saint Petersburg. This setting is characteristic of the opulent realism that dominated stage design in the late nineteenth century. (Photograph reprinted from Mary Clarke and Clement Crisp, *Ballet: An Illustrated History,* New York, 1973, p. 78.)

ries of Émile Zola and the staging practices of George II, duke of Saxe-Meiningen, was absorbed with inserting unimaginative literalness into ballet. As a result, the exotic and atmospheric settings of the Romantic era's ballets were now created with painstaking realism upon the stage, which tended to overwhelm the production and rob it of the sensuality and emotion that had enhanced earlier productions. In Italy, allegorical, topical ballet-spectacles such as *Excelsior* (1881) were produced, whose scenes included the "Palace of Telegraphy" in Washington, D.C., and the Mount Cenis Tunnel. The style and technique of late nineteenth-century scenography allowed for amazing illusionism in the creation of realistic scenery. This was perfect for the naturalistic theater but was inappropriate for the staging of Romantic-era ballet.

Unified Art. Toward the end of the nineteenth century, a new aesthetic of stage design was developed by Swiss designer Adolphe Appia and English designer Gordon Craig. Basically, they called for simplification of the stage and the depiction of setting through suggestive rather than naturalistic imagery. Appia, especially, proposed a stage setting that would unify the stage floor, the two-dimensional scenic space, and the three-dimensional performer. This approach was stimulated in large part by the theories of German opera composer Richard Wagner. Wagner's concept of the *Gesamtkunstwerk,* or unified artwork, suggested that all elements of the performance be equal and unified. Although Appia had little opportunity to put his ideas into practice and did no work on conventional ballet, his ideas were to have a profound effect upon twentieth-century design in general, and upon much of the dance design of the Ballets Russes.

Appia achieved much of his goal through the effective use of light and shadow, now possible with electric lighting. Though many of his theories and designs were created with the operas of Richard Wagner in mind, he actually realized little of his visionary work. His most fruitful efforts came in his collaboration with Émile Jaques-Dalcroze. For Jaques-Dalcroze's school in Hellerau, Germany, Appia designed the first theater in modern times without a proscenium—just a rectangular space with the stage at one end. The stage did not have conventional scenery but consisted of platforms and steps that could be arranged in any configuration—what Appia referred to as "rhythmic space"—and was surrounded by translucent walls lighted by incandescent lamps behind the walls. The influence of Appia and Craig has been felt throughout the twentieth century, although it took some time for their ideas to become widely accepted. [*See the entries on Appia and Craig.*]

In the world of ballet, the change in scenographic ideas was to come from the Ballets Russes of Serge Diaghilev in the first decade of the twentieth century. Although the change was a movement away from the Romantic realism of the previous century, it was not directly inspired by Appia and Craig. It came instead from the easel painters, from the indigenous art of Russia, and from the emergence of the avant-garde.

Easel Painters. Nineteenth-century Russian ballet never felt the influence of theatrical naturalism, and though it suffered many of the same problems as the rest of European Romantic-era ballet, it also had two very fine designers who rose above the general mediocrity: M. A. Shishkov and Alexandre Benois. Furthermore, in at least two theaters in Russia at the end of the nineteenth century, easel painters were beginning to be employed as stage decorators. (The tradition for at least a century had been to use scene painters who had become craftsmen instead of using creative artists.) A leader in this trend was Savva Mamontov, a wealthy arts patron, who built his own opera theater and employed the Russian painters Viktor Vasnetzov, Mikhail Vroubel, and Konstantin Korovin, among others, to design operas in the 1890s. Meanwhile at the Moscow Art Theater—the home of Russian playwright Anton Chekhov and the birthplace of modern naturalistic acting—Konstantin Stanislavsky and Vladimir Nemirovich-Danchenko employed such painters as Viktor Simov, Nikolai Krimov, and Mstislav Dobujinsky to create settings. Mamontov felt that scenery was more than background and that it should be instrumental in establishing the style and mood of a ballet. As a result, the scenographer in Russia was to rise to a position equal to that of the choreographer and the librettist.

In 1898, with the financial assistance of Mamontov, art lover Serge Diaghilev founded the magazine *Mir iskusstva* (The World of Art), which presented the rediscovery of the great heritage of traditional Russian art. It also introduced Western innovations to the Russian art world—specifically symbolism, Art Nouveau, and the academic schools of Germany and France. The contributors to the journal, which was published until 1904, included Léon Bakst, Alexandre Benois, Konstantin Korovin, and Valentin Serov.

The ferment of ideas created by *Mir iskusstva* had a profound effect on ballet and design in general. Most notably there was an emphasis on the unification of all the elements of performance into a single, interrelated whole—essentially the idea expressed by Wagner and Appia. In 1904, the revolutionary choreographer Michel Fokine submitted a scenario for a ballet on *Daphnis et Chloë* (never produced), in which he wrote, "In place of the traditional dualism, the ballet must have complete unity of expression, a unity which is made up of a harmonious blending of the three elements—music, painting and the plastic art." While it is arguable that this unity existed throughout the Renaissance, it was virtually nonexistent by the late nineteenth century, and sets, costumes, and choreography for the same production often appeared to evolve out of different aesthetics. The unified artistic approach championed by Wagner and Appia was probably first seen in dance in the Benois-designed production of *Le Pavillon d'Armide* (1907) at the Maryinsky Theater in Saint Petersburg.

Serge Diaghilev and the Ballets Russes. In 1909, Diaghilev brought a program of opera and dance to Paris, and the Ballets Russes company was born. The first season included *Le Pavillon d'Armide* (Benois), but much of the design was by Léon Bakst and the overall impression of Parisian audiences was of a stage overwhelmed by vibrant color and the line and form of Art Nouveau. The nineteenth-century palette had consisted essentially of muted colors, with settings often purposely darkened in imitation of the old masters. Even the symbolists of the 1880s and 1890s, who had abandoned naturalistic color schemes, worked primarily with soft, mood-evoking colors. In using easel painters instead of scene painters, color in Diaghilev's productions assumed a symbolic value over the previous style of functional naturalism; with the designs of Bakst, influenced by Oriental motifs and Russian peasant sources (a palette of red, orange, yellow, and green), ballet design was freed from representational art.

This initial outburst of energy by the artists of the Ballets Russes had its climax in the 1910 season, with the production of *Schéhérazade*. Designed by Bakst, this ballet was an Oriental fantasy, with bold juxtapositions of brilliant reds, greens, blues, and touches of yellow, pink, and orange. Bakst's biographer, the critic André Levinson, wrote in 1923, "It is a decor animated by whirling forces whose unity penetrates the surface. This splendor of glowing colors, this outpouring of sensuality, demands action and superabundance of passionate ecstasy that can find satisfaction only in rivers of blood." With this production, any vestiges of romantic realism were effectively banished. Realistic landscapes and interiors became a thing of the past. Bakst saw stage design as a sensual, tactile experience with the body as the organizing element. Moreover, *Schéhérazade* seemed to establish the ideal of collaboration as paramount. Critic Camille Mauclair in his review claimed that the ballet was a "dream-like spectacle beside which the Wagnerian synthesis itself is but a clumsy barbarism." As later critics would note, however, it seemed to augur not Wagner's *Gesamtkunstwerk* as much as it heralded the dominance of the designer over the dancer.

The striking use of color—as continued in the work of Natalia Goncharova and Mikhail Larionov—and the general boldness of the sets altered the relationship between setting and costume. The costume was made to work harmoniously with the setting and, in many cases, the designs of the Ballets Russes virtually fused the two together so that the costumes might be seen as moving fragments of scenery. For such visual unity to be achieved, costumes and sets were usually designed by the same person. The dominance of the decor in these productions led to new roles for the painter; several libretti for Diaghilev's ballets were consequently written by designers. More importantly, the decor literally influenced the movement. The classical vocabulary was often inappropriate for the Art Nouveau lines and exotic color of the Ballets Russes artists, so Bakst and Benois advised Fokine on incorporating Isadora Duncan's style of movement into his choreography. One designer, Larionov, did in fact step over into choreography in the production of *Le Chout* (1921).

Petrouchka (1911), with libretto and decor by Benois, is

generally considered the best example of the collaborative process and unification of elements by the Ballets Russes, incorporating Benois's traditionalism with the emerging interest in Russian folk art, color symbolism, and realism. Although Benois held the title of artistic director of the Ballets Russes, his aesthetic style was essentially aristocratic and traditional, and he was at his best when working with eighteenth-century material rather than the newer work of the company. Many of his settings, in fact, are reminiscent of the rococo paintings of Watteau. As a result he became increasingly out of step with Diaghilev's changing ideas; he left the company in 1912.

The other main designer of the Ballets Russes' early years was Nikolai Roerich. He had a great knowledge of historical Russia and his designs of bleak landscapes, colored in earth tones, seemed primitive and mysterious. His best-known work was for Nijinsky's *Le Sacre du Printemps* (1913).

The next major artists to work for the Ballets Russes were husband and wife Mikhail Larionov and Natalia Goncharova. Diaghilev first used Goncharova in 1914 for *Le Coq d'Or* and employed her husband the following year. Influenced by cubism and futurism, Larionov founded his own movement called rayonism, based on his idea that visual perception is based on the sum of all light rays emitted by an object. The paintings by Goncharova and Larinov were characterized by rays of color arranged in dynamic patterns. This is clearly seen in Larionov's setting for *Le Chout.* With *Le Coq d'Or,* however, Goncharova abandoned rayonism and returned to Russian primitive art, inspired by early Russian chapbooks. This combina-

SCENIC DESIGN. Inspired by the indigenous arts of her homeland, Natalia Goncharova used characteristic Russian motifs in her design for the City Square in Diaghilev's production of *Le Coq d'Or* (1914), first performed at the Paris Opera. (Photograph from the Dance Collection, New York Public Library for the Performing Arts.)

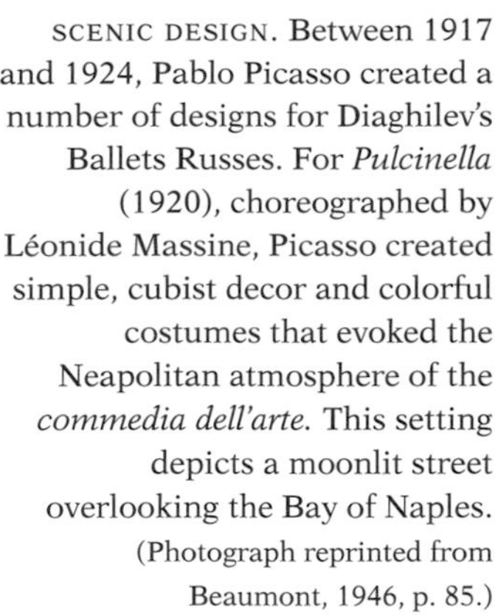

SCENIC DESIGN. Between 1917 and 1924, Pablo Picasso created a number of designs for Diaghilev's Ballets Russes. For *Pulcinella* (1920), choreographed by Léonide Massine, Picasso created simple, cubist decor and colorful costumes that evoked the Neapolitan atmosphere of the *commedia dell'arte.* This setting depicts a moonlit street overlooking the Bay of Naples. (Photograph reprinted from Beaumont, 1946, p. 85.)

tion of neoprimitivism and brilliant color continued through the work of both artists and provided a bridge between Russian traditional art and modern art—perhaps best seen in Goncharova's set for Stravinsky's *The Firebird* (1926), with its act 2 backdrop of onion-domed churches arranged not in linear perspective but in a geometric, almost cubist, composition. Larionov is also credited with introducing a sense of the grotesque and the absurd into the work of the Ballets Russes. [*See* Goncharova; Larinov.]

Picasso and design. Until 1917, Diaghlev had used only one non-Russian painter, but the 1917 season brought several new artists to the ballet stage. By far the most significant production of the season was *Parade,* with sets by Pablo Picasso. It was, in a sense, the next logical step. The colors of Bakst had released the stage from its representational grip; the cubo-futurist elements introduced by Goncharova and Larionov continued this trend while also freeing the decor from its folklore context. Picasso saw *Parade* as an opportunity to incorporate the elements of time and movement into a formal artistic conception—an idea that had been essential to the futurists and to the painter Marcel Duchamp. In this ballet, Picasso sought a means of fully integrating the visual aesthetic of cubism with the demands of the plastic stage and spent several months with the company in Rome studying ballet movement. [*See* Parade; *and the entry on Picasso.*]

Cubism was not a mere abstraction of reality, nor was it an attempt to manifest subconscious states of mind as certain earlier avant-garde movements had done. Rather, cubism sought to alter the spectator's perceptions, by fragmenting the visual image into a geometrical form, as if an object were being viewed from several perspectives. With the collage phase of cubism (the use of found materials glued to art boards), the representational aspect of art was denied even further owing to an emphasis on the reality of the materials and so on the art object itself.

Picasso's stage curtain for *Parade* harked back to his pre-cubist period; it was essentially narrative, reminiscent of nineteenth-century act drops. His stage set was depicted in an architectonic, cubist style, but it was essentially background—in the way traditional ballet scenery had always functioned. The integration of all the elements came in the costumes of the two Managers, creating a link from the decor to the performers. The costumes were three-dimensional cubist creations and appeared to be moving scenery. More significantly, they determined the movement of the performers. In the words of French author Jean Cocteau, the awkward movement caused by the wooden frames of the costumes "far from hampering the choreographer, obliged him to break with the ancient formulae and to seek inspiration not in the things that move, but in the things round which we move, and which move according to the rhythm of our steps." Thus, the idea, begun a decade earlier, of the decor influencing the choreography reached a peak in *Parade* when the costume-decor became one with the performer.

This concept was taken even further by Picasso in the 1924 production of *Mercure* by Les Soirées de Paris. In this production the costumes were designed in specific relation to the decor—they "fit," as it were, into specific visual points of the setting. Setting and performer became unified in a total design, the epitome of the designer's ballet.

SCENIC DESIGN. Fernand Léger's setting for *La Création du Monde* (1923), presented by Les Ballets Suédois at the Théâtre des Champs-Élysées, Paris. (Photograph reprinted from Beaumont, 1946, p. 99.)

In 1924 the Ballets Russes also staged what might best be described as an abstract ballet or, more simply, a light show. While in Rome earlier that year, Diaghilev had invited two of the Italian futurists, Fortunato Depero and Giacomo Balla to work with him. Depero designed a production of Stravinsky's *Rossignol,* using futurist images but in a conventional manner. Balla, however, chose to put the ideas of Enrico Prampolini's 1915 manifesto, "Futurist Scenography," to work. Prampolini had stated:

> The stage will no longer be a colored backdrop but a *colorless electromechanical architecture, powerfully vitalized by chromatic emanations from a luminous source,* produced by electric reflectors with multicolored panes of glass, arranged, coordinated analogically with the psyche of each scene. With the luminous irradiations of these beams, of these planes of colored lights, the dynamic combinations will give marvelous results of mutual permeation, of intersection of lights and shadows.

Balla took *Fireworks,* composed by Igor Stravinsky, created a stage of irregular geometric forms, painted a variety of colors (including some small brightly painted translucent forms that were lighted from within), and played light over these forms for the five-minute duration of the piece. The result was an abstract performance in which light, rather than dancers, was the performer.

It had been the 1917 season when Diaghilev had not only opened ballet to the modern artists of Europe but firmly established ballet as a painter's theater. In the following years, the painters Georges Braque, Giorgio de'Chirico, Sonia and Robert Delaunay, André Derain, Raoul Dufy, Max Ernst, Marie Laurencin, Henri Matisse, Joan Mirò, Georges Rouault, and Maurice Utrillo all designed scenery for the Ballets Russes. The integration, however, of scenography, choreography, libretto, and music was, for the most part, lost, since few of the painters explored the medium of the stage as Picasso had done. Instead, the stage became a very large canvas, and decor reverted to painted background—though painted in the various styles of twentieth-century modern art.

Constructivism. Diaghilev continued his quest for the new and, in 1927, introduced Western audiences to Russian constructivist design; he produced *La Chatte,* with scenery by Naum Gabo and Anton Pevsner, and *Le Pas d'Acier,* a Soviet ballet with designs by Yuri Yakulov.

Constructivism was a Russian art movement that spread during the early Soviet era of the 1920s to European theater music, and literature. Drawing on concepts from the futurists and cubists (although vociferously rejecting these earlier movements), the initial ideas were stated in the "Realistic Manifesto" of 1920 by Gabo and Pevsner. *"The realization of our perceptions of the world in the forms of space and time is the only aim of our pictorial and plastic art,"* they announced. "We affirm *in these arts a new element the kinetic rhythms as the basic forms of our perception of real time."* Constructivist art was to be fitted into the new technological society (and into the new Soviet state); it generally emphasized structure and movement. In theatrical design, it was manifested as skeletal, nonobjective settings, frequently with moving parts.

The setting for *La Chatte* consisted of boxes and geometrical forms made of translucent material, which reflected and refracted light, set against a backdrop and a ground cloth of black vinyl. *Le Pas d'Acier* consisted of a multilevel scaffold with levels connected by ladders and ramps, including some on wheels. One of the most significant elements of constructivist design was the elimination of the open, flat stage floor. The dancers moved around and through objects or danced on several levels.

The use of nonobjective forms as a design element and light as a performer was further exploited in a 1928 Ballets Russes production of *Ode,* with designs by Pavel Tchelitchev. All the lighting came from onstage: pale blue scrims in front of the lights diffused the light, creating an azure glow over the whole stage. Upstage, dolls were placed in an inverted V formation to create a false perspective. Film projections of chalk drawings swirled over the stage. The dancers were connected by ropes to one another and to parts of the scenery. As they pulled upon the ropes, webs and webbing were created. Some of these effects anticipated the later work by the Bauhaus and by Alwin Nikolais.

Later Innovations. Concurrent with the later work of the Ballets Russes in Paris was Les Ballets Suédois, founded in 1920 by Rolf de Maré. Maré, like Diaghilev, primarily used designers from the Paris school of painters, including Andrée Parr, Jean Hugo, Fernand Léger, Giorgio de'Chirico, Francis Picabia, and Pierre Bonnard. Les Ballets Suédois was decidedly more adventurous in its choice of material than the Ballets Russes. In terms of design, its most significant productions were probably *Skating Rink* and *La Création du Monde,* with sets by Léger, and *Relâche,* with sets by Picabia. The design for *Skating Rink* consisted of a curved white background with abstract, two-dimensional, colored forms set against the upper part and the dancers silhouetted against the lower. For *La Création du Monde,* Léger used a motif of African masks, although all the design elements—clouds, mountains, and the masks themselves—were reduced to almost abstract geometric forms. The mountains and clouds were painted on the backdrop and on hanging flats; three gods, twenty-five-feet tall, moved in front of the backdrop on rails; twelve-foot-high demi gods, in the form of costumed actors on stilts, moved in front of the gods and, on the stage plane, moved animals and plants (costumed actors) and humans. The stage became a series of horizontal planes, and the two-dimensional nature of the costume-sets caused the performers to blend in with the setting; it was all one.

Picabia was a Dadaist, and *Relâche,* which he also wrote, was a Dadaist *antiballet.* It is difficult to talk of Dadaist theory, since the Dadaists ridiculed such approaches to their work, but in essence they were interested in destroying the accepted boundaries and conventions of all art and performance. The setting for *Relâche* was a backdrop of some four hundred metal disks, each with a light, forming a huge reflector, whose lights shone directly at the audience. The two acts were separated by the film *Entr'acte* by René Clair. Although the ballet nominally occurred on the stage, it also encompassed, at least by implication, the entire auditorium—thus prefiguring much post–World War II theater staging.

SCENIC DESIGN. Pavel Tchelitichev's constructivist-influenced set for *Ode* (1928), choreographed by Léonide Massine and produced by Diaghilev's company. By echoing the costumes of the female dancers with mannequins suspended on ropes, Tchelitchev created an eerie visual effect. Some of his lighting innovations for the ballet included projecting lights and time-lapse films onto onstage screens. (Photograph reprinted from Beaumont, 1946, p. 125.)

Not only in Paris were theater artists interested in the dynamic qualities of space and the incorporation of movement into art. Dance was a logical proving ground for these artists. Because conventional dance required the open space of the stage and because many of the artists were interested in creating sculptural, volumetric, three-dimensional settings, limited possibilities existed for collaboration.

Alexandra Exter, working in Russia, is a good example. In the words of historian John Bowlt, Exter was "one of the few members of the Russian avant-garde who was able to transcend the confines of the pictorial surface and to organize forms in their interaction with space." Exter was interested in the rhythmic quality she felt was inherent in various materials and the way these affected movement and perception. She created a style that has been described as a lyrical version of cubism and constructivism. Although she worked on some dance, most of her work was with the Kamerny Theater, a theatrical company. Exter, however, had a strong influence on designers who designed scenery for ballet, including Tchelitchev.

The Bauhaus and design. The interaction of the human figure with space was nowhere more extensively studied than at the Bauhaus, which was founded as a design academy for art and architecture by Walter Gropius in Germany from 1919 to 1933 (and afterward in Chicago). The dance experiments at the Bauhaus were largely the work of Oskar Schlemmer. Although most of his design falls technically in the realm of costume, it is more properly considered as moving scenery, so fully were the performers integrated with the surrounding space. In Schlemmer's essay "Man and Art Figure," he outlined some of his principles:

> Man, the human organism, stands in the cubical, abstract space of the stage. Man and Space. Each has different laws of order. Whose shall prevail? Either abstract space is adapted, in deference to natural man, and transformed back into nature or the imitation of nature [as] happens in the theater of illusionistic realism . . . or natural man, in deference to abstract space, is recast to fit its mold [as] happens on the abstract stage. . . . *Man as Dancer . . . obeys the law of the body as well as the law of space.*

In Schlemmer's *Triadic Ballet* and in a series of other works and experiments—"Space Dance," "Form Dance," "Gesture Dance," and a series of pantomimes—he transformed the body through geometric costumes, which indicated the body's range and volume of movement and the extension of its lines into space. Other members of the Bauhaus created performances that were, in essence, dances although not always identified as such; notable among these was Alexander Schawinsky's *Circus*.

The fascination with mechanization and abstraction was taken to its logical extreme in dance with two pieces by Kurt Schmidt: in *Mechanical Ballet,* abstract jointed figurines were moved about the stage by unseen dancers, creating the effect of automatons; *Man + Machine,* which was never performed, was more like a puppet play for abstract figures. [*See* Bauhaus, Dance and the.]

SCENIC DESIGN. The Russian-American artist and designer Eugene Berman rejected the geometric, abstract tendencies of the 1920s and 1930s and instead sought to create realms of magical illusion in his stage settings. His design for the tomb scene in Antony Tudor's *The Tragedy of Romeo and Juliet* (1943) is typical of his best work. (Photograph from the Dance Collection, New York Public Library for the Performing Arts.)

Mainstream dance. Most of the radical experimentation of the years between the world wars had little effect on mainstream dance or theater and, by the 1930s, the energy and quest for new forms (which had informed much of the previous four decades) was dissipated. With the death of Serge Diaghilev in 1929, the Ballets Russes went through a series of upheavals and factional splits. The company, ultimately directed by Léonide Massine, continued the practice of using artists to create decor, and through the 1930s and 1940s the designers included Christian Bérard, Eugene Berman, Marc Chagall, and Salvador Dali, as well as Derain, Dufy, Matisse, Miró, and Tchelitchev. All these artists created beautiful and spectacular designs, but they were essentially large easel paintings that provided a backdrop for the dance. Nowhere is this better demonstrated than in the late ballet designs by Picasso (for example, *Chant Funèbre* [1954] or *Icare* [1962]), for which he simply enlarged existing drawings.

Of the designers of mainstream dance during this period—Bérard, Berman, and Tchelitchev—all were members of the neoromantic school influenced by Picasso's early twentieth-century Blue and Rose Periods. Bérard had inherited the tradition of *le treteau nu* ("bare stage"), propounded by stage director and theoretician Jacques Copeau. The roots of the empty stage are to be found in the work of Appia and in the nineteenth- and early twentieth-century attempts to recreate the open stage of the Elizabethans. By the 1930s, however, many French designers were beginning to adorn the bare stage with some few decorative elements, and Bérard falls into this category. Nonetheless, his designs are simple, elegant, and suggestive, almost ethereal. At times he even simplified the decor into nothing but black drapes. His most notable designs were for *Cotillon, Seventh Symphony,* and *Symphonie Fantastique.*

Berman had been overwhelmed by his first visit to Italy, and virtually all his painting and design portrays a dreamlike vision of Italian Renaissance and Baroque style. Like Bérard, his designs have a simple quality to them—but they also have one of modern theater's most distinctive personal styles. Among his major works were *The Devil's Holiday* (1939), *Romeo and Juliet* (1943), and *Concerto Barocco* (1941).

Tchelitchev's early designs, especially for costumes, were generally based on spiral or circular patterns, with bold color contrasts and the elimination of horizontal planes and angles, thus creating a sense of movement. His work on *Ode* showed the influence of constructivism and the Bauhaus. His later work was lighter and simplified, as in neoromantic style, and it revealed his fascination with light and color. His major works after *Ode* include *Errante* (1933), *Orpheus and Eurydice* (1936), *Nobilissima Visione* (1938), *Concerto* (1942), and *Apollon Musagète* (1942), in which the scene change is achieved solely through a change in lighting. Although the use of light as a major design element can be dated from Appia and the *fin de siècle* dance productions of Loie Fuller, it has precedents in some of the work already discussed; the modern use of light as a design element in ballet can in fact be seen to derive from the later work of Tchelitchev. [*See the entry on Tchelitchev.*]

Modern dance. For modern dance, which was developing in the 1920s and 1930s, new approaches to dance design emerged. Partly for economic reasons and partly for aesthetics, modern dance rejected the prettified, painterly, decorated stage; most early modern dance occurred on a bare stage.

In 1935, modern dance pioneer Martha Graham asked the American abstract sculptor Isamu Noguchi to create a setting for her performance of *Frontier (Perspective No. 1).* The stage set consisted of a short fence and a V-shaped rope extending out from the fence and disappearing into the flyspace. This was the start of one of the great choreographer-designer collaborations of all time and led to some three dozen designs. The most significant aspect of Graham's choice is that Noguchi was a sculptor, not an easel painter. Noguchi's sets consisted primarily of objects—basically abstract, although often suggestive and symbolic—around which Graham choreographed her dances. Writing about *Frontier,* Noguchi noted: "Space became a volume to be dealt with sculpturally." Graham's dances would be totally inappropriate in front of a painted drop; they are focused on and created around sculptural objects. Noguchi's suggestive settings (such as the farmyard in *Appalachian Spring* [1944], in which the enclosed yard is depicted by a fragment of fence rail and a stump and the house by part of a peaked roof, a clapboard wall, a bench, and a fine-lined rocking chair) are harbingers of the dance and theater designs of Oliver Smith and Jo Mielziner. Others sets, such as the one used in *Seraphic Dialogue* (1955) with its three constructions of thin metal rods, were reminiscent of constructivism.

Noguchi also designed for the ballets of George Balanchine; for the Ballet Society's *Orpheus* (1948), the sudden zigzag descent of a white silk curtain was dramatic enough in context to elicit gasps from the audience. [*See the entry on Noguchi.*]

In the post–World War II era, some of the most significant developments in design (not only in dance but in all performance) was found in the work of Alwin Nikolais and Merce Cunningham. Anna Halprin also made significant contributions.

Scenography by Nikolais is constructed out of light and costumes—there is virtually no scenery as such—yet the result is a stage totally consumed by visual imagery. Nikolais operates from a theory of *decentralization*—meaning that no object, whether narrative, image, or dancer, should occupy the center or focus of attention. The stage

SCENIC DESIGN. For Merce Cunningham's *Rainforest* (1968), Andy Warhol designed a set consisting of silvery, air-and-helium-filled pillows that drifted about the stage. Here, Barbara Dilley and Cunningham navigate the set. (Photograph by Oscar Bailey; from the Cunningham Dance Foundation, New York.)

space becomes a microcosm of Nikolais's vision of the universe expressed, metaphorically, in movement, time, space, color, form, light, and sound. The dancers are usually encased in stretch jersey constructions or, as in the case of *Tent,* the elastic fabric is spread over all or part of the stage. The movement of the dancers within and under the material, combined with the use of ever-changing light and projections, creates an overwhelming visual image. All other elements of the dance are subsumed in this scenographic display. It is a form sometimes referred to as "total theater" and sometimes as "mixed media." As Nikolais uses it, it has its roots in Loie Fuller's 1890s use of light and material; Erwin Piscator's 1920s theatrical productions in Germany, which used projections and film; the 1930s dances of Mary Wigman and Ruth Page, who used costumes as an environment for the dancer; and Bauhaus work of Oskar Schlemmer.

Merce Cunningham's approach to dance design has been shaped largely by the theories of modern composer John Cage, whose interest in chance and indeterminacy inform his own work. Cunningham choreographs his dances independent of the score or the design; when all three elements are combined, any correlation among them is random, and the dancers must respond as necessary. For example, in Cunningham's *Rainforest* (1968), Andy Warhol designed an environment of air-and helium-filled mylar pillows that floated about randomly. It was an unpredictable set that functioned independently of the dancers, yet the dancers had to respond to any pillows in their line of movement. For *Tread* (1970), Bruce Nauman arranged standing fans along the downstage edge of the stage that seemed to function as an actual barrier to audience perception.

Cunningham has worked primarily with Robert Rauschenberg and Jasper Johns, as well as Remy Charlip and Frank Stella. The settings sometimes function as sculptural elements, as Noguchi's sets did for Graham (for whom Cunningham had danced before starting his own company); more often they are closer to props than set pieces and function either as objects with which the dancers operate or as objects in counterpoint or juxtaposition to the dancers. In *Story* (1963, costumes and decor by Rauschenberg), one segment called "Object" consisted of the dancers moving or carrying an object that was newly created for each performance.

For Cunningham, sometimes the nature or mood of the settings suggested the dance titles, such as *Summerspace* (1960), which had no objective reference to summer. Perhaps most important in Cunningham's work has been his relationship to space. By eliminating a central focus, he essentially destroyed the traditional organization of stage space; this was further enhanced by moving his dances out of theaters—out of proscenium stages—and into nontraditional spaces such as art galleries, in which the performance space is structured, if at all, by the performance and not by stage architecture or conventional design.

Anna Halprin's work led to an exploration of space in which she did not create settings in any traditional sense but used objects to transform space and to inform the movement of the dancers. This began with her *Birds of America* (1957); she explained that she was unhappy with the space: "I put a bamboo pole in everybody's hands. . . . The poles were very long and they created their own spatial environment. . . . I became preoccupied with movement in relation to space." For *Five-Legged Stool* (1961), the audience was in the center and the performance moved around and through them. *Esposizione* (1964) was performed at the Venice Opera House; to destroy the proscenium and allow the dance to move through the whole theater space, Halprin stretched a cargo net over the stage opening. Not only did this allow an integration with audience space, but it allowed for the vertical movement of the dancers.

Postmodern dance. Postmodern dance, which was begun in the early 1960s by many of Cunningham's and Halprin's dancers, generally eschewed decor but continued the exploration of nontraditional space and the creation of environments. The Judson Dance Theatre—the originators of postmodern dance—performed in the open space of Judson Memorial Church. Other performances were given in art galleries and lofts. In the late 1960s some choreographers, notably Trisha Brown and Joan Jonas, began to perform in found spaces outdoors and to construct environments in which to create dances.

In Brown's series of *"Equipment" Dances* (1968–1971), walls (both the outside of buildings and the inside of rooms) became the setting as dancers, using ropes, harnesses, and other equipment, defied gravity and danced on the walls. (This has been further explored, with greater scenic spectacle, by the Multigravitational Experiment Group.) For *Rummage Sale and the Floor of the Forest* (1971), a pipe gridwork was suspended above a standing audience. The pipes were threaded through the arms and legs of various pieces of clothing, and the performers moved over the gridwork, climbing in and out of the clothes. *Roof Piece* (1971) was staged on rooftops over a twelve-block area of New York's Soho district. The setting was what is called a "found environment," nothing is created; it uses available space as is.

The found environment is, however, the ultimate destruction of the proscenium frame, since the setting is not even a particular roof, but, from the spectator's perception, the entire skyline of New York. This idea also was taken up by Joan Jonas. She was interested in the effect of distance on the perception of space and movement and has used large open spaces such as beaches (*Beach Piece II,* 1971; *Sound Delay,* 1970) or landfill in lower Manhattan (*Delay Delay,* 1972).

The ultimate environmental dance concept, however, may have been Meredith Monk's *Vessel* (1971). Monk is concerned with blending movement, light, costume, film, sound, and environment into a unified production; many of her productions were created for what she calls "specific sites," existing architectural space or natural environments. For example, Monk created works to move through the spaces of the American Museum of Natural History *(Tour: Dedicated to Dinosaurs)* and the Guggenheim Museum (*Juice,* 1969), both in New York City. *Vessel* was a three-part performance that took place over two nights. Part one occurred in Monk's loft. Spectators then boarded a bus that took them to the Performing Garage for part two. Part three took place the following night in a parking lot. Not only did each nontraditional space in-

SCENIC DESIGN. Dancers performed Trisha Brown's *Roof Piece* (1971) atop various buildings in Soho. The cityscape of lower Manhattan, dominated by looming watertowers, served as the work's backdrop. (Photograph © 1973 by Babette Mangolte; used by permission.)

form perceptions of the particular section, but the somewhat processional nature of the total piece—reminiscent of certain medieval and Renaissance productions—affected perceptions of the total work. By spreading the performance over two days and the space of New York City, Monk seemed to be attempting to incorporate everyday life and the design of the urban environment into the production. [*See the entry on Monk.*]

Since the 1970s, other dances have been performed on rafts on lakes, rolling lawns, and city streets; there is no longer any inappropriate space. In all these cases, there was no creation of decor in the traditional sense. Rather, new relationships between the audience and the performer were created to foster new perceptions of dance and space.

Ironically, the postmodern dancers have come almost full circle—back to the concept of design—although their collaborators in the contemporary art world have created settings more conceptual than decorative. Rauschenberg has designed for Trisha Brown, and architect Frank Gehry designed a multilevel platform and hurricane-fence construction for Lucinda Childs's *Available Light*.

Modern ballet. Concurrent with modern and postmodern developments has been the ongoing tradition of classical ballet. The difficulty in designing anew for the classics—not only in dance but in theater as well—is in making them visually and stylistically relevant while adhering to the original spirit. The ballets may date from the nineteenth century, but they often involve subject matter from earlier times. In a piece like *Giselle,* for ex-

SCENIC DESIGN. Agnes de Mille's *Fall River Legend* (1948) tells the story of Lizzie Borden, a New England woman who was accused, tried, and acquitted of killing her father and her stepmother in 1892. Oliver Smith's fragmented architectural setting suggests a world torn apart by psychic conflict. Seen here are Diana Krupska (left) as the Accused and Muriel Bentley as the Stepmother. (Photograph from the Dance Collection, New York Public Library for the Performing Arts.)

ample, the job is to create a twentieth-century version of a nineteenth-century view of a medieval setting. Designers in the post–World War II era who have worked in this classical tradition include Michael Ayrton, Jean Carzou, Nicholas Georgiadis, Leslie Hurry, Oliver Messel, and Lila de Nobili.

Modern ballet design has been eclectic, showing the whole range of mid-twentieth-century design. Beginning with Oliver Smith, there was the use of the fragmented, suggestive setting, in which a few fragments or elements suggested a more realistic setting. Notable among these were *Fall River Legend* (1948), *Rodeo* (1942), and *Fancy Free* (1944). This idea became more abstracted in the work of Anton Clavé in which chairs, ladders, and scaffolds became scenery and props hung from ropes, as in *Carmen* (1949).

Although the painted background continued to dominate, ballet designers became more interested in textures. This led to the use of unconventional materials to line the stage space or to include in painted designs. The dominant trend, however, was toward the sculptural and structural set. With obvious precedents in constructivism and the designs of Noguchi, the sculptural decor creates a three-dimensional environment. The dancer moves in relation to an object. The style of recent years has been to create forms out of industrial and pedestrian materials; scaffolding, pipe grids, raw wood, and the like have comprised the designer's material, a trend popularized in theater and opera by designer Ming Cho Lee. Notable designers in this style include Nadine Baylis and Rouben Ter-Arutunian.

Sheer spectacle has become an aesthetic in some ballets. One of the most notable examples is Maurice Béjart's Ballets du XXe Siècle, Brussels. His designers have included Dali, Bernard Daydé, Joelle Roustand, and Roger Bernard. The style is best described as eclectic, with various productions including projections, circus motifs, Renaissance entry wagons, and psychedelic imagery, as well as some conventional elements. Most important is the location of the performances, which has included tents and arenas. Some works of the Joffrey Ballet, such as *Astarte*, fall into the same category, but on a smaller scale.

Today's Design Trends. As modern dance and ballet cross boundaries with increasing frequency, design for dance has simplified somewhat and become more austere. If there is a current trend beyond eclecticism, it is in the use of simple bands or swaths of color, as seen in recent designs by Ming Cho Lee and Santo Loquasto; the stage becomes a statement through the use of color, but the real design is in the lighting.

Simply put, there is no single style of design in contemporary dance (nor in theater or opera). Scenic designers, working in the dance, have sought ways to serve the performance simply, without intruding on the primary element of the dancer. Whatever the success of these designs, little of the structured and collaborative meshing of ideas that had its climax in the Diaghilev era is still in evidence. There is, however, a resurgence of artists working for the stage. The contemporary generation of artists tends to be neither easel painters nor sculptors but conceptual artists, architects, or performers in their own right. But the problems remain unchanged; when asked about his approach to Trisha Brown's *Set and Reset,* Rauschenberg replied that he faced "the usual problem—how to fill the space but not trip the dancers."

[*See also* Ballet de Cour; Designing for Dance; Masque and Antimasque; Orchestra; *and* Theaters for Dance. *In addition to the figures already cross-referenced above, many of the principal designers and choreographers mentioned herein are the subjects of independent entries.*]

BIBLIOGRAPHY

Amberg, George. *Art in Modern Ballet.* New York, 1946.

Anatomy of an Illusion: Studies in Nineteenth-Century Scene Design; Lectures of the Fourth International Congress on Theatre Research, Amsterdam, 1965. Amsterdam, 1969.

Baur-Heinhold, Margarete. *The Baroque Theatre.* London, 1967.

Beaton, Cecil. "Designing for Ballet." *Dance Index* 5 (August 1946): 184–204.

Beaumont, Cyril W. *Ballet Design: Past and Present.* London, 1946.

Bland, Alexander. "Recent Ballet Design." *Ballet Annual* 17 (1963): 58–61.

Bowlt, John E. *Stage Designs and the Russian Avant-Garde, 1911–1929.* Washington, D.C., 1976.

Bowlt, John E. *Russian Stage Design: Scenic Invention, 1900–1930.* Jackson, Miss., 1982.

Buckle, Richard. *Modern Ballet Design.* London, 1955.

Carroll, Noël, et al. "Post-Modern Dance." *Drama Review* 19 (March 1975): 3–51.

Clarke, Mary, and Clement Crisp. *Design for Ballet.* New York, 1978.

Cohen, Selma Jeanne, ed. *Dance as a Theatre Art.* New York, 1974.

Dance, Theatre, Opera: Costume and Decor Designs, Sculpture, Photographs, and Books. New York, 1977. Exhibition catalogue.

Delarue, Allison. "The Stage and Ballet Designs of Eugene Berman." *Dance Index* 5 (February 1946): 4–24.

Gascoigne, Bamber. *World Theatre: An Illustrated History.* Boston, 1968.

Hainaux, René. *Stage Design throughout the World.* 3 vols. Brussels and New York, 1957–1976.

McNamara, Brooks. "Vessel: The Scenography of Meredith Monk." *Drama Review* 16 (March 1972): 87–103.

The Next Wave Catalog. Brooklyn, 1983.

Nicoll, Allardyce. *The Development of the Theatre.* 5th ed., rev. New York, 1967.

Rainer, Yvonne. "Ann Halprin." *Tulane Drama Review* 10 (Winter 1965): 142–166.

Rischbeiter, Henning. *Art and the Stage in the Twentieth Century.* Translated by Michael Bullock. Greenwich, Conn., 1968.

Russian Stage and Costume Designs for the Ballet, Opera, and Theatre. Washington, D.C., 1967.

Scholz, Janos, ed. *Baroque and Romantic Stage Design.* New York, 1949.

"Sets: Painted Drops and Fabulous Props." *Theatre Crafts* (September 1973).

Smith, Karen, et al. "The New Dance." *Drama Review* 16 (September 1972): 115–153.

Spencer, Charles, et al. *The World of Serge Diaghilev.* Chicago, 1974.
Strong, Roy. *Splendour at Court: Renaissance Spectacle and Illusion.* Boston, 1973.
Ter-Arutunian, Rouben. "In Search of Design." *Dance Perspectives,* no. 28 (Winter 1966).
Ter-Arutunian, Rouben. "Decor for Dance." In *Contemporary Stage Design, U.S.A.,* edited by Elizabeth B. Burdick et al. New York, 1975.
Williams, Peter. *Masterpieces of Ballet Design.* Oxford, 1981.
Windham, Donald. "The Stage and Ballet Designs of Pavel Tchelitchew." *Dance Index* 3 (January-February 1944): 4–32.

ARNOLD ARONSON

SCHALL, CLAUS (Claus Nielsen Schall; born 28 April 1757 in Copenhagen, died 9 August 1835 in Copenhagen), Danish composer, dancer, and violinist. Schall joined the Royal Theater in Copenhagen in 1772 as a dancer and in 1779 became a member of the court chapel. When the Italian dancer and choreographer Vincenzo Galeotti was engaged in 1775 by the Royal Theater, he recognized Schall's ability immediately, appointing him *répétiteur* and conductor of ballet music at the Royal Theater in 1775. In the late 1780s Schall traveled; in 1792 he returned to Copenhagen and was given Johann Ernst Hartmann's position as concert master at the Opera, under the well-known German composers Johann Schulz and Friedrich Kunzen. In 1795 he became composer for the Royal Ballet and *Hofdansemusikkompositør.* In 1818, after Schall visited Paris for the second time, he was appointed music director of the Copenhagen Opera. Although he had stopped composing, he remained there until 1834.

Schall is the first native Danish composer of importance. He achieved great popularity as a conductor, composer, and violinist. Apart from a few theory classes with Schulz and Hartmann, he was self-taught. Although clearly influenced by French composers, his style reflects Christoph Willibald Gluck's assimilation to the "national" school of music created in the second half of the eighteenth century by the German composers Johann Naumann, Hartmann, Schulz, and Kunzen. In purely technical terms, Schall's compositions ignore the rules of harmony and counterpoint, but his melodic sense and musical power compensate for this. Schall's musical production includes several song plays the most famous is *Chinafarerne* (The China Travelers; 1792), with text by Peter Andreas Heiberg; about thirty ballets, ranging from light *divertissements* to full-length tragedies; numerous *entrées;* cantatas; much chamber music; and a large amount of popular dance music. Most of his ballet and dance music was published for piano or in instrumental parts by his own publishing house.

For about forty years Schall was Galeotti's consistent musical collaborator, and Schall's composition marks a high point in the early history of ballet music. The music for *Kjærligheds og Mistankens Magt* (The Power of Love and Suspicion; 1780) is the earliest example that we have and was obviously inspired by French *opéra comique.* In *Laurette* (1785) we find a more dramatic tone, showing a knowledge of the melodramatic illustrative style derived from the melodramas of Georg Benda. The music for *Afguden på Ceylon* (The Idol in Ceylon; 1788) represents the key work of Schall's early musical style. A well-defined structure, popular singable melodies, tone pictures, and cheerful dances characterize the score. Around 1800 Schall's style, influenced by the developing tide of musical sensitivity and romanticism, became more passionate and lyrical, to match Galeotti's great pantomimic works.

Lagertha (1801) was a turning point in Danish ballet, the first Nordic ballet built on material from the nation's legendary age. Schall's music also breaks new ground: the endeavor to find a dramatic quality for the highly passionate pantomime resulted in music with strong rhythmic motifs, sensitive, psychologically determined melodies, and melodramatic tone pictures, creating a fluid accompaniment with tragic power that builds on the established forms of the eighteenth century, such as the *gavotte, menuet,* and *allemande.* Both melodically and harmonically, Schall sometimes worked in a minor Nordic mood that stemmed from the old ballads. Reflecting the consciousness of the age in terms of the integration of art forms, Schall also used chorus and vocal soloists in the music for *Lagertha.* His serious tone became of great importance for later Danish composers; August Bournonville referred his composers to Schall's scores when a composition in the Nordic style was required.

Many fruitful years followed, with *Sigrid* (1802, choreography by Laurent), *Rolf Blaaskæg* (Bluebeard; 1808), *Romeo og Giulietta* (1811), and *Macbeth* (1816) being Schall's most important larger works among the series of pastorals and tableaux.

[*For related discussion, see also* Bournonville Composers.]

BIBLIOGRAPHY

Abrahamsen, Erik. "Den musikalske Bournonville." In *Den Kongelige Danske Ballet,* edited by Svend Kragh-Jacobsen and Torben Krogh. Copenhagen, 1952.
Bournonville, August. *My Theatre Life* (1848–1878). Translated and edited by Patricia McAndrew. Middletown, Conn., 1979.
Bruun, Kai. *Dansk musiks historie fra Holberg-tiden til Carl Nielsen.* 2 vols. Copenhagen, 1969.
Friedrich, Julius. "Claus Schall als dramatischer Komponist." Ph.D. diss., University of Berlin, 1930.
LaPointe, Janice D. M. "Creative Integration: A Selective Study of August Bournonville and His Musical Collaborators." *Dance Research Annual* 16 (1987): 87–97.
Schiørring, Nils. *Musikkens historie i Danmark,* vol. 2, *1750–1870.* Copenhagen, 1978.

OLE NØRLYNG

SCHANNE, MARGRETHE (Margrethe Marie Sophie Schanne; born 21 November 1921 in Copenhagen), Danish dancer. Schanne was considered the greatest Sylphide of her time and hence a personification of the Romantic ballerina. There was a Romantic tradition behind Schanne. She was schooled at the Royal Ballet from 1930 to 1940, her most important teacher being the Bournonville specialist, Valborg Borchsenius. The Sylphide tradition—which went back through Ellen Price in an unbroken line to Bournonville's favorite dancer, Juliette Price—was handed over to her, and Schanne was the right one to take over the heritage.

Schanne already showed lightness and poetry in her debut as a Butterfly in the Harald Lander reconstruction of Bournonville's *The Valkyrie* on 29 September 1939. Other Bournonville parts in her repertory were Edouard (1945) in *Far from Denmark,* Eleonora (1951) in *Kermesse in Bruges,* Victorine (1953) in *Konservatoriet,* and Rosita (1956) in *Far from Denmark.* In the Bournonville repertory her foremost contribution remains the lead in *La Sylphide,* which she danced from 1945 to 1966, seemingly unchangeable in her soulful art and the expressiveness of her dark eyes. The same ethereal and moving qualities were to be found in her second main Romantic role, Giselle, which she danced beginning in 1951.

By that time Schanne had studied abroad with Lubov Egorova and Boris Kniaseff, and in 1947 she had been a guest with the Ballet des Champs-Élysées, all of which contributed to her classical style and dramatic characterization. This made her the ideal interpreter of George Balanchine's *Night Shadow,* introduced to the Danish public in 1955. She was also the witty center of Anton Dolin's *Pas de Quatre.*

Schanne's last major part—displaying her wide dramatic range—was the title role in Elsa-Marianne von Rosen's *Irene Holm,* in 1963. Based on a short story by Herman Bang, it depicts the misery of an obscure ballet teacher and former dancer. The role gave Schanne the opportunity to demonstrate her finest qualities: soulfulness, romantic longings, expressive mimicry, and a pure technique. She retired from the Royal Danish Ballet in 1966.

BIBLIOGRAPHY

Anderson, Jack, and George Dorris. "A Conversation with Svend Kragh-Jacobsen." *Ballet Review* 5.4 (1975–1976): 1–20.

Chujoy, Anatole. "Great Romantic Ballerina." *Dance News* (February 1966): 5.

Hering, Doris. "The Danes." *Dance Magazine* (November 1956): 14–17, 50–52.

Kragh-Jacobsen, Svend. *Twenty Solodancers of the Royal Danish Ballet.* Copenhagen, 1965.

Roberts, Sonia. "Margrethe Schanne of the Royal Danish Ballet." *Ballet Today* (October 1961): 25–27.

HENRIK LUNDGREN

SCHAUFUSS FAMILY. Danish family dynasty of dancers. Family dynasties have always been characteristic of ballet in Denmark. The Schaufuss family, comprising Frank Schaufuss, his wife, Mona Vangsaae, and their son, Peter Schaufuss, is one such dynasty of dancers, choreographers, and ballet directors who have elevated the ballet tradition in Denmark and, in particular, the prominence of the Royal Danish Ballet.

Frank Schaufuss (born 13 December 1921 in Copenhagen) belonged to the group of male dancers trained by Harald Lander, who impressed the world when it discovered the Royal Danish Ballet around 1950. Schaufuss entered the ballet school of the Royal Theater in Copenhagen in 1931; he became a member of the company in 1941 and a principal dancer in 1949. He was tall, handsome, and a fine partner. He danced the Hussar when Léonide Massine staged *Le Beau Danube* in Copenhagen in 1948, and he had his most important part as Mercutio in *Romeo and Juliet,* which Frederick Ashton created for the Royal Danish Ballet in 1955. Schaufuss choreographed a few ballets of minor importance and was director of the Royal Danish Ballet from 1956 to 1958. Beginning in 1969 he ran a private school in Copenhagen and in 1974 and 1975 was ballet master of the Royal Opera Ballet in Stockholm.

Mona Vangsaae (born 29 April 1920 in Copenhagen, died 17 May 1983 in Copenhagen), was also a Lander pupil and one of the leading ballerinas of the Royal Danish Ballet in the 1940s and 1950s. Vangsaae entered the ballet school in 1926 and became a member of the company in 1938 and a principal dancer in 1942; she retired in 1962. She was trained in the Bournonville tradition, but it was choreographers from outside the company who gave her the parts that made her a great artist, parts that combined the lyrical with the dramatic. Other choreographers appreciated her great temperament and her humor, and they understood her talent to radiate eroticism. She was the Street Dancer in Léonide Massine's *Le Beau Danube* in 1948 and the Beloved in his *Episodes of an Artist's Life (Symphonie Fantastique),* also in 1948. Both Nini Theilade and George Balanchine used her erotic-dramatic personality in *Metaphor* in 1950 and as the Coquet in *The Sleepwalker* in 1955. In 1957 Birgit Cullberg created *Moon Reindeer* for her, and she danced the part with a moving, poetic feeling, building toward the tragic ending. Two years before she had reached the peak of her career when Frederick Ashton had created the role of Juliet in *Romeo and Juliet* for her.

Apart from these parts in the modern repertory, Vangsaae covered the classical ballets ranging from the works of August Bournonville, dancing in *Konservatoriet* and as Teresina in *Napoli,* to *Chopiniana (Les Sylphides),* to the international classics, such as Aurora in *Aurora's*

Wedding and Myrtha in *Giselle*. She choreographed a few unimportant ballets but had success in London as a Bournonville producer, staging *Napoli*, a *divertissement*, in 1971 for the London Festival Ballet and *Konservatoriet* in 1973 for the London Festival Ballet and in 1982 for the Royal Ballet. A well-respected teacher, she helped her son with his successful Bournonville productions in Germany, France, and Canada. Mona Vangsaae and Frank Schaufuss divorced after they had both left the theater. [*See* Royal Danish Ballet.]

Peter Schaufuss (born 26 April 1949 in Copenhagen) has the greatest artistic range in the family. He entered the ballet school in Copenhagen when he was six years old; Stanley Williams and Vera Volkova were his most important teachers. Schaufuss made his debut in 1967 in the *Don Quixote* pas de deux, but he did not wait quietly for new challenges at home. He went abroad, where he became an important international dancer. Over the years, however, he has nurtured a distinctive love for the Danish ballet tradition. In 1967 and 1968 Schaufuss was for two periods with the National Ballet of Canada in Toronto, and after a few more years in Copenhagen he joined the London Festival Ballet as a principal. From 1974 to 1977 he was a principal dancer with the New York City Ballet and afterward had close connections to the National Ballet of Canada and the London Festival Ballet, where he became artistic director in 1984. In 1990 he left the London Festival Ballet (renamed the English National Ballet) to become director of the German Opera Ballet in Berlin.

SCHAUFUSS FAMILY. Peter Schaufuss and Vanessa Harwood as Siegfried and Odile in Erik Bruhn's 1977 production of *Swan Lake* for the National Ballet of Canada. (Photograph © 1977 by Jack Vartoogian; used by permission.)

SCHAUFUSS FAMILY. Mona Vangsaae and Frank Schaufuss in the title roles of Birger Bartholin's *Romeo and Juliet*, set to Tchaikovsky's music in 1938. Almost twenty years later, Vangsaae created the role of Juliet in Ashton's production for the Royal Danish Ballet in 1955. (Photograph from the Dance Collection, New York Public Library for the Performing Arts.)

A classical dancer with a superb technique, Schaufuss received a silver medal at the International Ballet Competition in Moscow in 1973. He has danced all the princes in the classical repertory as well as the *demi-caractère* parts of Franz in *Coppélia* and both Colas and Alain in *La Fille Mal Gardée*. His range encompasses even the tragic Petrouchka. Over the years he has thus developed into an interesting character dancer with both nerve and temperament. As a dancer he has constantly sought new challenges, and modern choreographers have created roles for him: George Balanchine in *Rapsodie Espagnole* and *The Steadfast Tin Soldier* (both 1975), Roland Petit in *Le Fantôme de l'Opéra* (1980), and Kenneth MacMillan in *Orpheus* (1982).

Schaufuss choreographed a few ballets at quite a young

age, but his most important contribution to ballet history has been as a Bournonville producer. Schaufuss's staging of *La Sylphide* for the London Festival Ballet in 1979 showed his personal relationship to the Bournonville tradition. He works directly with the sources, the music as well as the choreography, updating and refreshing the ballets while treating Bournonville's ideas with respect and clarity. He has a sense of how to make Bournonville international without betraying the original spirit of his work. With *Napoli,* staged in Toronto in 1981, and *A Folk Tale,* performed in Berlin in 1983, he showed the same ability to enliven a performance and to make the classics new by exposing their feelings and dramatic tension.

Schaufuss is an intelligent, dynamic, and outgoing ballet personality whose appearances on television have enriched the public's understanding of dance. In 1984 he made four programs for British Broadcasting Corporation (BBC) Television about the male dancer. In his first season as director of the London Festival Ballet, he persuaded Frederick Ashton to restage the *Romeo and Juliet* he had created for the Danes—and that had made the careers of Schaufuss's parents—in 1955. In 1994 Peter Schaufuss left Berlin to become artistic director for the Royal Danish Ballet. Unfortunately his stay was not a success and he left after only a year. He went on working with the company, however, bringing Fredrick Ashton's *Romeo and Juliet* back to Copenhagen in 1996, where he also staged the full-length ballet *Hamlet.*

[*See also* London Festival Ballet *and* National Ballet of Canada.]

BIBLIOGRAPHY

Aschengreen, Erik. "Schaufuss, Peter." In *Dansk biografisk leksikon.* 3d ed. Copenhagen, 1979–.

Dodd, Craig. *Peter Schaufuss.* London, 1985.

Hering, Doris. "The Royal Danish Ballet and Copenhagen." *Dance Magazine* (July 1956): 14–19.

Kaplan, Larry. "Peter Schaufuss." *Ballet Review* 22 (Winter 1994): 15–17.

Kragh-Jacobsen, Svend, and Torben Krogh, eds. *Den Kongelige Danske Ballet.* Copenhagen, 1952.

Maynard, Olga. "Peter Schaufuss." *Dance Magazine* (September 1974): 36–39.

Merrett, Sue. "Spotlight on Peter Schaufuss." *The Dancing Times* (November 1991): 124–125.

Schaufuss, Peter. "All in the Danish Tradition." *Dance and Dancers* (July 1978): 25–29.

Willis, Margaret E. "The Two Sides of Peter Schaufuss." *Dance Magazine* (December 1987): 56–59.

ERIK ASCHENGREEN

SCHAYK, TOER VAN (born 28 September 1936 in Amsterdam), Dutch dancer, choreographer, designer, and sculptor. Toer van Schayk studied ballet with Sonia Gaskell, in whose Netherlands Ballet he made his debut as a dancer (1955–1959); he also studied painting and sculpture at the Academy for the Arts in the Hague (1958–1965). As soloist with the Dutch National Ballet (1965–1976), he was celebrated for his expressive and sensitive interpretations in roles such as the lead in in Rudi van Dantzig's *Monument for a Dead Boy* (1965). In the 1970s he became, with van Dantzig and Hans van Manen, a resident choreographer of the Dutch National Ballet and won an international reputation. He is also one of the foremost Dutch stage designers, particularly for all of his own ballets and those by van Dantzig. As a painter and sculptor he has had exhibitions in Amsterdam, Athens, London, and New York.

Van Schayk's choreographic approach is very plastic, often combining dance and mime and using his dancers as moving sculptures. His emphasis on the expression of emotions is similar to van Dantzig's, but van Schayk's expressionism is not so tormented. His dance images are instead impressionistic, with a fluid, ethereal quality and sketchlike composition. The content of his ballets is often enigmatic, usually with undertones of anxiety. They are often elegies about the lack of contact and communication, sometimes with a dry, ironic sense of humor, as in *Voor, Tijdens en Na het Feest* (Before, During, and After the Party; 1972), set to music by Gilius van Bergeijk.

Van Schayk's interests in various periods of dance history have often been reflected in his works. The martial dances of ancient Greece, for example, have provided inspiration for no fewer than four ballets: *Pyrrhic Dances* (1974), to music by Geoffrey Grey; *Pyrrhic Dances II* (1977), to music by Lully, Couperin, and others; *Pyrrhic Dances III* (1980), to music by Alban Berg; and *Pyrrhic Dances IV* (1991), to music by Furrer and Liberda. Van Schayk's *Eerste Lugtige Plaatsing* (First Aerial Position; 1976), set to music by Louis Spohr, is a direct reference to the advent of the Romantic ballet in the 1830s, when ballerinas first rose, aerially, on pointe. Similarly, van Schayk's *Jeux* (1977) and *Faun* (1978), set to the scores by Claude Debussy, are direct references to the ballets created by Vaslav Nijinsky for Diaghilev's Ballets Russes in the 1910s. (Rudolf Nureyev created the title role of *Faun*, imbuing it with an animal magnetism evocative of Nijinsky.)

In collaboration with Rudi van Dantzig and Hans van Manen, his colleagues in the Dutch National Ballet, van Schayk contributed to the creation of *Collective Symphony* (1975), set to music by Igor Stravinsky. This led a few years later to creation of another important collaborative work with van Dantzig, *Life* (1979), set to music by various composers and taking as its theme the oppression of liberty. The strong social focus of this work was echoed in van Schayk's first full-length ballet, *Landschap* (Landscape; 1982), also set to a musical collage by various composers, which dealt with warfare and environmental pollution.

Other works created by van Schayk for the Dutch National Ballet include *Onvoltooid Verleden Tijd* (Imperfect Past Tense; 1971), to music by György Ligeti; *Eight Madrigals* (1975), to music by Carlo Gesualdo; *Chiaroscuro* (1980), to music by Gesualdo and Jan van Vlijmen; *Dodeneiland* (Island of Death; 1983), to music by Sergei Rachmaninov; *Seventh Symphony* (1986), to music by Beethoven; *Het Mythische Voorwendsel* (The Mythical Pretext; 1987), to music by Béla Bartók; *Mozart Requiem* (1990); *Stilleven wit Plein* (Still Life with White Square; 1992), to music by Arnold Schoenberg; and *De Omkeerbaarheid van Roest* (The Reversibility of Rust; 1994), set to a musical collage.

[*See also* Dutch National Ballet.]

BIBLIOGRAPHY

Schaik, Eva van. "Toer van Schayk." *Ballett International* 11 (June–July 1988): 52–59.

Utrecht, Luuk. *Het Nationale Ballet 25 jaar: De Geschiedenis van Het Nationale Ballet van 1961 tot 1986*. Amsterdam, 1987.

LUUK UTRECHT

SCHÉHÉRAZADE. Ballet in one act. Choreography: Michel Fokine. Music: Nikolai Rimsky-Korsakov. Libretto, scenery, and costumes: Léon Bakst. First performance: 4 June 1910, Théâtre de l'Opéra, Paris, Ballets Russes de Serge Diaghilev. Principals: Ida Rubinstein (Zobéïde), Vaslav Nijinsky (The Favorite Slave), Aleksei Bulgakov (Shah Shahryar), Enrico Cecchetti (The Chief Eunuch), Sofia Feodorova, Vera Fokina, Bronislava Nijinska, Ludmilla Schollar, and Elena Poliakova (Odalisques).

During more than three decades of performance *Schéhérazade* was identified with the notion of Russian ballet by audiences around the world. Considered the epitome of Serge Diaghilev's Orientalism, this one-act choreographic drama created an instant sensation when it was first presented at the Paris Opera, and again in London. Léon Bakst's vivid palette for the decor immediately influenced fashion and interior decoration as well as stage design.

The ballet's libretto is of uncertain provenance; Diaghilev's attribution of it to Bakst was disputed by Alexandre Benois. It probably developed in general discussions among all Diaghilev's "cabinet," with Michel Fokine also contributing ideas. Based on the first story of A *Thousand and One Nights*, the action depicts harem wives and black slaves indulging in an orgy, led by Zobéïde, the Shah's favorite wife, and her Favorite Slave. Upon the Shah's discovery of the scene, the wives and slaves are slaughtered. Ida Rubinstein's coolly aristocratic mime as Zobéïde contrasted sharply with Vaslav Nijinsky's pantherine presence. Rubinstein's role was later performed with great success by Tamara Karsavina and Lubov Tchernicheva. Nijinsky's role (sometimes called the Golden Slave, because of the golden costume) was later essayed by others, but his astonishingly sensual performance was never equaled.

Staged in pseudo-Oriental style before Fokine had studied authentic Eastern dance, the choreography was noted for its application of Fokine's reforms. It used the whole body in naturalistic mime; plot action was integrated with the dances; and asymmetry featured in the whirling bacchanal.

Schéhérazade remained popular in the Ballets Russes repertory until Diaghilev's death, even though the impresario eventually repudiated the work that had helped to make his reputation. It was often revived into the 1950s, and again in 1995 in a production mounted by Andris Liepa and Isabelle Fokine, but today it seems tame, and its virtues are not immediately obvious to the modern viewer.

[*See also the entries on the principal figures mentioned herein.*]

BIBLIOGRAPHY

Beaumont, Cyril W. *Complete Book of Ballets*. Rev. ed. London, 1951.

Buckle, Richard. *Diaghilev*. New York, 1979.

Fokine, Michel. *Memoirs of a Ballet Master*. Translated by Vitale Fokine. Edited by Anatole Chujoy. London, 1961.

Garafola, Lynn. *Diaghilev's Ballets Russes*. New York, 1989.

Kirstein, Lincoln. *Movement and Metaphor: Four Centuries of Ballet*. New York, 1970.

Nijinska, Bronislava. *Early Memoirs*. Translated and edited by Irina Nijinska and Jean Rawlinson. New York, 1981.

Pruzhan, Irina. *Léon Bakst: Set and Costume Designs, Book Illustrations, Paintings, and Graphic Works*. Translated by Arthur Shkarovsky-Raffé. Middlesex, 1986.

Vaughan, David. "Fokine in the Contemporary Repertory." *Ballet Review* 7.2–3 (1978–1979): 19–27.

SUZANNE CARBONNEAU

SCHĒMA. The ancient Greek word *schēma* (plural, *schēmata*) was used as a technical term in oratory, music, and dance. In its earliest dance contexts, it can be translated as "dance figure" or "design," but on occasion it approximates "dance step." *Schēmata* were not limited to movements of the feet but included the head, torso, arms, and the whole body, as in Xenophon's *Symposium*.

The early Greek dramatists choreographed and performed in productions of their own plays. Thespis and Pratinas, two figures of early Greek drama, were well known for their dancing prowess. Originality in the design of the dances was praised, and the early fifth-century BCE tragedians Phrynichus and Aeschylus prided themselves on inventing their own *schēmata* and teaching them to the choruses.

Descriptions of dancing in late fifth-century comedies and a satyr play suggest that *schēmata* continued to be numerous and included energetic movements. Philocleon in Aristophanes' *Wasps* drunkenly imitates tragic *schēmata* with spins and kicks. The farmer chorus in his *Peace* cannot repress their kicks, and in Euripides' *Cyclops*, the one-eyed monster will not eat the satyrs because he fears they will perform their leaping *schēmata* in his stomach.

Ancient commentators Athenaeus (*Deipnosophists* 1.21, 14.629–630) and Pollux furnished long lists of terms that they categorized as orchestic, or dance, *schēmata*. Some modern scholars have accepted these as a codification of the actual movements that the fifth-century BCE choreographers used for their choral designs. The names of the terms are descriptive and suggest jumps, leaps, turns, hand gestures, or group formations. Although steps similar to those described in the lists may have been used in fifth-century choral dances, the organization of the festivals where the dramatic competitions took place did not create a need for a standardized system of *schēmata*. Since a play was assured of only one performance (the competition), there was no need for a codified vocabulary. With a chorus of amateurs chosen from the citizenry, a playwright could assume that the play would not be performed again with the same chorus members. Only repertory companies, with professional chorus members who performed the same material again and again, required a set movement vocabulary. Such companies did not appear until the fourth century BCE.

Plutarch (c.50–c.120 CE) in his philosophical essay "Quaestiones convivales" identifies *schēma, deixis,* and *phora* as the three components of dance. In Plutarch's treatise, *deixis* may mean "pointing," "indication," or even "portrayal"; *phora* may be translated as "motion" or "carriage"; and *schēma* as "posture," "gesture," or "figure," among other possibilities. The overlapping and elusive meanings of his terms have confused modern scholars who have interpreted the essay as a technical analysis rather than as a philosophical inquiry.

[*See also* Greece, *article on* Dance in Ancient Greece.]

BIBLIOGRAPHY

Lawler, Lillian B. "*Phora, Schēma, Deixis* in the Greek Dance." *Transactions and Proceedings of the American Philological Association* 85 (1954): 148–158.

Smigel, Elizabeth [Libby]. "Redefinitions of the Fifth-Century Greek Chorus Using a Methodology Applied to Aristophanes' *Thesmophoriazusae*." Master's thesis, York University, 1982.

LIBBY SMIGEL

SCHILLING, TOM (born 23 January 1928 in Esperstedt, Germany), German dancer, choreographer, and ballet director. Beginning in 1941 Tom Schilling studied at the ballet school of the Dessau Theater. At the end of 1945 he went to Dresden as a soloist; there he met Gret Palucca and Dore Hoyer. In 1946 he moved to Leipzig as a dancer and studied techniques of expressive dance with Mary Wigman. In 1953, after a number of choreographic experiments, he was invited to become ballet master at the German National Theater in Weimar. There, along with large-scale productions such as *Gayané* (1953), *The Fountain of Bakhchisarai* (1955), and *The Flames of Paris* (1954), he created the first of the small chamber dances he still prefers. Back in Dresden he turned theory into practice in *Abraxas* (1957), *Die Nachtigall* (music by Otto Reinhold, 1958), and other ballets, attempting to synthesize modern dance, ballet, and his own worldview.

Of great significance was his 1965 move to East Berlin's Komische Oper Berlin, which was directed by Walter Felsenstein. There Schilling developed his own type of dance theater, in which traditional ballet forms are critically reevaluated and represented in a modern idiom. Examples are *Romeo and Juliet* (1972), with Romeo as a fisherman and Juliet as the daughter of a rich count; *Swan Lake* (1978), based on the original libretto, but departing from the original choreography by Petipa and Ivanov; and *A New Midsummer Night's Dream* (music by Georg Katzer, 1981). He brought new subjects to the ballet stage: *Der Doppelgänger* (music by Fritz Geissler) in 1969; in 1975, in collaboration with his ballet master and librettist Bernd Köllinger, *Schwarze Vögel* (Blackbird) (music by Katzer), which deals with the historical theme of the German peasants' war; and in 1983, *Wahlverwandtschaften* (Elective Affinities) (music by Franz Schubert), based on Goethe's novel about marriage and a love affair.

Schilling's smaller works were often as successful as his many attempts to revive full-length ballets or to develop them in a contemporary mode. *La Mer* (music by Claude Debussy), which premiered in 1968 at the ballet competition in Varna, has since entered the international repertory. A dialogue between tennis and dance, *Match* (music by Siegfried Matthus, 1971) is one of the most popular ballet miniatures created in East Germany. Since that time, the Komische Oper has performed Schilling's works at several international dance festivals, including the Edinburgh Festival in 1984 and Interballet '85 in Budapest. Companies in other cities, including Munich, West Berlin, and Düsseldorf-Duisburg, have also acquired his choreography.

BIBLIOGRAPHY

Köllinger, Bernd. *Tanztheater: Tom Schilling und die zeitgenössische Choreographie*. Berlin, 1983.

Regitz, Hartmut. "Die 'Schwarzen Vögel' an der Berliner Komischen Oper." *Das Tanzarchiv* 23 (November 1975): 368–370.

HARTMUT REGITZ

SCHNEITZHOEFFER, JEAN (Jean-Madeleine-Marie Schneitzhoeffer; born c.13 October 1785 in Toulouse, died 4 October 1852 in Paris), French musician and composer. The son of an oboe player at the Paris Opera, Schneitzhoeffer studied harmony and composition under Charles-Simon Catel at the Conservatoire. He was timpanist in the orchestra at the Opera from 1816 until 1820 and at the King's Chapel from 1816 until 1823. Upon the death of Martin Joseph Adrien, Schneitzhoeffer was named his successor in the post of chorus master at the Opera, a position he held until 1840. In 1827 he became *professeur de solfège* at the Conservatoire, and from 1831 until 1851 he was *professeur des choeurs des femmes.* In 1840 he was named a Chevalier de la Légion d'Honneur. He died in an asylum in Montmartre in 1852.

During the last years of the Napoleonic era Schneitzhoeffer composed numerous overtures, symphonies, and other instrumental works, but his most important achievement consists of the music for six ballets that he composed for the Opera. Of these, *La Sylphide* was of greatest significance—French Romantic ballet's first masterpiece. Schneitzhoeffer made his debut as a composer of ballet music with *Proserpine* (1818). The musical style is based on Luigi Cherubini's and Gaspare Spontini's classicism and also on the more popular tone of the *opéra comique* of the period. In accordance with accepted practice the score contains borrowings from, among others, Haydn, Mozart *(The Marriage of Figaro),* and Cherubini.

Following a break of six years, Schneitzhoeffer composed the music for the ballet *Zémire et Azor* (1824). He achieved great success with the music for *Mars et Vénus* (1826). The style of his music had become lighter; the many short motifs remind one of Daniel Auber. Schneitzhoeffer reveals himself—not least in the graceful use of wind and string solos in the *divertissements*—to be a child of the Restoration taste for the virtuoso. While the music for the pantomime scenes is characterized by borrowed melodies and mimetic effects, the dance music is strictly structured in eight-bar groups, with a simple melody and an accentuated rhythm.

The music for *La Sylphide* (1832) brought Schneitzhoeffer great critical recognition. The score is extensive, the orchestra large, and the instrumentation varied. The traditional overture portends the atmosphere of the ballet: somber brass, deep strings, and tympani rolls emphasize the melancholy aspects of the story. The melody "La Strega" (The Witch), made famous by Paganini in his variations, is used in the ballet itself as the witches' leitmotif. The Sylphide, by contrast, is illustrated by a hovering string theme. The tone throughout is vivid, light, and lyrical, and the Scottish setting is musically accentuated by frequent use of British folk tunes and bagpipes. If the music for the pantomime scenes suffers to some extent from lack of musical substance, Schneitzhoeffer shows himself to be a capable composer of dance music—for example, in the piquant opening solo and in the grand pas de trois for the Sylphide, James, and Effy in act 1. The witch music in act 2 is interesting in its use of a theme from Bach's *Well-Tempered Clavier* for a grand fugue corresponding to the witches' entry. The moonlit forest romance of act 2 is depicted by harp, string tremoli, and a flowing adagio melody. As an illustration of James's unhappiness upon the death of the Sylphide, Schneitzhoeffer uses Christoph Willibald Gluck's melody from *Orphée et Euridice,* "J'ai perdu mon Euridice." The music for *La Sylphide* is characterized by exciting ideas, vigor, and color. The romantic mood-imagery and theatrical effectiveness are paramount, and as such the music is a direct predecessor of Adolphe Adam's score for *Giselle.*

Schneitzhoeffer's ballet music also includes the scores of *Le Séducteur au Village* (1818, choreography by Monsieur Albert), *Le Sicilien, ou L'Amour Peintre* (1827, choreography by Monsieur Albert and Anatole Petit), and *La Tempête, ou L'Île de Génies* (1834, choreography by Adolphe Nourrit and Jean Coralli), as well as a *grand pas de deux* for Mademoiselle Fitzjames. He collaborated on the music for the tragédie lyrique *Pharamond* and left an unfinished opera, *Sardanapale.*

[*See also* Sylphide, La.]

BIBLIOGRAPHY

Castil-Blaze. *L'Académie Impériale de Musique de 1645 à 1855.* Vol. 2. Paris, 1855.

Comettant, Oscar. *Musique et musiciens.* Paris, 1862.

Constant, Pierre. *La Conservatoire Nationale de Musique et de déclamation.* Paris, 1900.

Fétis, François-Joseph. *Biographie universelle des musiciens.* Paris, 1875.

Gautier, Théophile, et al. *Les beautés de l'Opéra.* Paris, 1845.

Gautier, Théophile. *Histoire de l'art dramatique en France depuis vingt-cinq ans.* 6 vols. Leipzig, 1858–1859.

Guest, Ivor. *The Romantic Ballet in Paris.* 2d rev. ed. London, 1980.

Obituary. *Gazette Musical de Paris* (10 October 1952).

OLE NØRLYNG

SCHOLLAR, LUDMILLA (Liudmila Frantsevna Shollar; born 15 March 1888 in Saint Petersburg, died 10 July 1978 in San Francisco), Russian-American ballet dancer and teacher. Trained by Michel Fokine and Klavdia Kulichevskaya at the Imperial Theater School in Saint Petersburg, Ludmilla Schollar entered the corps de ballet of the Maryinsky Theater upon her graduation in 1906. Between 1909 and 1914, she divided her time between the regular winter seasons at the Maryinsky and the spring and summer Saisons Russes presented by the Ballets Russes de Serge Diaghilev in Paris. Favored by Fokine, she created important solo roles in many of his ballets, including Estrella in *Le Carnaval* (1910), an Odalisque in *Schéhérazade* (1910), and the Street Dancer in *Petrouchka* (1911). She also appeared as one of the two women in Vaslav Nijinsky's *Jeux* (1913).

Upon the outbreak of World War I, Schollar returned to Saint Petersburg to serve as a Red Cross nurse. While ministering to soldiers in the Russian Army, she suffered a serious wound to an arm but continued her duties nevertheless. Later, she was awarded the Medal of Saint George for her courage.

After the war, Schollar rejoined the Ballets Russes in 1921, dancing the Fairy of the Hummingbirds and her popular White Cat variation in Diaghilev's production of *The Sleeping Princess* at London's Alhambra Theatre (1921/22). Dismissed from the company as the result of a labor dispute in 1925, Schollar and her husband, Anatole Vilzak, went to the Teatro Colón in Buenos Aires, where they appeared together in a number of Fokine ballets. In 1928, Schollar became a principal dancer with the Ida Rubinstein company, creating the role of the Fiancée in Bronislava Nijinska's *Le Baiser de la Fée*. Subsequently, in addition to performing with Rubinstein, she danced with the Monte Carlo Opera and with Nijinska's Théâtre de Danse.

Immigrating to the United States in 1936, Schollar taught at the School of American Ballet, the Ballet Theatre School, and the Washington School of Ballet, in addition to conducting a school in New York with her husband. A superb teaching team, the couple joined the staff of the San Francisco Ballet School in 1966.

BIBLIOGRAPHY

Buckle, Richard. *Nijinsky*. London, 1971.

Denny, Carol H. "Viva Vilzak: On His Toes at Eighty-Six." *San Francisco Sunday Examiner and Chronicle* (31 January 1982).

Krasovskaya, Vera. *Russkii baletnyi teatr nachala dvadtatogo veka*, vol. 2, *Tantsovshchiki*. Leningrad, 1972.

Moore, Lillian. "Diaghileff Teachers in America: A Study in Constructive Guidance." *Ballet Annual* 10 (1956): 75–77.

Nijinska, Bronislava. *Early Memoirs*. Translated and edited by Irina Nijinska and Jean Rawlinson. New York, 1981.

LYNN GARAFOLA

SCHÖNBERG, BESSIE (born 27 December 1906 in Hanover, Germany, died 14 May 1997 in Bronxville, New York), one of the foremost dance educators and teachers of choreography in the United States. At ninety, Shönberg conducted dance composition courses, led workshops, and advised choreographers who sought her discerning eye.

Growing up in Dresden, Schönberg studied Dalcroze eurhythmics but was discouraged from considering a career in dance by her conservative father, a civil engineer. Her first serious dance studies began after she came to the United States in 1926. Schönberg's American mother, Rose Elizabeth McGrew, who had separated from her husband, headed the voice and opera workshop at the University of Oregon. Schönberg enrolled in the university's arts program and was enthralled by the just-developing ideas and technique of Martha Graham, introduced at the university when Martha Hill came to teach there.

Hill returned to New York City in 1929 to join the all-female company Graham was forming, and Schönberg accompanied her, securing a scholarship to the Neighborhood Playhouse (where Graham taught) and a place in the company. Between 1929 and 1931, she performed in such epochal Graham works as *Heretic* (1929) and *Primitive Mysteries* (1931). Along with Neighborhood Playhouse students and faculty, she also appeared in various symphonic dance dramas staged by Playhouse co-director Irene Lewisohn (with music provided by the Cleveland Orchestra).

A knee injury halted Schönberg's performing career and diverted her into teaching. Between 1933 and 1935, she worked as Hill's assistant at Bennington College in Bennington, Vermont, where she finished her own degree; she also taught at the Bennington summer school and festival from its inception in 1934 (through 1941). Other early employers included Briarcliff Junior College.

In 1934 she embarked on a harmonious fifty-year marriage with Dimitry Varley, and in 1938 began an equally durable association with Sarah Lawrence College in Bronxville, New York. She first taught dance classes and then, in 1941, took over the chairmanship of the dance department, a position she held until her retirement in 1975.

Schönberg brought luminaries of modern dance as guest teachers to the unorthodox liberal arts college, and, with colleagues such as musicians Ruth and Norman Lloyd, developed a curriculum and an approach to teaching, especially of dance composition. Not wishing to impose her own style or taste, she devised what she described as increasingly complex "problems to solve with movement, time, energy. . . ." With beginners, she once said, her role was "to lead the path toward exploration, toward excursion, toward courage, toward daring, toward taking chances." With some of these same words, she urged professional choreographers toward greater experimentation. Former students, such as Meredith Monk, have spoken gratefully of Schönberg's extraordinary ability to guide them toward what she deduced they were trying to create.

Since her retirement from Sarah Lawrence, Schönberg taught composition at the London School of Contemporary Dance, the Laban Centre (London), and the Dance Theatre of Harlem (1986–1992). In 1992 she joined the dance faculty of the Juilliard School. Dance Theater Workshop regularly hosted her workshops for selected choreographers beginning in 1981, and Jacob's Pillow in 1980. In 1988 she became artistic adviser to The Yard, on Martha's Vineyard, where choreographers develop dances during summer residencies.

Dance Theater Workshop paid her homage in 1984 by naming its annual New York Dance and Performance Awards, the Bessies, after her. She was one of the first recipients of a National Endowment for the Arts Master

Teachers/Mentors grant in 1993 and, along with her first modern dance teacher, Martha Hill Davies, was presented in 1994 with an Ernie, an award established by Dance/USA to acknowledge the field's "unsung heroes." Schönberg is also known for her English translation (1937) of Curt Sachs's *World History of Dance.*

BIBLIOGRAPHY

Jowitt, Deborah. "A Conversation with Bessie Schönberg." *Ballet Review* 9 (Spring 1981): 31–63.

Schönberg, Bessie. "A Lifetime of Dance." *Performing Arts Journal* 4.1–2 (1979): 106–117.

DEBORAH JOWITT

SCHOOLING, ELISABETH (born 27 April 1915 in London), British dancer and teacher. A dancer with a wonderful flair for comedy, Schooling was one of the original members of the Ballet Rambert. From her earliest performances in 1930 to her departure for Australia in 1947 with choreographer Frank Staff, then her husband, and a group of the company's dancers, she danced in nearly every work in the repertory, creating roles in sixteen of them.

Many of the ballets in which she gave her most memorable performances are now lost; she was often the Wife in Frederick Ashton's chic, mysterious *Les Masques,* the Fille au Bar in Ninette de Valois's *Bar aux Folies-Bergère,* and Hebe in Antony Tudor's *The Descent of Hebe,* a work Marie Rambert described as "altogether ravishing." Schooling also danced in many ballets, new then, that are still performed—Ashton's *Façade;* Tudor's *Jardin aux Lilas, Gala Performance,* and *The Judgment of Paris*—and in some that were then already recognized masterpieces—*Le Carnaval, Les Sylphides,* and *Le Spectre de la Rose.* She also appeared in the London company of George Balanchine's Ballets 1933 and in West End productions of *The Tales of Hoffmann* and *The Glass Slipper* during World War II.

In later years, Schooling applied her exceptional memory to the restaging of old works. With William Chappell she mounted Vaslav Nijinsky's *L'Après-midi d'un Faune* for the Joffrey Ballet and London Festival Ballet and for the film *Nijinsky* (1980); with Sally Gilmour she taught Ashton's *Capriol Suite* to Ballet Rambert in 1983. On her own she mounted works by Andrée Howard and Frank Staff for Sadler's Wells Royal Ballet, for the Mercury Ballet in New York City, and for various schools in England. She also briefly ran her own school in Devon.

BIBLIOGRAPHY

Bradley, Lionel. *Sixteen Years of Ballet Rambert.* London, 1946.

Clarke, Mary. *Dancers of Mercury: The Story of Ballet Rambert.* London, 1962.

Noble, Peter, ed. *British Ballet.* London, 1949.

Rambert: A Celebration. Compiled by Jane Prichard. London, 1996.

BARBARA NEWMAN

SCHOOP, TRUDI (born 9 October 1903 in Zurich), Swiss dancer, teacher, choreographer, and dance therapist. At the age of sixteen, having had no training in dance, Trudi Schoop announced that she wanted to become a dancer. Even her understanding family reacted to her pronouncement with amusement. Nevertheless, only a few months later, at the Pfauentheater in Zurich, Schoop presented a program of dances composed of movements derived exclusively from her own fantasies and intuition. The evening was a major success, marred only by the fact that the audience sometimes laughed unexpectedly, at inappropriate moments. Over the next few years, Schoop performed in Switzerland and Germany while continuing her training in classical and modern technique, especially in the school of Ellen Tells, a disciple of Isadora Duncan. In 1926, Schoop opened her own school in Zurich and experimented with her first choreographies at the municipal theater.

Schoop's dance evenings were always very successful, but she was frequently disappointed to find that dances she intended to be perceived as pure expressions of beauty and deep seriousness instead aroused merriment from the audience. Although such experiences were initially painful, they ultimately gave her the courage to accept her comic talent and to work toward becoming a dance comedienne. By the 1930s she had developed her skills in both dance and pantomime and had made a successful entrée into dance theater, which was then very much in vogue.

In the figure of Fridolin, which she created, Schoop combined the essential sadness of the human condition with such gaiety and openness to life that critics always drew comparisons to the figure of the Little Tramp, created by Charlie Chaplin. Schoop created a number of Fridolin pieces for her own dance group, which she called Fridolin en Route, and in 1932 their performances took second prize at a Paris choreography competition, right behind Kurt Jooss's masterpiece, *The Green Table.* Through extensive tours with her troupe, Schoop became well known in Europe and the United States. During World War II she remained in Switzerland, where she performed in the Cornichon, the most spirited antifascist cabaret in the country, but she resumed touring as soon as hostilities ceased. In 1947, after many years of restless wandering, she settled in the United States, making her home in Los Angeles.

In California Schoop began her second career, which grew out of her earlier activity and which evolved in much the same way as her dance career. Again guided by her creative intuition, she developed methods of reaching out to mentally ill people, many of whom had completely closed themselves off from the world around them. As a pioneer in the then emerging field of dance therapy,

SCHOOP. Eugene Hari and Ruth Mata augmented their dance training by studying mime with Schoop in Zurich. Having come to the United States in 1937 with Schoop's company, they later became well known as the dance-mime duo of Mata and Hari, touring extensively and appearing frequently on television during the 1950s. Among their most popular numbers was "Carnegie Hall," pictured here, in which they portrayed a couple arriving at a concert and then imitated all the members of the orchestra. (Photograph from a private collection.)

Schoop succeeded, through movement and body expression, in opening paths to minds closed to customary avenues of communication, thereby breaking through the fearful isolation of mental patients and enabling them to accept rather than shrink from human contact.

[*See also* Dance and Movement Therapy.]

BIBLIOGRAPHY

Levy, Fran. "Trudi Schoop." In Levy's *Dance-Movement Therapy.* Reston, Va., 1988.

Pastori, Jean-Pierre. *Dance and Ballet in Switzerland.* Translated by Jacqueline Gartmann. 2d ed., rev. and enl. Zurich, 1989.

Roberts, Stephanie. "Trudi Schoop Beyond Dance: Mime Turned Therapist." *Dance Magazine* (October 1979): 86–91.

Schoop, Trudi, and Peggy Mitchell. *Won't You Join the Dance? A Dancer's Essay into the Treatment of Psychosis.* New York, 1974.

Young, Therese A. "Trudi Schoop: From Dance Mime to Dance Therapy." Master's thesis, Texas Women's University, 1986.

RICHARD MERZ
Translated from German

SCHUMAN, WILLIAM (William Howard Schuman; born 4 August 1910 in New York City, died 15 February 1992 in New York City), American composer and teacher. Although Schuman's family was not especially musical, as a boy he took violin lessons, and in high school he composed popular songs in collaboration with Frank Loesser. In 1930, while studying business at New York University, he attended an all-Wagner concert conducted by Arturo Toscanini and immediately enrolled in the Malkin Conservatory. To prepare himself for a teaching career, he attended Columbia University's Teachers College (B.A. 1935, M.A. 1937) but also studied conducting at the Salzburg Mozarteum (1935) and composition with Roy Harris (1936–1938). Although he had worked as an arranger for jazz bands while a student, Schuman soon devoted himself to classical music. His theater music especially reveals his understanding of jazz.

In 1935 Schuman began teaching at Sarah Lawrence College, working to integrate music into the liberal arts curriculum rather than teaching it in isolation from the other arts. Although not then involved in dance, he often included dance works on the tours of the chorus, which he directed. In 1945 he became president of the Juilliard School, where he once again brought about sweeping reforms in how music was taught, especially through his Literature and Materials of Music program. That same year he wrote *Undertow,* his first ballet, and was established as one of the leading American composers and teachers.

In 1951, after he had composed one ballet for Antony Tudor and two for Martha Graham, Schuman invited Martha Hill to head a new dance division at Juilliard with a faculty including Tudor, Graham, Agnes de Mille, Doris Humphrey, José Limón, and Ann Hutchinson. This innovative program of bringing together some of the most important figures in ballet and modern dance—and expecting students to become proficient in both—while including composition and notation in the curriculum had an enormous impact on the teaching of dance long after Schuman resigned from Juilliard to succeed General Maxwell D. Taylor as president of Lincoln Center in 1962.

At Lincoln Center, Schuman oversaw the opening of each division of the complex with the exception, ironically, of the new Juilliard quarters (which opened last). During his seven-year tenure, he stressed the center's role as an educational and cultural force in the community. He encouraged active sponsorship of dance, drama, film, and chamber music as well as opera and orchestral music; he developed an elaborate educational program involving the city schools; and he planned inventive summer programs to bring new audiences to the center. He resigned in 1968 over basic disagreements with the executive committee about the funding of cultural and educational programs, which gave the center an active role in developing the arts rather than passively presenting them. After he left Lincoln Center, Schuman devoted himself primarily to composing and to promoting American music while also retaining his interest in dance.

Schuman's first composition for dance, *Undertow*, was for Tudor. Its premiere, by Ballet Theatre, was on 10 April 1945 at the Metropolitan Opera House. The strong dramatic score, conducted by Antal Dorati, combined powerful dissonant harmonies with a slightly off-key lyricism, contributing significantly to Tudor's grimly effective study of an alienated killer in a slum society. Later that year a considerably revised concert version was presented by Alfred Wallenstein and the Los Angeles Philharmonic.

Schuman's four other works for dance were all for Martha Graham. His long melodic lines (often combined polyphonically), rhythmic exuberance, and strong triadic harmonies meshed well with Graham's world of emotional intensity and complex mythic structures. *Night Journey* was Graham's meditation on the Oedipus-Jocasta story. At the 3 May 1947 premiere at Harvard University, members of the Boston Symphony were conducted by Louis Horst. Afterward Schuman commented that "modern dance suffers from the insufficient tonal range its limited budgets permit. For this reason the music for modern choreography often sounds inadequate and places modern dance at a disadvantage when compared with the musical resources usually available to ballet companies." As if to address this, his and Graham's next collaboration, *Judith* (4 January 1950), which he called "a choreographic poem for orchestra," was designed for solo dancer and symphony orchestra on a commission from the Louisville Orchestra. Isamu Noguchi's set situated the orchestra, under Robert Whitney, at the back of the stage behind a great translucent curtain. Schuman unified the work's episodes by using a limited number of themes and harmonic devices. Asked if *Judith* showed the influence of jazz, he retorted, "That's no influence—that's jazz." *Undertow* and *Judith* have remained his most durable theatrical scores. *Voyage* (17 May 1953; later called *Theatre for a Voyage*) had Graham dancing erotically with three men to Schuman's chamber orchestra version of a 1953 cycle for piano also called *Voyage*. In *The Witch of Endor* (1965), Graham again danced with Bertram Ross and Robert Cohan (as the Witch, King Saul, and David), but in this much darker work, Schuman showed his more dramatic side.

Although Schuman wrote no other ballet scores, his concert works have been drawn on occasionally for dance because his style was naturally dramatic and he understood what it takes to achieve an effective collaboration in which music and dance play equally important roles.

BIBLIOGRAPHY

Schreiber, Flora-Rheta, and Vincent Persichetti. *William Schuman*. New York, 1954.

Young, Edgar B. *Lincoln Center: The Building of an Institution*. New York, 1980.

GEORGE DORRIS

SCHWARZ FAMILY, French family of ballet dancers and teachers, most of whom were active in the Paris Opera Ballet.

Jean Schwarz (born 31 December 1884 in Paris, died 6 February 1936 in Paris) was a dancer at the Opera from 1896 to 1909, when he began teaching and lecturing. He married an actress, Nelly Nibert, and fathered four daughters: Nelly, Solange, Jane, and Christiane. When he and his wife divorced, his sister Jeanne became surrogate mother to his girls.

Jeanne Schwarz (born 22 July 1887 in Paris, died November 1970 in Paris), was herself a star at the Opera. She entered the Paris Opera Ballet School in 1897, when she was ten, and was graduated in 1903. She became a *première danseuse* in 1917 and a *danseuse étoile* in 1919. After almost ten years at the pinnacle of her profession, she retired from the stage in 1928 and turned her energies to the classroom. Best known for her teaching at the Opéra-Comique (1935–1951), she also taught a class at the Conservatoire de Musique. In 1967, she was awarded the Medaille de Vermeil in recognition of her contributions to the art of dance.

Encouraged by their father and their aunt, all four of Jean Schwarz's daughters became dancers. **Nelly Schwarz** (born 26 March 1909 in Berck, Pas-de-Calais) entered the Paris Opera Ballet School in 1920 and joined the company in 1925. She achieved the rank of *petit sujet* in 1937 and, after dancing for ten years, retired to teach in 1947. Jane Schwarz, better known as **Jhanyne Schwarz** (born 17 March 1912 in Asnières), entered the ballet school at the Opera in 1923, joined the company in 1926, and was promoted to *grand sujet* in 1937. Having begun a teaching career in 1950, she retired from the company in 1952. Christiane Schwarz, better known as **Juanina Schwarz** (born 29 April 1914 in Asnières), began her training at the ballet school at the Opera in 1926. She left in 1932 to join the ballet company at the Opéra-Comique, where she was a soloist until 1946. During her performing years she created numerous roles in ballets by Constantin Tcherkas and took part in revivals of many older works.

Solange Schwarz (born 12 November 1910 in Paris) became the best known of all the Schwarz sisters. She entered the Paris Opera Ballet School in 1920, joined the company upon her graduation in 1924, and was promoted to *grand sujet* in 1929. In 1932 she left the Opera to join the ballet company of the Opéra-Comique as *danseuse étoile*. In 1937, after five years at the Opéra-Comique—where she shared the stage with her sister Juanina—she returned to the Opera as a *grand sujet* at the request of the director, Jacques Rouché, who particularly wanted her to dance Swanilda in Paul Larthe's production of *Coppélia.* She was promoted to *première danseuse* soon after her successful performances in that role and was finally elevated to *danseuse étoile* in 1940.

In 1945, when the Paris Opera Ballet was temporarily disbanded, Schwarz joined Les Ballets de Champs-Élysées, directed by Roland Petit. In 1948 she rejoined the company at the Opéra-Comique, remaining there until 1951. In 1952 she was a guest artist with the Grand Ballet de Marquis de Cuevas, and in 1954 she danced as a guest for the first season of Les Ballets de l'Étoile, founded by Maurice Béjart and Jean Laurent.

Early in her career with the Paris Opera Ballet, Schwarz created roles in Michel Fokine's *La Rêve de Marquis* (1921), Bronislava Nijinska's *Les Rencontres* (1925), Léo Staats's *Le Triomphe de l'Amour* (1925), and Serge Lifar's *Bacchus et Ariane* (1931). Later she created roles in two important works by Albert Aveline, *Le Festin de l'Araignée* and *La Chartreuse de Parme* (both 1939), and in numerous works by Lifar, including *Alexandre le Grand* (1937), *Entre Deux Rondes* (1940), *Le Chevalier et la Damoiselle* (1941), *Joan de Zarissa* (1942), and *Suite en Blanc* (1943). Lifar danced as her partner in many of these works.

At the Opéra-Comique, Schwarz created roles in ballets made for her by another frequent partner, Constantin Tcherkas, including *La Pantoufle de Vair* (1932), *Le Cygne* (1935), and *La Rosière du Village* (1936), and by Jean-Jacques Etchévery, including *Les Heures* (1949), *Paris-Magic* (1949), and *Concerto* (1950). She also created the role of Nina in Léonide Massine's *La Valse* (1950). For Les Ballets de l'Étoile, she created roles in Maurice Béjart's *La Lettre* and Yves Brieux's *Le Jugement de Pâris* (both 1954).

To the disappointment of the public, Schwarz retired from the stage while still at the peak of her powers. She gave a memorable farewell performance at the Paris Opera on 17 January 1957, dancing in *Suite en Blanc* and *Coppélia,* ballets that provided her with two of her best roles. Reviewing this performance, the critic Jacques Bourgeois praised Schwarz's "admirably precise technique, the extreme finesse of her *batterie,* her nervous pointes" and stated, unequivocally, that she had "the most beautiful feet in the world" and "incomparable arms" (*Arts,* 23 January 1957). After leaving the stage, Schwarz took over the classes of her aunt, Jeanne Schwarz, at the Conservatoire de Musique in Paris and taught there for the next twenty years. In 1979 she moved with her family to the south of France.

BIBLIOGRAPHY

Dolin, Anton. "Solange Schwarz: An Appreciation." *The Dancing Times* (July 1938): 398–399.

Fumet, Stanislas. "De la poésie de la danse à sa littérature." *Formes et couleurs* 10.4 (1948): 19–26.

Guest, Ivor. *Le ballet de l'Opéra de Paris.* Paris, 1976.

Hering, Doris. "'We Talked about It So Much.'" *Dance Magazine* (July 1961): 46–51.

Laurent, Jean. "Solange Schwartz." In *Quinze danseurs et danseuses,* by Jean Arnaud-Durand et al. Paris, 1948.

"Portrait of Miss Jo." *Ballet Ballyhoo* 1 (Fall 1977): 4–5.

Schwarz, Jean. "Méthode de la danse classique." *Archives internationales de la danse* (November 1935): 3–4.

Schwarz, Solange. "Le neveu de Lully." *La danse* (March 1957).

Schwarze, Richard F. "Hermene Schwarz." *Dance Magazine* (March 1987): 107.

Vaillat, Léandre. *La danse à l'Opéra de Paris.* Paris, 1951.

MONIQUE BABSKY
Translated from French

SCHWEIZER MILCHMÄDCHEN, DAS. *See* Swiss Milkmaid, The.

SCOTT, MARGARET (born 26 April 1922 in Johannesburg), South African dancer, teacher, choreographer, and administrator. Scott studied privately in South Africa, then in London at the Sadler's Wells School from 1939 through 1940. She stayed in London during World War II and danced in Sadler's Wells Ballet (1940–1941) and then joined the Ballet Rambert where she was a principal from 1941 through 1948.

In 1947 Scott traveled to Australia with the Ballet Rambert and remained there when its tour ended. In Australia she performed with the National Theatre Ballet Company for whom she also reproduced *Peter and the Wolf* in 1950. She returned to London in 1952 and was one of six dancers, including Kenneth MacMillan, who were invited by John Cranko to join an experimental dance group that performed Cranko's choreography at Henley-on-Thames and at Benjamin Britten's Aldeburgh Festival.

Rejoining the Ballet Rambert as ballet mistress and assistant to Madame Rambert, Scott also directed the company on tour. In 1953 she returned to Australia and taught privately for Paul Hammond and his wife Peggy Sager, while they were on tour with Edouard Borovansky. Later she opened her own school in Melbourne.

In preparation for the formation of the Australian Ballet, Scott was commissioned to organize and conduct interim classes for dancers from the defunct Borovansky Ballet and from overseas. With the addition of three principals, these dancers formed the nucleus of the Australian Ballet Company under Peggy van Praagh in 1962.

Scott's next undertaking was to plan and found the Australian Ballet School in 1964, which she directed until her retirement in 1990. She choreographed several ballets, notably *Recollections of a Beloved Place* (to Tchaikovsky's *Souvenir of Florence*) for Ballet Victoria in 1975, and she has worked with a number of leading creators including

Cranko, Frederick Ashton, Ninette de Valois, Robert Helpmann, Antony Tudor, and MacMillan.

In the administrative field she has headed an official delegation to China, hosting the return visits in 1975 and 1976, and was a member of the jury at the Moscow International Ballet Competitions (1981 and 1985) and of several boards. She is married to Dr. Derek Benton, Director and Research Professor at the Howard Florey Institute in Melbourne, and has two sons.

[*See also* Australian Ballet.]

BIBLIOGRAPHY

Laughlin, Patricia, and Brian McInerney. "Dame Margaret Scott." *Dance Australia,* no. 5 (September–November 1981): 9–12.

Ruskin, Pamela. *Invitation to the Dance: The Story of the Australian Ballet School.* Sydney, 1989.

Ruskin, Pamela. "A Tribute to Dame Margaret." *Dance Australia,* no. 46 (February–March 1990): 23–25.

INTERVIEW. Dame Margaret Scott, by Michelle Potter (April 1993) National Library of Australia, Canberra (TRC 2928).

GEOFFREY WILLIAM HUTTON
Amended by Michelle Potter

SCOTTISH BALLET. Robert Cohan mounted a contemporary version of *A Midsummer Night's Dream* for the company in 1993. Noriko Ohara and Lloyd Embleton danced the roles of Titania and Oberon. (Photograph © by Bill Cooper; used by permission.)

SCOTTISH BALLET. Established in Glasgow in 1969, the Scottish Ballet evolved from Britain's first regional dance company, Western Theatre Ballet. This Bristol-based company had been founded in 1957 by Elizabeth West, a dancer-actor and theater choreographer, and Peter Darrell, an original member of the Sadler's Wells Theatre Ballet. Dance theater—that is, dance combined with drama, performed by dancer-actors—had been a vital ingredient of the artistic ethos of this company from its beginning.

The first performance by Western Theatre Ballet, given at Dartington Hall, Devon, on 24 June 1957, included a work characteristic of the new company's aims: Darrell's *The Prisoners,* set to music by Béla Bartók, dealt with seduction, betrayal, and murder. Strongly influenced by the *nouvelle vague* (new wave) of 1950s French cinema, Darrell hoped to invigorate British dance with choreographic realism as powerful as that shown in films and on stage. For many years he was the only British choreographer to invite collaboration from contemporary playwrights: John Mortimer for *Home* (1965), dealing with mental illness, and David Rudkin for *Sun into Darkness* (1966), the first full-length British ballet with a contemporary theme, including ritual rape and murder.

Other important works demonstrating Darrell's concern to relate to modern-day affairs were *A Wedding Present* (1962), dealing with homosexuality; *Mods and Rockers* (1963), set to music by the Beatles; and *Jeux* (1963), a reworking of themes used by Vaslav Nijinsky in his 1913 ballet to the score by Claude Debussy. Equally valuable additions to the repertory were ballets choreographed by Laverne Meyer, Jack Carter, Ray Powell, and Peter Wright, and in the late 1960s the company presented the British premieres of two remarkably powerful works: Kenneth MacMillan's *Las Hermanas* (1966), and Flemming Flindt's *The Lesson* (1967).

Western Theatre Ballet had initially struggled for survival, but by the early 1960s it had received wide recognition; an extended season in Brussels had been followed by appearances at the Edinburgh International Festival and at the Jacob's Pillow Dance Festival in the United States. Tragically, Elizabeth West had been killed in a Swiss avalanche in 1962, and Darrell had assumed sole directorship of the company. In 1969, he accepted the challenge of moving it to Scotland as a way of achieving financial security.

Although the ethos of the Scottish Ballet—called Scottish Theatre Ballet until 1974—was similar to that of Western Theatre Ballet, its status as a national company brought new demands. The repertory was expanded to include some of the classics as well as original full-length and one-act ballets. The company continued to tour England and to make numerous appearances in Scotland, performing not only in the major cities but in many smaller towns, often in schools and city halls. The Scottish Ballet had become a pioneering company, developing and educating its new audiences.

Between 1969 and 1979, the company expanded from twenty to nearly fifty dancers; international tours were made throughout Europe and Australasia; and such artists as Margot Fonteyn, Rudolf Nureyev, and Natalia Makarova were frequent guests. These were the company's golden years, shaped by Darrell's personal vision and amazingly eclectic artistic output: *Beauty and the Beast* (1969), to a commissioned score by Thea Musgrave; *Giselle* (1971), staged by Joyce Graeme but reworked dramatically by Darrell; *Tales of Hoffmann* (1972); *The Nutcracker* (1973); *Mary, Queen of Scots* (1976), to a commissioned score by John McCabe; *Swan Lake* (1977), radically reinterpreted; and *Cinderella* (1979), set to music by Gioacchino Rossini. The only other full-length works to enter the repertory were two classics by August Bournonville: *La Sylphide,* staged in 1973, and *Napoli,* added in 1978. However, a large number of shorter ballets were mounted, including works by John Neumeier, Rudi van Danzig, Maurice Béjart, Jack Carter, Walter Gore, Andrée Howard, John Cranko, Antony Tudor, Jiří Kylián, and, of course, Darrell himself. Choreographic talent for the future was nutured through annual workshops, with the results often incorporated into the touring schedule.

Financial constraints imposed in 1979 reduced the size of the Scottish Ballet to fewer than forty dancers, cut back touring, and severely restricted new creations. Only three major works were added to the repertory in the next six years. In 1980 and 1985, Darrell produced his last two major works, *Chéri* and *Carmen,* for the Edinburgh International Festival, and in 1982 John Cranko's *Romeo and Juliet* was staged. In the mid-1980s, Darrell suffered increasing ill health, and he died in 1987 at the age of fifty-eight; his contribution to the formation and growth of a ballet company has few parallels in modern times. [*See the entry on Darrell.*]

Darrell's death occurred just as a new position of chief executive—with control over the artistic director—was being created. Darrell's muse and the company's principal ballerina, Elaine MacDonald, initially took over the artistic reins, but her position was made untenable. Nanette Glushak, as guest director during the 1989/90 season, breathed new life into the company and brought the first works by George Balanchine into the repertory, but her artistic and directoral freedom were likewise compromised. Renowned former dancer Galina Samsova became artistic director in 1991. Her productions of *The Sleeping Beauty* (1994) and *Swan Lake* (1995) were both critically pilloried for an absence of dramatic integrity. The company is currently seen to lack identity and direction, choosing largely to ignore its distinguished heritage but having found nothing valid with which to replace it.

BIBLIOGRAPHY

Anderson, Robin. "The Scottish Ballet." In *Twentieth-Century Dance in Britain,* edited by Joan W. White. London, 1985.

Bowen, Christopher. "Company at the Crossroads." *Dance and Dancers* (January 1990): 22–23.

Brinson, Peter, and Clement Crisp. *Ballet for All.* London, 1970.

Goodwin, Noël. *A Ballet for Scotland.* Edinburgh, 1979.

Percival, John. *Modern Ballet.* Rev. ed. London, 1980.

"Peter Darrell Talks to D. & D." *Dance and Dancers* (June 1979): 22–24.

West, Geoffrey. "The Darrell Legacy at Scottish Ballet." *Dance Now* (Winter 1994): 29–37.

GEOFFREY WEST

SCULPTURE. *See* Artists and Dance.

SEGUIDILLAS. One of the oldest dance and song forms in Spain, the *seguidilla* in the sixteenth century was a popular favorite and was therefore incorporated into most of the plays of the period. Derivative dances survive today among Spain's regional dances. The most famous form is the *seguidillas sevillanas,* more familiarly known as the *sevillanas,* the regional dance of Seville. Affectionately known as the "mother of Spanish dance," the *sevillanas* is usually the first dance taught in a dance academy. To expatriate Spaniards, the *sevillanas* arouses strong passion for the homeland, and everyone dances it with varying degrees of proficiency.

The *seguidillas manchegas,* the other well-known variety, exists as both a regional dance from La Mancha, in southeast Castile, and as one of the dances of the *escuela bolera.* Both are danced to the same music.

Seguidillas and *boleros* use similar steps, but they are distinguished by the number of strophes per line in the song accompanying the dance. Whereas the *sevillanas* in its regional form has four *coplas* (verses), the *sevillanas boleras* (danced to the same tune) has only three. The *sevillanas* is extremely popular, but only a few dancers perform the *sevillanas boleras,* because of its technical difficulty. Castanets accompany both dances. Many regional variations of *seguidillas* exist and are usually danced by couples, with partners using *pasadas* (passing steps) to change places with each other throughout the dance.

[*See also* Bolero; Escuela Bolera.]

BIBLIOGRAPHY

Actas del II congreso de folclore Andaluz: Danza, música e indumentaria tradicional. Seville, 1988.

Armstrong, Lucile. *Dances of Spain.* London, 1950.

Caballero Bonald, José Manuel. *El baile andaluz.* Barcelona, 1957.

García Matos, Manuel. *Danzas populares de España: Andalucía.* Madrid, 1971.

Iza Zamácola, Juan Antonio de. *Colección de las mejores coplas de seguidillas, tiranas y polos que se han compuesto para cantar a la guitarra.* Madrid, 1790.

Valdenebro, Pepa Guerra. *Así canta y baila Andalucía.* Malaga, 1987.

PHILIPPA HEALE

SEMENOVA, MARINA (Marina Timofeevna Semyonova; born 30 May [12 June] 1908 in Saint Petersburg), Russian dancer, teacher, and coach. Semenova studied at the Petrograd ballet school between 1909 and 1925 under Agrippina Vaganova. While still a student, Semenova appeared as the Queen of the Dryads in *Don Quixote* and as Princess Florine in *The Sleeping Beauty.* Ever sensitive to the individuality and idiosyncracies of her pupils, for Semenova's graduation performance Vaganova chose the ballet *La Source,* in Achille Coppini's version; it contained the role of the fairy Naila, which called for a powerful technique, surging energy, inpetuosity, and speed. She could not have made a better choice; Semenova displayed her mastery of a striking range of dance movements, a fine musicality, and total aplomb. Upon graduation she was invited by Leningrad's Theater of Opera and Ballet to be a soloist. There, under Vaganova's expert guidance, Semenova made rapid progress in mastering the established classical repertory.

SEMENOVA. In 1926, Semenova appeared as Nikia in *La Bayadère* at the State Academic Theater for Opera and Ballet in Leningrad. The dramatic intensity of the early scenes in this ballet and the classical nobility of the later ones made Nikia, the doomed temple dancer, an ideal vehicle for her. (Photograph from the Dance Collection, New York Public Library for the Performing Arts.)

Semenova felt equally at home in dramatic, grotesque, and lyrical roles. In the course of five successive seasons in Leningrad she appeared as Odette-Odile (*Swan Lake* in 1926), Nikia (*La Bayadère* in 1926), Princess Aurora (*The Sleeping Beauty* in 1927), the Tsar-Maiden (*The Little Humpbacked Horse* in 1928), Aspicia (*La Fille du Pharaon* in 1928), and Raymonda (*Raymonda* in 1929). Semenova's appearance as Odette-Odile marked the start of a new interpretation of this classical character. As interpreted by her, the frail swan-maiden acquired a dynamic and determined quality. Nikia's tragic Snake Dance as performed by Semenova in *La Bayadère* took on the quality of high drama. Stefan Zweig (1928), who saw her in action on the stage in those days, wrote, "When she steps onto the stage with her nature-given gait, which her training only polished, and suddenly soars up in a wild leap, the impression is that of a storm suddenly splitting the quiet of a humdrum existence."

In 1930 Semenova became *prima ballerina* of the Bolshoi Theater in Moscow. She continued to dance the roles that had brought her into prominence, adding a number of new ones, including Kitri *(Don Quixote),* Esmeralda, and Giselle. Semenova invested her Princess Aurora in *The Sleeping Beauty* with a sense of expectation that anticipated the solemn pas de deux in the third act of the ballet. The fact that Aurora, a passive character in the libretto, in Semenova's interpretation seemed to have become mistress of her own fate, thereby contradicting the submissiveness of a fairy-tale heroine, generated a great deal of controversy. But Semenova argued that Tchaikovsky's optimistic music gave her a right to this interpretation.

In *Giselle* Semenova took issue with her predecessors, insisting on a new ideal of the beautiful, one more in harmony with the spirit of the times. In her interpretation, the romantic and sad image of Giselle took on a more down-to-earth quality, an acquired will and determination. For Semenova's Giselle the moral purity of feelings was of paramount value, not submission to a predestined fate. Her Giselle perished, shocked out of life by human cruelty and duplicity. Thus, Giselle, having lived for her ideal of beauty, was able to defeat evil. Semenova presented her interpretation of Giselle to Paris audiences during her guest appearances in 1935 and was acclaimed as ranking next to Anna Pavlova and Olga Spessivtseva.

Semenova always sought to project a complete, integrated image. One example was her Raymonda, a role she danced for more than twenty years. Through all the five variations-monologues Semenova projected the same proud image, at once chaste and exalted. In *La Esmeralda* she romanticized Esmeralda, seeing her, above all, as a gifted dancer. This approach helped her to highlight the dominant theme of the ballet: the tragedy of a talent that was never realized.

During her first season in Moscow, Semenova danced Tao-Hoa in *The Red Poppy,* a ballet choreographed by Vasily Tikhomirov and Lev Lashchilin. In 1933 she appeared as Mireille de Poitiers in Vasily Vainonen's *The Flames of Paris.* Appearing as the Court Actress in the scene at Versailles, Semenova conveyed the refined beauty and splendor of rococo style, but as soon as the mythological ballet was over she transformed herself into a woman in love who lives through the tragedy of losing her loved one and who is now fully determined to fight. In the finale of the ballet Semenova displayed a fiery temperament and a sense of heroic drama when, dressed in a red tutu, javelin in hand, and helmeted as a Roman legionnaire, she impersonated Liberty in the climactic scene, Triumph of the Republic.

On another occasion Semenova displayed her gift of impersonation and her ability to live her roles when she created the role of Polina in *The Prisoner of the Caucasus* (1938), choreographed by Rostislav Zakharov. The Actress, whose prototype was the great Russian ballerina Avdotia Istomina, appeared as both a woman whose talent and future could be bought and sold as she changed hands, and a gifted dancer who projected an image of innocence and chastity. Semenova's interpretation of the Actress, who was forced to deceive and "act" in life and who was sincere and exalted only on the stage, was noted for an admirable sense of measure, taste, and style.

Semenova's Pannochka in the ballet *Taras Bulba,* choreographed by Zakharov in 1941, was a ravishing Polish beauty with graceful but imperious gestures and a proud, regal bearing. In the ballet *Mistress into Maid,* choreographed by Zakharov in 1946, Lisa, a nobleman's daughter, disguises herself as a peasant girl, Akulina. Semenova transformed herself, with a subtle sense of humor and grace, to convey the endearing simplicity and essential goodness of a Russian peasant girl. Semenova was again a comic actress as Mirandolina in the ballet of the same name, choreographed by Vainonen and Sergei Vasilenko in 1949. Following the canons of the dramatic ballet of Carlo Goldoni's day, she conducted dramatic dialogues, changing from dancing to mimed, histrionic recitative and back again, in a natural and organic manner.

The role of Cinderella in the ballet of the same name by Zakharov was one of Semenova's creations in the postwar period (1947). In the ball scenes her dancing struck just the right festive note on which the choreographer had built his concept, and matched the light intonations of Prokofiev's music, with its sad overtones. Semenova caused the sounds of music to come alive in her plastique. Significantly, Prokofiev said after watching Semenova as

SEMENOVA. As Princess Aurora, surrounded by the cavaliers who attend her in the Rose Adagio, from the 1927 production of *The Sleeping Beauty* at the State Academic Theater for Opera and Ballet in Leningrad. (Photograph from the Dance Collection, New York Public Library for the Performing Arts.)

Cinderella, "That is exactly how I heard my Cinderella" (quoted in Ivanova, 1965).

Semenova's last role was as Queen of the Ball in Zakharov's 1949 ballet *The Bronze Horseman.* It is fair to say that Semenova, who began her career as Odette-Odile and ended it as Queen of the Ball, was an unsurpassed performer of the Russian national repertory. Since her retirement in 1952 Semenova has been a leading teacher and *répétiteur* of the Bolshoi Ballet. She has groomed to stardom Marina Kondratieva, Nina Timofeyeva, Svetlana Adyrkhaeva, Nina Sorokina, Nadezhda Pavlova, and Nina Semizorova, to name but a few leading ballerinas. As a teacher Semenova seeks to instill in her pupils an unerring sense of natural plastique, which was her own hallmark. She gets her pupils to execute each combination of steps logically and with precision, in keeping with the canons of classical dance and the academic purity of its language. As *répétiteur* Semenova has helped many ballerinas to prepare their leading roles. Apart from her work at the Bolshoi Theater, Semenova holds a professorship at the Lunacharsky Theater Technicum, where she lectures on the training of classical dance teachers, thereby carrying on the tradition of her own teacher, Agrippina Vaganova.

Winner of the State Prize of the USSR in 1941, Semenova was awarded the title of People's Artist of the USSR in 1975 and Hero of Socialist Labor in 1988.

BIBLIOGRAPHY

Barnes, Clive. "Kirov Ballet Backdrop." *Dance Magazine* (September 1961): 40–47.

Ivanova, Svetlana. *Marina Semenova* (in Russian). Moscow, 1965.

Karp, P. M. *Marina Semenova.* Moscow, 1988.

Smakov, Gennady. *The Great Russian Dancers.* New York, 1984.
Swift, Mary Grace. *The Art of the Dance in the U.S.S.R.* Notre Dame, 1968.
Uralskaya, Valeria. "Magiya vdokhnovennogo tantsa." *Sovetskii balet,* no. 1 (1983).
Vaganova, Agrippina. *Stati, vospominaniia, dokumenty.* Leningrad and Moscow, 1958.
Volkov, Nikolai D. "Marina Semenova." In *The Soviet Ballet,* by Yuri Slonimsky et al. New York, 1947.
Willis, Margaret E. "Marina Semyonova: The Vaganova Link." *Dance Magazine* (February 1991): 58–61.
Zweig, Stefan. "A Journey into Russia." *Krasnaia gazeta* (26 November 1928).

VALERIA I. URALSKAYA
Translated from Russian

SEMYONOVA, MARINA. *See* Semenova, Marina.

SEN, SASWATI (born 25 August 1953 in Chittaranjan, West Bengal), Indian dancer, teacher, and choreographer. Sen began studying *kathak* dance at the age of seven under Reba Vudyarthi, a leading teacher of the Lucknow *gharānā* at the Kathak Kendra school in Delhi. She soon drew the attention of the school's masters with her natural talent for dance and was selected for intensive training by Birju Maharaj, with whom she is still associated as his assistant in teaching and choreography. She also earned a master's degree in anthropology from Delhi University.

Sen has devoted her career to *kathak,* giving solo performances and taking part in group choreographic works by Birju Maharaj at Kathak Kendra, a training center affiliated with the Central Sangeet Natak Akademi. She is both a senior teacher there and a lead dancer in the school's performing company.

Sen appeared in Satyajit Ray's film *Shataranj ke khilari,* dancing in a work choreographed by Birju Maharaj. She has received critical acclaim in lead roles in such dance dramas as *Krishnayana, Roopamati Baz Bahadur, Gīta Govinda,* and *Katha Raghunath Ki.* For the past twenty years she has partnered Birju Maharaj in many national and international dance festivals. She also gives solo performances and has done some independent choreography.

Sen's dancing is marked by an impeccable sense of *tāla* (rhythmic cycle) and *laya* (pulse). Her lines are clear and graceful and her stances arresting, reminiscent of the poses seen in Rajput and Mughal miniature paintings. Her facial expressions are gentle, sober, and delicate. Her dancing has a quicksilver quality polished over the years, representing the best of the Lucknow *gharānā* of Birju Maharaj.

Sen's younger sister Bhaswati Sen is also a gifted dancer and choreographer, and the sisters have appeared together in works choreographed by Bhaswati. They are noted for their excellent technique and the uniformity of their movements and expressions.

Sen lives in Delhi, where she is on the staff of Kathak Kendra. She has received the Sanskriti award from Sanskriti Pratishthan in New Delhi.

BIBLIOGRAPHY

Kothari, Sunil. *Kathak: Indian Classical Dance Art.* New Delhi, 1989.
Lequeux, Alain-Paul. "Cercle, et points de repère indiens." *Pour la Danse* (November 1981): 20–25.
Massey, Reginald. "Saswati Sen." *The Dancing Times* (October 1994): 57.

SUNIL KOTHARI

SENEGAL. *See* Sub-Saharan Africa, *overview article. See also* National Ballet of Senegal.

SERAPHIC DIALOGUE. Choreography: Martha Graham. Music: Norman Dello Joio. Scenery: Isamu Noguchi. Costumes: Martha Graham. Lighting: Jean Rosenthal. First performance: 8 May 1955, ANTA Theater, New York City, Martha Graham Dance Company. Principals: Linda Margolies (Joan), Patricia Birch (Joan as Maid), Mary Hinkson (Joan as Warrior), Matt Turney (Joan as Martyr), Bertram Ross (Saint Michael).

Seraphic Dialogue developed from a solo, *The Triumph of Saint Joan,* commissioned, along with Dello Joio's score, by the Louisville Arts Council. The solo was first performed by Graham with the Louisville Symphony Orchestra (5 December 1950), with a set by Frederick Kiesler. Graham included material from this dance in *Seraphic Dialogue.*

The central figure of Joan, at the moment of her transfiguration, recalls stages in her life. Each of her solos presages a dance by one of her three aspects, who sit, cloaked and waiting. Saint Michael is framed at the rear in a gold-wire structure, from which he descends, with his attendants, Saint Catherine and Saint Margaret, to bless, summon, and encourage. At the end, Joan takes her place beside him.

The "Warrior section" eventually became a duet, with Saint Michael endowing Joan as Warrior with a large golden-wire sword and the will to use it. During this tour, Helen McGehee assumed the role of the Warrior and played it for many years, while Mary Hinkson became associated with the role of the Maid.

BIBLIOGRAPHY

Reynolds, Nancy, and Susan Reimer-Torn. *Dance Classics.* Pennington, N.J., 1991.

FILM. Dave Wilson, *Seraphic Dialogue* (1969).

DEBORAH JOWITT

SERBIA. *See* Yugoslavia.

SEREGI, LÁSZLÓ (born 12 December 1929 in Budapest), Hungarian dancer, choreographer, and ballet director. Seregi graduated from the Budapest School of Applied Arts and studied folk dance with Iván Szabó in the Army Artistic Ensemble and classical ballet under Marcella Nádasi. He became a dancer of the Budapest Opera Ballet in 1957, ballet master in 1967, and choreographer in 1975; he was artistic director between 1977 and 1983.

Among his first works for the army ensemble was *Morning in the Camp,* to music by G. Barta (1953). After creating several minor ballet interludes for operas, he choreographed all the dance scenes in Joseph Kozma's opera *Electronic Love* (1953) and the jazzy dance of the film *Girl Danced into Life* in 1964. His two outstanding ballet scenes for opera—"Walpurgis Night" for *Faust* (1966) and "Venus's Grotto" for *Tannhäuser* (1967)—displayed great talent.

Seregi was then commissioned to produce a full-length ballet. He chose Aram Khachaturian's *Spartacus,* which was produced with tremendous success in 1968 on the stage of the Budapest Opera. Here he incorporated much of the art of ballet seen until then in Hungary, such as Gyula Harangozó's national style, the monumentality of Soviet drama ballet, and the expressive trends of Hungarian folk dance art, combining these with a high degree of musicality, set design, and dramaturgy and a feeling for modern dance. The first act, a drama of revolutionary heroism, is seen through the eyes of Spartacus; the second is shown from Crassus's perspective and has an epic narrative character; the third is Flavia's view of the events couched in a lyrical rendering. This was the first ballet by a Hungarian choreographer to depict a revolutionary hero. Among the many powerful scenes, the Bell Dance in Crassus's summer palace and Flavia's farewell duet with Spartacus are real gems of Hungarian choreographic art.

After this event, which may be considered a turning point in Hungarian ballet, Seregi took on one of his greatest ventures. He rechoreographed Béla Bartók's *The Miraculous Mandarin* and *The Wooden Prince* in 1970, the twenty-fifth anniversary of the composer's death. The wooden puppet, suggesting the alienation of the creator from his creation, was portrayed as a rival turning into an enemy, danced with less angularity and more flexibility than a human adversary. Employing a neoclassical style of dancing, Seregi emphasized what is universally valid in the story instead of the national character of this fairy tale. *The Miraculous Mandarin* also was stripped of its oriental color to stress general human qualities in settings suggesting the horizons of a metropolis rather than the walls of a low tavern, in an interplay of light and shade. The choreographic idiom was a combination of modern realistic and naturalistic elements, converging in a final pose reminiscent of Michelangelo's *Pietà.*

Seregi's next bold move was to turn Léo Delibes's *Sylvia* into a modern ballet comedy parodying the mannerisms of nineteenth-century dancers. It has two parallel plots, one occurring in real life and the other in rehearsal—a kind of play within a play bubbling with humor.

The Cedar Tree, to music by Frigyes Hidas (1975), is a series of scenes inspired by the great master of modern Hungarian painting, Tivadar Csontváry Kosztka, whose work is associated with the eastern Mediterranean in its themes and lively colors. Seregi reached beyond the painter's creativity and personal tragedy to depict in seven dance scenes the universal and perennial issue of the artist's fate. After a study tour in the United States in 1976, Seregi, inspired by Leonard Bernstein's music, created *Serenade,* five scenes of merry and sad encounters for five couples, ending in a grand dance together, the whole set in the neoclassical idiom. Another work inspired by Bernstein was *On the Town* (1977), three episodes in the style of a Broadway revue.

The year 1976 saw Seregi's *Chamber Music No. 1* (music by Paul Hindemith), a rivalry between two ballerinas without a plot but with deep emotional content choreographed for dancers of brilliant technique. His *Variations on a Nursery Song,* to music by Ernő Dohnányi (1978) depicts five older couples remembering their childhood and youth in playful scenes, even when reflecting life-and-death issues of the past. In 1981 Seregi rechoreographed *The Wooden Prince* in Budapest and *The Miraculous Mandarin* in New Mexico for his own ensemble. In the former he again stressed the folk and national character of the plot; his new *Mandarin* reassumed a certain oriental touch in an otherwise realistic metropolitan setting.

Seregi scored another success in the Madách Theater with his choreography for the musical *Cats;* its Budapest premiere in 1983 was the first production after New York and London. *The Wooden Prince* was filmed for television in 1969, as was *Sylvia,* under the title *From Rehearsal to Premiere,* in 1974. A film biography of Seregi, *The Dances Were Choreographed by László Seregi,* was produced in 1974. His Bartók ballets were presented in West Germany in 1972, 1973, and 1974; *Spartacus* in Berlin in 1973; and *Sylvia* in Vienna (1973) and Zurich (1975). Among Seregi's awards are the Decor Erkel Prize (1962), the Austrian Great Order of Merit (1976), and the Kossuth Prize (1980). In 1994 Seregi premiered his new Shakespearean ballet, *The Taming of the Shrew,* 11 and 12 June 1994, to music by Károly Goldmark.

BIBLIOGRAPHY

Kun, Zsuzsa. "Budapest and Pécs." *Hungarian Music News,* no. 6 (1976): 5–6.

Koegler, Horst. "The Hungarian State Ballet at the Budapest Opera House." *Dance and Dancers* (August 1973): 52–56.

Koegler, Horst. "The Hungarian State Ballet." *Dance and Dancers* (September 1975): 38–40.
Koegler, Horst. "Seregi, László." In *Balettlexikon*. Budapest, 1977.
Körtvélyes, Géza, and György Lőrinc. *The Budapest Ballet: The Ballet Ensemble of the Hungarian State Opera House*. 2 vols. Translated by Gedeon P. Dienes and Éva Rácz. Budapest, 1971–1981.
Körtvélyes, Géza. "Seregi-Evening." Program. Budapest, 1977.
Staud, Géza, ed. *A Budapesti Operaház 100 éve*. Budapest, 1984.

GÉZA KÖRTVÉLYES

SERENADE. Ballet in four movements. Choreography: George Balanchine. Music: Petr Ilich Tchaikovsky; Serenade in C, for string orchestra, op. 48 ("Serenade for Strings"). First performance: 10 June 1934, at Woodland, the estate of Felix Warburg, near White Plains, New York, by students of the School of American Ballet, wearing rehearsal costumes. Restaged by the Producing Company of the School of American Ballet, 8 December 1934, Avery Memorial Theater, Hartford, Connecticut, with students wearing costumes designed by William B. Okie, Jr. First professional performance: 2 March 1935, Adelphi Theater, New York, American Ballet. Scenery: Gaston Longchamp. Costumes: Jean Lurçat. Principals: Holly Howard, Kathryn Mullowny, Heidi Vosseler, Charles Laskey.

Serenade, the first work George Balanchine mounted on American dancers, was designed as a graduation exercise for the first students of the School of American Ballet. By creating challenging, expressive choreography for each of the ballet's members, Balanchine diminished the hierarchical importance of the soloist roles, thus fashioning his first plotless work for the corps de ballet. It is a work about breadth of movement and sustained phrasing with professionally trained dancers as protagonists.

The ballet's structure appears to be almost a stream of consciousness, with an unpredictable ebbing and flowing of movement ideas and phrases. Fortuitious accidents that occurred during the ballet's creation (e.g., a girl falling or arriving late) were incorporated in the action without apparent reason. Yet the choreography, like the music (which is built on a descending C-major scale), is constructed logically and simply by the accumulative impact of shifting pattern and design. The dramatic undercurrents of loss and yearning, plus the references to romantic images in such ballets as *Giselle* and *Swan Lake*, are not its subject matter but its atmosphere; the exploration of space by the community of dancers is the ballet's true theme.

In early productions of *Serenade* Balanchine used only the first three movements of Tchaikovsky's score: Sonatina, Waltz, and Elegy. At the first performance by the American Ballet in March 1935, the dancers of the Sonatina included Leda Anchutina, Holly Howard, Elise

SERENADE. Members of the female ensemble of the Dance Theatre of Harlem in a 1979 performance. (Photograph © 1979 by Jack Vartoogian; used by permission. Choreography by George Balanchine © The George Balanchine Trust.)

Reiman, and Elena de Rivas; the Waltz was led by Anchutina, Howard, Gisella Caccialanza (billed as Sylvia Giselle), Helen Leitch, and Annabelle Lyon; and the principal dancers of the Elegy were Howard, Kathryn Mullowny, Heidi Vosseler, and Charles Laskey. In 1940, for a production by the Ballet Russe de Monte Carlo featuring Marie-Jeanne, Balanchine reworked some of the solo parts and inserted an abbreviated form of the fourth movement of Tchaikovsky's Serenade, the Tema Russo, before the final Elegy. This new movement, called the Russian Dance, was performed by a ballerina and four demi-soloists. Balanchine lengthened it in the 1960s, restoring all the previous cuts, by employing a recapitulation of themes.

Since 1936, *Serenade* has been performed without scenery and has thus been dependent on costumes and lighting to establish its mysterious, romantic atmosphere. For the 1941 production by American Ballet Caravan, costumes were designed by Candido Portinari. For subsequent productions by New York City Ballet, lighting schemes were designed by Jean Rosenthal (1948) and Ronald Bates (1964). Certainly the most effective change of design, however, occurred in 1952, when the tunics worn by women in earlier productions were replaced by long, flowing dresses of pale blue tulle designed by Barbara Karinska.

Serenade is, by default, the signature work of New York City Ballet, and it has rarely been absent from the repertory. Since its premiere some sixty years ago it has been staged by companies large and small throughout the world. The opening tableau of seventeen women standing quietly, with feet precisely aligned, right arms outstretched, and palms turned upward, is an unforgettable image, and the moment when they suddenly and simultaneously open their feet into ballet's first position has caused countless audiences to catch a breath in anticipation of the dance to follow.

BIBLIOGRAPHY

Balanchine, George, with Francis Mason. *Balanchine's Complete Stories of the Great Ballets.* Rev. and enl. ed. Garden City, N.Y., 1977.

Choreography by George Balanchine: A Catalogue of Works. New York, 1984.

Croce, Arlene. "*Serenade:* In the Beginning." In *Allegro,* edited by Thomas W. Schoff. New York, 1993.

Daniels, Don. "Academy: The New World of *Serenade.*" *Ballet Review* 5.1 (1975–1976): 1–12.

Fleming, Bruce. "Balanchine's *Serenade* as a Modernist Work." In *Looking at Ballet: Ashton and Balanchine,* compiled by Jane B. Roberts and David Vaughan. Studies in Dance History, vol. 3.2. Pennington, N.J., 1993.

Hofmeister, Eleni Bookis. "Balanchine and Humphrey: Comparing *Serenade* and *Passacaglia.*" *Choreography and Dance* 3.3 (1993): 13–30.

Kaplan, Larry. "Corps Choreography by Balanchine." *Ballet Review* 15 (Winter 1988): 64–75.

Kirstein, Lincoln. *Thirty Years: The New York City Ballet.* New York, 1978.

Reynolds, Nancy. *Repertory in Review: Forty Years of the New York City Ballet.* New York, 1977.

Reynolds, Nancy. "Balanchine: An Introduction to the Ballets." *Dance Notation Journal* 6 (Winter–Spring 1988–1989): 15–74.

Siegel, Marcia B. *Two American Dance Classics.* Essays from the Faculty, Sarah Lawrence College, vol. 4.1. Bronxville, N.Y., 1978.

VIDEOTAPE. "Three by Balanchine," *Dance in America* (WNET-TV, New York, 1975), available in the Dance Collection, New York Public Library for the Performing Arts.

REBA ANN ADLER

SERGEYEV, KONSTANTIN (Konstantin Mikhailovich Sergeev; born 20 February [5 March] 1910 in Saint Petersburg, died 1 April 1992 in Saint Petersburg), Russian ballet dancer and choreographer. After starting his training in evening courses offered by the Leningrad ballet school, Sergeyev studied at the school itself under Vladimir Ponomarev, graduating in 1930. In 1928 and 1929 he was *premier danseur* in Iosif Kshessinsky's company, touring the Soviet Union. From 1930 to 1961 he was the leading male dancer of the Kirov Ballet, in both the classical and modern repertories, and from 1960 to 1970 he was the chief choreographer. From 1973 to 1982 he was the artistic director of the Leningrad Choreographic Institute.

An impeccable classical dancer, Sergeyev had a vivid lyrical individuality and poetic looks. He subordinated his brilliant virtuosic technique to the creation of character and mood. He was in his element in lyrical roles and unsurpassed in romantic ballets. A subtle interpreter of Tchaikovsky's lyrical music, he revealed the composer's heroes: *Swan Lake*'s Siegfried, veiled in a haze of elegiac sorrow; the refined Désiré, the prince who anxiously enters adulthood in *The Sleeping Beauty.* Creating the poetic portraits of Siegfried, Désiré, Albrecht in *Giselle,* Jean de Brienne in *Raymonda,* and the Poet in *Chopiniana,* he formed his own style and tradition, which were taken over by dancers of succeeding generations. He was also inimitably individual in roles outside the type he usually portrayed, such as Basil in Marius Petipa's *Don Quixote,* and the roles he created, such as Antoine Mistral in Vasily Vainonen's *The Flames of Paris* (1932), Frondoso in Vakhtang Chabukiani's *Laurencia* (1939), or Ostap in Rostislav Zakharov's *Taras Bulba* (1941). *Romeo and Juliet,* choreographed by Leonid Lavrovsky in 1940, was the peak of the legendary partnership of Sergeyev and Galina Ulanova. His Romeo was the personification of romantic love and youth. His Vatslav in Zakharov's *The Fountain of Bakhchisarai* (1934) was full of reverential and chivalrous love for Maria, danced by Ulanova. The complex character of Lucien in Zakharov's *Lost Illusions* (1935) was remarkable for its deep psychological content.

SERGEYEV. As Prince Désiré, with Natalia Dudinskaya as Aurora, in *The Sleeping Beauty* at the State Academic Theater for Opera and Ballet, Leningrad, 1932. (Photograph from the Dance Collection, New York Public Library for the Performing Arts.)

Sergeyev took part in almost all the Kirov's experimental productions from the 1930s through the 1950s; the lyrical dancer became an actor in the best tragic style. The postwar period witnessed not only the beginning of his work as a choreographer but also the creation of many new and complex characters, such as the mischievous and derisive Prince in his own version of *Cinderella* (1946), the nimble Good Lad in Fedor Lopukhov's *Spring Fairy Tale* (1947), the brave hunter Ali-Batyr in Leonid Yakobson's ballet of the same name (1950), the passionate Andrei in Boris Fenster's *Taras Bulba* (1955), the youth Lenny in his own *Path of Thunder* (1957), and Arbenin in Fenster's *Masquerade* (1960). Sergeyev's quest to master acting culminated in the role of Aleksandr Pushkin's Evgeny in Zakharov's *The Bronze Horseman* (1949). All these roles demanded a variety of psychological nuances and subtle internal and external transformations.

Sergeyev's work as a choreographer began in 1946 with *Cinderella*. The lucid and poetic fairy tale, cast within the traditions of the Russian school, announced a new trend in Soviet choreography. In *Cinderella* Sergeyev met Natalia Dudinskaya (who became his wife), and the new classical partnership united two dancers of different but complementary personalities and talents. The pinnacle of the partnership was *Path of Thunder*, based on the novel by Peter Abrahams. Its numerous dances portrayed contemporary Africa, real and poetic, passionate and mundane; classical dance was blended with South African folk art, and the protagonists spoke the poetic language of dance. In *The Distant Planet* (1963), to music by Boris Maizel, Sergeyev described, through the medium of virtuosic classical dance, the determination and courage of a man who ventured into outer space. *Hamlet* (1970), to music by Nikolai Chervinsky, was a notable event in Shakespearean ballet. *Levsha* (The Left-hander, 1976), to music by Boris Aleksandrov, was a narrative of the kindness, faithfulness, and talent of the Russian people. *The Legend of Joan of Arc* (1980), to music by Nikolai Peiko, was staged by Sergeyev at the Stanislavsky and Nemirovich-Danchenko Musical Theater.

Sergeyev contributed greatly to preserving classical masterpieces as both a dancer and a choreographer. His versions of *Raymonda* (1948), *Swan Lake* (1950), and *The Sleeping Beauty* (1952), on which he worked as artistic director and choreographer, are very close to the originals, a model of a careful and professional approach to the classics. They have remained in the repertory of the Kirov for more than forty years. In 1973 Sergeyev revived on the Leningrad stage another Petipa masterpiece, *Le Corsaire*. Concert activities also occupied an important place in his work as a dancer and choreographer.

After 1973 Sergeyev was artistic director of the Leningrad Choreographic Institute and continued to stage ballets for the Kirov. In 1990 he was invited to stage his version of *Swan Lake* for the Boston Ballet. Expressing the new mood of international cooperation, he had a Soviet dancer partner an American at each performance. Sergeyev was named People's Artist of the USSR in 1957 and was a four-time winner of the State Prize of the USSR.

BIBLIOGRAPHY

Bogdanov-Berezovskii, V. M. *K. M. Sergeev* (in Russian). Leningrad, 1951.

Iving, Victor. "Konstantin Sergeyev." In *The Soviet Ballet*, by Yuri Slonimsky et al. New York, 1947.

Joel, Lydia. "A Friendly Visit." *Dance Magazine* (November 1964): 18–21, 68–69.

Lvov-Anokhin, Boris. "Sergeyev in Giselle" (in Russian). *Neva*, no. 7 (1951).

Prokhorova, Valentina. *Konstantin Sergeev* (in Russian). Leningrad, 1974.

Roslavleva, Natalia. *Era of the Russian Ballet* (1966). New York, 1979.

Smakov, Gennady. *The Great Russian Dancers*. New York, 1984.

Swift, Mary Grace. *The Art of the Dance in the U.S.S.R.* Notre Dame, 1968.

VALENTINA V. PROKHOROVA
Translated from Russian

SERRANO, LUPE (Guadalupe Serrano; born 7 December 1930 in Santiago, Chile), American dancer and teacher. Of Mexican parentage, Serrano began dance lessons at the age of four in Chile. She moved to Mexico City at the age of twelve and took classes with Nelsi Dambre, making her stage debut in 1944 with the Mexico City Ballet. When that company was disbanded, she joined the newly formed Ballet Nelsi Dambre. In 1951, Serrano became a soloist with the Ballet Russe de Monte

Carlo, and in 1952 she joined the company of Igor Schwezoff, which toured South America as Ballet Concerts. After joining Ballet Theatre in 1953, she rose to ballerina rank. In 1958 and 1959 she also danced feature roles with the Metropolitan Opera Ballet, appearing in their first-ever ballet evening and in the operas *La Gioconda* and *Die Fledermaus*.

Serrano created roles with Ballet Theatre that included Elena in Eugene Loring's *Capital of the World* (1953), a role in Herbert Ross's *Paean* (1957), the Courtesan in Agnes de Mille's *Sebastian* (1957), and Ellida in Birgit Cullberg's *Lady from the Sea* (1960). A ballerina of considerable virtuosity and charm, Serrano formed rewarding partnerships with Erik Bruhn and, later, Royes Fernandez. She achieved particular success as the Saracen girl, Clorinda, in William Dollar's *The Duel*, where her taut, highly dramatic dancing made a vivid impression. Her wide repertory also included *Theme and Variations*, *Les Sylphides*, *Caprichos*, *Fall River Legend*, and *Las Hermanas*. She distinguished herself in *Giselle* and in David Blair's production of the full-length *Swan Lake*, but it is perhaps in her bravura performances of classical pas de deux such as those from *Don Quixote* and *Swan Lake*, act 3 (the "Black Swan"), that Serrano remains most memorable.

Following her retirement as a dancer in 1971, Serrano taught for three years at the National Academy of the Arts in Champaign, Illinois. In 1975 she headed the apprentice program of the School of the Pennsylvania Ballet in Philadelphia, and in 1981 she became the school's director. In 1988 Serrano moved to Washington, D.C., and joined the faculty of the Washington Ballet as artistic associate.

BIBLIOGRAPHY

Garcia-Barrio, Constance. "Lupe Serrano: She Shoots for Stars." *Dance Teacher Now* 5 (January–February 1983): 4–8.

Goodman, Saul. *Dancers You Should Know: Twenty Biographies*. New York, 1964.

ARCHIVE. Dance Collection, New York Public Library for the Performing Arts.

PATRICIA BARNES

SETTERFIELD, VALDA (born 17 September 1934 in Margate), English dancer, actress, and teacher. Setterfield began her studies in ballet with Marie Rambert and Audrey de Vos in London, performing as an apprentice with Ballet Rambert. She toured Italy in a revue in 1956 and immigrated to the United States in 1958. There she performed with James Waring (1958–1962), Katherine Litz (1959), Merce Cunningham (1960–1961 and 1965–1974), Yvonne Rainer (1971–1972), and Grand Union (1976). She is married to the choreographer David Gordon and has appeared in his work since he began choreographing.

Setterfield is known principally for her work in the Cunningham and Gordon companies. Some of her roles with Cunningham were in *Walkaround Time*, *Landrover*, *Signals*, and *Changing Steps*. She appeared in many of Gordon's Pick-Up Company works, including *The Matter*, *Chair*, *Not Necessarily Recognizable Objectives*, *Trying Times*, and *A Plain Romance Explained*, as well as in *The Photographer* (1983), a theater piece with music by Philip Glass for which Gordon did the choreography. She appeared in Bryan de Palma's film *The Wedding Party* (1966) and Rainer's *Lives of Performers* (1972) and *Kristina Talking Pictures* (1976). She has also taken roles in two films by Woody Allen, *Mighty Aphrodite* (1995) and *Everyone Says I Love You* (1996).

Setterfield has said that she thinks of herself as "a very, very finely honed tool who will render other people's work faithfully and without distortion, [a] vessel through

SETTERFIELD. David Gordon's multipart 1988 work *United States* included a lengthy solo for Valda Setterfield (seen here in a studio shot) in its New England section, set to a recorded reading by poet Robert Frost. (Photograph by Andrew Eccles; used by permission of David Gordon/Pick Up Co.)

which . . . material is transmitted to a group of other people, visually." An extraordinarily serene and meticulous dancer, she is a unique presence in the New York dance world and was one of the first recipients of a Bessie (New York Dance and Performance) award, in 1984. She is also noted for her ability as an actress and for her distinctive speaking voice, employed in the dialogues with Gordon in *Not Necessarily Recognizable Objectives* and the narration for his *Murder,* for American Ballet Theatre in 1986. The latter was included in Gordon's "Made in USA" in the public television series *Dance in America* for WNET in 1987, together with *Valda and Misha,* created for Setterfield and Mikhail Baryshnikov. In 1991 she appeared as Marcel Duchamp in Gordon's *The Mysteries and What's So Funny?,* and in 1992 she joined Baryshnikov's White Oak Dance Project, touring Europe and Japan in works by Gordon and Paul Taylor.

Setterfield has also acted in works by directors Robert Wilson, Richard Foreman, and JoAnne Akalaitis, and in Caryl Churchill's *The Skriker* at the Public Theater (1995). She has performed in several works by her son Ain Gordon, and won an Obie award for her role in Ain and David Gordon's *The Family Business,* which was produced at many venues in New York City and in Los Angeles (1994–1996).

BIBLIOGRAPHY

Newman, Barbara. "Speaking of Dance: Valda Setterfield" (parts 1–2). *The Dancing Times* (November–December 1985).

AMANDA SMITH

SEYMOUR. With Christopher Gable in Kenneth MacMillan's *The Invitation* (1960). The role of the Girl in this ballet offered Seymour opportunities to display the dramatic lyricism that propelled her to stardom. (Photograph from the Dance Collection, New York Public Library for the Performing Arts.)

SEYMOUR, LYNN (Berta Lynn Springbett; born 8 March 1939 in Wainwright, Alberta), Canadian dancer and choreographer. Seymour studied dancing in Vancouver and auditioned for the Sadler's Wells Ballet in 1953, when the company was touring Canada. Acceptance brought two years study at the Sadler's Wells Ballet School; in November 1956 she joined the Covent Garden Opera Ballet and then transferred to Sadler's Wells Theatre Ballet. Her gifts—a strong musicality and lyricism—were immediately recognized, and with Kenneth MacMillan's *The Burrow* (1958) there began a twenty-year association in which Seymour was the choreographer's muse.

Seymour danced her first *Swan Lake* in 1959, on tour with the company in Australia, and at Covent Garden. In 1960 came *Giselle,* and a role in which MacMillan clearly identified the melting beauty of the young dancer's style: The Fiancé in *Le Baiser de la Fée* for the Royal Ballet at Covent Garden. At this time Seymour was shuttling between both halves of the Royal Ballet, making her Opera House debut as Cinderella (by Frederick Ashton, in 1960), and dancing her first Aurora with the touring company. MacMillan's next role for her, the Girl in *The Invitation,* revealed her expressive intensity as a dance actress and also confirmed a partnership with Christopher Gable. Ashton made *The Two Pigeons* for them in 1961. There followed a period marred by injury: Seymour's sometimes uncertain health was a recurrent source of sadness throughout her career.

In 1962 she transferred to the Royal Ballet at Covent Garden and gained a large new repertory. In 1965 she was MacMillan's Juliet (the roles of the young lovers were created for Seymour and Gable, although assumed at the first performance by Fonteyn and Nureyev). When, in the following year, MacMillan accepted an invitation to direct the ballet at the Deutsche Oper, Berlin, Seymour went with him as ballerina. Major roles created for her there included the original, one-act *Anastasia,* and new productions by MacMillan of *Swan Lake* and *The Sleeping Beauty.* Her twin sons were born in Berlin in 1958. In the following year Seymour made guest appearances with the National Ballet of Canada (in Roland Petit's *Kraanerg*), with the London Festival Ballet, and with the Felix Blaska troupe in Paris.

Seymour rejoined the Royal Ballet in autumn 1970, made guest appearances with the Alvin Ailey American Dance Theater in New York in *Flowers* (inspired by Janis Joplin), and in July 1971 triumphed in the full-length *Anastasia,* which MacMillan staged at Covent Garden. Her third son was born in 1974, following her second marriage; her return to dancing in 1975, in *Anastasia,* revealed an artist in peak form. During the next two years her roles included an astonishing rendering of MacMillan's *Manon,* Ashton's *Four Brahms Waltzes in the Manner of Isadora Duncan* (1975–1976), and Natalia in Ashton's *A Month in the Country.* With American Ballet Theatre in 1976 she danced the leading roles in Antony Tudor's *Pillar of Fire* and *Romeo and Juliet,* as well as Odette-Odile in *Swan Lake.*

Seymour made her first choreography in collaboration with Robert North, *Gladly, Sadly, Badly, Madly,* for London Contemporary Dance Theatre. She also produced *Rashomon* for Sadler's Wells Theatre Ballet, and *Leda and the Swan* for BBC-TV. Roles in 1977 included Katherine in Cranko's *Shrew* and both Carabosse and Aurora in *The Sleeping Beauty.* She created two more ballets, *The Court of Love* (1977) and *Intimate Letters* (1978) for Sadler's Wells Royal Ballet, and she danced in Paris with Nureyev and in Chicago with Peter Schaufuss. Her last role for MacMillan was Baroness Mary Vetsera in *Mayerling,* with the Royal Ballet, February 1978. In that year Seymour was invited to Munich to direct the Bavarian State Opera Ballet, and she took up her duties as ballerina and director-choreographer in December 1978. Plagued by administrative problems and by injury, she resigned after a year, and her projected return to the Royal Ballet was delayed by continued ill health. In January 1981 Seymour announced her retirement, a process charted in a revealing television documentary, *When the Dancing Had to Stop,* directed for BBC-TV by Vanya Kewley (1981).

During the 1980s Seymour maintained a connection with ballet, teaching, making occasional guest appearances, and creating choreography, including *Basket* for Sadler's Wells Royal Ballet and *Wolfie* for Rambert Dance Company. In 1988 she joined London Festival Ballet and made a return to a major role by appearing as Tatyana in Cranko's *Onegin.* In the following year she repeated this interpretation and appeared in the company's newly acquired version of MacMillan's one-act *Anastasia*—and was once again a superior expressive artist in the title role.

The unconventional image sometimes projected of Lynn Seymour, and the publicity accorded her private life, never obscured the beauty of her dancing, nor its power to express emotion and drama. Her battle with her body—an instrument capable of the most exquisite and the most searing effects—was conducted in public; her unwillingness to compromise with her art, her exceptional intelligence, and her musicality, as well as her inability to give audiences anything less than the absolute best of which her body was capable, often pitched her performances on the edge of physical and emotional daring. There resulted unforgettable and often unrivaled interpretations of many roles.

BIBLIOGRAPHY

Austin, Richard. *Lynn Seymour.* London, 1980.
Crickmay, Anthony, and Clement Crisp. *Lynn Seymour.* London, 1980.
Seymour, Lynn. *Lynn.* London, 1984.
Vaughan, David. *Lynn Seymour.* Brooklyn, 1976.

VIDEOTAPE. Vanya Kewley, "When the Dancing Had to Stop" (BBC1, London, 1981).

CLEMENT CRISP

SHAKER DANCE. The American Shakers, one of the few Christian sects opposed to Christianity's generally negative attitude toward dance, elevated dance and song to the highest place in their ritual life. Because a relatively extensive amount of documentation of Shaker society exists, it is possible to reconstruct the development of Shaker dancing—its form, its function, and the beliefs associated with it. Studying the history of Shaker dance provides insight into how dance can become a symbol within a culture as well as a symbol of a culture to outsiders.

The Shakers, whose formal name was the United Society of Believers in Christ's Second Appearing, originated as an offshoot of Quakerism (the Society of Friends) in mid-eighteenth-century England. Ann Lee (1736–1784), later known as Mother Ann, emerged as the leader; she and eight of her followers transplanted Shakerism to America in 1774. They believed that the second coming of Christ had been ushered in through Mother Ann and that therefore the millennium had arrived, bringing a new world with new rules. Mother Ann condemned sexuality; thus celibacy, the social division of the sexes, and an ascetic way of life became basic religious principles of the Shakers, who also believed in the equality of the sexes. Their way of life mirrored their theology of a dual male-female godhead.

To separate themselves from the corrupting nature of the outside world, the Shakers formed their own self-sufficient villages. At their peak, they had nineteen communities in New England, New York, Ohio, and Kentucky, with a combined population of approximately six thousand; they had an estimated total of twenty-three thousand adherents (called Believers) over the duration of the sect's existence. Today only a few Shakers remain in two villages. Although renowned in the outside world for the integrity and ingenuity of their products, their household furnishings and agricultural implements, Shakers were probably best known for their dance.

Shaker dance began to develop in the earliest phase of the religion, when converts were often overcome by ecstatic fervor, accompanied by involuntary convulsive movement. Because of this behavior they were derisively called "shaking Quakers" by outsiders, but the name was soon appropriated by the Believers themselves.

Being led against one's will into bizarre tremblings, jumpings, and whirlings was interpreted by the Shakers as a sign of spiritual influence, but it was also considered to be a mortifying experience. Soon, however, they began to perform such shaking movements deliberately. Mother Ann's successor, Father James Whittaker, according to oral tradition, said that dancing was "the greatest gift of God that ever was made known to man for the perfection of the soul"; Calvin Green, an early elder, remarked that dancing helped people to "keep down the life of the flesh."

By 1787 the Shakers began to settle down to build their villages. Their ecstatic exercises also began to settle down: rather than continuing the individualistic, undisciplined movements characteristic of Shaker dancing until that time, Father Joseph Meacham, a new leader who was to organize the Shaker social and economic structure, actually choreographed a dance for their ritual. Called the Square Order Shuffle, or Holy Order, this dance was a prototype for many to follow. In it, the worshipers formed rows of men and women on separate sides of the room, either facing their leaders, the singers, or each other. The dance consisted of the ranks going back and forth, in a series of three steps back to the beginning place, turn, three steps backward, turn, three steps forward, and then three steps backward, punctuated with shuffling in place. This dance in particular was a popular subject for several nineteenth-century artists.

Around 1790 the society went through a period of strict discipline. The Turning Shuffle, a slow, mortifying dance, was introduced; this dance involved making a very slow shuffling turn, often with knees bent until the fingers touched the floor. Elder Green claimed that "I scarcely ever felt so distressing a cross as to attempt it." In 1796 dancing ceased, only to be reintroduced a year and a half

SHAKER DANCE. With hands extended to shake off the sins of the world, rows of men and women dance as part of a worship service. Note the starkness of the meeting room—unadorned windows, a few movable benches, and rows of pegs holding the cloaks and hats of the Believers. This early nineteenth-century print shows an outsider observing the ritual; her fashionable dress offers a contrast to the simple clothes of the Believers. (Photograph from the Dance Collection, New York Public Library for the Performing Arts.)

later as a means of invigorating the ritual. The Shakers also began to seek new explanations for their dancing. They invoked biblical justifications and advocated dancing as an expression of joy or as a sign of spiritual "gifts."

From about 1811 into the 1830s Shaker dance forms proliferated. Many of them were lively and had complicated floor plans, often resembling military drills. The worshipers also began to motion or pantomime song lyrics. The gestures, movements, and spatial patterns of the dances were often given explicit symbolic meanings. For example, the overall shaking of the body was reduced to a shaking of the hands, sometimes interpreted as "shaking off the sins of the world." Later, rather than shaking with the palms downward, the gesture became one of palms-up shaking inward, which was interpreted as a means of waving love toward oneself.

In 1837 a major revival of spiritual fervor began. During this "Era of Manifestations" (also known as "Mother Ann's Work") the Shakers received an outpouring of spiritual "gifts," many of which took the form of new and elaborate rituals involving dances and other forms of symbolic movements. These movements included the "whirling gift," a series of rapid revolutions in place, and walking the "Narrow Path."

Social and physical control were linked symbolically in the Shaker dance, with its neat rows and circles, narrow paths, measured steps, and moving and singing in unison; its physical separation of the sexes and of the leaders from the masses, as well as its spatial arrangement by age, mirrored the sect's social structure and worldview. By being in order in the dance, the worshipers not only symbolized the ideal of order, they helped to achieve it. Ecstatic outbursts too were given their place; this form of worship was called a "Shaker high," the "back manner," or "promiscuous" dancing. Shaker life was a balancing of control and religious ecstasy, and so was their dancing.

For most of the Shakers' history the Sunday worship service was open to the public, partially in the hope of attracting converts. These services became a tourist attraction in nineteenth-century America. Visitors' reactions varied over the years and in different villages, but most were extremely negative. The dancing was called a humiliating spectacle, a degradation, and shocking; it was even compared to behavior in an insane asylum. The characteristic shaking-hand gesture reminded some visitors of "rheumatic kangaroos," "penguins in procession," or "dogs splashing in water." Nonetheless, some felt "enchantment" and "celestial rapture" while watching the dancing and found the movements graceful and dignified. Few had a neutral opinion of the activity; dancing as worship was foreign to most spectators, and the Shaker combination of fervor and asceticism was a particular puzzle. Parodies of Shaker dance also began to appear on the popular stage.

By the second half of the nineteenth century, dancing began to be discontinued and the marches became very slow and orderly. Gradually, as the Shaker population aged (without sex or procreation, members joined only as converts), the marches too disappeared.

Today many people know about the Shaker dance through the imaginary version that Doris Humphrey choreographed as *The Shakers* in 1930, using nineteenth-century prints of Shaker dances as inspiration. Martha Graham's *Appalachian Spring* also reveals some indirect Shaker inspiration, in that composer Aaron Copland incorporated the melody from the Shaker song "Simple Gifts" into the score. Graham's dance story is not about the Shakers, but the piece capitalizes on the symbolism of Shaker music as a comment on the austerity and sexual ambivalence expressed in the frontier wedding that the dance depicts. Although Shaker dance was a shock to most outsiders in the past, in the mid-twentieth century the Shakers' practice of using dance as worship became a positive model for the return of dance to Christian churches through the liturgical dance movement.

[*See also* Christianity and Dance.]

BIBLIOGRAPHY

Andrews, Edward D. *The Gift to Be Simple: Songs, Dances, and Rituals of the American Shakers.* New York, 1940.

Andrews, Edward D. "The Dance in Shaker Ritual." In *Chronicles of the American Dance: From the Shakers to Martha Graham,* edited by Paul Magriel. New York, 1948.

Evanchuk, Robin. "Problems in Reconstructing a Shaker Religious Dance Ritual." *Journal of the Association of Graduate Dance Ethologists* 1 (Fall-Winter 1977–1978): 11–23.

Patterson, Daniel W. *The Shaker Spiritual.* Princeton, 1978.

Youngerman, Suzanne. "'Shaking Is No Foolish Play': An Anthropological Perspective on the American Shakers—Person, Time, Space, and Dance-Ritual." Ph.D. diss., Columbia University, 1983.

SUZANNE YOUNGERMAN

SHAKERS, THE. Full title: *The Shakers (Dance of the Chosen).* Choreography: Doris Humphrey. Music: Pauline Lawrence, improvisations on authentic hymn tunes. First performance: 12 November 1930, Hunter College, New York City. Principals: Doris Humphrey, Charles Weidman, and Concert Group.

The American sect of Shaker Christians, led by the visionary eldress Mother Ann Lee, established several communities in the nineteenth century. Their utopian regimen, based on a withdrawal from the secular life, strict segregation of the sexes, and a purging of sin through ecstatic dancing, singing, and prayer, provided Doris Humphrey with a dramatic framework for her developing ideas about the sources of dance movement. She said years later that the Shakers appealed to her because they believed dancing was "a joyful thing to be rendered to the Lord for their own salvation."

When she choreographed *The Shakers,* she had never seen a Shaker service, but from woodcuts and verbal descriptions she derived the basic earthward "shaking" motions and the uplifted, praising gestures that formed the two opposing physical states between which the tension of the dance was suspended. The dance is not a literal recreation of a Shaker service, but a theatrical glimpse of its progression, brilliantly rising through a series of climaxes to an exalted release.

The Shakers was perennially popular in the repertory of Humphrey-Weidman, and Doris Humphrey used it as a training piece in her repertory classes. Because of its documentary flavor and its theatrical accessibility, it is probably the most frequently performed of Humphrey's pieces today.

BIBLIOGRAPHY

Andrews, Edward D. *The Gift to Be Simple: Songs, Dances, and Rituals of the American Shakers.* New York, 1940.

Andrews, Edward D. *The People Called Shakers.* New York, 1953.

Humphrey, Doris. *Doris Humphrey, an Artist First: An Autobiography.* Edited by Selma Jeanne Cohen. Middletown, Conn., 1977.

Reynolds, Nancy, and Susan Reimer-Torn. *Dance Classics.* Pennington, N.J., 1991.

Siegel, Marcia B. *Days on Earth: The Dance of Doris Humphrey.* New Haven, 1987.

Youngerman, Suzanne. "The Translation of a Culture into Choreography: A Study of Doris Humphrey's 'The Shakers' Based on Laban-analysis." *CORD Dance Research Annual* 9 (1978): 93–110.

FILM. Thomas Bouchard, *The Shakers* (1940).

MARCIA B. SIEGEL

SHAKESPEARE AND DANCE. *See* Great Britain, *article on* Theatrical Dance, 1460–1660.

SHAMANISM. The term *shaman* is derived from the Tungusic *šaman,* which can be traced through the Prakrit *śamana,* a term for a Buddhist monk, to the Sanskrit *śramaṇa,* meaning "the one who practices asceticism." Shamaṇism predated the organized world religions and usually accompanied animism and animatism. The term was used by early Russian writers to denote a priest or priestess of northern Eurasian, especially the Altaic-speaking peoples of North and Central Asia.

The shaman's religious duties were to link this world to the unseen; to induce a state of trance or possession in which the soul would leave the body to travel in space, either in this world or another; to call on the appropriate spirits to manifest their intentions; and to counsel the people, make divinations and prophecies, perform miracles, cure diseases, reverse bad luck and prolong good, find missing objects, change the identity of things, placate dead souls, and control natural and unnatural phenomena. Nowadays the term *shamanism* is applied loosely to any mystic magico-religious cult that shares some of the original beliefs and practices of this prototype.

Shamans believe that each phenomenon of the universe is governed by a distinct force, which has both a benevolent and a malevolent element. These individual forces are controlled by the shaman through rituals so that the beneficial element is more frequently exercised for the benefit of humans.

A person becomes a shaman when called by the spirits, by inheritance, or through a voluntary quest. Most typically, the future shaman receives the calling from one or more spirits (who later become his guardian spirits) in a form of "shamanic illness," the symptoms of which resemble psychosis. In a hallucinatory state, the candidate begins to see the spirits, and the shamanic journey commences. The aspirant experiences a symbolic death as an ordinary person, retrogresses to the point of origin in utter chaos, and is then reborn through a religious initiation. During this time the future shaman gains the sacred knowledge of the universe—its origin, structure, and rules of operation. This initiation is followed by a long period of apprenticeship under master shamans.

Shamanic rituals are performed to create, temporarily, some sacred time and space within transitory time and space. The shaman, the ritual objects, and the clients and participants, after a period of purification by observing strict taboos, reverse the process of the birth of the universe to retrogress to the point of origin, the void. The core of the ritual is the trance—the possession—of the shaman, who uses his or her own body as a medium between the sacred and profane worlds. This state is induced through sensory stimuli (including the use of psychoactive substances)—by dancing, singing, chanting, drinking, eating, and smoking—aided by such magico-religious linking objects as bells, drums, fans, costumes, swords, mirrors, tree branches, spirit paintings, masks, or puppets. This aspect of the ritual is believed to be an important source for the development of artistic activities.

One of the most fundamental aspects of the ritual is the dancing of the shaman, who often spins to the left to enter the state of trance possession, to be transformed into a god. This may be said to imitate the motion of the birth of the universe from the void. Cosmic rules operate in this dance, the sacred knowledge having been acquired by the shaman during the long period of training. The purpose of the shaman's dance, then, is to journey to the sacred from the ordinary world by regressing to his or her primordial void. His or her void reflects the macrocosmic void, which is the origin of the universe and the deities. Thus, with this dance, the microcosmic entity becomes one with the macrocosmic whole to give birth to a god to be manifested.

[*See also* Russia, *article on* Siberian Dance Traditions.]

BIBLIOGRAPHY

Blacker, Carmen. *The Catalpa Bow: A Study of Shamanistic Practices in Japan.* London, 1975.

Eliade, Mircea. *Shamanism: Archaic Techniques of Ecstasy.* Translated by Willard R. Trask. New York, 1964.

Kim, Theresa Ki-ja. "The Relationship between Shamanic Ritual and the Korean Masked Dance-Drama: The Journey Motif to Chaos/Darkness/Void." Ph.D. diss., New York University, 1988.

Michael, Henry N., ed. *Studies in Siberian Shamanism.* Toronto, 1963.

THERESA KI-JA KIM

SHANGANA-TSONGA DANCE. A Bantu people numbering approximately three million, the Shangana-Tsonga live on both sides of the national boundary between Mozambique and South Africa. Dance is essential to their ritual and social life. As they mature, individuals learn the dances performed by their elders.

Much Tsonga dancing features exaggerated raising of the knees, relaxed up-and-down swinging of the arms, hand-clapping, rhythmic hip movements, mimicry of personalities during improvisation, the waving of hyena-tail whisks or knobkerries (from Hottentot, *kirri,* "a club"), and a basic pattern of fast footwork against slower trunk and head movements. Dancers stand in a line and, following cues from the lead drummer, move forward guided by the music's sectional structure.

The girls' *khomba* initiation rites feature *ku khana* ("joy dancing") to mark the novices' assembly, dispatch to the river where the ceremony takes place, and return home. Two special preritual dances are the *nanayila,* performed in a circle with wooden hatchets in hand and metal whistles held between the teeth, and the *managa,* a duet performed by dancers wearing grass skirts. At the river, participants perform nine secret mimes that simulate the pounding of maize (corn), the gathering of firewood, and other women's chores.

The boys' *xigubu* drumming school features *xifase* competitive dancing, performed by teams of youngsters on moonlit nights and involving a chain of partner changing. The boys' secret circumcision rites *(murhundzu)* feature the *hogo* marching dance, performed by several hundred novices on their way to the lodge in the bush. There, the *mayimayiwane* dance mimics the waddling chameleon, who changes color, much as the initiates change from red ochre body paint to white ochre as they go from boyhood to manhood. Many Tsonga dance terms have ideophonic names, such as *kanya-kanya* (used in the *mayimayiwane* dance) and *kotla-kotla,* which means "the leg rattles" that imitate the sounds.

At social beer-drinks for adults, men perform *xichaya-chaya* dancing, with humorous trotting steps. Women perform *xilala,* with their numerous copper leg bangles jingling on the downbeat. Both men and women dance the *muchongolo* (*ku chongolo* means "to stamp"), the Tsonga national dance, which features high jumps and baton-wielding. The most important Tsonga beer-drink dance is the men and women's *rhambela phikezano,* a competitive team dance, which is both uniformed and rehearsed by each chief to represent his court. Sent as display at rival courts, these dances bring prestige to a musical chief and enlarge his constituency by attracting new residents.

SHANGANA-TSONGA DANCE. This group is performing the *makwaya,* a singing and miming dance. As the dancers advance behind their leader, they perform the characteristic action of slapping their fists and stamping in quick rhythm. (Photograph by Merlyn Severn; reprinted by permission from Hugh Tracey, *African Dances of the Witwatersrand Gold Mines,* Johannesburg, 1952, p. 100.)

Power is also expressed through exorcism dances, where charismatic medicine men acquire wealth through healing and where women find solidarity through possession cults. Exorcism dancing features either *xidzimba* rhythms from the neighboring Shona or *mandhlozi* rhythms from the neighboring Zulu, depending on the shaman's diagnosis and prescription. Women are the main cultists; possession brings vacation from chores as well as gifts and attention from husbands who fear unplacated spirits.

Tsonga dance is multidimensional; it constitutes drama, social commentary, and ritual. It unites music, motion, and social action. In many ways, it symbolizes Tsonga values and worldview.

[*For related discussion, see* South Africa, *article on* Indigenous Dance; Southern Africa; *and* Sub-Saharan Africa.]

BIBLIOGRAPHY

Johnston, Thomas F. "Possession Music of the Shangana-Tsonga." *African Music* 5.2 (1972): 10–22.

Johnston, Thomas F. "The Cultural Role of Tsonga Beer-Drink Music." *Yearbook of the International Folk Music Council* 5 (1973).

Johnston, Thomas F. "The Social Determinants of Tsonga Musical Behavior." *International Review of the Aesthetics and Sociology of Music* 4.1 (1973).

Johnston, Thomas F. "Tsonga Musical Performance in Cultural Perspective." *Anthropos* 70 (1975).

Johnston, Thomas F. "Structure in Tsonga Music: An Analysis in Social Terms." *Journal of African Studies* 3 (Spring 1976).

Johnston, Thomas F. "The Secret Music of Nhanga Rites." *Anthropos* 77 (1982).

Johnston, Thomas F. "The Integrative Role of Dance in Shangana-Tsonga Social Institutions." In *Dance: Current Selected Research*, vol. 1, edited by Lynnette Y. Overby and James H. Humphrey. New York, 1989.

THOMAS F. JOHNSTON

SHANKAR, UDAY (born 8 December 1900 in Rajasthan, India; died 26 September 1977 in Calcutta). Indian dancer, choreographer, producer, and educator. Uday Shankar is the founder of India's modern dance, a creative genius who brought the first Indian dance company to the West. He was born in Udaipur, where his father, a Sanskrit scholar, had entered princely service, eventually becoming prime minister of Jhalawar State. Shankar's mother was the daughter of a Bengali landowner who had settled near Benaras. Shankar had six brothers, of whom four survived to adulthood, and the youngest is the sitarist Ravi Shankar.

At age twenty, Shankar was called by his father from his studies at the J. J. School of Arts in Bombay to go to London and help produce shows in aid of Indian soldiers wounded in World War I. There, Shankar enrolled at the Royal College of Arts to study painting. Though praised by its head, Sir William Rothenstein, young Shankar was wooed away by ballerina Anna Pavlova to compose two Indian dances for her *Oriental Impressions* (1923). *A Hindu Wedding* and *Krishna and Radha*, in which he danced with Pavlova, were based on paintings and sculptures that Shankar had seen in British museum collections. The success of these dances persuaded Pavlova to invite Shankar to join her company for an American tour sponsored by impresario Sol Hurok, during which Shankar learned about touring companies and Western stagecraft.

On their return to London, Shankar left Pavlova's company to follow her advice about founding an Indian ballet troupe, moving to Paris to further his career. Dancing with various European partners, to whom he taught his evolving style, he found a partner in Simkie (Simone Barbier) and a patron in Alice Boner, a Swiss sculptor. With Boner he sailed to India in January 1930 for a year of courting potential Indian patrons, viewing dances ranging from *kathakaḷi* to tribal, and discovering India's heritage in sculptures, frescoes, and religious sites. The *kathakaḷi* master Shankaran Namboodiri became his guru and, after several triumphant performances in Calcutta, the eminent musician Timir Baran agreed to become his new company's music director, along with Vishnudass Shirali, who was waiting for them in Paris. Lacking female dancers of proper status for the company, Shankar chose his cousin, Kanaklata, and his brothers; with his mother, they sailed for Paris. Their first performance was 3 March 1931 at the Théâtre des Champs-Élysées, and its success led to performances in Europe and Hurok-sponsored American tours for 1932/33, 1934, and 1937/38, as well as tours in Canada, Europe, East Asia, and the Middle East. The Uday Shankar Company of Hindu Dancers and Musicians gave about 890 shows in thirty countries in seven years.

In 1938, Shankar disbanded his company and created the Uday Shankar India Culture Centre at Almora, in the foothills of the Himalayas. He engaged four gurus, Shankaran Namboodiri for *kathakaḷi*, Amobi Singh for Manipuri, Kundappa Pillai for *bharata nāṭyam*, and Ustad Allauddin Khan for music. With lead dancer Zohra Mumtaz (later Segal), he created a five-year curriculum in dance, teaching the creative dance course himself; he brought in eminent artists and speakers and attracted students from India and other parts of the world. His India Culture Centre Company toured India every winter, presenting new choreography, including *Rhythm of Life*, *Labour and Machinery*, and a *Rāmāyaṇa* shadow play. The regular and the summer courses enrolled Indian and international students, some of whom became leaders in India's performing arts after World War II, including dancer and choreographer Narendra Sharma, dance troupe director Sachin Shankar, folk museum founder Devilal Samar (from Udaipur), and the founder of Delhi's Triveni

Kala Kendra. The India Culture Centre was an ideal combination of traditional Indian training and modern workshops, but it was closed in 1942, when its troupe, teachers, and students dispersed because of the war.

After marrying Amala Nandi, a leading dancer in his company, he moved to Madras to make his only film, *Kalpana,* at Gemini Studios; it had innovative sets, newly trained dancers and musicians, and his wife Amala as the female star. Completed in 1948, the film was shown in India and abroad—with high praise for the dance sections and mixed reviews for a purportedly autobiographical story of a young man's idealistic vision shattered by reality, counterpoised by two women contending for his attentions. In the 1950s he and Amala moved to Calcutta, where they raised two children: Ananda Shankar, now a composer and dance company director with his wife Tanusree; and Mamata Shankar, a dance director and film actress. After India's independence, Uday Shankar toured in China, Europe, and the United States with new companies. With his wife Amala he opened the Uday Shankar Culture Centre in Calcutta, and he created several new dances, including *The Life of the Buddha* and *Shankarscope,* a mixed-media production, combining dance and film.

SHANKAR. A studio portrait of Shankar, c.1929. (Photograph by Lipnitzki, Paris © Lipnitski-Viollet; used by permission; from the collection of Amala Shankar; courtesy of Joan Erdman.)

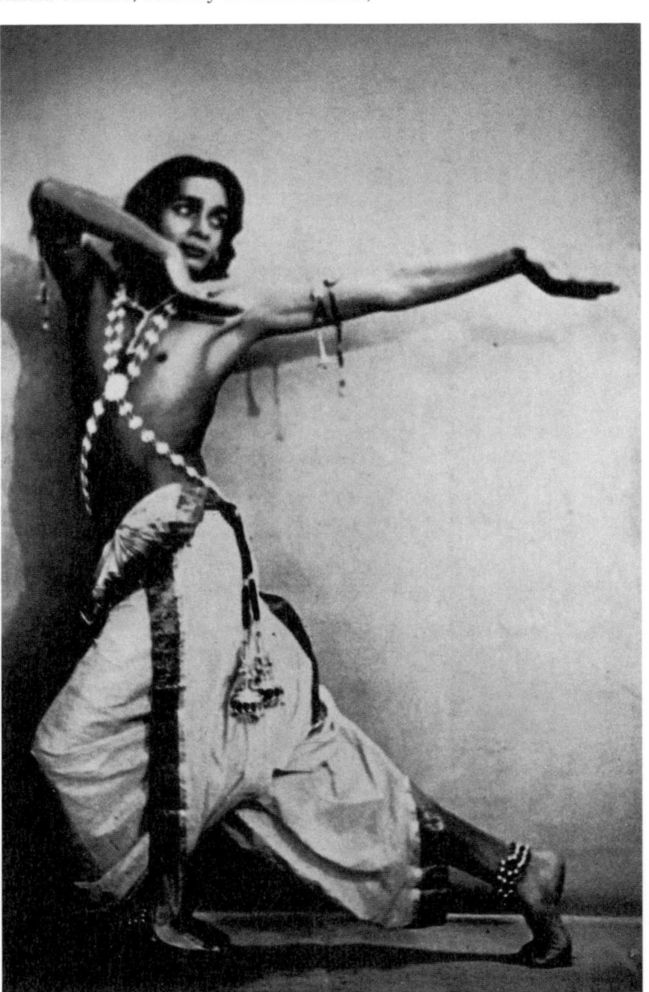

Shankar's contribution to Indian dance was a creative style with a new grammar that derived inspiration from classical forms as well as from folk dance. His fascination with the dramatic aspects of production was accompanied by a mastery of the mechanical in staging and timing. Shankar created magical spectacles of color, rhythm, and light, with themes that were initially mythological and folkloric but that were later political and social. His ability to produce dramatic staging and lighting, to construct costumes derived from authentic Indian arts, to rivet audiences on his magnificent appearance, and to capture the Indian spirit in innovative choreography make him not only a model for his times but an inspiration to generations in India today—many of whom are moving beyond the traditional to new dance and beyond classical solos to ensemble choreography.

BIBLIOGRAPHY

Bowers, Faubion. "India and Her Dance Art Today." *Dance Magazine* (November 1951): 19–25, 40–44.

Erdman, Joan L. "Performance as Translation: Uday Shankar in the West." *The Drama Review* 31/1 (Spring 1987): 64–88.

Khokar, Mohan, *His Dance, His Life. A Portrait of Uday Shankar.* New Delhi: Himalayan Books, 1983.

Kothari, Sunil, and Mohan Khokar, eds. *Uday Shankar.* New Delhi, 1983.

Segal, Zohra. "Shankar's Ballet." *Natya* 7 (December 1963): 22–24.

JOAN L. ERDMAN

SHARMA, UMA (born in Delhi, India), Indian dancer and choreographer. Uma Sharma was trained from childhood in *kathak* dance by Shambhu Maharaj and Sundarprasad. With natural talent and hard work, she soon received acclaim for her performances. She was born into a brahman family, a social division in which women usually do not become professional performers, but her parents encouraged both her and her sister to study dance and music. Uma Sharma is also a gifted vocalist; along with Urmila Nagar, she is the foremost female *kathak* performer who accompanies her dancing with singing.

Going beyond the solo *kathak* repertory, Sharma made an intensive study of the *rās līlā* dance drama of Braj and Mathura, exploring its *kathak* elements. She studied its technical aspects with the legendary Rasadhari Ladlisharanji and with Rasadhari Devaki Nandanji. In Delhi, she not only presented traditional *rās līlā* works but also choreographed her own dances based on the tradition.

Her choreography has also included works based on the lyrics of Suradas and of the *ashtachhap sakha* poets of the Vaiṣṇava Hindu sect, who worship Kṛṣṇa. She created the dance drama *Suradas* for the Shri Ram Bharatiya Kala Kendra company. She also choreographed *Indarsabha* and a contemporary dance drama, *Stree.*

It is as a solo dancer, however, that Sharma has established herself in the world of *kathak.* Her *abhinaya* (expressive dances) are appreciated by connoisseurs for their spontaneous, imaginative quality. To the dances known as *upaj ang* (improvisations to lyrics)—including texts from Urdu poetry—she brings skill with *sañchari bhāvas*, the symbolic associations which amplify the meaning of the lyrics and give them an extra dimension. Sharma sings the lyrics in a melodious voice while she enacts them expressively with consummate artistry; she is able to establish instant rapport with audiences. She has produced a thirteen-part television serial, *Naina,* using lyrics of Indian poets.

Sharma has been honored with the Padamshri award of the government of India, with an award from the Central Sangeet Natak Akademi, and with other awards from cultural organizations. She has participated in dance festivals both in India and abroad. She runs an academy in Delhi, the Uma Sharma School of Dance and Bharatiya Sangeet Sadan, where she trains young dancers.

SHARMA. An acclaimed dancer and singer in the solo *kathak* tradition, Sharma is pictured here in a dance drama with her partner Birju Maharaj. (Photograph from the Dance Collection, New York Public Library for the Performing Arts.)

BIBLIOGRAPHY

Kothari, Sunil. *Kathak: Indian Classical Dance Art.* New Delhi, 1989.
Najan, Nala. "The Little Clay Cart." *Arabesque* 16.6 (1991): 4–5.

SUNIL KOTHARI

SHARP, CECIL (Cecil James Sharp; born 22 November 1859 in London, died 23 June 1924 in London), musician and collector of English folk dances and songs. Sharp is renowned for beginning the revival of English folk dance and song. He was born in London; his father was a merchant, and his mother was deeply interested in music. Sharp was educated at Uppingham and at Clare College, Cambridge. He spent some years in Australia before returning to England, where he married a childhood friend, Constance Dorothea Birch. He taught music and became principal of the Hampstead Conservatoire of Music in London.

In 1899 Sharp saw his first Morris dance at Headington, Oxford, and in 1903 he heard his first folk song, "The Seeds of Love," sung by a gardener, John England, in Somerset. These events settled his future.

Sharp noted and studied Morris, sword, and country dances from many parts of England. His research into the history of the dance and its traditions made him a scholar; his musicianship and experience as a teacher enabled him to pass on the techniques of the dance to a demonstration team he collected from among friends who shared his enthusiasm. Among the many benefits of his work are the survival of the Morris and other dances that were disappearing in many parts of the country where they had once flourished. Generations of dancers derive both their knowledge and their practice from Sharp's pioneering work, which also stimulated the revival of John Playford's seventeenth-century publications on English folk music.

From 1914 to 1919 Sharp traveled in the United States with his colleague, Maud Karpeles (1885–1976). Their collection of songs from the Appalachian Mountains brought to light a wealth of songs and dances, some of which were still known in England. Others had been brought by early settlers from the British Isles and had been lost or forgotten in their places of origin.

At his death in 1924, Sharp left printed collections of songs and dances. The English Folk Dance and Song Society's London headquarters is named after him. Dancers and singers still make use of music he saved from oblivion.

Among Sharp's publications are *English Folk Song: Some Conclusions, Folk Singing in Schools,* and *Folk Dancing in Elementary and Secondary Schools,* all published in 1912, and *The Dance: An Historical Survey of Dancing in Europe* (with A. P. Oppé), published in 1924. He published many other books and articles on country dances, as well as collections of songs.

[*For related discussion see* Great Britain, *article on* English Traditional Dance.]

BIBLIOGRAPHY

Buckland, Theresa Jill. "Traditional Dance Scholarship in the United Kingdom." In *Dance: A Multicultural Perspective,* edited by Janet Adshead. Guildford, 1986.

Dommett, Roy. "How Did You Think It Was? The Political Background to the Folk Revival, 1903–1912." *Country Dance and Song,* no. 11–12 (1981): 47–52.

Karpeles, Maud. *Cecil Sharp: His Life and Work.* Chicago, 1967.

Keller, Kate Van Winkle, and Genevieve Shimer. *The Playford Ball: 103 Early Country Dances, 1651–1820, as Interpreted by Cecil Sharp and His Followers.* 2d ed. Northampton, Mass., 1994.

Palmer, Roy. "Some Sharp Words." *English Dance and Song* 55 (Summer 1993): 2–3.

Sharp, Cecil, and Herbert C. Macilwaine. *The Morris Book.* 5 vols. London, 1909–1913. 2d ed. London, 1912–1924.

Sharp, Cecil, et al. *The Country Dance Book.* 6 vols. London, 1909–1927.

Sharp, Cecil. *The Sword Dances of Northern England.* 3 vols. London, 1912–1913. 2d ed. London, 1951.

Shimer, Genevieve. "English Country Dances: Cecil Sharp (1859–1924): and John Playford (1623–c. 1687)." *Country Dance and Song,* no. 13 (November 1983): 24–30.

Szczelkun, Stefan A. *The Conspiracy of Good Taste: William Morris, Cecil Sharp, Clough Williams-Ellis, and the Repression of Working-Class Culture in the Twentieth Century.* London, 1993.

Townsend, A. D. "Cecil James Sharp as a Collector and Editor of Traditional Dance." *Traditional Dance* 5–6 (1988): 53–76.

URSULA VAUGHAN WILLIAMS

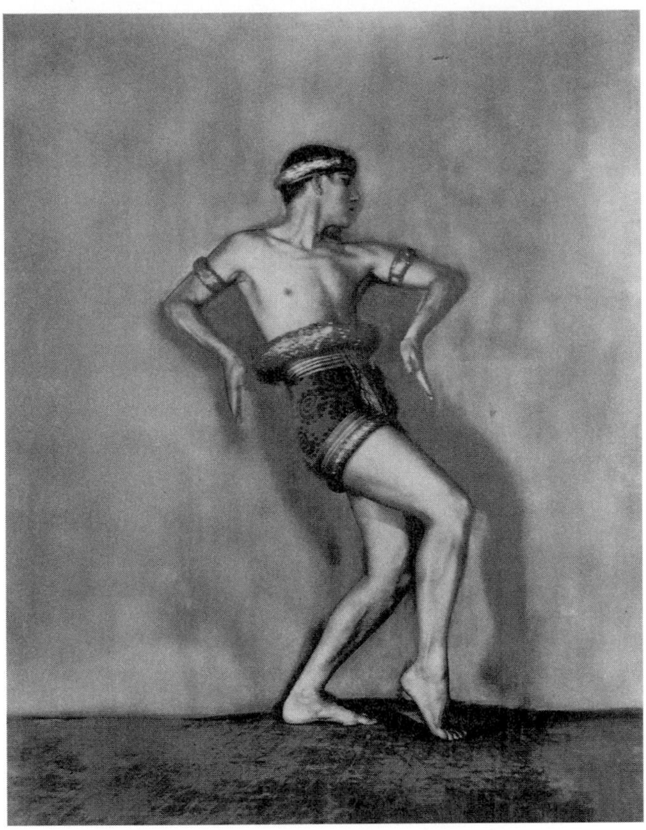

SHAWN. From the 1910s through the 1930s, Shawn created many solos for himself in different guises. This pose is from his *Gnossienne,* c.1919. (Photograph from the archives at Jacob's Pillow, Becket, Massachusetts.)

SHAWN, TED (Edwin Meyers Shawn; born 21 October 1891 in Kansas City, Missouri, died 9 January 1972 in Orlando, Florida), American vaudeville and concert dancer, choreographer, and teacher. Shawn can be described as the first American male in serious dance to acquire worldwide recognition; he danced in the United States, Canada, Cuba, Australia, Germany, England, Switzerland, and in many countries of Asia. Involved in dance entities called Ruth St. Denis, Ted Shawn and the Denishawn Dancers (1914–1931), Ted Shawn and His Men Dancers (1933–1940), and the Jacob's Pillow Dance Festival (1940–1972), he was a choreographer, teacher, lecturer, and impresario, as well as a dancer for almost sixty years. Also a prolific writer, Shawn championed his educational and artistic views with commitment. The critic John Martin best summed up his complex personality:

> Keen of wit, caustic of tongue, avid of interest, terrifically temperamental, of inexhaustible energy, tenacious, aggressive, indomitable, he was obviously of the stuff to break down barriers and become the first male dancer in America to achieve a position of influence and importance. (Martin, 1936)

Shawn recorded that he entered the University of Denver (Colorado) intending to become a minister but abandoned his studies after a serious illness left his legs temporarily paralyzed. His dance career began when he took his first ballet lessons to strengthen his weakened muscles. Then in 1911 he saw Ruth St. Denis in a vaudeville performance of *Egypta,* and his future was determined. He made his professional debut in 1913, demonstrating ballroom dances with his partner, Norma Gould.

After a move to Los Angeles, California, Shawn taught dancing, appeared in the dance movie *Dance of the Ages* for the Thomas A. Edison Company, and began to create his own dances in a free style. During a tour with Gould to New York in January 1914, he auditioned for St. Denis. Engaged as her partner, he joined her in a midwestern tour, during which they were married, on 13 August 1914; thereafter they toured with her company to the West Coast, and Shawn choreographed their first duet together in *Arabic Suite.*

In 1915 Shawn and St. Denis founded the first Denishawn school in Los Angeles, under the name of the Ruth

St. Denis School of the Dance and Its Related Arts. From 1915 to 1921 they maintained the school, choreographed their own dance programs, and toured American vaudeville and concert stages with their company. At times the indefatigable Shawn ran his own school, appeared in more movies, and, after he had served in the army, choreographed several vaudeville-circuit acts for Denishawn performers. The productions most notable of these were *Julnar of the Sea* (Pantages circuit, November 1919 to March 1921), *Xochitl,* with Martha Graham (Pantages, 1921), and *Les Mystères Dionysiaques* (Pantages, 1920). His own cross-country tour of 1921—Ted Shawn, assisted by Graham, Betty May, Dorothea Bowen, Charles Weidman, and Louis Horst as musical director—was the first Denishawn group in New York and thus initiated the international development of the Denishawn school and company. There followed, beginning in 1922, three concert tours of the United States with the Ruth St. Denis, Ted Shawn and the Denishawn Dancers and then, in 1925–1926, the fifteen-month tour that brought the first U.S. dance company to Asia.

Shawn wielded incalculable influences on the American modern dancers Graham, Weidman, and Doris Humphrey,

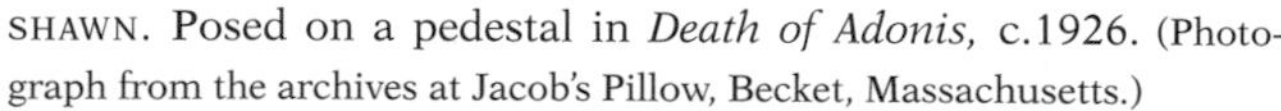
SHAWN. Posed on a pedestal in *Death of Adonis,* c.1926. (Photograph from the archives at Jacob's Pillow, Becket, Massachusetts.)

SHAWN. While on tour in Seville, Shawn acquired this bullfighter's costume from a *torero* superstitious about a tear in one pant leg. Shawn wore it in his *Cuadro Flamenco,* a humorous, Spanish-style piece created for the Denishawn ensemble. (Photograph c.1926 by White Studio, New York; from the archives at Jacob's Pillow, Becket, Massachusetts.)

who were his students at the Denishawn school and coperformers in his Denishawn company from 1916 to 1928. Because he did most of the teaching, choreographed most of the dances, scheduled the tours, and managed the myriad details demanded by the large organization Denishawn had become, Shawn's importance as a role model was profound. To the dance just being raised from the vaudeville to the concert stage and being upgraded from an entertainment to a serious art, Shawn, with St. Denis, provided a rare ambience of professionalism.

With the exceptions inevitable in reaction to such controversial dancing, contemporary reviewers praised Shawn for both his dancing and his choreography, which was based on Delsarte fundamentals and a firm belief in the eclecticism of the art of dance. During the existence of Denishawn, from 1914 to 1931, Shawn choreographed 185 dances and nine major ballets, co-created three other ballets with St. Denis, and performed in most of these works. His most famous solos during these years were a Grecian sculpture plastique entitled *The Death of Adonis,* the *Japanese Spear Dance*, the *Invocation to the Thunderbird, Flamenco Dances,* and *The Cosmic Dance of Siva*. The ballet *Xochitl* and his 1924 Hopi Indian dances titled *The Feather of the Dawn,* featuring Louise Brooks, reflected his lifelong interest in Native Americana.

Although annual tours brought large sums of money to Denishawn, St. Denis and Shawn were always plagued by a lack of funds. Their personal lifestyle was not extravagant; most of what they earned went into expensive new productions. They commissioned settings and music and insisted on individually designed and fitted costumes of the finest materials, often with intricate handwork and ethnic ornamentation. During their Asian tour, they purchased entire Japanese, Chinese, and Burmese ballets, complete with wigs, jewelry, costumes, props, and backdrops. They acquired similar necessities for their own Javanese and East Indian works. Much of their fame, indeed, rested on such theatrical color and perfection of detail. In those days, no government or corporation grants were available for dance. Everything, therefore, that Shawn as manager needed to support two consecutive companies and schools had to be earned by those companies and schools. In his obituary on the front page of the *New York Times,* he is quoted as having said, "I have been burdened all the time with the simple fight for survival."

Although Denishawn failed to survive the breakup of the Shawns' marriage and the breakup of the American economy in 1929, the Ted Shawn drive to dance soon found another vehicle for expression. In seven performing seasons, from 1933 to 1940, Shawn led, performed with, and choreographed for his second American dance group, Ted Shawn and His Men Dancers. Based at his home near Lee, Massachusetts—a retreat, school, and summer theater called Jacob's Pillow—the group was put together by Shawn with the express purpose of getting the male dancer accepted in American serious dance. Toward that end, he created fifty-seven ensemble or solo dances and six ballets for himself and this company. Shawn, Barton Mumaw, Frank Overlees, Wilbur McCormack, Dennis Landers, Fred Hearn, Foster Fitz-Simons, and Frank and John Delmar were major performers during the existence of the company.

Shawn also carried dancing for men into nearby Springfield College and Nashville's Peabody College in Tennessee. Tea-lecture-demonstrations, offered at Jacob's Pillow during summers of preparation for winter tours, developed into an annual migration of dance spectators there, a phenomenon that continues. The School of Dance for Men officially opened in the summer of 1936; by then the company had established itself and was appearing in Philadelphia's Robin Hood Dell, accompanied by the Philadelphia Orchestra.

Although the Men Dancers sometimes met opposition to male dancing, Shawn successfully presented a four-part program designed to be both artistic and aggressive. He carried over music visualizations developed by St. Denis and himself, his own solos, and some religious dances from Denishawn, but early in the company's history he began to stress "masculine" movement in program sections such as Play and Labor Dances, with music and accompaniment by Jess Meeker. That emphasis was developed the next season (1934/35) into a section called Primitive Rhythms, a display of strength that invariably moved audiences: *Ponca Indian Dance* (Shawn/Meeker), *Sinhalese Devil Dance* (Shawn/Vaughan), and *Maori War Haka* (Shawn/Meeker), *Hopi Indian Eagle Dance* (Shawn/Cadman) and *Dyak Spear Dance* (Shawn/Meeker).

SHAWN. In his dances, Shawn turned repeatedly to the use of Native American themes and imagery. He is pictured here, c.1930, in his solo *Invocation to the Thunderbird.* (Photograph by Robertson, Berlin; from the archives at Jacob's Pillow, Becket, Massachusetts.)

SHAWN. Ted Shawn's Men Dancers in his *Kinetic Molpai* (1935). Based on Delsartean principles of natural human movement, this was perhaps Shawn's most successful ensemble work. (Photograph from the Dance Collection, New York Public Library for the Performing Arts.)

A long work entitled *Labor Symphony* (Shawn/Meeker), first performed in 1934, was boldly pantomimic, as its subtitles suggest: "Labor of the Fields," "Labor of the Forests," "Labor of the Sea," and "Mechanized Labor." In spring 1935 the group went on tour to London, first at His Majesty's Theatre, then extended at the Apollo Theatre.

Later in 1935 Shawn choreographed what was perhaps his greatest and most characteristic work for the Men Dancers, *Kinetic Molpai,* with music again by Meeker. Shawn made dances solidly based on Delsartean principles of dance naturally growing out of the human body as it moved and naturally containing meaning as it unfolded. *Kinetic Molpai* summed up the possibilities of the moving human body, both alone and intermeshing in an ensemble group. Created in an abstract, impersonal style, this dance was divided into seven sections that flowed into each other: "Strife and Oppositions," "Solvent, Dynamic Contrasts," "Resilience and Successions," "Unfolding and Folding," "Dirge and Limbo," and "Surge and Apotheosis," with Shawn participating both as soloist and member of the ensemble. Its power has been verified by the reception of its reconstructions by Norman Walker at Jacob's Pillow in 1962 and by Alvin Ailey in 1972.

Evening-length works choreographed around a single theme followed. In 1937 there was *O, Libertad!,* a search for liberty through the depiction of American life and legend. The past was represented in *Noche Triste de Montezuma, Los Hermanos Penitentes, Peonage, Hacendado de California,* and *The Forty Niners.* The present was made up of two sections. The first, "Olympiad," contained *The Banner Bearer,* choreography by Mumaw; *The Cheer Leaders,* choreography by Landers; *Boxing,* choreography by McCormack; and *Basketball,* choreography by Landers. The second, "War," contained *Call to Arms, No Man's Land, Return of the Hero, The Jazz Decade, Modernism, Credo,* and *March of the Veterans of the Future Wars.* As the finale for this statement on America, Shawn inserted *Kinetic Molpai* as his best expression of the future.

Similarly, Shawn prepared two evening-length works for his final tours of the Men Dancers. The 1938 *Dance of the Ages* (choreography by Shawn, with accompaniment by Meeker) was a four-part symphonic work based on the elements of fire, water, earth, and air, leading to a finale on Shawn's fifth element, creativity. For the 1939/40 season Shawn compiled *The Dome,* with one part composed of music visualizations and another of well-loved dances from the group's past.

Shawn danced for the last time onstage in August 1964, in the Ted Shawn Theater at Jacob's Pillow, during the celebration of the fiftieth anniversary of his marriage to St. Denis. The famous pair briefly reunited to perform *Siddhas of the Upper Air,* a duo specially created for this occasion. Only six months before his death at the age of eighty, Shawn was still teaching classes at the Pillow.

Of the vast number of works Shawn created, few have been seen in recent years. *Japanese Spear Dance* and *Gnossienne* were revived by the Joyce Trisler Company in 1976; his *Five American Sketches: Danse Américaine, Around the Hall in Texas, Gringo Tango, Pasquinade,* and *Boston Fancy 1854* were reconstructed by Jane Sherman for the Vanaver Caravan in 1982; his *Polonaise* has been performed by Les Grands Ballets Canadiens; and various works have been included on programs by the Marion Rice Dancers. Mumaw has danced Shawn's *Gnossienne, Pierrot in the Dead City* (also revived for Richard Cragun in 1982), *Cutting the Sugar Cane, Mevlevi Dervish, The Di-*

vine Idiot, Four Dances Based on American Folk Music, and what Shawn called his favorite solo, *O Brother Sun and Sister Moon* (a study of Saint Francis of Assisi).

At the invitation of the Lyon (France) Biennale de Danse for its September 1990 festival of "An American Story," Sherman reconstructed a Denishawn program of St. Denis, Shawn, and Humphrey dances. Those by Shawn were *Floor Plastique* (group), *Choeur Dansé* (trio for women), *Serenata Morisca* (solo for Graham), *Tillers of the Soil* (group, co-created with St. Denis), and *Danse Américaine* (solo for Weidman), *Around the Hall in Texas* (duet), *Gringo Tango* (duet), and *Boston Fancy 1854* (group) from *Five American Sketches.* These works remain in the repertory of the Denishawn Repertory Dancers of the Center Dance Collective and the Vanaver Caravan, who appeared at the National Museum of Dance, Saratoga, New York, on 14 July 1991 and at Jacob's Pillow 28–29 August 1991 at the centennial celebration of Shawn's birth.

Charged with messages, and offering a deliberately eclectic style that borrowed from every Western and ethnic movement encountered in the course of endless travels, Shawn's idiosyncratic choreography remains controversial, but its liberating effect on dance as a male activity does not. Writing in the *New York Times* after Shawn's death in 1972, critic Clive Barnes supplied the most appropriate epitaph for Shawn's work: "There is not a modern dancer in the world today who cannot trace his pedagogical heritage to Shawn."

[*See also* Denishawn *and the entry on St. Denis.*]

BIBLIOGRAPHY

Brady, Susan, ed. *After the Dance: Documents of Ruth St. Denis and Ted Shawn.* Performing Arts Resources, vol. 20. New York, 1997.

Jowitt, Deborah. "Jacob's Pillow '66: Microcosm of Dance." *Dance Scope* (Fall 1966): 19–24.

Martin, John. *America Dancing.* New York, 1936.

Phillips, McCandlish. Obituary. *New York Times* (10 January 1972).

Schlundt, Christena L. *A Chronology of the Professional Appearances of the American Dancers Ruth St. Denis and Ted Shawn, 1906–1932.* New York, 1962.

Schlundt, Christena L. *The Professional Appearances of Ted Shawn and His Men Dancers: A Chronology and an Index of Dances, 1933–1940.* New York, 1967.

Schlundt, Christena L. "Ted Shawn's *Kinetic Molpai* (1935)." In *Pipers Enzyklopädie des Musiktheaters,* vol. 5. Munich, 1986.

Shawn, Ted. "Fundamentalism in the Dance." *Denishawn Magazine* 1 (Spring 1925): 12–16.

Shawn, Ted. *The American Ballet.* New York, 1926.

Shawn, Ted. *Gods Who Dance.* New York, 1929.

Shawn, Ted. *Fundamentals of a Dance Education.* Girard, Kansas, 1937.

Shawn, Ted. *Every Little Movement: A Book about François Delsarte.* Pittsfield, Mass., 1954.

Shawn, Ted, with Gray Poole. *One Thousand and One Night Stands.* Garden City, N.Y., 1960.

Sherman, Jane. *The Drama of Denishawn Dance.* Middletown, Conn., 1979.

Sherman, Jane. *Denishawn: The Enduring Influence.* Boston, 1983.

Sherman, Jane, and Barton Mumaw. *Barton Mumaw, Dancer: From Denishawn to Jacob's Pillow and Beyond.* New York, 1986.

Terry, Walter. *Ted Shawn: Father of American Dance.* New York, 1976.

FILM. *The Men Who Danced: Ted Shawn and His Dancers* (1985).

ARCHIVE. Denishawn Collection and Ted Shawn Collection, New York Public Library for the Performing Arts. Ruth St. Denis Collection, Special Collections, Library, University of California, Los Angeles, Calif.

CHRISTENA L. SCHLUNDT

SHCHEDRIN, RODION (Rodion Konstantinovich Shchedrin; born 16 December 1932), composer and pianist. Shchedrin graduated in 1955 from the Moscow Conservatory, where he had studied composition with Yuri Shaporin and piano with Yakov Flier. As a composer Shchedrin has achieved fame for his idiosyncratic musical style, well-chosen themes, and broad range of musical forms. He composed the scores for five ballets, all of which have been performed in Russia and other countries, including Bulgaria, Germany, Cuba, Poland, Czechoslovakia, Yugoslavia, Brazil, Italy, Peru, and Finland. The ballets had a considerable impact on the worlds of theater and music, and with his deep understanding of the art Shchedrin helped to develop modern ballet. Many of his creations were prompted and inspired by his wife, Maya Plisetskaya, an outstanding ballerina who for many years was not only his leading dancer but also his choreographer. Shchedrin's ballets, a fusion of compelling music and serious drama, are very theatrical and danceable.

The folk comedy and fantasy *The Little Humpbacked Horse* received its first performance in 1960 at the Bolshoi Theater, in a rechoreographed version by Aleksandr Radunsky after Arthur Saint-Léon's nineteenth-century original. Shchedrin's ability to convey comedy and satire through music is one of his strengths. The score for *Carmen Suite,* premiered in 1967 at the Bolshoi with choreography by Alberto Alonso, is largely based on Georges Bizet's opera *Carmen.* Shchedrin followed Bizet's musical ideas in character portrayal but brought out the choreographic side of the opera, reworking the music to heighten the dramatic conflict of the original. Shchedrin radically rearranged Bizet's music, often changing the ideas, tone, rhythm, tempo, and register, and replacing the full symphony orchestra with a string orchestra and an enlarged percussion section.

In 1972 at the Bolshoi *Anna Karenina* was first presented, with choreography by Plisetskaya, Natalia Ryzhenko, and Vladimir Smirnov-Golovanov. Shchedrin called the ballet "lyric scenes," thus concentrating on only one facet of the original, the heroine's personal conflict. The story is unified less by character portraits or changes of mood as by symphonic continuity. The conflict is resolved through the heroine's efforts to overcome her inner torment in the face of turbulent external events. Thematic and formal elements from instrumental works by Tchaikovsky, composed in the period described by the novel, are organically woven into the modern texture of the score. But Shchedrin treats even Tchaikovsky's music in his own way, giving it a contemporaneity in keeping with the fast tempo of modern life. *The Seagull,* choreographed by Plisetskaya in 1980 for the Bolshoi, captures the mood of Anton Chekhov's play with subtle shades of emotion and an uneasy anticipation of the tragic finale. Although it has great freedom, the score is a strictly disciplined symphonic series of twenty-four preludes, three interludes, and a postlude. The music presents the lives of the protagonists polyphonically, without sharp contrasts or clashes because there is no spiritual contact among the characters, and therein lies the drama. The score of another tale from Chekhov, *The Lady with a Lapdog,* was choreographed by Plisetskaya in 1985 for the Bolshoi. It is piercingly lyrical, full of gentle sadness; there are none of the explosions and contrasts typical of Shchedrin's works. The ballet's music is heartfelt and penetrating, its beauty delicate and fragile. The chamberlike intimacy of Chekhov's tone is stressed by the composer's choice of instrumentation—besides the strings it includes only two oboes (one of them further changed to *cor anglais*), two French horns, and a celesta.

Shchedrin was named People's Artist of the USSR in 1981, and won the USSR State Prize in 1972 and the Lenin Prize in 1984.

[*See also* Little Humpbacked Horse, The.]

BIBLIOGRAPHY

Gaylin, Jed. "Late Soviet Composition." Master's thesis, Peabody Conservatory of Music, 1995.

Likhacheva, Irina. *Muzykalnyi teatr Rodiona Shchedrina.* Moscow, 1977.

Paisov, Yuri. *Khor v tvorchestve Rodiona Shchedrina.* Moscow, 1992.

Rodion Shchedrin: A Complete Catalog. Milan, 1992.

Tarakanov, Mikhail. *Tvorchestvo Rodion Shchedrina.* Moscow, 1980.

ELENA N. KURILENKO
Translated from Russian

SHEARER, MOIRA (Moira Shearer King; born 17 January 1926 in Dunfermline, Scotland), dancer. A ballerina of fragile beauty and crystalline style, Shearer began her training in Rhodesia at the age of six with Ethel Lacey, a pupil of Enrico Cecchetti, and continued it in London from the age of ten; her teachers there were Flora Fairbairn and Nikolai Legat and his wife, Nadine Nicolaeva. Shearer studied briefly at the Sadler's Wells Ballet School in 1940 and then joined Mona Inglesby's newly formed International Ballet in 1941. There she danced featured parts in *Aurora's Wedding* and *Le Carnaval* before entering the corps of the Sadler's Wells Ballet in 1942. Her light, strong technique and engaging manner carried her straight into solo roles, such as the pas de deux in *Les Patineurs,* the Polka in *Façade,* and the Waltz in *Les Sylphides,* as well as several small created parts: the flirtatious pas de trois in Ninette de Valois's *Promenade* (1943) and, more important, Pride in Frederick Ashton's *The Quest* (1943), which provided her first critical success.

Never again anonymous, although still in the corps of *Apparitions, Les Rendezvous,* and *Hamlet,* among others, Shearer enlarged her repertory steadily and with growing assurance. She danced the Young Girl in *Le Spectre de la Rose* and Chiarina in *Le Carnaval* with delicate charm and created a touchingly innocent Lover in Robert Helpmann's *Miracle in the Gorbals* (1944). In 1946 she confirmed her new title of ballerina with debuts in *The Sleeping Beauty, Coppélia,* and *Swan Lake* that displayed technical brilliance and emotional subtlety. The same year she shared the creation of *Symphonic Variations* with the company's purest classicists; for the women of the original cast, Ashton chose Margot Fonteyn, the striking, red-haired Shearer, and the fair Pamela May, a trio of ballerinas of exceptional beauty and harmonious musicality.

Shearer left the Sadler's Wells Ballet for six months to take the leading role in *The Red Shoes,* perhaps the most popular dance film ever made and an introduction for

MOIRA SHEARER. A studio portrait in costume for *Giselle,* c.1948. (Photograph © by Maurice Seymour; used by permission.)

thousands to classical ballet. [*See* Red Shoes, The.] When she returned to her great classical roles, Léonide Massine selected her for the original Sadler's Wells casts of *La Boutique Fantasque,* in which she played the Can-Can Dancer opposite the choreographer, and *Mam'zelle Angot,* both of which he staged in 1947. The following year Shearer made a distinctive debut in *Giselle,* inspired and guided by Tamara Karsavina's coaching, and created the title role in Ashton's *Cinderella,* replacing the injured Fonteyn. She would also succeed Fonteyn in the challenging intricacies of *Scènes de Ballet* and *Ballet Imperial* and as the forlorn Julia in *A Wedding Bouquet.*

In 1952, having danced Roland Petit's *Carmen* in Paris and completed two more films, *The Tales of Hoffmann* and *The Story of Three Loves* (both choreographed by Ashton), Shearer became a guest artist with the Sadler's Wells Ballet for a single season. Then, only ten years after joining the company, she left it to pursue an acting career. In 1954 she danced her last performance, in *Le Spectre de la Rose* with London's Festival Ballet. More than thirty years later, in 1987, Shearer returned to dancing briefly in the television production of *A Simple Man,* choreographed by Gillian Lynne for Northern Ballet Theatre.

BIBLIOGRAPHY

Gruen, John. *People Who Dance: Twenty-two Dancers Tell Their Own Stories.* Princeton, N.J., 1988.

Newman, Barbara. *Striking a Balance: Dancers Talk about Dancing.* Rev. ed. New York, 1992.

Nugent, Ann. "Moira Shearer." *Dance Gazette* (July 1985): 36–38.

Shearer, Moira. *Balletmaster: A Dancer's View of George Balanchine.* London, 1986.

BARBARA NEWMAN

SYBIL SHEARER. A studio portrait taken during the 1940s. Shearer was one of the few modern dancers of her era who was able to hold an audience spellbound throughout a program composed entirely of solos. (Photograph by Earle Forbes; from the Dance Collection, New York Public Library for the Performing Arts.)

SHEARER, SYBIL (born c.1918 in Toronto), dancer and choreographer. Shearer does not consider herself a modern dancer, but instead a participant in the wide field of "all dance." She has adapted ballet's standard vocabulary, including pointe work, merged it with mainstream modern dance movements, and added a wide range of her own movement inventions. Her technical range and strength create an effect of great space and epic ideas.

Shearer's subjects come from her own experience. Many of her dances express her affinity for nature and her sensitivity to human emotions. Dance critic John Martin wrote, "She has an uncanny penetration into things that lie below the surface of experience. She has danced into existence a world of her own." Her serious point of view mingles with a sense of comedy.

Shearer began taking dance lessons as a child. After graduating from Skidmore College, she enrolled in the summer dance course at Bennington College, where she studied primarily with Doris Humphrey and Charles Weidman and later joined their company as a soloist. In 1941 she was an assistant to Agnes de Mille, and then she became a solo artist, gaining immediate recognition. In 1942 Martin wrote in the *New York Times* that she had made the most promising debut of the year.

In 1943 Shearer left New York and chose to settle near Chicago because she considered the Midwest "a place to expand." She concentrated on choreographing and dancing solo concerts. Although she confined most of her activities to suburban Chicago, the world of the arts recognized her importance. Audiences arrived from everywhere whenever she announced a program.

In the late 1950s Shearer began to work with a group, showing a talent for designing group movement. She created several evening-long group works, mainly suites of dances.

Shearer's longtime interest in cinematic dance culminated in 1976 in a collaboration with filmmaker Helen Morrison on the creation of *A Sheaf of Dreams,* a one-hour film with a background of Brahms music. For this, Shearer choreographed and danced a number of episodes, personal dreams woven into a flow of the seasons. In the 1980s Shearer worked on a project involving the creating of a group dance for cinema, designing it through the lens of the camera. She created one piece in this manner, then turned to other interests.

In 1986 Shearer gave up public appearances, although she still danced and created works privately. She launched a career as dance critic, writing iconoclastic essays for *Ballet Review.*

Shearer's solo concerts, created in the late 1940s and in the 1950s and performed throughout the United States, include *Let the Heavens Open That the Earth May Shine; In a Vacuum; O, Lost, and Prophecy; In the Cool of the Garden; In Thee Is Joy; Arise and Dance; As the Twig Is Bent;* and *Shades before Mars.* She also performed suites of solos, one identified only by number, and *Once upon a Time,* a suite of dances identified by whimsically named females.

Shearer's full-evening works with a group were *Within This Thicket,* set to music by Béla Bartók (1959), *Fables and Proverbs* (1961), *The Reflection in the Puddle Is Mine* (1963), *In Place of Opinions* (1964), *The Return of the Herd* (1965), and *Spells and Rituals* (1971).

In 1990 Shearer founded the Morrison-Shearer Charitable Foundation. It awards grants to arts activities and maintains the Morrison-Shearer Museum and Archives in Northbrook, Illinois, which houses Helen Morrison's photographs and films, in addition to the records of Shearer's dance career and writings. The Morrison films are of Shearer dancing from the 1950s through the 1970s.

BIBLIOGRAPHY

de Mille, Agnes. *Dance to the Piper.* Boston, 1952.

Denby, Edwin. *Looking at the Dance* (1949). New York, 1968.

Martin, John. *Book of the Dance.* New York, 1963.

Martin, John. *Sybil Shearer.* Palatine, Ill., 1965.

Shearer, Sybil, et al. "A Sybil Shearer Sampler." *Ballet Review* 12 (Fall 1984): 22–40.

Sorell, Walter. *Dance in Its Time.* Garden City, N.Y., 1981.

Terry, Walter. *I Was There: Selected Dance Reviews and Articles, 1936–1976.* Edited by Andrew Mark Wentink. New York, 1978.

Turner, Margery J. *New Dance: Approaches to Nonliteral Choreography.* Pittsburgh, 1971.

Vaughan, David. "Sybil Shearer." *Dance and Dancers* (July 1966).

ANN BARZEL

SHIGEYAMA FAMILY, one of Japan's extant branches of the Ōkura school of *kyōgen.* The Shigeyamas, one of the most popular and innovative troupes of *kyōgen* actors, today dominate traditional and experimental *kyōgen* in the Kamigata region of Japan, which includes the cities of Kyoto, Nara, Osaka, and Kobe. In the twentieth century the family has produced two renowned performers, the brothers Shigeyama Sennojō II and Shigeyama Sensaku IV.

History. In 1830 the Ōkura school headmaster designated the Shigeyama Sengorō family to carry on the Kyoto court and temple *kyōgen* traditions. Although they were vassals of Naosuke Ii of Hikone, the Shigeyamas continued to train amateurs and to perform at temple and shrine festivals.

Along with the Nomura family, the Shigeyamas were instrumental in gaining recognition for *kyōgen* as a potent art form independent of its cousin, *nō,* provoking a post–World War II boom that is still cresting. Shigeyama Sensaku II (1864–1950) believed in offering *kyōgen* plays as dedicatory services at Shintō temples and shrines, producing the Hundred Shrine and Temple Dedicatory Pilgrimage in the Kyoto region from 1937 to 1948. Shigeyama Sensaku III (1896–1986) was a great popularizer of postwar *kyōgen* in Kyoto. His carefree, elegant style won him many admirers in his later years. He was designated a National Living Treasure by the Japanese government in 1976 and was elected to membership in the Japan Arts Academy in 1979. He continued performing until his death, at age eighty-nine.

The Shigeyamas bring a broad, almost slapstick, sensibility to *kyōgen,* believing that the ancient comedies' true audience is the common people. They are proud of their family's "tofu-ism"—their belief that *kyōgen* should be as simple and unassuming, but also as popular, as soybean curd (a staple, in other words, of Japan's entertainment diet). While some critics, including some fellow *kyōgen* actors, decry such modernizing as pandering, Shigeyama-lovers delight in the family's easily understood and tremendously entertaining farce. Today, the Shigeyama family is represented by the brothers Sensaku IV and Sennojō II, their four sons, and their five grandsons.

Shigeyama Sensaku IV (born 18 December 1919 in Kyoto) was given the name Shime at birth but took the traditional honorific name Shigeyama Sengorō XII in 1966 and his present honorific name in 1994. He and his brother, now Shigeyama Sennojō II, achieved early fame as "little sprout stars," but Sensaku was an indifferent *kyōgen* student. He admits having turned back to *kyōgen* when he realized that there was nothing else at which he was capable of excelling. He and Sennojō continued their family tradition of popularizing *kyōgen,* entertaining at shrine and temple festivals, on tours to rural junior high schools (appearing in as many as a thousand plays a year), in the low-priced "townsmen's *kyōgen*" sponsored by the city of Kyoto since 1957, and at the nightly Gion Corner potpourris of traditional arts (from 1969 onward).

Sensaku supplemented his traditional *kyōgen* performances with appearances on television, in modern plays, and in experimental works by Takechi Tetsuji, including the French farce *Susugigawa* (The Henpecked Husband, 1953) and the Japanese folk play *Hikoichi Banashi* (The Tale of Hikoichi, 1955).

SHIGEYAMA FAMILY. Shigeyama Sengoro XII (Sensaku IV) boasting as he rides an unruly horse in *Shidohōgaku*. (Photograph by Osamu Muranaka; used by permission; courtesy of Jonah Salz.)

Sensaku's portrayals of gravelly voiced commoners have endeared him to millions. He is said to be a "natural" *kyōgen* actor, who merely needs to set foot on the stage to create *kyōgen*. His characters are so alive with basic fears and hungers—for food, drink, pleasure—that he carries his audiences along with him across the centuries, creating the feeling that this is indeed what medieval servants must have been like. His signature role is that of the lazy, sake-loving servant Tarō Kaja, to which role Sensaku brings an unassuming, timeless sensuality. His *Kirokuda, Suotoshi,* and *Bo Shibari* are simple, vibrant interpretations of the quintessential servant.

Like his father Sensaku III a decade earlier, Sensaku was designated a National Living Treasure in 1989 and elected into the Japan Arts Academy in 1991. He received the name Sensaku IV in a series of well-received 1994 performances that reflected the strengths of the entire Shigeyama family. Having reached the pinnacle of success as a *kyōgen* actor, Sensaku has turned his attention to performing with his sons and training his grandsons and the extended family of professional disciples to carry on the Shigeyama tradition.

Shigeyama Sennojō II (born 14 October 1923 in Kyoto), whose birthname was Shigeyama Masatsugu, has made his reputation as an experimenter in new and adapted *kyōgen* and as a devoted opponent of the tyranny of traditional custom in the worlds of *kyōgen* and *nō*.

Sennojō showed an early aptitude for *kyōgen,* debuting at age three. Because his future as a *kyōgen* performer was not assured, however, he became involved in *kabuki,* folk opera, and modern theater. Sennojō apprenticed himself to Takechi Tetsuji, an innovative director of *kabuki* and modern theater. His portrayal of the hapless husband in Kinoshita Junji's sentimental folk tale *Yūzuru* (Evening Crane) was well received, and he toured the play throughout Japan for many years. Sennojō credits his ability to go beyond classical *kyōgen* form to playwright Kinoshita's advice to him: "*Forget* you are a *kyōgen* actor."

Sennojō's beautiful voice and physical grace have been admired in such plays as *Hanago* and *Tsukimizato* (The Moon-Viewing Blind Man) and on a recording of folk songs and romantic ballads. As the Shigeyama family scribe, he has corrected mistakes in the *kyōgen* texts,

SHIGEYAMA FAMILY. In this scene from the play *Kamabara* (Suicide by Sickle), Shigeyama Sennojō II portrays a henpecked husband who attempts to kill himself with a farming implement and is restrained by his wife. (Photograph by Osamu Muranaka; used by permission; courtesy of Jonah Salz.)

transferring his father's careful calligraphy to computer. As an actor, he attempts to make the medieval characters come alive. With both text and performance, Sennojō struggles with the question of how much he can make comprehensible to a modern audience while retaining the classical style.

Besides engaging in efforts to resuscitate *kyōgen*'s fortunes after World War II, Sennojō and his brother Shigeyama Sensaku IV experimented in numerous intergenre performances, including puppet theater, dance, opera, Mishima Yukio's modern *nō* plays, and, in 1964, some *kabuki* performances—for which experimentation they were nearly expelled from the *nō–kyōgen* world. Sennojō continues to work in radio and television and as a director of opera, modern drama, and fusion forms and to speak out against the autocratic restrictions of the *iemoto* (headmaster) system. When he turned sixty he staged his own "funeral recital," a satire on the expense and emptiness of customary rites. In 1991 he performed a show in Tokyo and Kyoto that was indicative of both his mastery of tradition and his radicalism: a solo performance of *Hitori Matsutake* (Hunting for Mushrooms), revived from an extant text, and a version of Samuel Beckett's *Krapp's Last Tape*, performed in clownish whiteface, with pantomime, and directed by his son Akira.

Akira has continued along his father's experimental path through acting in plays by Beckett, W. B. Yeats, and Woody Allen in Kyoto's Noho Theater Group; teaching non-Japanese artists in Kyoto and abroad; producing a "comparative" clown tour with clowns from Kiev; and directing opera and theater. Akira's traditional and experimental works have been performed to great acclaim at the Edinburgh Fringe Festival (1982) and the Avignon International Theater Festival (1994).

[*See also* Kyōgen.]

BIBLIOGRAPHY

Gondo Yoshikazu, ed. *Otofushūgi: Shigeyama-ke monogotari.* Kyoto, 1994.

Salz, Jonah. "Roles of Passage: Coming of Age as a Japanese Kyogen Actor." Ph.D. diss., New York University, 1996.

Shigeyama Sennojō. *Kyōgen banashi.* Tokyo, 1983.

Shigeyama Sennojō. *Kyōgen yakusha.* Tokyo, 1987.

Shigeyama Sensaku. *Kyōgen hachijūgonen.* Tokyo, 1984.

RECORDING. Shigeyama Sennojō. *Sennojō: Kyōgen kayōsen* (Osaka, 1987).

JONAH SALZ

SHIKHAT. *See* Morocco.

SHIMAI are short dances based on movements used in Japanese *nō* plays. The history, principal schools, categories, and other aspects of *shimai* are the same as for *nō* theater.

Shimai possess a highly codified vocabulary of movement patterns called *kata,* a word roughly meaning "forms in time or space"; the arrangement or sequence of *kata* is called *kumiawase.* In the *kumiawase,* the same *kata* are used repeatedly, for there is conscious use of a limited number of movements. The development of *nō* under the influence of Zen Buddhism led to the expression of spiritual matters through simple means of suggestion and understatement in refined and abstract forms reduced to bare essentials.

Shimai movement emphasizes slow, sustained walking; smooth turns; rhythmic stamping; and manipulation of props (fans, swords, sticks) and of the sleeves of the kimono. There are also a few spectacular jumps for warrior and demon roles. The most characteristic movement of *shimai* is the manner of walking called *hakobi,* in which the dancer slides his whole foot forward, then lifts it in a straight line while maintaining heel contact; he then lowers the whole foot as a new step is taken. A performer's skill is determined by how well he executes *hakobi.*

Each *shimai* is a distillation of the main theme of the play on which it is based with at least one distinctive movement-metaphor to identify it. *Shimai* are performed to sung texts, with the first few lines taken by the dancer and the remainder by a chorus. Sometimes, they are also accompanied by a *hayashi,* the *nō* flute and drum ensemble.

One major difference between dances within *nō* plays and *shimai* is that the latter are performed *suuodori,* that is, wearing only a formal kimono and *hakama* (full, skirt-like trousers). It is considered more difficult to perform *suuodori* because the performer must portray character and emotion with only his dancing, acting, and singing skills—that is, without being able to rely on the masks and costumes used in *nō.*

Traditionally, *shimai* are danced by *nō* performers; training starts at an early age. In recent years, amateur performance of *shimai* has become a popular hobby for wealthy middle-aged men and women.

The Japanese concept of *ki,* or energy, is important in *shimai. Ki* is a complex word with several meanings, ranging from everyday human energy to the spirit or universal power in nature. In *shimai* as in Zen meditation and the martial art aikido, the gathering and control of energy in the lower abdomen near the center of gravity appears to give the body more substance and weight. At the same time, the performer imagines the *ki* emanating from the center of the body in all directions. To project great energy while being relaxed and centered requires extraordinary concentration and self-control, and this ability to project one's spirit becomes the ultimate in simplicity and the highest skill attainable in the performance of *shimai.*

[*See also* Nō.]

BIBLIOGRAPHY

Bethe, Monica, and Karen Brazell. *Nō as Performance: An Analysis of the Kuse Scene of Yamamba.* Ithaca, N.Y., 1978.

Keene, Donald. *Nō: The Classical Theatre of Japan.* New York, 1966.

Wolz, Carl. "The Spirit of Zen in Noh Dance." *CORD Dance Research Annual* 8 (1977): 55–64.

CARL WOLZ

SHINPA. *See* Hanako; Yakko and Kawakami.

SHINTŌ. *See* Kagura.

SHISHIMAI ("lion dance") is a popular genre of folk dance found throughout Japan. *Shishimai* differ greatly according to local traditions. The basic form involves the donning of a lion mask (these also vary considerably from region to region and town to town) and dancing to a rhythmical accompaniment provided either by musicians or by the dancers themselves. In some places the mask may represent a dragon, deer, boar, or bear, but the dances are nevertheless usually referred to as lion dances. When tigers are represented, however, the performance is called "tiger dance" *(toramai).*

Shishimai are known to have been performed in such ancient Japanese theatrical dance types as *gigaku, bugaku,* and *sangaku;* various examples of *shishimai* seen today appear to have their antecedents in these old styles. *Shishimai* have a close relationship with folk religion, and the dances are almost always performed at religious festivals in connection with exorcisms, purification rites, memorial services for the dead, ceremonies to prevent fires, and so forth. They are believed to have evolved from animistic beliefs, the lion being considered an especially auspicious beast. Lions are not indigenous to Japan, and their representation in the arts derives from Chinese models.

There are two main categories of *shishimai,* each with myriad variations. In the first, each dancer wears a lion mask that completely covers his head; he has a drum at his abdomen that he beats with a stick in either hand. Anywhere from two to a dozen or more similarly garbed dancers will perform, often going from door to door through the village streets. They may be accompanied by colorfully costumed musicians playing flute, drums, or the *sasara,* a type of bamboo clacker.

In the second type, two performers may depict the animal—one the forepart, the other the rear—or the torso of the lion may be represented by a voluminous cloth under which a large group of dancers moves, their legs giving the beast a caterpillar-like appearance.

Lion dances exist in both *nō* and *kabuki,* where they form an important part of the repertory. In these dance genres, where they have been highly developed as sophisticated theatrical dances and have shed their folk aspects, they are called *shakkyō mono. Shakkyō* means "stone bridge," and the lion dance has taken this name in *nō* because it occurs at a stone bridge in a *nō* play of that name. Among the many *kabuki* dances based on *shishimai* are popular works such as *Renjishi* and *Kagamijishi.*

SHISHIMAI. Ichikawa Ennosuke II in *Kagamijishi* (The Mirror Lion), a *shakkyō mono* lion dance created in the 1890s. In the second half of this piece, a beautiful girl is transformed into the spirit of a playful lion and performs the dance pictured here. (Photograph courtesy of Samuel L. Leiter.)

[*For related discussion, see* Bugaku; Gigaku; Kabuki Theater; *and* Nō.]

BIBLIOGRAPHY

Kawatake Shigetoshi, ed. *Geinō jiten.* Tokyo, 1953.

Leiter, Samuel L. *Kabuki Encyclopedia: An English-Language Adaptation of "Kabuki Jiten."* Westport, Conn., 1979.

SAMUEL L. LEITER

SHOES. *See* Footwear.

SHOSTAKOVICH, DMITRI (Dmitri Dmitrievich Shostakovich; born 25 September [8 October] 1906 in Saint Petersburg, died 9 August 1975 in Moscow), Russian composer. Although a prolific composer of dramatic music (he provided scores for more than thirty films and a dozen stage plays as well as four operas), Shostakovich composed no music for dance after reaching the age of thirty, his three ballets of the early 1930s having been received by Soviet critics and authorities with great hostility. All of them date from the last years of the "idealistic" phase of Soviet cultural life, when many artists identified enthusiastically with the task of building a revolutionary social order. These were also years of great openness to the music of the Western avant-garde. During his student period and immediately thereafter, Shostakovich would have been able to hear in Leningrad recent and important works by Arnold Schoenberg, Alban Berg, Paul Hindemith, Darius Milhaud, and others, and he would have been aware of the legacy of experimentation inherited from before the Revolution, when Russian composers had already begun to explore atonality, futurism, and the use of microtones. Indeed, it is not uncharacteristic of early Soviet cultural life that the political department of the State Music Publishing House (Muzgiz) was for some years directed by Nikolai Roslavets, the pioneer of serialism in Russia.

Divisions soon developed, however, among the modernist composers, with their ears open to the West, the older and more conservative nationalist school, and the "proletarian" group, which included not only the composers of utilitarian and agitprop music but also those who distrusted most classical music, past and present, as elitist and irrelevant to the class struggle. The conflict between modernists and proletarians was at its height in the late 1920s. Shostakovich's concert works of this period, the Second Symphony (*To October,* 1927) and the Third (*The First of May,* 1929), found temporary acceptance with both modernists and proletarians. The former welcomed their dissonance, their brilliant (even lurid) scoring, their powerful rhythmic impetus, and their kinship with advanced Western music of the time, as models of truly revolutionary symphonic thinking. The latter doubtless saw their ferocious impact as an apt metaphor for the advance of socialism; both works have propagandizing choral finales that would have confirmed this view. When such music was allied to the specific scenario of a ballet, however, its ambiguous humor and wild energy were found disconcerting or doctrinally questionable.

The plot of *The Golden Age*—choreographed by Leonid Yakobson, Vasily Vainonen, Vladimir Chesnakov, and E. Kaplan and premiered in Leningrad on 26 October 1930—was conceived as a lighthearted satire on the capitalist West. A Soviet football team visiting a Western city gets into a fight with a group of fascist thugs; some of the Russian players are arrested, but they are rescued by sympathetic workers, with whom they unite in a dance glorifying labor. The music is colorful, vigorous, and exuberantly witty, but it was criticized as eccentric, exaggerated, and grotesque, an unsuitable portrayal of the Soviet people, with too much emphasis given to the depiction of capitalists. Shostakovich's humor was too equivocal for the Soviet authorities; for example, in act 3, a meeting of the League of Nations (the subject of much odium in Russia at the time) was accompanied not by sinister or satirically pompous music but by a cheerful, if absurd and derisive, polka that soon became very popular. Worse, the score incorporated Shostakovich's demurely flippant orchestration of Vincent Youmans's "Tea for Two." This, too, became so popular that Shostakovich was soon obliged to disown it; it was perhaps hard to distinguish whether his mockery of Western popular music was dismissive or wittily affectionate. [*See* Golden Age, The.]

Such ambiguities also led to the denunciation of Shostakovich's next ballet, *The Bolt,* staged by Fedor Lopukhov in Leningrad on 8 April 1931. It concerns the attempts of petty-bourgeois saboteurs to disrupt Soviet industry, foiled by members of the Soviet youth organization Komsomol. Again, what should have been the heroic figures were thought to have been caricatured in Shostakovich's music, which continues the style of *The Golden Age,* although with heavier and more mechanical rhythms reflecting the industrial setting; even the overture and the final "affirmative" general dance and apotheosis have a driven, feverish quality that could scarcely be seen as an adequate representation of socialist optimism. Both ballets were later disavowed by Shostakovich, but it is significant that he spoke of them merely as "gross failures from the dramatic [rather than ideological] point of view" (Shostakovich, 1984).

Shostakovich did not return to composing music for dance for four years, during which time the conflict between modernists and proletarians was officially brought to an end in 1932 by a Party Resolution that disbanded the warring factions and established instead a single Union of Soviet Composers under close ideological supervision. His opera *Lady Macbeth of the Mtsensk District* (1934) received a triumphant welcome from the Russian public and widespread attention in the West, and a mixed though largely respectful response from Soviet critics. Then, on 28 January 1936, *Pravda* published a virulent attack on the opera, which Stalin had seen for the first time a few days earlier and violently disliked. A week later Shostakovich's recently premiered ballet *The Bright Stream* (also known as *The Limpid Stream*)—staged by Lopukhov in Leningrad on 4 June 1935 and in Moscow on 30 November 1935—was tarred with the same brush in

Pravda. Its ostensible subject was life on a collective farm, but the gist of the plot was the standard farcical situation of a lustful husband seeking a rendezvous with a prospective mistress, only to be confronted with his wife in disguise; the ironic targets of the music now included the revered classics of Russian ballet music. Lopukhov, already much criticized for the modernism of his choreography, was dismissed from his position as director of the Maly (now Modest Mussorgsky) Theater. Shostakovich was disgraced, and although the cloud over his reputation was somewhat dispelled two years later by the Fifth Symphony (subtitled "a Soviet artist's response to justified criticism"), he composed no more ballets; a later project for a ballet on the life of the nineteenth-century poet Mikhail Lermontov came to nothing.

Shostakovich continued to be regarded with suspicion and hostility by the authorities for many years. The disturbing, double-edged ambiguity that had inspired the denunciations of his ballet scores was to become, for the remainder of his composing life, an essential element in his vocabulary, subversive or expressively enriching according to the political standpoint of the listener.

Many of Shostakovich's concert works have been used by Soviet and Western choreographers. They include the following ballets: Léonide Massine's *Rouge et Noir: L'Étrange Farandole* (1939; First Symphony) and *Leningrad Symphony* (1945; Seventh Symphony); Norman Morrice's *The Wise Monkeys* (1960; First Piano Concerto); Igor Belsky's *Seventh Symphony* (1961; first movement of the Seventh Symphony) and *Eleventh Symphony* (1966; Eleventh Symphony); Asaf Messerer's *Leçon de Danse* (1961; movements from Ballet Suites 1–3, with music from other composers, later danced to Shostakovich's music only); John Cranko's *The Catalyst* (1961; First Piano Concerto); Konstantin Boyarsky's *The Young Lady and the Hooligan* (1962; movements from *The Bolt* and *The Bright Stream*); Kenneth MacMillan's *Symphony* (1962; First Symphony) and *Concerto* (1966; Second Piano Concerto); Ray Powell's *Just for Fun* (1962; movements from Ballet Suites 1–4); Peter van Dyk's *Ninth Symphony* (1964; Ninth Symphony); Alan Carter's *Tenth Symphony* (1967; Tenth Symphony); Arthur Mitchell's *Fête Noire* (1971; Second Piano Concerto); David Drew's *Sacred Circles* (1973; Piano Quintet); Simon Mottram's *In Concert* (1974; First Piano Concerto); Valery Panov's *The Idiot* (1979; various works) and *Hamlet* (1984; music from the film); André Prokovsky's *The Storm* (1981; various works); Mark Morris's *Vestige* (1984; movements from the Cello Sonata in D); Robert North's *Der Schlaf der Vernunft* (1986); and Maurice Béjart's *Trois Études pour Alexandre* (1987).

BIBLIOGRAPHY

Bogdanova, Alla. *Opery i balety Shostakovicha.* Moscow, 1979.

Hulme, Derek C. *Dmitri Shostakovich: A Catalogue, Bibliography, and Discography.* 2d ed. Oxford, 1991.

Kay, Norman. *Shostakovich.* London, 1971.

Kennicott, Philip. "Dance Music: The Young Dmitri." *Dance Magazine* (February 1990).

Lopukhov, Fedor. *Shestdesiat let v balete.* Moscow, 1966.

Noriss, Christopher. *Shostakovich: The Man and the Music.* London, 1982.

Roseberry, Eric. *Shostakovich: His Life and Times.* New York, 1981.

Schwarz, Boris. *Music and Musical Life in Soviet Russia, 1917–1970.* London, 1972.

Shneerson, Grigorii M. *D. Shostakovich: Stati i materialy.* Moscow, 1976.

Shostakovich, Dmitri. *Testimony: The Memoirs of Dmitri Shostakovich.* Translated by Antonina W. Bouis. Edited by Solomon Volkov. 2d ed. New York, 1984.

Swift, Mary Grace. *The Art of the Dance in the U.S.S.R.* Notre Dame, 1968.

MICHAEL OLIVER

SHURALE. Dance work in three acts and four scenes, originally created by Leonid Zhukov in 1941 under the title *Shurale;* later performed under the title *Ali-Batyr* by Leonid Yakobson.

Shurale. Choreography: Leonid Zhukov and Gay Tagirov. Music: Farid Yarullin. Libretto: A. Faisi and Leonid Yakobson. Scenery: P. Speransky. First Performance: 12 March 1945, M. Dzhalil Theater of Opera and Ballet, Kazan. Principals: A. Gazulina (Syuimbike), G. Akhtyamov (Ali-Batyr), V. Romanyuk (Shurale).

Ali-Batyr. Choreography: Leonid Yakobson. Music: Farid Yarullin, revised instrumentation by V. Vlasov and V. Fereh. Scenery and costumes: L. Milchin and I. Vano. First performance: 28 May 1950, Leningrad, Kirov Opera and Ballet Theater. Principals: Alla Shelest, Natalia Dudinskaya, and Inna Zubkovskaya (Syuimbike), Boris Bregvadze, Konstantin Sergeyev, and Askold Makarov (Ali-Batyr), Igor Belsky and Robert Gerbek (Shurale).

The ballet was created in Kazan in 1941 but got only as far as the dress rehearsal before war intervened, postponing its debut until 1945. After the revised version of 1950, the ballet was performed again on 1 January 1955 under the title *Shurale* at one of the Bolshoi Theater's subsidiaries in Moscow. The choreographer was Leonid Yakobson, and scenery and costumes were by L. Milchin. The role of Syuimbike was performed by Maya Plisetskaya, the role of Ali-Batyr by Yuri Kondratov, and the role of Shurale by Vladimir Levashev. On the same stage in 1960 Syuimbike was played by Marina Kondratieva, Ali-Batyr by Vladimir Vasiliev, and Shurale again by Levashev. The ballet was staged in many towns and cities throughout the Soviet Union and in Eastern Europe.

The libretto of *Shurale* was based on the eponymous classical poem by the Tatar poet Gabdulla Tukai. The ballet's creators embroidered it with the motifs of Tatar folk tales and created a highly original work. The plot was simple. Having wandered deep into a forest, the hunter Ali-

Batyr sees a flock of birds descend on a clearing and turn into maidens. The wood demon Shurale tries to capture the bird-maiden Syuimbike, but Ali-Batyr saves the girl. Upon waking, she recognizes her rescuer and consents to be his wife.

The wedding is to take place in the village and the people rejoice. However, Syuimbike misses her friends and flies away; the scene shifts to Shurale's forest realm. The demon Shurale once again tries to capture Syuimbike, but Ali-Batyr, who has been pursuing him, sets fire to the forest. He throws Shurale into the fire, where he and his retinue perish. Syuimbike returns to the village with Ali-Batyr and the wedding celebrations begin again.

Shurale left an indelible mark on the development of Soviet choreography in that it outlined new paths in the search for expressive imagery. "The music of *Shurale* is rewarding material for a choreographer. Melodic and colorful, it is rooted in Tatar folklore. . . . The group wedding dances overwhelm the audience with an abundance of rhythms, forms, moods. . . . But perhaps the best aspect of the ballet's music is its vividness in defining character" (Dobrovolskaya, 1968). The ballet's choreographer, Yakobson (1950), recalled, "My task was a matter of delineating all the characters solely in the idiom of dance; to achieve unity of content, music, and plastique; to erase the difference between the dancing and the pantomime; to blend the two principles of dance language into a single whole. In other words, I sought to assert the principle of symphonism in choreography."

BIBLIOGRAPHY

Bogdanov-Berezovskii, V. M. "Ali-Batyr." *Vecherny Leningrad* (26 June 1950).

Dobrovolskaya, Galina N. *Baletmeister Leonid Iakobson.* Leningrad, 1968.

Martin, John. "Ballet at the Bolshoi Accents Bravura Style." *New York Times* (24 June 1956).

Roslavleva, Natalia. *Era of the Russian Ballet.* London, 1966.

Yakobson, Leonid. "My Work with *Shuraleh*" (in Russian). *Sovetskaia muzyka,* no. 9 (1989); no. 6 (1991).

GALINA A. GULYAEVA
Translated from Russian

SIBERIA. *See* Russia, *article on* Siberian Dance Traditions.

SIBLEY, ANTOINETTE (born 27 February 1939 in Bromley, England), British dancer. Sibley is often considered the quintessential example of the English style in ballet. A dancer of the purest line and technique, she was refined, reticent, elegant, and supremely musical.

Having already studied ballet, tap, and musical comedy dancing for five years at the Arts Educational School, Sibley entered the Royal Ballet School with a scholarship at the age of ten. She progressed straight through the Lower and Upper Schools (she was the first English ballerina to do so) and graduated into the Royal Ballet corps de ballet in 1956, the product of instruction by Winifred Edwards, Pamela May, and Ailne Phillips.

Her first solo roles—the Fairy of the Crystal Fountain and the Bluebird pas de deux in *The Sleeping Beauty* —showed her quick, neat attack and sparkling personality to great advantage. In the year between her promotion to soloist in 1959 and to principal in 1960, her first performances of Swanilda, the lead in *Ballet Imperial,* the Polka in *Façade,* and the White Couple pas de deux in *Les Patineurs* revealed a true ballerina in the making. She also danced her first *Swan Lake* in 1959—after only two performances on tour, she made a triumphant Covent Garden debut on twelve hours' notice, partnered and coached by Michael Somes (to whom she was married from 1964 to 1973). She took full command of the classical repertory with subsequent debuts as Aurora and Giselle.

In Tamara Karsavina's book *Classical Ballet and the Flow of Movement* (1962), photographs capture Sibley's

SIBLEY. As Titania in Frederick Ashton's *The Dream* (1964), with Anthony Dowell as Oberon and Alexander Grant as Bottom the weaver, temporarily transformed into an ass. (Photograph by Anthony Crickmay; used by permission of the Board of Trustees of the Theatre Museum, London.)

impeccable form and placement at this age, as the solo created for her by Frederick Ashton in his pas de quatre (1963) for *Swan Lake* captured her witty stylishness. *The Dream* (1964), her first important creation for Ashton—who conjured a signature role for her in the quicksilver Titania—launched her partnership with Anthony Dowell. Paired by their perfect proportions and matching musical impulses, Sibley and Dowell achieved an ideal balance temperamentally, with his natural gravity anchoring her more mercurial quality.

Classicism personified in *Symphonic Variations,* Sibley flowered dramatically into a tempestuous Juliet, a radiant Cinderella, an unearthly Firebird, and a beguiling Clara in Rudolf Nureyev's *The Nutcracker.* She inspired passionate choreography from Kenneth MacMillan, most notably the title role in *Manon* (1974), and a gallery of creations from Ashton that included Dorabella in *Enigma Variations,* Friday's Child in *Jazz Calendar*—with Nureyev, a frequent partner—and the serenely abstract *Monotones I.*

Sibley appeared in the first Royal Ballet casts of Jerome Robbins's *Dances at a Gathering, In the Night,* and *Afternoon of a Faun;* was named a Commander of the Order of the British Empire in 1973 for services to ballet; danced with Mikhail Baryshnikov in the film *The Turning Point* (1978); and then—plagued by recurrent injury—retired temporarily in 1979. After returning to the Royal Ballet as a guest artist in 1981, she created the glamorous La Capricciosa in Ashton's *Varii Capricci* (1983), made her debut as Natalia Petrovna in *A Month in the Country,* and reestablished herself as Titania, Manon, Cinderella, and the company's most enchanting ballerina. In 1991, Sibley became president of the Royal Academy of Dancing, succeeding Margot Fonteyn, and in 1996 she was honored with the title of Dame Commander of the Order of the British Empire.

BIBLIOGRAPHY

Cargill, Mary. "Talking to Antoinette Sibley." *Dance View* 10 (Winter 1993): 40–43.

Crisp, Clement. "Antoinette Sibley, C.B.E." *Dance Gazette* (October 1991): 17–19.

Harris, Dale. *Antoinette Sibley.* Brooklyn, 1976.

Manning, Emma. "Life's Labours Loved." *Dance Australia* (February–March 1995): 32–35.

Newman, Barbara. *Antoinette Sibley: Reflections of a Ballerina.* London, 1986.

Newman, Barbara. *Striking a Balance: Dancers Talk about Dancing.* Rev. ed. New York, 1992.

Ostlere, Hilary. "Meet the New President: Antoinette Sibley." *Dance Magazine* (January 1993): 46–47.

BARBARA NEWMAN

SIDDIQUI, NAHID (born 1956 in Karachi), Pakistani dancer and choreographer. Siddiqui's father, Mohammad Bashir Siddiqui, was a government civil servant, and her mother, Talat Siddiqui, was an actress and singer. Nahid started her *kathak* training under Maharaj Ghulam Hussain Kathak at the age of fifteen: she remains his most successful student. She studied under Maharaj for seven years.

Siddiqui established herself as Pakistan's most promising proponent of *kathak.* While studying under Maharaj at the Alhamra Arts Academy in Lahore, she impressed the director, who was assembling a troupe to publicize Pakistan's culture abroad. She danced with this company for a few months, also performing for television. She gained the admiration of Zia Mohiyuddin, director of the PIA Arts Academy in Karachi, a cultural academy for promoting Pakistan International Airlines. On his request she joined the Academy and was soon stunning audiences all over the world with her folk and *kathak* dance performances. The next year she married Zia Mohiyuddin. In 1976 she began to appear in weekly solo dance performances in a television series, *Payal.* In 1978, after its twelfth episode, the show was banned by the military government. The PIA Arts Academy had closed about a year earlier and Zia Mohiyuddin had emigrated to London, where Siddiqui now joined him.

As a result of *Payal,* Siddiqui had no trouble attracting students to her *kathak* classes in England. Within a year she was performing regularly all over the world. In 1980 she went to India to study under Birju Maharaj for six months, and since then she has returned there every year for a few months.

Siddiqui has received more awards than any other Pakistani dancer. In 1991 she received the Time-Out Award at the National Theater in London and the International Umbrella Award for dance. In 1993 she received the Digital Dance Award for a dance-drama, *Timecycle.* In 1992 she received the Faiz Foundation Award, and in 1994, the Pride of Performance Award from the Pakistan government.

Siddiqui has broken away from most Hindu aspects of the *kathak* repertory taught in India. Her strong sense of identity as a Muslim is reflected in her choreography, all of which draws on the works of Muslim poets, musicians, and mystics, such as Amīr Khusraw, Fā'iz Aḥmad Fā'iz, and Jalāl al-Dīn Rūmī. In 1991 she formed her own company and has choreographed several innovative dances for it. Supported by grants, she has traveled and conducted research in order to enlarge her repertory. In Turkey she explored ancient Sufi texts, particularly the works of Rūmī, and studied the whirling dervishes who were inspired by him. Her research culminated in an award-winning dance, *Tihai,* first performed in London's Palace Theatre and then throughout Britain, Holland, and Italy. The music incorporates Turkish rhythms using the violin, *tabla,* piano, and a twelfth-century instrument, the *ney.* Another powerful work, *Dancing in the Mist,* links the *faqirs*, or ascetics, of the Punjab to the dervishes of Turkey. In addition to her fascination with Islamic mysticism and appreciation for Sufi music and dance, another motive behind choreographing these dances may have been to establish the long-standing connection of dance with Islam, and thereby to increase the acceptance of dance in Pakistan.

Since the advent of a more liberal government in 1988, Siddiqui has gradually increased her presence in Pakistan. She now spends six months a year there, holding workshops and performances and making plans for establishing a dance institute. The turnout at her workshops and performances has been excellent, and prospects for raising adequate financing for her dance school through private sponsors and student fees seem bright.

BIBLIOGRAPHY

Husain, Marjorie. "Dancing in the Dark." *Dawn Tuesday Review* (7–13 February 1995).

INTERVIEW. Nahid Siddiqui, by Shayma Saiyid (Lahore, January 1995).

SHAYMA SAIYID

SIKINNIS. The *sikinnis* was a revel dance performed by the chorus in ancient Greek satyr plays. The Greeks believed that satyrs—mythological creatures who were half man and half goat—danced the *sikinnis* when they participated in riotous drunken revels honoring the god Dionysus. Because the creatures had a reputation for lewd, drunken, and playful behavior, their *sikinnis* dance was also regarded as lascivious and wild. Plato felt that such dancing in imitation of the satyrs' rites was a practice unfit for the Greek citizen.

The chorus members in traditional satyr plays were all costumed as satyrs. In the one extant play (Euripides' *Cyclops*), Silenus refers to the dancing entrance of his satyr band as a *sikinnis* and likens it to the *kōmos* they danced in procession for Dionysus. Apparently, later in the play the satyrs dance a *kōmos* revel dance with the Cyclops. The *sikinnis*, then, must have been closely akin to the *kōmos*. Satyr plays were also a vehicle for burlesquing traditional mythological themes, so it is likely that the satyr choral dances parodied more serious or noble dances.

The origins of the *sikinnis* are unclear. Some Roman sources suggest that the dance developed in Crete from the wild and clamorous leaping dances that the mythological Curetes performed to drown out the cries of the infant Zeus; others indicate that the dance may have originated in Phrygia in Asia Minor, perhaps in secret rites honoring Dionysus. Modern scholars believe that the word *sikinnis* had Thraco-Phrygian origins, from a root meaning "to leap."

Although Roman commentators had never seen the *sikinnis*, they testified that it was a rapid dance that never slowed. They regarded the *sikinnis*, *kordax*, and *emmeleia* as three Greek theatrical dances, each performed in a particular genre of dramatic poetry: the *sikinnis* in satyr play, the *kordax* in comedy, and the *emmeleia* in tragedy.

[*For related discussion, see* Choral Dancing, Dithyramb; *and* Hyporchēma. *See also* Greece, *article on* Dance in Ancient Greece.]

BIBLIOGRAPHY

Athenaeus. *Deipnosophists* 1.20, 14.629–630.

Euripides. *Cyclops* 37–40, 495–502.

Lawler, Lillian B. *The Dance of the Ancient Greek Theatre.* Iowa City, 1964.

Lucian. *On the Dance* 22.

Plato. *Laws* 815.

LIBBY SMIGEL

SIKKIM. A state of India since 1975, Sikkim is bordered by Tibet to the north, Nepal to the west, Bhutan to the east, and West Bengal state to the southeast. Its population is about 300,000. Three principal ethnic groups inhabit Sikkim, the indigenous Lepchas, Bhotias (Tibetans), and Nepalese; only 10 to 15 percent of the population is Lepcha. The state religion is Buddhism, even though the Nepalese, who constitute 70 to 75 percent of the population, are Hindu. This article focuses on the dance and drama of the indigenous Lepchas.

The Lepchas are of Mongolian descent and probably came originally from Assam. Today they tend to live in the isolated northern area of Sikkim, close to Mount Kanchenjunga, farming and raising animals. The traditional Lepcha dress for men is the *pagi*, a knee-length piece of striped cotton fabric which is wrapped around the body, leaving the arms free; it is fastened on the right shoulder with a bamboo pin and generally tied around the waist. The men often wear caps decorated with multicolored feathers. The traditional dress for women is the *tugu*, a loose blouse, and a lower garment, the *dom dyam*, a piece of cloth tied at the waist. The daily dress of the women may also be a *bakku*, a full-length sleeveless, double-breasted wrap dress worn over a long-sleeved blouse, the *lako*. During traditional dances, the blouse's sleeves are unfolded and hang several inches below the hands, giving the impression of flowing scarves. Married women wear a multicolored striped apron. For festive occasions women wear an abundance of jewelry—necklaces of semiprecious and precious stones and gold and silver, with amulets attached, bracelets, and earrings. The men also wear earrings. Traditionally both men and women had long plaited hair, interwoven with ribbons on festive days; today most men wear their hair short.

The Lepchas have two types of dance traditions, folk and religious. Folk dancing usually occurs during socioreligious festivals, such as weddings, name-givings, changes of the seasons, and historically important dates. In general, the performers wear everyday dress, although more colorful and of better quality. The folk dances, which mostly consist of technically uncomplicated repetitive steps, can be categorized as nature, agricultural, warrior, historical, and mythological dances.

In a nature dance the dancers imitate some creature such as an insect or a deer. When imitating an insect, the performers first rub their feet together once, then rub their hands (substituting for the insect's front feet), and then turn to the right. They then repeat the movements and turn to the left. All ages participate in this dance, which is often accompanied by singing, continuous clapping, and the music of the flute, drum, and metal gong.

Agricultural dances are performed by a group of men and women singing together. In one such dance, the steps imitate the planting of a field, with dancers moving three steps forward, balancing on one foot, then three steps back, balancing on the other foot; then all turn to the left and repeat the pattern.

The warrior dance is performed only by men, who carry swords and shields or bows and arrows. Accompanied by a drum, the dancers are divided into two groups who imitate attack and counterattack. A common movement is four steps toward each other and then four steps back, with jumping, bending and other expressive movements throughout.

Historical dances, performed by men and women, depict particular events. These dances are often similar to the warrior dance, as many of the events portrayed are renowned battles.

All ages participate in mythological dances, dramatizations of Lepcha folk tales. The actors not only portray the characters but also symbolize trees, rivers, and other aspects of nature.

The religious dance, performed exclusively by Buddhist monks, is called the *cham.* It is a dance drama performed in a stately manner, reflecting the meditation practice of the Buddhists. The *cham* begins with the monks, wearing their robes and ceremonial headdresses, coming from within the monastery and forming a large circle in the monastery courtyard. After the circle is completed, the main dancers go to the center of the circle and begin the ceremony. There are 108 steps, repeated over and over, mostly in a circular pattern. The *cham* is a difficult dance to learn and perform, since it requires tremendous concentration and balance to sustain the slow, deliberate steps. Cymbals, pole drum, and *rgya-gling,* a type of shawm, accompany the dance. Scriptural texts presenting Buddhist teachings are read periodically during the dance, describing the symbolism and function of the ceremony.

One of the most impressive aspects of the *cham* is the costumes worn by the main dancers. Their elaborately brocaded long robes are decorated with flowing scarves and an apron upon which is painted a protective, wrathful deity. The dancers wear huge, colorful masks, also wrathful in expression. In Buddhism, a non-theistic religion, a deity represents a state of mind; these protective deities often symbolize the dispelling of negative energies and the inviting in of positive, benevolent ones.

[*For related discussion, see* India.]

BIBLIOGRAPHY

Chopra, P. N. *Sikkim.* New Delhi, 1979.

Das, Amal Kumar. *The Lepchas of Darjeeling District.* Calcutta, 1962.

Gowloog, Rip Roshina. *Lingthem Revisited: Social Changes in a Lepcha Village of North Sikkim.* New Delhi, 1995.

Kotturan, George. *The Himalayan Gateway.* New Delhi, 1983.

Lama, Mahendra P., ed. *Sikkim: Society, Polity, Economy, Environment.* New Delhi, 1994.

Shukla, Satyendra R. *Sikkim: The Story of Integration.* New Delhi, 1976.

Siiger, Halfdan. *The Lepchas: Culture and Religion of a Himalayan People.* Copenhagen, 1967–.

FILM. Fred Lieberman and Michael Moore, *Traditional Music and Dance of Sikkim* (1977).

ELIZABETH GOLDBLATT

SIMONE, KIRSTEN (born 1 July 1934 in Copenhagen), Danish dancer, mime, and teacher. In June 1945, the eleven-year-old Simone went, by herself, to an audition for the ballet school of the Royal Theater in Copenhagen. Having studied privately with Dagny Jensen, she was found to be well prepared and was accepted into the school, where she became a diligent student. Determined to succeed, she progressed steadily through the curriculum, eventually becoming the pupil and protégée of Vera Volkova, an internationally recognized authority on the Russian school of ballet. Simone was invited to become a member of the Royal Danish Ballet in 1952, was promoted to *solodanser* (soloist, or principal dancer) in 1956, and was named *førstesolodanser* (equivalent to *prima ballerina*) in 1966.

The first of the Danish ballerinas fully to master Russian schooling, Simone displayed a secure technique, a clearly classical style, and a gentle, radiant presence in works such as *Les Sylphides, The Sleeping Beauty, Giselle,* and *Swan Lake.* In contrast to her roles in the classical repertory, which were characterized by a certain coolness and remoteness, she also eventually became identified with dramatic roles in two contemporary masterpieces, making a smolderingly erotic Carmen in the Roland Petit work and a vehement Miss Julie in the Birgit Cullberg ballet. She also danced in a number of Balanchine works mounted for the Royal Danish Ballet, including *Apollo, The Four Temperaments,* and *Symphony in C.* In all her roles—whether as Balanchine's Sleepwalker in *Night Shadow (La Sonnambula),* as Frederick Ashton's Juliet, or

SIMONE. As Carmen, Simone entices Erik Bruhn as Don José in Roland Petit's *Carmen*, mounted for the Royal Danish Ballet in 1960. In addition to such erotically charged roles as Carmen, Simone excelled in lighter fare, such as The Sweet Young Thing in John Cranko's *Secrets* (1958). (Photograph by Rigmor Mydtskov; from the Archives and Library of the Royal Theater, Copenhagen.

as Petit's Roxanne in *Cyrano de Bergerac*—her pale, Nordic beauty added piquancy to her performance.

Although Simone was most at home in the international repertory, she danced many of the Bournonville heroines, from Hilda in *A Folk Tale,* in which she made her professional debut in 1952, to principal parts in *La Sylphide* (1956), *Konservatoriet* (1956), and *Flower Festival in Genzano* (1963). In 1965, while the company was on tour in New York, she learned that King Frederick IX of Denmark had named her a Knight of the Order of Dannebrog. The following year, with her promotion to *førstesolodanser* and her starring role in the Walt Disney film *Ballerina,* her career reached its zenith, and it seemed that the years ahead held promise of her dancing many performances as a mature artist in a variety of roles.

This promise was not fulfilled. After Flemming Flindt assumed the position of ballet master of the Royal Danish Ballet in 1966, Simone's career gradually went into decline, for Flindt came to prefer a repertory of modern works for which her classical style was ill suited. She did create the role of the glamorous villainess Milady in his production of *The Three Musketeers* in 1966, and in 1967 she created Tadea in Elsa-Marianne von Rosen's *Don Juan* and danced the leads in the Bournonville ballets *Napoli* and *La Ventana.* Thereafter, however, she performed only rarely, despite her continuing popularity with the Danish critics and public, and very few new roles were available to her. Notable exceptions were roles in two Balanchine ballets, *Donizetti Variations* and *Serenade,* mounted in 1968 and 1969, respectively, and the principal part in a new version of Harald Lander's *Fest-Polonaise* in 1970.

In 1976, at age forty-two, Simone entered a new phase of her career as a mime and character dancer in the Bournonville repertory. She has since been widely praised for the charm and poignancy of her Louise in *The King's Volunteers on Amager* and for her lusty wit as Madame von Everdingen, the rich widow in *Kermesse in Bruges.* By the mid-1980s she had been awarded the most coveted roles in the Danish mime repertory: Muri, the troll queen, in *A Folk Tale,* and Madge, the witch, in *La Sylphide.* In 1990 she appeared as Frigga in the reconstruction of *The Lay of Thrym,* which had not been performed at the Royal Theater since 1905.

Over the course of her long career as dancer, mime, and teacher, Simone has often appeared outside Denmark, notably in the United Kingdom, the United States, Italy, and Germany. She appeared as guest artist with the Edinburgh International Ballet, Ruth Page's Chicago Opera Ballet, the Bolshoi Ballet, American Ballet Theatre, and London Festival Ballet. In Copenhagen, she currently teaches at both the Royal Theater and the Royal Danish Ballet School.

BIBLIOGRAPHY

Aschengreen, Erik. "Kirsten Simone." *Les saisons de la danse* (March 1971). Includes a checklist of roles and activities.

Aschengreen, Erik. "The Royal Danish Ballet Season of 1954–1955." *Dance Chronicle* 18.3 (1995): 419–426.

Kragh-Jacobsen, Svend. "Kirsten Simone." In Kragh-Jacobsen's *Twenty Solodancers of the Royal Danish Ballet.* Copenhagen, 1965. Includes photographs by Mogens von Haven. Also published in Danish.

Poesio, Giannandrea. "Kirsten Simone Talks about Bournonville Training and Style." *The Dancing Times* (July 1994): 974–975.

Terry, Walter. "Royal Mime." *Ballet News* 1 (June 1980): 13–17.

Tobias, Tobi. "In Praise of Older Women." *Dance Magazine* (November 1982): 55–59.

FILM. *Ballerina* (1966). Walt Disney Studios.

ARCHIVES. Materials pertaining to Simone's career can be found in the archives of the Royal Theater, Copenhagen, and in the Harvard Theatre Collection, Harvard University, Cambridge, Massachusetts.

CLAUDE CONYERS

SIMS, SANDMAN (Howard Sims; born 24 January 1917 in Los Angeles), American sand and tap dancer. As the name "Sandman" suggests, Howard Sims was the foremost sand dancer in the United States. An old and distinctly African-American tap style, sand dancing produces its rhythmic percussions from the gritty sounds that the soles of shoes make while swhishing on a light layer of sand. Sims (one of ten children) began dancing with his brothers on street corners when he was a very small child. As a young man he was strongly influenced by the dancers Jack Williams and "Tiajuana" Pete, and he greatly admired the artistry of Bill ("Bojangles") Robinson.

After working as a boxer and dancer in California, Sims traveled the Cuba-Mexico club circuit as a sand and tap dancer. In 1946 he went east, to New York City, where he met and came to greatly admire the work of Chuck Green. On the East Coast, Sandman danced in various clubs and theaters, managing to perform even during the great tap drought of the 1950s and 1960s because of his unique sand specialty. During the 1960s he worked at the famed Apollo Theater in Harlem, sometimes as a dancer but most often as the comic who pulled struggling performers offstage during the theater's infamous Amateur Nights. In 1968 Sims was a favorite performer in Letitia Jay's Tap Happenings, after which he toured widely in the United States, Africa, and Europe, both with The Hoofers and as a solo specialty.

Sims had a strong, vigorous tap style—body hunkered over, knees bent, feet digging into the floor—and his sand dance was characterized by clear, quick rhythms and subtle nuances. As the featured narrator in George T. Nierenberg's film *No Maps on My Taps,* Sims made memorable observations about the art of tap. "The man who improvises is a free man," he said. "The feet are a set of drums: the heels are the bass, the toes the melody, and you get off rim shots (like the drumming technique) with the sides of the foot, while sand is the sound of brushes on snare drums." He was a featured dancer and actor in the 1989 film *Tap,* starring Gregory Hines, who looks upon Sims as one of his most important mentors. Certainly Sandman's expertise has kept alive the art of sand dancing, a fascinating tap form that he has passed on to younger generations of tap dancers so that they can take it into the future.

ARCHIVES. Tap Dance Clipping File, Dance Collection, New York Public Library for the Performing Arts. George T. Nierenberg Productions, New York.

FILM AND VIDEOTAPE. George T. Nierenberg, *No Maps on My Taps* (1979). "Tap," *Dance in America* (WNET-TV, New York, 1989). *Tap* (Orion Pictures, 1989).

SALLY R. SOMMER

SINGH, BIPIN (known as Guru Bipin Singh; born 23 August 1919 in Silhat, Assam), Indian dancer, choreographer, and teacher. Born into a family of traditional dancers, Bipin Singh was trained in the Manipuri school of dance by his mother. He later moved to Imphal, Manipur, to study, receiving intensive training from Amudon, Sharma, Atombi, Singh, and several *rāsadhārīs* (dance masters). He also studied music and learned to play the *pung,* the Manipuri drum.

Singh moved to Calcutta in the early 1940s and later joined Madame Menaka's company in Bombay. After starting to teach, he collaborated with the Jhaveri Sisters in shaping the contemporary neoclassical Manipuri repertory of solo, duo, and group dances. He condensed the traditional night-long dance dramas into a form suitable for presentation on urban stages. Performed with the Jhaveri Sisters, his works became popular throughout India. Singh drew inspiration from the great corpus of Manipuri dance works and movement sequences and added sophistication and imaginative touches. His condensed versions of the *rās līlā* dance dramas drew attention to their more important elements. He has choreographed more than seventy solo works and dance dramas, which are in the repertories of the Jhaveri Sisters and the company Manipuri Nartanalaya.

Singh's wife, Kalavati Devi, is also a traditional Manipuri dancer, well versed in singing, dancing, and playing the *pung.* She has choreographed dance dramas both alone and in collaboration with Singh. Their daughter Bimbavati is another gifted dancer.

Singh and Darshana Jhaveri edited several books on Manipuri dance, and he has also authored treatises on Manipuri music. His research has related the Vaishnava *saṅgīt* texts with the *kīrtana* tradition of Bengal and the works of Bengali poets in discussions of the songs used as texts in Manipuri dance.

Among Singh's honors are the Central Sangeet Natak Akademi award, the Kalidas Sanman, and others. He lives in Calcutta, where he continues to choreograph and edit books.

BIBLIOGRAPHY

Bipinsingh, Guru. "The Rasleela of Manipur." *Quarterly Journal of the National Centre for the Performing Arts* 3 (September 1974): 27–36.

Bipinsingh, Guru. "Manipuri Dance: Tradition and Future." *Journal of the Department of Dance* (Rabindra Bharati University, Calcutta) 1 (1982): 35–38.

Jhaveri, Darsana, comp. *Guru Bipin Singh: Achievements and Accomplishments.* Bombay, 1991.

Jhaveri, Nayana. *Guru Bipin Singh.* Calcutta, 1979.

Jhaveri, Susheel, ed. *In Appreciation of Guru Bipin Singh.* Bombay, 1989.

SUNIL KOTHARI

SIRETTA, DAN (born 19 July 1940 in Brooklyn, New York), American dancer and choreographer. Siretta studied modern dance and ballet at New York's High School of Performing Arts and at the Juilliard School; he also studied ballet with Elizabeth Anderson-Ivantzova, Antony Tudor, and Margaret Craske, modern dance with Merce Cunningham, and tap and ballroom dancing with Jimmy Trainor. Siretta began his dancing career in musicals and was encouraged to begin choreographing in 1971 by John Neville, the star of *Lolita, My Love,* when both Danny Daniels and Jack Cole quit the show. Siretta took over; the show closed out of town, but he continued to choreograph in summer stock and for television, and in 1973 he staged a new touring production of *No, No, Nanette,* starring Ruby Keeler.

For fifteen years, starting in 1975, Siretta was resident choreographer and artistic director of the Goodspeed Opera House in East Haddam, Connecticut, where he played an important part in the movement to revive classic American musical comedies in versions as authentic as possible. Siretta's great contribution to such shows as Jerome Kern's *Very Good Eddie, Oh, Boy!,* and *Sweet Adeline,* George and Ira Gershwin's *Tip Toes, Lady, Be Good!,* and *Oh, Kay!,* Louis Hirsch's *Going Up,* Walter Donaldson's *Whoopee,* Vincent Youmans's *Hit the Deck,* George M. Cohan's *Little Johnny Jones,* and Bert Kalmar's *The 5 O'Clock Girl* was his perception that the style of the dance numbers in such shows in their original productions must have been derived from the ballroom dance of the time. Thus, "I've Got to Dance" in *Very Good Eddie* was based on a combination of the body positions of the maxixe with the one-step and the Castle Walk. Even if not demonstrably authentic, this and other numbers using the same kind of material added to the correct period flavor of the shows. Siretta also choreographed brilliant tap numbers for most of the shows. At Goodspeed, he also choreographed the original production of *Annie,* in 1976.

Several of the Goodspeed shows played on Broadway and had national tours, with varying degrees of success. Siretta went on to choreograph the 1990 Broadway revival of the Gershwins' *Oh, Kay!* with a black cast. In London, he restaged *Very Good Eddie* in 1976 and a new production of Sandy Wilson's *The Boy Friend* in 1983. In 1987 he choreographed *Three Gershwin Preludes* for Mikhail Baryshnikov and a small group for an award-winning show in the PBS (Public Broadcasting Service) *Great Performances* series. In 1992 he choreographed *Indian Summer* for the Calgary Ballet (Canada), based on the 1930s big band music of Earl ("Fatha") Hines.

In 1991 he staged the musical numbers for the New York City Opera production of Frank Loesser's *Most Happy Fella,* and in 1993 Emmerich Kálmán's operetta *The Gypsy Princess* for the Orange County Performing Arts Center in California. At the Long Wharf Theater in New Haven, Connecticut, he choreographed *I'll Be Seeing You, Pal Joey,* and a musical version of *Pride and Prejudice.* He has also directed and choreographed many industrial shows.

In the way that he layers one pattern over another and, as dance writer Arlene Croce observed, sets the stage "flowing with rhythms and cross-rhythms," as well as his sheer inventiveness in the matter of steps, Siretta is a choreographer worthy of being named with the best of his contemporaries, not only in musical comedy but in dance as a whole.

BIBLIOGRAPHY

Croce, Arlene. "Soundtracks." In Croce's *Going to the Dance.* New York, 1982.

Vaughan, David. "Dan Siretta: Rediscovering the American Musical." *Dance Magazine* (February 1978): 58–62.

Vaughan, David. "Very Good Siretta." *Ballet News* 1 (January–February 1980): 26–28.

DAVID VAUGHAN

SITARA DEVI (Dhanalakshmi Maharaj; born October 1925 in Banaras), Indian dancer. The daughter of Sukhdev Maharaj, a court musician in Nepal, Sitara Devi was trained in classical *kathak* dance from early childhood, along with her sister Alaknanda and her brothers Chaube Maharaj and Pande; another sister, Tara, was trained as a musician. In teaching dance to his children, Sukhdev went against the socioreligious strictures of his conservative Brahman family, who ostracized him and his children. He persisted, however, requesting Achhan Maharaj, father of the great dancer–choreographer Birju Maharaj, to undertake the children's training. Later, Sitara Devi studied under Shambhu Maharaj and Lachhu Maharaj, acquiring the subtleties of the Lucknow *gharānā,* or the Lucknow school of *kathak.*

Sitara Devi is naturally gifted, and her dancing is zestful and fiery. Her professional name, Sitara, means "star," and her stage presence reflects it; bubbling with enthusiasm, she establishes instant rapport with audiences. She dances with abandon, and her uninhibited performing style is extremely popular in India. She has a vast repertory and excels in both *nṛtta* (pure dance) and *abhinaya* (mime and expressive dance).

Until the late 1950s Sitara Devi acted in films with great success, working for Ranjit Studios in Bombay for some years. Her best-known films include *Holi, Dhiraj, Roti, Halchal,* and *Phool.* She contributed imaginative choreography to the film *Lekh.* She left her acting career, however, to concentrate on classical dance.

After a first marriage to the film producer K. Asif, Sitara Devi was remarried to an engineer; their son Ranjit Barot is a well-known jazz percussionist. She also adopted her brother's two daughters Jayantimala and Priyamala and trained them in her style of dancing.

Sitara Devi received the Padamshri award from the government of India, the Kalidasa Sanman, and the Central Sangeet Natak Akademi awards for her services to the world of dance. A film on her life was made by the Films Division of the government of India. She lives in Bombay and continues to delight dance fans with her lively performances, even at an advanced age, winning admiration for her love of life and dance.

BIBLIOGRAPHY

Hall, Fernau. "News from the World." *Ballet Today* (March 1956): 6–7.
Kothari, Sunil. *Kathak: Indian Classical Dance Art.* New Delhi, 1989.
Misra, Susheela. *Some Dancers of India.* New Delhi, 1992.

SUNIL KOTHARI

SKEAPING, MARY (born 15 December 1902 in Woodford, England, died 9 February 1984 in London), dancer, choreographer, teacher, and international authority on seventeenth-, eighteenth-, and nineteenth-century ballet. Skeaping came from a family of musicians, painters, and sculptors, and her approach to dancing was influenced by all of these artistic disciplines.

Her early schooling introduced her to a variety of dance traditions. Among her teachers were the Italian dancer and mime Francesca Zanfretta; the Russian émigrés Laurent Novikoff, Vera Trefilova, and Lubov Egorova; Rudolf Laban; and Margaret Craske, an outstanding English dance teacher. She was one of the earliest members of the Cecchetti Society, to which she maintained a deep loyalty all her life. Skeaping made her debut with Pavlova's company in London in 1925, subsequently dancing with the Nemchinova-Dolin Ballet among others. She spent World War II teaching in South Africa.

Her national and international reputation developed significantly after her dancing days were over, beginning with her staging of the dancers for the film *The Little Ballerina* in 1947. She was ballet mistress of the Sadler's Wells Ballet at Covent Garden, London, from 1949 to 1951, and was responsible for *The Sleeping Beauty* on BBC television in 1951, the first live television transmission of a full-length classical ballet.

Skeaping was director from 1953 to 1962 of the Royal Swedish Ballet in Stockholm, where she produced notable and musically distinguished versions of *Giselle* and *Swan Lake,* as well as *The Sleeping Beauty,* productions she developed later in both Europe and the Americas. In particular, her production of *Giselle* for the London Festival Ballet in 1971 was regarded as definitive. She persuaded Antony Tudor to return to Europe in 1963 to create the most substantial of his later ballets for the Royal Swedish Ballet.

Skeaping's work with the Swedish company enormously enhanced its national and international reputation. From 1956 almost to the day of her death, she and her Swedish dancers gradually established Stockholm as a world center for the creation and study of seventeenth- and eighteenth-century theatrical dance styles, especially the court ballet of seventeenth-century France. This was made possible not only through her own ability as a dance scholar and the support of the Royal Opera House and Royal Swedish Ballet in Stockholm, but also through the archival excellence of the Royal Library and the accident of the perfectly preserved stage machinery and building of the Drottningholm Court Theater outside Stockholm. This included the scenery and costumes of many of Gluck's operas, dating from the reign of the Swedish king Gustavus III in the late eighteenth century. At Drottningholm, using appropriate period lighting and stage effects with her own remarkable choreography in each style, Skeaping created an astonishing series of ballets, bringing to life on stage the historical development of classical ballet from mid-seventeenth-century *ballet de cour (Cupid Out of His Humour)* to the pre-Romantic ballet of the early nineteenth century *(The Return of Springtime).*

In Britain, Skeaping's achievements in historical choreography never achieved the recognition they were given in Sweden, and it was only through her production of *Giselle* in 1971 that she achieved recognition as a leading producer/choreographer of Romantic and Russian classical ballet. Her historical work, however, was extended in Britain through her association with the Royal Ballet's educational section, Ballet for All, directed by Peter Brinson. For the small group of up to six dancers (sometimes only four) and with one or two actors and a pianist, she created from 1965 to 1971 a range of dances from the late sixteenth century to her first version of *The Return of Springtime.* The most important of these was an extract from the fourth part of *Le Ballet de la Nuit,* using the original words and music, which announced the young Louis XIV as the Sun King in 1653; *The Loves of Mars and Venus,* recalling John Weaver's creation of the first *ballet d'action* at Drury Lane Theatre, London, in 1717; a solo for a shepherdess in the style of Jean-Georges Noverre's *Les Petits Riens,* to music by Mozart (1778); and Filippo Taglioni's ballet, *The Return of Springtime,* created in Stockholm in 1918. This last was first staged in Britain with only three dancers (Zephyr, Cupid, and Flora) on 10 September 1965. The following year its full version was presented at Drottningholm on 31 August as part of the theater's bicentennial celebration.

In a similar way, Skeaping worked out some of her choreography and ideas for *Giselle* with the dancers of Ballet for All. She was able to develop her late sixteenth-century dances into a long and striking sequence at the court of Henry VIII in the film *Anne of the Thousand Days* (1970), with Richard Burton as the king.

Skeaping's work with Ballet for All illustrated some of her remarkable personal characteristics: deep historical knowledge based on careful research, generosity in the use of this knowledge, and disinterest in personal reward or fame. What mattered to her was the opportunity to do work she believed in and the chance to create with others who approached work in a similar way and who respected her integrity.

She was made a Member of the Order of the British Empire (MBE) in 1958. From Sweden she received the Order of Vasa (1961), the Carina Ari Medal (1971), and the Royal Gold Medal as the personal gift of the king (1981). Much of her work was filmed, including her creations for Drottningholm. She wrote "Ballet under Three Crowns" in *Dance Perspectives* (1967), *Balett på Stockholmsoperas* with Anna Greta Ståhle (1979), and a translation and annotation, published posthumously, of Gennaro Magri's *Trattato teorico-prattico di Ballo,* printed in Italy in 1778.

[*See also* Sweden, *article on* Theatrical Dance since 1900.]

BIBLIOGRAPHY. Very little has been written about Mary Skeaping. Apart from her own books, the best, necessarily brief, account of her life and work is by Peter Brinson in Skeaping's translation of Gennaro Magri, *Theoretical and Practical Treatise on Dancing* (London, 1988). The most effective records are films of her productions made by Swedish television. A documentary of Skeaping's life was produced for Swedish television in 1984 by G. Andersson and V. Aberle. The reader may also consult the following:

Anastos, Peter. "A Conversation with Mary Skeaping." *Ballet Review* 6.1 (1977–1978): 17–28.

Guest, Ann Hutchinson. "Mary Skeaping." *Dance Chronicle* 7.4 (1984–1985): 484–488.

Harris-Warrick, Rebecca. "Translating Magri." *Dance Chronicle* 12.1 (1989): 140–148.

Koegler, Horst. "The Northern Heirs of Noverre." *Dance and Dancers* (February 1987): 24–26.

Skeaping, Mary. "Ballet under the Three Crowns." *Dance Perspectives,* no. 32 (1967).

Skeaping, Mary, and Anna Greta Ståhle. *Balett på Stockholmsoperan.* Stockholm, 1979.

Woodruff, Dianne L. "On Composing a Period Ballet: A Chat with Mary Skeaping." *Dance Scope* 4 (Spring 1970): 18–25.

PETER BRINSON

SKIBINE, GEORGE (Iurii Borisovich Skibin; born 30 January 1920 in Yasnaya Polyana, Russia, died 14 June 1981 in Dallas, Texas), dancer and choreographer. Skibine was one of the few Romantic dancers of the period after World War II, and a genuine Prince Charming of the ballet of his time. He was tall and elegant, with a handsome face lit up by intensely blue eyes. His most famous roles were the Poet in *La Sonnambula,* the Slave in *Sebastian,* and the tragic king in *Doña Inés de Castro,* as well as Romeo, Daphnis, and other legendary lovers.

The son of dancer Boris Skibine, a member of the Ballets Russes, George (or Youra, as he was known to his friends) was raised in Paris, where he made his debut at sixteen as a can-can dancer at the Bal Tabarin. His teachers were Olga Preobrajenska, Julia Sedova, and Alexandre Volinine. His first triumph came in the role of the Stag in Léonide Massine's *Seventh Symphony* (1938) for the Ballet Russe de Monte Carlo.

After World War II began, Skibine left France and toured with Colonel de Basil's Ballets Russes in Australia and Latin America. He finally reached New York, where he became one of the soloists of Ballet Theatre in 1941. With Alicia Markova he created Massine's *Aleko.* In 1942 he joined the U.S. Army and returned to Europe, participating in the Normandy invasion. After the war he re-

SKIBINE. With Marjorie Tallchief in a pas de deux from his ballet *Le Prince du Désert,* set to a score by Jean-Michel Damase for Le Grand Ballet du Marquis de Cuevas in 1955. (Photograph by Studio Liseg, Paris; from the archives at Jacob's Pillow, Becket, Massachusetts.)

turned to dancing and began a brilliant European career with Le Grand Ballet du Marquis de Cuevas in 1947. He and his wife, Marjorie Tallchief, were ideal partners and the parents of twins, George and Alexander.

In 1949 Skibine created his first choreographic work, *Une Tragédie à Verone,* for the marquis's troupe, and danced it with Ethéry Pagava. It was followed by *Annabel Lee* (1952), *Idylle* (1954), and *Le Prisonnier du Caucase.*

In 1958 Skibine became ballet master and star dancer with the Paris Opera, where he mounted *Daphnis et Chloé,* with sets by Marc Chagall, and Jolivet's *Concerto* for the Opéra-Comique in Paris. From 1964 to 1966 he was the artistic director of the Harkness Ballet; afterward he worked for a period as a freelance choreographer. In 1969 he settled in the United States, where he directed the Civic Ballet and the Dance Academy in Dallas, Texas. Although he is an American citizen, Skibine's art belongs above all to France, the country of his childhood and his early successes.

BIBLIOGRAPHY

Anastos, Peter. "A Conversation with George Skibine." *Ballet Review* 10 (Spring 1982): 68–97.

Glotz, Michel. *George Skibine.* Paris, 1953.

Lidova, Irène. "George Skibine." *Saisons de la danse,* no. 132 (March 1981): 45.

IRÈNE LIDOVA
Translated from French

SKINNER RELEASING TECHNIQUE. *See* Body Therapies, *article on* Skinner Releasing Technique.

SKIRT DANCE. The skirt dance was first introduced around 1876 in British music halls as a solo dance performed by a woman. English choreographer John D'Auban had created the dance for his sister, Marietta, in a production of Charles Lecocq's *La Fille de Mademoiselle Angot.* Whereas some spectators saw the dance as a frivolous waste of time, others admired its graceful quality of movement. Its chief innovator was ballet dancer Kate Vaughan, who, at the Gaity Theatre in London, started to wear a long, flowing skirt instead of a short, stiff tutu. Writers began to call this new dance, in which the dancer delicately used a skirt to frame her body, the skirt dance.

Even though most of the footwork consisted of ballet steps, the skirt dance was not difficult to perform. Because of the length of the skirt, intricate legwork was hidden from the audience's view. A ballet dancer who wore a short tutu was able to show off her artistry and mastery of complex ballet steps. The skirt dancer, on the other hand, was able to conceal her lack of proficiency and dexterity in ballet, and this was why the skirt dance became so popular. Music hall audiences did not appreciate the ballet dancer's "feats and stunts," but the skirt dancer enchanted them with her simple but decorous and skillful skirt manipulations, patterned with gentle gliding across the stage and usually performed to waltz music.

This "modern" dance became the most popular stage dance in music and variety halls in England and the United States from 1888 until about 1910. Music hall producers slipped a skirt dance into a sketch or pantomime whenever they could. Many female performers, including singers and seriocomic actresses, performed some sort of skirt dance as part of their acts, eventually altering the original look of the dance; what began as a serene floating across the dance floor developed into a vulgar stage romp, with high-kicking legs and rustling petticoats.

The skirt dance was performed not only on the stage but also in the ballroom, where it was danced discreetly by sophisticated, society-minded women. It became an accepted social dance because it provided a way in which young girls could be trained to be graceful. At private girls' schools, the skirt dance was taught specifically for that purpose and remained as part of the curriculum for a few years after it ceased to be a popular stage dance.

In the early 1900s the popularity of the skirt dance diminished; the use of the skirt to frame the body was no longer a novelty, and too many dancers had imitated the original form and altered the prudent and stately appearance of the dance. It also ceased to be a solo dance; in its decline the skirt dance was performed by four girls. No longer could it hold the interest of music and variety hall audiences, who wanted to see more girls—and more pairs of legs.

[*For related discussion, see* Music Hall, *article on* British Traditions.]

BIBLIOGRAPHY

Fellom, Martie. "Kate Vaughan: The First Skirt Dancer." In *Proceedings of the Ninth Annual Conference, Society of Dance History Scholars, City College, City University of New York, 14–17 February 1986,* compiled by Christena L. Schlundt. Riverside, Calif., 1986.

Flitch, J.E. Crawford. *Modern Dancing and Dancers.* London, 1912.

Lamb, William. *How and What to Dance.* New York, 1903.

"The Real Skirt Dance." *The Sun* (23 March 1890).

MARTIE FELLOM

SLAVENSKA, MIA (Mia Fedora Dragica Čorak; born 1916 in Brod-na Savi), dancer, teacher, choreographer, and director. Slavenska was born to Milan Čorak, a Croatian pharmacist, and Hedda Palme, daughter of an industrialist of German-Slovak ancestry. Slavenska studied ballet in Zagreb with Josephine Weiss and Margarita Froman and was a child star with the Yugoslav National Opera in Zagreb from the age of seven. Later, she took lessons in Vienna, studying ballet with Leopold Dubois (whom she credited with teaching her "the meaning of classicism") and modern dance with Gertrud Kraus. She then studied in Paris with the Maryinsky-trained Mathilde Kshessinska, Lubov Egorova, and Olga Preobrajenska.

From 1930 to 1933, Slavenska was *prima ballerina* of the Yugoslav National Opera at Zagreb. She spent 1933 and 1934 in Paris with the Opéra Russe. In 1936 she won first prize at the Dance Olympics in Berlin; this was followed by guest appearances in Paris and a tour of Europe and North Africa with her own group. She starred with Serge Lifar, Yvette Chauviré, and Janine Charrat in the 1937 J. A. Benoît-Levy film *La Mort du Cygne,* choreographed by Lifar. Slavenska joined the Ballet Russe de Monte Carlo and toured Europe and the Americas with that company from 1938 to 1941.

In 1942 Slavenska settled permanently in the United States, marrying Kurt Neumann, a political scientist and dance administrator, in 1946, and becoming a citizen in 1947. She developed into one of the strongest technicians of her generation, particularly in *terre-à-terre* work. In her mature years she studied with Vincenzo Celli. Her dancing had great clarity, controlled energy, and stamina. Her balances became legendary. Well-formed, though her legs were not long, she was a beauty who exuded glamor in the classics—such as *Giselle, Coppélia, The Nutcracker, Swan Lake,* and *Don Quixote*—and in works by Ballet Russe choreographers Bronislava Nijinska, Léonide Massine, George Balanchine, and Lifar.

After 1942, Slavenska spent her time in the United States and abroad with her own touring groups (Slavenska and Company, Ballet Variante, Slavenska-Franklin Ballet), which she directed, danced in, and for which she choreographed. However, she continued to appear in ballerina roles with such companies as the Ballet Russe de Monte Carlo, Ballet Theatre, London Festival Ballet, the Metropolitan Opera, and Ruth Page's Chicago Opera Ballet, as well as dancing with symphony orchestras and in summer stock musicals.

Initially, Slavenska was considered suited for worldly rather than spiritual roles, but as her talent matured she became an actress and stylist of wide range. The triumph of her last dancing years was as Blanche Dubois opposite Frederick Franklin's Stanley Kowalski in Valerie Bettis's choreographic version of *A Streetcar Named Desire,* premiered by the Slavenska-Franklin Ballet in 1952. In 1958, Slavenska and Andre Eglevsky appeared with the Joffrey Ballet in Boston, and she also danced in the Saint Louis Municipal Opera's production of *Die Fledermaus.* From 1959 to 1962 she directed the Fort Worth Ballet Arts in Texas, for which she choreographed *Chiaroscuro.*

Slavenska retired from performing in 1963 and concentrated on teaching, first in New York, where she was sought by Yvonne Rainer and other postmodern dancers of the Judson Church group; she then taught in Los Angeles at the California Institute of the Arts, the University of California at Los Angeles, and her own school. She has written an autobiography, which is as yet unpublished.

BIBLIOGRAPHY

Anderson, Jack. *The One and Only: The Ballet Russe de Monte Carlo.* New York, 1981.

Denby, Edwin. *Looking at the Dance* (1949). New York, 1968.

Sorley Walker, Kathrine. *De Basil's Ballets Russes.* London, 1982 and New York, 1983.

Swisher, Viola Hegyi. "Mia Slavenska: A Study in Contrasts." *Dance Magazine* 47 (March 1973): 55–68.

Tallman, Margaret. "Dancescape: Mia Slavenska." *Dance Magazine* (August 1990): 9.

ARCHIVE. Dance Collection, New York Public Library for the Performing Arts.

GEORGE JACKSON

SLEEPING BEAUTY, THE. [*This entry consists of two articles on ballets choreographed to Petr Ilich Tchaikovsky's score: the first is a description of Marius Petipa's original production; the second is a survey of later productions.*]

Petipa Production

Russian title: *Spiashchaia Krasavitsa.* French title: *La Belle au Bois Dormant.* Ballet in three acts, with a prologue and apotheosis. Choreography: Marius Petipa (Enrico Cecchetti, Bluebird pas de deux); Music: Petr Ilich Tchaikovsky. Libretto: Ivan Vsevolozhsky. Scenery: Heinrich Levogt, Ivan Andreyev, Konstantin Ivanov, Matvei Shishov, Mikhail Bocharov. Costumes: Ivan Vsevolozhsky. First performance: 3 [15] January 1890, Maryinsky Theater, Saint Petersburg. Principals: Carlotta Brianza (Princess Aurora), Pavel Gerdt (Prince Désiré), Marie Petipa (Lilac Fairy), Enrico Cecchetti (Carabosse and The Bluebird), Varvara Nikitina (Princess Florine).

In a letter to Tchaikovsky dated 13 May 1888, Ivan Vsevolozhsky wrote, "I have thought of writing a libretto based on Perrault's story 'La Belle au Bois Dormant.' I want to do the *mise-en-scène* in the style of Louis XIV. Here one can give full rein to one's musical imagination and create melodies in the spirit of Lully, Bach, Rameau, and so on. If the idea appeals to you, why don't you undertake the composition of the music?" Vsevolozhsky's libretto was based on only the first part of Charles Perrault's fairy tale, but it proved sufficient to support a full-length ballet, complete with a Prologue and Apotheosis. Each of the ballet's three acts had a brief plot pretext; the action as conceived by the librettist was to unfold as a slow panorama of processions, magic transformations, and a garland of various dances. The idea appealed to Tchaikovsky, as it offered a chance to universalize images, characters, and situations poetically, and the eighteenth-century stylization proved a suitable frame for a balletic symphonic poem. *The Sleeping Beauty* was the high point of ballet in the latter half of the nineteenth century and the peak of Marius Petipa's distinguished career.

During the many years that Petipa had been forced to use the music of Cesare Pugni and Léon Minkus, who were the official composers for the Imperial ballet, he had carefully stored away experience in the symphonization of ballet. When he met Tchaikovsky he was quick to appreciate the important implications of the *Sleeping Beauty* project, and as they discussed the planned scenario Petipa thought in images in which the fundamentals of music and dance were indissolubly merged. Subordinating to the music the crystalized structural forms of contemporary choreography, Petipa breathed life into and spiritualized them. The ballet was built on the principles of the symphonic development of the action. Each of its acts, like the movements of a symphony, was closed in form and could be appraised at its true worth only in relation to the other acts. Only then could one appreciate the dominant message of the ballet: the triumph of good and love over evil and vindictiveness.

For his part Tchaikovsky valued Petipa as a partner. Aware that the development of ballet dramaturgy followed its own rules and principles, he willingly relied on the experience of the venerable choreographer. As a result, the form of *The Sleeping Beauty* became closer to that of a symphony than a drama. The climaxes of the plot were subordinated to the logic and dynamics of the music. Each act had its own epicenter in a musical climax that did not necessarily coincide with a climax of the plot. In the prologue, the adagio and variations of the fairies bringing gifts to the newborn Aurora constitute the peak of the symphonic elaboration of the theme. The climax of the first act is represented by the adagio of Aurora with the four princes. In the second act it is the "Dance of the Nymphs" that has its own focal point in the adagio for Prince Désiré and Aurora. In the third act the climax is represented by the grand *pas de deux* of the protagonists. These central moments of the musical dance action of the ballet were dominated by one and the same theme—love as the source of life and its chief motive force—with different facets of it being presented at a given point in time. It is precisely the complex coincidence of the musical and dance climaxes that made *The Sleeping Beauty* a superlative artistic creation.

In his scenario Petipa laconically outlined the boundaries between different segments of the theme, sometimes also predetermining the character of the dances. The objectives he defined in each episode, for all their brevity of statement, were precise and in their totality exhaustive in detail. Nevertheless, Tchaikovsky's music came as a revelation to Petipa. It gave him what he had long been looking for but could not find: the metaphorical poetry of images, with their multiplicity of meanings, and the overall imagery of an entire ballet. Within the music Petipa found completely new forms for the realization of his original ideas and new expressive possibilities in the vocabulary of classical dance. A jealous custodian of the methods he himself had canonized, Petipa decided on innovations that were in perfect harmony with the symmetry and the

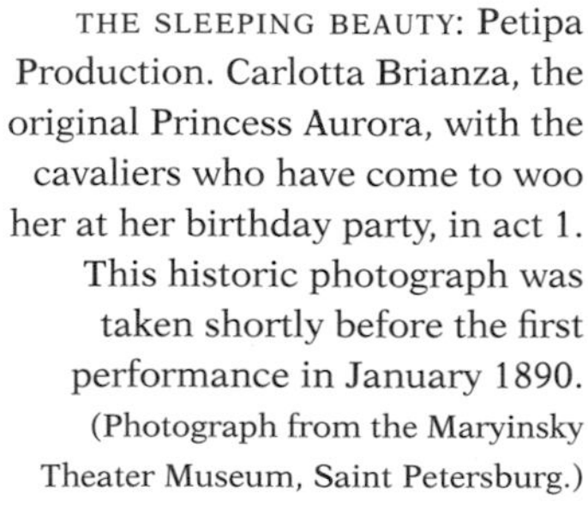

THE SLEEPING BEAUTY: Petipa Production. Carlotta Brianza, the original Princess Aurora, with the cavaliers who have come to woo her at her birthday party, in act 1. This historic photograph was taken shortly before the first performance in January 1890. (Photograph from the Maryinsky Theater Museum, Saint Petersburg.)

order of the dance design, the frontal quality of dance compositions and groupings, and the completeness of dance phrases.

The adagio of the fairies that climaxed the prologue conjured up musical images of childhood, with its naive and joyful perception of the world. The flowing melodiousness of the cradle-adagio suggested that the world is beautiful, not yet clouded by anxieties and troubles. The variations of the fairies branched off from the adagio.

- The tender theme of the first variation was like the awakening of a spring morning, when the ear catches the unclear calls of reality. Petipa softened the Carnation Fairy's *taqueterie* (sharp steps on pointe) by a lulling smoothness of *port de bras*. The florid design of the dance covered the stage in every direction and on the last inquiring note drew itself up in a quivering arabesque, which created the image of a blossoming flower gently swaying on a slender stem.
- The music of the second variation, marked by Petipa in his planned scenario *coulante* ("flowing," "fluid"), caused the dancer to make lashing *ronds de jambe* that whipped the air while her arms quickly opened up above her head.
- The music of the third variation suggested the rustle of spilling grain, and in the dance the movements of the legs modified the staccato quality of the music: the arms incessantly lashed in a capricious pattern, strewing invisible crumbs or shaking drops of dew.
- The clear, resonant whistling and the ethereal flight in the musical characterization of the fourth variation caused the dancer to run across the stage with a mincing, twittering step. Now she folded her arms at her mouth as if wishing to make her inaudible song carry far; now she opened them the way a bird opens its wings, only to fold them again and put them behind her back.
- Petipa marked the fifth variation *échevelée* ("disheveled"), and in Tchaikovsky's music it suggests the suddenness of a summer cloudburst, at once threatening and cheerful. In accordance with the noisy flow of the music, Petipa built the dance on a sharp alternation of movements. The arms tense, with index fingers stretched out and pointing, they cut through the air like flashing lightning.
- The final link in this chain is the *voluptueuse* variation of the Lilac Fairy, a joyful exultant waltz giving rise to a majestic flowing dance. The gay bustle of the "sharp and animated" coda naturally crowned the cluster of variations.

A slow exposition precedes the variations. In a processional march ladies, nobles, and pages fill the palace hall; the major-domo, Catalabutte, looks over the lists of invited fairies and becomes extremely pompous at the entrance of the king and his queen to the strains of solemn music. Following the adagio of the fairies comes the entrance of the fairy Carabosse, at which point the icy breath of winter and death sweep through the music. The grotesque appearance of the evil fairy combines the comic and the fearful. The angular, shrewish old woman mimics the fairies, calling to mind the images of their dances as if distorted by an ugly, spiteful grimace. Carabosse's retinue of freaks, monsters, and rats collects in a gloomy circle around her when she herself breaks into a dance. Monotonously whirling and heavily swinging her body, Carabosse seems to trample underfoot the joyful dances of the good fairies, and her retinue echoes the malicious dance-song accompanied by the same monotonous swaying.

The end of the prologue bridges the first climax and the first aspect of the theme common to the entire ballet. At this point, in the most appropriate way possible, comes a quick succession of short pantomimic moments: the fairies comfort the King and his Queen, the King pardons Catalabutte, then orders the destruction of all needles and spindles in the realm.

The climax of the first act was prepared and completed in the same unhurried way. After the opening comic scene of knitting women, Petipa suggested that Tchaikovsky should provide a peasant waltz, transferring the pantomime into the sphere of dance. Thanks to the music, this transitional movement was converted into an independent dance miniature that became one of Petipa's best creations, the "Garland Dance." Its composition repeats that of many of Petipa's previous corps de ballet ensembles. All is subordinated to the strict symmetry of lines that are converging, diverging, crossing, and swirling in large and small spirals. The dance theme has its own set of harmonic designs; they emerge as combinations of falling and rising figures of the corps de ballet and children (pupils of the theater school). A familiar device, to be sure, but set to Tchaikovsky's music it produced new artistic effects: Petipa's garlands and baskets of flowers are raised, lowered, and swung around by the dancers to create the image of a spring garden in bloom.

The entrance of pages and maids of honor precedes the appearance of Princess Aurora. Petipa's habit of arranging a ceremonial entrance for a ballerina proved to be entirely appropriate. Descending the last step of the grand staircase Aurora begins to dance for the gathering, and her dance seems to illuminate them with the sunrays of daybreak. The music and the dance generalize the motifs of coquetry and shyness, fusing them into a multilayered metaphor of love that underlies life, a young girl's awakening, and daybreak. Petipa matched the standard of Tchaikovsky's creation in the entrance dance of Aurora, her adagio with the four princes, and her variation. For Petipa the word *performance* was identified not with an actor's expressiveness as understood in the dramatic theater, but with the expressiveness of the performing musician—the instrumentalist or vocalist.

Petipa built Aurora's dance with the four princes, the Rose Adagio, as an instrumental ensemble, using the architectonics of his usual *pas d'action.* The dance seems to radiate from a center inside concentric rings. The center is the ballerina's role, comparable to that of a solo instrument in an orchestra. Aurora's dance expresses in general terms the dominant idea, relying, in both a literal and a figurative sense, on the accompaniment of the princes. These five form the adagio's basis, which in turn is framed by a less mobile background consisting of four maids of honor, four "young girls" with lutes, and eight pages with *pochettes* (pocket-sized stringed instruments). The ornamental design of the group changes only upon the completion of passages in the ballerina's dance, forming a kind of harmonic background for the complex, contrapuntal structures of the adagio. Finally, the last circle—the sitting, standing, kneeling, and semirecumbent figures of the king, queen, court servants, and peasants—forms a living but immobile frame for this all-encompassing choreographic picture.

The role of Aurora is dominated by the motif of the *attitude;* standing on pointe in this pose the dancer softly rests her arm on that of a partner. Keeping her balance she hardly moves her body, while the second and then the third and the fourth partners offer her in turn their support. The stately and feminine pose of the *attitude* is repeated four times toward the end of the adagio, only now each partner slowly turns the ballerina as he walks around her. The serenely flowing, upward thrusting lines of Aurora's *attitude* suggest her quiet and happy confidence. The same fluidity and completeness mark the phrasing of Aurora's variation, but the variation individualizes her character in a more concrete way than the adagio. Petipa found for her a charming "everyday" touch within the limits of the rigorously selected devices of classical dance: in the middle of a gay dance Aurora suddenly stops in fifth position and decorously folds her arms in front of her, as if she were a little girl eager to play pranks but suddenly remembering good manners.

In this episode the theme of love predominates, but it differs from the love theme of the prologue. Now, childhood is over; youth has begun, full of strength and eager to come into its own. After the culmination of this theme, the antagonistic theme of the fairy Carabosse enters. When Aurora falls, enveloped by the magic sleep, Petipa stops the dance, letting the composer and the stage designer have the floor. A forest of green trees slowly grows upward as the Lilac Fairy moves fluidly through it, guarding the silence suggested by the music.

The scene of Prince Désiré's hunt opens the second act. A sequence of old dances ends with the entrance of peasants, who blend idyllically with the courtiers in a *farandole.* The dance as the supreme expression of the feelings of the protagonists comes into its own when the composer and the choreographer return to the main theme of the ballet. The Lilac Fairy appears to Prince Désiré to show him a vision of the sleeping Aurora. The love theme enters to motivate the action, as the feeling becomes more definite, now that it has a goal to pursue. The image of the pursuit of an unattainable object is incarnated by Petipa in the adagio of the principals, accompanied by the corps de ballet of nymphs. The clarity and optimism of the adagio could be called classical insofar as the term denotes impeccable, perfect examples of any art.

Suddenly the vision is broken, Aurora disappears, and the nymphs fly away. The dance again retreats before the music and the decor: the Lilac Fairy and Prince Désiré glide in a barque toward the enchanted castle. Once reached, the Prince races up the steps as the curtain falls. Then begins the musical entr'acte, in which the choreographer deferentially yielded primacy to the composer.

The theme of feeling originated in the music-dance climax (adagio) of the first and second acts. However, the symphonic treatment of this theme does not coincide with the climax of the plot—the Prince's battle against the monsters and the awakening of the Princess—but occurs in the third act, which crowns the complex and perfect edifice of the ballet-symphony. The adagio of the hero and heroine, where the theme of love reaches its completion, is the natural culmination. Feeling here finds maturity and fullness. The principal motive-force of life, it is identified in its flowering with the summer flowering of nature. The triumph of this theme is consolidated by the *divertissement,* which is built on the principle of the suite: each section of the suite develops the dominant theme of the ballet with a choreographic miniature, a figurative "roll-call" of all the motifs that have already appeared in the ballet.

- Childhood with its joys and transient sorrows is evoked again in the dance of Tom Thumb and His Brothers and in the duet of Little Red Riding Hood and the Wolf.
- Open, youthful feelings blossom in the pas de deux of Princess Florine and the Bluebird, and are amusingly refracted in the amorous quarrel of the White Cat and Puss-in-Boots.
- A kind of musical *entrée* takes place in the separate variations of the four fairies of precious stones and metals; these form a glittering background for the suite, held together by their recapitulations as they prepare for the adagio of Aurora and Prince Charming.

The fourth adagio completes the central theme of love, becoming the focus of its expression in dance. The motif of the *attitude,* already established as characteristic of Aurora, here receives its maximum development, growing out of the floating, fluid poses, and appears as the stable origin of the dazzling pirouettes. Love's inexhaustible optimism is revealed in the solemn, measured rhythm of the passages and transitions and in the proud, calm affirmation of the central musical-choreographic theme of the entire production. The apotheosis of the love of Aurora and Prince Désiré is also the apotheosis of the symphonic dance imagery attained by Tchaikovsky and Petipa.

More than one hundred years have elapsed since the first performance of *The Sleeping Beauty.* Since then the ballet has been staged by major theaters throughout the world that have a suitably sized stage and a troupe of adequate standard to attempt the production. New scenery and costumes have been created for these productions. For some of them, plot situations of the original production have been altered and some of the scenes, such as that of the knitting women at the beginning of act 1, cut. Passages of music, like the entr'acte of act 2, have also been cut. Mime passages and character and *demi-caractère* dances have been modified. But in all productions, however different they might be from the original Saint Petersburg performance, classical dance, above all the musical-choreographic climaxes of each of the acts, has been left intact.

At the Maryinsky Theater, where *The Sleeping Beauty* had its premiere, the ballet was completely revived by Aleksandr Gorsky in 1914, with scenery by Konstantin Korovin, and by Fedor Lopukhov, who inserted a few new episodes, in 1922, again using Korovin's scenery. In 1952 Konstantin Sergeyev introduced his own versions of the prologue entrance of the Lilac Fairy's retinue and the act 2 hunt scenes and adagio of Aurora and Désiré.

The Sleeping Beauty was first performed at the Bolshoi Theater in 1899, when Gorsky transferred to Moscow Petipa's original production; the scenery and costumes for the production were designed by Anatoly Geltser and Karl Walz. In 1924 the ballet was revived by Vasily Tikhomirov and in 1936 by Asaf Messerer and Aleksandr Chekrygin. In 1952 it was revived by Mikhail Gabovich and Messerer. Yuri Grigorovich provided two different versions of the ballet, in 1963 and in 1973; the scenery on both occasions was designed by Simon Virsaladze.

BIBLIOGRAPHY

Bakhrushin, Yuri. "Balety Chaikovskogo i ikh stsenicheskaia istoriia." In *Chaikovskii i teatr,* edited by A. I. Shaverdiana. Moscow, 1940.

Beaumont, Cyril W. *Complete Book of Ballets.* Rev. ed. London, 1951.

Brown, David. "Tchaikovsky's Ballets: *The Sleeping Beauty.*" *Dance Now* 2 (Summer 1993): 34–41.

Davydova, Kseniia, ed. *Muzykalnoe nasledie Chaikovskogo.* Moscow, 1958.

Guest, Ivor. "An Earlier 'Sleeping Beauty': 'La belle au bois dormant' in the Eighteen Thirties." *Ballet* 12 (April 1952): 36–42.

Guest, Ivor. "The Alhambra Ballet." *Dance Perspectives,* no. 4 (1959).

Kashkin, Nikolai. *Vospominaniia o P.I. Chaikovskom.* Moscow, 1896.

Krasovskaya, Vera. *Russkii baletnyi teatr vtoroi poloviny deviatnadtsatogo veka.* Leningrad, 1963.

Krasovskaya, Vera. "Marius Petipa and *The Sleeping Beauty.*" Translated by Cynthia Read. *Dance Perspectives,* no. 49 (1972).

Krasovskaya, Vera. *Istoriia russkogo baleta.* Leningrad, 1978.

Legat, Nikolai. *The Story of the Russian School.* Translated by Paul Dukes. London, 1932.

Maynard, Olga. "*The Sleeping Beauty:* An Historical Survey." *Dance Magazine* (December 1972): 43–66.

Nocilov, N. I. "Tchaikovsky's Ballets." In *P. I. Chaikovskii na stsene teatra opery i baleta imeni S. M. Kirova,* edited by Aleksandr Brodskii. Leningrad, 1941.

Scholl, Tim. *From Petipa to Balanchine: Classical Revival and the Modernization of Ballet.* New York, 1994.

Shiriaev, Aleksandr. *St. Petersburg Ballet: Memoirs of a Maryinsky Theater Actor.* Leningrad, 1941.

Slonimsky, Yuri. *P. I. Chaikovskii i baletnyi teatr ego vremeni.* Moscow, 1956.

Smakov, Gennady. "Marius Petipa and the Creation of *The Sleeping Beauty.*" In *One Hundred Years of Russian Ballet, 1830–1930,* edited by Nancy Van Norman Baer. New York, 1989.

Tchaikovsky, Petr Ilich. *Correspondence with P. I. Jurgensen.* Moscow, 1952.

Tchaikovsky, Petr Ilich. *Polnoe sobranie sochenii.* Edited by Boris Asafiev. Moscow, 1955.

Tchaikovsky, Petr Ilich. *To My Best Friend: Correspondence between Tchaikovsky and Nadezhda von Meck, 1876–1878.* Translated by Galina von Meck, Oxford, 1993.

Wiley, Roland John. *Tchaikovsky's Ballets: "Swan Lake," "Sleeping Beauty," "Nutcracker."* Oxford, 1985.

Wiley, Roland John, trans. and ed. *A Century of Russian Ballet: Documents and Accounts, 1810–1910.* Oxford, 1990. Includes the libretti for *The Sleeping Beauty,* comments by German Laroche and Alexandre Benois, and a review by Konstantin Skalkovsky.

Wiley, Roland John. "Musical Form in *The Sleeping Beauty.*" *Dance,* no. 16 (October 1990): 31–34.

VERA M. KRASOVSKAYA
Translated from Russian

Later Productions

Although the theme of *The Sleeping Beauty* was treated by Western choreographers prior to the Russian version of 1890 by Marius Petipa and Petr Ilich Tchaikovsky—one example is Jean-Louis Aumer's *La Belle au Bois Dormant* (Paris Opera, 1829)—not one of these works was fated to enjoy the longevity of the Russian version. Petipa's masterwork was first staged in the West at the Teatro alla Scala, Milan, in 1896 by Giorgio Saracco, with Carlotta Brianza re-creating the role of Aurora. Americans saw the ballet for the first time in 1916, in a fifty-minute abridged version presented by Anna Pavlova, with choreography by Ivan Clustine, at the Hippodrome in New York City. Apart from its brevity, this production was notable for its scenery and costumes by Léon Bakst (some of which were later used by Diaghilev's Ballets Russes) and for its enormous number of supernumeraries, a characteristic common to the Hippodrome's offerings. All four scenes of the original were presented in abbreviated form, with the occasional use of a narrator to explain the action. Pavlova

THE SLEEPING BEAUTY: Later Productions. In 1934, Colonel W. de Basil's Ballets Russes de Monte Carlo presented a revival of *Aurora's Wedding,* a pastiche of *divertissements* from *The Sleeping Beauty,* mostly from the last act. Pictured here are Alexandra Danilova, David Lichine, and the full company in the finale of a 1936 performance. The backdrop was designed by Alexandre Bakst. (Photograph from the Dance Collection, New York Public Library for the Performing Arts.)

danced the title role opposite Alexandre Volinine and transformed the wedding pas de deux into a stately *gavotte* executed in heeled shoes.

After having established himself as the apostle of the avant-garde, impresario Serge Diaghilev decided to present *The Sleeping Beauty* as his sole new offering in the 1921 season; this must have seemed as radical a step for him as his modernist experiments had been. Although the ballet was little known in the West, it was recognized as part of the Russian repertory against which Michel Fokine had successfully rebelled. Furthermore, in London, where Diaghilev proposed to present it, it was handicapped by the long association of its theme with traditional English pantomime. Diaghilev may have chosen to change its 1921 title to *The Sleeping Princess* to lessen this association, though he testily claimed to have done so because there were no beauties in his company.

Having made up his mind to espouse the classicism he had once despised, Diaghilev did so with enthusiasm. He engaged Nicholas Sergeyev, a former dancer and ballet master of Russia's Maryinsky Ballet, to reconstruct Petipa's choreography from Stepanov notation. Bronislava Nijinska was charged with the task of choreographing a new *pas d'action* and dances for the hunting scene in act 2, as well as new *divertissements* for the wedding scene. Among the latter was "Innocent Ivan and His Brothers" (also called "The Three Ivans"), a character dance in Russian peasant style performed to the coda from the *grand pas de deux.* Though some observers criticized this dance as incongruous to the courtly setting of the ballet, it became an audience favorite and was revived in many later productions. Nijinska also added the fairy tale of Bluebeard, Ariana, and Sister Anne. In addition, she choreographed several dances from *The Nutcracker* that had been interpolated by Diaghilev and by composer Igor Stravinsky, who worked on the score. The Lilac Fairy danced the Sugarplum Fairy's variation in the prologue, while in the wedding scene *The Nutcracker*'s "Arabian Dance" became a mini-drama for Schéhérazade, the Shah, and his brother; the "Chinese Dance" was recast as a pas de trois for two Porcelain Princesses and a Mandarin. The ballet's design was entrusted to Léon Bakst, who assiduously researched the seventeenth- and eighteenth-century theatrical designs of the Bibiena family in the Bibliothèque Nationale in Paris.

For this ballet, Diaghilev engaged a number of dancers from the Maryinsky Ballet who had fled Russia after the 1917 Revolution. Olga Spessivtseva danced Aurora, alternating with Lubov Egorova, Lydia Lopokova, and Vera Trefilova. Pierre Vladimiroff and Anatole Vilzak alternated as the Prince. Lopokova, who also shared the role of the Lilac Fairy with Nijinska, danced the Bluebird pas de deux with Stanislas Idzikowski. Although Diaghilev had wanted Carlotta Brianza to dance Aurora, she preferred to play the fairy Carabosse, a role later assumed by its creator, Enrico Cecchetti, for a single performance in celebration of the fiftieth anniversary of his stage career.

The ballet was co-produced by Diaghilev and Sir Oswald Stoll at London's Alhambra Theatre. Both hoped that it would rival the successful musical *Chu Chin Chow,* or at least prove a viable competitor to the pantomimes that proliferated during the holiday season. The ballet's

THE SLEEPING BEAUTY: Later Productions. In 1941, the newly formed Ballet Theatre also presented a program of *divertissements* from *The Sleeping Beauty,* mounted for the company by Anton Dolin under the title *Princess Aurora.* Seen here in the title role is Nora Kaye in a 1947 performance. She is partnered in the Rose Adagio by (from left to right) Hugh Laing, Michael Maule, Harry Asmus, and Marvin Krauter. (Photograph © by Fred Fehl; used by permission.)

first performance on 2 November 1921 was, however, marred by mechanical mishaps; the foliage failed to rise at the Lilac Fairy's command, and the gauzes of the panorama piled up into a shapeless jumble—aside from these blemishes, the production was acclaimed as a visual feast. Unfortunately, this approbation did not extend to the action, which the critics found tedious and devoid of dramatic interest. Although some viewers were able to appreciate the fine classical dancing, others found that they missed the spicier meat of Diaghilev's modernist experiments. The ballet ran until February 1922, with full houses during its final performances, but was deemed a failure because it had fallen far short of its projected six-month run and had resulted in financial loss for both Diaghilev and Stoll. [*See* Ballets Russes de Serge Diaghilev.]

Diaghilev did manage to salvage a one-act ballet variously titled *Le Mariage de la Belle au Bois Dormant, Le Mariage d'Aurore,* or *Aurora's Wedding.* Composed mainly of *divertissements* from the wedding scene, it was first presented at the Paris Opera on 18 May 1922 with Vera Trefilova in the title role. Since Bakst's sets had been sequestered by Stoll, it was danced against Alexandre Benois's backdrop for Fokine's *Le Pavillon d'Armide.*

Colonel Wassily de Basil's Ballets Russes de Monte-Carlo, one of the heirs of the Diaghilev company, premiered *Le Mariage d'Aurore* in a slightly revised form in Philadelphia in 1934. This version was augmented by the fairies' solos from the prologue, and the Sugarplum Fairy variation was given to Aurora. Nijinska's Porcelain Princesses and Three Ivans were retained, but the story of Bluebeard and Ariana was transmogrified into a pas de trois for Florestan and His Sisters or for Ariana and Her Brothers, depending on the cast available.

The first full-length version of the ballet in the United States was staged by Catherine Littlefield (who may have seen the de Basil version) for the Philadelphia Ballet in 1937. A more widely traveled American incarnation was Ballet Theatre's *Princess Aurora,* which consisted of the fairies' variations from the prologue, the Rose Adagio from act 1, and a selection of wedding *divertissements,* highlighted by the Bluebird pas de deux. First staged by Anton Dolin after Petipa in 1941, *Princess Aurora* was extensively revised by George Balanchine in 1949. Over the years a succession of ballerinas undertook the demanding role of Aurora, among them Irina Baronova, Alicia Markova, Alicia Alonso, Nora Kaye, and Nana Gollner. The critic Edwin Denby saw this ballet as an active means of educating the American public to the appreciation of classical dancing. As early as 1944, he noted that viewers no longer waited solely for the virtuosic thrills of the Rose Adagio and the Bluebird pas de deux but demonstrated an equal enjoyment of the other dances: proof, he felt, that Americans were ready for longer versions of the classics.

For the British, *The Sleeping Beauty* became a sort of talisman. At the invitation of Ninette de Valois, Nicholas Sergeyev staged it for the Vic-Wells Ballet in 1939, making an effort to restore it to its original form by reinstating Diaghilev's cuts and deleting the interpolated dances. At de Valois's request Nadia Benois, the niece of Alexandre, designed sets and costumes that were simpler and lighter than those of Bakst, though some observers found them lacking in glitter and grandeur. The cast was led by the nineteen-year-old Margot Fonteyn, with Robert Helpmann as her Prince. The production, the company's most ambitious undertaking to date, was a great success with the public.

When, as Sadler's Wells, the company was invited to open the postwar 1946 season at the Royal Opera House, Covent Garden, it chose *The Sleeping Beauty* to celebrate the occasion. New sets and costumes by Oliver Messel gave this production a satisfying air of grandeur. The choreography was supplemented by Frederick Ashton, who created a new "Garland Dance" for act 1 and a pas de trois for Florestan and His Sisters in act 3, while de Valois staged a new version of "The Three Ivans" and the *polonaise.* Fonteyn repeated her triumph as Aurora, displaying a radiance that endeared her to audiences, while Helpmann demonstrated his dramatic versatility by doubling the roles of the Prince and Carabosse.

The Sleeping Beauty was instrumental in the Sadler's Wells Ballet's conquest of the New World in 1949. Fonteyn, as Aurora, was recognized as a ballerina of international standing, and the company as a whole won praise for its classical purity, musicality, and grand manner. *The Sleeping Beauty* was not forgotten after the company became Britain's Royal Ballet; on the contrary, it has been repeatedly revived. In 1968, for example, a new production directed by Peter Wright set it in the medieval period rather than in the seventeenth century, and Ashton created a new Awakening pas de deux for Aurora and her Prince after the spell has been broken.

A certain degree of innovation was introduced by three productions in the early 1990s. Helgi Tomasson's version for the San Francisco Ballet (1990) was set in seventeenth- and eighteenth-century Russia—that is, Russia before and after westernization. In recognition of the increased capacities of male ballet dancers, Tomasson introduced a dance for Aurora's four suitors in act 1 and expanded the act 3 pas de quatre of the Diamond, Sapphire, Gold, and Silver fairies into a pas de six by adding two cavaliers. Crediting part of his inspiration to the cartoonist Winsor McCay, Roland Petit lent a comic-book ambience to his 1990 staging for the Ballet National de Marseille Roland Petit. Aurora's father became a cigar-chomping Groucho Marx–like figure presiding over a court of circus clowns. Aurora herself was somewhat overshadowed by the glamorous Carabosse, played by Zizi Jeanmaire, whose witty solo turns included a Charlie Chaplin impersonation. In 1991, Peter Martins staged a streamlined *Sleeping Beauty* for New York City Ballet, using slide projections on a scrim to achieve spatial and temporal transitions.

The Sleeping Beauty is now recognized as a major test-piece of a company's classical training, and it is performed in its entirety throughout the world. Unlike its counterparts *Swan Lake* and *The Nutcracker,* it has remained relatively free of attempts to reinterpret it in the light of modern psychological findings. Perhaps it owes its stability to the truth of its original story, a truth that is at once simple, telling, and timeless.

THE SLEEPING BEAUTY: Later Productions. Nicholas Sergeyev's full-length production of *The Sleeping Beauty* for the Sadler's Wells Ballet was first performed at the Royal Opera House, Covent Garden, in February 1946. It has remained in the repertory of the Royal Ballet ever since. Pictured here is Deanne Bergsma (aloft) as the Lilac Fairy in a 1960s performance. This scene occurs at the end of the prologue, "The Christening," after the benevolent fairies have bestowed their gifts on the infant princess. (Photograph by Houston Rogers; used by permission of the Board of Trustees of the Theatre Museum, London.)

BIBLIOGRAPHY

Bland, Alexander. *The Royal Ballet: The First Fifty Years.* London, 1981.

Buckle, Richard. *Diaghilev.* New York, 1979.

Cohen, Selma Jeanne, and A. J. Pischl. "American Ballet Theatre, 1940–1960." *Dance Perspectives,* no. 6 (1960).

Gruen, John. "NYCB's Long-Awaited Nod to Petipa: Peter Martins Tackles *The Sleeping Beauty.*" *Dance Magazine* (April 1991): 38–41.

Jordan, Stephanie. "Ashton and *The Sleeping Beauty.*" *Dance Now* 2 (Summer 1993): 43–49.

Kisselgoff, Anna. "A Vision of Beauty." *Ballet Review* 20 (Winter 1992): 18–31.

Koegler, Horst. "Timeless, Uncritical, Opulent, Equivocal." *Ballett International* (June 1995): 40–45.

Lopukhov, Fedor, and Boris Asafiev. "Annals of *The Sleeping Beauty.*" *Ballet Review* 5.4 (1975–1976): 21–43.

Macaulay, Alastair. "The Big Sleep." *The Dancing Times* (May 1990): 805–808.

Macdonald, Nesta. *Diaghilev Observed by Critics in England and the United States, 1911–1929.* New York, 1975.

Money, Keith. *Anna Pavlova: Her Life and Art.* New York, 1982.

Scholl, Tim. "Anticipating a New 'Sleeping Beauty.' " *Ballet Review* 19 (Spring 1991): 43–45.

Sorley Walker, Kathrine. *De Basil's Ballets Russes.* New York, 1983.

Vaughan, David. "Annals of *The Sleeping Beauty:* ABT, 1987." *Ballet Review* 15 (Summer 1987): 107–113.

Vaughan, David. "Peter, Petipa, and Peter Ilyitch." *Ballet Review* 19 (Summer 1991): 23–27.

SUSAN AU

SLONIMSKY, YURI (Iurii Iosifovich Slonimskii; born 13 March 1902 in Saint Petersburg, died 23 April 1978 in Leningrad), dance critic, librettist, teacher, and theorist. Slonimsky was one of the founders of ballet criticism in the Soviet Union and was also actively involved with the practical side of ballet theater. While attending the School of Russian Drama in Petrograd (Saint Petersburg) in 1918, Slonimsky took private dance lessons from students of the ballet school, among them outstanding future choreographers such as Vasily Vainonen and George Balanchine.

Slonimsky made his debut as a ballet critic in 1919, while still a student in the law department of Petrograd University. He ultimately wrote more than four hundred articles on ballet. Slonimsky the critic closely followed the contemporary ballet scene and took great interest in the history and theory of ballet. In his historical and theoretical writings he consistently advocated the idea that dancing itself is the dominant means of expression in ballet and that sentiment and feeling are its specific content, enabling it to reflect the real world. Slonimsky proposed and developed the concept of "choreographic dramaturgy," defining it as a synthesis of libretto, musical score, and dance. In his article "On Ballet Dramaturgy" he concluded that "dance is the criterion in selecting suitable material for dramatic ballets. Anything that is unnatural, artificial, and spurious from the standpoint of artistic truth and verity is unfit for ballet." Slonimsky looked at the entire history of ballet production in the light of this concept. In his works dealing with the history of ballet he concentrated on choreographers such as Charles Didelot and Marius Petipa. He wrote monographs and extensive articles on *La Fille Mal Gardée, La Sylphide, Giselle, Swan Lake,* and *Raymonda.*

Slonimsky was the author of many ballet libretti, notable among which were those for Boris Fenster's *Youth,* Konstantin Sergeyev's *Path of Thunder,* Petr Gusev's *Seven Beauties,* Igor Belsky's *The Coast of Hope* and *Icarus,* and Kasyan Goleizovsky's *Leili and Medzhnun.* He was also a teacher of ballet history. From 1932 onward he taught at the Leningrad Ballet School. In collaboration with Ivan Sollertinsky he compiled a number of syllabi in different disciplines for use at the school. He coauthored the textbook *Fundamentals of Character Dance* with Andrei Lopukhov (1939). In 1937 he joined forces with Fedor Lopukhov in organizing a choreography department at the Leningrad Ballet School, the first of its kind in the history of Soviet ballet, where he lectured on the analysis of ballet productions. In 1922 and 1924, and again between 1932 and 1961, Slonimsky was on the staff of the Leningrad Institute of the History of the Arts (now the Institute of Theater, Music, and Cinematography). In 1959 he was given an honorary doctorate at the Paris Université de la Danse, and from 1962 onward he held a professorship at the department of choreography at the Leningrad Conservatory.

BIBLIOGRAPHY

Cohen, Selma Jeanne. "Yuri Slonimsky." *Dance Chronicle* 2.2 (1978): 148–156.

Slonimsky, Yuri. *The Soviet Ballet.* New York, 1947.

Slonimsky, Yuri. *P. I. Chaikovskii i baletnyi teatr ego vremeni* (Tchaikovsky and the Ballet Theater of His Time). Moscow, 1956.

Slonimsky, Yuri. *Didelot: Vekhi tvorcheskoi biografii* (Didelot: A Lifetime of Creativity). Moscow, 1958.

Slonimsky, Yuri. *V chest' tantsa* (In Honor of Dance). Moscow, 1968.

Slonimsky, Yuri. *Giselle: Etudy* (Giselle: A Study). Leningrad, 1969.

Slonimsky, Yuri. *Baletnie stroki Pushkina* (Balletic Lines in Pushkin). Leningrad, 1974.

Slonimsky, Yuri. *Dramaturgia baletnogo teatra, XIX veka* (Dramaturgy in Nineteenth-Century Ballet Theater). Moscow, 1977.

Oleg A. Petrov
Translated from Russian

SLOVAKIA. *See* Czech Republic and Slovak Republic.

SLOVAK NATIONAL THEATER BALLET. Foreign theater companies brought ballet to Slovakia and to Bratislava in the nineteenth century. The birth of local Slovak ballet, however, was connected to the founding of the Slovak National Theater in Bratislava in 1920. The first ballet production, in 1920, was *Coppélia,* with choreography by a Czech, Václav Kalina. The original seven-member company expanded to thirty dancers after the arrival in 1923 of the Italian director Achille Viscusi, who gave the ballet a firm technical base. The conservative repertory of the Viscusi era, which lasted until 1931, consisted mostly of traditional works and the ballet pantomimes of Oskar Nedbal. Over the course of the 1930s various Czech choreographers directed the company, and the ballet performed primarily *divertissements* for opera and operetta. During the existence of the Slovak state during World War II, the company was directed by the Russian Maksimilijan Froman, a former member of Diaghilev's Ballets Russes and Anna Pavlova's company. Froman enriched the repertory with such works as *The Sleeping Beauty, Raymonda,* and several ballets by Michel Fokine.

The company's postwar development was connected to Czech choreographers Rudolf Macharovský and Stanislav Remar. As ballet director from 1948 to 1955, Remar staged several Soviet dance dramas as well as the first national Slovak ballets, Tibor Andrašovan's *Orpheus and Eurydice* in 1949 and *Song of Peace* in 1950. After Remar, the soloist and first Slovak choreographer, Jozef Zajko, became director. He staged the second full-length Slovak ballet, *Knight's Ballad,* in 1960 (music by Šimon Jurovský). Another Slovak choreographer, Karol Tóth, a graduate of Moscow's State Institute of Theatre Arts, took over in 1961 and built up a wide and varied repertory. Among his best productions were *Path of Thunder* in 1961 (music by Kara-Karajev) and *Rite of Spring* in 1964 (music by Igor Stravinsky).

By the end of the 1960s the company was weakened by the departure of many members to foreign engagements but was then consolidated and rejuvenated under the directorship of Boris Slovák. After 1980 it was again directed by Tóth, who shared the choreography with Zajko, Jozef Dolinský, and various guest choreographers, such as Cuban choreographer Iván Tenorio. In 1990 the critic Emil Bartko became director of the ballet, which under his leadership staged new productions featuring the creations of younger choreographers, such as Libor Vaculík and Ondrej Šoth.

[*See also* Czech Republic and Slovak Republic, *article on* Theatrical Dance.]

BIBLIOGRAPHY

Jaczová, Eva. *Balet Slovenského národného divadla.* Bratislava, 1971.
Masko, Robert. "Slovak National Theater Ballet." *Dance Magazine* (October 1995): 104–105.
Tanec/Dance. Prague, 1991.

VLADIMÍR VAŠUT
Translated from Czech

SLOVENIA. *See* Yugoslavia, *article on* Theatrical Dance since 1991.

SMITH, GEORGE WASHINGTON (born c.1820 in Philadelphia, died 18 February 1899 in Philadelphia), American dancer and choreographer. Like his namesake, George Washington Smith earned a first place in history: that of the first American-born *premier danseur.* Over the course of a sixty-year career as a performer, ballet master, choreographer, and teacher, Smith partnered many of the leading ballerinas who appeared in the United States, introduced many staples of the Romantic repertory to American audiences as well as producing his own choreography in the Romantic style, and extended his talents to the related arts of pantomime, opera, circus, and social dancing.

He made his first appearances as a clog and hornpipe dancer in Philadelphia in the 1830s. The advent of the legendary ballerina Fanny Elssler changed his life. He joined her company, probably in 1841, the second year of her triumphal American tour, and studied with her partner James Sylvain, who taught him not only academic ballet technique but also the standardized role of Harlequin, which he later performed in pantomimes. Elssler gave Smith a deep appreciation of Spanish dancing, which he studied intensively, performed, and frequently utilized in his own choreography.

After leaving Elssler's company, Smith worked in pantomimes such as *Mazulme, or The Black Raven of the Tombs,* to which he returned again and again. He then probably accompanied a fellow Philadelphian, Mary Ann Lee, to Paris, where she studied in 1844 and 1845 with Jean Coralli. Smith was her partner when she returned to the United States to tour with a repertory of Romantic ballets such as *La Fille du Danube* and *La Jolie Fille de Gand.* The pair staged the first American production of *Giselle* in Boston on 1 January 1846, with themselves in the leading roles.

SMITH. A portrait of Smith in Spanish costume. (Photograph from the Dance Collection, New York Public Library for the Performing Arts.)

In 1847 Smith was engaged by the Bowery Theater in New York, where he staged *Giselle* and *Nathalie* (the latter from Elssler's repertory), and partnered Julia Turnbull and Giovanna Ciocca. An engagement in 1850 at the newly opened Brougham's Lyceum in New York brought him a new partner, Louise Ducy-Barre from the Paris Opera.

He was entrusted in 1851 with the difficult task of staging ballets for the American debut of Lola Montez and, apparently, was fairly successful in concealing her deficiencies as a dancer. His *Bloomer Polka,* created for her corps de ballet, won notice as a satire of current fashion.

He struck up a more satisfying partnership in 1853 with the Spanish dancer Pepita Soto. For her he staged *La*

Maja de Seville, first performed on 11 May 1853, which he was to revive repeatedly for other ballerinas. The two also formed a prestigious connection with the renowned opera singers Giulia Grisi and Giovanni Mario; besides presenting incidental dances in operas, they also performed ballet *divertissements* on the singers' nights off.

On 22 May 1855 Smith and Soto presented the first American production of *La Péri* in New York. Smith then returned to pantomime, including *Mazulme,* then rejoined Ducy-Barre for a tour of the American South, followed by an engagement in New York. His ballet *Mose's* [*sic*] *Dream,* presented at the Bowery Theater on 15 June 1857, showed a freer use of imagination than his earlier, more conventional Romantic choreography; it prefigured the ballet spectacles of his later years.

He was in Europe probably during 1857 and 1858, then returned to the United States and joined Domenico Ronzani's ballet company in Philadelphia in June 1859. There, at the age of about forty, he attained his peak as a premier danseur, performing Gringoire (Jules Perrot's own role) in Ronzani's authoritative restaging of Perrot's *Esmeralda,* and Conrad in *Le Corsaire.*

In 1861 he became the ballet master of Frank Rivers's Melodeon Company, producing among other works dances for the extravaganza *The Seven Sisters.* He later staged dances for similar spectacles, among them *The Forty Thieves* and a revival of *The Naiad Queen;* he also supervised several productions of *The Black Crook.* In the 1870s he staged circus dances and marches for Barnum's Roman Hippodrome.

Smith married Mary Coffee in 1854; the couple had ten children. He danced for many years, possibly until as late as 1876. Active also as a teacher throughout his life, in 1881 he opened a studio in Philadelphia, where he taught both ballet and ballroom dancing. One of his most promising pupils was his son Joseph (1875–1932), who, like his father, enjoyed a varied and successful stage career. George Washington Smith left behind a notebook, begun around 1848, that recorded his choreography for various ensemble dances in words, stick figures, and diagrams of floor patterns.

BIBLIOGRAPHY. To date, the only extended monograph on Smith, but one essential to any student of his life and work, is Lillian Moore's "George Washington Smith," *Dance Index* 4 (June–August 1945): 88–135, reprinted in *Chronicles of the American Dance: From the Shakers to Martha Graham,* edited by Paul Magriel (New York, 1948).

SUSAN AU

SMITH, OLIVER (born 13 February 1918 in Waupun, Wisconsin, died in 1994), American stage designer, theatrical producer, and ballet director. As stage designer, producer, and co-director of Ballet Theatre from 1945 to 1980, and again from 1990 onward, Oliver Smith had a manifold effect on the substance as well as the appearance of the burgeoning American ballet and theater traditions. In his own designs for the dance stage he has been identified with a subject matter and style that are specifically American; as an administrator, he helped shape the stylistic eclecticism of American Ballet Theatre.

Smith's first stage designs came about when friends in the Ballet Russe de Monte Carlo encouraged the young painter to try his hand at scenery for Léonide Massine's *Saratoga* (1941). The following year he designed the wide-open prairie spaces of Agnes de Mille's *Rodeo.* A new and different aspect of Americana was given vivid theatrical life in Smith's first work for Ballet Theatre, the landmark collaboration with Leonard Bernstein and Jerome Robbins on *Fancy Free* (1944). The streamlined bar, the tilted lamppost, and the random lights of looming skyscraper windows provided an essential ambience for the jazzy urban idyll of three sailors picking up girls on a summer night—and did it with such suggestive economy that a nearly open stage was reserved for dancing. His skeletal house frame for de Mille's *Fall River Legend* (1948) provided both exterior and interior settings, starkly evocative against a dark sky.

The huge success of *Fancy Free* led the collaborators to expand their work into a Broadway musical, *On the Town,* with Smith as producer as well as set designer. Launched on a Broadway career, he went on to design such shows as *My Fair Lady, West Side Story,* and *Camelot.* Extremely prolific, he designed more than four hundred productions in all areas of dance, theater, and film.

BIBLIOGRAPHY

Barret, Dorothy. "Man Behind the Scenes." *Dance Magazine* (March 1946): 23.

Current Biography (September 1961). Includes an extensive list of works through 1960.

"A Man for All Seasons." *Time* (19 March 1965).

Smith, Oliver. "Ballet Design." *Dance News Annual* (1953): 92–103.

CLAUDIA ROTH PIERPONT

ŠMOK, PAVEL (born 22 October 1927 in Levoča, Czechoslovakia), Czech dancer and choreographer. Šmok began his professional ballet career at an age usually coinciding with a dancer's peak. Before graduating from the dance department of the Prague Conservatory at twenty-six, he finished four semesters at the Prague Technical College and led a short but successful acting career in the Prague E. F. Burian Theater and in films. As a solo dancer of a *demi-caractère* type he danced with the Military Artistic Company of Vít Nejedlý and in the Military Opera (1952–1955), and for another three years in Pilsen, dancing among other roles, Vatslav in *The Fountain of Bakhchisarai* (music by Boris Asafiev), Marko in the

Ochrid Legend (music by Stevan Hristić), and Petia in *Youth* (music by Michail I. Chulaki).

A serious spinal operation sped up Šmok's decision to dedicate himself to choreography. In 1958 he became the *chef de ballet* and choreographer at the state theater in Ústí and Labem, posts he held until 1961. After a somewhat tame beginning he demonstrated his choreographic ability in an expressive production of Victor Bruns's *New Odyssey* (1960). As choreographer in Ostrava from 1961 to 1964, Šmok further freed his imagination from established stereotypes. In Karel Kupka's *Picassiana,* televised locally in 1963, Šmok defined his individual style.

In 1964, together with choreographer Luboš Ogoun and dance critic Vladimír Vašut, Šmok cofounded the independent Studio Ballet Prague, a creative laboratory for contemporary Czechoslovak ballet. Šmok choreographed several new works for the company, and from 1968 to 1970 he served as its director. The outstanding achievement from this period was *Intimate Letters,* performed in 1968 to Leoš Janáček's String Quartet no. 2. After the dissolution of Ballet Prague in 1970, Šmok, together with the core of the company, moved to Switzerland, where he became ballet master of the Basel Ballet. On his return to Czechoslovakia in 1973, he worked as a freelance choreographer, and from 1975 to 1979 he worked for the Prague City Theaters, where in 1977 and 1987 he produced, with a small group of dancers in the Rokoko Theater, evenings of short ballets titled collectively *Contrasts* and *Balletograms.* In 1980 this group became the Prague Chamber Ballet with Šmok as choreographer and artistic director.

In the 1960s, Šmok's works were harsh and hard-edged, full of unexpected contrasts, contentious knots, and athletic movement vocabulary; the dominating aspect was an intellectual creative will and a constructivist ingenuity. The turning point in terms of style came in 1968 with *Intimate Letters,* in which the form—previously aggressive and ostentatious—began to be overshadowed by the content. The movement lost its angularity and the lines became softer and suppler, round and "singing." A further artistic development was evident in Šmok's staging of Antonín Dvořák's *American Quartet* in 1977; it was a tender and simple, purely continuous movement flow in perfect harmony with the music. To Šmok's "quartet file" were later added *Kreutzer Sonata* (1978), set to Janáček's String Quartet no. 1, and *From My Life* (1983), set to Bedřich Smetana's String Quartet no. 1. Both were poetic and dramatic works. Also remarkably dramatic was Šmok's version of Arnold Schoenberg's *Transfigured Night* (1986), and two works choreographed to music by Dvořák: *The Wild Dove* (1993), set to the symphonic poem of the same name, and *Stabat* (1995), set to the first part of the cantata *Stabat Mater.*

Šmok has created more than a hundred ballets, both full length and shorter, of varied character and type; two-thirds of these were done to the music of Czech and Slovak composers, and approximately twenty-five were presented to new scores. Since the end of the 1960s he has been not only the most prolific but also the most individual and the most "Czech" of the local choreographers.

Often invited abroad, Šmok created choreography for companies throughout Germany, in the former Soviet Union, and in Poland and Austria. In 1978 he choreographed Smetana's *Bartered Bride* at the Metropolitan Opera in New York, and a humorous work, *Pavel's Piece,* was choreographed to Mozart's Violin Concerto no. 3 and performed at the American Dance Festival in Durham, North Carolina, in 1988. Šmok has also done guest work for television and film studios, often assuming the dual role of director. From among his television choreographies, Šmok has received prizes for *Understudy* to music by Franz von Suppé, at Montreux in 1978, and for Igor Stravinsky's *The Soldier's Tale* in 1982 and *The Nightingale's Song* in 1983, both at the Golden Prague Festival. In

ŠMOK. Members of the Prague Chamber Ballet in Šmok's *Kreutzer Sonata* (1978). (Photograph courtesy of Vladimír Vašut.)

ŠMOK. Members of the Prague Chamber Ballet in Šmok's *The Wild Dove* (1993), set to music by Dvořák. Throughout his career, Šmok has found inspiration in the music of Czech composers. (Photograph by Ivan Drábek; courtesy of Vladimír Vašut.)

1990, after the so-called Velvet Revolution, Šmok was made a professor on the music faculty of the Prague Academy of Arts.

[*See also* Czech Republic and Slovak Republic, *article on* Theatrical Dance.]

BIBLIOGRAPHY

Hertling, Nele. "Dance Observations between East and West." *Ballet International* 13 (December 1990): 10–13.

Schmidová, Lidka. *Československý balet.* Prague, 1962.

Studio Balet Praha. Mexico City, 1968. In Spanish and English.

Vašut, Vladimír. "Šmok." *Divadlo* 1 (1964).

Vašut, Vladimír. "Prága Balett." *Tánctudományi tanulmánok* (1975): 95–112.

Vašut, Vladimír. "O jednom choreografovi." *Scéna* 7–8 (1978).

Vladimír Vašut
Translated from Czech

SNOEK, HANS (Johanna de Vries-Snoek; born 29 December 1910 in Geertruidenberg, The Netherlands), Dutch dancer, choreographer, and ballet director. Snoek began her dance training at the Folkwang Schule in Essen, Germany. Back in Holland, she started her own school and danced for a short time with the Netherlands Ballet, as well as giving dance recitals of her own. During the German occupation of World War II her dance career stopped temporarily.

After the war Snoek founded a professional dance company for children, the Scapino Ballet (now known as Scapino Rotterdam), and remained its director for twenty-five years. She always had a comprehensive interest in all forms of art. Famous for her never-ending stream of ideas and her boundless energy, she succeeded in persuading many painters, writers, composers, and choreographers to work for her company and got the government to give it financial support.

During the first years of Scapino's existence, Snoek danced many roles and choreographed several ballets, the most important being *De Gouden Zwaan* (The Golden Swan), *De Toverfluit* (The Magic Flute), and *De Pascha en de Beer* (The Pascha and the Bear). She also founded and directed a school for amateurs and a professional dance academy bearing the Scapino name. After her retirement in 1970, she devoted her time to another of her ideals: a theater for children, an aim that was fulfilled in 1976.

Hans Snoek has been lavishly honored for her many services. In 1960 she was given the royal distinction of Knight in the Orde van Oranje-Nassau, being promoted in 1970 to Officer. She received the Leuve Medal of the City of Rotterdam and the first prize for activities in youth theater, which thereafter was called the Hans Snoek Prize.

[*See also* Scapino Rotterdam.]

BIBLIOGRAPHY

Schaik, Eva van. *Op gespannen voet: Geschiedenis van de Nederlandse theaterdans vanaf 1900.* Haarlem, 1981.

Snoek, Hans. *Dance and Ballet.* Amsterdam, 1956.

Voeten, Jessica. *Scapino.* Amsterdam, 1985.

Ine Rietstap

SOCIAL DANCE. [*To discuss the role of social and recreational dance in Western culture, this entry comprises four articles:*

Court and Social Dance before 1800
Nineteenth-Century Social Dance
Twentieth-Century Social Dance before 1960
Twentieth-Century Social Dance since 1960

These articles are supplemented by numerous entries on specific social dances that appear throughout the encyclopedia.]

Court and Social Dance before 1800

Although social dancing has never been the exclusive property of the upper classes, the investigation of social dance before 1800 must focus on the dances of the courts, the nobility, gentry, and well-to-do citizens, for which written documentation exists, in many instances coupled with choreographic notations. While many of the social dances of the lower classes are known by name, the details of their execution—step sequences, pattern, and content—are nebulous at best; this repertory was transmitted mainly in an oral tradition that, although long and venerable, eludes the grasp of precise scholarship.

Social dancing in most cultures is a choreographic activity devoid of ritual meaning (such as dances that incite to war, honor a deity, exorcise demons, or ask for rain, victory, fertility, etc.). It is a form of relaxation after a day's work, a celebration, an expression of *joie de vivre.* It is an orderly, rhythmic activity that allows the participation of all—men and women, young and old, either jointly or in separate groups. It is healthful exercise. It entertains the onlookers and creates a sense of belonging among the participants.

Social dancing can be simple and easygoing or complex and physically demanding. It can be improvised on the spot, led by a musician or dancer whose song or steps are imitated by the rest of the company; it can consist of a sequence of known figures or step-units that the dancers combine according to their personal preference or ability (e.g., the sixteenth-century *galliards, canarios*, and *passamezzos* or the nineteenth-century waltzes and polkas), or it can be preset, that is, fully choreographed by a dancing master, learned in private, and subsequently performed in the ballroom. In every instance social dancing allows the participants to display themselves to best advantage: "as diamonds mov'd more sparkling do appear," as John Davies wrote in his poem *Orchestra* in 1596. Men can show their strength and agility, women their grace, and together they may enjoy the delights of dancing with and for one another.

Our understanding of the techniques of social dance during the 350 years before 1800 for which documentation exists is derived from the primary sources—the dance instruction books, which over time provide increasingly detailed information about the execution of individual steps, their combinations into dance phrases, and the structure of complete choreographies. That the manuals also deal extensively with the codes of accepted behavior on and away from the dance floor and with style and gesture makes them rich sources of information about the social graces of a given period; they rank in importance with the courtesy literature and books on education in conveying information about the post-medieval past.

In social dance, as in any other form of communal artistic expression, each generation creates its own materials and vocabulary; yet, despite stylistic changes, certain fundamental elements remain constant. One such constant is the interaction of men and women on the dance floor. As Thoinot Arbeau observed in his 1588 dance manual *Orchésographie,* "Naturally the male and female seek one another, [and] a mistress is won by the good temper and grace displayed while dancing" (Arbeau, trans. Evans, 1948, p. 12). Medieval and more recent folk traditions do include dances in which the sexes are separated—men dancing with men, women with women—but many of these dances have their roots in ancient religious rites rather than in social dance.

Choreographic shapes provide another constant. Throughout the history of Western social dancing, regardless of time or place, three major categories repeat themselves again and again: line and circle dances, processional dances, and figure dances. Each of these fulfills a specific, definable function.

Line and Circle Dances. Line and particularly circle dances create a sense of unity and community. As Davies (1596, stanza 110) put it,

> All as one in measure do agree,
> Observing perfect uniformity;
> All turn together, all together trace,
> And all together honour and embrace.

The energy of the dance flows from person to person through their linked hands. Line and circle dances are the most relaxed of the social dances; the onlookers' attention is focused not on individual participants but on the group as a whole; steps tend to be few and simple; figures are rare and interrupt the directional continuity only momentarily.

In the Middle Ages, the prime examples of this type of group choreography were the *carole* and the less securely documented *farandole.* In the fifteenth century, the *bassadanza alla fila* appears to have continued the tradition, and further testimony to the form's long-livedness is given by the many round and linear dances depicted in the iconography of the fourteenth and fifteenth centuries. Most of the French *branles* of the late sixteenth century (contained in Arbeau, trans. Evans, 1948) follow the same

SOCIAL DANCE: Court and Social Dance before 1800. Many court dances were danced by one couple at a time, as seen in this detail from a seventeenth-century French engraving, *The Ball,* by Abraham Bosse. (Metropolitan Museum of Art, New York; The Elisha Whittelsey Fund, 1951 [no. 51.501.2268]; used by permission.)

pattern, and reports from Spain attest to the presence of circular *zarabandas.* [*See* Sarabande.] John Playford and his contemporaries in seventeenth-century England created country dances in the round "for as many as will," and the Baroque version of the *branle* flourished at the court of Louis XIV (see the Israel Silvestre plate in Hilton, 1981, p. 14). From eighteenth-century America comes documentation of a "democratic" version of the minuet, danced by a large company in a circle.

Processional Dances. The processional dances emphasize courtly formality. Here, an unlimited number of couples proceed, one behind the other, through the allotted space; the order of rank is strictly maintained. Processional dances were popular from the late Middle Ages to the middle of the seventeenth century. They are absent from the repertory of the eighteenth century but reappear in the grand marches and group polonaises of the nineteenth century.

The main representatives of the processional genre before 1800 are the Burgundian *bassedanse* (fourteenth to sixteenth centuries), the *pavane* (sixteenth to early seventeenth century), and the English measure or *almaine* (late sixteenth to mid-seventeenth century). These last seem to have been somewhat lighter than either the *bassedanse* or *pavane,* and they frequently incorporated simple figures such as place changes, two-hand turns, "sett and turne," and so on. Yet the *bassedanse* and the *pavane* also allowed variety in their step sequences. [*See* Bassedanse *and* Pavan.] In the *bassedanse* this was achieved by means of a complex and carefully thought out system of step groupings *(mesures)* that, while maintaining the processional nature of the choreographies, gave each its own expressive quality. According to Arbeau, the *pavane* was often enlivened by the insertion of accelerated steps:

> Some dancers divide up the double step that follows the two single steps; for in place of the double that occupies four bars notated in four semibreves [roughly equivalent to whole notes], they make it into eight white minims or sixteen black minims [roughly equivalent to half notes and quarter notes] and consequently execute several steps, passages, and flourishes that retain the same cadence and occupy the same amount of time, and such subdivisions and lightly executed foot movements moderate the gravity of the pavane.
>
> (*Orchésographie,* 1588, folio 33)

Customarily, the slow processional stepping dances were followed by quick after-dances: for example, Antonio Cornazano, in his *Libro dell'arte del danzare* (1455–1465), couples the *bassadanza* with a *saltarello;* Arbeau couples the *pavane* with a *galliarde* or a *tordion* (which Arbeau calls a *galliarde par terre*). The processional arrangement of the dancers was not affected by the change of meter and tempo. [*See* Galliard; Saltarello; *and* Tordion.]

Not strictly processional but possibly descended from the earlier processional dances are the English longways "for as many as will" of the seventeenth and early eighteenth centuries. In these, too, an unlimited number of couples set themselves up one behind the other in strict hierarchy of rank. Although many of these choreographies, all of which belong to the country dance genre, begin with a short processional passage ("up a double, back a double, that againe"), their emphasis is on the figures, on an internal progression of the couples down and back up the set while the group as a whole remains stationary. In these English longways the processional type of social dance merges with the third main choreographic category, the figure dances. [*See* Country Dance *and* Longways.]

Figure Dances. From the fifteenth century onward, figure dances are common in dance manuals and dance collections. By definition, all figure dances consist of a succession of ingeniously conceived floor patterns, some purely ornamental in nature, others clearly expressive of a dramatic idea or theme. The hundreds of extant figure dances prior to 1800 can be divided into two distinct groups: performance pieces and participation pieces.

Performance pieces are figure dances designed for soloists or a small ensemble (usually two to eight performers, though sometimes more) and were intended for presentation by courtly dancers, at times assisted by professionals. The category includes the Italian *bassadanze, balli,* and *balletti* of the early Renaissance; *galliardes, passamezzos, pavaniglias*, and *cascardas* (also frequently called *balli* or *balletti*) of the sixteenth century; and *menuets, allemandes, bourrées, sarabandes, gigues,* and *rigaudons* of the Baroque period. The most illustrious choreographers of each successive era—from Domenico da Piacenza and Guglielmo Ebreo to Fabritio Caroso and Cesare Negri, Raoul-Auger Feuillet, Guillaume-Louis Pecour, Mister Isaac, Anthony L'Abbé, and Gennaro Magri—delighted in the creation of such performance pieces, in which the carrier of the activity was the individual dancer, who was given the opportunity to show technical prowess, strength and stamina, grace, poise, and expressiveness.

Because of their technical complexity and the intricacies of their floor patterns, choreographies of this type had to be prepared ahead of presentation time under the guidance of a dancing master, who was often also the choreographer. Many of the patterns stem from a standard repertory of figures: one- and two-hand turns, place changes, S-curves, figure eights, diagonals, winding lines, and circles are present everywhere. The placement of these figures into the space varies from one period to the next.

Most Renaissance figure dances were choreographed with a surrounding audience in mind; they tended to be concentric and could be watched from any place in the ballroom. Some especially attractive choreographies took into account the spectators seated in balconies and galleries: for example, the star and chain patterns of Caroso's "Il Contrapasso Nuovo" (in his *Il ballarino,* 1581 and later editions) and Playford's "Gathering Peascods" (*The English Dancing Master,* 1651) are most advantageously seen from above.

The figure dances of the Baroque era, on the other hand, were composed around a central axis whose orientation point was the "presence": the king, queen, or other ranking personage presiding over the festive event. Entrances and opening and concluding bows were invariably directed toward the presence; the symmetrical configurations were designed for viewing from "the top of the hall" (as in the Baroque figure dances notated in the extant printed and manuscript sources).

Participation dances—that is, figure dances for any number of persons, usually paired in couples—are exemplified by the English country dances and their French counterparts, the *contredanses* (It., *contradanze*). These emphasize floor patterns over steps, as can be seen in the verbal descriptions in Playford and in the various Thompson publications from the mid-eighteenth century, as well as in the Baroque linear notations of choreographies by Feuillet, Dezais, Claude-Marc Magny, and others (regarding the steps to be used, see the introduction to Feuillet's *Recüeil de contredances,* 1706). Because of their relative simplicity, country dances and *contredanses* required little or no preparation outside the ballroom. Only the first two couples who began the action needed to know the figures; the rest of the company could—and was expected to—learn each dance simply by observing the activity at the top.

Between the virtuoso performance pieces and the figure dances for a large company fall the country dances for a set number of performers. Four in a square, six in a circle or in longways formation, and eight in a circle or a square are the most frequent constellations. (The term *square dance* was first used by Playford in the 1651 edition of *The English Dancing Master.*) As in the longways "for as many as will," the steps are kept simple, while the figures show considerable variety. Once established, the tradition of the square dance and the cotillon (early examples of which appeared in the Annual Collections of France in the early eighteenth century; see Brainard, 1986) remained unbroken through the nineteenth century and into the present. The tradition survives in a revival form in Britain, in the contras of New England, in the French-Canadian *contredanses,* and in the square dances popular throughout the United States. [*See* Annual Collections *and* Cotillon.]

Social Dance and the Other Arts. In the three and a half centuries of documented social dancing before 1800, the technique and style of dancing evolved along with the musical accompaniment. The history of dance music is a matter of musicological record: its development proceeds from the earliest notated one- and two-part dance pieces of the thirteenth century through *bassedanse* and *ballo* improvisation by loud and soft Renaissance bands, through the collections of printed dance music for lute, keyboard, and ensembles of various kinds (compiled by Pierre Attaingnant, Ottaviano Petrucci, Tylman Susato, Michael Praetorius, and others), to the splendid sonorities of Baroque orchestras. [*See the entry on Praetorius.*]

As both a pastime and an art, social dancing adhered to the same aesthetic matrices that governed music, poetry, and the decorative arts. As aesthetic concepts changed, so did dance. In the early Renaissance, the tenuous gentleness of Burgundian dancing contrasted with the gaiety and lightness of Italian dances; both were superseded by the assertive vigor of the dances of the late sixteenth century. This in turn was gradually replaced by the delicate yet assured grace of the Baroque—the mental and physical poise (equilibrium) that made even the most difficult step-sequences appear effortless. In the second half of the eighteenth century, the social dances began to show a tendency toward greater simplicity; the split between the ballroom and the stage was by then practically complete.

[*See also* Ballet Technique, History of, *article on* French Court Dance; Renaissance Dance Technique; *and* Technical Manuals, *article on* Publications, 1440–1725.]

BIBLIOGRAPHY

Arbeau, Thoinot. *Orchésographie et traicte en forme de dialogve, par leqvel tovtes personnes pevvent facilement apprendre & practiquer l'honneste exercice des dances.* Langres, 1588, 1589. Reprinted with expanded title, Langres, 1596. Translated into English as *Orchesography* by Mary Stewart Evans. New York, 1948. Reprint with corrections, a new introduction, and notes by Julia Sutton. New York, 1967.

Blume, Friedrich. *Studien zur Vorgeschichte der Orchestersuite im 15. und 16. Jahrhundert* (1925). Hildesheim, 1973.

Brainard, Ingrid. "Der Höfische Tanz: Darstellende Kunst und Höfische Repräsentation." In *Europäische Hofkultur im 16. und 17. Jahrhundert,* edited by August Buck et al. Hamburg, 1981.

Brainard, Ingrid. "Modes, Manners, Movement: The Interaction of Dance and Dress from the Late Middle Ages to the Renaissance." In *Proceedings of the Sixth Annual Conference, Society of Dance History Scholars, the Ohio State University, 11–13 February 1983,* compiled by Christena L. Schlundt. Milwaukee, 1983.

Brainard, Ingrid. "The Art of Courtly Dancing in Transition: Nürnberg, Germ.Nat.Mus.Hs.8842, a Hitherto Unknown German Dance Source." In *Crossroads of Medieval Civilization: The City of Regensburg and Its Intellectual Milieu,* edited by Edelgard E. DuBruck and Karl Heinz Göller. Detroit, 1984.

Brainard, Ingrid. "New Dances for the Ball: The Annual Collections of France and England in the Eighteenth Century." *Early Music* 14.2 (1986): 164–173.

Brainard, Ingrid. "Sir John Davies' *Orchestra* as a Dance Historical Source". In *Songs of the Dove and the Nightingale. Sacred and Secular Music c.900–c.1600,* edited by Greta Mary Hair and Robyn E. Smith, pp. 176–212. Sydney, 1994.

Buckman, Peter. *Let's Dance: Social, Ballroom, and Folk Dancing.* New York, 1979.

Caroso, Fabritio. *Della Nobiltà di Dame.* 1600, 1605. Reissued as *Raccolta di variji balli.* Rome, 1630. Translated into English as *Nobiltà di Dame* by Julia Sutton, Oxford, 1986. Reprint, New York, 1995.

Carter, Françoise. "Dance as a Moral Exercise." In *Guglielmo Ebreo da Pesaro e la danza nelle corti italiane del XV secolo,* edited by Maurizio Padovan. Pisa, 1990.

Corti, Gino. "Cinque balli toscani del cinquecento." *Rivista Italiana di Musicologia* 12.1 (1977): 73–82.

Cottis, Anne. "Women and Dancing after the Restoration." *Historical Dance* 2.6 (1988–1991): 16–20.

Cunningham, James P. *Dancing in the Inns of Court.* London, 1965.

Davies, Sir John. *Orchestra, or, A Poem of Dancing* (1596). London, 1945.

Emmerson, George S. *A Social History of Scottish Dance. Ane Celestial Recreation.* Montreal and London, 1972.

Gerbes, Angelika. "Gottfried Taubert on Social and Theatrical Dance of the Early Eighteenth Century." Ph.D. diss., Ohio State University, 1972.

Gingell, Jane. "Spanish Dance in the Golden Age: The Dance Text of Juan Antonio Jaque." In *Dance in Hispanic Cultures: Proceedings of the Fourteenth Annual Conference, Society of Dance History Scholars, New World School of the Arts, Miami, Florida, 8–10 February 1991,* compiled by Christena L. Schlundt. Riverside, Calif., 1991.

Goff, Moira. "'The Art of Dancing, Demonstrated by Characters and Figures': French and English Sources for Court and Theatre Dance, 1700–1750." *The British Library Journal* 21.2 (Autumn 1995): 202–231.

Guglielmo Ebreo da Pesaro. *On the Practice or Art of Dancing.* Translated and edited by Barbara Sparti. Oxford, 1993.

Harris-Warrick, Rebecca. "Ballroom Dancing at the Court of Louis XIV." *Early Music* 14.1 (1986): 41–49.

Hilton, Wendy. *Dance of Court and Theatre: The French Noble Style, 1690–1725.* Princeton, 1981.

Hilton, Wendy. "Dances to Music by Jean-Baptiste Lully." *Early Music* 14.1 (1986): 51–63.

Hudson, Richard. *The Allemande, the Balletto, and the Tanz.* Cambridge, 1986.

Ingber, Judith Brin. "Jewish Wedding Dances of Europe During the Middle Ages and the Renaissance." In *Proceedings of the Fifth Annual Conference, Society of Dance History Scholars, Harvard University, 13–15 February 1982,* compiled by Christena L. Schlundt. Riverside, Calif., 1982.

Jenyns, Soame. *The Art of Dancing. A Poem in Three Cantos.* London?, 1729.

Jones, Pamela. "Spectacle in Milan: Cesare Negri's Torch Dances." *Early Music* 14.2 (1986): 182–198.

Jones, Pamela. "The Relation between Music and Dance in Cesare Negri's 'Le gratie d'amore' (1602)." 2 vols. Ph.D. diss., University of London, 1988.

Little, Meredith Ellis. "Dance under Louis XIV and XV." *Early Music* 3 (October 1975): 331–340.

Little, Meredith Ellis. "French Court Dance in Germany at the Time of Johann Sebastian Bach: *La Bourgogne* in Paris and Leipzig." In *Report of the Twelfth Congress. International Musicological Society* (Berkeley 1977), edited by Daniel Heartz and Bonnie C. Wade, pp. 730–734. Kassel, 1981.

Marsh, Carol G. "French Court Dance in England, 1706–1740: A Study of the Sources." Ph.D. diss., City University of New York, 1985.

McGee, Timothy J. *Medieval Instrumental Dances.* Bloomington, 1989.

Mullally, Robert. "More about the Measures." *Early Music* 22.3 (1994): 417–438.

Nettl, Paul. *The Story of Dance Music.* New York, 1947.

Padovan, Maurizio. "La danza di corte del XV secolo nei documenti iconografici di area italiana." In *Guglielmo Ebreo da Pesaro e la danza nelle corti italiane del XV secolo,* edited by Maurizio Padovan. Pisa, 1990.

Polk, Keith. "Flemish Wind Bands in the Late Middle Ages: A Study in Improvisatory Performance Practices." Ph.D. diss., University of California, Berkeley, 1968.

Pontremoli, Alessandro, and Patrizia La Rocca. *Il ballare lombardo: Teoria e prassi coreutica nella festa di corte del XV secolo.* Milan, 1987.

Ralph, Richard. *The Life and Works of John Weaver.* London, 1985.

Ramos Smith, Maya. *La danza en México durante la época colonial.* Mexico City, 1979.

Reichart, Sarah Bennett. "The Influence of Eighteenth-Century Social Dance on the Viennese Classical Style." Ph.D. diss., City University of New York, 1984.

Reichart, Sarah Bennett. "The Thuillier Contredanses." In *The Myriad Faces of Dance: Proceedings of the Eighth Annual Conference, Society of Dance History Scholars, University of New Mexico, 15–17 February 1985,* compiled by Christena L. Schlundt. Riverside, Calif., 1985.

Rimmer, Joan. "Foreign Elements in Irish Eighteenth-Century Dance Music." *Historical Dance* 2.4 (1984–1985): 28–35.

Rimmer, Joan. "Dance and Dance Music in the Netherlands in the Eighteenth Century." *Early Music* 14.2 (1986): 209–219.

Rubin, Dorothy. "English Measures and Country Dances: A Comparison." In *The Myriad Faces of Dance: Proceedings of the Eighth Annual Conference, Society of Dance History Scholars, University of New Mexico, 15–17 February 1985,* compiled by Christena L. Schlundt. Riverside, Calif., 1985.

Russell, Craig H. "Lully and French Dance in Imperial Spain: The Long Road from Versailles to Veracruz." In *Dance in Hispanic Cultures: Proceedings of the Fourteenth Annual Conference, Society of Dance History Scholars, New World School of the Arts, Miami, Florida, 8–10 February 1991*, compiled by Christena L. Schlundt. Riverside, Calif., 1991.

Russell, Tilden A. "The Unconventional Dance Minuet: Choreographies of the Menuet d'Exaudet." *Acta Musicologica* 64.2 (1992): 118–138.

Saftien, Volker. Ars Saltandi: *Der Europäische Gesellschaftstanz im Zeitalter der Renaissance und des Barock*. Hildesheim, 1994.

Skeaping, Mary. "Ballet under the Three Crowns." *Dance Perspectives*, no. 32 (1967).

Smith, A. William, trans. and ed. *Fifteenth-Century Dance and Music: The Complete Transcribed Italian Treatises and Collections in the Tradition of Domenico da Piacenza*. 2 vols. Stuyvesant, N.Y., 1995.

Smith, Judy, and Ian Gatiss. "What Did Prince Henry Do with His Feet on Sunday 19 August 1604?" *Early Music* 14.2 (1986): 199–207.

Sparti, Barbara. "Style and Performance in the Social Dances of the Italian Renaissance: Ornamentation, Improvisation, Variation, and Virtuosity." In *Proceedings of the Ninth Annual Conference, Society of Dance History Scholars, City College, City University of New York, 14–17 February 1986*, compiled by Christena L. Schlundt. Riverside, Calif., 1986.

Sparti, Barbara. "Rôti Bouilli: Take Two. 'El Gioioso Fiorito.'" *Studi musicali* 24.2 (1995): 231–261.

Squire, Geoffrey. *Dress and Society, 1560–1970*. New York, 1974.

Stokes, James, and Ingrid Brainard. "'The Olde Measures' in the West Country: John Willoughby's Manuscript." *REED Newsletter* 17.2 (1992): 1–11.

Sutton, Julia. "Triple Pavans: Clues to Some Mysteries in Sixteenth-Century Dance." *Early Music* 14.2 (1986): 174–181.

Taubert, Karl Heinz. *Höfische Tänze: Ihre Geschichte und Choreographie*. Mainz, 1968.

Taubert, Karl Heinz. *Die Anglaise . . . mit dem Portefeuille Englischer Tänze von Joseph Lanz*. Zurich, 1983.

Wagner, Ann. "The Significance of Dance in Sixteenth-Century Courtesy Literature." Ph.D. diss., University of Minnesota, 1980.

Ward, John M. "The English Measure." *Early Music* 14.1 (1986): 15–21.

Ward, John M. "Apropos 'The Olde Measures.'" *REED Newsletter* 18.1 (1993): 2–21.

Wilson, D. R. "Dancing in the Inns of Court." *Historical Dance* 2.5 (1986–1987): 3–16.

INGRID BRAINARD

Nineteenth-Century Social Dance

Sweeping demographic and political changes in nineteenth-century Europe and the United States brought about significant changes in artistic and expressive forms, including dance. Instigated by the development of free enterprise, capitalism, and finally industrialization, this upheaval culminated in the major restructuring of society. Worldwide, the social revolution challenged traditional hierarchical authorities of church and state and irrevocably changed western European communities by altering family, intimate associations, and the polity. The city—bonding a crowd of strangers—loomed as symbol and sign of changing social relationships and patterns of gathering. People recommitted with conscious effort to their families, intimate associations, and religious and governmental structures in order to assert their visibility and power against the threat of machines and factories, clock time and workday schedules, and bureaucratic power structures and loss of autonomy. Associated with this tumultuous period were changes in cultural values that affected expressive forms of interpersonal communication and social rituals reflecting deep social and family relationships. Among the changes in expressive forms were those in dancing.

Dance theorists like Jean-Georges Noverre (1727–1807) and later Carlo Blasis (1803–1878) had already drawn attention to the differences in practice and performance between choreographies danced on the stage and what was conventionally termed "private dancing," choreographies performed in the ballrooms of private homes and salons. The theatrical necessities of dancing on the stage—for example, projection, narrative pantomime, and more comprehensive training—were thought inappropriate to private dancing.

By the first quarter of the nineteenth century, there was an international community of professional dance teachers (who had included the Londoner Thomas Wilson and later the American Charles Durang, the Frenchman Henri Cellarius, and the Englishman turned American Allen Dodworth) as well as physical educators, all of whom were patronized by the bourgeoisie and whose numbers steadily increased, and all of whom had an effect on the definition of private dancing. In the eighteenth century, private dancing had assumed classical training and a knowledge of choreographies for the private ballroom; it served an elite, literate, and reasonably stable population. By the mid-nineteenth century, new masters of dancing with training from classical dance academies (like the Frenchmen Henri Cellarius and Eugène Coulon, both of whom traveled internationally) found burgeoning commercial opportunities in the new cosmopolitan urban environments, where diverse and mobile populations were ready for popular entertainments and to believe the promises of business success and instant social status. These instructors focused not on the separation of theatrical and private standards for dance performance (a separation that was not argued by the 1840s) but on bringing the edifying influences, the reformative attributes and civilizing refinements of society—"the art of dancing"—to broader populations.

Several international developments contributed to the shaping of nineteenth-century social dance. Among them were new dance forms, developments in music for social dance, and the professionalization of dance instruction.

Dance Forms. Nineteenth-century social dance is commonly characterized by a specific repertory of dances. A selection of these dances, with the approximate dates of their rise to broad popularity and their vagaries of spelling, includes the *valtz à trois-tèmps* (c.1800), the galop or *galopade* (c.1829), the *quadrille* (c.1810), the Lancers (c.1817), the Caledonians (c.1820s), the *valse à deux-tèmps* (c.1830s), the polka (theatrical version, c.1840), the *polonez,* or polonaise (c.1830s), the mazurka (c.1830s), the *varsoviana* (c.1853), the Cellarius, or mazurka waltz (c.1830s), the *redowa* (c.1840s), the *cotillion* (new version, c.1830s), the *Schottische* (c.1840s), the Circassian Circle (c.1850s–1860s), and the *maxixe* (c.1890). Many of these dances appeared in several variations; for instance, waltzes were distinctive for the type of steps they employed, and the *redowa* is a waltz form. Some of these dances compounded their forms to produce ever "newer" dances and variations, such as the polka-quadrille.

Social dances of the period reflected contemporary preoccupations, such as reinstatement of national boundaries through the performance of national dances and music; demonstration of sexual roles through various elements of closed couple dancing; and the dangers of uncontrolled emotion through their juxtaposition with sentiment and proper courtship behaviors. These preoccupations provide clues to the function of expressive postures and gestures and of the reasons for their arrangement in the larger choreography of social dance events. Various ideas about practices in couple dancing, for instance, reflect the century's changing ideas about gender roles and the expression and reading of feelings between individuals who now do not know each other as well as they might have in the past. Furthermore, the Romantic movement promoted interest in the past, in feelings of nostalgia, in exoticism, and in folklore study of the arts and philosophy. Early folklorists of the nineteenth century, such as the German brothers Grimm, Jacob Ludwig Carl and Wilhelm Carl, and Sir Walter Scott were particularly interested in the origins of peasant dances and participated in bringing them to the attention of the fashionable world through their research and writings. Exotic and "original" (untouched by modern civilization) dances bolstered the nationalist sentiments that prevailed throughout Europe.

Revolution in Styles and Techniques. Late seventeenth- and eighteenth-century court dance emphasized classical canons of body placement, steps, and spatial patterns ranging from the simple to the complex. Court dance codified a technique for presenting the body in public—the foundation of "polite" behavior—which became increasingly popular throughout the eighteenth century. In the late eighteenth and the early nineteenth century, this technique evolved into the Romantic ballet. It also remained the foundation for nineteenth-century private dancing.

The rationalization of body movement known as the classical style had always required specialized training. Because only the elite had the money and the time for such training, popular dances usually emphasized the spatial figures and general shape of the classical dances over the subtleties of body placement and step vocabulary. The nineteenth-century stylistic "revolution" in social dance reflected this contrast, shifting the emphasis of social dance instruction away from intricate classical steps and patterns toward the precisely executed collective figure, that is, from individual to group expression. Ironically, the dance revolution also paralleled a change in economic conditions that encouraged the emulation of the upper classes and that made it financially expeditious to pursue dance instruction as a means of joining "the right" (commercially viable) social class.

New York society dancing master William B. DeGarmo gave some idea of the development of this "revolution" in social dancing in his *The Dance of Society* (1875), observing that before the Civil War in the United States, dancers learned the classical steps, whereas after the war, the dances of society became differentiated from those of the theater. While some ballroom dancers might be trained in the classical postures, positions, and steps, others might be taught no more than the *pas marché* ("walking step"). According to DeGarmo, contemporary social dancing consisted of "movements at once easy, natural, modest and graceful," which afforded "an exercise sufficiently agreeable to render it conducive to health and pleasure." Theatrical dancing befitted "the genius of Taglioni, Elssler, Grisi, Cerrito and Vestris" and required "in its classic poses, poetical movement, and almost supernatural strength and agility, too much study and strain, even with the most naturally gifted, to admit of its performance off the stage, without considering whether it were expedient or desirable." DeGarmo recalled that twenty-five years earlier the distinction between the dance of the theater and the dance of society had been less clear: "*Entrechats, pas de bourrées, pas de basques, petits battements, pirouettes, chassés, jetés, assemblés,* etc. were then used as quadrille steps, instead of the *pas marché,* which has since been in vogue." It should be noted that printed dance manuals stressed the figures, the order and definition of larger spatial maneuverings, and not classical technique because it was difficult to notate classical steps in words and communicate a sense of verisimilitude.

Anticipating the problems that a popular audience would have in learning ballet steps, the Parisian dancing master Cellarius echoed Blasis on the separation of theatrical and social dance styles. Cellarius de-emphasized practiced "presentation" or performance of classical steps in social dance. The steps and deportment of the dancers were less important than was the ability to convey a sense of smoothness and equilibrium in dancing that often required rapid changes in direction, shifts in step patterns, and management of ladies' gowns.

Other contrasts, too, characterized attitudes toward social dancing in the mid-nineteenth century. The classical, controlled, and closed shape of the square vied with the Romantic, expanded, and dynamic shape of the circle and coupled partners. The classical aesthetic present in the geometric division of space and time patterns in "square" dancing opposed the Romantic aesthetic present in the potentially intoxicating momentum of circle dancing. Durang observed that in new combinations of dances like the polka-quadrille, the music encouraged waltz and polka steps between and during the old figures of the set quadrilles. The polka-quadrille permitted the newest music to enter into the older dance forms, whose repetitive figures were more familiar and controlled the movement of the dancers.

Major Developments in Music for Social Dance. As classical musical instruction and musical instruments became more widely available and more affordable to the middle class, the number of orchestras and bands outside of aristocratic circles grew dramatically. These new musical groups played at large public events, such as the Promenade Concerts at London's Drury Lane and at concerts held at the pleasure gardens in London, Vienna, Copenhagen, and Paris and in German beer gardens and dance halls. Public concerts in the nineteenth century brought the new dance music to the masses, in contrast to eighteenth-century chamber ensembles, often composed of gentlemen musicians, which had played for a select and private company. With warm and captivating melodic lines, played on new instruments like the piano and keyed brass, romantic music for the new dances—waltzes, polonaises, polkas, and mazurkas—enchanted the new concert audiences and dancers and challenged the new composers and conductors of light music, such as the Frenchmen Louis Jullien (1812–1860) and Philippe Musard (1793–1859), the Austrians Johann Strauss (1804–1849) and his sons, Johann the younger (1825–1899), Josef (1827–1870), and Eduard (1835–1916), and their compatriot Joseph Lanner (1801–1843).

During this time, the growth of music publishing houses and music publications made printed music, especially inexpensive sheet music, available to more people. The most popular and fashionable dance music might be

SOCIAL DANCE: Nineteenth Century. The formality of the quadrille, a popular nineteenth-century social dance, as depicted in *Dance of Society* (1875), a treatise by New York dancing master William DeGarmo. (Dance Collection, New York Public Library for the Performing Arts.)

heard even in remote areas. Tours by band and orchestra leaders, including members of the Strauss family and the flamboyant Jullien, helped to popularize their own compositions and other dance music. Also popular were dance arrangements of serious music, including opera themes such as the waltzes and polonaises from Mikhail Glinka's *A Life for the Tsar* (1836) and Petr Tchaikovsky's *Eugene Onegin* (1877).

Professionalization of Dance Teachers. The simplification of dance styles made life easier for the social dancer, but it created serious problems for the dancing master, who, like other artists, had for centuries been in the service of royal courts and the social elite. Without patrons, the livelihood of dancing masters was threatened. The expansion of free enterprise throughout the nineteenth century, and the class disruptions that resulted from it, created economic and social flux—both opportunity and disaster. Public access to dance teachers' "trade secrets," now printed in dance manuals, further reduced their opportunities. To expand their clientele, dance teachers began to emphasize the moral, physically corrective, and novel aspects of their arts. De-emphasis of classical dance technique in social dancing did not mean that the "principles of dancing," the philosophical core of the profession, were to be disregarded. Learning to control the parts of the body was morally valuable and physiologically sound.

Revolutionary wars at the end of the eighteenth century in Europe and America and later nineteenth-century wars in Europe, such as the Crimean War and the Franco-Prussian War, greatly altered the business of teaching dancing. Besides disrupting the court and state academies where the dance masters taught, war also brought a wave of newcomers to the profession: displaced aristocrats, deprived of other means of support, were forced to consider teaching the genteel arts. The numbers of uncredentialed dancing teachers and consequent public fear of social contamination and seduction by unprincipled perpetrators of fraud eventually led to the protective regulation of the teaching profession and the certification of those who were trained or had equivalent professional experience. One example illustrates the international dimension of the cooperative movement to certify dance teachers. On the title page of the new American translation of his *Grammar of the Art of Dancing* (1905), German Friedrich Albert Zorn listed himself as "teacher of Dancing at the Imperial Russian Richelieu-Gymnasium, Odessa, and Member of the German Academy of the Art of Teaching Dancing," and he dedicated the book to the American National Association of Masters of Dancing, United States and Canada.

Improvements in mechanical printing processes made dance publications easier and faster to produce and thus more profitable. New forms of transportation like the steamboat and the train sped and expanded dissemination of dance publications, thereby enabling them to reach wider audiences. As advertising and marketing became more sophisticated, knowledge of dancing and dances reached the public through printed broadsides, newspapers, and magazines. Mail-order houses made the accouterments of the ballroom—ready-made ball gowns and suits, floor treatments, imported decorations, and specialized furniture—widely available for home and club. As national copyright laws extended more comprehensively to verbal descriptions and schematic renderings of social dances as well as to music, the efforts of dancing masters were protected and rewarded. Fundamental in this communication process were homogenized standards for dance teachers and dance forms through which "social dance" became a language and an accepted aspect of international social life.

At the end of the century, the newly defined "social dance" united with other cultural interests: social reform, physical education, recreation, medicine, and nationalistic ceremonies. These connections created new contexts for dancing in society and so promoted the twentieth-century configurations of social dance. Because overlapping generations and more traditional communities continued to retain their own performance elements and occasions for dancing, many aspects of nineteenth-century social dance survived well into the twentieth century.

[*See also* Ball; Cotillon; Polka; Quadrille; *and* Waltz.]

BIBLIOGRAPHY

Blasis, Carlo. *The Code of Terpsichore: A Practical and Historical Treatise on the Ballet, Dancing, and Pantomime.* London, 1828.

DeGarmo, William B. *The Dance of Society.* New York, 1875.

Dodworth, Allen. *Dancing and Its Relations to Education and Social Life.* New York, 1885.

Emmerson, George S. *A Social History of Scottish Dance.* London, 1972.

O'Neil, Rosetta. "The Dodworth Family and Ballroom Dancing in New York." In *Chronicles of the American Dance: From the Shakers to Martha Graham,* edited by Paul Magriel. New York, 1948.

Richardson, Philip. *The Social Dances of the Nineteenth Century in England.* London, 1960.

Schneider, Gretchen. "Using Nineteenth-Century American Social Dance Manuals." *Dance Research Journal* 14.1–2 (1981–1982): 39–42.

Zorn, Friedrich Albert. *Grammatik der Tanzkunst, theoretischer und praktischer: Unterricht in der Tanzkunst und Tanzschreibkunst, oder, Choregraphie.* Leipzig, 1887. Translated by Benjamin P. Coates as *Grammar of the Art of Dancing* (Boston, 1905).

Gretchen Schneider

Twentieth-Century Social Dance before 1960

As commonly used, the term *social dance* describes partnered dancing to musical accompaniment by men and women in contemporary dress on celebratory, secular occasions. These occasions are observed in a variety of settings ranging from the informal house party to the most formal ballroom gala. They involve a variety of dances with a generally agreed upon vocabulary of steps that may be combined at will by the individual couples.

With few exceptions social dances, like folk melodies, are unattributable. They arise from among the more robust, less constrained layers of society to find general acceptance. Almost without exception, these dances, starting with the waltz in the eighteenth century, have been initially denounced for their uninhibitedness by the more conservative elements of the society and just as inevitably have been accepted by them. The resistance arises from the implicit and sometimes blatant demonstrations that these dances make about changing sexual relationships between men and women.

Developed by those on the bottom rungs of the social ladder, social dances are less bound by what is considered acceptable public expression and indicate a change—often a disturbing one—to those charged with maintaining public morals. Denunciations and at times prohibitions by social arbiters, churches, local governments, schools, and established dance teachers are an almost certain sign that the dance embodies a valid social expression.

The popularity of these dances varies widely. Most have a brief vogue like the *maxixe* and the Twist and then disappear. Others such as the fox trot and tango achieve the status of classics and are added to the standard curricula of dance schools. Unlike folk dances, which remain embedded in the culture from which they arise, social dances readily cross national borders and achieve international acceptance. Thus wherever ballroom dancing exists, the Germanic waltz, the American fox trot, and the Argentine tango are found in the repertory of accomplished social dancers.

The first recognized social dance, the waltz, appeared in Austria and Germany toward the end of the eighteenth century, coincident with eroding European monarchical power. The waltz derived from a turning dance known as a *Ländler,* which had been popular for centuries in the countryside. The waltz departed radically from the aristocratic practice of confining participants to intricate and controlled patterns executed at arm's length. In the waltz, each couple embraced and varied the pattern of dance steps to suit themselves. Social dancing arose as an urban custom, which reflected the growing economic and political power of the middle class. Such dancing eventually replaced formal, court-derived dance, but it had little or no effect on country or folk dance. [*See* Waltz.]

While social dancing broke with the imposed restraint of aristocratic dance, it retained the idea of dancing as a civilizing force in the society. For the greater part of the nineteenth century and well into the twentieth, deportment and dance instruction were given equal emphasis.

Instruction and Values. In the United States, Allen Dodworth and his family were the most important teachers of social dance. The Dodworth Academy opened in 1842 and continued active instruction until 1920 in New York City. The system of instruction was codified by Dodworth in 1885 in his *Dancing and Its Relation to Education and Social Life, With a New Method of Instruction Including a Complete Guide to the Cotillion (German) with 250 Figures.* He considered dance instruction to be a means of instilling values that included personal morals as well as social manners; he insisted that the dancing school was "not a place of amusement."

During his fifty years of teaching, Dodworth steadfastly resisted the introduction of "vulgar" elements onto the dance floor. His first *bête noire* was the polka, which was introduced to the United States about 1840; he deplored its grotesque gyrations and continued to defend the inherent worth of cotillions as expressions of proper training and character. [*See* Polka.]

When Dodworth died in 1896, he was succeeded by his nephew, T. George Dodworth, who assumed direction of the academy and revised his uncle's manual in 1905. The standards of behavior were still maintained, although they came under assault by the pre–World War I dance craze that included the introduction of the Turkey Trot, Bunny Hug, and Camel Walk. Traditional dance teachers formed the New York Society of Teachers of Dancing, with Dodworth as its president. The stated aim of the group was to standardize dance instruction, but its real purpose was to ban the new and "vulgar" dances and customs, such as "cutting in," from the ballroom. The latter innovation deftly evaded the social control of the dance card that young ladies carried, on which only the names of approved partners were to be entered dance by dance. Dodworth finally closed the academy in 1920, with the arrival of the jazz age.

The idea of deportment, however attenuated, lingered on among socially approved dance schools, such as that of William deRham in New York. Until the decline of closed-couple "touch" dancing and the rise of detached singles' dancing in the 1960s, he cautioned his young charges not to abandon their female partners until the latter acquired another partner or got married. In contemporary society, however, the idea of dancing as a primarily pleasurable activity superseded the older notion of dance instruction as an educational instrument for inculcating social values.

Dancing Cheek to Cheek. At the turn of the twentieth century, the established dances were the waltz, the two-step, the schottische, the polka, and the Lancers. The two-step, inspired by the marching cadences of John Philip

SOCIAL DANCE: Twentieth Century. A studio portrait of Irene and Vernon Castle. Admired for their elegance and refined manners, the Castles popularized ballroom dancing during the pre–World War I era. (Photograph by Hill Studio, New York; from the Dance Collection, New York Public Library for the Performing Arts.)

Sousa, was especially popular in the United States. While couples embraced quite naturally while performing them, social convention dictated that the embrace not be too close. Even during the vigorous two-step, couples were expected to keep their exuberance under proper control.

The ragtime rhythm that was developed in the Storeyville district of New Orleans during this time posed a distinct challenge to the existing decorum of the ballroom floor. It featured rhythmic accent on the offbeat and spawned a menagerie of animal-titled dances that dispensed with conventional propriety on the dance floor. The Bunny Hug, Turkey Trot, Grizzly Bear, Kangaroo Dip, Camel Walk, and the Snake thrust couples tightly together in athletic embraces.

Instead of the approved positions of the woman's hand on the man's shoulder and the man's hand on the woman's waist, men and women clung to one another's necks and shoulders, bringing them cheek to cheek. They no longer glided across the floor but jogged energetically.

The Grizzly Bear was perhaps the most uninhibited of the dances. The man draws his partner to him with his right arm around her waist and supports the back of her head with the left palm. She responds by sliding her right arm up the middle of his back and the other over his shoulder and around his neck. The alternate clasp has the man wrap the left arm around her neck while still circling the waist with his right. She responds by hooking her hands over his shoulders as if she were preparing to do a chin-up. The tussling pair sets off in a rapid sequence of eight short steps forward, ending with a slightly off-balance sway. Recovering quickly, they repeat the sequence but conclude with a bent-knee dip.

The most prominent ballroom dancers of the second decade of the century were Irene and Vernon Castle. Their lyrical and restrained approach to dancing avoided the more extreme displays seen elsewhere, but they did dance cheek to cheek. As dancing began to extend from private homes and the ballrooms of the rich into clubs and hotels, the Castles gave the movement further impetus by popularizing the late-afternoon tea dance. These *thés dansants,* as they were called, gained an enormous following. Demonstrators of the latest dances like the Castles appeared in the major hotels of Europe and the Americas. [*See the entry on the Castles.*]

Among these demonstrators were Moses Teichman and Rodolfo Guglielmi. Teichman changed his name to Arthur Murray and created a home instruction manual that could be ordered by mail. It offered to teach anyone how to dance in the privacy of his or her own home simply by following the pattern of left and right steps printed in the booklet. [*See the entry on Murray.*] Guglielmi danced on the screen silver as Rudolph Valentino, infusing the tango with smoldering passion.

During this dance-fevered age prior to World War I, dance studios proliferated and prospered. In 1913, one of the few identifiably authored dances appeared and gained the status of a classic. Harry Fox, appearing on Broadway in the *Ziegfeld Follies,* created a dance routine. When it was slowed down by dance teacher Oscar Duryea, it won permanent acceptance as the fox trot.

The move toward less-inhibited social dancing continued after World War I, reflecting the growing independence of women in the society. The seemingly frail, dependent Victorian woman who took to her bed with unexplained maladies was being replaced by the woman seeking horizons outside the home. For women, acquiring the vote, full property rights, and a foothold in the world of commerce accompanied the shedding of bustles, waist clinchers, and layer upon layer of cumbersome clothing. The gliding look of a dance floor in the age of propriety gave way to the bouncy, rollicking appearance of a roomful of couples.

In addition to clothing changes, the average woman began to make a variety of cosmetic changes. These included the frank use of lipstick, rouge, eye makeup, powders, hair coloring, beauty patches, fingernail polish, and moisturizing creams. Once considered the tools of the demimondaine, these beauty aids gradually came into general use without any pejorative implication. The most striking change occurred when long hair was abandoned in favor of the short or "bobbed" style. It was the most radical cosmetic change witnessed in several centuries.

The boyish look that resulted was also reflected in clothing. The normal feminine curves were deemphasized or actively suppressed in favor of a prepubescent look. Skirts were hiked up to the knee, the waistline was dropped to the hip, and sleeves were reduced to a minimum. Rolled silk stockings in pale colors shimmered on legs in high-heeled pumps. Thus dramatically revealed, the limbs were perfectly suited to the arm-swinging, kicking dance that dominated the jazz age: the Charleston.

The Charleston came to widespread attention as part of a 1923 black revue, *Runnin' Wild,* that played on Broadway. Its most characteristic gesture was the rapid closing and spreading of the knees from a crouched position. Arms were simultaneously crossed and uncrossed to touch the opposite knees and be drawn outward and inward with them. In the closed portion of the dance when couples embraced, the torsos rocked buoyantly together, but in a moment dancers would separate to face one another again, kicking one leg straight out while swinging the arms in the opposite direction. Kicks and swings would alternate from one side to the other vigorously. It was jazz-inspired movement and the music was provided by white musicians who tailored the jazz they heard in black clubs to suit a white audience.

SOCIAL DANCE: Twentieth Century. Three dancers performing a characteristic Charleston slide, c.1928. (Photograph from the collection of Sally R. Sommer and William G. Sommer.)

The Charleston was openly flirtatious, with its peekaboo, now-you-see-it-now-you-don't opening and closing of the legs. The liberated limbs that tossed and kicked had a reckless insouciance. The young woman was being openly daring and suggesting her independence from the restraints of clothing and custom that would have made such a dance impossible only a few years before. Other popular dances like the Black Bottom and the Varsity Drag shared a similar energetic impudence.

International Influences. After World War I, elation with peace was mixed with the restraint of Prohibition. Alcoholic beverages, banned after 16 January 1920 from legal manufacture or sale in the United States (by the Eighteenth Amendment and the Volstead Act), became a passionately sought-after commodity. Those who could afford to lived in postwar Europe and vacationed abroad; in the process, they may have learned the tango in Paris, where it had become enormously popular.

The tango had originated in the slums of Buenos Aires. The songs that accompanied it related tales of violence, despair, and disappointment in love. Its slow opening is followed by a heavy second beat and two slightly lighter but stately beats, reflecting the underlying sense of danger, sadness, or apprehension that infuses the songs. Partners facing one another in a conventional waltz posture are light-years away from the tender swaying of the waltz. In the tango, they are like two adversaries locked together in a contest, thrusting legs between one another's and withdrawing as quickly as a fencer might. They stalk side by side to offer a brief pause in the competition. Then it is quickly resumed as the partners each hook one foot in the other's, slightly off the floor, and momentarily rock provocatively. It is a combative dance elegantly encasing the war between the sexes in ritual movement. [*See* Tango.]

Thirsty visitors to Cuba discovered the rumba in Havana; it quickly established itself on ballroom floors. While the upper body is held fairly rigid, the hips roll sinuously, giving the rumba its special piquancy. Unlike the tango, which covers a lot of floor space, the rumba confines itself to a relatively small, boxy area within which the couple moves with suggestive undulations.

The continuing development of jazz, from turn-of-the-century ragtime to big-band swing arrangements, was reflected on the dance floor by a proliferation of dances that arose from the Lindy Hop. The Lindy Hop originated in the Savoy Ballroom in Manhattan's Harlem. Its name refers to aviator Charles Lindbergh's solo flight in 1927, his "hop" across the Atlantic from New York to Paris.

A group of dancers calling themselves the "Four Hundred" (a spoof on Lady Astor's society gatherings) gathered at the Savoy on Tuesday evenings, adding acrobatic footwork to jazz-inspired moves for the Lindy Hop. In the dance, the man's right hand is placed on the woman's waist, and the couple hooks the free hands. A gentle push with the man's right hand sends the woman swinging outward, and she is brought back with a tug on the hooked hand. Variations can involve turns in place as each partner continues to hold one hand—or even both—of the other. As the dance became more popular, combinations proliferated and became even more complex, with the woman leaving her feet to swing high in the air or to slide under the man's legs. Examples of the more acrobatic versions of the dance can be seen in movie musicals of the 1930s and 1940s and on reruns of 1950s and 1960s television shows, such as *American Bandstand*. [*See* Lindy Hop.]

The ballroom style was brought to its highest level in the dancing of Fred Astaire and Ginger Rogers. While they used jazz rhythms, they eschewed the more ungainly tosses and catches of jitterbug devotees. They represented the elegant approach that the Castles had brought to the dance-fevered years prior to World War I.

SOCIAL DANCE: Twentieth Century. Theatricalized performances of social dances in the late twentieth century have revived popular interest in learning the fox trot, waltz, tango, and other ballroom dances. Artistic directors of American Ballroom Theater Pierre Dulaine and Yvonne Marceau appear here in their popular number "The Continental." (Photograph from the archives at Jacob's Pillow, Becket, Massachusetts.

SOCIAL DANCE: Twentieth Century. Acrobatic partnering became characteristic of the Lindy Hop after Frankie Manning created the first airstep c.1935. Here, couples demonstrate spectacular Lindy aerials in a competition. (Photograph from the Dance Collection, New York Public Library for the Performing Arts.)

In the 1940s and 1950s a flood of Latin-inspired dances like the mambo, cha-cha, samba, *merengue,* and *bossa nova* joined the established tango and rumba. These dances had the excitement of rapid rhythm dancing but did not require the almost gymnastic ability that was necessary for the more demanding jitterbug routines. [*See* Samba.]

With the advent of rock-and-roll music in the 1950s, by the 1960s, a new era of nontouch dancing opened. The Twist was the first of the new dances to gain wide acceptance. It was quickly followed by the Frug, the Monkey, the Swim, the Mashed Potato, and dozens of others that appeared and disappeared with regularity.

A new cycle of touch dancing based on the Lindy Hop emerged from Latin clubs in New York City. The leading dance was called the Hustle. With the return of closed-couple touch dancing in the 1970s, classic dances such as the fox trot also made a reappearance, although nontouch dancing dominated discos. When discos (dance clubs that used disc recordings, or records) began to spread from their home base in Paris during the 1960s, they definitively ended the existence of the big bands; those of Benny

Goodman, Tommy Dorsey, Glenn Miller, and Artie Shaw had accompanied social dancing in nightclubs and on records from the swing era of the 1930s through the transitional 1950s.

Professional and Competitive Dancing. While there has always been a wide gulf between professional ballroom dancers and amateurs, these distinctions were formalized by various national associations that set standards, certified classifications, and authorized and graded competitions. In the United States, the National Council of Dance Teacher Organizations sets the standards. The Imperial Society of Teachers of Dancing performs a similar function in England and sets the most universally accepted curriculum in the international style.

Competitions are held regularly. While couples may specialize, to be judged general champions they must include selections from a wide variety of styles.

From its start as a rebellion against the formality of court dancing, social dancing has evolved its own rigorous standards professionally. Of course, competitive dancers represent only a small proportion of social dancers. [*See* Ballroom Dance Competition.] Many more recreational dancers simply enjoy dancing at social functions. For them, the rules are meant to be broken imaginatively. It is from such experimentation that new dances emerge and are perfected in their presentation by the professionals. The process spawns many new dances regularly. The vast majority of these never become generally popular. The exceptions are those that become classics. In each case, though, the dance is an expression of social relations between men and women.

[*See also* United States of America, *overview article and article on* African-American Social Dance. *For related discussion, see* Dance Marathons *and* Round Dancing.]

BIBLIOGRAPHY

Dawson, Jim. *The Twist: The Story of the Song That Changed the World.* Boston, 1995.

Malnig, Julie. *Dancing Till Dawn: A Century of Exhibition Ballroom Dancing.* New York, 1992.

McDonagh, Don. *Dance Fever.* New York, 1979.

McDonagh, Don. "The Evolution of Social Dancing." In *Dance.* New York, 1986. Exhibition catalog, Metropolitan Museum of Art.

Richardson, Philip. *A History of English Ballroom Dancing.* London, 1946.

DON MCDONAGH

Twentieth-Century Social Dance since 1960

In the forty years from 1960 to the end of the century, American dance continued to absorb dance rhythms, movements, and attitudes from the numerous cultural groups that made up its ever-varying population. Following a well-established pattern of diffusion, American social dances originated in urban African-American or Hispanic communities, spread to mainstream America, and then to the world. Pushing this rapid growth were television broadcasts and the distribution of recordings (tape cassettes, records, and compact discs). By far the most crucial aspect of this expansion was the development of the music-video industry, which began in the early 1980s.

Some characteristics of 1960s dances were the limited use of space, with partners facing each other and moving separately, yet dancing in rapport with each other. Body positioning emphasized slightly bent knees that gently bounced, flexible torsos with hips twisted, arms and hands gesturing, and heads nodding or swung in opposition to the arms. The rise of the civil rights and antiwar movements encouraged more group dancing, in which each participant moved individually yet was a part of the throng. Rock-and-roll (a 1950s version of the 1940s jitterbug, which came from the 1930s Lindy Hop) dances were still performed, and closed-couple dancing was done in situations celebrating formal events, such as weddings, proms, or charity balls. In darkened clubs or at parties, couples pressed against each other, twined thighs, and "slow" danced or "dirty" danced to lyrical love ballads sung in tight harmony by groups like the O'Jays.

In 1959, Hank Ballard and the Midnighters recorded "Twist" for King Records. When performing the song live, Ballard and the Midnighters twisted their hips from side to side. Ballard says he is unsure about where they first saw these movements, but the kids (urban African-American youth in their teens and twenties) were already twisting. Twisting hips have always been important in

SOCIAL DANCE: Twentieth Century. A couple doing the Twist in the early 1960s. (Photograph from the Dance Collection, New York Public Library for the Performing Arts.)

African-American vernacular dance, and given the exchanges of song and movement that always occur between singers and their audiences, it is easy to understand how twisting got transformed into a singular dance when the right song arrived.

In 1960 Chubby Checker re-recorded "Twist," copying Ballard's original precisely, even in his vocal intonations. It rose to first place on *Billboard*'s pop-music chart and Checker's name became synonymous with the Twist. What Checker added to his recording were dance instructions: dancers were to twist their feet as if putting out a cigarette and move their hips as if drying off their buttocks on a towel. Performing on television shows such as Dick Clark's *American Bandstand* and *The Ed Sullivan Show,* Checker made the dance accessible to millions of Americans, then to a worldwide public.

The Twist quickly became a worldwide dance craze. The appeal was its utter simplicity; it could be done by anyone, regardless of dancing ability, age, or economic class. It could be danced alone, with a partner, or in a group. The rich and fashionable twisted in clubs like New York's Peppermint Lounge, teenagers twisted on the beach, children twisted in the schoolyard, and "Twisters" danced in Tokyo, Paris, London, and Rio.

By 1964, however, the Twist was supplanted by a series of pantomime dances, such as the Skate, the Swim, the Chicken, and the Pony (to name a few of hundreds). In the Skate, for example, dancers glided their feet as if skating; in the Swim they basically stood in one place, shaking their hips as they made swimming motions with their arms.

Certainly these dances paralleled, and were inspired by, the stylish routines of the singing groups of Motown Records, which had been choreographed by tap dancer Cholly Atkins (a partner of Honi Coles in the tap duo Coles & Atkins). Creating routines for such world-popular groups as Smokey Robinson and the Miracles, the Temptations, and Gladys Knight and the Pips, Atkins developed a style he called "vocal choreography." Because singers had to be able to reach the microphones, Atkins devised dances that kept the performers swaying or bouncing in place as their feet repeated little step-tap/step-tap combinations, and when the singers moved, they were precise and controlled. Atkins always incorporated bits and pieces of older social dances; then fusing highly syncopated small steps and turns with hand gestures that underscored the rhythms, words, and attitudes of the songs, Atkins created the high-energy dances of Motown. In their famous song "Stop in the Name of Love," the Supremes caused audience frenzy merely by stretching out one arm, palm facing out in the gesture "Stop!"—while continuing cute little hip bops. If Atkins's routines were copied by the fans, they provided him with the raw material of witty gestures that kept social dance fresh.

SOCIAL DANCE: Twentieth Century. In the early 1960s, young people still enjoyed dancing cheek-to-cheek, as shown in this 1962 photograph taken at Windham High School, Windham, Maine. (Photograph © 1963 by Stanley Aldrich; used by permission.)

Contrasting with the tightly structured routines of the Motown singers was the raw energy of James Brown's dancing. Brown's style was imitated by younger, energetic, inner-city youth. A personal variation on be-bop or "scat" dancing of the 1940s and 1950s, Brown's greatly admired, energetic dancing featured fast footwork, with rapidly pedalling cross-steps, punctuated by lightning-quick half-split drops to the floor.

Concurrently, fed by maturing baby boomers, civil rights, black consciousness, and anti–Vietnam War movements were growing in the 1960s. People wanted to return to their roots, and African-inspired dances that emphasized loose and flexible spins (the Watusi, the Jerk) became popular. Folk songs and rock-and-roll were the musical styles of choice when "flower children" massed together for "love-in" celebrations of semipolitical events. At the August 1969 Woodstock Music and Art Fair, film clips show people dancing separately in mixed, democratic groups, basically staying in place, bouncing and twisting their hips, and twirling their arms around their bodies or above their heads, with some pantomiming the Jerk.

As the 1970s approached, a new musical style evolved from the full-blown synthesized sounds of Motown productions. Disco music was geared for the burgeoning discothèques opening across the United States. Electronically engineered for vinyl records and big sound systems, disco music was structured around a driving, easy-to-follow 4/4 beat, topped with high, synthesized instrumentals of strings and brass, with a wailing vocal line of repeated vocal incantations.

Dance activity centered around the discothèque or club. Clubs could be small and unpretentious, but most tried to manufacture a spacious, glamorous ambience. The prototypical disco club was "2001" in Brooklyn, which was featured in the movie *Saturday Night Fever* (1977). The club created a flashy otherworldly environment with smoke and fog machines, reflective mirrored balls, banks of blinking lights, a plexiglass dance floor illuminated from underneath, translucent wall panels pulsing with colored lights, and loud music booming from huge speakers. A DJ (disc jockey) played specially formatted, long-playing, fifteen-minute dance records that had longer rhythm sections and shorter vocal interludes. Spinning two turntables, the DJ made smooth transitions from one record to the next, mixing nonstop consistent beats that propelled the dancing. By 1977, more than fifteen thousand discos were operating throughout the United States; by the end of the decade, discos like Tramps and "2001" were franchised; most large motels and hotels across the country ran discos in their basements.

In 1975, when Van McCoy recorded "The Hustle," its immediate success highlighted Hustle dances that were the staple of the disco scene. The basic structure of the Latino-inspired partner Hustle looks like the Lindy Hop cut to half time. Starting in a closed-couple position, partners maintain a one-handed or two-handed hold. A basic push-pull pattern was established in which the woman is spun outward, then pulled back in toward her partner. The various arm wraps, twirls, and lifts could become exceedingly elaborate, resulting in dozens of Hustle variations (a perusal of three disco dance books yields nineteen partner Hustles and nine line Hustles). The disco line dance (one popular version may be seen in *Saturday Night Fever*) was the 1970s update of such 1950s line dances as the Madison and the Stroll. In turn, those 1950s dances had updated and simplified line dances from the 1940s and 1930s. Accompanying the disco craze were numerous regional and national television dance shows, such as *Solid Gold, Soul Train,* and *American Bandstand,* which were first broadcast across America and then Europe.

Toward the end of the 1970s, in opposition to the high-tech slickness of disco, hip-hop dance and rap/scratchin' music erupted. In the same way that graffiti suddenly splashed across walls and subway cars in New York City, hip-hop dancing broke out in parks and on sidewalks. Hip-hop culture (an amalgam of graphic art, dance, poetry, and music) had been developing since the late 1960s in New York City's South Bronx neighborhoods, which were then populated by Hispanics and African Americans. That the *capoeira,* an Angolan-Brazilian martial-arts dance seen throughout South America and the Caribbean, influenced Breaking (break dancing) is revealed in the slashing legwork and emphasis on placing the body upside down. Breaking—as well as Electric Boogie and Popping and Locking (the latter two are West Coast variations of Electric Boogie)—are difficult, exciting, virtuosic, and best done by young, strong males. Called "B" boys, they danced on the break in the music, expanding the idea of breakaway improvisations into a solo dance form.

Performed in a circle by groups (crews) of young dancers, the dancer moves to the circle's center in response to a challenge—one after another or sometimes two at a time. The dancer enters with an oblique, sideways traveling step; then he dives ("breaks") to the floor to execute spins on shoulders, buttocks, or back; he ends in a "freeze," as he twists his legs in pretzel forms. Then he exits the circle.

In Popping and Locking (body popping) the body is segmented, and movement seems to ricochet through the torso and limbs in sharp fragments, locking the joints or muscle groups in millisecond freezes. The Electric Boogie is more fluid and frenetic, and motion races through the body in quicker fragments or smoother waves. By the mid-1980s rap music rather than hip-hop dancing dominated street music, and through the medium of music videos and movies, rap music and hip-hop dancing were disseminated around the world.

At the same time, a smaller slam dance craze developed

SOCIAL DANCE: Twentieth Century. Swirling vapors and a luminous floor were typical of the glitzy atmosphere discothèques provided in the late 1970s and early 1980s. (Photograph by Carolyn Schultz; reprinted from Deats, 1979.)

among American white youths who were copying the fashion of English punks: they wore combat boots, torn jeans, metal-studded dog collars and bracelets, and plaid shirts; they sported shaved heads. Slam dancing, or moshing, in the 1980s was directly descended from punk Pogo dancing. To the aggressive harshness of "hard-core" music (about 160 beats per minute), the dancers jumped up and down (it was like hopping on a pogo stick) to a rapid beat of about 180 per minute. The slam dancer moved to a similar tempo, but he stomped around in the "pit" (an area just in front of the stage designated for slamming), thrashing his arms, elbows out, and head down. Then he slammed or collided into another dancer. One mosher compared it to the thrill of the football tackle or scrum in rugby. Indeed, one function seemed to be males bonding in a ritualized, rough dance-sport, and perhaps because of their generally lighter body weight, few women mosh. One variation is "stage diving": one dancer after another dives off the stage and crash lands on the crowd standing below, trusting that the crowd will catch him and keep him from injury. The crowd cushions the landing, catching the weight on their backs, then passes the diver over their head through the crowd. The dive is reminiscent of the final act of some of the punk or heavy metal bands, where at the concert's end the performers ecstatically destroyed their clothing and instruments and threw the pieces, then themselves, into the crowd. By the end of the 1980s, slam dancing had diminished in popularity, and moshing tended to be done mostly by adolescents in smaller cities or suburban centers.

Concurrently in the 1980s, and in stark contradiction to street dancing, country-western couple dances, such as the Tucson Swing or the C&W Two-Step, and line-couple dances, such as Cotton Eyed Joe or the Texas Ten-Step, enjoyed a surge of popularity. Country-western bars and honky-tonks soon opened across the United States, featuring live bands, which attracted dancers. Then, as the 1980s merged into the 1990s, line dancing became enormously popular. For America's growing population of older single people with leisure time, it offered an ideal social dance situation. These dances were easy to learn and do, since often a caller gave instructions, the music was lively, the dancer could have the pleasure of being part of a group—yet the line allowed each person to remain an individual and dance at his or her own level of expertise.

The pervasive influence of Jamaican reggae music and its rhythms on American social dance began in the 1970s; it kept growing throughout the 1980s. By the beginning of the 1990s, reggae had not only changed the syncopations and tempos of a large segment of hip-hop music and dancing, it had become established as a viable musical form. American interpretations of Jamaican dance concentrated on lower-body motions, hip-and-buttock rotations (called "winding"), and loose rubber-legging, thus deemphasizing movement in the upper torso. Reggae dance had blended easily with indigenous dances like the Funky Butt, the Mooch, and the Grind, which had been around since the beginning of the 1900s. In Washington, D.C., Go-Go, a reggae-inspired music-and-dance form, emerged; in 1988, Chuck Brown's song "The Funky Butt," along with its dance of the same name, became nationally popular.

In the late 1980s and early 1990s, reggae dances such as Bogolo, Peppa Seed, Santa Barbara, Butterfly, Tootsie-Roll, and Skettle enjoyed popularity, as did a free-style, sexy dance called Dance Hall or Ragamuffin. In Miami and the eastern seaboard cities of Baltimore and Atlanta, another music-dance mode was also emerging, known as "Bass" (Miami Bass, Atlanta Bass, etc.). In this form, deep bass notes override the other musical elements. Computer created and digitally engineered in the studio, Bass music stimulated new speaker and soundboard designs that could accommodate the heavy, booming bass, reproducing and amplifying it without distortion.

This driving bass line fused with the powerful accentuation of pelvic thrusts and rotations. Male-female partner dancing and touch dancing became popular once again—but *not* in the previously acceptable configurations. Rarely touching hands, partners twined thighs, danced pelvis to pelvis, knees bent, with elaborate pelvic rotations, while their upper torso tilted away from each other. Or they danced snuggled together, her back and buttocks nestled against the front of his body, grinding to the bass beats. Called "Freestyle," "Freaking," or "Booty" dancing, this style is frankly sensual and tends to be done primarily by adolescents and young adults in the dark environment of their clubs and private parties—emphasizing a primary function of social dancing: to bring the sexes together for safe physical flirtations in public, social situations.

The brief appearance of the lambada in the early 1990s highlighted a growing attraction to Latino and Caribbean-inspired musical rhythms. The lambada was little more than a stripped-down version of some elements of the merengue. A manufactured dance, it had been brought from Brazil to France to America by two French entrepreneurs. Based on the classic step pattern 1-2-3-hold, 1-2-3-hold, done to a quick 4/4 tempo, the lambada featured pelvis-to-pelvis, thigh-twined positions that were already entrenched among younger American dancers; for salsa or merengue dancers, the lambada was merely another variation on what they already knew. For them, the lambada did not sizzle. Advertized as "hot" and "safe sex," the lambada mostly appealed to the middle-aged dancers in the dance studios. The lambada was popular for only a few months and never really heated up the dance floors.

The popularity of the Macarena proved, once again, that the tradition of line dancing in America remains stable. The typical line dance is performed to a 4/4 tempo, and has quarter- or half-turns that face the dancers in various directions, so that they can repeat the phrase. What makes these dances engaging to do are the idiosyncratic interpretations each dancer can bring to the steps. The Macarena is no exception.

The Macarena hit in late 1993, in California first, then Florida and New York City. The Macarena has two sources, and these two traditions became confused. The very simple line dance is as American as the Madison, Stroll, Bus Stop, Electric Slide, country-western line dances, and especially the Hokey Pokey, which the Macarena most strongly resembles. The music derives from a Cuban musical-rhythmical style of the 1960s, which also had a line dance that had, no doubt, come to Cuba from the American cousins. According to a knowledgeable, irate reader of the *New York Times* (Letters to the Editor: 9 September 1996), "El Mozambique" had been created by Pello el Afrakan; it was later reborn as "Azucar" in the 1980s and recorded by the dance band Ritmo Oriental. The music traveled to Spain, where it was simplified and recorded by the singing duo Los Del Rio; subsequently, it became a European hit. In the United States, the most popular remix of Los Del Rio was made by the Bayside Boys, and this is the version most often played for the dance.

In 1996, the Macarena publicity buzz was at its highest pitch, because the dance was done at both the Democratic and the Republican national presidential conventions, a testament to its easiness. In a repeated phrase of sixteen counts, the dancer stays in place shaking the hips to a simple 4/4 tempo. The arms alternate, first right then left: arms stretch out, palm up, palm down; touch the shoulders, sides of the head, front of the hips, and then the buttocks. Swing the hips three times; quarter-turn or half-turn; yell "Hey, Macarena!" and begin again.

Line dancing is a comforting group activity; it may be traced back to the ancient serpentine lines and the circle dances that lie at the heart of social dance activities. In the United States, line dancing probably was influenced by marching bands and cheerleading; undeniably, the chorus lines of Broadway and Hollywood took line dancing to the farthest extremes. Remaining popular, line dancing's current manifestations are sports' half-time entertainments and national cheerleading competitions.

Dance clubs are both those that are fashionable, where people go to see and be seen, and those where serious dancers go to dance. Usually these are two separate places, but the same place can host a different crowd and have a different purpose on different nights of the week. Clubs, however, have been the institutions of learning for popular dance. There have always been groups of committed social dancers who go to clubs to work on their craft, rather than to drink, take drugs, or pick up partners. They keep standards high and set models for new dancers. During the 1980s and 1990s, House music and dance developed in Chicago and New York City. Masters of mixing,

SOCIAL DANCE: Twentieth Century. Barbara Tucker and Brahams ("Bravo") La Fortune, two dedicated New York club dancers who have developed highly individual, virtuosic styles of movement. (Photograph © 1995 by Andrew Eccles; used by permission.)

the DJs manipulated four turntables, CD (compact disc) players, DAT (digital audiotape), reel-to-reel and cassette tapes, drum machines, keyboards, and created dance music (about 120–127 beats per minute). Smoother and more fluid than rap music, House music and dancing assimilated varied styles. Performed to House music in crowded conditions, for example, Breaking elements were smoothed, softened, and transformed. Dances could be done alone, with a partner or a group, or in competitive circles. Movement was reined in to fit into smaller spaces; dancers vaulted down to the floor in quickly rebounding dives; footwork was fast, confined to little space, and played at the edge of balance. Mostly called "FreeStyle," the dances were individualistic and mutated too quickly to acquire a name. However, Lofting, Diving, Whacking, Fast Footwork, Voguing, hip-hop/House are some of the associated dance names. Everything from famous television cartoons, advertisements, motion pictures, and martial-arts films was recycled, satirized, and commented upon in these dances. Unfortunately, in the last part of the 1990s, in response to some club violence, municipal governments began indiscriminately closing *all* clubs, denying access to everyone because of the transgressions of a few.

As the 1990s drew to a close, the influence of Latino rhythms was escalating. In major cities like New York, Miami, and Los Angeles, salsa dancing was becoming popular once again, as it had been in the 1950s, and elements of the mambo and merengue were being recycled through other popular dance forms. Reflecting the increasing demographics from Latino and Caribbean immigration to the United States that is projected for the twenty-first century, the Latino connection may well continue to flavor American, and then worldwide, popular dancing in upcoming decades.

BIBLIOGRAPHY

Deats, Randy. *Dancing Disco.* WGBH Educational Foundation, 1979.

Emery, Lynn Fauley. *Black Dance.* Rev. ed. Princeton, 1988.

Henry, Tricia. *Break All Rules: Punk Rock and the Making of a Style.* Ann Arbor, 1989.

Malnig, Julie. *Dancing till Dawn.* Storrs, Conn., 1992.

Malone, Jacqui. *Steppin' on the Blues.* Urbana, Ill., 1996.

Sommer, Sally. "Check Your Body at the Door." *Dance Ink* (Winter 1994).

Sommer, Sally. "DOA: Lambada in America." *Village Voice* (30 January 1990), p. 91.

Sommer, Sally. "House You." *Village Voice* (25 April 1995), pp. 87–94.

Sommer, Sally R. "Night in the Slammer." *Village Voice* (18 January 1993), pp. 29–31.

Stearns, Marshall, and Jean Stearns. *Jazz Dance.* Rev. ed. New York, 1994.

Villari, Jack, and Kathleen Villari. *The Official Guide to Disco Dance Steps.* New Brunswick, N.J., 1978.

FILMS AND VIDEOTAPES. *Beat Street* (1986). Margaret Selby, *Everybody Dance Now!* (WNET-TV, New York, 1991). *History of Rock 'n Roll* (WGBH-TV, Boston, 1996). *Saturday Night Fever* (1977). *Searching for the Perfect Beat* (Channel 4, London, 1993). Mura Dehn, *The Spirit Moves* (© Eiko and Koma, held in the Dance Collection of the New York Public Library). Ron Mann, *Twist* (Sphinx Films, Newline [video]; Oktober Film, New York [film], 1994). Art Cromwell, *Watch Me Move* (KCET-TV, Los Angeles, 1989).

SALLY R. SOMMER

SOKOLOVA, LYDIA (Hilda Munnings; born 4 March 1896 in Wanstead, Essex, died 5 February 1974 in Sevenoaks, Kent), English dancer, teacher, and writer. Born Hilda Munnings, Lydia Sokolova was listed as Muningsova with Serge Diaghilev's company in 1913 and 1914; in 1915 Diaghilev changed her name to Lydia Sokolova. Trained at Stedman's Academy and by Mikhail Mordkin, Anna Pavlova, Aleksandr Shiriaev, Ivan Clustine, and Enrico Cecchetti, Sokolova made her professional debut in the corps de ballet of *Alice in Wonderland* at the Savoy Theatre in 1910. She joined Mordkin's All-Star Imperial Russian Ballet for a United States tour in 1911 and 1912, and Theodore Koslov's company for a London engagement and tour of Germany and Austria-Hungary in 1912 and 1913.

In 1913 Sokolova was taken into Diaghilev's Ballets Russes, and with a few interruptions (a wartime separation, which she spent dancing in various shows in London, 1914–1915; brief participation in Léonide Massine's London programs, and other small ventures, 1922–1923; later periods of illness) she remained with the company until its dissolution in 1929. Though she worked under all of Diaghilev's major choreographers, Sokolova is identified, and identified herself, as a Massine dancer, part of that generation of witty, vigorous actor-dancers, including Lydia Lopokova, Stanislas Idzikowski, and Leon Woizikowski, who dominated the company in the years immediately after World War I. "I responded to [Massine's] type of movement," she wrote in *Dancing for Diaghilev,* "because the whole system of it seemed to be part of me."

In keeping with Massine's style, Sokolova was essentially a character dancer—indeed, the company's foremost female character dancer in the early 1920s—her chief gifts being strength, vivacity, dramatic piquancy (particularly in comic and grotesque roles), and endurance. She was habitually given taxing assignments, the prime example being her most famous role, the Chosen Virgin in Massine's *Le Sacre du Printemps* (1920). Further roles created on her by Massine were the Tarantella Dancer in *La Boutique Fantasque* (1919), Death in *Le Chant du Rossignol* (1920), the Tarantella Dancer in *Le Astuzie Femminili* (1920), and the Friend in *Les Matelots* (1925). The role of the Miller's Wife in Massine's *Le Tricorne* (1919) was also created on her and danced by her with tremendous success, but it was first performed by Tamara Karsavina.

Other roles originated by Sokolova were the Apple Woman in Nijinsky's *Till Eulenspiegel* (1916), the Gray Girl in Nijinska's *Les Biches* (1924), Perlouse in Nijinska's *Le Train Bleu* (1924), the Nurse in Nijinska and Balanchine's *Romeo and Juliet* (1926), and Goddess in Balanchine's *Triumph of Neptune* (1926). Her repertory included, in addition, Ta-Hor in *Cléopâtre,* Papillon and Columbine in *Le Carnaval,* the Ballerina in *Petrouchka,* the leader of the Bacchantes in *Narcisse,* Chloé in *Daphnis et Chloé,* Felicità in *Les Femmes de Bonne Humeur,* Kikimora in *Contes Russes,* Pimpinella in *Pulcinella,* the Cherry Blossom Fairy and Red Riding Hood in *The Sleeping Princess,* the Hostess in *Les Biches,* and the Peasant Woman in *Barabau.*

After the disbanding of the Diaghilev company in 1929, Sokolova danced little. In July 1962 she returned to the stage to take the role of the Marquise Silvestra in the Royal Ballet's revival of *Les Femmes de Bonne Humeur* (The Good-Humored Ladies). Otherwise her ballet-related activities were confined primarily to teaching, arranging dances for various programs, and, in later years, assisting the Royal Academy of Dancing and producing an occasional article or lecture on the Diaghilev period. In 1960, with the help of Richard Buckle, she published her *Dancing for Diaghilev,* one of the very best of the Ballets Russes memoirs: a sane and, at the same time, highly atmospheric account, full of bright detail and offering a fairer, more credible portrait of Diaghilev than can be found elsewhere. Sokolova was not, as is often claimed, the first English dancer in the Diaghilev company (Hilda Bewicke preceded her), but she was the first English star of the company and thereby helped to persuade the English and other publics that balletic skill was not an exclusively Russian gift.

BIBLIOGRAPHY

Buckle, Richard. *In the Wake of Diaghilev.* New York, 1983.

Garafola, Lynn. *Diaghilev's Ballets Russes.* New York, 1989.

Sokolova, Lydia. "The Rôle." In *Footnotes to the Ballet,* edited by Caryl Brahms. New York, 1936.

Sokolova, Lydia. *Dancing for Diaghilev.* Edited by Richard Buckle. London, 1960.

JOAN ACOCELLA

SOKOLOW, ANNA (born 9 February 1910 in Hartford), American dancer, teacher, and choreographer. Sokolow, the daughter of Russian immigrants, grew up on the Lower East Side of New York City. She first studied dance with Elsa Phol at the Emanuel Sisterhood Settlement House. Then, from the age of fifteen, she studied at the Neighborhood Playhouse with Blanche Talmud and Bird Larson, and later with Martha Graham and Louis Horst. Also at the Playhouse, she took classes in acting, music, painting, and stage design, and she performed with the Playhouse's Junior Players. From 1938 to 1939 Sokolow studied ballet with Margaret Curtis at the Metropolitan Opera Ballet School.

Sokolow was a member of Graham's company between 1930 and 1938, concurrently working as Horst's assistant in his choreography classes at the Playhouse. Her technique remained rooted in Graham throughout her career. Sokolow began presenting her own work in the early 1930s. Her company, the Dance Unit, performed for labor unions and workers' organizations under the auspices of the Workers' Dance League. Sokolow's work of this period reflected the social concerns of Depression-era America and the turbulent political situation in Europe from an openly Left perspective, often with a satiric edge. Works included *Strange American Funeral* (1935) to music by Elie Siegmeister; 1935; *Four Little Salon Pieces* (1936), to music by Dmitri Shostakovich; *Slaughter of the Innocents* (1937), to music by Alex North; and *Facade* (1937), also to music by North and created while Sokolow was a summer fellow at Bennington College.

In 1939 Sokolow and a company of twelve traveled to Mexico for a short engagement. Their performances sparked great interest in modern dance. At the invitation of the Ministry of Public Education, Sokolow stayed for eight months to teach, choreograph, and organize Mexico's first modern dance company. The fifteen dancers were, and some still are, affectionately referred to as "Sokolovas" although they never appeared under that name on any program. Later, the nucleus of this company became part of a larger group, La Paloma Azul (The Blue Dove). For the next nine years, Sokolow spent more than six months of each year working in Mexico.

Sokolow entered a new phase of her career in 1953 with *Lyric Suite,* to music by Alban Berg. It was the first of many works she would do about the alienation and despair of modern urban life. She brought the experience of over twenty years of solo dancing to the development of each characterization in *Lyric Suite.* The choreography, like the music, is in suite form. There is no narrative line. The parts are related by the underlying emotional pull of the work. In 1955 Sokolow created *Rooms,* her brilliant masterwork set to music by Kenyon Hopkins. Although similar in format, *Rooms* has a much clearer narrative line, creating a dramatic whole. The dance is performed with chairs onstage, each chair representing a character in his or her isolated city room.

Her comic work, *A Short Lecture and Demonstration on the Evolution of Ragtime as Presented by Jelly Roll Morton* (1952), to music by Morton, was done for a Danny Daniels concert and was later toured by Agnes de Mille's company. In 1954, retired from performing, Sokolow re-formed her company in the United States. Other works of this period included *Poem* (1956), to music by Aleksandr Scriabin; *Metamorphosis* (1957), to music by Hopkins; *Season for*

SOKOLOW. A dramatic moment in the second section, "The Beast Is in the Garden," of Sokolow's solo *The Exile* (1939). (Photograph © by Barbara Morgan; used by permission of the Barbara Morgan Archives, Hastings-on-Hudson, New York.)

Six (1958), to music by Teo Macero; and *Dreams* (1961), to music by Anton Webern, Macero, and Johann Sebastian Bach. She returned to Mexico in 1960 to stage *Opus '60,* to music by Macero, and in 1961 to stage *Dreams* and *Musical Offering,* the latter to music by Bach, for Bellas Artes.

At the behest of the American Fund for Israel Institutions Sokolow went to Israel in 1953 to teach and professionalize a fledgling Yemenite dance company, Inbal Dance Theater. Thus began another period of regular commuting to a foreign country to teach and choreograph. Increasingly interested in integrating dance, drama, and music, in 1962 Sokolow founded Lyric Theatre in Israel with ten actor-dancers. This was the prototype of Sokolow's subsequent American companies of various names, including, since 1971, Anna Sokolow's Players Project. Works for those groups and others included *Ballade* (1964), to music by Scriabin; *Odes* (1964), to music by Alexander Boskovich, revised in 1965 to music by Edgard Varèse; *Opus '65,* to music by Macero, for the Joffrey Ballet; *Time + 6,* (1966) to music by Macero, for the Boston Ballet; *Memories* (1967), to music by Macero, revised in 1968 to music by Tadeusz Baird; *Tribute* (1968), to music by Bach, in memory of Martin Luther King, Jr; *Echoes* (1969), to music by John Weinzweig, for the Juilliard Dance Ensemble; *Act Without Words, No. 1* (1969), to music by Joel Thome; *Scenes from the Music of Charles Ives* (1971), for the Juilliard Dance Ensemble; *Magritte, Magritte* (1972), to music by Scriabin, Maurice Ravel, Franz Liszt, Erik Satie, and Thome; *Moods* (1975), to music by György Ligeti, for Contemporary Dance System; *La Noche de los Mayas* (1977), to music by Silvestre Revueltas, for the Sophie Maslow Dance Company; and *Homage to Edgar Allan Poe* (1985), to music by Sergei Rachmaninov.

Sokolow has choreographed such television and Broadway shows as *Street Scene* in 1947, *Regina* in 1949, *Camino Real* in 1953 and *Candide* in 1956. She also has choreographed or directed many off-Broadway and regional productions. She did the original choreography for the musical *Hair* but withdrew before it opened. She has taught at American Theater Wing, School of American Ballet, Connecticut College Summer School of Dance, Juilliard, and at other schools and universities around the world. A noted teacher of movement to actors, Sokolow has taught at the Actors Studio and the Herbert Berghof School of Acting. Her works, among the most popular in the modern dance repertory, have been performed throughout the United States and Europe, as well as in Mexico, Israel, Peru, Venezuela, Australia, and China. She currently teaches and choreographs in New York City.

Among the many honors and awards Sokolow has received are the Aztec Eagle Honor (the highest civilian honor awarded in Mexico to a foreigner) in 1988, the Samuel Scripps Award in 1991, and admission into the American Academy of Arts and Letters in 1993.

BIBLIOGRAPHY

"Anna Sokolow." *Dance Magazine* (March 1962): 34.

Beck, Jill. "Anna Sokolow's *Scenes from the Music of Charles Ives:* A Critical Analysis." *Dance Notation Journal* 3 (Spring 1985): 9–67.

Bissell, Robyn. "*Rooms:* An Analysis." *Dance Notation Journal* 1 (January 1983): 18–34.

Cook, Ray, and Ann Hutchinson Guest, eds. "*Ballade.*" Yverdon, Switzerland, 1993.

Current Biography. New York, 1969.

Lloyd, Margaret. *The Borzoi Book of Modern Dance.* New York, 1949.

Reynolds, Nancy, and Susan Reimer-Torn. "Rooms." In *Dance Classics.* Pennington, N.J., 1991.

Schmitz, Nancy Brooks. "Catherine Littlefield and Anna Sokolow: Artists Reflecting Society in the 1930s." In *Dance: Current Selected Research,* vol. 1, edited by Lynnette Y. Overby and James H. Humphrey. New York, 1989.

Siegel, Marcia B. "Anna Sokolow (Rooms)." In Siegel's *The Shapes of Change.* New York, 1979.

Sokolow, Anna. "The Rebel and the Bourgeois." In *The Modern Dance: Seven Statements of Belief,* edited by Selma Jeanne Cohen. Middletown, Conn., 1966.

Sokolow, Anna. *Ballade.* Philadelphia, 1993.

Stodelle, Ernestine. "Anna Sokolow, Spokesman for the Psyche." *Ballet Review* 23 (Spring 1995): 33–39.

Warren, Larry. *Anna Sokolow: The Rebellious Spirit.* Princeton, 1991.

DARCY HALL

SOLOMON ISLANDS. *See* Melanesia.

SOLOVIEV, YURI (Iurii Vladimirovich Solov'ev; born 10 August 1940 in Leningrad, died 12 January 1977 in Leningrad), dancer. Soloviev graduated from the Leningrad Choreographic Institute, where he studied under Boris Shavrov, in 1958 and immediately joined the

Kirov Ballet, remaining with the company until his death, purportedly by suicide. His virile and soaring style was tempered with lyricism and sincerity. The major roles in his career were those that symbolized the character of the Russian people, such as the creative artisan Danila in Yuri Grigorovich's *The Stone Flower* (1957), the patriotic Fisherman in Igor Belsky's *The Coast of Hope* (1959), and the Young Man in his *Leningrad Symphony* (1961). Soloviev danced in most premieres and revivals at the theater, portraying the Prince in Konstantin Sergeyev's *Cinderella* in 1945 and Man in his *Distant Planet* (1963), the Brave Warrior in Leonid Yakobson's *Land of Miracles* (1967), and the title role in Belsky's *Icarus* (1974), among others. He also commanded a full repertory of classical roles. Famed primarily as a brilliant virtuoso, Soloviev was not known initially for expressiveness, but his spectacular success in the character role of God in Natalia Kasatkina and Vladimir Vasiliov's *The Creation of the World* (1971) evidenced a talent for grotesque dance and comedy. The range and power of Soloviev's style conveyed especially well the drama and uplifting heroism of *Leningrad Symphony*. His portrayal of the courageous fighter, an indomitable champion of his country, was among the highest achievements of Soviet performing arts.

SOLOVIEV. Famed for his extraordinary elevation and *ballon*, Soloviev excelled in such demanding solos as that of the Bluebird in *The Sleeping Beauty*. (Photograph from the Dance Collection, New York Public Library for the Performing Arts.)

Soloviev's awards included first prize of the International Festival of Youth and Students in Vienna in 1959, the Nijinsky Prize in Paris in 1963, first prize of the International Festival of Dance in Paris in 1965, and People's Artist of the USSR in 1973.

BIBLIOGRAPHY

Krasovskaya, Vera. "Iurii Solov'ev." *Sovetskii balet*, no. 3 (1983).

Lin'kova, L. "Iuri Solov'ev." In *Leningradskii balet segodnia*, vol. 1, edited by V. V. Chistiakova. Leningrad, 1967.

Sinclair, Janet, and Leo Kersley. "Interview with Yuri Soloviev." *Ballet Today* (October 1961): 14–16.

Smakov, Gennady. *The Great Russian Dancers*. New York, 1984.

ARKADY A. SOKOLOV-KAMINSKY
Translated from Russian

SOMES, MICHAEL (born 28 September 1917 in Horsley, England, died 19 November 1994 in London), British dancer and teacher. Somes began his ballet studies with Katherine Blott and Édouard Espinosa and won the first male scholarship to the Sadler's Wells Ballet School in 1934. He joined the Vic-Wells (now the Royal) Ballet in 1936; except for a period of military service (1941–1945), he remained with the company until 1984. He first came to public notice in 1937, leading the corps de ballet in the original cast of *Les Patineurs* and as the original Guy in *A Wedding Bouquet*. A year later, in *Horoscope*, Frederick Ashton paired him with Margot Fonteyn for the first time and entrusted him with his first leading role, thus both defining and foretelling his future. Somes and Fonteyn together created the principal roles in Ashton's *Dante Sonata* and *The Wise Virgins* (1940), and then in *Symphonic Variations* (1946).

Somes's ballet *Summer Interlude* (1950) for the Sadler's Wells Theatre Ballet was his sole attempt at choreography; he was seriously interested only in dancing. When Robert Helpmann resigned from the Sadler's Wells Ballet in 1950, Somes succeeded him as the company's principal male dancer and Fonteyn's regular partner. In their many performances of *Swan Lake, Giselle, The Sleeping Beauty,* and *Les Sylphides,* he emerged as a true *premier danseur noble,* a model of aristocratic deportment, personal modesty, and accomplished technique. He also partnered Moira Shearer, Beryl Grey, Pamela May, Violetta Elvin, and Svetlana Beriosova and danced a broad range of roles from the Red Knight in *Checkmate* to Ivan Tsarevitch—a haunting and still unsurpassed interpretation—in *The Firebird*. It was with Fonteyn, however, in the classics and in roles created for him by Ashton—in *Cinderella, Daphnis and Chloe, Ondine,* and *Scènes de Ballet,* to name four of more than fifteen—that his strength, romantic ardor, and sensitive musicality shone most brightly.

SOMES. A stalwart partner to Margot Fonteyn, Somes is pictured here with her in costume for the Black Swan pas de deux from *Swan Lake,* 1945. (Photograph from the Dance Collection, New York Public Library for the Performing Arts.)

Somes was named a Commander of the Order of the British Empire in 1959 and retired from dancing two years later. He continued to perform mime roles, however, lending his dramatic authority to two that he created: Lord Capulet in Kenneth MacMillan's *Romeo and Juliet* and the Father in Ashton's *Marguerite and Armand.* As both an assistant director of the Royal Ballet from 1962 to 1970 and principal *répétiteur* (rehearsal director) from 1970 to 1974, he had particular responsibility for the Ashton repertory and made an incalculable contribution to the continued excellence of the company for more than twenty years. He successfully applied his experience and his own high standard of performance to all his teaching and coaching. Without vanity or exaggeration, and to the company's great good fortune, he described himself as "a perfectionist . . . [who] demands similar perfection from all the dancers in the Royal Ballet." After leaving the company in 1984, Somes taught pas de deux classes at the Royal Ballet School and staged productions of Ashton ballets for various companies.

BIBLIOGRAPHY

Anthony, Gordon. "Michael Somes." In Anthony's *A Camera at the Ballet: Pioneer Dancers of the Royal Ballet.* Newton Abbot, 1975.

Brinson, Peter. "A Life of Dance: Michael Somes." *Opera House* (May 1995): 42–43.

Clarke, Mary. *The Sadler's Wells Ballet.* New York, 1955.

Fisher, Hugh. *Michael Somes.* Dancers of Today, no. 7. London, 1955.

Gruen, John. *The Private World of Ballet.* New York, 1975.

Monahan, James. "Michael Somes." *The Dancing Times* (November 1984): 130–131.

Newman, Barbara. *Antoinette Sibley: Reflections of a Ballerina.* London, 1986.

BARBARA NEWMAN

SOMNAMBULE, LA. Full title: *La Somnambule, ou L'Arrivée d'un Nouveau Seigneur.* Choreography: Jean-Louis Aumer. Music: Ferdinand Hérold. Libretto: Eugène Scribe. Scenery: Pierre Ciceri. Costumes: Hippolyte Lecomte. First performance: 19 September 1827, Théâtre de l'Académie Royale de Musique, Paris. Principals: Pauline Montessu (Thérèse), Ferdinand (Edmond), Amélie Legallois (Gertrude), Louis Montjoie (Saint-Rambert).

The workings of the unconscious mind during sleep fascinated Romantic-era artists. Henry Fuseli's painting *The Nightmare* (c.1790) depicts some of the horrors that may reveal themselves during sleep. William Shakespeare's plays of two centuries earlier were much esteemed by the Romantics, especially the role of a famous sleepwalker, Lady Macbeth.

In contrast with these dark images, Aumer's *La Somnambule* presents an uncomplicated world where sleepwalking is a temporary aberration and sunrise vanquishes all darkness, whether of the physical world or of the spirit. Unlike full-blown Romantic ballets like *La Sylphide,* it evinces no desire to escape the here and now. A cautionary tale rather than a fantasy, it deals with problems of this world: the frailty of a woman's reputation and the necessity for faith in a higher justice.

Thérèse, the sleepwalker of the title, is led by her malady to the village inn and to the bedroom of Saint-Rambert, the new lord of the manor. Although he discreetly leaves when he realizes that she is asleep, her presence there scandalizes the villagers, who have come to pay their respects to him. Edmond, Thérèse's fiancé, immediately breaks off their engagement and vows to marry Gertrude, the widow who owns the inn. But she, too, is compromised, for her shawl is found in Saint-Rambert's room. At this climactic moment, Thérèse is seen wending her way perilously along the edge of the roof, fast asleep. This evidence convinces Edmond of her innocence, and the sleepwalker awakes to her own wedding.

La Somnambule plays upon a favorite Romantic dichotomy, that of the pure and innocent female (epitomized by Théophile Gautier's "Christian" dancer, Marie Taglioni) and the worldly and experienced woman (Gautier's "pagan" dancer, Fanny Elssler). In Filippo Taglioni's seminal *La Sylphide,* these two poles were cast in terms of spirit and flesh, and the hero's choice of the otherworldly sylphide led ultimately to tragedy. In *La Somnambule,* purity wins not only a moral victory but the promise of domestic happiness. This theme evidently appealed to August Bournonville, who staged his own version of the ballet in Copenhagen in 1829.

Dramatic rather than choreographic values apparently dominated this ballet, although observers commented on the innovation of raising the curtain on a dance already in progress. The scenario represents the first venture into ballet by Eugène Scribe, already a well-known and prolific French playwright.

BIBLIOGRAPHY

Guest, Ivor. *The Ballet of the Second Empire.* London, 1974.

Guest, Ivor. *The Romantic Ballet in Paris.* 2d rev. ed. London, 1980.

Scribe, Eugène. *La Somnambule, ou, L'arrivée d'un nouveau seigneur.* Paris, 1827.

SUSAN AU

SONNAMBULA, LA. Original title: *The Night Shadow.* Choreography: George Balanchine. Music: Vittorio Rieti, orchestrated and arranged from operas by Vincenzo Bellini, including *La Sonnambula, I Puritani, Norma,* and *I Capuletti ed i Montecchi.* Libretto: Vittorio Rieti. Scenery and costumes: Dorothea Tanning. First performance: 27 February 1946, City Center of Music and Drama, New York, Ballet Russe de Monte Carlo. Principals: Alexandra Danilova (The Sleepwalker), Nicholas Magallanes (The Poet), Maria Tallchief (The Coquette), Michel Katcharoff (The Host).

Concise yet powerfully theatrical, charged with an atmosphere that is often called melodramatic, *La Sonnambula* is a departure from the neoclassical ballets that have become Balanchine's hallmark. In the year of its creation, however—during which Balanchine's *Four Temperaments* also had its premiere—it was more accessible and appealing to audiences accustomed to story ballets and spectacle.

Although John Martin, reviewing its 1960 revival, found it reminiscent of the "ballet russe epoch," *La Sonnambula* actually derives from an earlier period. Its precursor, Jean-Louis Aumer's *La Somnambule* (1827), inspired Vincenzo Bellini's opera *La Sonnambula,* which in turn supplied part of the score adapted by Rieti for Balanchine's ballet. Balanchine's plot is less intricate than Aumer's, but the four leading characters in both ballets bear affinities to one another: the sleepwalking heroine, her young lover, the older man whose actions crucially affect them, and the worldly woman who becomes the heroine's rival.

Balanchine's ballet is set at a masked ball given by the Host and the Coquette in the garden of a great mansion. After an entertainment by fantastically costumed dancers, the guests go to supper, leaving the Poet and the Coquette alone. Their initial attraction is thwarted by the Host, who

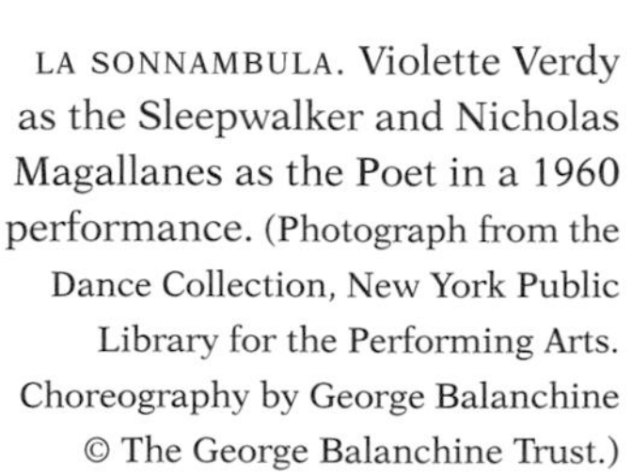

LA SONNAMBULA. Violette Verdy as the Sleepwalker and Nicholas Magallanes as the Poet in a 1960 performance. (Photograph from the Dance Collection, New York Public Library for the Performing Arts. Choreography by George Balanchine © The George Balanchine Trust.)

takes the Coquette away. Suddenly a beautiful white-clad woman appears, walking in her sleep and bearing a candle. The Poet attempts in vain to wake her. The jealous Coquette, seeing them together, informs the Host, who stabs the Poet. Before the startled eyes of the guests, the Sleepwalker returns, still asleep, to bear his body away.

Unlike Aumer, who closed his ballet with the unambiguous triumph of virtue, Balanchine makes no moral statement. The ending of *La Sonnambula* bears a kinship, however, to Romantic-era ballets such as *La Sylphide,* which depict the futility of mortal yearnings for the supernatural. Balanchine's Sleepwalker indeed has an otherworldly aura: moving weightlessly on pointe, she seems to waft in the breeze of the Poet's movements. The ballet's unearthly conclusion, in which nothing is seen but the light of the Sleepwalker's candle rising from one window to another, reinforces the perception that the ballet takes place in a world only superficially like our own.

BIBLIOGRAPHY

Anderson, Jack. *The One and Only: The Ballet Russe de Monte Carlo.* New York, 1981.

Balanchine, George, with Francis Mason. *Balanchine's Complete Stories of the Great Ballets.* Rev. and enl. ed. Garden City, N.Y., 1977.

Barnes, Clive. "Night Shadow." *Dance and Dancers* (December 1960): 15–17.

Beaumont, Cyril W. *Ballets of Today: Being a Second Supplement to the Complete Book of Ballets.* London, 1954.

Beaumont, Cyril W. *Ballets Past and Present: Being a Third Supplement to the Complete Book of Ballets.* London, 1955.

Choreography by George Balanchine: A Catalogue of Works. New York, 1984.

Kirstein, Lincoln. *Movement and Metaphor: Four Centuries of Ballet.* New York, 1970.

Reynolds, Nancy. *Repertory in Review: Forty Years of the New York City Ballet.* New York, 1977.

Shaw, Alan J. "Balanchine's Angelic Messenger." *Ballet Review* 17 (Winter 1990): 56–61.

SUSAN AU

SOTHO DANCE. *See* South Africa, *article on* Indigenous Dance.

SOUDEIKINE, SERGE (Sergei Iur'evich Sudeikin; born 19 March 1882 in Smolensk, Russia, died 12 August 1946 in Nyack, New York), Russian-American scenery and costume designer. From 1897 to 1909 Soudeikine attended the Moscow Institute of Painting, Sculpture, and Architecture, where he studied principally under Konstantine Korovin and established close contact first with the neonationalist colony at Abramtsevo, and then with the *Mir iskusstva* (World of Art) group. In 1906, at the invitation of Serge Diaghilev, Soudeikine traveled to Paris in connection with the Russian section of the Salon d'Automne. The following year he took part in the "Blue Rose" exhibition in Moscow. By 1908 Soudeikine had moved away from his early symbolist style to a more primitivist one; and in 1909 he settled in Saint Petersburg where he enrolled at the Academy of Arts. In 1911 Soudeikine designed wall panels for the Stray Dog cabaret; in 1913 he designed sets and costumes for Diaghilev's production of *La Tragédie de Salomé* in Paris, the first of the many stage presentations that Soudeikine ultimately designed in Russia, Europe and the United States. He emigrated to Paris in 1920 and settled in New York in 1922. During the 1920s he worked for Nikita Baliev's Chauve-Souris cabaret, designed several productions for the Metropolitan Opera (among them *Le Rossignol,* 1926), and painted portraits, especially of dancers and actors.

Soudeikine was a prolific designer in the 1910s and 1920s, collaborating with Baliev, Diaghilev, Nikolai Evreinov, Aleksandr Tairov and other impresarios, although he is remembered more as a designer of cabarets than of ballets. However, his sets and costumes for Florent Schmitt's *La Tragédie de Salomé,* choreographed by Boris Romanov for Diaghilev in 1913, are among his memorable contributions. According to Valerian Svetlov, Soudeikin managed to evoke the spirit of malevolence and mysticism, especially through his costume for Salomé (Kogan, 1975, p. 74). From the decadent colors of dark blue and gold to the rose that Soudeikine painted on Salomé's knee at each performance, the presentation impressed the audience with its brooding exoticism.

[*For related discussion, see* Costume in Western Traditions, *overview article; and* Scenic Design.]

BIBLIOGRAPHY

Kogan, Dora. *Sergei Iurevich Sudeikin* (in Russian). Moscow, 1974.

Lobanov-Rostovsky, N. D. "Russian Painters and the Stage." *Transactions* 2 (1968): 133–210.

Sullivan, Lawrence. "Nikita Baliev's Le Théâtre de la Chauve-Souris: An Avant-Garde Theater." *Dance Research Journal* 18.2 (1987): 17–29.

Sullivan, Lawrence. "Sergei Soudeikine, 1882–1946: A Chronological Checklist and Bibliography." *Bulletin of Bibliography* 46 (June 1989): 67–75.

ARCHIVES. Bakhrushin Museum, Moscow. Mr. and Mrs. N. D. Lobanov-Rostovsky, London.

JOHN E. BOWLT

SOURITZ, ELIZABETH (Elizaveta Iakovlevna Surits; born 25 February 1923 in Berlin), Russian critic and dance historian. Souritz completed her studies with Yuri Slonimsky at the Lunacharsky State Institute of Theater Art (GITIS) in Moscow in 1949. She received the degree of Candidate of the Science of Art in 1970. From 1960 to 1964 she worked at the State Central Theater Library in Moscow; in 1964 she became head of the dance section of the Moscow Institute for the History of the Arts.

Souritz has written regularly for the journals *Theater* and *Soviet Ballet* (later *Ballet*), contributed major articles on ballet in many countries to the *Great Soviet Encyclopedia,* and written a number of entries for the Soviet *Ballet Encyclopedia,* serving also on its editorial board. Her work also appears in anthologies, such as *Music and Choreography of Contemporary Ballet,* for which she wrote on George Balanchine.

For the 1986 seminar "Ausdruckstanz," held in Bayreuth, Germany, Souritz read an important paper on exponents of expressive dance in the Soviet Union, artists who were until then unknown in the West. For the international conference "Dance Scholarship Today," held in 1988 in Essen, Germany, she reported on the state of research and publication in her country.

Souritz's first book was *All about Ballet* (1966). She is best known, however, for her work on the early years of Soviet dance. *Choreographic Art of the 1920s* (1979) perceptively delineated the experimental styles of that period and offered detailed analyses of the works of Aleksandr Gorsky, Kasyan Goleizovsky, and Fedor Lopukhov. Her article "Soviet Ballet of the 1920s and the Influence of Constructivism" appeared in the journal *Soviet Union* (Arizona State University) in 1980. Her extended book on the dance of the period appeared in Russia in 1989. Translated into English as *Soviet Choreographers in the 1920s,* it was published the following year in the United States where it was awarded the de la Torre Bueno Prize for the year's most distinguished original work of dance scholarship.

BIBLIOGRAPHY

Sasportes, José. "Revolutionary Soviet Dance." *Dance Chronicle* 14.1 (1991): 108–111.

Souritz, Elizabeth. *Soviet Choreographers in the 1920s.* Translated by Lynn Visson. Durham, N.C., 1990.

Souritz, Elizabeth. "Moscow's Island of Dance, 1934–1941." *Dance Chronicle* 17.1 (1994): 1–92.

SELMA JEANNE COHEN

SOUTH AFRICA. [*This entry comprises three articles on dance in the Republic of South Africa:*

Indigenous Dance
Ballet
Contemporary Theatrical Dance

For further discussion of indigenous dance, see Southern Africa. *For further discussion of theatrical dance, see the entries on individual companies, choreographers, and dancers.*]

Indigenous Dance

The pro-Afrikaner Nationalist party began its rise to power in South Africa in the 1920s, bringing with it policies of racial segregation that by the late 1940s had solidified into an elaborate system of laws enforcing strict *apartheid* ("separation") of "Europeans" (i.e., whites) and "non-Europeans," a broad grouping of peoples that included "Coloureds" (people of mixed race), Indians, and Bantu. The Bantu tribes, the indigenous peoples of the region, were officially classified by four major language groups: Nguni (north and south), Sotho (north and south), Tsonga, and Venda. Since the defeat of the Nationalist party in 1994 and the establishment of a democratic government under Nelson Mandela, these classifications are no longer officially used. Nevertheless, they remain useful, because they were for many years employed by scholars engaged in studying the music and dance of indigenous peoples, and they thus can still be found in the literature.

The Nguni tribes of South Africa include the Zulu, Swazi, Xhosa, and northern Ndebele; the Sotho tribes include the Tswana, Lovedu, Pedi, and Kgaga; the Tsonga and the Venda are large independent tribes. These peoples are not strictly confined to the present-day Republic of South Africa. Some of them also live in neighboring countries: Shangana-Tsonga in Mozambique, Tswana in Botswana, Sotho in Lesotho, Swazi in Swaziland, and Venda in the independent republic of Venda (established in 1979). The principal indigenous peoples of South Africa are those of the Nguni and Sotho language groups, which are discussed herein. [*For related discussion, see* Shangana-Tsonga Dance; Venda Dance.]

Since the 1940s, the indigenous dance traditions of South Africa have been preserved through the institution of "mine dances," regularly scheduled performances by tribal teams in dance arenas constructed at the gold mines in the Witwatersrand, a region near Johannesburg. Such teams also often appear in other public arenas and stadiums.

General Characteristics. Apart from the Shangana-Tsonga and some Venda and Pedi (northern Sotho) dances, most dances of indigenous peoples in the Republic of South Africa have a fairly slow tempo, especially in comparison with the dances of central Africa. The body generally moves as a single unit; body parts are not often moved in isolation. Drumming is important in dances of possession or trance throughout South Africa. This importance is reflected in the terms denoting mediumistic diviners, which all include the root *-goma,* meaning "a drum"—Zulu *isangoma,* Sotho *makomane,* and Tsonga and Venda *mungomane.* Elaborate grass costumes and masks are widely used in South African initiation rites.

Many of the men's dances described in this article are seen in both rural-traditional and urban settings. In the urban, they are performed by teams of migrant workers, whose performance is often superior to those seen in their homeland because the migrants have more opportunity to rehearse. The best known of these may be the dances performed by the gold miners of Witwatersrand.

SOUTH AFRICA: Indigenous Dance. This team of Zulu dancers, preparing to perform a rain dance, was photographed at the Zulu Cavalcade in the Green Point Stadium in Cape Town in 1969. Kneeling in line formation, the dancers are beginning their dance song, accompanied by drummers (upper right). Their team costumes feature Angora goatskin wristbands and armbands. Small, token Zulu shields and decorated "dance sticks," to be used in the dance, are arrayed before the performers. (Photograph used by permission of the Cape Newspaper Picture Service.)

Nguni Dance. The Nguni are by far the largest of the four language groups, with about fourteen million in South Africa, Swaziland, and neighboring countries. They comprise the Zulu, Swazi, Xhosa, and northern Ndebele. The most striking characteristic of their dances is that communal dancers usually sing their own music; furthermore, although ankle rattles and hand-clapping were sometimes added, the traditional basis of collective music making was usually the unaccompanied dance song. Improvised drums are now a part of their communal dancing (Rycroft, 1980).

Most Nguni-speaking peoples perform the *indlamu* in various local styles. The *indlamu* is performed by a team of young men, in single or double line, under the control of a leader who determines the start and end of the routine. The unified and concerted stamping of alternating feet on the ground is the typical action of the dance. Perfect unison, each dancer not only performing as an individual but also as part of a figure, is expected of the team.

The most important Zulu dances were the men's team dances and the wedding dances (Tracey, 1948, 1952, 1971). The team dances were related to the warriors' dances performed in the past by young men to help ensure that their group could move as one body, consolidating their action as a team. The main characteristic of these dances is the stamping of alternating feet. The stamps had a number of variations: the leg could be raised forward in a high kick before bringing the foot down, or the knee could be raised and the leg swung backward with a piston accent before stamping, with the aim of making the ground shake on communal impact. The Zulu said they sounded "like the waves of the sea pounding along the shore" when they danced. The dance was performed in three main parts—entry and preparation, followed by two dance routines. The entry usually consisted of a double file of half-crouching men circling around the dance area before lining up. The dancers then sat on the ground shouting traditional cries while the leader performed solos in front of them. Then the dance proper started when the leader rushed forward and stamped on the ground, and the whole group sprang into action, using dance shields and sticks in concerted movements. The dance routine had a dramatic climax, such as falling to the ground prone or prostrate.

In the wedding dances, the antagonism between the two parties—bride's and bridegroom's—was expressed by an elaborate dancing competition. The dancing differed on each occasion, but there was a typical pattern. The bride's party, the male dancers in a line with the women behind them, started by performing quick, spirited backward and forward movements. Toward the end of this dance, the dancers formed two files, circled outward away from each other, wheeled back, crossed in the center, and formed into a line to end their movement. In front of this stationary line, the young men of the party then danced solos. Next, the groom's party performed a special dance choreographed for the occasion. At first the men were in front with the women behind; later the women came through the men's ranks and danced in front of them, retiring to their original position at the end of the movement. The young girls paraded in front of the men, modestly walking up and down the length of the line and disappearing again to the rear. In the wedding dances the men's actions were vigorous and violent, while the women's steps were demure and pleasant (Krige, 1936; Tracey, 1948; Erasmus, 1975; Harper, 1981).

An important feature of much Xhosa men's dancing is a distinctive shaking of the body, in which the thorax undulates rapidly so that the whole length of the spine appears to be rippling. This action may be accompanied by a number of other movements. In the *umteyo,* the shaking dance of youths not yet initiated into adulthood, the dancers alternated the weight from one leg to the other, and the knee of the supporting leg moved rapidly forward and backward, emphasizing the rippling of the thorax and the furious tinkling of the small bells worn strapped across the chest. The dance was performed in double files and usually in four stages: the dancers advanced; they retired; they stood their ground, marking time on alternate feet; and finally they brought the performance to a close with a kind of genuflection (Tracey, 1952). During the dance, the concertina player walked up and down between the two files of dancers. The whistle player, who controlled the dance, remained in the middle of the group.

In the *umdudo* men's dance, which derived its name from its first movement, the shaking of the body was used only in the third movement. It was so pronounced that the skin worn by the dancer on his shoulders often stretched out horizontally behind him, and the bead necklaces likewise flew out in front. The dance was accompanied by women striking hard, dried bullock skins with sticks, in unison. In the first movement, the men lined up in several lines of about ten men each; they then threw the left foot forward and struck the ground with a resounding stamp, flexing the body forward at the same time. In unison, they returned to the original erect position and repeated the step three or four times. This was followed by a like number of vertical jumps, marking the end of the first movement. The second movement was more spirited, and only the younger and more active men engaged in it. The leader broke away from the line and moved quickly about with each leg advanced alternately, each step being initiated by a short hop; he was followed by the other dancers in single file. There were no limits as to the space within which the dancers performed, and the leader made intricate patterns. At the end of the movement the dancers broke up into several groups and performed the shaking movement described above (Soga, 1931).

In another dance, the *xhensa,* performed by adult men, the rippling action was performed in a circle. The dancers directed their attention inward toward the center of the ring, or stared vacantly as if in a trance, producing a guttural roar. Tracey (1952) described this dance as "a continual shaking by a closely packed circle of gyrating and grunting dancers."

The movements performed by circumcised youths in the *abakweta* dance were much more restricted. Their dance dress consisted of palm leaves made into a heavy, stiff skirt wrapped a number of times around the waist, which restricted the movement of the entire body, along with a face-concealing headdress, having long slender twigs affixed on each side, like a grasshopper's antennae. The dancers simultaneously bent the upper torso forward and the lower torso backward from the waist, throwing the antennae forward to touch the ground gracefully. Apart from this restricted action, movement was confined almost entirely to the lower limbs.

SOUTH AFRICA: Indigenous Dance. A dance team of the Xhosa tribe performs the *umteyo,* the shaking dance of the *amakwenkwe,* young men not yet initiated into adulthood. The dancers wear traditional dance skirts and Angora goatskin leggings. At the center of the group is the whistle player, who controls the dance. During the rippling motion characteristic of the dance, one leg is held up while the other shakes at the knee and the thorax quivers, causing vibration of the bells strung across the dancer's body. (Photograph by Merlyn Severn; reprinted by permission from Tracey, 1952, p. 63.)

SOUTH AFRICA: Indigenous Dance. The leader of a dance team of the Pedi tribe, a northern Sotho group indigenous to the Northern Province of modern-day South Africa. He is performing the *muchongolo*, or pipe dance, common among northern Sotho peoples. He wears a single ostrich feather in each armband, decorative strips of cloth and fur, and leg rattles made of wild fruit shells strung onto light sticks and strapped around his calves. He carries a spare metal pipe in his left hand. (Photograph by Merlyn Severn; reprinted by permission from Tracey, 1952, p. 81.)

Sotho Dance. The Sotho are divided into a southern subgroup who live largely in Lesotho, and a northern subgroup in the former province of Transvaal. The northern and southern Sotho dances are quite different. The characteristic northern Sotho dance form is the circle moving counterclockwise; in contrast, southern Sotho dances are commonly performed in straight lines, and stamping provides an important percussive element in the music (Tracey, 1952; Blacking, 1980).

Common among the northern Sotho were reed pipe dances performed by men. For the *muchongolo* dance, each dancer played a single pipe; the dance was also accompanied by an ensemble of four drums played by women, around which the dancers gyrated in a counterclockwise direction, enhancing the rhythm with leg rattles strapped onto their calves (Tracey, 1952). Among the Lovedu, a northern Sotho tribe, private individuals sent well-rehearsed reed-pipe teams to friends or relatives to express sympathy or to announce a death as well as to celebrate a marriage or the setting up of a new home. The host and guest teams competed, but neither ended as victor or vanquished; the competitive element was present merely to heighten the enjoyment of the dance. The objects were self-expression, without stress on individual performance, and entertainment (Krige and Krige, 1943).

Among the northern Sotho, dances that involved difficult physical feats were often part of the girls' initiation ceremonies. A Kgaga girl, for example, had to hop like a frog with a stick behind her knees or dance on one leg with the other pulled up (Hammond-Tooke, 1981). Lovedu girls danced bending forward while crouching deeply, with the arms held above the head for balance (Krige and Krige, 1943).

Mohobelo, the men's stamping dance of the southern Sotho, was characterized by long striding steps between stamps. It included a number of set movements or routines. The dancers started in a file, sliding and striding, moving along sinuously to the sound of hissing. When within the dance area, they formed into lines and performed high kicks, raising the knee waist-high and then throwing the foot head-high. In the second movement, the distinctive feature was fast leaping and twisting in the air. In the third movement, they performed sinuous hand actions with fingers either extended or tightly flexed with the palm open. The musical accompaniment consisted of response songs; the leader started the song in solo fashion while the others sang the refrain to punctuate the leader's verses. The performance was sometimes interspersed with solo dancing (Tracey, 1952, 1971; Guma, 1967; Adams, 1980).

The distinctive feature of several girls' and women's dances among the southern Sotho was that the whole dance was performed by women kneeling in a line. The knees beat the ground as the body rose and fell. This movement was accompanied by lateral and upward sweeps of the hands. As the dance continued, the pace quickened, going faster and faster until the dancers brought it to a climax by flinging their fully extended arms upward and straightening their bodies. The dancers were supported by a chorus of women standing behind them, who encouraged them and explained the dance through topical song lyrics (Ashton, 1952; Adams, 1980).

SOUTH AFRICA: Indigenous Dance. (*opposite page*) A southern Sotho dance team performing movements of the *mohobelo,* a stamping and striding dance. (*above*) The *bahobela,* the high-striding kick typical of the opening movement. Only the dance leader (in front) and the two men second and third from right are at the top of the kick. The dancers wear headdresses made of ostrich feathers and carry square-headed knobkerries. (*below*) In the *molapo,* the second movement, the dancers leap and twist to an accelerated tempo. (Photographs by Merlyn Severn; reprinted by permission from Tracey, 1952, pp. 73 and 77.) ▶

SOUTH AFRICA: Indigenous Dance. Gumboot dancing, said to have been invented by Zulu workers on the docks in Durban, is one of the most popular of South Africa's indigenous dance types. Based on the percussive possibilities of rubber Wellington boots (called *isicathulo* in Zulu), which make a sharp sound when stamped or slapped, it is frequently performed in a theatrical setting. This group of youngsters appeared on the program billed as *Africa Pride II* in Soweto in 1994. (Photograph by John Hogg; used by permission.)

Indigenous and Traditional Dance Today. For most of the twentieth century, there were in South Africa two official national languages: English and Afrikaans. Today, the "rainbow nation" has eleven official languages—Zulu, Xhosa, English, Afrikaans, Ndebele, Venda, Tsonga, Tswana, Northern Sotho, Southern Sotho, and Mswati (Swazi)—along with accompanying cultural Heritage Trust's annual national traditional dance knockouts, indigenous dance is categorized as AmaXhosa, BaPedi, VhaVenda, AmaZulu, XiTsonga, AmaNdebele, BaSotho, BaTswana, and AmaSwazi. In the former homeland of Transkei, the Transkei Traditional Music Association, based in Umtata, fosters traditional dancers threatened by urbanization.

Theatricalized social and traditional dance forms include *marabi*, *iscathamiya* (a choral tradition that fuses Western elements with traditional African forms), gumboot dancing (a worker's dance), and *mapantsula* (township jive). The *toyi-toyi*, which originated in guerilla training camps in neighboring countries, surfaced in South Africa in the mid-1980s as a "war dance" that could be effectively performed in protest marches and at trade union rallies. While it has been transformed into a dance of celebration, it also is used in community theater to promote women's rights and AIDS education and to fight child abuse. The *toyi-toyi* and other above-mentioned dances were featured in Mbongeni Ngema's musical *Sarafina!* (1987), which subsequently became a Broadway show and a Hollywood film. Traditional and urban dance in their own right are also making a serious transition to the stage. In September 1996, the Dance Factory's annual Arts Alive festival included an "African night," featuring theatricalized versions of traditional and urban dances.

BIBLIOGRAPHY

Adams, C. R. "Lesotho: Basotho Music." In *The New Grove Dictionary of Music and Musicians*. London, 1980.

Ashton, Hugh. *The Basuto*. London, 1952.

Blacking, John. "Musical Expeditions of the Venda." *African Music* 3.1 (1962): 54–78.

Blacking, John. "An Introduction to Venda Traditional Dances." *Dance Studies* 2 (1977): 34–56.

Blacking, John. "Trends in the Black Music of South Africa, 1959–1969." In *Musics of Many Cultures*, edited by Elizabeth May. Berkeley, 1980.

Cook, P. A. W. *Social Organisation and Ceremonial Institutions of the Bomvana*. Cape Town, 1931.

Erasmus, J. "Music, Song, and Dance of the South African Bantu." *Bantu* 22.8 (1975): 1–33.

Grau, Andrée. "Some Problems in the Analysis of Dance Style, with Special Reference to the Venda of South Africa." Master's thesis, Queen's University of Belfast, 1979.

Guma, S. M. *The Form, Content, and Technique of Traditional Literature in Southern Sotho*. Pretoria, 1967.

Hammond-Tooke, W. David. *The Bantu-Speaking Peoples of South Africa*. London, 1974.

Hammond-Tooke, W. David. *Boundaries and Beliefs: The Structure of a Sotho World View*. Johannesburg, 1981.

Harper, Peggy. "Dance." In *The Cambridge Encyclopedia of Africa*. Cambridge, 1981.

Krige, Eileen J. *The Social System of the Zulus*. London, 1936.

Krige, Eileen J., and J. D. Krige. *The Realm of a Rain-Queen: A Study of the Pattern of Lovedu Society*. Cape Town, 1943.

Mokhali, A. G. *Basuto Music and Dancing.* Roma, Lesotho, 1966.
Rycroft, D. K. "Nguni Music." In *The New Grove Dictionary of Music and Musicians.* London, 1980.
Soga, J. Henderson. *The Ama-Xhosa: Life and Customs.* London, 1931.
Tracey, Hugh T. *Zulu Paradox.* Johannesburg, 1948.
Tracey, Hugh T. *African Dances of the Witwatersrand Gold Mines.* Johannesburg, 1952.
Tracey, Hugh T. "Dances of Aborigenes." In *Standard Encyclopaedia of Southern Africa.* Cape Town, 1970–.

ANDRÉE GRAU
Amended by Adrienne Sichel

Ballet

Ballet has been part of the theatrical tradition of South Africa since the early nineteenth century, when three-act ballets with specially composed music were presented in Cape Town between 1802 and 1820. The creators of these ballets, which were probably closer to opera than to ballet as we think of it today, were of diverse nationalities, as can be seen from the names found in theatrical records, including Jan Ludwig Petersen, a Dutch ballet master; Charles-Etienne Boniface, a French librettist; and Carl Frederick Lemming, a Danish composer. Some of the themes of these ballets were drawn from Greek legends, always a popular source for theatrical spectacles, but in 1831 one notable ballet was presented that had a decidedly local theme: *Jack at the Cape, or All Alive among the Hottentots,* was performed before a backdrop of Table Mountain, the famous mountain that itself provides a dramatic backdrop for the city of Cape Town.

All this took place less than two hundred years after Jan van Riebeeck established a supply post at the Cape of Good Hope for the Dutch East India Company in 1652 and thus created the first permanent European settlement in southern Africa. Descendants of the original Dutch settlers, the Boers (literally, "farmers"), developed the Afrikaner language and culture and established new farms and settlements throughout the region. British settlement and influence increased steadily until 1815, when control of the Cape Colony officially passed from the Dutch to the British, resulting in the Great Trek some twenty years later when the Boers migrated north and east to found Natal, the Transvaal, and the Orange Free State.

Throughout the nineteenth century Cape Town considered itself very much a European city, and its inhabitants maintained a strong interest in European trends and fashions. They were, however, sorely deprived of theatrical performances of dance. The only professional dancers known to have visited the colony at this time came from Mauritius in 1848, when they presented a performance of Spanish dances of the Romantic period, such as the cachucha of Andalusia and the bolero of Cadiz. Strong disapproval from the Calvinist Dutch Reformed Church stifled any further growth of dance in the last decades of the century, when the only evidence of dance lies in reports of solo dances such as the hornpipe.

In the early years of the twentieth century, however, things began to change. After the Boer War of 1899–1902, the Transvaal and the Orange Free State became British colonies, joining the Cape Colony and Natal, and in 1909 the South Africa Act joined all four colonies in the Union of South Africa. One result of these momentous military and political events was that several dancing teachers from Great Britain immigrated to South Africa, set up schools of dancing, and began to train pupils. The earliest teachers of note came from London, where they had studied with R. M. Compton: Helen Webb, who went to Cape Town in 1912, and Madge Mann, who went to Johannesburg in 1914.

The dancing of this period was known as "fancy dancing," and it was only later, after pupils of the Webb School had gone abroad to study and had returned home, that matters improved. They came back to South Africa with sound training in the principles of classical ballet and with a strong appreciation for the performance style of Russian companies they had seen in Europe. As a result, local stage presentations of classical ballets were vastly improved, as local dancers were immeasurably strengthened by the training now available from local teachers. Here again, the influence was British. In Johannesburg, Ivy Conmee returned from London to teach the method of the Association of Operatic Dancing of Great Britain, later to be known as the Royal Academy of Dancing (RAD). Also in Johannesburg was Marjorie Sturman, an exceptionally fine and influential teacher who first taught the Cecchetti method and then the RAD method. In Cape Town, Webb's pupil Maude Lloyd was the first to return, in 1927, with some knowledge of the Cecchetti method, which she had learned from her studies with Marie Rambert in London.

The Cecchetti method was formally introduced to South Africa the following year, in 1928, when Margaret Craske visited the country with the specific purpose of founding the Imperial Society of Teachers of Dancing, Overseas Branch. With her pupil Dulcie Howes, newly returned to Cape Town from Anna Pavlova's company, she journeyed to Johannesburg to found the society and thus ensure that the Cecchetti method of ballet technique would be formally and properly taught. Consequently, with a number of teachers now firmly grounded in both the RAD method and the Cecchetti method, South Africa became a ballet stronghold.

Returning to Cape Town, Howes moved her private studio to the College of Music at the University of Cape Town (UCT) in 1934 and formed, distinct from her school, the UCT Ballet Company, the oldest ballet company in South Africa and the only one with an unbroken tradition of performing. Howes produced her own ballets and later introduced the classics into the repertory. The strength of her company was that it included professional dancers capable of meeting the artistic demands of leading roles in the classical repertory. Drawn mainly from the staff of her school, her principal dancers were well seasoned by their experiences in such London-based companies as the Vic-Wells Ballet and Ballet Rambert, and they did much to raise the standards of ballet performance in South Africa.

Another Webb pupil, Cecily Robinson, was the first to stage Russian ballets in South Africa. She had danced with the Woizikowski and de Basil companies, after a brief stint with Ballet Rambert. Having suffered an injury during a performance, she returned to Cape Town in 1938 and started the Cape Town Ballet Club, where she staged ballets by Petipa and Fokine. Her early struggles to present ballet to local audiences can only be imagined from the historical record that the first South African performance of *Les Sylphides* shared the program with a Boris Karloff horror film.

By the late 1930s South Africa had seen several Russian ballet companies, which had toured the main provincial centers. The first was Anna Pavlova's, in the 1925/26 season. Preceded by her reputation as a great ballet star, Pavlova received widespread press coverage and drew a large public, stimulating interest in ballet throughout the country. Almost a decade later, in 1934, the Levitov Russian Ballet toured the country. Among its dancers was the South African Eileen Keegan, who was to return to Durban to present the first ballet performances there. In 1936, the Ballets de Monte-Carlo, headed by René Blum, also made a tour of the country. In addition to its stars, Vera Nemchinova, Anatole Vilzak, and Nana Gollner, the company included Yvonne Blake, a pupil of Dulcie Howes, who had been rehearsed by Fokine in his ballets. She too was to contribute to the improvement of local performance standards when she returned to Cape Town in 1939.

SOUTH AFRICA: Ballet. John Cranko mounted *Tritsch-Tratsch* to the lively music of Johann Strauss the younger for the University of Cape Town Ballet in 1946 and restaged it the next year for Sadler's Wells Theatre Ballet in London, creating yet another strong tie between these two companies. Elaine Fifield is seen here in the Sadler's Wells production. (Photograph by Gordon Anthony; used by permission of the Board of Trustees of the Theatre Museum, London.)

Having presented the first local production of Fokine's *Les Sylphides* under the banner of the Ballet Club in Cape Town in 1938, Cecily Robinson followed it with a production of the second act of *Swan Lake,* based on Ivanov's choreography, in 1940. Subsequently, in 1947, after the Ballet Club had become the South African National Ballet, Alexis Rassine returned to Cape Town from London to produce and dance in the second act of *Giselle* on a stage in the City Hall.

A complete performance of *Giselle* was seen for the first time by South African audiences in 1949, when Alicia Markova and Anton Dolin toured South Africa and Southern Rhodesia (now Zimbabwe). The National Ballet and the UCT Ballet joined forces to present an unforgettable season at the Alhambra Theatre in Cape Town. Dolin called the combined company "the best corps de ballets we have ever danced with." For this special season, Pamela Chrimes staged Ninette de Valois's *The Haunted Ballroom,* and Cecily Robinson staged Fokine's *Polovtsian Dances* from *Prince Igor,* both seen for the first time in South Africa. Following the success of this season in Cape Town, Markova and Dolin appeared as guest artists with the Johannesburg Festival Ballet, staging and dancing in three famous "white ballets": the second act of *Giselle,* the second act of *Swan Lake,* and *Les Sylphides.* Before leaving Johannesburg, Dolin also taught Marjorie Sturman his staging of the first act of *Giselle.* The influence of the Markova-Dolin seasons in South Africa was widespread, causing another wave of balletomania to sweep the country.

In Cape Town, the National Ballet was slowly losing force and was disbanded in the early 1950s. Aside from its contribution to South African culture, however, it is significant on an international level in having provided a proving ground for choreographers Alfred Rodrigues and John Cranko, both of whom made their first ballets for the company: *Danse Macabre,* to music by Camille Saint-Saëns, was choreographed by Rodrigues in 1939; *The Soldier's Tale,* to Igor Stravinsky's score, was made by Cranko in 1944.

In the Transvaal, local ballet companies came and went, as numerous performing groups were founded, flourished for a while, and ultimately collapsed for lack of support. In Johannesburg in the 1940s Madge Mann had a company called Les Danseuses, and Pretoria had its Ballet Club for some years. The Johannesburg Festival Ballet, founded by Marjorie Sturman, Poppy Frames, and Ivy Conmee in 1946, lasted more than a decade, until it was disbanded in 1957. Shorter-lived was the Johannesburg

SOUTH AFRICA: Ballet. In 1964, Galina Samsova appeared with the newly formed PACT Ballet in Johannesburg as a guest artist in *Swan Lake*. Partnered by Gary Burne, the company's ballet master and *premier danseur,* she danced ten performances within eleven days. Samsova subsequently returned often to perform in South Africa. (Photograph by Oostuvsen; courtesy of Claude Conyers.)

Ballet Theatre, founded in 1947 by Joyce van Geems, a Capetonian recently returned from the Ballet Russe de Monte Carlo, and Faith de Villiers, a dynamic Johannesburg teacher; their company lasted only a couple of seasons. Somewhat more successful was Frank Staff's South African Ballet Company, which lasted three years, from 1955 until 1958, and provided the multitalented Staff with the opportunity to create a number of original works. In 1959 the Johannesburg City Ballet was founded, at the suggestion of Yvonne Mounsey, with support from the Johannesburg City Council and other teachers and dancers in the city. Happily, it would prove to be the last of the short-lived companies.

In 1961, after many years as a sovereign state of the British Commonwealth, South Africa became an independent republic, and the ensuing rise of nationalism led to major programs of government support for all the performing arts in all four provinces of the nation. Having had, for more than a hundred and fifty years, no ballet company that could be called fully professional, South Africa was, in 1963, suddenly given four companies, one for each province. Performing arts councils, or boards, were formed in each province, and the ballet companies were named accordingly: the one in Johannesburg, based on the Johannesburg City Ballet, was called PACT Ballet; the one in Cape Town, founded on the UCT Ballet, was called CAPAB Ballet; in Durban, the capital city of Natal, a new company called NAPAC Ballet was formed; and in Bloemfontein, the capital city of the Orange Free State, PACOFS Ballet came into being. The only two that survive to the present day are the companies of the Performing Arts Council of the Transvaal (PACT) and the Cape Performing Arts Board (CAPAB), the latter being the more successful because of the excellent and stable direction provided in its early years by Dulcie Howes. She appointed Frank Staff resident choreographer in 1964 and handed over the artistic directorship to David Poole on her retirement in 1967. With firm leadership, excellent productions, and high standards of training, Poole created a company of international stature.

In the early years, under Howes, the UCT Ballet presented original ballets by Howes, Cranko, and many local choreographers. Cecily Robinson and Pamela Chrimes brought in works from the international repertory such as *Swan Lake, Le Carnaval, Les Sylphides,* and *The Haunted Ballroom.* In 1952 Poole was to increase the British influence on the company by bringing from London Frederick Ashton's *Les Rendezvous,* John Cranko's *Sea Change* and *Beauty and the Beast,* and his own production of *The Nutcracker,* act 2. Adding to the classics in the repertory, Chrimes staged *Coppélia* in 1953, and Petrus Bosman mounted *Petrouchka* in 1955. These were followed by full-

SOUTH AFRICA: Ballet. In Françoise Adret's production of *Cinderella* for PACT Ballet in 1966, Gillian Joubert (center) portrayed the Stepmother. Kenn Jones (left) and Frank Staff (right) were the Stepsisters. Costumes were designed by Chris van den Berg. (Photograph by Tommy Murray; courtesy of Claude Conyers.)

length productions by Poole of *The Nutcracker* (1959), *Sylvia* (1961), and *The Snow Queen* (1961). Among other South Africans who danced as guest artists were Nadia Nerina, Alexis Rassine, Maryon Lane, and Toby Fine. The Cape Town company developed along very firm lines because of its connection with the Sadler's Wells Ballet, whose standards of production became part of CAPAB Ballet's heritage.

CAPAB Ballet's repertory is an eclectic one that has been fashioned by a number of choreographers over the years. Using Prokofieff's score, Frank Staff produced *Romeo and Juliet,* the company's first original full-length ballet, in November 1964. Since that time the repertory has been enriched by such works as Richard Glasstone's *Mandoline* (1967) and *Ritual* (1971); Gary Burne's *Variations within Space* (1971); David Poole's *A Midsummer Night's Dream* (1970) and *The Rain Queen* (1973); and Veronica Paeper's *Don Quixote* (1981), *Orpheus in the Underworld* (1982), *The Merry Widow* (1988), and *Sylvia in Hollywood* (1993). Along with numerous other works by these choreographers, the CAPAB repertory includes dances made by other South African choreographers, including Lindy Raizenberg, Eduard Greyling, Norman Furber, Marina Keet, Audrey King, and Pamela Chrimes. Visiting choreographers and producers such as Attilio Labis, Alfred Rodrigues, Petrus Bosman, Anna Markard, and André Prokovsky have either mounted their own works or staged ballets by such luminaries as Ashton, Bournonville, Cranko, de Valois, Dolin, Fokine, Jooss, and Macmillan. [*See* CAPAB Ballet.]

SOUTH AFRICA: Ballet. Nicholas Beriozoff's 1980 production of *Romeo and Juliet* for PACT Ballet featured Stephen Jefferies and Dawn Weller in the title roles. Jefferies appeared as a guest artist from the Royal Ballet in London. (Photograph © by Nan Melville; used by permission.)

SOUTH AFRICA: Ballet. David Poole mounted *The Firebird* for CAPAB Ballet in 1965 and periodically revived and refreshed it for the next twenty-five years. This studio portrait of Elizabeth Triegaardt as the Firebird and Keith Mackintosh as Ivan Tsarevich was made for the 1980 revival. (Photograph by James de Villiers; courtesy of the Cape Town City Ballet.)

Historically, the first government-sponsored ballet performance in South Africa was PACT Ballet's *Giselle* in April 1963, with Yvette Chauviré as guest artist, partnered by Gary Burne, then the company's ballet master and principal dancer. These performances were presented jointly by the Performing Arts Council of the Transvaal (PACT) and Johannesburg City Ballet, under the name of Ballet Transvaal. Vera Volkova was then invited to work with the company and to stage *Swan Lake,* with guest ballerina Beryl Grey alternating with Phyllis Spira, the newly appointed *prima ballerina* of the company, both partnered by Burne. Early in 1964 Faith de Villiers was named artistic manager of the company, which was renamed PACT Ballet, with Marjorie Sturman as honorary consultant. In 1965 Frank Staff became resident choreographer and producer.

SOUTH AFRICA: Ballet. Phyllis Spira danced leading roles with both PACT Ballet and CAPAB Ballet, excelling in such classic works as *The Sleeping Beauty.* She is seen here as Princess Aurora, with Eduard Greyling as Prince Florimund, in the 1984 production mounted by CAPAB Ballet. (Photograph by James de Villiers; courtesy of the Cape Town City Ballet.)

For a number of years PACT Ballet was handicapped by a lack of continuity in artistic direction, undergoing six changes of leadership in the first two decades of its existence. The most successful directorships during these years were perhaps those of Faith de Villiers, from 1964 to 1968, and of Denise Schultz and Louis Godfrey, who jointly shared the post from 1973 to 1978. De Villiers, the company's first artistic manager, began to build a strong repertory, presenting *Coppélia,* as staged by Alexander Bennett, in 1965 and *Cinderella,* in a lavish production mounted by Françoise Adret, in 1966. These works were augmented by Walter Gore's *Nutcracker,* Roland Petit's *Carmen,* and two classic works by Frederick Ashton, *Façade* and *Les Patineurs,* as well as numerous works by South African choreographers: de Villiers herself, Yvonne Mounsey, Audrey King, Lorna Haupt, and Frank Staff. In the mid-1970s Denise Schultz and Louis Godfrey also had a successful period of company management, highlighted by Nicolas Beriosoff's productions of *The Nutcracker, Schéhérazade,* and *Romeo and Juliet.*

Finally, in the early 1980s, a measure of stability was achieved when artistic directorship of the company was undertaken by the current prima ballerina Dawn Weller. She has continued the company tradition of mounting such classics as *Swan Lake* and *La Sylphide,* of maintaining a close relationship with the Royal Ballet in England, and of bringing in guest artists and choreographers from the leading companies in Europe. In 1996, she was responsible for staging a full-length *La Bayadère,* one of the few such productions to be mounted outside Russia. [*See* PACT Ballet.]

Ballet Natal, later called NAPAC Ballet, began modestly with a program arranged by Dorothy McNair and John Pygram that was presented at seven school performances. Its first full program was produced in 1964 and included *Les Sylphides,* staged by McNair, who also choreographed an original ballet, *Test Match,* using music by Prokofiev. During the following two years, Gwynne Ashton, an Australian teacher working in Johannesburg since 1952, served as ballet mistress. In 1965 Frank Staff choreographed *Apollo 65,* with Veronica Paeper and Owen Murray in the principal roles, and *Swan Lake,* act 2, was given with Galina Samsova as guest artist. In 1966 the company joined forces with the Rhodesian National Ballet for a season and invited Johannesburg's PACT Ballet to make its first tour to Natal with its new production of *Coppélia.*

When the company became NAPAC Ballet in 1968, Dudley Davies was appointed ballet master, in association with his wife, Patricia Miller. They remained, in various capacities, until 1976, when the company was disbanded,

SOUTH AFRICA: Ballet. Tanja Graafland, with members of the ensemble, in George Balanchine's *Rubies,* staged for PACT Ballet by Patricia Neary in 1994. (Photograph by Edzard Meyberg; courtesy of PACT Ballet. Choreography by George Balanchine © The George Balanchine Trust.)

SOUTH AFRICA: Ballet. Veronica Paeper, director of the Cape Town City Ballet, is South Africa's most prolific choreographer. Among numerous full-length works mounted for the Cape Town company is her 1995 production of *Spartacus.* This scene shows members of the male ensemble as slaves performing armed combat for the amusement of their Roman captors. (Photograph by Pat Bromilow-Downing; used by permission.)

chiefly because of a lack of public support. During their tenure, however, NAPAC Ballet enjoyed several notable successes. Miller restaged John Cranko's *Beauty and the Beast,* a ballet in which she had created the role of Beauty, and Davies mounted several major classics, including *Giselle,* in which Merle Park and Donald Macleary appeared as guest artists in 1968. In 1974 Macleary again danced in *Giselle,* partnering Margaret Barbieri in her triumphant return to her hometown of Durban, where she received standing ovations from local audiences. Her performances broke all box-office records in Durban. Similarly, Dawn Weller's appearances in *Coppélia* in 1975 were greeted by Durban audiences with great appreciation and enthusiasm for a hometown girl who had achieved stardom as a ballerina.

In the Orange Free State, a stronghold of Afrikaner culture and the Dutch Reformed Church, ballet has never flourished to the extent that it has in other provinces of South Africa. Still, PACOFS Ballet can lay a legitimate claim to a significant place in the country's history of theatrical dance. It was directed by Frank Staff in the last years of his life, 1969 to 1971, and provided him with the opportunity to create two original works: *Séance,* set to music by Benjamin Britten, and *Mantis Moon,* with music by Hans Maske, based on a Bushman legend. [*See the entry on Staff.*]

An interesting aspect of all these ballet companies is the inclusion of Spanish dance in their repertories. This was a direct result of the tours of Luisillo and his company beginning in 1957 and of the formation of the Spanish Dance Society in 1965. The popularity of Spanish dance with South African audiences led the Spanish Dance Society to develop a syllabus and a method of teaching Spanish dance that is now taught in a number of other countries, including Spain. Over the years, performances of Spanish dance have been frequently presented in all of South Africa's major cities. In Johannesburg, PACT presented the Mercedes Molina Company with Enrique Segovia; in Cape Town, Marina Keet choreographed numerous productions for CAPAB and the UCT Ballet and, in 1981, Mavis Becker founded the Danza Lorca, a Spanish dance company, bringing illustrious dancers to perform with her, such as José Antonio (Ruiz); and in Durban, Joy Shearer and Paco Morell often choreographed and danced their own works for NAPAC, while Theo Dantes and Bernie Lyle presented performances of Spanish dance.

Political events in South Africa during the early 1990s have had and will continue to have a direct effect on ballet in South Africa. In the wake of the downfall of the Nationalist party, with its policies of racial *apartheid* ("separateness"), and the rise of a democratic government under the leadership of Nelson Mandela, a new national identity emerged. As South Africa realized itself as a "rainbow nation" of many peoples with many kinds of performing arts, the future of state-subsidized ballet companies came under increasing scrutiny and became the subject of heated debate. Predictions ranged across the spectrum, from the total demise of classical ballet in South Africa to the possibility of a single, large, government-funded national company.

A White Paper on the Arts was finally adopted by parliament late in 1996. This document outlined government involvement and policy toward all artistic endeavors. Specifically, the provincial arts councils will continue to be subsidized, but at decreasing levels, until 1999, after which only their core structures and service departments will receive funding from the central government. The performing companies sponsored by the arts councils are envisaged as being restructured into independent entities deriving funding from private, municipal, and provincial sources as well as from a new government agency, the National Arts Council.

BIBLIOGRAPHY

Borland, Eve. "CAPAB and PACT Ballet South Africa." *Dance Gazette* (March 1985): 29–32.

Cooper, Montgomery, and Jane Allyn. *Dance for Life: Ballet in South Africa.* Cape Town, 1980.

Glasser, Sylvia. "Is Dance Political Movement?" *Journal for the Anthropological Study of Human Movement* 6 (Spring 1991): 112–122.

Glasser, Sylvia. "Dancing in South Africa, Pre and Post Apartheid" (parts 1–2). *DCA News* (Winter 1995–Spring 1996).

Glasstone, Richard. "The Cape Ballet." *The Dancing Times* (September 1994): 1153–1157.

Grut, Marina. *The History of Ballet in South Africa.* Cape Town, 1981.

Hagemann, Fred. "The Politics of Dance in South Africa." *Ballett International* 13 (January 1990): 137–146.

Hagemann, Fred. "Having a Place in the World." *Ballett International* 15 (September 1992): 18–21.

Homzie, Hillary. "Pomare Travels to South Africa." *Dance Magazine* (August 1992): 12–13.

Larlham, Peter. *Black Theater, Dance, and Ritual in South Africa.* Ann Arbor, 1985.

Nelan, Rose. "Rewriting the Present." *Dance Magazine* (February 1989): 54–58.

Scimone, Diana. "Changes in South Africa." *Dance Teacher Now* 14 (April 1992): 52–57.

Sichel, Adrienne. "Healing Fractured Psyches through Dance: On the Divergent South African Dance Culture." *Ballett International* 14 (November 1991): 9–13.

South African Music Encyclopedia. Cape Town, 1979–.

Williams, Peter. "The Awakening Peninsula." *Dance and Dancers* (May 1975): 19–25.

Marina Grut
Amended by Jonathan Hurwitz

Contemporary Theatrical Dance

Following the formalities at his inauguration in the Union Building Gardens in Pretoria on 19 May 1996, President Nelson Mandela danced with the jubilant masses. The rhythmic dance of celebration by this revered elder statesman, who had been imprisoned by South Africa's Nationalist government for twenty-seven years, set the tone for the rest of the day's events, which united a racially and culturally divided population. The "rainbow nation" was born that day, and central to its birth were South African

SOUTH AFRICA: Contemporary Theatrical Dance. *Total Eclipse,* a full-evening dance work, was presented during the PACT Dance Company's first season in Pretoria, in April 1992. Choreographed by company director Esther Nasser, it was both a critical and a popular success. (Photograph by Edzard Meyberg; courtesy of PACT Dance Company.)

artists who had identified with the political struggle leading to it. Many of them participated in the concert of music and dance that was televised to a nation that had just miraculously escaped a prophesied bloodbath. Reflecting the theme "Many Cultures, One Nation," the concert included classical ballet, traditional and urban African dance styles, and contemporary dance in all its many facets.

For more than four decades, South Africans had lived with *apartheid,* the system of legalized racial segregation initiated by the Nationalist government when it came to power in 1948. This system, with its concepts of "homelands" and "separate development," had segregated and disenfranchised millions of people. It had also divided and isolated dance forms. During the years of *apartheid* (an Afkrikaans word meaning "separateness"), everyone could sing, dance, make music, and write plays (subject to government censorship) as long as blacks and whites did not do any of these things together or for mixed audiences.

Worldwide disapproval of *apartheid* and the consequent international boycott of South Africa resulted in cultural isolation that was particularly damaging to the development of contemporary dance in South Africa, which began in earnest only in the mid-1970s. Ironically, there was one positive effect of this cultural isolation. It forced visionary teachers, dancers, and choreographers to invent new teaching techniques and to develop new aesthetics drawn from a richly complex, dynamic, multicultural heritage. This often entailed breaking the law and taking physical risks. Theaters were only totally desegregated in the early 1980s, and it was a criminal offense for dancers of different races to share studios or stages.

The launch of South Africa's Dance Umbrella in association with Friends of the Ballet in February 1988 provided a free, safe, politically acceptable platform for black teacher-choreographers from Soweto, like Afro-jazz pioneer Carly Dibakoane, to share a stage with their white counterparts from Johannesburg. This festival—linked to Phillip Stein's AA Life Vita dance awards, now funded by the First National Bank (FNB)—remains a free platform to develop all contemporary South African dance forms and has spawned equivalents in other major cities: Dance Indaba in Cape Town, Dance Shongololo in Durban, Dance Umdudo in Grahamstown (in the Eastern Cape), and Dance Moketi (replacing Dance Kopana) in Bloemfontein. In 1994, the FNB–Vita Young Choreographer's Grant for two commissioned works was introduced and has since enriched the South African repertory.

When discussing dance in South Africa it is essential to set it into a basic sociopolitical context. The past three and a half centuries of its history were marked by colonial influences and occupations by Portugal, England, France, and Holland, culminating in the twentieth century with republican and liberation struggles. Indigenous peoples were either annihilated or repressed. The importation of slaves from Malaysia, the waves of immigrants from England, and the large-scale introduction of indentured laborers from India, coupled with migrations and invasions of African tribes, also had a profound influence. This legacy of political and cultural domination and fragmentation is detectable in South Africa's dance culture. Running parallel to a rich tradition of indigenous African dance—and related urban forms and styles that developed in the gold mines of the Transvaal and in urban townships (ghettos)—lies a history of classical ballet, ballroom, Spanish, and Indian classical dance performed by both professional and semiprofessional companies. Ballroom dancing is the third biggest sport in South Africa, a sports-crazy country.

SOUTH AFRICA: Contemporary Theatrical Dance. In Johannesburg, Sylvia Glasser made *Tranceformations* for her Moving into Dance Company in 1993. Vincent Mantsoe, pictured here with masked members of the ensemble, danced a leading role. (Photograph © by John Hogg; used by permission.)

Contemporary South African theatrical dance, which has weathered years of debate on Eurocentric versus Afrocentric art and training, harnesses all these influences and histories. Modern dance techniques were brought to this country from Europe and the United States mainly by women who traveled. Among the most significant figures in a history that has yet to be written were teachers such as Teda de Moor, Sheila Wartski, and Peggy Harper, who taught Graham technique in South Africa in the 1940s, 1950s, and 1960s. Harper left her homeland in the 1950s, when she clashed with the government for working with people of color, and became a respected African dance scholar and choreographer working in Nigeria, Ghana, and Zimbabwe. Since the 1960s, the Laban method has been taught extensively in university drama departments, where many academics and contemporary dance pioneers have trained. Chief among these is Professor Gary Gordon of the Dance Department at Rhodes University in Grahamstown, who started the influential First Physical Theatre Company in 1993.

Although the University of Cape Town (UCT) Ballet School, founded by Dulcie Howes in 1931, has always focused on classical ballet, Howes played a significant role in the sociocultural history of dance in South Africa because she found ways to beat the race laws. [*See* CAPAB Ballet.] "Coloured" dancers (people of mixed race) were trained at UCT, but, because of the laws of the land, on graduation they had to leave the country to dance professionally. Vincent Hantam, a star of the Scottish Ballet, who returned to South Africa in the 1990s, and Augustus van Heerden, dance master of the Dance Theatre of Harlem, were among generations of black dancers who had careers abroad, if they were lucky. A notable exception to the rule is Christopher Kindo, a dancer of Malay, Indian, and West African slave descent, who has made a successful career in South Africa.

In the late 1970s, Kindo left Cape Town with van Heerden to join the Boston Ballet, but after a time in North America he became homesick, and, after a stint at the Martha Graham School in New York, he returned to Cape Town and joined the Jazzart school, which had been founded by UCT graduate Sonje Mayo. When Mayo left for Johannesburg in 1978 to form the Mayo Modern Dance Ensemble, Jazzart, the country's oldest modern dance company, became the Sue Parker Jazzart Contemporary Dance Company. Subsequently, under Val Steyn, it was known as the Jazzart Contemporary Dance Company (1982–1986) and then, under Alfred Hinkel, as the Jazzart Dance Theatre Company (1986–1992). In 1992 the company became the modern dance department of the Cape Performing Arts Board (CAPAB). In the meantime, when the race laws were changed, Kindo had joined CAPAB Ballet and the Natal Performing Arts Council (NAPAC) Dance Company and had been employed as a dance captain at Sun City (South Africa's answer to Las Vegas, located in the then homeland of Bophuthatswana). Finally, in 1988, Kindo became a founding member of the Performing Arts Council of the Transvaal (PACT) Dance Company and its first dance master. He has since emerged as one of South Africa's foremost cross-cultural choreographers and is currently the associate director of Adele Blank's Free Flight Dance Company in Johannesburg.

SOUTH AFRICA: Contemporary Theatrical Dance. Dawn Langdown's *Soe Loep Ons*, created for the Jazzart Dance Theatre Company, was performed in December 1993 by Heinrich Reisenhofer (jumping) and Simpiwe Magazi at the Victoria and Albert Waterfront Amphitheatre in Cape Town. (Photograph by Anton Feun; courtesy of the Jazzart Dance Theatre Company.)

Much has changed in South Africa since its first democratic elections on 27 April 1994 brought the African National Congress into power. Of principal importance, a government of national unity was established, and in support of this goal the geopolitical structure of the country was reorganized. South Africa is now divided into nine provinces instead of the former four. The Transvaal was subdivided into Gauteng, North-West Province, Northern Province, and Mpumalanga; the Orange Free State be-

SOUTH AFRICA: Contemporary Theatrical Dance. Actor Jay Pather and members of the Jazzart Dance Theatre Company in a performance of Alfred Hinkel's *Medea* at the Market Theatre in Johannesburg in February 1995. (Photograph by Ruphin Coudyzer; courtesy of the Jazzart Dance Theatre Company.)

came simply the Free State; Natal became KwaZulu-Natal; and the Cape Province was subdivided into the Eastern Cape, the Western Cape, and the Northern Cape.

This provincial restructuring has also affected the arts. At the national level there is a Department of the Arts and Culture. Each province also has a department responsible for the arts and cultural heritage. By democratic process in November 1996, a National Arts Council, based on models from Europe and on the National Endowment for the Arts in the United States, was elected. It convened for the first time on 1 April 1997. In October 1996, the government of Gauteng (a Tswana word meaning "gold"), representing Pretoria, Johannesburg, and Soweto, had been the first provincial government to set up an interim arts and culture council to formulate policy and to elect a representative to send to the national council.

During the years of *apartheid,* arts funding in South Africa was administered and dispensed by the five performing arts councils and boards (in the Cape Province, Natal, Orange Free State, Transvaal, and Bophuthatswana). In the new dispensation, formulated in a hotly debated white paper released in June 1996, all art forms will have an equal opportunity to access funding. In effect, the state-funded ballet and dance companies will come to the end of decades of privilege and will be totally phased out by 1999. The state-built opera houses in Pretoria, Bloemfontein, Durban, and Cape Town will still receive funds, but they will cease to function as arts council production houses and will instead become presenters.

Major changes in companies supported by provincial arts councils began to occur as early as 1995. In the North-West Province, the neoclassical Bop Dance Company, which had been directed by David Krugel (now in Cape Town running Batho Dance) and which had been supported by the Bophuthatswana Performing Arts Council, was disbanded in 1995; the new North-West Arts Council turned it into a company specializing in ballroom and Latin American dances. In Gauteng, PACT Ballet, directed by Dawn Weller, and PACT Dance Company, directed by Esther Nasser, were given a period of grace, but in November 1996 they became autonomous companies, each with its own governing board, and, upon expiration of their contracts in September 1997, both will be renamed to reflect their new identities. The PACT Ballet School, founded in 1994 to train black children, will also change its name. In Cape Town, CAPAB Ballet, directed by Veronica Paeper, and CAPAB Jazzart Dance Theatre, directed by Alfred Hinkel, also became independent companies. In April 1997, CAPAB Ballet changed its name to Cape Town City Ballet.

In Durban, KwaZulu-Natal, the former Natal Performing Arts Council (NAPAC) was transformed into the Playhouse Company in January 1995 and has been struggling to find a way to survive once guaranteed funding dries up. The Playhouse Company has a very active, community-oriented dance department (linked to the organization's education and development department), which includes two contemporary dance companies: the Playhouse Dance Company and the Siwela Sonke Dance Company. The former, which was founded by Ashley Killar as NAPAC Dance Company in 1985, is now directed by Mark Hawkins. The latter, a successor to Alfred Hinkel's short-lived Phenduka Dance Company, was begun in 1994, when Hinkel was again seconded from Cape Town, as a unique training course drawing on the region's Zulu and classical Indian dance heritage. Launched in 1996, it is now directed by Jay Pather.

The Dance Factory, which is arguably the continent's only theater venue devoted entirely to contemporary dance, was founded in Johannesburg in 1992 by an association of concerned dancers, teachers, and choreographers from town and township to create a communal dance space that would also attract audiences. With support from the Johannesburg City Council, this dance center, directed by Suzette Le Seuer, is now housed in a converted garage workshop. It is a major presenter and training facility. International guest artists have included the Senegalese dancer and teacher Germaine Acogny, teachers from the Dance Theatre of Harlem, and New York's Bebe Miller, Donald Byrd / The Group, and Blondell Cummings.

Contemporary dance in South Africa is really in the first flush of its development. Dance Alliance, founded in Johannesburg, in the early 1990s to mobilize the dance community and to lobby politicians, has played a significant networking role. Another major developmental force has been the Pretoria Technikon Dance Department, which started out in 1982 to train ballet teachers. From its inception, under UCT graduate Susan Botha, it took the lone initiative to promote and teach contemporary dance choreography and musical theater. Under Vicki Karras, it has introduced South Africa's first dance-degree course, which will produce its first graduates in 1998. Since 1987 the Technikon has hosted the biennial Sanlam Ballet Competition, which became an international event in 1989.

SOUTH AFRICA: Contemporary Theatrical Dance. Alethea Knight and Gladys Agulhas in Robyn Orlin's *As Fall Women, So Fall Women,* choreographed in 1995 for the PACT Dance Company. (Photograph by Edzard Meyberg; courtesy of the PACT Dance Company.)

SOUTH AFRICA: Contemporary Theatrical Dance. Selva Hannam and Boyzie Cekwana in his *Lonely Won't Leave Me Alone,* mounted in 1995 for the Playhouse Dance Company in Durban. (Photograph by Val Adamson; courtesy of the Playhouse Dance Company.)

Other major training facilities are Sylvia Glasser's Afrocentric Moving into Dance Company (formed in 1978), which instituted its historic Community Dance Teachers Course in 1991, and the Johannesburg Dance Foundation (JDF), formerly Equinoxe Dance Theatre, established in 1980 by Corinna Lowry and Grayham Davies. The JDF, which has an extensive educational outreach program, also houses the Johannesburg Dance Theatre and JDF Ensemble. The Johannesburg Youth Ballet, begun in 1976 by Audrey King for all South Africans, regardless of race, is still functioning. The National School of the Arts now teaches contemporary dance as a matriculation subject in a syllabus set by Sonje Mayo.

Individual teachers and choreographers like Adele Blank, Sharon Friedman, Gisela Taeger-Berger, Tossie van Tonder, Esther Nasser, Geoffrey Sutherland, Frederick Hagemann, Gillian Joubert, Ken Yeatman, Dawn Langdown, John Linden, Arlene Westyergaard, Jeannette Ginslov, Henri Noppe, Eugene Berry, Jill Waterman, Marlene Blom, Debbie Rakusin, and Robyn Orlin have made important contributions across the country. Orlin, an idiosyncratic choreographer (influenced by Pina Bausch) and a performance artist, has choreographed extensively in South Africa and for Zimbabwe's Tumbuka Dance Company. In 1983, she started South Africa's first black contemporary dance company, the Federated Union of Black Arts (FUBA) Dance Company, and in the mid-1980s

SOUTH AFRICA: Contemporary Theatrical Dance. The Playhouse Dance Company in Sonje Mayo's *Soul of Africa,* created in 1995, with costumes designed by Andrew Botha. In 1996, Mayo created *Viva Afrika Borwa* for PACT Ballet, set to a commissioned score by South African composer Dean Hart. (Photograph by Val Adamson; courtesy of the Playhouse Dance Company.)

she founded the now defunct City and Theatre Dance Company before leaving South Africa to take up a Fulbright scholarship to study for her master's degree at the School of the Art Institute of Chicago.

Apart from Carly Dibakoane (a FUBA and Moving into Dance dancer), who directs the Soweto Community Dance Project in Meadowlands, Soweto has other notable pioneers, most of whom have attended the American Dance Festival's International Choreographers Program, in Durham, North Carolina. Nomsa Kupi Manaka founded the now defunct Soyikwa Institute of African Theatre's Pan African Dance Project. Jackie Mbuyiselwa runs the Soweto Dance Theatre, a company and school based at the YMCA in Orlando East Soweto. Ballet-trained Isabelle Doll (formerly a Sun City Dancer) started the Afro-fusion Soweto Street Beat Company at the Orlando West Swimming Pool. Subsequently relocated in Atlanta, Georgia, this company still considers itself a South African troupe. Its choreography and teaching methods fuse West African, South African, and Western influences and rhythms.

Africa is a continent where dance is indivisible from music and from life itself. Therefore the role of the African dancer-choreographer-musician creating for the stage is a multifaceted one. It carries with it elements of the shaman, the storyteller, the healer, the teacher, the poet, the cultural activist, and the entertainer.

These qualities are to be detected in work by South Africans making their mark nationally and internationally. Chief among them are the JDF graduate Boyzie Ntselileko Cekwana, the Playhouse Dance Company's first choreographer in residence (until March 1996), and Moving into Dance graduate Vincent Sekwati Mantsoe. Both Sowetan dancer-choreographers were recipients of FNB–Vita grants and the Standard Bank National Arts Festival's Young Artist Awards for dance in 1995 and 1996, respectively. Previously honored choreographers who have had their work performed on this national platform in Grahamstown were Lindy Raizenberg (1984), Gary Gordon (1989), and Robyn Orlin (1990). Both Mantsoe and Cekwana received important commissions from the African Odyssey Festival presented by the Kennedy Center in Washington, D.C., in the spring of 1997. The Dance Theatre of Harlem performed Mantsoe's *Sasanka* (Pride) in April and the Washington Ballet premiered Cekwana's *Savannah* in May.

As resources become available and creative movement is taught in regular schools, dance activities across the cultural spectrum will escalate throughout South Africa. What we have seen so far is just the beginning of what the "rhythm nation" has to offer the world.

BIBLIOGRAPHY

Glasser, Sylvia. "Is Dance Political Movement?" *Journal for the Anthropological Study of Human Movement* 6 (Spring 1991): 112–122.

Glasser, Sylvia. "Dancing in South Africa, Pre and Post Apartheid" (parts 1 and 2). *DCA News* (Winter 1995–Spring 1996).

Hagemann, Fred. "The Politics of Dance in South Africa." *Ballett International* 13 (January 1990): 137–146.

Hagemann, Fred. "Having a Place in the World." *Ballett International* 15 (September 1992): 18–21.

Sichel, Adrienne. "Healing Fractured Psyches through Dance: On the Divergent South African Dance Culture." *Ballett International* 14 (November 1991): 9–13.

ADRIENNE SICHEL

SOUTHERN AFRICA. The region known as southern Africa extends from Namibia on the Atlantic coast through Botswana, Zimbabwe, Malawi, and Swaziland to Mozambique on the Indian Ocean and to South Africa on the southern tip of the continent. The documentation of dance here, although slightly better than that of Central and East Africa, is nevertheless incidental to reports on music or social life. Detailed references can be found in the works of Hugh Tracey and Andrew Tracey on the Chopi of Mozambique and in those of Lorna Marshall and Richard Katz on the !Kung San (Bushmen) of Botswana. Other groups such as the Swazi, Shona, and Shangana-Tsonga are also fairly well documented, but many groups have not been studied in detail. Exceptions are provided by Nadia Nahumck Chilkovsky, who made choreographic comments and notations of the *ngodo* dances of the Chopi, and Dora Frankel and Andrée Grau, who notated the dances of the Venda.

Southern Africa shares several characteristics with the rest of the continent. Dance is a constant accompaniment to most social gatherings as well as to many religious rites. It is integrated into everyday life and is often used to provide ethical instruction as well as entertainment. Among the Shona of Zimbabwe, for example, dances are considered tests of general intelligence. A child's performance is thought to indicate whether he or she will become a competent adult. Through dancing, a child is introduced to society beyond the family group. Large, enthusiastic dances may be an important factor in attracting potential residents to a village. Most dances are exclusively male or female, although members of the opposite sex may participate in an accompanying role. For example, women may provide the vocal accompaniment and clapping for the men's dance, or men may play instruments for the women's dance. The music tends to be quite repetitive, employed primarily to provide a strict metrical foundation for the more syncopated activities of the dance routine.

The most commonly observed dance formations are, as in Central and East Africa, the single or double line and the circle moving in a counterclockwise direction. The carved wooden masks associated with Central and West Africa do not penetrate farther south than the upper Zambezi Basin, but grass masks are commonly used in initiation dances. Competitive dances and associated dance clubs, which originated in the coastal towns of Kenya and Tanzania and spread southward, are also found in Malawi. Some dance events are carefully organized; others, especially community gatherings such as banana-beer–drinking sessions, are informal, with individuals rising to dance as they feel moved and for as long as they wish. Team competitions have been regularly held in the dance arenas of the Witwatersrand gold mines since the early 1940s. The "mine dances" are hugely popular with both performers and audiences.

The most striking characteristic of southern African choreography is the prevalence of team dances composed of carefully measured movements performed in strict unison. Similar to the military drills once used to discipline young men, these dances are often athletic displays and include tumbling or acrobatics, requiring much skill and energy. A team of dancers rehearses arduously to attain the desired group coordination and precision. The Shangaan *muchongolo* dance drills, for example, are usually led and managed by an elderly man, but the dance steps are chosen by group consensus. A common practice is to have two types of leaders—a "manager" who deals with organizational aspects (attendance at rehearsals, punctuality, distribution of beer after rehearsals, and choice of costumes) and "artistic directors" of both music and dance. The music director is responsible for starting and stopping each dance, choosing and often leading songs and seeing that they are correctly performed, checking that the musical instruments are properly tuned, and supervising the coordination of song and dance. The director of dance supervises the choice of variations, demonstrates and teaches the steps, and checks that the performance is up to the expected high standard of unison. Occasionally, individual dancers break away from the formation and move forward to display their virtuosity.

Team dances are often characterized by stamping actions in perfect unison. The manner of raising the leg before stamping the foot varies, but the important factor is a high kick that gives strength to the blow; when a great number of dancers perform together, the ground shakes perceptibly with the impact. These stamping dances are found especially among the Nguni-speaking people—Zulu, Xhosa, Swazi (Swati), and Ndebele—and the closely related Tsonga (Shangaan).

All team dances are performed in set routines that together constitute the complete dance, the most complicated and elaborate being the *ngodo* dances of the Chopi of Mozambique. Performed to the sound of xylophones, *ngodo* were composed of a number of distinct movements, each with its own music, song, and dance, and each lasting one to six minutes. A full performance consists of eight to fifteen parts and lasts some forty-five minutes. Each dancer carries a long shield in his left hand and a spear in his right. Many of the dance actions resemble warlike maneuvers; attacks are feinted as the shields are twirled vigorously in front of the body, overhead, and downward, ultimately striking the ground with a resounding thump. Jumps and kicks vary in height and speed but

SOUTHERN AFRICA. Since 1886, when gold was discovered in South Africa, men from all over southern Africa have gone to work in the mines near Johannesburg. There they formed tribal dance teams and participated in competitive performances in specially constructed dance arenas. These four men are members of a large dance team of the Chopi tribe in Mozambique. They are performing *kukavula,* a concerted leap into the air that occurs during one of the sections of the *ngodo* orchestral dance for which the Chopi are famous. (Photograph by Merlyn Severn; reprinted by permission from Tracey, 1952, p. 134.)

always start with the dancer raising his right knee and then kicking the left leg high at the peak of the ascending motion. In between energetic sections, dancers adopt a swaying step, moving slowly from one foot to the other to recuperate. Precision is of great importance. Being out of step, even slightly, or making a mistake provokes laughter among the spectators. To offset the expected perfection of the team, some dancers may have the role of clowns, doing everything wrong.

The Shangana-Tsonga of Mozambique and South Africa also use shields, which they hit with dance batons or sticks to punctuate the action of the *muchongolo* dance. *Muchongolo* dancers are allowed choreographic freedom and exercise the wildest fancies in their costumes. They enter the dance ground somersaulting, walking on their hands, or performing other remarkable movement—always in perfect rhythm to the drums—before forming lines in front of the drums. A dance has four or five sections, each signaled by a change in drumming or by the leader's whistle or horn. The general aim of the dance is to execute unusual and apparently spontaneous movements with perfect uniformity. Dancers might throw themselves onto their faces and bounce along the ground on their hands and the tips of their toes. They might turn cartwheels and finish in couples, with one partner standing or sitting on the other's back. A sudden hiatus in the drumming might initiate staccato stamping accompanied by intermittent slapping of the shields, followed by somersaults; when the stamping resumed, spectators might expect another somersault, but instead the dancers might fall flat on their backs. The greater the element of surprise and spontaneity, the more the dancers are acclaimed. The performance also includes humorous mime, and one of the aims of the team is to devise as many comical situations as possible.

Shields and sticks are also used by the Swazi people of Swaziland and South Africa, especially during the dances held for the Incwala (kingship ceremony). The shields can be turned in a quick movement, or the sticks can be suddenly pointed at the ground. The men dance in a vast crescent facing the king's *kraal* (compound), swaying rhythmically until all, as one man, abruptly take a long step forward with the right foot, while women and girls dance toward and then away from the crescent.

The team dances of southern Africa usually play a sociopolitical role. Relationships between chiefs and villages are expressed in the rivalry of dance and orchestral groups. Headmen and chiefs occasionally assemble groups of musicians and dancers in competitive display, entertaining visiting dignitaries at home courts and sending uniformed teams to compete against those of political rivals. The sponsorship of teams usually entails providing beer and sometimes food to refresh the dancers after rehearsals (which may go on for weeks), as well as providing costumes, transport, or whatever is considered necessary to ensure the success of the performance.

Although team dances prevail in southern Africa, dancers do not lose their individuality. The freedom to improvise is, however, limited; teams aim to produce an

SOUTHERN AFRICA. At a "mine dance" performance in the late 1940s, this team of Ngoni tribesmen from Nyasaland (present-day Malawi) appeared in a circle dance, or round dance. The team leader leaps into the circle formed by seated dancers; three men dressed as women stand in the center. Having left their families at home, some of the miners perform the female roles that women would normally play. (Photograph by Merlyn Severn; reprinted by permission from Tracey, 1952, p. 57.)

overpowering effect with dozens if not hundreds of dancers performing the same movements. Nonetheless, as a Swazi dancer told Hilda Kuper (1952), "A person always dances alone, but stands with others." Most spectators can discern the originality and excellence of individuals among the crowd.

Other dances in the repertory allow more freedom. The team dances, which are carefully worked out and rehearsed before performances, emphasize creativity and invention in choreography and composition; other dances stress these qualities in improvisation and performance. Originality is highly valued.

Reed-pipe dances are popular in southern Africa. Single reed styles, in which each player-dancer plays a single note on his pipe, are found especially among the Pedi, Sotho, and Venda of South Africa and among the Tswana of Botswana and the North-West Province in South Africa. Panpipes are used as accompaniment among the Nyungwe of Mozambique. The Tswana have a reed-pipe dance in which each man plays a single end-blown pipe while performing steps or actions as he circles slowly in a counterclockwise direction. The musician-dancers provide the melody by blowing their pipes according to the principle of polyrhythm; no two pipes of different pitch play in unison.

The Nyungwe panpipes performance consists of four main parts: a panpipes part with voiced notes, a women's choir, the dancing, and the lead singer. The panpipes players dance fixed, named steps while continuing to play. The choice of dance steps is made by the lead singer, who introduces a new step in one of his phrases to warn the dancers of an imminent change. The other dancers follow, but the unison of the panpipes dance is different from

SOUTHERN AFRICA. Both tumbling and miming are features of the dances of the Ndau and Tswa tribes of Mozambique. These two Tswa tribesmen are miming a scene known to all gold miners, breaking a rock underground with a jackhammer. Comedy is introduced as the miner tries to hold his "jackhammer" down by sitting on it. The dancers' white leggings and wristbands are made of Angora goatskin. (Photograph by Merlyn Severn; reprinted by permission from Tracey, 1952, p. 113.)

SOUTHERN AFRICA. A group of Xhosa dancers in South Africa perform the *xhensa,* the shaking dance of the *amadoda,* men who have been fully initiated into adulthood. The dancers gyrate in a circle while their music makers clap and sing the dance song. The violent shaking characteristic of the dance is indicated by the waving pattern of the leather thongs suspended from the leading dancer's neck. (Photograph by Merlyn Severn; reprinted by permission from Tracey, 1952, p. 57.)

that of the team dances. Group coordination exists, but it is of another order: the dancers do not try to imitate the leader or copy his movements exactly, and each dancer has a wider range of acceptable variation. Most steps consist of twenty-four pulses and are repeated once, although some may vary the second time through. The dancers crouch slightly; the more enthusiastic the dancer, the lower the position. Each dancer wears a rattle on his right leg and stamps the ground with the right foot before shifting the weight onto the left foot. While the lead singer is performing, the dancers walk around, keeping the circle formation, sometimes with one hand on the shoulder of the man ahead. When the group dance starts again, they turn toward the center of the circle and either put the right foot forward or stay in the circular line and stamp the right foot in place.

The general use of the body in southern African choreography differs from that in Central and East Africa, where particular body parts are often isolated and emphasized. The Swazi royal daughters glided forward and back, swinging their hips, during the Incwala kingship ceremony; and Chopi women moved their shoulders up and down in some dances to represent the flapping of a bird's wings. Isolations are sometimes used as an incongruous movement to make a "dance joke." For example, among the Shona, a dancer may swivel her hips in an overtly sexual manner in the middle of a performance before resuming her dance. The joke may take other shapes, such as suddenly dropping to the knees and hopping along the floor in time to the music and then leaping back. To use the body as a whole, however, does not mean to use it stiffly. Dancers in southern Africa can twist and turn their bodies with great fluidity, although they do not usually isolate body parts by moving them in opposite directions. Here, too, leg movements seem to be more important than in Central and East Africa.

The !Kung San of Botswana, Namibia, and South Africa form a distinct choreographic group, similar in some ways to the so-called Pygmies of Central Africa. They have dances exclusively for women, as part of the girls' first menstruation ceremony, or exclusively for men, as part of the initiation rites for boys, but these segregated dances occur only once every few years. Most !Kung San dances exclude no one: octogenarians dance along with small children. The most common dance, which researchers have labeled a "medicine" or "healing" dance, provides preventive treatment as well as cure. It is performed regularly, not necessarily because someone is sick, but as an aspect of normal socialization. Also important in the !Kung's formal movement repertory are numerous miming movements used to portray animals in dramas, such as a play about the hunting of a gemsbok or its killing by a lion.

[*See also* !Kung San Dance; Shangana-Tsonga Dance; Venda Dance; *and* South Africa, *article on* Indigenous Dance. *For general discussion, see* Sub-Saharan Africa.]

SOUTHERN AFRICA. A group of men of the Tswana tribe, from the region of Botswana near the Northern Province of South Africa, performing *kubina dithlaka,* the pipe dance. Each dancer has his own pipe; each pipe produces only one note, which is added to the melody of the accompaniment at appropriate moments. The dance itself is a simple shuffling in a circle, and the dancers make no attempt at special dress. (Photograph by Merlyn Severn; reprinted by permission from Tracey, 1952, p. 84.)

SOUTHERN AFRICA. The !Kung-San people inhabit the Kalahari Desert region of Botswana, Namibia, and South Africa. In this medicine dance, the dancers circle about the seated groups, who clap and sing. One woman (second in line) and two young boys have joined the dancing men. Some people rest in the shade of the tree. (Photograph reprinted from Marshall, 1969.)

BIBLIOGRAPHY

Asante, Kariamu Welsh. "The Jerusarema Dance of Zimbabwe." *Journal of Black Studies* 15 (June 1985): 381–403.

Ballantine, Christopher J. "Tswana Pipe Melody." *African Music* 3.4 (1965): 52–57.

Bastin, Marie-Louise. "Musical Instruments, Songs, and Dances of the Chokwe." *African Music* 7.2 (1992): 23–44.

Berliner, Paul. *The Soul of Mbira*. Berkeley, 1978.

Blacking, John. "An Introduction to Venda Traditional Dances." *Dance Studies* 2 (1977): 34–56.

Blacking, John. "Trends in the Black Music of South Africa, 1959–1969." In *Musics of Many Cultures*, edited by Elizabeth May. Berkeley, 1980.

Burnett-van Tonder, Cora. *Sosio-etniese danse van die Venda-vrou*. Pretoria, 1987.

Carter, G., and P. A. Gardner. "The Incwala Festival in Swaziland." *Geographical Magazine* 30.7 (1957–1958): 263–272.

Cartmel-Robinson, S. "The Lupanda Dance." *Nyasaland Journal* 15.2 (1962): 20–22.

Chilivumbo, Alifeyo. "Malawi's Lively Art Form: Chiwoda Dancers Mirror Their Changing World in a Traditional Frame." *Africa Report* 16.7 (1971): 16–18.

Chilivumbo, Alifeyo. "Vimbudza or Mashame: A Mystic Therapy." *African Music* 5.2 (1972): 6–9.

Doke, Clement M. "Games, Plays, and Dances of the !Khomany Bushmen." *Bantu Studies* 10 (1936): 461–471.

Earthy, E. Dora. "Notes on Some Agricultural Rites Practised by the Valenge and Vachopi (Portguese East Africa)." *Bantu Studies* 2 (1926): 193–198, 265–267.

Friedson, Steven M. *Dancing Prophets*. Chicago, 1996.

Gelfand, Michael. *Growing Up in Shona Society*. Salisbury, 1979.

Grau, Andrée. "Dance Scholarship in Southern Africa." In *Beyond Performance: Dance Scholarship Today*, edited by Susan Au and Frank-Manuel Peter. Berlin, 1989.

Grau, Andrée. "Some Problems in the Analysis of Dance Style, with Special Reference to the Venda of South Africa." *The Choreologist* 40 (Summer 1990): 5–13.

Johnston, Thomas F. "Possession Music of the Shangana-Tsonga." *African Music* 5.2 (1972): 10–22.

Johnston, Thomas F. "The Cultural Role of Tsonga Beer Drinking Music." *Yearbook of the International Folk Music Council* 5 (1973a): 132–155.

Johnston, Thomas F. "Folk Dances of the Tsonga." *Viltis* (1973b): 5–19.

Johnston, Thomas F. "The Integrative Role of Dance in Shangana-Tsonga Social Institutions." In *Dance: Current Selected Research*, vol. 1, edited by Lynnette Y. Overby and James H. Humphrey. New York, 1989.

Junod, Henri A. *The Life of a South African Tribe*. New York, 1962.

Katz, Richard. *Boiling Energy: Community Healing among the Kalahari Kung*. Cambridge, Mass., 1982.

Kuper, Hilda. *The Swazi*. London, 1952.

Kuper, Hilda. "Incwala in Swaziland: Celebration of Growth and Kingship." *African Arts* 1.3 (1968): 56–59, 90.

Lancaster, Chet S. *The Goba of the Zambezi*. Norman, Okla., 1931.

Mair, Lucy P. "A Yao Girl's Initiation." *Man* 50 (1951): 60–63.

Marshall, Lorna. "The Medicine Dance of the !Kung Bushmen." *Africa* 39 (1969): 347–381.

Moyana, Toby T. "Muchongoyo: A Shangani Dance." *African Arts* 9.2 (1976): 40–42.

Parry, H. N. "The Nyau Dance." *The Dancing Times* (June 1944): 402–404.

Read, Margaret. *Children and Their Fathers: Growing Up among the Ngoni of Nyasaland*. London, 1959.

Schadeberg, Jürgen. *The Kalahari Bushmen Dance*. London, 1982.

Schaeffner, André. *Le sistre et le hochet: Musique, théâtre et danse dans les sociétés africaines*. Paris, 1990.

Schapera, Isaac. *The Khoisan People of South Africa*. London, 1930.

Sugawara, Kazuyoshi. "Interactional Aspects of the Body in Co-Presence: Observations on the Central Kalahari San." In *Culture Embodied,* edited by Michael Moerman and Masaichi Nomura. Senri Ethnological Studies, no. 27. Osaka, 1990.

Taylor, G. A. "Some Mashona Songs and Dances." *Nada* 4 (1926): 38–42.

Thompson-Drewal, Margaret. "Films on Music and Dance in Southern Africa." *Dance Research Journal* 12 (Fall–Winter 1979–1980): 30–33.

Tracey, Andrew T. N. "The Nyanga Panpipe Dance." *African Music* 5.1 (1971): 73–89.

Tracey, Andrew T. N. *A Companion to the Films "Mgodo wa Mbanguzi" and "Mgodo wa Mkandeni."* Johannesburg, 1976.

Tracey, Hugh T. *Chopi Musicians: Their Music, Poetry, and Instruments.* London, 1948.

Tracey, Hugh T. *African Dances of the Witwatersrand Gold Mines.* Johannesburg, 1952.

Tracey, Hugh T. "Dances of Aborigines." In *Standard Encyclopaedia of Southern Africa.* Cape Town, 1970–.

Twala, R. G. "Uhmlanga (Reed) Ceremony of the Swazi Maidens." *African Studies* 11.3 (1952): 93–104.

JOHN BLACKING

SPAGNOLETTA. The origins of the *spagnoletta* (Sp., *españoleta*), a flirtatious couple dance popular in the sixteenth century, are unknown. Four to six figures are danced to a single popular (fast triple) tune. There are only five extant choreographies: four in Fabritio Caroso's manuals (1581, 1600), in which one version is for a trio and one is "in the style of Madrid" (the implications of which are not defined); the fifth is in one of the English so-called Manuscripts of the Inns of Court (Bodleian MS Douce 280, John Ramsey, *Practise for Dauncinge,* c.1578), which is without music or step descriptions. A two-couple *spagnoletto* in duple in Cesare Negri's collection (1602) reveals no direct relationship to Caroso's dances and also seems indistinguishable from Negri's other two-couple dances.

There are no other known choreographies in print or manuscript. The *spagnoletta* is mentioned by Filippo Alessandri (1620), but not by F[rançois] de Lauze (1623) or Marin Mersenne (1636). Juan de Esquivel Navarro cites it in 1642 as one of the old dances still done in *saraos* ("soirées") and *máscaras* ("masques") "for his majesty and other princes." Choreographies in "Spanish" style abound in the publications of the eighteenth century, but none has been found set to the well-known *spagnoletta* tune, even in Spanish or Portuguese sources.

Except for the tune (which also formed the basis for many vocal and instrumental variations in the seventeenth century), Caroso treats his four *spagnolettas* as *cascarda/saltarello* types, with their standard figures, such as passages traversing the floor side by side, playful movements facing or turning away from and back to each other, and with the standard step patterns of fast triple dances (e.g., *seguiti spezzati, fioretti, passi minimi*). His *spagnoletta*s in no way resemble Ramsey's description (see above), which calls for the man to "heave up ye woman" in his arms, and the woman to "heave upp ye man, honor & soe ende" (there is no way of knowing whether this lusty gesture resembles any authentic Spanish dance of the time).

Despite the name, only two of Caroso's four versions even briefly use the canary steps that authorities of the period perceived as Spanish. Because some *cascardas* also use canary steps, however, this usage does not authenticate Spanish origins, but at most some kind of exoticism. There is, however, a musical relation between the third strain of the *spagnoletta* music and standard contemporary canaries, both melodically and in the short tonic-dominant ostinato bass. It is there, in fact, that canary steps and choreographic patterns occasionally occur. Thus, it is known that Caroso recognized the *spagnoletta*'s partial musical relationship to the canary, but he treated it choreographically largely as a *cascarda/saltarello* type.

Twentieth-century sources (Italian only) merely cite the dance. Some of these writings are questionable for their propagandistic purpose (under Mussolini) of reviving old Italian dances. However, the best say that nothing is now known of the dance but its name (in some areas). Significantly, all the modern sources see it as a folk dance. Thus, although it seems to have arisen from obscurity and returned to it, charming variants remain from its courtly heyday.

BIBLIOGRAPHY: SOURCES

Alessandri, Filippo degli. *Discorso sopra il ballo.* Terni, 1620.

Caroso, Fabritio. *Il ballarino* (1581). Facsimile reprint, New York, 1967.

Caroso, Fabritio. *Nobiltà di dame.* Venice, 1600, 1605. Facsimile reprint, Bologna, 1970. Reissued with order of illustrations changed as *Raccolta di varij balli.* Rome, 1630. Translated into English with eight introductory chapters by Julia Sutton, the music transcribed by F. Marian Walker. Oxford, 1986. Reprint with a step manual in Labanotation by Rachelle Palnick Tsachor and Julia Sutton, New York, 1995.

Esquivel Navarro, Juan de. *Discursos sobre el arte del dancado* (1642). Facsimile reprint, Madrid, 1947.

Jacobilli, Ludovico. *Modo di ballare.* Circa 1615. Manuscript located in Foligno, Biblioteca Jacobilli, AIII.19, ff.102–104.

Manuscript of the Inns of Court. Located in Bodleian Library, Bodleian, Douce 280, ff.66av–66bv (202v–203v).

Praetorius, Michael. *Terpsichore.* Wolfenbüttel, 1612. Facsimile reprint of text only in *Gesamtausgabe der musikalischen Werke.* Vol. 15. Edited by Friedrich Blume et al. Wolfenbüttel, 1928–1960.

BIBLIOGRAPHY: OTHER STUDIES

Commune di Roma Assessorato all Cultura. *La danza tradizionale in Italia, mostra documentaria.* Rome, 1981. Includes a lengthy bibliography of popular (i.e., folk) dances in Italy.

Esses, Maurice. *Dance and Instrumental Diferencias in Spain during the Seventeenth and Early Eighteenth Centuries.* Stuyvesant, N.Y., 1992.

Hudson, Richard. "Spagnoletta." In *The New Grove Dictionary of Music and Musicians.* London, 1980.

JULIA SUTTON

SPAIN. [*To survey the dance traditions of Spain, this entry comprises four articles:*

Dance Traditions before 1700
Social and Theatrical Dance, 1700–1862
Theatrical Dance since 1862
Dance Research and Publication

See also Basque Dance; Bolero; Escuela Bolera; *and* Flamenco Dance. *For further discussion, see the entries on individual companies, choreographers, and dancers.*]

Dance Traditions before 1700

As a Carthaginian outpost in the third century BCE, Spain was famous for the *puellae gaditanae,* Celtic-Iberian dancing girls whose graceful, seductive dances were performed for war, peace, worship, love, and entertainment. Spain's Roman conquerors sent Spanish dance choirs to Rome; even then, Spain's dances featured complex footwork, hip movements, and shell castanets. When Christianity triumphed in Spain in the third century CE, Iberian dances penetrated the churches, cemeteries, and saints' feasts. Dance declined under the Visigoths, who followed the Romans as conquerors in Spain, and male mimes became the dominant entertainers. The eighth-century Moorish conquest introduced a court and culture that appreciated Spanish dance and that contributed its own rhythms and complex spatial designs. Moorish influence in music, costume, language, and art survived the completion of the Christian reconquest of Spain in 1492. The arrival of Gypsy bands in the 1400s had introduced additional Eastern influences to popular dance.

Throughout the medieval period, *juglares* (itinerant entertainers) took mime, dance, satire, poetry, song, and puppetry from town to town. Male and female *juglares* entertained both rich and poor, with some serving noblemen or city governments. With characters such as shepherds or villagers, performances typically included satire, slapstick, and acrobatics. The religious plays and fables of the fifteenth and sixteenth centuries reflected the influence of this theater by incorporating pastoral themes, popular characters, song, and dance.

In the late medieval and early Renaissance periods, a literary form called the *danza* emerged. Focusing on religious themes, the *danzas* were performed within the church, usually by villagers and shepherds. Two examples of this *danza* are the fourteenth-century "Danza General," a version of the Dance of Death, by the *converso* Rabbi Sem Tob (Shem Tov, who became the Christian Rabí don Santo), and the sixteenth-century "Danza del Santissimo Nacimiento de Nuestro Señor," by Pedro Suárez de Robles. The latter work was the culmination of Spain's ancient Christmas dances, which are mentioned as early as the mid-thirteenth century by King Alfonso X.

Sixteenth-century Spanish theater retained and expanded the role of dance. Many plays opened and closed with lively, often acrobatic dances performed by groups of popular characters. These dances may have begun with the performers joining hands in a ring dance, but the development of the choreographies often included leaping, jumping, tumbling, arm gestures, exaggerated facial expressions, running, and whirling. Finales of pastoral plays featured verse compositions with refrains and simple choreographies. Danced play interludes led to the literary form called the *baile* or *baile entremesado.* Often the main attraction for the public, the baile featured humor, song, and dance, unrelated to the main plot. Dramatists of the era, including Quevedo Villegas and Miguel de Cervantes, specialized in writing the texts for these incidental works.

Under the Hispanic church liturgy, which evolved during the Moorish domination, Corpus Christi and other religious feasts were celebrated with dance. The churches of Seville and Toledo presented their finest choirboys, called *los seises,* ("the sixes"), in elegant, pavane-like choreographies at the altars of the cathedrals. The institution of *los seises* evolved as a group of eight to twelve select choristers, some as young as eight, who were chosen for the quality of their voices and were fully supported and educated at the expense of the local cathedral chapter. Their activities included daily altar duties and a rigorous school program that focused on music and religious education. For major processional feasts such as Corpus Christi, the Feast of the Immaculate Conception, and celebrations of royal visits, *los seises* performed dances to music written especially for them by their own music masters. Until the late sixteenth century, they also performed in Christmas plays dressed as little shepherds or angels and were directed by professional actors. Documentation exists indicating that they received some training from dancing masters hired by the church to rehearse them for their Corpus Christi performances. The dancing of *los seises* continues to this day in Seville, although the youngsters are no longer supported or educated by the cathedral council but are chosen from among talented boys attending local schools. Valencia featured similar performances in the sixteenth century, and more dramatic dances may have preceded the courtly works performed later in the Golden Age of the sixteenth and seventeenth centuries.

For major processions, Spain's city councils commissioned professional dancers for works based on religious, classical, or national themes. These ballets were independent works, featuring eight to twenty characters, spectacularly costumed; the ballets were performed within the cathedral and outdoors, along the processional route. These dances had no sung or written text, but drew on both popular and courtly dances to produce lively choreographies appealing to all social classes. A regular component of these festivals was the *morisca,* a sword dance based on the ancient dance called "Moros y Cristianos."

The dance commemorated the centuries-long struggle (from 711 to 1492) between Christians and Muslims in Spain.

Following the Moorish period, Spain's princes were educated in the social dances of the court, and Arab dancing girls were popular with the Christian nobility. In the fifteenth and sixteenth centuries, noblemen displayed their strength, agility, and grace through dance. Under Philip IV, from 1621 to 1665, dance and courtly behavior were so important as to form almost a religious code. A century later, Bartholomé Ferriol y Boxeraus commented, in his *Reglas útiles para los aficionados a danzar,* that courtiers had to master the art of dance, and that Philip V founded three academies where masters were employed to teach this discipline.

Among the entertainments at the Spanish court was the *sarao:* "the gathering of ladies and gentlemen in a principal and memorable festivity, especially in the palaces of kings and great lords, where the necessary seating is placed in a large, decorated hall: . . . one dances to the sound of many musical instruments, and also it is customary to have vocal music" (Covarrubias, 1611). Probably choreographed by the lord's dancing master, the *sarao* combined dance with music and drama and was usually performed by nobles dressed in magnificent costumes. The Spanish *sarao* apparently focused even less on plot line than did its Italian equivalents, and the emphasis was on brilliant execution of a variety of dance forms, perhaps with an allegorical theme as a loose organizing principle.

Dramatic courtly entertainments called *máscaras* (a type of masque) required clear characterization, costuming, and the wearing of masks. Some were performed on horseback, as were the choreographed bullfights and jousts of the period. By the late seventeenth century, the *máscara* may have evolved away from its original intent, losing its dramatic focus. *Máscaras* and *saraos* involved grand processional entries, each couple honoring the king or host and following complex rules of courtesy. The king himself often danced, along with the queen and courtiers. Sometimes, younger members of the court presented entertainments for the adults, and new dances sometimes premiered on these occasions. The novelty of staging and costuming was always intrinsic to the event's success, however.

Spanish dance manuals record close parallels with the mainstream of European Renaissance court dance. An Italian influence dominated in Castile and Andalusia, while the Cervera dance manuscript (c.1468) indicates French influence in Catalonia. A Castilian translation of Cesare Negri's *Le gratie d'amore* appeared in 1630. Dancing master Esquivel Navarro, in his *Discursos sobre el arte del danzado* (1642), commented on several Italian masters in Madrid who had conformed their teaching to that of Antonio de Almenda and Francisco Ramos, the outstanding Spanish masters of the age. Spain contributed several dances to European courts and theater and also brought exotically costumed New World dances from her conquered territories in the Americas. Spanish clothing was fashionable throughout Europe, and the farthingale skirt and stiff ladies' bodice shaped stylistic and movement possibilities during the sixteenth century.

In music, as in dance, Spain exchanged influences with her neighbors and with the New World, contributing her name to the popular Renaissance song "La Spagna." Spanish dance music, flavored with Moorish rhythms and harmonies, could be vocal or instrumental, and song texts from stage works often referred to dancing. Instrumental accompaniment for dance included the vihuela, rebec, guitar, tambourine, kettle drum, pipe and drum, timpanum, lute, bells, timbrel, harp, viol, and violin. Much dance music was based on tunes that were familiar to all who performed and heard them, and the themes could be treated improvisationally. Although much of this music was not written down, some dance music of the Spanish Renaissance can be found in Spain's archives. Although great rhythmic variety is evident, triple meters dominate. Singing, reminiscent of Moorish prayer chants, led to the emergence of the popular *cante jondo* ("deep song") of southern Spain.

The dancing master, who educated both the nobility and the middle class in social dance and comportment, was an important figure in Golden Age Spain, and even earlier, in the Middle Ages. Among his dance disciples, Esquivel lists state officials, court constables, public scribes, merchants, painters, jurists, silversmiths, and military men. To guard against those traces of disrepute that clung to the dance, the academies Esquivel describes taught only men, although women were permitted as occasional observers. Esquivel went to excessive lengths to distance himself from crude popular dance, and from the people associated with it, in order to establish his respectability. Mixing the sexes, apparently, was too risky for so delicate a situation. Ladies, it is assumed from other sources, were taught at home or at separate schools.

Popular dance flourished in the Renaissance. For example, merchants' fairs concluded at night with dancing and revelry. To ensure the proper solemnity at the death of royalty, Seville's government had to issue decrees prohibiting such irrepressible amusements as music and dance. Heat waves were endured by sharing dinner, songs, and dances by the riverside, well into the night. Some dances passed to the upper classes, but in their popular versions, they included stamping, acrobatic contortions, running, leaping, tumbling, hand clapping, castanet playing, and singing. The courtly versions of these dances, while refined for the tastes of the aristocracy, were appreciated for the variety of movement they offered, with kicks, jumps, and even special sorts of bows adopted from the popular works. From this period came the Andalusian seguidilla, related to a particular form of poetic and musical refrain, with all the complexity and grace that typifies the popular dances of southern Spain.

Among the most notorious of Spanish dance was the *zarabanda* (saraband), whose reputed lewdness has left many records of the dance in the form of moralists' attacks. It was described as "gay and lascivious because it is done with waggings of the body, and the arms making more gestures, sounding the castanets" (Covarrubias, 1611). Despite official prohibitions, the *zarabanda* was so popular—especially in its birthplace, Andalusia—that it made its way into Seville's Corpus Christi procession in the late sixteenth century.

Ordinary people learned these dances largely, it seems, from imitation, observing friends and family at home, in cafés, and at fiestas. Esquivel disdained those dancing masters who carried their guitars or violins from tavern to café to plaza, offering public dance lessons for whatever money was tossed into their cap. He accused them of ignoring dance fundamentals, lacking personal authority, and deceiving people into taking dance lessons at bargain prices. These wandering masters probably played an important role in the spread of popular dances from region to region and from class to class. In addition to these dancing masters, actors also knew a wide range of popular and court dances, and the theater served as another medium of stylistic and regional diffusion. Popular dances featuring lively movement, and often with a story line, fell into the category of *danzas de cascabeles* ("dances of little bells"), referring to the bells sewn into the dancers' costumes. The term identified some of the lively, dramatic dances commissioned for public festivals.

The question of popular dance versus courtly dance leads to the linguistic issue of Spain's two words for dance—*baile* and *danza.* Further investigation of these terms—their usage and meaning in the Golden Age—is warranted, but some tentative distinctions may be suggested here. The term *baile* seems to have indicated popular dancing, with its wilder movements, including the arms and torso, while *danza* was used more often to refer to aristocratic dances of a graver and more cultured style, primarily restricted to leg movements. The term *baile* also was used most frequently to refer to the actual performance or activity of dancing, while *danza* referred to the dance piece itself. The word *baile* was most often used for a dance inserted into a play, and *danza* referred to independent dance works, created by choreographers, rather than by theater directors or playwrights.

Definitions provided in the old dictionaries link *baylar* with capers, jumps, arm gestures, and twisting movements. The word *danzar* is defined as dancing with gravity, to instrumental rhythms, with order, with schooling, and with education in the precepts. The linguistic distinction between popular and aristocratic dance is strongly suggested here, although the definitions themselves make use of the two terms, indicating that they were also used correlatively. In Emilio Cotarelo y Mori's roster of dance types, some are called *bailes* while others are called *danzas* (Cotarelo, 1911). These dances fall roughly into popular and courtly forms, although many began as popular *bailes* and, after courtly adoption and transformation, entered the category of *danzas,* while retaining a popular version.

BIBLIOGRAPHY

Barrera y Leirado, Gayetano Alberto de la. *Catálogo del Teatro Español.* Madrid, 1860.

Borrow, George. *The Zincali: An Account of the Gypsies of Spain.* London, 1841.

Brooks, Lynn Matluck. "Los Seises in the Golden Age of Seville." *Dance Chronicle* 5.2 (1982): 121–155.

Brooks, Lynn Matluck. *The Dances of the Processions of Seville in Spain's Golden Age.* Kassel, 1988.

Brooks, Lynn Matluck. "Cosmic Imagery in the Religious Dances of Seville's Golden Age." *Choreography and Dance* 3.4 (1994): 17–27.

Capmany, Aurelio. "El baile y la danza." In *Folklore y costumbres de España,* vol. 2, edited by Francisco Carreras y Candi. Barcelona, 1934.

Castellanos de Losada, Basilio Sebastián. *Discursos histórico-arqueológicos sobre el orígen, progresos, y decadencia de la música y baile español.* Madrid, 1854.

Chase, Gilbert. *The Music of Spain.* New York, 1959.

Cotarelo y Mori, Emilio. *Colección de entremeses, loas, bailes, jácaras, y mojigangas.* Madrid, 1911.

Covarrubias, Sebastian de. *Tesoro de la lengua castellana o española.* Madrid, 1611.

Davillier, Baron Charles. *Spain.* Translated by John Thomson. New York, 1876.

Esquivel Navarro, Juan de. *Discursos sobre el arte del dancado* (1642). Madrid, 1947.

Esses, Maurice. *Dance and Instrumental Diferencias in Spain during the Seventeenth and Early Eighteenth Centuries.* Stuyvesant, N.Y., 1992.

García Matos, Manuel. "Cante flamenco: Algunos de sus presuntos origenes." *Anuario Musical* 5 (1950): 97–124.

González Climent, Anselmo. *Flamencologia.* Madrid, 1955.

González Climent, Anselmo. *Bibliografía flamenca.* Madrid, 1965.

González Climent, Anselmo, and José Blas Vega. *Segunda bibliografía flamenca.* Malaga, 1966.

Grande, Félix. *Memoria del flamenco.* 2 vols. Madrid, 1979.

Inglehearn, Madeleine. "A Dancing Master in the Early Seventeenth Century." *The Dancing Times* (April 1993): 670–671.

Lewis, Daniel, ed. *Dance in Hispanic Cultures.* Yverdon, Switz., 1994.

Machado y Alvarez, Antonio. *Colección de cantes flamencos: Recogidos y anotados por Demofilo [pseud.].* Seville, 1881.

Márban Escobar, Edilberto. *El teatro español medieval y del renacimiento.* Madrid, 1971.

Meri, La [Russell Meriwether Hughes]. *Spanish Dancing* (1948). Pittsfield, Mass., 1967.

Molina Fajardo, Eduardo. *Manuel de Falla y el "Cante Jondo."* Granada, 1962.

Molina, Ricardo, and Antonio Mairena. *Mundo y formas del cante flamenco.* 2d ed. Seville, 1971.

Pohren, D. E. *Lives and Legends of Flamenco.* Madrid, 1964.

Pohren, D. E. *The Art of Flamenco.* Seville, 1972.

Rey, Juan José. *Danzas cantadas en el renacimiento español.* Santiago de Campostela, 1978.

Sánchez Romero, José. *Castilla: La copla, el baile, y el refrán.* Madrid, 1972.

Shergold, N. D. *A History of the Spanish Stage from Medieval Times until the End of the Seventeenth Century.* Oxford, 1967.

Stark, Alan. "What Steps Did the Spaniards Take in the Dance?" In *Proceedings of the Fourteenth Annual Conference, Society of Dance History Scholars, New World School of the Arts, Miami, Florida, 8–10 February 1991,* compiled by Christena L. Schlundt. Riverside, Calif., 1991.

Starkie, Walter. *Spain: A Musician's Journey through Time and Space.* 2 vols. Geneva, 1958.

Triana, Fernando el de [Rodríguez Gómez, Fernando]. *Arte y artistas flamencos.* 2d ed. Madrid, 1952.

LYNN MATLUCK BROOKS

Social and Theatrical Dance, 1700–1862

Many references to *danzas* and *bailes* (two generic terms for dance) are found in the works of dramatists of Spain's Golden Age (sixteenth and seventeenth centuries). The existence of plays with titles such as *La escuela de danza* by Navarrete y Ribera (c.1592–1652), *El maestro de danza* by Lope de Vega (1562–1635), and another with the same title by Calderón de la Barca (1600–1681), indicate the popularity of dance. *Maestros de danzas* ("dancing masters") were hired to arrange dances for plays as early as 1540; the importance of dance as a social grace among the upper classes also necessitated the services of a dancing master. If a dance teacher were not available, dance manuals were used.

SPAIN: Social and Theatrical Dance, 1700–1862. A woodcut illustrating how to dance the minuet from Pablo Minguet e Irol's *Arte de danzar à la francesa,* published in Madrid in 1737. (Courtesy of Mary Ann O'Brian Malkin.)

SPAIN: Social and Theatrical Dance, 1700–1862. An early nineteenth-century engraving of a male *bolero* dancer. He is wearing a streamlined version of eighteenth-century costume, including flat slippers instead of shoes with heels. (*Colección general de los trages que en actualidad se usan en España,* 1804.)

Spain was one of the first countries to record its social dances in a system of dance notation, and notation was to be an important element in dance manuals of the eighteenth century. The first Spanish book devoted entirely to dance was *Discursos sobre el arte de danzado* (1642) by Juan de Esquivel Navarro, dancing master to Philip IV. The next dance book, by Bartolemé Ferriol y Boxeraus, did not appear until a century later in 1745. Pablo Minguet e Irol, a famous engraver as well as an author and translator, published works on a wide range of subjects; his dance books included several important works which incorporated the French dance notation of Raoul-Auger Feuillet. Other dance works included a manuscript work by Juan Antonio Jaque and published books by Felipe Roxo de Flores (1793), Don Preciso (pseudonym of J. A. Iza Zamacola y Ozerin) (1796), Cairón (1820), and Biosca (1832).

The literature of the late eighteenth century reflected changes in dance genres, with the publication of books on the technique or "science" of playing castanets. This was inspired by the introduction of a new dance, the *bolero* (believed to have been created by either Sebastián Cerezo or Antón Boliche in 1780), as well as by the *seguidillas* and *fandango*; manuals also included introduced French and Italian ballet techniques. The *seguidillas,* one of the oldest and most popular dances of the Spanish people, was featured frequently in the works of Golden Age playwrights. The *fandango*, another favorite dance of the people, was a dance whose propriety, like that of the *zarabanda* (saraband) at an earlier date, was questioned by the authorities.

The introduction of the *bolero* into the ballrooms of society was seen as a measure to counteract the invasion of foreign dances under the influence of the Bourbon dynasty. Because it was important for young ladies to know the bolero, dancing masters were in great demand, and bolero schools existed in towns as far-flung as Madrid, Cadiz, Seville, Córdoba, and Murcia. These schools were not only important for the upper ranks of society but were also frequented by the lower classes, who learned dance in order to perform in theatres and taverns.

The repertory of the dancing schools included not only variants of the *seguidillas* and *bolero* but also dances such as the *olé, vito, manola, jaleo de Xerez, caracoles, peteneras,* and *zapateados* (the last three should not be confused with modern flamenco dances bearing the same names). Some of the dances were performed as solos, but most were for a man and a woman performing as a pair, with opportunities for each to demonstrate virtuosity.

These school dances are variously referred to as *bailes de la academia* or *bailes de la escuela, escuela bolera, bailes de palillos* or more recently, *bailes de candil,* the last referring to the fact that in taverns and patios the dances were lit by hanging oil lamps. These dances were eventually to share performing honors in the *cafés cantantes* (cafes featuring flamenco) in which flamenco became a professional art form.

SPAIN: Social and Theatrical Dance, 1700–1862. In the nineteenth century, Spanish dancers often performed theatrical versions of their national dances on stages well beyond the borders of Spain. *(left)* Felix García and Manuela Perea (known as La Nena) in the *Bolero de la Caleta,* which they first danced in London on 10 April 1845. *(right)* Pepita de Oliva, a dancer who appeared in many European countries, was depicted in 1853 wearing a Spanish costume and playing castanets. (Photographs from the Dance Collection, New York Public Libray for the Performing Arts)

The science of playing castanets (considered an essential accompaniment for the dances of the *escuela bolera*) was a much easier subject to write about than actual dance movements. Consequently numerous works, varying in tone from serious or moralistic to jocular, appeared under real or pseudonymous authorship.

The era of Romantic ballet saw a vogue for national dances, which were inserted into many ballets and *divertissements.* Paris took to heart the Spanish dancers who appeared in 1833; Dolores Serral, Mariano Camprubí, Francisco Font, and Manuela Dubinon were the first Spanish dancers to cross the border over the next twenty years and captivate audiences not only in Paris but in other French cities, London, Copenhagen, and around Europe.

The Spanish visitors made an enormous impact on the ballet world. Fanny Elssler's performance of the *cachucha* in *Le Diable Boiteux,* fiery and voluptuous, thrilled audiences in Europe and America. Elssler modeled the dance on traditional *escuela bolera* steps, and her success inspired many other ballet dancers to tackle the Spanish idiom. Audiences' enthusiasm for these dances encouraged other Spaniards to follow in the steps of Serral, Camprubí, and their partners. Audiences thrilled to the art of Manuela Perea (known as La Nena), Josefa Vargas, Petra Cámara, and Pepita de Oliva. Many prints of the Romantic era show the Spanish idiom; Édouard Manet immortalized the 1862 company of Camprubí in two paintings that bring to life the color and vitality of the Spanish dancers.

[*See also* Bolero; Castanets; Escuela Bolera; *and* Seguidillas.]

BIBLIOGRAPHY

Blas Vega, José. *Los cafés cantantes de Sevilla.* Madrid, 1987.

Cairón, Antonio. *Compendio de las principales reglas del baile.* Madrid, 1820.

Derra de Moroda, Friderica. "A Spanish Book of 1758: Another Eighteenth-Century Book Discovery." *The Dancing Times* (July 1931): 336–338.

Fernández de Rojas, Juan. *Crotalogía o ciencia de las castañuelas.* Barcelona, 1792.

Ferriol y Boxeraus, Bartolomé. *Reglas utiles para los aficionados a danzar.* Capua, 1745.

Gingell, Jane. "Spanish Dance in the Golden Age: The Dance Text of Juan Antonio Jaque." In *Proceedings of the Fourteenth Annual Conference, Society of Dance History Scholars, New World School of the Arts, Miami, Florida, 8–10 February 1991,* compiled by Christena L. Schlundt. Riverside, Calif., 1991.

Guest, Ann Hutchinson. *Fanny Elssler's Cachucha.* New York, 1981.

Guest, Ivor. *Fanny Elssler.* London, 1970.

Guest, Ivor. *The Romantic Ballet in England.* London, 1972.

Guest, Ivor. *The Romantic Ballet in Paris.* 2d rev. ed. London, 1980.

Guest, Ivor, trans. and ed. "Théophile Gautier on Spanish Dancing." *Dance Chronicle* 10.1 (1987): 1–104.

Ivanova, Anna. *The Dance in Spain.* New York, 1970.

Iza Zamácola, Juan Antonio de. *Elementos de la ciencia contradanzaria.* Madrid, 1796.

Lewis, Daniel, ed. *Dance in Hispanic Cultures.* Yverdon, Switz., 1994.

Llorens, Pilar, et al. *História de la danza en Cataluña.* Barcelona, 1987.

Matteo. *The Language of Spanish Dance.* Norman, Okla., 1990.

Meri, La [Russell Meriwether Hughes]. *Spanish Dancing* (1948). Pittsfield, Mass., 1967.

Minguet e Irol, Pablo. *Breve tratado de los passos del danzar a la española.* Madrid, 1764.

Pericet Blanco, Eloy. "Influencia andaluza en la Escuela Bolera." In *Actas del II congreso de folclore Andaluz: Danza, música e indumentaria tradicional.* Seville, 1988.

Rojo de Flores, Felipe. *Tratado de recreación instructiva sobre la danza: Su invención y diferencias.* Madrid, 1793.

Ruyter, Nancy Lee Chalfa. "Satirical Dance Texts as Historical Sources: Two Examples from Spain." *Cairón,* no. 1 (1995): 73–84.

Suárez-Pajares, Javier, and Xoán M. Carreira. *The Origins of the Bolero School.* Studies in Dance History, vol. 4.1. Pennington, N.J., 1993.

Udaeta, José de. *La castañuela española: Origen y evolución.* Barcelona, 1989.

PHILIPPA HEALE

Theatrical Dance Since 1862

In the latter half of the nineteenth century, flamenco began its transition from an intimate mode of expression to a professional art form. In 1862 the French writer Davillier described performances of flamenco and Andalusian dances presented for tourists in Granada; in 1866 the first publicized flamenco performance took place in Seville. In the popular *café cantantes* flamenco became a stage art, and dances from the *escuela bolera* were eventually performed there as well. These clubs proliferated throughout the country until the 1920s and were responsible for introducing the public to many of flamenco's outstanding artists. During this time, often referred to as "the golden age of flamenco," much of its dance technique and repertory were established. La Macarrona, El Estampío and Frasquillo, among others, achieved renown for their mastery of rhythmic footwork. The *bata de cola's* long train was introduced and created new movement possibilities for female dancers. Modern-day *tablaos* descend from the *café cantantes;* the best of them continue to be a proving ground for young talent. The popularity enjoyed by flamenco and Andalusian dances also meant that they were often added to plays and light operas *(zarzuelas)* as notes of local color. During the later nineteenth century, dance continued to flourish in Barcelona's Teatro Principal and Teatro del Liceo, the Teatro Real in Madrid, and many theaters in Seville, where ballet was presented regularly. The Liceo and the Real had corps de ballets, and the Real had its own school.

Escuela bolera teachers incorporated ballet barre and center exercises in their classes, and the dancers' technique improved. In Seville Angel Pericet Carmona opened his first school in 1897, later moving to Madrid and founding a dynasty of respected *escuela bolera* teachers and performers, carried on to this day by his grandchildren. In 1942 he and his son Angel Pericet Jiménez published the first *escuela bolera* curriculum. [*See* Bolero; Escuela Bolera; *and* Pericet Family.]

Artists from the Liceo such as Rosita Mauri or Ricard Moragas—*premier danseur* as well as a composer and director—became famous throughout Europe. Mauri was named an *étoile* at the Paris Opera, where he performed from 1878 to 1907. Teachers Pauleta Pamiés and Juan Magriñá were instrumental in promoting dance in Barcelona. A distinguished performer and choreographer, in 1932 Magriñá began to present solo recitals, a novel enterprise in the city at that time. He continued his independent performing career with many partners, among them María de Avila, Aurora Pons, and Rosita Segovia, even after he was named *premier danseur* and ballet master at the Liceo in 1939. He was resident choreographer at the theater until his retirement in 1976.

Creative individuals rather than systematic schools of dance have often been responsible for the evolution of dance as a theatrical art form in Spain. The artistry of exceptional performers and choreographers, who carefully polished for the concert stage dances that had long been acclaimed in more intimate settings, brought Spanish dance international recognition and appreciation. Antonia Mercé, called La Argentina (1890–1936), was a pioneer in this respect. A gifted performer with enormous stage presence and excellent technique, she included in her repertory not only flamenco and adaptations of traditional Spanish dances but also pieces set to music for her by composers Isaac Albéniz, Enrique Granados, and Manuel de Falla, among others. These were presented in programs of short works she performed throughout Europe and the Americas in solo concerts, and, beginning in 1929, with her ensemble, the first Spanish repertory dance company. This formula would be repeated successfully over the years by many dancer-choreographers and

SPAIN: Theatrical Dance since 1862. During the first two decades of the twentieth century, flamenco experienced a rebirth and moved from the music hall to the concert stage. A corresponding shift of style emerged, including an enlargement of gesture and an increasing awareness of spatial patterns and scenic design. Rosario's Spanish Dance Company, pictured here in the 1950s, was one of a number of Spanish troupes that toured Europe. (Photograph by Annemarie Heinrich; used by permission.)

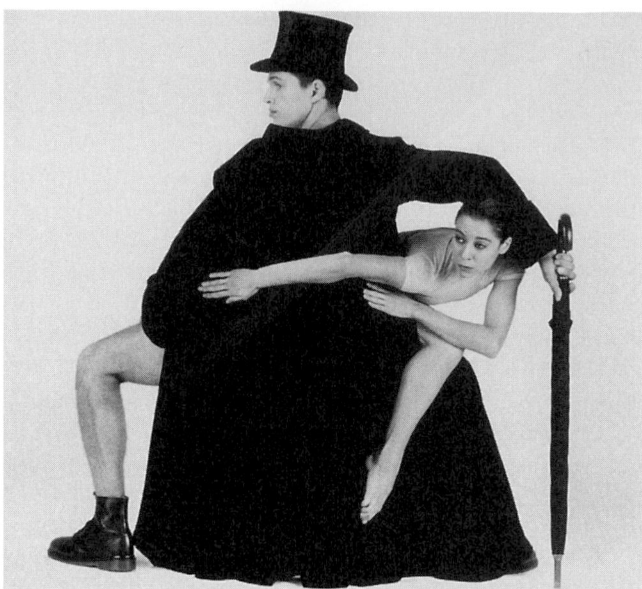

SPAIN: Theatrical Dance since 1862. A studio portrait of Ruth Maroto and Thomas Klein of the Compañía Nacional de Danza in Nacho Duato's *Alone for a Second,* set to music by Erik Satie. (Photograph © by Jorge Represa; used by permission.)

represented a definitive step toward formalizing Spanish dance as a theatrical art. [*See* Flamenco Dance *and the entry on La Argentina.*]

During this period, the interpreter Pastora Imperio premiered Falla's *El Amor Brujo* (Love, the Magician; 1915), the first flamenco ballet as well as the first orchestration of flamenco rhythms. That year Serge Diaghilev and the Ballets Russes visited Spain. Captivated by flamenco music and dance, he added Falla's *Le Tricorne* to his company's repertory in 1917.

Argentina, Vicente Escudero, Argentinita (Encarnación López) and her sister Pilar López, Antonio Ruiz (first with his partner Rosario and later with his own company), Mariemma, Teresa and Luisillo, and Carmen Amaya are some of the outstanding performers who toured extensively from the 1920s through the 1960s with their companies. Many established contact with leading cultural and intellectual figures of their day, resulting in rewarding collaborative efforts. Carmen Amaya's fierce sense of rhythm and driving footwork changed established concepts about flamenco dance for women. These companies provided opportunities to explore new choreographic and musical structures and trained many young artists, such as Antonio Gades, José Greco, Manolo Vargas, and Roberto Ximénez, who all began their careers with Pilar López. [*See* Ximénez-Vargas Ballet Español *and the entries on Amaya, Antonio and Rosario, Escudero, Gades, Greco, López, and Luisillo.*]

In 1973 Gades premiered an innovative, austere, and powerful choreographic version of Federico García Lorca's *Blood Wedding,* later taken to the screen by filmmaker Carlos Saura as part of a trilogy with *Carmen* and *El Amor Brujo.* Saura produced two dance-related films on his own, *Sevillanas* (1992) and *Flamenco* (1995). Other innovative choreographers include Mario Maya, José Granero, José Antonio, and the late Rafael Aguilar.

In 1978 the Spanish Ministry of Culture founded the Ballet Nacional Español, a national ensemble presenting Spanish classical, regional, and flamenco dance. The following year the Ballet Nacional Clásico was created. The former was directed by Gades, while Victor Ullate—formerly a star in Maurice Béjart's company—headed the ballet company. Both directors stepped down in 1983 when the ministry announced that the distinguished ballet teacher María de Avila would assume responsibility for both groups. Under Avila's direction the ballet company added works by George Balanchine and Antony Tudor to its repertory. In 1984 the Ballet Nacional de España premiered José Granero's *Medea,* a landmark in the genre of flamenco dance drama. In August 1986 María de Avila resigned as director and dancer-choreographer José Antonio (Ruiz) assumed leadership of the Spanish dance company. Since 1993 it has been directed jointly by Aurora Pons, Nana Lorca, and Victoria Eugenia.

Maya Plisetskaya was invited to head the ballet company, now known as the Ballet del Teatro Lírico Nacional, with Ray Barra as associate director. In June 1990 the young dancer-choreographer Nacho Duato assumed directorship of the latter, which under the new name Compañía Nacional de Danza performs a contemporary repertory with works by Jiří Kylián, Hans van Manen, William Forsythe, Duato, and others.

The lack of a national classical ballet company is a controversial subject. It remains to be seen whether Madrid's Teatro Real, due to reopen as an opera house in 1997, and Barcelona's Teatro del Liceo, destroyed by fire in 1993, will have resident ballets. Several private ballet companies exist in Spain, the most outstanding being the Ballet de Victor Ullate, founded in 1988, followed by Bilbao's Ballet de Euskadi and the Ballet de Zaragoza.

In the 1990s a new generation of flamenco artists have given the genre a more contemporary look. Their dance training often includes ballet, jazz, and modern dance, and the results can be seen in the spectacular technique of many young performers. Names such as Antonio Canales, Joaquín Cortés, Antonio Márquez, and Lola Greco, among many others, have joined those of such respected figures as Antonio Gades and Cristina Hoyos. The fusion of flamenco with other Mediterranean musical styles and the addition of percussion, flute, electric bass, and violin to traditional accompaniment have also influenced contemporary flamenco dance.

Tórtola Valencia's exotic and individualistic dance portraits, performed at home and abroad, won her a place among the earliest exponents of modern dance in Spain from 1909 to 1930, but only during the past twenty-five years has Spanish contemporary dance really come into its own. Teachers such as Anna Maleras in Barcelona, and Carmen Senra and Carl Paris in Madrid introduced modern dance technique to Spain. The Institut de Teatro de Barcelona's diploma program in contemporary dance helped to create a strong nucleus of dancers and choreographers in Catalonia. Cesc Gelabert, Angels Margarit-Mudances, Danat Dansa, Ramón Oller-Metros, Mal Pelo, and Juan Carlos García-Lanónima Imperial in Barcelona, along with Valencia's Ananda Dansa and Madrid's 10 y 10 Danza, are some of established companies and choreographers winning recognition both in Spain and abroad. Contemporary dance activity has also increased recently in the Basque country and Andalusia. The Centro Andaluz de Danza was founded in Seville in 1994. Nevertheless, many dancers from Spain must find creative outlets and employment with foreign contemporary dance and ballet companies and will most likely continue to do so until there is an adequate support structure for dance in Spain.

[*See also* Ballet Nacional Español *and the entries on Duato and Gelabert.*]

BIBLIOGRAPHY

Antonia Mercé "La Argentina": Homenaje en su centenario, 1890–1990. Madrid, 1990.

Blas Vega, José. *Diccionario enciclopédico ilustrado del flamenco.* 2d ed. Madrid, 1990.

Bourio, Juan María. *Colección Juan María Bourio.* Madrid, 1992.

Encuentro internacional "La Escuela Bolera." Madrid, 1992.

García Otzet, Montse. "La danza contemporánea de Cataluña ha cumplido veinte años." Program, Madrid en Danza festival. Madrid, 1990.

Koegler, Horst. *The Concise Oxford Dictionary of Ballet.* 2d ed. Oxford, 1987.

Llorens, Pilar, et al. *História de la danza en Cataluña.* Barcelona, 1987.

LAURA KUMIN

Dance Research and Publication

Dance manuscripts first appeared in Spain in the fourteenth century; the oldest is *El libre vermell de Montserrat.* An anonymous book published around 1496 in Cervera, Catalonia, *Manuscrit de Cervera,* is one of the first known notation books. In the following century, two anonymous manuscripts were written, *Manuscrit de Tarrago* and *Arte para aprender a danzar, aunque mal se puede aprender con sólo leer.* In the seventeenth century one of the most important of all Spanish dance books, *Discursos sobre el arte del danzado* (1642), was written by Juan de Esquivel Navarro.

In the eighteenth century the production of dance

SPAIN: Theatrical Dance since 1860. Members of the all-male Catalan dance-theater company La Fura dels Baus during a performance of their evening-length *Sur O/Sur* on a sound stage in Queens, New York City, in 1991. The group, whose name means "the scum of the sewers," creates violent, ritualistic spectacles set to industrial rock music that surround and assault the audience. The work pictured involved quantities of raw meat, animal blood, sawdust, crushed chalk, and water, and several crude vehicles like those seen here; the piece evoked images of riots, primeval war, and sacrifice. (Photograph © 1991 by Jack Vartoogian; used by permission.)

books increased. The most important are *Reglas utiles para los aficionados a danzar* (1745) by Bartolomé Ferriol y Boxeraus; *Breve tratado de los passos del danzar a la española* (1764) by Pablo Minguet e Irol; *Crotalogía o ciencia de las castañuelas* (1792) by Juan Fernández de Rojas; *Tratado de recreación instructiva sobre la danza: Su invención y diferencias* (1793) by Felipe Rojo de Flores; and the best known, *Elementos de la ciencia contradanzaria* (1796) by Juan Antonio de Iza Zamácola. Unfortunately, many of the dance manuscripts of the past were burned by the Inquisition, and others were lost through neglect.

During the nineteenth century the *escuela bolera* flourished. The most important books of this era are *Las castañuelas* (1879) by Francisco Asenjo y Barbieri, and *Compendio de las principales reglas del baile* (1820) by Antonio Cairón. Many books of historical importance can be found in the Barbieri Collection in the National Library in Madrid.

At the beginning of the twentieth century appeared *Colleción de entremeses, loas, bailes, jácares y mojigangas del siglo XVI al XVIII* (1911) by Emilio Cotarelo y Mori, and *Tratado de bailes españoles* (1912) by José Otero Aranda, a compilation of popular and flamenco dances. In the mid-twentieth century, two ballet lovers who lived in Barcelona wrote extensively about dance: Alfonso Puig authored *Ballet y baile español* (1951); Sebastiàn Gasch published *De la danza* (1946), establishing the guidelines for dance historiography. The important folklorist Aurelio Capmany produced several books, notably the two-volume *La dansa a Catalunya* (1930–1953) and *El ball i la dansa popular a Catalunya* (1948). Part of Alfonso Puig's papers are in Palau Güell at the Institut del Teatre in Barcelona. Since then hardly anything has been published, and in Spain there is no single publisher who specializes in dance.

Research and Criticism. Until the mid-1990s, there were no degree programs in dance at the university level in Spain, but legislation mandated that these would be provided. The University of Alcalá de Henares (Madrid) began a degree program in 1995–1996. There are also people in Spain doing postgraduate courses in related fields or pursuing dance studies abroad. There had also been no specialized journal, but the University of Alcalá de Henares has begun a publication named *Cairón*.

Historically, Spain has not had a ballet tradition, and for this reason media, book publication, and audiovisual material in the field are in their infancy compared to other countries. Before the 1980s, the Spanish press covered only foreign companies touring in Spain and flamenco performances. After two state dance companies were created—Ballet Nacional de España and Compañía Nacional de Danza—press coverage increased. In the late 1980s cultural sections began to appear in newspapers, including features on dance. The only recognized dance critic of the 1950s and 1960s was Edgar Neville of *ABC* newspaper in Madrid. In Spain, dance criticism has usually been conflated with theater and music criticism, but there are notable exceptions. In *El país* the criticism of Roger Salas appears regularly. In Catalonia's *Avui*, Xavier Perez, the theater critic, covers dance events. In *Vanguardia*, Marjolin van der Meer is the critic and sometimes reports on premieres in the rest of Europe. Montse García Otzet comments on dance for *El periodico* and *El país*. In Madrid, Julio Bravo has been the dance critic of the *ABC* since 1986, Julia Martin for *El mundo* since 1989, and Delfí Colomé and Estrella Casero-García for *Diario 16*. In northern Spain's *El correo español*, the music and opera critic, Carmelo Errecacho, is also the dance critic, and there is an annual special section written by Cosme Berañano. In Andalusia, only *Diario 16* has a dance critic, Marta Carrasco Benítez.

Generally, dance information in Spain has increased in recent years, especially in Seville after Expo 92, as a result of the summer festivals Festival de Música y Danza and Festival de Danza Itálica. Flamenco is an exception: for the past twenty-five years it has had a daily section in many newspapers.

There are only two dance magazines. *Ballet 2000*, the Spanish version of Italy's *Balletto oggi*, comes out bimonthly and is coordinated by Roger Salas; *Por la danza*, edited by the Professional Dance Association in Madrid, also appears every two months.

MARTA CARRASCO BENÍTEZ and NÈLIDA MONÉS I MESTRE

ŠPAREMBLEK, MILKO (born 1 December 1928 in Farnaves, Slovenia), dancer and choreographer. Šparemblek studied at the Zagreb Ballet School with Ana Roje and Oskar Harmoš after studying comparative literature and Slavic linguistics. His fondness for dance led him into it as a career. In 1951, as corps dancer and soloist with the National Theater, he danced such varied roles as Romeo in Prokofiev's *Romeo and Juliet*, the Prince in *Eine Mittelalterliche Liebe*, and the Miller in *Le Tricorne*.

In 1953 he went to Paris, where he worked with Olga Preobrajenska and Serge Peretti, danced with Janine Charrat, Maurice Béjart, and Ludmilla Tcherina, and became a member of the Yugoslav core of the Miškovic Troupe. His 1957 libretto for the ballet *L'Échelle*, to music by Zdenko Turjak, demonstrated creative talent. Immediately thereafter he presented his first choreographic work, *Quatuor*, to music by Raffaello de Banfield, in which he danced with Tessa Beaumont, Veronika Mlakar, and Vasilij Sulić. Such works as *Der Mann vor dem Spiegel*, to music by Milka Kelemen, *Die Sieben Todsunden* (The Seven Deadly Sins), to music by Kurt Weill, *Orfeo*, to music by Carlo Monteverdi, and *Siegfried-Idyll*, to music by

Richard Wagner, were all works typical of modern dance theater.

In 1963 and 1964 Šparemblek served as ballet master and deputy director of the Ballet du XXe Siècle in Brussels. He spent the next five years as a choreographer, composer, and director for companies, festivals, and television productions and as a designer of sets, costumes, and lighting. Starting in 1970, Šparemblek spent four years as artistic director of the Ballet Gulbenkian in Lisbon; for three of those years he also choreographed ballets for New York's Metropolitan Opera.

In 1975 Šparemblek choreographed his first ballet evening in Zagreb; the program included *Opus 43,* to music by Ludwig van Beethoven, *Sonata,* to music by Claude Debussy—in a premiere with Maja Srbljenović and Stefan Furijan—and *Trionfi di Afrodite,* to music by Carl Orff. The public and the dance world alike responded enthusiastically to his work. He was equally successful in Ljubljana in 1977 with *Magnificat,* a dance work based on the hymnal themes from Johann Sebastian Bach's oratorio, and with the premiere of *Duett,* to music by Anton Webern, op. 6, 10, danced by Lane Stranić and Vojko Vidmar, with costumes by Maria Kobi. Late in the fall of 1977 he produced the Zagreb premieres of *Die Sieben Todsünden, Visage,* to music by Luciano Berio, and *Psalmensymphonie,* to music by Igor Stravinsky.

From 1977 to 1980 Šparemblek was ballet director in Lyon, where his productions included *Chants de l'Amour et de la Mort,* inspired by Gustav Mahler's songs of a traveling apprentice—"Lieder eines fahrenden Gesellen" and "Des Knaben Wunderhorn"—and his song-symphony *Das Lied von der Erde.* An expanded version of the evening-length work, under the Croatian title *Pjesme Ljubavi i Smrti,* was performed at the Zagreb National Theater on 24 April, 1981, with sets by Šparemblek and costumes by Ika Škomrlj. Gustaf Mahler, danced by Stefan Furijan, witness and victim in this deathly dance of life, was led from the prologue through thirteen episodes to an epilogue by the Lady in Red, alias Death, danced by Maja Srbljenović. Šparemblek's ability to develop the eloquence of tensions and resolutions in his dancers is superb. Lidija Mila was perfect as the unfortunate Girl Clown, as was Irena Pasarić in the tragic role of the Fiancée. This existential work was awarded the choreography prize at the Ninth Yugoslav Ballet Biennial of Ljubljana.

On 22 April 1982, Šparemblek presented *Dragi Miha* (Dear Michael), a farce for one dancer and five percussion musicians, danced by Vojko Vidmar, at the Ljubljana Cankarjev Dom. At the Ljubljana Opera House on 25 June 1983, *Pulcinella* and *The Soldier's Tale* were performed under the aegis of the Igor Stravinsky Ballet Theater. The adaptation, staging, and choreography were by Šparemblek, and the costumes by Škomrlj; Gabor Tasfi played Pulcinella and Vojko Vidmar the Soldier. Šparemblek's first appearance as a choreographer at the Belgrade National Theater came with *Catulli Carmina* and *Trionfi di Afrodite,* both to music by Carl Orff. In 1986, collaborating with Frano Parac, Šparemblek choreographed *Carmina Krleziana,* dedicated to Croatian poet Miroslav Krleza, for the Croatian National Theater's 125th Jubilee. In 1991 the ballet company of the Teatro San Carlo performed Šparemblek's *Sinfonia dei Salmi* to the music of Stravinsky. For the Nationaltheater Zagreb in 1990, he presented his full-evening ballet *Amadeus Monument* to the music of Wolfgang Amadeus Mozart.

Šparemblek created two dance films for television, *Enigma Gallus* (1989), to the music of Gallus Carniolus, and *Objem* (1995), to the music of Vojko Vidmar-Portrait, both presented in Ljubljana.

BIBLIOGRAPHY

Boutwell, Jane. "Prime Mover." *Opera News* (9 January 1971).

Hering, Doris. "Two by Šparemblek." *Dance Magazine* (November 1970): 77–80.

"Milko Šparemblek Talks about Himself and Europe." *Dance News* (October 1967): 4.

Van Gelder, Lindsay. "Daily Closeup: The Commuter." *New York Post* (21 September 1970).

PIA MLAKAR and PINO MLAKAR
Translated from German

SPARTACUS. Russian title: *Spartak.* Ballet in four acts and nine scenes. Choreography: Leonid Yakobson. Music: Aram Khachaturian. Libretto: Nikolai Volkov. Scenery and costumes: Vera Khodasevich. First performance: 27 December 1956, Kirov Theater, Leningrad, Kirov Ballet. Principals: Askold Makarov (Spartacus), Inna Zubkovskaya (Phrygia), Alla Shelest (Aegina), Robert Gerbek (Crassus).

The slave rebellion led by Spartacus and its suppression by troops under Crassus were real events in the history of Rome in the first century BCE. In the ballet *Spartacus,* the conflict between cruelty and violence and noble ideas and moral integrity is revealed in mass scenes (the gladiators' conspiracy, the feast, the battle scenes, Crassus's triumph) and in the solos of the protagonists: the brave Spartacus; the treacherous hetaera Aegina, who helps Crassus to encircle the rebels' camp by subterfuge; and Phrygia, Spartacus's beloved and faithful wife who laments the hero's death in the finale.

A new production of *Spartacus* was presented at the Bolshoi Theater on 9 April 1968, with libretto and choreography by Yuri Grigorovich, sets and costumes by Simon Virsaladze, and Gennady Rozhdestvensky conducting. At that performance Vladimir Vasiliev danced Spartacus, Ekaterina Maximova was Phrygia, Nina Timofeyeva was Aegina, and Maris Liepa played Crassus. This production was awarded the Lenin Prize and has been staged in many countries of the world.

Grigorovich renounced the luxuriant stage scenery and the meticulous details of the action of the earlier version. His ballet has a historically authentic but generalized and austere decor that corresponds to the heroic and tragic events of the action and the drama of Khachaturian's music. The contrasting mass scenes, based on dance similar to symphonic music in structure and development, alternate with solo "monologues" by the protagonists. Dance metaphors are liberally used. Every act ends in a symbolic scene. In the first act it may be called "A Thrust to Freedom," in the second act, "A Stronghold," and in the finale of the third act, which is a requiem for the fallen Spartacus, a series of moving symbolic scenes evoke associations with the finest masterpieces of world art (e.g., *Pietà, Deposition from the Cross*). Remaining within the limits of classical dance, Grigorovich created contrasting choreographic images of enslavement and freedom.

The ballet has been produced by other Russian and eastern European choreographers, has been seen worldwide, and remains in active repertory up to the present day.

BIBLIOGRAPHY

Alovert, Nina. "The Soviet Dance Theater of Yuri Grigorovich." *Dance Magazine* (December 1987): 39–42.

Balanchine, George, with Francis Mason. *Balanchine's Complete Stories of the Great Ballets.* Rev. and enl. ed. Garden City, N.Y., 1977.

Dorris, George. "Music for Spectacle." *Ballet Review* 6.1 (1977): 45–55.

Goodwin, Noël. "Grigorovich's *Spartacus.*" *Dance News* (September 1969): 6.

Greskovic, Robert. "The Grigorovich Factor and the Bolshoi." *Ballet Review* 5.2 (1975–1976): 1–10.

Grigorovich, Yuri, and Victor V. Vanslov. *The Authorized Bolshoi Ballet Book of Spartacus.* Translated by Tim Coey. Neptune City, N.J., 1990.

Haskell, Arnold L. "Russian Logbook" (parts 1–3). *The Dancing Times* (June-September 1962).

Parker, Ralph. "*Spartacus* and Plisetskaya." *Dance Magazine* (September 1962): 30–35.

Roslavleva, Natalia. "The Bolshoi's *Spartacus.*" *The Dancing Times* (June 1969): 463.

Tigranov, Georgii. *Balety A. Khachaturiana.* 2d ed. Moscow, 1974.

Vanslov, Victor V. *Balety Grigorovicha i problemy khoreografii.* 2d ed. Moscow, 1971.

VICTOR V. VANSLOV
Translated from Russian

SPESSIVTSEVA, OLGA (Ol'ga Aleksandrovna Spesivtseva, also known as Olga Spessiva; born 18 [6] July 1895 in Rostov; died 16 September 1991 in New York State), Russian dancer. A student at the Imperial Theater School in Saint Petersburg, Olga Spessivtseva joined the company of the Maryinsky Theater in 1913. She came to the attention of the public and of such critics as Valerian Svetlov and Akim Volynsky, and in 1916 she was made soloist, performing *La Bayadère* to great acclaim. In the same year she joined Diaghilev's Ballets Russes for a tour of the United States, gracefully depicting a young girl lost in a dream, opposite the light, leaping *spectre de la rose* danced by Vaslav Nijinsky.

Back at the Maryinsky, Spessivtseva appeared in ballets of the repertory, notably *Esmeralda* and *Giselle.* Her success was remarkable, and she was named *prima ballerina* in 1920. On 2 November 1921, in London, she danced with the Ballets Russes in the role of Aurora in *The Sleeping Princess.* The *Daily Express* praised "the new first dancer, as incorporeal as a genuine fairy." She perfected her technique with Enrico Cecchetti and returned to Russia, where she worked with Agrippina Vaganova before leaving her country permanently in 1924. Jacques Rouché, director of the Paris Opera, offered her a contract as *première danseuse étoile*. She danced in *Giselle, Suite de Danses* (choreography by Ivan Clustine), and *La Péri* (choreography by Léo Staats), and created roles in *Soir de Fête* (Staats) and *Les Rencontres* (choreography by Bronislava Nijinska). In 1927 she accompanied the Ballets Russes to Italy, performing with Serge Lifar in *Les Sylphides, The Firebird,* and *Le Mariage d'Aurore.* Her partner later told how the director in Turin conducted the variation in *Swan Lake* too slowly, but Spessivtseva maintained miraculous balance, leaving viewers amazed. On 30 April, she performed in the premiere of George Balanchine's *La Chatte* in Monte Carlo. She was praised for it, but she seemed to value neither the choreography nor the geometric costume, and she abandoned the role on the pretext of a foot injury.

In 1928 Spessivtseva danced *La Tragédie de Salomé* (choreography by Nicola Guerra) at the Opera, and met the choreographer Boris Kniaseff, who saw in her an unsurpassed exemplar of pure classicism. In 1929 she triumphed in *Swan Lake* at Covent Garden. She was on the verge of signing a new contract with the Ballets Russes, but Diaghilev's death intervened. On 30 December at the Opera, Spessivtseva and Serge Peretti embodied *Les Créatures de Prométhée* (choreography by Lifar). In 1931 she was Ariane, the frail and pathetic lover of Bacchus, danced by Lifar. In 1932 the couple danced *Giselle* to great popular and critical acclaim.

After this, Spessivtseva left the Opera permanently. She triumphed again in *Giselle* at the Savoy Theatre in London with Anton Dolin, toured South America with Michel Fokine in 1933, and in 1934 toured Australia at the invitation of Victor Dandré, who was reestablishing the Pavlova Company. She met Fokine in New York, with a view to establishing a ballet company. Upon her return to Paris she gave her last French recital at the Opéra-Comique in June 1935.

In 1937 Spessivtseva went to Buenos Aires for a short season, then returned to France with the intention of opening a school, but she left Europe when World War II

SPESSIVTSEVA. A studio portrait in costume for *Giselle,* act 2. The purity of line and delicacy of demeanor evident in this photograph indicate that Spessivtseva's fame as a supreme interpreter of Giselle was entirely justified. (Photograph by Studio-Lipnitzki, Paris © Lipnitzki-Viollet, used by permission.)

broke out. She settled in New York and participated as an adviser in the activities of Ballet Theatre. Mental illness had troubled her since 1934, and she was hospitalized from 1942 to 1963. She was released as cured and spent her later years at Valley Cottage, supported by the Tolstoi Foundation.

Photographs of Spessivtseva show a serious face with regular features, a body with a perfect line, delicate arms, and long legs, producing arabesques of infinite purity. Her contemporaries admired her ethereal movement and supernatural lightness, her incomparable *développé,* her immense, sad eyes, and the internal clarity that transfigured her dance. A few simple steps in the second act of *Giselle*—a fifth position on pointe, a *glissade,* and an *assemblé*—led André Levinson to write, "The poetic utilization of this sequence is so perfect that we feel invaded by a sweet and heart-rending exaltation." She worked tirelessly and was endowed with remarkable muscular strength. She was an ideal partner, according to Lifar; her extraordinary ease, simplicity, and naturalness conquered the hearts of dancers who saw her rehearse the role of Aurora, according to Boris Kochno. She loved the classical style and revealed its superiority to both artists and the public. She did not like Fokine's modernism and felt alien to the ballets of Léonide Massine and Nijinska; she complied with reservations with the angular gestures of Balanchine's neoclassicism, but she surrendered to the creative power of Lifar.

It has been said that Spessivtseva was not much of a musician, but she was sensitive to the music of the body, a trait she owed to Isadora Duncan. Whether interpreting Esmeralda or La Chatte, the Princess Aurora or Salomé, the Péri or Ariane, she aroused passionate admiration. Her seeming fragility, air of melancholy, incorporeality, and the contradictions of her tormented soul made her an ideal Romantic dancer and above all a stunning Giselle. At the end of the dramatic mad scene, her discordant steps expressed the fatal break; the supernatural world that welcomes her perhaps represented the only refuge in which her wounded spirit could survive. Lifar said that she always lived between dream and reality.

BIBLIOGRAPHY

Christout, Marie-Françoise. "Hommage à Olga Spessivtseva." *Saisons de la danse,* no. 229 (November 1991): 40–41.

Dolin, Anton. *The Sleeping Ballerina: The Story of Olga Spessivtseva.* London, 1966.

Fern, Dale. "Spessivtseva" (parts 1–3). *Dance Magazine* (April–July 1960).

Ilyin, Eugene K. "Tragedy of a Living 'Giselle': The Story of Olga Spessivtseva." *Dance Magazine* (June 1954): 21–23, 54–55.

Kniaseff, Boris. "Reminiscences: In the Footsteps of Olga Spessivtseva" (parts 1–3). *Ballet Today* (July–October 1957).

Krasovskaya, Vera. *Russkii baletnyi teatr nachala dvadtatogo veka,* vol. 2, *Tantsovshchiki.* Leningrad, 1972.

Levinson, André. *Les visages de la danse.* Paris, 1933.

Lifar, Serge. *The Three Graces: Anna Pavlova, Tamara Karsavina, Olga Spessivtzeva.* Translated by Gerard Hopkins. London, 1959.

Pask, Edward H. "Three Ballerinas." In Pask's *Enter the Colonies Dancing.* Melbourne, 1979.

Shaïkevitch, André. *Olga Spessivtseva.* Paris, 1954.

Smakov, Gennady. *The Great Russian Dancers.* New York, 1984.

Spessivtseva, Olga. *The Technique for the Ballet Artiste.* London, 1967.

JEANNINE DORVANE
Translated from French

SPINDRIFT. Choreography: Paul Taylor. Music: Arnold Schoenberg, String Quartet Concerto, after George Frideric Handel's Concerto Grosso (op. 6, no. 7). Design: Santo Loquasto. Lighting: David A. Finn. First performance: 8 July 1993, Page Auditorium, Duke University, Durham, North Carolina, Paul Taylor Dance Company. Dancers: Andrew Asnes, Sandra Stone, Mary Cochran, Patrick Corbin, Francie Huber, Denise Roberts, Hernando Cortez, David Grenke, Thomas Patrick, Rachel Berman

Benz. (At the premiere, Stone danced her own role and that of the injured Angela Vaillancourt.)

The most vivid realization of *Spindrift*'s title occurs in the prologue. Against a backdrop of swirling clouds and tranquil sea, a cluster of dancers dip and sway in canon to the sound of waves lapping on the shore. Thereafter, the sea becomes a metaphor for both motion and transience. Time and tide become potent symbols for Paul Taylor's reflections on the ebb and flow of relationships—both real and idealized—and on life itself.

Taylor's theme of retrospection is further supported by his choice of Schoenberg's String Quartet Concerto (1933) as accompaniment for *Spindrift*'s four main sections. The concerto was a reworking of music by George Frideric Handel, dating from 1739, and it was one of several transcriptions of pre-twentieth-century scores that the composer made after his early 1900s' explorations of atonal music. Thus, the concerto was a response to Schoenberg's own past and to the classical music canon. Taylor also revisits former territory in *Spindrift*. The prologue acknowledges the naturalism of America's first modern dances—specifically Doris Humphrey's *Water Study* (1928)—as well as Taylor's own early explorations of posture and gesture, most notably in *Seven New Dances* (1957). As with *Esplanade* (1975), *Airs* (1978), *Mercuric Tidings* (1982), and *Syzygy* (1987), in *Spindrift* natural phenomena are transformed into theatrical form. Where *Esplanade* was inspired by the bustle of pedestrian activity near Taylor's Broadway studio, *Spindrift* draws upon the forces surrounding his Long Island beach house. Spatial patterns make overt reference to eddies, breaking waves, and seaspray, and the dancers' movements sometimes imply those of sea lions and other marine life.

As the slow, undulating prologue ends, the dancers reform downstage into two distinct groups of five women and four men. Their dispersal reveals a lone dancer (Andrew Asnes) who emerges like some evolutionary creature by rolling, crawling, and finally standing between them. He becomes the focus of *Spindrift*'s four main sections; his relationships with various members of the two groups and with an aloof, fleeting figure (Angela Vaillancourt) provide both the thematic and structural progression of the work.

One of the most striking features of *Spindrift* is its asymmetry. Movements and phrasing correspond with the irregular rhythms and sectioning of the music, and whorls of dance energy are interspersed by moments of calm. Moreover, Taylor highlights the dissonances of Schoenberg's transcription of Handel (unlike the dance-music harmonies in *Aureole* [1962] and *Airs*, which both were set to Handel scores). In these two earlier works, a hands-on-hips motif accompanies skimming sideways steps and squat jumps, and a distorted version of this recurs in *Spindrift*. Indeed, Taylor's oblique, one-handed version becomes a key motif in the first movement. It is embellished by the dancers crossing one leg in front of the other and leaning to one side, thus reinforcing the angularity of the motif. As Schoenberg's music begins, the motif is used as a formal greeting between Asnes and the two groups of dancers. Initially, their movements are conversational but, after only a few measures of the largo-allegro, the orchestration starts to shift key abruptly and the soloist-group interchange begins to fracture too. (The largo and the allegro form two separate sections in Handel's original score, but they were elided by both Schoenberg and Taylor.)

While certain gestures and steps in *Spindrift* recall previous Taylor choreography, Taylor has discovered a new sense of impulse and phrasing from Schoenberg's music. It is most marked in the second-movement largo, where Asnes performs the same forward *dévelopées* and promenades as Taylor performed in the *Aureole* Larghetto. The extreme twists of Asnes's chevron-like torso and the accentuated backward tilts that accompany many of his traveling steps, however, produce a taut, off-balance quality—in stark opposition to the smooth, seamless lyricism of *Aureole.*

Taylor highlights further tensions in the third movement, set to Schoenberg's allegretto grazioso. Here, the relationship between Asnes and the other dancers is confrontational. Alternating male/female groups encircle him menacingly, and two duets (with David Grenke and Patrick Corbin) are physically combative. At the end of this section, the tensions—both musical and choreographic—are resolved temporarily and for the first time in the work, Asnes becomes part of the group. The final movement, a mornpipe-moderato, begins with the dancers performing a *manège* of *jetés* and spins around the stage. A series of virtuoso solos and duets follows, and the breathless sweep of the dancers' entrances and exits recalls *Aureole*'s joyous finale.

Such accord is short-lived, however. As the dissonances in Schoenberg's music return, Asnes becomes separated again from the other dancers. He attempts to rejoin them but, one by one, they take his hand in a gesture of farewell and leave the stage. His isolation is further reinforced by Vaillancourt who, like some unattainable ideal, circles around him and then disappears. To the last muted chords of Schoenberg's music, Asnes reaches out into the now-empty space, and the themes of difference and distance, which have been underscored throughout *Spindrift,* become crystallized in this final image.

Reviews of the premiere at the 1993 American Dance Festival and of performances in New York in October 1993 focused on the parallels between *Spindrift*'s male soloist/ensemble divide and Taylor's working relationship with his present company. Some critics also suggested a connection between the red trim on Santo Loquasto's pastel-colored costumes and AIDS-awareness ribbons—prompted in part by the death of Christopher Gillis (one of Taylor's finest and longest-serving dancers) in August 1993—but it has been refuted by Taylor. More specifically, *Spindrift* can be seen as a summation of Taylor's key works and of his choreography for particular dancers. Yet his treatment of the past is never nostalgic. On the contrary, *Spindrift*'s most profound statement seems to be that it is only through reconciling the past that we are able to move forward constructively—and in the case of Taylor—creatively. That his choreography has evolved over four decades and through four distinct groups of dancers offers testimony to this concept.

BIBLIOGRAPHY

Berman, Janice. "A Solo Baryshnikov and a Splendid Spindrift." *Newsday* (October 1993).

Jowitt, Deborah. "Paul's People." *Village Voice* (9 November 1993).

Kisselgoff, Anna. "Free Association in Technicolor from Paul Taylor." *New York Times* (12 July 1993).

Kisselgoff, Anna. "Solitude and Memory by a Brooding Sea." *New York Times* (28 October 1993).

Teachout, Terry. "Paul Taylor Tackles AIDS & Much More." *Daily News* (28 October 1993).

Tobias, Tobi. "Past Recall." *New York* (15 November 1993).

ANGELA KANE

SPOERLI. One of Spoerli's earliest successes as a ballet master was his production of *Giselle, oder Die Wilis* for the Basel Ballet in 1976. He restored some musical passages from the original score and strengthened the dramatic structure of the plot by adding a brief prologue in which the wilis danced in their graveyard just before dawn. Seen here in act 1, during a 1983 performance, are Philippe Anota as Albrecht and Catherine Zerara as Giselle. (Photograph by Peter Schnetz; from the Dance Collection, New York Public Library for the Performing Arts.)

SPOERLI, HEINZ (Heinz Spörli; born 8 July 1940 in Basel, Switzerland), ballet dancer, choreographer, and company director. In recent decades, Switzerland has produced a number of outstanding dance personalities, but the first and only Swiss to make a name for himself as a significant choreographer is Heinz Spoerli. Based for many years in his home town of Basel (1973–1991), then in Düsseldorf, Germany (1991–1996), and currently in Zurich, Spoerli has created a large and impressive body of works, many of which have been mounted for companies in such cities as Stuttgart, Berlin, Vienna, Tel Aviv, Paris, Helsinki, Stockholm, Lisbon, Milan, Beijing, and Hong Kong. He has also produced a sizeable body of work for Swiss, German, Czech, French, and Austrian television.

Spoerli received his early training in Basel from Walter Kleiber, then studied in New York at the School of American Ballet and the American Ballet Center (the Joffrey Ballet School) and in England at the London Dance Centre. He made his professional debut in 1960 as a dancer with the Basel Ballet, then under the direction of Vaslav Orlikovsky. After three years with Orlikovsky's troupe, dancing in operas and in occasional productions of the Russian ballet classics, Spoerli moved to Germany and joined the Cologne State Opera Ballet, directed by Todd Bolender. There he appeared in a varied repertory of works by George Balanchine, Maurice Béjart, John Cranko, Agnes de Mille, and Harald Lander. Having developed both a secure technique and a strong stage personality, he was hired as a soloist by the Royal Winnipeg Ballet in 1966 and then by Les Grands Ballets Canadiens, in Montreal, in 1967. He remained with the Montreal company until 1971, dancing featured or leading roles in both classical and modern works by such choreographers as Anton Dolin, David Lichine, Fernand Nault, Richard Kuch, and John Butler. In 1971, he returned to Switzerland and joined the Ballet du Grand Théâtre de Genève, then directed by Alfonso Catá under the aegis of George Balanchine. While in Geneva, he made his first major ballet, *Le Chemin* (1972), set to a specially commissioned score by Eric Gaudibert.

In 1973, Spoerli was engaged as resident choreographer for the Basel Ballet, and in a remarkably short time he built an interestingly eclectic repertory and put together an ensemble that became a versatile and capable instrument for his choreographies. His first major production was *A Midsummer Night's Dream* (1976), a full-evening work designed for dancers, singers, and actors and mounted to inaugurate Basel's elegant new civic theater. Almost from the beginning of his tenure, Spoerli distinguished himself as a creator of dance works ranging from charming, intimate ballets to dramatic pas de deux to provocative, avant-garde theater pieces to full-scale, often spectacular productions of the classics. He was named ballet director of the Basel Municipal Theater in 1978. By the time he left this post in 1991, he had created more than seventy works for the Basel Ballet.

Spoerli has dealt extensively with the repertory of *ballets d'action,* always taking great care that the story is clearly told and the characters appropriately presented through the dance. Particularly impressive examples of his success in story telling and characterization are his *Romeo and Juliet* (1977) and *Coppélia* (1984). Less convincing was his 1983 choreography for Gluck's opera *Orpheus und Eurydike,* in which the dancing, although powerful, bore a questionable relationship to the music. Spoerli scored an unqualified triumph, however, with his production of *La Fille Mal Gardée,* performed for the first time by the Paris Opera Ballet in 1981. The lighthearted story of Lise and Colas, combining romantic lyricism, gaiety, and whimsical comedy, proved to be ideally suited to Spoerli's own cheerful temperament. His unexpected casting of the virtuoso dancer Patrick Dupond in the comic role of Alain also proved to make an ideal match of role and performer.

As a choreographer, Spoerli is not among the innovators who invent new vocabularies of movement. His works are solidly grounded in the vocabulary of classical ballet, and they demand a high level of technical and stylistic mastery from their performers. Nevertheless, Spoerli does not use the vocabulary of academic dance merely to conform to tradition; he often uses it in unexpected ways and frequently invests it with fresh choreographic idioms and phrasings of his own. In mounting such classic works as *Giselle* (1976) and *The Nutcracker* (1979), for example, he made dances in a lively, modern fashion while maintaining complete respect for the traditional style of the original models.

In his own creations, Spoerli has over the years shown great versatility and daring in his experiments both with subject matter and with styles of dance. In *Chäs* (1978)—the title is the Swiss-German word for "cheese"—he combined Swiss folk music and Alpine customs with dancing on point, low-comedy routines, and virtuosic technical

SPOERLI. Scene 4 of Spoerli's *La Belle Vie* (1989) takes place in a ballet studio at the turn of the century, evoking images from the paintings of Edgar Degas. Created for the Basel Ballet, it was set to music by Jacques Offenbach and was based on a libretto by Wolfgang Oberrender. Scenery was designed by Walter Perdacher, costumes by Martin Rupprecht. Despite the optimistic title, the romantic costumes, and the lighthearted music, the work was a grim psychological drama of a dysfunctional family. (Photograph © by Gundel Kilian; used by permission.)

display. In *Thundermove* (1979), he parodied the modern obsession with competitive sport in a dynamic work of raw energy and athleticism. In *Oktett* (1982), he created a scenic-optical movement reminiscent of the work of Alwin Nikolais. In his *John Falstaff* (1984), Spoerli defied the cliché that only young, slender men can express themselves in dance by creating a role for himself (he is rather plump) and another for Hans van Manen, who danced the title role of the old, fat nobleman. Turning in yet another stylistic direction, Spoerli created an answer to the New Age dance happening with his choreography for *Orpheus* (1988), set to a score by Hans Werner Henze.

Throughout his career, Spoerli has used musical compositions of every style, ranging from Bach and Vivaldi to Arthur Honegger and Steve Reich. He has been criticized for sometimes departing far from the spirit of the music, and for burdening his work with vague ideas or subject matter, but he always choreographs with an uncommon feel for musical phrasing and with a decided flair for flowing movement sequences. When the choreographic event unfolds totally in accord with the musical composition, as, for example, in his *Verklärte Nacht* (1982), set to Arnold Schoenberg's haunting score, the result is a work of profound dance and musical urgency.

In the autumn of 1991 Spoerli left Basel to become director of the Ballett der Deutsche Oper am Rhein, the resident company for Düsseldorf and Duisberg, Germany. The large roster of this company, which boasted some seventy dancers, almost twice as many as the Basel Ballet, afforded Spoerli opportunities to make ballets on a grander scale than ever before. In 1993 he created his version of *Goldberg Variations* and mounted new versions of his productions of *Giselle* and *The Firebird.* A highlight of 1994 was a new version, his third, of *A Midsummer Night's Dream,* set to a score consisting of the familiar music of Felix Mendelssohn augmented by music composed by Philip Glass and Steve Reich. Other works mounted for the Ballett der Deutsche Oper am Rhein include *Verklärte Nacht* and *Die Josephslegende* as well as such classics as *The Nutcracker, La Fille Mal Gardée, Swan Lake,* and *The Sleeping Beauty.*

In 1995 Spoerli returned to the Basel Ballet to choreograph the world premiere of *Ippolito,* set to an original score by the Swiss composer Rolf Urs Ringger. This work, like many of Spoerli's ballets, was also filmed for Swiss television. Perhaps the largest television audience for his choreography, however, was composed of viewers of the 1995 New Year's Eve concert by the Vienna Philharmonic Orchestra. Broadcast worldwide on the first of January 1996, this concert included dances made by Spoerli for members of the Vienna State Opera Ballet. Tradition demanded that one of them be set to Johann Strauss's famous waltz "An der Schönen Blauen Donau" (On the Beautiful Blue Danube).

SPOERLI. Olivier Lucea and Stephane Dalle happily suspended in the midst of Spoerli's *Goldberg Variations,* created for the Ballett der Deutsche Oper am Rhein. With simple unitard costumes designed by Kekso Dekker, this work was premiered in Düsseldorf in March 1993 and in Duisberg in April 1995. Upon returning to Switzerland, Spoerli immediately mounted it for the Zurich Ballet in September 1996. (Photograph by © Gundel Kilian; used by permission.)

Returning to Germany, Spoerli made his last work for the Ballet der Deutsche Oper am Rhein the following March. Presented as a new form of dance, it was entitled *. . . und Farben, die mitten in die Brust leuchten* (. . . and colors, which glow in the center of her bosom), and it was set to a score of musical pieces by Krzysztof Penderecki, John Dowland, Julia Wolfe, Ludwig Senfl, Giovanni Battista Pergolesi, Henryk Mikolaj Gorecki, Dave Heath, Luca Marenzio, Michael Gordon, and Dave Land. One could call it a story ballet without a story as well as an abstract ballet full of action and significance. A work filled with references and allusions, playfully light, and fraught with meaning, it cast a mysterious spell over its viewers.

The following summer, upon completion of his contract in Düsseldorf, Spoerli returned to Switzerland once more, to assume the post of director of the Zurich Ballet. His first major production for this company was his fourth version of *A Midsummer Night's Dream,* presented in October 1996. No longer content with simply telling the story by means of dance, Spoerli caught the essence of it, the confusions of identity and of the senses, into a kind of dreamlike action, leaving audiences to wonder if they have seen a story ballet, a play, a rehearsal of a work in progress, a piece of abstract choreography, or all of them in one.

Among the honors and awards bestowed on Spoerli are the Hans-Reinhart-Ring, given by the Swiss Gesellschaft für Theaterkultur in 1982; the arts prize of the City of Basel, awarded in 1991; and the Jacob-Burckhardt Prize, also given by the City of Basel, in 1995.

[*See also* Basel Ballet; Switzerland; *and* Television, *article on* Dance on Television in Europe.]

BIBLIOGRAPHY

Como, William. "Heinz Spoerli and the Basel Ballet: Alpine Treasure." *Dance Magazine* (January 1983): 58–61.

Eckert, Heinz. *Heinz Spoerlis Basler Ballett.* Basel, 1991.

Flury, Philipp, and Peter Kaufmann. *Heinz Spoerli: Ballett-Faszination.* 2d ed. Zurich, 1996. Includes a complete catalog of Spoerli's works to 1996.

Merz, Richard. "Getanzte Farbklänge bunte Musikbewegung." *Neue Zürcher Zeitung* (25 March 1996).

Pastori, Jean-Pierre. *Dance and Ballet in Switzerland.* Translated by Jacqueline Gartmann. 2d ed., rev. and enl. Zurich, 1989.

Pellaton, Ursula. "Heinz Spoerlis *Goldberg-Variationen* in Lausanne." *Tanz und Gymnastik* 51.3 (1995): 28–30.

Robertson, Alan. "Perfect Timing." *Ballet News* (January 1983): 24–26.

Schmidt, Jochen. "It's the Way That You Tell It!" *Ballett International* 11 (March 1988): 16–21.

Sikes, Richard, ed. *Heinz Spoerli und das Basler Ballett.* Basel, 1985.

Sorell, Walter. "Heinz Spoerli Talks of Swiss Ballet." *Dance News* (November 1977): 9.

Vollmer, Horst. "A Plea for More Independence: A Conversation with Heinz Spoerli." *Ballet International/Tanz Aktuell* (March 1994): 32–36.

RICHARD MERZ
Translated from German
Amended by Claude Conyers

SPOHR, ARNOLD (Arnold Theodore Spohr; born 26 December 1927 in Rhein, Saskatchewan), Canadian dancer, choreographer, and company director. Arnold Spohr began ballet studies in his late teens in Winnipeg, Manitoba, with Gweneth Lloyd and Betty Farrally; later he trained with various teachers in London, New York, and Los Angeles. He joined the Winnipeg Ballet, a semiprofessional company directed by Lloyd and Farrally, in 1945, and when it became a fully professional company in 1947 he was promoted to principal dancer, at age nineteen. After the Winnipeg Ballet was granted a royal charter in 1953, Spohr found himself leading a company with the imposing name of the Royal Winnipeg Ballet. Notable for his gifts as a partner, he created roles in numerous ballets by Lloyd and others. He also danced in musicals and television productions, often in his own choreography. A high point of his performing career occurred in 1956, when he was invited to partner Alicia Markova in a London revival of *Where the Rainbow Ends.*

Spohr began to choreograph for the Winnipeg Ballet in 1950. His first work, *Ballet Premier,* was set to music by Felix Mendelssohn. This was followed by *Intermède* (1951), to music by Domenico Cimarosa; *Children of Men* (1953), to music by César Franck; *E Minor* (1958), to music by Frédéric Chopin; and *Hansel and Gretel* (1960), to music drawn from the opera by Englebert Humperdinck.

SPOHR. With Eva von Gencsy in an *apache* dance, c.1950, with the Royal Winnipeg Ballet. Tight trousers, an open shirt, and a silk neckerchief were *de rigueur* items of *apache*-style costumes for men in the 1950s, as were a slit skirt and fishnet hose for women. (Photograph by Phillips-Gutkin; courtesy of the Royal Winnipeg Ballet.)

After a disastrous fire in 1954, which destroyed the company's home, performances by the Royal Winnipeg Ballet were suspended until 1956. Revival of the company and reconstruction of the repertory were slow. In 1958 Spohr was invited to become interim director of the company, following the sudden departure of Benjamin Harkarvy. Spohr's success soon led to a permanent appointment as the first native-born—and eventually the longest-serving—director of a major Canadian ballet company. Spohr remained in the post for thirty years, until his retirement in 1988.

With vision and energy, Spohr revived the company after a period of financial and artistic crisis, and he is held principally responsible for its popular success within Canada and abroad. Although he himself soon ceased to choreograph, despite encouraging critical response, he searched widely to find new works for the company's repertory. He tended to concentrate on the works of choreographers whom he particularly favored, including

Brian Macdonald, Norbert Vesak, John Neumeier, and Oscar Araiz, a practice that sometimes drew criticism.

Following a tradition established by the company's founders, Lloyd and Farrally, Spohr built a repertory clearly designed to please a wide range of audience tastes. Other than *The Nutcracker,* mounted by John Neumeier in 1972, the Royal Winnipeg Ballet generally performed mixed bills of short works that balanced romanticism, drama, humor, and high spirits. During the 1980s, however, the advent of Evelyn Hart as a ballerina of exceptional talent led to full-scale productions of *Romeo and Juliet* (1981), *Giselle* (1983), and *Swan Lake* (1988).

Spohr was also active until 1981 as one of the heads of the Banff Centre School of Fine Arts summer dance program in Alberta. Since his retirement in 1988, when he was named artistic director emeritus of the Royal Winnipeg Ballet, he has continued to teach privately, and since 1994 he has been associate director, on a seasonal basis, of Ballet Jorgen, a small company dedicated to the development of young dancers. Among Spohr's many honors are the Order of Canada (1967), a *Dance Magazine* Award (1982), and the Diplôme d'Honneur of the Canadian Conference of the Arts (1983).

[*See also* Royal Winnipeg Ballet.]

BIBLIOGRAPHY

Crabb, Michael. "Family Man: Arnold Spohr." *Ballet News* 5 (April 1984): 17–21.

Dafoe, Christopher. *Dancing through Time: The First Fifty Years of Canada's Royal Winnipeg Ballet.* Winnipeg, 1991.

Maynard, Olga. "Idea, Image, and Purpose: Ballet in Canada Today." *Dance Magazine* (April 1971): 32–65.

Windreich, Leland. "Out of the Prairies." *Dance and Dancers* (September 1972).

Wyman, Max. *Dance Canada: An Illustrated History.* Vancouver, 1989.

MICHAEL CRABB

SPORTS. *See* Dance as Sport.

SQUARE DANCING. A North American social dance in which a prominent portion of the interaction between dancers is performed in a formation approximating the shape of a square, the term *square dance* can also refer to the event at which such dances are featured. During the last century, several different types of dances found in the United States have been called "square dances" by writers and historians. This has resulted in some confusion about the relationship between these dance forms and their development.

The legacy of three major types of square dance can be found in the United States today: Northeastern, Southeastern, and Western. There have been many regional and local variants, but all derive from at least one of the major types. Tracing the history of square dance forms earlier than the late nineteenth century is problematic because written sources are limited. There are descriptions in travelers' accounts of visits to various regions, regional literature, and advertisements and instructional materials hawking the skills of itinerant dancing masters. But the roots of the American square dance are embedded in community dance traditions that are not well represented in written documents. Oral history materials and a broad understanding of performance traditions and their transmission play a critical role in reconstructing the development of square dance forms and their role in community life.

Northeastern Square Dance or Quadrille. The Northeastern square dance is a descendant of the French cotillon and quadrille. These dances institutionalized the square dance formation in the European ballroom dance repertory. They spread to America via dancing masters and well-traveled individuals, and by the late eighteenth century the energetic cotillon was a regular part of social dance programs in North America. In the first quarter of the nineteenth century it was replaced by the quadrille, which was a refinement of the figures and patterns danced in the cotillon. The quadrille attained such popularity that it soon eclipsed the longways dances that had been the mainstay of American dancing assemblies for decades. In the northeastern United States and throughout the more populated areas along the eastern seaboard, the quadrille was introduced into social and metropolitan centers and then disseminated to smaller outlying communities. Through generations of community performance, the quadrille was adapted to changing aesthetic and social values.

The original quadrille introduced to North America consisted of five parts—often called a change—that were danced to different tunes and separated by a brief break. It was danced by four couples in a square formation; the head couple was positioned with their backs to the musicians or the head of the dance hall. After formal bows and curtsies to partners and corners, they most often began the first change by dancing with the couple opposite them in the set. A caller generally prompted each figure with minimal explanation. Over the years, many communities shortened the quadrille to three, and sometimes two, parts.

In New England, nineteenth-century enthusiasm for the quadrille continued unabated into the twentieth century. Folk dance educator Elizabeth Burchenal did much of her early collecting in New England, especially in Maine, during the first decades of the twentieth century. She recorded many quadrilles and firsthand accounts of community social dancing. Burchenal was among the first educators to introduce the quadrille as well as American circle and longways dances into the panoply of international folk dances used in physical education and recreation programs. The quadrille also remained a favorite in parts of New Hampshire and Vermont, where many communities had a predilection for the longways contradance (Tolman and Page, 1937). A folk dance revival movement in New England in the late 1960s and 1970s sparked widespread interest in the contra dance, yet old-time callers continued to feature a significant number of quadrilles at dances through this period of revival fervor.

The quadrille also took root in New York and other northeastern states and spread westward with nineteenth-century settlers and travelers. In the late 1910s and early 1920s, educator Grace Laura Ryan found that the quadrille was the most common dance in rural Michigan communities, many of which were populated by families that had migrated west from New York and the New England states (Ryan, 1926). She incorporated many of the dances she collected into her nationwide teaching of recreational folk dance. In the mid-1920s, automobile mogul Henry Ford generated tremendous publicity by underwriting a crusade to revive the old-time dancing. Ford looked outside his native Michigan, however, and imported a dance caller from Massachusetts to lead those efforts. The quadrille was the cornerstone of Ford's revival dance repertory, which later expanded to include many singing-call square dances popularized by radio "barn-dance" programs in the 1920s and 1930s.

From the 1920s onward, other social dances became increasingly popular and eclipsed the quadrille in many community social dance traditions. Round dances such as the two-step, waltz, and polka became more regularly featured elements of dance events. In many areas, this resulted in a pattern of three round dances alternating with three changes of a quadrille. Today, this pattern continues in community dance events in some areas of the northeastern and midwestern United States, and perhaps elsewhere.

In other communities, where singing-call dances and what came to be known as the "modern Western square dance" became increasingly popular after the 1930s, the quadrille was danced only occasionally. Today, the quadrille is still danced in many communities that perform a variety of social dances, including other types of square dances, while the modern Western square dance has become the exclusive focus of a separate recreational movement that does not mix older square dances into its programs. [*See* Cotillon; Longways; *and* Quadrille.]

Southeastern Square Dance. The Southeastern square dance has traditionally been rooted in the Appalachian mountains and surrounding lowlands, an area extending roughly from southwestern Pennsylvania south through Georgia and Alabama. The dance form was apparently known to the earliest settlers who established their homesteads along the isolated mountain hollows. Firsthand written accounts and oral history indicate that the oldest form of traditional dancing found in the region was a circle formed by a varying number of couples. Before the 1920s, this dance did not have a special name in most areas. It was usually referred to simply as "dancing." The term *square dance* was known but did not refer to the shape of the larger set. Instead, it described the small square formed by two couples as they danced together on the circumference of the circle.

The structure of patterns and figures in the Southeastern square dance has always varied by region and, in some cases, from one community to the next. Basically, couples joined together in as large a circle as could be accommodated in a given performance space. The dance began with a group figure, such as circling left or right, in which everyone could participate. The first couple, generally designated beforehand by the dancers, then traveled to their right to visit the second couple and danced a certain figure with them. The first couple then traveled around the circle, visiting every couple in turn and dancing the same figure with each of them. When the first couple reached the original position, the entire circle danced a group figure together. Then the second couple proceeded to visit each couple in turn, dancing the same figure with them. The basic structure consisted of these two alternating segments: (1) a group figure for the entire circle, and (2) one couple traveling around the circle to visit all the other couples.

In this older form, only one couple traveled at a time. The other, inactive dancers watched the two active couples perform the visiting figure, listened to the music, flirted with their partners, and sometimes did rhythmic, solo step dancing to display artistic skill and inspiration. A caller—who was often one of the dancers—generally prompted the dance figures, sometimes interspersing verbal patter between movement instructions.

A common variation of this circle form also began with a group figure. But the visiting sequence, instead of commencing with only one couple traveling, was initiated by every other couple simultaneously. The result of this multiple-couple visiting was that everyone was immediately involved in dancing in a small square subset of two couples around the circumference of the circle. The entire circle remained active throughout the alternation of group and two-couple figures. The history and distribution of this circle-form variation have not been thoroughly researched; it seems likely that it was preceded by the single-couple visitation form in most parts of the southeastern United States. It is known, however, that the variation was danced in North Carolina by the 1920s and 1930s and was the centerpiece of folk dance revival activities around Asheville, North Carolina.

In contrast, the multiple-couple visitation was unknown in older Kentucky tradition. It was apparently introduced into folk dance instruction at Berea College in the 1940s, probably by recreation programs leader Frank Smith. Smith was a native of England, but his experience in the folk school movement in both Denmark and North Carolina shaped much of the dance and folk game repertory he later taught to a generation of recreation specialists. The multiple-couple visiting pattern subsequently spread in Kentucky and into other parts of the United States via recreational folk dance classes, instruction manuals, and revival folk dance and music festivals. Recreational folk dance specialists began to call this dance form "Big Set," "Big Circle," or "Appalachian Circle." This newer circle variation was adopted by some communities that had no active dance tradition. It is unclear, however, whether the newer, multiple-couple visiting form supplanted the older, single-couple visiting form in communities with ongoing dance traditions.

Cecil Sharp's influence. The recreational folk dance movement in the United States has helped to disseminate the southeastern square dance outside its native communities and has also been partly responsible for some of the confusion over square dance history. In 1917 Cecil Sharp, an English collector of folk songs and folk dances, observed the older circle form performed at the Pine Mountain Settlement School and other eastern Kentucky mountain communities. In the following year Sharp published instructions for the dance under the name *running set.* This name was invented by Sharp. He further proposed that the running set was a survival of ancient English dancing—with roots in primitive religious ceremonies—that had been preserved in the isolated Appalachian Mountains by descendants of English settlers. Much of his argument was based on similarities between Appalachian dance figures and old English children's games and on the absence of ballroom courtesy movements that became common in England by the seventeenth century. Sharp's explanations were adopted by folk dance educators and their students without question.

However, a number of factors undermine Sharp's claims. First, English people did not constitute the majority of original settlers in the areas of southern Appalachia where he observed dancing; many settlers were already second- or third-generation Americans from Scotch-Irish and German backgrounds as well as some English, French Huguenots, and others. Second, the dance figure patterns so similar to old English children's games are also found in many other parts of northern and western Europe. The southeastern square dance is apparently an Americanized form developed from shared European patterns and aesthetics that were shaped by immigration and frontier experience in the New World. Although studies of other aspects of southern Appalachian folk culture suggest a blending of Scotch-Irish heritage, the relative influence of specific European dance cultures on the square dance has not been established.

Sharp's publication on the running set played an important role in the popularization of the Southeastern square dance as a dance in four-couple square formation. Al-

SQUARE DANCING. Dancers in fancy dress performing a figure at an outdoor venue in San Antonio, Texas. (Photograph by Elicson Photographer, San Antonio, Texas; from the Dance Collection, New York Public Library for the Performing Arts.)

though he stated clearly that the traditional form was a circle, he suggested that four couples was the "most effective" number of dancers for a set because it enabled everyone to progress around the circle relatively quickly and kept inactive time to a minimum. Sharp cared about documenting the traditional form, but his goals as an educator also included producing practical instructions for use in participatory classes and demonstration groups. In the 1930s, Sharp's assistant, Maud Karpeles, published additional figures for the running set but indiscriminantly included many figures from the Northeastern square dance that were unrelated to the traditional Southeastern form and repertory. By the late 1930s and early 1940s, many prominent folk dance educators had mistakenly institutionalized the so-called running set into their curricula as a four-couple square form.

Other factors also contributed to this association of a four-couple square with the Southeastern dance tradition. In the 1920s and 1930s, radio "barn-dance" programs gained tremendous popularity and, in effect, marketed an image of the rural Southeastern square dance to a mass audience. Exhibition dance groups were developed to perform on these live broadcasts. They danced in four-couple sets and often featured rhythmic step dancing, which was especially audible to a radio audience. Patter and singing calls were generally used for dances. Why the four-couple square, rather than the older circle form, was featured on the radio barn-dance programs is not clear.

Today, there is tremendous variation in the mixture of dances performed from one community to the next. The multiple-couple visiting pattern performed in four-couple squares or a large circle is more common than the old Southeastern square dance with single-couple visiting. Other types of square dances, including singing-call and modern western squares are also danced in some areas. The popularity of round dances such as the one-step, two-step, and waltz as well as clogging has also influenced the programs of many community dance events.

Western Square Dance. In the 1920s and 1930s an image of the Western square dance became fixed in the popular imagination. This owed initially to the efforts of folk dance educators and recreation specialists who popularized the Western square dance as an authentic piece of cowboy culture and American heritage. The form that became known as the Western square dance was essentially the alternation of group figure and single-couple visiting found in the southeast, performed in a four-couple set.

The Southeastern square dance moved westward with settlers, first to parts of the region now considered the midwestern United States and later through most of the territories west of the Mississippi River. There are records of the Southeastern circle form in some western regions, but by the late nineteenth century the four-couple square was most common. The transition from dancing the alternating group figure and single-couple visiting pattern in a circle to dancing it in a four-couple set has not been fully documented, but it appears to have occurred during the first generation of migration to western territories.

While this Western square dance was indeed a staple of community dance repertories in many regions of the western United States, it was not the only square dance known. The quadrille was also popular in many areas throughout the nineteenth century and remained part of local repertories until World War I. The quadrille, one of the most popular social dances of the time, was disseminated via dance events held at dance halls, saloons, and other public sites; by the interaction between travelers and settlers already familiar with the dance from their previous places of residence; and, in larger population centers, through the instruction of dancing teachers. Variants of the standard quadrille, such as the northeastern square dance that incorporated regionalized choreography and performance style, and a shortened number of parts, also spread westward with the migration of settlers.

Which square dance form was present in a community depended on a number of factors, including the repertory that settlers brought with them from their previous homes, the proximity of local musicians and callers, the frequency of community dance events, and the influence of popular culture forms in the community. Some communities knew only the Western square dance or the quadrille; many knew both forms and contributed to the blending of elements from the two square dances.

In many western regions, community dance traditions began to wane after World War I, but beginning in the 1920s a number of interrelated factors contributed to the revival of interest in square dancing. The spread of nationwide broadcasts of radio barn-dance programs, along with record companies' growing interest in recording and marketing a variety of regional and ethnic musical styles, highlighted traditional dance music over the airwaves. By the late 1920s and early 1930s, the instructional and promotional materials disseminated as part of Ford's old-time dancing revival campaign reached an ever-increasing number of local communities. Also, the incorporation of folk dance materials into physical education and recreation programs, which had begun before World War I, was continued and became more firmly established. This helped to foster a new dimension in the public attitude toward old-time dancing. Traditionally, dancing was fun and a favorite means of social and artistic fellowship. As a result of the new programs, dancing became a means of individual expression and rhythmic exercise in keeping with the progressive educational philosophy of the time. This trend in physical education reached its zenith in the 1940s and 1950s. By the latter part of the period, the

Western square dance had supplanted European folk dances as the mainstay of American recreation programs.

Lloyd Shaw's work. An educator from Colorado, Lloyd Shaw, was instrumental in developing the Western square dance into an educational resource for a broad constituency. In the 1930s, Shaw collected the square dance patterns and calls integral to dance traditions in his region. He then taught them to his students, whose repertory had been limited to European folk dances and the few American forms (primarily quadrilles and singing games) then available in printed teaching materials.

Shaw's ambitions reached beyond home-grown recreation, however; he trained exhibition dance teams and took them to festivals, contests, and educational conferences to demonstrate their "cowboy dances." Shaw used the framework of the traditional western square dance but changed the older participatory patterns into one better suited to formal display. He added new variations to the traditional figures and introduced the idea of all four couples dancing throughout the dance, with no inactive time. This was in contrast to the traditional Western form, based on the Southeastern pattern of one couple visiting each other couple in turn, while the rest of the set watched, flirted, or did some fancy stepping.

Shaw wanted to challenge his dancers to master more complicated routines danced at a very quick tempo. He also introduced the use of four different figures in a single dance, with each visiting couple starting a new pattern. In general, Shaw believed that repetition was too boring for an audience to watch. Many of the local old-timers disliked such changes in the traditional forms and aesthetics, but Shaw had untraditional goals. While he was interested in integrating American dance forms into folk dance education, he also wanted to mold expert square dancers whose expertise extended beyond the confines of any single traditional community.

Shaw's efforts received much attention in educational circles, and he began to give training seminars for teachers. During World War II, recreation specialists were employed to teach square dancing to the troops and to groups at home. Although not all the dancing taught was Shaw's modern Western style, square dancing became further entrenched in the popular consciousness as the archetypal American folk dance. After the war there was an explosion of interest in organized Western square dancing and clubs formed all over the country.

Square dance clubs. In the late 1940s the development of square dance recreational clubs in many parts of the United States was integral to the building of new community ties in a nation rediscovering peace. Initially, most of the square dance clubs drew on either the regional square dance forms that had been previously known in the area (few, if any, areas of the country were without active community dance traditions until the 1920s) or the square dance forms taught by community recreation specialists, such as those who worked for Works Progress Administration programs during the 1930s.

By the early 1950s, however, there was a growing movement to standardize the recreational square dance repertory using Shaw's modern version of the western square dance as a base. Another significant change was a shift away from the relatively informal, dancer-run clubs to caller-run clubs that instituted a formal system of classes for training new dancers. Simultaneously, more products and services were developed for the square dance market. For example, a growing number of professional callers arose around the country. The record industry responded to the new custom of using recordings of square dance calls and music by marketing specialized recordings. In addition, clothing designers and manufacturers expanded their lines of sewing patterns and ready-made costumes featuring western-style dress, a new trademark of what came to be known as the "modern" Western square dance clubs.

By the 1950s, professional callers had helped to increase the modern Western square dance repertory at such a fast rate that those who wished to dance occasionally in a local club could not keep up with the expanding number of figures. Modern Western square dancing increasingly became recreation for only the most devoted hobbyists. The need for formal instruction changed the fundamental nature of square dancing for many people who initially enjoyed the community fellowship in a noncompetitive environment.

By the 1960s, formal criteria were established by national square dance organizations (that served the modern western square dance hobbyists exclusively), grouping square dance figures into different levels of achievement (such as "mainstream" and "advanced"). Formal qualifications for callers were also established for every level. This structure continues today in the modern Western square dance movement throughout the United States and many other countries. Consequently, what has developed as the modern Western square dance since the 1950s is a choreographic form and type of social recreation distinct from any of the older, regionally based square dance traditions found in the United States.

The modern Western square dance is confined to recreational clubs organized expressly for the purpose of learning and performing this type of dance. Independent of these clubs, however, many communities across the United States still participate in older styles of the square dance that have roots in the regional culture and community tradition.

BIBLIOGRAPHY

Craig, Jenifer Pashkowski. "Contemporary Accounts of Dance from the American West in the Nineteenth Century." Ph.D. diss., University of Southern California, 1982.

Dalsemer, Robert G. *West Virginia Square Dances.* New York, 1982.
Damon, S. Foster. *The History of Square-Dancing.* Worcester, Mass., 1952.
Jennewein, J. Leonard. *Dakota Square Dance Book and Instructor's Manual.* Huron, S. Dak., 1950.
Kartchner, Kenner C. *Frontier Fiddler: The Life of a Northern Arizona Pioneer.* Tucson, 1990.
Kimball, James. "Country Dancing in Central and Western New York State." *New York Folklore* 14 (1988).
Matthews, Gail V. S. "Cutting a Dido: A Dancer's Eye View of Mountain Dance in Haywood County, N.C." Master's thesis, Indiana University, 1983.
Ryan, Grace L. *Music for Dances of Our Pioneers.* New York, 1926.
Sanders, Olcott. "The Texas Cattle Country and Cowboy Square Dance." *Journal of the International Folk Music Council* 3 (1951).
Shaw, Lloyd. *Cowboy Dances.* Caldwell, Idaho, 1940.
Spalding, Susan Eike, and Jane Harris Woodside, eds. *Communities in Motion: Dance, Community, and Tradition in America's Southeast and Beyond.* Westport, Conn., 1995.
Tolman, Beth, and Ralph Page. *The Country Dance Book.* New York, 1937.
Tyler, Paul Leslie. "'Sets on the Floor': Social Dance as an Emblem of Community in Rural Indiana." Ph.D. diss., Indiana University, 1992.

LEEELLEN FRIEDLAND

SRI LANKA. *See* Kandyan Dance; Kandy Perahera; Kohomba Kandariya; Tovil; *and* Ves Dance. *See also* Costume in Asian Traditions; Mask and Makeup, *article on* Asian Traditions.

SRIMPI. *See* Indonesia, *article on* Javanese Dance Traditions.

STAATS, LÉO (born 26 November 1877 in Paris, died 15 February 1952 in Paris), French ballet dancer, teacher, and choreographer. After entering the Paris Opera Ballet School, Staats became a pupil of Louis Mérante and Joseph Hansen, who was first ballet master at the Opera. He joined the company in 1893 and was promoted to demi-soloist *(petit sujet)* in 1898. Characterized as "an agile, nimble dancer with good leaps" by Léandre Vaillat, Staats was also a skilled partner and was frequently cast opposite Carlotta Zambelli, then a rising star in the company. When Hansen died in 1907, André Messager, director of the Opera, named Staats to replace him on 1 January 1908.

Staats's first important creation was *Javotte* (1909), set to a score by Camille Saint-Saëns and J. L. Croze, which he danced with Zambelli. He produced nearly fifty works for the Paris Opera Ballet at the Palais Garnier, while working from time to time for other theaters. In 1909, for example, he accepted the offer of Jacques Rouché, then the director of the Théâtre des Arts, of a post as artistic director, which he held until 1914. During this period he produced dances for numerous productions, including *Fêtes d'Hébé* and *España* (both 1911) with Albert Aveline as guest artist. Expert in character dances, Staats prepared highly complicated sequences of steps meticulously embellished with authentic stylistic details. He was also a specialist in reproducing steps and figures from dances of the eighteenth century. His ballets were pleasant, unpretentious, and full of *joie de vivre.*

Staats was drafted during World War I, but during furloughs he managed to produce several ballets for the Opera (of which Jacques Rouché was by then director), including *Contes de Ma Mère l'Oye* (1915), to music by Maurice Ravel, and *Les Abeilles* (1916), set for Jeanne Schwarz to music by Igor Stravinsky. Upon his release from military service, he returned to the Opera and remained there until 1926. His first major work after the war was a production of *Sylvia* (1919) for Carlotta Zambelli, Albert Aveline, and Jeanne Schwarz. This was followed by *Antar* (1921), created for Camille Bos to the music of Gabriel Dupont, a young composer who died during the war, and *Maimouna* (1921), set for Camille Bos and Aida Boni to music by Gabriel Grovlez. He also choreographed a ballet for Jeanne Schwarz and Anna Johnsson in Hector Berlioz's opera *Les Troyens* (1921). He himself danced in *Frivolant* in 1922.

The following years were the most prolific of Staats's career. In 1923 he produced *La Nuit Ensorcelée,* to music by Frédéric Chopin and with scenery by Léon Bakst, and *Cydalise et le Chèvre-pied,* to music by Gabriel Pierné, with Zambelli and Aveline in the leading roles. In 1924 he produced *Nerta* for Jeanne Schwarz, *Siang-Sin* for Camille Bos and Serge Peretti, and *Istar* for Ida Rubinstein, among other works. A highlight of 1925 was his production of *Soir de Fête,* set to music by Léo Delibes and Léon Minkus, which was danced by Olga Spessivtseva, then a guest artist at the Opera, and Gustave Ricaux. (This work was revived in 1975 by Staats's pupil Christiane Vaussard.) In 1926 Staats topped his previous success by inventing the *grand défilé du corps de ballet,* an occasion when the entire ballet company of the Paris Opera takes the stage. Setting his production to music from Richard Wagner's opera *Tannhäuser,* he established a tradition of spectacular display that has been cherished by Parisian audiences ever since.

Under contract to produce ballets for the Roxy Theatre in New York, Staats left Paris after presenting the *défilé* at the Opera. From New York, he wrote to Jacques Rouché:

> At the Roxy, the famous American music hall, there are five shows a day, with a new show every week. There are a hundred applicants for every dancer's position. My ballets are beginning to be appreciated. Some of them have two-week runs.

Staats returned to Paris in 1928, opened a school, and resumed his post as ballet master at the Opera. His later ballets were less inspired than his earlier works, however, and less appealing to the Opera audiences, who were being educated to other styles by the new artistic director of the ballet company, Serge Lifar, hired in 1929.

Writing on the occasion of the Paris Opera centennial, Olivier Merlin described Staats as "a man of character, warm in his relationships, endowed with an exuberant imagination, who became an excellent choreographer after having been a dancer of pleasant proportions" (Merlin, 1975). He also noted that Staats was better in composition than in pure technique and added that he had "created the most striking ballets of recent times." Today, apart from *Soir de Fête,* which is performed by students at the Paris Opera Ballet School, nothing remains of these "striking ballets," as none was ever notated or filmed.

BIBLIOGRAPHY

Barzel, Ann. "European Dance Teachers in the United States." *Dance Index* 3 (April–June 1944): 56–100.

Dorris, George. "Léo Staats at the Roxy, 1926–1928." *Dance Research* 13 (Summer 1995): 84–99.

Garafola, Lynn. "Forgotten Interlude." *Dance Research* 13 (Summer 1995): 59–83.

Guest, Ivor. "Carlotta Zambelli" (parts 1–2). *Dance Magazine* (February–March 1974).

Guest, Ivor. *Le ballet de l'Opéra de Paris.* Paris, 1976.

Merlin, Olivier. *L'Opéra de Paris.* Paris, 1975.

Vaillat, Léandre. *Ballets de l'Opéra de Paris (ballets dans les opéras—nouveaux ballets).* Paris, 1947.

Vaillat, Léandre. *La danse à l'Opéra de Paris.* Paris, 1951.

ARCHIVE. Walter Toscanini Collection of Research Materials in Dance, New York Public Library for the Performing Arts.

MONIQUE BABSKY
Translated from French

STAFF, FRANK (Frank Cedric Staff; born 15 June 1918 in Kimberley, South Africa, died 10 May 1971 in Bloemfontein), ballet dancer, choreographer, and producer. Having moved from the mining town of Kimberley, Staff received his early training in ballet in Cape Town with Helen Webb and Maude Lloyd, who had trained in London with Marie Rambert. When Lloyd returned to London in 1933 to resume her performing career, she encouraged her young pupil to follow her. He soon did so, and not long after his arrival in England he was invited to join Rambert's Ballet Club, where Lloyd was a ballerina. During the next few years Staff worked with the Rambert company and with the Vic-Wells Ballet as both dancer and choreographer.

For the Ballet Club in 1938 Staff choreographed his first work, *The Tartans,* a pas de trois on a Scottish theme to music by William Boyce, which he danced with Elisabeth Schooling and Anthony Kelly. He scored his first big success as a choreographer the next year, 1939, with *Czernyana,* a suite of dances to piano studies by Carl Czerny: some of the pieces were satirical and witty, others lyrical and romantic; all together, audiences found them charming. A sequel, *Czernyana II,* followed in 1941 and proved to be just as popular as the original. In between the two came a remarkably clever version of *Peter and the Wolf* (1940). Commenting on the first performances, Marie Rambert noted that "Sally Gilmour was the enchanting Duck and Celia Franca a brilliant Bird" and said that "audiences laughed a great deal and felt happy for an hour" (Rambert, 1972, p. 171).

Debonair, handsome, and technically versatile, Staff inherited many of Hugh Laing's roles in the Rambert repertory. He remained with Ballet Rambert until 1945, except for seasons with the Vic-Wells Ballet (1934/35, 1938/39) and a brief stint with the London Ballet in 1940 (which later in that year was combined with the Rambert company). His repertory as a dancer was large and varied, ranging from the Lover in Antony Tudor's *Jardin aux Lilas* to Harlequin in Fokine's *Le Carnaval.* For the Vic-Wells Ballet he created several memorable roles, including Hornblower in Ninette de Valois's *The Rake's Progress* (1935) and Cupid in Frederick Ashton's *Cupid and Psyche* (1939). For Ballet Rambert in 1940 he created the role of Julien, the Boy, in Andrée Howard's *La Fête Étrange* and choreographed an abstract version of Sir Edward Elgar's *Enigma Variations* as well as a work set to Glazunov's *The Seasons.* Upon completion of his war service in 1945, he returned to this company to choreograph *Un Songe,* set to music by Guillaume Lekeu.

In 1946, with his first wife, Elisabeth Schooling, Staff returned to South Africa and joined, for one season, the South African National Ballet in Cape Town. There he produced and danced in several of his own ballets—*Peter and the Wolf,* set to the familiar Prokofiev score; *Variations on a Theme by Haydn,* to music by Brahms; and *Romeo and Juliet,* to a Tchaikovsky score—as well as mounting versions of Nijinsky's *L'Après-midi d'un Faune* and Howard's *Death and the Maiden.*

Returning to Britain, Staff served from 1947 to 1948 as resident choreographer of the Metropolitan Ballet, for which he choreographed *Fanciulla delle Rose,* to music by Anton Arensky, and *The Lovers' Gallery,* to music by Lennox Berkeley. *Fanciulla delle Rose* was created expressly for the youthful Svetlana Beriosova, who is said to have danced it exquisitely. Staff then toured Australia with Ballet Rambert in 1948 and the United States and Canada with the Sadler's Wells Ballet in 1949. In 1950 he was appointed ballet master to a company at the Empire Cinema in London, for which he choreographed *Frankie and Johnny.* He also worked for brief periods with the Ballets des Champs-Élysées in Paris, with the San Francisco Ballet, and with musical productions on Broadway and in London's West End.

Staff returned to his homeland, South Africa, in 1953. Two years later, in 1955, after completing several commissions in musical theater, he founded a ballet company of his own in Johannesburg, the South African Ballet Company. By the time this company folded in 1958 he had choreographed some twenty ballets for it, as well as staging musicals such as *Irma La Douce.* When the South African government created four professional ballet companies in 1963, Staff staged some of his ballets for the Cape Town company, known alternatively as the University of Cape Town (UCT) Ballet or as CAPAB Ballet (i.e., the ballet company of the Cape Performing Arts Board). Appointed resident choreographer of this company in 1964, he staged a version of Prokofiev's *Romeo and Juliet* and a psychological drama, *Transfigured Night,* to Schoenberg's score, that he based on a true story reported in a U.S. newspaper.

Leaving the Cape Province in 1965, Staff would spend the remaining years of his life working with the government-sponsored ballet companies in each of the other three provinces of South Africa: Natal, the Transvaal, and the Orange Free State. For the NAPAC company in Durban, the capital city of Natal, he produced three ballets in 1965, among them *Apollo 65,* set to music by Benjamin Britten. Moving on to the Transvaal in 1966, he worked until 1968 as resident producer and choreographer with PACT Ballet in Johannesburg, where he created seven ballets. Notable among them were *Spanish Encounter* (1966), a romantic abstraction to music for classical guitar by Joaquín Rodrigo; *Five Faces of Eurydice* (1966), set to music by Stephen O'Reilly and described in the program notes as "a good-humoured ballet in five visions"; *Czernyana III* (1966), the third recension of his first big hit; and *Raka* (1967), a three-act ballet set to a score by Graham Newcater and based on an epic poem by N. P. van Wyk Louw. During his tenure with PACT Ballet, Staff also created two especially memorable characters in his performances as Doctor Coppélius, the disappointed toymaker in *Coppélia,* and as one of the Stepsisters in *Cinderella;* the former role gave him scope to be both witty and affecting, the latter allowed him to be outrageously funny.

In 1969 Staff moved again, to Bloemfontein in the Orange Free State, where he was appointed artistic director of PACOFS Ballet. For this small company he staged intimate works such as *Mantis Moon,* based on a Bushman legend and set to music by Hans Maske, and *Séance,* derived from Menotti's opera *The Medium* but using music by Benjamin Britten. At the time of his death in 1971, Staff was working on a full-length ballet for the Republic Festival, *The Rain Queen,* set to a score by Graham Newcater and based on an African legend. In homage to Staff, this work was rechoreographed in 1973 by David Poole for CAPAB Ballet, since the PACOFS company had been disbanded after Staff's death.

Of all Staff's work, *Peter and the Wolf* is the most likely to endure. Bearing the subtitle *A Fable without a Moral* and exhibiting the wit and whimsy that mark so much of his oeuvre, Staff's *Peter* is now generally recognized as the most successful of the numerous choreographies that have been set to the well-known and frequently performed Prokofiev score. It has been restaged for Northern Dance Theatre, later Northern Ballet Theatre, in Manchester and by the Sadler's Wells Royal Ballet, now known as the Birmingham Royal Ballet. Other works by Staff have been revived in South Africa by his fourth wife, the former dancer Veronica Paeper. Known as South Africa's most prolific choreographer, she has served as director of CAPAB Ballet (now Cape Town City Ballet) since 1991.

[*See also* CAPAB Ballet; PACT Ballet; *and* South Africa, *article on* Ballet.]

BIBLIOGRAPHY

Beaumont, Cyril W. *Supplement to Complete Book of Ballets.* London, 1942.

Cooper, Montgomery, and Jane Allyn. *Dance for Life: Ballet in South Africa.* Cape Town, 1980.

Grut, Marina. *The History of Ballet in South Africa.* Cape Town, 1981.

Hobbes, Tarquin. "Born under Mercury." *Ballet* 2 (July 1946): 57–59.

Kersley, Leo. "Frank Staff." *The Dancing Times* (June 1971): 481–483.

Rambert, Marie. *Quicksilver: The Autobiography of Marie Rambert.* London, 1972.

MARINA GRUT
Amended by Claude Conyers

STAGE SPACE. *See* Orchestra *and* Theaters for Dance.

STANISLAVSKY NEMIROVICH-DANCHENKO MUSICAL THEATER. *See* Russia, *article on* Secondary and Provincial Dance Companies.

STARZER, JOSEPH (also known as Franz Starzer; born 1726 or 1727 in Austria, died 22 April 1787 in Vienna), Austrian violinist and composer. Very little is known about Starzer's background. He joined the orchestra of the new French Theater (Burgtheater) in Vienna as a violinist, probably in 1752. Ballet sections were included in the theater's productions, and Starzer was known as a composer of airs for the ballet. In 1758–1759 he joined the Vienna ballet master Franz Hilverding at the Russian imperial court. He became concert master and introduced Austrian preclassical symphonies and concertos. Besides composing for Hilverding, he also worked with the choreographers Francesco Calzevaro, Gaetano Cesare, and Pierre Granger.

Starzer returned to Vienna in 1768 and in the following years he worked with the two greatest ballet masters of the time, Jean-Georges Noverre (*Don Quixote,* 1768; *Roger et Bradamante,* 1771; *Adèle de Ponthieu,* 1773; *Les Horaces et les Curiaces,* 1774) and Gaspero Angiolini (*Il Cid,* 1774; *Les Moissonneurs,* 1775; *Teseo in Creta,* 1775).

Starzer composed numerous symphonies, vocal works and chamber music, but little of this survives, and his reputation rests on his ballet music. He was perhaps Noverre's best musical collaborator. His music shows the development of ballet from a free series of pantomimic character dances or *divertissements* to the dramatically integrated *ballet d'action.*

The music for Hilverding's ballets shows the emergence of a pantomimic form relevant to the story. *Don Quixote* consists of a free sequence of dances with roots in the dance suite, a series of gavotte, bourrée, minuet, and so on. More conscious musical characterization begins to appear in *Roger et Bradamante;* the number of instruments used is unusually large, with flutes, oboes, bassoons, and strings augmented by brass instruments and Turkish percussion. In the ballets which followed, the old dances were dramatized, while elements from Neapolitan opera—recitativo, accompagnato, aria, and finali—are noticeable in the music. The expression is deepened by recurring rhythmic motifs.

Starzer had great skill in adapting music to dance figures and stage action. His many dance pieces—a full-length ballet consisted often of more than thirty separate numbers—reveal a wide range. Many folk themes appear in his works. Like other Viennese ballet composers, Starzer frequently reused his pieces; occasionally he also borrowed from other composers. Mozart in return used an entire series of numbers by Starzer in his opera *Lucio Silla* (1772).

[*See also the entries on Hilverding and Noverre.*]

BIBLIOGRAPHY

Abert, Hermann. "J. G. Noverre und sein Einfluss auf die dramatische Ballettkomposition." *Jahrbuch der Musikbibliothek Peters* 15 (1908): 29–45.

Braun, Lisbeth. "Die Ballettkomposition von Joseph Starzer." *Studien zur Musikwissenschaft* 13 (1926): 38–56.

Brown, Bruce Alan. *Gluck and the French Theatre in Vienna.* Oxford, 1991.

Haas, Robert. "Der Wiener Bühnentanz von 1740 bis 1767." *Jahrbuch der Musikbibliothek Peters* 44 (1937): 77–93.

Lynham, Deryck. *The Chevalier Noverre: Father of Modern Ballet.* London, 1950.

Schmid, E. F. "Gluck-Starzer-Mozart." *Zeitschrift für Musik* 104 (1937).

Winter, Marian Hannah. *The Pre-Romantic Ballet.* London, 1974.

OLE NØRLYNG

STEPANOV NOTATION. Vladimir Ivanovich Stepanov (1866–1896), a dancer in the Imperial Ballet of the Maryinsky Theater, was the first person to base a movement notation system on an anatomical analysis of movement and to use music notes as his basic signs. While at the Maryinsky Theater, Stepanov attended lectures on anatomy at a hospital. Combining what he learned with his knowledge of music, he developed a system of notation suitable for movement in general, not geared specifically to dance. Because his system was applied to classical ballet the incorrect impression has been given that it was based on or limited to this dance form.

STEPANOV NOTATION. On a modified musical staff with two lines for torso, three lines for arms, and four lines for legs, Stepanov used signs similar to musical notes, as seen in this example of two measures in 4/4 time. The movements for the right and left limbs are shown by the stem directions on each note, downward for right and upward for left. (Photograph reprinted from W. J. Stépanow, *Alphabet des mouvements du corps humain,* Paris, 1892, p.57.)

Stepanov traveled to Paris, where, in 1892, he published *Alphabet des mouvements du corps humain.* In 1893 a committee of dancers and choreographers thoroughly examined his system, which was subsequently introduced into the curriculum of the Imperial Ballet School in Saint Petersburg. He was later sent to Moscow to introduce his system there. When poor health from his days in Paris brought on Stepanov's early death at the age of twenty-nine, Aleksandr Gorsky became responsible for carrying on the system and published several pamphlets in 1899. Several notators were trained, notably Nicholas Sergeyev, who became *régisseur* and whose responsibility it was to contribute to and be in charge of the resulting scores. It is because of these scores, which Sergeyev used in the 1930s to reconstruct the great full-length classical ballets, that Stepanov's system is of interest today. The scores are in the Harvard Theatre Collection.

Stepanov's system had been used to record the Marius Petipa repertory, which was based on the familiar ballet vocabulary. With Michel Fokine's introduction of a wider range in movement, in particular the use of torso and head, recording choreography became a more complex affair for which no one had been trained. Stepanov's system was blamed as being inadequate and interest in it dropped. Then, Léonide Massine gave it a renewed term of service. (He had learned the system while a student at the Imperial School in Moscow.) When Massine decided that the balletic heritage limited creativity and that a new approach to choreography was essential, he concentrated on basic movements stemming from the anatomical structure of the body. He used Stepanov's system as the tool with which to record the movement sequences and studies he developed.

Stepanov used music notes with their established time values, modifying them with square heads to indicate contact with the ground (support). The modified music staff consists of two horizontal lines at the top for the body (torso), three lines in the middle for the arms, and four lines at the bottom for the legs. The placement of the notes on the lines and the spaces on the staff indicate direction and level for the first-degree parts (torso, whole arm, whole leg). The movements of the second-degree parts (chest, lower arm, lower leg) are shown by signs drawn on the stem of the music note. For third-degree parts (head, hand, foot), indications are placed next to the note, at the left. Right and left limbs are shown by the stem of the note: a downward stem indicates right, an upward stem left.

For direction, the zero point (the normal position in standing for the torso, arms, and legs) is established at a different location for each section of the staff. From that point, the indication of the directions forward, sideward, and backward progresses upward or downward on the staff; each progression is an increase in level. Diagonal directions are indicated by the addition of signs for abduction and adduction to forward, sideward, or backward. Indications for turning and direction faced in the room are written with numbers above the section for the legs. Step direction (transference of weight) is shown by a preparatory leg gesture into the desired direction; this indication is tied with a dotted horizontal bow to the following step sign. Floor plans, drawn from the audience's point of view, use a circle or a white pin to represent a female dancer and a cross or a black pin to represent a male. Arrows indicate the direction of travel.

[*See also* Notation.]

BIBLIOGRAPHY

Gorsky, Aleksandr. *Two Essays on Stepanov Dance Notation.* Translated by Roland John Wiley. New York, 1978.

Guest, Ann Hutchinson. *Choreo-Graphics: A Comparison of Dance Notation Systems from the Fifteenth Century to the Present.* New York, 1989.

Stepanov, Vladimir. *Alphabet of Movements of the Human Body* (1892). Translated by Raymond Lister. New York, 1969.

ANN HUTCHINSON GUEST

STEP DANCING. [*This entry comprises two articles on the traditional form of solo dance known as step dancing. The first article presents step dancing in Great Britain and Ireland; the second discusses step dancing in Cape Breton, Nova Scotia.*]

Step Dancing in Great Britain and Ireland

Step dancing is a traditional form of solo dance known in several distinct but related styles in the British Isles and North America. Extremely nimble footwork is common to all forms of step dancing, and most are also performed essentially in place, using limited forward-and-back or side-to-side steps, always returning to an original floor position. Much step dancing also belongs to the larger world family of percussive dances, including tap and some North Indian dance styles, in which the feet sound out the dance rhythms on the floor. However, there is no firm dividing line between hard-shoe and soft-shoe dancing in the British Isles, since many steps are common to both. Step-dance steps also appears outside the context of solo dancing in reels and other set dances.

Sound production in many forms of step dancing is aided by hard-soled footwear. In some parts of the British Isles, where step dancing shows great regional variation, step dancers simply wear shoes with hard leather soles. In other areas, including Ireland, hard-shoe step dances were traditionally performed in shoes to which cobblers or farriers had added thick pads of hammered-down nails or cleats at the toe and heel; such shoes eventually evolved into the tap shoes worn by stage dancers. Modern Irish step dancers wear specialized versions of these traditional shoes that replace the nails with very thick flared taps of compressed wood or fiberglass at the toe, and with fiberglass heels, which make the loud and distinct sounds they need to compete with amplified music.

In those areas (usually coastal) where wooden-soled clogs were worn, dancers discovered centuries ago that such shoes made a splendid rattle on hard surfaces, and dancing in clogs became widespread. The irons with which English clogs were shod also produced sparks on flagstone floors, which added to the appeal of this form of dance. In the north of England, where step dancing is still often performed in wooden-soled clogs, it is often called clog dancing or, in a popularized stage version, the "Lancashire Clog Dance." The term *clogging,* however, is never used to refer to dancing in clog-wearing areas, where *to clog* means to resole a wooden-soled shoe. A dance of the clogging type was formerly often taught in English dance schools as the Lancashire Hornpipe, together with a group of other "national" dances, including the Irish Jig, the Highland Fling, and the Dutch Dance (which was actually not a traditional dance, but derived from a stage show, *Miss Hook of Holland*). The distinctive clogs of England (including a special light dance clog that dispensed with irons and was particularly used for dancing on a mat of wooden lathes) were probably developed from indigenous patterns, and not borrowed from Flanders, as has often been suggested.

Though step dancing existed in other parts of England, it was not widely known until recent years. The modern revival of interest was concentrated originally in the Newcastle area, where step dancing was taught at local academies and where Jackie Toaduff became the first well-known modern virtuoso. During the 1950s members of the English Folk Song and Dance Society realized that a large body of traditional dances had never been explored; their research led to the notation and filming of dances from all regions of the British Isles.

Many of the form's individual steps derive originally from traditional social dances, particularly reels. Some scholars believe that the anglaise, a rather uncommon dance in the baroque suite, was originally a stepping dance, but no notation of it survives. Traditional dances that incorporate stepping include the Brixham Reel, the Dorset Four-Hand Reel, and the Wiltshire Six-Hand Reel in southern England, and the Square Eight, the Three-Hand Reel, and "Down Back o' t' Shoddy" in the north. Also noteworthy are the Morris jigs of the Cotswolds and the South Midlands, which are ideal examples of the steps of a group dance being rearranged for solo display. Conversely, some teams of northwestern Morris and northeastern sword dancers have over the years incorporated steps of the clog dance into their choreography.

There appear to be two main forms of step dancing. The first consists of a sequence of steps with no particular pattern, and which cannot be traced to any form of social dance; this form is common among the traveling peoples (who include true ethnic Gypsies, or Rom, among other nomadic groups in the British Isles). The second and more common form features a definite pattern of six bars of stepping commencing with the left foot, followed by a two-bar closing step called a break. This sequence is followed by six bars of the same step on the other foot, closing with the same break. Another step is then begun on the left foot, and the pattern continues throughout the dance. This pattern is a development from the country-dance step pattern codified by Baroque dance masters. The steps themselves can be divided into two varieties, one done largely on the ball of the foot (shuffles), and the other done on the whole foot, sometimes called "heel and toe." In some areas, both styles are performed in clog dancing, and are sometimes even combined in the same dance.

Forms of step dancing vary considerably throughout Britain and Ireland. In Scotland some dances, such as the "Earl of Errol" and the Lancashire Hornpipe, are purely stepping dances, and some reels ("The Drunken Skipper," for example) consist largely of the shuffle type of step. The "Highland Fling" and the sword dances, among others, tend to be rigidly codified for competitions; some steps that were once used have been proscribed and forgotten.

Irish step dancing makes a stronger distinction between hard-shoe and soft-shoe dances. In Ireland the abundance of dancing groups, the prevalence of competitions, and a patriotic attitude toward the native culture have ensured the continued practice of the traditional dances, and rivalries among villages are still common. Nonetheless, *sean nós* ("old style") Irish step dance—weighted, close to the floor, and unspectacular—is ever rarer, having been displaced by the virtuosic complexity, rigid carriage, and exaggerated aerial maneuvers of the competition style.

In Wales one clog dance, known as the Shepherd's Dance, is done with a broomstick or a lighted candle, or

STEP DANCING IN GREAT BRITAIN AND IRELAND. James Keane, age seventy-nine, of Labasheeda, county Clare, dancing "The Priest in His Boots," an old solo jig he learned as a boy from Jack Spelsey, an elderly neighbor; the dance was formerly popular in Clare. Keane was traditional Irish step dancer in residence at the University of Limerick (1996–1997), the first such appointment in the world. He is pictured here teaching a class at the university's Irish World Music Centre in 1996. (Photograph by Catherine E. Foley; used by permission.)

both. Dancing over a broom is common in all parts of England and the Channel Islands, and snuffing a candle by jumping and hitting soles together on the wick without touching the wax is a favorite pub pastime. The dance is also performed with a step similar to the Russian *prisiadka,* with the dancer crouching and kicking out each foot in turn.

Between 1880 and 1930 many clog dancing contests were held, each with an impressive title, so that virtually every one of the old dancers could claim to be a world champion. With the revival of the competitions at folk festivals, many dancers are busy improving old steps and creating new ones. Thus it becomes difficult for the dance scholar to distinguish between what is original and what is new; those who dance for display guard their steps as jealously as did earlier generations. Step dancing is believed to have influenced the development of tap dancing in the United States; there is also a unique form of step dancing called *clogging* performed in Appalachia. Step dance traditions continue in the Irish and Scottish immigrant communities in the United States, both as social dances and in competitions. Strong and distinct traditions of step dancing also flourish in Cape Breton and Quebec in Canada.

STEP DANCING IN GREAT BRITAIN AND IRELAND. Laura Mulqueen, age fifteen, of Clonoughter, Clonlare, county Clare, a student at the O'Rourke School of Irish Dance, Limerick, in a solo soft-shoe reel, photographed during a class in 1996 at the Na Piarsaigh Athletic Association Club, Caherdavin, Limerick. The heavily embroidered and appliquéd velvet costume, with its stiffened front panels and broad, stiff sash, is a highly exaggerated version of traditional dress worn only for competition. (Photograph by Catherine E. Foley; used by permission.)

[*See also* Great Britain, *articles on* English Traditional Dance *and* Scottish Folk and Traditional Dance; *and* Ireland, *article on* Traditional Dance. *For related discussion, see* Clogging; Hornpipe; Jig; Morris Dance; Reel; *and* Sword Dance.]

BIBLIOGRAPHY

Clifton, Peter, and Anne-Marie Hulme. "Solo Step Dancing within Living Memory in North Norfolk." *Traditional Dance* 1 (1982): 29–58.

Flaherty, E. "Memories of a Lanchashire Clog Dancer." *English Dance and Song* 30 (1968).

Flett, J. F., and T. M. Flett. *Traditional Step-Dancing in Lakeland.* London, 1979.

Hardy, Thomas. "The Fiddler of the Reels." In Hardy's *Life's Little Ironies.* New York, 1894.

Metherell, Chris. *An Introductory Bibliography on Clog and Step Dance.* Vaughan Williams Memorial Library Leaflet, no. 22. London, 1994.

Pilling, Julian Oliver. "The Lancashire Clog Dance." *Folk Music Journal* 1.3 (1967): 158–179.

Pilling, Julian Oliver. "Step Dancing." In *Sixty Years of Folk.* London, 1971.

Pilling, Julian Oliver. *Down Back o' t' Shoddy.* London, 1973.

Sherry, S. "Lancashire Clog Dancing, Part 2." *Folk Music Journal* (1971).

Steele, S. "Lancashire Clog Dancing, Part 1." *Folk Music Journal* (1971).

JULIAN OLIVIER PILLING

Step Dancing in Cape Breton

Cape Breton, an island separated by a narrow strait from the northern tip of Nova Scotia, Canada's easternmost mainland province, is home to a distinct step-dancing tradition rooted in a cultural heritage brought to the island by Scottish Gaels in the nineteenth century. It is the primary dance form of a larger artistic whole, which also includes Gaelic singing, storytelling, fiddling, and piping. Gaelic society's art forms have always been an integral part of everyday life in Cape Breton, in a rural setting largely isolated from mainstream influences.

The majority of the island's Scottish immigrants arrived between 1802 and 1847, when an estimated thirty thousand Highlanders acquired land holdings. Most of the pioneers came as a result of the extensive social, economic,

STEP DANCING IN CAPE BRETON. No Cape Breton wedding would be complete without step dancing. *(left)* Ronald (Raghnall Aonghais Raghaill) MacEachen (age eighty-five) dances with his son Angus at a 1954 wedding in Port Hawkesbury, Nova Scotia. While usually only one person dances at a time, a dancer may coax another out on the floor in this way, by taking the other's hands and doing a few steps together before retiring. *(right)* Chris Rankin MacMaster dancing at the same wedding reception. Traditional step dance, which requires very little space, is ideally suited to this kind of parlor setting. The vocabulary of steps is nearly identical for both sexes. (Photographs from the collection of Kay MacEachen.)

cultural, and religious changes then occurring in Scottish society. The pattern of Highland immigration to Cape Breton was striking in that the Gaels' new communities largely mirrored those they left behind in Scotland. Most established new settlements in homogeneous groups that reflected their geographic origin in the Highlands and the Hebrides, their religion, and their family ties.

The absence of Cape Breton–style step dancing from modern Scotland's dance scene has led to much conjecture in Scotland over the form's origins. Little recorded documentation for its existence is available through historical sources, though descriptions of dances written by travelers to the Highlands in the eighteenth century do match characteristics of Cape Breton step dance. Today, step dancing is done either as a solo form or as part of the Cape Breton Square Set, a derivative of the quadrille or Lancers that came to Cape Breton early in the twentieth century. Step dancing is also part of the Scotch Four, a set dance now seldom seen except onstage. The Square Set incorporates solo reel steps and "shuffling" steps in jig time (6/8). Solo step dancing is performed to a sequence of strathspey and reel. The strathspey is sometimes called a "dance strathspey," to distinguish it from what is commonly understood to be strathspey tempo and rhythm in Scotland (slower and less fiercely syncopated than the Cape Breton version).

In step dancing some steps can be identified partly with the sounds they make. The most basic steps (the word *step* in this sense meaning a whole phrase) incorporate simple heel-toe action. Basic reel steps involve six or eight sounds that correspond to the beats in each bar of music. While performing a step, the dancer's weight-bearing foot helps to maintain balance but has its own role to play in adding certain sounds. Good dancers keep their heels off the floor, with most of the body weight on the balls of the feet. It is also important to "hold yourself well," which means with hands comfortably at the sides, face looking straight ahead, and with little movement or action above the knees. This is not to suggest a ramrod posture, however, as dancers should be relaxed, yet lively. In this the Cape Breton style is close to Irish *sean nós* ("old-style") step dancing, and very different from the exaggeratedly stiff carriage of modern Irish competition step dance.

It is common practice in Cape Breton step dancing to repeat each step (i.e., phrase), usually in multiples of two, on both the left and right foot, to coincide with the structure of the tune. Seasoned dancers will consistently perform certain steps to certain tunes but will also extemporize variations on the basic steps in response to the musician, adding, for example, extra "triplets"—flourishes that substitute three sounds, where normally they would make one—in imitation of the ornaments typical of Cape Breton's distinctive style of fiddling. Traditionally, the most admired dancers are not necessarily those with the widest vocabulary of steps but those with a total mastery of a smaller number, the ability to improvise effective variations on their steps, and a recognizable personal style.

The tradition places great emphasis on precision timing, mastery of which is impossible without a profound intuitive knowledge of the music. In Gaelic, a construction with the preposition *ann* ("in") expresses the concept of having a quality or trait; hence the idiom corresponding to "he is musical" is *tha ceol ann* (literally, "there is music in him"). It is much more common to hear Cape Bretoners say in English "the music is in him," than "he is musical." This reflects the Gael's traditional belief, inherited by today's largely English-speaking population, that music is innate. Above all, the dancer must be in tune with the fiddler. So intimate is the relationship between dancer and fiddler that the fiddler's music is said to give the dancer the "lift" he or she needs, and vice versa. Since step dancing is a percussive dance form, it is in a sense almost a dialogue between two musicians, and it is not uncommon for a dancer to become completely absorbed in the steps and the music, although at certain social occasions (and in stage performances) the rapport with the audience is also important.

"The music to me, always dictated what I did with my feet, as opposed to a programmed dance where step number one followed step number two," said Diane MacIsaac Miller, of New Waterford, in an interview in 1987 (MacGillivray, 1988). Most dancers concur that following a pattern too closely will rob the dancer of feeling, individuality, and joy—important characteristics of Cape Breton step dance. The freedom of this dance form is likely a result of the informal setting in which dancers traditionally learned their art. There are accounts of early "dancing masters" in Cape Breton during pioneer times but ensuing generations, until the 1970s, were generally void of any formal dance instruction. Most dancers say they just picked up the steps by watching. "There was none of this teaching business," said Aggie (MacLean) MacLennan of Benacadie. "We got out there and did what we did and added to it as we went along" (MacGillivray, 1988). The social setting, the element of improvisation, and the individualistic nature of the art distinguish it strongly from modern Highland dancing (which is also known on the island) and again from Irish and Irish-American step dance, both highly regulated and choreographed competitive forms.

After 1970, with concerts and public performance opportunities on the rise, the level of innovation has increased. Dancers have more readily invented steps, combined certain steps, and incorporated steps from other areas, such as Prince Edward Island and the Ottawa Valley. Excellent dancers, however, are able to keep the time-honored elements of Cape Breton step dance intact, while incorporating new steps and even using taps on their shoes (a good example is Father Angus Alex MacDonnell of Deepdale, Inverness County). Although step dancing does appear onstage, the community of dancers in Cape Breton does not depend on the stage, and many of the greatest dancers have never performed before a paying audience.

According to Frank Rhodes, who visited Cape Breton in 1957, the set dances brought to Cape Breton from Scotland were eight-handed reels *(ruidhle mór)* and four-handed reels *(ruidhle ceathrar)*. Memories of older Gaels confirm that the eight-handed reel and the four-handed reel—also known as the Scotch Four or Single Four—were commonly danced before the arrival of quadrilles or the modern Square Set. Strathspey and reel music were both part of the Scotch Four, while the eight-handed reel used only reels. Both incorporated setting (in-place) and traveling steps. The eight-handed reel is only a vague memory, but the Scotch Four is still performed today, although more commonly on stage than at social dances or house parties.

The fiddle was, and is, the most common instrument for dance, but in some communities the pipes were common for both solo and set dances. Traditional pipe music for dancing had a sense of rhythm and timing very different from the military-style piping that is pervasive today. When instruments were absent, which was often the case, Gaels danced to *puirt-a-beul* or mouth music (unaccompanied vocal music for dance). These tunes have Gaelic lyrics and make great use of Gaelic vocables (rhythmical syllables) in their choruses. [*See* Folk Dance Sounds.] Typical *puirt-a-beul* in Cape Breton includes "Calum Crubach" (Lame Malcolm), a very popular strathspey for dancing, and the reel "Muilean Dubh" (The Black Mill). Gaels in Cape Breton also "jigged" a tune, or mimicked the notes vocally without using words. The Gaelic word for this is *canntaireachd,* a term also used for a precise system of oral transmission for pipe music. Buddy MacMaster, of Judique, one of the most respected living Cape Breton fiddlers, learned some of his tunes from his mother's jigging. As a young girl, expert step dancer Minnie (Beaton) MacMaster, of Mabou and Troy, danced more often to her mother's jigging than to a fiddle.

Interest in learning to dance is more widespread than ever before. The demand for teachers is great throughout North America and in Scotland. Today, it is more common for students to learn in classes to taped music rather than to *puirt-a-beul* or jigging. Important elements of musicality and enjoyment, however, remain sacred and have not changed since the arrival of the Gaels to the New World.

BIBLIOGRAPHY

Fergusson, Donald A. *Beyond the Hebrides.* Halifax, Nova Scotia, 1977.

Gibson, John. "Traditional Piping in Nova Scotia." In *Celtic Languages and Celtic Peoples.* Halifax, Nova Scotia, 1989.

MacGillivray, Allister. *A Cape Breton Ceilidh.* Sydney, Nova Scotia, 1988.

MacLeod, Angus. *The Songs of Duncan Ban Macintyre.* Edinburgh, 1952.

Moore, Maggie. "Scottish Step Dancing." In *Program for the Nineteenth Annual Washington Irish Folk Festival.* Washington, D.C., 1995.

Rhodes, F. "Dancing in Cape Breton Island, Nova Scotia." Appendix to *Traditional Dancing in Scotland* by J. F. Flett and T. M. Flett. London, 1964.

INTERVIEWS. Harvey Beaton, 1997; Willie Fraser, 1991; Buddy MacMaster, 1991; Minne MacMaster and Margaret Ann Beaton, 1995.

FRANCES MACEACHEN

STILT-DANCING. *For discussion of stilt-dancing in African dance traditions, see* Mask and Makeup, *article on* African Traditions.

STONE FLOWER, THE. Russian title: *Kamennyi Tsvetok*. Ballet in three acts, eight scenes, and a prologue. Choreography: Leonid Lavrovsky. Music: Sergei Prokofiev. Libretto: Sergei Prokofiev, based on Pavel Bazhov's story, "The Malachite Casket," drawn from fairy tales from the Urals. Scenery and costumes: Tatiana Strazhenetskaya. First performance: 12 February 1954, Bolshoi Theater, Moscow, Bolshoi Ballet. Principals: Galina Ulanova (Katerina), Vladimir Preobrazhensky (Danila), Maya Plisetskaya (Mistress of the Copper Mountain), Aleksei Yermolayev (Severyan).

The ballet begins with the stone carver, Danila of the Urals, searching for the Stone Flower, a symbol of beauty and consummate art. He is imprisoned in the magic realm of the Mistress of the Copper Mountain, where he proceeds to work on a malachite casket. The bailiff, Severyan, attempts to seduce Danila's fiancée, Katerina. Severyan pursues her, but at the will of the enraged Mistress of the Copper Mountain, he is engulfed by the earth. The love of Katerina and Danila stirs the stone heart of the Mistress of the Copper Mountain, and she releases Danila, who has learned the great mystery of artistic creation.

The second production of *The Stone Flower* was significant to Soviet ballet. It was presented at the Kirov Theater in Leningrad on 25 April 1957, with choreography by Yuri Grigorovich and decor by Simon Virsaladze. Irina Kolpakova danced the role of Katerina; Aleksandr Gribov, Danila; Alla Osipenko, Mistress of the Copper Mountain; and Anatoly Gridin, Severyan. This production, in its congruity to the imagery, modernity, and innovation of Prokofiev's music, marked a turning point from excessive dramatization of choreography and from realism onstage to dance patterns that relied on a wealth of choreographic forms and vocabulary.

The ballet was Grigorovich's debut as a choreographer. He used a variety of forms of symphonic dance, his intention being not to stage dances as they are in real life, but to portray real life through the medium of dance. Accordingly, for example, he presented a betrothal and a fair through dance, not literally. The choreography was based on classical dance enriched with Russian national motifs, with acrobatic elements added for the Mistress of the Copper Mountain. The ballet has since been staged in many Russian cities and abroad.

BIBLIOGRAPHY

Balanchine, George, with Francis Mason. *Balanchine's Complete Stories of the Great Ballets*. Rev. and enl. ed. Garden City, N.Y., 1977.

Devereux, Tony. "The Stone Flower Stories." *The Dancing Times* (July 1993): 994–997.

Dorris, George. "Music for Spectacle." *Ballet Review* 6.1 (1977): 45–55.

Karp, Poel M., and S.Y. Levin. *Kamennyi tsvetok S. S. Prokof'eva*. Leningrad, 1963.

Lopukhov, Fedor. "Yuri Grigorovich's *Stone Flower*." *Dance News* (July 1979): 1.

Percival, John. "Grigorovich of the Bolshoi." *Dance and Dancers* (September 1989): 10–13.

Vanslov, Victor V. *Balety Grigorovicha i problemy khoreografii*. 2d ed. Moscow, 1971.

VICTOR V. VANSLOV
Translated from Russian